T0328932

Routledge Handbook of Football Business and Management

Football is the world's most valuable sport, generating bigger revenues, as well as being watched and played by more people, than any other. It is virtually impossible to understand the business of sport without understanding the football industry. This book surveys contemporary football in unparalleled breadth and depth.

Presenting critical insights from world-leading football scholars and introducing football's key organisations, leagues and emerging nations, it explores key themes from governance and law to strategy and finance, as well as cutting-edge topics such as analytics, digital media, and the women's game.

This is essential reading for all students, researchers and practitioners working in football, sport business, sport management or mainstream business and management.

Simon Chadwick is Professor of Sports Enterprise at Salford University Manchester, UK, where he is also Co-Director of the Centre for Sports Business. He is also a Founding Director of the China Soccer Observatory at the University of Nottingham, UK and regularly works with organisations in football across the world, including clubs, federations, commercial partners, event organisers, and governments. He tweets: @Prof_Chadwick

Daniel Parnell is Senior Lecturer in Business Management at Manchester Metropolitan University, UK. Dan's research is across three areas; policy and politics, management and change (individual, community and organisational), across elite sport. He currently works with a number of professional sport clubs and national governing bodies in England and internationally. He has worked with several English Premier League and Football League Clubs, the Premier League, Football League, and the Football Foundation.

Paul Widdop is Senior Research Fellow in Sport Business at Leeds Beckett University, UK. His research explores social and economic networks on the consumption and production of Sport. He has published widely in areas of sport and popular culture including articles in *Journal of Consumer Culture, Cultural Sociology, Cultural Trends, Political Behaviour, Electoral Studies*, and *Leisure Sciences*.

Christos Anagnostopoulos is Assistant Professor in Sport Business Management at University of Central Lancashire, Cyprus, where he also serves as the Co-Director of the Centre for Entrepreneurship. Christos is also an adjunct Associate Professor in Sport Management at Molde University College, Norway. His research interests lie in corporate social responsibility, governance, and more recently entrepreneurship and positive organisational behaviour in sport. Christos serves as an elected member-at-large at the European Association for Sport Management, as well as at the editorial boards of the *European Sport Management Quarterly, Sport, Business and Management: An International Journal, International Journal of Sport Communication, Journal of Global Sport Management*, and the *International Journal of Sport Management*.

Routledge Handbook of Football Business and Management

Edited by
Simon Chadwick, Daniel Parnell,
Paul Widdop and Christos Anagnostopoulos

Routledge
Taylor & Francis Group

LONDON AND NEW YORK

First published 2019 by Routledge

2 Park Square, Milton Park, Abingdon, Oxon, OX14 4RN
605 Third Avenue, New York, NY 10017

Routledge is an imprint of the Taylor & Francis Group, an informa business

First issued in paperback 2020

British Library Cataloguing-in-Publication Data
A catalogue record for this book is available from the British Library

Library of Congress Cataloging-in-Publication Data
A catalog record has been requested for this book

ISBN: 978-1-138-57907-1 (hbk)
ISBN: 978-0-367-73246-2 (pbk)

Typeset in Bembo
by Deanta Global Publishing Services, Chennai, India

Contents

List of contributors   *ix*

Acknowledgements   *xx*

1 Introduction to the handbook of football business and management   1
   Simon Chadwick, Daniel Parnell, Paul Widdop, and Christos Anagnostopoulos

2 A framework for diversification decisions in professional football   3
   Sascha L. Schmidt and Florian Holzmayer

3 Global football: Defining the rules of the changing game   20
   Remco M. Beek, Martijn Ernest, and Jos Verschueren

4 Structures and policies at the main European football leagues:
   Evolution and recent changes   33
   Juan Luis Paramio-Salcines and Ramón Llopis-Goig

5 Points, pounds, and politics in the governance of football   44
   Hallgeir Gammelsæter

6 Contemporary issues in the management of grassroots football   56
   Jimmy O'Gorman, Danny Fitzpatrick, Jonathan Sibley,
   Matthew Hindmarsh, Zora Saskova, and Dan Parnell

7 Football law   71
   Richard Parrish and Adam Pendlebury

8 Football and marketing   88
   Argyro Elisavet Manoli and James Andrew Kenyon

9 Digital and social media   101
   Alex Fenton and Boris Helleu

Contents

10 Corporate social responsibility (CSR) in football:
Exploring modes of CSR implementation 114
*Geraldine Zeimers, Christos Anagnostopoulos,
Thierry Zintz, and Annick Willem*

11 Agents and intermediaries 131
Giambattista Rossi

12 Managing performance in elite professional football 144
Barry Drust, Andy O'Boyle, and Mark Gillett

13 The sporting director: Exploring current practice
and challenges within elite football 155
Daniel Parnell, Ryan Groom, Paul Widdop, and Sara Ward

14 Strategic management in football organisations 171
Mikkel Draebye

15 Finance and accounting in football 186
Rob Wilson and Daniel Plumley

16 Sponsorships, stadia, and naming rights 199
Leah Gillooly and Dominic Medway

17 Venue management in football 209
Eric C. Schwarz

18 Human resource management in football 220
Jonathan Lord

19 Fans, spectators, consumers in football 232
Petros Parganas

20 Sports business analytics: The past, the present and the future 246
Ian G. McHale

21 Leagues, tournaments, and competitions 258
Thadeu Gasparetto and Angel Barajas

22 Football, networks, and relationships 273
Anna Gerke and Hagen Wäsche

23 Leveraging football events 282
Vitor Sobral, Sheranne Fairley, and Danny O'Brien

24 The labour markets of professional football players   294
    Jean-François Brocard and Christophe Lepetit

25 Value management in football: A framework to
    develop and analyse competitive advantage   308
    Harald Dolles and Sten Söderman

26 Supply chain management in professional football   319
    Birnir Egilsson

27 Risk and crisis management   334
    Dominic Elliott

28 Women and football   351
    Sue Bridgewater

29 Managing match officials: The influence of business and
    the impact of finance in an era of Premier League dominance   366
    Tom Webb

30 Perspectives on ethics and integrity in football   376
    Simon Gardiner

31 Talent management   388
    Richard P. Bailey, Rob J. Bailey, and Nick Levett

32 Retailing in the football industry   400
    Dimitrios Kolyperas and Leigh Sparks

33 Sport licenced products in the football industry   412
    Dimitra Papadimitriou and Artemisia Apostolopoulou

34 FIFA   423
    Tom Bason, Paul Salisbury, and Simon Gérard

35 UEFA   441
    Kenneth Cortsen

36 CONMEBOL: South American Confederation of Football   459
    *Renan Petersen-Wagner, Alberto Reinaldo Reppold Filho,
    Cássia Damiani, Felipe Magno and Felippe Marchetti*

37 Asian Football Confederation   473
    N. David Pifer

Contents

38 Confederation of African Football   485
    Michael M. Goldman and Mlondi Mashinini

39 CONCACAF   497
    Dr Joel Rookwood and Dr Glaucio Scremin

40 Oceania Football Confederation   511
    Geoff Dickson and Sean Phelps

41 Football in China   522
    Simon Chadwick and Jonathan Sullivan

42 Business and governance of football in Qatar   539
    Mahfoud Amara and Ahmed Al-Emadi

43 Football in Brazil   547
    Leonardo José Mataruna-Dos-Santos, Daniel Range,
    André Luiz Pereira Guimarães, Luis Antonio Verdini de Carvalho,
    and Carlos Eugenio Zardini Filho

44 Football in Turkey   564
    Cem Tinaz, Emir Güney, and Ahmet Talimciler

45 Management of football in India   577
    Gautam Ahuja and Eric C. Schwarz

46 Soccer in the United States   590
    Clinton J. Warren and Kwame J.A. Agyemang

47 The rise and rise of the world's favourite sport   601
    Simon Chadwick, Daniel Parnell, Paul Widdop,
    and Christos Anagnostopoulos

Index   607

List of contributors

Gautam Ahuja is Research Officer with the Ministry of Youth Affairs and Sports under the Government of India. Gautam has been working on various projects dealing with preparation of elite athletes for the major competitions including the Olympic Games.

Ahmed Al-Emadi is Dean of College of Education at Qatar University and Associate Professor in Sport Management. Ahmed has taught many courses in his major such as sports management, sports facilities, sport sociology, and research methods. He has contributed to regional and international publication in the area of sport in general and sports management in particular. He is affiliated to a number of international and national associations related to his major.

Kwame J.A. Agyemang is Associate Professor of Sport Management at Louisiana State University (LSU). His research attempts to better understand a range of issues related to how social actors create, preserve, disrupt, and change institutions. His research has been published in various sport management- and general management-related journals.

Mahfoud Amara joined Qatar University in the fall of 2015. He is currently Director of Sport Science Program at the College of Arts and Sciences, Qatar University. Before joining Qatar University, he was Assistant Professor in Sport Policy and Management and Deputy Director of the Centre for Olympic Studies at Loughborough University. Amara published a number of papers and chapters on sport business, culture, and politics.

Artemisia Apostolopoulou is University Professor in the Department of Sport Management at Robert Morris University, USA. She conducts research on branding and brand extension strategies of sport organizations, sport sponsorship, and the consumption and value of sport licensed products. Her work has appeared in many peer reviewed journals including the *European Sport Management Quarterly, Journal of Brand Management, Journal of Marketing Communications, and Sport Marketing Quarterly*.

Richard Bailey leads research at the International Council of Sport Science and Physical Education, the worldwide umbrella body for sports science and education organisations. Before this position, he was Founding Chair of Sport and Education at the University of Birmingham, UK. He is the author/editor of 30 books and more than 120 research articles. His current research focuses on exercise neuroscience, and theories of embodiment.

Rob J. Bailey is Director of Five Lines Consulting, which is a business consultancy that provides strategic, financial and commercial advice within the sport and leisure sectors. He has been an industry consultant since 1994. Rob was previously a Director at KPMG, and prior to that he was a Senior Manager at Deloitte. Rob is a part-time football coach at a professional football club.

Angel Barajas is Professor and Head of the Department of Finance at the St Petersburg School of Economics of Management (NRU Higher School of Economics). Moreover, he is the Academic Supervisor of the ID Lab (NRU Higher School of Economics – Perm Campus). He was the Director of the MBA in Sport at University of Vigo from 2012 until 2016. He is Researcher for the Spanish Economic Observatory of Sport. His research interests include investment valuation, intellectual capital, and finance of sports.

Tom Bason is Lecturer in Sport Management at Coventry University and PhD candidate at Manchester Metropolitan University where he is supervised by Professor Jonathan Grix. Tom's research interests relate to sport mega-events, and in particular the ways in which bids for such events can be leveraged for positive benefits.

Remco M. Beek is Associate Professor at the Rotterdam University of Applied Science and PhD-candidate at the Rotterdam School of Management, Erasmus University Rotterdam. His research focuses on the impact of hallmark events on commercial partners, rights holders, and society. Actual research topics cover the decision-making process of sponsorship relationships, the legacy of hallmark events, and risk management of events.

Sue Bridgewater is Professor of Sports Marketing and Director of the Centre for Sports Business at Liverpool University Management School. She is Non Exec Director of the League Managers Association Institute, a member of UEFA's Research Grants Jury, and researches the role of women in football on behalf of Women in Football.

Jean-François Brocard (PhD Economics, University of Limoges) is Associate Professor of Economics at the University of Limoges, where he's a member of the Centre de Droit et d'Economie du Sport (CDES). He is the Secretary General of both the International Association of Sports Economists (IASE) and the French Seminar of "Dynamique Economique du Sport" (DESport).

Luis Antonio Verdini de Carvalho is Professor of Football at the Federal University of Rio de Janeiro (UFRJ). He has an MA degree in Physical Education by UFRJ. Specialised in soccer and sports training. He has sports management degree by FIFA/FGV and football management by National Football Federation – CBF. He was coach and physical trainer of the Brazilian National Football Team U20.

Kenneth Cortsen co-founded of the Department of Sport Management at UCN in Denmark and is a Visiting Professor at University of San Francisco and DIS, Copenhagen. Cortsen does sports business research, lectures, and consults for organisations in Denmark and abroad. Cortsen also coaches (UEFA A-license) in the Danish football club Aalborg BK/AaB.

Cássia Damiani is Senior Lecturer at the Institute of Physical Education and Sports of the Federal University of Ceará, Brazil. She was Special Advisor and Director of Planning and Strategic Management of the Brazilian Ministry of Sports, from 2005 to 2016, and research member of the Center for Olympic and Paralympic Studies. Her area of research is on sport policy.

Geoff Dickson is a leading member of the Australian and New Zealand sport management academic community. His research interests are expansive – interorganisational relationships and sport governance, event impacts and legacies, volunteers, sponsorship, ambush marketing, and consumer behaviour. He has supervised nearly 30 honours, MA and PhD theses.

Harald Dolles is Professor in Sport Management at Molde University College, Molde (Norway). Harald is immediate past chair of the EURAM Strategic Interest Group on "Managing Sport" and frequently contributes to the scientific development in the fields of sports management and international business, most recently with Egilsson on "sports expatriates" (Research Handbook of Expatriates, Edward Elgar, 2017).

Mikkel Draebye is SDA Professor of Strategy and Entrepreneurship at SDA Bocconi School of Management, Milan. He has been teaching Strategic Planning in Sports Organisation in various MA programmes since 1998. He has been UEFA Kiss Expert since 2008 and has conducted a variety of strategy workshops with federations, clubs, and leagues.

Barry Drust is Professor of Applied Exercise Physiology at Liverpool John Moores University. He has published over 150 peer reviewed research articles associated with understanding high performance in football. In addition to his academic background is his applied experience providing consultancy services to professional teams in both the UK and internationally.

Birnir Egilsson is PhD student and Lecturer at Molde University College, Specialised University in Logistics, Molde (Norway). His main research interest is the operations management of professional institutions in sports. His PhD thesis focuses on football, looking into the various supply chains of professional football clubs with the purpose of understanding if, why, and how football clubs utilise supply chain management strategies and practices. Other research interests relate to migration and integration issues within the supply chain of talents.

Dominic Elliott is Professor of Business Continuity and Strategic Management at Liverpool University. He is interested in how organisational success is achieved and, on the downside, how organisations deal with minor and major interruptions that are an inevitable part of life. He has worked with organisations including BP, Coca Cola, the Government of Lesotho, IBM, Merrill Lynch, BNP-Paribas, RBS, ShopDirect, Speedyhire, Health and Safety Executive, Royal Mail, and Emirates.

Martijn Ernest (Tongeren, 1993) is Head of Research and Development at the International Football Business Institute (IFBI). Due to his academic background – an MA in History at the KU Leuven and Postgraduate in Sports Management at the Vrije Universiteit Brussel – he has the ability to process information in an unconventional way, adjusted to the high-demanding needs of the football business industry. As Head of Research, it is his responsibility to guarantee the quality of IFBI-related research and projects.

Sheranne Fairley is Senior Lecturer at The University of Queensland Business School. Her research interests include sport and event tourism, event leveraging, and volunteerism. She is an Associate Editor of *Sport Management Review* and *Leisure Sciences*.

Alex Fenton is practitioner and researcher in the areas of digital business, social media marketing and sport. His research primarily focusses on the use of digital technology for sports fans and fan engagement including digital media, digital business models, virtual reality, online communities, and gamification. Alex has won numerous industry and teaching awards and has published in some of the world's top publications.

Alberto Reinaldo Reppold Filho is Professor at the School of Physical Education, Physiotherapy and Dance of the Federal University of Rio Grande do Sul, Brazil, where he also acts as Coordinator of the Center for Olympic and Paralympic Studies. His area of research is on the legacy of sports mega-events and policy for elite sport in Brazil.

Danny Fitzpatrick is a Lecturer in Politics at Aston University. Danny's main research interests are in the study of regulation, the politics of sport, and theories of state transformation. His book, *The Politics of UK Regulation: Between Tradition, Contingency and Crisis*, was published by Palgrave in 2016.

Carlos Eugênio Nardini Filho is a civil servant at the Brazilian Ministry of Sport. In 2016, as a Chevening Scholar (UK Government scholarship for future leaders) he concluded an MA in Sport Management at Coventry University. Carlos also holds another MA degree in Physical Education from University of Brasília (2013)

Hallgeir Gammelsæter is Professor in Social Change, Organization and Management at Molde University College – Specialized University in Logistics. Besides sport studies, he has published research on organisation change, management in professional organisations, knowledge diffusion, and innovation in private and public institutions. He has authored and co-authored several Norwegian books as well as *The Organization and Governance of Top Football Across Europe: An institutional Perspective* (2011, Routledge).

Simon Gardiner is Professor of International Sports Law and has been an active researcher in the area of sports law for over 25 years. His particular research interests include sports governance and the regulation of sports-related corruption, racism in sport, and labour law issues concerning athlete mobility. He has been involved in funded research projects including with the European Union.

Thadeu Gasparetto has a PhD in Education, Sport and Health from the University of Vigo (2017). Currently, he works as Senior Lecturer at National Research University Higher School of Economics (St Petersburg, Russia). He has an MA degree in Sports Business Management at University of Vigo (2014) and a BA degree in Physical Education at Federal University of Juiz de Fora (2012). His research lines lie on Sports Economics and Management, focusing on broadcast demand, competitive balance, demand for tickets, and design of sports leagues.

Anna Gerke is Associate Professor at Audencia Business School in Paris in the department of management. Her research focuses on organisational theory, innovation, and economic geography notably in the context of sport organisations. Anna is head of the Specialised Master of Management of Sport Organisations.

Simon Gerard is Lecturer in Sport Management at the Coventry University in the UK. His research interests relate to sport governance, institutional change, and disability sports. Simon is also a research associate in the Olympic Chair in Management of Sport Organisations (Université catholique de Louvain, Belgium)

Mark Gillett has extensive experience in sports medicine both as a clinician and as head of performance at a football club. Expertise developed in both elite basketball (British basketball) and elite football (Chelsea FC and West Bromich Albion FC) have provided Mark with a unique skill set that supports the leadership of a multi-disciplinary high-performance team. Mark is currently the Director of Performance at West Bromich Albion FC.

Leah Gillooly is Senior Lecturer in Sports Marketing at Manchester Metropolitan University. Her research interests focus on the brand-building effectiveness of sports sponsorship, brand image transfer, and sponsorship activation. She has published her work in journals including *Urban Geography*, *Journal of Marketing Communications*, and *Journal of Marketing Management*.

Michael Goldman teaches, researches, and consults within a number of marketing-related themes, including marketing strategy, sport marketing, sport business development and sales, branding, and sponsorship. He is based at the University of San Francisco, while also working with the University of Pretoria's Gordon Institute of Business Science in South Africa.

André Luiz Pereira Guimarães is Associated Professor of Didactics in UFRRJ (Universidade Rural do Rio de Janeiro) and Sports Training Methods in UNIABEU (Centro Universitário Abeu). He is also a PhD candidate in sociology and sport management at ULISBOA (Universidade de Lisboa).

Emir Güney is a graduate of Global and International Affairs Dual Diploma Program co-owned by Boğaziçi University and SUNY Binghamton and a PhD candidate at Marmara University Sports Management Program. Since 2010, he has worked as Director of Sports Studies Research Centre at Kadir Has University.

Ryan Groom is Program Director for the MA/MSc Exercise and Sports degrees at Manchester Metropolitan University. His research focuses on the use of social theory to explore power, identity, and interaction in elite sports contexts. Ryan was a co-editor for Research Methods in Sports Coaching and Learning in Sports Coaching.

Boris Helleu recent research deals with digitalisation of fan experience. On a daily basis, he shares his international sports marketing and economy press review on his twitter account (@bhelleu). He also runs a blog dedicated to sports marketing (Hell of a Sport).

Matthew Hindmarsh is a PhD student undertaking research into the practice of sponsorship within grassroots football. His scholarly interests are wide-reaching and include all things football and sport business related, but more specifically focus on the financing and development of non-profit sport clubs and the promotion of small businesses.

Florian Holzmayer is a doctoral student and research assistant at the Center for Sports and Management (CSM) at WHU since 2016. One of his key research areas is "Corporate Diversification in Professional Football." He studied business administration at WHU, ESADE, and LSE followed by several years at Simon-Kucher & Company.

Jamie Kenyon is a Lecturer in Sport Management at Loughborough University. His research interests include managing community and volunteer sports organisations, marketing and relationship management in sport, and the impacts and legacies of sports mega-events.

Dimitrios Kolyperas is Lecturer of Sport Marketing at Stirling Management School, University of Stirling, UK. Dimitrios holds an MBA from Cardiff University and completed his PhD at University of Stirling in 2012. Dimitrios is Program Director of BA sport studies and Marketing in Singapore Institute of Management.

Ramón Llopis-Goig is Senior Lecturer at the University of Valencia, Spain. He has been Visiting Scholar Research at the University of Leicester (UK), at the European University Institute (Florence, Italy), and at the International Olympic Committee for Olympic Studies Centre (Lausanne, Switzerland).

Christophe Lepetit is Head of economic studies and partnerships of the Centre de Droit et d'Economie du Sport (CDES). He is specialised in economic impact analysis of mega-sporting events about which he has written several articles in national and international reviews. He is a member of the board of the French financial monitoring of professional football (DNCG).

Nick Levett is Head of Talent and Performance for UK Coaching, helping to develop coaches at all levels in the player pathway up to international youth teams. He previously worked at the Football Association for 14 years and was National Development Manager for Youth Football and Talent Identification Manager.

Jonathan Lord is Lecturer in Human Resource Management and Employment Law. He has previously been HR Director, Manager, and Consultant, working across all three sectors. Specifically, Jonathan has worked within the transport and construction industries, as well as carrying out HR projects within the public and voluntary sector. Jonathan has a Doctorate qualification, which involved researching the purpose of employment tribunals and their effectiveness.

Felipe Magno is a Bachelor of Physical Education and Sport and Master in Human Movement Studies at the Federal University of Rio Grande do Sul, Brazil, where he is currently a PhD student in production engineering at the School of Engineering. His area of research is on the social impact of sports mega-events in Brazil.

Argyro Elisavet Manoli is Lecturer in Sports Marketing and Communications at Loughborough University. Her research interests include marketing communications management practices – such as IMC, branding, and CSR promotion in football – and, match-fixing and economic mismanagement in Greek football clubs.

Felippe Marchetti is a Bachelor of Physical Education and Sport at the Federal University of Rio Grande do Sul, Brazil, and Master in Sport Management at the University of Oporto, Portugal. He is currently a PhD student in Human Movement Sciences. His area of research is on the economic sustainability of football stadiums.

Mlondi Mashinini operates at the confluence of sports, business, and technology. He is a founding partner of FanBase Analytics, a leading data insights and sports business consultancy. He has worked across Europe, the US, and Africa, including with the NFL's Kansas City Chiefs and Real Madrid's football and basketball clubs.

Leonardo Jose Mataruna-Dos-Santos is Assistant Professor (College of Business Administration, American University in the Emirates – Dubai) and Associated Research at Coventry University –

CTPSR (Marie Currie Fellow – EU/FP7/UK). He has a PhD from Gama Filho University (Brazil) focusing on innovation in sport. He is commentator of SPORTV Channel and Physical Education Teacher.

Ian McHale is Chair in Sports Analytics at the University of Liverpool Management School. His research interests include statistics in sport and the analysis of gambling markets and various gambling issues. He was founding Chair of the Statistics in Sport Section of the Royal Statistical Society, and was co-creator of the EA SPORTS Player Performance Indicator, the official player rating system of the Barclays Premier League.

Dominic Medway is Professor of Marketing in the Institute of Place Management at Manchester Metropolitan University. His research focuses on the complexity of interactions between places and spaces and those who produce, manage and consume them. Dominic has published in leading academic journals, including *European Journal of Marketing and Marketing Theory*.

Andy O'Boyle has over ten years of experience working in professional football. During this time his roles have ranged from the day-to-day planning and delivery of high-performance programmes for elite players (both senior professionals and young players undertaking developmental programmes) to the strategic leadership and management of sport science programmes. He is currently Head of Elite Performance at The Premier League.

Danny O'Brien is Associate Professor, Sport Management, in the Bond Business School, Bond University, Australia. He is Visiting Scholar at both the Center for Surf Research at San Diego State University and the Plymouth Sustainability and Surfing Research Group at Plymouth University, UK. Danny's research interests are in sport-for-development and community-building through sport.

Jimmy O'Gorman is Senior Lecturer in Sports Management, Development and Coaching at Edge Hill University. Jimmy's main research interests are on the enactment and implementation of sports policy, the welfare and wellbeing of sports workers, and the development of youth football. Jimmy has undertaken consultation projects with the Football Association and local authority sport development organisations. He has edited a special issue titled: Junior and Youth Grassroots Football Culture published by Routledge in 2017.

Dimitra Papadimitriou is Assistant Professor in the Department of Business Administration at the University of Patras, Greece. She conducts research on service quality management, destination brand management, and sport consumer behavior in the sponsorship and licensing domains. Her work has appeared in many peer reviewed journals including the European Sport Management Quarterly, Journal of Business and Industrial Marketing, Journal of Travel Research, and Sport Management Review.

Luis Paramio-Salcines is Senior Lecturer at Universidad Autonoma de Madrid, Spain. His principal scholarly interest includes sport facilities and event management, commercial development and accessibility provision of stadia, the economic impact of sport events, and corporate social responsibility in sport.

Petros Parganas holds an MBA and DBA from the Edinburgh Business School, Heriot-Watt University, UK, and currently leads the digital analytics football department at Adidas. Prior to that he was teaching sport marketing courses at various universities and colleges. He is a member of the Marketing and Sports Unit at the Athens Institute for Education and Research as well as the Hellenic Management Association. His principal research interests include sport brand management, fan engagement, and social media. His academic research has appeared in various journals including *European Sport Management Quarterly, Journal of Brand Management, Journal of Strategic Marketing, Sport, Business & Management* and *International Journal of Sports Marketing & Sponsorship.*

Richard Parrish is Jean Monnet Chair of EU Sports Law and Policy and the Director of the Centre for Sports Law Research at Edge Hill University. He has held a number of senior advisory positions relevant to sport including membership of the European Commission's High Level Expert Group on Sport Diplomacy, the Commission's Group of Independent Sports Experts, and Specialist Adviser to the House of Lords Inquiry into Grassroots Sport and the EU.

Adam Pendlebury is Senior Lecturer in Law at Edge Hill University with teaching specialisms in Torts, Sports Law and Media Law. His research interest is in sports law, in particular, the regulation of misconduct. He has published in peer reviewed journals, given papers at a number of international conferences, and is connected to key sports law networks. As the coordinator of the Centre for Sports Law Research at Edge Hill, Adam has assisted in the organising of a number of sports law events.

Sean Phelps is a graduate of Florida State University. Sean's research interests focus on organisational theory and organisational behaviour. His research has been published in *Sport Management Review, European Sport Management Quarterly, International Journal of Sport Management and Marketing,* and the *International Journal of Sport Marketing and Sponsorship.*

N. David Pifer obtained his PhD from the University of Georgia and currently serves as Assistant Professor of Sport Management at Texas Tech University in Lubbock, Texas. Dr Pifer's research focuses broadly on financial and economic aspects of sport, but more specifically on sports analytics and how individuals and organisations can use data and statistical techniques to make more informed decisions.

Daniel Plumley joined the teaching team at Sheffield Hallam University in 2011. His main research interests are in the finance and governance of professional team sports and his PhD focused on measuring financial and sporting performance in English professional football. Dan has published widely on holistic performance measurement in professional football.

Daniel Range graduated from the London School of Economics in 2003 and has worked at Coventry University since 2007. Here he obtained an MA in Community Cohesion Management and is currently working towards his PhD. He is part of the Research Group of Sport for Peace and Development.

Giambattista Rossi is Lecturer Birkbeck University of London, where he is responsible for a course module on sport labour markets. Giambattista investigates the role of sport agents, third-party ownership in football, athletes' remuneration and their economic value, team performance, and individual athletes' contract duration.

Joel Rookwood is Senior Lecturer in sports business management at UCLAN, UK. His research interests include football mega-events, management, enterprise, fandom, social development, and politics, areas in which he has published widely. Joel has visited 165 countries, including every nation of the Americas and every CONCACAF member country.

Paul Salisbury is Senior Lecturer in Sport Management at Coventry University in the UK. He has also held management positions in academia and in the sports sector. Paul's research interests surround sport policy and governance, especially as they relate to sports mega-events. He has been a recipient of the International Olympic Committee's Advanced Research Grant.

Zora Saskova is a PhD researcher at Ulster University. Her ethnographic research explores the ways in which the myriad, complex issues emanating from post-conflict Sierra Leone might impact the extent to which footballers from the country have sought a career abroad. The study also investigates an emerging football migration network between Sierra Leone and Scandinavia.

Sascha L. Schmidt is Senior Professor and Director of the Center for Sports and Management at WHU. "Future of Sports" is his key research area. Prior to his professorship he worked as entrepreneur and as a consultant with McKinsey, and he studied at the universities of Essen, Zurich, St. Gallen, Harvard Business School, and EBS.

Eric C. Schwarz has been a sport business management academician and administrator since 2000 in the US, Australia, and China. He currently is Senior Lecturer in Sport Management, Chair of the Postgraduate Courses in Sport Business and Integrity, and the College of Sport and Exercise Science's Director of Teaching and Learning.

Glaucio Scremin is a life-long learner, an award-winning teacher and scholar, and Associate Professor of Sport Management at the University of West Georgia, US. He investigates the attitudes and perceptions of sport fans. More specifically, he seeks to understand the influence of fan motives on team identity and loyalty.

Jonathan Sibley teaching responsibilities include the delivery of event management lectures and seminars at postgraduate and undergraduate levels as well as supervising dissertations specialising in sports events. In addition, he also contributed to regional workforce development courses in Qatar in preparation for the 2022 FIFA World Cup. Prior to undertaking a career in higher education Jonathan worked at an English professional football club; within this role, he was responsible for all aspects of community engagement. He has recently begun a PhD; the focus of which is ethical governance in English football.

Vitor Sobral is a PhD candidate at University of Queensland. He lectures on international sport and events at University of Queensland and Bond University. He previously worked as a football journalist and covered several major football events, including two Men's and Women's FIFA World Cups and UEFA Euro 2012.

Sten Soderman is Professor Emeritus of International Business at Stockholm Business School, Stockholm University and affiliated researcher at Centre for Sports and Business, Stockholm School of Economics Institute for Research. His research interests are focused on market strategy development and implementation.

Leigh Sparks is Professor of Retail Studies and Deputy Principle at University of Stirling, Scotland, UK. Leigh has been Director of the Institute for Retail Studies and the Dean of the Faculty of Management, and Editor of the leading European retail journal (*The International Review of Retail, Distribution and Consumer Research*, published by Taylor and Francis).

Jonathan Sullivan is Director of the China Policy Institute at the University of Nottingham, and co-founder of the China Soccer Observatory.

Ahmet Talimciler Talimciler graduated from the Sociology Department at Ege University Literature Faculty in 1994. Talimciler became an associate professor in 2011 still teaches at the Literature Faculty, Department of Sociology at Ege University. He has four books on sports media and sociology topics.

Cem Tinaz is Director of the School of Sports Sciences and Technology at Istanbul Bilgi University and a board member of the Turkish Tennis Federation. He has published in the areas of sport policy, sport event management, and sport sponsorship. He has participated as tournament coordinator, director, and marketing manager in many international sport events.

Jos Verschueren is Programme Director Sports Management at Vrije Universiteit Brussel (Brussels Free University – Belgium) in the Faculty of Physical Education and Physiotherapy within the Department of Sports Policy and Management. He is also the founder and manager of the Sport Management Knowledge Centre at the same university and founder of the International Football Business Institute. He has over 15 years of consulting and academic business experience in sports marketing and communication, sports partnership branding, and sports business and management.

Renan Petersen-Wagner is Senior Lecturer in Sport Business and Marketing at Leeds Beckett University, his research interest lies in the cultural consumption of sport, in particular football and the Olympic Games, the Global South, and Critical Social Theory. His research has appeared in *Current Sociology, International Review for the Sociology of Sport*, and the *Journal of Sport & Social Issues*.

Sara Ward joined MMU's Business School in 2008 and heads executive education for the Faculty of Business and Law. Sara specialises in football and sport governance and her current research interests are focused on English and German football clubs, predominantly looking at the supporter ownership business model.

Clint Warren is Assistant Professor of Sport Management in the School of Kinesiology & Recreation at Illinois State University. He earned his PhD from the University of Minnesota, and since that time his research has focused on sport service innovation, value co-creation, ticket sales and service strategy, and ticket sales management. He has a specific interest in examining these, and other, topics in the context of soccer in the United States.

Hagen Wäsche is Senior Lecturer at the Department of Sports and Sports Science at the Karlsruhe Institute of Technology. His research interests lie in the fields of sport management, organisation theory, sport sociology, and the analysis of networks in sport.

Tom Webb is Senior Lecturer in the Department of Sport and Exercise Science at the University of Portsmouth. He writes widely on sports match officials, is author of the book *Elite Soccer*

Referees: Officiating in the Premier League, La Liga and Serie A (2017) and coordinator of the Referee and Match Official Research Network.

Annick Willem is Professor of Sport Management at Ghent University. She is holder of the Olympic Chair Henri de Baillet Latour and Jacques Rogge. Her research interests include interorganisational relationships in public and non-profit sports and knowledge management.

Rob Wilson is the subject head for sport business management at Sheffield Hallam University. His PhD focused on the factors affecting financial performance in professional team sports and he has numerous publications in the sport management field, particularly the financial health and competitive balance of professional football.

Géraldine Zeimers is a PhD candidate in Sport Management at the Université catholique de Louvain and Ghent University. Her research examines implementation of social responsibility practices by non-profit sport organisations. She explores the interaction dynamic involved in managing collaboration among non-profit organisations.

Thierry Zintz is Professor Sport Management at the Université catholique de Louvain. He is holder of the Olympic Chair Henri de Baillet Latour and Jacques Rogge. He investigates good governance and change management in international and national sports governing bodies.

Acknowledgements

The editors would like to thank Taylor and Francis for accepting our proposal to compile this book, and then for publishing it. Specifically, we reserve special mention for Routledge's Sport, Leisure and Tourism team. Particularly, our good friend Simon Whitmore has proven yet again to be a great supporter of academic writing about sport. Otherwise, we send our sincerest thanks to the chapter authors, each of whom worked diligently and professionally to deliver their work – well done all!

Simon salutes his younger, fitter, better looking co-editors, and thanks Barbara and Tom for continuing to tolerate his endless chatter and scribble about football. For me, it's been almost 25 years of researching and writing in this field – it remains an endless source of interest and opportunity. Thankfully, there is now a community of like-minded professionals around to support and sustain our contributions.

Dan would like to express his sincere gratitude to the wide-ranging sterling contributors from around the world. In a time of increasing pressures in academia, taking the time and commitment to see-through such high-quality chapters is a tremendous effort and pays testament to the incredible and collegiate scholars operating in the football research – thank you. This extends to the editorial team for their ongoing support and diligence, notably Simon who provided the impetus to approach the handbook conception – thank you all. Also, thank you to Manchester Metropolitan University and my colleagues in the Business School for their ongoing support. And finally, Sarah, Niamh, George, and Betty for providing their best support anyone can ask for – a loving family.

Paul is grateful to the large number of leading researchers who gave their time to join us in producing this handbook, a football degree in a book. Collating the efforts of a large and diverse group of scholars is a difficult task and we hope that this book is a fitting tribute to the excellence and generosity of our authors. Gratitude goes out to the Sports Business group and wider School of Sport at Leeds Beckett University. Thanks also to Simon Whitmore and the hidden network of individuals at Routledge, whose support has been brilliant throughout. To my fellow co-authors, what a time it was. Finally, to my family, Jayne, Heidi, Paddy, Elsie, and Betsy, thank you for your unconditional love and support. Family, Football, and Work – the holy trinity.

Christos would like to thank the "dream team" of contributors that brought this volume to life. His gratitude goes out to the three co-editors for the work they have done and continue to do together, especially to Simon whose influence on his career – as his MA tutor, PhD supervisor, colleague, but also co-author in several scholarly studies – is immeasurable. Special thanks to Molde University College that afforded him the time and resources to travel around the world and meet most of the contributors in this handbook. A huge "Thank You" for the endless patience, support and love of his wife Demetra; unfortunately for her, this handbook will bring even more "football discussions" into the house! Inevitable, if one considers that their 15-month-old son, Charis' first ever word was "GOAL".

Introduction to the handbook of football business and management

Simon Chadwick, Daniel Parnell, Paul Widdop,
and Christos Anagnostopoulos

Football is commonly referred to as the global game, which is a testament to the sport's enduring appeal. Many countries claim to have been the originators of football as we now know it, though it is over the last 150 years that the sport which most of us are familiar with has emerged and developed. Initially, football was predominantly a socio-cultural phenomenon in the way that it drew people and communities together under a common identity. As the twentieth century progressed and professional sport took hold, management in football became a key consideration for participants and observers of the game. Later, the influence of North American capitalism began to exert its influence such that, by the end of the twentieth century, the likes of television rights, sponsorships, and club ownership began to fundamentally change the nature and organisation of the sport. And as the twenty-first century matures, there are new issues and challenges, not least those brought about by globalisation, and by ongoing concerns about governance in football. Yet among these many and varied changes to the game, there is still great affection for it among fans; its relationship with the media remains symbiotic; governments still recognise its importance; and businesses know it makes good commercial sense to be involved with it.

Now more than ever, good management is required to ensure that football remains robust and relevant. Rapid societal and technological changes mean that the sport now has serious competition for its dominance of the sport, leisure and entertainment narratives. At the same time, the level of scrutiny that football is now exposed to ensures that decisions made on everything from event-bidding to the signing of sponsorship contracts are examined at an almost forensic level of detail. There are new challenges too, not least in the growing influence of states and corporations on football. With elite professional clubs increasingly owned by American investors, Asian governments or those intent on building franchise networks, this potentially has profound consequences for everything from player transfer markets through to branding, marketing, and financial decisions. At the same time, the lifeblood of the sport – players and fans – continue to occupy a prominent position in football's landscape. Fans are consuming it in new and different ways, whilst retaining the fervency and strength of their team affiliations. Players are always in demand; spotting, acquiring, retaining, and rewarding them are arguably now bigger challenges than ever before.

In this context, there has arguably never been a more important time for managers in football, especially given the additional business pressures that clubs, representative associations and other related organisations must contend with. As such, the purpose of this book is to highlight and analyse the most important issues facing the sport. Drawing from their extensive experience of the game (as players, fans, advisers, consultants, researchers, and observers), the editors have drawn together a group of leading writers who examine the sport's most salient issues and challenges using a combination of academic and practical insights. We deliberately adopt a business and management approach in the book which, whilst addressing commercial aspects of football, nevertheless acknowledges and embraces its socio-political dimensions too. As such, the reader will find that the book covers fields such as sponsorship, agents, and social media, while also addressing grassroots football and governing bodies.

The book is targeted at students and staff studying or working on football and sport business management programmes in universities across the world. Given the book's multi-disciplinary nature, we also believe that it may also be of interest to event management, sport studies, sport sciences, and sociology of sport students and staff. Other programmes, which contain sport management or business modules are also likely to find considerable relevance in the work presented here. Furthermore, we envisage the book being of interest to people working in football, and to people generally who have an interest in the sport. As such, we have sought to ensure that the content of it is as accessible to as wide a range of audiences as possible. This has been achieved through, for example, the examination of prominent issues, and the use of appropriate case material.

To further supplement the readings in this book, the reader's attention is drawn to the Twitter timelines for each of the editors:

- Simon Chadwick @Prof_Chadwick
- Dan Parnell @parnell_daniel
- Paul Widdop @Fire_and_Skill
- Christos Anagnostopoulos @chrisanagno

In addition, readers may find the following are activities, in which members of the editorial team are engaged, to be helpful:

- Football Collective https://footballcollective.org.uk
- China Soccer Observatory http://www.nottingham.ac.uk/iaps/cso/index.aspx

A framework for diversification decisions in professional football

Sascha L. Schmidt and Florian Holzmayer

Introduction

The burgeoning European football market has provoked increasing competition between clubs for further growth. Besides strengthening the core football business, new related revenue sources will be decisive for the future growth of football clubs. *Digitalisation* offers numerous opportunities for a football club's growth portfolio as it entails new technologies and changing consumer behaviour. These opportunities, however, also increase the complexity for clubs to act in a changing environment. As such, they may lead the clubs to advanced management requirements in terms of corporate strategy, which is defined as "the scope of the firm in terms of the industries and markets in which it competes" (Grant, 2016).

In order to ensure competitive longevity, a structured strategy development approach has become inevitable for football clubs. The implementation of such an approach entails two main aspects. First, a football club is required to answer the crucial strategic question – where to compete? (Grant, 2016). From a corporate perspective, this means finding the right level of *related* versus *unrelated diversification*. The level of relatedness must be examined in terms of business activities and geographical reach. Second, clubs need to consciously manage a portfolio of growth initiatives that leverage and combine its existing resources with those that are newly acquired. This structural approach will support clubs in countering the interdependency of financial and sportive performance in football.

Evidence suggests the existence of an upwards trend between financial and sportive performance in professional football (Szymanski and Smith, 1997; Dobson and Goddard, 2011). As such, superior financial resources increase the likelihood of higher sportive performance through, for instance, investments into new players. At the same time, sportive performance has a positive impact on a club's revenues (Dobson and Goddard, 2011; Rohde and Breuer, 2016). However, sportive underperformance may lead to a downward spiral. As a result, professional football clubs attempt to reduce the interdependency of financial and sportive performance. New digital business models help to decouple earnings from football success and enable a broader risk distribution. In this respect, professional clubs are on the verge of reinventing themselves and taking on the structure of corporate organisations that operate in a diverse range of businesses.

In order to guide football clubs in their growth development, we introduce the *Growth Strategy (GS) framework*, which is rooted in diversification literature (e.g., Rumelt, 1974; 1982; Palepu, 1985; Chatterjee and Wernerfelt, 1991; Vachani, 1991; Markides and Williamson, 1994; Kumar, 2013; Kim, Hoskisson, and Lee, 2015). Overall, the 3×3 matrix entails nine distinct principal strategies along the two dimensions – *business proximity* and *regionality*. The GS framework is intended to support football clubs in making profound decisions about where to allocate their resources and select the most suitable diversification path in order to stimulate further growth. Case examples illustrate the applicability of the GS framework.

This chapter is divided into six sections. After the introduction, we review the characteristics and recent developments of the European football industry followed by a discussion about the impact of digitalisation on football market growth. Next, we derive learnings from diversification theory. These provide the basis for developing the GS framework, for which we then define principal strategies for each cell and illustrate their applicability with case examples. Subsequently, we describe diversification paths within the GS framework. Finally, we discuss the contribution and limitations of the GS framework and provide an outlook for future research based on our work.

The European football industry

The European football industry is governed by the Union of European Football Associations (UEFA), which embodies one of the most significant members of the Federation of International Football Associations (FIFA). Among a range of activities, UEFA is responsible for delivering some of the world's most prestigious football competitions. At the international level, it organises the UEFA European Championship for national teams, which is regarded as one of the most viewed TV broadcasts worldwide (e.g., Schreyer, Schmidt, and Torgler, 2017). At the club level, the UEFA organises the UEFA Champions League (CL), which has enjoyed enormous success from a commercial and broadcasting perspective (Drut and Raballand, 2012). In the CL, the top football clubs in Europe stand in direct competition and earn large payouts (Peeters, 2011), regardless of whether or not they perform well in the competition (Pawlowski, Breuer, and Hovemann, 2010). Regular appearance in the CL not only benefits clubs financially, but also the leagues through exposure as they compete in major international TV markets. Clubs from the big five European leagues (i.e., English Premier League, German Bundesliga, Spanish LaLiga, Italian Serie A, and French Lique 1), in particular, have profited as they are consistently part of the CL.

The big five European leagues have been consistently growing by almost 30 per cent over four seasons reaching revenues of €13.6 billion in 2015/16 (Deloitte, 2016; 2017). Today, and according to Deloitte's (2017) latest reports, competition occurs mainly between the clubs' core businesses, comprising broadcasting (49 per cent), commercial (34 per cent) and match day revenues (17 per cent). Broadcasting represents the major income source and is fuelled by recently renewed national TV contracts in the UK, Spain, Italy, and Germany (Deloitte, 2017). Although the core national market remains the most important revenue source for European clubs, the share of international revenues is growing quickly. For example, in the 2013–2016 cycle almost 60 per cent of broadcasting revenues in the English Premier League (EPL) could be accounted to national TV contracts. Yet, "EPL revenues generated from international media rights have become an increasingly important source of income" (Schreyer, Schmidt, and Torgler, 2016c), growing from 24 per cent to more than 40 per cent of broadcasting revenues from the 2004–2007 to the 2013–2016 cycle (Schreyer, Schmidt, and Torgler, 2016c; UEFA, 2016).

However, for clubs, achieving additional revenue growth is difficult, because they do not have full managerial control over the product they offer. In competitive sports systems,[1] clubs need each other to produce football (Cairns, Jennett, and Sloane, 1986). This means that on the one hand, clubs must cooperate. On the other hand, they stand in direct sportive competition. Contrary to typical economic activity where businesses do not necessarily rely on cooperation, in competitive sports systems "the greater the economic collusion and the more the sporting competition the greater the profits" (Neale, 1964). This phenomenon has attracted much research as it is unique to sports business. Scholars have, therefore, explored the role of the determinants in shaping the demand for the product, which might be the drivers for revenues in turn. These might include, inter alia, the competitive balance within a league and the resulting game outcome uncertainty,[2] or the role of superstars (e.g., Brandes, Franck, and Nüesch, 2008). Such determinants, however, are difficult to manage as they cannot be influenced directly by the clubs. In fact, even if they were to be controlled for, physical assets such as a club's stadium capacity might present boundaries, while the number of TV viewers will not increase endlessly. Hence, the current growth development in the core football business might be opposed to limits at some point.

Within this competitive landscape, clubs must identify new investments outside their core business in order to compete for the attention of the football fan. Additionally, clubs may advance their core business internationally. For both aspects, football clubs hold a distinct advantage as compared to other companies in the entertainment industry: They enjoy oligopolistic access to the game of football and its resources.

The impact of digitalisation on European football

According to representatives from the football business in Germany, Austria, and Switzerland, digitalisation is identified as the main driver for future growth in the football market (Schmidt and Eberhard, 2016). In our view, digitalisation entails two key factors that impact the core football business: new technologies, and changing consumer behaviour. These, in turn, lead to an acceleration of the clubs' internationalisation, and the emergence of new digital business models related or unrelated to the existing core business.

New technologies such as cloud computing or integrated software solutions (i.e., club management systems), and their appropriate application, are critical for successful growth (Schmidt and Krause, 2017). These have already and will continue to further strengthen the process efficiency and effectiveness of the core football business. Moreover, new technologies have created new opportunities for the management of customer relationships and the handling of substantial amounts of data (Schmidt and Eberhard, 2016). For example, the use of *big data* has revolutionised football itself. In just minutes, football players can create more than seven million data points with only three balls (Curtis, 2014). The availability of datasets has led to the employment of data scientists, who can interpret and process the information into key insights for on- and off-pitch strategic purposes.

In addition, new technologies impact the football spectator experience and multiplied "the possibilities of enjoying sports content" (Evens and Lefever, 2011). They fundamentally changed the game experience for the fan. For instance, augmented reality or virtual reality goggles enable a fan to see the 360-degree perspective of a player or a referee and might make it possible to project the stadium experience into the living room, soon. Real-time statistics, super slow motion, video highlights, or interactive content further improved the fan experience during gameplay. In the future, fans might be able to choose a camera on their favourite player's jersey via smart glasses or contact lenses using eye movements, whilst also reviewing the specific fitness and performance statistics of a player[3]. Experts see the sports industry in a pioneer role to introduce "yet unforeseen digital technologies" (Merkel, Schmidt, and Schreyer, 2016).

Besides the emergence of new technologies, consumer behaviour has changed. *Digital natives* have grown up with the Internet and manage their daily business on smart devices. They outnumbered traditional consumers in 2013 and will overtake digital converts soon (PWC, 2014), becoming the most important football consumers in the near future. Nowadays, fans leave digital footprints in all their online activities, making them transparent in terms of personal data. This encourages clubs to create individualised, custom-tailored content that is distributed "across as many multi-media platforms as possible" (Santomier and Hogan, 2013). Hereby, data mining and CRM systems are once more important to predict distinct behavioural patterns and to hold the attention of their fans while competing with other leisure and entertainment providers.

Since the Internet unlocks new sales channels to distribute content around the world with very limited marginal costs, internationalisation in football has been facilitated and accelerated. As a result, we have seen strong growth rates of new international broadcasting contracts in England, Germany, and Italy (Deloitte, 2016, 2017). This is not surprising since digital natives are often also fans without borders, following their second- or third-favourite club abroad. The variety of digital news and the increased mobility provide them with a feeling of greater proximity to their favourite international clubs. In the past, fans had to purchase a newspaper in order to discover how their favourite team abroad had performed. Today, fans can track scores, monitor newsfeeds, and watch video streams live.

Fans without borders can also follow their chosen stars, look for rare sports events, or hold a personal connection to their preferred team abroad (Schmidt and Schreyer, 2012). Following superstars via social media and other digital channels plays an important role for fans without borders. Evidence suggests "a positive effect of superstar characteristics and role model perception on team identification" (Hoegele, Schmidt, and Torgler, 2014). Fans are willing to spend money on merchandise or broadcasting offerings for their cross-border favourites even if they might not regularly be onsite for home matches. Clubs seek to endear to their fans abroad by creating an integrated digital fan experience, thus strengthening the fan bond and increasing fan loyalty. Manchester United can be named as best practice example in responding to changed consumer behaviour with its recently launched digital app that will broadcast its own MUTV channel and content across 165 countries (Cohen, 2017). Other clubs like Schalke 04, Manchester City, or Ajax Amsterdam have entered the emerging *e-sports* business to extent their reach internationally.

Insights from diversification theory

The choice of business portfolio is a critical part of a corporate strategy (Markides and Williamson, 1994). This is due the fact that a diversified portfolio can offer many benefits but also serious costs implications. For this choice, digitalisation offers enormous growth opportunities for a football club that maximises potential benefits. However, given that clubs have only limited resources to invest into growth initiatives, it is crucial to decide on where to compete. This entails answering questions of where and to what extent to diversify when choosing among different business opportunities. Limited diversification entails the challenge of risk concentration, especially in a money intensive business such as football where sportive underperformance can provoke a financial downward spiral. Certainly, there is no "one size fits all" solution to cope with digitalisation. However, a clear guidance for categorising and deciding on corporate diversification, "i.e., decisions on the entry into new lines of activity," (Speckbacher, Neumann, and Hoffmann, 2015) is central for the growth of a club.

Diversification has been examined from portfolio and strategic management perspectives. Drawing on modern portfolio theory (MPT), diversification is identified as the underlying factor in the context of portfolio selection (Markowitz, 1952). MPT outlines the importance of choosing assets that are diversified and not positively correlated. The aim is to maximise return and minimise risk. From a strategic management perspective, Wu (2013) states, "firms diversify in order to leverage firm-specific resources for which factor markets are imperfect". This is in line with the resource-based view suggested by Penrose (1959) and Teece (1982) and further supported by Datta, Rajagopalan, and Rasheed (1991). This school of thought summarises potential benefits from diversification literature as performance improvements from scale and scope economies, and skill synergies. In contrast, it can also be associated with costs from bureaucracy, control, and resource inefficiencies.

Decades of research on diversification have examined influential factors and motives for diversification decisions. Building on Dhir and Dhir (2015), these include, inter alia, resources (e.g., Chatterjee and Wernerfelt, 1991; Miller, 2004; Sakhartov and Folta, 2014), geography and environment (e.g., Chakrabarti, Singh and Mahmood, 2007; Mayer and Whittington, 2003; Diestre and Rajagopalan, 2011; Kim, Hoskisson, and Lee, 2015), competition (e.g., Wiersema and Bowen, 2008; Lien and Klein, 2013), technological changes (e.g., Lu and Beamish, 2004; Lange, Boivie, and Henderson, 2009), leadership characteristics (e.g., Jensen and Zajac, 2004), risk (e.g., Montgomery and Singh, 1984; Wang and Barney, 2006), dynamic capabilities (e.g., Døving and Gooderham, 2008), ownership (e.g., Alessandri and Seth, 2014), or diversification experiences (e.g., Mayer, Stadler, and Hautz, 2015) of a firm.

Diversification choices

Besides examining these factors and motives, research on diversification distinguishes between the choice of relatedness, entry options and entry decisions for a firm, which can be classified as *level, mode,* and *type of diversification* (Dhir and Dhir, 2015). The level of diversification comprises the spectrum from related to unrelated diversification (e.g., Rumelt, 1974; Palepu, 1985; Chatterjee and Wernerfelt, 1991; Vachani, 1991; Kumar, 2013). While the level of diversification considers corporate decisions on where to compete, the type and mode of diversification focus on how to compete concerning the implementation aspects of diversification. Accordingly, the mode of diversification defines entry or execution forms of diversification through internal development, alliances, and acquisitions (e.g., Villalonga and McGahan, 2005; Yin and Shanley, 2008). Finally, the type of diversification refers to horizontal, vertical, concentric, and conglomerate diversification moves (e.g., Ansoff, 1965).

Scholars such as Lubatkin (1983), Montgomery (1985), and Palepu (1985) have argued "that the primary determinant of firm performance is not the extent of diversification [e.g., diversification versus focus], but the direction or relatedness in diversification" (Park, 2002). Thereby, when deciding on its corporate strategy, a firm needs to differentiate between relatedness in terms of business activities (e.g., product or business unit) and relatedness in terms of geography (Vachani, 1991). Corporate strategy-making should therefore consider two levels of diversification relatedness: *business proximity* and *regionality*.

The Growth Strategy (GS) framework

Founded on learnings from diversification theory, we establish the Growth Strategy (GS) framework. The framework's first dimension, business proximity, entails *core, related,* or *unrelated* business activities. The second dimension, regionality, entails a football club's business activities in *national, close-by,* or *global* geographical region(s). This framework addresses a current lack of go-to guidelines for corporate strategy considerations regarding emerging digitalisation opportunities. Existing strategy frameworks, for example, by Ansoff (1957, 1958), Ayal and Zif (1979),

Ade (1993), Kotler (1999) or Gupta and Govindarajan (2000), are mainly concerned with the product-market level and thus, do not offer these go-to guidelines for corporate strategy accordingly.

The business proximity dimension

Diversification decisions are central to capture, evaluate, and structure new growth opportunities in the football market. Thereby, the strength of the existing core business determines these decisions, since it provides the funding for (un)related diversification decisions. We define the core business of a professional football club as the classical football department, which builds on revenues from broadcasting, commercial and match-day activities. Referring to Teece (1982), this "core business may provide critical resources to a related segment in the form of knowledge and human capital" (Kumar, 2013). Hence, it represents the starting point for relatedness decisions. We therefore label the first divide within the business proximity dimension of our GS framework as *core*.

Related versus unrelated diversification of business activities

Many scientific studies have identified the competitive advantages of related diversification over unrelated diversification of business activities. The competitive advantages include growth, profitability, firm value, or costs benefits (e.g., Rumelt, 1974; 1982; Palepu, 1985; Markides and Williamson, 1994; Sakhartov and Folta, 2014; 2015). These benefits are explained by synergies in resources from economies of scope (e.g., Teece, 1980; 1982), R&D aspects or resource sharing (e.g., Wan, 2005; Lim, Das, and Das, 2009) and resource redeployment (e.g., Sakhartov and Folta, 2014; 2015). In addition, some scholars state that even related diversification helps to minimise risks (e.g., Lubatkin and Chatterjee, 1994). Even though most scholars favour related diversification in terms of business activities, Kumar (2013) highlights "productivity shifts and the concomitant subsidisation of the core business" as substantial costs beside complexity considerations (Zhou, 2011). However, for football clubs, synergy generation and risk minimisation through related diversification seem in particular attractive with their dependency on sportive performance in the core business.

In addition to the output differentials of related and unrelated diversification, resource *input* also influences the level of diversification. In particular, intangible assets, external financial resources, and a surplus of physical resources are connected to increased related diversification (Chatterjee and Wernerfelt, 1991). This emphasises the importance of the current and future resource endowment when deciding on related diversification moves. For football clubs, the existence of physical assets such as stadiums, training facilities or business areas offer many opportunities for related diversification entries. Moreover, knowledge-based resources like databases on customer behaviour taken from ticketing and merchandising sales can be used for cross- and upselling purposes of football-related products and services. Interestingly, successful firms find an expansion formula over time that allows them to predict and repeat related moves (Zook and Allen, 2003). With this repeatability, a club can grow systematically and make use of learning effects. We therefore name *related* business activities as the second divide along the business proximity dimension.

In comparison, unrelated diversification is associated with more destructive effects but might provide interesting aspects in the football market context. Although some scholars have found beneficial financial economies (e.g., Hill and Hoskisson, 1987) from unrelated diversification, evidence suggests that it might lead to lower performance (e.g., Ramanujam and Varadarajan, 1989; Chatterjee and Wernerfelt, 1991; Palich, Cardinal, and Miller, 2000) due to higher learning costs and weaker scope economies (Kumar, 2013). However, given the volatility of the foot-ball market, a move into an unrelated business could be beneficial to hedge periods of sportive and subsequently financial underperformance – assuming that financial resources from the broadcasting and commercial activities at the core can be made available. Thereby, such unrelated diversification would need a clear plan and leadership with a careful consideration of all stakeholders, options, and eventualities (Zook and Allen, 2010). In order to incorporate these considerations into the GS framework, we label the third divide within the business proximity dimension as *unrelated*.

The regionality dimension

In management literature, the performance effect of geographic diversification over time has been an intensively discussed topic (e.g., Vachani, 1991; Kim, Hoskisson, and Lee, 2015; Patel, Criaco, and Naldi, 2016). Taking a resource-based view, it is argued that firms can already have positive performance effects in early stages of international expansion due to firm specific advantages from the home market. In contrast, the organational learning theory advocates for performance increases in a later stage from learning effects and exploration of new resources (Kim, Hoskisson, and Lee, 2015). Other scholars highlight the negative effects of geographic diversification (e.g., Patel, Criaco, and Naldi, 2016). Importantly, the geographic relatedness between countries is underlined as a crucial factor when deciding on the level of geographic diversification (Vachani, 1991). Although the overall necessity to grow due to the increasing competition pushes clubs to extend their core business into foreign markets, their national football business still remains the most important revenue source. Hence, the *national* region represents the starting point for geographic expansion and will present the first divide within the regionality dimension of our GS framework.

Related versus unrelated geographic diversification

When diversifying geographically, clubs need to review the characteristics of potential markets, as well as its endogenous aspects. According to Vachani (1991), the geographic relatedness of diversification including the physical and cultural proximity between regions is a critical characteristic to consider. Yet, the economic development of the regions can also play a crucial role. In terms of its endogenous aspects, a firm needs to review its resources and capabilities as "firms choose to globally diversify based on their firm attributes" (Chang et al., 2016).

Evidence suggests that related geographic diversification is more profitable than its unrelated counterpart. This is due to a range of benefits including less complex operations (Ronen and Shenkar, 1985), more spillover effects (Daniels and Radebaugh, 1989), lower coordination costs (Grant, 1987) and more similarities between intangible assets and the target country's characteristics (Vachani, 1989). Regions with low cultural, administrative/political, geographic, and economic distances (Ghemawat, 2001) compared to the home market seem to be attractive for geographical expansion of football clubs. It enables them to utilise and reinforce the strength of the national business. As such, we label *close-by* regions as the second divide within the regionality dimension.

However, digital sales and social media channels diminish national borders and enable clubs to not only consider close-by regions for geographical diversification but also the global market. To further internationalise, a step-by-step geographic expansion, starting with a low-commitment expansion into related markets and increasing gradually in terms of commitment and geographical distance is suggested (Johanson and Vahlne, 1977). Johanson and Vahlne (2009) emphasise the business network that a firm acts in as key for its internationalisation process. It is argued that this network is borderless and it is important to strengthen the position within the network. The football market can be perceived as a similar network when thinking about attracting new fans around the globe.

In order to gain additional merchandise and broadcasting revenues internationally, European clubs already compete through international tours (van Overloop, 2015), establishing local offices or international cooperation agreements. During the preseason 2017/18, more than 26 European top clubs were touring across North America, Asia and Australia led by 11 British and five German clubs (Burson-Marsteller, 2017). Leading clubs, such as Bayern Munich, FC Barcelona, Real Madrid, and Manchester United installed local offices on these continents in order to drive the expansion of their core business internationally (Lakhani, et al., 2016; Marsden, 2016; Schmidt, 2017). While local offices and staff can be afforded by the top clubs, those with fewer (financial) resources typically compete by signing international cooperation agreements with local partners. For instance, several Bundesliga clubs closed partnerships with Chinese football clubs (1. FC Cologne, Hamburger SV) or built local Chinese youth academies in Germany (Eintracht Frankfurt) (HSV, 2016; 1. FC Köln, 2017; Eintracht Frankfurt, 2017). To account for these internationalisation efforts of football clubs on a global scale, a third regional divide within the regionality dimensions is named *global* region(s).

In summary, the GS framework is a corporate strategy tool. It consists of a 3×3 matrix with nine distinct principal strategies for growth (see Figure 2.1) along the dimensions of business proximity and regionality. The former consists of core, related, and unrelated business activities and the latter of national, close-by, and global region(s) for geographic diversification.

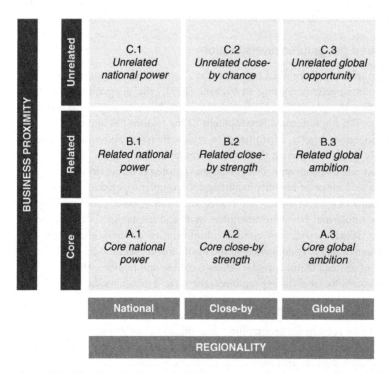

Figure 2.1　The Growth Strategy (GS) Framework for European Football Clubs

Portfolio growth options

Each of the nine cells of the GS framework entails a distinct portfolio growth option. These options include different levels of risk and return. For each cell of the framework, a principal strategy can be defined and illustrated with case examples.

Figure 2.1 cell A.1: A *core national power* strategy focuses on the core football business in the region of origin. It could cover improvements of the existing core business through new technologies such as cloud computing or integrated software solutions, or infrastructure investments in a smart stadium or innovative training facilities. For example, Borussia Dortmund and TSG Hoffenheim installed the so-called Footbonaut, a training machine used to systematically improve players' ball control at speed and in short-spaces (Zhu, et al., 2015).

Figure 2.1 cell A.2: A *core close-by strength* strategy extends the football core business towards neighbouring regions. It could imply a partnership agreement with a smaller club to identify, train, and shape new football talent. For example, Chelsea FC unofficially cooperates with Dutch club Vitesse Arnheim. Youth players from London are lent to Arnheim to ensure they receive playing time, and in best case, the market value of players increases (Conn, 2017). Bundesliga club RB Leipzig operates a similar cooperation with its partner club RB Salzburg in Austria.

Figure 2.1 cell A.3: A *core global ambition* strategy expands the core business to distant regions such as the opening of international offices. For example, FC Barcelona toured the entire U.S. East Coast and opened an outpost in New York City in 2016 with plans to introduce further offices around the world (Marsden, 2016). With this strategy, the club geographically entered a less known territory away from its home and close-by regions, whilst promoting its core football business through additional merchandising sales or new sponsoring agreements. Another example of a core global ambition strategy is Manchester United's launch of a new digital app, which will broadcast MUTV, the club's dedicated television channel, to 165 countries. The main aim of this strategy is to capitalise on untapped revenue potential by increasing its merchandise sales across their 659 million followers worldwide (Cohen, 2017).

Figure 2.1 cell B.1: A *related national power* strategy entails business activities in the home region that are related to the core football business such as the construction of a new multi-purpose high-tech stadium. Examples of these include the plans of football club Tottenham Hotspur to provide a fully customisable home to host also American football games from the NFL. In the future, the club is even flirting with the idea of cross-discipline offerings (Vrentas, 2017). In addition, top clubs increasingly invest into the opening of attractions (e.g., museums, stadium tours, or escape rooms – an interactive game through which visitors need to crack different puzzles to solve an overall case) at their stadiums or the surrounding facilities. Besides European top clubs, smaller clubs like Athletic Club Bilbao or Olympique de Marseille recently inaugurated museums or announced plans to do so (KPMG, 2017).

Figure 2.1 cell B.2: A *related close-by strength* strategy comprises related business activities in neighbouring regions. For example, European clubs such as Schalke 04, VfL Wolfsburg, AS Rome, Manchester City, FC Valencia, Sporting Lisbon, Ajax Amsterdam, Paris Saint-Germain, and Besiktas Istanbul have expanded into e-sports competitions. Each of these clubs has established e-sports teams that compete against each other in the football simulation game FIFA. These tournaments are often organised by the clubs themselves in close-by European markets.

Figure 2.1 cell B.3: A *related global ambition* strategy covers related business activities on a global scale. This strategic approach relates, for instance, to investments in ventures that are concerned with sports technology around the globe. For instance, Arsenal FC recently announced a collaboration with corporate innovation specialist L Marks for the launch of an Arsenal Innovation Lab. The idea is to work closely with start-ups to identify ground-breaking new fan experiences and move the club's international business forward. Although based in London, the ten-week start-up accelerator program is open for teams around the globe (Claxton, 2017). Another example is provided by Schalke 04, who entered the League of Legends e-sports market by acquiring and rebranding the e-sports team Element in 2016 (Wolf, 2016). This move into the world's most popular strategy game provides Schalke 04 access to a global fan base and is still related to the core business, given professional e-sports teams need to be managed in a similar fashion to that employed for their professional football teams (e.g., training, nutrition, sponsoring, and merchandising).

Figure 2.1 cell C.1: An *unrelated national power* strategy entails a completely new business activity in the home region that is not related to the existing football core business. For instance, a football club could invest into a new national sports league (e.g., drone racing, e-sports) or acquire shares of a national technology start-up. The unrelated investment would have the character of a business option that neither requires much financial resources nor top management attention but would spread the risk within the business portfolio. In case the new business is successful, the club would participate with its shares; in case of failure, the financial loss would be limited.

Figure 2.1 cell C.2: An *unrelated close-by chance* strategy comprises a business activity unrelated to the core business with a focus on neighbouring regions. Building on the example from cell C.1 in the GS framework, a football club could invest into a new European sports league or acquire shares of a European technology start-up. This unrelated investment would work like a business option for the club as outlined for cell C.1.

Figure 2.1 cell C.3: An *unrelated global opportunity* strategy includes a business activity in faraway regions. At the same time, this business activity would have no direct link to the existing core business, maximising the risk distribution and independency from the core business. Analogue to cells C.1 and C.2, the football club could invest into a new global sports league or acquire shares of a technology start-up active in distant markets.

Diversification paths

Taking a strategic perspective, the GS framework equips a club with the means to map and incorporate growth initiatives from digitalisation. The starting point for all diversification considerations should be the core national football business (Figure 2.1 cell A.1), generating the major part of revenues that are crucial for diversification activities. At the same time, the dependency on sportive performance remains strong with most of a club's activities in the core national market. To expand outside this market, a professional football club can explore various diversification paths within the GS framework (see Figure 2.2). There are two generic diversification paths that start from the core national football business.

Path 1: A club might advance along the regionality dimension and decide to internationalise into close-by regions or even capture global opportunities to extend the core business. Here, familiarity with markets plays the most important role as it facilitates market-entry efforts. However, the further the business is extended beyond national borders the more the club taps into new ground, while at the same time hedges against volatilities on the national market.

Path 2: A club might choose to diversify by moving along the business proximity dimension into related or unrelated business activities. Within related opportunities, the club can leverage existing skills from the core business as it remains within the sports industry but moves outside the football market. With unrelated business activities, a club attains a more balanced level of overall risk distribution as unrelated business activities are not correlated to the core football business. As a result, the dependency on sportive performance is reduced.

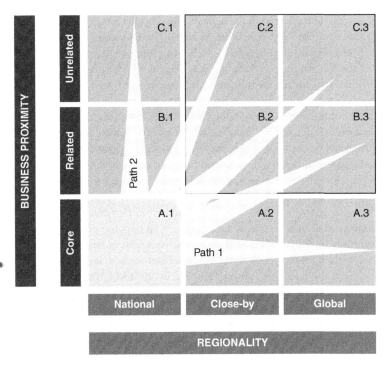

Figure 2.2 Diversification Paths Within the GS Framework

Since there is no "one size fits all" approach to diversification, each club needs to consider an individual path to growth. The two illustrated generic diversification paths are suitable for clubs that have exploited their core national business and start to seek out first options to grow outside their current competitive arena. Top European clubs, such as Manchester United, Real Madrid, FC Barcelona or Bayern Munich, face rather saturated home markets and have therefore already started to diversify into new businesses and geographies. Hence, opportunities away from their core business and national market (see Figure 2.2 cells B.2, B.3, C.2 and C.3) become more attractive for further diversification and growth. In doing so, lower revenues from the core business in periods of underperformance can be hedged with contributions from related or unrelated business activities on international markets. However, a diversified portfolio of business activities per se is not a guarantee for financial success. It is complex to manage and requires a lot of management attention. As such, it involves constant examination in terms of, inter alia, realised synergies from economies of scope and scale, risk reduction, and potential inefficiencies.

Contribution and outlook

Deducted from diversification theory, the GS framework aims to support football clubs in reducing complexity resulting from almost unlimited digitalisation opportunities in terms of new technologies and changing consumer behaviour. In turn, these accelerate the clubs' internationalisation, and create new digital business models. The GS framework should help in making profound decisions from a corporate level on where to compete within these opportunities. Thereby, the 3×3-matrix improves resource allocation within a club's business portfolio along the business proximity and regionality dimensions. Clubs shall identify growth opportunities along nine principal strategies and various diversification paths that can be implemented with the underlying resources of a club.

Conclusively, it advances existing diversification frameworks focused on the product-market level (e.g., Ansoff, 1957; 1958; Ayal and Zif, 1979; Ade, 1993; Kotler, 1999; Gupta and Govindarajan, 2000) by allowing to sort in the digitalisation opportunities from a corporate perspective.

Besides the benefits of the GS framework, there are also limitations that need to be mentioned. The GS framework is a tool for the identification and evaluation of strategic diversification options. It might primarily assist football clubs from the big five European leagues that have already reached a certain level of maturity and professionalism. For less advanced clubs with very limited financial resources, focusing on the core business might be of first strategic priority, instead of seeking out related or unrelated business opportunities nationally or internationally. Further, the GS framework does not address the question of how to compete in a new business or geographic field since it concentrates on principal strategies on the corporate level. Hence, it is not concerned with the respective diversification type (e.g., horizontal or vertical) and mode (e.g., internal development, alliance, or acquisitions) that would need to be considered for implementation measures. In addition, the GS framework shall only be the starting point for an ongoing portfolio review process. The aim is to obtain a balanced portfolio of growth initiatives while constantly questioning borders and barriers within and on the periphery of the club's business activities.

With regards to future research, we see three areas to empirically test and further develop the GS framework: First, the output perspective of diversification strategies for football clubs needs further consideration. An empirical analysis of the short- and long-term performance implications as well as cost effects from related or unrelated diversification decisions by football clubs with regards to business proximity and regionality would be insightful. Second, the current diversification approaches of football clubs have to be examined empirically from an input perspective. The resource classification used by Chatterjee and Wernerfelt (1991) in terms of physical resources, intangible assets, and financial resources and its impact on the level of diversification might provide a starting point. As such, it may be adapted to the football market context. Insights could aid understanding as to why clubs diversify in different manners with their underlying resources. Third, the impact of diversification strategies (e.g., through learnings from related or unrelated diversification) on the core business needs empirical investigation. At the same time, the effects of increasing complexity in managing a diversified business portfolio should be examined.

Notes

1 Each of the big five European leagues involves 18 to 20 clubs, which play each other twice per season, resulting in 34 to 38 games for each club from August to May. As they are open league systems, promotion and relegation from the second divisions is possible. In addition, national cup competitions involving clubs from a country's different leagues are organised on a knockout basis (e.g., FA Cup, Copa del Rey de Fútbol or DFB-Pokal).

2 The role of game outcome uncertainty in shaping the demand for professional football has been examined recently (e.g., Cox, 2015; Pérez, Puente, and Rodríguez, 2017; Scelles, 2017; Schreyer, Schmidt, and Torgler, 2016a; 2016b; 2016c; 2017).

3 It is worth noting, that the increasing use of these new technologies is also likely to have a significant impact on future stadium attendance demand. In fact, as Schreyer und Däuper (2017) observe, in the German Bundesliga, the second most-attended professional sporting league in the world (DFL, 2017), currently about every tenth ticket sold remains unused and this number is likely to further increase as technology changes the way fans consume the game.

References

1. FC Köln (2017) *Der 1. FC Köln besucht China.* [online] Retrieved from: https://fc.de/fc-info/news/detailseite/details/der-1-fc-koeln-besucht-china/

Ade, S. (1993) Market concentration versus market diversification and internationalization. Implications for MNE performance. *International Marketing Review*, [e-journal] 10(2), 40–59. [online] Retrieved from: http://dx.doi.org/10.1108/02651339310032543

Alessandri, T.M. and Seth, A. (2014) The effects of managerial ownership on international and business diversification. Balancing incentives and risks. *Strategic Management Journal*, [e-journal] 35(13), 2064–2075. [online] Retrieved from: http://dx.doi.org/10.1002/smj.2222

Ansoff, H.I. (1957) Strategies for diversification. *Harvard Business Review*, 35(5), 113–124.

Ansoff, H.I. (1958) A model for diversification. *Management Science*, 4(4), 392–414.

Ansoff, H.I. (1965) *Corporate Strategy. An Analytical Approach to Business Policy for Growth And Expansion*. New York, NY: McGraw Hill Book Co.

Ayal, I. and Zif, J. (1979) Market expansion strategies in multinational marketing. *Journal of Marketing*, [e-journal] 43(2), 84–94. [online] Retrieved from: http://dx.doi.org/10.2307/1250744

Brandes, L., Franck, E., and Nüesch, S. (2008) Local heroes and superstars. An empirical analysis of star attraction in German soccer. *Journal of Sports Economics*, [e-journal] 9(3), 266–286. [online] Retrieved from: http://dx.doi.org/10.1007/978-3-8350-5429-5_3

Burson-Marsteller (2017) *Planet Football Report. Strategies for International Success*. Brussels: Burson-Marsteller.

Cairns, J., Jennett, N., and Sloane, P.J. (1986) The economics of professional team sports. A survey of theory and evidence. *Journal of Economic Studies*, 13(1), 3–80.

Chakrabarti, A., Singh, K., and Mahmood, I. (2007) Diversification and performance. Evidence from East Asian firms. *Strategic Management Journal*, [e-journal] 28(2), 101–120. [online] Retrieved from: http://dx.doi.org/10.1002/smj.572

Chang, S., Kogut, B., and Yang, J.-S. (2016) Global diversification discount and its discontents. A bit of self-selection makes a world of difference. *Strategic Management Journal*, (11), 2254. [online] Retrieved from: http://dx.doi.org/10.1002/smj.2574

Chatterjee, S. and Wernerfelt, B. (1991) The link between resources and type of diversification. Theory and evidence. *Strategic Management Journal*, [e-journal] 12(1), 33–48. [online] Retrieved from: http://dx.doi.org/10.1002/smj.4250120104

Claxton, D. (2017) *Arsenal FC launches its own innovation lab for startups*. [online] Retrieved from: https://www.sporttechie.com/arsenal-fc-launches-innovation-lab-startups/

Cohen, J. (2017) *How Manchester United is leading the way when it comes to digital and commercial innovation in football*. [online] Retrieved from: http://www.independent.co.uk/sport/football/news-and-comment/manchester-united-leading-digital-commercial-sina-weibo-mutv-a7595371.html

Conn, D. (2017) *How Chelsea's links to Vitesse Arnhem run deeper than the public was told*. [online] Retrieved from: https://www.theguardian.com/football/2017/feb/28/chelsea-vitesse-arnhem-links-deeper-public-told

Cox, A. (2015) Spectator demand, uncertainty of results, and public interest. Evidence from the English Premier League. *Journal of Sports Economics*. [online] Retrieved from: http://dx.doi.org/10.1177/1527002515619655

Curtis, S. (2014) *Germany's World Cup tactics: shaped by data*. [online] Retrieved from: http://www.telegraph.co.uk/technology/news/10959864/Germanys-World-Cup-tactics-shaped-by-data.html

Daniels, J.P. and Radebaugh, L.H. (1989) *International Business: Environments and Operations*. Reading, MA: Addison-Wesley.

Datta, D.K., Rajagopalan, N., and Rasheed, A. M.A. (1991). Diversification and performance. Critical review and future directions. *Journal of Management Studies*, (5), 529–258. [online] Retrieved from: http://dx.doi.org/10.1111/j.1467-6486.1991.tb00767.x

Deloitte (2016) *Annual Review of Football Finance 2016. Reboot*. London, UK.

Deloitte (2017) *Annual Review of Football Finance 2017. Ahead of the Curve*. London, UK.

DFL (2017) *Report 2017*. Deutsche Fussball Liga [DFL]: Frankfurt am Main, Germany.

Dhir, S. and Dhir, S. (2015) Diversification. Literature review and issues. *Strategic Change*, [e-journal] 24(6), pp. 569–588. [online] Retrieved from: http://dx.doi.org/10.1002/jsc.2042

Diestre, L. and Rajagopalan, N. (2011) An environmental perspective on diversification. The effects of chemical relatedness and regulatory sanctions. *Academy of Management Journal*, [e-journal] 54(1), 97–115. [online] Retrieved from: http://dx.doi.org/10.5465/AMJ.2011.59215087

Dobson, S. and Goddard, J. (2011) *The Economics of Football*. Cambridge: Cambridge University Press.

Døving, E. and Gooderham, P. N. (2008) Dynamic capabilities as antecedents of the scope of related diversification. The case of small firm accountancy practices. *Strategic Management Journal*, [e-journal] 29(8), 841–857. http://dx.doi.org/10.1002/smj.683

Drut, B. and Raballand, G. (2012) Why does financial regulation matter for European professional football clubs? *International Journal of Sport Management and Marketing 2*, [e-journal] 11(1–2), 73–88. http://dx.doi.org/10.1504/IJSMM.2012.045488

Eintracht Frankfurt (2017) *Eintracht Frankfurt setzt auf Dreieich.* [online] Retrieved from: http://www.eintracht.de/news/artikel/eintracht-frankfurt-setzt-auf-dreieich-60558/

Evens, T. and Lefever, K. (2011) Watching the football game: broadcasting rights for the European digital television market. *Journal of Sport and Social Issues*, [e-journal] 35(1), pp. 33–49. [online] Retrieved from: http://dx.doi.org/10.1177/0193723510396665.

Ghemawat, P. (2001) Distance still matters. *Harvard Business Review*, 79(8), 137–147.

Grant, R.M. (1987) Multinationality and performance among British manufacturing companies. *Journal of International Business Studies*, [e-journal] 18(3), 79–89. [online] Retrieved from: http://dx.doi.org/10.1057/palgrave.jibs.8490413

Grant, R.M. (2016) *Contemporary Strategy Analysis:* John Wiley & Sons.

Gupta, A.K. and Govindarajan, V. (2000) Managing global expansion. A conceptual framework. *Business Horizons*, [e-journal] 43(2), 45–54. [online] Retrieved from: http://dx.doi.org/10.1016/S0007-6813(00)88560-2.

Hill, C.W.L. and Hoskisson, R.E. (1987) Strategy and structure in the multiproduct firm. *The Academy of Management Review*, [e-journal] 12(2), 331–341. [online] Retrieved from: http://dx.doi.org/10.5465/AMR.1987.4307949

Hoegele, D., Schmidt, S.L., and Torgler, B. (2014) Superstars as drivers of organizational identification. Empirical findings from professional soccer. *Psychology & Marketing*, [e-journal] 31(9), 736–757. [online] Retrieved from: http://dx.doi.org/10.1002/mar.20731

HSV (2016) *Hamburger SV vereinbart Kooperation mit chinesischem Top-Club SIPG.* [online] Retrieved from: https://www.hsv.de/news/meldungen/allgemein/august2016/hamburger-sv-vereinbart-kooperation-mit-chinesischem-top-club-sipg/

Jensen, M. and Zajac, E. J. (2004) Corporate elites and corporate strategy. How demographic preferences and structural position shape the scope of the firm. *Strategic Management Journal*, [e-journal] 25(6), 507–524. [online] Retrieved from: http://dx.doi.org/10.1002/smj.393

Johanson, J. and Vahlne, J.-E. (1977) The internationalization process of the firm - A model of knowledge development and increasing foreign market commitments. *Journal of International Business Studies*, [e-journal] 8(1), 23–32. [online] Retrieved from: http://dx.doi.org/10.1057/palgrave.jibs.8490676

Johanson, J. and Vahlne, J.-E. (2009) The Uppsala internationalization process model revisited: From liability of foreignness to liability of outsidership. *Journal of International Business Studies*, [e-journal] 40(9), 1411–1431. [online] Retrieved from: http://dx.doi.org/10.1057/jibs.2009.24

Kim, H., Hoskisson, R.E., and Lee, S.-H. (2015) Why strategic factor markets matter: "New" multinationals' geographic diversification and firm profitability. *Strategic Management Journal*, [e-journal] 36(4), 518–536. [online] Retrieved from: http://dx.doi.org/10.1002/smj.2229

Kotler, P. (1999) Kotler on *Marketing: How to Create, Win, and Dominate Markets. Reading*, Simon & Schuster Inc.

KPMG (2017) Football-themed attractions: opening up a new revenue source for clubs. [online] Retrieved from: https://www.footballbenchmark.com/football_themed_attractions

Kumar, M.S. (2013) The costs of related diversification. The impact of the core business on the productivity of related segments. *Organization Science*, [e-journal] 24(6), 1827–1846. [online] Retrieved from: http://dx.doi.org/10.1287/orsc.1120.0812

Lakhani, K., Schmidt, S.L., Norris, M., and Herman, K. (2016) *Bayern Munich in China.* Harvard Business School Case 617–025, Boston, MA.

Lange, D., Boivie, S. and Henderson, A. D. (2009) The parenting paradox. How multibusiness diversifiers endorse disruptive technologies while their corporate children struggle. *Academy of Management Journal*, [e-journal] 52(1), 179–198. [online] Retrieved from: http://dx.doi.org/10.5465/AMJ.2009.36462006

Lien, L. B. and Klein, P. G. (2013) Can the survivor principle survive diversification? *Organization Science*, [e-journal] 24(5), 1478–1494. [online] Retrieved from: http://dx.doi.org/10.1287/orsc.1120.0793

Lim, E. N.-K., Das, S. S., and Das, A. (2009) Diversification strategy, capital structure, and the Asian financial crisis (1997–1998). Evidence from Singapore firms. *Strategic Management Journal*, [e-journal] 30(6), 577–594. [online] Retrieved from: http://dx.doi.org/10.1002/smj.752

Lu, J.W. and Beamish, P.W. (2004) International diversification and firm performance. The S-curve hypothesis. *Academy of Management Journal*, [e-journal] 47(4), pp. 598–609. [online] Retrieved from: http://dx.doi.org/10.2307/20159604

Lubatkin, M. (1983) Mergers and the performance of the acquiring firm. *The Academy of Management Review*, [e-journal] 8(2), 218–225. [online] Retrieved from: http://dx.doi.org/10.2307/257748

Lubatkin, M. and Chatterjee, S. (1994) Extending modern portfolio theory into the domain of corporate diversification. Does it apply? *Academy of Management Journal*, [e-journal] 37(1), 109–136. [online] Retrieved from: http://dx.doi.org/10.2307/256772

Markides, C.C. and Williamson, P.J. (1994) Related diversification, core competences and corporate performance. *Strategic Management Journal*, [e-journal] 15(S2), 149–165. [online] Retrieved from: http://dx.doi.org/10.1002/smj.4250151010

Markowitz, H. (1952) Portfolio selection. *The Journal of Finance*, [e-journal] 7(1), 77–91. [online] Retrieved from: http://dx.doi.org/10.1111/j.1540-6261.1952.tb01525.x.

Marsden, S. (2016) *Barcelona to open New York office to increase business in United States.* [online] Retrieved from: http://www.espnfc.com/barcelona/story/2942635/barcelona-to-open-new-york-office-to-increase-business-in-united-states

Mayer, M. and Whittington, R. (2003) Diversification in context. A cross-national and cross-temporal extension. *Strategic Management Journal*, [e-journal] 24(8), 773–781. [online] Retrieved from: http://dx.doi.org/10.1002/smj.334

Mayer, M.C.J., Stadler, C., and Hautz, J. (2015) The relationship between product and international diversification. The role of experience. *Strategic Management Journal*, [e-journal] 36(10), 1458–1468. [online] Retrieved from: http://dx.doi.org/10.1002/smj.2296

Merkel, S., Schmidt, S.L., and Schreyer, D. (2016) The future of professional football: A Delphi-based perspective of German experts on probable versus surprising scenarios. *Sport, Business and Management: An International Journal*, [e-journal] 6(3), 295–319. [online] Retrieved from: http://dx.doi.org/10.1108/SBM-10-2014-0043

Miller, D.J. (2004) Firms' technological resources and the performance effects of diversification. A longitudinal study. *Strategic Management Journal*, [e-journal] 25(11), 1097–1119. [online] Retrieved from: http://dx.doi.org/10.1002/smj.411

Montgomery, C.A. (1985) Product-market diversification and market power. *Academy of Management Journal*, [e-journal] 28(4), 789–798. [online] Retrieved from: http://dx.doi.org/10.2307/256237

Montgomery, C.A. and Singh, H. (1984) Diversification strategy and systematic risk. *Strategic Management Journal*, [e-journal] 5(2), 181–191. [online] Retrieved from: http://dx.doi.org/10.1002/smj.4250050208

Neale, W.C. (1964) The peculiar economics of professional sports. *The Quarterly Journal of Economics*, [e-journal] 78(1), pp. 1–14. [online] Retrieved from: http://dx.doi.org/10.2307/1880543

Palepu, K. (1985) Diversification strategy, profit performance and the entropy measure. *Strategic Management Journal*, [e-journal] 6(3), 239–255. [online] Retrieved from: http://dx.doi.org/10.1002/smj.4250060305

Palich, L.E., Cardinal, L.B., and Miller, C.C. (2000) Curvilinearity in the diversification–performance linkage. An examination of over three decades of research. *Strategic Management Journal*, [e-journal] 21(2), 155–174. [online] Retrieved from: http://dx.doi.org/10.1002/(SICI)1097-0266(200002)21:23.0.CO;2-2

Park, C. (2002) The effects of prior performance on the choice between related and unrelated acquisitions. Implications for the performance consequences of diversification strategy. *Journal of Management Studies*, [e-journal] 39(7), 1003–1019. [online] Retrieved from: http://dx.doi.org/10.1111/1467-6486.00321

Patel, P.C., Criaco, G. and Naldi, L. (2016) Geographic diversification and the survival of born-globals. *Journal of Management.* [online] Retrieved from: http://dx.doi.org/10.1177/0149206316635251

Pawlowski, T., Breuer, C. and Hovemann, A. (2010) Top clubs' performance and the competitive situation in European domestic football competitions. *Journal of Sports Economics*, 11(2), 186–202.

Peeters, T. (2011) Broadcast rights and competitive balance in European soccer. *International Journal of Sport Finance*, 6(1), 23–39.

Penrose, E.T. (1959) *The Theory of the Growth of the Firm.* Oxford, UK: Oxford University Press.

Pérez, L., Puente, V., and Rodríguez, P. (2017) Factors determining TV soccer viewing. Does uncertainty of outcome really matter? *International Journal of Sport Finance*, 12(2), 124–139.

PWC (2014) *Football's digital transformation. Growth opportunities for football clubs in the digital age.*

Ramanujam, V. and Varadarajan, P. (1989) Research on corporate diversification: A synthesis. *Strategic Management Journal*, [e-journal] 10(6), 523–551. [online] Retrieved from: http://dx.doi.org/10.1002/smj.4250100603

Rohde, M. and Breuer, C. (2016) Europe's elite football: financial growth, sporting success, transfer investment, and private majority Investors. *International Journal of Financial Studies*, [e-journal] 4(12). [online] Retrieved from: http://dx.doi.org/10.3390/ijfs4020012

Ronen, S. and Shenkar, O. (1985) Clustering countries on attitudinal dimensions. A review and synthesis. *The Academy of Management Review*, 435–454. [online] Retrieved from: http://dx.doi.org/10.5465/AMR.1985.4278955

Rumelt, R.P. (1974) *Strategy, Structure, and Economic Performance*. Cambridge, MA: Harvard University Press.

Rumelt, R.P. (1982) Diversification strategy and profitability. *Strategic Management Journal*, [e-journal] 3(4), 359–369. [online] Retrieved from: http://dx.doi.org/10.1002/smj.4250030407

Sakhartov, A.V. and Folta, T.B. (2014) Resource relatedness, redeployability, and firm value. *Strategic Management Journal*, [e-journal] 35(12), 1781–1797. [online] Retrieved from: http://dx.doi.org/10.1002/smj.2182.

Sakhartov, A.V. and Folta, T.B. (2015) Getting beyond relatedness as a driver of corporate value. *Strategic Management Journal*, [e-journal] 36(13), 1939–1959. [online] Retrieved from: http://dx.doi.org/10.1002/smj.2327

Santomier, J. and Hogan, P. (2013) Social media and prosumerism: implications for sport marketing research. In: S. Söderman, and H. Dolles (eds.). *Handbook of Research on Sport and Business* (pp. 179–201). Cheltenham, Gloucestershire: Edward Elgar Publishing.

Scelles, N. (2017) Star quality and competitive balance? Television audience demand for English Premier League football reconsidered. *Applied Economics Letters*, 1–4. pp. 179–201 http://dx.doi.org/10.1080/13504851.2017.1282125

Schmidt, S. L. (2017) Bayern Munich's strategy to enter the Chinese market. [online] Retrieved from: https://cpianalysis.org/2017/08/01/bayern-munichs-strategy-to-enter-the-chinese-market/

Schmidt, S.L. and Eberhard, K. (2016) *SPOAC Sportbusiness-Studie 2016*. Düsseldorf/Vallendar.

Schmidt, S.L. and Krause, F. (2017) *SPOAC Sportbusiness-Studie 2017*. Düsseldorf/Vallendar.

Schmidt, S.L. and Schreyer, D. (2012) Press Conference: MasterCard report on 'Fans Without Borders,' Munich.

Schreyer, D. and Däuper, D. (2017) Determinants of spectator no-show behavior: Empirical evidence from the German Bundesliga. *Mimeo*.

Schreyer, D., Schmidt, S.L. and Torgler, B. (2016a) Against all odds? Exploring the role of game outcome uncertainty in season ticket holders' stadium attendance demand. *Journal of Economic Psychology*, [e-journal] 56, 192–217. [online] Retrieved from: http://dx.doi.org/10.1016/j.joep.2016.07.006

Schreyer, D., Schmidt, S.L., and Torgler, B. (2016b) Game outcome uncertainty and television audience demand. New Evidence from German Football. *German Economic Review*, 1–22. [online] Retrieved from: http://dx.doi.org/10.1111/geer.12120

Schreyer, D., Schmidt, S.L., and Torgler, B. (2016c) Game outcome uncertainty in the English Premier League. Do German fans care? *Journal of Sports Economics*, 1–20. [online] Retrieved from: http://dx.doi.org/10.1177/1527002516673406

Schreyer, D., Schmidt, S.L., and Torgler, B. (2017) Game outcome uncertainty and the demand for international football games. Evidence from the German TV market. *The Journal of Media Economics*, [e-journal] 30(1), 31–45. [online] Retrieved from: http://dx.doi.org/10.1080/08997764.2017.1281818

Speckbacher, G., Neumann, K., and Hoffmann, W.H. (2015) Resource relatedness and the mode of entry into new businesses. Internal resource accumulation vs. access by collaborative arrangement. *Strategic Management Journal*, [e-journal] 36(11), 1675–1687. [online] Retrieved from: http://dx.doi.org/10.1002/smj.2305

Szymanski, S. and Smith, R. (1997) The English football industry. Profit, performance and industrial structure. *International Review of Applied Economics*, [e-journal] 11(1), pp. 135–153. [online] Retrieved from: http://dx.doi.org/10.1080/02692179700000008

Teece, D.J. (1980) Economies of scope and the scope of the enterprise. *Journal of Economic Behavior & Organization*, [e-journal] 1(3), 223–247. [online] Retrieved from: http://dx.doi.org/10.1016/0167-2681(80)90002-5

Teece, D.J. (1982) Towards an economic theory of the multiproduct firm. *Journal of Economic Behavior & Organization*, [e-journal] 3(1), 39–63. [online] Retrieved from: http://dx.doi.org/10.1016/0167-2681(82)90003-8

UEFA (2016) *The European club footballing landscape. Club licensing benchmarking report financial year 2015.*

Vachani, S. (1989) Implications of environmental differences on strategies of multinationals' manufacturing subsidiaries. *Vikalpa*, [e-journal] 14(3), 3–12. [online] Retrieved from: http://dx.doi.org/10.1177/0256090919890302

Vachani, S. (1991) Distinguishing between related and unrelated international geographic diversification. A comprehensive measure of global diversification. *Journal of International Business Studies*, [e-journal] 22(2), 307–322. [online] Retrieved from: http://dx.doi.org/10.1057/palgrave.jibs.8490305

van Overloop, P.C. (2015) *Internationalisierung professioneller Fußballclubs: Grundlagen, Status quo und Erklärung aus Sicht des internationalen Managements.* Wiesbaden: Springer-Verlag.

Villalonga, B. and McGahan, A.M. (2005) The choice among acquisitions, alliances, and divestitures. *Strategic Management Journal*, [e-journal] 26(13), 1183–1208. [online] Retrieved from: http://dx.doi.org/10.1002/smj.493

Vrentas, J. (2017) Tottenham wants to be the NFL's Premier League team. [online] Retrieved from: https://www.si.com/nfl/2017/08/11/tottenham-hotspur-nfl-partnership

Wan, W.P. (2005) Country resource environments, firm capabilities, and corporate diversification strategies. *Journal of Management Studies*, [e-journal] 42(1), 161–182. [online] Retrieved from: http://dx.doi.org/10.1111/j.1467-6486.2005.00492.x

Wang, H.C. and Barney, J.B. (2006) Employee incentives to make firm-specific investments. Implications for resource-based theories of corporate diversification. *The Academy of Management Review*, [e-journal] 31(2), 466–476. [online] Retrieved from: http://dx.doi.org/10.5465/AMR.2006.20208691

Wiersema, M.F. and Bowen, H.P. (2008) Corporate diversification. The impact of foreign competition, industry globalization, and product diversification. *Strategic Management Journal*, [e-journal] 29(2), 115–132. [online] Retrieved from: http://dx.doi.org/10.1002/smj.653

Wolf, J. (2016) *Schalke 04 buys, renames League of Legends team.* [online] Retrieved from: http://www.espn.com/esports/story/_/id/15559925/schalke-04-announces-purchase-renaming-league-legends-team-elements

Wu, B. (2013) Opportunity costs, industry dynamics, and corporate diversification. Evidence from the cardiovascular medical device industry, 1976–2004. *Strategic Management Journal*, [e-journal] 34(11), 1265–1287. [online] Retrieved from: http://dx.doi.org/10.1002/smj.2069

Yin, X. and Shanley, M. (2008) Industry determinants of the "merger versus alliance" decision. *The Academy of Management Review*, [e-journal] 33(2), 473–491. [online] Retrieved from: http://dx.doi.org/10.5465/AMR.2008.31193515

Zhu, F., Lakhani, K.R., Schmidt, S.L., and Herman, K. (2015) *TSG Hoffenheim: Football in the age of analytics.* Harvard Business School Case 616-010, Boston, MA.

Zhou, Y. M. (2011) Synergy, coordination costs, and diversification choices. *Strategic Management Journal*, [e-journal] 32(6), 624–639. [online] Retrieved from: http://dx.doi.org/10.1002/smj.889

Zook, C. and Allen, J. (2003) Growth outside the core. *Harvard Business Review*, 81(12), 66–75.

Zook, C. and Allen, J. (2001) *Profit from the core. A return to growth in turbulent times. Reprint* 2010: Harvard Business School Press Boston, MA.

3

Global football

Defining the rules of the changing game

Remco M. Beek, Martijn Ernest, and Jos Verschueren

Introduction: The phenomenon of globalisation

For decades, the term globalisation has been a buzzword with which to describe the integrations of markets and the benefits and dis-benefits of our present economic relationships. Several contributions were made to categorise the history of globalisation over the course of 200,000 years and multiple organising principles were used, mainly related to economics or by the definition of trade (Baldwin, 2016). The new globalisation is driven by information technology, which has radically reduced the cost of moving ideas across borders (Baldwin, 2016). In order to understand the actual and upcoming dynamics, it is relevant to briefly outline the dynamics of globalisation in order to integrate these patterns in the context of football.

Baldwin (2016) extrapolated two stages of globalisation. First, around 1820, trade costs fell, which drove "unbundling" of production and consumption. Nearly all economists and scholars of globalisation have noted that the economy was globalised by the early twentieth century. As European countries colonised Asia and sub-Saharan Africa, they turned their colonies into suppliers of raw materials for European manufacturers, as well as markets for European goods. Meanwhile, the economies of the colonisers were also becoming free-trade zones for each other (Saval, 2017). Production clustered locally as markets expanded globally, as this micro-clustering sparked innovation. Multinational corporations were prominent in the economic landscape and became significant investors in and exploiters of knowledge (Little, Go, and Poon, 2017).

The second stage occurred around 1990 when communication costs fell and the information and communication technologies (ICT) revolution and wage gap drove unbundling of G7 factories (this was the start of new globalisation). High-tech nations moved operations to low-wage nations and ICT broke the monopoly that G7 labour had on G7 knowhow. With the reduction of transaction costs as a recent driver of globalisation, production or supply "chains" were replaced by much more densely networked patterns (Little et al., 2017). This enabled innovation in the development of new business models and relationships with new sectorial and regional strategies in response to the demand for a global approach to positioning within global networks (Little et al., 2017).

Globalisation is inevitable in a world of modern communications that cannot be un-invented, but it will not be possible to combine globalisation with a small-state approach

(The Economist, 2016). Individuals, communities, and corporations can appeal directly to supra-national entities, creating a diffusion of state power in areas such as trade, security, and environment through the emergence of transnational corporations operating in internationalised financial and labour markets (Little et al., 2017).

Globalisation of football

The game of football has come a long way since English villagers began kicking around pigs' bladders in the Middle Ages. Football began to spread internationally during the heyday of the British Empire, but the sport's globalisation went into reverse in the interlude between World Wars I and II, as authorities restricted the international transfer of players (Ghemawat, 2007).

Ghemawat (2007) outlined five parallels of football's global progress and many economic indicators of globalisation. First, there was a peak before World War I, followed by a reversal during and between the two world wars, and then a revival after World War II. Second, globalisation remained, in many respects, uneven and incomplete. In the case of football, this can be explained by the failure to gain traction in the United States, the world's largest sports market. Third, cross-border differences featuring cultural, administrative, geographic, and economic differences between countries are highlighted in the football context as well. This could be illustrated by the role that Latin cultures, temperate climates, and threshold levels of economic development play in explaining various countries' success in the FIFA rankings. Furthermore, the strategies that football clubs have followed exhibit a range of approaches for dealing with the differences between locations, related to forging a local identity or aggregate across borders. The final parallel is the negative portents about globalisation fuelling debates about whether it stalls or goes into reverse.

However, the business of football should not be considered independently of the major challenges facing the world in which sports may have a facilitating role. The shift towards hosting international hallmark events in emerging destinations such as South Africa (2010 FIFA World Cup™), Brazil (2014 FIFA World Cup™), Russia (2018 FIFA World Cup™) and Qatar (2022 FIFA World Cup™) raises challenges on the alignment with modernisation and neoliberal globalisation approaches (Beek and Go, 2017). Moreover, the impact of multinational organisations such as FIFA is stated in relation to state powers since laws changed in host countries because of organising these hallmark events. In the case of the 2014 World Cup, for example, the Brazilian President Dilma Rousseff signed a law that allows the sale of beer at football matches, reversing existing legislation in accordance with FIFA requirements (BBC, 2017a). Therefore, the political spectrum is crucial to understanding the process of globalisation in the context of football.

Stages of globalisation in football

In order to understand the developments in the playground of football, we clarify the phenomenon of globalisation in the context of football. In addition to the first process of internationalisation within football in the early 1900s, four main "globalisation stages" could be offered: geographical globalisation (Globalisation 1.0), commercial globalisation (Globalisation 2.0), digital globalisation (Globalisation 3.0) and social globalisation (Globalisation 4.0). Over the last decades, these much-discussed trends within international football are considered more important than others in fundamentally changing the game. However, it seems relevant to include these patterns in order to understand the challenges ahead, realising that these stages are continuous processes, without evident origin or expected ending.

Globalisation 1.0: Geographical globalisation

The first official international game was played between England and Scotland on the afternoon of Saturday, December 2, 1872. Four thousand spectators saw the teams draw 0–0 at Glasgow's West of Scotland Cricket Club (*The Guardian*, 2016). Football's global spread was both encouraged and hampered by Britain's empire, most often in locations where Britain's influence was through trade (such as Central America, South America, and Europe) rather than conquest (Pearson, 2017). In countries subject to acute British imperial muscle (such as South Africa, Australia, and New Zealand), football never really took hold as a truly popular sport since cricket and rugby became the sports of the people (Tomlinson, 2011). The FIFA World Cup in 1930 was the first world championship for men's national association football teams. It took place in Uruguay from 13–30 July 1930 with 13 teams: seven from South America, four from Europe, and two from North America. The first pan-European football tournament was held in France in 1960.

The immigration of South American football players, especially to Spanish and Italian leagues, was explained by the historically talented South American players, the linguistic and cultural link because of the Spanish colonial past (except Brazil) and perceived styles (skill, flamboyance, and the like) that were better suited to the playing styles of Italy and Spain than to those of northern Europe (Maguire and Pearton, 2000). The concept of globalisation is an active ingredient in most analyses of player migration. However, Taylor (2007) argued that footballer migration is by no means a new phenomenon and should not be isolated from the general trends and patterns of migrations. Three sets of determinants (economic, cultural, and institutional/structural) have influenced and stimulated the movement of football labour and are crucial for understanding why players move around the globe. The movement of footballers from country to country and from continent to continent is much more than the product of the current economic and power relations of world football. It reflects a "complex set of linkages between specific countries, or sets of countries, linkages that often have deep social, cultural and historical roots" (Taylor, 2006). Poli (2010) contributed to this idea by concluding that the creation of economic opportunities is intrinsically linked to the characteristics of the actors involved (such as their biographies, linguistic skills, trust relationships) within the development of transfer networks.

Globalisation 2.0: Commercial globalisation

A new set of social and cultural relations have arisen, notably featuring the greater migration of elite labour, a gradual proliferation of continental and global competitions, astronomical rises in elite player salaries, new media outlets for football (satellite television, club television stations, the Internet, etc.), and new forms of cultural encoding of football through these media (Giulianotti, 2002). In line with the professionalisation of football towards an industry, sponsorship relationships started as transactional approaches, in addition to the philanthropic origins, and football organisations shifted from local institutions to global brands.

Although football was first broadcast on television in 1937, with the FA Cup final between Sunderland and Preston North End, the role of television was limited until the 1960s. Clubs refused to let cameras onto their grounds for fear of declining attendances (Sondaal, 2013). In 1964, an agreement was reached between the BBC and the Football League whereby £5,000 would be divided equally between all 92 Football League teams to allow the broadcast of extended highlights of football matches on the programme Match of the Day. By the 1980s, however, negotiations for a new contract took place in a changed environment, due to a combination of Prime Minister Margaret Thatcher's deregulation policies, growing television ownership, English football's global popularity, and developments in satellite television (Sondaal, 2013).

In addition to the stated private investments in football to gain shares and (partial) ownership in a football club, several examples indicated this commercial globalisation from a business investor's perspective. In order to understand these patterns, it is relevant to briefly indicate the case of investments made in Brazilian football. Since football became big business in the 1990s, several companies have invested heavily in Brazil. Private equity firm Hicks, Muse, Tate & Furst was one of these investors with radical ideas, as the firm's president Charles Tate mentioned that "soccer in Brazil is like baseball, basketball and football put together in the USA" (Romero, 1999). The transaction with the Corinthians club gave the company all licensing rights to the club's name, enabling it to sell items like caps or T-shirts emblazoned with the Corinthians insignia as well as the opportunity to negotiate deals for the TV broadcast of games. At that time, Hicks, Muse, Tate & Furst had already entered into pay-tv ventures in Brazil and in neighbouring Argentina that could facilitate such deals. Over the years, other companies such as Bank of America and ISL invested, and lost, hundreds of millions of dollars in storied clubs such as Vasco da Gama, Flamengo and Corinthians (Antunes, 2012). Almost all have fled, with no desire to come back. According to Ghemawat (2007), the story of Hicks, Muse, Tate & Furst's investment in Brazil also illustrates what is "probably the most common bias in evaluating cross-border strategies: an emphasis on 'size-ism', which fails to appreciate the persistence of differences between countries".

Some football clubs were originally founded by another commercial organisation; for example, the professional Dutch football club PSV was started in 1913 to serve the needs for activities for Philips employees (PSV, 2017). Some other clubs were founded as a result of interference of Western football clubs. For example, Ajax Cape Town was formed in 1999 as the Dutch football club AFC Ajax expanded its worldwide talent-feeder network to South Africa (Ajax CT, 2017). These clubs supported society, shared knowledge, trained football and management skills, and aimed to spot new talent for the parent club. Furthermore, in order to offer fans around the world the opportunity to see their beloved team play live and to promote the club's brand, clubs routinely travelled to financially lucrative places to play games during the preseason, such as the International Champions Cup (Sondaal, 2013).

Globalisation 3.0: Digital globalisation

The emergence of information and communication technologies, coupled with a globalising society, has resulted in network-centric marketing, causing corporate sponsors to be active in redrawing multiple boundaries. Internal restructuring, combined with international strategies, strategic alliances, and collaboration with a variety of societal stakeholders, has proven increasingly important to enhance sponsors' reputations. In an increasingly globalised, connected, and media-intensive world, one of the most challenging tasks managers face is the implementation of effective ICT strategies.

In addition to the impact of satellite television, new technological innovations radically changed the media landscape. In addition to the worldwide commercialisation and developments of the Internet in the late 1990s, the first years of the new century were marked by the establishment of online social networks with Facebook (since February 2004), Twitter (since March 2006), WhatsApp (since January 2008), Instagram (since October 2010), and Snapchat (since September 2011). These innovations extended media and marketing communications as they shifted consumer behaviours away from personal computers, via laptops and tablets, to mobile devices (Parganas, Anagnostopoulos, and Chadwick, 2015). Moreover, it enabled football fans worldwide to watch games and interact with other fans. The more physical communities of the football clubs were transformed into digital communities in which the content of football drove the interaction between the members of the tribes (Parganas, Anagnostopoulos, and Chadwick, 2017).

The opportunities to connect the world with the live streams of football games shifted the model of free public viewing on television to the first types of decoded pay-tv. Moreover, at this stage, multiple digital innovations were made in the football industry, including LED-boarding on the pitch, virtual advertising during the matches, and online communication. Most of these innovations created new forms of existing aspects (such as hardcopy advertising and hardcopy magazines moving to virtual advertising and online content, respectively). At the stage of digital globalisation, the digital gamification of football also started, resulting in a variety of games including FIFA (since 1993) and Pro Evolution Soccer (since 2001). However, what started as casual gaming was actually the start of the growing phenomenon of e-sports as well. Other forms of simulation (such as football analysis) also grew rapidly, enabling football clubs to improve tactical (on-field) aspects. Thus began a long process of incorporating the technological opportunities in the game by, for example, goal-line technology and video assistance referee (VAR).

Globalisation 4.0: Social globalisation

The ways in which supporters talk about football and "consume" the game indicate the dynamics of football in transnational networks and identified social movements in the new media age (Millward, 2011). Digital communication has forced organisations to redefine interaction with their communities and new efforts to enlarge sense of belonging and fan experiences (during the game as well as in and out of the stadium).

The social impact of influencers and the increasing technological opportunities have fundamentally changed the game. Whereas celebrity endorsement started as a way of connecting a celebrity (such as an athlete or artist) to a brand, with influencer marketing the influencer is perceived to be the creator of the entire content. Nevertheless, branded content is where branded content interferes with credibility and authenticity. Football is a context in which these social interactions with influencers as role models will also become more dominant and complex. The impact on social media of Francesco Totti's farewell from AS Roma after 25 years was impressive and broke the club's digital records on Facebook, Twitter, Instagram, Snapchat, YouTube and AS Roma's website. With 8.8 million Facebook followers – which is only a fraction of the social following database compared to clubs such as FC Barcelona and Real Madrid (102 million followers) or Manchester United (73 million followers), Roma out-performed every team in the world in terms of Facebook videos during that period of time (Rogers, 2017). The tribute to the talismanic Totti highlights the global impact of influencer marketing.

In line with the battle for football talent and in their search for authenticity, sports brands are looking for the "next big thing" to promote their products. While Neymar had only just turned 13 when Nike signed him in 2009, Shane Kluivert is now the youngest player to have signed an endorsement agreement. The nine-year-old son of retired Dutch football icon Patrick Kluivert switched from Paris Saint-Germain to FC Barcelona (both Nike sponsored) and continues his development as a football talent in addition to already being an impactful influencer. He has a global reach on social media, with 178,000 followers on Instagram and over 50,000 YouTube subscriptions to his personal channel (BBCb, 2017).

Community formation is driven by community members engaging, participating, and feeling supported by strong networks to form strong communities and tribes (Misener and Mason, 2010). These communities and tribes raise the complexity of the unique characteristics of a person and the interactions of a person as a component of a group. Moreover, this complex interaction is also driven by the various roles a person may have, such as a consumer, employee, or volunteer. Cultural dimensions, group behaviour, tribes, and networks are commonly used to draw tendencies among individual behaviours. Several contributions have sought to define the spectator identities in football including diversity on sense of belonging (Giulianotti, 2002) with interplay of identity, time boundaries, geographic constraints, level of attachment, the degree of fan-like behaviour, and the primary form of self-identification (Hunt et al., 1999; Sullivan, 2004). It seems relevant to reconsider the taxonomy of fandom in perspective of the new dynamics on geographical, commercial, digital, and social aspects in order to define marketing opportunities. Moreover, football clubs are investing in databases to have a more detailed understanding of the fan base, enabling them to explore new commercial possibilities.

In line with the service-dominant logic and the related integrative approach of value co-creation (Vargo and Lusch, 2008), new dimensions of engagement marketing by virtual extensions (such as virtual reality) were introduced to get access to exclusive content. Organisations shift from selling products and services towards creating detailed data profiles, knowing that the individual consumer becomes more valuable. Regulations on increasing interactions with spectators during the game have changed to create new ways of fan engagement. The debut of "Ref Cam" by ESPN came in the football match between MLS All Stars and AS Roma in 2013; four years later, FOX Sports enhanced the MLS All-Star Game with Real Madrid with "Ref Cam" (FoxSports, 2017). Following applications of technological capabilities in other sports (such as ice hockey, American Football and rugby), unique content was created by player cameras during a (friendly) match between Legends Real Madrid and AS Roma (Matthews, 2017). Indeed, Intel planned to showcase Intel TrueVR during the 2018 Olympic Winter Games in PyeongChang (Grant and Novy-Williams, 2017), while TAG Heuer Connected showed the use of smartwatches during football games in the Premier League and Bundesliga (Shaw, 2016).

The future dynamics of global football

According to the phenomenon of globalisation and its development within the context of sports, five patterns can be identified: global outlook with fidelity to local roots, changing commercial partnerships, changing media landscape, cultural battles within the playground of football, and attractiveness of the game. These are crucial ingredients in understanding the future dynamics of global football, representing challenges and dilemmas for the industry.

Pattern I: Global outlook with fidelity to local roots

Professional sports clubs need to clearly define what they are (identity), who they want to target (segmentation and targeting), how they want to be perceived and how they differentiate themselves from the other main competitors (positioning) (Bodet, 2010). As suggested by Sondaal (2013), there is a need for a global outlook with fidelity to local roots. What role is to be played by the vast majority of "local" clubs that are incapable of hiring global stars (Alvito, 2007)?

The dilemma of the identity of the football club is reflected in the rare emergence of the truly "global" team: Many players still play in their host nation and host-nation players are often awarded the accolade of club captain. This can be illustrated best by the 15 greatest performing European football clubs of 2017 (based on the UEFA coefficient season 2016/2017), which include Real Madrid (captained by Spain's Sergio Ramos), Juventus (Italy's Gianluigi Buffon), Club Atlético de Madrid (Spain's Gabi), Manchester United (England's Wayne Rooney), FC Barcelona (Spain's Andrés Iniesta), FC Bayern Munich (Germany's Philipp Lahm), Borussia

Dortmund (Germany's Marcel Schmelzer), Olympique Lyonnais (France's Maxime Gonalons), AFC Ajax (Dutch Davy Klaassen), Sevilla FC (Spain's Vincente Iborra), and RC Celta de Vigo (Spain's Hugo Mallo). These "home" players are typically viewed as the "heart" of the team. Only AS Monaco (Colombia's Radamel Falcao), Leicester City FC (Jamaica's Wes Morgan) and Paris Saint-Germain FC (Brazil's Thiago Silva) had captains who were not from the club's home country. This supports the argument of football clubs practising cultural "globalisation", meaning they accord status to symbolic local or national figures and recruits "foreign" players from culturally similar nations, at the same time as they seek to build global recognition.

Football clubs should determine their core values and higher purpose in order to strengthen the engagement of the community members and sense of belonging in the "glocal" tribes. In this foreign–familiarity continuum, trust is a crucial ingredient. Studies on place and identity in football cultures (e.g., Edensor and Millington, 2008) suggest that place-based sporting histories, practices, and identities matter more than ever, resonating culturally in an age of global communications, information, and capital flows. It is of importance here how these histories and practices, and the places and spaces tied to them, are being reworked, reordered, and, most critically, privileged by and through media according to differing hierarchies of symbolic value (Ruddock et al., 2010).

The case of the Maracanã stadium in Brazil indicated multiple aspects of the bright and dark sides of globalisation in the football context. Despite the centrality of the Estádio Mario Filho (Maracanã) stadium in the sporting landscape of Brazil and Rio de Janeiro, the shifting political economy of global sport in the 1990s positioned the Maracanã outside the realm of international competitions (Gaffney, 2010). Beginning in 1998 and continuing today, the Maracanã has undergone a series of major reforms in order to bring it into compliance with international regulations towards a Euro-American style of spectatorship. Before it was eliminated in 2005, a section of the stadium was known as the "geral", a low-lying area of concrete that encircled the field. This "populist heart of the stadium was a functional and symbolic space that allowed for the inclusion of all social sectors in public life to participate in Brazil's most popular form of leisure in its most iconographic stadium because of the low ticket prices" (Gaffney, 2010). As it illustrates several described dynamics, the pressure of global forces on local identity and the impact of society are obvious in this case.

Pattern II: Changing commercial partnerships

A geopolitical shift is underway that has not been seen since the end of the Cold War, moving from a unipolar world with one superpower to a multipolar one. This new world order has many great powers that will need to work together in order to avoid friction and conflict on trade and currency, on economics and finance (WEF, 2017). These changing powers will affect the sporting and football industries as well, since the challenges of the football context cannot be viewed independently from the dynamics in the world. New opportunities arise to collaborate within international partnerships in an effort to identify, where appropriate, the reputation-reality gap and manage the brand reputation as football organisation or stakeholder (sponsors, host cities, governments, etc.). These changing powers by new stakeholders are illustrated best by the case of City Football Group. This holding company now administrates six association football clubs under the ownership of Abu Dhabi United Group (ADUG): Manchester City FC, New York City FC, Melbourne City FC, Yokohama F. Marinos, Club Atlético Torque, and Girona FC (Tremlett, 2017).

The impact of globalisation is more sudden, more individual, more unpredictable, and more uncontrollable (Baldwin, 2016). Therefore, the role of the football club in the (local) society should surpass corporate social responsibility, since the contribution to the world is increasingly important to the members of the community. FC Barcelona and Arsenal recently announced their intentions to be of value for the stakeholders in innovative ways. Both clubs presented – separately from each other – two concepts that had distinct similarities: the Barça Innovation Hub and the Arsenal Innovation Lab. The Barça Innovation Hub is a platform for research, development, training, and innovation that aims to help change the world through sporting excellence via knowledge and innovation as a powerful brand with worldwide impact and one of the leading sports organisation regarding talent and knowledge (Barça Innovation Hub, 2017). The Arsenal Innovation Lab aims to identify smart-thinking businesses and help them identify ground-breaking ideas to take Arsenal forwards in a partnership with L Marks (Arsenal, 2017).

Pattern III: Changing media landscape

Due to the changing media landscape, the impact of the media will shift as well, since new ways of communication and sharing of content between consumers and organisations will enable new dynamics in the reality–reputation gap. Therefore, sponsorship partnerships help overcome the gap among stakeholders between perceived reality and obtained reality. The projected and perceived image, as well as the destination's reputation, can be clarified as potential gaps between these aspects. It is important to understand the opportunities and the risks in increased digital media usage, so that both industry and users can learn how best to exploit the benefits while mitigating the negative effects (WEF, 2016). Wagg (2007) illustrated these dynamics by the vital myths in global sport and popular culture: the myths of the celebrity and of the football manager. As they are endowed via the media with special significance and unusual powers, the actual skills cannot be known, only believed, which makes both celebrity and football management socially constructed (Wagg, 2007). The changing media landscape affects the reality–reputation gap, which designs new opportunities and risks for the football industry.

In the nexus of branded content and user-generated content, sponsorship partnerships become increasingly important in the marketing domain to leverage engagement and conversations with stakeholders through meaningful content. For example, it has been suggested that new media powers such as Amazon, Google, Apple, Facebook, and Netflix will join the broadcasting battle in the Premier League (Sweney, 2017). Moreover, illustrating the changing media landscape, the live streaming sports network Stadium partnered with Twitter and Facebook to offer live streamed sports (Perez, 2017); Amazon won the battle with Twitter for the livestream rights of the NFL (Rovell, 2017); Snapchat signed partnerships with the NFL, MLB, NBA, Formula 1, and Wimbledon (Edmondson, 2017); and the Champions League shifted from the public network to pay-tv in Spain, Great Britain, and Germany (Sportcal, 2017). Furthermore, e-sports has experienced massive global growth over the past few years, with major investments from blue-chip sponsors, game publishers, and media companies, as well as sports leagues and teams (Nielsen, 2017). In understanding e-sports and its potential related to the football industry, it is crucial to distinguish gamification of football with professional gaming of, for example, League of Legends and the growing interaction on new media platforms like Twitch.

As digital engagement became key in order to engage customers, upcoming technological innovations in relation to artificial intelligence, blockchain, and 3D printing will undeniably impact the football industry in the years to come and shift the value propositions of rights holders and their partners (PWC, 2015).

Pattern IV: Cultural battles within the playground of football

In the next few years, cultural conflicts will be expressed in the context of football, both within the borders of a nation as well as in the international playing field. These conflicts will follow the political and social dynamics within and across nations and religions. The rivalry between FC Barcelona and Real Madrid reflects a broader antipathy of the media and citizens in Madrid towards the Catalans in general and FC Barcelona in particular, and vice versa (Ball, 2002). The recent political and social dynamics in relation to the potential independence of Catalonia have affected the tensions between the fans of both football clubs, as well as the support of the national team.

In addition, Great Britain leaving the European Union is suggested to have far-reaching effects on sports, especially in case of labour conditions and business investments of non-British organisations. This new Britain's status as a member of the European Union might have both positive and negative effects on the national football industry and the global brand of the English football clubs and sponsors (Aarons, 2016). Moreover, the upcoming 2022 FIFA World Cup™ in Qatar has raised questions about alcohol being banned from stadiums and streets because of cultural and legal principles in the conservative Middle Eastern country (Payne, 2016). With Budweiser as a major sponsor of that event, the cultural clash between FIFA and Qatar's strict cultural norms might not end like the FIFA's push in Brazil to adjust legislation on alcohol for the 2014 World Cup. This is especially the case since FIFA already made an exception for the host country of the tournament being played in the winter, with a break during the regular season of the clubs, instead of the regular summer edition at the end of the club season.

The globalisation of football enables intercultural encounters of people within destinations, between destinations as well as among organisations with different cultures and structures. Despite the positives of this pattern, these dynamics will challenge the football industry as well. History has shown the impact of these aspects by means of political boycott, political conflict, and hierarchy of power (for example, players of German club Hertha BSC kneeling in support of NFL protests for tolerance and against discrimination (Uersfeld, 2017)). This form of social-cultural risk (for example, social support and cultural differences) was relevant in the conflict between Papiss Cissé and the English football club Newcastle United. The Senegal striker had complained that Newcastle's new four-year, £24m sponsorship with a payday loan company called Wonga offended his Muslim faith and personal beliefs (*The Guardian*, 2013). He objected on religious and ethical grounds that he would not wear Wonga-branded clothes. Under Sharia Law, a Muslim is not allowed to benefit from lending money or receiving money from someone – that is, earning interest is not allowed. Wonga's annual percentage rate is over 4,000 per cent. A few weeks after leaving the preseason training camp, Cissé and the club agreed on the terms of wearing these shirts (Taylor, 2013).

In addition to the cultural conflicts, the process of globalisation will have an impact on legal aspects as well, including labour rights, contract rights, transfer windows, television rights, and financial agreements (such as investments, ownership, taxes) among the cultural and political spheres of influence. For example, although Brazilian child-labour laws prevent anyone under the age of 14 from working, foreign clubs have the alternative of "hiring" a player's entire family, who move along with the star player (Alvito, 2007).

Pattern V: Attractiveness of the game

The integration of football into the global economy represents a double challenge for all those involved with the sport and for the future of the sport itself. As Croci and Ammirante (1999, p. 501) stated, on the one hand, "all of these developments constitute new exciting and profitable opportunities, at least for a few people". On the other hand, "they risk destroying all the identities and traditions that football has long embodied and that have been at the base of its appeal". However, this process started decades ago, and new opportunities in the actual stage of globalisation bring new dimensions that will radically affect the football context.

Another example of this pattern is that the substantially Western-dominated powers of sport circulating around the globe will create new dominant practice and expressions by cultural adaptions (for example, English Premier League in the Asian context) and hybridised local forms of global sport such as Indian Premier League cricket. The latter illustrates perhaps the most tangible example yet of a genuine political and economic shift in the power relations of a major sport from West to East (Rowe and Gilmour, 2009). The rise of the Indian economy, combined with the nation's population and its elevation of cricket above all other sports, has placed India at the centre of the sport. The same tendency might occur in case of an exceptional growing popularity of the local clubs and global world-class football players in the Chinese Super League exceed the interests in the English Premier League by Asian football fans (and investors). At the beginning of 2017, Chinese clubs were breaking transfer records and international football players quadrupled their wages and became some of the biggest stars in a continent of four billion people (Price, 2017). Moreover, only seven football teams are among the world's 50 most valuable sports teams (Manchester United, Barcelona, Real Madrid, Bayern Munich, Manchester City, Arsenal, and Chelsea), in contrast to teams of strong global sport competitions like the NFL, the NBA, and MLB (Badenhausen, 2017).

While globalisation will affect both men's and women's football, it is considered less evident that globalisation transforms cultural values within football, especially when it comes to gender roles (Eliasson, 2009). However, a new agreement between Norway's football association and the country's international players will lead to men and women receiving the same financial compensation for representing their country, with the men making a financial contribution to the women's team in this historic deal (Wrack, 2017). Moreover, the aging population generates new opportunities for the football industry, with a significantly growing new type of the game: walking football (Ramaswamy, 2016). Nevertheless, the incredible growth of women football is the focus of gender and the interference of Asian investors in European clubs impact the changing powers by new stakeholders. The competition with other sports and other types of entertainment in this era brings football into perspective, as there is, and will be, no unequal spread of interest in football around the world. With the aim of raising value for the sport's fans, new strategies are required to reach new fans and create more intense relationships with present fans. There is a need for football clubs to avoid becoming the equivalent of a city in which residents move from the city centre because there are too many tourists. The same might occur in stadia where loyal fans feel less devoted to the club during matches when there is a higher proportion of day-visitors from abroad. Football clubs must realise the impact of change in ownership and spectators of the club in relation to not only identity and atmosphere, but to competitiveness between teams, level of attractiveness, and sense of belonging within the communities of the football industry.

Football's long-term hope is that the magnificence of a performance and the excitement of its unpredictability will protect it from the problems that commodification inevitably brings (Croci and Ammirante, 1999). The main question of global football is whether the game being played is the finite one or the infinite one. A finite game is played for the purpose of winning, while an infinite game is played for the purpose of continuing the play (Carse, 1986).

References

Aarons, E. (2016, June 24) Brexit vote: what does it mean for professional sport in the UK? *The Guardian.* [online] Retrieved from: https://www.theguardian.com/uk news/2016/jun/24/brexit-vote-what-does-it-mean-professional-sport-eu

Ajax, C.T. (2017) History. [online] Retrievedfrom: http://www.ajaxct.co.za/theclub/history

Antunes, A. (2012, December 19) It's official: It's official: Brazil's days as the world's ultimate soccer power are over. *Forbes.* [online] Retrieved from: https://www.forbes.com/sites/andersonantunes/2012/12/19/its-official-brazils-days-as-the-worlds-ultimate-soccer-power-are-over/#7117cc722543

Arsenal (2017) Arsenal Innovation Lab. [online] Retrieved from: arsenalinnovationlab.com

Badenhausen, K. (2017, July 12) Full list: The world's 50 most valuable sports teams 2017. *Forbes.* [online]. Retrieved from: https://www.forbes.com/sites/kurtbadenhausen/2017/07/12/full-list-the-worlds-50--most-valuable-sports-teams-2017/#3dc98cb4a05c

Baldwin, R. (2016) *The Great Convergence.* Cambridge, MA: Harvard University Press.

Ball, P. (2002, April 21). Mucho morbo. *The Guardian.* [online] Retrieved from: https://www.theguardian.com/football/2002/apr/21/championsleague.sport.

Barça Innovation Hub (2017) About Barça Innovation Hub. [online] Retrieved from: barcainnovationhub.com

BBC (2017a, July 26) Shane Kluivert: Patrick Kluivert's nine-year-old son signs Nike deal. BBC. [online] Retrieved from: http://www.bbc.com/sport/football/40732508.

BBC (2017b, April 14) AC Milan: Silvio Berlusconi sells Italian giants to Chinese investors. BBC. [online] Retrieved from: http://www.bbc.com/sport/football/39591910

Beek R.M. and Go F.M. (2017) Legacy of Hallmark Events: Cross-Cultural Analysis Among Emerging Destinations. In: Little S., Go F., Poon TC. (eds.). *Global Innovation and Entrepreneurship.* Cham: Palgrave Macmillan.

Carse, J.P. (1986) *Finite and Infinite Games.* New York: The Free Press.

Croci, O. and Ammirante, J. (1999) Soccer in the age of globalization. *Peace Review, 11*(4), 499–504.

Edmondson, L. (2017, July 13) F1 enters partnership with Snapchat. *ESPN.* [online] Retrieved from: http://www.espn.com/f1/story/_/id/19986945/f1-enters-partnership-snapchat

Eliasson, A. (2009) The European football market, globalization and mobility among players. *Soccer & Society,* 10(3–4), 386–397.

Edensor, T. and Millington, S. (2008) "This is Our City": branding football and local embeddedness. *Global Networks,* 8(2), 172–193.

FoxSports (2017, July 20) Global Soccer Icons Ronaldo, Villa, Bale & Kaka Collide at 2017 MLS All-Star Game on FS1. [online] Retrieved from: http://www.foxsports.com/presspass/latest-news/2017/07/20/global-soccer-icons-ronaldo-villa-bale-kaka-collide-2017-mls-star-game-fs1

Gaffney, C. (2010) Mega-events and socio-spatial dynamics in Rio de Janeiro, 1919–2016. *Journal of Latin American Geography,* 9(1), 7–29.

Ghemawat, P. (2007) *Redefining Global Strategy.* Boston: Harvard Business School Press.

Giulianotti, R. (2002) Supporters, followers, fans, and flaneurs: a taxonomy of spectator identities in football. *Journal of sport and social issues,* 26(1), 25–46.

Grant, N. and Novy-Williams, E. (2017, June 21) Intel will sponsor the Olympics to showcase virtual reality tech. *Bloomberg.* [online] Retrieved from: https://www.bloomberg.com/news/articles/2017-06-21/intel-will-sponsor-the-olympics-to-showcase-virtual-reality-tech

Hunt, K., Bristol, T., and Bashaw, E. (1999) A conceptual approach to satisfying sports fans. *Journal of Service Marketing,* 13(6), 439–452.

Little, S.E., Go, F.M., and Poon, T.S.C. (2017) *Global Innovation and Entrepreneurship: Challenges and Experiences from East and West.* Cham: Palgrave Macmillan.

Maguire, J. and Pearton, R. (2000) Global sport and the migration patterns of France '98 World Cup finals players: Some preliminary observations. *Soccer & Society,* 1(1), 175–189.

Matthews, D. (2017, June 13) Ex-Real Madrid star Roberto Carlos wears a body-cam for legends game with Roma, giving fans a never-before-seen view of playing at the Bernabeu. *MailOnline.* [online] Retrieved from: http://www.dailymail.co.uk/sport/football/article-4600740/Real-Madrid-v-Roma-legends-Roberto-Carlos-wears-body-cam.html

Millward, P. (2011) *The Global Football League: Transnational Networks, Social Movements and Sport in the New Media Age.* Basingstoke: Palgrave Macmillan.

Misener, L. and Mason, D. (2010) Towards a community centred approach to corporate community involvement in the sporting events agenda. *Journal of Management & Organization,* 16(4), 495–514.

Nielsen (2017, August 17) Nielsen launches new e-sports business to help define and quantify value for the competitive gaming marketing. [online] Retrieved from: http://www.nielsen.com/eu/en/press-room/2017/nielsen-launches-new-esports-business-to-help-define-and-quantify-competitive-gaming.html

Parganas, P., Anagnostopoulos, C., and Chadwick, S. (2017) Effects of social media interactions on brand associations: A comparative study of soccer fan clubs. *International Journal of Sport Marketing & Sponsorship*, 18(2), 149–165.

Parganas, P., Anagnostopoulos, C., and Chadwick, S. (2015) "You'll never tweet alone": Managing sports brands through social media. *Journal of Brand Management*, 22(7), 551–568.

Payne, M. (2016, November 9) Alcohol banned from stadiums, streets at 2022 World Cup in Qatar. *The Washington Post*. [online] Retrieved from: https://www.washingtonpost.com/news/early-lead/wp/2016/11/09/alcohol-banned-from-stadiums-streets-a-2022-world-cup-in-qatar/?utm_term=.ee72bbe4de9d

Pearson, S. (2017) Soccer origins, growth and history of the game. [online] Retrieved from: http://www.thepeoplehistory.com/soccerhistory.html

Perez, S. (2017, August 24) Stadium's live-streamed sports and original programming comes to Twitter. *TechCrunch*. [online] Retrieved from: https://techcrunch.com/2017/08/24/stadiums-live-streamed-sports-and-original-programming-comes-to-twitter/?guccounter=1

Poli, R. (2010) Understanding globalization through football: The new international division of labour, migratory channels and transnational trade circuits. *International Review for the Sociology of Sport*, 45(4), 491–506.

Price, S. (2017, January 5) Why Chinese clubs are breaking transfer records – and why players are wise to go. *The Guardian*. [online] Retrieved from: https://www.theguardian.com/football/these-football-times/2017/jan/05/china-chinese-super-league-oscar-carlos-tevez

PSV (2017) History. [online] Retrieved from: http://www.psv.nl/english-psv/club/history-1/history.htm

PWC (2015) Blockchain – an opportunity for energy producers and consumers? [online] Retrieved from: https://www.pwc.com/gx/en/industries/assets/pwc-blockchain-opportunity-for-energy-producers-and-consumers.pdf

Ramaswamy, C. (2016, October 12) You'll never walk alone: the rise of walking football. *The Guardian*. [online] Retrieved from: https://www.theguardian.com/football/shortcuts/2016/oct/12/walking-football-rules-what-you-need-to-know-fa

Rogers, P. (2017, June 2) How AS Roma, with 8.8m Facebook fans, generated over 70m video views in 5 days. [online] Retrieved from: https://www.linkedin.com/pulse/how-roma-88m-facebook-fans-generated-over-70m-video-views-paul-rogers

Romero, S. (1999, May 11) International Business; Making Brazilian Soccer a Bigger Deal. *NY Times*. [online] Retrieved from: http://www.nytimes.com/1999/05/11/business/international-business-making-brazilian-soccer-a-bigger-deal.html

Rovell, D. (2017, April 5) Sources: Amazon wins rights to live-stream Thursday Night Football. *ESPN*. [online] Retrieved from: http://www.espn.com/nfl/story/_/id/19078771/amazon-wins-rights-livestream-nfl-thursday-night-football-replacing-twitter

Rowe, D. and Gilmour, C. (2009) Global sport: where wembley way meets Bollywood boulevard. *Continuum*, 23(2), 171–182.

Ruddock, A., Hutchins, B., and Rowe, D. (2010) Contradictions in media sport culture: the reinscription of football supporter traditions through online media. *European Journal of Cultural Studies*, 13(3), 323–339.

Saval, N. (2017, July 14). Globalisation: the rise and fall of an idea that swept the world. *The Guardian*. [online] Retrieved from: https://www.theguardian.com/world/2017/jul/14/globalisation-the-rise-and-fall-of-a-idea-that-swept-the-world

Shaw, S.G. (2016, August 15) English Premier League refs getting smartwatches this season. *Sports Illustrated*. [online] Retrieved from: https://www.si.com/tech-media/2016/08/15/tag-heuer-english-premier-league-referees-smartwatch

Sondaal, T. (2013) Football's grobalization or globalization? The lessons of Liverpool Football Club's evolution in the Premier League era. *Soccer & Society*, 14(4), 485–501.

Sportcal (2017, June 23) Mediapro and BeIN land exclusive Champions League rights in Spain. [online] Retrieved from: http://www.sportcal.com/News/FeaturedNews/111511

Sullivan, M. (2004) Sport marketing. In Beech, J. and Chadwick, S. *The business of sport management*. Harlow: Financial Times Prentice Hall, 64–76.

Sweney, M. (2017, August 11) Sky faces paying extra £1.8bn for Premier League broadcast rights. *The Guardian*. [online] Retrieved from: https://www.theguardian.com/media/2017/aug/11/premier-league-broadcast-battle-hots-up-as-sky-face-doling-out-extra-600m

Taylor, L. (2013, July 25) Papiss Cissé stands down in Wonga row and agrees to wear branded kit. *The Guardian*. [online] Retrieved from: https://www.theguardian.com/football/2013/jul/25/papiss-cisse-newcastle-wonga-row

Taylor, M. (2007) Football, migration and globalization: the perspective of history. *Idrottsforum.org*. [online] Retrieved from: http://www. idrottsforum. org/articles/taylor/taylor070314.html

Taylor, M. (2006) Global players? Football, migration and globalization, c. 1930–2000. *Historical Social Research/Historische Sozialforschung*, 7–30.

The Guardian (2016, November 11) The first official fixture between England and Scotland – archive 1892. *The Guardian*. [online] Retrieved from: https://www.theguardian.com/football/2016/nov/11/england-scotland-first-football-fixture-1872

The Guardian (2013, July 17) Papiss Cissé refuses to wear Newcastle's Wonga-branded shirt. *The Guardian*. [online] Retrieved from: https://www.theguardian.com/football/2013/jul/17/papiss-cisse-newcastle-wonga-shirt

Tomlinson, A. (2011). *The World Atlas of Sport: Who Plays What, Where and Why*. Brighton, Myriad Editions.

Tremlett, G. (2017). Manchester City's plan for global domination. *The Guardian*. [online] Retrieved from: https://www.theguardian.com/news/2017/dec/15/manchester-city-football-group-ferran-soriano

Uersfeld, S. (2017, October 14) Hertha Berlin players support NFL protests before Bundesliga game. *ESPN*. [online] Retrieved from: http://www.espnfc.com/hertha-berlin/story/3228844/hertha-berlin-players-support-nfl-protests-before-bundesliga-game

Vargo, S.L. and Lusch, R.F. (2008) Service-dominant logic: continuing the evolution. *Journal of the Academy of Marketing Science*, 36(1), 1–10.

Wagg, S. (2007) Angels of us all? Football management, globalization and the politics of celebrity. *Soccer & Society*, 8(4), 440–58.

WEF (2016) Impact of digital media on individuals, organizations and society. *World Economic Forum*. [online] Retrieved from: http://reports.weforum.org/human-implications-of-digital-media-2016/section-3-impact-of-digital-media-on-individuals-organizations-and-society/

WEF (2017) World Economic Forum Annual Meeting 2017; The biggest stories from Davos 2017. *World Economic Forum*. [online] Retrieved from: https://www.weforum.org/agenda/2017/01/the-biggest-stories-from-davos-2017

Wrack, S. (2017, October 17) Norway's historic pay deal for women's team shows it can be done. *The Guardian*. [online] Retrieved from: https://www.theguardian.com/football/blog/2017/oct/17/norway-historic-pay-deal-for-womens-team-shows-it-can-be-done

4

Structures and policies at the main European football leagues

Evolution and recent changes

Juan Luis Paramio-Salcines and Ramón Llopis-Goig

Introduction

Over the last several decades, the European football industry has experienced wide-reaching, ongoing transformations in its organisational and regulatory structures and policies (Arnaut, 2006; Holt, 2007; García, 2011, 2017). These transformations of European football have contributed, among other factors, to set up a more horizontal model of stakeholder networks, replacing the traditional pyramidal and hierarchised centrality of the national and international governing bodies in the football structures. These changes have also involved the professional footballers' fight against the regulations of their working conditions (e.g., the highly influential Bosman case in 1995); the clubs' contestation of the legitimacy of the national and international governing bodies; and not least, the changing relationship between clubs and one of the main stakeholders as represented by existing and prospective fans (García, 2017; García, and Welford, 2015). As the FREE project (Football Research in an Enlarged Europe) revealed (FREE, 2015), there are increasing demands in favour of promoting more effectively the engagement of fans in the governance of football across Europe.

Accordingly, the primary thrust of this chapter is to analyse how these changes in the main European football leagues have influenced fans' participation and engagement in football management and governance and their reactions to those extensive modifications. These concerns will help delineate and frame the structures and policies expected for professional clubs, a framework that will be used to guide our analysis throughout the chapter.

The remainder of the chapter proceeds as follows. The next section focuses on understanding the recent chronicle of structures and policies in the European football industry, mainly in relation to three central issues: (a) ownership and management models of football clubs across top European leagues; (b) level of participation and engagement of fans in the management of their clubs, and (c) how fans have either accepted or rejected those transformations since the 1990s. This section includes a commentary of the transfer of the Brazilian striker Neymar Jr. from the Spanish LaLiga club Barcelona FC to the French Ligue 1 club Paris Saint-Germain. Finally, the chapter draws a conclusion and offers suggestions as to what lessons can be learned from the discussion of the broad governance issues examined. Our analysis builds on the review of official reports and regulations from the EU, UEFA (the European football governing body), and the main top leagues complemented by the Deloitte Football Money League, the CIES Football Observatory and the FREE project reports. Considering that most football studies have mainly focused on a single country and professional league, much of the work incorporated here follows a comparative, interdisciplinary, pan-European perspective (e.g., Hughson et al., 2017).

Recent changes in structures and policies in European football

Changes in the European model of professional football are best understood in terms of their connections with economic, legal, social, sporting, and technological factors. Although there is neither an EU Constitution nor a common European sport policy yet, the EU institutions and laws in conjunction with UEFA, have exerted substantial influence over European football structures and policies. To illustrate this argument, "whilst the European Union has no power to regulate directly on football structures, its policies have had a profound impact on the governance of the beautiful game" (García, 2011, p. 32). García went even further to state the real influence of the EU laws on the governance of football saying that "European Union policies have empowered [to certain extent] stakeholders in football governance, undermining the vertical channels of authority featured in the traditional pyramid of European football" (García, 2011, p. 33; see also García, 2007, 2017). This situation has forced the EU institutions in conjunction with a myriad of football governing bodies "to establish new frameworks of cooperation with the European Union and with clubs, leagues and players, and the raising of standards of governance of the game" (UEFA, 2015a).

First, and considering the lack of uniformity and conflicting policies in terms of governance, regulatory structures and policies affecting multiple stakeholders and financial management at European level, normative pressures have gradually developed in a piecemeal fashion over the last decades with direct and indirect influence on European football structures and policies. UEFA has launched different key regulations such as the Club Licensing System – launched originally in 2004 and subsequently revised over the years – and the Financial Fair Play regulations, approved in 2010 (UEFA, 2015b). Those regulations outline the minimum sporting, infrastructure, personnel, and administrative, legal, and financial criteria to be fulfilled by a club (license applicant) in order to be granted a license by a UEFA member association or its affiliated league (licensor) to enter into UEFA club competitions. In line with the recommendations from the influential Independent European Sport Review (IESR) in 2006 (Arnaut, 2006), these UEFA regulations have increasingly mandated implementing (a) good governance practices; (b) increased economic and financial accountability for their leagues and clubs; and (c) encouragement of fans' participation in the governance of their clubs, while taking into account the demands and needs of all types of home and away fans of those clubs that take part in domestic and European clubs competitions. To follow suit with those regulations, all the top five European football leagues (i.e., the English Premier League (EPL), the German Bundesliga, the Spanish LaLiga, the French Ligue 1, and the Italian Serie A) have introduced their own licensing system for their domestic competitions, with the German Bundesliga being regarded as a benchmark example in financial stability, good governance (Deloitte, 2017, 2018; Bundesliga, 2017), and a "harmonious relationship between clubs and their fans" (Merkel, 2012, p. 306).

Football clubs were the second stakeholders to challenge the centrality of the governing bodies in the football structures. Because of the transformation of European football into a 1990s global media spectacle, clubs realised their economic potential and demanded a part of the revenues generated by the liberalisation and deregulation of the broadcasting sector.

As noted, the coincidental establishment of a new league structure at European level – UEFA's Champions League – and at national level – the English Premier League–in 1992 marked a new era in European football (Peeters and Szymanski, 2014). These new league structures have run in parallel to the increasing and irreversible commodification and commercialisation of the whole of European football and of the top five European leagues in particular (see Baroncelli and Caruso, 2011; Hamil, et al., 2010 for the Italian football, Senaux, 2011 for the French football, Morrow, 2011 for the EPL; Wilkesmann, Blutner, and Müller, 2011; Merkel, 2012 for the German Bundesliga; Gómez, Martí, and Bofarul Mollo, 2011; Gay de Liébana, 2016; Llopis-Goig, 2015 for the Spanish football).

One direct effect of the UCL is that it has strengthened UEFA's position in European football. Likewise, the increasing influence of elite football clubs was the background in which the G-14 – an independent organisation of top European football clubs – was created in 2000. Neither football governing body – UEFA or FIFA – ever recognised it as a valid entity and, in 2002, clubs created the European Club Forum (ECF), which included 102 clubs, to give a voice to them (Holt, 2007). Afterward, the G-14 was finally dissolved (under the former UEFA presidency of Michel Platini) and the clubs created the new European Club Association (ECA), which was accepted by UEFA as the legitimate representative of professional football clubs.

The influence of the EU institutions has also affected football players' working conditions. Despite some pressure from football trade unions in countries like England, France, and Spain to improve players' working conditions, players used to have little say. The Bosman case, however, marked another milestone in European football and helped directly modify, not without some resistance from main clubs over the years, the bases that had previously articulated professional players' working conditions. This significant case forced UEFA not only to abide by EU labour rights on the issue of working mobility, but also contributed to increasing the trading of players at an international level (Gammelsæter and Senaux, 2011). Since the Bosman case, clubs have also devoted more funds to sign players, an exercise that directly contributed to increasing the financial debts of clubs. The escalating transfer fees paid by the main European clubs to players (Figure 4.1) may have direct consequences on the structures and policies as well as on the economic and financial viability of the European football industry for years to come (Armstrong, 2017; Laurens, 2017; Malyon, 2017; Poli, Ravenel, and Besson, 2017).

While professional clubs, leagues, and professional players have been enhanced in their roles as relevant stakeholders at domestic and European levels, an emerging challenge is how to engage and promote more effectively all their fans in the governance and management of the main European leagues and their clubs. Despite the fact that the IESR report made a call to the European football governing bodies to establish a pan-European football fans organisation, such a body still needs to be set up. As part of the corporate social responsibility (CSR) approach applied to professional football management (see Chapter 10 in this handbook), there is a need to integrate those groups traditionally considered outside of the game such as people with disabilities and elderly people, regarded as "new" market segments worthy of further attention from the European football industry. CSR and good corporate governance in football require the incorporation of the fans' perspective – as key stakeholders in the process – in order to guarantee the clubs' own sustainability and survival (Paramio-Salcines, Babiak, and Walters, 2013). In the meantime, UEFA helped to establish a pan-European advocacy organisation CAFÉ (Centre for Access to Football in Europe) in 2009 to enhance the rights of fans with disabilities, while in major leagues like the EPL, NADS (nowadays Level Playing Field (LPF)) was set up in 1998. Like the NADS (LPF), the German association of disabled fans and disability officers within their clubs (*Bundesbehindertenfanarbeitsgemeinschaft*) (BBAG) was created in 1999 (Paramio-Salcines, Kitchin, and Downs, 2018). To enhance the relationship between clubs

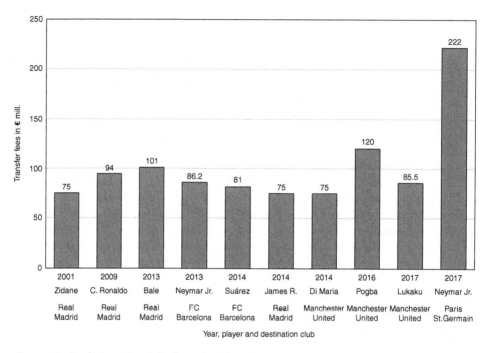

Figure 4.1 Evolution of transfer fees of professional football players from 2001 to 2017
Source: Authors.

and their fan base, two new managerial positions, the Supporter Liaison Officer (SLO) and the Disability Access Officer (DAO) (UEFA&CAFÉ, 2017) have also been created.

Unfortunately, despite the progress made, different academics have been sceptical about some of the most visible effects of the abovementioned transformations regarding the structures and policies of European football. A number of authors (e.g., Acero, Serrano, and Dimitropoulos, 2017; Gay de Liébana, 2016; Peeters and Szymanski, 2014) have argued that a side effect of this economic growth has been a sustained and growing financial polarisation between large and small clubs. For instance, Deloitte offers compelling figures when it estimates that the revenue ratio between the top-earning and bottom-earning clubs in the top European 20 in 1997 was 3.2:1, and which has now increased to 4:1 (Deloitte, 2017, 2018); this trend is more acute in the cases of FC Barcelona and Real Madrid, in LaLiga clubs and to a lesser degree, among the EPL clubs (Gay de Liébana, 2016).

To date, academic literature on European football governance has focused on the analysis of the financial situation of European football clubs in general (Peeters and Szymanski, 2014; Acero, Serrano, and Dimitropoulos, 2017 or Deloitte Football League reports over the last two decades) and to the financial state of Spanish football clubs (Gay de Liébana, 2016); or the Italian football clubs (Baroncelli and Lago, 2006; Hamil, et al., 2010) in particular. Other studies have examined the types of ownership and management models of European football clubs (Holt, 2007; Hassan and Hamil, 2010) and their influence on the financial performance in the main European football leagues (Acero, Serrano, and Dimitropoulos, 2017); the effects of transfer spending on players on the management of clubs (Gay de Liébana, 2016); the relationships and level of representation of fans within their clubs in different European football leagues (Cleland, 2010; García and Welford, 2015; García, et al., 2017; Llopis-Goig, 2015; Merkel, 2012; Kennedy and Kennedy, 2012; Welford, García, and Smith, 2015); the type and demographic and social profiles of existing and prospective fans who attend live matches in three of the main leagues in Europe (Paramio-Salcines, Downs, and Grady, 2014; Paramio-Salcines, Kitchin, and Downs, 2018). Apart from this, the EU institutions, central government bodies (see DCMS, 2016 in the UK) along with academics have also shown great interest in the study of how those ongoing policy changes may be affecting the relations of fans with European football stakeholders in a plethora of significant interrelated governance factors.

Evolution of ownership and management models of European football clubs

Back in 2006, those changes in structures and policies in European football clearly affected the ownership and management models of top European football clubs. To this end, the IESR report clearly stated that "no single model (*of ownership, control and management*, emphasis added) provides a water-tight solution to safeguard the interest of football" (Arnaut, 2006, p. 75). This report expressed some concerns about the way the main European football club's leagues were owned and managed, and warned all the stakeholders involved in European football that "there is a real risk that ownership of football clubs will pass into the wrong hands, the true values of the sport will be eroded, and the public will become increasingly disaffected with the 'beautiful game'" (Arnaut, 2006, p. 14).

Since then, academic research on this critical issue across Europe has drawn the attention of sport management scholars worldwide as a special issue of *Soccer&Society* shows (Hassan and Hamil, 2010). This study shows that it is almost impossible to establish a common and ideal ownership and management model among the top European football leagues. Apart from this, it was found that the club ownership structure varies from the more predominantly "limited company model" (represented historically by the English Premier League, and followed suit from the 1990s by the French Ligue 1 and Italian Serie A clubs and by the majority of Spanish LaLiga clubs and by German Bundesliga clubs) to the less prevalent member clubs or registered association club (four of the 20 clubs in LaLiga still have this legal structure – Real Madrid FC, FC Barcelona, Athletic de Bilbao and CA Osasuna – along with some German Bundesliga clubs). In the case of the French Ligue 1 clubs, the Spanish LaLiga clubs and the Italian Serie A clubs, this limited company model emerged after legislative pressure from the European Commission and from their central government legislation to address severe financial problems of most of clubs and to regulate the legal ownership structure of professional clubs (in the Spanish case, the 1990 Sport Act, in France the Act 99-1124 and in Italy, the Act 91/1981). As a result, these three countries have transformed the legal structure of their clubs – traditionally non-profit members' associations – and have become limited company clubs (private limited companies); (*Sociedades Anónimas Deportivas*) (SAD) in Spain, (except the four clubs mentioned before which represents an "*exception to the rule*" with the rest of top European leagues) (Gómez, Martí and Bofarull Mollo, 2011), professional sport limited company (*Société Anonyme Sportive Professionnelle*) (SASP) in France (Senaux, 2011) and in Italy Serie A clubs have evolved into "for profit entertainment companies" (Baroncelli and Caruso, 2011; Hamil, et al., 2010; Doidge, 2015, 2017). The German case is interesting as the change came from the General Assembly of the German Football Association (FA) in 1998, when this governing body allowed football clubs to transform their traditional club structure to become joint stock companies by demanding that the association retain 50 per cent plus one voting right (see more details of the German club ownership and management model, in Wilkesmann, Blutner, and Müller, 2011; Merkel, 2012). After all, the German case remains distinctive as there is no common model as in France or Spain and thereafter, German clubs were able to become public limited companies (AG) (FC Bayern Munich), limited liability companies (GmbH) (Hertha Berlin or Vfl Wolfsburg, among others), or limited partnerships with share capital (KGaA). Since the establishment of the EPL in 1992, the transformation of English clubs into limited companies has clearly consolidated (Hassan and Hamil, 2010; Morrow, 2011), not without substantial debate and criticism around "foreign ownership" and fans' reactions (Kennedy and Kennedy, 2012; Nauright and Ramfjord, 2010; DCMS, 2016).

The relationships between fans and clubs in European football

The ongoing transformations in the organisational and regulatory structures and policies of European football have had an impact on the relationships between clubs and their fans. This is mainly due to a growing concern that the increasing commodification of football might be having harmful effects on its social dimension (Conn, 1997; Giulianotti, 2005). This could lead to a loss of connection between clubs and their fans. As a result, a number of authors have suggested the need to restart this connection by allowing fans a greater say in the governance structures of the game as legitimate stakeholders (García and Welford, 2015; García, et al., 2017; Llopis-Goig, 2015).

The terms "fan" and "supporter" have been commonly used as synonyms in the literature on football cultures and management. In this discussion, authors refer to individuals, who follow or have an interest in a particular football club. This interest is dependent on the differences in degrees of engagement with their clubs among fans/supporters, terms as customers, stakeholders or shareholders will be more accurate (see Chapter 19 in this handbook). The term "customers" refers to those fans or supporters who simply follow their team by attending matches, buying merchandise, or through the media (Giulianotti, 2002). These fans do not show a keen interest in becoming involved in the management of clubs, in contrast to those who are generally known as stakeholders; i.e., those who form associations in order to have a formal dialogue with their clubs.

Apart from the terminological classification of fans, there is no common typology that describes the type, demographic and social profiles of traditional and prospective fans at European football clubs. Researchers have used different typologies in order to gain an under-standing of fans' behaviour. Two approaches frequently quoted in football literature are active versus passive fandom classification or "traditional consumer" versus fan dichotomy (Giulianotti, 2002). It is also more relevant nowadays to examine how traditional and prospective fans have valued and reacted in favour or against the ownership and management models across the top leagues in Europe and the relationship of fans with those governing bodies and their clubs over the last two decades.

Fans have organised their support for decades as they gathered to discuss the game through-out the week (Doidge, 2015, 2017). Such practices started in the 1920s in England. In Germany and Italy, the trend started after the Second World War, while in Spain this occurred after the Civil War (Llopis-Goig, 2015). Football clubs have historically made little effort to involve sup-porters in the governance of clubs beyond their role as fans or customers (Cleland, 2010). In fact, most clubs maintained a paternalistic approach to their fans, they usually did not call for representation in the clubs' structures, and few fans gained access to the club board. Although the conflicts between fans and clubs increased throughout the 1970s, there were few examples of politically inspired groups of fans in football before the 1990s (Doidge, 2017).

By the 1980s, fans felt that they were being neglected and ignored by clubs and the game's authorities, and they began to devise ways that forced them to be recognised. Since there was a feeling that media portrayed them negatively – there was an increase in hooliganism and extreme political adscription in the 1980s – they reacted by developing fanzines where they could share their fears and ideas about the game (Cleland, 2010). For instance, the Heysel tragedy acted as a catalyst for more politically active fans to form the Football Supporters' Association (FSA) in 1985. The FSA was a bottom-up organisation founded by a group of supporters in Liverpool to contribute to the management of football and to help fight against violence and hooliganism. Later on, the Independent Supporters Associations (ISAs) were created to represent the interests of supporters and establish direct relations with their own clubs. These became "the dominant form of organised fandom in English football in the 1990s" (Nash, 2000, p. 466).

The commercial changes in football in the 1990s have transformed the sport into a global media spectacle, while fans began to organise around issues affecting their clubs: the increase in ticket prices, stadium redevelopments and relocations, the rights of access to stadia by people with disabilities, and anti-racism initiatives. These changes transformed the membership model and augmented fan activism across Europe; a range of independent and politically oriented fan groups emerged to contest the development of the game (Doidge, 2017). It is true that many of them are happy to remain football consumers, but others have become "active" fans, challenging their clubs' executive board and trying to influence the way in which these clubs have been managed (Cleland, 2010; Merkel, 2012). As mentioned earlier, football fans and groups are heterogeneous and have many different rationales.

An illustration of fans' opinions and attitudes towards current football is provided by the results of a survey carried out in 2014 by the FREE project (FREE, 2015). This study shows that more than a half of both British and Spanish fans stated that as supporters, they should have a say in the club's affairs. The scores were lower in Italy and France and got the minimum share in Germany with only three out of ten fans (Table 4.1). Similarly, eight in ten Spanish fans answered that club owners/chairpersons see and treat supporters as nothing more than customers. In the rest of the big five countries, the figures ranged from seven in ten in the UK to four in ten in Germany. Not surprisingly, more than seven in ten Italian, Spanish, and French fans stated that football is in need of more regulation by the authorities. The study also revealed that the percentages were much lower in Germany and the UK.

In the meantime, several studies (Paramio-Salcines, Grady, and Downs, 2014; Welford, García, and Smith, 2015; García et al., 2017) put forward that key actors in the European football industry must implement policies to grow the customer base of the game. Such policies should aim at attracting and retaining people with different types of disabilities and the increasing aged population, along with their friends, families, and carers, who have gradually become the irresistible force of the new marketplace. Within this context, the European football industry should broaden the traditional base of fans and now include the aforementioned customer groups, described as the "new generation of sport consumers". It is unfortunate that these groups of fans have been largely ignored by the three of the most profitable, most competitive, and highly supported professional football leagues in Europe (i.e., EPL, the Bundesliga, and LaLiga). Instead, preference

Table 4.1 Football fans' opinions and attitudes in the main top European Leagues

	Germany	France	Italy	Spain	UK
As a supporter, I believe I should have a say on the affairs of the club	31.4	43.9	45.9	57.1	59.2
Club owners/presidents see and treat supporters like me as nothing more than customers	44.9	62.0	53.7	79.8	67.7
Football is in need of more regulation by the authorities	41.8	72.9	80.9	76.9	60.3

Unit: percentage of agree and strongly agree. Base: respondents who like football.

Source: Adapted from the FREE project (FREE project, 2015).

has been given to other groups such as youngsters, families, and other minorities. For instance, the EPL revealed that 40 percent of attendees to their matches were fans between 18 and 34 years old, with attendance among adult fans decreasing as from the age of 41 (EPL, 2016). Still, it is a daunting task to estimate the type, demographic, and social profiles as well as an accurate number of elderly and/or fans with different types of disabilities who regularly attend matches at stadia at any of the three leagues mentioned. There are more compelling economic, social, managerial, and sport arguments that support that accessibility and inclusion for those groups make a good business case (Paramio-Salcines, Kitchin, and Downs, 2018), though this has not been extensively studied in the football industry.

Case study: The transfer of Neymar Jr. and its side effects on the structures and policies in European football

Since the Bosman case, clubs have devoted more funds to recruiting players, which contributed to increasing the financial debts of many clubs. Football authorities like UEFA have already expressed their concern about this operational change in the transfer market and the inflated player costs and salaries, admitting the inflationary effect of the transfer of players. Meanwhile, the new commercially driven owners are looking to generate commercial revenues through football. Therefore, the transfer player market analysis has attracted the attention of the CIES Football Observatory (Poli, Ravenel, and Besson, 2017), of academics and of the international press, especially after the transfer of Neymar Jr. This case can be linked to the exponential and sustained increase in revenues of top clubs in Europe over the last two decades (Deloitte, 2017, 2018), to the business model of contemporary football of which LaLiga clubs FC Barcelona and Real Madrid FC has been benchmark over the last decade (Gay de Liébana, 2016), and to the desire of the current chairman of Paris Saint-Germain, Nasser Al-Khelaifi, to emulate the successful football model of both Spanish clubs by signing outstanding players to build their team.

Against this situation, it is also necessary to consider the UEFA Financial Fair Play regulations where the football governing body clearly demands football clubs to live within their means – placing restrictions on permitted levels of debt – and not to spend more of their turnover on signing players, a situation that is not completely new. To put this transfer in an economic context, the 2018 Deloitte Money League report estimated that FC Barcelona revenues, ranked third in the table, for 2016/2017, were €648.3 million, while Paris Saint-Germain revenues, ranked seventh, were €486.2 million (Deloitte, 2018). Neymar Jr.'s five-year contract was expected to bring around €55 million a year before taxes, meaning that the total deal, spread over the course of a five-year contract, could cost €90 million annually. This transfer fee, as well as the contract, marked a milestone, as it was the highest transfer fee paid for any professional football player at any level for the period 2010–2017 (Poli, Ravenel, and Besson, 2017).

As one might expect, the departure of such an iconic player, on 7 August 2017, after FC Barcelona played a preseason match against the Brazilian Serie A club, Chapacoense, brought public criticism against the player from a group of FC Barcelona fans who did not approve of the transfer. Many FC Barcelona fans questioned his transfer during the abovementioned match, some of them shouting "Neymar muérete" ("Neymar die"). From a sociological and managerial perspective, it is worth analysing the extreme reactions of contemporary fans who more often go beyond how fans feel betrayed by their loved players. As Figure 4.1 shows, the money spent by the main European clubs for the transfer of players over the last decades has grown from €8.5 million paid in 1988 to about €222 million paid for the transfer of Neymar Jr. (Poli, Ravenel, and Besson, 2017). The chairperson of Paris Saint-Germain Al-Khelaifi had decided to buy Neymar Jr. from one of their main competitors in Europe, FC Barcelona, as a critical factor to the economic, commercial, and sporting success of the club. Apart from this, the transfer of Neymar Jr. could illustrate the use of an iconic player to increase the global brand of the club. However, the massive investment made by Paris Saint-Germain since the Sheik Mohammed Al Thani, current Amir of Qatar, took over the control of the club in 2011, estimated at nearly one billion euros, has contributed to raising major concerns over its effects on the structures and policies in European football in coming years. In this respect, Malyon (2017) raised concerns by saying: "Neymar's move from Barcelona to PSG is an era-defining transfer – it will alter the European footballing landscape forever." These changes will impact European football structures and policies.

Conclusions

The present chapter highlighted that launching of a range of policy statements, regulations, and rules by the EU institutions, the UEFA, and the European leagues – chief among them the Bosman case ruling on players' mobility, the UEFA Club Licensing system and Financial Fair Play – demonstrates the growing interest of the EU institutions and European football bodies in improving the governance and management of football across Europe.

European clubs' revenues have clearly escalated and they are expected to increase substantially over the coming decades; however, some questions about how this increase in revenues will benefit the governance of clubs and how the reactions of fans to these transformations remain unanswered. Some fans agree with the evolution of governance of most European clubs, whilst most criticism comes from existing fans who seem clearly disenchanted with the game. A related side effect of this economic growth is that it has also contributed to undermining the much-desired competitive balance between leagues and clubs across Europe and within national competitions. It is still a challenge to ensure an adequate level of competitive balance in the main European football leagues, and above all, to manage the increased commercialisation and commodification of football and their effects and types of responses and reactions to both processes among fans. The evidence shows that some of the aforementioned and consolidated trends in the European football sector are still today far from the recommendations of the IESR report and the more recent UEFA financial, managerial, and legal regulations (i.e., the Club Licensing and Financial Fair Play). Looking at the near future, relevant stakeholders in the European football industry, such as national governing bodies as well as professional clubs, should respond to the needs and expectations of all types of fans.

References

Acero, I., Serrano, R., and Dimitropoulos, P. (2017) Ownership structure and financial performance in European football. *Corporate Governance: The International Journal of Business in Society*, 17(3), 511–523. https://doi.org/10.1108/CG-07-2016-0146

Arnaut, J. (2006) *Independent European Sport Review, A report by José Luis Arnaut.* [online] Retrieved from: http://www.independentfootballreview.com/doc/A3619.pdf

Armstrong, M. (2017) 30 years of soccer transfers: boy that escalated quickly. *Statista.* [online[Retrieved from: https://www.statista.com/chart/10527/30-years-of-soccer-transfers/

Baroncelli, A. and Lago, U. (2006) Italian football. *Journal of Sports Economics*, 7(1), 13–28.

Baroncelli, A. and Caruso, R. (2011) The organization and economics of Italian top football. In: H. Gammelsaeter and B. Senaux, B. (eds.). *The Organization and Governance of Top Football Across Europe: An Institutional Perspective* (pp. 168–181). Oxford: Routledge.

Bundesliga (2017) *Bundesliga Report 2017. The Economic State of German Professional Football.* Frankfurt/Main: DFL Deutsche FuBball Liga Gmbh.

Cleland, J. (2010) From passive to active: the changing relationship between supporters and football clubs. *Soccer & Society*, 11(5), 537–552

Conn, D. (1997) *The Football Business: Fair Game in the 1990s?* Edinburgh, Scotland: Mainstream.

Deloitte (2017) *Planet Football. Football Money League.* Manchester: Sports Business Group.

Deloitte (2018) *Rising Stars.* Manchester: Sports Business Group.

Department for Culture, Media and Sport (DCMS) (2016) Government expert working group on football supporter ownership and engagement. [online] Retrieved from: https://www.gov.uk/government/publications/government-expert-working-group-on-football-supporter-ownership-and-engagement

Doidge, M. (2015) *Football Italia: Italian Football in an Age of Globalisation.* London: Bloomsbury

Doidge, M. (2017) Democracy and supporter ownership. In: J. Hughson, K. Moore, R. Spaaij, and J. Maguire, J. (eds.). *Routledge Handbook of Football Studies* (pp. 336–347). London: Routledge.

English Premier League (EPL) (2016) Premier League handbook season 2016/17. [online] Retrieved from: https://www.premierleague.com/publications

Football Research in an Enlarge Europe (FREE) (2015) *Free policy brief no. 2: Football stakeholders & governance.* European Commission. Available at: http://www.free-project.eu/documents-free/Forms/FREE%20Policy%20Brief%202%20-%20Governance.pdf (Accessed 30 August 2017).

Gammelsaeter, H. and Senaux, B. (2011) *The Organization and Governance of Top Football Across Europe: An Institutional Perspective.* Oxford: Routledge.

García, B. (2007) The independent European sport review: half full or half empty?. *Entertainment and Sports Law Journal*, 4(3), 5. DOI: http://doi.org/10.16997/eslj.82

García, B. (2011) The influence of the EU on the governance of football. In: H. Gammelsaeter and B. Senaux (eds.). *The Organization and Governance of Top Football Across Europe: An Institutional Perspective* (pp. 32–45). Oxford: Routledge.

García, B. (2017) Football and governance. In: J. Hughson, K. Moore, R. Spaaij. and J. Maguire, J. (eds.). *Routledge Handbook of Football Studies* (pp. 99–110). London: Routledge.

García, B. and Welford, J. (2015) Supporters and football governance, from customers to stakeholders. A literature review and agenda for research. *Sport Management Review*, 18, 517–528.

García, B., de Wolff, M., Welford, J. and Smith, B. (2017) Facilitating inclusivity and broadening understanding of access at football clubs: the role of disabled supporter associations. *European Sport Management Quarterly*, 17(2), 226–43.

Gay de Liébana, J.M. (2016) *La gran burbuja del fútbol.* Barcelona: Conecta.

Giulianotti, R. (2002) Supporters, followers, fans and flaneurs: A taxonomy of spectator identities in football. *Journal of Sport and Social Issues*, 26(1), 25–46

Giulianotti, R. (2005) Sport spectators and the social consequences of commodification: critical perspectives from Scottish football. *Journal of Sport and Social Issues*, 29(4), 386–410.

Gómez, S., Martí, C., and Bofarull Mollo, C. (2011) Commercialisation and transformation in Spanish top football. In: H. Gammelsaeter and B. Senaux (eds.). *The Organization and Governance of Top Football Across Europe: An Institutional Perspective* (pp. 182–194). Oxford: Routledge.

Hassan, D. and Hamil, S. (2010) Who owns football? The governance and management of the club game worldwide. *Soccer & Society*, 11(4), 343–353.

Hamil, S., Morrow, S, Idle, C., Rossi, G., and Faccendini, S. (2010) The governance and regulation of Italian football. *Soccer & Society*, 11(4), 373–413.

Holt, M. (2007) The ownership and control of elite club competition in European football. *Soccer & Society*, 8(1), 50–67.

Hughson, J., Moore, K., Spaaij, R., and Maguire, J. (2017) *Routledge Handbook of Football Studies.* London: Routledge.

Kennedy, P. and Kennedy, D. (2012) Football supporters and the commercialization of football: comparative responses across Europe. *Soccer &Society*, 13(3), 327–340.

Laurens, J. (2017) Neymar: how the record-breaking €222m move to PSG unfolded. *The Guardian*. 4 August. [online] Retrieved from: https://www.theguardian.com/football/2017/aug/04/neymar-how-record-breaking-move-to-psg-unfolded

Llopis-Goig, R. (2015) *Spanish Football and Social Change. Sociological Investigations.* London: Palgrave-Macmillan.

Malyon, E. (2017) Neymar's move from Barcelona to PSG is an era-defining transfer – it will alter the European footballing landscape forever. *The Guardian*, 2 August. [online] Retrieved from: http://www.

independent.co.uk/sport/football/transfers/neymar-transfer-news-psg-barcelona-200m-cost-fee-real-madrid-weak-a7868806.html

Merkel, U. (2012) Football fans and clubs in Germany: conflicts, crises and compromises. *Soccer &Society*, 13(3), 359–376.

Morrow, S. (2011) History, longevity, and change. Football in England and Scotland. In: H. Gammelsaeter and B. Senaux (eds.). 2011. *The Organization and Governance of Top Football Across Europe: An Institutional Perspective* (pp. 46–61). Oxford: Routledge.

Nash, R. (2000) Contestation in modern English professional football: the Independence Supporters Association movement. *International Review for the Sociology of Sport*, 35(4), 464–486.

Nauright, J. and Ramfjord, J. (2010) Who owns England´s game? American professional sporting influences and foreign ownership in the Premier League. *Soccer & Society*, 11(4), 428–441.

Paramio-Salcines, J. L., Babiak, K., and Walters, G. (2013) *Routledge Handbook of Sport and Corporate Social Responsibility.* London: Routledge.

Paramio-Salcines, J.L., Grady, J., and Downs, P. (2014) Growing the football game: the increasing economic and social relevance of older fans and those with disabilities in the European football industry. *Soccer &Society*, 15(6), 864–882. DOI:10.1080/14660970.2014.92062

Paramio-Salcines, J.L., Kitchin, P., and Downs, P. (2018) Promoting universal accessibility for disabled and older fans to European stadia: a holistic journey sequence approach (HOPES). In: D. Hassan (ed.). *Managing Sport Business*, (2nd ed.)., (pp. 530–560). London: Routledge.

Peeters, T. and Szymanski, S. (2014) Financial fair play in European football. *Economic Policy*, 29(78), 343–390.

Poli, R., Ravenel, L., and Besson, R. (2017) Transfer market analysis: tracking the money (2010–2017). CIES Football Observatory Monthly Report, n° 27, September. [online] Retrieved from: http://www.football-observatory.com/IMG/sites/mr/mr27/en/phone/index.html

Senaux, B. (2011) The regulated commercialization of French football. In: H. Gammelsaeter and B. Senaux (eds), *The Organization and Governance of Top Football Across Europe: An Institutional Perspective* (pp. 123–137). Oxford: Routledge.

UEFA (2015a) *UEFA Club licensing and financial fair play regulations.* UEFA: Nyon. [online] Retrieved from: http://www.uefa.com/MultimediaFiles/Download/Tech/uefaorg/General/02/26/77/91/2267791_DOWNLOAD.pdf

UEFA (2015b) *Club Licensing. 10 years on … Evolvement of the club licensing system since its introduction in 2004.* UEFA: Nyon. [online] Retrieved from: http://www.uefa.com/MultimediaFiles/Download/uefaorg/FinancialFairPlay/02/32/60/65/2326065_DOWNLOAD.pdf

UEFA & CAFÉ (2017) *Disability access officer handbook.* UEFA: Nyon. [online] Retrieved from: https://www.uefa.com/MultimediaFiles/Download/uefaorg/General/02/50/38/59/2503859_DOWNLOAD.pdf

Welford, J., García, B., and Smith, B. (2015) A "healthy" future? Supporters´ perceptions of the current state of English football. *Soccer &Society*, 16(2–3), 322–343.

Wilkesmann, U., Blutner, D., and Müller, C. (2011) German football. Organising for the European top. In: H. Gammelsaeter and B. Senaux (eds.). *The Organization and Governance of Top Football Across Europe: An Institutional Perspective* (pp. 138–153). Oxford: Routledge.

5

Points, pounds, and politics in the governance of football

Hallgeir Gammelsæter

Introduction

What is football? We may have different views of what football is, or what it should be, or where current developments takes it. Analysing that is exactly what this chapter is about. To be more precise, it is about how we could and, perhaps should, analyse it. How to understand what it is and where it is going or should be going. I do not assert that there is a final answer to these questions, but to govern football one must have an idea of where to go.

In this chapter, I depart from an observation that I think is widely shared. It is that, in the past, football developed as an autonomous sport with its own integrated set of ideas (logic) and a pyramid of governing bodies. While the pyramid is still in place, this structure now staggers as commercial and state actors increasingly have cast their eyes, and logic, and money on football.

A question such as "how should football be governed more effectively?" may seem uncontroversial, but the stance here is that governance structures necessarily serve somebody more than it benefits others. Therefore, the issue of governance is a question of whose interest football should serve most. Whose football should football's governance structure realise? Disregarding this question does not make football less political. While sport frequently profiles itself as a-political, I claim that it is not. It is highly political, and can never be neutral or a-political. The institutional approach posits diverse institutional logics, in part hinging on diverse interests in society, against each other. The attraction of football exposes it to many stakeholders that struggle to define it and benefit from it. How does this shape the governance of football and its development?

In the next section, I briefly outline the basics of the institutional framework, using examples from football to illustrate its applicability to studying football. I move on to address the concept of governance, showing its relevance for conceptualising football's development. In the following three sections, I draw an ideal typical outline of three institutional logics relevant for the analysis of football governance; the definitional elements of football as a game; the ideas driving the sphere of business; and the central elements of the state. All of these are related to observations of present-day football. In the end, I wrap up the discussion by pointing out how the governance of football and its development is subject to competing logics.

As will become clear, I understand the institutional framework used in this chapter as a cultural model. This means that football is conceptualised as socially constructed, and consequently it is different "things" in different cultures. To simplify the analysis, the main cultural reference point in this chapter is European football.

The institutional organisation of human activity

Imagine that society can be divided to separate sections or spheres of human activity. Be it family life, school, subsistence, religion, politics, defense, leisure and sport, etc. These spheres of life have to be organised and even if this organising obviously changes through time and across cultures, it is likely that there will be differences across the spheres. To take an example, it is possible to see politics organised a bit like a family with a family head distributing political roles among the family clan. This "principle" even has a name, nepotism. In most contemporary societies, this way of politics is considered unacceptable and ineffective, at least by the masses. On the contrary, politics should be democratic and based on elections and referenda among the populace. While present-day families are perhaps more participative than they were in times past, and some may practice "referenda" to decide the next holiday destination or the Saturday night menu, the principle that families have natural heads, still often husbands, that distribute roles and duties is far more acceptable and used than it is in politics. As this example shows, despite some exception and experiment, the used principles of how to organise human activities are different across different spheres of society. For good reason, one might add, because it makes sense to us.

Institutional organisation sociology departs from the idea that it is adequate to study society as diverse spheres or domains of activity. These spheres institutionalise their unique ways of organising, as indicated by concepts such as institutional pillars (Scott, 2001) and institutional orders (Friedland and Alford, 1991; Thornton, Ocasio, and Lounsbury, 2012). Whilst there is no agreement on what the spheres of society are, this is perhaps the least important. What is important is the usefulness of the analytic approach in describing and explaining differences of organising across spheres, roughly defined, and why and how they change.

Besides the idea of institutional domains, institutional theory assumes that we as human beings construct our social life. It is not entirely given that nepotism does not work effectively in politics (or football for that matter) or that families could not be democratic. Rather, what we experience as realities, or rational, is socially constructed, so societies may experiment with how to organise politics and families and sport and arrive at different solutions that are all seen as rational. The plural is important here, because, as we know, diverse groups of people construct diverse meanings of what constitutes, for instance, football as a game or how to govern it.

In a more condensed parlance, we may say that the theoretical model of institutionalism is that diverse organising principles, practices, and symbols, all socially constructed through time, institutionalise the governance of diverse spheres of life. Despite exceptions and similarities, we still do not run the government in the same way we run the family, sport in the same way we run the church, and working life as if it were football. Moreover, the way we organise these spheres of life, sport again being a good example, also differs across territories and nations.

Nevertheless, "underneath" the observable in each of these (and other) spheres of social life are institutional logics, the collective ideas that underpin actual governance. Institutional logics are "composed" of patterns of cultural assumptions, values, beliefs and symbols, and material practices which provide meaning to the way we organise time, space, and our daily activities within them (cf. Thornton and Ocasio, 2008). If one looks closely, football is very rich on assumptions, values, beliefs, symbols, and language and material practices. Football is embedded and suffused in its logics. There would be no football without it.

Whilst it is fair to say that we do organise diverse spheres of life differently, it is likewise a fact that we, as individuals, endlessly move across these spheres, because we occupy roles in most of them, as family members, citizens, customers, employers, employees, fans, etc. Social spheres are not isolated from each other and although organising principles, practices, and symbols are institutionalised as being rational, they are still susceptible to social reconstruction and change. Meaning production is never-ending, even if most of the time we seem to reproduce the status quo. However, football is a good example that stability and institutionalisation often go hand in hand with reconstruction and change. While the game itself has not changed much the last decade, the governance of it certainly has. The tournaments, the governing bodies, the policies, and the interdependence and interaction between diverse bodies have changed much (cf. Gammelsæter and Senaux, 2011; Garcia, 2007) and is still being transformed.

Change typically happens because the spheres are interdependent and their borders permeable. This means that they are being subjected to each other's standards. A very good football example is the Bosman case, which can be seen as a clash between the institution of sport, represented by UEFA, and the institution of government, represented by the EU commission. To hyperbolise, before Bosman football was defined as sport, while after it was defined as working life. The Bosman case was over the definition of professional sport exercise. Was it to be understood as a regular employer–employee relationship and regulated as such, or was sport too specific to be subject to ordinary working life? Should society keep admitting sport the right to bind professional athletes to clubs and contracts they cannot leave?

According to contemporary sport law, the Belgian player Jean-Marc Bosman was perhaps correctly treated as a footballer, but he found his rights as a citizen violated by the same law. The European court supported this view and judged in the favour of Bosman. Despite efforts to do so (Garcia, 2007), in the end, sport (UEFA) could not run away from the verdict because sport and football depend on governments. The sphere of sport relies on governments for security, regulation, and revenue. As a result, the relationship between players and clubs changed, leaving the professional players in a position in which they were acknowledged as employees.

However, such changes do normally not lead to diverse spheres collapsing into one. Their dominating institutional logics still separate them. If they do not, it does not make sense to regard them as different spheres and institutions. For football (and sport) the question is whether it is in fact separate from other spheres or if its patterns of cultural assumptions, values, beliefs, symbols, and organisational practices are the same as in the spheres of government, business, family, or other spheres. Is it unique?

Governance and football

The issue of spheres being separate and having unique logics obviously relates to how the activities of a sphere are being regulated and governed. Governance and government are often seen as twin concepts. Government entails the notion that a governing body can define and control its sphere. In the past, this was perhaps the case for nations but also for football. Football affairs were dealt with by its national (football associations), regional (the confederations), and international (FIFA) governments. While this formal pyramid is still in place, it is relevant to ask the question: do these football-specific bodies any longer define and control the domain of football?

The concept of governance is a response to the observation that governments increasingly are not in control. Instead, governing bodies have to compete, adjust, and cooperate with other organisations and groups and hence the structure and changes of a domain, including its borders, are subject to contestation and negotiation. This is the case in football where the traditional top-down hierarchies of "governments" far from control their sport any more (cf. Henry and Lee, 2004). On the contrary, football is changing through interaction in a complex web of stakeholders who make claims on it. Again, the Bosman case outlined above is a good illustration. The governing bodies of football were not able to control its domain because the professionalisation of football meant that it was increasingly perceived as business (certainly by the EU commission), and as businesses are regulated by states; thus, the EU Court of Justice ruled there be no exception for professional sport. What happened was that one of the spheres football depended on (the state) intervened in football's domain.

Relating this back to institutional logics, the governments of sport increasingly had to deal with the logics of competing spheres, the logic of EU regulation being one of them. Government had to give way to governance. Today, the field of football is highly subjected to contestation and negotiation. Take the Financial Fair Play scheme that was launched by UEFA to regulate professional clubs' revenue streams and hopefully curb the widening financial gap between clubs in Europe (UEFA, 2011). To be able to enforce such a scheme, UEFA is highly dependent on political and public support and to be in accord with the regulations of business. Simultaneously, those forces that contest the scheme, notably big leagues and club owners, may be willing to exploit loopholes and bypass the regulation (e.g., Geey, 2011; Preuss, Haugen, and Schubert, 2014). Cases, such as the transfer of Neymar from FC Barcelona to Paris Saint-Germain in the summer of 2017, nicely illustrate that governance of present-day football is beyond the control of the football governing bodies.

Thus, governance has a highly political dimension. Who owns football? Who defines and directs its future? Which logics are relevant in defining it, and what rules apply? To understand football's past, present, and future one has to understand the politics of football governance.

Related to this is the understanding of how football's governing bodies are designed and how these operate. In the institutional view, this is much a question about what organising principles, practices, and symbols are institutionalised and whether football's diverse stakeholders see them as being effective and rational. What are the legitimated strategies, actions, structures, and systems created by football's mandated organisations and directors (cf. Ferkins, Shilbury, and McDonald, 2005)? Does the exposed version of football governance live up to the current standards of corporate social responsibility (e.g. Breitbarth, Walzel, Anagnostopoulos, and van Eekeren, 2015) or "good governance" (e.g. Geeraert, Alm, and Groll, 2014); that is, "the accepted norms or values for the just means of allocation of resources, and profits or losses (financial or other) and of the conduct of processes involved in the management and direction of organisations" (Henry and Lee, 2004, p. 26)? If football's governance structure is not considered rational any more, there will be stakeholders working to change it (cf. Lawrence and Suddaby, 2006).

The move from government to governance, from defining and controlling its domain to having to fight and negotiate to remain in its centre is a signal that there is controversy and ongoing redefinition of the predominant institutional logic(s) of the sphere of football. In recent years, FIFA and UEFA have been under increasing and unprecedented attack for not keeping current standards of good governance. Moreover, national FAs, leagues, and clubs have to fight to keep up their legitimacy among the public and their own fans. In the press, examples flourish,[1] reflecting a public debate that is no longer confined to the game and what happens on the pitch, but embracing issues of governance, many of which leave the sport not as the beautiful game anymore but as a "cut-throat, ruthless and results-based industry" (Kelly, 2017, p. 151). The stark contrasts with the ancient ideals of the sport and with contemporary ideals of good governance, transparency, democracy, and corporate social responsibility leave the governing bodies of football in a weak position and with the risk that the sport (in its current form) loses its appeal to the public.

Figure 5.1 Sport governance across interdependent and potentially conflictual institutional relationships
Source: Adapted from Gammelsæter, H. (2016).

Figure 5.1 illustrates how sport is conceptualised as interdependent with other ideal typical spheres or institutions in society (sport may be seen as dependent on other institutions as well, such as family and science, but to avoid complicating the analysis we confine ourselves to these which are pertinent), all potentially in conflict and with diverse core ideas in which their rules of the game are rooted. The action of sport and sports organisations results from the interplay and tensions across these institutions, and questions may be asked about where football is heading within this triangle. Has it transformed from being a sport with its own inherent logic and powerful governments to pure commercial industry or a blend of industry and international politics where stakeholders outside football's governing bodies drive its development? Is the governance structure of football hollowed out to the extent that it merely window dresses the mix of commercialism and politics of present-day football? Has the domain of football as a sport collapsed?

The institutional logics of football

A sport is a (socially) constructed game with an appeal to challenging the human body and mind (and sometimes the animal body and mind, like in horse racing). Competition is a means to extracting the best of effort. Certainly, sport may produce diverse external benefits, be it religious ritual, health, social integration and discipline, national unity, entertainment, or revenue generation. To understand its core nature, however, I think we have to ask what motivates athletes, or what motivated athletes to engage in the sport before they became professional. I think this has not changed much. Footballers typically develop from childhood, and the sport heavily relies on kids and youngsters who enjoy playing and winning and master their trade. The game is for them an absorbing activity that is enjoyed for its own sake to the extent it becomes central to their identity. This is not to deny that athletes may have extrinsic reasons for engaging in sport, such as high salaries and status, but the principal reasons for engaging in it at an early stage are intrinsic and autotelic. For the athlete, the value arises in the participation and excelling in the sport itself (Walsh and Giulianotti, 2007). They cannot *not* practice the sport.

This likens elite sport much more to art and music than to the jobs most of us occupy; jobs we perhaps did not anticipate or start training for until our late teenage years, at best. We can only imagine what football (or other sports) would be like with a similar training and recruitment system. For now, and still, the football industry stands on the shoulders of grassroots football, which it has in part industrialised by the means of scouting and academy training. However, an education where hardly any of the students qualify for a professional job (e.g. Conn, 2017; Platts, 2012) is unlikely to be accepted outside of sport, and it would not be viable unless it floated on intrinsic motivation and respect for the dreams of kids and youngsters.

Another feature that defines football is the fine weighing of competition and cooperation, where each is dependent on the other (Chadwick, 2009). Both are indispensable but too much of the one will harm the other. The competition in sport is not such that you may gobble up and do away with your contenders. Sport competitions are collective and meaningless without contenders. Despite the claim that "the winner takes it all" winners and losers start competing with a fresh start every new season (in fact, every week). Likewise, the competition must be trustworthy and its integrity not "tainted" by agreements behind the scene, whether it is caused by fixing, multi-club ownership or other forms of cooperation or cheating that is not levelling the playing field. Moreover, competition should be balanced and ensure uncertainty of outcome, leaving a fair chance for everybody to beat his or her contestant. If not, it is assumed the sport will lose its attraction (Szymanski, 2001).

The nature of the sport is also such that the individual game relies on the tournament and history of past games to have value. Individual games, some of which evoke rivalry and attract immense attention would fall short of attracting many spectators unless they were played in the context of a tournament and its history. This translates into an inescapable interdependent relationship between football clubs (and between national associations). This tricky issue is solved differently in the European and US versions of team sport (cf. Smith and Stewart, 2010), but it cannot escape the issue of collective regulation versus individual freedom. Without regulation, fair play would be impossible. However, the idea of fair play is a social construction so how much and by what means the sport should be regulated is typically subject to debate – the debate over governance.

Another defining feature of football is its zero sum characteristic (Gammelsæter, 2013). A maximum amount of points is allocated among the teams every season (this point is in part thwarted when teams are awarded three points for a win, one for a draw and zero for a lost game, but this does not basically change the validity of the argument). This is irrespective of the quality of the play, the salaries of the players, the spectacle on the stands, the leadership abilities of management, etc. The point system is non-pecuniary and valid across big and small leagues, and it makes football intelligible and accessible despite its complicated and puzzling nature in terms of understanding cause-effect relationships. One might add the confinement that teams may not at any time field more than 11 players, which has dramatic effects in terms of enhancing the chances of the small towards the big, David towards Goliath. This makes football a powerful medium through which places and nations may expand pride and identity, hence the loyal fan base of many clubs and nations. Maybe it is this blend of opportunity, simplicity, and complication that makes football so attractive to so many people?

Like any social construction football is susceptible to reconstruction and change because it is not crystal clear among stakeholders what it is that constitutes the core of football and, even more so, how the sport is preserved and improved. On the one hand, football is different things to different people. On the other, football may not be anything. Yes, it has perhaps elements of religion, family, politics, business, etc., but that does not mean it can be reduced to any of these. I think the elements outlined above are some of the most defining features of football, and if I am right, governance concerns exactly if and how stakeholders are able to preserve and buttress such defining elements. Governance would be much easier if the stakeholders agreed on what organising principles, practices and symbols are rational for football, but the attraction of football, and I should add intrinsic dynamics in the sport itself, complicate such agreement.

Football, like all competition sport, is progressive, and chasing sporting excellence is costly. This intrinsic dynamic complicates agreement on what football is. The thirst for increasing income seems to be infinite. To expand the sport, football early turned to public bodies and business to finance its growth. Over the past 150 years or so, football has transformed from being local and regional to attracting international and global interest; from being amateur to increasing professionalisation; and from organisation structures rooted in mutuality to a commercial industry characterised by huge financial gaps across clubs and nations. From an institutional perspective, it is relevant to ask how football has exposed itself along the road to the logics of its main funding sources and how the interaction with other spheres of society has influenced its understanding of what football is and should be (Gammelsæter and Senaux, 2011).

Football and the institutional logics of business

If the sphere of sport has its defining features, the same goes for business. What is the meaning of the sphere of business? There may be diverging views on whether profit is the aim of the firm, or if it is merely the means by which firms fulfil more decent aims, such as producing goods and satisfying human needs. In any case, profit-making or maximisation is key to business, and the motor behind the neo-liberal capitalist economy that embraces sport (Coakley, 2011). Profit-making fuels expansion of production and increasing consumption. To make profit, firms need sellable products, whether they are tangible or not, and to achieve this they must communicate the quality, price, and advantages of their commodities to potential customers (Walsh and Giulianotti, 2001). Businesses that are not making profit go into bankruptcy (or are acquired by competitors).

As we know, the sphere of business has responded positively to football's invitation to expand its budget. If we put aside benefactors, the approaches of the business sphere to football have been several. One is to capitalise on football's outreach to their potential customers, in particular since the age of TV-broadcasting, by using clubs and players to brand its products or the name of the company, hence improving its profits through marketing (sponsorship) [see Chapter 8 in this Handbook]. This model may seem innocent because it has no ownership implications, but given the importance of sponsors' money, it harbours the danger that sponsors influence the club's decisions to align with sponsor's perspectives, which may diverge from the perspectives of other stakeholders.

Another model is incorporating football clubs as limited liability companies with a shareholder structure, which divides the profit and share value among those that own the shares. In continental Europe, corporatisation of clubs has increased over recent decades, and regulation has become more lenient (Gammelsæter and Senaux, 2011). In England, where clubs have been limited liability companies for generations, restriction on dividend payments to owners has not been effectively enforced since the 1980s (Morrow, 2011), hence clubs have been floated and shares have changed hands like in any other commercial industry. In accord with business logic, mutuality principles are less influential and football sees more and more clubs being transformed into for-profit companies.

If business is about making profit, then it follows that commercial owners in football will bring in their expertise to commodify football as a commercial product, and do their best to achieve return on investment. This is not easy in a sport where there are few winners and many losers. "The winner takes it all" rule is offset with the "winners' curse" (Rosenbaum and Swindell, 2002) and win maximisation being more important than profit maximisation (Garcia-del-Barrio and Szymanski, 2009). With the hard competition for the best players to stake a place in the top, costs are going up but without guaranteeing success and return on investment. More points do not always translate into more pounds on the margin. It is no wonder owners of rich football clubs prefer uneven distribution of league revenue.

In industries where the profit margin is low due to many actors and hard competition, rationalisation often takes the form of bigger actors acquiring the smaller to obtain economies of scale and higher profit. This kind of measure goes against the David versus Goliath opportunities in football described above. Restriction on participation is realised in the US oligarchic franchise system where the number of competitors is strictly controlled with the aim to reap profit from the sport.[2] While closed-league oligarchy is perhaps effective in balancing competition and cooperation, it happens at the expense of the many to the profit of the few. Needless to say, the US closed-league model is socially constructed too, but that does not prove European fans, politicians, or UEFA will accept it. However, a European closed Super League has been on the agenda for almost two decades (Holt, 2007), so efforts to change football to align better with a business logic have emerged already.

What has been seen in European football over a long period is the gradual abandonment of solidarity principles, most notably materialised in the allocation of broadcasting revenue and prize money across leagues and clubs. The development has been unambiguously towards less redistribution and greater dividends to clubs in the upper echelons of national leagues, which are the same clubs that qualify for the European Champions League and reap the benefits of this lucrative tournament. The consequence is the further widening of the gap between big and small clubs (and football nations), but also a system that corresponds better with the business logic because, relatively speaking, the top clubs are paid better for the points and fortify their position in the top. The for-profit logic is changing football.

Football and the institutional logics of the state

What is the meaning of states? An ideal typical answer is that states should deliver crucial political goods such as human security, rule of law, political participation, and welfare services (Rotberg, 2003). Defence, education, and health systems, however good they are, are witness of such objectives, and most states support sport as contributing to these aims. While intuitively intelligible, security and wellbeing are almost "catch-all" aims, which for sport is something like a double-edged sword. On the one hand, sport fits into so many of a state's policies: prepare soldiers and police, educate and discipline the young, promote social and ethnic integration, build national pride and identity, enhance trade and tourism etc. Given sport's infinite thirst for more funding, its versatility may seem like a huge benefit. It has a lot to offer in exchange for public funding. On the other hand, as outlined above, all of these functions are externalities to sport and in practice, they may sometimes conflict. The aims of the athletes, their coaches and support staff is not to implement public policy. Their motivation is to excel in the sport and if state funding or regulation thwart this aim it may come at a huge cost.

I described earlier how Bosman capitalised on the logic of the state to improve his position as an athlete and how this changed the conditions of professional football. The case led to a heated situation between the EU (EU commission) and the football associations, as if it was a wake-up call for the coming of governance at the expense of government in the field of sport.

EU policies undermined the vertical channels of government in football and empowered stakeholders such as players and clubs, which had a weak position in the traditional pyramid (Garcia, 2011). However, it also prompted renewed cooperation between EU and football authorities and the first EU policy paper on sport addressing sport's economic and social role in Europe (European Commission, 2007, Garcia, 2007; 2011).

Nevertheless, the EU's economic policy, rooted in the principle of free movement of goods, services, people, and capital to boost the gross domestic product (and presumed wellbeing for Europeans) may privilege some stakeholders over others and restrain the development of effective sport policy at EU and national levels. Is the state throwing sport in the hands of business, or is it using its regulating power to defend sport towards the excesses of the market? The routes to wellbeing are contested, and if governance rather than government is the manner through which the future is shaped, football's authorities should engage in politics and negotiation to influence the direction of regulation and resource allocation.

One of the privileges of the state is to regulate the market and redistribute income among its citizens. It is beyond doubt that currently regulation is perhaps the biggest challenge in football. In the current situation, there is less of cooperation and competition alike. Both suffer. It has been claimed that the recent developments in football have led to financial doping (Olsson, 2011; Iorwerth, Tomkins and Riley, 2017), a situation whereby clubs use money they have not earned on the football activity or activities related to it. This situation has widened the financial gap between clubs and increased the chance of the richest few to win at home and qualifying for European tournaments where they earn even more money. Another consequence is that the uncertainty of outcome is undermined (Iorwerth et al., 2017).

It is interesting that while the business logic has transformed football, football authorities seem not to have approached the state, notably the EU, forcefully to aid in regulating the football industry. Although licencing regulation introduced by football's governing bodies has not proved effective, there are few signs that UEFA has the capability and appetite to do whatever is needed to fight financial doping and protect the spirit of football (Iorwerth et al., 2017). There is an interesting similarity here with the situation that precipitated the establishment of the World Anti-Doping Agency (WADA) for medical doping back in 1999. With the Festina doping scandal in cycling as a backdrop, increasing discontent with the International Olympic Committee (IOC) as the anti-doping body culminated in a coup by European sport ministers that insisted anti-doping must be fought by a body independent of the sport establishment (Hanstad et al., 2008). The ongoing corruption scandals in FIFA and UEFA, starting in 2016, is surely not second to the disclosure of doping in cycling. It precipitated the ousting of presidents Sepp Blatter and Michel Platini and led to the indictment of several directors, and an inquiry into the conduct of the incumbent presidents is ongoing. Will the state intervene in financial doping in the same way it intervened in anti-doping when IOC failed to pass the legitimacy test, the test of good governance?

Governance under competing logics – a final discussion

Studying football governance from an institutional logics perspective has the unequivocal advantage of asking questions about the assumptions governing bodies and stakeholders pursue. The institutional logics perspective is as a meta-theoretical framework for analysing relationships among institutions, organisations, and individuals in social systems (Thornton et al., 2012), such as in sport. This means that institutional change can be studied vertically as well as horizontally, at the macro and meso as well as the micro level. Importantly, this may help us relate actual cases, decisions, and strategies to their broader meaning and long-term effects. While theorising topics such as good governance and corporate social responsibility, to name a few examples, may be important, the institutional logics framework digs deeper and knocks harder on the nerves of the object under study. To illustrate, CSR initiatives may well increase concomitantly with increased brutalisation of the industry (Calvin, 2017; Kelly, 2017), and conforming to good governance principles may appear as a rather passive response to institutional pressures (DiMaggio, 1988; Oliver, 1991). In fact, employing codes of ethics may become an institutionalised practice that confers legitimacy on the organisation while the organisation distances itself further from the moral foundation of the codes (Long and Driscoll, 2008).

In this treatment, we have posited that football authorities, business, and state powers are separate yet interdependent spheres, but at the same time interdependent and in potential conflict. With the expansion of professionalisation and commercialisation, this situation has intensified and football's authorities do not control their domain. Hence, governance has replaced government and football's governing bodies have increasingly been exposed to, and embraced the logic of business. More than ever the race for trophies is a race for the big money, putting decision-makers in a compelling situation where they keep arm's length from the regulation powers of the state. This has effects for the way football is organised and managed, for the ownership of clubs, the club's access to tournaments and fans' access to watching them, the fixtures, recruitment patterns and devices, the salaries of players, ticket prices, revenue generation and (re)distribution of revenues – in essence, almost every aspect of the game. Football is being reconstructed before our eyes, largely without any intervention from public authorities, which might have slowed down the transformation, or any defenders of the football logic. It is more likely the State has facilitated the transformation. Seemingly, football is currently a big success, but simultaneously football as we know it might be on the brink of losing itself.

Notes

1 Cf. for instance the sport/football section of sites such as *The Guardian, Inside World Football, The Conversation*.
2 Closed leagues are not untried in the European context. In France, for instance, the "Group of authorised clubs" existing between 1944 and 1969, was closed to amateur sides (Senaux, 2011).

References

Breitbarth, T., Walzel, S., Anagnostopoulos, C., and van Eekeren, F. (2015) Corporate social responsibility and governance in sport: "Oh, the things you can find, if you don't stay behind!" *Corporate Governance. The International Journal of Business in Society*, 15(2), 254–273.
Calvin, M. (2017) *No Hunger in Paradise: The Players. The Journey. The Dream*. London: Cornerstone.
Chadwick, S. (2009) From outside lane to inside track: Sport management research in the twenty-first century. *Management Decision*, 47, 191–203.
Coakley, J. (2011) Ideology doesn't just happen: sports and neoliberalism, *Journal of ALESDE*, 1, 67–84.
Conn, D. (2017) "Football's biggest issue": the struggle facing boys rejected by academies. *The Guardian*,. [online] Retrieved from:https://www.theguardian.com/football/2017/oct/06/football-biggest-issue-boys-rejected-academies
DiMaggio, P. (1988) "Interest and Agency in Institutional Theory". In L.G. Zucker (ed.). *Institutional Patterns and Organizations: Culture and Environments*. Cambridge, Mass.: Ballinger European Commission, (2007) *White Paper on Sport*, 11 July 2007.
Ferkins, L., Shilbury, D., and MacDonald, G. (2005) The role of the board in building strategic capability: towards an integrated model of sport governance research, *Sport Management Review*, 8, 195–225.

Friedland, R. and Alford, R. R. (1991) Bringing society back in: symbols, practices, and institutional contradictions. In: W.W. Powell and P. DiMaggio. (eds.). *The New Institutionalism in Organizational Theory*. Chicago: The University of Chicago Press.

Gammelsæter, H. (2013) Leader succession and effectiveness in team sport. A critical review of the coach succession literature. *Sport, Business and Management: An International Journal*, 3, 285–296.

Gammelsæter, H. and Senaux, B. (eds.) (2011) *The Organisation and Governance of Top Football Across Europe. An Institutional Perspective*. New York: Routledge.

García, B. (2007) UEFA and the European Union: from confrontation to cooperation. *Journal of Contemporary European Research*, 3, 202–223.

Garcia-del-Barrio, P. and Szymanski, S. (2009) Goal! Profit maximization versus win maximization in soccer. *Review of Industrial Organization*, 34, 45–68.

Garcia, B. (2011). The influence of the EU on the governance of football. In: Gammelsæter, H. and B. Senaux (eds.). *The Organisation and Governance of Top Football Across Europe: An institutional Perspective*. New York: Routledge.

Geey, D. (2011) The UEFA Financial Fair Play rules: a difficult balancing act, *Entertainment and Sports Law Journal*, 9(1). [online] Retrieved from: https://www.entsportslawjournal.com/articles/10.16997/eslj.30/

Geeraert, A., Alm, J., and Groll, M. (2014) Good governance in international sport organizations: an analysis of the 35 Olympic sport governing bodies, *International Journal of Sport Policy and Politics*, 6, 281–306.

Hanstad, D.V., Smith, A., and Waddington, I. (2008) The establishment of the world anti-doping agency: A study of the management of organization change and unplanned outcomes. *International Review for the Sociology of Sport*, 43, 227–249.

Henry I. and Lee, P.C. (2004) Governance and ethics. In: Chadwick, S. and Beech J. (eds.). *The Business of Sport Management*. Harlow: Pearson.

Holt, M. (2007), The ownership and control of elite club competition in European football, *Soccer & Society*, 8, 50–67.

Iorwerth, H., Tomkins, P., and Riley, G. (2017) Financial doping in the English Premier League. *Sport, Ethics and Philosophy*. DOI:10.1080/17511321.2017.1351484

Kelly, S. (2017) *The Role of the Professional Football Manager*. London: Routledge.

Lawrence, T.B. and Suddaby, R. (2006) Institutions and institutional work. In: R. Greenwood, C. Oliver, K. Sahlin-Andersson, and R. Suddaby (eds.). *The Handbook of Organizational Institutionalism*. London: Sage.

Long, B.S. and Driscoll, C., (2008) Codes of ethics and the pursuit of organizational legitimacy: theoretical and empirical contributions. *Journal of Business Ethics*, 77, 173–189, DOI 10.1007/s10551-006-9307-y

Morrow, S. (2011), History, longevity and change: football in England and Scotland. In: Gammelsæter, H. and B. Senaux (eds.). *The Organisation and Governance of Top Football Across Europe: An Institutional Perspective*. New York: Routledge.

Oliver, C. (1991) Strategic responses to institutional processes. *Academy of Management Review*, 16, 145–179.

Olsson, L.-C. (2011), "Decisive moment in UEFA". In: Gammelsæter, H. and B. Senaux (eds.). *The Organization and Governance of Top Football Across Europe: An Institutional Perspective*. New York: Routledge.

Platts, C. (2012) Education and Welfare in Professional Football Academies and Centres of Excellence: A Sociological Study. Unpublished doctoral dissertation. University of Chester, United Kingdom.

Preuss, H., Haugen, K.K., and Schubert, M. (2014) UEFA financial fair play: the curse of regulation. *European Journal of Sport Studies*, 2, 33–51

Rosentraub, M.S. and Swindell, D. (2002) Negotiating games: cities, sports, and the winner's curse. *Journal of Sport Management*, 16, 18–35.

Rotberg R., (2003) *When States Fail: Causes and Consequences*. Princeton University Press.

Scott, W.R. (2001) *Institutions and Organizations* (2nd ed.). Thousand Oaks: Sage.

Senaux, B. (2011), The regulated commercialization of French football. In: Gammelsæter, H. and B. Senaux (eds.). *The Organisation and Governance of Top Football Across Europe: An Institutional Perspective*. New York: Routledge.

Smith, A. and Stewart, R. (2010) The special features of sport: a critical revisit. *Sport Management Review*, 13, 1–13

Szymanski, S. (2001), Income inequality, competitive balance and the attractiveness of team sports: some evidence and a natural experiment from English soccer. *The Economic Journal*, 111, 69–84.

Thornton, P.H., and Ocasio, W. (2008) Institutional logics. In: R. Greenwood, C. Oliver, K. Sahlin-Andersson and R. Suddaby (eds.). *The Handbook of Organizational Institutionalism*. London: Sage

Thornton, P.H., Ocasio, W., and Lounsbury, M. (2012) *The Institutional Logics Perspective. A New Approach to Culture, Structure, and Process*. Oxford: Oxford University Press

UEFA (2011) Securing a long-term balance, *UEFA Direct*, No. 105 – 01-02/2011, 12–13.

Walsh, A.J. and Giulianotti, R. (2001) This sporting mammon. a normative critique of the commodification of sport. *Journal of the Philosophy of Sport*, 28, 53–77.

Walsh, A. and Giulianotti, R. (2007) *Ethics, Money and Sport. This Sporting Mammon*. London: Routledge.

6

Contemporary issues in the management of grassroots football

Jimmy O'Gorman, Danny Fitzpatrick, Jonathan Sibley,
Matthew Hindmarsh, Zora Saskova, and Dan Parnell

Introduction

Grassroots football is a global activity spanning villages in South Asia through to multi-use games areas in Europe. Much has been written on a variety of matters relating to the governance (Hassan and Hamil, 2010; Gammelsæter and Senaux, 2011) and management (Chadwick and Hamil, 2010) of football at the elite level. Other work has focused on the organisational, cultural, and environmental dimensions of elite youth player development (Manley, Roderick, and Parker, 2016; Relvas et al., 2010). Yet the players, coaches, and adults who are the focus of such work will have at some point participated in, and had their formative experiences shaped by, grassroots football. The preoccupation with elite youth level players and the governance of professional football has been accompanied by a relative academic neglect of grassroots football.

In very many countries, most people who play football are children and adolescents who participate in various youth and junior grassroots settings, with varying degrees of formality, and for a whole range of purposes and motivations. Data obtained by FIFA (2007) from its 207 member associations estimated that 265 million people play football in organised settings worldwide. Of which 9.4 million youths under the age of 18 were formally registered with football clubs. Such figures do not include those that engage in forms of football that could be considered grassroots in less formally organised settings (e.g., jumpers for goalposts, street football). Within the context of changing leisure and sporting habits, particularly in Westernised countries (Harris, Nichols, and Taylor, 2017), these informal forms of participating in grassroots football appear to be dwindling, and the propensity to engage in, and formalise aspects of informal engagement with grassroots football appear to be increasing. These changing trends and the scale and scope of grassroots football presents challenges to the governing bodies and organisations that seek to manage this part of the game. It is therefore difficult to clarify the boundaries and vagaries of grassroots football. UEFA (2018) notes that grassroots football is played by the masses at a level where participation and a love of the game are the driving forces and is "all football that is non-professional and non-elite". This includes, but is not limited to, children's football, schools and youth football, amateur football, football for disabled players, football for veterans, and walking football. Whilst we recognise football provision that may be considered grassroots may also exist within the boundaries of corporate social responsibility (CSR) and international development (see O'Gorman and Rookwood, 2016), for the purposes of this chapter, we focus on issues relating to the increasing propensity to "manage" a variety of aspects of grassroots football. Therefore, we adopt a definition to focus on the spectrum of organised football outside of the professional game, incorporating three distinct but inter-related levels: youth and junior football (boys and girls under 18), community football (male and female amateur leagues and organised small sided competitions) and non-league or feeder league football (adult amateur / semi-professional in the football pyramid below professional level).

Some might argue that this academic bias is not surprising, though as the football historian James Walvin (2001, p. 252) noted at length, the significance of grassroots football is crucial because

> there is another football story to tell; about ordinary, run-of-the-mill football, about boys in the park, schoolchildren driven to games by parents, older men (long past their prime) struggling on bleary-eyed Sunday mornings to recapture their footballing best, and millions more simply kicking a ball against a back wall. It is generally untold because it is part and parcel of the world we live in. We see it, know it, have taken part in it, as children, parents, as players or as spectators. At this level, football is just another feature of life's weekly routines and scarcely warrants a passing thought. Yet it is this massive, incalculable substratum of popular football that sustains the professional game; the millions of ordinary players who nurture the national (and global) interest in the high-powered, commercially driven world of successful professional soccer. More than that, this popular attachment to the game takes us right back to the origins of the game itself. This is how football has always been; a simplicity and ease of play embedded deep in the routines and habits of ordinary people. That is why the game of football remains the people's game, however lavish and often absurd the antics of the wealthy minority.

For Walvin, and perhaps many others, grassroots football is the lifeblood of the professional game. It provides the foundations upon which future playing talent, coaches, and officials are introduced to the game and developed (O'Gorman, 2016; Breuer and Nowy, 2018), and contributes to the development and increasing commercialisation and professionalisation of professional football (O'Gorman, 2016). Whilst such processes arguably appear to be fuelling an ever-increasing divide between grassroots football and the professional parts of the game, in management and governance terms, the more organised, structured, and sustainable grassroots provision is, the more likely the sustainability of the whole game (Breuer and Nowy, 2018). Yet knowledge and understanding of the connections between professional and grassroots football remain largely underdeveloped.

This chapter is split into four sections. The first provides an insight into the management of the European grassroots game in the context of increasing managerialism and New Public Management, drawing on examples of grassroots club development in England. The second explores the potential impact of the economic downturn on grassroots football in England. The third discusses the sponsorship of grassroots football in England. The last section identifies new trends in participation from 11-aside to five-aside football and Futsal in England.

Management of grassroots football in Europe

In Europe, the governance and management of the entire game is predicated upon a pyramid through with UEFA located at the summit, and national member associations beneath it through to the largely voluntarily organised grassroots, amateur, junior clubs and competitions. This hierarchical arrangement is supported by internal vertical solidarity (usually in the form of funding) which is filtered through to the grassroots aimed at protecting the sustainability of the whole game (Breuer and Nowy, 2018). In recent times, the governing bodies of football have begun to recognise that the professional game requires a strong foundation if it is to continue to prosper (UEFA, 2013; Wicker et al., 2013; Vos et al., 2013). These developments have been shaped in the context of private sector managerial tools and principles being adopted by European public sector organisations aimed at improving the effectiveness and efficiency (Hood, 1995; London, 2002) of voluntary/third sector organisations such as grassroots football clubs (Lusted and O'Gorman, 2010). In sport, public sector organisations have sought to instil managerialism in their own and third sector clubs, by locating decision-making with professionally trained workforces and the employment of managers (Parker, 2002). Managerialism here is synonymous with New Public Management, based on reforms to move from a traditional Weberian/bureaucratic model to a customer-oriented and flexible management style grounded in private sector approaches (Esposito, Ferlie, and Gaeta, 2017; Pollitt, 2013). Managerialism is associated with the integration of business principles and practices, such as the use of performance indicators and target setting in monitoring and prioritising outputs over processes, cost-efficiency and increased productivity, external accountability, benchmarking, and performance management (Deem and Brehony, 2005).

In this context, governing bodies of football have sought to develop strategies to enhance the management of provision to ensure the grassroots game better supports the foundations of the football pyramid. The organisational capacity (Balduck, Lucidarme, Marlier, and Willem, 2015; Breuer and Nowy, 2018) of grassroots football clubs has been one area that governing bodies have sought develop and manage. To this end, UEFA developed a "Grassroots Charter," to which all 53-member associations have become signatories (UEFA, 2014). UEFA provides financial and logistical support for grassroots development across all national associations based on a range of measurable criteria based on the following questions: does the national association under review have a focus on increasing the number of registered players? Are specific efforts being made to retain players as they approach adulthood? Does the association operate an inclusive and comprehensive grassroots programme which effectively provides footballing opportunities for everyone?

A star system ascertains three levels of recognition: bronze for a basic level of grassroots programming, silver for advanced level, and gold for the national associations where top-quality grassroots programmes, conforming to UEFA's benchmarks, are being implemented under five headings: Growth, Retention, Education, Always Fair Play, and Terms (UEFA, 2014). To achieve UEFA recognition, a national association is required to demonstrate that a grassroots programme forms part of a national football development strategy. Each association is required to have a committee and a manager or director who is responsible for grassroots football, a dedicated budget specifically assigned to grassroots football and the administrative costs of organising and running it, coherent targets and objectives for development, and clear codes of conduct in achieving objectives of social value, including the eradication of racist behaviour, bigotry, and discrimination (UEFA, 2014).

One such example is the "The FA Charter Standard Clubs" programme, established in 2001. To manage and govern the grassroots game more effectively, the English Football Association (FA) changed the structure and purpose of County FAs (regional football associations responsible for the local organisation grassroots football in England) in the 1990s from purely legislative and administrative voluntary led bodies, to limited companies with full-time professional paid staff (Howie and Allison, 2016). Set within the context of the modernisation agenda for community sport organisations in the UK, grassroots football clubs were encouraged to adopt more business-like and managerial practices to enhance the quality of their provision. This was supported by a newly professionalised workforce in the form of football development officers (Lusted and O'Gorman, 2010). Fundamental to the strategy were the implementation of basic operating standards. Grassroots football clubs were required to devise and implement club development plans to increase the quality of their provision for their end users (participants). This was achieved by screening background checks and the gaining of qualifications for coaches, implementing codes of conduct; continual professional development plans for coaches; partnerships and links with schools; adopting small sided games, and devising strategies for increasing opportunities for girls and disability football (Howie and Allison, 2016). It is claimed that the implementation of the Charter Standard has increased the quality of provision and sustainability of grassroots clubs in England (The FA, 2015; Howie and Allsion, 2016) given that 75 per cent of all youth football teams had a qualified coach, and 80 per cent of all youth and junior football is played in Charter Standard clubs. Management challenges do remain, however. Increasing demands on volunteers have caused some resistance (Lusted and O'Gorman, 2010). Many volunteers in grassroots football clubs lacked the required skill sets and experience to deal with the reforms of managerialism and formalisation of roles (Harris, Mori, and Collins, 2009), and often lacked access to resources and time in which to carry out required duties (O'Gorman, 2012). These issues have also impacted on the recruitment and retention of volunteers with the skill sets and the capacity to operate more professionally (Ferkins and Shilbury, 2015). In an era of austerity that compromises the financial integrity of clubs, these are intractable problems faced by governing bodies in seeking to manage the grassroots game more effectively. Moreover, the imposition of performance indicators within a managerialist approach tend to distort outputs and can be counterproductive to achieving programme aims (O'Gorman, 2011; Nichols et al., 2016) and have led some scholars to question New Public Management techniques as an effective tool for grassroots sport in Europe (Fahlen, 2017). These issues are particularly acute in the policy area of community sport, whereby grassroots football is perceived as an important vehicle through which governments seek to achieve a whole range of social outcomes (e.g., improved community cohesion, positive youth development, enhanced social inclusion, and improved health and wellbeing) in many countries.

Challenges and trends in the management of English grassroots football in the context of an economic downturn

Despite the intentions of football organisations and governing bodies implementing managerialism and New Public Management techniques to incentivise stakeholders in grassroots football to systematically increase participation in organised and formal contexts, English grassroots football has witnessed a gradual decline with consequences for funding from central government. Whilst there has been a reported modest growth in the participation of women and disability players, addressing the perennial participation problems of getting young girls into football and reducing drop-off among boys entering adolescence (Temple and Crane, 2016) continue to prove elusive. In 2014, Sport England imposed a £1.6 million cut from the £30 million four-year investment on the FA. At the time, poor weather conditions and facilities and increased costs for clubs and the end-user (i.e., players) were attributed as factors influencing this decline.

As part of community sport, grassroots football remains on the periphery of and subject to policy decisions in other more significant policy areas. Much of this decline has taken place within the context of austerity driven policies driven initially by the Conservative Party-led coalition government of 2010–2015 in response to (real and perceived) "debt" incurred by the previous Labour Party government. Drastic cuts to public spending, including a raft of financial austerity measures in its *Comprehensive Spending Review* imposed £81 billion cuts to government departments. Subsequent budgetary constraints on local authorities have resulted in an expenditure decrease for non-discretionary services including "sport development and community recreation" (Widdop et al., 2017). In a period of continued austerity, or what some term "super austerity" (Lowndes and Gardner, 2016; Parnell, Spracklen, and Millward, 2016), more than other sports, football clubs at the grassroots level may face the greatest repercussions, given that it depends heavily upon local authority provisions such as pitch hire and maintenance (Widdop et al., 2017). With local authorities across the UK increasingly trying to protect core services, as a result of government cuts, many have subsequently increased council pitch fees and reduced the costs of maintenance (Widdop et al., 2017). An example of this trend is evident on the Wirral – a borough in the North West of England – that has witnessed significant increases in expenditure from grassroots football clubs directed toward the payment of pitch fees. Whilst adult category A pitch fees have soared from £220 in 2004 to £549 in 2016, junior category A pitch fees have also grown from £115 to £292, evidencing increases of 150 per cent and 153 per cent over 12 years (Wirral Borough Council, 2015). Such hikes in expenditure, both here and elsewhere, merely add to the clubs' growing financial conundrum in a bid to survive. The reliance on local authority provision for facilities is compounded by the majority of pitches being grass based. For example, in 2014, there were 639 publicly available artificial grass pitches in England, as compared to 3,735 in the World Cup winning nation, Germany (Gibson, 2014).

Financial redistribution to grassroots football, particularly in relation to facility development, maintenance, and management has been a contentious issue, especially when considered in juxtaposition to the financial excesses of The Premier League (King, 2014). The Football Foundation receives £12m a year each from The FA and The Premier League and £10m from the government (Gibson, 2014) and supports the development of local facilities through a competitive bidding process engaged in by grassroots clubs. The Premier League has also committed £1bn of its £5.5bn three-year TV contracts in community and grassroots initiatives (Gibson, 2015). To this end, The Premier League has recently financed 300 facility projects, 69 artificial grass pitches, 112 grass pitches, and 54 changing rooms through The Premier League & The FA Facilities Fund (www.premierleague.com).

The FA Premier League also part fund The FA's Parklife Project, which represents national governing bodies' attempts to respond to the changing dynamics of grassroots football by coordinating the increasing trend towards informalisation and individualisation of participation. Established in November 2016, The FA (in partnership with Sport England, the Department of Culture, Media and Sport, The FA Premier League, Football Foundation, and selected local authorities) dedicated a five-year investment of £230 million to develop up to 120 football hubs complete with new 3G pitches, changing facilities, and clubhouses across 30 of the country's biggest town and cities. The selection of the new football hubs is determined through a tendering process; Sheffield was selected as the initial pathfinder local authority, followed by Liverpool and West London. Only local authorities with a current population exceeding 200,000, who can raise a minimum of 40 per cent partnership funding of total capital costs are eligible (Sport England, 2017).

The Parklife Project also signals an extension of a professionalised, commercial, and strategic approach by The FA to grassroots football in The FA 'Charter for Quality' in 1997 (Howie and Allison, 2016). In the tendering process explicit consideration was "given to the factors which will support a more commercially focussed offer to drive income generation and help make the model sustainable" (Sport England, 2017, p. 2). The project seeks to emulate the business model adopted by private football facility companies: the vision is for football hubs that could host a mixture of school and community sessions during the day and profit-making "pay as you play" sessions in the evening accompanied by revenue-generating bars and refreshment facilities (Gibson, 2014).

The Parklife Project has been generally well received as a belated recognition that there has been a historic failure to invest satisfactorily in the infrastructure of grassroots football (Gibson, 2014). Although touted as a significant investment, the initiative represents a reallocation of public resources. The £230m investment is designed to ameliorate the fiscal shortfall created by the squeeze on local authority budgets and the consequential pressure this has placed on the maintenance of the existing football facilities stock. Moreover, in seeking to achieve cost efficiencies by investing in centralised "hubs" that almost exclusively rely on artificial grass pitches (to be used for a mix of different formats), Parklife may signal the end-game for mass participation in competitive adult 11-a-side football. Although local authorities are warned against using the sale of existing playing fields to raise the £400,000 needed to apply for the Parklife Project, this is permissible if it is rationalised in a Playing Pitch Strategy. The Parklife Project risks exacerbating existing geographical disparities; major towns and cities will see significant improvements in football facilities (with additional opportunities for the development of coaching and refereeing) that are likely to sustain, if not necessarily improve, existing participation rates. However, other smaller and more rural local authority areas are likely to languish. Therefore, while the strapline may be "Football for All," the Parklife Project will create discernible winners and losers.

Grassroots football and its sponsorship in England

Whilst the largely altruistic outlook of grassroots football clubs may be at odds with making profit, as a first requirement they must be financially sustainable (Nowy et al., 2015) if they are to meet their own objectives and contribute effectively to social policy goals. Grassroots football clubs in Europe, are likely to report notoriously low financial resources and financial problems (Breuer et al., 2015; Wicker and Breuer, 2014). Critical here, is the ability to diversify revenue sources and acquire resources (Millar and Doherty, 2016; Wicker and Breuer, 2013), particularly in times of austerity. Wicker and Breuer (2011), for example, identify grassroots clubs' desire to forge or strengthen collaborations with local organisations across their community as one core channel used to procure additional funds. One popular way to raise revenue has traditionally been through sponsorship sources. Sponsorship is thus claimed to have become an increasingly critical pillar of a grassroots sport clubs' propensity to look past their core revenue stream of membership fees to achieve survival and attain their objectives (Cousens and Barnes, 2009; Misener and Doherty, 2014). Yet, when compared to similar socio-economic developed countries, the UK seems to trail behind in the amount private sector investment contributes to community sports club revenue. Whereas nations such as Canada and Belgium note sponsorship generates 15 per cent (Gumulka et al., 2005) and 13.3 per cent (Vos et al., 2011) respectively of all club finance, it is alarming that in the UK sponsorship accounts for merely 3 per cent of income (Downer and Talbot, 2011). Grassroots football clubs in England typically secure an average of £1,200 through sponsorship per annum (ibid). Although imprudent to draw direct comparisons from polar extremes, in a business sense, instances such as Manchester United generating sponsorship revenues of £162.3 million in 2017 (Manchester United, 2017) exemplifies a vivid picture of an ever-expanding chasm between the wealthy, at the top, and the pauperised, at the bottom of the English football pyramid (Roberts, 2017). Such disparities could indeed be attributable to several reasons, including deviations in what reports constitute as sponsorship and cultural differences in how sport operates at the grassroots level. Nevertheless, it could alternatively be because both UK clubs and, more conceivably businesses, adjudge grassroots sponsorship not as viable as other sources of income or promotional tools. This is particularly prevalent in tough economic times, during which revenue from sponsorship in grassroots sport typically reduces (Wicker, Breuer, and Hennigs, 2012).

To this end, a vicious cycle appears to currently engulf the grassroots football sponsorship milieu. On one side, grassroots football clubs wish to increase their revenue through sponsorship, to at least in the first instance break even and ensure financial sustainability. On the other, companies now, more than ever, appear reluctant to invest in grassroots football clubs for returns that are hard to measure. Empirical investigation into the objectives both football clubs and businesses pursue from their involvement in football sponsorship at the grassroots level would thus act as a notable starting point. Indeed, this work has primarily revolved around only one half of the sponsorship dyad – the sponsee – and should thus take into account the sponsors perspective also. How grassroots football sponsorship is tackled and managed during times of financial hardship, and the critical success factors, which ensure fruitful long-withstanding partnerships, is further crucial. These phenomena have thus far received a dearth of, or indeed, no scholastic attention.

New and emerging trends in grassroots football participation in England

In part, the socio-political context shaping the decline in local authority provision, the changing nature of leisure and sporting habits and increasing commercialisation have contributed to an evolving mixed economy of provision for grassroots football in England. These developments have also raised some management issues for the stakeholders involved, to which this chapter now turns.

Despite the fiscal pressures of austerity, football remains the most popular team sport in England (The FA, 2015); 1.8 million participate in it on a weekly basis (Sport England, 2017). These headline figures mask the changing dynamics of grassroots football, however. The traditional organisation and management of grassroots football in England has centred upon provision and opportunities for 11-a-side competitions. Though we lack accurate longitudinal data, both quantitative (The FA, 2004; 2015) and qualitative research (Lusted, 2009; Koutrou, Pappous, and Horne, 2016), indicate a progressive decline in the number of people playing 11-a-side football on a regular basis since the late 1970s. This downward trend has accelerated in the last decade. Between 2005 and 2015, the number of people playing affiliated 11-a-side football fell by 180,000 (The FA, 2015). Moreover, the frequency of participation is also decreasing; the average squad size increased from 18 to 24 between 2010 and 2015, suggesting that even those who are still playing are doing so less often (The FA, 2015). The growing popularity of small-sided games (including five-a-side, seven-a-side, Futsal and mini-soccer) has mitigated (and perhaps contributed to) the drop-off in 11-a-side participation in this period. The emergence and growth of private and commercial operated small-sided football facilities, beyond the affiliated control of The FA, has been one of the key trends of grassroots football in recent years (Lusted, 2009). Due to its more informal, flexible, and episodic nature, reliable evidence on the participation numbers for these small-sided formats is difficult to capture. The FA (2014) estimates that approximately 1.5 million play some type of small-sided game each week; with around 30,000 teams playing in organised and competitive leagues as well as more informal, recreational participation. The realisation of these broader socio-political challenges to traditional football participation is something that The FA has come to accept rather than seek to overcome. As former FA senior official, Adrian Bevington, observed: "It is being recognised and needs to be further recognised that people are increasingly not able to dedicate all Sunday morning or afternoon to playing a game" (cited in Foster, 2017).

Despite some initial resistance to change, the transition to smaller-sided games in organised and formalised settings for children, at youth and junior level (O'Gorman and Greenough, 2016) has been led by investment into a number of strategies by The FA to improve coaching standards and provision for young people (Howie and Allison, 2016). Due in large part, to the perceived developmental benefits small-sided formats have become the staple of junior grass-roots football in England under the ages of ten (Amatria et al., 2016). Notwithstanding this investment, The FA has played a rather marginal role in facilitating the growth of small-side football formats for adults. Many officials within The FA (at least county level) were initially very sceptical about any deviation of funding away from "proper" 11-a-side football. (Stevens and Watkins-Mathys, 2006). It is only in the last five years that The FA has sought to respond to the changing trends in participation and "tap into" this new market and better understand the needs and drivers of its participants.

The inertia by The FA in responding to changing participation demands and patterns, and the increasing retreat of local authority provision, in part has seen small-sided football provision driven by the market imperatives of supply and demand. Research with key public and private stakeholders in the funding, facilitation, and delivery of small-sided football suggested that commercial imperatives would and should determine the location of facilities, akin to health and fitness clubs (Stevens and Watkins-Mathys, 2006). Three main private football companies – Powerleague, Goals Soccer Centres, and PlayFootball – have emerged and effectively colonised the market for small-sided football. Expansion of these private football providers was rapid from the mid-2000s but has since plateaued as these companies seek to consolidate the market having "cherry-picked" the most profitable locations near large urban centres. The commercialisation of grassroots football (especially in terms of the small-sided formats) has been driven by and in response to the increasing individualised nature of sports and leisure participation (Harris, Nichols, and Taylor, 2017), and has led to innovative approaches that seek to maximise flexibility while maintaining a level of sociability. Various types of informal "flexi-football," "kickabouts," and "turn up and play" sessions marketed under different names and delivered in local contexts are now common in different county FAs. Akin to similar initiatives in other national contexts, such as Football Fitness in Denmark, the focus here is on the promotion of health, enjoyment, and personal development, rather than skills or tactics per se (Bennike, Wikman, and Ottesen, 2014). Small-sided football could potentially be included in the same category as other self-organised individual sports with a large degree of organisational flexibility (Laub, 2013). The wider societal implications of this shift away from conventional 11-a-side, as well as for public health outcomes and the viability of volunteer-led grassroots football, is not yet fully understood.

The emergence of Futsal in England

Futsal is one such small-sided variant of football that is now played worldwide at amateur, semi-professional, and professional levels (Moore and Radford, 2014). The origins of the sport can be traced back to a YMCA in Montevideo in Uruguay in the 1930s; however, the game was quickly adopted by Uruguay's neighbours Brazil, in the 1930s/1940s where it was developed from a recreational game into a more organised form with a uniform set of rules (Berdejo-del-Fresno, 2014; Moore and Radford, 2014). Originally, it was played indoors on a basketball court-sized pitch with five players on each team, using field hockey-sized goals and a smaller ball with reduced bounce (Berdejo-del-Fresno, 2014). The sport has been popular in South America and Portugal since its conception where it is known as "futebol de salao," which can be translated from Portuguese as "hall football" (Moore and Radford, 2014). Futsal is stated to be the World's fastest growing indoor sport and in the last decade, the sport has developed significantly in Asian countries such as Iran, Japan, and Kuwait (Berdejo-del-Fresno, 2014). FIFA standardised the sport in the 1980s and branded it the official version of "5-a-side" to create a structure to allow Futsal to develop worldwide (Moore and Radford, 2014). Although some modest forms of the original governing bodies/institutions remain, Futsal is governed by FIFA and is the de facto guardian of the sport worldwide. The sport is now structured similarly to football, through the international federation and regional governing bodies with worldwide competitions such as the UEFA Futsal European Championships and FIFA World Cup (Moore and Radford, 2014).

Similar to other countries across the globe, Futsal is increasing in popularity in England. The definition of Futsal as small-sided football is consolidated with its inclusion within the Small-Sided Football Strategy 2013–2017 (The FA, no date), as part of wider FA targets and goals for increasing participation in adult small-sided football. Moore and Radford (2014) highlighted additional opportunities for participation in Futsal, including The FA Futsal Fives, The FA Youth Festival, FA National Under 18s Championships, the @Futsal Leagues, the British Universities and Colleges Sport (BUCS) Championship, and the Football League Trust Futsal League. The FA Futsal Fives shares similarities with the FA Futsal Cup and in relation to the FA Youth Festival and U18s Championship a new £300,000 fund has been launched, with the aim at developing Futsal within youth football leagues, youth Futsal leagues, and colleges and sixth forms (the FA, no date). In addition, the venues where the @Futsal Leagues were hosted are still operating and commercial leagues and opportunities to participate in Futsal are still available in these locations (PlayFootball, 2018). In relation to the BUCS Championship, Futsal is one of the newest league sports comprising four pre-mier leagues, including 148 men's teams and 75 women's teams. In addition to the league structure, The BUCS Football Development is also responsible for the development of Futsal within universities, working in partnership with the FA to provide students with opportu-nities to access the sport. Futsal is also part of the BUCS international programme and is played at European University Competitions (British Universities & Colleges Sport, 2018). The significance of the contribution of BUCS to the development of Futsal participation should not be ignored as Moore and Radford (2014) identified that BUCS provided com-petition for 55 per cent of the participation in Futsol in the UK. Whilst this has in some ways protected Futsal from being disregarded; the conglomeration of small-sided football has also stifled the opportunity to monitor, track, and evaluate the growth of Futsal in England at a grassroots level. In addition, reference to Futsal as a tool to aid in recruitment, retention, and skill development, for the benefit of the 11-a-side game is suggestive of a subservient position for Futsal within the governance structure of The FA. Despite these issues, it is acknowledged by the national governing body that Futsal is very much a game in its own right (The FA, no date).

It is recognised that Futsal faces many of the same challenges and barriers to participation as grassroots football. These include "poor facilities," the increased cost to use facilities, and reduced maintenance of facilities (Moore and Radford, 2014). The data relating to participation in Futsal is sparse – an issue which should be of concern for The FA as the sport's governing body with a remit to both increase participation at a grassroots level and achieve international success. The possibilities of Futsal becoming an Olympic sport and the trend for sports fans becoming increasingly interested in shorter and quicker formats of traditional sports are key trends that The FA may wish to capitalise on. In addition, Futsal may also become an increasingly attractive alternative to football in the context of urbanisation and a lack of space for recreational play; such factors were at the origins of the sport in South America. If this is to be the future of the sport, both Futsal and The FA will be ideally positioned to address the challenges facing current grassroots participation as well as meeting the needs of future generations of participants and consumers. However, as grassroots Futsal continues to develop and increase in popularity in England, it will be interesting to note the extent to which governing bodies may continue to pursue the inclusion of Futsal as part of grassroots football development as a political strategy within the continued imposition of managerialism techniques. Whilst it remains under the stewardship of The FA, it may be forced to remain as a subservient tool for recruitment and skill development within the 11-a-side game.

An insight into grassroots football in the third world: Sierra Leone

Sierra Leone is a small country on the Sub-Saharan African west coast, which continuously languishes at the bottom of the Human Development Index, with around 75 per cent of the population living in poverty. Football was introduced by British colonisers at the turn of the twentieth century and quickly became popular among underprivileged youth (M'bayo, 2017). Since independence in 1961, the organisation and provision of football continues to be dysfunctional. Despite this, football is considered to be the national sport in the country. Compared to Ghana and Nigeria with whom it shares a similar history and geographic location and where football has experienced, without major difficulties, steady progress (Darby, 2016; Poli, 2006), in Sierra Leone, football development, and sport in general, has suffered from under-investment, mismanagement, and conflicting personal agendas from both the Sierra Leonean Football Association (SLFA) and the Ministry of Sport (M'bayo, 2017). What's more, the decade-long civil war lasting from 1991–2002 during which Sierra Leone experienced total social and economic collapse, also had a destructive impact on the football infrastructure and left the country without pitches, equipment, or qualified coaches. Regardless of the pitiful condition of the game, football still holds significant importance for Sierra Leoneans and helps to bind the society together. The significance of the game is evident from the fact that football games were one of the very rare times during the war when people dared to gather (Van der Niet, 2010).

As a consequence of football's popularity and the fact that it is a relatively inexpensive way to mobilise a large number of people, the game is utilised by international NGOs, such as Play31 and Football for A New Tomorrow, which use it as a tool to achieve their objectives (Van der Niet, 2010; Dyck, 2011). For example, after the war, football was used in peacebuilding interventions for the rehabilitation of child and youth ex-combatants and for the purpose of community reconciliation. More recently, football was employed to challenge the social stigma of Ebola survivors and reintegrate them back to the society as they were shunned by their communities for fear of reoccurrence of the disease. Similarly, for disabled people in Sierra Leone, who comprise around ten per cent of the population, football is also used to help them gain recognition from their communities. One such initiative is FC Polio, a football team composed of amputees and Polio survivors who engage with the game as part of their efforts to demonstrate to other Sierra Leoneans that they are a valuable part of society. Football programmes also attract many children as the provided football equipment is a scarce and expensive commodity in the country. Even if people can afford to buy boots or balls, the sandy gravelly pitches significantly decrease the lifespan of any equipment. An average ball that would usually last for a few years in European conditions gets spoiled on the rough Sierra Leonean pitches within four to five months. Thus, football is often played with homemade or old deflated balls by children wearing slippers or barefooted. Yet, the harsh reality does not prevent Sierra Leonean youth to have big football dreams.

For many, football is a symbol of hope. Despite the fact that Sierra Leone has not produced many big football names or never won any major football competition nor qualified for the FIFA World Cup, many young men see football as their only way out of the poverty. However, only a very small fraction will ever get a chance to chase their dream and go abroad. No matter how talented a player might be, the opportunities are highly limited. The players are also held back by the fact that the Sierra Leonean domestic league has not been played for the last five years and as such they are lacking a platform to demonstrate their capabilities. The league's interruption was partly caused by the recent Ebola epidemic (2014–15), when playing football or any other collective sport was banned for safety reasons for over a year, but it remains suspended by internal wrangles, conflicting personal interests, corruption, and issues between the SLFA and the Ministry of Sport (M'bayo, 2017). With the resumption of the country's Premier League unlikely to occur in the short term, the only way football talent is nurtured is through grassroots football. Today, the sole football competition played in the country comprises various community matches and tournaments played in the capital, Freetown, as well as the small rural villages. Without any organisational structure or support, members of local communities raise funds for football games to be played and for the footballers to bolster their livelihoods. Although they do not receive any salary or compensation from their clubs, the players still treat football as their job.

Conclusion

In this chapter, we have sought to illustrate the increasing importance of grassroots football as a development tool to a range of stakeholders, and ongoing attempts to shape the management of its provision specifically in England. We have noted, somewhat paradoxically, these processes appear to be taking place at a time when grassroots and elite football are becoming increasingly polarised. We have also problematised the implementation of managerialism and new public management techniques in attempts to increasingly influence grassroots stakeholders to engage in activities that comply with football's governing bodies' and nation states' goals for grassroots football contribution to other agendas. However, as we note, these processes appear to be taking place at a time of continued austerity, a mixed economy of provision and changing trends in participation in different formats of grassroots football, increasing commercialisation, changing leisure and sporting preferences, and sustained reduction in state financial support for grassroots football pitches. The question for grassroots football is whether the strategies and investment by governing bodies will be sufficient not only for grassroots football to contribute to the sustainability of the football pyramid, but whether it can even survive and adapt to such trends and for whom. If not, we can only expect existing conditions to prevail, that is, postponed matches, poor experiences, risings costs, declining participation, inequality in playing opportunities, and little hope for supporting talent development and identification. The extent to which these issues shape how, and in what ways, grassroots football is managed in England, Europe, and beyond in the future require further empirical investigation.

References

Amatria, M., Lapresa, D., Arana, J., Anguera, M.T., and Garzón, B. (2016) Optimization of game formats in U-10 soccer using logistic regression analysis. *Journal of Human Kinetics*, 54(1), 163–171.

Balduck, A.L., Lucidarme, S., Marlier, M., and Willem, A. (2015) Organizational capacity and organizational ambition in nonprofit and voluntary sports clubs. *VOLUNTAS: International Journal of Voluntary and Nonprofit Organizations*, 26(5), 2023–2043.

Bennike, S., Wikman, J.M., and Ottesen, L.S. (2014) Football Fitness – a new version of football? A concept for adult players in Danish football clubs, *Scandinavian Journal of Medicine and Science in Sport*, 24(1), 138–146.

Berdejo-del-Fresno, D (2014) A Review about Futsal. *American Journal of Sports Science and Medicine*, 2(3), 70.

Breuer, C., Hoekman, R., Nagel, S., and van der Werff, H. (2015) Sport clubs in Europe. Switzerland: Springer.

Breuer, C. and Nowy, T. (2018) *European grassroots football. The Global Football Industry: Marketing Perspectives*. London: Routledge.

British Universities & Colleges Sport (2018) About Futsal. [online] Retrieved from: www.bucs.org.uk/page.asp?section=20284&sectionTitle=About+Futsal

Chadwick, S. and Hamil, S. (2010) *Managing Football*. London: Routledge.

Cousens, L. and Barnes, M. (2009) Sport delivery in a highly socialized environment: a case study of embeddedness. *Journal of Sport Management*, 23(5), 574–590.

Darby, P. (2016) Football and identity politics in Ghana. In: A. Bairner, J. Kelly, and J.W. Lee (eds.). *Routledge Handbook of Sport and Politics* (pp. 137–149). London, UK: Taylor & Francis Ltd.

Deem, R. and Brehony, K.J. (2005) Management as ideology: the case of 'new managerialism' in higher education. *Oxford Review of Education*, 31(2), 217–235.

Dyck, C.B. (2011) Football and post-war reintegration: exploring the role of sport in DDR processes in Sierra Leone. *Third World Quarterly*, 395–415.

Downer, J. and Talbot, N. (2011) *Survey of Sports Clubs 2011: A Review of Clubs, Facility Access, Finances, Challenges and Opportunities*. London: The Sport and Recreation Alliance.

Esposito, G., Ferlie, E., and Gaeta, G.L. (2017). The European public sectors in the age of managerialism. *Politics*, 1–20.

Fahlén, J. (2017) The trust–mistrust dynamic in the public governance of sport: exploring the legitimacy of performance measurement systems through end-users' perceptions. *International Journal of Sport Policy and Politics*, 9(4), 707–722.

Ferkins, L. and Shilbury, D. (2015) The stakeholder dilemma in sport governance: Toward the notion of "stakeowner". *Journal of Sport Management*, 29(1), 93–108.

FIFA, 'FIFA Magazine: Big Count (2007). Retrieved from: http://www.fifa.com/mm/document/fifafacts/bcoffsurv/emaga_9384_10704.pdf

Foster, R. (2017) 'From five-a-side to Futsal and Star Sixes: how football's small forms went big', [online] 28 March, 2017, *The Guardian*. Retrieved from: https://www.theguardian.com/football/the-agony-and-the-ecstasy/2017/mar/28/five-a-side-Futsal-star-sixes-football-tournament

Gammelsæter, H. and Senaux, B. (eds) (2011) *The Organisation and Governance of Top Football Across Europe: An Institutional Perspective*. London: Routledge.

Gibson, O. (2014) FA reveals its 2020 vision: football hubs and 3G pitches for all. [online] 10 October 2014, *The Guardian*. Retrieved from: https://www.theguardian.com/football/2014/oct/10/fa-football-hubs-3g-pitches-grassroots

Gibson, O. (2015) Premier League promises to share £1bn of TV deal with English football. [online] 26 March 2015, *The Guardian*. Retrieved from: https://www.theguardian.com/football/2015/mar/26/premier-league-richard-scudamore-sky-deal

Gumulka, G., Barr, C., Lasby, D., and Brownlee, B. (2005) Understanding the Capacity of Sport and Recreation Organizations: A synthesis of Findings from the National Survey of Nonprofit and Voluntary Organizations and the National Survey of Giving, Volunteering and Participating. Ontario: Imagine Canada.

Hassan, D. and Hamil, S. (2010) Models of football governance and management in international sport. *Soccer & Society*, 11(4), 343–353.

Harris, S., Nichols, G., and Taylor, M. (2017) Bowling even more alone: trends towards individual participation in sport. *European Sport Management Quarterly*, 17(3), 290–311.

Harris, S., Mori, K., and Collins, M. (2009) Great expectations: voluntary sports clubs and their role in delivering national policy for English sport. *VOLUNTAS: International Journal of Voluntary and Nonprofit Organizations*, 20(4), 405.

Hood, C. (1995) Contemporary public management: a new global paradigm?. *Public Policy and Administration*, 10(2), 104–117.

Howie, L. and Allison, W. (2016) The English Football Association Charter for Quality: the development of junior and youth grassroots football in England. *Soccer & Society*, 17(6), 800–809.

King, A. (2014) Why England fails. *Sport in Society*, 17(2), 233–253.

Koutrou, N., Pappous, A., and Horne, R. (2016) Keeping up the Participation Levels in adult 11 V 11 football in Kent. University of Kent.

Laub T.B. (2011) Sports participation in Denmark 2011 – National survey – English version. Copenhagen: Danish Institute for Sports Studies, 2013.

London, R. (2002) Tools for governing: privatization, public-private partnerships and entrepreneurial management. *Public Administration Review*, 62(1), 118–123.

Lowndes, V. and Gardner, A. (2016) Local governance under the Conservatives: super-austerity, devolution and the 'smarter state'. *Local Government Studies*, 42(3), 357–375.

Lusted, J. (2009) Playing games with 'race': understanding resistance to 'race' equality initiatives in English local football governance. *Soccer & Society*, 10(6), 722–739.

Lusted, J. and O'Gorman, J. (2010) The impact of New Labour's modernisation agenda on the English grass-roots football workforce. *Managing Leisure*, 15(1–2), 140–154.

Manchester United (2017) *Manchester United plc. United States Securities and Exchange Commission*. Washington, D.C.

M'bayo, T. E. (2017) The politics of football in post-colonial Sierra Leone. In B. Elsey and S. G. Pugliese (eds), *Football and the Boundaries of History: Critical Studies in Soccer* (pp. 267–294). New York: Palgrave Macmillan.

Manley, A., Roderick, M., and Parker, A. (2016) Disciplinary mechanisms and the discourse of identity: The creation of 'silence' in an elite sports academy. *Culture and Organization*, 22(3), 221–244.

Millar, P. and Doherty, A. (2016) Capacity building in nonprofit sport organizations: development of a process model. *Sport Management Review*, 19(4), 365–377.

Misener, K. and Doherty, A. (2014) In support of sport: Examining the relationship between community sport organizations and sponsors. *Sport Management Review*, 17(4), 493–506.

Moore, R. and Radford, J. (2014) Is Futsal kicking off in England?: a baseline participation study of Futsal. *American Journal of Sports Science and Medicine*, 2(3), 117–22.

Nichols, G., Grix, J., Ferguson, G., and Griffiths, M. (2016). How sport governance impacted on Olympic legacy: A study of unintended consequences and the 'Sport Makers' volunteering programme. *Managing Sport and Leisure*, 21(2), 61–74.

Nowy, T., Wicker, P., Feiler, S., and Breuer, C. (2015) Organizational performance of nonprofit and for-profit sport organizations. *European Sport Management Quarterly*, 15(2), 155–175.

O'Gorman, J. (2011) Where is the implementation in sport policy and programme analysis? The English Football Association's Charter Standard as an illustration. *International Journal of Sport Policy and Politics*, 3(1), 85–108.

O'Gorman, J. (2012) The changing nature of sports volunteering: modernization, policy and practice. In: Hamil, Sean, David Hassan, and Jim Lusted, (eds.). *Managing Sport: Social and Cultural Perspectives*. London: Routledge.

O'Gorman, J. (2016) Introduction: developing the research agenda in junior and youth grassroots football culture. *Soccer & Society*, 17(6), 793–799.

O'Gorman, J. and Greenough, K. (2016) Children's voices in mini soccer: an exploration of critical incidents. *Soccer & Society*, 17(6), 810–826.

O'Gorman, J. and Rookwood, J. (2016) Football and international social development. In: J. Hughson, K. Moore, K, R. Spaaij, and J. Maguire (eds.). *Routledge Handbook of Football Studies*. London: Routledge.

Parker, M. (2002) *Against Management*. Oxford: Polity.

Parnell, D., Cope, E., Bailey, R., and Widdop, P. (2016) Sport policy and English primary physical education: The role of professional football clubs in outsourcing. *Sport in Society*, 20(2), 292–302.

PlayFootball. (2018) Swindon Indoor, My Centre. [online] Retrieved from: www.playfootball.net/swindon-indoor

Pollitt, C. (2013) The evolving narratives of public management reform: 40 years of reform white papers in the UK. *Public Management Review*, 15(6), 899–922.

Poli, R. (2006) Migrations and trade of African football players: historic, geographical and cultural aspects. *Afrika Spectrum*, 393–414.

Relvas, H., Littlewood, M., Nesti, M., Gilbourne, D., and Richardson, D. (2010) Organizational structures and working practices in elite European Professional Football Clubs: Understanding the relationship between youth and professional domains. *European Sport Management Quarterly*, 10(2), 165–187.

Roberts, K. (2017) Sport in Europe's era of austerity: crisis or adaptation? *International Journal of Sociology and Social Policy*, 3(1/2), 123–130.

Sport England (2017) Parklife Football Hubs National Programme. Retrieved from: https://www.sportengland.org/media/12134/parklife-football-hub-prospectus-july-2017.pdf

Stevens, A. and Watkins-Mathys, L. (2006) The FA's role in developing five-a-side football: Strategic alliances with stakeholders. *Managing Leisure*, 11(3), 186–202.

Temple, Viviene A., and Jeff R. Crane. (2016) A systematic review of drop-out from organized soccer among children and adolescents. *Soccer & Society*, 17(6), 856–881.

The Football Association (2004) *Annual Review 2004-2005*. London: The Football Association.

The Football Association. (2015) *The FA National Game Strategy for Participation and Development, 2015–2019*. Burton: The Football Association, 2015.

UEFA. (2013) Full House for Grassroots Charter. [online] Retrieved from: http://www.uefa.com/insideuefa/football-development/technical/grassroots/news/newsid=1916605.html#/grassroots+landmark+reached

UEFA. (2014) Grassroots Newsletter, no.15. [online] Retrieved from: http://www.uefa.com/MultimediaFiles/Download/EuroExperience/uefaorg/Grassroots/02/10/87/26/2108726_DOWNLOAD.pdf

UEFA. (2018) [online] Retrieved from: https://www.uefa.com/insideuefa/football-development/technical/grassroots/index.html

Van der Niet, A. (2010) Football in post-Conflict Sierra Leone. *African Historical Review*, 42(2) 48–60.

Vos, S., Breesch, D., Kesenne, S., Van Hoecke, J., Vanreusel, B., and Scheerder, J. (2011) Governmental subsidies and coercive isomorphism: Evidence from sports clubs and their resource dependencies. *European Journal for Sport and Society*, 8(4), 257–280.

Vos, S., Wicker, P., Breuer, C., and Scheerder, J. (2013) Sports policy systems in regulated Rhineland welfare states: Similarities and differences in financial structures of sports clubs. *International Journal of Sport policy and Politics*, 5(1), 55–71.

Walvin, J. (2001) *The Only Game*. Oxford: Blackwell.

Wicker, P. and Breuer, C. (2011) Scarcity of resources in German non-profit sport clubs. *Sport Management Review*, 14, 188–201.

Wicker, P., Breuer, C., and Hennigs, B. (2012) Understanding the interactions among revenue categories using elasticity measures – Evidence from a longitudinal sample of non-profit sport clubs in Germany. *Sport Management Review*, 15(3), 318–329.

Wicker, P., Vos, S., Scheerder, J., and Breuer, C. (2013) The link between resource problems and interorganisational relationships: a quantitative study of Western European sport clubs. *Managing Leisure*, 18(1), 31–45.

Wicker, P. and Breuer, C. (2013) Understanding the importance of organizational resources to explain organizational problems: Evidence from nonprofit sport clubs in Germany. *VOLUNTAS: International Journal of Voluntary and Nonprofit Organizations*, 24(2), 461–484.

Wicker, P., and Breuer, C. (2014) Examining the financial condition of sport governing bodies: The effects of revenue diversification and organizational success factors. *VOLUNTAS: International Journal of Voluntary and Nonprofit Organizations*, 25(4), 929–948.

Widdop, P., King, N., Parnell, D., Cutts, D., and Millward, P. (2017) Austerity, policy and sport participation in England. *International Journal of Sport Policy and Politics*, 10(1), 1–18.

Wirral Borough Council. (2015) Retrieved from: https://www.wirral.gov.uk/about-council/performance-and-spending/fees-and-charges

7

Football law

Richard Parrish and Adam Pendlebury

Introduction

The existence of a body of law identifiable as *football law* is contested. As Grayson argued, "no subject exists which jurisprudentially can be called sports law" (Grayson, 1994: xxxvii). By extension, Grayson would deny the existence of the even more discrete area of football law. Grayson favoured the label "sport and the law" reflecting his view that "[e]ach area of law applicable to sport does not differ from how it is found in any other social or jurisprudential category" (Grayson, 1994, p. xxxvii). Beloff et al. disagree. They claim that "the law is now beginning to treat sporting activity, sporting bodies and the resolution of disputes in sport, differently from other activities or bodies. Discrete doctrines are gradually taking shape in the sporting field, which are not found elsewhere" (Beloff et al., 2012: 4). Our approach finds favour with James (2017), albeit in an adapted form, who highlights two sources of sports law, and by extension football law, one operating within a public legal sphere, the other in the private sphere (James, 2017, pp. 3–24).

The public face of football law refers not only to the influence of nation state governments, parliaments and courts on football, but also the activities of international organisations such as the European Union and the Council of Europe. The football related legislation, jurisprudence and activity of these bodies generates *national football law*, *EU football law* and *international football law* respectively.

The private face of football law refers to the statutes and regulations of the competent football authorities and the jurisprudence of the various dispute resolution bodies operating at domestic (for example national association), continental (UEFA and its equivalents) and global (FIFA and Court of Arbitration for Sport) levels. This gives rise to *domestic football law*, *continental football law* and *global football law*. It has become fashionable to refer to this collective body of private sports law as the *lex sportiva*, an essentially private contractual order established between sporting bodies and those subject to their sporting jurisdiction.

These labels are contested, and we acknowledge that as an alternative we could have chosen to reject the *football law* label and refer instead to the *law relating to football*. This would then have taken us on either a vertical rule-led thematic investigation of how law and private regulation affects aspects of football governance (such as labour market regulation), or a more purist horizontal inquiry examining how each category of law (such as criminal and EU law) is applied to football contexts. Our approach does not reject these methods, it merely offers a typology for understanding the complex interplay between the public and private actors whose activities shape football's regulatory environment.

In doing so, our approach assists with the exploration of perhaps the most fundamental question facing football law: can the public and private faces of football law co-exist or does the involvement of the former undermine the autonomy and specificity of the latter? It is our contention that far from treating football activities in the same way as other sectors, the public face of football law is receptive to claims that the football industry is "special."

The private face of football law

Domestic football law

Domestic football law, like its global and continental counterparts discussed below, relates to the private law relating to football. In England, this relates to the rules, regulations, and decisions of three main entities. The English Football Association (FA), The English Football League (EFL), and the English Premier League (EPL) have varying influences over the regulation of English football. One of the key challenges for football lawyers is to understand which of the entities has jurisdiction over a particular matter. This section of the chapter will focus on the actual disputes which may occur in English football which when heard before the respective panels gives rise to a body of domestic football law. It will focus in detail on the roles of the FA and the EPL. It is sufficient for the purpose of this contribution to say that the EFL deals with breaches of FL rules and applies *inter alia* to clubs, players, officials, owners, and directors whose clubs are competing in the EFL.

The rules, regulations, and disciplinary decisions of the FA make up the vast majority of English domestic football law. The FA is granted exclusive rights by FIFA to regulate football in England which allows the FA to deal with disciplinary issues. The English FA is also able to regulate the activities of the EPL and EFL as well as of participants and clubs. On certain matters, the FA may defer disciplinary powers to the EPL or EFL but ultimately, it retains the control over English domestic football. The terms of the contract between the member club and the organisation will evidently include a disciplinary code. Misconducts of which the respective disciplinary body would act upon include: acts of violence against participants, match officials or supporters; the use of indecent or insulting words against participants, match officials or supporters or; bringing the sport into disrepute; corruption; financial rule infringements including, *inter alia*, financial fair play (FFP) rules and entering into administration; and failing to fulfil a fixture. Typically, the sanctions for such offences include disqualification; suspension; points deductions; warnings; fines; and permanent exclusion.

Professional football in England has developed dispute resolution mechanisms to deal with the multi-faceted nature of the disciplinary issues that may arise. As mentioned above, the type of dispute will govern which regulations apply and impact upon the judicial body that hears the case. However, taken as a whole, the dispute resolution mechanism forms a complete code by which all disputes are resolved within football.

The Football Association Judicial Panel is established by the FA Council as the group of individuals from which regulatory commissions and appeal boards will be drawn by the Judicial Panel chairman or in his absence, his nominee, to hear cases or appeals in connection with disciplinary and other regulatory processes of the FA. The Football Association Regulatory Commission and the appeal boards in the cases before them are drawn from members of the

Judicial Panel. Issues pertaining to misconduct, contrary to Rule E1(a) of the FA regulations will fall exclusively within the FA's remit. Rule E1(a) concerns incidents that infringe the actual Laws of the Game. Other types of misconduct include, *inter alia*: a) violent conduct; b) bringing the game into disrepute; c) threatening, abusive, indecent, or insulting words or behaviour; d) discrimination; e) taking bribes; f) illegal betting. In these cases, the FA shall have the power to take disciplinary action but it may not be an elite power.

In dealing with misconduct listed a–d above, the key provisions are E3(1) and E3(2) of the FA rules. The 2017/18 version of the rules read as follows:

> (1) A Participant shall at all times act in the best interests of the game and shall not act in any manner which is improper or brings the game into disrepute or use any one, or a combination of, violent conduct, serious foul play, threatening, abusive, indecent or insulting words or behaviour. (2) A breach of Rule E3(1) is an "Aggravated Breach" where it includes a reference, whether express or implied, to any one or more of the following: ethnic origin, colour, race, nationality, religion or belief, gender, gender reassignment, sexual orientation or disability. These provisions are wide enough in scope to encompass a wide range of different offences.

In dealing with an alleged offence the role of the regulatory commission is not to usurp the role of the referee, so if, for example, a referee issues a caution then no other punishment can be issued. However, the FA can increase a player's suspension if the circumstances of the incident under review are truly exceptional, such that the standard punishment should not be applied or the standard punishment would be clearly insufficient. *FA v Thatcher*[1] provides an example of truly exceptional circumstances. After elbowing his opponent Pedro Mendes (Portsmouth Football Club) and rendering him unconscious, Ben Thatcher (Manchester City Football Club) was only cautioned by the match official and in ordinary circumstances, this would bring an end to the matter. However, this incident was held to be sufficiently grave to warrant an additional sanction being imposed. The Regulatory Commission decided to impose an eight-match suspension on Thatcher with a further 15 matches suspended. The further 15 match suspended sentence meant that any subsequent issues of misconduct would lead to a total sanction of 23 matches for the initial misconduct which further evidences the exceptional and gravity circumstances of the incident.

The preceding paragraph explored the role the Regulatory Commission plays when infringements are sanctioned on the field of play. This next section discusses incidents on the field of play that were not dealt with by match officials, but were caught on video. An example of a retrospective charge concerns the case of *FA v Terry*.[2] After an alleged racially motivated insulting comment by John Terry (Chelsea Football Club) towards his opponent Anton Ferdinand (Queens Park Rangers Football Club), the FA charged Terry with misconduct pursuant to r.E.3(1) of its rules and regulations, which included a reference to the ethnic origin and/or colour and/or race of Ferdinand within the meaning of r.E.3(2). Terry was found guilty of misconduct. He had a four match suspension imposed upon him and was fined £220,000. Following *FA v Terry*, the FA amended its rules relating to aggravated misconduct with r.E3(3) increasing the minimum sanction to five matches.[3]

Misconduct involving media comments or comments made on social networking sites are again charged under FA r.E3(1). Should the offence have aggravating features it will also infringe FA r.E3(2). Until relatively recently, the most common type of media misconduct concerned managers and their post-match criticisms of match officials. However, in recent years the advent of social networking sites has given rise to a number of disciplinary infringements in football.

The rules of the FA that govern the sanctioning of aggravated breaches via social media do not necessarily require the commission to consider the imposition of a five-match playing suspension. The pertinent direction is contained in r.E3(4ii) which in effect means that the commission has discretion in sanctioning aggravated breaches as was highlighted in *FA v Sagbo*[4] and *FA v Assou-Ekotto*[5] where suspensions of two and three matches respectively where imposed. These two cases made it abundantly clear that playing suspensions are likely to be attached to aggravated misconduct irrespective of the fact they take place via social media. Further evidence of this can be taken from the commission's approach to sanctioning in *FA v Balotelli*[6] in which the Panel stated there would be an "expectation of a sporting sanction" in relation to issues concerning aggravated misconduct. Though, not operating a system of binding precedent, it is clear that previous authorities provide persuasive principles.

The FA has a number of rules relating to betting and integrity which affect all players, managers, coaches, club medical staff, and other participants (e.g., directors, licensed agents). Rule E5 regulates integrity matters such as influencing the result of a game or competition. This can include issues such as intentionally performing below standard or taking bribes to manipulate results or competitions. Rule E8 addresses betting and the provision of inside information. Ahead of the 2014/2015 English Football season, this rule was amended with effect that an employee of any club participating in the English football league or four leagues below it, cannot place a bet, directly or indirectly, on any world football event.[7]

Disciplinary issues which fall within the jurisdiction of the EPL will be heard before the FA EPL Disciplinary Commissions. As a general rule, facts or matters giving rise to alleged misconduct under r.E1(b) to (f) inclusive of the FA rules, which also give rise to an alleged breach of the rules and/or regulations of the EPL, shall be dealt with under the EPL disciplinary rules. There are certain disciplinary issues that are solely violations of EPL rules. Evidently, these will be dealt with by the EPL. For example, EPL rules exist to regulate matters specific to Premier League clubs which are not covered by FA rules. These include issues such as making illegal approaches to players registered at another club,[8] the prohibition on third party influence over clubs[9] and specific sanctions for a club or its parent undertaking suffering an event of insolvency.[10] The key jurisdictional point here is that this type of misconduct, at the time, only infringed EPL rules so the EPL disciplinary commission dealt with the cases.

Challenges to the decisions of football disciplinary bodies in England are extremely rare. However, the rules of the FA and EPL do stipulate that challenges to decisions can be made by way of arbitration. FA arbitration is dealt with under Rule K which stipulates that any challenge to the FA rules and regulations, including disciplinary, should be dealt with by arbitration and the role of arbitration is supervisory.[11] Similarly, challenges to EPL disciplinary commission decisions shall be dealt with by arbitration.[12]

Continental football law

Continental football, at a European level, concerns the rules, regulations, and decisions of UEFA. In essence, its jurisdiction is over UEFA club and international competitions. According to Article 32 of the UEFA Statutes, UEFA has two disciplinary bodies – the Control, Ethics and Disciplinary Body and the Appeals Body. UEFA disciplinary inspectors represent UEFA in proceedings before the disciplinary bodies. These authorities are independent within the organisation, and its members are bound by UEFA's rules and regulations. The Control, Ethics and Disciplinary Body deal with disciplinary cases, both on and off the field, which arise from the UEFA Statutes, regulations, and decisions of UEFA that do not fall within another committee or body's competence. The Control, Ethics and Disciplinary Body decide on the halting of proceedings; acquittals; convictions; and the dismissal or acceptance of protests. It also rules on eligibility to play and the admission of clubs to UEFA competitions. The Appeals Body handles appeals against disciplinary decisions taken by the Control, Ethics and Disciplinary Body. It either confirms, amends, or revokes the contested decision. Any final appeal of UEFA decisions can be referred to the Court of Arbitration for Sport (CAS) which highlights how continental football law feeds into global football law. Articles 11–16 of UEFA disciplinary regulations 2017 refers to the specific disciplinary offences. They include general principles of conduct, integrity of matches and competitions, match-fixing, doping, racism, other discriminatory conduct and propaganda, misconduct of players and officials, and order and security at UEFA competition matches.

In addition to the aforementioned disciplinary bodies, the UEFA Club Financial Control Body (CFCB) has the important role of overseeing the application of the UEFA Club Licensing and Financial Fair Play Regulations. The CFCB is an Organ for the Administration of Justice and may impose disciplinary measures in the event of non-fulfilment of the requirements set out in the UEFA Club Licensing and Financial Fair Play Regulations. Its final decisions may only be appealed before the CAS. Importantly, the CFCB is competent to determine whether licensors (national associations) and licence applicants (clubs) have fulfilled the licensing criteria or the FFP requirements[13] and to decide on cases relating to club eligibility for the UEFA club competitions. With regards to eligibility for the UEFA club competitions, this has included issues relating to the interpretation of Article 5 of the UEFA Champions League regulations with regards to multiple club ownership and the integrity of the competition.[14]

Global football law

Global football law is applied by two bodies: FIFA and CAS. The statutes, regulations and decisions of FIFA's two alternative dispute resolution (ADR) bodies forms the basis of global football law. This is because FIFA is competent to regulate the game globally and all those subject to its jurisdiction must comply with its decisions, including those handed down by its dispute resolution bodies. Furthermore, FIFA statutes and regulations, particularly the FIFA Regulations on the Status and Transfer of Players (RSTP), are routinely interpreted by CAS, the so-called global court for sport and CAS is competent to hear appeals from the decisions of FIFA's ADR bodies. Taken together, the decisions of FIFA and CAS form the cornerstone of global football law.

The current FIFA dispute resolution system has its origins in the 2001 agreement between FIFA, UEFA, and the European Commission, the terms of which allowed the Commission to close its investigation into the operation of the international transfer system for players.[15] From FIFA's perspective, the dispute resolution system is designed to provide in-house solutions to international disputes, with all the attendant advantages of ADR, including expedited and affordable sporting justice. However, it should be noted that international employment-related disputes can still be heard in ordinary courts.[16] This is an exception to FIFA's general rule that "recourse to ordinary courts of law is prohibited"[17] and is a product of the 2001 agreement.

FIFA operates two dispute resolution bodies: the Players' Status Committee (PSC) and the Dispute Resolution Chamber (DRC), although the later can be considered to fall under the "umbrella" of the former (de Weger, 2008, p. 1). Both are dispute resolution bodies and not arbitral tribunals meaning that enforcement of decisions is secured through the statutes and regulations of FIFA. If a party appeals a decision of the PSC or the DRC to CAS, which is a recognised arbitral tribunal, then decisions can be legally enforced as per the requirements of the New York Convention on the Recognition and Enforcement of Foreign Arbitral Awards 1958.

Typically, the types of disputes heard by these bodies include international employment-related disputes between a club and a player, disputes between clubs and players in relation to the maintenance of contractual stability, international employment-related disputes between a club or an association and a coach, disputes relating training compensation and the solidarity mechanism and other disputes between clubs belonging to different associations (Ongaro and Cavaliero, 2013, pp. 77–112). The PSC and the DRC adjudicate in the presence of three members although provision is made for a single judge to sit. Compliance with the decisions of these two bodies is by way of the FIFA Disciplinary Code.

At the pinnacle of global football law lies the CAS, an arbitral tribunal competent to hear appeals from FIFA's dispute resolution bodies. Based in Lausanne, Switzerland, the CAS statutes entered into force in 1984. Initially proposed by the International Olympic Committee (IOC), the establishment of the CAS reflected the IOC's desire for sports-related disputes to be resolved, not through litigation, but through sports-specific arbitration.

The CAS has approximately 300 arbitrators drawn from countries worldwide and in the region of 300 cases are registered with it every year. Hearings are usually before a panel of three arbitrators with each party to the dispute selecting an arbitrator from the CAS list and the panel members, or the president of the relevant CAS division, then selecting a chair.

Most international sports federations, including football, grant jurisdiction to the CAS to be the final dispute resolution body in sport. Cases are referred via the ordinary or appeals procedures, denoted by an O or A in the case citation. The Ordinary Arbitration Procedure is a voluntary but ultimately binding first instance procedure with the jurisdiction of CAS emanating from a contract or a sports regulation. The subject matter for this procedure can relate to any dispute that is sports related, such as one emanating from an employment or sponsorship contract or a civil tort. The bulk of the CAS workload comes from the Appeal Arbitration Procedure which governs appeals from the dispute resolution chambers of signatory sports bodies. In football, these appeals are referred from the relevant FIFA body and tend to involve issues relating to transfers, the payment of training compensation, and doping sanctions. In addition to the above two procedures, the CAS operates an Ad hoc Division that sits during the staging of major sporting events including the FIFA World Cup and the UEFA European Championships. The CAS also offers mediation services.

Decisions of the CAS are binding on the parties and are legally enforceable by the parties to the dispute. CAS decisions can be reviewed by the Swiss Federal Tribunal with the grounds for review limited to procedural flaws and in exceptional cases to substantive review if the award is contrary to Swiss public policy.

The CAS has emerged as an important source of the so-called *lex sportiva*. This contested term (Foster, 2005) refers to the body of decisions that derive from the interpretation and application of sports regulations and the selection of best practice that guides the future conduct of all sports bodies and stakeholders thus encouraging harmonised standards across sports. In doing so, the CAS has applied general standards that are common to most legal systems to cases before it, including legal certainty, the presumption against retroactivity, the protection of legitimate expectations, the prohibition of arbitrariness, and proportionality. It has also developed sports-specific standards such as the non-reviewability of referee's decisions, the strict liability principle in doping cases, and the principle of comfortable satisfaction as the standard of proof for sporting disciplinary offences (Beloff et al., 2012, p. 308–309). The *lex sportiva* is an essentially private order based on contract which is designed to be autonomous from national courts but which is, as explained above, reviewable and enforceable in national courts.

The impact of CAS jurisprudence on football has been substantial. For example, CAS cases have shaped football regulations concerning the ownership of football clubs, the consequences for unilateral termination of employment contracts, the scope of unilateral options clauses, doping provisions and sanctions, hooliganism, match-fixing, player release rules, and the protection of minors (Wild, 2012). In recent years, the CAS has also heard cases involving good governance in football, for example hearing the appeals brought by Joseph Blatter[18] and Michel Platini in the aftermath of the FIFA governance scandal.

Whilst the CAS has been praised for finding speedy and cost-effective solutions tailored to the specific requirements of sport, it has also attracted criticism. Throughout its history the CAS has had to rebut allegations that the organisation lacks the requisite independence from the sports movement to be an impartial arbitral tribunal[19] or that the arbitration clauses are unfairly imposed on athletes.[20] It has also faced criticisms that rather than establishing predictable jurisprudence, its decision making varies and is inconsistent with EU law. This criticism was levelled at the CAS following the different approaches it adopted to two broadly similar cases involving footballers unilaterally terminating their employment contracts with their clubs under the terms of Article 17 of the FIFA Regulations on the Status and Transfer of Players (Parrish 2015; Pearson, 2015). Whereas in *Webster*, the CAS determined that the player must compensate his club a sum equivalent to the residual value of his contract, in *Matuzalem* the CAS adopted the so-called "positive interest" principle to require the player to compensate the club for all quantifiable losses.[21] Unable to settle such a large sum[22] and facing a suspension until he did so, Matuzalem successfully appealed the CAS judgment to the Swiss Federal Tribunal. In March 2012, it found that the CAS award was contrary to public policy and should be annulled.[23]

The public face of football law

National football law

This section of the chapter explores the concepts of English national football law. In order to answer the question raised earlier, as to whether the public and private faces of football law coexist or whether the involvement of the former undermines the autonomy and specificity of the latter, this section will also draw on the wider national sports law jurisprudence in order to tease out the impact, if any, on football. England does operate a non-interventionist and non-consolidated sports model. This model implies an "arms-length") role for the state in sport in which sports are organized by the sports bodies and, unlike states such as France, there is no specific sports law statute (Parrish and Pendlebury, 2013, pp. 342). As a result, the UK Parliament has tended to adopt a light touch approach to the regulation of sport in general, though, during the last three decades of the twentieth century there were a number of pieces of legislation that impacted directly on English football. For example, The Safety of Sports Grounds Act 1975 provides for licensing of sports grounds and The Football Spectators Act 1989 (s8) established the Football Licensing Authority (now the Sports Ground Safety Authority) which is required to operate a licensing scheme to regulate the spectator viewing accommodation at English Premier and Football League Grounds.

The legislature responded to public disorder at football matches by enacting, *inter alia*, the 1985 Sporting Events (Control of Alcohol) Act (as amended 1992), the Football Spectators Act of 1989 which provides for a system of Football Banning Orders as a means of controlling spectator behaviour, and the Football Offences Act 1991 which establishes specific football-related offences of throwing missiles (s2), racist or indecent chanting (s3), and entering the playing area without lawful excuse (s4). Essentially the above "football law statutes" provide a framework for the regulation of crowd safety and crowd disorder. Parliament has not sought to regulate directly non-spectator issues pertaining to football but sports law statutes such as the Gambling Act quite clearly have the potential to impact on football by making cheating at gambling and assisting another person to cheat at gambling an offence (s42(1)). Despite there not being any convictions as yet for football's participants and stakeholders, this is an example of where a source of national sports law can overlap with domestic sports law and by analogy national football law with domestic football law. The criminal convictions in 2011 of Pakistani cricketers Salman Butt, Mohammad Amir, and Mohammad Asif, intertwining with the private disciplinary sanctions serves as an example to those convicted of FA regulatory offences, relating to betting, integrity, or match fixing that they could also be subject to the criminal law.

Despite some role being played by Parliament in national football/sports law, the development of this source of law has been achieved through the decisions of the courts. There has already been detailed analysis of the typology of national sports law (Parrish and Pendlebury, 2013), so this section, whilst revisiting some of the key points, will focus attention on the question of whether decisions of national courts impact upon the autonomy and specificity of football.

The use of the law of tort to secure compensation for injuries is the most commonly occurring example of national sports law in action. (James, 2017, pp. 75–121). If catastrophic injury is caused, then there is the potential for an aggrieved party to bring a legal action against the alleged wrongdoer. By far the most frequently utilised tortious action is brought in the law of negligence. Since the seminal case of *Condon v Basi*,[24] which involved a participant successfully suing an opponent for a late, high, and dangerous tackle in an amateur football match, the growth in litigation has been rapid. In addition to participant/participant litigation, negligence actions for injuries caused on the field of play have been brought against match officials,[25] governing bodies,[26] and organisers of the event.[27] It is, however, important to note that the courts have understood that in fast-moving sports it is inevitable that there will be injury-causing contacts that occur outside of rules of the game and, therefore, the threshold for liability is high.[28]

The England and Wales Court of Appeal in *Caldwell* was referring to a claim by a participant but the same approach has been adopted in relation to other areas of sporting liability. In particular the match official liability case of *Smoldon v Whitworth & Nolan*,[29] in which the Court of Appeal stated at page 139 that a referee: "could not be properly held liable for errors of judgment, oversights or lapses of which any referee might be guilty in the context of a fast-moving and vigorous contest."

In applying this approach to football, it can be argued that a mistimed tackle will not necessarily reach the threshold for negligence liability to be established. The tackle may constitute a foul, but if it was only an error of judgement or through lack of skill, liability will not arise (see *Elliot v Saunders*). Only where a tackle is late, high, and significantly misjudged will it amount to negligent conduct.[30] This approach of the Court of Appeal to sport means that deference is given to bodies such as the FA to deal with foul play unless it crosses the high threshold to establishing negligence liability. Further, match officials, following rules and protocols should not be deterred from officiating. One area of the law of negligence that has had the biggest impact on the private face of sport in general is governing body liability. The national sports law decision of *Watson v British Boxing Board of Control*[31] established that a sport's governing body owes a duty of care to its participants in relation to the medical protocols contained in the regulations. This is clearly an example of the public face of sports law impacting upon the private, as bodies such as the FA are under a duty to ensure that participants are given appropriate medical treatment and examination on suffering injury. One particular example is the introduction of the FA's new guidelines for assessing and dealing with a concussion. In our view, cases such as *Watson* are good example of the public face of football law impacting positively on the private face.

The approach of the English criminal law in relation to acts of violence on the sports field is one of the best examples of the specificity of sport and the courts respecting the autonomy of sport. It is only in the most serious cases that criminal prosecutions will be warranted. This is most apparent in professional football where there have only been a handful of successful prosecutions.[32] These have included attacks on supporters,[33] fighting with one's own teammate[34] and gratuitous "off-the-ball" violence against an opponent.[35] Even in amateur football, the criminal law is reserved for the most severe of incidents. On-the-ball incidents with close proximity to the play are unlikely to result in criminality. The Court of Appeal in the leading case of *R v Barnes*[36] summarises this non-interventionist approach:

> In determining what the approach of the courts should be, the starting point is the fact that most organised sports have their own disciplinary procedures for enforcing their particular rules and standards of conduct … A criminal prosecution should be reserved for those situations where the conduct is sufficiently grave to be properly categorised as criminal.[37]

The *Barnes* case (at paragraph 15) expressly accepts the concept of playing culture which is a principle specific to sport. It allows for acts of injury-causing foul play to be included within the boundaries of legal consent to criminal assault. The approach of the England and Wales Court of Appeal clearly allows for football to be afforded special treatment and is an example of a football exception to the general law of the land. The court recognises that sports such as football have their own disciplinary bodies, which means they are respecting the autonomy and specificity of football. The *FA v Thatcher* case mentioned above shows the importance of responsible regulation of sports-field violence. Following a number of complaints, Greater Manchester Police (GMP) launched an investigation into the incident. In an unprecedented move, GMP waited for the outcome of the FA regulatory commission before deciding whether to pass the file onto the Crown Prosecution Service (CPS) (James, 2008: 771–772). Given the fact they chose not to proceed in the case, the sanction must have been seen as sufficient. It provides a further example of the state not encroaching upon the private regulatory sphere in circumstances in which it is perceived that justice is achieved.

The English common law doctrine of restraint of trade provides an avenue through which the decisions of a domestic football body can be challenged, and this has given rise to another area of national football law. This doctrine asserts that rules or actions restraining trade (meaning denying or restricting the opportunity to earn a living) are void unless they can be justified.[38] Traditionally, governing bodies have argued that restraints are justified *inter alia* with reference to the need to: promote competitive balance; incentivise youth development; encourage solidarity between participants; maintain the integrity, stability, and proper functioning of competitions; protect national teams; and maintain the commercial viability of sport. The doctrine requires that restraints are reasonable not only in the interests of the parties imposing the rule, but also in the wider public interest. Restraint of trade has been raised by both clubs and players. In *Stevenage Borough Football Club v Football League Ltd*[39] a football club finished top of the Conference, which normally would have led to it joining the Third Division of the Football League. However, the club did not at the relevant dates satisfy the Football League's criteria for admission to the league, which included matters relating to its ground and to financial matters. The club expected to meet the requirements by the time the season started. It sued the league for declarations that the criteria were unlawful because they were an unreasonable restraint of trade. This challenge was unsuccessful and is another example of national football law recognising the specificity of football and autonomy of football. Relief was refused on the grounds of delay and prejudice to third parties. The court was sensitive to the need for arrangements to be fixed and administered in an orderly way to the benefit of other affected clubs.

Eastham v Newcastle United FC[40] *is* an example of national football law impacting on the absolute autonomy of the EFL and FA in relation to certain aspects of the English football transfer system. In this case an English professional footballer sued his club, the Football Association and the Football League for a declaration that their retention and transfer system was an unlawful restraint of trade. The system, in effect, allowed for a club to retain a player at the end of his contract on less advantageous terms. The club only had to pay a FL minimum wage and crucially did not even have to pick the player to play. If a player wished to move to another club he could not do so unless the club agreed to release him on a free transfer or come to an agreement with another club to pay a transfer fee. The court held that the "retain" aspect of the transfer system was void. Therefore, the FL had to amend its rules as a result of a decision of a court. However, specificity of football was still respected by the court and transfer fees for players under contract survived.

EU football law

The EU has exerted a significant influence on European and global football governance largely through the manner in which EU Treaty provisions regulating the freedom of movement of people and services and those regulating fair competition in the single market have been applied to the sector.

These provisions are general in nature and are aimed at regulating the conduct of economically active actors, such as workers, and undertakings. They were written and refined without consideration for the specific characteristics of the football sector, particularly given that at its inception the EU Treaty did not list sport as one of its competences. As sport, and particularly the football industry, began to internationalise and commercialise, it became only a matter of time before EU law was applied to the activities of the sector.

A series of European Court judgments and European Commission decisions have defined the relationship between the football sector and EU law, and this activity has drawn the criticism from some sports, including the football authorities FIFA and UEFA, that in treating the football sector in the same way as any other, EU law has failed to recognise the autonomy and specificities of sport. In other words, as the football sector, and sport more generally, operate under market conditions that are different to those found in "normal" industries, the self-regulation of sport should be preferred.

Initially, this was the approach favoured by the EU. In *Walrave*, the Court of Justice declared that sport was subject to European law only in so far as it constitutes an economic activity and that rules motivated by purely sporting interest fell outside the scope of the Treaty.[41] This approach offered sport a wide margin of appreciation in terms of its relationship with EU law (Parrish and Miettinen, 2008).

The relative stability of the sporting exception was challenged two decades later when the court delivered its judgment in *Bosman*.[42] In the case, the court rejected arguments based on *Walrave* that the operation of the international transfer system for players and the use of nationality quotas in European club football should be excluded from the reach of EU law. Following the ruling, players at the end of their contracts were free to transfer to another club in another EU member state without a transfer fee being payable, and in doing so they were able to take up employment without the restrictive effects of nationality quotas being felt. The impact of the judgment on football has been profound (Duval and Van Rompuy, 2016).

The *Bosman* judgment highlighted the importance of EU law, not only to European football but football globally. Following the judgment, the European Commission received a series of complaints from private parties regarding alleged ongoing restrictive practices in the operation of the international transfer system for football players (Van den Bogaert, 2005). In 1998 the European Commission issued to FIFA a statement of objections resulting in FIFA making amendments to the global transfer rules.[43] A similar Commission investigation resulted in amendments being made to FIFA's worldwide player agent regulations.[44]

Various aspects of the FIFA regulations governing transfers have been tested, either directly or indirectly, against the requirements of EU law. For example, in *Lehtonen*, the Court of Justice established that whilst transfer windows amounted to a restriction on a workers freedom of movement, they could, subject to them being non-discriminatory and proportionate, be compatible with EU law because late transfers could call into question the proper functioning of sporting competition.[45] Furthermore, in *Bernard* the Court held that a system of training compensation in sport which restricts the freedom of movement of players could be justified with reference to the objective of educating and training young players.[46]

The approach of the European Court to sports cases was further refined in the case of *Meca-Medina*, the first case in which the Court expressly applied the competition law provisions of the Treaty to sporting rules, in this case anti-doping rules.[47] The judgment is notable for its forthright rejection of the *Walrave* defence and for this reason the judgment did not find favour with the football authorities (Infantino, 2006). Despite finding against the complainants, two professional swimmers sanctioned for doping violations, the Court established that:

> it is apparent that the mere fact that a rule is purely sporting in nature does not have the effect of removing from the scope of the Treaty the person engaging in the activity governed by that rule or the body which has laid it down.[48]

This means that contested sporting rules need to be assessed against the requirements of EU law, an approach critics argue invites litigation and causes legal uncertainty. Importantly however, the court accompanied this statement by asserting that not all contested sporting rules are capable of amounting to a restriction of competition, or by extension, free movement. In coming to this assessment, the court found that:

> account must first of all be taken of the overall context in which the decision of the association of undertakings was taken or produces its effects and, more specifically, of its objectives. It has then to be considered whether the consequential effects restrictive of competition are inherent in the pursuit of those objectives ... and are proportionate to them.[49]

This approach had, in fact, found similar expression in an earlier case involving selection rules in judo and the right to provide services.[50]

The *Bosman* and *Meca-Medina* judgments were influential in convincing the sports movement that the EU Treaty should be amended so that the EU institutions, specifically the court and commission, were required to take the specificity of sport into account in the exercise of their powers, particularly those relating to free movement and competition. A campaign, led by the IOC, resulted in the adoption of Article 165 of the Treaty on the Functioning of the European Union (García and Weatherill, 2012). Entering into force in 2009, Article 165 requests that they take into account "the specific nature of sport." This statement was the breakthrough the sports movement wanted but opinion differs on its significance. Given the paucity of post-Article 165 sports-related jurisprudence, it is not yet clear whether reference to "taking account of the specific nature of sport" is a horizontal obligation which applies to the exercise of other EU powers such as free movement and competition law. If not, these provisions will trump the sporting provisions and the quest for greater legal protection for sport will be defeated.

Ultimately, that issue is for the Court and, to some extent, the Commission to decide. However, the significance of the debate should not be overstated as the pre-165 jurisprudence of the Court and decisional practice of the Commission points to a sympathetic treatment of sporting rules and practices. That is not to say, however, that the EU has not exerted a significant influence on football governance in Europe. In that connection, it is possible to present a brief typology of sporting rules that (1) are not considered restrictive of free movement and competition laws (2) may amount to restrictions in EU law but are capable of justification or exemption and (3) are generally not permitted under EU law. Caution should be exercised when employing this typology as each new case brought before the Court and Commission will need to be assessed on a case-by-case basis as made clear by the Court in *Meca-Medina*.

Rules that are not considered restrictive of free movement and competition laws include nationality restrictions in the composition of national team sports,[51] rules relating to selection criteria,[52] rules preventing multiple club ownership,[53] and proportionate doping sanctions.[54]

Rules that are considered restrictive of free movement and competition but which are capable of justification/exemption include the FIFA regulations governing training compensation,[55] the operation of transfer windows,[56] rules regulating players' agents,[57] the collective sale of broadcasting rights,[58] and the listing of major events on free-to-air television.[59]

Rules currently prohibited by EU law include nationality restrictions in club sport,[60] discrimination against non-EU sportspersons protected under the terms of association agreements,[61] rules protecting sports bodies from competition,[62] national territorial exclusivity in sale of media rights and the use of licenses protecting this model.[63]

In addition to the above, the Commission has investigated the granting of state aid to sports organisations and has, in a line of decisions, declared admissible state-funded projects, such as the construction of multifunctional arenas, which are capable of hosting different cultural events or which improve facilities with a view to encouraging high levels of public participation in sport.[64] The Commission has also approved French state aid measures granted to football clubs in order to host the 2016 Euro Championship and Dutch measures that supported clubs in financial difficulties in the Netherlands (Cattaneo, 2018).[65] However, the commission has required a number of Spanish clubs, including Real Madrid and Barcelona, to repay aid received from local and national governments.[66]

Important issues yet to receive systematic treatment by EU law concern, *inter alia*, rules governing the release of players for international duty,[67] the use of locally trained player rules in European football, FFP and similar licensing requirements, salary caps, FIFA's prohibition on the third-party ownership (TPO) of players, and the vexed issue of rules discouraging football clubs from entering new national markets either temporarily or permanently.

A final influence of the EU on football governance concerns its role in encouraging social dialogue between the various football stakeholders. Since the judgment in *Bosman*, the commission has encouraged the football stakeholders to resolve disputes within the sector through stakeholder dialogue which is supported by the EU Treaty.[68] A Social Dialogue Committee for European Professional Football was established in 2008 and in 2012 it concluded its first agreement on minimum conditions in player contracts.[69]

International football law

The term international sports law gives rise to different interpretations. For example, Nafziger and Ross (2011) in their *Handbook on International Sports Law* refer to it in a way we, the authors, would understand the term global sports law. We posit a different interpretation favoured by

James, (2017: 20) that it is a distinct source of sports law. With that in mind, we distinguish international football law from global football law.

International sports law and as a result, international football law, is very much formed through international organisations of which states are members, as opposed to the contractual source of global sports law. The Council of Europe's conventions provide the only direct source of international football law. For example, the *European Convention on Spectator Violence* was drafted by the Council of Europe as a response to the Heysel stadium disaster of 1985. The need for the treaty was the frequency of football matches between national and club teams from Council of Europe states. Its aim is to get organisations and authorities to work together to ensure safety and orderly conduct at sporting events. There is also an aim to prevent and control violence and misbehaviour by spectators at football matches through the coordination of policies and the actions of government departments and public agencies against these problems and the possibility of setting up coordinating bodies to do this. Though not binding on the UK, it has shaped the direction of nation football law in its statutory regulation of football hooliganism. (James, 2017: 22). *The Anti-Doping Convention* 1989, though not directed specifically to football can be seen as the driver behind the World Anti-Doping Agency WADA, which football's private regulatory bodies are signatories to. *The Convention on the Manipulation of Sports Competitions* 2014, is again of general applicability to sport but its aims, of preventing, detecting, and sanctioning national or international manipulation of matches together with its vision to promote cooperation, quite clearly apply to football.

The non-sports related *European Convention on Human Rights (ECHR)* has played only a marginal role in creating an international football law. The convention's institutions have engaged with football only fleetingly and in any case, unlike the European Union institutions, have tended to side with football's governing bodies. An example of this is in relation to the football transfer system. In *X v Netherlands*,[70] the now abolished European Commission of Human Rights determined that Article 4 ECHR – freedom from forced or compulsory labour – was not infringed by football's transfer system. The decision was predicated on the basis that professional football players chose to enter the profession freely, in full knowledge of the rules relating to transfers between clubs, and that the requirement that a fee be paid was an "inconvenience" rather than being oppressive. This is very much in contrast to the European football law case of *Bosman* mentioned above.

The recent European Court of Human Rights case of *Mutu v Switzerland*[71] has elevated the perceived importance of the ECHR in creating international football law. This case concerns a complaint by a professional footballer of the unfairness of proceedings before the CAS and of a lack of impartiality and independence of that court and its arbitrators. Following a positive drugs test, Mutu was ordered by FIFA to pay about 17 million euros in damages to Chelsea Football Club for unilateral breach, without just cause, of the employment contract that he had concluded the previous year. The CAS upheld that decision, and the applicant's application to the Swiss Federal Court for review was dismissed in 2010. The European Court of Human Rights ruled that the CAS is a genuine arbitration tribunal and that such sports jurisdiction is necessary for uniformity in sport. This is further corroboration that public face of international football law respects the autonomy of the private face of global football law.

Conclusions

In the above, we have presented a typology for unpacking and understanding the term "football law." We argue that football law can be understood as comprising two dimensions – a private and public sphere. The private sphere is an essentially contractual order regulating the private relationships between the football stakeholders. Within this system is a network of alternative dispute resolution bodies that seek to resolve football-related disputes within the "football family." At the pinnacle of this system is CAS, the global and supreme arbitral tribunal of sport.

The sophistication of the private face of football law lends support to the argument that football, and sport more generally, should be self-regulating. The argument goes that interference from public authorities, such as governments, parliaments, and courts, should be resisted as it risks undermining the autonomy and specificity of sport and it disturbs the proper functioning of what is a global industry.

Our investigation has revealed that far from the public face of football law undermining the autonomy and specificity of the football sector, ordinary courts, in particular, have generally been quite reluctant to intervene in football disputes and where they have, particularly at EU level, the specificities of the sector have been acknowledged.

Our view is that a complete detachment of private football law from public oversight is not desirable. Governance failures in football, the rise of new economically active stakeholders and the increasingly important quasi-public social functions that football plays, highlights the need for public scrutiny of football practices. Whilst self-regulation is to be preferred given the benefits this brings to both the private stakeholders and the public taxpayers, this autonomy should be conditioned on the football authorities committing to the highest standards of governance, including ensuring effective stakeholder representation in decision-making and guaranteeing independent, high-quality and consistent dispute resolution systems. The football authorities have, in recent decades, made important strides to deliver this agenda, but this has been done in either the shadow of the law or indeed as a consequence of activity in the courtroom.

Notes

1 Independent Disciplinary Commission, 12 September 2006.
2 *FA v Terry* Independent Disciplinary Commission, 24–27 September.
3 See *FA v Anelka* Independent Disciplinary Commission, 3 March 2014.
4 *FA v Sagbo* Independent Appeal Commission 12 June 2014.
5 *FA v Assou-Ekotto* Independent Disciplinary Commission 19 September 2014.
6 *FA v Balotelli* Independent Disciplinary Commission 18 December 2014.
7 *FA v Joseph Barton* 26 April 2017 Independent Disciplinary Commission.
8 *Football Association Premier League LTD vAshley Cole, Chelsea Football Club and Jose Mourinho*, 1 June 2005.
9 *Football Association Premier League LTD v West Ham United*, 27 April 2007.
10 *Football Association Premier League LTD v Portsmouth FC*, 17 March 2010.
11 *West Ham United LTD v FA*.
12 See *Sheffield United FC LTD v FA Premier League LTD* [2007] ISLR, SLR 77.
13 *Manchester City FC – Settlement Agreement* – May 2014.
14 Case AC-01/2017 Rasenballs Sport Leipzig GMBH FC Red Bull Salzburg GMBH.
15 Letter from Mario Monti to Joseph S. Blatter, D/000258 (5 March 2001); See also European Commission. (2002), Commission Closes Investigations into FIFA Regulations on International Football Transfers, IP/02/824 (Brussels 5 June 2002).
16 Article 22, *FIFA Regulations on the Status and Transfer of Players*, 2016 edition.
17 Article 59(2), *FIFA Statutes*, April 2016 edition.
18 CAS 2016/A/4501 *Joseph S. Blatter v FIFA*, 4 December 2016.
19 See Decision of the Swiss Federal Tribunal, 4P.217/1992, *Gundel v FEI* ATF 119 II 271, 15 March 1993. In *Lazutina* and *Danilova*, the Swiss Federal Tribunal acknowledged that post *Gundel* structure of CAS guaranteed the independence and impartiality of the CAS. See, CAS 2002/A/370 *Lazutina v IOC* & CAS 2002/A/371 *Danilova v IOC*.
20 See Claudia Pechstein's unsuccessful attempts to annul a CAS award at the Swiss Federal Tribunal: Case 4A_612/2009, 10 February 2010 and Case 4A_144/2010, 28 September 2010.

21 See cases: CAS 2007/A/1298 *Wigan Athletic FC v/ Heart of Midlothian* & CAS 2007/A/1299 *Heart of Midlothian v/ Webster & Wigan Athletic FC* & CAS 2007/A/1300 *Webster v/ Heart of Midlothian*, award of 30 January 2008 & CAS 2008/A/1519 *FC Shakhtar Donetsk (Ukraine) v/ Mr. Matuzalem Francelino da Silva (Brazil) & Real Zaragoza SAD (Spain) & FIFA* CAS 2008/A/1520 – *Mr. Matuzalem Francelino da Silva (Brazil) & Real Zaragoza SAD (Spain) v/ FC Shakhtar Donetsk (Ukraine) & FIFA*.

22 €11,858,934 plus interest of 5 per cent until the debt was settled.

23 Case 4A_558/2011.

24 [1985] 1 WLR 866.

25 *Vowles v Evans and the Welsh Rugby Union Ltd* [2003] EWCA Civ 318.

26 *Watson v British Boxing Board of Control* [2001] QB 1134.

27 *Wattleworth v Goodwood Road Racing Company Ltd & Ors*, [2004] EWHC 140.

28 *Caldwell v. Maguire and Fitzgerald* [2001] EWCA 1054 at paragraph 11.

29 [1997] P.I.Q.R. P133.

30 *McCord v Swansea City Football Club* [1997] *The Times*, February 11, *Watson v Gray and Huddersfield Football Club* [1998] *The Times*, November 26 and *Gaynor v Blackpool Football Club* [2002] CLY 3280.

31 [2001] QB 1134.

32 See below for an example of an *on-the-ball* prosecution.

33 *R v Cantona* (1995) *The Times*, 25 March.

34 *R v Bowyer* (Unreported) Magistrates' Court (Newcastle), 5 July 2005.

35 *R v Kamara* (1988) *The Times*, 15 April.

36 [2004] EWCA Crim.

37 Ibid at para.5 per Lord Woolf.

38 *Nordenfelt v Maxim Nordenfelt Guns* [1894] AC 535.

39 *Stevenage Borough Football Club Ltd v Football League Ltd* (1997) 9 Admin LR 109.

40 *Eastham v Newcastle United FC Ltd* [1964] Ch 413.

41 *Walrave and Koch* (C-36/74) [1974] ECR 1405 paragraphs 4 and 8.

42 *Union Royale Belge Sociétés de Football Association and others v Bosman and others* (C-415/93) [1995] ECR I-4921.

43 European Commission (2002), Commission Closes Investigations into FIFA Regulations on International Football Transfers, IP/02/824, 05 June 2002.

44 The matter was ultimately the decided by the Court of Justice in Case T-193/02, *Laurent Piau v Commission of the European Communities* [2005] ECR II-209.

45 *Lehtonen v Federation Royale Belge des Societes de Basket-Ball ASBL* (C-176/96) [2000] ECR I-2681, paragraph 54.

46 Case C-325/08, *Olympique Lyonnais v Olivier Bernard and Newcastle United* [2010] ECR I-2177.

47 *David Meca-Medina and Igor Macjen v Commission* (Case C-519/04 P) [2006] ECR I-6991.

48 *David Meca-Medina and Igor Macjen v Commission* (Case C-519/04 P) [2006] ECR I-6991, paragraph 27.

49 *Meca-Medina* [2006] ECR I-6991 paragraph 42.

50 *Deliège v Ligue francophone de Judo et disciplines Associeés Asb* (Joined cases C-51/96 and C-191/97) [2000] ECR I-2549.

51 *Walrave* [1974] ECR 1405.

52 *Deliège* [2000] ECR I-2549.

53 Decision in Case COMP/37 806 *ENIC/UEFA*. See Commission Press Release IP/02/942, 27. June 2002, 'Commission closes investigation into UEFA rule on multiple ownership of football clubs'.

54 *Meca-Medina* [2006] ECR I-6991.

55 Case C-325/08, *Olympique Lyonnais SASP v Olivier Bernard and Newcastle UFC* [2010], ECR I-02177.

56 *Lehtonen* [2000] ECR I-2681.

57 Case T-193/02, *Laurent Piau v Commission of the European Communities* [2005] ECR II-209. It should be noted that since this judgment an entirely new set of regulations have been issued by FIFA.

58 See cases: UEFA Champions League Decision 2003/778 OJ 2003 L291/25. Bundesliga Decision 2005/396 OJ 2005 L134/46. Football Association Premier League Decision C(2006) 868.

59 Joined Cases C-201/11 P, C-204/11 P and C-205/11 P, *UEFA and FIFA v Commission* [2013], ECR 2013 -00000.

60 *Bosman* [1995] ECR I-4921.

61 See cases: Case C-438/00 *Deutscher Handballbund v Kolpak* [2003] ECR I-4135. Case C-265/03 *Simutenkov* [2005] ECR I-2579. Case C-152/08 *Real Sociedad de Fútbol SAD, Nihat Kahveci v Consejo Superior de Deportes, Real Federación Española de Fútbol*.

62 European Commission, Press Release IP/01/1523. Commission closes its investigation into Formula One and other four-wheel motor sports, 30 October 2001. See also Case C-49/07, *Motosykletistiki Omospondia Ellados NPID (MOTOE) v Elliniko Dimosio*, [2008], ECR I-04863. See also Case AT.40208, International Skating Union's Eligibility rules, 08/12/2017, C(2017) 8240 final.

63 Cases C-403/08 and C-429/08. *Football Association Premier League and Others v QC Leisure and Others Karen Murphy v Media Protection Services Ltd* [2011] ECR I-09083.

64 See cases: Commission Decision of 20 March 2013 on State aid SA.35135 (2012/N) – Germany Multifunktionsarena der Stadt Erfurt; Commission Decision of 20 March 2013 on State aid SA.35440 (2012/N) – Germany Multifunktionsarena der Stadt Jena; Commission Decision of 2 May 2013 on State aid SA.33618 (2012/C) which Sweden is planning to implement for Uppsala arena; Commission Decision of 20 November 2013 on State aid SA.37109 (2013/N) – Belgium Football stadiums in Flanders.

65 See Decision of the Commission on Aide d'Etat SA 35501 (2013/N) – France Financement de la construction et de la rénovation des stades pour l'EURO, 2016 C(2013) 9103 final.

66 European Commission (2016), State aid: Commission decides Spanish professional football clubs have to pay back incompatible aid, Brussels, 4 July 16, IP/16/2401.

67 A case relating to this was removed from the Court register by order of the President of the Court of 25 November 2008. See Case C-243/06 *SA Sporting du Pays de Charleroi, G-14 Groupment des Clubs de Football Européens v Fédération Internationale de Football Association (FIFA)* reference for a preliminary ruling from the Tribunal de Commerce de Charleroi lodged on 30 May 2006.

68 Articles 152–155 of the TFEU.

69 Agreement regarding the minimum requirements for standard player contracts in the professional football sector in the European Union and the rest of the UEFA territory, 19 April 2012, http://www.ecaeurope.com/Documents/Dialogue%20social%20IX%20Final%20Version.pdf

70 Application 9322/81, X v Netherlands, European Commission of Human Rights' Decision of 3 May 1983, (1983) 32 DR 274.

71 *Mutu v. Switzerland* (no. 40575/10).

References

Beloff, M. Kerr, T. Demetriou, M., and Beloff, R. (2012) *Sports Law*. Oxford: Hart Publishing.

Cattaneo. A. (2018) State aid and sport. In: Anderson, J. Parrish, R., and García, B. (eds.). *Research Handbook on European Union Sports Law and Policy*. Cheltenham: Edward Elgar.

De Weger, F. (2008) *The Jurisprudence of the FIFA Dispute Resolution Chamber*, The Hague: TMC Asser Press.

Duval, A. and Van Rompuy, B. (eds.) (2016) *The Legacy of Bosman: Revisiting the Relationship between EU Law and Sport*. The Hague: Springer.

Foster, K. (2005) Lex sportiva and lex ludica: the court of arbitration for sport's jurisprudence, *The Entertainment and Sports Law Journal*, 3(2), 2.

García, B and Weatherill, S. (2012) Engaging with the EU in order to minimise its impact: sport and the negotiation of the Treaty of Lisbon, *Journal of European Public Policy*, 19(2), 238–256.

Grayson, E. (1994) *Sport and the Law*, 2nd ed. London: Butterworth & Co.

Infantino, G. (2006) Meca-Medina: a step backwards for the European sports model and specificity of sport, (UEFA Paper, 02/10/2006). [online] Retrieved from: http://www.uefa.com/MultimediaFiles/Download/uefa/KeyTopics/480401_DOWNLOAD.pdf

James, M. (2008) Sports participation and the criminal law, In: Lewis, A. and Taylor, J. (eds.). *Sport: Law and Practice*, 2nd edition. London: Bloomsbury.

James, M. (2017) *Sports Law*. Basingstoke: Palgrave Macmillan.

Nafziger, J.A.R. and Ross, S.F. (eds.) (2011) *Handbook on International Sports Law*. Cheltenham: Edward Elgar Publishing.

Ongaro, O. and Cavaliero, M. (2013) Dispute Resolution at the Federation Internationale de Football Association and its Judicial Bodies. In: Colucci, M and Jones, K. (eds.). *International and Comparative Sports Justice, European Sports Law and Policy Bulletin*, 1–2013, 77–112.

Parrish, R. and Miettinen, S. (2008) *The Sporting Exception in European Union Law*. The Hague: TMC Asser Press.

Parrish, R. (2015) Article 17 of the FIFA regulations on the status and transfer of players: compatibility with EU law, *Maastricht Journal of European and Comparative Law*, 22(2) 256–282.

Parrish, R. and Pendlebury, A. (2013) International and comparative sports justice: England. *European Sports Law and Policy Bulletin*, 1, 97–127.

Pearson, G. (2015) Sporting justifications under EU free movement and competition law: the case of the football "transfer system". *European Law Journal*, 3, 220–238.

Van den Bogaert, S, (2005) *Practical Regulation of the Mobility of Sportsmen in the EU Post Bosman*. The Hague: Kluwer Law International, p. 224.

Wild, A. (2012) *CAS and Football: Landmark Cases*. The Hague: Springer. p. 272.

8

Football and marketing

Argyro Elisavet Manoli and James Andrew Kenyon

Introduction

From football's traditional, working-class cultural heritage and roots, to its present arrangement as a multibillion, global enterprise, the financial, organisational, and cultural transformation of the professional game over the past three decades has been prodigious. In that time, Europe's top football clubs have grown to become "transnational business corporations" (Walsh and Giulianotti, 2001, p. 55), functioning collectively as a significant feature of the "postmodern entertainment industry" (Fürtjes, 2014, p. 593), which operate in, and draw diverse revenue streams from, multiple domestic and international markets (see, for example, Downward, 2014). From the 1960s – when English clubs found it necessary to begin diversifying their sources of revenue in response to the increased expenditure associated with gentrifying stadia (Taylor, 1971), the end of the transfer-and-restraint system, and the lifting of the maximum wage (Downward, 2014; Fürtjes, 2014) – through the 1970s, when "corporate sponsorship increased significantly, as firms sought more direct identification (with clubs)" (Andreff and Staudohar, 2000, p. 259), to the present day, in which collective club revenues across Europe equalled €24.6 billion in 2015/16 (Deloitte, 2017), football's vast transformation would not have been possible had it not explored, developed, and enhanced its relationship with the broadcast media. Indeed, of the 12 per cent growth in European club revenues between the 2014/15 and 2015/16 seasons, 59 per cent of this was due to increased income from broadcasting rights (Deloitte, 2017). Overall, growth in media incomes – primarily since the start of the English Premier League (EPL) in 1992 – accounts for a significant part of the massive transformation of the football industry, and such revenues have long since surmounted more traditional sources of income – i.e., live attendances – and both revealed and augmented revenue-generating opportunities in new and existing markets.

It is through its relationship with the media that football has managed to capitalise on an inherent marketing advantage to evoke strong emotions in its fans, and in doing so encourage loyalty, allegiance, and devotion. As such, football and its numerous brands (i.e., players, clubs, federations, national associations, sponsors, etc.) have expanded their reaches internationally, creating wider supporter bases in more diverse markets than the more traditional local sources. While the same could be argued for many other industry sectors, such as the wider entertainment industry, it is football's cultural, geographical, and often political extensions that, one could argue, put it in a favourable position from a marketing perspective (Conn, 2004; Fawbert, 2017). Football has managed to capitalise upon this inherent marketing advantage and utilise its unique relationship with the media in order to both cope with marketplace changes and challenges, and more importantly to *succeed*, often "paving the way" for wider sport-marketing management. Football's marketing advantage, as it were, and the way in which this has been leveraged will be discussed in detail below, employing relevant case studies to better illustrate the issues highlighted. Finally, this chapter draws attention to those areas in need of further scholarly attention.

Football's marketing advantage

To better understand the relationship between football and marketing, it is first worth exploring more broadly what marketing is. Marketing is concerned with customers – that is, creating and keeping customers – and communicating to them why they should choose one particular product or service over another. More specifically, an oft-cited definition is that of the American Marketing Association Board of Directors (2013) that describes marketing as:

> … the activity, set of institutions, and processes for creating, communicating, delivering, and exchanging offerings that have value for customers, clients, partners, and society at large.

Though its origins are often associated with sales-function and transactional-related approaches that date back to before the industrial revolution, with the emergence of the *marketing mix* throughout the mid-twentieth century, popularised by McCarthy's (1964) *4Ps*, marketing was, during this time, characterised by more product- and service-centric approaches, with a concentration on profit-related goals (Varey, 2002; Kamboj and Raham, 2015). In the present, however, and in response to rapidly changing marketplaces, continual re-adjustment of demand and supply, rapid technological advances, the multiplication of media, and widespread globalisation, marketing has evolved into a brand-centric and loyal consumer-focused managerial process (Kotler, 1977; Webster, 2002; Morosan et al., 2014; Homburg et al., 2015; Baker and Magnini, 2016). It is these two processes that give football an additional advantage in developing and harvesting its relationship with marketing. Football, as with any sport, has the power to evoke strong emotions in its fans, thus building loyalty (Conn, 2004; Fawbert, 2017). Yet, unlike other sectors, its aforementioned cultural, geographical, and often political extensions can often provide football brands with a "head start" in marketing, specifically with regard to building *brand equity*.

Brand equity has been described as "a set of brand assets and liabilities linked to a brand, its name and symbol, that add to or subtract from the value provided by a product or service to a firm and/or to that firm's customers" (Aaker, 1991, p. 15). For the sake of clarity, and given the context of this chapter, we might instead consider *brand equity* in a football context as: a set of brand assets and liabilities linked to a football club (or player), its name and logo, that add to or subtract from the value provided by said club (or player) and/or its supporters. Thus, it can be considered "the 'added value' endowed to a [football club or player] in the thoughts, words, and actions of consumers" (Keller, 2006, p. 546). The four dimensions of brand equity according to Aaker (1991) and Keller (1993) include *brand awareness, brand associations, perceived quality* and *brand loyalty*.

Brand awareness refers to a brand's presence in consumers' minds, asking both whether and to what extent a consumer is aware that the brand exists, and is thus able to recall and recognise it. For example, in the football context, *brand awareness* represents the ability of individuals to recognise a football club's (or player's) key characteristics, such as names, badges, colours, locations, etc. It would also be demonstrated if, when individuals are asked to name a football club or player, a particular club or player is mentioned over another. While preference to supporting a particular club or player is not expected, brand awareness suggests that the brand is in fact present to some extent in individuals' minds. For example, based on a study on the brands of two of the most prominent footballers in the world, Cristiano Ronaldo and Lionel Messi, data analytics company Nielsen Sport (2014) found that in the 15 markets examined, the overall brand awareness of Ronaldo and Messi was 94 per cent and 87 per cent respectively within the sample examined. That would suggest that despite their positive, negative, or neutral perceptions of the players, and their interest or lack thereof in the clubs where these players ply their trade, or even the sport of football overall, the vast majority of the participants were aware of these players' brands. While this study was conducted on only 15 markets, using a relatively limited research sample, preventing in this way any generalisation to the whole populations of the countries involved or to other countries not examined, it does suggest that the brands of the two players have a high level of recognition. Hoyer and Brown (1990) argue that brand awareness is the easiest dimension a brand can influence through advertising and promotion. Unlike other sectors, football has been on the receiving end of "free advertising" through regular, multiple and often lengthy mentions in the media. Daily updates on football results and stories on a regional, national and international level are common in print, broadcast and online media worldwide, providing football with "free" publicity across these formats (Manoli, 2017). As media sources proliferate, and the demand for football grows, "free advertising" flourishes, providing football brands with an advantage in building awareness around the globe.

The second dimension of brand equity, *brand associations*, represents the various meanings of a brand for the consumer, encompassing the traits and characteristics that consumers associate with it. In other words, *brand associations* comprise the different consumers' perceptions of the brand, and thus include various levels of favourability, strength, and uniqueness, while including negative, positive, and neutral attributes and attitudes. The benefits individuals associate with a brand include all functional, experiential, and symbolic aspects. Brand associations in the football context would refer to the image or perceptions individuals have for a club or a player. Some might exhibit a preference for a particular club or player, often demonstrated through professed fandom, while some might display entirely opposite perceptions, including antipathy and animosity for the same clubs and players, occasionally shown through excessive gestures. While extreme cases of both professed fandom, such as tattooing one's body with a football club's emblem or a player's face, or declared animosity toward a club or player, played out through social media exchanges (see, for example, Cleland, 2014) or through more zealous cases of fan disorder, violence, and hooliganism among supporters of rival clubs (see, for example, Rookwood 2010, 2014; Rookwood and Pearson, 2012), are not foreign to the world of football, such cases are less likely to be observed in brands outside of the football and wider sports industries.

Even on a less extreme nature, brand associations, formed due to the experiential and symbolic nature of football, are of great importance to football marketing. Following a commissioned study conducted by Kantar Media (2012), Manchester United FC, one of the biggest global football club brands argued that they have a "following" of 659 million people worldwide. These include all individuals that demonstrate positive associations with the club, even if they do not identify Manchester United as their favourite team. While the study does not present the number of people who claimed to have negative perceptions of the club, it could be argued that there exists a number of individuals that share unfavourable brand associations with Manchester United also. Even though the same could be claimed for any brand, it is the number of individuals that form any meanings, positive or negative, for football brands, as well as the intensity these meanings have, that sets football apart. Although an in-depth discussion on football brand meanings would encompass areas of culture, history, geography, politics, psychology, and sociology, grasping the breadth of football brands and their meanings to supporters is exemplified in the following quote from Fawbert (2017, p. 279):

> Nobody's spreading their grandfather's ashes down the central aisle of Tesco's [supermarket]. But, every day of the week somebody is spreading someone's ashes on a football pitch in England … it is more like a disciple going to a temple.

Broadly, it is such strong and meaningful associations created by football brands that countenance the industry's aforementioned marketing advantage. More specifically, the benefits that football fans might attribute to particular clubs or players can often be experiential and/or symbolic, originating from their feelings when they are "consuming" the brand (i.e., watching a football match or a particular player in action) and/or how that reflects on them. As a result, the excitement of a football fan when "consuming" something produced by their favourite club, by buying a match-day ticket, watching a match on TV, visiting the stadium, purchasing a branded mug, or even liking a Facebook post of their team, as well as their view on how this "consumption" echoes in them, might differ from the benefits the same individual would ascribe to another brand (for example, drinking Coca-Cola or Pepsi). One could argue that from all aspects of brand associations that Aaker (1991) and Keller (1993) examined, it is the uniqueness element that sets football and other sports apart from most brands. As both these authors argue, in order for a brand to have a sustainable competitive advantage, the consumers need to be provided with a compelling reason for buying into that brand. In the context of retail branding, this might occur through extensive direct comparisons with competitors (for example, Apple's "Get a Mac" advertising campaign conducted between 2006 and 2009 which played on the perceived weaknesses of non-Mac PCs, particularly Microsoft Windows-based machines) or implicitly through emphasis on a brand's unique selling proposition (for example, Apple's "Think Different" slogan between 1997 and 2002 aimed to communicate to customers that they were buying into a company at the forefront of technology).

However, and despite the brand's emphasised functional, experiential, or image benefits, unless there is a complete lack of competitors, some shared direct or abstract associations among brands are to be expected. In the football's context, brands consider themselves unique, offering a selling proposition and a set of benefits that are inimitable and thus incomparable to any of the other brands in the same category. While the functionality is rarely discussed, it is the experiential and image benefits that football brands highlight without nevertheless making a direct or indirect comparison with their competitors. In fact, despite the on-the-pitch emphasis on competition, brand comparisons are not a common phenomenon off-the-pitch among football brands. Yet, brand associations, and consequently *brand loyalty*, are built based on this uniqueness that fans assign to particular football brands.

Overall, as Fawbert's (2017) quote above highlights, it is these intense and unique benefits, or even detriments, that football brands are associated with in consumers' minds, which form the basis of football marketing.

The third and fourth dimensions of brand equity, *perceived quality* and *brand loyalty*, better illustrate football's marketing advantage. Perceived quality refers to a consumer's perceptions of the overall quality of a brand and its subjective superiority over available alternatives. For football consumers, the perceived quality of their favourite team is what encourages their support and viewing it as superior to any other football team available. Perceived quality is not to be mistaken with objective quality, which focuses on the technical, measurable, and verifiable aspects of a brand (see, for example, Mitra and Golder, 2006). Instead, perceived quality is the subjective judgement of a consumer, which might include some quality control measures of the intrinsic attributes of a brand (e.g., its appearance), but is mostly formed from the assessment of its extrinsic aspects, such as its brand associations. In other words, a decision on perceived quality in football is not made on the objective superiority of a club or a player, but on its intrinsic and extrinsic attributes, such as a player's physical appearance, a club's colours, or the brand meaning that the club or individual might have in fans' minds. While the perceived quality of football brands is a subjective concept and thus difficult to generalise or measure universally, based on the strength and uniqueness of football brand associations discussed above, their corresponding perceived quality is partially to blame for the excessive pricing strategies of various football brands (Nash, 2001).

As Aaker (1991) argued, the perceived quality of a brand is a valuable positioning characteristic or advantage that allows the brand the option to charge a premium price. In the context of professional football, it can be suggested that perceived quality has in fact been valued as significantly advantageous for football brands, which have correspondingly raised the prices of their products and services. One of the most common examples used to illustrate this price rise based on the perceived quality of the brand, is again the case of EPL clubs. As various authors have argued (e.g., Doczi and Toth, 2009; Williams, 2012), the EPL consists of clubs that have taken their perceived quality into consideration when designing their pricing strategies, especially with regard to match-day tickets. While these clubs' pricing strategies are expected to affect the satisfaction of their fans (Biscaia et al., 2013), EPL clubs have succeeded in attracting audiences of more than 13.5 million people to their matches for the 2016/17 season, corresponding to an average capacity/stadium utilisation of 96 per cent (Deloitte, 2017, p. 30). Even though the processes and strategies followed for a price to be set extend beyond the assessment of the perceived quality of a brand, the subjective judgement of the consumer/supporter is valued as a key element in the potential success of a brand and its acquirement and attainment of the fourth and final dimension of brand equity, *brand loyalty*.

Brand loyalty, describes a consumer's attachment and commitment to a brand that can be manifested both attitudinally and behaviourally. The former suggests that individuals have the intention to be loyal to a brand, while the latter indicates that they are demonstrating such loyalty by purchasing it. While all consumers demonstrate a level of loyalty to their preferred brands, sport brands in general, and football brands in particular, are often presented with high levels of brand loyalty, based on the strong and unique associations and meanings they can maintain in their supporters' minds. As Bridgewater and Stray (2002) argued, these meanings or values that football supporters associate with their preferred brands include their nostalgic importance, social entertainment, and community role. It is in fact these associations that maintain the brand loyalty in high levels, even when the subjective quality of the service received is not equally high (e.g., attending a football match in which the supported team lose). In other words, while team success can have a strong emotional impact on the supporters of a club, which in turn might result in them demonstrating their brand loyalty behaviourally through purchasing merchandise items, and thus engaging further with the brand in question, it is not a decisive factor of their attitudinal loyalty towards their preferred football club. As studies on fandom suggest, attitudinal brand loyalty in football brands, for example, a football club, can be significantly high even when the club under question is not successful, if other factors, such as team identification are also high (Campbell, Aiken, and Kent, 2004). The fact that football brand loyalty can remain at high levels even when performance is relatively low, is better illustrated by Brand Finance's (2017) report, which assesses the value of major football brands. In that report, they evaluated that Manchester United as the strongest football brand in the world, worth approximately $1.7 billion, despite the club's ranking of sixth in the EPL table in the 2016/17 season, capping a poor run of final league standings in recent years compared to the 1990s and 2000s (the last league title won by the club was in 2012/2013).

The importance of brand loyalty lies in the lack of a tight correlation between success and loyalty, underlying once again the inherent marketing advantage that football has over other industries. As such, and knowing that once a supporter/customer has been exposed to the brand, thus beginning their journey up the loyalty ladder (Narayandas, 2005), their progression from prospect to advocate is rather quick, through the brand equity dimensions discussed above. Most importantly, however, and due to football's marketing advantage and the consequent high switching cost between different football brands (Manoli, 2014), once an individual has become a fan/customer of a football brand, and thus has climbed the first step of the loyalty ladder, the possibility of them selecting a different football brand in the future is reduced. Despite the importance of this inherent marketing advantage, football would not have managed to build its current status as "*the most popular sport worldwide*" (FIFA 2017), had it not formed and developed marketing management practices that seize its advantage and foster its growth both in terms of popularity and commerciality. These practices, as well as the importance they bear in today's demanding marketplace, are examined below in more detail.

Football marketing management

Perhaps the best way to illustrate how football has utilised its inherent marketing advantage, and thus how football marketing management has been conducted, is through an examination of the development of its relationship with the media. Football, through its remarkable exploitation of its symbiotic relationship with the media, not only achieved significant financial profits, but also, most importantly, succeeded in gaining wide-ranging increased exposure through them, that has in turn allowed for football brands to be broadcasted and promoted worldwide. By doing so, football has tapped into an immense, international pool of prospective loyal consumers, who, due to football's marketing advantage of evoking strong emotions, can begin to climb the loyalty ladder of football brands. As the switching cost between football brands is considerably high, once the first step of this ladder is climbed and individuals become supporters of a brand, football often gains their loyalty for life. It could be argued that it is the way in which football has utilised its relationship with the media in order to capitalise on its inherent marketing advantage that has in fact shaped today's flourishing football marketing landscape. This relationship is illustrated in Figure 8.1 and can be better elucidated in the case study that follows.

Case study: The English Premier League

English football, and in particular its top division, the EPL, is considered one of the fastest growing industry sectors in the UK, with a remarkable growth difference when compared to any other UK sport (Deloitte Sports Business Group, 2016). Yet the significant growth in audiences, popularity, and subsequent brand recognition of the EPL and its constituent clubs would not have been possible had there not been a reciprocal relationship between the EPL and the broadcast media (most notably, Sky). The way in which this relationship has developed from the EPL's inaugural season in 1992 to the present day, has worked to re-position the media in the wider ecosystem of the football industry from a mere intermediary between football and its supporters/consumers, as it was in English football prior to the start of the EPL, to a key supplier, as is shown in Figure 8.1. Apart from the significant monetary value of this relationship (see Table 8.1, for

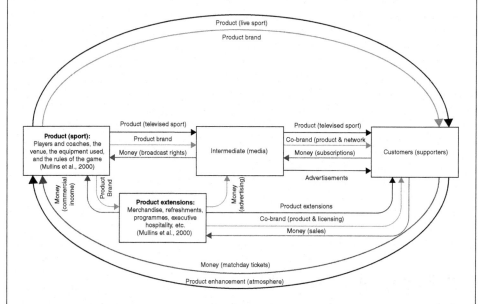

Figure 8.1   Football's unique marketing/media relationship (adapted from Manoli, 2014, p. 10)

example) that has allowed football to improve and grow, the media's main benefit to football has been the exposure it has provided. By televising football's main product, live matches, the media have allowed for a global audience to be exposed to the sport, capturing in this way their attention and potentially long-term interest. FIFA (n.d.) reports that the 2014 World Cup final was watched by 1.013 billion people who tuned in to watch, or consume, football through the media. In other words, football was able to reach over one billion people, who were exposed and thus given the opportunity to consume and potentially enjoy the sport which would not have been possible without the assistance of the media. The extent of such media coverage (and for other mega-events, such the Olympic Games), 'simply cannot be reliably achieved by other means short of natural disasters or wars' (Black, 2007, p. 264). In marketing terms, this symbiotic relationship has allowed football an immense, international pool of prospective loyal consumers, while making football brands some of the most recognisable in the world.

Table 8.1 Broadcast Rights Fees for the English Premier League, 1992 to the present day

Year	1992	1997	2001	2004	2007	2010	2013	2016
Main broadcaster	BSkyB	BSkyB	BSkyB	BSkyB	BSkyB Setanta/ ESPN	BSkyB Setanta/ ESPN	BSkyB BT	Sky<?>BT
Length of contract (years)	5	4	4	3	3	3	3	3
Rights fee (£m)	191.5	670	1100	1024	1706	1782	3018	5136
Annual rights fee (£m)	38.3	167.5	275	341	569	594	1006	1712
Live matches per season	60	60	66	138	138	138	154	168
Fees per live match (£m)	0.64	2.79	4.16	2.47	4.12	4.30	6.53	10.2

Sources: Cox, 2012; Downward, 2014; Taylor & Gratton, 2002.

As the above case study has demonstrated, football marketing management has been able to exploit both its inherent marketing advantage and its symbiotic relationship with the media in order to further flourish. Taking the rapidly changing marketplace into consideration, football's marketing landscape can be expected to also transform, presenting football with both opportunities to further develop and challenges to be faced. First, the multiplication of media that has occurred in the past ten years is expected to intensify, with new and social media often replacing traditional media in sports communication (Manoli, 2017). These new media call for user content creation, publishing, and promotion, which in turn can revolutionise the way in which communication and brand management occurs (Berthon et al., 2012). As a result, and based on this "horizontal revolution" where the users can communicate with other users directly, while potentially excluding the brand owner/manager from the overall communication process, users or audiences have an increasing power over the way in which a brand is communicated and consumed (see, for example, Kaplan and Haenlein, 2010). In fact, as new forms of media are introduced, and more overlapping occurs among different stakeholder groups (e.g., employees become customers), the power relations between audiences and brand owners/managers change, with more power invested in the various audiences of each brand. This power lies in the ability to influence other audiences through the use of their word-of-mouth, which when communicated electronically can spread faster and more globally, potentially affecting the views and thus the brand reception of various other audiences of the brand. As a result, brand management can no longer be considered a controlled process in which the brand owner is able to design and manage the brand in hand, since part of this process is in fact occurring while the audience is interacting with the brand or with other brand users. The brand's image and associations are therefore co-created during these interactions that help each member of an audience reach their own understanding of what the brand stands for. The brand owner can still aim to influence the functional image of their brand by highlighting its key attributes, such as a football club's history, connection with the local community or titles won, however, the hedonic image of the brand tends to be affected by user-generated content. This hedonic brand image – the image that is linked with feelings and emotions – is further exaggerated in the case of football, due to its natural marketing advantage, which could potentially lead in amplified deviations in terms of *brand image*. It is these deviations in brand image and their link or lack thereof with the *brand identity* of a football brand that are presenting football marketing management with its biggest challenge thus far: achieving brand consistency. As recent studies on brand consistency and coherency in sports have argued (Kenyon et al., 2018), such a task might prove more demanding in the future, since boundaries worldwide are eliminated, making a global audience the potential audience for any football brand, paired with the increasing overlapping of stakeholders and the overall philosophy of sharing using the multiple user-controlled media. This challenge can be better illustrated in the following case study.

Case study: Exploring the brand consistency of the EPL's "Big Four" in foreign markets

Brand image: the total impression of an organisation, product, or place in consumers' minds (Aaker, 1991), or "the characteristics or attributes through which customers evaluate the brand and compare it to others" (Bodet, Meurgey, and Lacassagne, 2009, p. 371).

Brand identity: "the processes by which brand owners and managers endeavour to convey the individuality and distinctiveness of their organisations and products" (Nandan, 2005, p. 265) which includes both "visual (tangible) components, such as a name, a logo, a theme, etc., and the brand's social and psychological (intangible) components" (Kenyon et al. 2018, p. 8) (Figure 8.2).

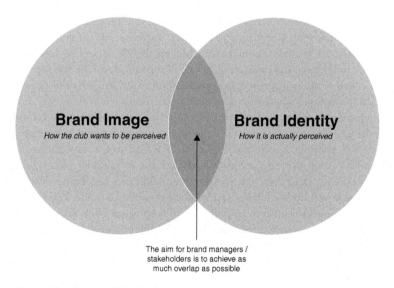

Figure 8.2 The brand identity/image link

In 2010, the Asia Pacific Journal of Marketing and Logistics published a study by Bodet and Chavanet, the purpose of which was to investigate the brand equity of English professional football clubs in foreign markets, namely China. Specifically, the research sought to investigate Keller's (1993) customer-based brand equity (CBBE), among Chinese supporters, of the EPL's so-called "Big Four," these being: Arsenal FC, Chelsea FC, Liverpool FC, and Manchester United. Among the various findings of the research, the authors present the strongest features of these clubs' brand images as follows: Arsenal FC was perceived as "young, dynamic, and sexy"; Chelsea FC as "rich, wealthy, and sometimes superficial"; Manchester United as "successful, aggressive, and dominant"; and Liverpool FC as "steady, honest, and pugnacious" (Bodet and Chavanet, 2010, p. 63). Yet, as the literature suggests, a "brand's identity – created and managed by the brand owner/manager – does not always correspond to the brand image as perceived by customers or broadcast by the media" (Kenyon et al., 2018, p. 6). Taking Liverpool FC as an example here, the brand image characteristic of the club being "pugnacious," meaning quick to argue or quarrel, does not coincide with the brand identity that the club have tried to create, both domestically and internationally, as being a family club (see Kenyon and Bodet, 2017). Similarly, it is unlikely that those responsible at Chelsea FC for the club's brand management set out to have their club perceived as superficial. If the brand consistency is to be achieved, therefore, those responsible for the brand management of these clubs must work to identify how and why these brand images are being engendered and then work to both mitigate these and promote their more desired brand identity characteristics. Interestingly, Bodet and Chavanet (2010) argue that the findings of their research suggest that the brand images of the clubs in question are influenced, in significant part, by the "image transfer from the players, the coach and even the chairman" (ibid, p. 63). If indeed then these clubs' brands are the product of interaction between the brand owner/manager and its stakeholders (the players, for example), the challenge for those responsible for the brand management of these clubs is addressing such issues with said stakeholders.

Conclusion and future research

In countries aiming to expand upon their own domestic sports industries, it is hardly surprising that football is seen as an appropriate avenue through which to achieve such aims. One only has to look to Qatar's hosting of the 2022 World Cup [see Chapter 41 in this Handbook], for example, or the ambitious target of Chinese President Xi Jinping who aims to have created an $800 billion sport industry in his country by 2025 (Chadwick, 2015) and a World Cup winning team by 2050 (Chadwick, 2017) [see Chapter 40 in this Handbook]. In achieving such aims, whether for Qatar or China, understanding the needs and wants of their customers and consumers, alongside the successful intermediation by the media, will be key in delivering successful versions of these stakeholders' visions.

More broadly, the growth of football's relationship with the media has not only benefited the two parties involved, but also created, shaped, and helped the development of new sub-sectors of the sports industry. Following the increasing global demand for football paired with the rapid multiplication of media, the broadcasting rights sub-sector was created, in which a number of broadcasters from both traditional media, such as TV and radio stations, and new media, like Amazon and Google, are expressing interest, bidding and buying the rights to broadcast football matches to be played to a worldwide audience (*The Guardian*, 2017). Apart from football clubs, federations, and media outlets, this sub-sector has also attracted the attention of intermediaries or outsourcing agencies, which assist in this bidding, buying and distribution process of broadcasting rights (Manoli and Hodgkinson, 2017). Marketing outsourcing overall and in particular the bidding, sale, and distribution of broadcasting rights are two important areas in football marketing that are still under-researched, despite their immense impact on the industry. With the demand for football ever increasing and new media outlets joining the broadcasting process, the future of this symbiotic relationship, how it is marketed, and its commercial implications are expected to be nothing but fascinating.

Finally, the aforementioned move away from its traditional, working-class cultural heritage and roots (e.g., Duke, 2002; Hognestad, 2012) toward a more commercially oriented structure has seen football's various bodies, and wider sport organisations for that matter, come to consider and manage themselves as brands in recent years, particularly in international markets (Bouchet, Hillairet, and Bodet, 2013; Bodet, Kenyon, and Ferrand 2018). For example, in those years, Asian markets have proved a particular target for European football brands, with their populous nations (e.g., almost 1.4 billion in China in 2016) and increasing levels of purchasing power, among other factors, proving a particular draw (Desbordes, 2012). In such markets, the regarding of football clubs as brands, and subsequent marketing of these brands has proven a successful strategy in "extend[ing] their visibility in new solvent markets" and generating international consumer bases (ibid, p. 10). Yet, in domestic markets, there is much evidence to suggest that football fans are often sceptical and sometimes resistant to marketing rhetoric (e.g., Chadwick and Beech, 2007; Chadwick and Holt, 2006; Giulianotti, 2005; Numerato, 2015); an approach which considers them as customers and consumers and no longer as fans (e.g., Oppenhuisen and van Zoonen, 2006). So, if understanding the needs and wants of customers and consumers is at the heart of successful marketing (Keller, 2006), but being identified in such a market-focused way is criticised by those very individuals regarded in such a way (Giulianotti, 2005) – who often see such approaches as exploitation of their communal identities (Kennedy and Kennedy, 2012) – how then are football clubs to proceed? With this question in mind, the challenges raised by domestic and international football marketing strategies – an issue of which some professional clubs do seem aware (see, for example, Kenyon and Bodet, 2017) – is an area in which future research might be aimed.

References

Aaker, D.A. (1991) *Managing Brand Equity*. New York, NY: The Free Press.
Andreff, W. and Staudohar, P.D. (2000) The evolving European model of professional sports finance. *Journal of Sports Economics*, 1(3), 257–276.
Baker, M.A., and Magnini, V.P. (2016) The evolution of services marketing, hospitality marketing and building the constituency model for hospitality marketing. *International Journal of Contemporary Hospitality Management*, 28(8), 1510–1534.
Berthon P.R., Pitt L.F., Plangger, K., and Shapiro, D. (2012) Marketing meets Web 2.0, social media, and creative consumers: implications for international marketing strategy, *Business Horizons*, 55(3), 261–271.
Biscaia, R., Correia, A., Rosado, A.F., Ross, S.D., and Maroco, J. (2013) Sport sponsorship: the relationship between team loyalty, sponsorship awareness, attitude toward the sponsor, and purchase intentions. *Journal of Sport Management*, 27(4), 288–302.
Black, D. (2007) The symbolic politics of sport mega-events: 2010 in comparative perspective. *Politikon*, 34(3), 261–276.
Bodet, G., Meurgey, B., and Lacassagne, M. F. (2009) Brand social representations: strategic perspectives for a fitness club. *International Journal of Sport Management and Marketing*, 5(4), 369–383.
Bodet, G. and Chanavat, N. (2010) Building global football brand equity. *Asia Pacific Journal of Marketing and Logistics*, 22(1), 55–66.
Bodet, G.S.P., Kenyon, J.A., and Ferrand, A. (2018) Appetite for or resistance to consumption relationships? A trans-European perspective on the marketization of football fan relationships. *Journal of Consumer Culture*, forthcoming.
Bouchet, P., Hillairet, D., and Bodet, G. (2013) *Sport Brands*. Oxford: Routledge.
Brand Finance®. (2017) *Football 50 2017*. London: Brand Finance®.
Bridgewater, S. and Stray, S. (2002) Brand values and a typology of premiership football fans. Working Paper. Coventry: Warwick Business School.
Campbell Jr, R.M., Aiken, D., and Kent, A. (2004) Beyond BIRGing and CORFing: Continuing the exploration of fan behavior. *Sport Marketing Quarterly*, 13(3), 151–157.
Chadwick, S., & Beech, J. (eds.). (2007) *The Marketing of Sport*. Harlow, UK: FT Prentice Hall.
Chadwick, S., & Holt, M. (2008) Releasing latent brand equity: the case of UEFA's Champions League. *The Marketing Review*, 8(2), 147–162.

Chadwick, S. (2015) China's strategy for sport yields intriguing research opportunities. *Sport, Business and Management: An International Journal*, 5(3).

Chadwick, S. (2017) A £198m transfer is not about football. It's about soft power. *The Guardian*. [online] Retrieved from: https://www.theguardian.com/commentisfree/2017/sep/01/neymar-transfer-barcelona-soft-power-asian-governments

Cleland, J. (2014) Racism, football fans, and online message boards: how social media has added a new dimension to racist discourse in English Football. *Journal of Sport and Social Issues*, 38(5), 415–431.

Conn, D. (2004) *The Beautiful Game? Searching for the Soul of Football*. London: Yellow Jersey Press.

Cox, A. (2012) Live broadcasting, gate revenue, and football club performance: Some evidence. *International Journal of the Economics of Business*, 19(1), 75–98.

Deloitte, (2017) *Annual Review of Football Finance*. London: Deloitte LLP.

Desbordes, M. (2012) *Marketing and Football*. Oxford: Routledge.

Dóczi, T. and Tóth, A.K. (2009) Football fandom in England: Old traditions and new tendencies. *International Quarterly of Sport Science*, 2, 30–41.

Downward, P. (2014) English professional football. In: J. Goddard and P. Sloane (eds.). *Handbook on the Economics of Professional Football* (pp. 277–297) Cheltenham: Edward Elgar.

Duke, V. (2002) Local tradition versus globalisation: resistance to the McDonaldisation and Disneyisation of professional football in England. *Football Studies*, 5(1), 5–23.

Fawbert, J. (2017) West Ham United in the Olympic Stadium: A Gramscian analysis of the rocky road to Stratford. In: P. Cohen and P. Watt (eds.). *London 2012 and the Post-Olympics City* (pp. 259–286). Palgrave Macmillan, London.

FIFA (2017) *FIFA Marketing Research*. [online] Retrieved from: http://www.fifa.com/about-fifa/news/y=2010/m=12/news=fifa-marketing-research-1354721.html

FIFA (n.d.) *2014 FIFA World Cup Brazil Television Audience Report*. [online] Retrieved from: https://resources.fifa.com/mm/document/affederation/tv/02/74/55/57/2014fwcbraziltvaudiencereport(draft5)(issuedate14.12.15)_neutral.pdf

Fürtjes, O. (2014) Football and its continuity as a classless mass phenomenon in Germany and England: rethinking the bourgeoisification of football crowds. *Soccer & Society*, 17(4), 588–609.

Giulianotti, R. (2005) Sport spectators and the social consequences of commodification: Critical perspectives from Scottish football. *Journal of Sport and Social Issues*, 29(4), 386–410.

Hognestad, H.K. (2012) Split loyalties: football is a community business. *Soccer & Society*, 13(3), 377–391.

Homburg, C., Vomberg, A., Enke, M., and Grimm, P.H. (2015) The loss of the marketing department's influence: is it really happening? And why worry. *Journal of the Academy of Marketing Science*, 43(1), 1–13.

Hoyer, W.D. and Brown, S.P. (1990) Effects of brand awareness on choice for a common, repeat-purchase product. *Journal of Consumer Research*, 17(2), 141–148.

Kamboj, S. and Rahman, Z. (2015) Marketing capabilities and firm performance: literature review and future research agenda. *International Journal of Productivity and Performance Management*, 64(8), 1041–1067.

Keller, K.L. (1993) Conceptualizing, measuring, and managing customer-based brand equity. *The Journal of Marketing*, 57(1), 1–22.

Keller, K.L. (2006). Measuring brand equity. In R. Grover & M. Vriens (eds.). *The Handbook of Marketing Research* (pp. 546–568). Thousand Oaks, CA: Sage.

Kennedy, P., and Kennedy, D. (2012) Football supporters and the commercialisation of football: Comparative responses across Europe. *Soccer & Society*, 13(3), 327–340.

Kenyon, J.A. and Bodet, G. (2017) Supporter engagement through social media: a case study of Liverpool Football Club. In: N. Chanavat, M. Desbordes, and N. Lorgnier (eds.). *Routledge Handbook of Football Marketing* (pp. 372–394). Oxon: Routledge.

Kenyon, J.A., Manoli, A.E., and Bodet, G. (2018) Brand consistency and coherency at the London 2012 Olympic Games. *Journal of Strategic Marketing*, 26, 6–18.

Kotler, P. (1977) From sales obsession to marketing effectiveness. *Harvard Business Review*, November–December, 67–75.

Manoli, A.E. (2014) The football industry through traditional management analysis. *Scandinavian Sport Studies Forum*, 5(1), 93–109.

Manoli, A.E. (2017) Media relations in English football clubs. In: J. J. Zhang and B.G. Pitts (eds.). *Contemporary Sport Marketing: Global Perspectives* (pp. 120–138). Oxon: Routledge.

Manoli, A.E. and Hodgkinson, I. R. (2017) Marketing outsourcing in the English Premier League: the rights holder/agency interface. *European Sport Management Quarterly*, 17(4), 436–456.

McCarthy, J.E. (1964) *Basic Marketing. A Managerial Approach*. Homewood, IL: Irwin.

Mitra, D. and Golder, P.N. (2006) How does objective quality affect perceived quality? Short-term effects, long-term effects, and asymmetries. *Marketing Science*, 25(3), 230–247. [online] Retrieved from: https://doi.org/10.1287/mksc.1050.0175

Morosan, C., T. Bowen, J., and Atwood, M. (2014) The evolution of marketing research. *International Journal of Contemporary Hospitality Management*, 26(5), 706–726.

Nandan, S. (2005) An exploration of the brand identity–brand image linkage: a communications perspective. *Journal of brand management*, 12(4), 264-278.

Narayandas, D. (2005) Building loyalty in business markets. *Harvard Business Review*, 83(9), 131–139.

Nash, R. (2001) English football fan groups in the 1990s: Class, representation and fan power. *Soccer & Society*, 2(1), 39–58.

Nielsen Sports (2014) *Messi vs. Ronaldo Who is the most marketable?* [online] Retrieved from: http://nielsensports.com/wp-content/uploads/2014/12/Messi-vs-Ronaldo.pdf

Numerato, D. (2015) Who says "no to modern football?" Italian supporters, reflexivity, and neo-liberalism. *Journal of Sport and Social Issues*, 39(2), 120–138.

Oppenhuisen, J., and van Zoonen, L. (2006) Supporters or customers? Fandom, marketing and the political economy of Dutch football. *Soccer & Society*, 7(1), 62–75.

Rookwood, J. (2010) "I smell the blood of an Englishman": Cardiff City, football disorder and Welsh nationalism. *The International Journal of Multidisciplinary Thought*, 1(1), 395–406.

Rookwood, J. (2014) Hooliganism. In: H. Copes and C. Forsyth (eds.). *Encyclopaedia of Social Deviance* (pp. 347–351). Thousand Oaks, CA: Sage.

Rookwood, J. and Pearson, G. (2012) The football hoolifan: positive fan attitudes to "hooliganism". *International Review for the Sociology of Sport*, 47(2), 147–162.

Taylor, I. (1971) Soccer consciousness and soccer hooliganism. In: S. Cohen (ed.). *Images of Deviance* (pp. 134–164). Harmmondsworth: Penguin.

Taylor, P. and Gratton, C. (2002) *The Economics of Sport and Recreation: An Economic Analysis*. Oxon: Routledge.

Varey, R.J. (2002) *Marketing Communications Principles and Practice*. London: Routledge.

Walsh, A.J. and Giulianotti, R. (2001) This sporting mammon! A normative critique of the commodification of sport. *Journal of the Philosophy of Sport*, 28(1), 53–77.

Webster, F.E. (2002) Marketing management in changing times. *Marketing Management*, 11(1). 18–23.

Williams, J. (2012) *Into the Red: Liverpool FC and the Changing Face of English Football*. Random House.

9

Digital and social media

Alex Fenton and Boris Helleu

Introduction

Football clubs have always had a fascinating relationship with digital and social media. Chadwick (2009) highlighted the opportunity open to clubs to use these technologies to help enhance their features, engage fans, and stay ahead of the game. Football clubs are examples of brands with large volumes of highly engaged fans. This provides an increasing and potentially lucrative opportunity to engage with fans locally and globally.

Digital and social media are proving to be disruptive for football clubs. They have been held responsible for the changing consumption behaviours of fans and also for distracting viewers from the game (Helleu, 2017). Commentators suggest this could impact on lucrative TV rights deals in the future (Gibson, 2016). There has been an increasing shift of sporting media consumption from TV to social media platforms such as Twitter, Facebook, Instagram, and YouTube. The use of multiple mobile devices whilst watching TV or a live match, has become commonplace. This practice, known as second and third screen viewing, continues to disrupt the way in which people consume and enjoy football (Miah, 2017, p. 240).

Fans who engage globally through social media with clubs and players demonstrate different levels of emotional involvement, commitment, and sense of community. The ubiquitous usage of social media by football clubs and fans globally (Cave and Miller, 2015; McCarthy et al., 2014) and its potential and disruptive effects provides the basis for this chapter. The traditional values and characters within the game can also view these technologies as a threat (Helleu, 2017). Clubs are at a critical crossroads where the business and management of football must stay ahead of the game. They need to learn more about how to use these technologies, avoid the pitfalls, and maximise the potential to enhance their brands. This chapter explores these opportunities and threats of this immense disruptive force on the beautiful game.

Football and digital media

In an article entitled "The Pub as a Virtual Football Fandom Venue: An Alternative to "Being there"?" Mike Weed (2007) tries to understand the deep nature of the sport spectator experience in a pub on the occasion of the World Cup 2002. He recalls that according to the current academic literature, there would be no more satisfactory experience for football fans than the live presence. The football fan is compared to the passionate tourist. Both of them are looking for the live experience: "I am there" or "I was there." Weed noted further that the stadium experience has become so lifeless that many fans prefer to go to the pub to consume. To watch a game at the pub may appear as an inevitably less satisfactory secondary experience. Yet Weed explains that the essence of the fan experience is not to be there but rather to share a common experience.

According to Weed (2007, p. 411): "*It would appear that 'spontaneous group association' is a key part of the sport spectating experience, and that the primary element of sports spectatorship can be redefined: rather than being about seeing the game, it is centred on sharing the experience.*" Weed published his work in 2007 on an observation, which dates back to 2002. At that time, Facebook, Twitter, Instagram, or Snapchat did not yet exist. Since then, according to a study from "We Are Social" (2017), there are more than three billion people active on social media. Facebook alone has more than two billion accounts with 700 million on Instagram, Twitter (328 million), and Snapchat (255 million). Social media enable a conversation within a community of peers around contents, these 3 Cs on their own are not enough to explain social media success in sport.

For that purpose, it is necessary to return to the work of Mike Weed. By wanting to reconsider the nature of fan experience 10 years ago and without knowing it, the author supplies a tool to analyse the motivations and the behaviour of the "millennial" fans. The football match generates strong feelings due to the uncertainty of results. Sports emotion is valuable only if it is shared and this is exactly the catalyst, which allows social media to be successful. Sports entertainment is not simply spectated, it is lived and interacted with by fans who are conversing and sharing their feelings with their community and the world (Gantz, 2013). Social media creates an opportunity for "*spontaneous group association,*" which is a disruptive way for digital fans to consume sports (Pegoraro, 2014; Sanderson, 2011). In the introduction of a special issue of *International Journal of Sport Communication* dedicated to new media and social networking, Clavio explains (2010, p. 393):

> Although the World Wide Web had gotten its start in the early 1990s, very few people would have predicted the seismic shifts that Web access and Web applications would have on the sport communication landscape. It is remarkable to think that common present-day communication methods and concepts such as blogging, Internet-enabled phones, online digital video, and social networking weren't part of the lexicon a decade ago.

If the experience of the spectator consists of sharing fan emotions at the expense of following the game, then social media works perfectly with sports entertainment. The "Know the Fan" report (2014) shows that although TV was the primary way to consume football, smartphones and social media were growing fast. 12 per cent of French fans used social media to consume sport in 2011, which grew to 21 per cent in 2014. Facebook was the most popular channel (79 per cent), followed by YouTube (52 per cent), Twitter (17 per cent), and Instagram (8 per cent). Fans use their second screen in order to read live text commentary, consume non-sports content, watch clips from other match, place a bet online, and share messages with friends.

In 2016 the summer Olympic games were the biggest moment of the year on Twitter. The 187 million tweets generated on the occasion of Olympics Games would have been seen more than 75 billion times. Football also generates large volumes of social media churn. Indeed, it has been present twice in the top three of the most commented moments during the games of Rio (the decisive penalty by Neymar in the final and his opening of the score). Furthermore, Euro 2016, where European countries compete to be crowned European champions, ranked fourth based on discussion subjects on Twitter.

Table 9.1 Some of the most commented upon sporting events on Twitter

Event	Year	Match	Score	Tweets (million)
World Cup	2014	semi-final, Brazil-Germany	1–7	35,6
World Cup	2014	final, Germany-Argentina	1–0	32,1
Super Bowl (NFL)	2017	New England Patriots-Atlanta Falcons	34–28	27,6
Euro 2016	2016	Fibal, Portugal-France	1–0	14,2
World Series (MLB)	2016	decisive 7th game, Chicago Cubs-Cleveland Indians	13–11	10,5
NBA Finals	2016	decisive 7th game, Cleveland Cavaliers-Golden State Warriors	93–89	8,4

Source: Twitter Blog (https://blog.twitter.com).

Table 9.2 Top 10 list of Football Clubs Digital Fanbase (millions)

Team	Country	Digital Community*	Facebook	Instagram	Twitter
FC Barcelona	Spain	206,7	102,6	50,7	40,8
Real Madrid	Spain	204,9	104,6	50,9	39,1
Manchester United	UK	111,8	73,6	18,2	13,1
Chelsea FC	UK	76,8	48	9,6	11,3
Arsenal	UK	63,3	38	9,7	10,3
FC Bayern München	Germany	61,2	42,4	10,2	4,8
Liverpool FC	UK	48,9	30	4,3	8,9
Juventus	Italy	45,4	30,1	7,3	5,5
Paris Saint-Germain	France	45,3	29,6	8,1	5,2
Manchester City	UK	43,4	25	4,9	8,2

* Facebook, Instagram, Twitter, Periscope, Google+, Youtube (Result Sports, 2017).

Social media allow new ways for clubs and fans to interact. Supporters are no longer in touch with their club for only 90 minutes, but every day, to reach exclusive content, behind the scenes information and relevant news. It is the connection, interaction and content that explains why so many fans follow football clubs on social media. Resultsports, a German agency of communication and digital marketing, created a world ranking of football clubs according to their digital fan base. The clubs are classified according to their number of subscribers on Facebook, Twitter, Instagram, YouTube, Periscope, and Google+. FC Barcelona and Real Madrid are the only clubs to accumulate more than 200 million social media accounts. This is significantly more than Manchester United's 111 million which completes the podium.

Four other English clubs appear in the top 10 (Chelsea, Arsenal, Liverpool, and Manchester City). We find also Paris Saint-Germain, Juventus and Bayern Munich in the top 10.

These big clubs are using the social networks for purposes of relationship marketing. Bayern Munich announced in February 2016 that the launch of a digital plan, which they highlighted, was a priority for the club. Stefan Mennerich, Director of IT and New Media said,

> The football business, via digitalisation is an international competition, and if we want to be able to compete against the big English and the big French and Spanish and Italian clubs, we have to be successful abroad as well. We see that the fans in China and the United States, that they love these Bavarian roots and we want to bring our history and our background to the fans in China and the United States, and we want to contextualise the content, that

means we want to be able to bring another content to a mobile phone user in Japan in the morning than to a desktop user in the evening in Brazil.

(Tewhatu, 2016)

Social media channels

The use of social media channels by football clubs and fans has grown considerably in recent years (McCarthy et al., 2014). The growth of mobile devices has further fuelled the use of social media through apps. Smartphones and social media offer opportunities for more interactive experiences for fans. Rowles (2017, p18) stated: "We have the opportunity to use mobile technologies creatively to deliver this value proposition via interaction." Successful social media channels increase fan engagement and ultimately make the brand of a football club better known.

Social media channels can be used to create online brand communities. The term brand communities was first introduced by Muniz and O'Guinn (2001). They defined and introduced the concept of brand communities to describe a community of admirers of a brand, set on a shared set of social relations but "not bound by geography." The authors noted the importance of brand communities built on social media and forums. Fans have been collaborating online for many years (Habibi et al., 2014). Increasingly, social media channels are being used to create brand communities by both football clubs and their fans.

Habibi et al. (ibid.) claimed to be the first authors to identify the differences between types of brand community by analysing social media brand communities. The authors found that social media based brand communities have great advantages compared to other types. These benefits included; attracting more people, being lower cost, and (crucially) people having to use their real identities compared to previous virtual communities such as forums where identities could be anonymised (Habibi et al., 2014). The use of real identities can also have an effect on the way in which people behave online. Another key difference is that social media channels are much more visual with people often including digital media photos and videos from their smartphones. These communities can be created by fans or by brands. Popp et al. (2016) concurred that social media brand communities are different. They also studied "anti-brand communities" on Facebook using a netnography (ethnography online) approach. They found that some football fans had set up anti-brand communities that allowed fans to dissociate from a brand. These communities such as "Anti Bayern!!!" were found to be "*important drivers in football-related anti-brand communities.*" These "Negative posts, media and comments lead to a reinterpretation of brand meaning" (Popp et al., 2016, p.1).

Social media content

Engaging digital content is the fuel that fires the social media channels of football clubs. This content comes in the shape of text, image, video, animation, or sound. The audience and platform selected, dictate the type of digital content to be produced. As technology has increased and new platforms and apps have arisen, so has the appetite for new kinds of social media content. Video content is increasingly popular with the majority of football clubs using this to show match highlights, interviews, and giving insights into their club. This content can be increasingly delivered by social media platforms including YouTube, Instagram, and Facebook. Some football clubs prefer to deliver video via Facebook and some prefer video platform YouTube. There are merits to each selected platform, but some consider YouTube to be the best way to deliver video and build an audience over time (McLaren, 2017). Dan McLaren of DigitalSport elaborates:

> Despite the current popularity of video on Facebook, Instagram and Snapchat the interaction is often fleeting and in that moment. YouTube has always been video first and is the 2nd most popular search engine in the world, but it tends to be the fans who utilise the platform best whilst clubs stick with where they have already grown audiences on Facebook.
>
> *(McLaren, 2017)*

In the age of web 2.0, fans are now equipped with powerful smartphones, which are quite capable of capturing all kinds of digital content including video clips and live streaming. This creates some challenges and opportunities for football clubs. For example, fans that create content are also engaging other fans, which can help to build the brand of clubs. However, there are also copyright issues and a lack of control for clubs who consider themselves "guardians of the brand" (McCarthy et al., 2014). In some cases, fans can create digital content and release club news on social media faster than the club is able to. Working with fans and key influencers to produce digital content and encouraging a positive co-creative relationship is key to progression and building the brand.

It is important to engage different audiences using the appropriate digital content. If content does not successfully engage different groups, then clubs run the risk of being crowded out of social media timelines. Social media algorithms are designed in such a way to deliver more of what people like. If fans are interacting with club content on social media, then this allows more content to rise to the surface. CEO of Seven League, Richard Ayers explains, "it's important from the club's perspective to have all those different types of people engaged because then the more people who are engaged the more it proves to the algorithm that there's a distribution of net worth." Social media content therefore can engage and build lasting relationships with fans. It can also engage fans globally and help clubs to stand out from the competition.

Social media fan segmentation

Segmenting fans is important in order for clubs to better understand and connect with their audience on social media platforms (Heinze et al., 2016). Fans can be segmented in lots of different ways including by location, loyalty, or gender. The idea of creating fan personas to represent different kinds of fan can help clubs to create the right digital content and campaigns to reach and engage them. Fan (or buyer) personas involve creating fictional characters, which represent different segments of fans.

Understanding fan behaviour and segments of fans provides "opportunities for club marketing managers to make use of increasingly sophisticated direct and database marketing techniques" (Fillis and Mackay, 2013). Manchester City social media manager Chris Parkes-Nield highlighted this opportunity, "You can put fans in a hierarchy based on how they are connected and therefore how you converse with them and what message you put across and what platforms to use." There have been various studies of football clubs, which have suggested different segments of fans. For example, Kantar's 2012 study found that football fans could be segmented into three categories based on their strength of connection to the club. These segments are:

- Core – those who state that it is their favourite club
- Current – those who support the club at all
- Followers – those who unprompted stated it was one of their favourite teams

Listening to fans and undertaking research can identify the different segments of fans within clubs. For example, for a segment of more weakly connected "followers" who may know less about the club, Richard Ayers explains that social media content would be "much more 'this is our background', 'here is where we came from', 'this is what a new fan does', and 'let me introduce you to the players' and building a relationship." Understanding different segments of fans and listening to what people are saying through social media is key to successful social media engagement.

Global fans and lurkers

Football clubs and players have many millions of social media followers from every corner of the globe. In February 2016, Christiano Ronaldo became the first athlete to reach 200 million combined followers across Twitter, Instagram, and Facebook. Brazilian superstar Neymar for example had approximately 170 million followers on his official Instagram, Twitter, and Facebook channels combined in 2017. These followers are international and they are often following several football clubs and players online. These more weakly connected followers have also been called lurkers and they present an opportunity for football clubs. Lurkers make up the largest percentage of any social media following. The majority of lurker followers do not tend to create digital content, they listen, but rarely interact with brands or other fans (Sun et al., 2014).

Engaging with the wider global fan base is important for football clubs in order to try and increase the connection to their club to become a more strongly connected fan. A stronger connection to a club potentially means more interaction on social media and more purchase of club merchandise. Importantly, a large base of followers and social media interactions is also an important signal for sponsors and potential partnerships. Valuations of football clubs can also take this into account. For example, KPMG valued 39 football clubs using financial information and also taking into account their popularity on social media (Chapman, 2017). Building and engaging a large global fan base on social media can also be an important factor in building new partnerships aside from attracting new fans from around the world.

Table 9.3 Top 10 list of Football Players Digital Fanbase (millions)

Name	Club	League	Total Digital Community	Facebook	Instagram	Twitter
Cristiano Ronaldo	Real Madrid	LaLiga	286	122,2	107,8	55,9
Neymar Junior	Paris Saint-Germain	Ligue 1	170	60,2	79,3	30,9
Leo Messi	FC Barcelona	LaLiga	166	89,1	77,2	
James Rodriguez	FC Bayern München	Bundesliga	78	32,3	32,6	13
Gareth Bale	Real Madrid	LaLiga	72	28,9	30,5	13,2
Andrés Iniesta	FC Barcelona	LaLiga	63	26,9	19	17,2
Mesut Özil	Arsenal	Premier League	61	31,7	13,3	16,5
Zlatan Ibrahimovic			58	26,7	26,7	4,4
Sergio Ramos	Real Madrid	LaLiga	53	23,4	18,7	11,3
Luis Suarez	FC Barcelona	LaLiga	53	18,8	23,6	10,3

(Result Sports, August 2017).

Clubs can engage with lurkers from around the world to potentially take advantage of this, but different social media channels are used around the world. Richard Ayers explains:

> If you're in Eastern Europe then Twitter is of very little use to you at all. That's actually also true in Germany. Facebook use is standard; that is going to get you the biggest audience. And that is true in most territories, except again if you go Eastern or Far East you start getting into VContact if it's Russian related or Soviet related or indeed, by the time you're out in China and other territories, you're usually on Weibo or possibly Tencent; Line if it's in Japan. The key is to research fans and platforms on an on going basis to reach a global audience.

Trolling and social media abuse

Aside from the positive interactions and relationships built on social media, there were also negatives. McKenna et al. (2016) highlighted that the growing Internet population has also attracted an increasing number of "trolls." These people disrupt and attack other individuals and brands in different ways through social media. A higher quantity of followers and higher brand exposure can also increase the amount of negative brand communications via social media (DeVries et al., 2012). Football clubs continue to learn more about how to use these technologies, avoid the pitfalls and maximise the potential to enhance their brands (Chadwick, 2009). Hayes and Carr (2015) found that organisations and PR professionals are increasingly trying to limit these negative communications. Damage to online reputation and brand can be limited by having a well thought out social media policy and training for staff. Understanding the intent of social media posts from abusive negativity to banter is also important. Cultural issues and sensitivities also need to be taken into account by football club social media managers who communicate with people around the world.

Football clubs are also increasingly accepting negativity on social media as part of the authenticity and transparency of communications. In a study of EPL clubs, McCarthy et al. (2014, p.192) found that, "all cases were slowly moving away from the lack of transparency in their dealings with fans, to a degree of openness." Football clubs were concerned about control over posts, which could negatively affect the brand. McCarthy et al. suggested that clubs are often uneasy about such transparency but Griffiths and Mclean (2015) found that increasingly, organisations are more open and are able to go "off script."

With the great openness and opportunity of social media platforms also comes challenges. Smartphones and social media apps make it quick and easy to post digital content. Accounts of footballing celebrities can reach many millions, which also presents opportunities for negative social media activity. There have been countless incidents when clubs, players and fans have become embroiled in an ill thought out social media posts. Deleting a controversial Tweet or account, even within seconds is no escape because journalists, bloggers and others take screenshots and respond immediately, which creates a news story.

Increasingly, football clubs offer training and social media guidelines for their staff. For players, fines and bans are often strongly enforced. Former players in the English Premier League, such as Rio Ferdinand and Joey Barton have been subject to social media incidents and fines. These players have also gained more followers because they are controversial. Clubs however want to reach their audiences by having a reputable, less controversial brand image to prevent brand damage and to appeal to a wider audience. As such, clubs increasingly issue social media policies, fines, and rules for players. A distinction can be drawn however between friendly banter and abusive posts from trolls, which can be vitriolic, and cause offence to individuals and weaken club brands. Banter and trolling between brands can also be a positive thing for raising brand awareness and exposure on social media. Given the large number of Retweets and Likes such social media posts can generate, brands can also use trolling and banter to their advantage to reach their buyer personas (Fenton and Chadwick, 2016).

Social media and sponsorship

The business model of professional football clubs is built on the income of broadcasting rights, match-day and commercial revenues from merchandise and sponsorship. For the biggest clubs, the commercial incomes weigh more than 40 per cent (see the 2017 edition of the Deloitte Football Money League). Sponsors of football clubs look for valuable association, notoriety, and public relations.

The objectives and techniques of sponsoring have also evolved with the emergence of new technologies. With new technologies, partnerships are becoming increasingly more immersive and rewarding. Football club brands are moving from a partnership of visibility (the presence of the brand on the jersey) to a partnership of the enhancement of the fan experience. If brands wish to be recognised for their commitment with a club, they also wish to be also perceived as the partners in the emotion. The sponsors try then to host to reward the community of fans. We identify three categories of public in order to lead a digital activation.

Influencers: an influencer is a person who by status, notoriety, digital activity, and thus the size of his community is considered able to change purchasing behaviours. The sponsors of club or event invite them on important games. In return, influencers broadcast contents on their digital platforms while emphasising the brand. For instance, during the 2017 French League Cup Final, the Professional Football League organised a Social Room in a Luxury Box. The Professional Football League received community managers from the partners of the cup and also influencer fans in order to make them live a "money can't buy" event. Through storytelling their own immersive experience on social media, influencers become the subtlest promoters of the sponsors thanks to user-generated branding (Geurin and Burch, 2017). YouTube fans are especially valued. Jamie Searle explains (2017):

> Perhaps surprisingly, the vast majority of online video consumed is alternative, fan based content and often driven by social influencers such as Calfreezy and the Sidemen, rather than match highlights. This includes highly relatable content such as fan punditry, goal challenges and soccer skills' demos. In fact, only 13 per cent of football video content consumed on YouTube is match highlights.

Millennial Fans: SociOL Room of the Olympique Lyonnais for its partner Hyundai consists in valuing not brand itself, the club, or the players but the fans (fans-centric strategy). The club and Hyundai invite fans to a connected luxury box and ask them to share their experience on their personal account. The fans have an all-access accreditation. From the arrival of the teams to the players after the game, the fans generate immersive and exclusive content. This digital activity can drain fans on the accounts of the main sponsor who can then go into a business relationship. For the club as for the brand, the activation allows the growth of the fan/prospects' community. So, Hyundai hopes to develop its notoriety and its brand preference. In 2015, 120,000 fans on average by match interacted with SociOL Room. The Facebook account passed from 100,000 fans to 264,000 (more than 360,000 this day). The total reach of the operations was two million of people with a rate of 15 per cent engagement on the contents and 10,000 new contacts were made for Hyundai.

Spectators: Orange (multinational telecommunications corporation) was a major partner of Euro 2016. The CEO of the operator had an objective to make of this event "the most connected Tournament of history." Orange installed 680 Wi-Fi hotspots in the fan zones of the host and also 35 4G antennas in 10 stadiums to allow 25,000 people to be connected at the same time. Beyond the technical partnership, Orange launched its sponsorship plan called "Orange Sponsors You." Thanks to a dedicated hashtag fans could light up the Eiffel Tower every evening with the colours of their national team. More than 20 million messages were sent.

Social and digital media can change the economy of football. Parganas, Liasko, and Anagnostopoulos (2017) found that the three main sources of club revenues (match day, broadcast and commercial) are positive drivers for Facebook followers. According to Nielsen, the 2017 match between Real Madrid and FC Barcelona generated more than $42.5 million in media value for sponsors. Half of the total sponsorship media value came from the live TV broadcast and 12 per cent came from social media, which is more than Print/Online coverage (Nielsen, 2017). In the UK, according to Nielsen, between 5 and 20 per cent of value generated for the sponsors comes from content released by the club on their social media. During the 2016–17 season, 62 per cent of value generated on social media was delivered by Facebook (Hurst and Plastiras, 2017).

The connected stadium

In 2012, Facebook released an infographic of the social landmarks around the world with check-in data. Seven stadiums and arenas were in the top 25, including Barcelona, which dominates the rankings. In the same year, three sports venues (the baseball stadiums of San Francisco Giants and the Los Angeles Dodgers and Staples Center in Los Angeles) were included in the top 10 list of places which were the most photographed on Instagram.

Because the fans want to capture their experience of the sports event, which they attend, they generate and share more with their smartphones and other devices. According to the Mobile Sports Report, during the 51th edition of the Super Bowl which took place in NRG stadium of Houston in 2017, 37.6 Terabytes (TB) of data were consumed (11.8 TB on the WiFi, 11 TB on the network Verizon, 9.8 TB on the network AT&T) (Kapustka, 2017). During the Barcelona v Manchester United match in Levi's Stadium of Santa-Clara during International Champion Cup of 2015, 2.62 TB of data was consumed on the WiFi of the stadium, 25,643 unique users connected to the WiFi with a peak of 18,322 connections just after the kick off.

Sports clubs wish to diversify their customer bases towards a younger and more family-based audience. Football clubs increasingly aim to create an enhanced entertainment experience alongside the match. In other words, it is not a question of simply going to see a match but creating an experience at the stadium. Clubs aim to fill the stadium not only with traditional supporters but also with new customers searching for comfort and for the quality of service.

At the beginning of 2017, Javier Tebas, the president of La Liga, explained:

> if there is no connectivity in stadium, we are going to lose spectators as "Millennials" need a second screen. Concerning the attendance, there are two [groups] whom we want to address: the women, who are at the moment a niche market, and the "Millennials," new generations, for whom the connectivity is very important.
>
> *(So Foot – CP, 2017)*

La Liga wishes all Spanish clubs could offer Wifi in their stadiums.

Table 9.4 Connected Stadium in MLS (2015)

Club	Stadium	Capacity	Wi-Fi	Distributed Antenna Systems (DAS)
Chicago Fire	Toyota Park	20 000	YES	NO (under construction)
Colombus Crew	Mapfre Stadium	20 145	NO	NO
D.C. United	RFK Stadium	45 596	Limited	NO
New England Revolution	Gillette Stadium	20 000	350+ access points	YES (AT&T, Sprint, Verizon)
New York Red Bulls	Red Bull Arena	25 189	YES	Unkown
Montreal Impact	Stade Saputo	20 521	YES	Unkown
New York City FC	Yankee Stadium	49 642	Limited	Yes
Orlando City SC	Citrus Bowl	70 000	NO	Under Construction
Philadelphia Union	PPL Park	18 500	NO	Unkown
Toronto FC	BMO Field	30 991	Unkown	Unkown
Colorado Rapids	DSG Park	18 086	No	No
FC Dallas	Toyota Stadium	21 193	NO	YES (AT&T)
Houston Dynamo	BBVA Compass Stadium	22 039	Limited	NO
Los Angeles Galaxy	StubHub Center	27 000	NO	YES
Portland Timbers	Providence Park	22 000	Limited	YES (AT&T, Verizon)
Real Salt Lake	Rio Tinto Stadium	20 507	YES	Unkown
San Jose Earthquakes	Avaya Stadium	18 000	180 access points	YES (under construction)
Seattle Sounders FC	CenturyLink Field	38 300	750+ access points	YES (AT&T, Verizon, Sprint, T-Mobile)
Sporting Kansas City	Sporting Park	18 467	160-200 access points	YES (AT&T, Sprint)
Vancouver Whitecaps FC	BC Place	21 000	800 access points	NO

(Mobile Sports Report, Stadium Tech Report Q2 2015).

The emergence of the connected stadiums and digital fans is not always received favourably by fans. The supporters of the PSV Eindhoven (Netherlands) brandished a banner "f*ck WiFi, support the team." A supporter of the OGC Nice (France) campaigned for stands which banned the social media selfie photograph. According to him: "the problem of people who have the head plunged into their smartphone remains a plague. I asked supporters present in South Stands to stop with this tourist's practice. During a game, it's better to sing and to support the team" (So Foot – AG, 2017).

The connected stadium and social media interactions are not always received well by the traditional fan. However, these continue to grow as part of the entertainment experience of football and drive towards encouraging new fans globally.

Conclusion

Digital media and new technologies can enhance and disrupt the football fan experience. The show is not just on the field but also on its second screen through billions of Internet connected devices. Social media channels and content are creating vast volumes of data and connecting fans from around the world. This creates opportunities and threats. In order to maximise the potential for digital and social media, football clubs should listen and interact with and use data to better understand fans. Segmenting fans and using the appropriate channels, content, and data is key. There is resistance from traditional fans to this disruption and people question the value of the vast millions of lurker fans.

Equally, there are challenges around the open nature of social media communications, meaning that trolls and online abuse can be an issue. Players and other staff are sometimes using social media channels to communicate directly with fans and this can cause delight and controversy. In order to prevent damage to their brands and maximise the potential for sponsorship, football clubs need to better understand and manage the potential of digital and social media. They need to have the appropriate skills and training in place. Aside from connecting with fans around the world, digital and social media can also play a key part in enhancing the in-stadium experience. The way in which football clubs evolve their relationship with digital and social media over the coming years will draw continued interest from fans, journalists, and researchers around the world.

References

Cave, A. and Miller, A. (2015) The importance of social media in sport. *The Telegraph*. [online]. Available at: http://www.telegraph.co.uk/investing/business-of-sport/social-media-in-sport/

Chadwick, S. (2009) From outside lane to inside track: sport management research in the twenty-first century. *Management Decision*, 47(1), 191–203 (doi: https://doi.org/10.1108/00251740910929786)

Chapman, B. (2017) *Manchester United overtake Real Madrid to become Europe's most valuable football club*. [online] The Independent. Available at: http://www.independent.co.uk/news/business/news/manchester-united-overtake-real-madrid-europes-most-valuable-football-club-kpmg-champions-league-a7764776.html [Accessed 22 Oct. 2017].

Clavio, G. (2010) Introduction to this special issue of IJSC on new media and social networking. *International Journal of Sport Communication*, 3 (4), 393–394. (doi: https://doi.org/10.1123/ijsc.3.4.393)

De Vries, L., Gensler, S., and Leeflang, P.S.H. (2012) Popularity of Brand Posts on Brand Fan Pages: An Investigation of the Effects of Social Media Marketing. *Journal of Interactive Marketing* (26), pp. 83–91, doi: 10.1016/j.intmar.2012.01.003

Deloitte, (2017) *Deloitte Football Money League 2017*. [online] Deloitte. Available at: https://www2.deloitte.com/uk/en/pages/sports-business-group/articles/deloitte-football-money-league.html [Accessed 22 October 2017].

Fenton, A. and Chadwick, S. (2016) Euro 2016 sponsors being ambushed on social media by "unofficial" brand. [online] The Conversation. https://theconversation.com/euro-2016-sponsors-being-ambushed-on-social-media-by-unofficial-brands-61880 [Accessed 22 October 2017].

Fillis, I. and Mackay, C. (2013) Moving beyond fan typologies: The impact of social integration on team loyalty in football, *Journal of Marketing Management*, 30 (3-4), 334–63, doi: 10.1080/0267257X.2013.813575

Gantz, W. (2013) Reflections on communication and sport: on fanship and social relationships. *Communication & Sport*, 1(1/2), 176–87. Published online before print 12 December 2012. doi: https://doi.org/10.1177/2167479512467446

Geurin, A.N. and Burch, L.M. (2017) User-generated branding via social media: an examination of six running brands. *Sport Management Review*, 20(3), 273–284. doi: 10.1016/j.smr.2016.09.001

Gibson, O. (2016) Is the unthinkable happening – are people finally switching the football off? *The Guardian*. [online]. Available at: https://www.theguardian.com/football/2016/oct/24/sky-sports-bt-sport-people-switching-football-off. [Accessed 22 October 2017].

Griffiths, M. and Mclean, R. (2015) Unleashing corporate communications via social media: A UK study of brand management and conversations with customers, *Journal of Customer Behaviour*, 14(2), 147–62. doi: 10.1362/147539215X14373846805789

Guardian Staff (2014) PSV Eindhoven fans protest against introduction of Wi-Fi at stadium. [online] *The Guardian*. Available at: https://www.theguardian.com/football/2014/aug/18/psv-fans-protest-against-wifi-access [Accessed 22 October 2017].

Habibi, M.R., Laroche, M., and Richard, M.-O. (2014) Brand communities based in social media: How unique are they? Evidence from two exemplary brand communities. *International Journal of Information Management*, 34(2),123–132. doi: 10.1016/j.ijinfomgt.2013.11.010

Hayes, R.A. and Carr, C.T. (2015) Does being social matter? effects of enabled commenting on credibility and brand attitude in social media, *Journal of Promotion Management*, 21(3), 371–90. doi: 10.1080/10496491.2015.1039178

Heinze, A., Fletcher, G., Rashid, T., and Cruz, A. (2016) *Digital and Social Media Marketing – A Results-Driven Approach*, Routledge.

Helleu, B. (2017) The other Field of Play: Football on Social Media. In N. Chanavat, M. Desbordes, and N. Lorgnier (eds), *Routledge Handbook of Football Marketing*. Routledge.

Hurst, C. and Plastiras, A. (2017) The rising importance of social media for football clubs. [online] Nielsen Sports. http://nielsensports.com/rising-importance-social-media-football-clubs [Accessed 22 October 2017].

Kantar. (2012) Manchester United Kantar Survey of fans. doi: 10.1016/B978-0-12-375674-9.10001-1

Kapustka, P. (2017) *Update: Super Bowl LI breaks 37 TB wireless mark.* [online] Mobile Sports Report. Available at: https://www.mobilesportsreport.com/2017/02/super-bowl-breaks-30-tb-wireless-mark/ [Accessed 22 October 2017].

Kapustka, P. (2015) *Futbol Fans like Wi-Fi: Barcelona vs. ManU match at Levi's Stadium uses 2.62 TB.* [online] Mobile Sports Report. Available at: https://www.mobilesportsreport.com/2015/07/futbol-fans-like-wi-fi-barcelona-vs-manu-match-at-levis-stadium-uses-2-62-tb/ [Accessed 22 October 2017].

McCarthy, J., Rowley, J., Ashworth, C.J., and Pioch, E. (2014) Managing brand presence through social media: the case of UK football clubs, *Internet Research*, 14(2), Emerald Group Publishing Limited, pp. 181–204 (doi: 10.1108/IntR-08-2012-0154).

McKenna, B., Vodanovich, S. and Fan, T. (2016) I heart you: how businesses are using social media to increase social capital. In *European, Mediterranean & Middle Eastern Conference on Information Systems (EMCIS)*, 2016-06-23-2016-06-24, Available at: https://ueaeprints.uea.ac.uk/59287/ [Accessed 22 Oct. 2017]

McLaren, D. (2017) *Our Top Insights Into Football Video on YouTube & Facebook.* [online] Digital Sport. Available at: https://digitalsport.co/our-top-insights-into-football-video-on-youtube-facebook [Accessed 22 October 2017].

Miah, A. (2017) *Sport 2.0 : Transforming sports for a digital world.* 1st ed. MIT Press.

Mobile Sports Report, (2015) *Stadium Tech Report. The baseball (and Soccer!) Issue.* [online] https://www.mobilesportsreport.com/report-downloads/ [Accessed 22 October 2017].

Muniz, A.M. and O'Guinn, T.C. (2001) Brand Community. *Journal of Consumer Research*, 27(4), 412–432. doi: 10.1086/319618

Nielsen, (2017) *New Media scores big returns for El Clasico sponsors.* [online] Nielsen. http://www.nielsen.com/us/en/insights/news/2017/new-media-scores-big-returns-for-el-clasico-sponsors.html?cid=socSprinklr-Nielsen [Accessed 22 October 2017].

Parganas, P., Liasko, R., and Anagnostopoulos, C. (2017) Scoring goals in multiple fields. Social media presence, on-field performance and commercial success in European professional football. *Sport, Business and Management: An International Journal*, 2(7), 197–215. doi: 10.1108/IJSMS-05-2017-087

Pegoraro, A. (2014) Twitter as disruptive innovation in sport communication. *Communication & Sport*, 2(2), 132–137. doi: 10.1177/2167479514527432

Perform, Kantar Media, Sport Business (2014) *Know The Fan, The Global Sport Media Consumption Report 2014, Global Overview.*

Popp, B., Germelmann, C.C., and Jung, B. (2016) We love to hate them! Social media-based anti-brand communities in professional football. *International Journal of Sports Marketing and Sponsorship*, 17(4), 349–67. doi: https://doi.org/10.1108/IJSMS-11-2016-018

Result Sport, (2017) *Global Digital Football Benchmarking Analysis, July 2017.* [online] Digtal Sports Media. Available at: http://digitale-sport-medien.com/global-digital-football-benchmarking-analysis-july-2017/ [Accessed 22 October 2017].

Rowles, D. (2017) *Mobile marketing : how mobile technology is revolutionizing marketing, communications, and advertising.* 2nd ed. Kogan Page.

Sanderson, J. (2011) *It's a Whole New Ball-game. How Social Media is Changing Sports.* New York: Hampton Press, INC.

Searle, J. (2017) *Why influencer football teams will change the face of football entertainment.* [online] Digital Sport. https://digitalsport.co/why-influencer-football-teams-will-change-the-face-of-football-entertainment [Accessed 22 October 2017].

Sun, N., Rau, P.P.L., and Ma, L. (2014) Understanding lurkers in online communities: A literature review, *Computers in Human Behavior* (38:September), Elsevier Ltd, 110–17. doi: 10.1016/j.chb.2014.05.022

So Foot – CP, (2017) *La Liga veut le wi-fi dans tous ses stades.* [online] So Foot. Available at: http://www.sofoot.com/la-liga-veut-le-wi-fi-dans-tous-ses-stades-438427.html [Accessed 22 October 2017].

So Foot – AG, (2017) *Selfies interdits dans une tribune à Nice ?.* [online] So Foot. Available at: http://www.sofoot.com/selfies-interdits-dans-une-tribune-a-nice-449116.html [Accessed 22 October 2017].

Tewhatu, M. (2016) *FC Bayern Munich set to revolutionise fan engagement.* [online] Digital Sport. Available at: https://digitalsport.co/fc-bayern-munich-set-to-revolutionise-fan-engagement [Accessed 22 October 2017].

We Are Social and Hootsuite, (2017) Digital in 2017 Global Overview. [online] Available at: https://wearesocial.com/special-reports/digital-in-2017-global-overview [Accessed 22 October 2017].

Weed, M. (2007) The Pub as a Virtual Football Fandom Venue: An Alternative to "Being there"?. *Soccer & Society*, 8(2/3), 399–414. doi: 10.1080/14660970701224665

Corporate social responsibility (CSR) in football

Exploring modes of CSR implementation

Geraldine Zeimers, Christos Anagnostopoulos,
Thierry Zintz, and Annick Willem

Introduction

Corporate social responsibility is developing to a considerable extent across business, sporting and, academic agendas. In its broader sense, CSR has emerged as an umbrella term that refers to "a concept whereby companies integrate social and environmental concerns in their business operations and in their interaction with their stakeholders on a voluntary basis" (European Commission, 2001). Indeed, CSR has become a taken-for-granted concept or "institution" within Western society (Bondy, Moon, and Matten, 2012) and has subsequently spread outside the classical business spheres. For example, we now even see non-profit organisations, such as national football federations and/or international football governing bodies, embracing the concept, both in practice and in rhetoric, despite its connotation with "corporate affairs."

More generally, in the field of sports, many studies have captured this relatively well-established engagement "to do good sport" by the sport industry (Breitbarth et al., 2015). The growing importance of the relatively recent CSR phenomenon in the sport industry worldwide has given rise to insights on the motives (Babiak and Wolfe, 2009), practices (Walker and Parent, 2010), communication (Kolyperas and Sparks, 2011), financial outcomes (Inoue, Mahan, and Kent, 2012), programme partners' evaluation (Kihl, Babiak, and Tainsky, 2014), or stakeholders' attitudes (Walker and Kent, 2009).

Professional sport clubs in Europe (Hamil, Walters, and Watson, 2010; Kolyperas and Sparks, 2011) and major league sports in North America (Babiak and Wolfe, 2009) are amongst the pioneering organisations in terms of addressing the issue of CSR in various ways (Walker and Parent, 2010). To date, however, football (or soccer) is the most represented sport in the scholarly activity of CSR, as a recent integrative review on the topic identified (see Walzel, Robertson, and Anagnostopoulos, 2018).

Against this background, the purpose of this chapter is to delineate the different types of organisational structures for managing CSR – or modes of implementation – within contemporary football. We examine three approaches (in-house, foundation, and collaboration) for managing CSR by using examples (as mini cases) from different types of football organisations across the globe. In doing so, we demonstrate the strategic and managerial (social as well as business) implications that each structural form entails. The chapter concludes with some key recommendations for practitioners seeking to develop CSR within the wider football industry.

Developments in the field of football-related CSR

In the football industry, CSR has become an important strategic issue, and more than just a business trend or an optional extra (Breitbarth and Harris, 2008; Walters and Chadwick, 2009; Kolyperas and Sparks, 2011). The literature currently provides contributions towards CSR theory and concepts that are broadly applicable to a wide range of industries. In the sporting context, studies have postulated that sport is a distinctively important industry within which to employ CSR-related business practices (Smith and Westerbeek, 2007). Babiak and Wolfe (2009) identified four factors in professional team sport that contribute to the practice of CSR: (a) passion among stakeholders, (b) the peculiar economic structure of leagues, (c) transparency of all aspects of the organisation's behaviour, and (d) the necessity for stakeholder management approaches.

Modern football and its unique characteristics for CSR

While football is not necessarily typical of all developments across the sporting world (Chadwick, 2009), it is also possible to pinpoint from the literature three interrelated and overlapping characteristics that support the development of CSR. First, the ever-increasing commercialisation of football has transformed the game into an industry in its own right (Beech and Chadwick, 2013). Various unethical practices (bribery, illegal gambling, match-fixing, unsocial labour conditions, etc.) have enhanced public attention on the side effects of commercialisation and resulted in increased social demands on football (Anagnostopoulos and Shilbury, 2013; Breitbarth et al., 2015).

Second, the strong connection to the community and the importance of stakeholder relationships in the football collaborative network created a favourable environment for CSR (Breitbarth and Harris, 2008; Hamil and Morrow, 2011; Walters and Chadwick, 2009). Morrow (2003) suggested that "the stakeholder concept has greater relevance for football clubs than for conventional businesses because of the particular features of certain football club stakeholders" (p. 43).

Third, football organisations evolve in an intensive media coverage climate, which has given a high degree of notoriety to football clubs and raised the importance of good reputation and positive brand image. Consequently, it is essential for football to adapt and to align to social responsibility principles (Anagnostopoulos and Shilbury, 2013; Blumrodt et al., 2013; Chadwick, 2009). In light of these characteristics, modern football organisations are favourably inclined to engage in CSR.

A descriptive snapshot of CSR undertakings in football

Over the past 10 years, the link between CSR and football has generated significant interest among sport management scholars as well as football governing bodies (Fédération Internationale de Football Association (FIFA), Union of European Football Associations (UEFA), European Club Association (ECA), etc.), all of which have attempted to capture the content of CSR–football engagement. While many football organisations have embraced the principles and practices of CSR, ranging from star players, professional football leagues, governing football bodies, mega football events, football clubs, and commercial stakeholders, sport scholars have principally investigated local and national organisations (Kolyperas, Morrow, and Sparks, 2015).

To date, the existing body of studies has mostly explored football in the United Kingdom (England and Scotland) and European (Spain, Switzerland, Italy, Turkey, Portugal, Belgium, Greece, Germany, and France) contexts, but also the United States and Asia (Breitbarth and Harris, 2008). England has the strongest institutionalised forms of CSR in European football (Hovemann et al., 2011; Walters and Tacon, 2011). Beyond local and national research, international and comparative country research (three notable exceptions being Breitbarth and Harris's (2008) comparative study across the USA, Japan, Germany, and England; Walters and Tacon's (2011) pan-European study; and Kolyperas and Sparks' (2011) G-25 football clubs) remains underdeveloped despite the widely recognised development of CSR practices around the globe.

A number of different types of CSR practices can be identified within the sport industry and football in particular. In their research commissioned by the Union of European Football Association (UEFA) to study CSR in European football, Walters and Tacon (2011) indicated that football clubs and federations are involved in a number of initiatives with various stakeholders, such as local communities, young people, schools, and employees. In this respect, Figure 10.1 points the strategic themes of CSR-football programmes. Integration, education, health and physical activity, and anti-discrimination represent the most common initiatives developed by the European Club Association (ECA)[1] football member clubs. Recent studies have pointed out the benefits (as well as the operational challenges) of football dealing with issues such as integration and social inclusion (e.g., Parnell et al., 2015), physical (e.g., Parnell et al., 2013; Pringle et al., 2014) and mental (e.g., Curran et al., 2017) health, as well as the need to become more strategic in health-related interventions (Lansley and Parnell, 2016). Furthermore, as illustrated by Figure 10.2, the target population has primarily been children and youth (59 per cent), while several initiatives have also an all-ages reach (33 per cent).

Kolyperas and Sparks (2011) identified that football clubs have moved beyond typical CSR expectations that are commonly addressed in other business sectors (such as mission, sustainability,

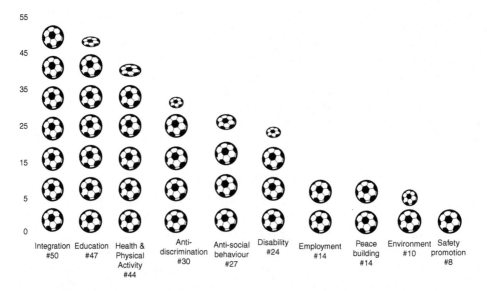

Figure 10.1   Strategic themes of CSR–football programmes
Source: 2016 ECA CSR Report.

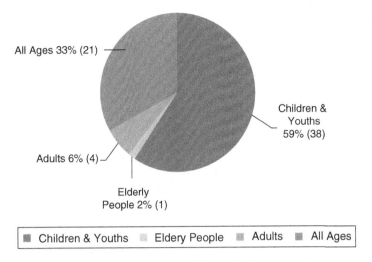

Figure 10.2 Target population of CSR–football programmes
Source: 2016 ECA CSR Report.

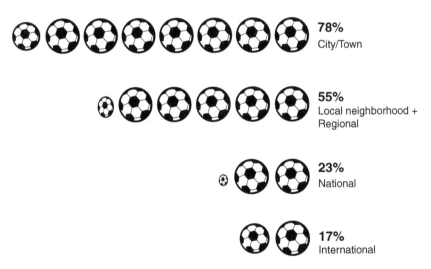

Figure 10.3 Geographical reach of CSR–football programmes
Source: 2016 ECA CSR Report.

and environmental conservation). Football clubs clearly take a position on both universal and context-specific concerns arising in society and the football sector more specifically.

The geographical reach of these initiatives taken by football organisations has generally occurred at all levels. In particular, Kulczycki and Koenigstorfer (2016) pointed to the importance of local context and geographical focus in CSR engagement. As Figure 10.3 indicates, CSR programmes have mostly been held at the level of the city or the town in which the football club resides and largely operate.

Increasingly, many football organisations are formalising their CSR programmes within their organisational structures (such as a specific budget, a formal strategy or dedicated individuals for CSR). Figure 10.4 appears to bear this out; it reveals that the budget allocated to CSR

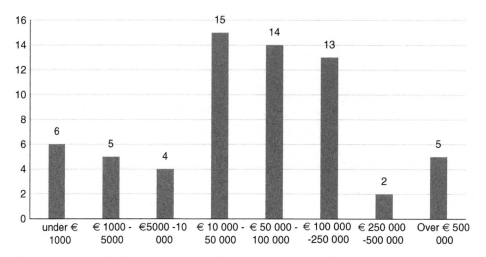

Figure 10.4 Budget of CSR–football programmes
Source: 2016 ECA CSR Report.

programmes by 23 per cent of the ECA's member clubs have had a budget ranging from €10,000 to €50,000, 22 use a budget of €50,000 to €100,000, while another 20 per cent deploy budgets of €100,000 to €250,000. This figure also shows that six clubs have a budget lower than €1000. In comparison, Walters and Tacon (2011) found that 53 per cent of the European national federations and 43 per cent of the European professional clubs had a budget for CSR activities. They also showed that many football clubs are funding CSR activity internally as only 25 per cent receive funding assistance through public and 34 per cent from other sources of funding (such as private partners engaging in CSR through sport). Many national federations receive financial support from UEFA.

In parallel, the growing influence of CSR in the football world is illustrated by the increasing influence of consulting agencies benchmarking (for example, Reponsiball by Schwery Consulting; Deloitte and Touche recommendations) and the rise of specific football-related CSR networks (such as the European Football and Development Network (EFDN)).

Professional football organisations concerned with developing CSR practices have inspired numerous studies on, *inter alia*, the motives (Hamil and Morrow, 2011; Kolyperas, Anagnostopoulos, Chadwick, and Sparks, 2016; Reiche, 2014), content (Reiche, 2014; Walters and Tacon, 2010), mode of implementation (Kolyperas et al., 2016), communication (Kolyperas and Sparks, 2011), and the evaluation (Breitbarth et al., 2011) and the perceptions and attitudes of key stakeholder's such as consumers and fans (Blumrodt et al., 2013; Kulcycki and Koenigstorefer, 2016).

CSR implementation and football

Despite numerous studies on the content and motives of CSR engagement, a number of sport studies have considered CSR from a more strategic management and a process-based perspective, broadening the scope of investigation to include issues of organisational change, forms and structures (Kolyperas et al., 2016; Morrow, 2012). CSR implementation[2] has emerged recently following the shift in CSR academic field toward a more strategic, practice-oriented research stream caused by practical challenges and greenwashing criticisms (Maon et al., 2010). This type of research focus investigates the complex strategic and cognitive process underlying the unfoldment of CSR principles and practices within organisations (Maon et al., 2010). For the purposes of the present chapter, we selectively reviewed the football-related CSR implementation body of literature.

Several general comments arose from this review on CSR implementation and football. First, the literature provides substantial, even disproportionate, findings on charitable foundations (Anagnostopoulos et al., 2017; Bingham and Walters, 2013; Walters, 2009), thus overlooking other implementation structures chosen by sport organisations to implement CSR (Husted, 2003). For instance, Kolyperas et al. (2016) described how some sporting organisations have altered their structure by establishing charitable foundations with the view to co-create CSR value. Eventually, these studies have suggested that sport organisations face challenges to manage the influential role of foundation managers, making the dynamics amongst organisational actors more complex (Anagnostopoulos et al., 2014) and more difficult to cope with risks related to the transformation of the community department into a foundation structure (Kolyperas et al., 2016).

Second, several step-based and stage-based CSR implementation models have been developed within the football context. Kolyperas et al. (2015) examined the progressive strategic and cultural organisational change required to embed CSR in football clubs. Similarly, Breitbarth and Rieth (2012) described key drivers for successful CSR implementation in German professional football and developed a 3S model of CSR integration. Walters and Anagnostopoulos (2012) designed a conceptual model that sets out the process of social partnership implementation (selection, design, management, and evaluation).

Third, most of these studies have focused on either the individual or organisational levels of analysis. For instance, an individual-level study has documented the decision-making process of CSR in football charitable foundations (Anagnostopoulos et al., 2014). However, "the organisational complexity, specifically related to CSR, is increasing as is the need to capture elements at both the cross-organisational and individual level" (Anagnostopoulos and Shilbury, 2013, p. 269). Moreover, research has yet to grasp this topic from a multilevel perspective that would reveal the dynamic interaction among individual, group, organisational, and inter-organisation levels (Zeimers et al., 2017).

Overall, these studies have highlighted the critical importance of positioning CSR implementation as a change process. As CSR develops, football organisations tend to alter their organisational structure, strategy and processes. The next section discusses the substantial challenges associated with CSR-related changes in organisation structure.

Husted's modes of CSR implementation

Organisations implementing CSR are likely to face a major strategic decision regarding how CSR activities should be structured. According to Husted (2003), this decision strongly influences the cost and the management of CSR (or "the cost side of CSR management"). For most organisations, CSR projects must be strategically aligned with the core mission of the organisation. The costs of implementing CSR activities should be minimised in relation to the overall return on investment (Husted, 2003).

Therefore, we draw on Husted's (2003) three forms of governance structures that impact upon how organisations manage CSR. While Husted referred to these structures as "issues of governance," we see them more as "modes of implementation." Beyond conceptual differences and/or used terminology, the three structures that Husted (2003) proposed enable discussion of CSR implementation in the football industry as a whole, thereby highlighting challenges for each mode as well as opportunities for optimising social and business benefits.

First, organisations *outsource CSR through charitable contributions*. Charitable contributions consist of the transfer of financial and/or other resources from an organisation to community and other social organisations that are experts in the problem at hand. There is an independent relationship between the "donor" and the "recipient" of the charitable contribution. The greatest advantage of this mode is that the organisation's involvement in the management of the project is usually minimal compared to the overall outcomes (Husted, 2003).

Second, organisations *internalise CSR through in-house projects*. The organisation allocates financial and other resources to the project, which is implemented through an organisational unit within the organisation. As such, the "donor" and the "recipient" are part of the same organisation. Although the costs of implementing an in-house project can be significant, its greatest advantage is that managers can strategically target resources to meet specific organisation and community needs (Husted, 2003).

Third, organisations enter *into a collaborative or partnership model*. Collaborative projects involve a partnership between the organisation and a non-profit partner, in which the former transfers resources to the latter in order to carry out CSR activities jointly. Here, the donor and recipient partner work together and jointly reap benefits from the CSR activity. In this case, both partners are potentially sharing resources and costs of the implementation (Husted, 2003).

Despite some subtle differences in the three modes of CSR implementation, each mode essentially presents elements, characteristics and processes evidenced in the other two. In other words, an in-house structure does not mean that the organisation is not involved in partnerships with other organisational entities. Similarly, many foundations are engaged in CSR activities in the same way as the first mode of implementation acts. For example, while the Manchester United Foundation is a company in its own right, it is actually comprised of two parts: The Manchester United Foundation is one company, but there is also Manchester United Foundation Trading, a company that does fundraising and commercial undertakings. However, the overarching aim of Manchester United Foundation Trading is that any profits go into the Manchester United Foundation. Given these complexities, readers should be cautioned in approaching the three modes of CSR implementation discussed here because there are no clear-cut boundaries amongst all three.

Empirical cases from football: Explaining the three modes of CSR implementation

This section draws on three mini-case studies, each of which reflects a specific mode of CSR implementation. First, the Celtic FC Foundation is an example of CSR efforts implemented by the sport industry from a foundation mode. Second, the case of the RBFA, the Belgian football federation, illustrates the in-house mode. Third, at the international level, the case of UEFA illuminates the collaborative model.

As shown in Table 10.1, the selected cases are different types of organisations (clubs and federations) from different settings (UK, Belgium, and Europe) and from different levels (local, national, and international), thereby providing cross-national and organisational perspectives of CSR implementation. These cases have been selected for their illustrative potential in light of the three-implementation modes framework presented in the previous section.

Table 10.1 Overview of the case studies

Case studies	Formed	Location	Club Ownership Structure	Financial Turnover	CSR programme	Board of Trustees	CSR budget	CSR initiatives
Celtic	1888	Glasgow, Scotland	Company	£90.6 million (in 2017)	Celtic Charity Fund	Celtic Football Club in the board	£10 million (in 2011)	Education, charity, health and social inclusion
URBSFA	1895	Brussels, Belgium	Not-for profit organisation	€60 million (in 2014)	CSR department	No board of trustees	Not available	Inclusion (homophobia, homeless and disability) and health issues
UEFA	1957	Nyon, Switzerland	Not-for profit organisation	€4.58 billion (in 2016)	FSR unit	Not in the board	0.7% budget €3,896,600 (FSR budget 2016)	Diversity, health, inclusion, fan dialogue, solidarity Environment, peace and reconciliation

Table developed from the organisations' websites and references (Walters & Anagnostopoulos, 2012; Kolyperas et al., 2015; Hamil and Morrow, 2012).

The Foundation case: Celtic FC Foundation

In Scottish football, the case of the Celtic FC provides interesting insights into the delivery of CSR initiatives through a separate foundation. At Celtic, philanthropy lies in the club's Irish identity and Catholic charity (Carr et al., 2000 cited in Hamil and Morrow, 2011). In the context of Scottish Football, football clubs were recognised formally as vehicles to deliver CSR through the Football in the Community (FITC) scheme, which progressively led to the development of FITC departments (Kolyperas et al., 2015 provided further details on the evolution of CSR in the Scottish football context). Recently, independent foundations, or community trusts, have been replacing the old CSR structures of FITC departments to boost the community work (Bingham and Walters, 2013; Kolyperas et al., 2015).

Celtic was the first club to experience this shift in 1995 when it introduced the Celtic Charity Fund structure, later complemented by the Celtic Foundation in 2006; both were established with the aim of uplifting Celtic's charitable traditions. These two units have been recently united to become a new stronger entity, Celtic FC Foundation. Celtic FC Foundation "upholds and promotes the charitable principles and heritage of Celtic Football Club" (www.charity.celticfc.net). The Celtic FC Foundation executes multifaceted CSR football-related initiatives (such as Celtic in the Community), inclusion, employability, educational, and diversionary initiatives (such as learning programmes and centres), health initiatives (for example, Celtic against Drugs), and its charitable engagement (through the Celtic Charity Fund). The Celtic FC Foundation also provides support in the form of delivery and/or partnership to external charities and other organisations that offer value in the community and whose principles fit within these key priority areas.

Hamil and Morrow (2011) reported that this separate structure was closely connected with the parent football club. Celtic provides financial donations and in-kind assistance to the Celtic Charity Fund through things like the involvement of its players, while its representative articulated the congruence in orientation: "There's a [separate] board of trustees [but it] is right to the core of Celtic and that's what differentiates us, I think, from most football clubs" (p. 158). This structure enabled the club to control its CSR activities, which are seen as an integral part of the business (Hamil and Morrow, 2011). Kolyperas and colleagues (2015) noted that Celtic (as well as the Rangers) seem to be moving progressively toward incorporating CSR principles in all levels of the organisation, perhaps due to their financial capability and social scale.

The in-house case: Belgium federation

The Royal Belgian Football Association (RBFA) is the national football federation in Belgium. Since 2008, its organisational structure has been composed of a Flemish-speaking wing, the VFV (*Voetbalfederatie Vlaanderen*), and a French-speaking wing, the ACFF (*Association des Clubs de Football Francophones*). The Pro League is responsible for the First and Second National Division Championships.

The RBFA has a long history of social responsibility dating back to 1986 with the "*Accion Diablos Rojos Casa Hogar*" during the Wold Cup in Mexico, where the team donated part of their bonus to help build a childcare institution in Toluca. In 2006, Open Stadium, a non-profit charitable organisation, with public and charitable support, was the social desk of Belgian football. In 2012, the RBFA, the Pro League, and the National League launched the Football + Foundation, a non-profit organisation responsible for football social matters. Similar to the English context, community work received significant support from public subsidies. In 2015, the Pro League stepped out from the foundation structure to become independent and create an autonomous social agenda for professional football.

In May 2016, the existing foundation structure was replaced by in-house structure (that is, a CSR department) in each football wing (the RBFA, Pro League, VFV, and ACFF) to incorporate more CSR principles into Belgian football and to advance CSR activity further. This department is organised like any other department. The CSR manager works under the event, CSR, security, and external relationship director. Meetings are frequently set up with the different CSR managers of the different entities (to build up a broader CSR department based on the CSR department per entity). In this case, the federation designs, develops, and executes the in-house CSR project alone and with the assistance of external partners. The CSR programmes have a separate budget. In order to meet these objectives, the RBFA invests in activities that help to address strategic social issues, particularly through partnerships with selected organisations. Over the years, it has developed CSR policies and collaborated with numerous social partners on inclusion (homophobia, homeless, diversity, and refugees) and health areas.[3] As such, this case raises the need to grasp the intra-organisational challenges related to the shift from one mode (foundation) to another (in-house). This case is also interesting because it involves both the in-house and collaborative mode.

The collaboration case: UEFA's football social responsibility

UEFA has addressed various social issues over the years, including racism, xenophobia, homophobia, reconciliation and peace, football for people with disabilities, violence, health, and humanitarian aid. In 2005, UEFA adopted a strategic approach to CSR (Aquilina and Gasser, 2011) that was characterised by the creation of the Fair Play and Social Responsibility Committee in 2007. The Football and Social Responsibility (FSR) unit is responsible for developing proposals that are then put forward to the Fair Play and Social Responsibility Committee (Walters and Anagnostopoulos, 2012). The FSR is a specialised office for social matters and aims to use the power of football and UEFA to build on football's role as a positive force in society, with the primary aim of strengthening the health and integrity of both European football and European society as a whole (UEFA, 2007).

UEFA has a formal commitment to allocate a minimum of 0.7 per cent of its annual revenue to social projects (Gasser, 2009). This investment falls into three categories: core partnerships, the Monaco award, and *ad hoc* donations. The six core partners are: the World Heart Federation (health and child obesity); Education4Peace (emotional health and behavioural awareness); Terre des Hommes (child exploitation and trafficking); the Cross Cultures Project Association (reconciliation and peace); Football Against Racism in Europe (FARE) (racism and discrimination); and Football for the Special Olympics (football for all, for people with learning difficulties to take part in sport). Alongside these, the World Wide Fund for nature (WWF), the International Committee of the Red Cross (ICRC), the Homeless World Cup, and the European Union (EU) have been among the partners of UEFA when dealing with social issues.

UEFA is the lead organisation in the partnership programme (Walters and Anagnostopoulos, 2012). UEFA requires that the projects carried out with partner organisations address problems that are significant in Europe, that focus on Europe, and that have a Europe-wide scope; be free of religious or political associations; and be delivered by an organisation with a credible reputation, through activities that are based on good practice and can demonstrate a sustainable impact (Walters and Anagnostopoulos, 2012). Each partnership is contractually bound to a duration of four-year. This contract sets out the scope of the partnership, the role and responsibilities of the partners, and the level of funding.

Despite this formal process, delivery of the projects is the responsibility of the partner organisation, which gives them significant autonomy in their decision-making. In turn, UEFA also provides an ongoing commitment to the projects by providing financial resources as well as knowledge sharing and project communication. The main point of contact for the partners is the FSR unit at UEFA, and frequency of contact varies between partners (Walters and Anagnostopoulos, 2012). This case is interesting because it involves both the in-house and collaborative modes.

Discussion on the three modes of CSR implementation

This section discusses the uniqueness, advantages, and challenges of each mode of implementation. In doing so, we also draw attention to the importance of decision-making in this mode of implementation, knowing that some football organisations do not always strategically define their implementation mode, which reveals failure in the strategic development of CSR. However, certain elements are relevant for understanding the decision of the organisation between the three modes.

To achieve this understanding, we suggest analysing each mode using comparative variables from the literature. According to Husted (2003), organisations that opt for CSR governance should take into account costs associated with governance tasks: coordination (autonomous and cooperative) and motivation (incentive intensity and administrative control). Moreover, while drawing on different theoretical approaches, Anagnostopoulos and Shilbury (2013) noted that three managerial challenges are at play when managers implement CSR: alignment of strategies, conflict, and access to resources. Therefore, borrowing from previous relevant literature (Anagnostopoulos and Shilbury, 2013; Husted, 2003), and using the micro cases discussed earlier, Table 10.2 depicts each of these managerial challenges for each mode of CSR implementation.

Given these managerial challenges, we now raise four main discussion points. First, collaboration is transversal. In other words, partnerships not only happen in the collaborative mode. Rather, football organisations are collaborating with numerous partners to fulfil their social engagement. In the case of UEFA, the social partnership refers to the classical mode of implementation described by Husted (2003), as it involves a sponsor (UEFA) and a recipient (the six core partners). Other studies have shown that other forms of collaboration exist to address social issues, with CSR through sport collaboration probably being the most popular. This involves the partnership between an organisation outside sport and one from within the sport sector (Dowling et al., 2013). Beyond such cross-sectoral collaboration, non-profit collaboration are also interesting configurations to consider in the future. These collaborations may involve collaboration between football federations (for example, between a football federation and a disability federation); among football clubs (for example, within the EFDN network or between a professional football club and an amateur football club); between football federation and sport clubs; among football clubs, the football league and the federation (Zeimers et al., 2017); between community football clubs and other non-profit organisations; or even between football foundations and non-profit organisations (Bingham and Walters, 2013).

Second, the cases chosen in this chapter have revealed that football organisations may not necessarily rely on a single structure. As noted earlier, Celtic, the RBFA, and UEFA have been adopting a specific mode of implementation, intermingled with another mode such as collaborations. While this choice might lead to more challenges, it also provides more assets and resources to the football organisations. This also suggests that, without the assistance of partner

Table 10.2 Key issues on the three modes of CSR implementation

Management challenges	Foundation	In-House	Collaboration
Coordination	• High autonomous coordination • Low cooperative coordination	• High cooperative coordination • Low autonomous coordination	Intermediate
Motivation	• High incentive intensity • Low administrative control	• Low administrative control • High incentive intensity	Intermediate
Strategic alignment	• Clear coherent alignment between the mission of the foundation and the business plan of the football club is difficult • Deeply embedded with each other's strategies: they have their own separate strategy, funding sources, partners, etc. • Collaboration is essential (working across organisational boundaries towards positive ends) (synergy and shared outcomes)	• Work under one overarching strategy • Working under one roof is no guarantee that it will be deeply embedded within the organisation strategy	• Strategic alignment is difficult due to the separate strategy and the different background of the partners (e.g., non-profit and for-profit collaboration) • A partnership agreement might secure formally the strategic alignment • The degree of fit between partners will influence the strategic alignment (synergy and shared outcomes)
Conflict	• Given their day-to-day responsibility and knowledge, foundation managers have an important role to play in avoiding conflicts between the entities. • In some cases, however, their power and responsibility is limited to influence on the good relationship. • Tensions can arise between the different entities from the feeling that the foundation is not valued for the business benefits they provide or from different understandings and perceptions • Allow the foundation to disengage from clubs' politics and conflicts but boomerang effects	• Overall, limited conflict is expected because the dynamic is different given that the department is not as independent as the foundation • Conflicts can eventually occur between the league and the federation when they share similar CSR programmes and structures	• Conflict can occur because the dynamic and the power is imbalanced (especially in cross-sectoral collaboration) • Boundary-spanning individuals are central in these issues. • Interpersonal trust to prevent tensions is critical • Partners selection is crucial for conflict avoidance (i.e., converging working cultures)

(continued)

Table 10.2 Continued

Management challenges	Foundation	In-House	Collaboration
Access to resources	• Challenge is to secure external funding • Foundation allows for better access to external resources to employ CSR initiatives • Either the "parent" football club acts as the primary donor of money and in-kind resources or, in some rare cases, the foundation does not receive resources from the football club (stability) • In this latter case, foundations are being more sustainable and independent • There might be a perception that the money goes to the club and not to serving the social aspect of CSR (e.g., local community)	• Challenge is to secure internal and external funding • It is more difficult to receive public funding in this setting because of the negative perceptions of the organisations or the legislation • There might be perceptions that the money goes to the club and not for serving the social aspect of CSR (e.g., local community) • Receive direct funding from the organisation, and will therefore never be autonomous • Bridge existing stakeholders and new partners around the federation	• Challenge is to secure internal and external funding for projects • Ideally, both partners share resources and contribute to the implementation of the programmes (and share the costs eventually)

Table developed from the existing studies (Husted, 2003; Walters and Anagnostopoulos, 2012; Kolyperas et al., 2015; Hamil and Morrow, 2012) as well as from the case studies.

organisations, the implementation of CSR is perhaps unrealistic for football organisations themselves via a CSR department alone.

Third, current studies have suggested a shift from in-house to foundation structure (Kolyperas et al., 2015; 2016). This contention builds on the increasing adoption of foundations in English football. This may be conflictual, as foundations and their founder football clubs do not automatically share common goals or stakeholder agendas (Anagnostopoulos and Shilbury, 2013). Another aspect consists of confirming that many clubs remain unclear in their decision to adopt a mode of implementation, as 24 per cent of the G-25 clubs do not have a specified (and transparent) delivery of CSR, and are therefore assumed to be driven by individual motivations and/or irregular organisational efforts (Kolyperas and Sparks, 2011). While this evolution more towards the foundation mode of implementation can be seen as a strategic evolution of CSR delivery, some cases, such as the RBFA, suggest that this trend is not automatic and that some football organisations inversely move from the foundation mode to the in-house one. As such, we can assume that one mode of implementation does not necessarily lead to a higher integrated CSR strategy. Indeed, CSR integration requires a strategic orientation at all levels of the organisation, and not only being restricted to the football club's charitable arm, which can often create a grey area (Kolyperas et al., 2015). Therefore, the organisational integration of CSR can occur through all forms and modes of implementation. As the RBFA case illustrates, the in-house mode also allows the integration of the CSR principles with the organisation.

Fourth, Kolyperas and colleagues (2015) compared CSR activities across clubs that have adopted a separate entity for CSR activity and others that exercise CSR from within the organisation. They found that football clubs with separate CSR structures show a greater CSR-related role, in that they spend more hours on community activity, team up with a greater number of community partners, and draw up more initiatives and support these initiatives with more staff compared to clubs that operate community departments as their CSR delivery agency. The establishment of foundations for delivering CSR reflects a broader trend in CSR implementation, not only in the case of football but also in many professional teams in the North American context (Babiak and Wolfe, 2009). Foundations and partnerships represent a move away from the philanthropic approach and, under these circumstances, it has been argued that the decision on how to govern the implementation of CSR becomes a strategy-led decision (Husted, 2003; Kolyperas et al., 2015), which can potentially lead to value co-creation through carefully crafted CSR programmes for the foundations and the "parent" clubs alike (Kolyperas et al., 2016).

Conclusions

By selectively, rather than exhaustively, drawing on CSR in football literature, we have illustrated that football organisations, clubs, and federations employ the three modes of CSR implementation, as described by Husted (2003). This framework is particularly relevant for examining how football organisations choose to organise CSR as it makes it possible to compare and contrast different types of CSR implementation modes. The variety of CSR structures identified above shows that CSR has developed differently across the examined cases. Different challenges of CSR engagement are apparent through these modes with regard to the comparative elements selected. Given the particular football setting, the implementation patterns and schemes chosen by organisations when engaging in CSR programmes raises important questions for sport practitioners and scholars.

Such analysis also provides practical implications for managers. First, selecting the mode of CSR implementation should be planned carefully, as the direction chosen by the organisation will inevitably affect its CSR orientation and integration. Therefore, managers should consider that the decision behind the mode of CSR implementation is strategic. Second, specific contextual circumstances may influence the implementation mode chosen (for example, English football context favours the foundation mode), before any strategic evaluation of the advantages and challenges attributed to each mode. Third, studies have also shown that changes occur from one mode to the other. These adaptations might influence the strategic alignment between the overall strategy of the organisation and the CSR strategy. In addition, this can also lead to misalignment between the organisation and its social partners. Fourth, the foundation and collaborative modes appear to be the most widespread in the football setting. However, while some clear-cut boundaries amongst all modes can be identified, the challenges can also overlap. Hence, managers should be aware of the complexities involved in delving into the three modes of implementation discussed in this chapter.

Notes

1 The European Club Association (ECA) is the sole, independent body directly representing football clubs at the European level. It replaces the G-14 Group and the European Club Forum, both of which were dissolved at the beginning of 2008. The ECA was recognised by UEFA and FIFA in a formal memorandum of understanding signed in 2008.

2 Although we specifically refer to CSR implementation, the heterogeneous terminologies (development, integration, and implementation) prevailing in the sport management literature have forced us to refer to the broader term of CSR implementation when reviewing existing sport studies on this area.

3 In parallel, the league is providing orientation to the football clubs by strategic plans, monitoring, and disseminating handbooks and organising workshops.

References

Aquilina and Gasser, P. (2011) "La stratégie de l'UEFA en matière de football et de responsabilité sociale". In Bayle E., Chappelet J.-L., Francois A., and Maltese L. (2011), *Sport et RSE, Vers un management responsable*, De Boeck.

Anagnostopoulos, C. and Shilbury, D. (2013) Implementing corporate social responsibility in English football: Towards multi-theoretical integration. *Sport, Business and Management: An International Journal*, 3(4), 268–84.

Anagnostopoulos, C., Byers, T., and Shilbury, D. (2014) Corporate social responsibility in professional team sport organisations: Towards a theory of decision-making. *European Sport Management Quarterly*, 14(3), 259–81.

Anagnostopoulos, C., Byers, T., and Kolyperas, D. (2017) Understanding strategic decision-making through a multi-paradigm perspective: The case of charitable foundations in English football. *Sport, Business and Management: An International Journal*, 7(1), 2–20.

Babiak, K. and Wolfe, R. (2009) Determinants of corporate social responsibility in professional sport: internal and external factors. *Journal of Sport Management*, 23, 717–42.

Beech, J. and Chadwick, S. (2013) *The Business of sport management*. Pearson Education Limited.

Bingham, T. and Walters, G. (2013) Financial sustainability within UK charities: Community sport trusts and corporate social responsibility partnerships. *VOLUNTAS: International Journal of Voluntary and Nonprofit Organizations*, 24(3), 606–29.

Blumrodt, J., Desbordes, M., and Bodin, D. (2013) Professional football clubs and corporate social responsibility. *Sport, Business and Management: An International Journal*, 3(3), 205–25.

Bondy, K., Moon, J., and Matten, D. (2012) An institution of corporate social responsibility (CSR) in multi-national corporations (MNCs): Form and implications. *Journal of Business Ethics*, 111(2), 281–99.

Breitbarth, T. and Harris, P. (2008) The role of corporate social responsibility in the football business: Towards the development of a conceptual model. *European Sport Management Quarterly*, 8(2), 179–206.

Breitbarth, T., Hovemann, G., and Walzel, S. (2011) Scoring strategy goals: Measuring corporate social responsibility in professional European football. *Thunderbird International Business Review*, 53(6), 721–37.

Breitbarth, T. and Rieth, L. (2012) Strategy, stakeholder, structure: key drivers for successful CSR integration in German professional football. *Contextualising Research in Sport: An International Perspective*, ATINER, Athens, 45–63.

Breitbarth, T., Walzel, S., Anagnostopoulos, C., and van Eeekeren, F. (2015) Corporate social responsibility and governance in sport: "Oh, the things you can find, if you don't stay behind!". *Corporate Governance*, 15(2), 254–73.

Carr, P., Findlay, J., Hamil, S., Hill, J., and Morrow, S. (2000) The Celtic trust. *Soccer and Society*, 1(3), 70–87.

Chadwick, S. (2009) From outside lane to inside track: sport management research in the twenty-first century. *Management Decision*, 47(1), 191–203.

Curran, K., Rosenbaum, S., Parnell, D., Stubbs, B., Pringle, A., and Hargreaves, J. (2017) Tackling mental health: the role of professional football clubs. *Sport in Society*, 20(2), 281–91.

Dowling, M., Robinson, L., and Washington, M. (2013) Taking advantage of the London 2012 Olympic games: corporate social responsibility through sport partnerships, *European Sport Management Quarterly*, 3(3), 269–92.

Gasser, P. (2009) From charity to strategy: UEFA's Football and Social Responsibility (FSR). In McDonald, S., Smith, A., and Westerbeek, H. (2009) Using Sport and Physical Activity (PA) in Corporate Social Responsibility Programs: An Analysis of Indexed Multinationals, in *Social responsibility and sustainability in sports*, Oviedo, Spain: Ediciones de la Universidad de Oviedo, pp. 111–134.

Hamil, S. and Morrow, S. (2011) Corporate social responsibility in the Scottish Premier League: Context and motivation. *European Sport Management Quarterly*, 11(2), 143–70.

Hamil, S., Walters, G., and Watson, L. (2010) The model of governance at FC Barcelona: balancing member democracy, commercial strategy, corporate social responsibility and sporting performance. *Soccer and Society*, 11(4), 475–504.

Hovemann, G., Breitbarth, T., and Walzel, S. (2011) Beyond sponsorship? Corporate social responsibility in English, German and Swiss top national league football clubs. *Journal of Sponsorship*, accepted for publication.

Husted, B. W. (2003) Governance choices for corporate social responsibility: to contribute, collaborate or internalize?. *Long Range Planning*, 36(5), 481–98.

Inoue, Y., Mahan, J. E., and Kent, A. (2012) Enhancing the benefits of professional sport philanthropy: The roles of corporate ability and communication strategies. *Sport Management Review*, 16(3), 314–25.

Kihl, L., Babiak, K., and Tainsky, S. (2014) Evaluating the implementation of a professional sport team's corporate community involvement initiative. *Journal of Sport Management*, 28(3), 324–37.

Kolyperas, D., Anagnostopoulos, C., Chadwick, S., and Sparks, L. (2016) Applying a communicating vessels framework to CSR value co-creation: empirical evidence from professional team sport organizations. *Journal of Sport Management*, 30(6), 702–19.

Kolyperas, D., Morrow, S., and Sparks, L. (2015) Developing CSR in professional football clubs: drivers and phases. *Corporate Governance*, 15(2), 177–95.

Kolyperas, D. and Sparks, L. (2011) Corporate Social Responsibility (CSR) communications in the G-25 football clubs. *International Journal of Sport Management and Marketing*, 10(1–2), 83–103.

Kulczycki, W. and Koenigstorfer, J. (2016) Doing good in the right place: city residents' evaluations of professional football teams' local (vs. distant) corporate social responsibility activities. *European Sport Management Quarterly*, 16(4), 502–24.

Lansley, S. and Parnell, D. (2016) Football for health: getting strategic. *Soccer and Society*, 17(2), 259–66

Maon, F., Lindgreen, A., and Swaen, V. (2010) Organizational Stages and Cultural Phases: A Critical Review and a Consolidative Model of Corporate Social Responsibility Development. *International Journal of Management Reviews*, 12(1), 20–38.

Morrow, S. (2003) *The people's game? Football, finance and society*. Basingstoke: Palgrave.

Morrow, S. (2012) Corporate social responsibility in sport. In L. Robinson, P. Chelladurai, G. Bodet, and P. Downward (eds), *Routledge Handbook of Sport Management*, (pp. 101–15). Oxon: Routledge

Parnell, D., Stratton G., Drust B., and Richardson D. (2013) Football in the community schemes: Exploring the effectiveness of an intervention in promoting healthful behaviour change. *Soccer and Society*, 14, 35–51.

Parnell, D., Pringle, A., Widdop, P., and Zwolinsky, S. (2015) Understanding football as a vehicle for enhancing social inclusion: Using an intervention mapping framework. *Social Inclusion*, 3(3), 158–66.

Pringle, A., Zwolinsky, S., McKenna. J., Robertson, S., Daly-Smith, A., and White, A. (2014) Health improvement for men and hard-to-engage-men delivered in English Premier League football clubs. *Health Education Research*, 29(3), 503–20.

Reiche, D. (2014) Drivers behind corporate social responsibility in the professional football sector: a case study of the German Bundesliga. *Soccer and Society*, 15(4), 472–502.

Smith, A. C. and Westerbeek, H. M. (2007) Sport as a vehicle for deploying corporate social responsibility. *Journal of Corporate Citizenship*, 25(1), 43–54.

Walker, M. and Parent, M. M. (2010) Toward an integrated framework of corporate social responsibility, responsiveness, and citizenship in sport. *Sport Management Review*, 13(3), 198–213.

Walker, M. and Kent, A. (2009) Do fans care? Assessing the influence of corporate social responsibility on consumer attitudes in the sport industry. *Journal of Sport Management*, 23(6), 743–69.

Walters, G. (2009) Corporate social responsibility through sport: The community sports trust model as a CSR delivery agency. *Journal of Corporate Citizenship*, (35).

Walters, G. and Tacon, R. (2010) Corporate social responsibility in sport: Stakeholder management in the UK football industry. *Journal of Management and Organization*, 16(4), 566–86.

Walters, G. and Tacon, R. (2011) Corporate social responsibility in European football. *Birkbeck Sport Business Centre Research Paper*, Vol. 4 No. 1, pp. 1–101.

Walters, G., and Chadwick, S. (2009) Corporate citizenship in football: delivering strategic benefits through stakeholder engagement. *Management Decision*, 47(1), 51–66.

Walters, G. and Anagnostopoulos, C. (2012) Implementing corporate social responsibility through social partnerships. *Business Ethics: A European Review*, 21(4), 417–33.

Walzel, S., Robertson, J., and Anagnostopoulos, C. (2018) Corporate social responsibility in professional team sports organizations: An integrative review. *Journal of Sport Management*. Forthcoming.

Zeimers, G., Anagnostopoulos, C., Zintz, T., and Willem, A. (2017) Teaming-up for social responsibility programs: the case of Belgian nonprofit sport organizations. Paper presented at the *North American Society for Sport Management* (NASSM). Denver, Colorado (USA), 30 May – 4 June 2017.

11

Agents and intermediaries

Giambattista Rossi

Football agents and intermediaries

In order to understand how and why the modern-day agent's industry developed we must first set out what is meant by the term "agent" in contrast to the synonym of intermediary. We therefore begin with a brief introduction to the differences between the two terms, charting how middlemen in the football market have flipped between the two terms over the last century, before going on to look at the historical development of their activities from the pre-war period through to the present day.

While the words agent and intermediary are used interchangeably in common parlance, there have traditionally been subtle differences between the two which can help us to explain the development of the industry (Frenkiel, 2014). In the business context, both terms are defined as professionals who act with or in between two or more trading parties for legitimate economics activities, illegitimate payments, or a combination of both, offered by a supplier to a consumer. However, while agents are legally authorised, through a legal mandate, to act on behalf of one of the two parties concluding a specific contract, intermediaries mainly carry out only material actions (establishing contracts, arranging meetings, etc.) in order to bring the contracting parties together as fixed by brokerage contracts (KEA et al., 2009). Specifically, while agents mainly centre their profession around the player's or athlete's representation and interests, intermediaries principally focuses on any sort of transactions involving players, clubs, and companies.

The transition of football agents from a social norm lacking any official status, to a coveted, legally recognised profession central to the operation of global football markets can be charted through four periods mirroring the dispersion of the game commercially and in parallel, liberalisation of the labour and transfer markets (Magee, 2002; Gouget and Primault, 2006):

- From the late nineteenth century to the late 1950s: scouting and intermediation on the behalf of clubs
- From the early 1960s to the mid 1990s: the representation of football players
- From the mid 1990s to the mid 2010s: the professionalisation of football agents
- From the mid 2010s to present days: the era of super agents and intermediaries.

From the late nineteenth century to the late 1950s: Scouting and intermediation on the behalf of clubs

Intermediaries in the football market have existed since the advent of professionalism, performing scouting and recruitment roles for clubs. As clubs developed, they internalised this activity and by developing their own scouting networks diminished the role of middlemen. These changes in the market led intermediaries to seek other roles and their position as middlemen working between players and clubs started to develop. Their initial role in the UK was largely confined to advising clubs on sourcing new football talent. Although the first case of professionalism in football dates back to 1876 with the transfer of the player James Lang to Sheffield Wednesday, the English FA sought to curb the use of professional players and it was almost a decade later in 1885 when they eventually reluctantly sanctioned professionalism. In this context, football intermediaries operated only on behalf of clubs to scout and recruit players (Roderick, 2001, p. 13).

In the UK, after the introduction of the "retain and transfer" system in 1893 which enabled football clubs to exercise a great degree of control over the movement of players (Magee, 2002), the early years of the twentieth century saw clubs beginning to take more responsibility for their own recruitment of players and intermediaries' activity was marginalised. The Football Association (FA) felt that intermediaries were against the ethos of football and disapproved of their activity so much that the activities of individuals who attempted to profit as the go-betweens of clubs and players were officially banned. However, despite clubs being regularly warned not to deal with intermediaries, there was still demand for their services (Taylor, 2005).

Regardless of their disputed image, the growth and increasing openness of the international transfer market offered an opportunity for intermediaries to start to gain both exposure and a prominent position in the development of football. From their inception, all of the professional leagues imported foreign players in accordance with the respective domestic transfer market restrictions (Taylor, 2006). Since the English FA was not a member of FIFA at that time, foreign clubs were not obliged to pay any transfer fees for players. Intermediaries appeared from abroad to collaborate with local intermediaries, who mainly operated domestically, in order to transfer British players overseas (Taylor, 2002). Consequently, intermediaries were not welcome and team managers did not want to deal with them.

By the end of WWII intermediaries were widespread throughout the main football markets. However, in general, players were not professionally advised in transfer deals or contract negotiations (Taylor, 1999). Players at that time were seen purely as a commodity without the proper labour legislation in place to protect their rights. Competition from foreign leagues with the strong desire to sign the most high-profile players offered appealing alternatives. In the UK, this situation was also aggravated by the presence of the maximum wage, which remained in place until 1961. Consequently, the best British players were not able to command fair-market compensation from their clubs. The top British players frequently moved to Italy in the 1950s and 1960s through intermediaries who became ever more closely embroiled in negotiations (Harding, 2004).

Within the football transfer markets, there was much collusion between clubs' managers and directors (Carter, 2006). Players' transfers were agreed at inflated fees in order to write money on their tax return. The actual fee would be recorded as much lower in the buying club's accounts and those parties involved in the deal would then split the extra cash and, sometimes, give a small part to the player. While in England club managers were the main drivers of the transfer market, in the rest of Europe club directors became prominent. The nature of the transfer market at that time has been criticised as being akin to slavery where players could be transferred to another club on the whim of their club chairman, while intermediaries acted as "human flesh brokers" (Wahl and Lanfranchi, 1995). From the mid-1950s, conflicts between players and clubs owners throughout Europe were regular and related to both demands for increased wages and transfers.

From the early 1960s to the mid 1990s: The representation of football players

By 1960 in England it had become apparent that the restrictions in the labour market were not conducive to keeping the best players, and the players' union, the PFA, chaired by player Jimmy Hill, was using its influence to campaign against the maximum wage and the "retain and transfer" system. The decision to abolish the maximum wage in 1961 balanced the bargaining power between players and clubs to the point where most athletes started negotiating their contracts with the assistance of personal representatives (Magee, 2002). Between 1960 and 1964, the wages of First Division players increased by 61 percent (Szymanski and Kuypers, 1999). Labour market liberalisation continued in 1963 when the High Court ruled in the George Eastham case that the "retain and transfer" system was illegal on the basis that it constituted an unjustifiable restraint of trade (Banks, 2002). Through this liberalisation, players began to redress the imbalance of power that had been a feature of their relationships with clubs. In making the transfers of players more flexible, leagues and football associations legitimatised the use of intermediaries. However, there were still restrictions on the movement of players as clubs could unilaterally extend players' registrations so long as terms equal to their previous contract were offered; in essence they could tie a player to the club for as long as the club was willing to pay for his services, irrespective of whether the player wished to remain at that club.

By the late 1960s, influenced by the general political climate as well as debates going on within sport in general and football in particular, football players in Europe also continued to readdress the power balance. This period of reform and liberalisation was replicated across many major footballing nations, often with governmental support (Marzola, 1981). However, while these reforms facilitated the movement of players domestically, their movement between national federations remained highly regulated. Concurrently, media interest in sports as part of regular television programming expanded very rapidly, bringing enormous amounts of revenue into the leagues. While sports governing bodies have been very keen to restrict the role of agents in all matters relating to the relationships between players and clubs, they have not sought to regulate their activity with third parties and therefore a role in arranging for players to benefit from sponsorship and endorsements has thrived with little or no interference. Recognising these commercial opportunities, the use of agents by players first flourished throughout the 1960s and 1970s.

By the late 1970s, with clubs increasingly looking at global markets, players were marketable beyond their national associations, and agents increasingly started to play an important role in this internationalisation. With different transfer regulations and labour market systems country by country, various information asymmetries arose; for clubs, it was still considerably difficult to obtain reliable information on the quality of players at both national and international levels and, even when this was available, their likely future performance was extremely difficult to assess. As McGovern (2002) outlines, patterns of migration within the football industry were mainly socially embedded along regional lines and appropriate economic evaluations of players were infeasible. In this environment, football agents slowly strengthened their position in the transfer market, establishing migration channels favoured by the loosening of transfer limitations on foreign players in different countries, such as England in 1978 and Italy in 1980, and the emergence of new markets following the fall of the Soviet Union block.

The dual factors of increased internationalisation and the related growth in media coverage combined with the reforms of the transfer market regulations meant that players could begin to exploit their talent in various ways. These combined factors led to wage increases throughout the world of football (Marzola, 1990). As the value of contracts increased, the profession of football agents became more lucrative and a new generation of agents emerged to mainly assist players with their endorsement contracts and provide legal advice to players (Minguella, 2008; Canovi and Mazzocchi, 2011; Caliendo, 2012): Dario Canovi and Antonio Caliendo in Italy, Norbert Pflippens and Wolfgang Fahrian in Germany, Dennis Roach and Mel Stein in England, Jose Minguella, Alberto Toldra, and Roberto Dale in Spain, and Bernard Généstar in France.

By the 1980s, agents in the UK transfer market were relatively commonplace, yet without official recognition by any football governing bodies, their activity was unregulated. Moreover, the absence of any supervision in transfer negotiations led to an opportunity for inappropriate behaviours to be undertaken by agents, managers, and football directors. The lack of accountability in the transfer market remained exposed to the presence of an unwritten code of conduct based on the bungs culture[1] within the football industry. In the early 1990s the involvement of some football managers, such as Brian Clough and Graham Taylor, in illicit payments received from agents in player transfers confirmed that the activity of football agents needed to be officially regulated by football governing bodies at national and international levels (Bower, 2007).

In 1994, FIFA formally recognised and regulated the activity of football agents with the first licensing system accepted by all football federations signalling the transformation of the activity of football agents into a profession. Finally, this formal recognition implied a more rigorous definition and regulation of the role, duties and responsibility of the agents whose license was officially issued by their national football association. This official recognition meant that some important figures who had long been involved in the football business in various guises could now be classified legitimately as stakeholders.

From the mid 1990s to the mid 2010s: The professionalisation of football agents

The Bosman ruling in 1995 fundamentally changed the way that football in Europe had operated. In the ruling, the ECJ afforded free agency to players once their contracts expired and guaranteed them freedom of movement within the EU in line with all other professions (Dubey, 2000). This new market scenario was favoured by the exponential revenue growth in the football industry resulting from greater competition and deregulation in the broadcasting market which meant that pay-tv incumbents were willing to pay a premium for rights to broadcast live premier league matches. This revenue filtered through to clubs, which in turn sought to employ the best players. Agents found themselves in a market that allowed them to fully exploit players' bargaining power and their transfer freedom across EU borders.

Clubs had to start fully dealing with players' representatives, who negotiated the best possible contracts for their clients as well as for themselves (Banks, 2002). With players able to move without a fee at the end of their contracts, the only way that clubs could recoup their investment in players was to sell them while they were still under contract. Conversely, if clubs wanted to retain players, whose contracts were due to expire, they would need to offer new contracts with improved terms before the current terms expired. Both situations represented lucrative bargaining positions for players and their agents. In the 2001/02 season, Premiership clubs spent £475 million on players' wages and £323 million on transfers according to Deloitte (2003). In that season, agents would have earned about £46 million. One Premier League financial director said, "there is nothing atypical about the amounts that English clubs pay agents. Every club has its own policies and indeed the levels would vary depending on the agent and the club's 'desperation' for a player" (Wild, 2003).

Recognising the opportunity to profit in the game, a new wave of agents entered the football industry from various business sectors. In England, for example, Jon Holmes used to be a life-insurance salesman; Eric Hall and Athol Still moved into football after representing performing artists; and Cyril Regis, Jasper Olson, and Barry Silkman were former professional players (Harding, 2004). By February 2001, there were 631 licensed agents worldwide and this number increased in the following years, when, under pressure from the EU Competition Commission, FIFA modified the rules governing the acquisition of an official license. In Europe alone, the number of football agents increased by about 1,000 per year equating to around 300 per cent (Poli, 2010c). In December 2009, there were 5,193 officially licensed agents worldwide.

Throughout the 1990s the role of agents was able to develop more fully and their activities on behalf of either players or clubs developed according to their own personal networks. Besides contract negotiations, the role played by agents encompasses the development of transnational networks which scout and train players. Once a talented player is identified, intermediaries organise short-term trials in clubs with which they have existing relationships. Europe-based agents often collaborate with "tipsters" living in particularly fertile markets who, in exchange for a regular salary or periodical commissions, scout local talent and organise tournaments, which their Europe-based partners then attend in order to finalise a deal (Poli, 2010a).

In an increasingly global world, massive investments in football networks are essential in order to recognise and attract the best players (Poli, 2010b). This requires that football agents have a deep and selective knowledge of professional football worldwide so as to be able to scout players on behalf of clubs (Pinna, 2006). Semens (2012) explains that while clubs have their own networks, well-connected agents can act as a link when club networks do not otherwise overlap. Agents are also responsible for the structure of migration channels conceived as information systems that guide labour migrations and govern entry into the foreign labour market. In the transfer market, they control the entry into the migration system and the flow dynamics by motivating players to migrate. In this context, as Poli (2010b) highlights, agents play a key role in manipulating the different steps of players' career trajectories and they can influence clubs' football strategies through their role in recruiting and buying players on the transfer market. These arrangements have been known to include a commission for the identifying agent should the player be sold on for a higher amount in future. This issue is increasingly important to the extent that, in recent years, there has been a proliferation of companies and investment funds whose main business is to invest in football players by buying and selling shares of their economic rights in exchange of financial profit. An established practice in South America, so-called Third Party Entitlement, TPE, has also been deployed in Africa and Europe, particularly when clubs cannot afford to invest in the recruitment of new players. Either setting up or actively taking part in TPE investments, the professional activity of football agents has now acquired an entrepreneurial dimension that goes beyond their historical roles and functions within the football labour markets.

On 3 June 2009, FIFA decided to conduct in-depth reform of the licensing system through a new approach based on the concept of intermediaries in order to overcome the deficiencies of the existing regulatory system (FIFA, 2015e). The member associations of FIFA acknowledged that almost three-quarters of international transfers were organised through unlicensed agents and they sought to deregulate the profession of agents through this new approach. The reform resulted from an extensive consultation process involving all stakeholders in football, except agents. Its proposal was to require clubs and players to record the use of any intermediary in a player transfer, and to regulate how such intermediaries were used. However, the new regulations, FIFA Regulations Working with Intermediaries (RWI), came into force on 1 April 2015 and no longer attempted to regulate access to the activity, but instead control the activity itself. With no direct link between football's governing bodies and the agents, any sanctions can only be enforced on players or clubs, whose responsibility it is to ensure that their selection of intermediary is behaving in an appropriate way. This radical change, approved by FIFA and supported by the main football stakeholders such as FIFPro, has widely affected the individual associations leaving a regulatory vacuum that is likely to impact on how the intermediary profession might change without a proper supervision and regulatory framework. Therefore, the inevitable result is that there is a huge diversity of national measures to govern the profession's activity (Martins, 2016).

From the mid 2010s to present days: The era of super agents and intermediaries

During the six years leading to the approval of the RWI, FIFA often pointed out that its intention was not to put in place a deregulation, but to switch the focus from agents to single football transactions. FIFA did not want to regulate intermediaries in the same way they attempted to regulate agents (Lombardi, 2016). FIFA in essence admitted defeat in its attempt to regulate players' agents, and it abandoned the agents' regulations in their entirely, discounting the recognition of the Licensed Players Agents as a profession (Bellia, 2016). The RWI are interesting in their approach as they now focus on the regulation of the transaction, rather than the regulations of the individual (agent). This radical change in FIFA's approach focuses more on monitoring the intermediaries' transactions rather than the formalities on their access to the profession as was the case before (Van Megen, 2016). Single transfers have now become the focus as FIFA has ultimately ceased to regulate the agents so abruptly. This new approach is consistent with the introduction of the Transfer Matching System in 2010, which is designed to regulate and monitor the international transfer of players.

Based on these premises, we can consider football players from a different perspective that highlights the football transfer activities as sources of added-value generation in financial terms. In the economic context of the transfer market, football players are not just workers under contract with a club, they are also commodities (Rossi et al., 2016). Theoretically, the resource-based view, RBV, suggests that they can be conceived of as strategic resources which help clubs to obtain a competitive advantage in their industry and generate value, thereby contributing to both the strategic and the financial viability of the club. According to the RBV, resources can be defined as those assets that are tied semi-permanently to the firm and, together with capabilities, are the foundation of the firm's long-term strategy since they are the primary source of profit (Amit and Schoemaker, 1993). These strategic resources are defined as valuable, rare, inimitable, and non-substitutable and any firm has then to identify how to generate, manage, and control them in order to establish and enhance its sustainable competitive advantage and, in turn, its profits (Barney, 1991). The RBV therefore helps us to understand the relationships between resources, capabilities, competitive advantage, and profitability and, as a consequence, can help with strategic planning. Additionally, the firm's returns from its resources depend not only on sustaining its competitive position over time, but also on its ability to appropriate these returns. The issue of appropriability concerns the allocation of rents where property rights are not fully defined.

It follows that different actors in football, including football intermediaries, create value-added chains in order to gain profit from the career trajectory of football players through their transfers between clubs (Poli, 2010). In the football context, since players are valuable, rare, inimitable, and non-substitutable for their clubs, clubs' actions in the transfer market, based on their scouting and recruitment process, can be thought of as representing the most important strategic decisions that have to be made. Indeed, contrary to other professional sports (e.g. rugby, basketball), football clubs buy out the contracts of players whose registration rights are owned by other clubs in an exchange for a negotiated amount of compensation. In operational terms, this financial element to labour market moves, which must be agreed in a relatively open market, has created opportunities for third parties to compete with clubs in the market to acquire these resources and extract economic rents for themselves.

Indeed, for a football intermediary, when it comes to assessing resources owned and controlled by third parties, their main asset is the network of personal relationships that they operate in. Built informally over time, and not governed by contracts, which could expire over time, agents use their networks to obtain information that can help them in making deals. In the context of the transfer market, third parties have helped to turn players into resources, either explicitly or implicitly and, in this respect, TPE investors buy a stake in the player's contract, which entitles them to a share of the financial benefit from a player's transfer. While football intermediaries are often involved in this, there are many other potential stakeholders for TPEs, including holding companies, investment funds, club shareholders and employees, football academies, and even football players and their relatives.

Given the competitive nature of the representation market, some intermediaries have found ways to differentiate themselves from the competition and to make their activity profitable, despite not controlling many resources, by their access to those resources. However, while players are advised by intermediaries, they are not controlled by them, or at least, intermediaries do not have the legal means to control the moves of players and since their relationships with players do not always involve a formal contract, these relationships with profitable clients might be vulnerable. However, intermediaries' revenues are tightly linked to the transfers they are involved with. By investing in TPEs, intermediaries have found a way to convert players into property-based resources, which can be protected and become a source of profit. In theoretical terms, intermediaries have taken advantage of the transfer system that was implemented by clubs under the same resource-based rationale since TPE is derived directly from this strategy. Investing formally in players thus gives intermediaries a competitive advantage in the market and the potential to profit from holding a share of a player's economic rights. This element characterises the so-called super agents and intermediaries together with their abilities to maximise their football networks potentials and capabilities to fully serve clubs and players in generating added-value to their transfer markets operations in terms of capital gains from transfers and contract renewals in salary terms (Widdop et al., 2016).

Despite the presence of high-profile intermediaries such as Jorge Mendes and Kia Joorabchian, most TPE investors, both natural and legal persons, are outsiders to the football world. This enables intermediaries to provide a dual role, one relatively official while the other is less transparent. First, intermediaries, as football insiders, are very often official members of the experts' commission set up by investors in order to give advice on which players should be targeted. Second, the central position of intermediaries in transfer deals also grants them the ideal role of ambassador. Indeed, third parties, although interested in the details and the conclusion of transfer deals, are not supposed to have an influence. In particular, they are not physically present around the negotiation table and have in turn to respect the deal as concluded by the negotiating participants. It is then very tempting to convince an intermediary to represent the interests of the third party during the negotiation or at least to communicate the information shared during the discussion. As clubs have clear incentives to keep third party shares down, intermediaries are the ideal partner for third parties. The conditions under which intermediaries can conduct such an emissary role are not always transparent, but the numerous ties between agents and third party owners of players' economic rights indicate that such relations exist.

From an intermediary's perspective, TPE has become a strategic investment tool to enter into transfer markets and compete directly with football clubs for the acquisition of football talent at all levels. As happens in many industries, intermediaries have acted as venture capital investors who are ready to support clubs in their transfer strategies and opportunistically exploit the recruitment and career development of football players who are seen as strategic resources.

Market concentration in the representation market across the big five leagues

In 2016, the big five European leagues together generated €13.4 billion in cumulative revenue, and spent €8.2 billion in wage costs and in estimated transfer fees in the region (Deloitte, 2017). With such fees being spent, the most relevant and influential football intermediaries are domiciled in these countries and operate within their professional leagues. The fees paid to agents are clearly significant sums of money. In England, both the Premier League (PL) and the Football League (FL) produce an annual report on the fees that clubs pay to agents, which shows that since the 2008/2009 football season roughly £980 million has been paid by the 92 professional English football clubs to football agents. This is aside from the huge sums estimated to be paid by players themselves. Since October 2010, the Transfer Matching System (TMS) has tracked all international football transfers and its Global Transfer Report states that between 2011 and 2016 $1,396 million were spent by clubs to pay intermediaries commission for their roles in international transfers (FIFA TMS, 2017).

By investigating the level of market concentration in the representation market in terms of market share and market power in 2016–2017, we are able to ascertain how the representation of players is distributed and how their market transfer evaluations are apportioned between agents. While market share is defined by the total percentage of professional players represented by an agent or an agency within the big five European leagues, the concept of market power is based on the total sum of the potential transfer market value of the players involved. This in turn gives us an indication of competitiveness within the market for agents and intermediaries.

In order to complete this analysis, data was collected on the main agent or intermediary for every player registered to a club in the big five European leagues and, where applicable, also on the second named agent. The potential transfer market value of each player was calculated based on an economic model that takes into consideration variables relative to players and their teams.

The actual market concentration can be seen in more detail in Figure 11.1. Indeed, 113 intermediaries or agencies represent half of the players' market share. On average, these agents manage the career of more than one football player in the big five, and one-quarter of the players are represented by 27 agencies, corresponding to roughly 2.8 per cent, on average, of the representation market in football. In terms of market power, half of the players' market value is managed by 71 individual intermediaries or agencies, 7.32 per cent on average during the season 2016/17, while one-quarter of players' market value is represented by only 17 agents on average, equal to 1.75 per cent of the representation market on average.

A more interesting insight is also to assess which agencies hold a dominant position in the big five leagues, both in terms of the market share and according to the average total amount of the estimated transfer value of their protégés. For this reason, the following analysis offers a detailed overview of the most influential agents and intermediaries, from both a numerical and a financial perspective, allowing also an assessment of the agencies which have been able to increase their market power and influence over the time period.

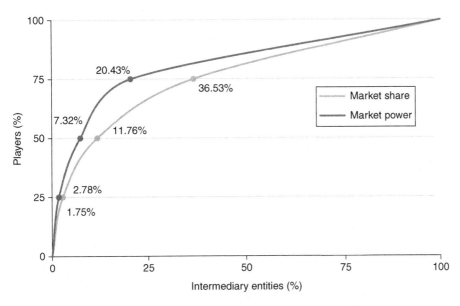

Figure 11.1 Market concentration in the big five in season 2016/2017

Table 11.1 Top 10 football agencies in with the highest market shares

Rank	Agency/Agent/Intermediary	Type	Market share %	Average number of represented players
1.	WMG (USA)	GG	1.97	49
2.	Sports Total (GER)	GS	1.36	34
3.	Stellar Group (UK)	GG	1.36	34
4.	Bahia Internacional (SPA)	GS	1.36	34
5.	Groupe USM (FRA)	GS	1.28	32
6.	Base Soccer (UK)	GS	1.2	30
7	Promoesport (SPA)	GS	1.2	30
8.	Rogon (GER)	GS	1.04	26
9.	Groupe USM (FRA)	GS	0.96	24
10.	Pastorello & Partners (ITA)	GS	0.92	23
Total			12.65	316

The 10 individual agencies with the most clients among the players in the big five leagues managed the careers of roughly 316 players, equal to 12.6 per cent of the players' market, as shown in the following Table 11.1. In terms of the typology of agencies, the top agencies are all global specialists, meaning that they focus predominantly on football representation and they operate at international level. The exception to this is WMG and Stellar Group which are involved in other commercial elements of sport and entertainment.

In the last five years, the agency has gone through an expansion process which will impact on its dominant presence in the representation market. In June 2013, WMG announced the appointment of highly rated consultants, including Chiel Dekker in Netherlands, and the agents Frederic Dobraje, Gregory Dakad, Cedric Mazet, and David Martinez in France (WMG, 2013). According to Mike Watts, WMG COO, "the appointment of these five consultants gives us a great opportunity to manage the careers of leading Ligue 1 and Eredivise players locally, which we see as a huge advantage for both the athletes and for Wasserman" (Long, 2013). In line with this expansion strategy, on 13 November 2014, WMG acquired the Dutch football agency Sport-Promotion founded and owned by Rob Jansen, one of the most respected agents in Europe, who currently represents International Dutch players such as Daley Blind, Marco Van Ginkel, Daryl Janmaat and Leroy Fer. Paul Martin, EVP managing executive for global football at WMG, said of the new collaboration: "the continued development of our European football practice is a priority for us and we firmly believe that this acquisition will enable us to go from strength to strength as we continue to grow our European presence" (WMG, 2014). In July 2016, Wasserman continued the expansion of its global football division with the acquisition of French-based agency, Mondial Promotion, which represents over 60 clients, including the likes of Didier Drogba, Diafra Sakho, Arouna Koné, Pape Souaré, Bafetimbi Gomis, Idrissa Gana Gueye, and Marouane Chamakh. This acquisition further adds to Wasserman's elite client base which already includes Ross Barkley, Steven Gerrard, Jordan Henderson, John Stones, Daley Blind, Chris Smalling, and Wilfried Bony, amongst others. Casey Wasserman, chairman and CEO, of Wasserman, said: "Mondial has done an incredible job dominating the French football market. Their impressive roster speaks for all the hard work Pierre, Etienne and Thierno have done and will significantly add to our portfolio. Our clients have always been our top priority," said Pierre Frelot, co-owner of Mondial. As part of Wasserman, we will now have access to a global wealth of services and opportunities for our clients and we look forward to doing great work together. (Heitner, 2016).

In Table 11.2, intermediaries are ranked in terms of market power measured by the yearly potential total amount of transfer fees that could have been generated by players represented by them. Amongst the top 10 agencies, an estimated €2.71 billion could have been generated in transfer fees. With a potential of €653 million, at the top of the rankings is Gestifute, the Portuguese agency run by Jorge Mendes that represents the archetype of the generation of super agents and intermediaries. In the last years, like few other prominent intermediaries, Mendes was quick to provide his services to the new flow of Chinese interest and money in football facilitating players' transfers to China and advising Chinese entrepreneurs on investing in European football. This market expansion became more evident when, Shangai Foyo, a company majority owned by Fosun, huge industrial, pharmaceutical and entertainment holdings, bought stakes in Gestifute's holding company Start followed by the launch of a marketing and football agency joint venture in Chinese football in January 2016 and by Fosun's acquisition of Wolverhampton

Table 11.2 Top 10 football agencies in with the highest market power

Rank	Agency/Agent/Intermediary	Type	Market power %	Represented players' total value estimation €m
1.	Gestifute (POR)	GS	4.41	653
2.	WMG (USA)	GG	2.62	388
3.	Stellar Group (ENG)	GS	1.93	285
4.	Maguire Tax & Legal (NDL)	GS	1.76	260
5.	Bahia Internacional (SPA)	GS	1.68	249
6.	Sports Total (GER)	GS	1.48	220
7.	Base Soccer (UK)	GS	1.22	181
8.	Euro Export Ass. e Prop. (BRA)	GS	1.08	160
9.	Pastorello & Partners (ITA)	GS	1.07	158
10.	Twenty Two (ARG)	GS	1.06	156
Total			18.31	2710

Wanderers five months later. Since 2001, Mendes has been able to obtain a privileged position via his connections to diverse groups (clubs, players, funding sources, scouts etc.), enabling him to collect more information than those outside of the network and therefore also exercise some influence over how that information is used and whose interests are served (Russo, 2014).

Conclusions

The evolution of the profession of agents and intermediaries has always been strongly linked with the reform of the football transfer market, the recognition of football players' working rights and the improvement of their working conditions. This aspect reveals that the profession of agents has emerged spontaneously in function of players' needs and ambitions to exploit their increasing bargaining power. In this context, agents have conquered a relevant market position that has led some of them to adopt abusive market power behaviour and illegal conducts within the transfer market, such as bribery, child trafficking, and tax evasion. The recent FIFA reform on agents represents the first attempt to regulate the profession in an inclusive manner, after a six-year period of consultation with the major football stakeholders.

With the introduction of the recent FIFA RWI, the concept of intermediation has become the centre of the regulation. It is not anymore solely players' rights and their interests alone but the entire transfer market and its stakeholders that need to be more accountable and transparent during the transfer activity with intermediaries. This change officially recognises that intermediaries are more than simple players' representatives as agents were supposed to be, but that their activity of intermediation also involves more services for clubs, players and leagues on transfer market issues and commercial opportunities. This new regulatory framework broadly regulated this profession at international level but it is highly fragmented and diversified at national level. This situation provides discrepancies and inconsistencies as intermediaries can operate in their country of origin but, at the same time, find regulatory limitations or hurdles to operate in other countries where they find more stringent regulations for their profession. At the moment, this heterogeneity of regulations represents the biggest challenge and it implies that this reform is far from being complete and perfect.

In relation with the FIFA RWI, it is also the increasing market power of the so-called super agents and intermediaries. We are assisting a superstars' effect in the market of intermediaries, wherein a few are strengthening their market position and domination through the leverage of their networks towards new business services and new markets. A ban on TPE is now current and ratified by FIFA, which controls every transfer through the TMS. However, it is hard to support that this ban is enough to limit the diffusion of this practice that leverages the influence of super agents within the transfer market. It is still early stage to assess whether the increasing power of super agents might create further market inefficiencies and integrity issues, but this represents an interesting topic that researchers might look at in the future.

Finally, the new FIFA RWI provides more transparency and, alongside the TMS, more information is now available regarding who the intermediaries are that are currently operating in the market and how much clubs remunerate them for their transfer market service. As clubs and players are required to be more responsible for allowing intermediaries to act on their behalves during the same transfer negotiations, i.e. double representation, this represents an opportunity for football stakeholders to be more aware of football intermediaries.

Note

1 This refers to the habit or tendency to facilitate a transfer deal using a secret financial incentive that is unauthorised and undisclosed to a club manager or any other decision maker within a football club.

References

Amit R. and Schoemaker, P. (1993) Strategic assets and organizational rent. *Strategic Management Journal.* 14(1), pp. 33–46.

Banks, S. (2002) *Going down: Football in crisis.* Edinburgh: Mainstream Publishing.

Barney, J. B. (1991) Firm resources and sustained competitive advantage. *Journal of Management.* Vol. 17(1), pp. 99–120.

Bellia, O. (2016) FIFA Regulations on Working with Intermediaries. Analysis from the perspective of the clubs. In: Colucci, M. (eds), *The FIFA Regulations on Working with Intermediaries: Implementation at National Level.* 2nd Edition. Salerno: Sports Law and Policy Centre, pp. 57–66.

Bower, T. (2007) *Broken Dreams: The Definitive Exposé of British Football Corruption* (updated version). London: Pocket Books.

Caliendo, A. (2012) *Nessuno prima di me. L'evoluzione del calcio e del procuratore sportivo.* Milan: Libreria dello Sport.

Canovi, D. and Mazzocchi, G. (2011) *Lo Stalliere del re. Fatti e misfatti di 30 anni di calcio.* Milan: Dalai Editore.

Carter, N. (2006) *The Football Manager: A history.* London: Routledge.

Davis, T. (2007) United States. In: Siekman, R.C.R., Parrish, R., Martins, R.B. and Soek, J. (eds), *Players' Agents Worldwide: Legal Aspects.* The Hague: T.M.C. Asser Press, pp. 655–92.

Deloitte (2017) *Deloitte Annual Review of Football Finance,* 26th Edition. Manchester: Deloitte.

Dubey, J. P. (2000) *La libre circulation des sportifs en Europe.* Bern: Staempfli.

FIFA TMS (2017) *Global Transfer Market Report 2017.* Zurich: FIFA.

Foot, J. (2006) *Calcio: A History of Italian Football.* London: Fourth Estate.

Frenkiel, S. (2014) *Une histoire des agents sportifs en France: Les imprésarios du football (1979–2014).* Neuchâtel: Editions CIES.

Gouget, J.J. and Primault, D. (2006) Les agents dans le sport professionnel: analyse économique. *Revue Juridique et Économique du Sport.* 81, 7–44.

Harding, J. (2004) It was my agent's idea. WSC When Saturday Comes [online]. 4 February 2004. Available from: http://www.wsc.co.uk/the-archive/102-Agents/2193-it-was-my-agents-idea [Accessed 1 May 2014].

Heitner, D. (2016) Wasserman adds 60 soccer clients through acquisition of Mondial Partners. Forbes [online]. Available from: https://www.forbes.com/sites/darrenheitner/2016/07/27/wassermans-acquisition-of-mondial-adds-1-billion-in-soccer-contracts-under-management/#4780ea436501 [accessed 21 November 2017].

Helyar, J. (1994) *Lords of the Realm: The Real History of Baseball.* New York: Villard.

KEA, CDES and EOSE (2009) Study on sport agents in the European Union. Brussels: Sport EC.

King, L. (1994) Remembrances of Bob Woolf, America's first sport agent. *Jeffrey S. Moorad Sports Law Journal.* 1(1), 3–5.

Lanfranchi, P. and Taylor, M. (2001) *Moving with the Ball: The Migration of Professional Footballers.* Oxford: Berg.

Lombardi, P. (2016) The FIFA Regulations on Working with Intermediaries. In: Colucci, M. (eds), *The FIFA Regulations on Working with Intermediaries: Implementation at National Level.* 2nd Edition. Salerno: Sports Law and Policy Centre, pp. 23–40.

Long, M. (2013) Wasserman expands European soccer practices. SportsPro [online]. Available from: www.sportspromedia.com/movers_and_shakers/wasserman_expands_european_soccer_practice [accessed 25 May 2015].

Magee, J. (2002) Shifting power balances of power in the new football economy. In: Sugden, J. and Tomlinson, A. (eds), *Power Games: A Critical Sociology of Sport.* London: Routledge, pp. 216–39.

Martins, R. (2016) FIFA Regulations on working with intermediaries: An analysis and opinion from the intermediaries' perspective. In: Colucci, M. (eds), *The FIFA Regulations on Working with Intermediaries: Implementation at National Level.* 2nd Edition. Salerno: Sports Law and Policy Centre, pp. 41–56.

Marzola, P. (1981) *Il Mercato del lavoro negli sports professionistici di squadra.* Ferrara: Editrice Universitaria.

Marque, A. (2012) Contrôle de l'activité d'agent sportif. In: Karaquillo, J. P. and Lagarde, F. (eds), *Agent sportif.* Paris: Juris Éditions, pp. 38–47.

Martins, R.B. (2008) European Football Agents Association wants to end malpractice in the international transfer of players. *The International Sports Law Journal.* 1–2, 96–99.

Marzola, P. (1981) *Il Mercato del lavoro negli sports professionistici di squadra.* Ferrara: Editrice Universitaria.

Marzola, P. (1990) *L'industria del calcio.* Roma: La Nuova Italia Scientifica.

Minguella, J. M. (2008) *Quasi tota la veritat*. Barcelona: Base.

McGovern, P. (2002) Globalization or internationalization? Foreign footballers in the English League, 1946-95. *Sociology*. 36(1), 23–42.

Pinna, A. (2006) The international supply of sport agent services. *International Sports Law Journal*. 1–2, 20–7.

Poli, R. (2010a) Agents and intermediaries. In: Hamil, S. and Chadwick, S. (eds) *Managing Football: An International Perspective*. Oxford: Elsevier Butterworth-Heinemann, pp. 201–16.

Poli, R. (2010b) Understanding globalisation through football: The new international division of labour, migratory channels and transnational trade circuits. *International Review for the Sociology of Sport*. 45(4), 491–506.

Poli, R. (2010c) *Le marché des footballeurs: Reseaux et circuitsdans l'économie globale*. Bern: Peter Lang.

Roderick, M. (2001) The role of agents in professional football, Singer and Friedlander's Review 2000-01 Season.

Rossi, G., Semens, A., and Brocard, J.F. (2016) *Sports Agents and Labour Markets: Evidence from world football*. London: Routledge.

Russo, P. (2014) *Gol di rapina: il lato oscuro del calcio globale*. Firenze: Edizioni Clichy.

Rosner, S. R. (2004) Conflicts of interests and the shifting paradigm of athlete representation. *UCLA Entertainment Law Review*. 11(2), 193–245.

Ruxin, R. (1993) *An Athlete's Guide to Agents*. Sudbury: Jones and Bartlett Publishers.

Semens, A. (2012) Bridge, Gate keepers, negotiator: The sport agent as entrepreneur. In: Ciletti, D and Chadwick, S. (eds), *Sports Entrepreneurship: Theory and Practice*. Morgantown: Fitness Information Technology, pp. 81–95.

Szymanski, S. and Kuypers, T. (1999) *Winners and Losers*. London: Penguin Books.

Taylor, M. (1999) No big deal. WSC When Saturday Comes [online], 14 November 1999. Available from: http://www.wsc.co.uk/the-archive/102-Agents/4042-no-big-deal [Accessed 18 June 2013].

Taylor, M. (2002) Work and play: The professional footballer in England c. 1900–1950. *The Sports Historian*. 22(1),16–43.

Taylor, M. (2005) *The leaguers – the making of professional football in England, 1900–1939*. Liverpool: Liverpool University Press.

Taylor, M. (2006) Global players? Football migration and globalization, c. 1930-2000. *Historical Social Research*. 31(6), 7–30.

Van Megen, W. (2016) FIFA Regulations on Working with Intermediaries. The Players' point of view. In: Colucci, M. (eds), *The FIFA Regulations on Working with Intermediaries: Implementation at National Level*. 2nd Edition. Salerno: Sports Law and Policy Centre, pp. 67–74.

Wahl, A. and Lanfranchi, P. (1995) *Les footballeurs français des années trente à nos jours*. Paris: La Vie Quotidienne Actuelle, Hachette.

Widdop, P., Parnell, D., and Ashgar, T. (2016) The networked rise and power of the football Super-Agent. The Football Collective – Bringing critical debate to our game [online], 27 September 2016. Available from: https://footballcollective.org.uk/2016/09/27/the-networked-rise-and-power-of-the-football-super-agent/ [Accessed 11 November 2017].

Wild, D. (2003) Agents net £50m from football. Accountancy Age [online], 20 November 2003. Available from: http://www.accountancyage.com/aa/news/1752064/agents-net-gbp50m-football [Accessed 8 April 2013].

WMG (2013) Wasserman expands football division. WMG [online]. Available from: www.wmgllc.com/wasserman-expands-football-division/ [Accessed 25 May 2015].

WMG (2014) Wasserman acquires Dutch football agency Sport-Promotion. WMG [online]. Available from: www.wmgllc.com/wasserman-acquires-football-agency-sport-promotion/ [Accessed 25 May 2015].

12

Managing performance in elite professional football

Barry Drust, Andy O'Boyle, and Mark Gillett

A basis for the need to understand football performance

Professional football as a sport has changed dramatically over the last 10–15 years. These developments are probably a consequence of multiple-factors (e.g. organisational and administrational reform, improvements in stadia etc.) that impact a diverse range of important operational factors. These off-field advances have resulted in substantial increases in the finance in the sport with modern clubs often reporting revenues of hundreds of millions of pounds (Deloitte, 2017). These finances and the profile that the sport offers those involved, have made the game a very attractive proposition for modern investors. Such changes have resulted in an increased interest in the administrative processes and management and leadership strategies that operate within elite football organisations (Crust and Lawrence, 2006).

One of the most important determining factors that drives the business side of football is the actual performance of the players and coaches within the organisation. These ultimately underpin the success of the team on the pitch. While success is frequently linked to the amount of money that an organisation spends (e.g. the top four clubs in the English Premier League are frequently the highest spenders in the league; Carmichael et al., 2011) there are examples in which teams have outperformed expectation (e.g. Leicester City FC winning the English Premier League in 2016). In these situations, it is less clear what other factors over finance may help explain such unpredicted events. This lack of insight emphasises the limited information that exists in the published literature around non-financial strategies that may help improve performance on the pitch. In addition to their underpinning performance, such strategies may also work to help protect the players' health and wellbeing in the longer term, thereby guarding the financial investment of the club. Such information is of obvious importance to individuals interested in the management and organisation of professional football given the direct impact it will have on the strategies used to plan, implement, and deliver an effective off-field strategy at executive level. This chapter will attempt to outline some of the considerations that may be associated with the support of performance in elite football. More specifically this chapter will attempt to:

1 Outline the potential role that performance support programmes based on sport science research can play in optimising performance in elite football

2   Explore the role that the performance director can play in the operational management of strategies that attempt to influence player performance.

Understanding football performance: The underpinnings of performance support programmes

Models that can be used to explain football performance are complex (Drust et al., 2007). It is generally agreed that football performance, at an individual player level, is a result of a combination of four interdependent areas: tactical knowledge, technical skill, physiological capabilities, and psychological skills.

While all these attributes are necessary for the elite performer it is clear that there is no one combination of these attributes that determines success. For example, it is easy to recognise players who have played at the elite level who are supremely technically gifted and those who are more recognised for their athletic abilities such as speed or strength while possessing limited skill. This makes the identification of talent and the prediction of performance much more difficult than in sports (e.g. endurance running) in which one attribute (i.e. physiological capacity) dominates. The successful outcome in the sport of football is also not, in most cases, determined by any one individual on a team but rather the contribution of each player's individual talents to the collective team effort. This further complicates our understanding of performance as the number of variables that may be related to any performance outcome are dramatically increased. These factors are also unlikely to be stable across different performances or time as they will be influenced by other situational variables such as the playing staff and the approach of the opposition. Such variability further compounds the difficulty in predicting the performance outcome.

Irrespective of the difficulty in identifying the important determinants of performance it is clear that any model that attempts to improve football performance needs to be multi-dimensional. As such the training and preparation strategies common within the game will

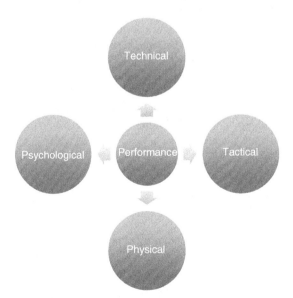

Figure 12.1   Diagrammatic representation of the factors that determine football performance at the individual player level

include both activities targeted at both the technical and tactical and physical/psychological demands of the sport. Modern fixture schedules within professional leagues are, however, incredibly demanding: it is not uncommon for a top-level team to play two games per week for the majority of the competitive season. This situation has been one factor in the involvement of non-technical/tactical experts in the areas of game preparation and performance. It is now far more common for clubs to operate with a diverse range of support staff who fulfil specialist roles related to the performance of both the individual and the team. Although these individuals can fulfil relatively diverse roles depending upon the club in question, they are frequently categorised broadly as "sport scientists." These staff together attempt to create frameworks of principles and practices that attempt to increase the likelihood that a given performance outcome (individual or team) will arise. Such frameworks not only draw on the experience and practical skills acquired by managers and coaches but also recognise that at times the scientific evidence base associated with the sport can be crucial.

Key areas for consideration in performance support programmes in football

Performance planning is ideally only one component of a holistic multi-disciplinary support system that is implemented within a specific football organisation. While communicating generic principles of a support strategy may be of some use to the interested reader, it should be stated from the outset that bespoke strategies individually tailored to each organisation offer the best chance of success. Such bespoke approaches are important if the chances of success are to be optimised. Effective performance support programmes will frequently include a number of areas of specific focus in an attempt to improve performance (Burgess and Drust, 2013). The four primary areas that determine performance are in turn frequently influenced by secondary considerations; for example, physical performance is impacted by the nutritional support of players. The role of effective strategies for injury management and prevention is also vital, as these can influence both individual player and team selection.

Figure 12.2 provides a representation of the major areas that are frequently included in performance support programmes within professional football clubs at the senior level. The attention given to any one area will be highly dependent on the characteristics of the practitioners developing the strategy (e.g., skill base, level of knowledge, personal philosophy) and the specific requirements of the individual players and the club. For example, successful teams that face larger numbers of fixtures in short time scales may strategically target physiological nutritional and psychological recovery strategies, while teams who compete in fewer competitive fixtures with poor fitness levels may concentrate on physiological development. Alternatively, teams who may

Figure 12.2 Common areas of focus for performance support programmes in elite adult football organisations

be performing poorly from a tactical perspective may place a great emphasis on understanding their approach to games through performance analysis. The most effective systems will integrate all these individual areas into a multi-disciplinary programme of player support. The potential areas of performance support in such multi-disciplinary programmes for players can be broadly defined into two key areas: (1) match preparation strategies and (2) strategies around the support of players for training.

Strategies for match preparation

Key activities on a match day primarily involve the preparation of players for the game, performance optimisation during the game, and then the initiation of the recovery process following the completion of the match. These areas require the co-ordination of various inputs that impact the physical, mental, nutritional, and tactical and technical considerations of the team. Another important contribution during the preparation for performance comes from the medical team at the club. These individuals are integral to not only supporting individual player preparation strategies that are medical in nature but also the on- and off-field management of any acute injuries that may occur in the game. It is now not uncommon for between five and 10 support staff to accompany the technical coaching team to a competitive fixture and play an important part in the attempt to deliver a winning performance on the field. Other requirements will include the planning and implementation of effective travel strategies. These may be especially important when the time between fixtures is short and the impact of travel fatigue and/or time zone shifts needs to be minimised. These travel strategies may also be developed to facilitate the recovery of the players after the game under such circumstances (e.g. modes of travel to encourage the use of compression garments, portable massage/electrotherapy, and sleep). This will especially be the case when the time between games is short (less than five to seven days).

Performance support priorities during training

Better preparation during training will result in players being more likely to withstand the demands of competition. The daily delivery of effective training sessions requires regular planning and communication to facilitate smooth programming on a week-to-week and day-to-day basis. This is largely determined by the competitive fixture programme that is relevant for the team in question. The overall plans for the squad can be influenced on an individual level by the specific performance requirements of individual players. These may be determined by factors such as individual weaknesses as a consequence of injury or the need to do additional training for those in the squad who are not regularly competing in the fixtures programme.

The development of the annual training plan is usually organised around two key periods; pre-season and the competitive season. For professional teams, the pre-season period typically ranges from six to 10 weeks in duration. The main challenge during this phase is to plan and deliver a training programme that balances the stress of training with the need for recovery. This is because the exposure of players to high volumes of training during this time period can lead to fatigue and burn out in the short term or during the season proper. As a consequence, any plan that is developed needs to be flexible in so far as it may need to be adapted at relatively short notice. Adopting a flexible approach to training does not however pose a major problem if the overall philosophy of the training plan is maintained.

In-season programming (once fixtures are determined) is largely dependent on the manager/ coach preference on training planning. The philosophy of performance staff is also influential at times when the relationship with the manager/coach is positive. As a result of these influences, the mutually agreed programme often strays from common theoretical planning models (Malone et al., 2014). This frequently leads to a different approach to that taken by practitioners working in sports where the competition schedule and athlete selection are more predictable, thus enabling the training program to be readily periodised. In leagues where games occur once per week, it is possible to assign types of training to various days of the week. For example, Table 2 outlines three possible weekly training scenarios during a week where matches occur on Sundays. Options 1 and 3 allow for a recovery on Monday followed by a day off, whereas Option 2 provides a day off after the game followed by a recovery/light tactical session. If the performance team, in conjunction with the manager, feel that an additional day off is required during the week, then Option 2 or Option 3 might be preferable. If this is not the case then Option 1 might be chosen.

Fundamental to informing the dynamic adaptations to planning strategies that often occur within football is the monitoring and analysis of the total weekly training and match loads, and the impact that these training loads have on individual players. An awareness of the relative "readiness" to play of each individual player within the squad for each given competitive fixture is probably one of the most crucial considerations for the modern performance strategy. This readiness is predominantly a function of the balance between the response to the physiological stress of training and the recovery from previous competitive matches and/or training sessions (Thorpe et al., 2015). Collecting and analysing objective data on these concepts can enable more informed judgements to be made about the relative status of a player. This may in theory help optimise team selection. These procedures become especially important when the team is required to play a large number of games within a short space of time and the rotation of the squad is essential. Effective data collection and analysis can also assist staff in maintaining players' fitness levels when they are not regularly starting in the team's competitive matches. It is also likely that such strategies can help inform the injury prevention strategies that may be in place within the club given that physical overload is an important risk factor for musculoskeletal injury (Drew and Finch, 2016).

The nature of the sport and the varied training requirements for players make the monitoring process within professional football complicated. There is no one method that is universally accepted as the "gold standard" for monitoring training and match loads. This frequently results in clubs using strategies that are determined by a delicate balance between the scientific rationale that supports a given approach and the practicality of applying this methodology in the real world. It is therefore common to see a number of different methods been employed with any given team to analyse the demands of training/matches. Certain principles should be important to the sports scientist irrespective of the method used. The principles of validity and reliability

Table 12.1 Possible examples of weekly in-season training schedules for a team that plays one game per week

Sunday	Monday	Tuesday	Wednesday	Thursday	Friday	Saturday
Game	Recovery	Off	Football Specific Conditioning	Tactical Training	Tactical Training	Tactical Training
Game	Off	Recovery/Tactical Training	Football Specific Conditioning	Off	Tactical Training	Tactical Training
Game	Recovery	Off	Football Specific Conditioning	Off	Tactical	Tactical Training

are clearly always important. It is also essential to not only consider the demands placed on players in the collection of the information but also the demands placed on support staff in terms of analysis time for the data. A clear decision should be made to only collect information if it can be effectively utilised by staff to improve the decision-making process concerning football-related decisions pertaining to players. Large amounts of erroneous data collection will only lead to player unrest, additional work for staff, and poor decisions. It also should be noted that effective monitoring can require data over long periods of time (in excess of three to six months). Such longitudinal information is important as it enables within-player comparisons to be made. These are undoubtedly the most sensitive in the detection of performance changes, player fatigue, or injury predisposition from the data that are available to staff within the football organisation.

The challenges associated with performance programmes in football

The impact of any performance intervention is a function of the applied practitioner(s) ability to take relevant scientific information and apply it within the environmental constraints of the organisation. Such constraints are a consequence of a large number of factors that include the culture of the club, the philosophy of the coaches, the attitude of the players, and the available resources. As a result, there is little consensus as to the specific nature of the operational processes used to support players and coaches at the elite level. The most effective programmes will therefore draw on the most relevant scientific evidence to inform activities and be highly specific to the environment in question. The philosophy of the manager/coach is perhaps the biggest influence on the performance strategy delivery within a team. The performance specialists are fundamentally a component of the team that works for the manager to fulfil the objectives of the club. As such, the performance team are obligated to adhere to the managerial instructions of the coach at all times. These directions can serve to either enhance or restrict delivery depending on the specific nature of the situation. This balance of operational power is infrequently recognised outside of football organisations despite it been fundamental to the day-to-day operation of the football activities for most teams.

Research into high-performance environments and other successful organisations highlight a number of concepts that seem important to successful interventions. These include culture, performance enablers (organisational factors), leadership, and characteristics of individuals (more individual factors; Sotiriadou, 2013). Little knowledge is available that explicitly presents data on the either the proficiency of individuals within applied science and football performance programmes in relevant skills or on how such concepts are actively strategically managed in teams of people in football from an organisational perspective. Inefficiency in these individual and organisational areas of practice may be just as harmful to the overall outcomes of applied performance support programmes as the inappropriate application of the theoretical content that is used to underpin performance solutions. More detail of the considerations in this area will be given in later sections.

A lack of clarity around the effectiveness of applied science and football support programmes, from both a performance outcome and effectiveness of delivery standpoint, must lead to questions around the impact of these structures on the football performance models. If these programmes fail to provide meaningful insights into performance and do not drive positive outcomes to marginal decisions, they can be considered little more than expensive job creation schemes. It may also suggest that such activity is merely a "folly" created to reflect the image that an organisation wishes to outwardly project about it's approach to underpinning player support processes. These programmes may also be associated with challenging operational issues associated with the "data tsunamis" and the associated management, access, and storage of data. Comprehensive evaluations of these issues are however inherently difficult to complete due to the complex nature of the network of factors that would need to be included if any appraisal of effectiveness was to be comprehensive. The de-limitation of these factors to performance-orientated criteria such as the impact of interventions on match performance still make effectiveness incredibly difficult to determine due to the problems associated with defining performance in a scientific context (e.g. individual versus team performance or tactical failure versus individual error; see the section "Understanding football performance"). These issues make effective evaluations of performance support programmes almost impossible from the organisational, logistical, and performance outcome perspective. This is probably the reason that such evaluations are not frequently attempted by applied practitioners within the sport despite their obvious importance to the understanding of the impact of their strategies.

Any uncertainty over the effectiveness of applied interventions may impact the philosophical approach and as a consequence the specific activities that are included in the support programmes implemented with players. High-performance football organisations operate under significant pressure. While innovation in the practical strategies used may have the potential to improve performance, untested protocols in the "real world" are also accompanied by risk. The balance between risk and reward is probably an important driver in the determination of which performance questions practitioners attempt to address. It is understandable that in this context, the potential impact of high-risk strategies may reduce performance support protocols to those which are relatively safe. Such low-risk protocols are unlikely to impact things such as the availability of a player or an individual's short-term performance potential (both important considerations in today's modern support programmes).

While this may ensure that players can play in games, such approaches may not be conducive to optimal preparation. This is because performance models that are inherently risk averse are unlikely to be associated with stimuli that may challenge a player physiologically and that will ultimately lead to athletic improvements (for example, training programmes that do not overload players will not result in physiological adaptations and in the long term improved physiological function). Such approaches may in fact be counter-productive to athletic excellence in the long term by under preparing players for the demands of competition and as a consequence exposing them to higher risks of injury that may be associated with under-conditioning.

Support programmes that do not challenge players with potentially useful, yet high risk strategies, may be one reason why applied performance support has gone a long way to gaining acceptance in the current climate. Unchallenging programmes will be both coach and player friendly and so will, in theory, be supported by such stakeholders as they simply maintain the status quo that exists within the organisation. If such strategies are common in football today it may not be surprising that performance support has expanded in such a way as it has over the preceding decade. This view may be unnecessarily pessimistic as it is feasible that the current state of performance support programmes are simply a reflection of the experience and real world learning of practitioners about what does and doesn't work within the organisational cultures that pervade such clubs and associations.

Frameworks for the delivery of performance services within football: The importance of the performance director

The nature of the performance requirements of the elite player may necessitate the involvement of a number of individuals in any support programme. These staff members frequently occupy specialist roles within the organisation. These roles commonly include strength and conditioning specialists (who may be predominantly gym based), fitness coaches (who may be field based), sport scientists, performance analysts, psychologists, and rehabilitation coaches (who focus on the return to fitness of recently injured players). In addition to these positions that are related to sport and exercise science, specialisms are a range of medical and health care professionals (e.g. doctor, physiotherapist, masseur, etc.). Another key human resource found in the majority of football clubs and organisations is the young trainee practitioner. "Applied science and football interns" are often recently qualified individuals from sport science-related degrees who are in the process of gaining experience of the work of sport science and medicine departments in a professional football club. These individuals, though not officially employed, have proved crucial in supporting the applied science and football expansion in organisations that are limited in their financial capabilities to employ specific staff. This increase in staff and the diversification of responsibilities is a significant departure from the strategies of the past that used to rely on a single individual to provide support in all of these areas. These individuals will fulfil specific roles within a complex organisational support structure aimed at the holistic support of the individuals within the team. An example staffing structure encapsulating all the aspects of performance delivery relevant to sport medicine and sports science for the team is illustrated in Figure 12.3 below.

Another roles, common in Olympic sports, broadly termed performance director, has appeared in the last five to 10 years or so alongside these specialist posts in football. This position broadly focuses on the management of the high-performance support team (Sotiriadou, 2013), bringing leadership and co-ordinated direction to the different components of a multi-disciplinary team and facilitating communication of significant performance issues to the organisation's hierarchy (executives, coaches, and players). It seems that one of the key drivers for these

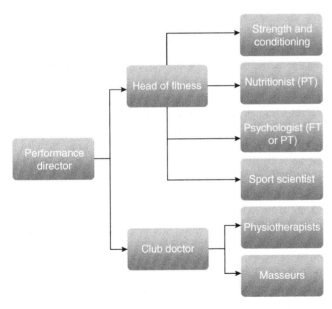

Figure 12.3 An example structure of a high-performance support team for an elite senior professional team in the English Premier League. It is not uncommon for these roles to be associated with multiple personnel in each area. Interns may be associated with day-to-day activities and be managed by full-time staff. These can range in number from a single individual to three to four people

roles is the potential constraint on performance that could originate from the complex organisational and inter-personal dynamics that typify contemporary support frameworks.

Sotiriadou (2013) has suggested that effective management and governance may be an important point of difference in the success of elite sporting organisations. These organisational influences that largely centre around the approaches by which individuals are led and managed have the potential to create frameworks that enable planning, execution, and monitoring of the systems and structures within the football club. For individuals such leadership can foster changes in attitudes and behaviours that may be fundamental in supporting performance as they inspire and challenge others to look beyond their own personal goals to a shared vision. Fletcher and Arnold (2011) support these ideas through empirical research by identifying vision, operations, people, and culture as key areas of consideration for the performance director in high-performance sport. This blend of leadership skill works to promote adaptive and constructive change (a strategy to compete and win) (longer-term objectives), as well as day-to-day management to provide order, consistency, and stability (immediate action orientation). This dual approach (operating "in the now" as well as creating longer-term strategy) would seem to be typified by "nested thinking" in which the day-to-day priorities are organised in relation to a more comprehensive, more enduring vision for the organisation.

The effectiveness of the performance director role is a function of a two main factors. Those associated with the "self" (i.e. the individual characteristics and approach of the person occupying the role) and the environmental factors that are operating within the sport (Arnold et al., 2015). These environmental factors can be further sub-divided into those that influence at both a proximal (within the organisation) and distal (those that exist within a broader framework, i.e. the sport, society etc.; Arnold et al., 2012) level.

Considerations associated with the "self" are under the direct control of an individual, and though clearly complex in nature, possess the potential to be a focus for individual change. Such change, in direct response to the challenges associated with the specific context of a performance director role, can be the platform for improvement in the "self" and the performance of the support systems in the organisation in question. Research that has investigated the important "self"-related factors for the performance director in Olympic sports has highlighted considerations such as personality, health, skill, and experience (Fletcher and Arnold, 2011). Other authors (Fletcher and Arnold, 2011) have identified the need for behaviours to be authentic – that is to say that key actions and approaches should reflect core values and inherently who they (the performance director) are. This does not necessarily negate the need at times to behave in negative ways as the "dark" behaviours often incorporated into the actions of key stakeholders in professional sport organisations are becoming increasingly recognised (Cruickshank and Collins, 2015).

The environment is clearly an important influence on the effectiveness of any performance director role as successful strategies are always context specific. Context clearly has the ability to directly impact the vision, operations, people, and culture – that is to say the factors that are frequently seen as the cornerstones of the role of the performance director. Such ideas are supported by a range of research studies that have investigated the role of the environment on the effectiveness of leadership and management strategies (Jones, 2002).

Framing the environment that is commonly observed in professional football organisations provides a useful starting point to describe the potential challenges to the function of performance directors in this world. Frequently professional football organisations are subject to frequent and rapid changes. This is typified by the short lifespan of the team's key staff, such as managers and coaches. This can result in these environments being chaotic, haphazard, and unpredictable. For example, little specific detail is often available around the specific job roles and responsibilities of performance staff. While this may limit bureaucracy (a potential advantage in fast-moving organisations), it may lead to role confusion, lack of identity (for the individuals involved), and/or role duplication and ineffectiveness (for the organisation). Such conditions may impact an individual's ability to perform as without shared visions around roles and behaviours the organisation may simply be left with multiple variably motivated individuals who are more focussed on "performance irrelevant and self-interested agendas" (Cruickshank and Collins, 2015) than a performance-focussed common purpose. The ability of the performance director to develop shared visions under such circumstances may be very difficult as the potential to move people beyond their own personal goals to simply survive in, and influence, the organisation is difficult.

Football organisations are also challenging for a performance director as a consequence of the complex de-centred power distribution. This complexity is not always clear from organisational charts that may illustrate relatively simple frameworks of stakeholders. The complexity itself is a product of the individuals who exert significant covert decision-making capabilities from less powerful positions. For example, players can be incredibly important drivers of behaviours and strategies despite not being located at key places in the organisational hierarchy. These power distributions may mean that operations and culture may be driven by agendas that are political in orientation rather than by rational performance-based decisions. This again would seem to be a direct challenge for the successful implementation of a performance director.

The traditional nature of the majority of football clubs can provide a further challenge to successful performance directing. It is not uncommon for the majority of the labour force within high performance teams in football to have their experience located exclusively in the football domain (i.e. ex-professional players, individuals who have only worked within football). This insularity can lead to a blinkered approach that only seeks to replicate strategies that originate in past experience. A lack of awareness of the potential effectiveness of the performance director (as they have not previously existed within the sport) may mean that such positions do not easily fit and operate within currently accepted organisational strategies. This may be especially pertinent in the contrast that may exist between the scope of planning typically expected by "traditionalists" within the game (i.e. relatively short term, informed by subjective feel, and reactive) and that usually preferred by performance directors (i.e. longer term, objectified, and planned).

The effective performance director will ultimately be able to dynamically manage themselves in response to the environment in which they are required to operate. In this sense they will, through reflective evaluation, modify, and if required, develop characteristics that enable them to influence the practices and individuals currently in use in the organisation in which they find themselves. Such dynamic and responsive processes are also vital in football as a consequence of the limited ability within the sport to utilise pre-fabricated strategies imported from other organisations. The successful performance director would also incorporate approaches that attempt to evaluate the effectiveness of such things within football organisations. Such evaluations would have the broad aim of attempting to ascertain if the "supporting infrastructure" around the high-performance support programme was "effective" in its general mission. It may also include attempts to understand ways in which the separate "teams" within the overall staffing structure may modify behaviour characteristics to help facilitate effectiveness. As such, these challenges represent the need to strike a balance between the idealistic principles of operation and the pragmatism of action in the real world. These organisational and social aspects of support programmes are seldom included in today's approaches within football despite their ability to clearly influence successful practice.

References

Arnold, R., Fletcher, B., and Molyneux, L. (2012) Performance leadership and management in elite sport: recommendations, advice and suggestions from national performance directors. *European Sport management Quarterly*, 12(4), 317–36.

Arnold, R., Fletcher, B., and Anderson, R. (2015) Leadership and management in elite sport: factors perceived to influence performance. *International Journal of Sports Science and Coaching*, 10(2–3), 386–407.

Burgess, D. and Drust, B. (2013) Developing a physiology based sport science support strategy. In: Williams, A.M. (ed.), *Science and Soccer*. Routledge, London, UK, pp. 223–50

Carmichael, F., McHale, I., and Thomas, D. (2011) Maintaining market position: team performance revenue and wage expenditure in the English Premier League. *Bulletin of Economic Research*, 63(4), 464–97.

Cruickshank, A. and Collins, D. (2015) Illuminating and applying "the dark side": insights from elite team leaders. *Journal of applied sports psychology*, 27(3), 249–67.

Crust, L. and Lawrence, I. (2006) A review of leadership in sport: implications for football management. *Athletic Insight*, 8(4), 28–48.

Deloitte (2017) *Annual Review of Football Finance*. Deloitte, London, UK.

Drew, M.K. and Finch, C.F. (2016) The relationship between training load an injury, illness and soreness: A systematic review and literature. *Sports Med*, 46(6), 861–3.

Drust, B., Atkinson, G., and Reilly, T. (2007) Future perspectives in the evaluation of the physiological demands of soccer. *Sports Med*, 37, 783–805.

Fletcher, D. and Arnold, R. (2011) A qualitative study of performance leadership and management in elite sport. *Journal of Applied Sports Psychology*, 23(2), 223–42.

Jones, G. (2002) Performance excellence: a personal perspective on the link between sport and business. *Journal of Applied Sports Psychology*, 14(4), 268–81.

Malone, J.J., Di Michele, R., Morgans, R., Burgess, D., Morton, J.P., and Drust, B. (2014). Seasonal Training Load Quantification in Elite English Premier League Soccer Players. *Int J Sports Physiol Perform*, 10(4), 488–97.

Sotiriadou, P. (2013) The roles of high performance directors within national sports oragnisations. In Sotiriadou, P. and De Bosscher, V. (eds), *Managing High Performance Sport*. Routledge, London, UK, pp. 1–15.

Thorpe, R.T., Strudwick, A.J., Buchheit, M., Atkinson, G. Drust, B., and Gregson, W. (2015) Monitoring fatigue during the in-season competitive phase in elite soccer players. *Int J Sports Physiol Perform*, 10(8), 958–64.

13

The sporting director
Exploring current practice and challenges within elite football

Daniel Parnell, Ryan Groom, Paul Widdop, and Sara Ward

Background

Over the past two decades, football has developed into a hyper-commodified multimillion-pound industry involving a range of stakeholders from investors, global media, sponsorships, and supporters (Kennedy, 2013). Football is well-recognised domain of popular culture (Parker, 1995), and attracts interests from millions of people worldwide. Governed internationally by FIFA (*Fédération Internationale de Football Association*), football is the world's most popular participation and spectator sport, with over 200 member countries (Jewell, 2009). Whilst many non-sporting and sporting industries across Europe have faced the consequences related to the global financial crisis (Parnell et al., 2017), the football industry has continued to deliver impressive revenue performance (Morrow, 2014). Between the period 2007–2013 club revenues increased, alongside developing substantial revenues (UEFA, 2013; Deloitte, 2015). Despite this buoyant economy, clubs have continued to place their financial sustainability at risk (Kennedy, 2013; Dimitropoulos et al., 2016). However, there is evidence to suggest that clubs often prioritise on-the-field success above financial performance (Dimitropoulos, 2011; Dimitropoulos and Tsagkanos, 2012). One strategy to create more sustainable football operations, embraced in European football but received more reluctantly in English football is the recruitment of a sporting director. This chapter aims to examine the current practice and challenges associated with the sporting director role in elite (i.e., the top two divisions, the English Premier League and English Championship League) football in England. Divided into three sections, this chapter firstly provides the background and context to the development of the sporting director role in England. Section two offers an analysis of semi-structured interviews which were conducted with sporting directors (or those within that senior role under another title) from within football in England, and, finally, section three offers several conclusions from the research and recommendations for future research.

As a business enterprise, football organisations need to perform competitively "on the pitch" (i.e., in football matches) and "in the boardroom" (i.e., financially) (Vaeyens et al., 2005; Slack and Parent, 2006). To explore the structure and organisation of any business is challenging; however, Mintzberg (1979) identified central processes of an organisation, which included an operating core, strategic apex, middle line, techno-structure, and support staff. This chapter seeks to apply these central processes to the football club contexts.

Mintzberg highlighted that work within these parts was based around one (or more) of the following five mechanisms: mutual adjustment, direct supervision, standardisation of work processes, standardisation of outputs, and standardisation of skills. Further, he noted that stability and effectiveness of organisations is based on notions of order, coherence, and consistency (Mintzberg, 1979). This provides links to elements of Total Quality Management (TQM), which aims to increase an organisation's quality and success through the participation, satisfaction, and commitment of all stakeholders (De Knop et al., 2004). It has been argued that the combined work of all relevant stakeholders of an organisation plays a key role in achieving aims and/or success (De Knop et al., 2004: Slack and Parent, 2006). Organisations appear to observe improved performance of their stakeholders through enhanced and effective management practices, such as organisational structure, quality management systems, and job role and satisfaction (De Knop et al., 2004). TQM appears a worthwhile consideration when exploring the sporting director context in the football industry given that it suggests that enhanced performance of employees can support the effectiveness of the organisation in achieving performance goals.

Decision-making structures such as executive boards are no-doubt important in developing behaviours, priorities, relationships, communication, and goals (Kikulis, Slack, and Hinings, 1995). Full commitment, shared values and goals must be clearly communicated and accepted by stakeholders (Slack and Parent, 2006), and to ensure they are clear on their expectations with respect to their contribution towards the goals of the organisation (Woodman and Hardy, 2001). Some of the challenges associated with this include community failures, ambiguity in the aim of the organisation, role clarity and structure, and the challenge of completing dual roles (Woodman and Hardy, 2001). This will be applied to the sporting director and football club context. Research in organisational studies has illustrated that higher-level decision-making and written procedures enhance communication and can increase an organisation's overall effectiveness (Wilkesmann and Blutner, 2002; Kimberly and Rottman, 1987). Similarly, in elite football clubs across Europe, research has demonstrated a number of different organisational structures that are utlised, yet issues concerning communication (specifically between the first team manager and youth departments) can significantly hamper the effectiveness of the football organisation (Relvas et al., 2010).

With a focus on either first team or academy business, and with poor organisational structures and processes, it has been argued that the hyper-commodification of football and a results/performance orientation has created a win at all costs environment (Gammelsæter and Jakobsen, 2008). This will most likely have an impact on a club's organisation, including factors such as autonomy, goal definition, targets, and performance measurement that contribute to the operating culture and the philosophy that underpins day-to-day working practice within a club (Gammelsæter and Jakobsen, 2008). As such, many clubs have become focused on first team performance. This has created a number of consequences, including increased focus on recruitment of players rather than development of youth players (Relvas et al., 2010). Moreover, the pressure and demand placed on first team managers to deliver instant success has created a revolving door culture in first team management. A recent report by the League Managers Association highlighted that English Premier League and Football League clubs employed an average of 12 managers between October 1997 and November 2017 (BBC, 2017). Indeed, first team managers appear to have burdened a significant responsibility of first team performance and the urgency to deliver success almost instantly. In her book on Football Management, Bridgewater (2010) highlighted the potential challenges of football managers, including identifying talent and managing up. It has been suggested that the sporting directors role is that of a conduit between the first team (and other departments, i.e., youth) and the chief executive officer (CEO), board, or chairman. This allows the first team manager (or head coach) to focus on the business of the first team and would hopefully contribute to a club where first team manager attrition was reduced. This is important, as analysis suggests that changing the manager might not be as beneficial as assumed by football decision-makers (Bridgewater, 2010). Despite this, the revolving door culture continues today, and as we write this chapter during the 2017–2018 football season, eight of 20 Premier League managers to start the season in August 2017 had lost their job by the end of January 2018 (i.e., Frank de Boer, Craig Shakespeare, Ronald Koeman, Slaven Bilic, Tony Pulis, Paul Clement, Mark Hughes, and Marco Silva).

The hyper-commodification of the game has no-doubt added to this increased scrutiny and pressure placed on first team managers. As clubs bolster their executive management functions from the CEO, through to marketing, the first team manager has more stakeholders to consider. One addition to this executive management is the sporting director, or director of football. Little is known around the role of sporting director in Europe or England, and there is very little research on the role in these contexts and globally. The sporting director role appears to vary from club to club, depending on the ideology of those at boardroom level. Broadly, in Europe the sporting director would lead on all business and operational aspects of the game, whilst the head coach would look after training of players (Bridgewater, 2010). However, English clubs appear to combine the role of head coach with the more traditional role associated with the first team manager, leaving them with much of the responsibility of identifying players and negotiating the signing of players, unlike their European counterparts (Bridgewater, 2010). Since the publication of Bridgewater's research in 2010, as a result of the competitive nature of football both on and off the pitch, clubs have developed strategies to enact an advantage over their competitors. Whilst in Europe professional football clubs have led the way in this strategy (i.e. the recruitment of a sporting director), football clubs in England have remained reluctant to embrace this change, with the first team manager maintaining their (or his) stature as leader of a club. Despite this, incremental TV revenues have seen the English Premier League grow as the world's most commercially valuable football league. This has attracted new ownership in clubs and a new rigor to protect these owners' investments. As such, more professional football clubs in England have adopted this position within their organisation, putting in place systems and processes that are more professional and systematic, rather than having decisions based on individual knowledge and feelings; one such example is recruitment. Indeed, there is greater emphasis on professionalisation and technical capital. This appears particularly important and suggests a change in the role of first team managers, helping address previously identified challenges (i.e. managing up, managing, and identifying talent) (Bridgewater, 2010).

Despite ongoing favour for the archetypal traditional football manager "the gaffer," who has overriding control over all footballing business at the club, an increasingly popular alternative to this traditional model of management, is a sporting director model. The role of the sporting director is yet to receive a clear consensus on the purpose and scope of the role, even the title itself has been used interchangeably with technical director, director of football, and head of football operations, all used to describe a broadly similar remit at different football clubs. For the purpose of consistency within this chapter, we refer to the sporting director, yet we will accept that each club is a unique context and operation, and therefore structures and titles may vary. Although a popular role across Europe, the adoption of the sporting director role in England has remained controversial, given the cultural and symbolic attachment to the role of the football manager.

The majority of clubs in the top leagues of Spain (e.g. Atletico Madrid), Italy (e.g. Juventus) and Germany (e.g., Bayern Munich) currently employ a sporting director; however, there is a growing number of English clubs utilising this position (Church, 2012). The growing influence of directors and owners of professional football clubs in England is currently attracting considerable media attention (Kelly and Harris, 2010). As such, the spotlight is on football clubs to enact operational changes to provide performance success on and off the pitch.

The sporting director role can cover a senior management role, with responsibility for the performance of various sporting departments that typically make up an elite professional football club. Theses sporting departments could include the first team, the academy, talent identification, and recruitment (i.e., scouting and associated processes), sport science and medical, performance analysis, etc. Through his work on the firing of head coaches, Nissen (2016) highlighted that the head coach–sporting director relationship is essential. This power relationship shifts dependent on on-field football performances. This is due to the role the sporting director plays with respect to human resource management. The sporting director ensures that an organisation is appropriately staffed, i.e. they are concerned with recruiting, selecting, and developing the people who are required to fill different roles in the organisation (Torrington, Hall, and Taylor, 2008; Nissen, 2016). Despite the relationship between the sporting director and head coach being explicitly about performance, when performance dips it is traditionally the head coach who is "blamed and fired," often at the hands of the sporting director (Nissen, 2016). Nissen (2016) advocates that head coaches should be fluent in the organisational structure of the club, and in the status, position, and culture created by the sporting director.

For the sporting director to deliver a strategic plan and operate as a custodian for the club's sporting performance, they often have responsibilities for these functions and the development of both day-to-day working culture and the playing style (sometimes referred to in England as the "DNA" or elsewhere, such as Spain, as the "Methodology") (Parnell, 2017). The sporting director will often act as the intermediary between the strategic apex of a football club's ownership and directors (i.e., the board, CEO, or chairman) and sporting departments (Relvas et al., 2010).

The sporting director's priorities may include supporting a number of department heads and assistants that contribute to the first team and academy departments and ensuring there are clear goals and communication processes. A failure to address these issues within elite football environments can negatively impact upon organisational effectiveness (Gibson and Groom, 2018; Relvas et al., 2010). In addition to attending to managerial and organisational issues highlighted by Bridgewater (2010), Gibson and Groom (2018) and Relvas et al. (2010) through "managing down," sporting directors are also responsible for developing a positive working relationship with the owners, chairman and board through the process of "managing-up," the identification and recruitment of the best talent (on and off the pitch), within budget and development of a club-wide football philosophy (culture) to support the clubs sporting strategy. The sporting director is often renowned (and judged) for their recruitment of players *into* and *out of* the club, and due to the increased financial resources within football, this role function is often highlighted by the media/press as the key success measure of the position (i.e., transfer fees paid and recouped based upon perceived player quality and value for money and overall profit/loss balances). Yet, the sporting director role often receives little attention for developing key mechanisms of the organisation related to work processes or skills (Mintzberg, 1979), or how they can attend to employer satisfaction from consistency, to goal clarity, to community (De Knop et al., 2004), and the ability of the sporting director to build, support, and develop organisational culture aligned to organisational objectives (Gibson and Groom, 2018). As a result of this, the recruitment of sporting directors may to lean towards candidates with a talent identification focus rather than a broader skill-set and capabilities associated with strategic and operational management.

The sporting director role is considered an essential role in European football clubs, yet still treated with suspicion by some in English football, a norm perpetuated by a suspicious media.

One experienced English Premier League manager branded the role "a joke." This appears to stem from incongruence between the power structure between the first team manager and sporting director (Edwards, 2014). Indeed, some managers may have found the new role a threat (James, 2013), particularly in terms of recruitment (Smith, 2014). Yet, it is the responsibility of the sporting director to ensure the club is at the forefront in terms of best practice, best recruitment, and most effective strategies. This allows the first team manager to primarily focus on man-managing the 25–30 players in the squad, taking training, picking the team, and selecting the right tactics. Despite the first team manager being the traditional leadership role in football (Molan et al., 2016), the sporting director is primarily in place to support them, and not, as misleadingly portrayed, to try to replace them. The following section of the chapter offers an analysis of semi-structured interviews which were conducted with sporting directors (or those within that senior role under another title) from within football in England and hopes to provide both industry and research considerations and recommendations.

Analysis

Through our roles working in elite sport and supporting senior sporting executives, we as authors of this chapter have been privileged to operate across various aspects of the elite football industry, covering areas as broad as ownership, governance, change management, corporate social responsibility, performance analysis, recruitment (executive, support staff and players), coach education, and (executive) mentorship. These experiences included applied research, full-time positions, and consultancy work with a number of English Premier League and Football League clubs. Within our position, to further understanding and assist in the education of the role, we have a responsibility to use the access and data we have accumulated responsibly. In this respect, we have ensured the contributors to this research are anonymous. Our intention with this chapter is to examine the current practice and challenges associated with the sporting director role in elite football in England to inform industry practice and future research. We hope this will prove informative and accessible for those in academia, the football industry, and broader football stakeholders. The primary source for the data presented within this chapter was collected between January and September 2017. The participants' identities are protected; however, we have provided an indication of the participants' experience for the reader to contextualise the data. All interviews (data N=10) were undertaken with sporting directors across English Premier League and English Championship football clubs. This examination of the sporting director role within football in England explored three key areas: (i) knowledge and understanding of the role, (ii) current practice across football contexts, and (iii) associated challenges within the role. As such, the following analysis is split into these three discrete areas.

Knowledge and understanding of the sporting director role

The role of the sporting director is difficult and challenging to define. There is clearly juxtaposition within the role, having different interpretations and symbolic attachment for different stakeholders in the production and consumption process, notably those within a club and those outside, namely media, commentators, and fans. We asked the participants about the title of the role and what the different variations meant to them:

> clubs and owners use all kinds of titles from Technical Director, Head of Football Operations, Director of Football, Head of Performance and the sporting director....
>
> *(Dave, director of football, Premier League club)*

The participants appear to share an indifference to the title of the role and the resultant perspectives of people:

> I don't get hung up on title…. Look, you can call it what you want. It doesn't matter too much as it's not the title it's the role you have [which is most important] ….
>
> *(Jonny, head of football operations, Premier League club)*

> I understand that some fella's just want the title, but for most of us it's the right job that matters. It's not the title, it's the actual role that counts.
>
> *(David, technical director, Premier League club)*

The title of the role does not appear to concern the majority of sporting directors interviewed. Despite this, variations did emerge during the discussions:

> I think that technical director is more limited to first team, academy and recruitment [department's], whereas the sporting director is much wider [looking after the entire sporting strategy/business] …
>
> Director of football or sporting director is the same for me because at Collington United [Premier League Club], I was director of football but I was doing exactly the same job as I was at Torrington Park FC [Premier League Club] being a sporting director. So it is the same thing.
>
> *(Rueben, sporting director, Premier League club)*

In an era of intense internal and external scrutiny faced by football clubs, these small variants undertook by those responsible for selecting the title of sporting director during their recruitment process, often CEO or boards or chairman of football clubs, may create unintended issues:

> Head of football operation is probably, either doing the role of the sporting director but the board do not want to deal with the aggravation of having a sporting director, having that title at the club they say that they are head of football operations so that the press will leave them alone.
>
> Sometimes the head of football operations has a lesser role he will not deal with the academy day-to-day, for instance, or academy recruitment, he will just deal with first team football matters. In most of the time, the individual will quite often report to the [first team] manager, whereas a sporting director will not report to the manager but will report to the board. So they are probably the biggest differences between head of football ops and sporting director.
>
> *(Jonny, head of football operations, Premier League club)*

The slight change in title of the sporting director may create issues for external stakeholders:

> It's ok to have the sporting director title, but when everyone thinks you have the full role and you don't, it can cause trouble. If the press and fans, or even just the lads in the academy think you have an influence on recruitment [i.e., transfer in and out of players], when you don't, then basically your head's on the line.
>
> At my last club, because no-one really knew who was in charge of transfers it ended up with other clubs and agents [i.e., intermediaries] getting caught between me, the chairman and the first team manager. It was a bit embarrassing and not good for business. This stuff has to come from the top and needs to be communicated.
>
> *(Jason, head of football operations, Football League club)*

Titles in the football industry can be confusing but providing that the functions and responsibilities are clearly understood within all of the football structure of the club then the title becomes less important. The titles only differ because of a lack of understanding or confusion about the implementation of the role.

(David, director of football, Premier League club)

There are many titles and yet there is little consistency in job descriptions. In my case I am vice chairman of football. I believe my job description is more important than the title. I also believe I am by definition the true sporting director …

… The technical director can mean anything, in some countries this can be the head coach (Director Tecnicos in Spain, Argentina). The guy who heads up the coaching staff (Entrenadors) in Holland it could mean a position above the head coach responsible for all of the technical department but working alongside the head coach (trainer). I am happy with the term director of football, it is a sport specific sporting director. Head of football operations is not a good descriptor and could be misleading as it implies a logistics role. In some clubs this is an executive level title for the club secretary which generally involves administration. Sporting director works perfectly for federations or governing bodies; providing it truly describes the person ultimately responsible for the sport.

(Carl, vice chairman of football, Premier League club)

The subtleties in the use of the title, the role, and the communication of the role can create misunderstanding with external stakeholders such as fans and the media (or even other clubs seeking to undertake a transfer). Job roles will be an important consideration for football clubs to address (De Knop et al., 2004). Woodman and Hardy (2001) conclude their research by stating that poor communication and blurred lines of roles and responsibilities are the main triggers for stress, ambiguity, role duplication, and repetition, which results in the failure of the organisation to achieve its strategic aims and objectives. It would be pertinent for football clubs to ensure clear communication of job-roles across internal functions to ensure organisational performance progress (Woodman and Hardy, 2001; Slack and Parent, 2006). Externally, this could point towards misunderstanding by the CEOs, boards and/or chairmen, undermining their authority and leadership of the club. Further, this could hamper football transfer business, whilst creating unnecessary questions related to responsibility and accountability at senior and executive board level (Kikulis, Slack, and Hinings, 1995). This also suggests that the lack of clarity in decision-making, job role, and communication could have consequences for job satisfaction and subsequently organisational performance (De Knop et al., 2004; Relvas et al., 2010).

Current practice across football contexts concerning the sporting director role

The following extract was shared by another sporting director interviewed, who had seen a wide variety of job roles undertaken personally and observed others within their network. During these questions, the participants spoke fluently about the "sporting director" job role and how it should be closely linked to senior leadership responsibilities:

the sporting director must carry the responsibility of balancing the risk/reward for the organisation – and as a senior executive or member of the board – with the medium to longer term in mind. They therefore have to work with a wider vision or philosophy – signed off by the board – as their framework to decision-making. Key components in this can be playing style, player development policy, club culture, and conduct.

(James, director of football, Football League club)

This corresponds with research undertaken by Relvas et al. (2010) who interviewed heads of youth development across 26 elite-level football clubs across Europe. He identified two organisational structures. One structure, evidenced in 18 football clubs, positions the sporting director as a link between the executive board and two distinct football environments (i.e., youth and professional). Relvas et al. (2010) highlighted that 14 of the football clubs (and sporting directors) he visited as part of his research placed greater emphasis on the professional (or first team) aspect and the rest of club worked around this. Our participants mostly highlighted that the sporting director usually works below the board

the sporting director should work with the first team manager, but sit above them in the hierarchy....

(Jonny, head of football operations, Premier League club)

You need to work below the CEO on all sporting aspects of the business. This is usually part of working with, but below the board.

(Thomas, director of football, Premier League club)

You need to be an ally of the first team manager, but above them in the hierarchy. You need to be able to work with them. This doesn't mean you need to be on the board.

(Santos, technical director, Football League club)

This offered a number of potential organisational structures for the sporting director. Accordingly to Mintzberg (1979), the sporting director would work middle-line, below the strategic apex (i.e., the board). Whilst this suggests that some operating within the industry are flexible provided the role is clear and a senior sporting position, others highlighted that there should be no compromise:

A director needs to sit on the board. A director is a director and clubs need to commit to that so you can do the job. I don't understand why anyone would take a [sporting] director role in title and not insist on being on the board.

(David, director of football, Premier League club)

Look you get different types of people in the industry. Some with a coaching background, some who have just done recruitment, and some who have just done operations roles. What you get is people who will take the title, and sometimes the role regardless of a seat on the board. They will be happy with that. That's just the nature of different types of people getting these jobs.

(Peter, head of football operations, Football League club)

In a football club, key decisions related to strategy are decided in the board room. If you don't sit round a table with the CEO and Director for Finance, how can you possibly ensure your strategy is presented correctly, to influence decisions, to ensure you get the support you need? You can't. You can't really lead properly as a sporting director without being on the board.

(David, director of football, Premier League club)

Relvas et al. (2010) identified one other structure evident in eight clubs across Europe. This structure included an executive board, but it was responsible for both youth and professional (first team) environments. This usually included two vice-presidents with respective responsibility for the football departments (i.e., one for youth and one for first team). Across our interviews there did not appear to be an overarching agreed expectation for the position of the sporting director within the organisational structure of a football club. That said, throughout our research, very few sporting directors held a board position. It would appear that the majority of decisions for football clubs reside within the strategic apex of football clubs with the CEO (board or chairman) (Mintzberg, 1979). Whilst, this leaves the sporting director in a middle-line position, it would place them above the first team manager.

In this situation, the sporting director would create the link between the first team manager and the board. Structurally, this could also result in an increased level of responsibility and accountability for a number of heads of department (e.g., recruitment, sport science, medical, performance analysis, etc.). Whilst this may soften the pressures placed on the first team manager (Bridgewater, 2010), it may also create skepticism surrounding the role of sporting director in the recruitment and release (firing) of the first team manager (Parnell, 2017). It is vital that clubs address robust communications coupled with clearly defined roles for football clubs to achieve high performance (Woodman and Hardy, 2001). It would appear pertinent to get deeper into the roles and responsibilities of the sporting director to understand this context further. This research project illustrated that whilst job titles and roles differed, the job role was the most important factor for consideration:

> At FC Conleone [European top division club] I was in charge of recruitment academy, player acquisition, and contract management but at Mollington FC [Premier League club] and Easthamton FC [Premier League club], I was in charge of all of this, plus academy scouting, sports science, medical, performance analysis and analytics, player welfare. I was also managing everything at the training ground, all the administration, the club secretary, pretty much everything. Which I did not do at FC Conleone.
>
> At Mollington FC, I was also heavily involved in commercial work, pre-season, which you do not do in French clubs because most clubs in France are not global brands and as soon as you start working in the Premier League, especially with the big clubs you are working within a global brand and you talking about different types of commercial deals and all these aspects.
>
> *(Rueben, sporting director, Premier League club)*

The sporting director can also be seen as someone who can link strategy and culture from the business side through to performance. Indeed, participants explained how different business models can impact upon the culture of a football club:

> The role of a sporting director is crucial in maintaining the club's culture, philosophy and strategy. It is important to lead and manage the heads of the performance department and sustain the clubs culture.
>
> A [first team] mangers job is win on Saturday. The sporting director is the global welfare of the performance environment and the clubs long-term sustainability.
>
> *(Peter, head of football operations, Football League club)*

I think it is about giving some guarantee that there is continuity in the club culture. I think that this is the main thing, stability in the culture and for me the culture in a football club involves business model and transfers. So do you sign players to win at all cost or stay in the division like the Crystal Palace model, to win at all cost which is the Chelsea, Manchester City or Manchester United model, or do you create a business model where you sign young players like the Tottenham business model or the Southampton business model or Dortmund business model?

So that is a big part of culture. Then what role do you give to the academy, that is part of the football culture, or the people that you hire is part of the football culture? … The Premier League and football is more and more about entertainment and results. The football fan based globally is so well educated that trying to win without entertaining is very difficult, especially at the top clubs.

The aspects make the culture of the football club, and the sporting director is there to make sure there is continuity in the culture. If there is one definition or summary of the job, it is having continuity in the culture of the football club. For me it is interesting to see some clubs losing their culture. Mainly because they have lost their business model, signing players for £40,000,000 at the age of 29 or 28. Clubs have to come back to what they are good at, and hiring good people allows you to change that culture back from where there has been a total strategy drift, and that is interesting to see when you look at clubs from the outside.

(Jonny, head of football operations, Premier League club)

There is clearly a variety of approaches to implement, but there is a common understanding that the sporting director job-role shifts across club contexts:

The role concerns recruitment, first team, sport science and medicine/medical, performance analysis, the u23s, academy and training ground. There will be people that say the role isn't just about recruitment and they are right. But if you get that wrong, you won't be in the job much longer.

(Thomas, director of football, Premier League club)

Several commentators explain the recruitment should not be the most important factor for a number of reason. However, every participant placed great emphasis on successful recruitment:

The most influential condition within the architecture is playing talent – for a number of reasons. Better players increase the potential of the team greater than any other component. They also carry the highest cost (and therefore risk to the business – typically 50–100+ per cent of turnover). This is, as a consequence the first consideration and the acquisition and management of this talent leads the agenda in regards to other functions in the sporting directors organisation.

(David, director of football, Premier League club)

I always say to people "you are only as good as your last signing" sadly. The culture in English football was so against the sporting director at the time, you are talking about 12 years ago when Tottenham Hotspur FC first appointed one, the press were very anti-sporting directors "it will never work in England bla, bla, bla, bla" but now everybody has got one. The focus is primarily recruitment.

(Rueben, sporting director, Premier League club)

There are two strategies in a football club: Firstly there has to be a business strategy which underpins the performance of the team. The more revenue generated, the better the investment can be in the team or the sport. The sporting director "directs the sport" and that should be everything to do with the sport. Using and selling players, hiring and firing managers and coaches, setting targets and objectives within the culture values and philosophy of the club and providing guardianship of that culture and those values. Where sports performance is concerned the true sporting director is the ultimate decision-maker and the holds responsibility and accountability for that performance. I think many incumbents of the role under this or any of the other titles rarely have this full level of responsibility. They are rarely board-level directors and most often the big decisions regarding players and coaches and budgets are made by other executives (CEOs) or owners/chairpersons. Big decisions made by inexperienced or non-sporting directors.

(Carl, vice chairman of football, Premier League club)

There appears to be a variety of job roles undertaken under the broad guise of the sporting director. The ambiguous transparent nature of the environments and job role appears fertile ground for misinformation, poor communication, and mistrust. All of which could hamper the progress and development of the sporting director, especially in forging the dyadic relationship with the first team manager, and the external perception of the role by fans and the media.

Associated challenges surrounding the sporting director role

This final section aims to provide a number of shared challenges associated with the sporting director role presently and in future. One major finding concerned the relationship between the sporting director and the first team manager:

The biggest challenge is that the industry gains a better understanding of the role. boards and owners appear to have difficulty understanding that what matters more are the functions and responsibilities of the role are more important than the title. If they first recognise the functions needed within their club then they will be able to devise a defined structure that they will be able to oversee knowing what the role entails. More help for the board/owner to understand the requirements will be necessary to achieve this.

(David, director of football, Premier League club)

Managers are fearful of their power being shifted at a club, Trust is the biggest fear. Not enough education given to chief executives and owners on how the sporting director can help a club and define the role. Opportunities to explain the role and current models at different clubs that are in operation.

(Thomas, director of football, Premier League club)

Football's conservatism, known as tradition has historically hindered progress on many fronts. In Britain the role of the "manager" has almost become a "cult" figure. It is perceived that these guys have some magic formula or secret algorithm for success. This adulation results in absolute power and ultimate decision-making being demanded by these big ego celebrities. Often this control is handed over by star-struck executives or owners. The biggest challenge for the development of true sporting directors in football is the cynicism for the role from both executives and "managers." This is slowly changing as ownership is transferring from local millionaire fans to billionaire business men who do not want one man with little or no business experience handling millions of pounds in funds. The longevity of the manger is decreasing year on year and most cannot expect to be in a job for over two years.

Managers are increasingly narrowly focussing on results and owners becoming increasingly impatient. The owner prefers to refer to his manager as head coach and is handing responsibility for the wider football operation, youth development, and the long-term future of the club to someone who is expected to stay longer term. These people are the pioneer sporting directors and their successes will determine the pace and trajectory of the profession.

(Carl, vice chairman of football, Premier League club)

Clarity around the job role appears to have added to the mistrust between the first team manager and sporting director. Clear communication in the recruitment of the sporting director from the apex of the organisation should bring clarity to job roles and organisational goals (Mintzbery, 1979). Indeed, with everyone in the club being unaware of the organisational goals it is likely to hamper quality management (De Knop et al., 2004). The absence of this communication and clarity may continue to hamper clubs with ambitions to enhance their operational performance (Woodman and Hardy, 2001). As such, first team manager scepticism may continue, resulting in the missed opportunity of an ally within the club, through a sporting director, and the continuation of the first team manager merry-go-round (Bridgewater, 2010). Finally, it appears pertinent to highlight comments that help understand the focus of the recruitment surrounding the role and the challenges in building an organisation prepared to achieve a long-term aim:

> There are sporting directors or directors of football in League Two. It is very different on the continent, the press and the fans, they look at signings obviously but the press don't come after sporting directors as they used to do in England at the time.
>
> But I didn't really care to be honest, sometimes it was frustrating but I didn't really care. The issue isn't when the fans judge you or the press judge you it's when the people who employ you start to listen to them. That is how you lose your job. But think that if you are getting influenced by taxi drivers and bloggers and whoever, probably you shouldn't run a football club. I've got nothing against taxi drivers, it's just an example [laughs].
>
> You cannot have a helicopter view because you need to get your hands dirty very often. But you can't have a view from too low because you forget the helicopter view. So you need to always find the right balance between short term, medium term, and long term.
>
> And when you are caught in the drama of running a Premier League club day-to-day, where at a top club you play between 50 and 60 games, without the friendlies and you deal with people getting knocked out of the World Cup and you need to deal with that or they get injured and you need to deal with that, sacking managers, appointing managers. The difficulty is always trying to find the balance between the three aspects: (1) short term, (2) medium term, and (3) long term.
>
> So that is the biggest challenge for a sporting director if you are day-to-day you don't think about the long term and if you are long term you don't think about the day-to-day. It's about finding the right balance. When I speak to Dave (Brailsford), it's that same thing in cycling, when I speak to Billy (Beane) it's the same thing in baseball. Whatever the sport it's always that same challenge.
>
> *(Rueben, sporting director, Premier League Club)*

This raises further concerns regarding the understanding of the sporting director role internally and externally. Specifically, it highlights the role of the media in being able to influence the strategic apex of an organisation. With the majority of sporting directors not on the board (as highlighted earlier) this raises an issue as their own role as middle-line may be jeopardised as a result of external influences (Mintzberg, 1979). Job stability would be crucial for successful performance of a sporting director; however, if they are not in the strategic decision-making positions they may hit barriers balancing the "day-to-day" against the long-term strategy of the organisation.

Conclusion and recommendations

This final section aims to offer the reader a number of conclusions from the research and recommendations for future research and industry practice. The analysis undertaken with sports directors created several issues for consideration, which are pertinent to conclude this chapter. These are not an exhaustive list of considerations, but those raised by the participants are valued and key for the ongoing discussion surrounding the sporting director role.

Key considerations:

- The title used for the sporting director role is flexible and the roles and tasks associated with the role are complex, interconnected, and varied;
- The job role varies across football clubs, and therefore the knowledge, expertise, and skill required to perform the role may vary. However, some level of sports-specific expertise is required within the role;
- Sporting directors currently do not always assume a board-level position. However, sporting directors are often required to influence senior executives and boardroom decision-making processes (managing both *up* and *down*);
- Internal and external stakeholders do not appear to fully understand the sporting director role and can lead to ambiguity both internally and externally to the organisation. Therefore, this needs to be clearly addressed and communicated.

It is unlikely that football will universally adopt the title sporting director and a set role function across all contexts. As such, it is crucial that the job role within each organisation must be explicit and effectively communicated both internally and externally to the organisation. From a practical perspective, incoming sporting directors must request clearly defined job-roles, areas of responsibility, and role performance criteria, upon which they may be judged. In addition, it is important to have clearly defined organisational structures that identify who the sporting director reports to and who the sporting director directly manages from a departmental and individual employee perspective. Those responsible for recruiting the sporting director must do so with a clearly defined remit and job description in place. In the absence of a consistent title, this is a necessity to ensure executive boards are in no doubt about the scope and goals of the job role (Kikulis, Slack, and Hinings, 1995). This directly relates the variance in job roles across football clubs. Any new or existing sporting director should seek clarity on their job-role and ensure the full-commitment of the executive board, gaining their commitment to the sporting strategy. The job role must be clearly communicated to ensure the support of all stakeholders internally (i.e. CEO, board members and chairman through to academy staff) and externally (i.e. fans and media). This may garner support and understanding during challenging times on and off the pitch when attempting to deliver the sporting strategy and help build relationships internally (notably the first team manager and sporting director) and externally.

We must also challenge senior executives in sport to move beyond a culture of sporting director performance assessments based principally on player recruitment in a simplistic and diminished chief scout model for senior executive work. Whilst football will remain a hyper-commodified industry, such endeavours may help manage the tension between performance in the present and long-term strategy. One outcome culminating from such approaches may be to create a tangible change in the high attrition rate of first team managers (as highlighted by Bridgewater, 2010).

Sporting directors appear to only rarely feature in the strategic apex of the football club (i.e., board level). This raises several issues, not least because the findings suggest that there is a lack of awareness and education surrounding the sporting director role at a CEO, board or chairman level. Currently, with sporting directors mainly assuming a middle-line position (according to Mintzberg, 1979), they are unable to influence and contribute to the key decision-making structures of a football club. Given the structure of football clubs, unless a sporting director resides within the strategic apex of an organisation, they would unlikely be able to positively influence Mintzberg's (1979) five mechanisms. The mechanisms that support the operations of an organisation and that can have consequences. Such consequences may impact upon the development and acceptance of behaviours (related to culture and TQM) (De Knop, 2004), relationships, ensuring clarity in communication and the development of organisation goal (Kikulis, Slack, and Hinings, 1995; Slack and Parent, 2006).

To further the professionlisation process of the role of sporting director within England, additional work is required to be undertaken in the following six key areas:

1 Conceptual clarity – clearly defined remit and role descriptors for the sporting director role for employers for employees;
2 Education – the further development of professional education and qualifications to support the sporting director role;
3 Recruitment and development pathways – the creation of clear career structures and pathways within sporting organisations for the recruitment and development of sporting directors;
4 Research – a distinct body of context-specific knowledge to inform the practices of the sporting director beyond existing disciplinary boundaries;
5 Regulation and support – an independent and inclusive professional membership body to support members;
6 Ethics and code of conduct – a clearly defined set of values and ethical principles to guide professional practice.

Acknowledgements

We would like to thank the sporting directors and football clubs for an insight into their working practice, experience, and expertise.

References

Austin, S. (2017) Interview with Parnell, D., 28 March. [online] Retrieved from: https://www.trainingground.guru/articles/sporting-director-footballs-most-misunderstood-job
BBC (2017) Sackings 'severely damaging' English football, says League Managers' Association. [online] Retrieved from: http://www.bbc.co.uk/sport/football/41954891
Bridgewater, S. (2010) *Football Management*. Warwick Business School. [online] Retrieved from: https://www.palgrave.com/gb/book/9780230238411?gclid=CjwKCAjw8O7bBRB0EiwAfbrThyfgExFNgkrJOnToxfpmo1TgRT-Dn1r9UgW8Dvm8suE4vCe8oVX2uhoCAncQAvD_BwE
Church, P. (2012) Technical Director Report. Professional Footballer's Association. pp. 70–98.
De Knop, P., Van Hoecke, J., and De Bosscher, V. (2004) Quality management in sports clubs. *Sport Management Review*, 7, 57–77.

Deloitte. (2015) Commercial breaks, Football Money League. Sports Business Group. [online] Retrieved from: https://www2.deloitte.com/content/dam/Deloitte/uk/Documents/sports-business-group/deloitte-football-money-league-2015.PDF

Dimitropoulos, P.E. (2011) Corporate governance and earnings management in the European football industry. *European Sport Management Quarterly*, 11(5), 495–523.

Dimitropoulos, P.E., and Tsagkanos, A. (2012) Financial performance and corporate governance in the European football industry. *International Journal of Sport Finance*, 7(4), 280–308.

Dimitropoulos, P., Leventis, S., and Dedoulis, E. (2016) Managing the European football industry: UEFA's regulatory intervention and the impact on accounting quality. *European Sport Management Quarterly*, 16(4), 459–86,

Edwards, R. (2014) The impossible job? How English football can learn to love the Director of Football. *FourFourTwo*. [online] Retrieved from: http://www.fourfourtwo.com/features/impossible-job-how-english-football-can-learn-love-director-football#:ItIHyQ7dYxbhcA

Gammelsæter, H. and Jakobsen, S. (2008) Models of organization in Norwegian professional soccer. *European Sport Management Quarterly*, 8(1), 1–25.

Gibson, L. and Groom, R. (2018) Ambiguity, manageability and the orchestration of organisational change: a case study of an English Premier League academy manager. *Sports Coaching Review*, 7(1), 23–44. DOI: 10.1080/21640629.2017.1317173

James, S. (2013) Angel or devil? How the sporting director is taking root in football. *The Guardian*. [online] Retrieved from: https://www.theguardian.com/football/2013/aug/30/sporting-director-tottenham

Jewell, R.T. (2009) Estimating demand for aggressive play: the case of English Premier League football. *International Journal of Sports Finance*, 4, 192–210.

Kelly, S. and Harris, J. (2010). Managers, directors and trust in professional football. *Sport in Society*, 13(3), 489–502.

Kennedy, P. (2013) Left wing' supporter movements and the political economy of football. *Soccer and Society*, 14(2), 277–290.

Kikulis, L., Slack, T., and Hinings, C. (1995) Toward and understanding of the role of agency and choice in the changing structure of Canada's national sport organizations. *Journal of Sport Management*, 9, 135–152.

Kimberley, J. and Rottman, D. (1987). Environment, organization and effectiveness: a biographical approach. *Journal of Management Studies*, 24, 595–622.

Mintzberg, H. (1979) *The Structuring of Organizations*. Englewood Cliffs, NJ: Prentice Hall.

Molan, C., Matthews, J., and Arnold, R. (2016) Leadership off the pitch: the role of the manager in semi-professional football. *European Sport Management Quarterly*, 16(3), 274–291.

Morrow, S. (2014) Financial fair play-implications for football club financial reporting. *The Institute of Chartered Accountants of Scotland*. [online] Retrieved from: http://icas.org.uk/Technical-Knowledge/Research/Publications/Financial-Fair-Play—Implications-forfootball-club-financial-reporting/

Nissen, R. (2016) Hired to be fired? Being a coach in Danish professional football. *International Journal of Sports Science and Coaching*, 11(2), 137–148.

Parker, A. (1995) Great expectations: grimness or glamour? The football apprentice in the 1990s. *The Sports Historian*, 15, 107–26.

Parnell, D., Spracken, K., and Willward, P. (2017) Sport management issues in an era of austerity. *European Sport Management Quarterly*, 17(1), 67–74.

Relvas, H., Littlewood, M., Nesti, M., Gilbourne, D., and Richardson, D. (2010) Organizational structures and working practices in elite European professional football clubs: understanding the relationship between youth and professional, *European Sport Management Quarterly*, 10(2),165–187.

Slack, T. and Parent, M. (2006) *Understanding Sport Organizations: The Application of Organization Theory*, (2nd ed.). Champaign, IL: Human Kinetics.

Smith, P. (2014) "Directors of football are just a joke" – QPR boss Harry Redknapp weighs in on Tottenham crisis. *The Evening Standard*. [online] Retrieved from: http://www.standard.co.uk/sport/football/directors-of-football-are-just-a-joke-qpr-boss-harry-redknapp-weighs-in-on-tottenham-crisis-9861012.html

Torrington D., Hall L., and Taylor S. (2008) *Human Resource Management* (7th ed.). Essex, UK: Pearson Education.

UEFA. (2013) *Licensed to Thrill*. Zurich: UEFA. [online] Retrieved from: https://www.uefa.com/MultimediaFiles/Download/uefaorg/FinancialFairPlay/01/99/91/07/1999107_DOWNLOAD.pdf.

Vaeyens, R., Coutts, A., and Philippaerts, R. (2005) Evaluation of the "under-21 rule": do young adult soccer players benefit? *Journal of Sports Sciences*, 23, 1003–1012.

Wilkesmann, U. and Blutner, D. (2002) Going public: the organizational restructuring of German football clubs. *Soccer & Society*, 3(2), 19–37.

Woodman, T. and Hardy, L. (2001) A case study of organizational stress in elite sport. *Journal of Applied Sport Psychology*, 13(2), 207–238.

Young, J. (2015) The rise and wane of the English-style manager (and what England will lose when they're gone. *Fusion*. [online] Retrieved from: http://fusion.net/story/125691/the-rise-and-wane-of-the-english-style-manager-and-what-england-will-lose-when-theyre-gone/

14

Strategic management in football organisations

Mikkel Draebye

Introduction

Management of football organisations, no matter whether it is a professional club, an amateur club, a league, or a governing body, is a complex affair:

A) Football organisations, because of the nature of the "product," are almost always *multi-business* organisations. In order to run a club on professional or semi-professional level, the organisation manages multiple value creating activities; The Team (for football results, prize money, and transfer profits), The Game Day Experience (for gate receipts/ticket/ subscription revenues), Sponsorships (for sponsor revenues and contributions), Web site / Fan Club (for co-marketing revenues, advertising, and engagement), Volunteering (for free helpers), Merchandising (for merchandising revenues). There can of course be other areas, but these are the typical ones. If football organisations are compared with similar-sized organisations in other industries – for example, in manufacturing or professional services – the complexity "gap" is enormous. A manufacturing company with 50 employees across production and administration, will almost never have to manage the amount of revenue streams (markets) that a small professional football club would need to manage, and that generates complexity.

B) Many football organisations have a "Political"/"Democratic" dimension since many are membership organisations, where members have voting rights and where governing committees and people are elected. This political dimension adds a layer of complexity that, again in contrast to many traditional small enterprises, is unique for football organisations.

C) It is often mentioned that complexity and uncertainty for football organisations is amplified because of the nature of the product, where the football results do not depend entirely on the team, but also on the opponent. This argument is weak. Compared to other industries where organisations are similarly subject to events beyond their control (competitor moves, changes in consumer preferences, changes in regulation, and changes in technology), football has traditionally been a quite stable environment to operate in. But there are things happening; for example, technology developments in (big) data analytics and advances in wearables and other technologies presents new opportunities and threats. Changes in regulatory frameworks and rule changes likewise are getting more and more frequent, so though football is still quite stable, managers must look out for uncertainty in addition to the complexity.

To manage business complexity with limited resources, which is the situation for many football organisations, tools are needed. One such tool is strategic management.

Strategic management is different from the normal day-to-day management of organisations in the fact that it is preoccupied with how best to meet the organisation's medium- and long-term objectives. There is evidence that without some kind of strategic management system, organisations find it difficult to allocate resources effectively and to efficiently coordinate their actions and efforts.

This role of strategic management as a tool for planning and coordination has played an important role in the success of individuals, teams, and organisations. Think of any successful football entity and you would find an organised approach to meeting specific goals as one of the main reasons behind that success. The same holds true for football organisations that cannot always rely on superior resources or pure luck; and by using a structured approach, they can increase their chances of success and reduce the time and effort it takes them to reach their objectives.

Strategic management can make three main contributions to football organisations, which we discuss in the following sections.[1]

Provide direction

Football organisations are unique in nature because, apart from managing various business and commercial properties, they are entrusted with developing and promoting their club and safeguarding the interests of various stakeholders. This dichotomy of interests creates an inherent risk that the various units and functions within the organisation might not always pull in the same direction in unison. For example, the people and units involved in organising women's football might act and communicate in ways which might prove counterproductive to what other units are doing. Another aspect of a lack of coherent direction involves the organisation following relatively divergent paths (or "zig zagging") in different time periods within a short time frame. Because many of the organisation's goals and objectives can only be attained in the long run, this lack of clear direction makes it difficult for the organisation to meet them efficiently. Strategic management allows the football organisation to chart out a coherent direction for the entire organisation and its various functional units.

Provide decision support

In recent times, football organisations have found themselves growing in size (in terms of strength of employees, volunteers, and service providers) to meet the demands of an increasingly commercial and professional football environment. As a result, the dynamics of decision-making within these organisations have become more complex.

In very small organisations (10 employees or fewer), decision-making is usually centralised with one person making all the decisions (facilitated by the knowledge of what everyone in the organisation is doing) and providing guidance to the other employees. But as organisations grow, it becomes increasingly difficult for leaders to retain the same degree of involvement without compromising the efficiency of the organisation. To avoid top management "overload," a certain level of explicit or implicit delegation to employees must take place. Since it is impossible to write detailed decision-making manuals and guidelines for each employee, "heuristic" decision-making support systems are needed to ensure that consistent decisions are made at all levels. Strategic management allows the football organisation to create such a support system. By having a formalised and documented strategic plan as a guide, employees at all levels in the organisation are more likely to make more coordinated and better aligned decisions on their own.

Provide coordination

Football organisations operate in a complex environment that includes a myriad of different stakeholders and various tangible and intangible resources. As evidenced with organisations in other sectors, football organisations can increase their chances of success by effectively allocating and organising available resources (infrastructure, finances, human resources, etc.) based on clearly defined strategic objectives. For example, if infrastructure development is an important objective in a particular period, then allocating superior resources that allow the responsible people and units the time and money to engage government agencies, apply for grants from international federations, plan investments, etc., will be a key to success even if it comes at the expense of other non-priority areas.

Strategic management allows the football organisation to plan and implement the effective utilisation of available resources to meet its defined objectives.

Strategic management systems

Strategic management systems usually refer to a set of ongoing and interconnected processes within an organisation that can be broadly grouped into the following elements:

Analysis – Strategic analysis is usually the starting point for strategic management and involves monitoring and analysing the internal and external situation of the organisation.

Planning – Strategic planning involves defining an organisation's strategy (or direction) and formulating goals, objectives, and action plans for pursuing that direction.

Implementation – Strategy implementation involves developing procedures and programmes, allocating resources, executing plans and controlling their performance.

The following diagram shows the various elements and processes involved in strategic management systems[2] (Figure 14.1).

While there are no universal rules on how structured and formalised these strategic management systems and processes need to be, a football organisation should ideally, however, have a system in place where a review of the organisation's strategic plans takes place every year, and where plans are updated such that the organisation always has targets for a three- to five-year time horizon.

Strategic management systems are simple and easy to put in place. They do not require a lot of investment in terms of capital, infrastructure, or technical know-how. All that is needed is the buy-in and support from the senior management of the organisation – in the case of a football organisation, its executive committee/board, the president and the general secretary/CEO.

If the football organisation doesn't already have a strategic management system in place, it might take a few years to find a system that truly fits the nature of the organisation and its operational cycles (usually the period of time between presidential elections or major competitions).

One of the reasons why the senior management at some football organisations is reluctant to introduce more structured strategic management systems is a perception that if the organisation

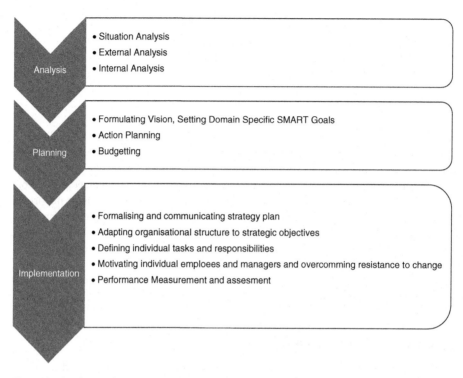

Figure 14.1 **Strategic management system**

fails to meet its stated objectives and goals in the short-term, it will be treated as a failure on the part of the president and/or the general secretary/CEO.

This perceived risk is based on an unsophisticated and old-fashioned outlook on management. Many great business leaders and managers have often had to present results, before their boards and shareholders, which were below expectations and did not meet an initial set of objectives. A strategic planning process, no matter how thoroughly prepared and well executed, cannot always foresee the changes in the internal and external environments that might affect the original plans.

The strategic management system should, therefore, allow contingency or emergent plans to be implemented to mitigate new threats (or exploit new opportunities).

Although strategic management systems are not difficult to set up, the strategic plans and actions that are developed are not always easy to implement. Strategic decisions can often encounter various types of resistance and must be accompanied by appropriate support systems.

Strategy analysis

As discussed in the previous section, strategic management of football organisations involves formulating specific and clearly articulated goals and objectives, designing action plans on how best to reach those goals and allocating resources to effectively implement those plans. The strategic management system would work best if these strategies and plans were based on a profound understanding of the organisation's external environment and an objective appraisal of its internal resources and capabilities. Many strategies fail because they do not properly take into account the various internal and external factors that might adversely affect their outcomes.

Like organisations in other domains, football organisations can also use a structured and thorough process of analysis to arrive at a better and actionable understanding of the environments in which they operate.

Strategic analysis can be thought of as the "ground work" that needs to be done before effective strategies can be formulated and implemented. It comprises three broad and interconnected steps: situation analysis, external analysis, and internal analysis. This chapter introduces these steps and the various tools that can be used for each of them.

Situational analysis

The starting point for any strategy formulation (or review) process is an assessment of the current situation in which the organisation finds itself in, within the broader context of its overarching goals (as laid down in its vision and mission statements). Situation analysis helps management define the overall scope of the strategy formulation process, both in terms of the issues it needs to address and its time horizon. Situation analysis involves defining the organisational context in which the strategy formulation process needs to operate, analysing the organisation's performance, and studying the problems and challenges that need to be solved.

The scope of the organisation's strategy formulation process is dependent on organisational boundaries or context within which the strategic management processes will operate and is an important element for situation analysis. The management team needs to clearly identify if the processes will encompass the whole organisation, its member organisations, or only include specific organisational functions and units. Explicating the context makes the strategy formulation process more focused by eliminating the need for analysis or strategies that are not relevant to the chosen context. For example, if one of the key objectives of the organisation is to boost the public image of a league or a federation, the strategies and plans formulated to meet that objective would require the involvement of various units like the competitions, grassroots development, communications, and marketing departments. Identifying this organisational context during situation analysis would allow for the necessary cross-functional analysis to be conducted, which in turn would result in the formulation of effective strategies.

Analysing performance

The past and current performance of the organisation in various areas provides a good indication of the situation it finds itself in and helps identify issues that need to be addressed.

Performance analysis in football organisations is more complex than in profit-maximising companies. Since the goal of most of these companies is to maximise shareholder value, performance can be easily measured in terms of economic and financial results – profits, return on investment, return on equity, etc. However, since most football organisations are not in the "business" of profit-maximisation, performance must be evaluated on the basis of the organisation's stated purpose and goals. The overall goals of a football organisation are usually articulated in its mission statement and reiterated through various other operational documents like strategic plans, annual reports, etc.

The strategy formulation or review process must depart from a thorough analysis of the actual fulfilment of these defined goals. The analysis must also determine how effectively and efficiently they are being fulfilled. Performance analysis typically involves studying various key performance indicators and comparing them with pre-determined targets or with previous results. Football organisations can also benchmark their results with those of similar organisations to understand how they are performing relatively.

External analysis

Football organisations, like organisations in all other domains, operate in an increasingly complex environment and are influenced by scores of diverse factors, many of which are interconnected. Therefore, as discussed earlier, formulation of effective strategies and plans require a profound understanding of the organisation's external environment and the various factors that can favourably or adversely affect their outcome. For football organisations, four main steps need to be considered as part of external analysis; we discuss these in the following sections.

Domain mapping

Domain mapping, an essential and often mandatory step in external analysis, involves identifying the core activity areas an organisation operates in, as it is typically the first step towards truly understanding the organisation's external environment. Since most of the areas the football organisations operate in are not "markets," they are referred to as "domains" instead of "business areas" or "business units" – terms that are frequently used in business/management literature.

A domain usually refers to an activity area which involves an exchange of goods, services and/or resources (tangible or intangible) between the organisation and a defined group of stakeholders.

Some of the domains that football organisations operate in are simple to identify and the exchange is clearly understood. For example, the sponsorship domain is a domain where the club or league exchange (rent or sell) space they own or control such as hoardings in stadiums, television graphics, players' jerseys, and website banners for a fee (cash or in-kind). The sponsor (a stakeholder) is a customer paying for a product/service, a defined sponsorship package that clearly describes rights and obligations.

Some other domains, for example, where the exchange, the beneficiary (or stakeholder), and the service are equally simple to identify are ticket sales, public fundraising, football academy and stadia certification. On the other hand, however, there are certain domains where the exchange is not inherently clear or obvious. For example, youth development might be one such domain, where the exchange, the service, or the value being created, is not readily attributable between the provider and the beneficiary.

Youth development can be thought of as the process of providing youngsters the opportunity to develop their abilities with the aim of pursuing the sport professionally and/or at an elite level. On deeper analysis, it appears that while the young player is the primary stakeholder in this process, there are other stakeholders (who can influence the domain) in the exchange like parents, schools, local governments, and also the teams that might use the player's services in the future. The exchange also, therefore, is not a direct transfer between the football organisation and the young player but happens through a series of direct or indirect value transfers.

As illustrated in these examples, an ideal starting point for understanding the external environment is by making a simple map of the domains in which the organisation is active (or could be active) and identifying the exchanges and stakeholders in each of them.

There are no fixed templates or blueprints for domain mapping in football organisations, but typically the organisation should list all the domains it is active (or could be active) in. A simplified example of domain mapping for a professional football club is listed below in Table 14.1.

Table 14.1 Examples of domains

Domain Category	Domain
Players	Talent scouting
	Academy
	Coaching and training
	Team and player management
Stadium and facilities	Stadium management
	Training facility management
	Medical center management
Tickets, rights and advertising	Game day revenue and experience
	Sponsorship and advertising
	Digital and TV rights
	Merchandising
Community and fans	Fans management
	Community and CSR
	Volunteer management

Source: Elaboration by author.

Having identified and mapped the domains, the management can classify them into priority and non-priority areas, based on the attention and focus each of them should receive. This would also allow coherent strategies and plans to be developed based on a clear understanding of the relative costs and benefits. After mapping the domains, a logical next step is to identify how the organisation can be successful in each of these domains. This can be done by analysing the key success factors of the domains.

Analysis of key success factors

Key success factors are those factors within a specific domain that determine how an organisation can succeed in that domain. Key success factors for a domain can be identified by finding the answers to two simple questions:

- What drives and determines the stakeholders' behaviour in that domain?
- How can the stakeholders' expectations be met (or, in cases where there is competition, better met)?
- Trying to understand the key success factors for the organisation's domains is often an insightful and interesting exercise which can, in many cases, improve internal analysis.

The ability of an organisation to efficiently execute its strategic plans and actions depends on the resources and capabilities at its disposal. Therefore, as discussed earlier, formulation of effective strategies and plans must depart from an objective appraisal of the organisation's internal resources and capabilities.

Football organisations can use the following tools for internal analysis.

Analysing resources and capabilities[3]

The most thoughtfully designed and well-articulated vision statements and objectives might amount to nothing if they are not grounded in reality. Sometimes, unrealistic goals and objectives can do more harm than good for the organisation by leading to a loss of faith and goodwill among internal and external stakeholders, because the organisation might run the risk of engaging in projects it does not have the resources or capabilities to see through.

Hence, before engaging in strategy formulation, the organisation must take clear stock of the resources and capabilities at its disposal – those that it can readily access and control.

Identification of resources and capabilities is usually pretty straightforward and most organisations have a fair knowledge, without formally taking stock, of the kind of resources that are available (or will be available) to them over the strategic management time frame. The organisation's resources can usually be categorised into four groups – financial resources, tangible assets, intangible assets, and human resources.

As indicated in Table 14.2, some of the resources available to the organisation can be directly measured through various metrics. The organisation's accounting, financial reporting, budgeting, and information systems determine how many and how detailed these metrics are. The organisation's income statement (or profit and loss statement) contains information about its revenue and fundraising levels and also its spending.

Assessment of strengths and weaknesses

To increase the possibility of success, strategies should leverage the areas where the organisation is strong and strengthen other areas where it is weak.

Internal analysis allows the organisation to evaluate its strengths and weaknesses. One way of objectively doing this is to map all the organisation's resources and capabilities on a strengths-weaknesses grid. In this method, all resources are scored and ranked on two dimensions – their importance and their relative strength.

Importance is linked to how valuable and important the resource is for success (usually following an analysis of key success factors). While there is no scientific way to score importance, it is recommended that more than one person assess the importance and an average (mathematical or mutually agreed) be applied to define the score.

Table 14.2 Typical resources football organisations possess

Financial resources	Tangible assets	Intangible assets	Human resources
Examples			
Cash reserves	Land	Brand	Skills and capabilities of
Future funding receivables	Buildings	Trademarks	employees
Revenue generated	Facilities	Reputation	Learning and idea-
Borrowing capacity	Equipment	Databases and contact information	generating potential of employees
		Network	
Metrics			
Revenues	Value of assets	Provide avenues for the older	Employee qualifications
Gross profit	Size and capacity	population to contribute	Pay rates
Cash flows	of facilities	to programmes as	Turnover
Credit rating		volunteers	

Relative strength refers to whether and how well the organisation excels at a certain resource or capability. For example, if the scoring is done on a scale of one to ten, a score of five might indicate that the organisation is about average at a certain resource or capability. Scoring of relative strengths, unlike that for scoring of importance, could be based on scientific methods because, whenever they involve measurable resource indicators, the scores could be a result of comparing the indicators (or benchmarking) with other comparable organisations.

In the example below, a sample list of resources and capabilities has been scored to illustrate the use of the strengths-weaknesses grid method.

After scoring, the resources are placed on a two-dimensional grid listing on the one dimension the strategic importance of the resource and on the other the relative strengths of the organisation[4] (see below example) (Figure 14.2).

The matrix is composed of four quadrants:

Key strengths: These are areas where the organisation has valuable resources and capabilities that are either unique to the organisation or where it is outscoring others.

Key weaknesses: These are areas that are actually important for the success of the organisation, but where the organisation is not performing as well as it should.

Superfluous strengths: These are areas where the organisation is strong, but which are largely irrelevant to the success of the organisation.

Area of irrelevance: These are areas where the organisation is weak, but also which are largely irrelevant to the success of the organisation.

The understanding of strengths and weaknesses is extremely relevant for assessing the solidity of strategies. Strategies that rely on areas where the organisation is generally weak are less likely to be successfully implemented and executed.

The analysis can also be used to assess the areas where internal development is required. The areas where the organisation is weak need to be addressed and there are usually two ways of doing it:

Building the capability internally – For example, football organisations can invest in building facilities, training employees, developing procedures, etc.

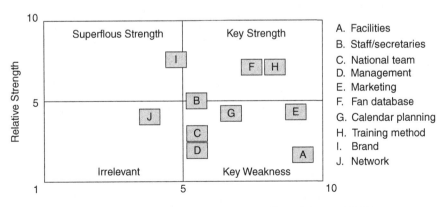

Figure 14.2 Importance-performance matrix (Martilla and James, 1977)

Source: Draebye/Raju.[a]

[a] Mikkel Draebye and P.N. Raju. *Strategic Management of Sports Governing Bodies*. Greyhouse Knowledge, 2012.

Outsourcing the task – For areas that require expertise beyond the core competence of the organisation or where internal capability cannot be easily built, organisations may choose to outsource activities to third-parties. For example, a lot of football organisations use the expertise of marketing agencies to facilitate sponsorship and other commercial deals.

Analysis of resource leverage

Internal analysis also provides the organisation with a better understanding of the resources and capabilities at its disposal that it has not yet fully utilised. In economics and management, this is often referred to as leverage and indicates the degree to which the organisation is utilising those resources and capabilities. For example, fans of a national team are an important resource of the corresponding national governing body in the sense that the organisation, through its owner-ship of the national team, has a privileged position in reaching and engaging the fans. At many football organisations, however, the fan base is usually under-leveraged, in terms of the value that is created for the organisation in comparison to the positive affiliation and identification the sport enjoys. Internal analysis allows for the identification of areas where revenues or other forms of value are being foregone, so that they can be better leveraged.

On its most basic level, the method of testing for leverage is nothing more than a brainstorm-ing tool. For each of the organisation's resources and capabilities (identified in the earlier steps), but most importantly for the ones where the organisation is relatively strong, the following questions need to be answered:

- Is the resource or capability being exploited fully in commercial terms?
- Is the resource or capability being exploited fully from an organisational efficiency point of view?

The first question relates to how well the various possible revenue streams are being utilised. For example, if the organisation has a website that generates a lot of traffic owing to certain unique features, how well is that traffic being exploited commercially in terms of advertis-ing, co-marketing, merchandising, ticket sales, etc.? The second question relates to whether an organisational resource or capability is being put to full use within the football organisation structure. For example, if a confederation or national association has invested in building a foot-ball management system, could this be used by its member organisations?

Strategic planning

Analysis of the organisation's current situation, its internal and external environments and the classification and prioritisation of the identified business issues serve as an important back-ground for the strategic planning process, which essentially consists of two main steps:

- Formulation of the vision, goals, and objectives.
- Design of an action plan for achieving the defined goals and objectives.

An important deliverable from the strategic planning process is a strategic plan, which is essen-tially a guiding document that outlines the organisation's direction and priorities for a defined time period. A strategic plan not only facilitates the effective use of the organisation's resources but also helps in building commitment from all its various stakeholders.

Strategic plans work best when the formulated vision, goals, and objectives are clearly articulated and the designed action plan is implementable and efficient.

Vision, goals, and objectives

There is often a lot of confusion among practitioners with the different terminologies used to describe an organisation's purpose and how those terms differ from one another. For example, the terms "mission" and "vision" have been used extensively in strategic planning at all types of organisations and an oft-repeated mistake is to confuse one with the other.

A mission, and a mission statement, is a short description of the organisation's *raison d'être*, i.e. its reason for existence. It should describe, in a few sentences, the main purpose of the organisation and its areas of activity. A mission statement is typically very broad and timeless. Therefore, organisations rarely change or rewrite their mission statements. On the other hand, a vision is a statement of intent which is valid for a specific time period. The vision statement is supposed to reflect where the organisation wants to be and what it wants to achieve by the end of that time period.

If the organisation wishes to increase its chances of efficiently and effectively utilising its resources towards the aim of fulfilling its mission on an ongoing basis, development of a vision statement is an absolute necessity. While developing a vision that truly reflects the organisation's potential can be a daunting task in itself, publishing and communicating the vision statement to all the various stakeholders can make the process even more "scary." But whether the organisation wishes to make its vision statement and strategic plan public or whether it chooses to use them as internal working documents is a matter of organisational temperament and culture.

The vision is usually general and has a typical duration of three to five years and can be seen as the slogan of that period's strategic plan. It is, therefore, common to see strategic plans named after the duration for which they are relevant, like "Vision 2020" or "Vision 2022." It is recommended that the vision be formulated only after goals, objectives, and actions have been developed. This will facilitate the definition of the overall intent of the organisation for the corresponding time period.

Linking goals and objectives to strategic issues

The process of formulating goals and objectives, linked to the identified strategic issues, is the starting point for the development of a strategic plan, which is nothing but a description of all the activities and actions the organisation needs to undertake to meet its defined objectives. The relationship between strategic issues and formulating goals and objectives is a much more direct one than with the vision. However, for the strategic plan to succeed, the formulated goals and objectives should be realistic and achievable.

Creating a strategy plan

Once the vision, goals, and objectives have been formulated, specific steps and activities needed to accomplish them have to be developed and documented. Although the development of an action plan can seem tedious and detailed, it plays a crucial role in the successful implementation of strategies and must not be ignored.

The process of developing an action plan typically involves identifying different action strategy options. It is often possible for an organisation to reach its objectives through different ways and means. Before choosing the appropriate actions to take, it is important to identify alternative actions to reach the objectives. This can be done through leveraging of the experience and ideas of employees and managers involved in the process, but also by looking at what other organisations have done in similar situations.

Resource requirements and budgeting

Based on the evaluation of the options available, the organisation will have chosen a series of actions aimed at meeting the identified goals and objectives. In order to verify whether the organisation will have the necessary financial resources to execute the plan, projections of the revenues, costs, and investments need to be inserted in the organisation's general budget in order to generate a consolidated budget. If the organisation's new consolidated budgets for the planning period are in equilibrium, i.e. the organisation has sufficient financial resources to execute the plan, the preliminary strategy plan can be finalised. If, on the other hand, the projected economic and financial effect of the action plan on the organisation's budget indicates losses, a need to use cash reserves or a need to take on new debt, the organisation must evaluate whether the plan is feasible or whether some initiatives need to be dropped.

After taking these considerations into account, a revised plan and consolidated budget can be made and finalised.

Finalising the strategy plan

Once the vision, goals, objectives, action plan, and budgets have been developed, they need to be compiled in the form of a formal strategic plan for the approval of the executive committee, board or general assembly. Although this can be done in many ways, it typically involves putting together a written document with the following broad structure:

- Foreword
- Introduction and background
- Mission, values, and vision
- Goals and actions

As discussed earlier, well-documented strategic plans not only facilitate the effective use of the organisation's resources but also help in building commitment from all its various stakeholders. In order that the strategic plans are used effectively by everyone, the strategic plan document needs to be accessible, readable, and well organised.

Implementation

The final and often most critical process in strategic management is the implementation of the formulated strategies and action plans. Strategy implementation is considered by many practitioners to be the most difficult component of the strategic management system.

While effective strategy implementation depends greatly on how well the strategies have been formulated, well-formulated strategies do not automatically translate into the desired results.

Management and research studies have shown that many organisations are unable to match effective strategies with the same level of effective execution.

Some of the reasons why a gap between strategy formulation and strategy implementation exists are:

- The strategies are not known or fully understood by those responsible for their implementation;
- There is a resistance to change within the organisation and among its various stakeholders. This could stem from various factors like neophobia – a fear of the loss of privileges – personal insecurities, etc.;
- There is a lack of clarity or experience with regards to the actual role that each individual or stakeholder needs to perform;
- The employees and stakeholders are not sufficiently motivated or incentivised to fully pursue the formulated strategies.

A common thread among all of these obstacles is the failure by management to fully understand that the organisations do not function by themselves, but through individuals (leaders, employees, volunteers, service providers, etc.). Strategy implementation, therefore, depends on how well these individuals are "activated" to produce the desired results for the organisation.

Effective "organisational activation" and, as a result, strategy implementation depends on 1) how effectively the plan is communicated and shared within the organisation and across stakeholders, 2) whether the strategy is supported by appropriate organisational structures, and 3) whether the people that have to move the implementation forward are made responsible, accountable, and are incentivised

Communicating the strategy plan

In today's open and connected world, communication is often inseparable from the effective implementation of strategies. It is, therefore, imperative for top management to ensure good communication with managers, employees, and other stakeholders.

Designing appropriate organisational structures

An organisation can be thought of as a cluster of various components aligned and working towards a common goal. For the smooth functioning of organisations, these components or functions should be based around common tasks, activities, domains, and/or capabilities. The structure of the organisation is the framework that defines the pattern of relationships among these various components. The existing or proposed organisational structure plays a major role in how well the strategies are executed and implemented. The organisational structures of football organisations should mirror the areas defined in their mission, vision, and strategy plans. This is in line with the accepted theoretical management thinking that "structure should follow strategy."

Designing individual performance appraisal and incentive systems

Just like overall strategic objectives can be translated into targets and budgets for individual functions and units, individual managers can also be assigned and made responsible for specific tasks and targets. A common tool used by many organisations to outline these responsibilities is Management by Objectives (or MBO, as it commonly referred). It involves assigning a number of annual objectives to key managers and employees. Depending on how the MBO system has been implemented, the goal or objective setting is often a participative process where the employees discuss targets assigned to them and provide periodic progress reports and feedback to their managers so that corrective actions can be taken, if required. These objectives are usually a starting point for the evaluation of individual performance whereby the employees are evaluated based on how well they meet the targets and objectives outlined at the beginning of the process. Individual performance is also often linked to bonuses and salaries at various business organisations. This system of incentivising employees based on their performance allows organisations to effectively activate their employees and meet their strategic goals and objectives. These types of performance-based remuneration systems are, however, not very common at football organisations and they must only be introduced if local labour laws allow them.

Governance

Strategic management systems need to be supported by appropriate governance systems. Most football organisations have both an administrative side (ceo/general secretary, managers, employees) and a political/representative/ownership side (president, executive committee, functional committees). In very politicised organisations, i.e., where the "presidential" side dominates, the risk of under-weighing and eschewing the focus on analysis, planning and long-term perspectives is increased. It is therefore useful to integrate a "strategic" perspective in the governance system. This can be done by clearly defining the role of different sides and institutionalising a planning orientation with fixed terms, deadlines, and strategic planning templates.

Innovation and entrepreneurship in football organisations

Strategic management is the bread and butter of success in football organisations. Ambitious but realistic goals, analysis-based decisions and plans together with continuous measurement and improvement systems, will put sports organisations in a position to increase their chances for *grinding* themselves to success. *But*, the world is changing. And the pace of change is picking up. From a technological, legal, and competitive perspective football organisations find themselves in what could be defined as a "turbulent environment." The insights modern data collection and analytics firms and techniques "promise" to provide to football organisations are enormous, disruptive, and very intriguing. Football leagues and clubs can now use demographics, income, and behavioural data to create heat-maps of where to place stadiums, where clubs in the leagues ideally should be placed, how many teams ideally should take part in the league, and which competition format would generate the highest stadium attendance. High-frequency GPS combined with pulse measures and accelerator sensors in players training gear can provide important information for training and injury prevention. Social media and other communication technologies allow for an unprecedented possibility to interact with fans and other stakeholders ... the possibilities are many. Unfortunately not all "innovations" bring value to the organisations. In fact, we know from research into new initiatives (start-ups, new product introductions, new process introductions) that failure rates are quite high (30–80 per cent depending on categories and studies). The dilemma for organisations is that in turbulent environments it dangerous NOT to experiment with innovation, but also risky to experiment too much. Not only because of the intrinsic failure risk of innovative projects, but also because "jumping" on too many fads could jeopardise the stability and long-term orientation that strategic management systems encourage.

The solution to the dilemma is "optimising" the strategic orientation of the organisation. Some organisations decide to spend a lot of resources on innovation and entrepreneurial initiatives. This is the case in the tech sector where companies like Google, Amazon, Facebook, Cisco, Apple, Samsung, etc. allocate lots of resources to R&D, innovation, business development, and mergers and acquisitions. Other organisations spend very little. There is no "blueprint" for how many resources football organisations ideally should allocate to entrepreneurial and innovative activities, but in today's turbulent environment, it should be something.

A starting point for organisations, is to develop an innovation strategy. This is best done by first assigning a director-level person to "own" the domain and after that, by applying innovation and entrepreneurship-specific analysis tools[5], defining a vision for which type of innovative organisation is appropriate in the specific context. Following the vision, different innovative initiatives can be launched. Though, as mentioned above, no general rule can be formulated, it could be useful for organisations to reflect on how much of their development budget is allocated to innovative projects and how much is used on managing the existing activities, and if investment in innovation is less than 5–10 per cent, it is probably too little.[6]

Conclusion

In the foregoing pages the basics of a strategic management system as it could be applied to organisations throughout the football family has been described. Not all organisations can (or should) apply fully formalised strategic planning systems, but moving towards a higher degree of formalisation and analysis-based decision-making is desirable.

Notes

1 For a more detailed description of the multiple roles of strategy for success see: Robert Grant: "Contemporary strategy analysis," 6th ed., Blackwell 2008, pp. 25–7.
2 For a more detailed description of strategy analysis applied to sports organisations see: Mikkel Draebye and P.N. Raju: "Strategic Management in Sports Governing Bodies", In: *Essays in Management*, Greyhouse Knowledge, 2012.
3 For a more complete introduction to strategy analysis from a resource-based perspective see: "Analyzing resources and capabilities," In: Robert Grant, *Contemporary Strategy Analysis*, 6th ed, Blackwell 2008, Ch 5 (pp. 123–68).
4 For a more detailed description of the logic behind this type of assessment see John A. Martilla and John C. James, *Journal of Marketing*, 41(1) (Jan. 1977), pp. 77–9 For a more complete introduction to strategy analysis from a resource-based perspective see: "Analyzing resources and capabilities," In: Robert Grant , *Contemporary Strategy Analysis*," 6th ed., Blackwell 2008, Ch 5 (pp. 123–68).
5 For an introduction to different approaches to innovation management see: Mikkel Draebye Draebye, M: " Return of the entrepreneur – towards a better corporate entrepreneurship definition and taxonomy," *Economia & Management*, No. 2, 2016.
6 For a tool to benchmark an organisation's innovation and entrepreneurial activities see: Duane Ireland, Donald F. Kuratko, and Michael H. Morris "A health audit for corporate entrepreneurship: innovation at all levels: part I," *Journal of Business Strategy*, 27(1) (January–February 2006).

Reference

Martilla, J.A. and James, J.C. (1977) Importance – performance analysis. *Journal of Marketing*, 41(1), 77–9.

15

Finance and accounting in football

Rob Wilson and Daniel Plumley

Introduction

During the last century, football has evolved from a noble sport – played for reasons of entertainment – to a major form of business. With globalisation (see Chapter 2 in this Handbook) there has been an accelerated period of growth in the development of the football industry, by reducing the barriers and differences between countries and emphasising the connections between them. This has led to the building of more than a game to form an industry that has global appeal and one that major commercial bodies seek to be part of. Consequently, such development has increased academic commentary on the financial elements of the game, particularly in European football where substantial increases in revenue have been well documented in recent years. Indeed, the European football market continues to show resistance to wider economic pressures, growing by almost 13 per cent to €24.6 billion in 2015/16. Despite this, the industry persists with the accumulation of debt, at individual club level, as costs continue to rise in line with, and in some cases more quickly than, increases in revenues. This imbalance between revenues and costs is pivotal to the research agenda in this field. The business of football is not ordinary. The emphasis on profit making, so often at the core of mainstream organisations, is routinely substituted with maximising on-field success. As such, football clubs have been leveraged by significant levels of debt – often in the form of "soft (or interest-free)" loans from their owners with a high proportion of club revenue normally spent on player acquisitions and wages. The advent of tougher regulatory practices such as Financial Fair Play encourages clubs to spend within their means or "break-even" seeks to redress this balance but, at the time of writing, is only in its infancy.

Against this backdrop, this chapter will consider the role that finance and accounting play in shaping the business of football, incorporating a number of key themes which include: regulatory frameworks and legal requirements, the balance between income and costs (including the asset valuation of players), exploring financial strategies and performance, and examining financial health through recognised industry techniques which enable us to evaluate the business performance of football clubs and the potential for future growth in the industry.

Regulatory frameworks and legal requirements

The international aspect of accounting is of vital importance to sport given that many areas of the industry are not confined strictly within UK businesses. Indeed, as mentioned above, the globalisation of sport, particularly the integration of various multinational and intercultural sponsors and broadcasters has provided a platform to establish and maintain a worldwide audience, putting international accounting and the financial performance of football clubs firmly in the spotlight. Yet the foundations for all clubs are the same. From a regulatory perspective, football clubs, along with general businesses, have to conform to a set of International Financial Reporting Standards (IFRSs) that have been established by the International Accounting Standards Board (IASB). Companies have been required to publish their financial statements using IFRSs rather than domestic standards since January 2005.

As Chopping (2010) simply puts it, financial statements are the accountant's summary of the performance of a company over a particular period and of its position at the end of that period. Performance in this sense means providing details of what money has been generated and what has been spent, leaving behind a profit or loss, and position refers to establishing the net worth of an organisation once all of the items that it owns and all of the items that it owes have been calculated. Such financial statements are prepared using a number of basic principles as defined by the IASB and are mandatory for all listed companies.

The Statement of Principles

The Statement of Principles describes fundamental rules but does not contain requirements on how financial statements should be prepared or presented; this is achieved under the requirements of company law and the accounting standards outlined above. However, the primary aim of the Statement of Principles is to help the respective accounting standard board(s) to review existing accounting standards and to develop new ones. The Statement of Principles contains and deals with the following key characteristics of accounting information:

- The objectives of financial statements;
- The qualitative characteristics of financial information;
- The elements of financial statements;
- Recognition in financial statements;
- Measurement in financial statements;
- Presentation of financial information;
- Accounting for interests in other entities.

Furthermore, it is vitally important, in the context of making effective business decisions, that the financial information used, or the way in which it is presented and recorded, is useful to the respective target audiences and various stakeholders. Financial information is deemed useful if it is:

- Relevant – Information has the ability to influence the economic decisions of users and is provided in a timely fashion to influence such decisions.
- Reliable – Information should be representationally faithful in a sense that it should report what it sets out to report or could be reasonably expected to represent.
- Comparable – Information enables users to compare the similarities and differences between financial information over time and against other entities.
- Understandable – Information can be perceived by users that have a reasonable knowledge of business, economic activities, and accounting.

The impact of a regulatory framework on football

History tells us that financial problems have been prevalent during the development of most professional team sports and professional football has not been an exemption. These problems have included issues such as tax avoidance, non-payment of liabilities, and creative accounting techniques. One such recent example witnessed a high-profile case in the English Premier League, where Newcastle United Football Club was accused by the tax authorities of extensive tax evasion on player transfers. The allegations suggested an elaborate scheme to evade income tax, VAT, and national insurance relating to the club's part in the transfers of players including Demba Ba, Moussa Sissoko, Papiss Cissé, Sylvain Marveaux, and Davide Santon. Her Majesty's Revenue and Customs (HMRC) said Newcastle had "systematically abused the tax system" with the use of "sham" contracts that disguised the true recipients of agents' fees. Newcastle United was not the only club indicted in the scheme but the case demonstrates the complex methods used by organisations to maintain strong profit margins or financial control, legal or otherwise. Without a strong regulatory framework it would be increasingly difficult to ensure that football clubs were playing by the rules.

Although some of the practices are improving based on the involvement of professional advisers, greater financial awareness and increased media interest, it is still conceivable that the unique nature of the football business and the increasing opportunities for money to be made will lead to further issues. The future development of accounting policies and regulatory frameworks will directly influence professional team sports as the two are inextricably linked, particularly within the United Kingdom (UK) where, for example, all companies are required to produce financial statements consistent with the regulatory framework in place. However, such frameworks have to be watertight so that they cannot be easily manipulated. The uniqueness of the football business is further underlined by an example from Italian football when Morrow (2006) investigated the effects of the so-called *salva calcio* decree in 2006, introduced by the Italian government. The decree effectively permitted clubs to amortise (gradually write off the initial cost of an asset, i.e. something that you own) the asset of players' registration rights over an arbitrary time period of 10 years rather than over the length of the players' contracts, thus improving clubs' reported financial position and performance.

Most issues with football and accounting (like the example above) are concerned with the valuation of player contracts and this is where we find evidence in relation to accounting principles. However, while we will discuss the valuation of players as assets to the football business in more detail later in the chapter, from a regulatory perspective, there has been one single piece of legislation that has become one of the most important changes to the world of sport business and in particular professional team sports. The method of reclassifying the way in which professional clubs could value their players and record them on the balance sheet, came about following the introduction of Financial Reporting Standard (FRS) 10. In time gone by, clubs had developed ways of including the costs and purchases of players without valuing them on the balance sheet, despite the fact that they were valuable assets. This is important when considering the characteristics of financial information mentioned earlier in the chapter. Such a practice was at direct odds with the concept of financial information being relevant, reliable, and understandable and it was clear that a regulatory change was necessary to try to combat this particular issue.

The introduction of FRS 10 provided a degree of consistency in the area of intangible assets, and comparisons between the financial results of professional sports teams can be now undertaken with greater confidence and a stronger level of comparability, as all clubs should be operating in the same way. Essentially, a fundamental principle of FRS 10 is that football clubs should record the player registration fee on their balance sheets as an amortised value based on the length of the player's contract (e.g., if a player is purchased for £50 million and signs a five-year contract, then the value recorded on the accounts is £10 million per annum for that particular player). This is similar to the concept of Net Book Value, which dictates that an asset is depreciated equally over the course of its useful life span whereby at the end of the time-period the asset holds no value to the business. Thus, at whichever point in time we are focusing on, the asset has a (net) value at that particular point.

Furthermore, owing to high-profile scandals and business collapses in recent years – witness the demise of a number of established football clubs such as Leeds United, Sheffield Wednesday, Portsmouth, and Coventry City for example – accounting bodies, accountants, institutional investors, and audit firms amongst others, have begun to place an increasing emphasis on "corporate governance" (see Hamil and Chadwick, 2010; Wilson, 2011). The Corporate Governance Code in the UK sets out standards of good practice for listed companies on issues related to board composition, shareholder relations, and accountability and audit matters. Whilst it is aimed at listed companies, the principles should apply to any organisation. Again, as with accounting policies, corporate governance is a global issue and many countries have developed their own ideas of corporate governance, some of which, the US's for example, are more rigid and rule-based than others. Sport organisations, much like any normal business, will have their own governance frameworks and these should conform to the principles of fairness, transparency, responsibility, independence, accountability, discipline, and social responsibility. The threat of litigation almost forces the larger-scale organisations to disclose how they consider corporate governance on an annual basis.

Income statements and balance sheets

As noted at the outset, each and every sport organisation has a responsibility to produce financial statements, the legal requirements for which will be determined by the nature of the company (i.e., whether they are a sole trader or a public company). There are two main financial statements that need to be drawn up by financial accountants: the *balance sheet* and *income statement*. The *balance sheet* provides a list of all assets owned by the business and all of the liabilities owed by a business at a specific point in time. It is often referred to as a "snapshot" of the financial position of the business at a specific moment in time (normally at the end of a financial year) and therefore is only really useful on the day on which it is produced.

The *income statement*, by contrast, provides a statement showing the profits (or losses) recognised during a period. The profit is calculated by deducting expenditure (including charges for capital maintenance) from the income generated during the accounting period, normally one calendar year. In simple terms, these documents help define a company's operations against the key financial equation: Assets – Liabilities = Capital.

It is worth mentioning here that "assets" are resources that the business owns, for example buildings, machinery, and vehicles. Such resources will be used by the business in its operations. There may also be bank balances and cash. These will hold the funds that the business needs to operate. However, the business may also owe money to its owners, other people, or organisations – these are called liabilities. A limited company will produce an income and expenditure statement for the period of one year. However, it is not uncommon for internal users to produce income statements on a quarterly or even monthly basis. Income statements that you come across are likely to be in annual reports and will therefore be for a 12-month period.

Asset valuation of players to the football business

For the purpose of this section, we use the UK for context in relation to how football players are recorded as assets to the business. Financial Reporting Standard 10 *Goodwill and Intangible Assets* sets out the principles of accounting for the measurement and recording of goodwill and intangible assets.

For clarity, goodwill is a long-term (or non-current) asset categorised as an intangible asset (for a definition of that, read on). Goodwill arises when a company acquires another entire business. The amount of goodwill is the cost to purchase the business minus the fair market value of the tangible assets, the intangible assets that can be identified, and the liabilities obtained in the purchase. A key component of goodwill is intangible assets. By definition, these are assets that you cannot necessarily touch. Examples of intangible assets will include copyrights, patents, mailing lists, trademarks, brand names, domain names, and so on. Often, the market value of an intangible asset is far greater than the market value of a company's tangible assets such as its buildings and equipment.

Based on this, the key objectives of FRS 10 is to ensure that:

- capitalised goodwill and intangible assets are charged in the income statement account in the periods in which they are depleted; and
- sufficient information is disclosed in the financial statements to enable users to determine the impact of goodwill and intangible assets on the financial position and performance of the reporting entity.

To take this all a stage further, one of the main issues surrounding accounting policies and professional football is the classification of football players, as assets to the football club, and therefore, their subsequent value to the business. The majority of sporting-related literature and accounting policies covers this issue (see, in particular, the work of Gerrard (2005) and Morrow (1996)). The former puts forward a resource-utilisation model of a professional sports team where teams optimise the stock of athletic resources (i.e., playing talent), subject to ownership preferences, over sporting and financial performance. Gerrard (2005) meanwhile, considers the theory surrounding a resource-based view (RBV) which emerged in the strategic management literature partly as a reaction to the more economics-based approaches in which the strategic decisions of firms are seen as primarily driven by competitive forces. The resource-utilisation model of a professional sports team consists of five basic relationships: (1) the team-owner objective function; (2) the sporting production function; (3) the profit function; (4) the revenue function; and (5) the cost function. All of these functions are subsequently translated into mathematical formulae before ordinary least squares (OLS) multiple regression is used, alongside performance ratio analysis, to determine the efficiency of the model.

The valuation of football players as assets has traditionally been a grey area when it comes to professional football clubs and the accounting literature, often due to the confusion surrounding which accounting practices should be followed. Using a more simplistic methodology than Gerrard (2005), Morrow (1996) considered whether the prospective services provided by a football player on behalf of the club holding his registration could be recognised as an accounting asset. This was based on the fundamentals of human resource accounting. Since the 1960s this type of accounting has been dominated by two issues: first, can human resources be satisfactorily defined and recognised as accounting assets and second, can a satisfactory valuation methodology be provided to reflect those assets? (Morrow, 1996). To bring this together, Morrow (1996) put forward four valuation methods in an attempt to answer such questions: (1) the historical cost model, (2) the earnings multiplier model, (3) the directors' valuation model and (4) the independent multiple player evaluation model. The consideration around these valuation methods is of particular relevance here as the value of assets (most normally in the form of players) to a professional football club will have some influence on the financial performance of the club in question. The valuation of assets (players) to a professional football club is particularly relevant if a club is in a perilous financial situation or close to liquidation or administration. Here, a club may wish to sell some of its most prized assets (players) to cover costs or to lower debt levels. Consequently, it is worth examining each of Morrow's valuation models in turn.

The historical cost model (method 1), involves capitalising players acquired by the club via the transfer market on the balance sheet at their cost of registration (capitalising simply means that the cost to acquire an asset is expensed over the life of that asset rather than in the period in which it occurs). The earnings multiplier model (method 2), involves applying a multiplier to a players' earnings to produce a current valuation of that player. The directors' valuation model (method 3) involves capitalising the players at a value provided by the chairperson and/or manager of the football club whilst the independent multiple player evaluation model (method 4), involves various informed and knowledgeable sources providing a value for the players of the club in question. The latter is based on a model set out by Biagoni and Ogan (1977; cited in Morrow, 1996) for valuing US professional team sports.

All of these methods have their respective strengths and weaknesses, although methods 3 and 4 become increasingly difficult to implement without internal access to a specific club and industry experts, or in most cases the chairperson and the manager. Furthermore, method 3 is likely to be far more susceptible to window dressing by management, as clubs are unlikely to wish to disclose a low valuation in respect of their players to the outside world. As a result, methods 1 and 2 present the most relevant approach to use when valuing football players as assets, although the earnings multiplier model (method 2) is also open to critique. It is also worth noting here that there is no universal acceptance of the theoretical conditions that would justify the use of wages and salaries as surrogate measures of human resource value that exist in practice (Morrow, 1996).

Similarly, Amir and Livne (2005) analysed the topic of accounting, valuation, and duration of football player contracts with reference to the guidelines outlined in FRS 10 and concluded that given the high degree of uncertainty associated with such contracts, it is not clear that this treatment is consistent with asset capitalisation criteria. Common to FRS 10 is the presumption that assets acquired in an arm's length transaction should be capitalised. The rationale behind this presumption is that the transaction price provides reliable evidence about the fair value of the acquired assets. However, this overlooks the possibility that certain fixed assets, tangible or intangible, represent speculative investments in that their recoverability and association with future economic benefits are highly uncertain. This is particularly relevant in relation to the nature of the professional football industry and it is possible to question the applicability of this presumption by demonstrating that the relationship between arm's length investment in player contracts by football companies and future benefits may be tenuous. FRS 10 requires that all purchased intangibles should be capitalised separately from goodwill and that all intangibles shall be amortised over their useful economic lives, unless useful life is indefinite, but the analysis here suggests that the rate of economic decline in the value of player contracts is higher than the rate of amortisation and impairment reported by sample firms under FRS 10.

This highlights how diverse an industry football is, compared to other areas of business, and how difficult it would be to compare football clubs to other businesses in other industries. At the outset there would be a differentiation between asset amortisation in football clubs compared to other businesses where assets are more tangible, meaning that what is being measured would not be like for like. Despite there being a regulating standard in place (FRS 10 in this instance) there would still be inconsistency in the reporting of asset valuation across industries, further highlighting the discrepancies within the conceptual framework for accounting.

Prior to FRS 10, UK football companies could elect between capitalisation and amortisation of players' transfers and immediate expensing of those transfers. As noted by Amir and Livne (2005) companies that elected the capitalisation method categorised player transfers as intangible assets and amortised these intangibles over the period of the contract. The introduction of FRS 10 has meant that football clubs can no longer exploit the vagueness that was present in regulatory guidance to immediately write transfer fees off as expenses. However, the case of unusual assets such as football player contracts makes it increasingly difficult to estimate useful economic life and amortisation. Consider, for example, Manchester City's acquisition of a young player with high potential such as Gabriel Jesus in 2016. He may be allowed time to develop early in his contract, and his skill set may diminish later in his career so that the net benefit obtained will be relatively small at the beginning and end of his playing career and highest in the middle years giving rise to a low-high-low pattern of amortisation. This makes it increasingly difficult to classify the exact value of intangible assets to a football company and the inconsistency that still surrounds accounting policies and principles further confuses the situation.

Certain methods of valuation offer a solution to the question "How much is this player worth at this moment in time", but whilst players are bought and sold in some sort of a market, certain methods do not always correspond to the financial meaning of the market. This is due to value of the market, or a specific player for example, changing over time. As club revenues, broadcasting deals and ticket prices have increased in professional football over the last twenty years, so too has the amount for which football players are bought and sold. Therefore, the value of player at a specific moment in time will not remain constant at a different point in time. Additionally, it is clear that there is work to be done to advance our understanding about the concept relating to the asset valuation of players in professional football and there is sparse academic literature, which covers it in recent time. Given that the nature of the industry has altered quite dramatically during the last decade, and club revenues and player transfer fees are at an all-time high, it is pertinent to revisit this topic of discussion moving forward to provide further insights into the current financial performance and positon of elite professional football clubs.

The role of finance linked to strategy

The problem with objectives

Sport teams have to balance multiple objectives (in most cases financial and sporting, but also social (see, Wilson and Anagnostopoulos, 2017)), and the very nature of professional football requires this same balance. However, there are also other factors that determine the objectives of professional sports teams that will have an impact on business and sporting performance. Primarily, in professional football clubs, there is a pragmatic problem with the objectives of owners, which could be further muddied by a change of ownership that may influence a change of business objectives over time. This is perhaps best evidenced by the case of Chelsea, Manchester City and Manchester United in English football. When Roman Abramovich purchased Chelsea FC in 2003 (at a time when there were no real financial restrictions or regulations on owner spending) he primarily invested money into securing the best playing talent in an attempt to improve sporting performance. A similar scenario occurred at Manchester City in 2008 when it was purchased by the Abu Dhabi Group although the introduction of FFP has since meant that Manchester City must now balance the books as well. The acquisition of Manchester United in 2005 by the Glazer family was slightly different as they purchased the club through a method of debt finance. It was suggested at the time that this was the first example of an American owner exerting profit maximisation principles on a UK professional sports team and Manchester United have since floated on the New York stock exchange in an attempt to raise further funds. Additionally, there has been recent investment from the Middle East and Asia into the game with Paris Saint-Germain currently owned effectively by a Qatari organisation that is state funded by the Qatari government, and several football clubs in England, Netherlands, and Spain have seen significant investment from Chinese business in recent years.

Given this context, it is difficult to ascertain definitively what the objectives of clubs truly are. It is not necessarily about trying to say that clubs are profit maximisers (i.e., prioritising financial performance and attempting to make a profit over prioritising sporting performance) or utility/win maximisers (i.e., prioritising sporting performance and wins on the pitch over financial performance), rather that they show the traits of these extremes to a greater or lesser extent. Debates around this topic can be discussed using examples such as Chelsea, Manchester City, Manchester United, and Paris Saint-Germain amongst others, although ownership investment and objectives in European football have been altered somewhat in recent years owing to the introduction of tighter financial regulation such as Financial Fair Play.

On-field/off-field performance dichotomy

Owing to the fact that contemporary sporting competition involves an abundance of statistics, football has become an ideal laboratory in which to test various economic theories (Sloane, 2015). Such statistics need not be exclusively confined to the field of play. Indeed, as the field of sports economics has grown, there has been increasing interest surrounding the off-field objectives and performance of, most notably, professional football clubs across Europe.

This interest has been stimulated, in part at least, by substantial increases in revenue in European football in recent years. In 2015/16 the cumulative revenue of the "big five" European leagues (the English Premier League in England, the Bundesliga in Germany, La Liga in Spain, Serie A in Italy and Ligue 1 in France) totalled €13.4 billion, driving the total value of European football market revenues to €24.6 billion (Deloitte, 2017). However, despite these positive revenue figures debt accumulation of European football clubs is an increasing source of concern for football authorities (Drut and Raballand, 2012). Of the five major European leagues, the English Premier League remains, by a distance, the highest revenue-generating league (€4.86 billion (£3.63 billion) in 2015/16). This figure is €2.15 billion more than the next best revenue-generating league in Europe (the Bundesliga in Germany), and during the last five years the EPL has established itself as the league with the highest turnover in world football. At individual club level, however, the figures are less positive. With reference to the EPL, financial data show that clubs are leveraged by significant levels of debt, often in the form of interest free loans from their owners. In 2016, the total debt of EPL clubs was £2.2 billion with "soft loans" from owners totalling £1.7 billion (Deloitte, 2017). Despite EPL clubs' revenue totalling £3.63 billion, clubs are spending £2.27 billion (63 per cent) on wages and academics have confirmed similar imbalances between revenue and costs for clubs across Europe in recent years.

In an attempt to address this imbalance, the Union of European Football Associations (UEFA) has introduced Financial Fair Play (FFP) regulations across the European game in an attempt to reduce the reliance on debt and borrowings and to make clubs spend within their means. The cornerstone of UEFA's FFP regulations is the breakeven requirement, which aims to help clubs across Europe achieve a more sustainable balance between their costs and revenues whilst also encouraging investment for the longer-term benefit of football. The regulations, applied in UEFA competitions for the first time in 2013/14, cover clubs' results from the 2011/12 and 2012/13 seasons and there have recently been high-profile examples of fines handed to clubs who have not fulfilled the break-even requirement such as Manchester City in England and Paris Saint-Germain in France.

The advent of UEFA FFP has brought about an increase in pressure on clubs to become more financially prudent and sustainable. Additionally, the effect of investment and ownership structure within clubs is also being analysed as part of FFP. Surrounding these areas is the issue of how we assess the long-term viability of professional sports leagues and the future proofing of individual businesses, as arguably, from a fundamental business position, professional sports teams should be looking to operate as sustainable businesses focusing on long-term growth as opposed to seeking short-term gain and trophy acquisition through immediate cash injections. The problem with sports teams, as noted in the section opening, is that they are ultimately guided by twin objectives. One is financial, in relation to business operations, and the other is sporting, in relation to on-pitch performance and trophy success. This strategic dilemma is a product of the phrase "peculiar economics" in relation to professional team sports. Central to this dilemma are the principles of competitive balance, uncertainty of outcome, and profit and utility maximisation; all underlying themes present in contemporary sports economics literature. In addition to measuring financial performance, the examination of the relationship between financial and sporting performance and whether or not the two concepts are interlinked or mutually exclusive is important.

Performance measurement

The unique nature of football means that performance measurement techniques, used in more general businesses, are not always the most appropriate tools for analysis. Consequently, this section, and the case study that follows, is based on the most up to date literature found in 2017. The primary aim of the case material was to develop an alternative method for analysing financial and sporting performance in English professional football clubs. There are many recognised techniques regarding financial analysis (ratio analysis being a principal example) yet that there is no set definition of which variables to actually measure.

It is clear that ratio analysis is an important tool for benchmarking and that it makes good business sense for organisations to benchmark themselves against their direct competitors. However, in the context of sport, and more specifically professional football, this is difficult to replicate. For example, both Manchester United and Brighton & Hove Albion were in the EPL in the 2017/18 season, yet it is unrealistic that the two clubs would be in direct competition in a financial context. Furthermore, the use of tools such as ratio analysis alone (even considering the case for benchmarking) may not tell the true story of performance for football clubs given that they operate under twin objectives.

Consequently, this section details an alternate approach to performance measurement in professional team sports and one which has been adapted and applied across other professional team sports including Rugby Union and Rugby League. Using football, and the EPL, as an example, the model builds on UEFA's approach to FFP, and can be used by academics, practitioners, and analysts to draw conclusions about club performance. It is important to note that the model is not used as a predictor for future performance, rather it is an analytical tool that can be used to check for performance health markers (both financial and sporting) to detect where clubs may be considered at risk. It outlines a composite index score that highlights

Table 15.1 Overall Performance Score: a hypothetical example

Dimension	Sub domain				Dimension		OPS
	Key Indicator	League ranking	Weight	Score	Score	Weight	
Financial	Total revenue	2	0.15	0.30			
	Pre-tax profit/(loss)	4	0.15	0.60			
	Net assets/(liabilities)	3	0.15	0.45	4.15	0.625	3.59
	Net funds/(debt)	8	0.15	1.20			
	Wages/turnover	4	0.40	1.60			
Sporting	League points	5	0.333	1.665			
	Total game variance	2	0.333	0.666	2.66	0.375	
	Attendance spread	1	0.333	0.333			

Adapted from Plumley, Wilson, and Shibli (2017).

how a club is performing in relation to its competitors. This composite index score is derived from eight variables (five financial and three sporting) which were developed during an initial pilot model, comprising 18 variables (nine financial and nine sporting). The initial model was tested using football club data and then the model was reduced by using a factor analysis which measured whether or not certain variables were strongly correlated with each other; i.e., it tested whether the same variables were double counted (for a more detailed account of how the model was produced you can read the full paper by Plumley, Wilson, and Shibli, 2017). The final Performance Assessment Model (PAM) is outlined in Table 15.1, where a hypothetical example is provided to show how it works in practice and to derive the final OPS (Overall Performance Score) for the football club.

Case study: Applying the PAM – an analysis of English football clubs since the inception of the EPL

The results include data from 21 clubs in total and covered the period 1992–2013. In relation to the OPS in Table 15.2 below a lower score is more desirable and a perfect score would be 1. The results indicate that Manchester United was the best performing club on average throughout the years studied. The club has recorded one of the largest net debt figures in recent years (primarily due to the levels of borrowing attached to the takeover of the club by the Glazer family in 2005), but its ability to generate revenue and profit remains unrivalled and its position at the top of the EPL and historically strong performance in both domestic and European cup competitions consolidates its position as the best performing club in England. A similar scenario can be found at Arsenal although its net debt figure has been one of the highest across all clubs since 2003. This debt must be considered in context, however. It was in large part due to the construction of a new stadium, which was necessary to help Arsenal bridge the gap to clubs with higher attendances such as Manchester United. Despite Chelsea ranking third for sporting performance, the club ranked sixth in relation to the overall performance. This was because of poorer financial performance, for which Chelsea ranked thirteenth. The three worst performing clubs in the study were Middlesbrough, Fulham, and Coventry City (see Table 15.2).

Table 15.2 Average OPS for all clubs 1992–2013

Rank	Club	Average finance score	Average sporting score	Average OPS
1	Manchester United	2.89	3.08	**2.96**
2	Arsenal	6.20	3.65	**5.24**
3	Tottenham Hotspur	5.10	8.16	6.25
4	Liverpool	8.27	6.30	**7.53**
5	Newcastle United	9.48	7.86	8.87
6	Chelsea	11.79	5.71	**9.51**
7	Aston Villa	9.30	12.24	**10.40**
8	Leeds United	9.36	12.81	**10.65**
9	West Ham United	10.72	11.37	**10.96**
10	Everton	11.49	11.97	**11.67**
11	Manchester City	12.23	10.79	**11.69**
12	Southampton	11.75	12.17	**11.91**
13	Sunderland	10.26	14.71	**11.93**
14	Bolton Wanderers	12.55	12.13	**12.39**
15	Leicester City	12.79	13.51	**13.06**
16	Charlton Athletic	13.17	13.03	**13.12**
17	Sheffield Wednesday	11.26	16.32	**13.16**
18	Blackburn Rovers	14.24	11.40	**13.17**
19	Middlesbrough	14.81	11.95	**13.74**
20	Fulham	16.25	11.67	**14.53**
21	Coventry City	15.57	15.25	**15.45**

Adapted from Plumley, Wilson, and Shibli (2017).

Further statistical analysis revealed a positive correlation between financial performance and sporting performance ($r = 0.44$). Whilst this is not a strong correlation in absolute terms, it is statistically significant ($p < 0.05$), which means that the probability of achieving a correlation coefficient of this magnitude by chance is remote. This, in turn, indicates the presence of a real relationship rather than a statistical quirk. Superficially at least, better financial health is moderately and positively associated with better sporting performance in the EPL.

A time series analysis for each club was also conducted and found evidence that, for the majority of clubs, overall performance, as measured using a mix of financial and sporting indicators, varies over time in cycles. Thus, football club performance often runs in cycles: Sometimes clubs have a successful period spanning a number of years before declining for a period of time.

Implications and the need for application

Success (in team sports) is a function of a strong stream of revenue primarily because teams have to pay the best wages to secure the best playing talent. As such, irrespective of what owner(s) actually want to do, they must balance the financial and sporting objectives of the club accordingly in order to maximise playing success. FFP regulations have had a further impact on financial development as it should force clubs to operate as sustainable businesses moving forward.

The findings suggest that financial and sporting performance are not dichotomous variables but a continuum along which clubs place themselves and move backwards and forwards to a greater or lesser extent. The aim of the model produced is not to attempt to predict future performance but to pinpoint health markers to ascertain warning signs for when clubs may appear to be performing badly. The model should be used to quantify club objectives and help analysts outline in what way clubs are performing based on economic principles. The model could also be used by governing bodies and decision-makers within respective sports in order to inform policy and set new regulations.

Summary

This chapter has introduced the concepts surrounding finance and accounting and the way in which they impact the business of professional football. Against the objectives of the chapter, readers should now understand and appreciate the importance of finance and accounting in football and the uniqueness of football compared to other mainstream businesses.

Finance and accounting in football is still very much, and will continue to be, an ongoing matter for sport managers and researchers. It should continue to consider how the role that finance plays links to strategy and the different techniques that can be used to measure performance against sport objectives. This, in turn, will allow football clubs to use financial information effectively, with the end goal of using good financial information and performance measurement techniques to drive strategic business decisions. Furthermore, the rapid rate of expansion and growth within the football industry during the last two decades means that the consideration of financial performance is even more important to football clubs.

This chapter has outlined the current position of finance and accounting within the football industry although it is clear that there is still further work required in the field to progress the research agenda. Future research should focus on how performance measurement models that utilise financial performance (like the one used in the case study) can be developed to focus on wider variables (e.g., corporate social responsibility (CSR), see Breitbarth, Hovemann, and Walzel, 2011; Breitbarth, Walzel, Anagnostopoulos, and van Eekeren, 2015) that also impact club performance so that the notion of viewing performance of football clubs in a more holistic style comes fully into focus.

References

Amir, E. and Livne, G. (2005) Accounting, valuation and duration of football player contracts. *Journal of Business Finance & Accounting*, 32(3–4), 549–86.

Breitbarth, T., Hovemann, G., and Walzel, S. (2011) Scoring strategy goals: Measuring corporate social responsibility in professional European football. *Thunderbird International Business Review*, 53(6), 721–37.

Breitbarth, T., Walzel, S., Anagnostopoulos, C., and van Eekeren, F. (2015) Corporate social responsibility and governance in sport: "Oh, the things you can find, if you don't stay behind!" *Corporate Governance*, 15(2), 254–273.

Chopping, D., (2010) *Applying GAAP 2010–11: A practical guide to financial reporting*. Wolters Kluwer Limited, Kingston upon Thames.

Deloitte, (2017) *Annual review of football finance: ahead of the curve*. Sport Business Group.

Drut, B., and Raballand, G. (2012) Why does financial regulation matter for European professional football clubs? *International Journal of Sport Management and Marketing*, 11(1–2), 73–88.

Gerrard, B. (2005) A resource-utilization model of organizational efficiency in professional sports teams. *Journal of Sport Management*, 19(2), 143–69.

Hamil, S. and Chadwick, S. (2010) *Managing Football*. Routledge, London.

Morrow, S. (1996) Football players as human assets. Measurement as the critical factor in asset recognition: a case study investigation. *Journal of Human Resource Costing & Accounting*, 1(1), 75–97.

Morrow, S. (2006) Impression management in football club financial reporting. *International Journal of Sport Finance*, 1(2), 96–108.

Plumley, D., Wilson, R., and Shibli, S. (2017) A Holistic Performance Assessment of English Premier League Football Clubs 1992–2013. *Journal of Applied Sport Management*, 9(1), 1–24.

Sloane, P.J. (2015) The economics of professional football revisited. *Scottish Journal of Political Economy*, 62(1), 1–7.

Wilson, R. and Anagnostopoulos, C. (2017) Editorial: Performance strategies for meeting multiple objectives: the case of professional sport teams. *Sport, Business and Management: An International Journal*, Vol. 7(2), 114–20.

Wilson, R. (2011) *Managing sport finance*. Taylor & Francis, London.

16

Sponsorships, stadia, and naming rights

Leah Gillooly and Dominic Medway

Introduction

On the 10 November 2011, Newcastle United Football Club announced that their stadium would officially be renamed from St James' Park to the Sports Direct Arena. This was deemed a temporary measure by the club's owners, who argued that the name change would signal the financial potential of Newcastle United Football Club to prospective sponsors, and that, in this respect, the St James' Park name was no longer "commercially attractive" (BBC, 2011a), were it ever thus. The move was met with disdain by some media commentators, with one suggesting that "it felt as if another sliver of football's soul had just been sold" (Conn, 2011). Even, the former club chairman, Freddy Shepherd, was critical, claiming:

> I don't think the fans will be very happy … St James' Park goes back hundreds of years … Fans in Newcastle, like myself, will always call it St James' Park anyway so anyone claiming the rights, it's not going to do them much good … .
>
> *(BBC, 2011b)*

Indeed, hours after the removal of the official St James' Park name from the stadium's perimeter wall, a fan had graffitied it back (*Mail Online*, 2012a), and others followed (*Mail Online*, 2012b). By October 2012, payday loan company Wonga.com became Newcastle United's main commercial sponsor and purchased the stadium naming rights. They subsequently announced that the St James' Park name would be restored as part of the deal (Edwards, 2012).

Sponsorship is "a cash or in-kind fee paid to a property (typically in sports, arts, entertainment, or causes) in return for access to the exploitable commercial potential of that property" (IEG, 2017a). Of the estimated $62.8 billion to be spent on sponsorship in 2017, sport accounts for approximately 70 per cent of this, making it the largest recipient of sponsorship worldwide (IEG, 2017a). Looking at the case of football, brands have an array of sponsorship options open to them, with the most prominent of these being kit sponsorships. In 2014, for example, English Premier League club Manchester United signed a seven-year kit sponsorship deal with car manufacturer Chevrolet worth $80 million per year. However, as the above debacle at Newcastle United Football Club indicates, also increasingly prevalent is sponsorship of stadia, or what is

199

termed: *naming rights sponsorship*. This involves an exchange of money in return for the right to name the stadium (Thornburg, 2002). Stadium naming rights are usually signed over for a longer period of time – for example, in 2012 the airline Emirates extended its naming rights deal for Arsenal's Emirates Stadium until 2028 (BBC, 2012). Such deals give sponsors the right to name a club's stadium after their brand, sometimes in a hybrid format, as is the case with Lancashire County Cricket Club's Emirates Old Trafford, or more usually as merely the "brand name" stadium, such as FC Köln's RheinEnergieStadion. A major advantage of stadia naming rights sponsorships is the significant volume of media exposure that they attract through mentions on live and highlighted television broadcasts, in print media, and online. The large volume of these "name checks" can contribute to the achievement of brand-name awareness, an important objective for corporate stadium naming rights sponsors (Hartland, Skinner, and Griffiths, 2005). Securing "buy in" from relevant media outlets to use the corporate name (particularly where this represents a change of name for an existing stadium) is crucial and often forms part of the responsibilities of the club as sponsorship rights holder. Minor commentator and journalist slips of the tongue aside, clubs have been largely successful in getting corporate stadium names into everyday media parlance.

This naming and renaming of football stadia and other sporting venues is certainly not a new phenomenon. Outside of football, for example, the practice can be traced back to 1971 when American Football team the New England Patriots granted Schaefer Brewing Company the right to name their stadium Schaefer Field in return for $150,000 (Crompton and Howard, 2003). Since then, the trend towards the corporate renaming of sports stadia, and what Boyd (2000) refers to as "selling home," has grown significantly, with many stadia, new and old, changing names in exchange for ever-growing sums of money. Focusing on the renaming of football stadia, naming rights confer on those stadia the label of "artefacts," that is, things that can be sold, marketed, and branded (Medway and Warnaby, 2014), reflecting Vuolteenaho and Kolamo's (2012, p. 145) observations that "English soccerscapes have been lately (re)textualised as 'landscape advertisements'." Indeed, by 2013, 14 out of the 18 stadia of German Bundesliga clubs had a corporate name (Woisetschläger, Haselhoff, and Backhaus, 2014). In England, seven of the 20 2017–2018 Premier League stadia bore a corporate sponsor name (Journey to the 92, 2017), although these are all newly built (or in the case of Bournemouth's Vitality Stadium, completely rebuilt), having been constructed post the Taylor Report (HMSO, 1990), which recommended new approaches to stadium and seating design following the Hillsborough Stadium disaster.

The case of Newcastle United Football Club discussed above also aptly illustrates one of the other (and arguably trickier) key challenges facing brands seeking to acquire and leverage the naming rights of football stadia: that is, gaining fan acceptance for the new, corporate name, particularly if it overwrites a previous moniker. Certainly, the most fan resistance to corporate renamings appears to have come in cases where a new name has been given to an older or long-established stadium (Crompton and Howard, 2003), such as Newcastle United's St James' Park. Potential sponsors may avoid renaming such stadia out of concerns over the damage fan protests might inflict on their corporate brand equity. Consequently, stadia with well-established, highly recognisable names are less likely to acquire naming rights deals, and sponsors are willing to pay more for naming rights for a new stadium (DeSchriver and Jensen, 2003). Equally, whilst all football clubs may be tempted to pursue corporate naming rights for their stadia, high-profile teams such as Manchester United have ruled out any corporate renaming of Old Trafford in order to preserve the tradition and the associations with which this name is imbued (Ogden, 2015).

This chapter will critically discuss current thinking in relation to corporate football stadium renaming through sponsorship, drawing on relevant theoretical frameworks and empirical findings, all illustrated by real-life examples. Issues of fan reactions towards corporate stadium names will be discussed, with a focus on appraising those factors, which impact likely acceptance or resistance. This is followed by a consideration of corporate stadium naming rights and issues of sponsorship fit. The chapter will conclude with implications for sponsors and clubs as the sponsorship rights holders and will present some relevant areas for future research to further our understanding of this growing practice in world football.

Fan reactions to corporate stadium names

Fan acceptance or resistance towards a corporate stadium naming rights sponsor has been explored through the lens of social identity theory (Tajfel, 1982; Woisetschläger, Haselhoff, and Backhaus, 2014). This states that fans feel connected to others in the "ingroup," which comprises fellow fans, and the club itself. In contrast, they may demonstrate resistance to "outgroup" members, such as new naming rights sponsors. Evidence of this was found by Woisetschläger, Haselhoff, and Backhaus (2014) in their survey of fans of German Bundesliga team Borussia Dortmund. Here, they found that more highly identified football fans are more resistant to corporate stadium naming rights sponsorships. Unlike other forms of sponsorship, naming rights sponsors are seen as having more calculative motives (Woisetschläger, Backhaus, and Cornwell, 2017). Therefore, it is likely that football fans will react differently to this form of sponsorship as they might see it as a threat to their group identity (Woisetschläger, Haselhoff, and Backhaus, 2014), leading them to enact forms of resistance such as hostility towards sponsors, anger, a perception of harm to the distinctiveness of a team (Reysen, Snider, and Branscombe, 2012), refusal to adopt the new name (Crompton and Howard, 2003) or the singing of songs relating to the old stadium (Woisetschläger, Haselhoff, and Backhaus, 2014). In their work on Borussia Dortmund, which had recently renamed its stadium in a corporate naming rights sponsorship deal, Woisetschläger, Haselhoff, and Backhaus (2014) also found that fans' high levels of identification with the region in which the club is located and negative attitudes towards commercialisation led to higher fan resistance to the naming rights sponsorship.

When considering the case of football clubs, many of which have deep roots and long histories in their towns, cities, and communities, it is unsurprising that the greatest fan resistance to stadium naming rights sponsorships concerns those which relate to longstanding, historic stadia (Crompton and Howard, 2003), as opposed to newly built stadia. Historic stadia were often named after the roads on which they were located or other local features (Bale, 1989). When such stadia change their name through corporate naming rights sponsorships, this local connection can appear to fans as being diluted (Edensor and Milington, 2008). In the case of historic stadia, fans also see corporate stadium naming rights sponsorship as a threat to their team's distinctiveness (Reysen, Snider, and Branscombe, 2012) as, rather than having their own unique and longstanding name, with roots in the club's geographic location and community, their team's stadium becomes merely one of many with a corporate name. This may be particularly exacerbated when corporate entities appropriate the naming rights of multiple venues to reflect their international reach and ambition as organisations. For example, the German insurance company Allianz has naming rights deals with numerous stadia worldwide, resulting in a plethora of similar stadium names including an Allianz Stadium in both Sydney and Turin (home of Juventus), Bayern Munich's Allianz Arena, Allianz Parque in Sao Paolo, Brazil, and Minnesota United FC's Allianz Field. It is therefore not difficult to see why corporate stadium naming rights sponsorship can be seen by fans to harm the distinctiveness of their club as the names appear relatively interchangeable, linked to seemingly placeless corporate sponsors (Edensor and Millington, 2008).

Boyd (2000) also refers to stadia as "memory places" – that is, sites at which events took place for which fans have (usually, but not exclusively) fond memories. These memories might include famous victories, promotions (or relegations), or more personal associations such as the site of one's first football match or recollections of attending that stadium in the past with family and loved ones. A former (non-corporate) name of a stadium can therefore act as a tie between those memories and the team (Boyd, 2000). When a corporate naming rights partner renames an existing stadium, any relationship between a former name for that venue and the memories this might evoke is threatened (Boyd, 2000). The Newcastle United example above exemplifies how this threat can generate fan resistance, and it is therefore unsurprising that most corporately named football stadia in the UK are newly built, such as Arsenal's Emirates Stadium and Brighton & Hove Albion's American Express Community Stadium.

In the case of newly built stadia, fan acceptance of naming rights sponsorship is likely to be higher because these stadia are often built on a new site, away from the historic stadium and therefore they are not (at least initially) considered by fans as memory places (Boyd, 2000), because no store of memories has yet been built up there. However, fans can still be resistant to naming rights sponsorship even for new stadia if they feel that it is in some way a threat to their club's identity or their self-identity as a fan of that club. For example, 85 per cent of Arsenal fans surveyed in 2003 were opposed to selling naming rights for the club's new stadium (Church and Penny, 2013). However, a 15-year naming rights deal was signed with the airline Emirates in 2004 (Church and Penny, 2013). The reactions of fans to such arrangements were not as extreme as those witnessed at Newcastle United. Nevertheless, Arsenal supporters have enacted some minor resistance to this corporate intervention by adopting their own terms for sections of the Emirates Stadium, which are based on names for stands at the club's historic Highbury venue, such as North Bank and Clock End (Church and Penny, 2013).

Whether or not fans choose to accept a new corporate name for their club's stadium can play an important role in the ultimate success of the naming rights sponsorship. Where fans routinely refuse to adopt a new stadium name, instead preferring to use a previous version, the sponsoring brand may lose some benefits, not only in terms of brand exposure, but also with regard to image transfer. Certainly, a refusal to accept and use the corporate name does not represent the ideal conditions for the transfer of fans' positive thoughts, feelings, and beliefs about their football club to a sponsor. Furthermore, despite the potential benefits of naming rights sponsorship in terms of brand awareness and associations, many sponsors are seeking to pursue sales-based objectives (Apostolopoulou and Papadimitriou, 2004). However, there is little existing evidence that naming rights sponsorships can influence fans' purchase intention towards a sponsor's products (Haan and Shank, 2004), particularly where fans have a strong sense of the club's history and tradition (Eddy, 2014). In this sense, naming rights are no different from other forms of sponsorship, in that their success relies not simply on acquiring the rights but also activating the sponsorship such that fans not only become aware of the new corporate name but also develop positive associations towards the sponsor (Donlan, 2014; Tripodi, and Hirons, 2009).

One of the most successful examples of this comes from outside of football, in the case of the O2 Arena. O2 has successfully activated its naming rights sponsorship through "Priority Tickets," whereby O2 customers are able to purchase tickets for events at the O2 Arena up to 48 hours in advance of them going on open sale. O2 customers also get access to VIP areas, plus discounts on food and drink at the venue (IEG, 2017b). Unfortunately, many football stadium naming rights sponsors fail to activate as effectively as they might do. While the frequent media exposure they gain from acquiring naming rights to football stadia will contribute to building their brand awareness, their lack of activation represents a missed opportunity to capitalise on these mentions, and thereby forge deeper and more meaningful relationships with fans (Vaswani, 2016).

Corporate stadium naming rights and sponsorship fit

Underpinning much of the decision as to whether fans will accept or resist a corporate stadium naming rights sponsor is the concept of sponsorship fit. The academic community is yet to agree on one universal definition of fit, but in a sports context, it can be thought of in terms of how logical it seems for a brand to sponsor a particular team (Olson and Thjømøe, 2011). As such, fit is often described in terms of functional/product-related fit or image-based fit (McDonald, 1991; Gwinner, 1997). For example, sporting goods retailer Dick's Sporting Goods are the naming rights sponsor for the US Major League Soccer team the Colorado Rapids, which has the stadium name, "Dick's Sporting Goods Park." This demonstrates functional fit through product category similarity. Others have suggested that sponsorship fit might also involve similarity in attitude, audience, and geographic location between the sponsor and the team (Olson and Thjømøe, 2011). As indicated above, this latter component of fit is supported in the case of corporate football stadium naming rights sponsors, with local sponsors more accepted than those from outside the club's region (Woisetschläger, Haselhoff, and Backhaus, 2014). Evidence of local companies seeking stadium naming rights sponsorship is found in the case of English Premier League club Swansea City. This team plays at the Liberty Stadium, named after Liberty Properties, a commercial property development company founded in Swansea in 1984 (BBC, 2005). In this case, the naming rights sponsorship appears more logical because the sponsor has a connection to the town or city, thus fostering fan acceptance of the new stadium name.

Clearly, not all potential football stadium naming rights sponsors can claim roots in a club's hometown/region and/or demonstrate functional (i.e., sport, or football-related in some way) fit. However, the multi-dimensional nature of fit means that even where geographic and functional fit are absent, fit can be emphasised in terms of a congruency of values between the sponsor and club. As an example, Austrian Bundesliga team Austria Vienna's stadium was renamed the Generali Arena in 2010 following a naming rights sponsorship deal with the insurance company Generali. While there is no functional or geographic fit between the Austrian club and the Italian insurance company, the naming rights deal is purportedly based around shared values of leadership, dynamism, and a hunger for success (Soccerex, 2010). Sometimes, this image-based fit is evident to fans and they are able to form positive beliefs about the naming rights sponsorship on this basis. In other cases, if clubs and sponsors present credible arguments (Samuelsen, Olsen, and Keller, 2015) in articulating the basis of fit or emphasising mutuality of benefit (Woisetschläger and Haselhoff, 2009) when a naming rights deal is announced, they may be able to create a positive response from fans, even if there is little actual evidence of this fit existing (Skard and Thorbjornsen, 2017). For example, in announcing a stadium naming rights sponsorship deal with energy and power generation company Talen Energy, the Vice President of Corporate Partnerships and Premium Seating for the MLS team Philadelphia Union declared on the club's website: "Our two companies share a level of commitment and passion that we want to utilise as our organization continues to grow. This is a mutually beneficial opportunity that we expect to fully capitalize on" (Philadelphia Union, 2015). Whilst such statements might, on the one hand, be viewed as mere corporate rhetoric, they also aim to reinforce amongst fans a view that the naming rights deal is a positive step for their club, which should help build their acceptance of the new stadium name.

The concept of fit in corporate football naming rights sponsorship is underpinned by schema congruity theory, which suggests that where fit between a corporate sponsor and the sponsored club is high, the transfer of image associations from the club to the sponsor will be enhanced (Gwinner and Eaton, 1999). Thus, good sponsorship fit can positively impact efforts by a sponsor to develop their brand image (Grohs and Reisinger, 2014), largely because that good fit is positively correlated with attitudes towards the sponsorship (Mazodier and Merunka, 2012; Simmons and Becker-Olsen, 2006); sponsor identification (Johar and Pham, 1999); attitude towards the sponsor (Bruhn and Holzer, 2015; Weeks, Cornwell, and Drennan, 2008; Becker-Olsen and Hill, 2006; Roy and Cornwell, 2003); and sponsor purchase intention (Speed and Thompson, 2000). Thus, whether that fit be functional, image-based or geographic it is important for football stadia naming rights sponsors to reinforce this fit amongst fans. This will help engender acceptance of the corporate stadium name and thus facilitate the achievement of a sponsor's objectives.

The transfer of associations from the football club to the corporate naming rights sponsor can be explained through models of brand image transfer (Gwinner, 1997, Smith, 2004). A considerable body of empirical evidence supports such a transfer of associations (Gwinner and Eaton, 1999; Nufer and Bühler, 2010; Grohs, 2015). More recently, researchers' attention has turned towards examining the extent to which associations can transfer in the opposite direction, from the sponsor to the club (Henseler, Wilson, and De Vreede, 2009; Tsiotsou, Alexandris, and Cornwell, 2014; Gross and Wiedmann, 2015; Kwon, Ratneshwar, and Kim, 2016), with high levels of perceived fit enhancing this transfer of associations (Gross and Wiedmann, 2015). Any perceived misfit between football club and naming rights holder may therefore harm fan/consumer evaluations of both the sponsor (Woisetschläger et al., 2010) and the club (Groza, Cobbs, and Schaefers, 2012).

Crucial, and where the case of football, and sports teams in general, differs from other vehicles for sponsorship such as music and arts venues, is the intense level of fan attachment to the clubs who are receiving sponsorship monies from corporate naming rights sponsors. If fans perceive that the naming rights sponsorship offers significant benefits to their club then this may enhance their perceptions of the sponsorship fit (Woisetschläger and Haselhoff, 2009). The ability of sport to engender connections between a team and its surrounding community, via shared history, goals, and fans' desire to belong (Gwinner and Swanson, 2003) may enhance the attachment a fan feels towards their club. As such, notions of power and ownership come to the fore regarding the issue of stadium naming. Like much other place branding, stadium naming is often a top-down decision-making process, with the views of stakeholders such as club owners and sponsors prioritised over those of fans (Aitken and Campelo, 2011). The lack of involvement of fans in stadium naming decisions thus may hinder the acceptance and sustainability of the name (Klijn, Eshuis, and Braun, 2012), particularly where the name is perceived to lack authenticity. Indeed, rather than fostering a sense of fan involvement, it has been suggested that the corporate naming of stadia sends out the message that fans are merely paying customers (Boyd, 2000).

Conclusion

In Western contexts, sponsorship has infiltrated every aspect of football over the last 40 years. In the English Football League, for example, sponsorship emerged in the late-1970s, with commercial brand names beginning to adorn team kits and players' shirts. By the late 1990s, some 20 years later, this practice had progressed to a new target: Namely, the physical structures of football stadia and the stands within them became fair game for corporate naming and renaming. The naming of Huddersfield Town's new ground "the Alfred McAlpine stadium" in 1994 represented a watershed moment in this sponsorship journey, with several more English Football League clubs soon following suit and adopting a corporate identity for their stadia, typically when newly built.

As evidenced in this chapter, a few studies have started to try and unpack the practice of corporate stadium renaming, looking broadly at fan reactions to it, as well as examining issues of fit in the context of stadium renaming (Eddy, 2014; Haan and Shank, 2004; Reysen, Snider, and Branscombe, 2012; Woisetschläger and Haselhoff, 2009; Woisetschläger, Haselhoff, and Backhaus, 2014). However, this existing work has been predominantly survey based and, for this reason, has arguably not really got "under the skin" of what changing a football stadium name to one with corporate associations really means socially, politically, and culturally for a club's fan base and the wider place and community in which it is embedded. We contend that more work is needed to understand these issues, ideally adopting a phenomenological and potentially quasi-ethnographic perspective. Getting close to fans through methods such as netnographies (Kozinets, 2002) of popular online platforms such as fan forums, Twitter feeds and Facebook groups, as well as more conventional focus groups and interviews with fans in person, and even just spending time with fans as a participant observer on match days, is likely to give greater insight into how they use, perform, and counter-perform stadium names in everyday life.

In particular, fans' non-usage of corporate stadium names is important because it emphasises issues of political resistance and contestation in their speech acts and discourse. If this resistance is occurring at a systemic level within a given fan base, it suggests that corporate naming practices could be relatively ineffective at getting those fans' buy-in and support, or engendering them with positive views about the corporate brand responsible for the naming act. It would also suggest that any potential transfer of love for a football team to love for its sponsoring brand is not happening. This chapter's discussion of fans' reactions to corporate stadium naming and renaming highlights a clear implication for both football clubs and (potential) naming rights sponsors, namely the importance of articulating the fit between the club and the naming rights sponsor in order to facilitate fan acceptance of the name. Where this fit does not logically exist or a basis for fit is not articulated, the naming rights sponsorship is less likely to succeed, thus harming the sponsor brand through lower return-on-investment. Similarly, the football club itself loses out in the case of unsuccessful naming rights sponsorship deals as they are less likely to be renewed and thus the club will face time and monetary costs in finding and negotiating with potential new sponsors.

Another potentially important area of research in relation to the corporate renaming of football stadia concerns the tensions and challenges that may arise when brands of international scope and coverage are applied to the unique fan geographies of individual football clubs. For example, many clubs in the English football league have a fan base which is strongly rooted within a particular town or city (Edensor and Millington, 2008), being made of people who live in that particular location and/or were born there. In these cases, it would be instructive to explore how easy it is for global brands to make a meaningful connection to a club and its fans at this local level, or what can be done to improve the chances of this occurring. Certainly, if a sense of emotional connection between brand, club, and fans is not fully realised, then it seems less likely that the potential sponsorship benefits of a stadium naming rights agreement can be successfully realised. Conversely, in those situations where a football club has itself become a global brand, with a dispersed, multi-national and multi-cultural fan base, then any sponsoring name applied to a football stadium may need to take this into account. For example, sponsors would have to consider carefully the economic traction of a corporate stadium name, not just in the immediate urban locale in which a football club is based, but more widely across the multiple jurisdictions in which its fans may be found.

In summary, whilst the corporate naming of football stadia is a practice that has been in evidence for the last 20 years in the English Football League, and longer in some other countries such as the US, there is still work to be done in fully understanding what this means for the business and management of football. We encourage others to examine and interrogate this fascinating new dimension to the "beautiful game's" brandscape.

References

Aitken, R. and Campelo, A. (2011) The four Rs of place branding. *Journal of Marketing Management*, 27(9–10), 913–933.

Apostolopoulou, A. and Papadimitriou, D. (2004) "Welcome Home": motivations and objectives of the 2004 Grand National Olympic sponsors. *Sport Marketing Quarterly*, 13(4), 180–192.

Bale, J. (1989) *Sports Geography*. London: Routledge.

BBC (2005) City stadium takes sponsor's name. [online] Retrieved from: http://news.bbc.co.uk/1/hi/wales/south_west/4352630.stm

BBC (2011a) Newcastle rename St James' Park the Sports Direct Arena. [online] Retrieved from: http://www.bbc.co.uk/sport/football/15668207

BBC (2011b) Freddy Shepherd says renaming St James' Park will deter investors. [online] Retrieved from: http://www.bbc.co.uk/sport/football/15672054

BBC (2012) Arsenal football club in £150m Emirates deal. [online] Retrieved from: http://www.bbc.co.uk/news/business-20464096

Becker-Olsen, K. and Hill, R. (2006) The impact of sponsor fit on brand equity: the case of nonprofit service providers. *Journal of Service Research*, 9(1), 73–83.

Boyd, J. (2000) Selling home: Corporate stadium names and the destruction of commemoration. *Journal of Applied Communication Research*, 28(4), 330–46.

Bruhn, M. and Holzer, M. (2015) The role of the fit construct and sponsorship portfolio size for event sponsorship success: a field study. *European Journal of Marketing*, 49(5/6), 874–893.

Church, A. and Penny, S. (2013) Power, space and the new stadium: the example of Arsenal Football Club. *Sport in Society*, 16(6), 819–834.

Conn, D. (2011) Newcastle stadium name-change lacks class and is unworthy of history. *The Guardian*. [online] Retrieved from: http://www.theguardian.com/football/blog/2011/nov/10/newcastle-united-st-james-renaming

Crompton, J. and Howard, D. (2003) The American experience with facility naming rights: opportunities for English professional football teams. *Managing Leisure*, 8(4), 212–226.

DeSchriver, T. and Jensen, P. (2003) What's in a name? Price variation in sport facility naming rights. *Eastern Economic Journal*, 29(3), 359–376.

Donlan, L. (2014) An empirical assessment of factors affecting the brand-building effectiveness of sponsorship. *Sport, Business and Management: An International Journal*, 4(1), 6–25.

Edensor, T. and Millington, S. (2008) "This is Our City": branding football and local embeddedness. *Global Networks*, 8(2), 172–193.

Eddy, T. (2014) Measuring effects of naming-rights sponsorships on college football fans' purchasing intentions. *Sport Management Review*, 17(3), 362–375.

Edwards, L. (2012) Newcastle United sponsorship deal with Wonga will see St James' Park reinstated as stadium name. *The Telegraph*. [online] Retrieved from: http://www.telegraph.co.uk/sport/football/teams/newcastle-united/9596399/Newcastle-United-sponsorship-deal-with-Wonga-will-see-St-James-Park-reinstated-as-stadium-name.html

Grohs, R. (2015) Drivers of brand image improvement in sports-event sponsorship. *International Journal of Advertising*, 35(3), 391–420.

Grohs, R. and Reisinger, H. (2014) Sponsorship effects on brand image: the role of exposure and activity involvement. *Journal of Business Research*, 67(5), 1018–1025.

Gross, P. and Wiedmann, K. (2015) The vigor of a disregarded ally in sponsorship: brand image transfer effects arising from a cosponsor. *Psychology & Marketing*, 32(11), 1079–1097.

Groza, M., Cobbs, J. and Schaefers, T. (2012) Managing a sponsored brand: the importance of sponsorship portfolio congruence. *International Journal of Advertising*, 31(1), 63–84.

Gwinner, K. (1997) A model of image creation and image transfer in event sponsorship. *International Marketing Review*, 14(3), 145–158.

Gwinner, K. and Eaton, J. (1999) Building brand image through event sponsorship: the role of image transfer. *Journal of Advertising*, 28(4), 47–57.

Gwinner, K. and Swanson, S. (2003) A model of fan identification: antecedents and sponsorship outcomes. *Journal of Services Marketing*, 17(3), 275–294.

Haan, P. and Shank, M. (2004) Consumers' perceptions of NFL stadium naming rights. *International Journal of Sports Marketing and Sponsorship*, 5(4), 25–37.

Hartland, T., Skinner, H., and Griffiths, A. (2005) Tries and conversions: are sports sponsors pursuing the right objectives? *International Journal of Sports Marketing & Sponsorship* 6(3), 164–173.

Henseler, J., Wilson, B., and De Vreede, D. (2009) Can sponsorships be harmful for events? Investigating the transfer of associations from sponsors to events. *International Journal of Sports Marketing and Sponsorship*, 10(3), 47–54.

HMSO (1990) The Hillsborough Stadium Disaster, 15 April 1989, Inquiry by the RT Hon Lord Justice Taylor, Final Report. [online] London: HMSO. Retrieved from: http://www.southyorks.police.uk/sites/default/files/hillsborough%20stadium%20disaster%20final%20report.pdf

IEG (2017a) IEG's Guide to Sponsorship. [online] Retrieved from: https://www.sponsorship.com/IEG/files/59/59ada496-cd2c-4ac2-9382-060d86fcbdc4.pdf

IEG (2017b) How O2 Is Using Sponsorship To Prevent Customer Churn. [online] Retrieved from: http://www.sponsorship.com/iegsr/2017/03/How-O2-Is-Using-Sponsorship-To-Prevent-Customer-Ch.aspx

Johar, G. and Pham, M. (1999) Relatedness, prominence, and constructive sponsor identification. *Journal of Marketing Research*, 36(3), 299–313.

Journey to the 92, (2017) Premier League Ground Guide. [online] Retrieved from: http://www.tothe92.co.uk/premguide.html

Klijn, E., Eshuis, J., and Braun, E. (2012) The influence of stakeholder involvement on the effectiveness of place branding. *Public Management Review*, 14(4), 499–519.

Kozinets, R.V. (2002) The field behind the screen: using netnography for marketing research in online communities. *Journal of Marketing Research*, 39(1), 61–72.

Kwon, E., Ratneshwar, S., and Kim, E. (2016) Brand image congruence through sponsorship of sporting events: a reinquiry of Gwinner and Eaton (1999). *Journal of Advertising*, 45(1), 130–138.

Mail Online (2012a) Toon fan charged following graffiti bid to reinstate iconic sign … hours after club tear it down. *Daily Mail.* [online] Retrieved from: http://www.dailymail.co.uk/sport/football/article-2102505/St-James-Park-sprayed-grafitti-sign-removal.html

Mail Online (2012b) Not again! Angry Newcastle fans return to reinstate iconic St James' Park sign. *Daily Mail.* [online] Retrieved from: http://www.dailymail.co.uk/sport/football/article-2103709/St-James-Park-graffiti-sprayed-Newcastle-again.html

Mazodier, M. and Merunka, D. (2012) Achieving brand loyalty through sponsorship: the role of fit and self-congruity. *Journal of the Academy of Marketing Science*, 40(6), 807–820.

McDonald, C. (1991) Sponsorship and the image of the sponsor. *European Journal of Marketing*, 25(11), 31–38.

Medway, D. and Warnaby, G. (2014) What's in a name? Place branding and toponymic commodification. *Environment and Planning A*, 46(1), 153–167.

Nufer, G. and Bühler, A. (2010) How effective is the sponsorship of global sports events? A comparison of the FIFA World Cups in 2006 and 1998. *International Journal of Sports Marketing and Sponsorship*, 11(4), 33–49.

Ogden, M. (2015) Manchester United rule out selling Old Trafford naming rights. *The Telegraph.* [online] Retrieved from: http://www.telegraph.co.uk/sport/football/teams/manchester-united/11594591/Manchester-United-rule-out-selling-Old-Trafford-naming-rights.html

Olson, E. and Thjømøe, H. (2011) Explaining and articulating the fit construct in sponsorship. *Journal of Advertising*, 40(1), 57–70.

Philadelphia Union (2015) Talen Energy Assumes Stadium Naming Rights. [online] Retrieved from: https://www.philadelphiaunion.com/post/2015/11/30/talen-energy-assumes-stadium-naming-rights

Reysen, S., Snider, J. and Branscombe, N. (2012) Corporate renaming of stadiums, team identification, and threat to distinctiveness. *Journal of Sport Management*, 26(4), 350–357.

Roy, D. and Cornwell, T. (2003) Brand equity's influence on responses to event sponsorships. *Journal of Product & Brand Management*, 12(6), 377–393.

Samuelsen, B., Olsen, L., and Keller, K. (2015) The multiple roles of fit between brand alliance partners in alliance attitude formation. *Marketing Letters*, 26(4), 619–629.

Simmons, C. and Becker-Olsen, K. (2006) Achieving marketing objectives through social sponsorships. *Journal of Marketing*, 70(4), 154–169.

Skard, S. and Thorbjornsen, H. (2017) Closed-ended and open-ended fit articulation: communication strategies for incongruent sponsorships. *European Journal of Marketing*, 51(7/8), 1414–1439.

Smith, G. (2004) Brand image transfer through sponsorship: a consumer learning perspective. *Journal of Marketing Management*, 20(3/4), 457–474.

Soccerex, (2010) Generali to sponsor Austria Vienna stadium. [online] Retrieved from: https://www.soccerex.com/insight/articles/2010/generali-to-sponsor-austria-vienna-stadium

Speed, R. and Thompson, P. (2000) Determinants of sports sponsorship response. *Journal of the Academy of Marketing Science*, 28(2), 226–238.

Tajfel, H. (1982). Social psychology of intergroup relations. *Annual Review of Psychology*, 33(1), 1–39.

Thornburg, R.H. (2002) Stadium naming rights: an assessment of the contract and trademark issues inherent to both professional and collegiate stadiums. *Virginia Sports & Entertainment Law Journal*, 2, 328–358.

Tripodi, J.A. and Hirons, M. (2009) Sponsorship leveraging case studies – Sydney 2000 Olympic Games. *Journal of Promotion Management*, 15(1/2), 118–136.

Tsiotsou, R., Alexandris, K., and Cornwell, T. (2014) Using evaluative conditioning to explain corporate co-branding in the context of sport sponsorship. *International Journal of Advertising*, 33(2), 295–327.

Vaswani, K. (2016) Opinion: Can King Power do a Leicester? [online] Retrieved from: http://www.prweek.com/article/1393903/opinion-king-power-leicester

Vuolteenaho, J. and Kolamo, S. (2012) *Textually produced landscape spectacles? A Debordian reading of Finnish namescapes and English soccerscapes*. Helsinki: Helsinki Collegium for Advanced Studies, (pp. 132–158).

Weeks, C., Cornwell, T., and Drennan, J. (2008) Leveraging sponsorships on the internet: activation, congruence, and articulation. *Psychology & Marketing*, 25(7), 637–654.

Woisetschläger, D., Backhaus, C., and Cornwell, T. (2017) Inferring corporate motives: how deal characteristics shape sponsorship perceptions. *Journal of Marketing*, 81(5), 121–141.

Woisetschläger, D., Eiting, A., Haselhoff, V., and Michaelis, M. (2010) Determinants and consequences of sponsorship fit: a study of fan perceptions. *Journal of Sponsorship*, 3(2), 169–180.

Woisetschläger, D. and Haselhoff, V. (2009) The name remains the same for fans' – why fans oppose naming right sponsorships. In: A. McGill and S. Shavitt (eds.). *NA-Advances in Consumer Research Volume 36* (pp. 775–776). Duluth, MN: Association for Consumer Research.

Woisetschläger, D., Haselhoff, V., and Backhaus, C. (2014) Fans' resistance to naming right sponsorships: why stadium names remain the same for fans. *European Journal of Marketing*, 48(7/8), 1487–1510.

17

Venue management in football

Eric C. Schwarz

Introduction

Football is big business globally! However, football cannot operate without having quality venues for training and games. This chapter on venue management in football looks at the business and management concepts inherent to quality management of football infrastructure. The chapter will start with a summary of the various ownership, organisational, human resource, financial, marketing, and operational management concepts inherent to managing football stadia. Next will be a look at the logistics issues to be considered for venue management for all events, including trainings, games, and alternative uses. Finally, will be a look at measuring performance in terms of financial and operational success.

While this is most certainly not a complete and comprehensive explanation of all the concepts of venue management in football, this chapter will provide a starting point for understanding the depth and breadth of responsibilities inherent to managing football venues. Perspectives on specific aspects of venue management in football will vary in terms of size and scope of football venues.

What is venue management?

Venue management refers to the maintenance and care of football facilities of all shapes and sizes – from local municipal pitches to large stadia; training grounds to large-scale football academies; and government-owned facilities to private enterprises. Regardless of the type of football venue, the goal of any manager is to organise and supervise the maintenance and operation of the football venue in an economically, socially, and environmentally responsible manner. Closely associated with venue management are venue operations, which for a football venue, involves maintaining, controlling, and improving organisational activities implemented to ensure the processes of producing and distributing core and ancillary football products and services to participants and spectators are accomplished in an efficient and effective manner (Schwarz, Hall, and Shibli, 2015). The intersection between venue management and venue operations is crucial for football facilities to ensure the safe and secure delivery of the sport and its associated services.

A football venue manager must understand a number of functions in order to be successful. Initially, they must understand the various ownership structures from a governance and business standpoint that they might be working under. Then there are the actual managerial functions inherent to venue operations, including organisational management, human resources, decision-making, operations planning, and implementation of operational functions (Schwarz, Hall, and Shibli, 2015). In addition, the football venue manager must also be able to oversee logistical functions for all football – and non-football–related events including trainings, games, and alternative uses. This may include marketing, risk assessments, security planning, scheduling, event bookings, sales, ticketing, box office management, food and beverage, merchandising, parking, and other assorted event management and facility service functions (Schwarz, Hall, and Shibli, 2015). Finally, the football venue manager must be able to measure the performance of all functions in terms of financial and operational success using benchmarks and performance management techniques (Schwarz, Hall, and Shibli, 2015).

Ownership structures

At the core of any football venue is the ownership structure in place. In looking at the ownership structure, there are two sub-structures to comprehend. First is the governance structure that dictates how the management and operational oversight of the venue are conducted and second is the business structure that drives the legal business status of the entity (Schwarz, Hall, and Shibli, 2015).

Football venue governance will usually fall under one of four governance structures: public governance, private governance, non-profit or voluntary governance, and governance by trust. Public football facilities operate under some variation of governmental or quasi-governmental oversight at any level (federal, regional, or local). Private football venue governance is run by an independent entity whose drive is commercial operations that generate profits. Non-profit governance, which also includes voluntary governance, are football facilities that are managed by volunteer executives and staff that operate the venue for the public benefit rather than for a profit. Finally, governance by trust is a unique ownership structure where a benefactor places a football venue into a trust that is managed by a trust manager who is assigned to ensure beneficiaries (customers, spectators, and participants) benefit from the services provided by the venue. Often these trusts are in the form of a charitable organisation, a non-profit without charitable status, or a public interest company.

From the business side, a football venue may have a structure as a sole proprietorship, a partnership, or a corporation. A sole proprietorship is the most basic business form because there is just one owner, which also means that a football venue manager in this case only has one person to answer to from a business standpoint. A partnership is where more than one individual is an owner. This becomes more complex for a football venue manager to work with because some of the partners will be general in nature and want to be fully involved in the day-to-day operations of the venue, with other being limited partners only concerned about their financial investment. The largest business structure is a corporation, which is created under the laws and regulations of governmental authority made up of a group of individuals who obtain a charter authorising them as a legal body to own and operate a football venue. The powers, rights, authority, and liabilities of the entity are distinct from the individuals making up the group, and the way in which the football venue manager must engage with the ownership will differ depending on the type of corporate structure that is in place. These can vary from traditional corporations to limited liability corporations to publicly traded corporations to non-profit corporations.

Regardless of the governance or business structure, the football venue manager must have a clear understanding of how to ensure organisational effectiveness through the achievement of outcomes inherent to a quality strategic planning process. There are many models of organisational effectiveness, but for a football venue, it is important to implement a contingency approach to management and operations since there is a wide variety of situations that can occur requiring flexibility to respond to specific sets of circumstances (Schwarz, Hall, and Shibli, 2015).

Organisational management

Regardless of the size or scope of any football venue, the human infrastructure is what helps bring the venue to life. The role of the venue manager in ensuring the proper organisational structure is put into place is vital to operating physical spaces and structures, as well as offering services and events to participants and spectators. The mission and vision of the venue owners, the service quality philosophy of the organisation, and the actual organisational structure put into operation drives the appropriate human infrastructure needed to manage a football venue (Schwarz, Hall, and Shibli, 2015).

As such, a football venue manager must understand the various management functions are roles. Let's start with the process of selecting and prioritising goals, objectives, and strategies through the planning process. It evolves through organising the assessment and delegation of resources to meet outcomes by leading and guiding staff to accomplish the required tasks and evaluate performance by monitoring the effective and efficient operation of the venue. This requires a football venue manager to be able to integrate the three major roles of organisational management: (1) developing interpersonal relationships through social interactions and (2) providing information through intelligence dissemination and overseeing dynamic collaborations through decision-making and problem-solving processes (Schwarz, Hall, and Shibli, 2015). This must be accomplished both upwards to ownership and to upper management, across similar management lines in other operational areas, and downward to various administrative and operational staff. This requires the football venue manager to be well versed in a variety of organisational behaviour characteristics, including personality, learning processes, attitudes, motivations, and perceptions. Beyond individual behaviours, venue managers must also be able to supervise and manage formal and informal group interactions to encourage teamwork across the organisation. Hence, the venue manager must also be able to demonstrate quality leadership skills to influence other members of the organisation to complete tasks, attain goals, and meet objectives by providing direction, managing conflict, taking risks, promoting an environment of trust, and driving towards success (Schwarz, Hall, and Shibli, 2015).

Human resource management

It is crucial for a venue manager to be well versed in human resource management. This is a function within a football venue related to the recruitment, training, and retention of personnel. Within a football venue, there are four general categories of human resources that a manager must be able to work with: professional staff, seasonal/part-time staff, volunteers, and customers/clients (Schwarz, Hall, and Shibli, 2015). Professional staff are hired to perform ongoing tasks such as pitch maintenance or infrastructure operations. This makes up the bulk of the full-time employees within a football venue. Seasonal or part-time staff are hired to perform specific tasks related to event operations and special functions. These may include ticket takers, ushers, security staff, and food service staff. Volunteers are non-employees that chose to become involved with a venue for no compensation to deliver a function that otherwise could not have been offered. This might include programs for raising money for charities or grassroots programming associated with the venue. Customers and clients such as participants or spectators provide both inputs and outputs for a football venue.

As with organisational management, understanding the individual differences between human resources is vital for success as a venue manager. A manager who is able to lead people is vital to the success of any venue. However, even more important is hiring the right people from the start. Football venues have intricate designs and a multitude of unique functions that require specialised skills and knowledge. Involvement in the creation of job descriptions, development of employee workplace manuals, recruiting and selecting employees, providing appropriate orientation and training programs, offering ongoing professional development, and evaluating employee performance are all requirements of a quality football venue manager.

Financial management

A quality football venue manager must also be well versed in financial management. The need to understand financial statements related to operations is vital for the quality management of a football venue. A balance sheet articulated the financial position of the venue; an income statement documents the profit or loss; a statement of cash flows shows the movement of cash in and out of the entity, and the statement of owner's equity looks at the value and retained earnings of the venue (Schwarz, Hall, and Shibli, 2015). Of most importance to the football venue manager is the income statement because it articulates the revenues coming into the venue and the expenses incurred in running the venue. This information is vital for the development of operational budgets, which are the forecasted income and expenditures expected over a given time. Budgets are maintained on a daily, weekly, monthly, quarterly, and annual basis, and the need to project budgets accurately for the proper management and operation of a facility is a crucial skill needed by any football venue manager (Schwarz, Hall, and Shibli, 2015).

In addition, it is necessary for football venue managers to expand those budgeting skills to project capital needs for improvements. Known as capital investment appraisal and budgeting, this is a process to plan for short- and long-term investments in fixed assets such as venue infrastructure, property improvements, and equipment upgrades (Schwarz, Hall, and Shibli, 2015). The ability to project these potential costs in advance and work with both management and ownership to maximise both existing capital and proposed capital investments is an important task to ensure meeting the strategic objectives and vision for the venue.

Logistics management

The ability to manage logistics is another crucial skill a football venue manager must have. Logistics management is a process of positioning resources to meet the user requirements of a football venue. The football venue manager is responsible for managing numerous products and services offered through the venue, and the manager must ensure that those products and services are in the right place at the right time to meet demand. Product and service management includes the products and services they have total control of (internal) and products and services they have limited control over (external) (Schwarz, Hall, and Shibli, 2015). Internal products include the venue itself – the playing surface and related equipment, seating, scoreboard/message boards, bathrooms, concession areas, and the general infrastructure. Internal services include maintenance, housekeeping, security, customer service, and first aid. External products include all aspects of the event taking place in the venue. External services are the added benefits provided by the event and other external entities to enhance the experience of the customer.

In addition, logistics management requires football venue managers to meet the needs and wants of customers by utilising resources available through supply chain management. A quality supply chain management process involves finding the best suppliers who can respond to the needs of the venue manager especially in the area of sourcing materials, equipment, and maintenance services (Schwarz, Hall, and Shibli, 2015). Having an effective supply chain also can reduce the need for the venue manager to reduce the amount of inventory they need to store and the number of full-time staff on payroll.

Finally, the venue manager also must constantly evaluate the life cycle of the football facility in terms of competition, saturation, and change. This is vital to maintaining appropriate levels of growth and maintenance throughout a time of maturity for the venue while avoiding decline and potential obsolescence of the football facility. As such, a high-quality logistics process can assist in the short- and long-term sustainability of the sport enterprise.

Operations management

In consideration of the previously mentioned skills, football venue managers must be able to engage in quality operational decision-making to solve problems and meet the strategic objectives set for the venue. This is the foundation for operations management, as the primary goal is to maintain quality experiences for users on a consistent basis in consideration of the resources available. With having a strong ownership and organisational structure, as well as being able to oversee human resource and financial functions in an efficient and effective manner, quality operations management is feasible. However, it is much more: It is also engaging in a process of continuous improvement to ensure strengths are enhanced, weaknesses are addressed, opportunities are taken advantage of, and threats are avoided.

Many football venue managers subscribe to a process of TQM (total quality management). This comprehensive and structured approach strives to improve the quality of all venue services through constant refinement via a planning, implementation, and evaluation process. Most effective in the areas of measuring customer service, human resource management, and marketing through public relations and the media, TQM seeks to provide a safe, efficient, and equitable operation of the football venue by providing and maintaining appropriate procedures for use and upkeep of facilities and equipment that contribute to the satisfaction of users. Operating procedures differ based on the various operations and services provided within a football venue, but the most common areas include plant operations, maintenance and repair, alterations management, inventory management, energy management, waste management and recycling, and environmental management including greening and sustainability (Schwarz, Hall, and Shibli, 2015).

From a service standpoint, areas such as ticketing, parking, custodial/housekeeping, and concessions may be managed in-house by the football venue manager or be outsourced, requiring the venue manager to work with outside vendors. The ticketing operation at a football venue facility can range from a small box office of one person selling tickets for general admission to an event to a full-service box office with a separate manager, paid staff, and relationships with secondary and tertiary ticketing services. Through ticketing, and by extension credentialing, this function allows a football venue manager to control admissions to events. As such, the venue manager must have a complete understanding of their inventory, or the number of seats available to a specific event. Seating capacities vary based on the type of event and have a direct effect on every operational function in the facility. A crowd for an opening training will be significantly smaller than that of a Champions League or FIFA World Cup match.

One such area would be parking. Football venues should offer enough parking for spectators, members, guest, employees, and management. The usual standard for a football stadium is one parking spot for every four seats if there is no mass transit to the facility, and less if there is mass transit available. Venue managers must have a parking and/or transportation plan integrated into the entire facility and event planning process. In some cases, parking may be outsourced to another company to manage, or if available, municipal parking garages may be utilised. Each football venue manager must weigh the pros and cons of parking, the potential revenue it can generate, and the additional responsibilities and liabilities that would be incurred to determine the best direction for the facility to take.

Another service affected by the size of crowds is the custodial and housekeeping functions. Football venue managers must ensure that their venue is clean and functional. Participants and spectators do not want to attend events as a facility that is dirty or where simple items such as soap, paper towels, and toilet paper are not readily available. The same is true with concessions, which are defined as a secondary business under contract or license from a primary business to exclusively operate and provide a specialised service. In football venues, the main two concessions areas are merchandising and food service. The major goals of both are to create a market demand for the products and services offered and increase the profitability and financial health of the entire venue. As with any other service, concessions can be outsourced or kept in-house. Most often, merchandising is an in-house function, where a majority of food service is outsourced – mainly because of the significant liability. This is because food and beverage services offer additional challenges related to the implementation of the planning process for preventing food safety problems related to the purchase, receiving, storage, preparation, cooking, packaging, transport, or display of food. Especially important to ensuring food safety and management is the concept of cleanliness and sanitation.

Event planning and management

A service area that is vital to football venue management success involves event planning and management. It is important to remember that no matter the size of the football venue, they need events, and events need venues. As such, football venue managers must implement their own sport event planning process as a part of its operations and management. The sport event planning process from the standpoint of a football venue involves the development of each football event (training, friendly match, league game, international tournament) from conceptualisation through activation to implementation and eventual evaluation as related to the infrastructure and support services offered (Schwarz, et al., 2017). This planning process involves setting objectives, conceptualising how the event will be implemented, and creating strategies for the event within the parameters of the infrastructure available at an affordable cost and in a manner that brings a positive image to all constituencies (Schwarz, et al., 2017). This requires the creation of feasibility studies and entering into negotiations to host an event. This may either be a part of a series of bid processes or through direct contact with an event promoter. A venue manager must also create a pro forma budget to anticipate what the general costs of hosting an event will be for the venue.

Once all terms are agreed upon, contracts are signed and pre-event preparation begins. The football venue manager works to ensure the event is presented and produced in a professional manner, as the appearance is a reflection on the football venue in the community. The venue manager also needs to ensure any processes implemented by the event do not damage the venue and have contingency plans in place for ensuring repair and restoration as quickly as possible post-event should damage occur. Venue managers must also be involved with activating the venue's event marketing plan, implementing and activating the event plan (set-up, pre-event, during the event, post-event, and breakdown), determining the level of involvement of facility personnel, coordinating tasks with unions and facility services (both in-house and outsourced), and preparing for any unexpected problems that may occur (Schwarz, et al., 2017). In addition, after the event has taken place, the football venue manager must engage in an evaluation process to determine the success of the event and improvements to be made when hosting future similar events.

Risk assessment and security planning

One of the most significant jobs before, during, and after an event hosted in a football venue is the assessment of risk and planning for security to manage risk. Risk is the possibility of loss from a threat. Risk increases as the consequences and probability of occurrence increases. Risk management is important to football venue managers in order to meet legal obligations, prevent financial loss, and ensure business continuity. An all-hazards approach must be employed when assessing potential threats and risks. This can include both man-made and natural events. Football venue managers face significant challenges in determining potential threats and must prepare for a wide range of possible incidents. In order to identify potential threats, football venue managers should conduct a risk assessment, which is the process of evaluating security-related risks from threats to an organisation, its assets, or personnel. The assessment process gathers critical information to aid the venue manager in the decision-making process related to specific assets and vulnerabilities inherent to the venue. This includes evaluating consequences, analysing risk levels, and providing countermeasure improvements in terms of the probability and consequence severity of a threat/risk (Schwarz, Hall, and Shibli, 2015). Venue managers also work to control risk through several strategies that may range from avoiding, transferring, reducing, or retaining risks.

As a result, football venue managers need to employ various security management systems to reduce risk and exposure to vulnerabilities. Venue managers have a range of responsibilities including keeping the football venue in safe repair, discovering potential hazards, and protecting users from foreseeable dangers. This requires a coordinated and collaborative effort from multiple stakeholders including individuals, government agencies, and private contractors to develop and implement venue emergency response plans for a range of activities including game-day operations, evacuation procedures, and incident responses to a variety of emergency scenarios up to and including terrorism. Implementing appropriate protective security measures will assist in detecting, deterring, and defending the football venue from attack or illegal activity. Standard protective security measures should be implemented on a permanent basis as routine inspection for a football venue including venue site design, safety, and sustainability; physical protection systems; perimeter and access control; communications; security personnel; training and exercise; crowd management; emergency management; and business continuity and recovery (Schwarz, Hall, and Shibli, 2015).

A hallmark example of quality risk assessment and security management was during the terrorist attacks in Paris, France on 15 November 2015. Among the various venues targeted by terrorists was the national football stadium of France, the Stade de France. One of the terrorists had a ticket to attend the France–Germany friendly match that was attended by 80,000 spectators including the French president (Robinson and Landauro, 2015). It was believed that his intention was to set off his suicide vest inside the stadium causing as much damage, destruction, and death as possible. It was also believed that this would create panic amongst other spectators who could have been also injured or killed through human crushing. Fortunately, the terrorist was prevented from entering the stadium due to security pat-down procedures being implemented at the entrance and the terrorist being refused entry into the venue. The terrorist eventually detonated their suicide vest outside the stadium. This, among other events on the evening across the city, resulted in further risk assessments being implemented to determine the best way to protect the spectators and game participants inside the venue. It was determined to evacuate the French president so he could coordinate a response to the emergency; continue the game but lock the stadium down; bring spectators onto the pitch after the game for a controlled evacuation once it was deemed safe to do; and keep the German team at the stadium overnight as their hotel had received a bomb threat (Robinson and Landauro, 2015).

Marketing management

In past generations of venue manager, the football venue manager was tasked with only managing the operations of a facility. In the 1990s and early 2000s, this changed drastically with venue managers expected to be actively engaged in marketing. The relationship between marketing and venue management stems from providing products and services that satisfy the needs, wants, and desires of the consumer. This requires the football venue manager to understand how to reach users – spectators and participants – through segmenting the population, targeting specific groups, positioning the football venue to influence potential customers to attend and/or use the facility, and then deliver on what is promised (Schwarz, et al., 2017). The football venue manager must also evaluate the venue itself and the competition in terms of a SWOT analysis – internal strengths and weakness of the football venue, and external opportunities and threats posed by competition and the environment (Schwarz, et al., 2017). Finally, the football venue manager must constantly evaluate a changing climate in terms of forecasting the factors that will have a direct effect on the internal and external functioning of the sport facility, such as the economy, societal change, politics, weather, and other uncontrollable factors (Schwarz, et al., 2017).

Venue managers are also actively engaged in the sales process on numerous inventories, including leasing/rental of the facility for events; ticketing and box office management; premium access (suites, club seating, public seating licenses/debentures); product branding through pouring rights and various promotional sales efforts, including advertising (signage and promotions) and sponsorships (naming rights and endorsements). With regard to the promotional aspects involved with marketing a football venue, the manager must understand all aspects of the promotional mix, including advertising, sponsorship, atmospherics, and public relations. Advertising partnerships need to match the venue's brand strategy. Football venue managers are involved with the management of sponsorships to ensure that the terms of the sponsorship are being upheld in terms of exclusivity, signage within the facility, implementation of promotional activities, and accuracy in the delivery of the corporate image and likeness. In terms of atmospherics, the venue manager must control the environment based on the needs and wants of the consumer – including temperature, lighting, sound, colour, and traffic flow.

One of the biggest marketing challenges for a football venue manager is public relations. While a major part of this work focuses on determining the best methods for getting information out to the public through various methods to enhance the image and awareness of the facility and the events being hosted, the relationship with the media is challenging. As the relationship with the media is crucial to how the brand of the football venue is articulated, the venue manager must implement numerous efforts to give the media more access than general customers. These may include press box/press row exclusively for the media; credentials for sideline/on-field access/locker room and behind-the-scenes access; areas for holding exclusive and group press conferences/interviews; and access to communications (phones/faxes/Internet technology) to file stories efficiently.

Hospitality and VIP management

One area that continues to evolve in football venue management is the area of hospitality and VIP management. The purpose of this area of venue management is to offer value-added experiences and amenities to the highest-end users during football events. This may include areas such as corporate/luxury boxes, private seat license and membership seating areas, specialised catering areas, and hosted experiences. For some of the largest football clubs in the world, hospitality and VIP services have created significant revenue and may result is as much as 25 per cent of a facility's operating income. For a club like Real Madrid that plays their home matches at the Estadio Bernabeu in downtown Madrid, the hospitality and VIP department offers both seasonal and match-day products to meet the needs of corporate clients and players' families. Their seasonal products are targeted to corporate clients for use during non-match day times throughout the year, offering exclusive and customised services and benefits across multiple areas of the stadium including outdoor luxury seating, Zen Market Restaurant, Area Blanca on the first Tier, second and third Tier Boxes, exclusive Tower Boxes, Puerta 57 restaurant seating, Asador de la Esquina restaurant seating, Real Café seating, and the Trophy Room (Real Madrid, 2017). On match days, the clientele is a mix of corporate clients and individuals wanting exclusive and customised services as part of their experience. These experiences are limited to the restaurants and specialised rooms, as boxes and luxury seating are purchased through memberships and corporate contracts.

Estadio Bernabeu and Real Madrid have four key performance indicators for hospitality and VIP management. The first is continuous adaptation and improvement to meet the ever-changing client needs and climate conditions through new products, visual changes, new services, catering enhancements, and top-quality customer service. The second is transforming to win in a volatile, uncertain, complex, and ambiguous (VUCA) world by bringing together the love the fans have for the brand through best industry practices and new technologies. The third is implementing innovation that will delight customers. The last is to be the best and portray excellence in all they do. This is all a strategic process that involves benchmarking via conducting a client analysis, redefining the products and services as needed, and pricing them to sell (Real Madrid, 2017).

Measuring and evaluating success

In consideration of this, it is important to close this chapter with an explanation of the responsibility a football venue manager has as related to the measuring and evaluating of success through benchmarking. Benchmarking is the process of comparing performance either in comparison with other football facilities or with previous performance of the football venue being measured (Schwarz, Hall, and Shibli, 2015). The main purpose of benchmarking is to determine whether the best course of action has been taken by the football venue manager regarding the decisions they have made across any function inherent to the venue. This feedback of performance serves as the foundation for measuring and evaluating success.

Performance management on a broader scale goes beyond benchmarking in three main ways. First, performance management aids football venue managers achieve better results through understanding the drivers of performance and how to influence them. The main drivers of performance, and hence the framework for key performance indicators (KPIs), are usually centred on data collected through research, reviewing the statistical performance of others and comparing to the performance of the venue, and an assessment of the processes being implemented by the football venue (Schwarz, et al., 2017). Second, quality performance management evaluation provides valid and reliable information beyond just the assumptions and postulations of the venue manager alone. Finally, when performance management becomes a part of the organisational culture of the football venue, clarity on the operational, business, and continuous improvement functions become an embedded part of the organisation, hence enhancing efficiency, effectiveness, equity, customer satisfaction, and service quality across the entire football venue operation (Schwarz, et al., 2017).

By definition, performance management in football venue management is taking action as a result of actual performances that make the outcomes for spectators and participants better than they otherwise would have been. Hence, it a process of improving venue performance by informing venue management decision-making with proper planning, realistic objectives, appropriate targets, quality measurements, and a process for review (Schwarz, et al., 2017). While managers often believe they know what is best for their venue, without evidence to guide decisions that demonstrate whether strategies and objectives are being realised, good management is not being employed. Furthermore, this evidence identifies financial and operational changes needed, validates decisions, demonstrates customer behaviour towards products and services, and identifies levels of services quality.

Conclusion

Football venue management involves the maintenance and care of facilities of all shapes and sizes. The goal of any football venue manager is to organise and supervise the maintenance and operation of the football venue in an economically, socially, and environmentally responsible manner. A football venue manager must understand a number of functions in order to be successful. They must first understand the ownership and governance structure of the venue they are managing, as that will directly influence organisational effectiveness and the strategic planning process. The football venue manager must also understand organisational management in terms of the human infrastructure that is available to operate the venue. The role of the venue manager in developing the appropriate organisational structure is vital to operating physical spaces and structures and offering services and events to participants and spectators. This requires football venue managers to understand a multitude of management functions including human resources, financial, logistics, operations, event planning, risk assessment, security planning, marketing, and ancillary operations.

Ultimately, the key to good football venue management is the ability to incorporate performance evidence into the decision-making process to maximise the quality management of football venues. While this chapter is most certainly not a complete and comprehensive explanation of all the concepts of venue management in football, benchmarking and performance management provide a focus for understanding the depth and breadth of responsibilities inherent to managing football venues. Perspectives on specific aspects of venue management in football will vary in terms of training facilities and grounds; privately owned and large-scale stadia; and government and community-owned facilities, to name but a few influencing factors. However, regardless of size or scope, good football venue management has its foundation in quality management measured through appropriate benchmarks and an appropriate performance management process.

References

Real Madrid (2017) Hospitality. *Real Madrid*. [online] Retrieved from: https://www.realmadrid.com/en/vip-area

Robinson, J. and Landauro, I. (2015) Paris attacks: suicide bomber was blocked from entering Stade de France. *wsj.com*. [online] Retrieved from: https://www.wsj.com/amp/articles/attacker-tried-to-enter-paris-stadium-but-was-turned-away-1447520571

Schwarz, E.C., Hall, S.A., and Shibli, S. (2015) *Sport Facility Operations Management: A Global Perspective* (2nd ed.). Oxford, UK: Routledge.

Schwarz, E.C., Westerbeek, H., Liu, D., Emery, P., and Turner, P. (2016) *Managing Sport Facilities and Major Events* (2nd ed.). Oxford, UK: Routledge.

18

Human resource management in football

Jonathan Lord

Introduction

Although football has managed to avoid the in-depth research into its internal human resource (HR) practices, the management of the people resource has always played a vital role, especially in the supervision of players and staff, the adoption of management styles, and the use of policies and procedures to support the growing commercial nature of football clubs. The use of the "moneyball" principle, now being implemented within sport, is one example as to the growing use of human resource management (HRM) practices to help improve the overall success of a football club.

From a historical perspective, "personnel" has always been integrated into the world of football in a non-systemic way, with managers and players bringing their extensive working backgrounds into the profession. Successful British football manager Sir Alex Ferguson states his dock-yard and trade union background were key educational tools that enabled him to become one of the best football managers and implement systems and processes throughout the whole club.

Now clubs are looking to use contemporary HRM theory, systems, and processes to support their development from the first team through to the commercial and community aspect of its operations. However, despite the increase in use of HRM practices there are still questions as to the reasons why normal HR practices are never questioned in football, yet are the subject of contentious debates in the field of HRM, particularly the public scrutiny of player performance. It is interesting to analyse whether the same practices would be effective in a typical non-football organisation and whether employees in other industries have the same desire to be recognised and rewarded for their performance.

The future for HRM – both inside and outside a sports context – will focus on people analytics, which uses data and analysis to understand an expansive range of issues related to employees, including recruitment and selection, performance management, leadership, and attendance. For employers, the key is to ensure decisions relating to recruitment and employee development are based on proven criteria. Companies who understand the benefits of this analysis, coupled with the way in which workforce metrics influence their bottom line and help to drive and predict future success, will have the edge over their competitors. This will

be discussed further in the chapter but it is worth noting that the football sector has utilised these types of systems for many years; for example, OPTA, a sports statistics company,
recorded around 1,500 "events" from every fixture. Professor Ian McHale from the University
of Salford co-created the EA SPORTS Player Performance Indicator, which uses statistical modelling (and not statistics) to identify not only the obvious statistics around goals and
passes but also whose contribution mattered more to their team over a season. For example,
the individual actions of a player (his/her passes, tackles, crosses, etc.) will affect the number
of shots his/her team has. In turn, the number of shots a team has, and how good those shots
are (the shot effectiveness) affects the number of goals that team scores. Lastly, the number of
goals scored by the two teams playing determines who wins the match. (This last part is rather
obvious, but nonetheless important to state!).

People analytics, also known as talent analytics or HR analytics, are very similar and refer
to the method of analytics that can assist managers to make decisions about their employees or
workforce. People analytics applies statistics, technology, and expertise to large sets of talent data,
which results in making better management and business decisions for an organisation that used
to be based on the old approaches of gut feeling which is no longer sufficient and replacing this
with computerised tests, database searches, and quantifiable performance metrics. Large corporations such as Google have invested heavily in this field, creating their own people analytics
team; it will be interesting to see whether this area of HRM will take off. However, for HR
traditionalists, it will be difficult to completely remove the necessity to get to know employees,
to find out what motivates them and actually talk. The success, performance, and competitiveness of football clubs or any other institution depends largely on the quality of the employees,
and having good HRM systems is integral to this. This chapter will review the background to
HRM, how HRM has become more involved in the world of sport, how football clubs and
organisations have adopted HR systems, and finally how a key element of HRM, leadership
style, has influenced the management of playing staff.

HRM: a historical context

According to Niven (1967, p. 1), the origins of "welfare personnel" can be traced back to the
latter part of the 1880s when a:

> ... handful of pioneer employers and welfare workers saw together the immediate need for
> improving working and social conditions through "industrial betterment."

Notable employers included the families of Cadbury and Rowntree who were intrinsically
linked to the Quaker tradition (McKenna and Beech, 2008). It is generally acknowledged
that working conditions during this period were particularly appalling, even in comparison to
today's worst standards (Foot and Hook, 2011). Although the government had tried to address
these issues through legislation (*Factories Act,* 1878) and also trade union members were elected
to the House of Commons to champion the causes of workers, it was enlightened employers
who wanted to improve working conditions for their employees through the adoption of various schemes, which dealt with unemployment, sick pay and subsidised housing for employees.
According to McKenna and Beech (2008), the motives of particular employers were questioned
as there was a general feeling of suspicion and scepticism of their practices, accusing employers
of introducing these schemes as an alternative to realistic wages, and also avoiding contact –
leading to possible disputes – with trade unions. Despite this scepticism, a number of organisations continued with this welfare policy, and it is generally acknowledged (see Niven, 1978) that

in 1896 the first 'personnel officer' was Miss Mary Wood who was appointed by Rowntrees in York. Her remit encompassed the wellbeing of women and children who were employed by the organisation, in particular monitoring and improving their health and behaviour.

Cadbury's was another company that had similar convictions of employee welfare, although their philosophy and approach was completely different to that of Rowntrees, who believed that the welfare of the workforce was the responsibility of each member of staff. In 1900, Edward Cadbury, spoke of the need to:

> ... develop the social and moral character of each worker ... the supreme principle has been that business efficiency and the welfare of employees are but different sides of the same problem.
>
> *(Niven 1978, p. 23)*

In 1913, a conference was called in York by Seebohm Rowntree, which was attended by 60 industrial welfare workers, resulting in the Welfare Workers' Association being formed, which eventually morphed into the modern day Chartered Institute of Personnel and Development (Foot and Hook, 2011).

At this key stage of "HRM," the first stages of personnel and government synergy emerged. During the First World War, the government had to utilise the best of resources, which included people, and also had to conform to the raft of recently introduced liberal employment legislation. As a result, the government established the Industrial Welfare Department under the auspices of the Ministry of Munitions, which had the responsibility for introducing new welfare and personnel policies by persuasion into factories (Foot and Hook, 1999). The Industrial Welfare Department ensured compulsory welfare workers in explosives factories and "strongly encouraged" them within munitions factories.

The period between the First World War and the Second World War saw personnel develop even further, although the need for efficient selection methods were omitted, possibly due to the high unemployment rate. The key development of personnel during this period was the emphasis on personnel administration, which involved supporting management in areas such as recruitment, discipline, time-keeping, payment systems, training, and keeping personnel records (McKenna and Beech, 2008).

The role of personnel developed further after the Second World War and into the 1950s to encompass areas such as salary administration, basic training, and advice on industrial relations. During this period, a growth in the labour market ensured that the various governments continued to support the rise of "personnel," with a particular interest in industrial relations. This can be attributed to a number of elements, including the shift from collective bargaining at industry level to company level, which required personnel workers to develop specialist skills in industrial relations (McKenna and Beech, 2008). With the increase in employment legislation in the 1960s and early 1970s, along with a high employment rate, there was an increase in activity around the core principles of personnel, specifically recruitment, selection, training, and remuneration. The practices of recruitment and selection were prompted by the shortages of labour and the need to attract and retain highly skilled staff. Training was regimented and systematically planned in accordance with the training boards, which, as previously stated, were created to fund and provide training within specific industries.

The establishment of training boards under the *Industrial Training Act* (1964), forced employers to dedicate time and resources to training. This resulted in training becoming another specialism within personnel, as well as other activities such as performance appraisal, management development, and "manpower" (sic) planning. As discussed earlier, the most significant development of employment law arrived in 1964, with the creation of Industrial Tribunals and their widening remit in 1968 to encompass other areas of the employment relationship.

This had a far-reaching impact upon the personnel worker, as the increase in employment legislation and the threat of Industrial Tribunals, meant that the personnel function often acted as a specialist adviser, ensuring that managers followed the prescriptive elements of employment legislation while trying to avoid the conflict being resolved within an Industrial Tribunal. Providing specialist advice on employment legislation became an important aspect of personnel, partly due to the severe consequences of not complying with employment legislation, and therefore required a highly skilled and well-trained person to carry out this specialised role.

The 1970s also saw an increase in trade union activity, which required personnel workers to develop another specialism, in the form of negotiation. This development also saw the position of the personnel worker shift from a tactical role towards a more strategic objective (McKenna and Beech, 2008). Throughout this period, despite the economic and political climate, the subject and practice of personnel management had secured a relatively low-status position within companies and educational institutions. According to Wood (1983), Bacon (2003) and Kelly (2003) the subject of personnel suffered from both an overall neglect of management as an academic discipline and the dominant position of industrial relations and collective bargaining. With the advent of the 1980s and the Conservative government, a new opening enabled personnel and contemporary HRM to come to fruition. Relevant factors included:

> ... growing national interest in new management methods to stimulate productivity, industrial performance and competitive advantage in the world economy; the swing in public opinion and national economic policy- away from labour collectivism and toward a neo-liberal policy of open markets and individualised employment relations.
>
> *(Boxall, Purcell, and Wright, 2007, p. 39)*

With this came an increase in the visibility of personnel, with senior personnel executives providing a contribution to the discussions around the company's future strategic direction, as well as setting and reviewing business objectives. In tandem with the increase in visibility of personnel came the recession of the 1980s, which had the double impact of high unemployment and a decrease in the power of the trade unions. With the introduction of new legislation, trade unions found it less effective to strike and employers could replace staff members quickly. The reduction in strength of the trade unions meant that the role of the personnel worker changed considerably. Detailed and time-consuming processes, based on collective bargaining and conflict management were replaced with rapid wage negotiations and swifter changes in necessary working practices:

> There was a move away from the traditional adversarial industrial relations of the 1970's towards an approach that sought to achieve excellence in the organisation through a committed workforce.
>
> *(McKenna and Beech 2008, p. 4)*

The 1990s heralded two major developments that affected the world of personnel. First, as mentioned previously, employment legislation empowered the individual employee and further reduced the power of the trade unions. Second, employers were required to develop new working practices to ensure they could meet the changing demands of a flexible workforce, which included an increase in the number of staff employed on a part-time or temporary contract, as well as a growth in the number of people working from home. Employers who had previously relied upon traditional employment practices had to suddenly meet the demands of a diverse workforce, which required the requisite skills to develop the appropriate policies, procedures, and mechanisms to manage these new working arrangements. McKenna and Beech (2002, p. 4) argue that:

> ... the early 1990s witnessed a change in emphasis. The reaction to individualism and unjustifiable greed of the 1980s made way for the spirit of consent and the value of teamwork. There was concern for core workers who are essential to the operation of the organisation since commitment is required from these workers. They are expected to be flexible about the hours they work and to work above and beyond their job descriptions. Wages tend to reflect the market rate rather than the rate determined by agreements with trade unions.

These changes ensured that personnel workers, who were now being labelled HR professionals due to the acceptance/embracing of human resource management by academics and leading businesses, had to develop a new set of skills and gain an array of competencies, which could support organisations in achieving their aims and objectives. The increase in importance/structure of personnel within academia and the business world was highlighted by the merger in 1994 of the Institute of Personnel Management (IPM) and the Institute of Training and Development (ITD). The new organisation was named the Institute of Personnel and Development (IPD), which was eventually granted a Charter by the privy council in 2000.

The historic development of HRM mirrors the progression of systems within the world of football, with players for decades adhering to a players' maximum wage and other collective arrangements that were bargained for by the players union. Since the Bosman ruling by the European Court of Justice in 1995, which adjudicated that clubs no longer had to pay transfer fees after the expiration of a player's contract, players have adopted a more independent approach to contract negotiation, particularly with an increase in use of agents. This has made it even more important to have a more engaging approach to human resources, less adversarial and more strategic.

Introduction of HRM into the world of sport

There has been a lack of intention to introduce welfare and HRM practices into sporting organisations, which could be attributed to the size of the organisation, its attitude towards limited resources, the culture of the short-termism, authoritarian ownership, and informal management practices (Beaver, 2002). It can be further attributed to the perceived importance of the sporting sector, as well as significant power, extent, appeal, and size of the industry (Boyle and Haynes, 2009; Smart, 2007). A third consideration has been the reliance upon the volunteers to historically undertake operational work within sporting organisations due to the psychological connections individuals have with their chosen institutions (Doherty, 1998).

Smith and Stewart (2010) simply state that although sport is another form of enterprise its product is "idiosyncratic" and requires a customised set of principles to establish an efficient way of working. Therefore, over the last 20 years, HRM has played an increasingly important role with specific responsibilities in creating competitive advantage with the human capital in their organisations. Ruta and Sala (2018) believe that HRM professionals have the ability to create competitive advantage with their human capital in organisations. This is implemented through the use of HRM practices such as organisational culture and behaviour, strategic leadership, talent management, and dealing with highly motivated people.

Utilising HRM practices such as these can be difficult, due to the primary focus of any sporting organisation being economic sustainability. However, it is no coincidence that the main costs of sporting organisations, sometimes up to 80 per cent, are associated with salaries for playing staff (Ruta and Sala, 2018). Although recruiting and retaining staff players and coaches can provide a competitive edge over rivals, it is just as important to have the right management team and processes in place for the organisation to operate effectively.

Even thought HRM can play a vital role in the effectiveness of sporting organisations operations, Cuskelly, G. et al. (2006) argue that given the substantial differences between sporting and other business organisations, modifications to generic HR practices have to be made. A lack of research into HRM within sporting organisations has also contributed to adapted practices, although the use of HR Business Partners enabled a more integrated approach to HRM, which required a "holistic" set of management functions to produce sustained, high-level performance from its staff.

To elicit maximum performance there are numerous organisational processes specific to HRM, which include (i) job design or the nature of the organisational task, including variety, quantity, autonomy, and interdependence, (ii) staffing and development, (iii) personnel evaluation, (iv) rewards, (v) communication, (vi) leader behaviour, (vii) power, including sources and uses of power and member involvement in decision-making, and (viii) conflict resolution.

These elements are vital in supporting an organisation's operations, however, the complexity of the sporting industry can affect the processes outlined above. Ruta and Sala (2018) state that although the sporting industry is generally international in scope, it has the added complications of varying from country to country. Therefore, organisations have to be able to deal with different governing bodies, laws and regulations, social and political sensitivities, as well as cultural differences of the playing staff. Sporting organisations are generally recognised to be undersized, despite their international operation and multinational firm status. For example, UEFA had a turnover in 2016/2017 of 2.84 billion euros but employed only 500 staff members. This family firm mentality can affect career progression, the implementation of formal policies and the promotion of a culture of meritocracy. The world of sport is a specialised industry and job applicants are generally appointed for their connections rather than ability to do the job (Ruta and Sala, 2018). The implementation of a clear HRM strategy can therefore support the recruitment and retention of playing staff, sustain economic viability as well as high organisational performance in a turbulent and changing sector.

The use of HRM in a sporting organisation should, however, extend beyond the traditional areas of HRM such as personnel selection, training, evaluating, and rewarding performance (Robbins, 1993; Slack, 1997) but should include all organisational processes influenced by HRM. One such strategy utilised in baseball was the "moneyball" principle which can potentially be applied to HRM innovation and competitive advantage (Wolfe, Wright, and Smart, 2006). A key aspect of this principle was the use of Sabermetrics, which uses statistical data to analyse baseball records and make determinations about player performance. The originator of Sabermetrics, Bill James, classified the process as the search for objective knowledge about baseball through using, "different, more detailed statistics ... that frequently create their own measures to analyse which players (or teams) are best." (Beneventano, Berger, and Weinberg, 2012, p. 1). Click (2006) confirm that the use of Sabermetrics provides an insight into baseball that other professionals are not able to ascertain. There are some critics of the system however, such as past baseball player Joe Morgan (Craggs, 2005) stating that statistics are only as good as the information input into the computer.

Wolfe et al. (2006) state their belief in the use of Sabermetrics and its insight into individual team and organisational performance. This has been incorporated into the world of HRM through HR Information Systems (HRISs), which have now become standard within large multinational corporations by storing a large amount of data on employees, across all jobs. This data can be described as an "alternative" to standard data that organisations have relied upon which can improve performance through recruitment and strategy via a less costly approach. Although it only remains less costly if competitors are utilising conventional criteria within the market.

The other concern around the use of Sabermetrics aligns with the point made earlier in the chapter around sport being a niche industry (Ruta and Sala, 2018). Within sport, Sabermetrics are able to isolate and measure an individual's performance, whereas in a conventional business setting it is far more difficult to silo a staff member's performance and measure this within the context of organisational performance. Replacing a staff member with a "substitute" as would happen in a sporting team, is not something that would generally happen or be acceptable in a regular business setting, neither is the measurement of teamwork in an organisation aligned to the pricing of a pork belly futures contract (Bryan and Rafferty, 2006).

Football's adoption of HRM

The increasing competition and financial consequences of poor performance within football has sharpened clubs' focus on the need to operate within a more strategic framework and less akin to small, family-run enterprises. Operating profits of £1.6 billion between 2013/14 – 2015/16 (Deloitte, 2017) highlight the importance of English Premier League clubs acquiring greater value and performance from their investment in both playing and non-playing staff (Gilmore, 2009). From a playing staff perspective, the increase in revenue from television rights, the reinvigoration of global competitions and the widening of football's appeal to wealthier, middle-class supporters (Gilmore, 2009) has resulted in the migration of highly paid, elite players. Salaries for premier league clubs in 2015/16 accounted for 64 per cent of overall turnover, which is sustainable if other costs and expenses are managed accordingly through the achievement of business goals that align with strategy and HRM practices (Beer et al., 1984). It also requires football clubs to apply human capital in the right way rather than align to strategic goals, with managers playing a key role in using the personal attributes of staff to sustain a competitive advantage. Gilmore's (2009, p. 468) case study on Bolton Wanderers Football Club (BWFC) highlights the success of operating within a budget whilst sustaining performance through the "acquisition and development of skilled staff, underpinned by supportive HRM practices, especially within the playing domain." BWFC had a clear "asset management strategy" to address the need for maintaining heightened competitiveness. This approach ensured that both playing and non-playing staff were considered to be a strategic resource and therefore both subject to similar HRM processes. Both sets of personnel were expected to "reach the next level" and a culture of innovation and continuous development throughout the club was engineered.

Other clubs have also recognised the importance of dedicated HR departments rather than existing employees having HR responsibilities as a secondary role. Manchester City Football Club (MCFC) established a HR department in 2009, after a review by the new owners identified 350 permanent staff, increasing to 1,100 on match days, working for the club (Sullivan, 2011). This resulted in creating a strategy of recruiting "the best people" who would remain at the club. The club has implemented a demarcation line though between playing and non-playing staff, which inevitably evolves around salaries. It is generally accepted that playing staff are dealt with as a separate entity as they have their own bargaining arrangements, and is a policy, which is not uncommon in other global businesses who adopt a more "person based pay," where salaries fluctuate based on organisational business strategy and culture (Lawler, 2000; Lee, Law, and Bobko, 1999). This in turn will support the recruitment and retention of high-performing staff who support organisational and HRM strategies (Gomez-Mejia and Blakin, 1992; Milkovitch and Newman, 2008).

As previously mentioned, HRISs are being more wildly used by clubs to recruit playing staff through an intelligence-based decision system constructed around analytical software of player attributes (Fernandez, 2017). Middlesbrough Football Club (MFC) utilise a "People Analytics" system to inform their transfer strategy. A more recent trend has been the introduction of "Talent identification software" which tries to ensure the club have right player for the right position at the right time, based on the player's physical, mental, and technical skills (Razali et al., 2017). Each playing position has a set of skills assigned that will be used to correlate against the right individual. Although this has a clear set of parameters to work within, the main problem sits with what has previously been raised as a concern with these systems, namely that the data is only as useful as the person inputting them, so data are still reliant upon human construction and interpretation.

Leadership style in football

An area identified as a key element of HRM in this chapter is the leadership and behaviour of managers. The English Premier League usually attracts media around the star players who are attracted to the EPL, but the raft of international managers appointed since the creation of the league has created discussion and debate around leadership within football clubs. In particularly during the 2015–16 and 2016–17 seasons, the appointment of Jose Mourinho (Manchester United), Pep Guardiola (Manchester City), Antonio Conte (Chelsea), and Jürgen Klopp (Liverpool) resulted in four of the top coaches in European football introducing their own style of management.

Football managers now earn the same – if not more than the stars of their team – and are treated in the same manner. What's more, they must achieve instant results or they are quickly relieved of their duties in ignominious fashion. The most successful premiership manager, Sir Alex Ferguson, always believed that a player should never earn more than a manager, as this could undermine their authority, which Ferguson based on fear and control (Elberse, 2013). When Manchester United's Wayne Rooney was offered a huge increase in wages, which usurped all players and the manager, Ferguson's initial response to the owners of the club was that no player should be paid more than a manager, something that resulted in an increase in Ferguson's salary. This is a sign of how managers within a football club now operate. They are more chief executives than football managers. They have to manage all aspects of the club, which not only include the playing staff but also the owners, and feel they deserve to be remunerated accordingly (Elberse, 2013).

The above-mentioned is something that brings into discussion the different management styles of the four Premier League managers mentioned earlier. Traditionally, managers in all walks-of-life have been pigeonholed into having one management style, from autocratic to *laissez-faire*. The growth and demand in football has resulted in managers educating themselves on the art of management, which usually stems from industry (Rock, 2007).

Jose Mourinho has stated he does not have a "style" but adopts differing approaches based on the situation(s) he operates in (Fenn, 2017). If he is managing a well-established team whom he expects to be, in what Dr Bruce Tuckman defined as the "Performing" stage, then he would adopt a confrontational style of management with high demands and expectations. If his team were relatively young, inexperienced and in transition (Tuckman's "Forming" stage), he would adopt a less confrontational style where he would nurture the players and let them learn their trade without the pressure of expectations. Mourinho, as with all great managers, understands that different individuals need different ways of being motivated and that getting to know the individual will enable him to manage the player better.

Pep Guardiola has the same passion and commitment as Mourinho but adopts a differing style based on total football philosophy and immaculate preparation. Whereas Mourinho would go out of his way to get to understand players and therefore control them emotionally, Guardiola believes in educating players, letting them think for themselves, allowing them certain freedoms once they have gained his trust. He is viewed more as an interventionist rather than a dictatorial coach. He is also a strategist, counting the great chess champion Garry Kasparov as a good friend, and someone who he can learn from and utilise strategic planning in his management of football teams. He is not afraid to ostracise players if they do not buy into the philosophy as Ronaldinho and Ibrahimović soon discovered (Perarnau, 2014).

Antonio Conte is renowned for being an old-fashioned type of manager, adopting a hard-line approach with expectations of hard work, loyalty and a respectable public image. Conte is similar to Guardiola in that he meticulously manages all aspects of footballers' lives, in particular, dietary requirements. Players Conte has managed have also pointed to the similarities between him and Ferguson, not just in their fiery natures but their belief in complacency being a disease. When a young Manchester United footballer requested a company car for playing a certain number of games for the first team (admittedly after being set up by his teammates), Ferguson chased Ryan Giggs out of his office, apoplectic with rage. A similar scenario happened whilst Conte was managing Juventus who had already won the league but were on 99 points with one match to go. Conte wanted to achieve 100 points in a season, but when he was interrupted during his pre-match team talk by a player enquiring about their bonuses, Conte reacted like Ferguson with a tirade that exemplified his unflinching desire to expect the best at all times, even when some managers would have been far more accommodating to a team that had already won the league. He also utilises an aggressive approach to team talks with players being singled out and objects thrown at them in the changing rooms. This is not someone who simply loses his cool, but a premeditated method of permeating his thoughts into a group of players who he knows will react positively to this form of management.

Jürgen Klopp is probably the most different of all three managers. Whereas Mourinho, Guardiola, and Conte understand the importance of managing upwards as well as down, Klopp is an individualist who invokes great loyalty and passion against adversity. In simple terms, he will challenge the board of directors just as much as those enemies outside of the club, and has based his management style around the clubs he has managed. With Dortmund and Liverpool, he espouses the fact that they are "outsider" clubs, big institutions with a rich history but not part of the corporate, unfriendly, sponsorship seeking establishments, which treat their fans like customers. This links with organisational behaviour and the cultural established by the leadership team. He is extremely frugal and prefers to buy conservatively, nurturing talent and spending wisely. He can be a fiery individual, mainly against other clubs and officials, but he is known to be extremely charismatic; something he deploys in his management of players, who seem to fight until the final minute of every match. This calls into question his ability to consistently manage big name players, although he could change his management style if required.

Analysing these different management styles, there are three similar traits running throughout Mourinho, Guardiola, Conte, and Klopp's approach to management. First, their ability to communicate. They have different styles of communicating from distributing well-thought-out post-it notes to players (Mourinho), putting an arm around players (Guardiola), throwing water bottles (Conte), and bear hugging a player (Klopp), but they are all aware of how important it is to communicate.

The second common theme is the ability to adapt to the situation. Conte compared his management style to that of a good tailor. Depending on the players one has available, and depending on their qualities, one has to put together a nice suit. All four managers have an understanding that you must fully understand your resources and position before deciding on your strategy (Stanco, 2017).

The third trait is their passion for football and winning mentality. All four managers are fiercely competitive and try to instil this into their teams. Guardiola will plan obsessively to ensure his teams are ready to win, Mourinho will agitate and cajole his team, Conte will drive his team through grit and determination, and Klopp will create a band of brothers who will run every last minute for him. All elements of leadership that fit within a strategic approach to managing human resources; that has probably always existed within football but only been recognised since the increased research into leadership and management styles.

Conclusion

This chapter reviewed the history of HRM and highlighted how sporting organisations have adopted various HRM processes into the running of their institutions. HRM has developed over the last 100 years from a supportive welfare approach to a more strategic as well as scientific approach to managing human resources. The increase in research into the field has resulted in HRM being more or less adopted as the norm within organisations (Beardwell, Holden, and Claydon, 2004) with strategic HRM becoming more and more influential in football clubs.

Analysing the effect of the utilisation of these HRM practices within football is difficult, as most of the research on HRM and performance is cross-sectional. Moreover, the process of analysing observations regarding a population at one specific point in time makes it difficult to be confident about cause and effect (Guest, 2011). The frequent change in leadership has also set up barriers in establishing a clear understanding of the short-, medium- and long-term HRM strategy. As a new coach enters the football club, a new set of values, culture, and management style is introduced, which usually takes time to implement and make an impact. Van der Heijden (2012) also highlights the intended (policy change) and unintended deviation (conflict, financial distress, injuries to playing staff) away from HRM strategies that can affect performance. The average term of the football managers in the top four leagues in England who were dismissed in 2016/17 was 423 days (Sky Sports, 2017), whilst the average manager has two jobs, across 1165 days and will take the helm for 91 games. In 1948, the average term for a football manager dismissed in that year was nearly 2,700 days. Clearly, the pressure of modern football with the extra pressure of getting into and remaining in the top tier is influencing owners to make drastic changes, or be seen to make changes to satisfy other stakeholders.

In terms of HRM, principles such as Sabermetrics and talent identification software will continue to be deployed depending on the propensity of coaching staff in favouring them and/ or other stakeholders within the club believing in their usefulness. Football clubs have tried to utilise HRM strategy in a more holistic manner, which supports the operational running of the club, providing foundations for the club to increase revenue as well as establish clear recruitment and retention strategies, which would not be affected by the constant change in coaches. HRM can act as a golden thread throughout football clubs, providing the stability for all staff employed that is required in a constantly changing, global sport.

References

Bacon, N. (2003) Human resource management and industrial relations. In: Ackers, P. and Wilkinson, A. (eds.). *Understanding Work and Employment: Industrial Relations in Transition.* Oxford: Oxford University Press.

Beardwell, I., Holden, L., and Claydon, T. (2004) *Human Resource Management: A Contemporary Approach.* London: Prentice Hall Financial Times.

Beaver, G. (2002) Strategy and management in the smaller enterprise. *Strat. Change*, 11, 175-181.

Beer, M., Spector B., Lawrence, P.R., Mills, D.Q., and Walton, R.E. (1984) *Managing Human Assets*. New York: The Free Press.

Beneventano, P., Berger, P. D., and Weinberg, B. D. (2012) Predicting run production and run prevention in baseball: the impact of Sabermetrics. *International Journal of Business, Humanities and Technology*, 2(4).

Boxall, P.F., Purcell, J. and Wright, P.M. (2007) *The Oxford Handbook of Human Resource Management*. Oxford: Oxford University Press.

Boyle, R. and Haynes, R. (2009) *Power Play: Sport, the Media and Popular Culture*. Edinburgh: Edinburgh University Press.

Bryan, D. and Rafferty, M. (2006) Can financial derivatives inform HRM? Lessons from Moneyball. *Human Resource Management*, 45, 667–671.

Click, J. (2006). What if Rickey Henderson had Pete Incaviglia's legs? In: J. Keri (ed.). *Baseball Between the Numbers: Why Everything You Know About The Game Is Wrong* (pp. 112–126). New York, NY: Basic Books.

Craggs, T. (2005) Say it ain't so, joe. *San Francisco News, Events, Restaurants, Music*. 6 July.

Cuskelly, G., Taylor, T., Hoye, R., and Darcy, S. (2006) Volunteer management practices and volunteer retention: a human resource management approach. *Sport Management Review*, Elsevier, 9(2), 141–163. DOI: 10.1016/S1441-3523(06)70023-7.

Doherty, A.J. (1998) Managing our human resources: a review of organisational behaviour in sport. *Sport Management Review*, 1(1), 1–24.

Elberse, A. and Ferguson, A. (2013) Ferguson's formula. *Harvard Business Review*, 91(10), 116–125.

Fenn, A. (2017) *Jose Mourinho's coaching secrets. FourFourTwo*. Department of Employment. London: HMSO.

Foot, M. and Hook, C. (1999) *Introducing Human Resource Management*, (2nd ed.). London: Financial Times Press.

Foot, M. and Hook, C. (2011) *Introducing Human Resource Management*, (6th ed.). London: Financial Times Press.

Gilmore, S. (2009) The importance of asset maximisation in football: towards the long-term gestation and maintenance of sustained high performance. *International Journal of Sports Science & Coaching*, 4(4), 465–488.

Gomez-Mejia, L.R. and Balkin, D.B. (1992). Determinants of faculty pay: an agency theory perspective. Academy of Management Journal, *35*(5), 921–955.

Kelly, J.E. (2003) *Rethinking Industrial Relations: Mobilisation, Collectivism and Long Waves: Mobilization, Collectivism and Long Waves. Routledge*. London: Routledge.

Lawler, E.E., III. (2000) *Rewarding Excellence: Pay Strategies for the New Economy*. San Francisco: Jossey-Bass Inc.

Lee, C., Law, K.S., and Bobko, P. (1999) The importance of justice perceptions on pay effectiveness: a two-year study of a skill-based pay plan. *Journal of Management*, 25(6), 851–873. DOI: https://doi.org/10.1016/S0149-2063(99)00029-X.

McKenna, E. and Beech, N. (2008) *Human Resource Management: A Concise Analysis*, (2nd ed.). Harlow: Pearson Education Limited.

Milkovich, G.T. and Newman, J.M. (2008) *Compensation* (9th ed.). McGraw-Hill, Irwin.

Niven, M. (1967) *Personnel Management: 1913–63: The Growth of Personnel Management and the Development of the Institute*. London: IPM.

Niven, M. (1978) *Personnel Management, 1913–63 (Management in Perspective)*. London: IPM.

Perarnau, M. (2014) *Pep Confidentia: Inside Pep Guardiola's First Season at Bayern Munich* (1st ed.). Edinburgh: Arena Sport.

Razali, N., N. Mustapha, A. Yatim, Faiz Ahmad, and Ab Aziz, Ruhaya (2017) Predicting player position for talent identification in association football. *IOP Conference Series: Materials Science and Engineering*, 226, 012087.

Rock, D. (2007) *Quiet leadership: help people think better – don't tell them what to do*. New York: Harper.

Ruta, D. and Sala, I. (2018) HRM in Sport Organizations. In: *HRM in Mission Driven Organizations*. Cham: Springer International Publishing, pp. 183–220.

Slack, T. (1997) *Understanding Sport Organisations: The Application of Organisation Theory*. IL: Human Kinetics.

Smart, B. (2007). Not playing around: global capitalism, modern sport and consumer culture. *Global Networks*, 7(2), 113–134.

Smith, A.C. and Stewart, B. (2010) The special features of sport: a critical revisit. *Sport Management Review*, 13(1), 1–13.

Sullivan, N (2011) Manchester City Football Club sets new goals for HR. *Employee Benefits*. 6 January.

Stanco, S. (2017) Antonio Conte in profile: 'He's like a tsunami, he drags everybody with him.' *Planet Football*. [online] Retrieved from: https://www.planetfootball.com/in-depth/qualities-make-antonio-conte-special-know-best/

Van Der Heijden L. (2012) Does HRM matter for professional soccer organizations? A research on the HRM-Performance relationship for PSO's. University of Twente: School of Management and Governance.

Wolfe, R., Wright, P.M., Smart, D.L. (2006) Radical HRM innovation and competitive advantage: the Moneyball story. *Human Resource Management*, 45(1), 111–145.

Wood, S. (1983) The study of management in British industrial relations. *British Journal of Industrial Relations*, 13(2), 51–61.

19

Fans, spectators, consumers in football

Petros Parganas

Introduction: Identifying the football customer

While marketing literature very often uses the terms 'customer' and 'consumer' interchangeably, a distinction between the two terms could be the following. A customer is generally viewed as an entity (e.g., person, company, organisation, etc.) that buys a specific product or service and may or may not use it, whereas a consumer generally makes use of a product or service in exchange for a payment. In this sense, we can distinguish between the following types of football 'followers':

- Customers: Entities (individuals or groups) who have an interest or agenda in a sport product or service. For instance, governments, media, or corporate sponsors show an interest in football products and services, but they are not consumers.
- Consumers: These are individuals or groups who use a football or football-related products and/or services in exchange for a direct (like cash to buy a ticket to a game) or indirect (like purchasing a television in which football is one form of entertainment) payment.

We can further distinguish among four categories of football consumers: The *football goods consumers*; that is, the buyers of memorabilia and licensed products and generally any physical product (equipment, books, merchandise, etc.) that is somehow related to football. Similarly, the *football services consumers* make use of a sport-related service or experience such educational activities, medical services, or even gambling. Notably, these consumers are not actively involved in football directly, unlike *football participants and volunteers* who include all amateur-level players and unpaid participants in football. The last category consists of *football supporters, spectators* and *fans*. Participants of this category are mainly (but not exclusively) interested in the elite or professional level of football.

Apparently, most sport participants and volunteers are sport fans as well, and also utilise different kinds of sporting goods and services. The activities of sport supporters, spectators, and fans include attendance at live sport, viewing sport on television or following their club through social media. However, this group of sport consumers is unique because of their intense use of sport products and services in ways that other, less intense or fanatical consumers do not use them. It is clear that the motives of sport supporters, spectators, and fans are the most complex, and need to be explored further. It is this last category that we will devote our attention to.

Football fans, whether local or international, form a major group of buying customers for the team sport product and are vitally important for the financial welfare of the team. This chapter explains the various factors that can influence their buying behaviours as well as their implications for the marketing strategies of the football clubs and organisations.

The football fan

Football fans are a distinct form of consumers as they display a bewildering array of values, attitudes, and behaviours. They are regarded as high-involvement costumers and are described as 'creatures tied for life to the club s/he first fell for as a child' (Kuper and Szymanski, 2009, p. 203). Sport club fans see their team as an extension of themselves, become loyal at an early age and rarely – if ever - change their loyalty in order to support a competitor team. The term 'fan', derived from the word 'fanatic', is used to describe individuals who willingly invest resources – either emotional or financial – in supporting their favourite sport team or club over a prolonged period of time, and their level of loyalty remains unaltered even when the clubs is not performing well. In the literature, several terms have arisen to define and describe a football (sports) fan, including for instance, fanatic, passionate partisan, highly committed fan, vested fan, die-hard fan, etc.

Fans vs. spectators

Not all fans are, however, equally passionate and fanatical, neither are they totally loyal or resistant to change. Some attend games on a regular basis, while others attend only on special occasions. Some display their fandom by watching football over television channels or increasingly engaging in online conversations over various online chat rooms and platforms. They experience football in different ways and use the team affiliation to meet a diverse range of needs. For this reason, it is advisable to establish a distinction between mere spectators and fans. Spectators are individuals who observe a sport and then forget about it. Spectators may not necessarily be fans. They remain rather passive in their interaction with the game, as they simply watch, analyse, and appreciate it, while fans are more intense in their interactions as they create and shape the experience of the game itself. Fans do not represent mere spectators but take part in the game and believe of themselves that their presence, engagement, and involvement affects their team's performance. They even think of ordinary spectators as intruders on their game and manifest their identification and attachment to their team by choosing friends of the same 'ideology', attending live matches at the stadium or collecting various team- and match-branded objects (memorabilia).

Fans' impact on football club revenues

From an *economic standpoint*, fans play an important role as far as the revenues of the sport teams are concerned. Besides their obvious impact on ticket sales and merchandising, fans have a large impact on the other streams of incomes such as sponsorship and media. This interrelation has been described as the virtuous cycle of revenue generation or the sport-media complex (Figure 19.1). Without fans, there would be no demand to show matches on TV and therefore no reason to pay the high broadcasting rights. Such high media exposure, besides being a significant revenue source and promotional tool for football clubs, allows them to become increasingly global in their appeal to audiences. As a result, the large amount of visibility and recognition

Figure 19.1   Graphical representation of the sport-media complex
Source: Parganas et al., 2017.

enables football clubs to become the vehicle for those multinational companies that want to expand their brand in foreign markets by becoming sponsors of famous football clubs. Thus, sponsorship deals become very lucrative for sport clubs. The subsequent influx of capital into the football club can be invested into new (and better) players, coaches, and facilities. All this, in turn, increases the quality of the product itself as well as the interest and size of the audiences, thereby feeding at the beginning of the loop.

The economic viewpoint suggests that all stakeholders involved in the transaction behave rationally and use sport products and services that meet their quality and value needs. However, this is not always (or perhaps never) true when talking about fans. Fans are more passionate than ordinary consumers and their purchase decisions are rarely made by financial and rational criteria. Football fans are motivated by a range of factors and reasons to attend games, buy merchandise, and follow their club on television or increasingly online. Football marketers need therefore to adopt a marketing perspective in order to appreciate the many factors that influence fans' behaviour and analyse the psychological, social, and cultural characteristics that shape their behaviour as consumers.

Understanding fan behaviour

In order to understand the nexus between sport marketing and consumer behaviour, Funk and James (2001) established the Psychological Continuum Model (PCM), a framework to organise literature from various academic disciplines to understand sport and event consumer behaviour. The PCM uses a vertical framework to characterise various psychological connections that individuals form with sport objects (e.g., sport, team, player, event, recreational activity) to explain the role of attitude formation and change that directs behaviours across a variety of consumption activities. Explaining the how and why of sport and event consumer behaviour, it discusses how personal, psychological, and environmental factors influence a wide range of sport consumption activities.

The PCM framework (Figure 19.2) states that, through the processing of internal and external inputs, individuals progress upward along the four psychological connection stages: awareness, attraction, attachment, and allegiance. As the individual progresses upwards to a higher floor, the psychological connection becomes incrementally stronger. The overall evaluation of

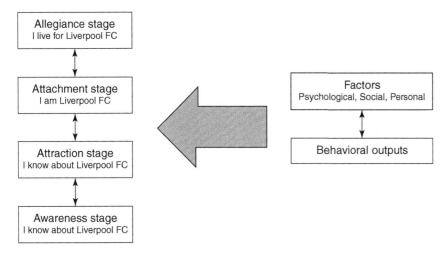

Figure 19.2   The Psychological Continuum Model (adapted from Funk and James, 2001)

a sport object at a specific stage is the product of the processing of personal, psychological, and environmental factors.

The first stage is the *awareness* stage. At this stage, an individual first learns about the existence of a certain sport, event, or team. The expression 'I know about Liverpool FC' best describes this stage. Awareness begins usually at an early age and stems from formal and informal channels such as parents, relatives, friends, media, etc.

In the *attraction* stage, the individual has formed a preference for or favourite sport, event, or team ('I like Liverpool FC'). During this stage, a psychological connection is formed based on whether a sport object provides opportunities to satisfy needs and receive desirable benefits. This psychological connection becomes stronger in the *attachment* stage. During this stage, an individual identifies with a team ('I am a Liverpool FC fan') and places functional, emotional, and symbolic meaning on the sport object. As the attachment processing continues, the individual reaches the final stage of the model, *allegiance* ('I live for Liverpool FC'). At this stage, the meaning becomes significantly stronger, more durable and stable, and guides the individual's activities and behaviour.

An individual may move upwards or downwards through the stages of the PCM or spend a varied amount of time in each of the stages. The mechanism that governs movement within the PCM framework is an internal process that is based on personal, psychological, and environmental factors that affect the motivation, experiences, and attitudes of individuals and result in different behavioural and psychological outputs. These factors are of importance to sport marketers in order to position and deliver an appropriate marketing mix for each consumer segment. For instance, during the awareness and attraction stage, promotional activities which focus on attributes and benefits of the sport object can easily address new and casual spectators and participants. However, as the individual moves upwards to the stages of attachment and allegiance, a different set of activities and strategies is needed to strengthen the functional, symbolic, and emotional meaning of a sport object; put differently, to increase their loyalty to the sport object.

Factors influencing sport consumption

There has been a considerable amount of research examining the various factors that influence sport fans in their consumption of sport products. The analysis of fans' behaviour cannot be split from the concept of commitment and loyalty to the club. Empirical analysis of motivational factors responsible for sport fandom include eustress, self-esteem, escape, entertainment, eco-nomic, aesthetic, group affiliation, and family needs (Wann, 1995). Even though the topic is complex, it plays a pivotal role in today's sport marketing environment. Sport marketers need to appreciate the many reasons why consumers are motivated to buy sport-related products and services and how different factors impact on their decisions. Given the complexity of the factors, it is difficult for sport marketers to draw a specific consumer profile. The next section examines sport consumer behaviour taking into account four categories of such factors: personal (physical), social, psychological, and external.

Personal

A sport fan's reasons for buying a sport product may be affected by an individual's characteristics and demographics. Such factors are related to gender, age, education, income, race as well as body and personality characteristics. Research suggests, for instance, that males are more likely to be motivated by economic factors to consume sport than females (Funk and James, 2004). Psychological factors (see psychological section) like escape, aesthetic pleasure, and self-esteem are also reasons higher regarded for males while females are more strongly motivated to con-sume sport for family, social, and body-related concerns (Shilbury et al., 2009). In addition, older people are less likely to follow a sport in order to address the desire of belonging to a group than younger fans; immigrants are more likely to follow a sport or team of their country of origin; while personality characteristics such as being open, shy, or quiet could explain why certain individuals prefer golf to football (Shilbury et al., 2009). Finally, individuals participate in sport for the possibility of gaining money through gambling (Wann, 1995).

Social

Spending time with family and friends may be one reason for an individual to follow a specific consumption pattern. In this case, the sports experience that allows a sport fan to fulfil family needs may be irrelevant as the primary aim is to spend some time with friends and relatives. Family and friends play a significant role when it comes to choosing a specific sport or team. Moreover, it can be argued that even TV or internet spectators also tend to view matches in the company of friends and/or family members either at home or at pubs and bars.

The need to belong to a group is another important aspect (Theodorakis et al., 2012; Wann, 1995). Individuals are motivated to identify with something bigger than themselves and feel part of a community that shares common values and beliefs. Related to this is the concept of peer group acceptance which suggests that if a consumer feels that friends and family approve of the following or supporting of a specific team, all constituents of the consumption experience will be viewed more favourably.

Sharing emotions in groups and feeling a spirit of community often means that sport fans exert 'tribal' behaviour and are not just consumers but also advocates of the team they support. A tribe is 'a network of heterogeneous persons in terms of gender, age, gender and income, who are linked by a shared passion or emotion' (Dionisio et al., 2008). Sport teams bring together people with varying socio-economic backgrounds, who share a bond. In football, for instance, the link that the tribe shares is the club – the love for the club and the team is where these collec-tive and passionate behavioural patterns originate. For example, rituals like pre- and post-game ceremonies are common practice in football (Dionisio et al., 2008). Fans wear the tribal colours (i.e., team shirts and scarves), sing tribal chants (i.e., team songs) and often have conflicts with other tribes (i.e., fans of other teams).

Psychological

Temporary escape from daily stress can be linked to professional team sport experience as a fan. People follow sport as an escape from their everyday demands and a distraction from their stressful lifestyle. That is, contrary to their usually highly organised and regulated working environment, sport gives spectators a place where they can shout and scream and even tell people explicitly and without censure – particularly the referee or the opponent's players – what they are thinking of them.

Sport elicits strong emotions. Particularly in team sports like football, the bond between the fan and the sports team is stronger than in any other industry. Fans often view football teams as an extension of themselves and often experience feelings of joy, pride, or even ecstasy, but also frustration and worry. For fans, team success is personal success and team failure is personal failure. The term vicarious achievement refers to a level of accomplishment that is felt second hand, through the success of someone else – a phenomenon known as basking in reflected glory (BIRG) (Cialdini et al., 1976). On the other hand, when an athlete or team fails, fans tend to distance themselves through a process labelled 'cutting off reflected failure' (CORF).

Entertainment is an important factor for both stadium attendees and supporters viewing the match through other means and serves also as a motivator for spectators and fan behaviour. The scale of many sporting venues, the sight of thousands of fans in club colours, or the aesthetic pleasure of watching a skilful and talented player fulfil such needs. In some sports, some sort of entertainment is provided during small or larger breaks (e.g., cheerleaders during time-outs in basketball).

Case study: Saving Spanish football club Real Oviedo from bankruptcy

In 2012, amidst the economic crisis that hit the country and consequently many football clubs, Spanish club Real Oviedo faced a sad end to 86 years of sporting history. With bankruptcy and extinction approaching fast, the debt-ridden football club has discovered a precious asset that may yet save it from doom: the loyalty of its fans. Thanks to a novel fundraising effort and a rampant social-media campaign, the third-tier club survived. The response from fans was overwhelming with thousands of them buying shares. 'There is a lot of excitement to save the club. All of us, from the fans all the way to the town mayor, are going to do what it takes to pull through,' lifelong fan Jose Garcia Ordonez told The Associated Press. 'The effort is coming from people with financial problems like so many are facing in this country. With 30, 40 euros they are doing what they can so that one day we can tell our children how we saved 86 years of history of the club of our parents and grandparents.' (Source: *The Independent*).

External

Even when fans are strongly connected to their club, they will not always regularly attend games or watch them on television. Their decisions to attend or view sport may be influenced by external factors, such as, for instance, the uncertainty of the outcome but also the likelihood of their team winning, the quality of the venue and facilities, financial reasons such as prices and income levels as well as the availability of alternative activities (James et al., 2006; Pritchard et al., 2009).

Some fans will be influenced by the anticipated closeness of the competition. Indeed, the uncertainty of the outcome is one of the key and distinctive characteristics of sports, compared to other industries. A close contest is expected to attract more viewers and fans tend to experience such contests more intensively. However, there are fans that are preoccupied with winning (Norris et al., 2014; Smith, 2008). Therefore, in general, winning teams and athletes will attract more spectators than losing teams and athletes. Since fans view team success as personal success, they are likely to attend or watch games more frequently if they believe their team has a strong chance of winning.

The features and quality of the facilities can have an impact on an individual's decision to attend a sport event, although arguably, football fans are expected to (and usually do) attend a game even under unfavourable circumstances (no sitting or parking conveniences, low-quality food and beverages, bad weather conditions, etc.) (Owen and Weatherston, 2004; Pritchard et al., 2009).

To some extent, the cost of attending a sport event can have an impact on the number of attendees, albeit evidence suggests that price increases have only minor effects because sport fans are unusually loyal consumers (a phenomenon called low elasticity of demand in economics) (Carmichael et al., 1999). The income levels of fans can have a direct effect on what kind of leisure they prefer. With sport being part of the wider entertainment industry, increased income levels usually mean greater availability of choices to participate in alternative leisure activities, such as travel, restaurants, and the theatre. The very availability of alternative leisure activities can explain a decline in attendance over a longer period of time (Smith, 2008).

Constraints

A number – if not all – of the previously mentioned factors can either facilitate or constrain movement between the different levels of the PCM framework (Funk and James, 2006). Personal constraints for example such as the age or health condition of an individual may prohibit him/her from visiting an event live. Good weather conditions may also be a problem if it means that people may be attracted to alternative leisure activities. Prevailing cultural norms and values that might inhibit patronage or social constraints, such as the influence of reference groups are other examples of barriers to repeat purchase behaviour (Lepisto and Hannaford, 1980). There are issues such as rejection of the consumer culture that football clubs operate or tribalism that excludes some sections of society. In fact, social networks and collective action constrain and facilitate behaviour so that rational choice is unthinkable (Cleland et al., 2018).

Understanding spectator behaviour

Many researchers have suggested different typologies of fans, recognising in each segment a particular behaviour (e.g., Hunt et al., 1999; Stewart et al., 2003; Tapp and Clowes, 2002). Although it is nearly impossible to describe the archetypal fan, motivational factors, such as the ones mentioned earlier in this chapter, or concepts like loyalty, value to the club, or behavioural characteristics, such as the number of games attended in a season, have been used to provide some categorisation of fans.

Other attempts have been made to categorise fans (spectators) from a sociological point of view (Giulianotti, 2002). Such attempts recognised the intensive hyper-commodification of football during the past decades and argued that the broad trend in sports identification is away from the *supporter* model (i.e., the traditional identification with local clubs) and toward the more detached, cool, consumer-orientated identification of the *flaneur*. That is, the process of commodification, which includes football's rapid increase in popularity, the stadiums' transformation into all-seating arenas, and the blurring of lines between broadcasters, sporting organisations, and digital platforms has an impact on spectator identities relative to their association with professional football clubs.

The most loyal fans go to the stadium just to see their favourite team contest the game. These fans, who are defined in the literature as *passionate partisans, fanatical* or *die-hard* fans, form the hard-core supporters base and their moods and identity are bound up with the successes and failures of their favourite team (Bristow and Sebastian, 2001; Hunt et al., 1999; Smith and Stewart, 1999; Tapp and Clowes, 2002). They express their love and loyalty even under inconvenient environmental circumstances (a rainy day, extreme cold, etc.), defend their club's history and tradition and are heavy purchasers of memorabilia and club merchandise. These fans feel as part of the team and exhibit a very strong emotional connection, reacting to events that happen to a player or team as if they happened to themselves.

The *reclusive partisan* has also a considerable amount of interest in the game and great levels of loyalty and commitment to their club, but s/he attends games in a less frequent manner (Smith and Stewart, 1999). As the passionate partisans, they have a strong desire to see their team win and their dominant concern is not the quality or closeness of the contest but rather the quality of their own team and the likelihood of success of their team.

Less loyal to their team, but equally driven by the desire to see their team win, are the *champ followers* (Smith and Stewart, 1999). These fans are usually non-attendees until their favourite team starts winning. These champ followers can become very vocal and demonstrative at the arena as they share some of the emotional highs and lows of the passionate partisan. They are, however, less reliable and fanatical and as soon their team begins to lose again, they will most probably return to their previous state of non-attendees.

Similar amounts of loyalty hold the fan segment called *theatergoers* (Smith and Stewart, 1999). These fans are committed to a particular team but are more interested in the game itself rather than driven by the desire to see their team win. They attend more frequently than the reclusive partisan, but less frequently than the passionate partisan as their primary motivation is entertainment. They are seeking a pleasurable experience, which involves not only a close and quality contest but also comfortable viewing conditions as well as the availability of complementary services, which, in turn, makes their experience more comfortable and enjoyable. As the likelihood of exciting and pleasurable contests increases, theatergoers are expected to attend more frequently but are unlikely to become regular patrons. With respect to their frequency of attendance, this fan segment has been described as either *casual* or *committed causal* fans.

Like the theatregoer, the *aficionado* will be attracted to games, which are expected to be exciting contests with high-quality players involved, showing only moderate concern about the success or failure of a particular team (Smith and Stewart, 1999). However, unlike most theatergoers, aficionados are not so much concerned about the closeness of the contest and the uncertainty of the game. They will attend games that provide high skill levels, tactical complexity and aesthetic pleasure, even if they are likely to be one sided or unexciting. The quality of the venue is of importance to the aficionado as long as it impacts upon the overall quality performance of the contest.

Table 19.1 summarises the abovementioned types of fans. Readers are, however, encouraged to access the literature at the end of this chapter for further and more detailed insights.

It is evident from the above discussion that the tribal, hard-core fan is but a minor figure in the sporting landscape. For example, although 3.2 billion people tuned in to the last World Cup, not every one of them is a football fan. Not all fans are equally passionate and not all fans identify with their team as strongly as others. In recent decades, a number of other fan segments have been identified, each having different motivations to attend a game as well as varying

Table 19.1 Categorisation of football fans

Super Fan

Loyalty	Fan categorization	Motivational factors
Strong team loyalty	Passionate Partisan (Smith & Stewart, 1999) Die-hard fan (Bristow & Sebastian, 2001) Fanatical (Hunt et al., 1999) Fanatics (Tapp & Clowes, 2002) Reclusive partisan (Smith & Stewart, 1999)	Emotions Group affiliation Vicarious achievement Likelihood of winning
Moderate team loyalty or loyalty related to team success	Committed casual fan (Hunt et al., 1999) Champ follower (Smith & Stewart, 1999) Theatregoer (Smith & Stewart, 1999) Regular supporter (Tapp & Clowes, 2002)	Entertainment Uncertainty of outcome Likelihood of winning
Low team loyalty but strong loyalty to the sport	Aficionado (Smith & Stewart, 1999) Casual supporter (Tapp & Clowes, 2002)	Uncertainty of outcome Quality of facilities Entertainment

Casual Fan

expectations of the sport experience. For example, while a *theatergoer* may welcome the new technological advancements in football such as the goal-line technology or the VAR (Video Assistant Referee) system, passionate and reclusive partisans are likely to view such adjustments as treachery, and in extreme cases sever their relationship with the game and the club. For the sport organisation, however, each of these segments has a unique value and the sport marketer must be aware of their characteristics in order to address their needs and desires in the most satisfactorily way.

It should be also clear that team loyalty has a significant positive impact on the fan's consumption behaviours and attitudes and generating increased levels of loyalty should be the primary goal of every sport team and marketer. Team loyalty is referred to or includes the concepts of fan allegiance, fan loyalty, fan support, team attachment, fan avidity, fan ship, fandom, and sport customer loyalty. High levels of loyalty lead to the irrational buying behaviour mentioned earlier because loyal fans view their expenditures on team merchandise as an avenue of supporting the team, as opposed to simply paying money in exchange for good or service (Bauer et al., 2008). For the same reason, loyal fans tend to support the sponsors of the team by preferring their products over their competitors or over sponsors of rival clubs. For a marketer, sports fans act in the same way as consumers of other brands and products, with the exception that sports fans exhibit greater amounts of loyalty towards their club (Meenaghan, 2011; Schlesinger and Gungerich, 2011). Having this in mind, marketing techniques and strategies can be designed and implemented accordingly. That is, by transferring the loyalty concept to fan behaviour, a sports marketer can segment fans by cultural, social and demographic attributes, articulate them to the corresponding behaviour, and define a specific marketing mix that suits best the business model of the club.

Future challenges and research opportunities

Football is big business, but it would be nothing without the fans supporting it. However, the world of football fans is changing. The rapidly evolving media landscape, the impact of new technologies, as well as globalisation and demographic changes, pose pressing questions about the future of football organisations and their fan bases. This section discusses some of the core trends that will shape the future of fans.

Changing demographics

A couple of decades ago, people would tend to follow sport clubs more locally. New technology has opened the possibility for football brands to acquire many millions of followers around the world. Because of the changing sports-media environment as well as the high penetration of social media, football's fan base has expanded into hundreds of millions worldwide. It has become more accessible, inclusive and appealing for international fans, women and families, inevitably resulting in an increasingly diversifying fan base. While football clubs and organisations are looking for ways to convert these huge followings into long-term customers, for fans it triggers a shift in the way they identify with football teams and athletes. For instance, females were a largely overlooked fan segment until recently (*The Future of the Sports Fan*, 2017). Roughly, women made up half of the global population, but only a small minority of fans. This, however, is about to change. Traditional gender roles are being questioned while football teams and sponsors realise the economic opportunity of female fans.

Therefore, as football marketers adapt to the changing nature of their fan base and ask themselves questions as to how better address their different needs, additional issues arise. That is, besides asking how to make the game more accessible and attractive to new fans, marketers must consider how existing fans may react to a more diverse fan base (*The Future of the Sports Fan*, 2017). For instance, the time zones and locations of the largest global fan bases are increasingly influencing when and where sports are scheduled. Furthermore, the increase in the number of fans comes not without tensions, even between members of the same fan community. A case in point are football giants FC Barcelona who saw fan protests over its deal with Qatar for what some considered were 'incompatible' values. A question, therefore, arises as to how far clubs will compromise their identity to resonate with new fans?

From passive to active

Arguably, fans have been never passive consumers. Psychologists suggest that their presence alone can influence athlete performance. Cheering has a positive effect, while jeering has a negative effect. Yet fans want to extend their influence beyond the duration of the football game. There are ongoing protests over ticket prices, ownership or broadcasting decisions. The rise of social media means fans are becoming far more integrated in the action. Social media provide a unique environment in which sports fans can not only amplify their sporting experiences but also encourage sports-related expressions and opinions. Fans produce and share media in extreme volumes, which become part of the event narrative. For instance, the World Cup of 2014 in Brazil attracted more than three billion viewers worldwide and was the biggest ever event for Twitter, with 672 million tweets sent. Every year's Champions League final becomes the most talked about event in social media. Fans are nowadays able to consume football 24/7, a trend not only likely to continue but to involve even larger amounts of fans. The challenge for marketers is therefore to find ways to attract and stimulate that interest.

What is more, fans are able to leverage their collective power and demonstrate their passion in new ways. They want to be involved in management decisions and express their contrast in issues like ticket prices or team ownership. Through participative platforms like social media, demonstrations are likely to become more organised, from ousting club owners to protesting misaligned sponsors. With access to myriad twitter feeds and other sources of information, fans not only have more power but more potential points of conflict and disgruntlement. Involving fans in the decision-making process might become tricky as their interests might be in conflict with the interests of a profit-maximisation club.

Case study: The failed Sky TV takeover of Manchester United

In an effort to fight back to the imposition of all-sitting stadia as well as huge increases in the cost of tickets, Manchester United fans formed IMUSA (Independent Manchester United Supporters Association) which, from its earliest days, launched campaigns in favour of standing, against further price increases as well as for supporters to gain democratic ownership of the club. IMUSA's 'high point' came with the defeat of the first takeover attempt of Manchester United Plc (the parent company of Manchester United football club) by BSkyB in 1998–1999. Supporters mounted a campaign largely focused on persuading the British government that the takeover would be bad for British football as well as the nascent satellite TV market and finally succeeded in preventing the sale of the club and stopping a corporation owned by Rupert Murdoch. Several years later, Manchester United was sold to the US-based Glazer family despite the opposition by many Manchester United fans. Several disaffected and disillusioned Manchester United fans reacted and formed a new fan-owned football club: FC United of Manchester (Source: *The Guardian*).

Technological advances

It becomes evident from the above discussion that fans are no longer just about watching and cheering. Technology is radically changing the relationship between fans and teams. Fans exhibit social and cultural attachment to clubs, which is increasingly common on a global scale as Internet growth continues to shape fandom. Empowered by social media, the amount of content produced by fans uploading video streams and images of live games – from smartphones inside the arena or interactions from home – will not only exceed the amount generated by official broadcasters but shared and viewed on a global scale. Mobile devices and augmented-reality will impact on the way fans consume sport as they will be able to participate, analyse, critique, deconstruct, and connect with their favourite players and teams in real time.

This, of course, will have an impact on the way sports marketers will design their strategies as they need to enhance experience and increase fan interaction by customising the use of technology within different settings. Technological advances, all-connected stadiums to bigger screens or virtual reality enable fans to explore new opportunities to personalise the experience and reach deeper immersion, whether at the venue or elsewhere. Finally, if we accept that participation is an important driver of fandom – an estimated 260 million people play football, while 1.2 billion play computer games, e-sports could become the world's most popular pastime, resulting in a totally new fan segment.

The football prosumer

The greater influence of sport fans, along with the changing demographics and the technological advances have resulted in better-informed and empowered individuals. Such individuals have been termed as 'prosumers' (Toffler, 1980). Toffler argued that one day, the functions of producers and consumers would not be clearly identifiable, and consumers would be actively involved in the design of products.

Global sport fans are both consumers and producers of products, often through the guidance of advertising and marketing personnel. The sport product goes beyond mere consumption and involves sharing emotions in groups, feeling a spirit of community as well as co-creation by consumers with respect to the product's meaning For instance, football fans inside stadiums produce choreographed, televised spectacles that attract other stadium fans and armchair viewers (Ritzer and Jurgenson, 2010).

With particular regard to the Net Generation, which grew up during the digital era, social media are making it possible for millions of sport fans to become prosumers. Such tools allow participants to consume (prosume) an event real time and become active recipients of information. Sport fans, for instance, are empowered to actively participate on sport-specific organisation or team wikis, blogs, and social media pages. In addition, immersive technologies are on their way to increase and enhance the experiences of sport fans regardless of their geographic location.

E-sports are further, contemporary spaces for prosumption, where sport fans consume (i.e., view content, buy gaming products) and produce (add content, making the action in e-sport games). As (sport) consumers are empowered by technological advances and seek to become part of the marketing process, they can be viewed as unpaid labour with significant implications for the global commercial sport system. Today's prosumers are actively using modern technologies to engage in increasing levels of collaboration and interactivity with organisations. Significant implications arise for sport marketers: They are not only urged to view fans as co-creators of the sport brand but also to try to connect consumers through the product itself rather than merely focus their marketing activities on the actual product or service.

Conclusion

Football is one of the most powerful forces in global culture. No other cultural property can move across languages and societies in such a magnitude, while very few businesses in the world are viewed with such personal identification by the consumer as football. Football fans can be regarded as the most essential part in the world of football business. They are deeply committed and have a long-term affiliation to a club, invest significant time and money resources in it and their level of loyalty remains unaltered even when their club is not performing well. Without fans, there would be no demand to show games on TV and pay for those rights. In fact, without game-attending fans clubs would have problems attracting sponsor. The initial driver for a sport club's growth should, therefore, be the development of a fan-base and the steady increase of their loyalty levels. Identifying the motivations and factors that influence football fans is pivotal for marketers to propose strategies in this peculiar market. However, the internationalisation and commercialisation of football imposes new challenges for marketers and researchers as well, as it leads to an ever more diverse fan base.

References

Bauer, H.H., Stokburger-Sauer, N.E., and Exler, S. (2008) Brand image and fan loyalty in professional team sport: a refined model and empirical assessment. *Journal of Sport Management*, 22(2), 205–226.

Bristow, D.N. and Sebastian, R.J. (2001) Holy cow! Wait 'til next year! A closer look at the brand loyalty of Chicago Cubs baseball fans. *Journal of Consumer Marketing*, 18(3), 256–275.

Carmichael, F., Millington, J., and Simmons, R. (1999) Elasticity of demand for Rugby League attendance and the impact of BskyB. *Applied Economics Letters*, 6(12),797–800.

Cialdini, R.B., Borden, R.J., Thorne, A., Walker, M. R., Freeman, S., and Sloan, L.R. (1976) Basking in reflected glory: three (football) field studies. *Journal of Personality and Social Psychology*, 34, 366–375.

Cleland, J., Doidge, M., Millward, P., and Widdop, P. (2018) *Collective Action and Football Fandom: A Relational Sociology Approach*. Palgrave Macmillan.

Dionisio, P., Leal, C., and Moutinho, L. (2008) Fandom affiliation and tribal behaviour: a sports marketing application. *Qualitative Market Research: An International Journal*, 11(1),17–39.

Funk, D. and James, J. (2001) The psychological continuum model: a conceptual framework for understanding and individual's psychological connection to sport. *Sport Management Review*, 4(2), 119–150.

Funk, D. and James, J. (2004) The Fan Attitude Network (FAN) Model: exploring attitude formation and change among sport consumers. *Sport Management Review*, 7(1), 1–26.

Funk, D. and James, J. (2006) Consumer loyalty: the meaning of attachment in the development of sport team allegiance. *Journal of Sport Management*, 20, 189–217.

Giulianotti, R. (2002) Supporters, followers, fans, and flaneurs: A taxonomy of spectator identities in football. *Journal of Sport and Social Issues*, 26(1), 25–46.

Hunt, K.A., Bristol, T., and Bashaw, E.R. (1999) A conceptual approach to classifying sports fans. *Journal of Services Marketing*, 13(6), 439–452.

James, J., Trail, G., Wann, D., Zhang, J., and Funk, D.C. (2006) Bringing parsimony to the study of sport consumer motivations: development of The Big 5. Symposium at the *North American Society for Sport Management Conference*, Kansas City, MO.

Kuper S. and Szymanski S. (2009) *Soccernomics*. New York: Nation Books.

Lepisto, L.R. and Hannaford, W.J. (1980) Purchase constraint analysis: an alternative perspective for marketers. *Journal of the Academy of Marketing Science*, 8(1), 12–25.

Meenaghan, T. (2001) Sponsorship and advertising: a comparison of consumer perceptions. *Psychology and Marketing*, 18(2), 191–215.

Norris, J.I., Wann, D.L. and Zapalac, R.K. (2014) Sport fan maximizing: following the best team or being the best fan? *Journal of Consumer Marketing*, 32(3), 157–166.

Owen, P.D. and Weatherston, C.R. (2004) Uncertainty of outcome, player quality and attendance at national provincial championship rugby union matches: an evaluation in light of the competition review. *Economic Papers*, 23, 301–324.

Parganas, P., Liasko, R. and Anagnostopoulos, C. (2017) Scoring goals in multiple fields Social media presence, on-field performance and commercial success in European professional football. *Sport, Business and Management: An International Journal*, 7(2),197–215

Pritchard, M., Funk, D.C., and Alexandris, K. (2009) Barriers to repeat patronage: the impact of spectator constraints. *European Journal of Marketing*, 43(1/2), 169–187.

Ritzer, G. and Jurgenson, N. (2010) Production, consumption, prosumption: the nature of capitalism in the age of the digital 'prosumer'. *Journal of Consumer Culture*, 10(1), 13–36.

Schlesinger, T. and Gungerich, M. (2011) Analysing sport sponsorship effectiveness – the influence of fan identification credibility and product-involvement. *International Journal of Sport Management and Marketing*, 9, 54–74.

Shilbury, D., Westerbeek, H., Quick, S., and Funk, D. (2009) *Strategic Sport Marketing*. Australia: Allen and Unwin.

Smith, A. (2008) *Introduction to Sport Marketing*. Oxford, UK: Elsevier.

Smith, A. and Stewart, B. (1999) *Sport Management: A Guide to Professional Practice*. Sydney: Allen and Unwin.

Stewart, B., Smith, A.C., and Nicholson, M. (2003) Sport consumer typologies: a critical review. *Sport Marketing Quarterly*, 12(4), 206–216.

Tapp, A. and Clowes, J. (2002) From "carefree casuals" to "professional wanderers": segmentation possibilities for football supporters. *European Journal of Marketing*, 36(11/12), 1248–1269.

The Future of the Sports Fan (2017) [online] Retrieved from: https://www.fotball.no/globalassets/dommer/the-future-sports-fan_spilleregler_english.pdf

Theodorakis, N., Wann, D., Nassis, P., and Luellen, D.B. (2012) The relationship between sport team identification and need to belong. *International Journal of Sport Management and Marketing*, 12(1/2), 25–38.

Toffler, A. (1980). *The Third Wave*. New York: William Morrow.

Wann, D.L. (1995) Preliminary validation of the sport fan motivation scale. *Journal of Sport and Social Issues*, 19, 377–396.

20

Sports business analytics

The past, the present and the future

Ian G. McHale

Introduction

In 1999 Paul DePodesta joined the Oakland Athletics, and together with Billy Beane, the pair are largely credited with helping the team reach the World Series playoffs in 2002 and 2003. Having a budget in the bottom three of teams in Major League Baseball and around a quarter that of the biggest team, the New York Yankees, the success came as a surprise to the whole of the baseball world, and was largely attributed to the use of analytics to gain an advantage over competitors in the employment market for baseball players. By identifying a skill that was undervalued in terms of its contribution to team success, the Athletics were able to compete at a much higher level than their budget should have made possible. The story became the subject of Michael Lewis's book *Moneyball* (Lewis, 2003), and was later immortalised on the silver screen in the film of the same name.

For analytics, the publication of *Moneyball* in 2003 was a turning point. In the years since its publication, we have entered the era of big data, and mega-corporations like Google, Facebook, Microsoft, and Twitter actively boast about using analytics as a tool to make better decisions across their businesses. As word spread, the analytics fever spread across sport. A notable example of analytics helping to gain an edge is that of the GB and Team Sky cycling teams. Since 2008, there has been the first ever British Tour de France winner (and subsequently several more), and a total of 24 gold medals at the 2008, 2012, and 2016 Olympic Games. Much of this success has been attributed to the team performance director/general manager, Sir Dave Brailsford, and his colleagues embracing the use of analytics in their search for "*marginal gains.*"

Today, analytics and the Moneyball concept is at the forefront of the minds of those in the business of sport, and those at teams and clubs across global sport as *the* example that making a difference is possible. Had it not happened at the Oakland Athletics, it may well have happened somewhere else in the world of sport, but those practising analytics in sport today are indebted to Michael Lewis and the visionaries at the Oakland Athletics who kick-started the analytics revolution.

In this chapter, I will describe what sports analytics is before providing some notable examples of sports analytics in practice. We will concern ourselves mostly with analytics being used to assess and improve team and/or player performances, though analytics should not be confined to this area and can and should be used to inform decision-making across a sports business. Marketing strategy, ticket pricing, and social media analysis are just some examples of areas in which analytics can help organisations. Let us first consider what analytics actually is.

What is analytics?

In some ways analytics is a rebranding of the subject disciple of statistics, and the basic idea of both areas is to make use of data in some way that helps understanding, and improves decision-making. The dictionary definition of analytics provided on Wikipedia is: "**Analytics** is the discovery, interpretation, and communication of meaningful patterns in data." The word "data" arises over and over again in definitions of analytics. A simpler description that I use is "analytics is the process of learning from data, to make better decisions." I like this description because it directly links data and decision-making. In sport, the decisions business managers, coaches, and team owners make are varied: from ticket pricing and forecasting demand, to how the organisation should manage its social media activity, to how much should be spent on advertising, to which players should be targeted and how much should we pay for them. Meaningful analytics should have direct consequences for decision-making.

Analytics is the process of turning data into something meaningful. To do this, we need tools, and there are many tools available to us to enable us to learn from data. The spectrum of tools ranges from simple descriptive statistics likes counts and averages, to fitting complex statistical models to make predictions about what might happen in the future. We use these tools, be they calculated averages or statistical models, to answer the questions we have, and/or learn what we can from the data.

What can we expect from analytics?

A somewhat common misconception is that by using analytics, your business, or sports team, is guaranteeing success. This is untrue because there are *externalities* which are out of the control of the business. Externalities may come in the form of a rival team being bought by a wealthy investor who is willing to fund the team's recruitment of the world's best players. No matter what clever analytics are employed, the monetary advantage is too big to breach.

One type of externality that makes guaranteed success impossible, is *noise*. Noise is a thorn in the side of forecasting in many facets of science – from the outcome of rolling a die, to modelling spread of disease across a population, to forecasting weather conditions – noise can make even the smartest people and most advanced models look seemingly poor. In sport, the outcome of a flip of a coin at the start of a Test match in cricket or an injury sustained to a star player, things THAT could not be known in advance, can have a negative (or sometimes positive) impact on the performance of a business or a team. The influence of noise affects the short-term more than the long-run and one can only assume that the effects of luck even out over time, but even Michael Lewis, the author of Moneyball said

> [Moneyball] was beautifully understood outside baseball, and by many baseball owners, [But there is] the inability, or refusal, to grab the most basic point—that it is about using statistical analysis to shift the odds [of winning baseball games] a bit in one's favor, not to achieve perfect certainty, which is impossible.

Lewis himself is admitting that employing analytics and making decisions backed by evidence are not going to result in a guaranteed success. Rather, analytics can increase the frequency with which good decisions are made, or even lower the frequency with which bad decisions are made.

Understanding that analytics will not guarantee success is just one aspect of appreciating the limitations of analytics. A second misconception is that decision-making can and should be solely driven by the results of analytics. In sport, this is especially true. Sports analytics cannot see everything; data sets do not capture all aspects of a situation. There should be a synergy between analysts and experienced industry insiders to get the best out of the findings of analytics. It should generate debate and conversation. A simple example might be of recruiting players for football clubs. Statistical models for rating players can be used to gain insight into how good a particular player is, and how good the player may be in the future, above and beyond what a traditional scout might be able to do. However, it is also the case that the scout will be able to 'see' things the data cannot. For example, the player may have a confrontational attitude towards his teammates or may get deflated and become less effective on the pitch up after playing a bad pass. The nature of these personality traits and a player's character cannot be detected in data, and so it is important to acknowledge that analytics will not replace experts, rather that the two should be used together to help make better, more informed, decisions.

The analytics process

Outside of sport and football, there are many textbooks discussing the analytics process, and ideally, the process will remain relatively unchanged by the industry in which analytics is being deployed. Zumel and Mount (2014) provide a continuing life-cycle of a data science project, and the practice of analytics in sport should be no different. The stages of the process are:

1   Define the problem: the first stage in analytics is to understand what the issue is. Describing manageable and realistic goals of a project are key to a successful analytics project. Understanding what stakeholders want, need and currently do can help gain trust and ultimately can help ensure that findings are acted upon.

2   Obtaining and processing data: it is vital to obtain data that are relevant to your goals, and that can help enlighten the issue into which you are investigating. It may be the case that the data you need do not exist. Further, it may be the case that obtaining the data you need would be too expensive. In this case, you may need to redefine your goals to take account of the data that are available. In sport, as data sets become ever larger, the processing, cleaning, storage, and management of data is becoming an increasingly more complex task and should not be taken lightly.

3   Selecting tools and building models: much like a carpenter must choose which tool to use for a particular job, an analyst must choose which tool to use to enlighten the issue at hand. It would be unwise for a carpenter to select a hammer as a tool when the problem is that a piece of wood needs to be cut in two, and there is very little point in an analyst employing complex statistical models to identify which player completed the most passes in a particular football match. The carpenter should clearly select a saw, whilst the analyst can solve his problem simply by counting. It should be noted that in sports analytics, there is a tendency to select the wrong tool. Too often analysts, and the media, equate counting with solving a problem that is inherently more complex than it may at first seem. For example, possession statistics in football, are interpreted incorrectly as answering the question "which team was the better in a match?" In fact, possession statistics turn out to explain surprisingly little about which team won the match. Possession statistics are more a reflection of which team went ahead in the game and conceded possession in order to increase the chances of

scoring on the break, whilst the team which fell behind puts more effort into attacking play in search of the equalising goal.

4   Interpretation and presentation of results: once a model has been fitted, evaluated, and checked for accuracy, the results should be carefully considered and interpreted in search of implications to decision-making. Ideally, this should be done with the participation of experts, decision-makers and the analyst(s).

5   Act upon the findings and evaluate: once all results have been interpreted and considered, a strategy for acting upon the implications of the work in decision-making should be sought. If acted upon, the results should be monitored and compared with previous performance to see if there is a positive or negative impact. There should be a back and forth between the decision-makers and analysts to continue to contribute to and improve the processes of the business.

These five steps in the analytics process will appear in most projects. But of these steps, perhaps the most underappreciated and difficult step in sports analytics is the interpretation of a piece of analytics. Consider an over-simplified example of aces in tennis and suppose that in a particular match Player A achieved five aces, whilst Player B achieved just one ace. Do these counts of aces reveal which of the two players is the better server? Despite aces often being quoted, and interpreted as differentiating between the players' serving abilities, they are flawed. Ignoring for a moment the small sample size, no account is taken of the number of first serves attempted. If you subsequently learned that Player A had attempted 90 first serves whilst Player B had served 50, would this change your opinion on the relative strengths of the two players' serving abilities? Now suppose that Player A is considered to be one of the best returners of serve in the world, whilst returning is a particular weakness for Player B. This information may completely reverse the identity of the player with the best serve. But we still do not actually know the answer using the counts of aces by the two players. To answer the question 'which player is the better server?,' we would have to employ a statistical model which could take account of the number of serves played by each player, and the strength of the opposition player's return of serve. Of course, how well a player serves is not just a case of estimating the probability of a particular player serving an ace. One might want to consider modelling the probability of a point being won on serve within a couple of shots (so that a player's general ability to play tennis once the point is underway is not conflated with the player's serving ability), as an improved measure of a player's serving ability. The point is, it is easy to assume that a statistic is telling you something that in fact, it is not.

Techniques for analytics

The previous example should demonstrate how the relatively simple question of which of two players is the better at serving can quickly turn into a complicated statistical problem. Identifying the tools required for a job requires a broad appreciation of what tools are available. It is not the purpose of this chapter to describe in full how to use all of the tools available, but rather, to highlight and comment on a small subset of the tools and techniques that are used more frequently than others.

Calculating *means* can go a long way in analytics. Especially when there are a lot of data. Descriptive statistics like means, standard deviations, minimums, and maximums, can help an analyst understand the data, and get a feel for the problem at hand. Calculating means of subsets of data can bring to light areas for further investigation. An example from golf is that the average driving distance of the top ten ranked golfers in the world is higher than those ranked between

11 and 20. Does this suggest that the old adage that "driving is for show, putting for dough," is misleading, or even worse, is the complete antithesis of the truth? Perhaps it does, and maybe someone should investigate this finding more.

Arguably the most commonly used tool in analytics is that of *regression*. Regression models quantify the relationship between a quantity of interest, called a dependent variable (e.g. win percentage of a baseball team), and other quantities, called independent variables or covariates (e.g. slugging average and on-base percentage). Regression can be used to tell us how the dependent variable moves with the covariates. Further, regression reveals the amount of change we can expect for given changes in the covariates. For example, how much might a baseball team's win percentage change if on-base percentage increases by 1 per cent. We will revisit this example later.

Survival analysis is used to explain the time until an event of interest. In sports like ice-hockey and football, survival modelling is particularly useful for modelling the time until the next score, and has been used in the literature to investigate issues like the impact of a red card on scoring rates (Vecer, Kopriva, and Ichiba, 2009).

Broadly speaking, the field of *machine learning* is concerned with the (semi)-automated selection, development, fitting, and monitoring of statistical models. In sport, it is increasingly being adopted in forecasting exercises (see, for example, Bunker and Thabtah, 2017) but also has the potential to be used in other areas (see, for example, Carey et al. 2016, who look at using machine learning to predict ratings of perceived exertion).

Markov Game models are a more advanced technique and have started to be used to better understand the contribution of actions and players in team sports. For example, Schulte et al. (2017), present a model to rate the actions of players in ice-hockey.

No one tool can be used for all of analytics and it is the task of the analyst to select the tool most suited to the problem at hand.

An ideology for sports analytics

Sports analytics is a practical subject, and results of analyses should ideally have practical implications. Given this is a relatively new area of application, and given that practitioners and decision-makers are still learning to trust analysts, it is especially important for researchers in the field to be pragmatic. It is perhaps reasonable to bear in mind two considerations for a piece of analysis:

i   The findings should impact results: there is no better way to grab the attention of a decision-maker than to suggest "do this, and results will improve." If this is not true, *selling* the analytics could be hard.

ii Consider whether the analytics are *predictive* in nature: there are many examples in sport of retrospective analytics that merely informs us of what has already happened. A simple example is that of possession statistics in football. They reveal what the state of affairs was in a match, but very little has been published about whether the possession statistics can be used to predict future performance. However, in sport, it is surely the case that we should be interested in statistics that tell us what performance we can expect in the future. The question recruitment departments are interested in is "what will the performance of this player be **next** year?" not "what was the performance of this player **last** year?"

To add to i. above, the research should, if implemented and acted upon correctly, inform and improve the strategy of the team.

Analytics in practice

In this section, we will take a look at some examples of sports analytics that have been used in practice, and some that are still to be adopted. We begin with an example from over fifty years ago, and one that should probably not be in a chapter advertising the merits of sports analytics …

The origins of the "long-ball"?

Sports analytics has only relatively recently come into the public consciousness. However, examples of analytics being used in sport date back much further into the past than *Moneyball*. Perhaps the most infamous case of analytics in sport is that of Charles Reep's analysis of passing sequences leading to goals in the 1960s. Reep was also responsible for research that had appeared in a paper published in the *Journal of the Royal Statistical Society* (Reep and Benjamin, 1968), so it was reasonable to assume that his analysis of passing sequences was sound and robust. However, this is a good example that as a reader and researcher, one should always question what you are being told.

Based on data collected from football games in the 1960s, Reep found that most goals in the matches he analysed were scored following passing sequences of three or fewer passes. He also noticed that most sequences of attacking play consisted of a very small number of passes. He concluded that attempting long sequences of passes was not as efficient, or as productive, as moving the ball as quickly as possible towards the opposition goal. It is said that this is where the "long-ball" style of play originated from, and in Jonathan Wilson's book *Inverting the Pyramid* (Wilson, 2009), Reep is held accountable for the England national team's style of play, and lack of success, for over half a century.

Wilson argues that there is a flaw in Reep's conclusion and demonstrates the flaw using the following argument. Reep found that 91.5 per cent of possessions in a game of football consist of three passes or fewer. If the length of a passing sequence (as measured by the number of passes) was independent of whether the possession would end in a goal, then it is reasonable to expect that (about) 91.5 per cent of all goals (from open play) would result from possessions of three passes or fewer. Further, if Reep's conclusion was true – that shorter passing sequences were more likely to result in goals, then the percentage of goals resulting from passing sequences of three passes or fewer would be *higher* than the 91.5 per cent. Unfortunately (for Reep, and for English football), just 80 per cent of goals resulted from moves of three passes or fewer. Not only do these figures put doubt on Reep's conclusions, but they are polar opposites and completely negate the advice that Reep gave clubs and the football world.

With hindsight, we can now see that the interpretation of Reep's analysis was unfortunately flawed. At the time, however, it did highlight to people in football that analysing data could be a useful thing to do. Even today, this is a challenge that faces analytics: getting people in sport to listen to, and act upon, findings from the analysis of data.

We can now revisit Reep's work, and the data he collected, and think about what conclusions can be made, and what future research might investigate. For example, the data suggested that in World Cup matches, the percentage of possessions consisting of higher numbers of passes was higher than in domestic league football. This hints at the idea that better quality players and teams may benefit more from longer passing sequences of play. As Wilson points out, players at lower levels may not be skilful enough to reap the benefits of playing a passing game, and in fact, may even suffer a detrimental effect due to a higher probability of making an error. Future research could look at what style of play suits a particular set of players, taking into account their skill levels. One might find that the long-ball is indeed an efficient strategy at some levels of football, but that at higher levels, the passing game is more useful.

Moneyball – what lessons can be learnt from baseball?

Having considered an example in which analytics may have failed sport, let us turn our attention to arguably the greatest success story of analytics in sport: Moneyball. There have been several academic papers appear since the years following the success of the Oakland Athletics. The first of these was Hakes and Sauer (2006), and their paper will help reveal what Moneyball actually is.

In the film, the Pythagorean formula receives a great deal of attention, relating win percentage to home runs and you may be forgiven for thinking this formula was the essence of Moneyball. In fact, it was not. The essential ingredient of Moneyball is an inefficiency in the employment market for baseball players. Hakes and Sauer (2006) demonstrate the existence of this inefficiency, and subsequently, show how it is corrected in the years following Moneyball. To do so, Hakes and Sauer first show how a team's performance (measured using win percentage) is related to the team's playing statistics (*slugging percentage* and *on-base percentage* being the two of particular interest). Using a regression model, they find that the influence of *on-base percentage* is over twice that of the influence of *slugging percentage*.

We learn of the inefficiency in the employment market for baseball players when Hakes and Sauer (2006) fit a second regression model exploring the relationship between players' salaries and the same two playing statistics, *slugging percentage* and *on-base percentage* (but this time at the player level). As Hakes and Sauer point out: "An efficient labor market for baseball players would, all other factors held constant, reward on-base percentage and slugging percentage in the same proportions that those statistics contribute to winning." However, the results of their second regression model show that the influence of slugging percentage is more than twice that of the influence of on-base percentage – the exact opposite of what should happen in an efficient market.

The Oakland Athletics noticed this inefficiency and are said to have changed their recruitment strategy to recruit players undervalued in the market and that were good at getting on-base, and not worry so much about the player's slugging percentage. For a few years it worked, but sure enough, the inefficiency soon began to disappear. Hakes and Sauer themselves find that this is the case, and most recently Brown, Link, and Rubin (2017) have shown that the inefficiency has been corrected.[1]

Perhaps the biggest finding from the Moneyball story is not of a team achieving unexpected success (given its payroll), but rather, that an inefficiency in an employment market lasted for so long. However, once the inefficiency was discovered, it soon disappeared, and within five years of recruiting players based on *on-base percentage*, the Oakland Athletics' secret was out and other teams changed their recruitment strategies and the Oakland Athletics returned to their status pre-Moneyball. One particularly nice interpretation, for analysts at least, is that the other teams learned of the contribution analytics could make and began recruiting analysts. The employment market for analysts is efficient, and the best went to the highest paying teams – and the equilibrium returned. In some ways, the recruitment of analysts is like the game-theory of the Cold-war. You have to build nuclear weapons to deter the enemy from deploying theirs, with the end result identical to neither country having nuclear weapons; you have to employ analysts to prevent opposition teams gaining an advantage, with the end result looking just like it was before any team employed analysts!

Can Moneyball happen again? Can it be done outside of baseball, in football? Some authors have looked into this. Weimar and Wicker (2017) seek inefficiencies in the German Bundesliga of the type detected in Hakes and Sauer (2006). Weimar and Wicker suggest that there may indeed be inefficiencies in that effort (measured by distance run and number of intensive runs) has a greater influence on team performance than it does on a player's salary. So, to answer the question of whether a football team can use the ideas of Moneyball to gain an edge, it all depends on whether the employment market for football players is efficient, and there is some evidence that inefficiencies may currently exist.

Expected goals

In football, the uptake of analytics is somewhat unknown, with the success of analytics even more uncertain. If there has been a club succeeding using analytics in the same way that the Oakland Athletics baseball team did in Moneyball, it is doing a very good job of hiding it. Figure 20.1 shows the League Points obtained by teams versus their relative wages. The relative wages are defined as the wages of a team in a particular season, divided by the average wages of all teams in the league in that season. In fact, other than for the outlier of Leicester City in the 2015–2016 season (the top left point), the relationship between wages and team performance (as measured by league points) has remained remarkably constant.

The evidence from Figure 20.1 suggests there has not been a Moneyball-like event in football. Instead, there is a gradual acceptance of analytics and that some new statistics are useful.

Within the media, most of the analytics we are presented with are still simply counting. There is nothing wrong with this in principal, but what is concerning is how the counting is interpreted. When discussing player transfers, players are often compared based on the number of goals they have scored, or their goals to shots conversion percentage with the intimation that the player with the most goals, or the higher conversion rate, is superior. We know only too well from the example above in which tennis players' serving ability was compared using the number of aces they served, that it is unlikely to be straightforward to answer the question: of two players, which is the better at scoring? Using total goals and/or shot conversion rate is

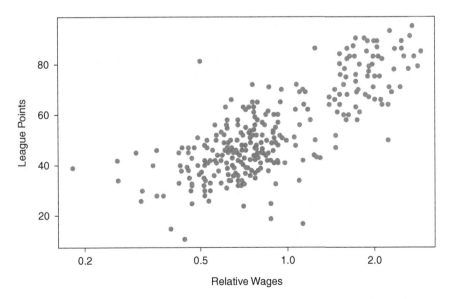

Figure 20.1   Relative wages (defined as the team's wages divided by the league average wages for that season) versus league points for teams in the English Premier League from the 2000/2001 season to the 2016/17 season

flawed in numerous ways: no account is taken for where the shots were taken from, no account is taken of the strength of the teams the two players are playing for, and no account is taken of how many shots the player took.

During the start of the 2017–2018 Premier League season, a statistic that has gained traction in both the industry and the media is that of *expected goals*, xG. The concept of expected goals has become increasingly popular in forecasting in football and is gradually being adopted as an alternative way to rate goal-scoring ability of teams and players. The idea is that there is more information about the quality of a team in counting the number of shots it generates, as opposed to the number of goals it scores. This is in part a consequence of football being such a low scoring game – noise plays a huge role in final score lines: a team can dominate a game without scoring and then concede a goal from a counter-attack.

To appreciate the logic behind, and information that is revealed by, expected goals, consider the game between Manchester City and West Ham United on 19 September 2015. West Ham won the game 2–1. If you knew nothing about football and were asked to rate these two teams, it would be reasonable to say that West Ham were the better team. However, Manchester City were the favourites for the title that season, so were in fact a very good team, whilst West Ham were likely to be mid-table come the end of the season. As such, the "truth" is that Manchester City were a much stronger side than West Ham United, but this is not revealed by the goals statistics. If you were looking for statistics to use to help forecast future match results, perhaps goal counts (for one match) are not as informative as we would like. In search of a statistic that is more helpful, we find that in the course of this particular match Manchester City had 26 shots whilst West Ham only had six. This is interesting – it is the complete opposite of the goal counts and Manchester City now look like the better team. It turns out that the total shots by each team is likely to be more revealing of the true relative qualities of the two sides.

In fact, we can get even more information out of shot data by knowing where the shots originated. A team generating shots from close range is likely to be better than one generating shots from outside the box. For the Manchester City vs West Ham United game, further digging reveals that City's shots tended to be of "high quality" (good opportunities with a high probability of being converted into a goal – but on this particular occasion were not), whilst West Ham United's shots were "low quality" from long range (with a low probability of being converted to a goal, but on this particular occasion were). To account for the location of each shot and build a more informative statistic than shot counts, we need a statistical model.

The statistical model used to calculate xG estimates the probability of a shot resulting in a goal. There is not one accepted model, but the general approach is to use the location of the shot plus some other pieces of information, like whether the shot was a header to estimate this probability. Kharrat, Lopez-Pena, and McHale (2018) present an expected goals model of this kind. The results of an expected goal model can be shown as a heatmap of the probability of a shot from open play (not a header) resulting in a goal. Such a plot is shown in Figure 20.2.

The darker areas are those with the highest probability of scoring a goal. It is as you would expect – as shots get further away from the goal, the lower the chance of the shot being a goal.

You can use this model to calculate the expected goals from a shot by each team in a match by summing up the probabilities of each shot resulting in a goal. This can also be done for a specific player, either in a match or over a longer period of time. For example, given the location of the shots during the match, we should have expected around 3.3 goals to City and 0.9 goals to West Ham. In other words, City were the dominant team but lost the game.

Expected goals explain future performance of players and teams better than the more traditional statistics of goals and shots counts. Monitoring of expected goals at the level of the team or the player, over the course of a season, should help a team better understand its own strengths

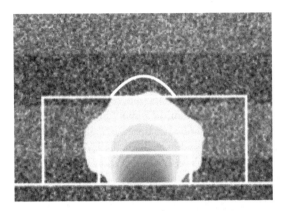

Figure 20.2   Heatmap of goal probability for an expected goals model

and the strengths of opposition teams. Indeed, it is a good sign for analytics that the media, fans, and analysts within clubs have accepted the use of expected goals as a more insightful source of information than simply using goals.

Plus-minus ratings

A core task of analytics within team sports is to understand player contributions to teams. A popular method to rate players for their contributions to their team's success in US sports has been the plus-minus player ratings system. First used in the 1950s in ice-hockey, but most often seen nowadays in basketball, the concept of plus-minus ratings is to measure a team's performance when a player is on the team and compare it to the team's performance when the same player is not on the team. In basketball, because there are so many changes to the team line-up during a game, this naïve plus-minus rating is informative. However, it is flawed in that no account is taken for the ability of the player's teammates, or of the opposition players. To deal with these difficulties, MacDonald (2012) uses regression models and presents ways in which the naïve plus-minus ratings can be adjusted for use in ice-hockey, and of course, this modified plus-minus rating system can be applied to basketball and football.

Recent developments in plus-minus ratings systems have focussed on using alternative metrics to measure team performance. The obvious way to measure team performance in basketball is points, whilst in football and ice-hockey it is goals. However, as discussed in the previous section on expected goals, because goals themselves are so low in number, using them to measure team performance can be misleading. As such, Kharrat, Lopez-Pena and McHale (2018) present a plus-minus ratings system using expected goals and the *target*.

Within basketball, plus-minus ratings are the norm within the media. Perhaps this will one day spread to football as the resulting player ratings reveal insights in to player abilities, without relying on large data sets revealing information on each and every event within a match. Nowadays of course, even richer data sets are available for analysis, and such big data are needed for the tools discussed in the next section.

Expected value of possession

The concept of expected value of possession[2] (EVP) was first introduced by Cervone et al. (2016). To calculate the expected value of a possession, Cervone et al. utilise player tracking data in basketball. In recent years, player tracking data has become available in ice-hockey and football, and the ideas introduced by Cervone et al. can be applied in these sports too.

The central idea of EVP is a simple one: given the location of the ball, the location of the players, and the history of how they got to this position, calculate the probability of the possession resulting in points. As the ball (or puck in ice-hockey) moves around, and the players also move around, this probability evolves. As the ball gets closer to the opposition goal (or basket) this probability typically increases, and as the ball moves further from the opposition goal it typically decreases. Complex spatio-temporal models, of the type described in Bornn et al. (2017), are used to estimate the probability of a possession ending in a goal, and once fitted, the EVP can be used to gain powerful insights into player decision-making, and player contributions to team success.

Assessing the decisions made by players reveals information unlike other player performance metrics, yet decision-making is surely a key attribute of a player's overall ability. For example, it is impressive if a basketball player has a three-point conversion rate of 40 per cent while marked by two opposition players, and it would seem reasonable for this star-three-point thrower to attempt to score. However, using the EVP framework, we might notice that during a particular possession that if the player were to pass to one of his teammates, the expected value would rise from $0.4 \times 3 = 1.2$, to $0.6 \times 3 = 1.8$. In this case, regardless of the outcome of the attempt, the player actually harmed his team's expected value of the possession. By comparing the expected value of possession for what a player chose to do (which teammate to pass to, where to dribble to, or whether to shoot) to the other options available to him, it is possible to measure how good, or bad, the player's decision-making is.

In addition to measuring a player's ability to make decisions that are beneficial to his team, the EVP concept can be used to directly measure a player's contribution to his team's play. Consider, for example, a possession which, at the moment a player receives the ball, has an EVP of 0.1 points. The player dribbles and then passes to a teammate in a better position, at which moment the EVP rises to 0.3 points. A simple interpretation is that the player has contributed $0.3 - 0.1 = 0.2$ expected points to his team. Summing these contributions up over a game or a season produces an entirely new, and unique, player ratings system.

Expected value of possession is a relatively new concept and, to date, it is unclear where it has been adopted and whether it has spread outside of basketball. There are obstacles to its widespread use in that to calculate EVP one not only needs to have access to player tracking data, which can be expensive, but also requires advanced expertise in statistical modelling. However, given its potential, and the unparalleled insight into player contributions through both on- and off-the-ball actions, it will almost certainly become a standard methodology within sports analytics.

Closing remarks

The adoption of analytics in sport has gathered pace in recent years. Some sports are more open to its use and benefits with success stories emanating from baseball and cycling in particular. Of course, we can never truly know how influential analytics is within a particular team, club, or organisation, or even what analytics are being used, since the competitive nature of sport means teams want to keep their advantage to themselves.

In this chapter, we have considered what analytics actually means, and described an ideology for the use of analytics, before looking at some examples of analytics in practice. Perhaps the biggest lesson from this chapter is to better understand what we can expect from analytics. Is adopting analytics going to guarantee success? No, it is not. But if done properly, it will help to make better decisions, and fewer poor decisions. These decisions will be backed by evidence and have a reasoned logic behind them. Too often in sport decision-makers are accused of making gut-feel, instinctive decisions that subsequently go wrong.

Although there has been much progress in people understanding that analytics can be a positive influence on a business, there are challenges to be overcome. Across many industries, analysts and statisticians have always faced, and will continue to face, a communication breakdown with non-quantitative people. In sport, if truth be told, this is particularly difficult to manage. Decision-makers are often ex-players, with little formal education and even less appreciation of mathematics. Helping people to understand a piece of analytics and persuading them to trust and act upon the results is a challenge that will perhaps forever face analytics.

Although a powerful tool, analytics cannot cover everything. Psychological aspects of player performance are, at present, not possible to assess using the data that are available. Will a prospective player gel with new teammates or settle in a new country? Such questions need the input of experts to inform recruitment decisions. As such, in sport, analytics and expert opinion should be used together, helping to enhance the success of the organisation.

Notes

1 With the caveat that this is only the case in the competitive marketplace for baseball player recruitment.
2 Cervone et al. (2016) talk about Expected Possession Value (EPV).

References

Bornn, L., Cervone, D., Franks, A., and Miller, A. (2017) Studying basketball through the lens of player tracking data. In: Albert, J., Glickman, M.E., Swartz, T.B., and Koning, R.H., (eds.). *Handbook of Statistical Methods and Analyses in Sports*. Chapman and Hall: Boca Raton, Florida.

Brown, D. T., Charles R. Link, and Seth L. Rubin. (2017) Moneyball after 10 Years: how have Major League Baseball salaries adjusted? *Journal of Sports Economics*, 18(8), 771–786.

Bunker, R.P. and Thabtah, F. (2017) A machine learning framework for sport result prediction. *Applied Computing and Informatics*. https://doi.org/10.1016/j.aci.2017.09.005

Carey, D., Ong, K., Morris, M., Crow, J. and Crossley, K. (2016) Predicting ratings of perceived exertion in Australian football players: methods for live estimation. *International Journal of Computer Science in Sport*, 15(2), 64–77.

Cervone, D., D'Amour, A., Bornn, L., and Goldsberry, K. (2016) A multiresolution stochastic process model for predicting basketball possession outcomes. *Journal of the American Statistical Association*, 111, 585–599.

Hakes, Jahn, K., and Raymond D. Sauer (2006) An economic evaluation of the moneyball hypothesis. *Journal of Economic Perspectives*, 20(3), 173–186.

Macdonald, B. (2012) Adjusted Plus-Minus for NHL players using ridge regression with goals, shots, Fenwick, and Corsi. *Journal of Quantitative Analysis in Sports*, 8(3), 1–24.

Reep, C., and Benjamin, B. (1968) Skill and chance in association football. *Journal of the Royal Statistical Society*, Series A (General), 131(4), 581–585. doi:10.2307/2343726

Kharrat, K., Lopez-Pena, J., and McHale, I.G. (2018) Plus-Minus ratings in soccer. Working paper.

Lewis, M. (2003) *Moneyball: The Art of Winning an Unfair Game*. Norton: New York.

Schulte, O., Khademi, M., Gholami, S. (2017) A Markov Game model for valuing actions, locations, and team performance in ice hockey. *Data Mining and Knowledge Discovery*, 31, 1735–1757.

Vecer, J., Kopriva, F., and Ichiba, T. (2009) Estimating the effect of the red card in soccer: when to commit an offense in exchange for preventing a goal opportunity. *Journal of Quantitative Analysis in Sports*, 5(1).

Weimar, D. and Wicker, P. (2014) Moneyball revisited: effort and team performance in professional soccer. *Journal of Sports Economics*, 18(2), 140–161.

Wilson, J. (2009). *Inverting the Pyramid: The History of Football Tactics*. Orion Books: London. pp. 138–144, 288–295, 301–303.

Zumel, N. and J. Mount (2014) Practical Data Science with R. Manning Publications: New York.

21

Leagues, tournaments, and competitions

Thadeu Gasparetto and Angel Barajas

Introduction

Professional football competitions are a major economic activity. Broadcasting rights and sponsorships contracts have been increasing season by season. In parallel, clubs are spending significant amounts of money on players year after year. Moreover, billions of euros have been invested in sports facilities and stadiums, seeking to extract the highest sports performance from the players and providing great experiences for supporters.

Millions of fans from all around the world follow football tournaments daily through the Internet, magazines, newspapers, radio, and television. Indeed, the consumption of information about football is massive and it is in the interests of all stakeholders to maintain the attractiveness of football competitions. Moreover, once a football match (or a tournament) is a proper "joint-product," as defined by Neale (1964) in his seminal paper, all interested parties should cooperate with each other and pursue fairness. In this case, fairness might be interpreted as all participants having similar schedules in terms of consecutive matches against strong (or weak) opponents, travel distances (i.e., successive games home or away), and some other sporting and geographical aspects.

Sports scheduling has achieved substantial growth over the last 15 years following the implementation of programming-based methods, such as constraint programming, decomposition, heuristic algorithms and integer programming. Noll (2003) highlights that although the organisation of sports leagues might be structured in several different ways, there are (at least) five types of decisions that clubs and league organisers must keep in mind: tournament format; hierarchy of quality between tournaments; multiplicity of leagues; membership conditions; and methods of governance. In this sense, football tournament organisers (i.e., Football Associations, Football Federations, Professional Football Leagues, etc.) should take into account these factors as well as satisfy some other requirements like the number of participants, geographical issues, fans behaviour, TV channels and sponsors' interests, security and fairness. Hence, scheduling is a complex task that researchers and decision-makers have been trying to resolve for some time.

The aim of the present chapter is to deliver an overview of professional football leagues, tournaments, and competitions. The first section is related to geographical issues, as professional football tournaments are usually organised taking into account geographical levels, like domestic (i.e., regional, national, etc.) and international (i.e., continental and world level) perspectives. Then, the most common competitive designs are explained – such as round robin and knockout championships – in the second section. The third section explains some of the main constraints of football scheduling such as breaks, travel distances, and carry-over effects. The fourth section describes scheduling optimisations, giving some real examples and their achievements. The last section is dedicated to the changes that professional football leagues have been making, finishing with some concluding remarks.

Geographical issues

Professional football is primarily organised along geographical lines. The governing body of football worldwide is the *Fédération Internationale de Football Association* (FIFA). Nowadays, 211 national affiliated associations are part of FIFA and they are divided into six continental confederations – the African (CAF), Asian (AFC), European (UEFA), North American and Caribbean (CONCACAF), Oceania (OFC), and South American (CONMEBOL) confederations. This structure represents the organisation of international football and it can be evidenced through the FIFA World Cup Qualifiers, where affiliated countries battle it out within each of the confederations for a place in the flagship tournament. On the other hand, domestic football around the world (football club perspective) has some other spatial scales, making it different contextually to the international one.

A domestic football market might be interpreted as all the activities, organisations and people related to football at a national level. In this sense, it comprises fans, players, agents, coaches, and other staff as well as football clubs, tournaments, TV channels, and League organisers. The national football associations are those organisations that control each domestic football market. However, although they follow several FIFA policies and rules, they enjoy autonomy in terms of structuring their own domestic market. Hence, several differences can be found when comparing two or more domestic football markets.

Several aspects make each domestic football market unique. In general, the most important national tournaments are organised by professional leagues. This is the case in countries such as England, Germany, and Spain (English Premier League, *Bundesliga*, and *La Liga*, respectively). In some other countries (i.e., Brazil and Chile), the respective national football association manages domestic leagues and cups. Nevertheless, professional minor levels (i.e., state or regional), also exist in some countries around the world, such as non-league clubs in the UK or Spain (i.e., Second Division B, Third Division and *Categorías Regionales* – Regional Divisions, in English). However, in both countries, these tournaments are considered semi-professional or even amateur tournaments.

The Brazilian football market offers an example of professional minor levels. The *Confederação Brasileira de Futebol* (CBF) is the Brazilian football association and the domestic governing body in Brazil. Nonetheless, 27 state football federations, each corresponding with a specific Brazilian state, compose the CBF. These state federations have several primary responsibilities, like club and player registrations as well as the annual organisation of their own competitions – *Campeonatos Estaduais* (State Championships). However, they have a certain degree of autonomy, as they can define the number of participants, scheduling, promotion, and relegation systems as well as other sporting aspects in these tournaments. A peculiar feature of the Brazilian State Championships is that clubs from different sporting levels may play against each other – currently, there are clubs from the First, Second, Third, Fourth, and even Non-Division teams competing for the title every year. However, all of them must be from the same state. These tournaments seem to be unbalanced – indeed, they are – but there are some cases where clubs from lower divisions have become the champions. To the best of our knowledge, there are no similar competitions that exist anywhere else in the world.

The Brazilian football market also has another peculiar tournament, called *Campeonatos Regionais* (Regional Championships). Clubs play The Regional Championships from the same region – Southeast, Northeast, North, Central West, or South. Although they do not have the same importance in the market nowadays, these championships represent an example of a professional football tournament at regional level.

Major League Soccer (MLS), comprising teams from the U.S and Canada, presents another geographic dimension in the organising of professional football tournaments. This league structure follows a similar framework laid down in other North American major leagues (NFL, NBA, MLB), whereby teams are segregated geographically into alternative confederations (leagues). However, despite this segregation, the clubs from one confederation play a match against all opponents from the other confederation during a regular season. Notwithstanding, the playoff stage is designed again by geographical criteria (confederation brackets). Only in the MLS Cup Final, do the winners of both confederations face off.

Design of competition

Professional football competitions may have several different designs. Although the kind of tournament often characterises the design of competition (i.e., round robin for leagues and knockout for cups), it is not a rule, there have been occasions where there have been both leagues and cups with round robin regular phases, plus playoff stages as well. The main concepts and features of round robin (RR), knockout, and RR plus playoffs are presented in the following subsections.

Round robin (RR)

Round robin is a tournament design where all teams play against all other opponents a fixed number of times. In a single round robin (SRR), every team meets every other team once, like in the Group Stage of the FIFA World Cup. Double round robin (DRR), the most popular design of competition in European football (Goossens and Spieksma, 2012a), is where all teams play twice against all other teams, once at each venue (one at home and one away). Some well-known professional football leagues such as the English Premier League, Spanish La Liga, German Bundesliga, Italian Serie A and French Ligue 1 use this design of competition. Other competition formats also exist, like triple and quadruple round robin, which have been employed in professional football leagues in countries with a lower number of clubs in the competition like Slovakia and Austria, respectively.

The "compact" schedule is a common characteristic among professional football leagues. Rasmussen and Trick (2008) define a schedule as compact when every team only plays once in every round. Although nowadays all European leagues have a compact schedule, Griggs and Rosa (1996) noted that both Dutch and Russian leagues had "relaxed" schedules in 1994/95 – when some teams played matches on "irregular" dates. The authors remark that geographical considerations explained the Russian case. However, exceptions may mostly be due to force majeure, but sometimes can be as a consequence of the participation of a team in international competitions. This usually creates some problems in finding a new date to recover the unplayed match. An additional problem is coordinating the matches of the national team with domestic competitions. This problem has been addressed with the setting of a common calendar for international matches.

Table 21.1 Symmetry schemes in a double round robin league with n = 20

Scheme	Opponent of club 20 in the first part					Opponent of club 20 in the second part				
English	1	2	3	...	19	19	1	2	...	17	18
French	1	2	3	...	19	2	3	4	...	19	1
Inverted	1	2	3	...	19	19	18	17	...	2	1
Mirroring	1	2	3	...	19	1	2	3	...	18	19

Source: Modified from Goossens and Spiekma (2012a).

Symmetry is another important component of round robin tournaments. The symmetry defines the order in which all of the matches will occur (fixtures) prior to the tournament. In this sense, the tournament is divided into equal parts, where each one could represent a single round robin championship. Goossens and Spieksma (2012a) remark that the most common symmetry schemes are English, French, Inverted, and Mirroring. Table 21.1 illustrates all of them in a double round robin league with *n* = 20.

In a round robin tournament with an odd number of participants, in every round one club does not play as a consequence of this uneven number of clubs. This no play in a slot (or round) is defined in the literature as a *bye*. For a comprehensive review of the round robin design of competition, see Rasmussen and Trick (2008).

Knockout

The knockout system is one of the most extensive competition designs among sports tournaments. Indeed, several championships exclusively adopt this competitive format in football, such as the Football Association (FA) Cup in the UK, *Copa del Rey* in Spain and *Coppa Italia* in Italy. In the European context, this kind of tournament (national cups) includes teams from lower divisions in the first rounds. After a certain stage, clubs from the top division enter into the competition. On some occasions, clubs taking part in international competitions start in more advanced rounds.

Knockout tournaments are those where the participants are paired at the beginning of the tournament and only the winner of each pair passes through to the subsequent round – where the remaining clubs will be paired again. This course is followed until the best team (which has won all the knockout rounds and won the final match) is declared the champion. In football, the winner in every round is usually defined after the result of a single match or through the aggregate result of home and away games. However, some other sports, like North American Major League baseball, often employ a *best-of-x* series of some odd *x*.

Brackets constitute the structure of knockout tournaments. According to Hennessy and Glickman (2016), the most common arrangements are Fixed Bracket and Adaptive Bracket. In the Fixed Bracket, the complete structure of the championship is known before it begins. In this sense, the clubs can identify in advance their possible opponents if they pass through to the subsequent round. On the other hand, the Adaptive Bracket rearranges the pairs in the subsequent round according to the winners and some predefined constraints.

Some researchers have analysed knockout tournaments over the last years. Baek, Yi, Park, and Kim (2013) describe universal statistics for the knockout design of competition, focusing on the relationship between competitiveness and prize money distribution. Moreover, some papers have been seeking ways to design optimal and/or fair knockout brackets, for example, Hennessy and Glickman (2016) and Prince, Smith, and Geunes (2013). The "optimal bracket" proposed by

Hennessy and Glickman (2016) is based on maximising the probability of the best team (player, in that case) becoming the champion. The bracket suggested by Prince, Smith, and Geunes (2013) is designed considering the following concept of *fair*: "A bracket is fair for a power set if and only if a team's probability of advancing in each round is no less than that of any team having a lower power ranking" (Prince, Smith, and Geunes, 2013, p. 322). In this sense, both papers aim to develop knockout brackets that increase the likelihood of success of the better clubs (players). Nevertheless, Aronshtam, Cohen, and Shrot (2017) mention a bracket manipulation in professional tennis that "under certain circumstances" tournament organisers may adjust the brackets in favour of a specific competitor. Hence, this might happen in professional football as well.

Therefore, a fair knockout tournament could be designed with a Randomly Generated Bracket, where before every round there is a draw of all participants (clubs qualified to the subsequent rounds) with no constraints. Through this approach, the brackets would be arranged randomly, with no bias. However, this may not be of interest to top clubs, as they would play with each other in the preliminary rounds and consequently some would be eliminated in the early stages, or to broadcasting rights owners or tournament organisers, if less popular clubs win through to advanced stages.

Round robin plus playoffs

Several professional tournaments employ a combination of round robin and knockout designs in their arrangements. Indeed, the well-known tournaments from both international and club perspectives are structured in this format: FIFA World Cup and UEFA Champions League, respectively.

Numerous designs employ RR plus playoff stages. The UEFA Champions League begins with some qualifying rounds of knockout matches, then a double round robin stage and finally the playoffs (starting in Round of 16). The FIFA World Cup has a group stage designed with a single round robin and then the playoff stage. In addition, there are competitions with different arrangements. The German *Bundesliga* employs promotion/relegation playoffs, where a club from the top tier faces another from the second tier in a knockout match in order to define who will play in the first division in the next season. Another alternative is that used in the Dutch *Eredivise*, where there is a playoff stage to define a participant for an international competition (Europa League). The MLS, as mentioned before, also employs a competitive format with a regular season followed by a playoff stage with the top clubs from each confederation.

Constraints in the scheduling

The scheduling of a professional football competition must set a number of constraints in order to make it as fair as possible. In this section, three of the most common constraints in professional football tournaments are analysed.

Breaks

Breaks are defined as the successive home (or away) matches. De Werra (1981) shows that in a single round robin tournament the minimal number of breaks is $n - 2$. Goossens and Spieksma (2012a) also show that for a double round robin championship employing an inverted scheme, $2n - 4$ breaks can be achieved, being the better solution. On the other hand, they remark that in a double round robin league where the structure does not consist of a two single-round robin design, the minimal number of breaks can be $n - 2$. Nonetheless, this structure is not usually used in professional football leagues. Hence, in every tournament with $n \neq 2$, breaks always happen.

In this sense, league organisers usually try to minimise the number of breaks through the maximum alternation of home and away matches for each participant or, at least, employing an "equitable schedule," where the total number of breaks is equally distributed among all competitors. Ribeiro (2012) explains two alternatives to minimise breaks: "First-schedule, then-break" and "First-break, then-schedule." The first approach consists in determining the matches that will be played in each round and then fixing the home–away pattern. The second strategy employs an inverted procedure, firstly defining a feasible home–away pattern and then determining the matches for each round.

Post and Woeginger (2006), Rasmussen and Trick (2007), and Brouwer, Post and, Woeginger (2008) are in favour of minimising the number of breaks. However, Urrutia and Ribeiro (2006) remark that a larger number of breaks may be useful in order to minimise travel distances, which represent another typical scheduling constraint.

Travel distances

Easton, Nemhauser, and Trick (2001) underlined for the first time the tournament-travelling problem. They identified travelling distances as a crucial issue for scheduling. In general, this problem consists in reducing the total distance travelled by all clubs, minimising both time and costs, but still providing fairness. However, other constraints should be considered when arranging travel distances, such as consecutive home or away games (breaks), number of clubs in the same city, the quality of successive opponents and the interests of broadcasting rights owners.

As each professional football tournament has numerous distinctive characteristics, an optimal solution to all of these seems *unlikely* to be achieved. However, researchers have been trying to solve this question considering particular competition designs. Uthus, Riddle, and Guesgen (2012) propose an iterative-deepening algorithm called the A★ approach to solve travelling problems in MLB. Anagnostopoulos, Michel, Hentenryck, and Vergados (2006), also analysing MLB, proposed a simulated annealing algorithm to generate schedules. Easton, Nemhauser, and Trick (2003) used combined integer programming to find an optimal solution for a double round robin tournament with $n = 8$. Cheung (2008) tried to solve the travelling problem through one-factorisation timetables finding optimal home–away distribution on a mirrored tournament with eight participants as well. Melo, Urrutia, and Ribeiro (2009) proposed and compared three integer-programming formulations to minimise travel distances in a single round robin tournament with predefined venues.

Considering these aforementioned points, league organisers, and decision-makers ought to take into account the particularities of their leagues and numerous other constraints (i.e., number of clubs, design of competition, rivalry, weather conditions, etc.) in order to generate a fairness schedule where the travel distances are as minimal as possible.

Carry-over effect

Russell (1980) is the first researcher to describe the carry-over effects in the literature. He defines the carry-over effect as follows:

> Each team is considered to have an effect on its opponents which carries over to the next match. If team A meets team B in one match and team C in the next, then it is reasonable that team A's performance against team C will have been affected by team B.
>
> *(Russel, 1980, p. 127)*

Like for other constraints, the structure (design of competition) and peculiarities (number of clubs, derbies, geographic issues, etc.) of each tournament make it difficult to find an optimal value for the carry-over effect. However, some researchers have been trying to discover its lower bound in some specific championships. Russel (1980) developed an algorithm for schedules where the number of participants is a power of two. Guedes and Ribeiro (2011) presented a solution to minimise carry-over effects in a tournament with 12 participants. In addition, Miyashiro and Matsui (2006) created an approach to minimise carry-over effects in tournaments that employ the Circle Method procedure. Nonetheless, Lambrechts et al. (2017) proved that this scheduling structure generates the maximum carry-over effect value.

Although the carry-over effect is mostly evidenced in body-contact sports (i.e., karate-do, judo, etc.), it has been an issue for sports management and, largely, for the scheduling of professional football as well. Indeed, Goossens and Spieksma (2012b) highlight that both Norwegian and Belgian top tiers had developed new scheduling approaches after some clubs complained about unbalanced schedules that influenced the results of those tournaments. On the other hand, based on those real cases, the authors have developed a methodology to measure the influence of the carry-over effect and, as a result, they evidenced that the carry-over effects were negligible over the 30 seasons analysed in the highest division in Belgium.

Scheduling optimisation

The scheduling process should take into account numerous requirements and constraints as well as the motivations of the interested stakeholders such as clubs, fans, TV companies, and sponsors. In recent years, manual scheduling has been replaced by computational optimisation methods in order to minimise the violation of constraints and with the aim of generating the fairest schedules. Although not all professional leagues or national football associations explain their scheduling strategies, some scholars have contributed to showing the development of scheduling in the scientific literature.

Schreuder (1992) published the first paper that describes a computational scheduling in professional football leagues. He explained that after the 1988/89 season, the Royal Dutch Football Association (KNVB) submitted a request to the Faculty of Applied Mathematics of the University of Twenty for the construction of a schedule for the Dutch Football League. The author scrutinised the problem and the mathematical formulation behind his approach in his paper. This paper has become the framework for further studies.

In this section, two real cases are described: the Brazilian League and the South American World Cup Qualifiers – an example of scheduling optimisation at both national and international level. Other examples can be found in the recent literature on professional leagues in different countries. Bartsh, Drexl, and Kröger (2006) present the case of Austria and Germany; Goossens and Spieksma (2009) study Belgium; Alarcón et al. (2017) analyse Chile; Recalde, Torres, and Vaca (2013) examine Ecuador; Rasmussen (2008) investigates Denmark; and Della Croce and Olivieri (2006) analyse the case of Italy.

Brazilian league

The Brazilian League is a double round robin tournament with 20 participants, similar to several European leagues. However, the competitive balance is significantly higher than some European championships (see Gasparetto and Barajas, 2016a). While in the European context there are some clubs (or a small group of teams) that often win their domestic leagues, in Brazil the rotation of championship winners is frequent. Moreover, a big club is regularly relegated to the Second Division – which would nowadays be unusual in Europe.

Ribeiro and Urrutia (2012) presented the formulation, implementation, and practical application of a schedule in the First and Second divisions of the Brazilian League, which they developed with the Brazilian Football Confederation. A peculiar feature in the Brazilian League is that there are several clubs from similar geographic locations, which makes the scheduling process even harder. They show that in the 2010 season, six clubs were from *São Paulo* state and other four from *Rio de Janeiro* state, among the 20 participants (half of the total). In this sense, besides the *classics games* (matches against clubs from the same city), the *regional games* (matches against clubs from the same state) are another important feature in schedule formulation. These matches are the most attractive ones – increasing both broadcasting and gate demand – but impose additional security constraints.

The approach given by Ribeiro and Urrutia (2012) consists in an integer programming formulation with three-stage decomposition. The clubs are paired according to geographic and sporting criteria, establishing the need for complementary pattern sets between them. In addition, some requirements from the broadcasting owners must be considered in the scheduling construction, such as best matches on weekends, no *Classics games* in the same round and a balanced spread of regional matches over the season. The home–away patterns are generated in Step 1 taking into account several predefined requirements. A significant number of them must be satisfied in order to achieve feasible solutions. The pattern sets (specifically the home–away pattern of each club) are inserted in Step 2. If some requirements are reached, Step 3 creates the final schedule considering the last constraints (Figure 21.1). As the whole process is conducted using a computer program, numerous solutions may be found in a short time. Notwithstanding, the optimal solution is chosen from them.

The optimisation process was validated comparing its results over two real seasons: 2005 and 2006. The new approach was considered much better than the previous one as it violated

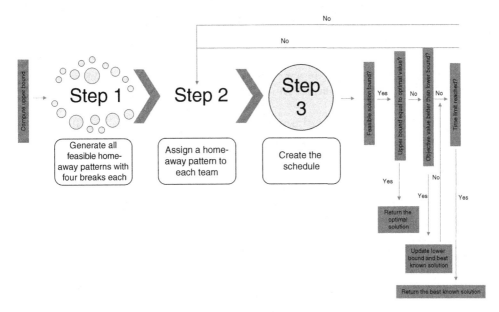

Figure 21.1 Flow chart of the three-stage decomposition approach
Source: adapted from Ribeiro and Urrutia (2012).

a lower number of requirements, reduced the number of breaks and increased the number of attractive matches that could be broadcast. The system was employed for the first time in a practical context creating the 2009 schedule. According to the authors, that tournament was the most attractive in recent times because four teams were in contention for the title in the last round. The system was employed again in the 2010 season and, despite the interruption of the tournament as a consequence of the FIFA World Cup and some additional constraints related to geographic issues, the league was decided again in the last round where three clubs could have become the champion until that match.

South American World Cup qualifiers

The South American qualifiers for the 2018 FIFA World Cup have the only computational scheduling in professional football at international level reported in the scientific literature. Indeed, Alarcón et al. (2017) comment on this scheduling optimisation in their paper, while Durán, Guajardo, and Sauré (2017) describe the whole process that was carried out.

The South American Football Confederation (CONMEBOL) organises its qualifying stage prior to each FIFA World Cup. For the last five South American qualifiers (between 1998 and 2014) the CONMEBOL employed a tournament with a double round robin design with a mirroring scheme symmetry where all ten national teams (country members) played against all their opponents once at home and once away. These qualification tournaments had 18 rounds (nine of FIFA's double rounds). The South American qualifiers extend over two to three years, thus after a double round, there is a long gap before the following one.

Some national members have complained about the scheme over the last years. Indeed, the previous South American qualifiers present numerous problems with the breaks distribution as well as unbalanced home–away patterns among the competitors. Thus, the CONMEBOL has invited all nation members to present proposals in order to define a new scheduling strategy for the next qualifiers (to the 2018 FIFA World Cup).

The methodology developed by Durán, Guajardo, and Sauré (2017) consists in an integer programming approach. The *balance constraints* are a major requirement which specify that in every double round all teams must play once at home and once away (to avoid the double round breaks that the nations complained of) and the home–away games should be distributed among the participants in a balanced way. To achieve this solution, the French scheme was chosen after testing some other symmetry schemes. Moreover, a random draw was employed in order to provide fairness.

The scheduling process developed by these authors was supported by Chile's Professional Football Association (ANFP). Although other nation members have presented different projects, this one was selected unanimously. This scheduling strategy was employed in the South American qualifiers to the 2018 FIFA World Cup, and two well-known players (Ronaldo and Forlán) were responsible for drawing the balls that randomly defined the position of each country in the schedule. The new schedule reduced the number of breaks to zero and balanced the distribution of home-away patterns among the participants.

In the quest for the best tournament

Professional football has changed throughout its history. A young football fan nowadays would not imagine that at the beginning of this sport there was no offside, players' substitutions, yellow and red cards, or numerous other features that are commonplace today. Football tournaments have been changing over the years as well. The most common change is in the number of participants. English football is used as an example: 12 teams played the first season of the English League (1888/1889), while in the Premier League period, 22 clubs played in its first season (1992/1993), and the current season (2017/2018) has 20 participants. This has also occurred in several European Leagues, like the Dutch, Italian, German, and Spanish ones. On the other hand, some other domestic leagues have changed the design of their competition as well. Gasparetto and Barajas (2016b) mention that the Brazilian League had several different competitive formats between 1959 and 2002 when the tournament was always decided with playoff stages (at least a final match) over those years. Nonetheless, the Brazilian Football Confederation decided to employ a double round robin design in its main domestic competition from the 2003 season.

The design of the most important international clubs' championship at European level has also changed several times. The first edition of the main European tournament − called the European Champion Clubs' Cup − was played in the season 1955/1956 by 16 teams in a knockout tournament design. The number of participants was increased in the following seasons, still maintaining the knockout design. It is interesting to remark that during some seasons the preliminary rounds were structured following geographic criteria. However, this tournament experimented with a huge change in the seasons 1991/1992 and 1992/1993. The group stage was adopted − after qualifying preliminary rounds − in the 1991/1992 edition and the tournament was rebranded as the UEFA Champions League in the subsequent season. In the group stage, the participants were divided into two groups of four clubs during these two seasons, but UEFA increased it progressively − to four groups in 1994/1995, to six groups in 1997/1998, and, finally, to eight groups in the 1999/2000 season. A detailed overview can be found on the UEFA site.[1]

The European Superleague that could have been

In 1998, Mediaset (an Italian mass media company) proposed the creation of a new tournament for European football − the European Superleague. The idea consisted in a closed championship involving the top European clubs − that is, employing the North-American system (closed leagues). Mediaset believed that the European Superleague could be a more balanced and interesting tournament for clubs, broadcasters, sponsors, and fans, consequently increasing the commercialisation, and enhancing revenue for all participants. This proposal was scrutinised by Hoehn and Szymanski (1999) and Vrooman (2007). Both papers suggested the adoption of this new tournament in the European context and even proposed possible structures and participants. Hoehn and Szymanski's (1999) suggestion comprised 60 participants from 28 different countries, while Vrooman's (2007) proposal included 30 clubs from eight UEFA nations.

One of the main assumptions behind the creation of the European Superleague is that the UEFA Champions League prizes were reducing the competitiveness among the domestic leagues. Indeed, it has been happening, as evidenced by Pawlowski, Breuer, and Hovemann (2010) and Peeters (2011). Nevertheless, the idea was never carried forward by UEFA. Both Hoehn and Szymanski's (1999) and Vrooman's (2007) suggestions included that a small number of UEFA members take part in this new tournament − UEFA has 55 members nowadays. In addition, the researchers remarked that clubs in the European Superleague must not participate in their domestic leagues, as happens with the UEFA Champions League. Then, however, UEFA could have several problems with its nation members because all the domestic leagues would lose importance without their best teams. Therefore, the structure of European football remains the same as before, UEFA being the European governing body on professional football, controlling its clubs' international competitions where the participants are qualified from their domestic leagues.

New horizons in European football?

If club tournaments in Europe have not changed dramatically, at the level of national teams UEFA has established an important reform in recent times. In 2017, UEFA confirmed the creation of the UEFA Nations League. This will be the first national teams' tournament using a common feature of clubs' leagues: promotion and relegation systems. The UEFA Nations League will be played during the seasons without official international tournaments (FIFA World Cup and UEFA European Championship). Then, the main idea is to replace the friendly matches that are habitually played on these FIFA dates, providing better and more competitive games to European national teams.

The league will be organised in four divisions (A, B, C, and D), where in its first season (2018/2019) all UEFA members are distributed according to their current European ranking position. Each division comprises four groups of three or four teams. The competitive design is a double round robin, where each team plays against all opponents twice – once at home, once away. The winner of each group in the divisions B, C, and D will be promoted to the upper tier, while the bottom team in each group in the divisions A, B, and C will be relegated. This flow is illustrated in Figure 21.2. The top four teams in division A will play the "Final Four" – a playoff stage that consists of semi-finals, a third-place match and a final match, which will decide the UEFA Nations League champion. The detailed information can be seen on the UEFA Nations League official website.[2]

The impact of the UEFA Nations League is unclear. Currently, national teams from different continental confederations use friendly matches to face each other. Moreover, the top national teams from other confederations usually play against the best European ones with the aim of testing their quality. However, with the creation of this new European tournament, these matches will not occur or will take place only rarely, hence decreasing the number of possible "competitive

Figure 21.2 Structure of UEFA Nations League
Source: Self-elaboration.

games" for those nations. An alternative for them could be to establish similar tournaments in each continental confederation. However, the other confederations have fewer members than UEFA and the travelling distances are higher than in Europe as well. An intercontinental tournament may also be designed for the top national teams. However, it could generate complaints from the less successful countries. The inclusion of all national teams would represent a world league without European national teams, but this kind of league seems to be unachievable.

Another important point is the relationship between clubs and national teams. Currently, football clubs often complain to their national federations when their best players get injuries in international matches. They argue that the club is responsible for hiring and paying the players' salaries and this kind of situation (injuries) is harmful for them. As the physical effort made by players in official tournaments is expected to be higher than in friendly matches, a higher number of injuries could occur. In this sense, more divergences between clubs and national federations might occur.

Evidently, UEFA wants the UEFA Nations League to be a successful tournament. However, are they prepared if this new tournament turns out to be more popular than the UEFA European Championship? This hypothesis may sound unlikely now, but it may happen. To take part in the UEFA European Championship, the national teams must have previously qualified, while all members will play the UEFA Nations League every competition. Moreover, although in the first season only the top 12 European national teams will play in Division A, the promotion and relegation system makes it possible, in the second season, for a less successful country to achieve the Final Four and, even, be the winner. In this sense, in a short competition, as the UEFA Nations League has been designed to be, several unexpected national teams might be successful and, consequently, the general interest can grow. On the other hand, the opposite situation may also happen. If the best European national teams neglect the tournament (i.e., problems with clubs, low interest of top players, aligning U-23 players, already qualified to World Cup or UEFA European Championship, etc.) and start to be relegated, the UEFA Nations League can reduce its relevance progressively. In any case, this new approach by UEFA also demonstrates its interest in finding new and attractive tournaments.

Final remarks

Some features of football tournaments such as geographical issues, the design of the competition, the most common constraints, the scheduling optimisation processes and changes in professional football competitions have been described in this chapter. All of these points and several other factors discussed above make the organisation of football tournaments a complex task. There followed a discussion about what is the best structure for a football league. Nonetheless, there is no best solution for all situations.

McGarry and Schutz (1997) compared the double round robin design with some knockout structures in order to find the best approach. Although they show that the round robin would be the most accurate method for ranking the participants, they comment that a double elimination knockout structure could perform better in some cases. At the same time, they identify the knockout system as the most suitable because it can efficiently rank the quality of the participants requiring relatively fewer matches (than a round robin). However, the paper only analyses tournaments with eight participants. This situation differs from most of the professional football leagues around the world. As essential elements such as fans' preferences and clubs, broadcasters', and sponsors' interests must be take into account when decision-makers are scheduling tournaments, it results in each competition being unique. Therefore, "optimal solutions" are specific for each tournament, not standard approaches.

The further consequences of the UEFA Nations League are now a new research line. Researchers may try to analyse the impacts of this tournament on European football as well as on the other national teams around the world. At the same time, further papers might examine the effects of changing the structure of the current club championships like the inclusion of MLS teams in the *Libertadores de América* Cup or increasing the number of participants in the FIFA Club World Cup. Moreover, a hypothetical World Football League played annually (as happens in professional volleyball) may be suggested and carefully scrutinised.

A theoretical dynamic schedule could be developed. In this speculative approach, the fixtures are not fixed as in current football tournaments. Employing some hard constraints like home–away patterns for all participants, equal distribution of breaks, non-consecutive derby matches, and maximum/minimum travel distance between *n* rounds, the sporting results from each round would provide the draw for the following round. If on the one hand, football clubs complain about this approach, because they would not be able to control the carry-over effects so well, on the other hand, this methodology could generate greater interest from fans due to its uncertainty, and the best match in each round could even be screened on television channels. However, this speculation must be better analysed before being acted upon.

As a final point, football tournament organisers should continue employing the most advanced computational techniques in order to enhance scheduling optimisations. A fair competition is essential for clubs, fans, sponsors, and broadcasters; therefore, it is always necessary to take into account the progress in this field.

Notes

1 For detailed information, see https://www.uefa.com/uefachampionsleague/history/index.html#.
2 http://www.uefa.com/uefanationsleague/#/.

References

Alarcón, F., Durán, G., Guajardo, M., Miranda, J., Muñoz, H., Ramírez, L., Ramírez, M., et al. (2017) Operations research transforms the scheduling of Chilean soccer leagues and South American World Cup qualifiers. *Interfaces*, 47(1), 52–69.

Anagnostopoulos, A., Michel, L., Van Hentenryck, P. and Vergados, Y. (2006). A simulated annealing approach to the traveling tournament problem. *Journal of Scheduling*, 9, 177–193.

Aronshtam, L., Cohen, H., and Shrot, T. (2017) Tennis manipulation: can we help Serena Williams win another tournament?: Or can we control a knockout tournament with reasonable complexity? *Annals of Mathematics and Artificial Intelligence*, 80, 153–169.

Baek, S.K., Yi, I.G., Park, H.J., and Kim, B.J. (2013) Universal statistics of the knockout tournament. *Scientific Reports*, 3 (3198), 1–6.

Bartsch, T., Drexl, A., and Kröger, S. (2006) Scheduling the professional soccer leagues of Austria and Germany. *Computers & Operations Research*, 33, 1907–1937.

Brouwer, A.E., Post, G., and Woeginger, G.J. (2008) Tight bounds for break minimization. *Journal of Combinatorial Theory, Series A*, 115, 1065–1068

Cheung, K.K.H. (2008) Solving mirrored traveling tournament problem benchmark instances with eight teams. *Discrete Optimization*, 5, 138–143.

Della Croce, F. and Oliveri, D. (2006) Scheduling the Italian Football League: an ILP-based approach. *Computers & Operations Research*, 33, 1963–1974.

De Werra, D. (1981) Scheduling in sports. *North-Holland Mathematics Studies*, 59, 381–395.

Durán, G., Guajardo, M., and Sauré, D. (2017). Scheduling the South American Qualifiers to the 2018 FIFA World Cup by integer programming. *European Journal of Operational Research*, 262, 1109–1115.

Easton, K., Nemhauser, G., and Trick, M. (2001) The travelling tournament problem: description and benchmarks. In: Walsh, T. (ed.). *Principles and Practice of Constraint Programming* (Volume 2239 of Lecture Notes in Computer Science, pp. 580–585). Berlin, Germany: Springer.

Easton, K., Nemhauser, G., and Trick, M. (2003) Solving the travelling tournament problem: a combined integer programming and constraint programming approach. In: Burke, E. and De Causmaecker P. (eds.). *Practice and Theory of Automated Timetabling IV.* PATAT 2002.) Lecture Notes in Computer Science, vol 2740). Springer, Berlin, Heidelberg.

Gasparetto, T. and Barajas, A. (2016a) Reanalizing the competitiveness in football leagues: accumulated points difference. *Revista de Administração de Empresas,* 56(3), 288–301.

Gasparetto, T. and Barajas, A. (2016b) Playoffs or just league: a debate in Brazilian football. *The Open Sports Sciences Journal,* 9 (Suppl-1), 94–103.

Goossens, D. and Spieksma, F. (2009) Scheduling the Belgium Soccer League. *Interfaces,* 39(2), 109–118.

Goossens, D. and Spieksma, F. (2012a) Soccer schedules in Europe: an overview. *Journal of Scheduling,* 15(5), 641–651.

Goossens, D. and Spieksma, F. (2012b) The carry-over effect does not influence football results. *Journal of Sports Economics,* 13(3), 288–305.

Griggs, T.S. and Rosa, A. (1996) A tour of European soccer schedules, or testing the popularity of GK2n. *Bulletin of the Institute of Combinatorics and its Applications,* 18, 65–68.

Guedes, A.C.B. and Ribeiro, C.C. (2011) A heuristic for minimizing weighted carry-over effects in round robin tournaments. *Journal of Scheduling,* 15, 655–667.

Hennessy, J. and Glickman, M. (2016) Bayesian optimal design of fixed knockout tournament brackets. *Journal of Quantitative Analysis in Sports,* 12(1), 1–15.

Hoehn, T. and Szymanski, S. (1999) The Americanization of European football. *Economic Policy,* 14(28), 204–240.

Lambrechts, E., Ficker, A.M.C., Goossens, D.R., and Spieksma, F.C.R. (2017). Round-robin tournaments generated by the Circle Method have maximum carry-over. *Mathematical Programming Series B.* doi:10.1007/s10107-017-1115-x

McGarry, T. and Schutz, R.W. (1997) Efficacy of traditional sport tournament structures. *Journal of the Operational Research Society,* 48, 65–74.

Melo, R.A., Urrutia, S. and Ribeiro, C.C. (2009) The traveling tournament problem with predefined venues. *Journal of Scheduling,* 12, 607–622.

Miyashiro, R. and Matsui, T. (2006) *Minimizing the carry-over effects value in a round robin tournament.* In Proceedings of the 6th International Conference on the Practice and Theory of Automated Timetabling (pp. 460–463). Brno, Czech Republic.

Neale, W.C. (1964) The peculiar economics of professional sports. *Quarterly Journal of Economics,* 78(1), 1–14.

Noll, R. (2003) The organization of sports leagues. *Oxford Review of Economic Policy,* 19(4), 530–551.

Pawlowski, T., Breuer, C., and Hovermann, A. (2010) Top clubs' performance and the competitive situation in European domestic football competitions. *Journal of Sports Economics,* 11(2), 186–202.

Peeters, T. (2011) Broadcast rights and competitive balance in European soccer. *International Journal of Sport Finance,* 6, 23–39.

Post, G. and Woeginger, G.J. (2006) Sports tournaments, home-away assignments, and the break minimization problem. *Discrete Optimization,* 3, 165–173.

Prince, M., Smith, J.C., and Geunes, J. (2013). Designing fair 8- and 16-team knockout tournaments. *IMA Journal of Management Mathematics,* 24, 321–336.

Rasmussen, R.V. (2008) Scheduling a triple round robin tournament for the best Danish soccer league. *European Journal of Operational Research,* 185, 795–810.

Rasmussen, R.V. and Trick, M.A. (2008). Round robin scheduling – a survey. *European Journal of Operational Research,* 188, 617–636.

Rasmussen, R.V. and Trick, M.A. (2007) A Benders approach for the constrained minimum break problem. *European Journal of Operational Research,* 177, 198–213.

Recalde, D., Torres, R., and Vaca, P. (2013) Scheduling the professional Ecuadorian football league by integer programming. *Computers & Operations Research,* 40, 2478–2484.

Ribeiro, C.C. (2012) Sports scheduling: problems and applications. *International Transactions in Operational Research,* 19, 201–226.

Ribeiro, C.C. and Urrutia, S. (2012) Scheduling the Brazilian soccer tournament: solution approach and practice. *Interfaces,* 42(3), 260–272.

Russell, K.G. (1980) Balancing carry-over effects in round robin tournaments. *Biometrika,* 67(1), 127–131.

Schreuder, J.A.M. (1992) Combinatorial aspects of construction of competition Dutch Professional Football Leagues. *Discrete Applied Mathematics,* 35, 301–312.

Urrutia, S. and Ribeiro, C.C. (2006) Maximizing breaks and bounding solutions to the mirrored traveling tournament problem. *Discrete Applied Mathematics*, 154, 1932–1938.

Uthus, D.C., Riddle, P.J., and Guesgen, H.W. (2012) Solving the traveling tournament problem with iterative-deepening A★. *Journal of Scheduling*, 15, 601–614.

Vrooman, J. (2007) Theory of the beautiful game: the unification of European football. *Scottish Journal of Political Economy*, 54(3), 314–354.

22

Football, networks, and relationships

Anna Gerke and Hagen Wäsche

Introduction

Networks are an institutional form of economic organisation besides the traditional forms of markets and hierarchies (Powell, 1990). Conceptually, networks are aggregates of bilateral relationships and exchanges that build up to networks, consisting of at least three actors. *Networks in itself* are characterised by blurred boundaries and an incidental development. They emerge incidentally through linkages between stakeholders. *Networks for itself* are consciously created, strategically formed, bounded, goal directed, and governed (Raab and Kenis, 2009). Often, they are temporary and based on complementary needs and interests of participating parties. Networks and inter-organisational relationships have become key success factors in the processes of value creation as illustrated for individual firms (Håkansson and Snehota, 2006), in supply chains (Borgatti and Li, 2009; Lazzarini, Chaddad, and Cook, 2001), and sport networks (Gerke, 2016; Wäsche and Woll, 2010; Woratschek, Horbel, and Popp, 2014).

In the context of football business, two types of networks are especially relevant: inter-organisational and intra-organisational networks (Wäsche, Dickson, Woll, and Brandes, 2017). Inter-organisational networks consist of organisations that are interlinked via multiple dyadic or multilateral relationships (Wäsche and Gerke, forthcoming). Examples in the field of football are stakeholder networks, sponsorship networks (Pieters, Knoben, and Pouwels, 2012), international player transfer networks among clubs, leagues/competition networks, football event networks, marketing networks, as well as football associations and clubs which form networks. Moreover, players' agents are important brokers who connect players and clubs and thereby form network structures. However, intra-organisational networks have to be considered also. Different units within an organisation, such as marketing, facility management, coaching and scouting, medical staff, fan ambassadors, and so forth form a diverse intra-organisational network of football teams, the interplay of which is key for economic and sporting success. Similarly, personal networks among staff, such as networks of information flow or advice-seeking networks are relevant intra-organisational networks. Last but not least, individual professional athletes are embedded in a personal network surrounding them that consists of coach(s), manager(s), assistants, medical staff, and as such form an intra-organisational network.

Table 22.1 Forms of football business networks depending on the type of network and the type of network formation.

| | | Type of Network | |
		Inter-organisational network	Intra-organisational network
Network formation	*Network in Itself*	Serendipitous network among organisations	Serendipitous network within organisations
	Network for Itself	Strategic network among organisations	Strategic network within organisations

Table 22.1 displays a typology of football business networks categorising four different forms of networks based on the type of network (inter-organisational or intra-organisational) and the way of network formation (network in itself and network for itself). This typology fulfils two purposes: first, it comprises all relevant forms of networks in football business and enables an understanding of their fundamental structural features. Second, the typology allows one to systematically analyse structural configurations in football business through the network perspective.

Finally, when analysing networks in football business one might be interested in the full network or in ego networks. In full networks, various characteristics at the network, subgroup, or individual level of all actors can be considered while ego networks focus solely on the network around a focal actor (ego) and the actors (alters) the ego has relations with.

Network-theoretical concepts and methods of Social Network Analysis (SNA) provide a wealth of opportunities to study and understand network structures in football (Wäsche et al. 2017). It enables an understanding of how relationships and networks come into being, how they are structured, and what the outcomes of networks are. Based on this understanding, network management and governance as well as strategic network development is fostered (Wäsche and Gerke, forthcoming).

This chapter will provide a comprehensive review of literature on sport and more specifically football business network research. Second, based on a network perspective we analyse the contemporary football business based on select cases and secondary data. Third, we will discuss research in football business networks, practical implications, and directions for future research.

Sport business networks

Literature in sport management covers a range of different kinds of sport networks: sport leagues, elite sport systems, sport tourism networks, sport event networks, sport clusters, sport incubators, to name but a few. All these types of networks present a group of organisations that are more or less connected and interdependent. Various dyadic relationships build up to networks as soon as one actor is involved in more than one dyadic relationship (Dickson, Arnold, and Chalip, 2005; Gerke et al., 2017).

To build on the theoretical framework introduced earlier we analyse those different kinds of networks with regards to networks *for itself* and networks *in itself*. To the sport networks *for itself* belong clearly sport leagues. Sport leagues are federated networks (Dickson et al., 2005; Waugh, Dickson, and Phelps, 2014) and can be open or closed networks depending on their relegation system. Members are the different sport clubs that depend on each other for the purpose of organising matches and championships. No single sport club can exist on its own as the club depends on the others to play.

Elite sport systems federate different organisations and actors to develop elite athletes and teams. According to De Bosscher, De Knop, van Bottenburg, Shibli, and Bingham (2009), there are nine pillars that constitute influencing factors for the sporting success of nations. Behind each pillar are organisations or smaller units of teams that need to work together, hence form a network. Those actors are financers, policymakers, grassroots sports, talent scouts, career support organisations, training facility managers, coaches, competition organisers, and research institutes (De Bosscher et al., 2009). Borders are less clear in this inter-organisational network though it corresponds to a network *in itself*. However, there are approaches to strategically organise such elite sport networks to foster innovation in elite sports (e.g., WISS-Netz, 2017).

Sport tourism networks consist of heterogeneous regional actors with different interests that are embedded in a network structure. These actors include tourism organisations, sport clubs, nature parks, sports rentals, sport facilities, tour operators, and others (Wäsche and Woll, 2013). Due to the heterogeneity of actors' nature and partially differing objectives, it is clear that also here we deal with a network *in itself*.

Sport event networks can be embedded in sport tourism networks (Werner, Dickson, and Hyde, 2015) which can be qualified as networks *for itself* as illustrated by Wäsche (2018) in the example of a small-scale sport event and its intentionally developed sport event network. Previous studies investigated topics such as knowledge transfer and the characteristics of inter-organisational relationships in such event networks. Ziakas and Costa (2010) investigated an event network of a host community's event portfolio and found that collaboration does not exist across all links within a network but that information-sharing is the most common link between network members. In addition to the strategically implemented event networks that are necessary for the organisation of an event, additional networks can emerge consisting of actors that were not initially included in the network (e.g., local media, local community, promoter). Hence, this can be qualified as a network *in itself* (Erickson and Kushner, 1999).

Sport clusters can be both networks *in itself* and networks *for itself*. Sport clusters are geographical concentrations of for-profit, non-profit, private, and public organisations with a shared interest in one particular or several similar sports (Gerke et al., 2017; Gerke, Desbordes, and Dickson, 2015). The cluster member organisations are interconnected through formal relationships (e.g., contractual relationships for business purposes) or informal relationships (e.g., knowledge sharing, friendship) (Gerke et al., 2017), and provide typically high levels of cognitive proximity (e.g., similar attitudes and managerial practices) and often high levels of organisational proximity (e.g., highly complementary business activities) (Gerke and Dalla Pria, 2017).

Sport incubators are per se networks *for itself* because start-up companies that become members are selected in a systematic process and boundaries are clearly identified. Beyond the start-up companies as members of sport incubators there are partners that become part of the sport incubator network (Wäsche, Gerke, and Giannakis, 2017). The selection process is less clear but the official affiliation with the incubator indicates also clear boundaries and conscious creation of this network. In addition, there are extended networks around incubators, which consist of a number of actors gravitating around the incubator including interested start-ups, interested partners, loose relationships to organisation to partner up occasionally. These satellite networks can be considered as networks *in itself*. The *ego network* of each start-up company, that is, the network of the start-up's stakeholders represents another network *in itself*. Here, as in many other instances, the network consists of other networks: a network of networks.

Football business networks

Inter-organisational football business networks

In terms of inter-organisational football business networks we can also distinguish sport networks *for itself* such as international football confederations, national football federations, and football leagues, but also networks *in itself* such as the network of linkages between a focal football club and its network of private (e.g., sponsors, hospitality providers, media) and public partners (e.g., city council, local associations) and other stakeholders (e.g., residents, local football clubs).

An interesting trend to notice is the increasing number of bilateral partnerships between small second-tier clubs and bigger first-tier clubs. This kind of bilateral partnerships are also called satellite clubs. Examples for satellite club relationships are numerous, Arsenal-KSK Beveren, Chelsea-PSV Eindhoven, Manchester United-Aarhus, to name but a few (Pellissier and Gerke, 2017). What is interesting from a network perspective is that the respective club-centred networks (i.e., the networks that are formed around one focal actor, here the club) of the two focal actors get an opportunity to interact and hence create a bigger network *in itself*. In this way, they might benefit from access to information and enhanced opportunities for exchange and cooperation, creating value for the involved actors.

Intra-organisational football business networks

Intra-organisational football business networks comprise individuals, groups, and units or departments within organisations. While sport organisations are usually hierarchically organised, the departments share knowledge, collaborate, or even compete (also in informal and lateral ways) and, as such, form an intra-organisational network (Tsai, 2002). On the individual level, personal networks include players, coaches, physiotherapists, fans, groupies, referees, and others. Moreover, managers and other club officials have their personal network that might be crucial for the economic and sport-related performance of the club. The theoretical framework of network *in itself* and networks *for itself* is also applicable. For example, the team of 11 players that is playing on the field is a team *for itself*, while the network surrounding a single player is a *network in itself* composed of a variety of actors (e.g., other players, physiotherapists, coaches, medical staff, personal trainer, family, friends) linked to the player through diverse links (e.g., formal, informal, professional, friendly). A club's fan base is a network *in itself* unless they are clearly identified as fan club members for example.

Analysis of contemporary football business through a network perspective

After having conducted an overview of sport business networks and more specifically football business networks, the next section analyses the case of a football club in terms of the four different types of networks that are illustrated in Table 22.1. We refer to the propositions of the sport value framework (SVF) (Woratschek, Horbel, and Popp, 2014) to illustrate value creation processes in these different forms of networks.

The SVF is based on the service dominant logic (SDL) that considers value as always co-created by value proposition providers (supplier) and beneficiary (customer) (Vargo and Lusch, 2004). SDL emphasises the use of operant resources (i.e., skills and knowledge) in contrast to operand resources (e.g., resources on which an act is performed). SDL provides a fundamentally different logic for value creation. SVF takes this theoretical approach to value creation and transfers it to the sport context. The result is the SVF, which comprises three levels of analysis and ten foundational premises (FPs). The three levels of analysis are: the intra-level (i.e., perspective of individual actors), micro-level (i.e., perspective of dyads or triads of actors), and the meso-level (i.e., the entire value co-creation system). The following sections analyse football club networks using some of the FPs of the SVF to explain value creation in the different forms of football club networks according to the network typology suggested in Table 22.1 (Woratschek et al., 2014; 2017).

Value creation in football club networks

Serendipitous networks within organisations. These are defined as intra-organisational networks that emerge incidentally and have blurred boundaries. Serendipitous networks within an organisation can be interpersonal networks or intergroup/interdepartmental networks. Interpersonal networks are for example athlete-centred ego networks, i.e., all actors surrounding an individual player including coaches, personal trainer, physiotherapists, medical staff, nutritionist, and/or other players. We could extend this serendipitous network beyond the organisation by including sponsors fans, agents, referees, recruiters, media representatives, journalists, lawyers, family members, friends, and other persons linked to the athlete but outside of the focal club. Network members apply their knowledge and expertise to help the athlete improving his or her performance; for example, the coach is applying his/her knowledge on training methods on the athlete.

Considering this kind of network, we can confirm FP1 from the SVF; stating that sporting activities are at the core of value creation in the context of serendipitous athlete-centred ego networks. The different networks members contribute to improving the athlete's performance or have an interest in the athlete performing. FP2 is based on the notion that service is the basis of exchange. The important nuance to understand here is that "service" is not equal to "services." A service means here applied knowledge and skill. So any interactional exchange is based on service provision, which means provision of applied knowledge and skills. This applied knowledge and skills can take the form of products or services. In terms of football, the player offers his/her knowledge and skills in football to the club and to spectators. Woratschek et al. (2014) argue that in the sport industry any type of value creation is dependent on some sporting activities, hence these are the fundamental basis (FP1). Service as applied knowledge and skills is the fundamental basis of exchange. Therefore, FP 2 "Service is the fundamental basis of exchange" (Woratschek et al., 2014, p. 19) is well illustrated in this example.

FP3 in SVF states: "Sport goods (products and services) are vehicles for service provision". In terms of a football club, this means that, for example, football players provide their applied knowledge by using a ball and football shoes. Entertainment – knowledge how to make people laugh or excited – is realised through the use of hospitality services, big video screens and other stadium-related animations.

Another form of serendipitous interpersonal networks is intra-team networks based on players' behaviour and tactics on the field. These are emergent during the play but can intensify over one or several season(s) of a football club. In the case of the VfB Stuttgart this had led to the designation of the "magic triangle" formed by three players excelling extraordinarily in their on-field interplay (VfB Stuttgart, 2017). A team of Portuguese researchers used SNA to analyse serendipitous intra-team networks emerging during on-field play on match days. They found that clusters emerge within the team and that centroid players contributed most to attacking processes. SNA seems to be a complementary tool to perform match analysis and help the coaches with information about the teammates' interactions in the game of football (Clemente et al., 2014).

Another study investigates interactions between football team members on the pitch using SNA. They look at group member attitudes towards cooperation, which are crucial for tactics, and hence value creation through high-quality football performance (Trequattrini, Lombardi, and Battista, 2015).

Interdepartmental networks within a football club can consist of the different club sections, for example, senior, women, youth, kids, and different sport sections. These different sections need to be coordinated and might have synergies or interactions, for example, shared resources (e.g., infrastructure, coaches, communication support) or knowledge sharing. Kolyperas et al. (2016) illustrate just that by offering empirical insights on value co-creation in the context of charitable organisations that have been established by their football clubs.

Strategic network within organisations. A strategic network within a football club on interpersonal level is the football team itself. The eleven players on the field, plus the substitute players form a by the coach strategically chosen team which is clearly defined. This kind of serendipitous network is fixed temporarily until a player leaves or joins the team for league football clubs and until the next championship for national football teams.

Strategic network among organisations. One typical strategic network among organisations in football and other team sports is the league. The football league links a defined number of clubs. Their interactions and interrelationships are clearly defined through a set of rules and regulations that determine the relegation and promotion system in open leagues and the barriers of entry in closed leagues. An example of research investigating a league network is Dickson et al.'s (2005) work on league expansion. This study is with the Victorian Football league but the network principle is the same as in European football leagues. Leagues create value through their members interaction on-field. The football matches are at the heart of value creation (FP1) because they evoke emotions, interest and excitement within the spectators. Based on this baseline other value generating activities can be developed (e.g., selling of TV rights and merchandising products).

Another study on sport leagues illustrates four levels of value creation for different target groups (Mason, 1999). Sport leagues, including football leagues, co-create value together with and for fans and spectators that attend the match in the stadium but also those that follow via media and those that purchase and merchandise products associated to clubs in the league. Second, the league co-creates value with the media through selling rights for broadcasting the games on television. It is co-creation because the media need the football league to get interesting content and the league needs the media to spotlight the league's main product: the football matches. Third, the clubs of a league co-create value with the local communities in which they are embedded through the construction of facilities and animating of local grassroots sport programmes. Last, leagues co-create value with corporations that sponsor the league or league members or even invest directly in sport entities (e.g., naming of stadium by large companies such as the Allianz Arena in Munich [see Chapter 16 in this Handbook]). All these examples illustrate co-creation of value as argued in FP4 ("Firms and customers can only offer value propositions") and FP5 ("Sport firms create value propositions mainly in the configuration of a value network") of the SVF. The role of supplier (firm) and customer is not fixed for every actor but can change depending on the interactional relationship and the angle that is analysed from. For example, fans can take the role of customers when they buy a ticket and come to the stadium to watch the match. However, they become "supplier" of good ambiance when they participate in chanting to create ambiance in the stadium (see also FP6: "Sport customers co-create value primarily by integrating resources from their social groups" and FP7: "Value is always co-created by firms, customers and other stakeholders") (Woratschek et al., 2014).

Another strategic network in football are national federations as boundaries are clearly identifiable and a clear governance is provided. National sport organisations or international sport confederations federate football clubs and coordinate and administer championships and football development on communal, departmental, regional, national, and international level. These are very large networks often with a lack of interaction and dynamics due to bureaucratic structures. Nevertheless, also in this case value is co-created through the interdependence of networks members in order to run competitions, at least within one divisional level (e.g., communal, regional).

Serendipitous network among organisations. Serendipitous networks between a football club – as focal actor – and other organisations emerge due to the entire stakeholder network of a football club. This includes the supply side of a football club: a football clubs' suppliers of sport equipment (e.g., tricots, footballs, protective gear), the owning or managing firm for training and match facilities (i.e., the stadium), the suppliers of food and drinks for the athletes, but also for the fans and spectators in the stadium, the provider of technology for training equipment, stadium equipment and digital technology, and others. On the other side is the customer of the football club, i.e., the fans and spectators that watch the football match in the stadium or via intermediaries that buy the broadcast rights (media), journalists that create content in the form of news about match results and analysis of matches for specialised reporting (FP7).

Discussion

Our analysis of football networks uses the typology of football business networks (Table 22.1) that distinguishes four different forms of networks in terms of type of network and type of network formation. The analysis show that there is a high variety of serendipitous networks in terms of networks within the organisation. However, there are also serendipitous networks amongst organisations (i.e., a football club and organisations outside of the football club) that have to be considered. When it comes to strategic networks regarding football clubs, there is a high diversity of strategic networks among organisations around a football club. Again, while probably less prevalent, strategic networks exist also within a football club organisation.

Moreover, it was shown that the network perspective enables a deeper understanding of value co-creation in the business of football. Applying the sport value framework to our typology of football business networks, a new perspective and understanding of the structure and processes of value co-creation (that unfolds in relations) opens up. While this perspective contributes to a theoretical understanding of network structures in football business, it also enables new approaches to empirical studies in the field of football business, combining this approach with methods of SNA.

Conclusion

This chapter sought to provide an overview of theoretical possibilities for practical existing networks in and around a football club as focal actor of the football industry. The value of this chapter is the exhaustive and systematic analysis of the network notion in the football context. Empirical examples are provided in an anecdotal manner and deserve more profound and in-depth investigation through future research.

References

Borgatti, S.P. and Li, X.U.N. (2009) On social network analysis in a supply chain context. *Journal of Supply Chain Management*, 45(2), 5–22. doi:10.1111/j.1745-493X.2009.03166.x

Clemente, F.M., Martins, F.M.L., Couceiro, M.S., Mendes, R.S. and Figueiredo, A.J. (2014) A network approach to characterize the teammates' interactions on football: a single match analysis/Uma abordagem através de métodos de network para caracterizar as interações entre futebolistas: análise de um jogo/Un enfoque usando los métodos de network para caracterizar las interacciones entre los jugadores: análisis de un juego. *Cuadernos de Psicología del Deporte*, (3), 141.

De Bosscher, V., De Knop, P., van Bottenburg, M., Shibli, S., and Bingham, J. (2009) Explaining international sporting success: an international comparison of elite sport systems and policies in six countries. *Sport Management Review*, 12(3), 113–136.

Dickson, G., Arnold, T., and Chalip, L. (2005) League Expansion and Interorganisational Power. *Sport Management Review*, 8(2), 145–165.

Erickson, G.S. and Kushner, R.J. (1999) Public event networks: an application of marketing theory to sporting events. *European Journal of Marketing*, 33(3/4), 348–365.

Gerke, A. (2016) Towards a network model of innovation in sport – the case of product innovation in nautical sport clusters. *Innovation: Management, Policy & Practice*, 18(3), 207–288.

Gerke, A., Babiak, K., Dickson, G., and Desbordes, M. (2017) Developmental processes and motivations for linkages in cross-sectoral sport clusters. *Sport Management Review*. forthcoming.

Gerke, A. and Dalla Pria, Y. (2017) Cluster concept: lessons for the sport sector? towards a two-step model of sport cluster development based on socioeconomic proximity *Journal of Sport Management*, forthcoming.

Gerke, A., Desbordes, M., and Dickson, G. (2015) Towards a sport cluster model: the ocean racing cluster in Brittany. *European Sport Management Quarterly*, 5(3), 343–363.

Håkansson, H. and Snehota, I. (2006) No business is an island: the network concept of business strategy. *Scandinavian Journal of Management*, 22(3), 256–270.

Kolyperas, D., Anagnostopoulos, C., Chadwick, S., and Sparks, L. (2016) Applying a communicating vessels framework to CSR value co-creation: empirical evidence from professional team sport organizations. *Journal of Sport Management*, 30(6), 702–719.

Lazzarini, S. G., Chaddad, F.R., and Cook, M.L. (2001) Integrating supply chain and network analyses: the study of netchains. *Chain and network science*, 7–22.

Mason, D.S. (1999) What is the sports product and who buys it? The marketing of professional sports leagues. *European Journal of Marketing*, (3/4), 402.

Pellissier, V. and Gerke, A. (2017) Enjeux des partenariats bilatéraux entre clubs de football professionnels. Unpublished thesis for Specialised Master Degree in Management of Sport Organisations Master thesis, Audencia Business School, Paris.

Pieters, M., Knoben, J., and Pouwels, M. (2012) A social network perspective on sport management: the effect of network embeddedness on the commercial performance of sport organizations. *Journal of Sport Management*, 26(5), 433–444.

Powell, W.W. (1990) Neither market nor hierarchy: network forms of organization. In: B.M. Staw and L.L. Cummings (eds.). *Research in Organizational Behaviour* (Vol. 12, pp. 295–336). Greenwhich, CT: JAI Press.

Raab, J. and Kenis, P. (2009) Heading toward a society of networks. *Journal of Management Inquiry*, 18(3), 198–210.

Tsai, W. (2002) Social structure of "coopetition" within a multiunit organization: coordination, competition, and intraorganizational knowledge sharing. *Organization Science*, 13(2), 179–190.

Trequattrini, R., Lombardi, R., and Battista, M. (2015) Network analysis and football team performance: a first application. *Team Performance Management*, 21(1/2), 85–110.

Vargo, S.L. and Lusch, R.F. (2004) Evolving to a new dominant logic for marketing. *Journal of Marketing*, 68, 1–17.

Vargo, S.L. and Lusch, R.F. (2017) *Service-dominant logic 2025*. *International Journal of Research in Marketing*, 34(1), 46–67.

Wäsche, H. (2018) The Social Capital Structure of a Small-Scale Sport Event: Configuration, Evolution, and Legacy (in review).

Wäsche, H., Dickson, G., Woll, A., and Brandes, U. (2017) Social network analysis in sport research: an emerging paradigm, *European Journal for Sport and Society*, 14(2), 138–165.

Wäsche, H. and Gerke, A. (forthcoming) Interorganisational network governance in sport. In: M. Winand and C. Anagnostopoulos (eds.). *Research Handbook on Sport Governance*. Cheltenham: Edward Elgar Publishing.

Wäsche, H. and Woll, A. (2010) Regional sports tourism networks: a conceptual framework. *Journal of Sport & Tourism*, 15(3), 191–214.

Wäsche, H. and Woll, A. (2013) Managing regional sports tourism networks: a network perspective. *European Sport Management Quarterly*, 13(4), 404–427.

Wäsche, H., Gerke, A., and Giannakis, M. (2017) The network structure of innovation – insights from a sport innovation incubator. Paper presented at the EASM, Bern, Switzerland.

Waugh, D., Dickson, G., and Phelps, S. (2014) The impact of member disaffiliation on the internal legitimacy of a federated network. *European Sport Management Quarterly*, 14(5), 538–555.

Werner, K., Dickson, G., and Hyde, K.F. (2015) Learning and knowledge transfer processes in a mega-events context: the case of the 2011 Rugby World Cup. *Tourism Management,* 48(Supplement C), 174–187.

WISS-Netz. (2017) WISS-Netz. [online] Retrieved from https://wiss-netz.de/

Woratschek, H., Horbel, C., and Popp, B. (2014) The sport value framework – a new fundamental logic for analyses in sport management. *European Sport Management Quarterly*, 14(1), 6–24.

Ziakas, V. and Costa, C. A. (2010) Explicating inter-organizational linkages of a host community's events network. *International Journal of Event and Festival Management*, 1(2), 132–147.

23

Leveraging football events

Vitor Sobral, Sheranne Fairley, and Danny O'Brien

Introduction

Events such as the FIFA World Cup, the UEFA European Championship, the AFC Asian Cup, and the UEFA Champions League final are all claimed to provide benefits to the cities and regions that host them. Government and football authorities argue that there are economic, political, cultural, and social benefits for a town, city, region, or nation that hosts a major football tournament or regular season club match (Cornelissen et al., 2011; Heere et al., 2013; Konecke et al., 2015). Like most events of significant scale, major football events are claimed to enhance tourism visitation, social benefits, soft power, economic activity, and even a host destination's image (Fairley et al., 2016; Brannagan and Rockwood, 2016; Kim and Morrison, 2005). However, simply hosting a football event does not mean that a host destination will automatically achieve positive tangible or intangible benefits (Chalip, 2004; O'Brien and Chalip, 2007; Ziakas, 2015). To maximise the likelihood of desired benefits materialising, a set of strategies should be implemented before, during, and after the event, in a process known as event leveraging (Chalip, 2004; Chalip, 2006). Successful event leveraging requires relevant stakeholders to work collaboratively together to achieve targeted outcomes (Chalip and McGuirty, 2004; Jago et al., 2003; O'Brien, 2006; 2007). This chapter starts by introducing the concept of event leveraging. Next, we explore stakeholder theory and discuss how relevant stakeholders should be identified. Then, we discuss attempts to leverage outcomes around various football events.

Event leveraging

Hosting an event is not enough to ensure desired benefits will eventuate (Horne and Manzenreiter, 2004; Cornelissen et al., 2011; Perna and Custodio, 2008). Event leveraging is the process by which the benefits of hosting an event are maximised through strategic planning before, during, and after the event (Chalip, 2004). Objectives must be set, relevant stakeholders consulted and identified, and strategies formulated to achieve certain outcomes well ahead of the event itself (Chalip, 2004; 2006; O'Brien and Chalip, 2007). Event leveraging strategies can link directly to the event itself, such as lengthening visitor stays or maximising tourism spend, or can be more targeted at longer-term, indirect benefits, such as upgrading communications and transport infrastructure, employment stimulation, or enhancing a host destination's image through the increased media attention that comes with hosting a large-scale event (Chalip, 2004). Other benefits might not be quite so tangible, but are potentially just as valuable, such as enhanced local and national identity, including a "feel good factor" or "communitas" that results from the event atmosphere or team performance, or improved international trade relations that may also lead to increased foreign investment and an opportunities to enhance the host destination's soft power and engage in public diplomacy (Allan et al., 2007; Cornelissen, 2008; Dauncey and Hare, 2000; Fairley et al., 2016 ; Grix and Brannagan, 2016; Maennig, 2007). When public money is being used to host events, taxpayers understandably question the benefits (Chalip, 2006). For instance, a new football stadium may be a long-term benefit for elite football competition, but there may be significant numbers of taxpayers who receive no real benefit from the new facility. This is why many scholars argue that hosting an event, particularly one that demands large-scale government investment and resources such as the FIFA World Cup, is not an efficient use of public money (Baade and Matheson, 2002; Matheson, 2009). However, if an event is strategically leveraged, in that plans are put in place with a view to producing wider benefits, then it is possible for event hosting to be a sound public investment (Chalip, 2006). To ensure that strategic plans are formulated and successfully implemented, it is important to identify and understand which stakeholders to engage to maximise chances of favourable outcomes (Chalip and McGuirty, 2004; Jago et al., 2003; O'Brien, 2006; 2007).

Stakeholder salience

In order to successfully leverage a football event, it is important to identify key stakeholders, and their motivations, concerns, and desired outcomes. Stakeholder theory is focused on agents who are affected by, or can cause effect on, a focal phenomenon (Freeman, 1984). In the case of a football event, the salience of stakeholders will depend on the leveraging objective being sought by event hosts. For instance, if a host destination is leveraging a football event for tourism gain, then regional and national tourism bodies, tourism businesses, and potential tourists could all be considered stakeholders. Stakeholder theory focuses "attention to the interests and well-being of those who can assist or hinder the achievement of the organisation's objectives" (Philips, Freeman, and Wicks, 2003 p. 481). One of the weaknesses of stakeholder theory is that when applied uncritically, it could refer to just about anyone in society, making it limitless and impractical (Philips et al., 2003). Mitchell, Agle, and Wood (1997) offer a practical framework for identifying which stakeholders are the most salient for given phenomenon based on legitimacy, power, and urgency. Legitimate stakeholders are those whose actions are describable, proper, and appropriate within socially constructed norms (Mitchell et al., 1997). When leveraging an international football event for tourism, the national or regional tourism body could be considered a legitimate stakeholder, as planning and implementing strategies for tourism without such a body becomes problematic, particularly when attempting to remain consistent with the host destination's overall tourism strategy. Attempting to do so without the involvement of an official tourism body would detract from the perceived legitimacy of the initiative and therefore, be catastrophic to the chances of leveraging success. Power relationships in this framework are concerned with those stakeholders able to achieve their preferred outcomes (Mitchell et al., 1997). When leveraging international football events for tourism, regional or national government can be considered powerful stakeholders, as they have the capability and authority to achieve preferred outcomes. Urgency refers to the time sensitivity and importance of the stakeholder's claim that demands immediate attention from the organisation manager (Mitchell et al., 1997). In the leveraging of an international football event for tourism for example, a major airline could be considered an urgent stakeholder as it has an immediate and important claim to the event, which may demand immediate attention, particularly if issues associated with the airline cause travel disruptions. When all three of these aspects – legitimacy, power, and urgency – are combined in a stakeholder, Mitchell et al. (1997) determine this to be a definitive stakeholder and one which requires careful attention from managers. However, stakeholders with one or two of these attributes may also warrant attention and if circumstances change, could become definitive stakeholders (Mitchell et al., 1997). For instance, if tourism business staff, who may be considered urgent stakeholders, decided to go on strike, their claim could also become legitimate, making them dependent stakeholders. If the staff combine with a powerful union that adds to their voice, then they fill all three categories and become definitive stakeholders. By understanding which stakeholders are most salient in different situations, the host destination has the best chance of leveraging the event to help ensure that the desired outcomes are achieved. There are several examples from past football events where this has and has not been achieved.

Economic impact

Authorities of host destinations, until recent years, have lauded the economic benefits of hosting events such as the FIFA World Cup or the UEFA European Championships. But evidence of direct economic benefits arising from events has been minimal and often proven the contrary, particularly when opportunity costs are considered (Szymanski, 2011). The 2002 FIFA World Cup was a prime example, with local Japanese governments suggesting the tournament would help regenerate their regions' economies, with investment in infrastructure (mostly event-related) acting as an economic multiplier (Horne and Manzenreiter, 2004). While there was an increase in the construction sector employment in the lead-up to the World Cup and an increase in television sales, the limited nature of both meant that even before the tournament began, Japanese authorities admitted the economic effect would be neutral. A similar disappointment in the lack of economic benefit from staging the 2002 World Cup was felt by co-host, South Korea (Kim and Petrick, 2005). For UEFA Euro 2004, the Portuguese Federal Government invested 964.4 million euros in developing roads, stadia, parking, and other amenities (Martins et al. 2004, as cited in Perna and Custodio, 2008). Despite this significant spending, the Portuguese preferred to focus on the global signals of modernity this would send, admitting they would not see an immediate return on this investment (Marivoet, 2006). In the case of stadia without regular tenants like Algarve, which cost 37.9 million euros and hosted just three matches during the tournament, it is difficult to foresee any net positive economic impact whatsoever (Perna and Custodio, 2008). Germany had the advantage of high-quality infrastructure well before the tournament but still used the 2006 World Cup as a catalyst for infrastructure improvements, which led to a small short-term increase in employment (Maennig, 2007). There were also developments and refurbishments to several of the country's stadia, but, with a significant portion of this paid for by private investors (Maennig, 2007), the negative economic impact on government was less pervasive than that felt by Portugal at Euro 2004. The other advantage for Germany in relation to stadia was that all were to be continually used in the aftermath of the event. Munich residents even gave approval for the city's Allianz Arena development, emphasising the importance of stakeholder collaboration (Ohmann et al., 2006). Despite this economic activity, the overall economic impact of the World Cup proved insignificant, even with a slight increase in retail, tourism, and employment (Maennig, 2007). South Africa spent 600 billion rand (GBP32 billion) on its infrastructure in the lead-up to the 2010 World Cup in the hope that it would lead to significant revenues and the creation of 415,000 jobs (Cornelissen, 2011). Ultimately, South African residents did not perceive an improvement in infrastructure or an economic improvement in the country post-2010 (Kaplanidou et al., 2013). Another issue raised by football event researchers is what Muller (2017) describes as event seizure, which is the overtaking of the initial event-leveraging priorities and objectives by others felt more necessary to the event's function and to the detriment of those initial objectives. Researchers use Russia's hosting of World Cup 2018 as a prime example. Russian authorities had initially intended to fast-track long-term infrastructure development in areas such as transport and tourism, with a focus in the less developed provincial capitals. However, as the Russian economy struggled and the delivery of event-specific infrastructure became more prominent, most of the resources were diverted to fulfilling World Cup-specific needs, rather than the initial development needs (Muller, 2017).

These examples demonstrate the difficulty in achieving net positive economic outcomes from hosting major football events. However, it is possible that football events that require less infrastructure investment, such as the UEFA Champions League final, may result in more positive direct economic outcomes. Regularly occurring football league matches may also provide economic opportunities for host destinations without the significant public expenditure of larger-scale events (Sparvero and Chalip, 2007; Konecke et al., 2015; Allan et al., 2007). For example, the regular season competition of Glasgow's (and Scotland's) two biggest football clubs, Celtic and Rangers (also known as the "Old Firm") are believed to provide an economic impact of 45.35 million pounds to Glasgow and Scotland – mostly through tourism (Allan et al., 2007). Similarly, through regular season competition, Bundesliga club, Kaiserslautern, has an estimated economic impact of 25.8 million euros, while the region enjoys a positive impact of 16.5 million euros (Konecke et al., 2015). This is not to suggest that there are no potential economic benefits associated with hosting major football events – it may be that these benefits are more indirect and difficult to measure, or it may be that some stakeholders benefit, while others do not.

Trade and investment

Hosting football events can also be accompanied by strategic leveraging initiatives for more long-term and less direct economic benefit, such as increased trade and investment for the host destination (Grix and Brannagan, 2016). Australia's hosting of the AFC Asian Cup focused on the more indirect benefit of establishing and enhancing trade relations with the country's Asian partners (Fairley et al., 2016). Specifically, the Australian Federal Government saw hosting the continent's most important and popular football event as an ideal opportunity to foster trade relations among important Asian partners, with three of the country's key export markets qualifying for the event: China, Japan, and South Korea. Collaborating closely with definitive stakeholders such as Australia's Department of Foreign Affairs and Trade, the Australian Trade Commission, as well as state governments, the organisers embarked on what was termed "football diplomacy" to establish networks across business and government. Enabling this was the creation of Match Australia, a program designed to "facilitate networking opportunities between Australian and Asian business" (Fairley et al., 2016, p. 7) during the tournament. Through this, a number of business delegations from across Asia were hosted by Australian officials at matches during the Asian Cup, facilitating these hoped-for networks and relationships, as well as consolidating recently signed free trade deals with South Korea, China, and Japan (Fairley et al., 2016; Murray, 2017). It is difficult to measure how successful this strategy was, but at the very least, it set the groundwork for business-relationship development and has the potential to lead to long-term outcomes for the host destination.

Australia also leveraged the 2015 AFC Asian Cup to send signals to its Asian audience that it is an open and willing trade partner. Another area in which Australia looked to leverage the hosting of the Asian Cup was for tourism development.

Tourism

When a destination is awarded the rights to host a major football event, one of the most commonly touted benefits is the increased tourism the destination will receive. For example, when Japan and South Korea were announced as co-hosts for the 2002 FIFA World Cup, there were predicted tourism benefits, particularly to areas in both countries that were previously unfamiliar to international tourists (Horne and Manzenreiter, 2004; Kim et al., 2006). Predictions proved wildly optimistic, with tourism numbers barely improving from the previous year. Some of the reasons identified for this unfulfilled outcome were distance, cost, security concerns, and even difficulty for Chinese visitors to obtain visas (Horne and Manzenreiter, 2004). There was no indication of a targeted and considered strategy to increase visitor numbers. Similarly, Portugal's hosting of the UEFA Euro 2004 also failed to live up to tourism expectations (Perna and Custodio, 2008). Perna and Custodio's (2008) study demonstrated a zero net economic impact for tourism in the Algarve region during the event compared to previous years. Tourism pricing, such as the price of accommodation, may rise during the event and compensate for the reduction in tourism numbers (Maennig, 2007).

While Perna and Custodio (2008) found an increase in per-bed revenue, the overall impact was negligible and did not recoup the 37.9 million euro investment from the Portuguese Federal Government, which was mostly spent on the stadium and associated infrastructure (Perna and Custodio, 2008).

Crowding that occurs in destinations because of large-scale events may lead to a "crowding out" effect, where potential visitors are put off by the large crowds, and locals may seek to escape the host destination during the event (Preuss, 2011). This was evident during the 2006 World Cup in Germany as local residents left the country and flocked to areas like Mallorca in record numbers (Maennig, 2007). "Time switching" may also occur – where potential tourists avoid the area during or around the event for fear of crowding (Maennig, 2007).

Setting up fan zones for supporters and tourists to experience the event outside the stadia has been a strategy used by multiple host destinations for World Cup events, such as South Korea in 2002, Germany 2006 and South Africa 2010 (Whang, 2004; Grix, 2012; Knott et al., 2016). Such fan events can help foster greater visitor spending on items like food and drink, as well as keeping tourists in the host destination even when they do not have a match ticket, all useful tactics for leveraging short-term, visitation-related event benefits (Chalip, 2004). But even when leveraging strategies are undertaken to entice and lengthen tourist stay, there are other external factors that could prevent event-related tourism, such as security fears. The hoped-for boost to tourist numbers in South Africa failed to materialise (Cornelissen et al., 2011), partly due to the perceived security risk of travelling in South Africa (Lepp and Gibson, 2011). This could have been addressed with greater promotion and media strategies which framed and focused on signalling South Africa as a safe tourist destination in the lead-up to the World Cup, rather than simply promoting the country as an exotic tourist location (Knott et al., 2016). For the 2015 AFC Asian Cup in Australia, local organisers devised international media strategies to increase event awareness and promote Australia as a tourism destination (Fairley et al., 2016). Both the tourism leveraging strategies of the 2010 World Cup and 2015 Asian Cup involved collaboration with definitive stakeholders. For example, the South African organisers worked closely with international media during the World Cup, local and regional tourism authorities, as did those in Australia during the Asian Cup (Knott et al., 2016; Fairley et al., 2016). However, the tourism benefits need not just be during the event itself. Indeed, the organisers in South Africa lamented the missed opportunity to take advantage of the tourism and media momentum created during the World Cup (Knott et al., 2016).

Image enhancement

The increased media attention and likely tourist flow in the lead-up to and during a football event gives the host destination an opportunity to present an image of itself through signalling (Grix, 2012; Preuss and Alfs, 2011). This is also known as media framing which is the "selection and salience" of certain aspects of reality from the communicator to a receiver who then interprets them (Entman, 1993). In the case of a football event, it is critical to consider how target audiences interpret messages (through images or language) about the host destination during broadcasts. To have the best chance of sending the destination's preferred message, organisers should adopt a media leveraging strategy referred to as "framing sponsorship" – the strategic attempt to have the media present an event through the sponsor's preferred frame (Van Gorp, 2007). South Korea used the attention of the 2002 World Cup opening ceremony to present itself as a modern, technologically advanced nation with deep traditions, while images of fans cheering the national team throughout the tournament went around the world, helping cement this message (Horne and Manzenreiter, 2004; Kim and Morrison, 2005). Portugal's hosting of UEFA Euro 2004 allowed the country to also present itself as a modern nation, focusing on creativity and efficiency. The organisers used a variety of strategies to send these signals, including the design of the tournament logo which featured Portuguese symbols presented in a more modern, creative way, and a focus on presenting the infrastructure as modern and efficient (Marivoet, 2006). This was most obvious in the design of Braga's Municipal Stadium, which was built in a quarry and has sheer rock faces at both ends of the ground, resulting in a unique image of creative engineering during the television broadcast, as well as for those in attendance. Such iconic buildings also create "urban impulses" for the city, something which may have been a missed opportunity in Germany, where stadia were described as "functional" (Maennig, 2007). Collaborating with local authorities was seen as a key driver to design such "iconic" stadia in Portugal (Maennig, 2007). To achieve this, Portuguese organisers worked closely with definitive stakeholders, such as the local football team and long-term tenant (Sporting Braga), the local council, national government, as well architecture and engineering firms. Braga's stadium is, however, a rare case of enhancing a host destination image simply through the football telecast. As football event guidelines stipulate how a broadcast should look, it can lead to uniformity and what is described as "placelessness," where there is nothing specific to determine where exactly the event is taking place (Higham and Hinch, 2006). As football grounds and broadcast production become more uniform across football events, this issue needs to be addressed by host destinations hoping to leverage football events for tourism and image enhancement.

To overcome "placelessness," event organisers need to devise strategies, such as having the city's name on advertising boards, which is now widely used at major tournaments, showcasing the city itself in the lead-up and during the breaks in play, or using imagery synonymous with the destination itself in the event logo (Green et al., 2003). In Germany the 2006 World Cup logo, consisting of friendly faces, formed part of an overall image-leveraging strategy. Its hosting of the tournament is seen as one of the most successful cases of using a football event for image enhancement, or in this case, altering an unsatisfactory global image (Maennig, 2007; Grix, 2012). Before the country was awarded the right to host the 2006 event, there was already a strategy in place to change Germany's image as cold and unfriendly to one that is more salubrious and creative (Grix, 2012). The media attention and expected tourism influx that would result from hosting the World Cup gave Germany a chance to turbocharge this long-term strategy.

By collaborating with definitive stakeholders, including national tourist boards, governments at all levels and volunteers, Germany successfully changed its image through messaging in the international media, using framing sponsorship. The leveraging strategies included a focus on being a hospitable and friendly host population, with volunteers trained in how to be "friendly" to international visitors and the implementation of a national "friendliness" campaign. Fan fests were set up across the country with a focus on creating a carnival atmosphere, linking to Germany's beer hall and communal celebratory traditions. Large-scale arts and culture programs were put on display, many with a World Cup theme to help present Germany as a fun and creative nation. The perceptions of local residents during the tournament, who described the event as a "great, friendly party" (Ohmann et al., 2006, p.141) helped cultivate this image. There was also a "Land of Ideas" campaign, set up before the World Cup bid, that aimed at producing an improved image by showcasing German culture, attracting tourists, and targeting foreign investment – an initiative that continued well beyond the tournament itself. The evidence of this successful reframing of Germany's global image was evident in media depictions of Germany that altered from one of cold efficiency to friendly and warm, particularly in the British media (Grix, 2012,) and from the perceptions of those visiting the country during the tournament (Florek et al., 2008). Confirming Germany's successful reimaging of itself was the country's significant improvement in the Anholt Nation Brand Index following the World Cup (Maennig, 2007).

For South Africa 2010, authorities embarked on a similar, image-altering strategy, albeit with more mixed success than Germany, four years prior. South Africa hoped to use its hosting of the 2010 World Cup to announce itself on the world stage, shed itself of a racist image linked to apartheid, and showcase a pan-African revival to a global audience (Lepp and Gibson, 2011). Understanding that the media was a definitive stakeholder in helping achieve this outcome, the organisers embarked on a strategy that included collaboration with tourism bodies to target key media outlets for pre-event tours. Some host cities also set up media centres outside the official FIFA zones (e.g. stadia) for non-accredited media, allowing them to access facilities, information, interviews, and sometimes special offers or excursions (Knott et al., 2016). Campaigns such as "Fly the Flag for SA," an initiative that encouraged South Africans to display the nation's flag where they could and included a choreographed dance, and "Football Fridays," a campaign encouraging South Africans to wear the national team's shirt on Friday, including at work, helped the media showcase a friendly, happy, united, and excited population and help differentiate it from the old apartheid image of South Africa. These strategies and the tournament itself attracted media that may not otherwise have visited South Africa, which enabled them to understand the country's context and deliver more authentic reports (Knott et al., 2016).

An improvement in South Africa's international image as modern and more positive was supported by Lepp and Gibson's (2011) study of United States' students' perceptions of the African nation pre- and post-World Cup. This was the case even for those that consumed few matches, emphasising the media attention a host receives outside the match broadcasts (Lepp and Gibson, 2011). Yet, that increased attention also focused on the country's problems in the lead-up to the event. Indeed, a lack of collaboration with definitive stakeholders across the African continent (Tichaawa and Bob, 2016) meant there was no strategic leveraging and the hoped-for change of existing undeveloped and primitive African stereotypes did not eventuate (Lepp and Gibson, 2011). This highlights the importance of leveraging and collaborating with stakeholders to achieve desired outcomes of hosting football events, even though there are occasions where fortune can deliver an unexpected benefit, it is important to understand that such outcomes are mere serendipity and cannot be guaranteed.

Social benefits

In 1998, France won the World Cup in Paris, sparking a mass celebration on the Champs-Elysees, bringing together people from the city's diverse population (Dauncey and Hare, 2000) who may not otherwise have encountered each other. The players that won the World Cup came from diverse ethnic backgrounds, such as Zinedine Zidane (Algerian), Marcel Desailly (Ghanian), and Youri Djorkaeff (Polish-Armenian). The image of people from diverse backgrounds joining together for the French cause allowed France to project a new, modern image of itself to both its own people and foreign publics. The event produced a social benefit of enabling French nationals from minority backgrounds, who may have felt excluded from mainstream French society, to feel more included and legitimised. The triumph also filled the nation with self-confidence that it could compete and win on the global stage (Dauncey and Hare, 2000). However, as Dauncey and Hare (2000) highlight, it is unlikely that these benefits would have eventuated had the French team lost a penalty shoot-out to Italy in the quarter-finals or even been beaten by Brazil in the final. More specifically, these hoped-for outcomes were generated by accident rather than design. While coach, Aime Jaquet, prepared his team for the tournament diligently, there is scant evidence of event-leveraging strategies from the organisers that specifically focused on the outcome of a more inclusive French society. This occurred through an uncontrollable variable, the French team's performance; this favourable outcome was thus, yet again, the result of serendipity, not strategy.

German authorities had a range of entertainment programs that included concerts and shows for both adults and children when it hosted the 2006 World Cup. This helped create a sense of "communitas" and strengthened community ties in host cities like Munich (Ohmann et al., 2006). Even the negative national identity aspects associated with football events, such as tensions between national groups or ethnicities, were temporarily suspended in Ohmann et al.'s (2006) study of Munich residents' perceptions of the 2006 World Cup. Hosting the 2010 World Cup in South Africa was positioned by organisers as an opportunity for nation building in a still divided country (Cornelissen, 2008; Gibson et al., 2014). While some initiatives such as "Football Fridays" and the international prestige from hosting a FIFA World Cup helped create a sense of national pride (Heere et al., 2013), there remains little evidence this led to an increase in social cohesion or social capital, which could be related to a lack of community involvement and stakeholder collaboration (Gibson et al., 2014).

However, for the 2015 AFC Asian Cup in Australia, multicultural engagement was determined as a strategic opportunity to be leveraged around the event. Specifically, the Local Organising Committee (LOC) developed strategies to engage the country's multicultural communities. The LOC's strategy included designing community events relevant to the Asian Cup, partnering with local multicultural media organisations, and appointing influential community ambassadors (Fairley, et al., 2016). The organisers also developed educational resources about the competing teams for primary schools. By identifying the definitive stakeholders, such as multicultural organisations, community influencers, and educators, the multicultural programs were deemed a huge success and seen as a major reason for the large turnout to matches not involving Australia (Fairley et al., 2016; Biron, 2015; Football Federation Australia, 2015). Australia's hosting of the 2015 AFC Asian Cup is a good example of how a football event can be leveraged to achieve positive social outcomes.

Soft power

Hosting football events, like the FIFA World Cup, have been used by some nations to enhance their soft power and achieve preferred foreign policy outcomes (Grix and Brannagan, 2016).

Soft power refers to, "the ability to affect others through the co-optive means of framing the agenda, persuading, and eliciting positive attraction in order to obtain preferred outcomes" (Nye, 2011, p. 21). The increased global attention of hosting a World Cup means the host destination can use the event to conduct public diplomacy, which is the cultivation of public opinion in other countries and building long-term relationships to help achieve preferred foreign policy outcomes (Cull, 2009). Grix and Brannagan (2016) suggest enhancing soft power through event hosting is based on five interlinked resources: culture (to make the state attractive); tourism (through multipliers, like visitor word of mouth); branding (selling the host, adding to international prestige); diplomacy (as an ice breaker or public diplomacy); and, trade (send a signal, building relationships). The discussion above has already highlighted how a football event host can leverage for culture, tourism, branding, and trade. In terms of public diplomacy, it needs to focus on cultivating its attractive qualities to foreign publics, as Germany did with the 2006 World Cup (Grix, 2012).

One region that has leveraged regular season football events to enhance its global image and its soft power is Catalonia (Xifra, 2009). Spanish giant, FC Barcelona, receives more attention than any Catalan institution and through its use of symbols and imagery (the away kit was recently designed in the style of the Catalan flag) has become synonymous with Catalan identity. Through this media attention, FC Barcelona has been used as a public diplomacy tool by Catalonia (Xifra, 2009) and may have even enhanced Catalan soft power by associating Barcelona's attractive qualities, such as its creative, attractive style of play, with that of the Catalan region. This also demonstrates the importance of working with a definitive stakeholder, such as FC Barcelona, which has power, legitimacy, and, in the case of Catalonia's image, urgency.

Yet, there are risks with using football events for soft power enhancement. Event upsets may offend or alienate foreign publics and lead to a loss of attraction (Brannagan and Giulianotti, 2014). This could be the situation Qatar faces as it prepares to host the 2022 World Cup, despite the nation's intention to use the tournament to signal to the world that it is peaceful, modern, innovative, and technologically advanced. Having the bid associated with FIFA's corruption scandal and the increased media attention highlighting the country's human rights issues, particularly concerning the conditions of World Cup construction workers, has the potential to upset, alienate, and offend parts of the world and lead to a loss of attraction among these populations (Brannagan and Giulianotti, 2014). To avoid this soft disempowerment, 2022 World Cup organisers will need to work with definitive stakeholders, such as influential international media outlets, and local firms and organisations associated with the event.

Conclusion

This chapter has demonstrated how football events can lead to positive benefits for host destinations, including societal, tourism, economic impact, trade and investment, image enhancement, and soft power. To create the optimal conditions for achieving these benefits, host city stakeholders must identify and collaborate closely with salient stakeholders to formulate and implement leveraging strategies to achieve targeted outcomes. Examples from the Germany 2006 World Cup, South Africa 2010 World Cup and Australia 2015 AFC Asian Cup demonstrate the benefits host destinations can reap from identifying and collaborating with salient stakeholders, to ensure strategies in the lead-up, during, and post-event stages achieve desired outcomes. Events like Germany 2006 were leveraged to successfully alter an unsatisfactory image, while South Africa and Australia boosted tourism and, in the latter case, also promoted long-term trade and investment through leveraging and stakeholder collaboration.

However, there are plenty of lessons showing the downside of not having, or poorly implementing, leveraging strategies, or neglecting stakeholders altogether. To be sure, there is evidence of host communities reaping benefits serendipitously without strategic leverage; but having a strategic leveraging plan founded upon deep stakeholder engagement and collaboration maximises the chances of achieving specific, targeted outcomes from hosting a major football event. For example, while Portugal managed to use UEFA Euro 2004 to portray itself as a creative, modern nation, its lack of a strategic approach and somewhat random spending on infrastructure failed to deliver other net long-term benefits. At this point, however, there is limited research into the long-term economic impact for a host destination from leveraging football events for developing trade relations and investment opportunities, as Australia attempted with the 2015 AFC Asian Cup. Evidence of a net positive economic impact was found in studies on regular season football events in Scotland and Germany, but a significant research gap remains in determining what other benefits such events can deliver to the host destination and what leveraging strategies can be used to maximise the chances of achieving desired outcomes. Understanding this will help identify and prioritise the definitive stakeholders needed for collaboration to ensure the successful implementation of leveraging strategies. Ultimately, football events inspire emotion and passion in millions across the world and are a powerful opportunity for host destinations to leverage desired outcomes, ideally for wider societal benefits.

References

Allan, G., Dunlop, S., and Swales, K. (2007) The economic impact of regular season sporting competitions: the Glasgow old firm football spectators as sports tourists. *Journal of Sport & Tourism*, 12(2), 63–97.

Baade, R. and Matheson, V. (2002) Bidding for the Olympics: fool's gold. In: M. Ibrahímo (ed.)., *Transatlantic Sport: The Comparative Economics of North American and European sports* (pp. 127–151). Cheltenham: Edward Elgar.

Biron, D. (2015) Football without enemies: the dual success of the Asian Cup. *The Conversation*. [online] Retrieved from: http://theconversation.com/football-without-enemies-the-dual-success-of-the-asian-cup-36888

Brannagan, P. and Giulianotti, R. (2014) Soft power and soft disempowerment: Qatar, global sport and football's 2022 World Cup finals. *Leisure Studies*, 34(6), 703–719.

Brannagan, P. and Rookwood, J. (2016) Sports mega-events, soft power and soft disempowerment: international supporters' perspectives on Qatar's acquisition of the 2022 FIFA World Cup finals. *International Journal of Sport Policy and Politics*, 8(2), 173–188.

Chalip, L. (2004) Beyond impact: a general model for sport event leverage. In: D. Ritchie (ed.), *Sport Tourism Interrelationships, Impacts and Issues*. Clevedon: Channel View Publications.

Chalip, L. (2006) Towards social leverage of sport events. *Journal of Sport & Tourism*, 11(2), 109–127.

Chalip, L. and McGuirty, J. (2004) Bundling sport events with the host destination. *Journal of Sport & Tourism*, 9(3), 267–282.

Cornelissen, S. (2008) Scripting the nation: sport, mega-events, foreign policy and state-building in post-apartheid South Africa. *Sport in Society*, 11(4), 481–493.

Cornelissen, S., Bob, U. and Swart, K. (2011) Towards redefining the concept of legacy in relation to sport mega-events: insights from the 2010 FIFA World Cup. *Development Southern Africa*, 28(3), 307–318.

Cull, N. (2009) How we got here. In: P. Seib (ed.), *Toward a New Public Diplomacy*. New York: Palgrave Macmillan, pp. 23–47.

Dauncey, H. and Hare, G. (2000) World Cup France '98: metaphors, meanings and values. *International Review for the Sociology of Sport*, 35(3), 331–347.

Entman, R. (1993) Framing: toward clarification of a fractured paradigm. *Journal of Communication*, 43(4), 51–58.

Fairley, S., Lovegrove, H., and Brown, M. (2016) Leveraging events to ensure enduring benefits: the legacy strategy of the 2015 AFC Asian Cup. *Sport Management Review*, 19(4), 466–474.

Florek, M., Breitbarth, T., and Conejo, F. (2008) Mega event = mega impact? Travelling fans' experience and perceptions of the 2006 FIFA World Cup host nation. *Journal of Sport & Tourism*, 13(3), 199–219.

Freeman, R. (1984) *Strategic Management: A Stakeholder Approach*. Boston: Pitman.

Football Federation Australia. (2015) *Asian Cup up for national multicultural awards.* [online] Retrieved from: https://www.myfootball.com.au/news/asian-cup-national-multicultural-awards

Gibson, H., Walker, M., Thapa, B., Kaplanidou, K., Geldenhuys, S., and Coetzee, W. (2014) Psychic income and social capital among host nation residents: a pre–post analysis of the 2010 FIFA World Cup in South Africa. *Tourism Management*, 44, 113–122.

Green, B., Costa, C., and Fitzgerald, M. (2003) Marketing the host city: analyzing exposure generated by a sport event. *International Journal of Sports Marketing and Sponsorship*, 4(4), 48–66.

Grix, J. (2012) "Image" leveraging and sports mega-events: Germany and the 2006 FIFA World Cup. *Journal of Sport & Tourism*, 17(4), 289–312.

Grix, J. and Brannagan, P. (2016) Of mechanisms and myths: conceptualising states' "soft power" strategies through sports mega-events. *Diplomacy & Statecraft*, 27(2), 251–272.

Heere, B., Walker, M., Gibson, H., Thapa, B., Geldenhuys, S., and Coetzee, W. (2013) The power of sport to unite a nation: the social value of the 2010 FIFA World Cup in South Africa. *European Sport Management Quarterly*, 13(4), 450–471.

Higham, J. and Hinch, T. (2006) Sport and tourism research: a geographic approach. *Journal of Sport & Tourism*, 11(1), 31–49.

Horne, J. and Manzenreiter, W. (2004) Accounting for mega-events. *International Review for the Sociology of Sport*, 39(2), 187–203.

Jago, L., Chalip, L., Brown, G., Mules, T., and Ali, S. (2003) Building events into destination branding: insights from experts. *Event Management*, 8(1), 3–14.

Kaplanidou, K., Karadakis, K., Gibson, H., Thapa, B., Walker, M., Geldenhuys, S., and Coetzee, W. (2013) Quality of life, event impacts, and mega-event support among south african residents before and after the 2010 FIFA World Cup. *Journal of Travel Research*, 52(5), 631–645.

Kim, H., Gursoy, D., and Lee, S. (2006) The impact of the 2002 World Cup on South Korea: comparisons of pre- and post-games. *Tourism Management*, 27(1), 86–96.

Kim, S. and Morrsion, A. (2005) Change of images of South Korea among foreign tourists after the 2002 FIFA World Cup. *Tourism Management*, 26(2), 233–247.

Kim, S. and Petrick, J. (2005) Residents' perceptions on impacts of the FIFA 2002 World Cup: the case of Seoul as a host city. *Tourism Management*, 26(1), 25–38.

Knott, B., Fyall, A., and Jones, I. (2016) Leveraging nation branding opportunities through sport mega-events. *International Journal of Culture, Tourism and Hospitality Research*, 10(1), 105–118.

Konecke, T., Preuss, H., and Schütte, N. (2015) Direct regional economic impact of Germany's 1. FC Kaiserslautern through participation in the 1. Bundesliga. *Soccer & Society*, 18(7), 988–1011.

Lepp, A. and Gibson, H. (2011) Reimaging a nation: South Africa and the 2010 FIFA World Cup. *Journal of Sport & Tourism*, 16(3), 211–230.

Maennig, W. (2007) One year later: a re-appraisal of the economics of the 2006 soccer World Cup. *SSRN Electronic Journal*. DOI: http://dx.doi.org/10.2139/ssrn.1520530

Marivoet, S. (2006) UEFA Euro 2004™ Portugal: the social construction of a sports mega-event and spectacle. *The Sociological Review*, 54(2), 127–143.

Martins, M. V., Tenreiro, F., Mendes, J., Jacinto, A., Ribeiro, J., Castro, A., ... & Perna, F. (2004). Avaliação do Impacto Económico do EURO 2004. *Relatório Final. Instituto Superior de Economia e Gestão.* Universidade Técnica de Lisboa.

Matheson, V. (2009) Economic multipliers and mega-event analysis. *International Journal of Sport Finance*, 4(1), 63–70.

Mitchell, R., Agle, B., and Wood, D. (1997) Toward a theory of stakeholder identification and salience: defining the principle of who and what really counts. *The Academy of Management Review*, 22(4), 853–886.

Muller, M. (2017) How mega-events capture their hosts: event seizure and the World Cup 2018 in Russia. *Urban Geography*, 38(8), 1113–1132.

Murray, S. (2017) Sports diplomacy in the Australian context: theory into strategy. *Politics & Policy*, 45(5), 841–861.

Nye, J. (2011) *The Future of Power.* New York: Public Affairs.

O'Brien, D. (2006) Event business leveraging The Sydney 2000 Olympic Games. *Annals of Tourism Research*, 33(1), 240–261.

O'Brien, D. (2007) Points of leverage: maximizing host community benefit from a regional surfing festival. *European Sport Management Quarterly*, 7(2), 141–165.

Ohmann, S., Jones, I., and Wilkes, K. (2006) The perceived social impacts of the 2006 Football World Cup on Munich residents. *Journal of Sport & Tourism*, 11(2), 129–152.

Perna, F. and Custodio, M. (2008) Importance of events in tourism: impacts of the UEFA-EURO 2004™ on the accommodation industry in Algarve, Portugal. *Anatolia*, 19(1), 5–22.

Phillips, R., Freeman, R., and Wicks, A. (2003) What stakeholder theory is not. *Business Ethics Quarterly*, 13(04), 479–502.

Preuss, H. (2011) A method for calculating the crowding-out effect in sport mega-event impact studies: the 2010 FIFA World Cup. *Development Southern Africa*, 28(3), 367–385.

Preuss, H. and Alfs, C. (2011) Signaling through the 2008 Beijing Olympics—using mega sport events to change the perception and image of the host. *European Sport Management Quarterly*, 11(1), 55–71.

Sparvero, E. and Chalip, L. (2007) Professional teams as leverageable assets: strategic creation of community value. *Sport Management Review*, 10(1), 1–30.

Szymanski, S. (2011) About winning: the political economy of awarding the World Cup and the Olympic Games. *SAIS Review*, 31(1), 87–97.

Tichaawa, T. and Bob, U. (2016) The African sport fan and a mega-event: implications for the Durban 2022 Commonwealth Games in South Africa. *African Journal of Hospitality, Tourism and Leisure*, 5(1), 1–13.

Van Gorp, B. (2007) The constructionist approach to framing: bringing culture back. *Journal of Communication*, 57(1), 60–78.

Whang, S. (2004) Football, fashion and fandom: sociological reflections on the 2002 World Cup and collective memories. In: W. Manzenreiter and J. Horne (ed.), *Football Goes East: Business, Culture and the People's Game in China, Japan and South Korea* (pp. 148–164). London: Routledge.

Xifra, J. (2009) Building sport countries' overseas identity and reputation: a case study of oublic paradiplomacy. *American Behavioral Scientist*, 53(4), 504–515.

Ziakas, V. (2015) For the benefit of all? Developing a critical perspective in mega-event leverage. *Leisure Studies*, 34(6), 689–702.

24

The labour markets of professional football players

Jean-François Brocard and Christophe Lepetit

Introduction

The labour market of professional football players has specific features, making it very peculiar to analyse. The application of classic economic theories is indeed inadequate when aiming at analysing the relationship between supply and demand in this one market. In particular, the traditional hypothesis made to describe classic labour markets (atomicity of buyers and sellers, homogeneous products, perfect information, no barriers to entry, etc.) are rarely observed in this market. The empirical analysis of the labour market of professional football players seems to validate another theory: the labour market segmentation originally developed by Doeringer and Piore in 1971. Indeed, according to this theory, a sole and homogeneous labour market does not exist, but rather several markets (or market segments) on which actors' behaviours and supply and demand adjustments mechanisms would substantially diverge.

A historical analysis of this labour market shows its high sensitivity to the level of dedicated regulation. In the past 20 years, a wide variety of deregulation decisions were made, either by the sports world itself or by national or international public regulators, which substantially impacted how the market operates. Among the main consequences are the large increase in international mobility of players and the talent concentration in the very best and wealthiest leagues and wealthy clubs. This deregulation trend also resulted in the emergence of several abuses such as the opacity surrounding the intermediaries' activities, or the development of mechanisms such as the Third-Party Ownership (TPO) in the transfer market.

The first widely acknowledged contribution to the football player's labour market literature was made by Sloane (1969). Ever since, it became a regular object of analysis for sports economists. First, because labour (of players) is the main input in the production function of clubs. The labour market then determines the talent allocation among clubs and leagues. The largely tested correlation between wage expenditure (which is a proxy of the amount of talent owned) and teams' performances (Szymanski, 2000) highlights how essential the labour market functioning is in understanding sports outcomes. Another important side of the literature tackles the moral hazard issue characterising the contract relationship between clubs and players. Indeed, the players' level of effort is difficult to assess for clubs, and shirking behaviour can occur implying that a player, purposely, does not perform to the best of his ability (Carmichael et al., 2012). Economists then test the relationship between the contracts offered to the player and his assessed performance (Feess et al., 2007; Frick, 2011; Rossi, 2012). The latest dedicated article on the topic suggests that the longer the contract the greater the tendency for players to shirk in the earlier part of the contract (Buraimo et al., 2015). This chapter will not directly tackle these questions.

Collecting data on this market has long been difficult, for it was hardly available or compiled. The situation progressively improved and the market is currently well documented with regular institutional reports providing official data, facilitating the research. The launching of the FIFA Transfer Matching System (TMS) – an online platform to record international players' transfers between clubs – in October 2010 was a clear step forward towards transparency and data availability on international transfers.

This chapter aims to establish how the regulation of the labour market of professional football players changed over time; review and update the characterisation of this market; and explain the financialisation of the market that endangers football's integrity.

Regulation evolution of the labour market of professional football players

On the football labour market, players supply their talent to demanding clubs. This market, once strongly regulated, was gradually deregulated at the end of the twentieth century.

The historic strong regulation of the market

In 1885 for the first time, the Football Association (FA) of England brought in the concept of a transfer when it introduced requirements for the registration with the federation of players who were going to be employed by clubs. Prior to this, players enjoyed a strong bargaining position enabling them to move from one club to another at any time (Magee, 2006). Under this so-called "retain-and-transfer" system, the Football Association required a player to be signed for a club for a full season and prevented his move to other clubs without the consent of the FA and the club (Morrow, 1999). All players' contracts were renewable annually at the club's discretion, and clubs were entitled to retain a player's registration even if his contract was not being renewed (Dobson and Goddart, 2001). This system was also introduced in France in 1925 (Lanfranchi and Wahl, 1998). Although the registration system was designed to protect smaller clubs (by preventing players from swapping clubs) it resulted in the "bought and sold" phenomenon and the creation of the transfer market, as the club was considered eligible for compensation for losing the player. Until 1959 in England, professional players were signed under one-year contracts with minimum and maximum salary terms. The incentive for players to seek to move was also restricted by the existence of a maximum wage, originally at $4 per week when it was introduced in 1901 (Dobson and Goddart, 2001). The maximum wage for footballers in England eventually rose to £20 prior to abolition in 1961. This meant that player salaries were just above wages earned by skilled engineers at the time (Frick and Simmonds, 2014). With the expiry of the contract, the club could retain the player offering them a minimum salary, transfer the player to another club for an agreed transfer fee, or cancel the player's registration to enable the latter to become a free agent. The club had total employment control over its players.

The continuous deregulation process

During the 1960s–1970s, the English Player's Union continued to question the transfer rules considering them restrictive. Even though players were granted a certain level of contractual freedom, their previous clubs were still entitled to receive a compensation fee for out-of-contract players. The maximum wage was also circumvented via proven and suspected cases of illegal payments to players and was abolished in 1961. In 1963, the English High Court declared that the retain-and-transfer system was "an unreasonable restraint of trade." France abolished all forms of compensation when the contract of the player expired as of 1969 (Lanfranchi and Wahl, 1998). The same took place in Germany in 1979.

It was, however, in 1995 with the intervention of the European Court of Justice in the Bosman case that the global transfer market was deeply transformed. Bosman was the opportunity for the court to acknowledge sport's specificities and consider its scope in relation to EU law (KEA and CDES, 2013). The final verdict abolished the retain clause for out-of-contract players, as well as the so-called 3+2 rule. The 3+2 rule was a nationality clause that limited the number of foreign players in a team (Kesenne, 2006). The decision in fact standardised transfer rules already adopted in some EU countries. The decision meant increased freedom for players to move with a radical change in recruitment patterns. It also forced international sporting bodies such as FIFA to review transfer rules and make them compatible with EU law on competition, on nationality (no discrimination) and on free movement of individuals. The current transfer system thus stems from an agreement reached in 2001 between FIFA, UEFA, and the European Commission, after consulting other football stakeholders (national associations, clubs associations, players unions, etc.). The impact of the Bosman rule was long debated among researchers. Some stated that the invariance principle would still apply, as the biggest clubs would still attract more talent (Kesenne, 1997). Others highlighted the risks related to this deregulation, focusing on the increasing disparities and their unfortunate consequences (Lavoie, 2000).

Characterisation of the market

The deregulation of the labour market had consequences on the functioning of the market. In particular, (a) it led to the expansion of the transfer market; (b) it promoted its segmentation, and (c) it facilitated its intermediation.

The expansion of the transfer market

The deregulation of the labour market combined with the liberalisation of several national audio-visual market (which allowed a huge increase of revenues for the major leagues) had consequences on the functioning of the market. The combination of these two movements of deregulation led to the economic boom of the labour market (KEA and CDES, 2013). Indeed, relying on the statistics collected by researchers or published by FIFA TMS, we observe the evolution of several variables, such as the number of transfers or the clubs' expenditures in the transfer market, which describes an expanding market.

The explanation of clubs' investments in talent is interpreted as an attempt on the part of the team to move towards its optimal position on a performance-profit frontier (Goddard, 2006). Dobson and Goddart (2001) compiled data on gross expenditures on transfers of English first division clubs from 1973 to 1999. Completing this database with the data on transfers published by Deloitte on a yearly basis, we can observe the historical evolution of the transfer fees paid by English first division clubs from 1973 to 2017 (Figure 24.1).

Before commenting on the evolution of this variable, and in order to widen the scope of the analysis, we can rely on the reports published by FIFA TMS. FIFA TMS has indeed provided extensive compiled data on international transfers since the service went live in 2008 and became mandatory in 2010. In particular, the publication of an annual global report on

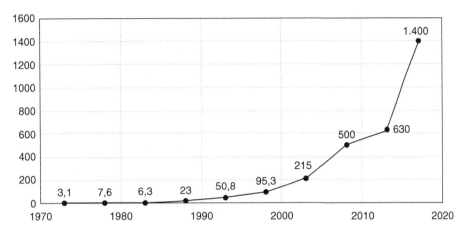

Figure 24.1 Transfer fees paid by English 1st Division clubs (in M£)
Source: Compiled data from Dobson and Goddart (2001) and Deloitte (2017).

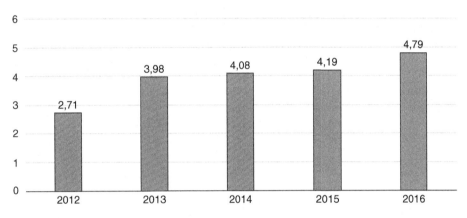

Figure 24.2 Total spending on transfer fees by year (billion $)
Source: FIFA TMS Global Transfer Market 2017.

international transfers helps in assessing the state of the market, providing both historical and geographical comparisons. However, it is worth noting that the following data only concern international transfers of players under running contracts.[1] As such, it does not take into account domestic transfers, which may account for 65 per cent of all transfers with fees (KEA and CDES, 2013). Moreover, the transfers of players under running contracts only represent 12 per cent of players' international movements (FIFA TMS, 2017) (Figure 24.2).

At $4.79 billion, spending on transfer fees has reached a new high. The 14.3 per cent increase from the previous year was the largest since 2013. Since October 2010, $22.67 billion was spent on transfer fees on international transfers. This global trend confirms the continuous growth observed in the English market. While the transfer market is increasing in value, we should also analyse its evolution in volume (Figure 24.3).

The number of international transfers completed each year has been increasing steadily, and a new record was also set in 2016 with 14,591 international transfers, 7.3 per cent more than in 2015.

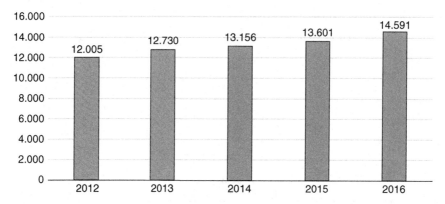

Figure 24.3 Total number of international transfers by year
Source: FIFA TMS Global Transfer Market 2017.

The segmentation of the labour market of professional football players

The labour market is often analysed through the prism of bargaining power that suppliers and demanders own. While clubs have long been mostly in charge, the removal of transfer fees and the potential severance notice consecutive to the Bosman case have given players signifi-cant bargaining power to increase their earnings (Magee and Sugden, 2002). As an illustration, comparing the 1996/1997–1998/1999 period with 1993/94–1995/96, Dobson and Goddard (2001) show increases in total team payrolls of 115 per cent and 79 per cent in tier 1 (English Premier League) and tier 2, respectively, of English football, based on Deloitte figures (Frick and Simmonds, 2014). Another illustration is given by the evolution of individual salaries in English football from 1961 to 2017 (Figure 24.4).

The average weekly wages earned by football players in the top division of English football rose from £20 in 1961 to £3,814 in 1996 and finally broke the £50,000 in 2017. We can espe-cially observe that the slope has clearly changed since the Bosman ruling in 1995. The increase in player salaries that has occurred since the 1995 Bosman ruling was facilitated by the removal of labour market restrictions but is largely a reflection of increased consumer demand to watch

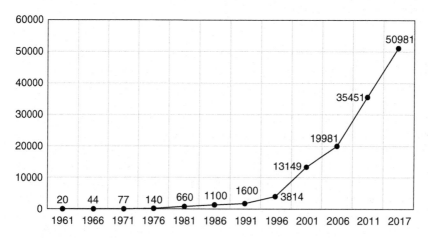

Figure 24.4 Average weekly wage in English football (in £)
Source: authors (compilation of data).

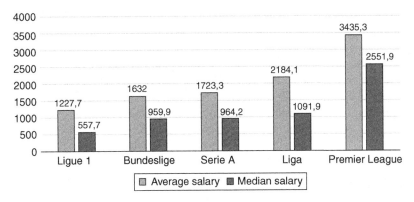

Figure 24.5 Average and median salaries in main European leagues in 2016/17 (in thousands of euros)

Source: Sporting Intelligence 2017 report, http://www.globalsportssalaries.com/

games either inside the stadium or in front of TV (or other media) (Frick and Simmonds, 2014). As soon as the players' salaries started to escalate, much of the surplus in fact shifted away from spectators towards the players (Dobson and Goddard, 1998).

Nevertheless, this bargaining power shift has to be put into perspective given the duality of the supply side of the labour market. Indeed, the "product" offered by the suppliers is not homogeneous. At the very least, we can clearly identify star players who belong to a separated segment of the market. Rosen (1981) provided a model that explains how small differences in the talent of manufacturers translate into much greater differences in their revenues. This is due to imperfect substitutability between labour suppliers. As a consequence, we observe that the deregulation offered, in fact, more market power to players on the top segment of the market (Magee, 2006). Indeed, the limited supply of superstar football players leads to an increased wage through monopsony rents (Garcia-del Barrio and Pujol, 2009). While superstars can extract bigger salaries thanks to the new structure of sport markets, average interchangeable players are indeed still dominated by clubs in the negotiation of playing contracts (Brocard and Cavagnac, 2017). Analysing the wages earned by football players in the Italian Serie A during the 2013/14 season, a group of superstars clearly emerges: the first 10 per cent earn at least €2 million (for a sample's average wage of €787,000), and the first 5 per cent earn at least five times more than the median earner (Carrieri et al., 2017). Additionally, the Gini index within the study sample is very high. The observed fact that average salaries are substantially higher than median salaries in most football leagues throughout the world and is further evidence of the concentration of revenues in the hands of a handful of star players (Figure 24.5).

While the supply side of the labour market is clearly segmented, we observe in parallel a large concentration of the talent in a handful of clubs and leagues (Goldblatt, 2007). In fact, the national markets that could accumulate the most resources from television and sponsorship could accumulate the most playing talent. As a consequence, since 2002, only 13 per cent of the quarterfinalist clubs in the UEFA Champions League do not come from one of the top five leagues (England, Germany, Spain, France, or Italy).

The generalised intermediation of the labour market

Another feature of the labour market of professional football players is the asymmetry of the information held by by both clubs and players. Indeed, players hold private information, which is not available without effort to clubs, such as their injury history or their expected salary. In parallel, players cannot easily access clubs' information such as their financial condition or their long-term projects. As a consequence, the labour market of football players is not the meeting place of suppliers and demanders. Indeed, the market is widely intermediated by a third party whose theoretical role is to solve these information issues by revealing private information helping to conclude deals (Brocard, 2012). This third party was long called "player agents" [see Chapter 11 in this handbook]. The first dedicated regulation was adopted by the FIFA Executive Committee in 1994, acknowledging the involvement of these actors in the allocation of talent among football clubs. The regulation has evolved ever since, and the latest framework lays down minimum standards and requirements as well as a registration system (Rossi, Semens, and Brocard, 2016). This new approach, based on the concept of "intermediaries," was aimed at overcoming the deficiencies of the previous regulatory system (FIFA, 2015).

One of the feature of the intermediation market in football is its concentration. Indeed, half of the 1,945 footballers of the main European leagues were represented by only the 83 top football agents and one-quarter were represented by only 24 of them (Poli and Rossi, 2012). Intermediaries are active during the negotiation of two different contracts more or less related to the labour market:

- They can first intervene in the negotiation of the transfer contract of a player and help either the buying or the selling club to conduct and conclude the deal. According to a TMS report, intermediaries were involved in 47.9 per cent of international transfers with fees in 2016. However, this evaluation seems to underestimate the real level of intermediation in the market, mainly because of the opacity which characterises the activity of intermediaries, and we claim that transfers with fees that do not involve an agent are in reality a small minority.
- Intermediaries are also largely involved in the negotiation of the labour contracts of players. Few empirical studies can support this claim. However, we note that in other sports leagues such as the French basketball top league, 86 per cent of the labour contracts signed between 2002 and 2010 involved an agent (Brocard and Cavagnac, 2017).

The level of intermediation is such that FIFA believed it relevant to ask their member associations to publish an annual report of the intermediaries' activity on their territory.

The intermediation has accompanied the increasing mobility of the football players.

Labour mobility: Acceleration and internationalisation

The historical analysis of the migration of professional football players reveals two main characteristics: the huge acceleration of the number of migrations and their internationalisation.

On the first point, Poli, Ravenel, and Besson (2017) showed the acceleration of migrations by establishing the percentage of new signings in squads. This indicator measures the percentage of players recruited by their employer club during the year of reference. In 2017, the share of new signings in the squads of clubs analysed (clubs belonging to 31 European first divisions) reached a new high with 44.8 per cent, which is more than eight points higher than in 2009. The most unstable league was the Portuguese Primeira Liga where new players represented a majority of the squad (57.6 per cent). Beyond this acceleration, the research produced by the Centre International d'Etudes du Sport (CIES) football observatory shows that the migration involves increasingly younger players. Thus, at an international level, the average age of expatriate football players reached a record low of 26.8 years in May 2017.

The growing internationalisation of the labour market is discussed in large detail in Szymanski and Kuypers (1999). Several quantitative studies illustrate this trend:

- The percentage of expatriate players in the 31 top division leagues of UEFA member associations has reached a new high in 2017 at 39.7 per cent, with a record in the Turkish Süper Lig (65.6 per cent). The evolution of the percentage of English players fielded in the English Premier League as well illustrates the growing internationalisation trend: from 55.37 per cent in 1999–2000 to 41.30 per cent in 2012–2013 (Buraimo et al., 2006).
- Poli et al. (2016) have shown that the percentage of expatriate football players has increased from 9.1 per cent to 46.7 per cent between 1985/86 and 2015/16 in the "big" five leagues.
- Poli et al. (2017), focusing on the nationality of migrant players, show that Brazil is the main country of origin of migrant players (with 1,202 expatriate football players), followed by France (781), and Argentina (753).

The impact of the combined acceleration and internationalisation of migrations has also been tackled in the literature. Economists have first tackled the question of the impact of the globalisation and opening up of the labour markets on the home country's economy, with mixed results. Milanovic (2005) empirically finds that it improved the competitiveness of national "small-country" teams, thanks to the skills and experience gained by their expatriate players. Frick (2009) finds divergent results. Another side of the literature focuses on the quality of the migrant players and indicates that the intensified competition on the labour markets resulted in higher productivity of subsequent market entrants (Jacobsen et al., 2013; Radoman, 2017). The current features of the labour market led to the development of actors' strategies that endanger football's integrity.

The financialisation of the labour market

The latest evolutions of the labour markets have had negative consequences, as the players have been converted into financial products. This can be illustrated by Third-Party Ownership practices and explained by the Resource-Based View (RBV) theory.

The player viewed as a resource

In recent years, in order to explain the uniqueness of firms, the academic focus has been set on the resources owned, controlled, and unavailable to others (Miller and Shamsie, 1996). The founding idea of viewing a firm as a bundle of resources was pioneered by Penrose in 1959. Penrose argued that it is the heterogeneity, not the homogeneity, of the productive services available from its resources that give each firm its unique character. The notion of firm's resources heterogeneity is the basis of the RBV of the firm. Resources are the foundation of the firm's long-term strategy because they are the primary source of profit for the firm (Amit and Schoemaker, 1993).

Football clubs turned their players into such strategic resources by developing the transfer market. Indeed, contrary to other professional sports (e.g., rugby, basketball), football clubs buy out players whose registration rights are owned by other clubs while their contract is still running. This leads to the payment of compensations whose amounts are negotiated over-the-counter. In this context, the conditions of clubs in financial and governance terms have created opportunities for intermediaries to become competitors with clubs in the market to extract economic rent. Some intermediaries actually managed to conquer these resources.

Indeed, when it comes to assessing resources owned and controlled by football agents, it becomes obvious that the main asset they own is the network of personal relationships they built over the time (Rossi, Semens, and Brocard, 2016). In fact, resources are either property based or knowledge based (Skilton, 2009).

Property-based resources are legally defined property rights held by the firm, and other firms are unable to appropriate theses rights unless they obtain the owner's permission. Property-based resources are protected by contracts, patents, or deeds of ownership. In contrast, knowledge-based resources such as technical expertise or good relationships with trade unions, are not protected by law, but they may still be difficult for other firms to access. It appears that the most important asset of football agents, i.e. their network, is in fact a knowledge-based resource which is not protected by contracts and which could fade and not be durable. Agents, recognising this weakness of their activity, sought solutions to develop their resources. In particular, players, as constituent of agents under the principal/agent framework are not strictly speaking resources of agents. Indeed, agents do not control players or, at least, they do not have legal means to do so, especially as many agents usually do not sign written contracts with players, which reduces even more the protection of their relationship with their profitable clients. However, agents' revenues are tightly linked to players they represent. As a first step, the strategy was then for agents to turn players into resources. In fact, according to the RBV theory, business strategy should be viewed as a quest for Ricardian rents, i.e., the returns to the resources, which confer a competitive advantage. Agents then needed to find a way to convert players into property-based resources, which could be protected and become a source of profit. Intermediaries, in fact, took advantage of the transfer system that was implemented by clubs under the same resource-based rationale. TPO derives directly from these actors' strategy. Indeed, through TPO agreements, players become the source of profit for the holders of economic rights. In other words, thanks to TPO, players become the resources that give actors a competitive advantage on the market.

"Third-Party-Ownership" as a pathological development of the labour market

The concept of TPO is based on the distinction between registration rights and economic rights. The former is understood to be the right of a club to register a player in the national association so that the player can be fielded for the club in different competitions organised by the national association. In this regard, jurisprudence of the Court of Arbitration for Sport (CAS) established that a player can only play for one club at a time; hence, registration rights "cannot be shared simultaneously among different clubs" (CASS, 2004). For both FIFA and CAS, registration rights have no economic value. In parallel, economic rights derive from the employment contract of the player. Indeed, the economic rights are considered as the net income resulting from the early termination of the employment agreement signed between the club and the football player. This includes any amount paid as compensation for the definitive or temporary transfer of the football player during the term of the employment agreement and are only valid and effective while the football player has a valid employment agreement with the club. TPO practices define the involvement of third parties in these players' economic rights.

TPO should be defined as "the entitlement to future transfer compensation of any party other than the two clubs transferring the registration of players from one to the other, with the exception of the players' training clubs as per the solidarity mechanism provided in the FIFA Regulation on the Status and Transfer of Players (RSTP)" (CDES and CIES, 2014). TPO arose as part of football clubs' need to finance the recruitment of sports talents and became more widespread in the 1980s and 1990s, with the development and the globalisation of football

(Brocard, 2015). Agents were at the core of the development of such practices, encouraging it for economic reasons and taking advantage of their intermediary role.

In France, FC Brest Armorique was the first club known to use TPO in 1986, when the club recruited two South-American players with the support of a pool of local investors united under the auspices of a company (Rossi, Semens, and Brocard, 2016). The French Professional League (LFP) sought to stop this practice in order to maintain the independence of its clubs and included a provision on TPO in its administrative regulations in the 1988–1989 season (Article 221). However, TPO practices only became globally prominent with the high-profile Tévez-Mascherano case in English Premier League.

TPO in England: The Tévez-Mascherano case

In the English Premier League (EPL), there was no express clause prohibiting TPO prior to a specific case involving Carlos Tévez and Javier Mascherano. The case had such a high profile that it had a significant impact on the regulations of players' transfers in the English football, i.e., a ban of TPO.

The facts

Carlos Tévez and Javier Mascherano, two Argentinian players, played for English club West Ham United in 2006. They were signed by West Ham from Brazilian club Corinthians.

The players' economic rights were held by two "third-parties," Media Sport Investments (MSI) and Just Sports, who contractually had exclusive power to decide on their transfer movements. The unusual contractual relationship between both players and the club came to light and an investigation was launched by the EPL. The players' TPC indeed contained a clause giving exclusive power to the third-party owners, MSI and Just Sports, to facilitate their transfers. West Ham United did not have a veto over this right and such a stipulation breached an EPL rule as it meant that outside parties had material influence over the decision-making of West Ham United.

On 27 April 2007, the club acknowledged having breached Rule B.13 of the EPL's rules[2] by failing to act with the "utmost good faith" in not disclosing the full nature of the deals. Moreover, the club was found to have breached Rule V.20[3] by entering into a contractual agreement with a third party who would have the right to exercise control over decisions concerning the future transfer and/or the termination of their contracts. West Ham United failed to disclose these details to the EPL, and so breached the rule, the purpose of which was to ensure that an outside party does not have the ability to influence team selection and potentially the outcome of a match. West Ham United received a fine of £5.5 million.

The EPL decided that from the beginning of the 2008/09 season an outright ban on TPO was required. While TPO practices have been banned in several leagues, they have thrived in other regions such as South-America or Southern Europe (Portugal, Spain, etc.). According to a study commissioned by FIFA, in 2013–2014, TPO's annual economic weight amounted to US$359.52 million, which represented 9.68 per cent of the global amount of transfer compensation on international transfers amounting to US$3.714 billion.

Via the circular n°1464 published in December 2014, FIFA whistled the end of TPO practices:

> No club or player shall enter into an agreement with a third party whereby a third party is being entitled to participate, either in full or in part, in compensation payable in relation to the future transfer of a player from one club to another, or is being assigned any rights in relation to a future transfer or transfer compensation.

In fact, FIFA acknowledges the fact that TPO could jeopardise football's governance, challenge the mechanisms of the transfer system, mitigate clubs' independence, reduce players' freedom of movement, and endanger football competitions' integrity.

The Neymar's case is an illustration of some of these risks. In 2013, Neymar transferred from Santos FC to FC Barcelona. The Brazilian club Santos FC only owned 55 per cent of the player's economic rights as the club had previously sold 45 per cent of Neymar's rights to external investors. The details of the transfer agreement are in question. FC Barcelona officially paid €57 million for Neymar – €17.1 million to his club Santos and €40 million to a company owned by the player's father called N&N. In fact, however, it is understood that as many as 12 contracts were exchanged. The Catalans had invested €86.2 million in the Brazilian forward, not to mention wages. The €86.2 million can be broken down as follows: €57.1 million for the transfer itself (of which €40 million went to N&N), €10 million as a signing-on fee, €2.7 million in commission to Neymar's father for the negotiation of the deal, €4 million to find new commercial partners for the club in Brazil, €2.5 million for Neymar's foundation, and €9.9 million in scouting and collaborative deals with Santos. This situation led to two separate cases, one carried out by the Spanish justice system for potential tax abuses, the other initiated by one of the Brazilian third-party involved in the player's economic rights.

The Neymar case in Brazil

When the deal is concluded, a third-party called DIS Group owns 40 per cent of the player's economic rights which entitles the group to 40 per cent of the total amount paid by the buying club to the selling club. In this transaction, DIS was given 40 per cent of the €17 million Santos received, which was considered by Santos as the amount that should be distributed among investors. But the investment company was claiming they were entitled to 40 per cent of the full €57 million which is the total amount paid in transfer fees for the player (not to mention the additional contracts). Interestingly enough, the company is also complaining on the grounds that it was excluded from the negotiations. "Real Madrid's offer was much better than Barca's, but DIS was never called to any of the negotiations with Madrid or Barca. The club did it all behind our backs," DIS representative Roberto Moreno said.[4]

This case is illustrative of the loss of independence of the club in its transfer strategy and the risk of tax abuses tied to transfer practices. It also questions the calculation of the transfer fee, which could be artificially reduced due to TPO practices while being the basis of the solidarity and training compensations (Brocard, 2016).

Conclusion

A historical analysis of this labour market shows its high sensitivity to the level of dedicated regulation. In the past 20 years, a wide variety of deregulation decisions were made, either by the sports world itself or by national or international public regulators, which substantially impacted how the market operates. Among the main consequences are the large increase in international mobility of players and the talent concentration. This deregulation trend also enabled some actors with sole-financial profitability objectives to get involved in the transfer market.

For these reasons, FIFPro (the international players' union), following the recommendations of a study conducted by the sports economist Professor Stefan Szymanski, filed in 2015 a legal action against FIFA, challenging the global transfer market system governed by FIFA's regulations as being anti-competitive, unjustified, and illegal. Even if FIFPro decided to drop the complaint in November 2017 for parallel political reasons, the original justifications of the complaint still apply. These elements all encourage the implementation of stricter regulations aimed at ensuring a proper functioning of the labour market of professional football players in order not to jeopardise the two main features of professional sports: the integrity and the uncertainty of sports competitions.

Notes

1 FIFA TMS also provides to national associations an online platform called DTMS dedicated to domestic transfers: https://www.fifatms.com/dtms/
2 Premier league handbook season 2007/08 – Rules – section B – The League "In all matters and transaction relating to the League each club shall behave toward each other club and the league with the utmost good faith."
3 "No Club shall enter into a contract which enables any other party to that contract to acquire the ability materially to influence its policies or the performance of its teams in League Matches or in any of the competitions set out in Rule E.10."
4 http://www.goal.com/en/news/12/spanish-football/2014/01/31/4585632/barcelona-to-face-neymar-court-case-in-brazil-lawyer-says

References

Amit, R. and Schoemaker, P. (1993) Strategic assets and organizational rent. *Strategic Management Journal*, 14, 33–46.

Brocard, J.F. (2012) *L'intermédiation du marché du travail des sportifs professionnels*. PhD dissertation. University of Limoges.

Brocard, J.F (2015) Transferts de joueurs et "third party ownership". *Reflets et perspectives de la vie économique*, 3, 57–69.

Brocard, J.F. (2016) Fallait-il interdire le TPO? *Jurisport*, 160.

Brocard, J.F and Cavagnac, M. (2017) Who should pay the sports agent's commission? An economic analysis of setting the legal rules in the regulation of matchmakers. *International Journal of Sport Finance*. 12. 65–88.

Buraimo, B., Simmons, R., and Szymanski, S. (2006) English football. *Journal of Sports Economics*, 7, 29–46.

Buraimo, B., Frick, B., Hickfang, M., and Simmons, R. (2015) The economics of long-term contracts in the footballers' labour market. *Scottish Journal of Political Economy*, 62, 8–24.

Carmichael, F., Rossi, G., and Simmons, R. (2012) *Contract Duration and Player Performance in Italian Football*. Work, Pensions and Labour Economics Study Group Conference, University of Sheffield, Sheffield, UK.

Carrieri, V., Principe, F., and Raitano, M. (2017) *What makes you "super-rich"? New evidence from an analysis of football players' earnings*. Working paper, Ruhr Economic Papers 681.

Dobson, S. and Goddard, J.A. (1998) Performance and revenue in professional league football: evidence from Granger causality tests. *Applied Economics*, 30–12, 1641–1651.

Dobson, S. and Goddard, J. (2001) *The Economics of Football*. Cambridge: Cambridge University Press.

Doeringer, P.B. and Piore M.J. (1971) *Internal Labor Markets and Manpower Analysis.* Lexington, Massachusetts: Health Lexington Books.

Feess, E., Frick, B., and Mühlheußer G. (2007) *Contract Duration and Player Performance: Empirical Evidence from German Soccer.* Faculty of Management and Economics, Witten/Herdecke University, Witten, Mimeo.

Feess, E. and Muehlheusser, G. (2003) Transfer fee regulations in European football. *European Economic Review*, 47, 645–658.

Frick, B. (2009) Globalization and factor mobility: the impact of the Bosman ruling on player migration in professional soccer. *Journal of Sports Economics*, 10, 88–106.

Frick, B. (2011) Performance, salaries and contract length: empirical evidence from German soccer. *International Journal of Sport Finance*, 6, 87–118.

Frick, B. and Simmonds, R. (2014) The Footballers' Labour Market after the Bosman Ruling. In: J. Goddart (ed.). *Handbook on the Economics of Professional Football.* Cheltenham. UK: Edward Elgar.

Garcia-del Barrio, P. and Pujol, F. (2009) The rationality of under-employing the best performing soccer players. *Labour*, 23, 397–419.

Goddard, J. (2006) The economics of soccer. In: W. Andreff (ed.). *Handbook of Sports Economics.* Cheltenham, UK Edward Elgar.

Goldblatt, D. (2007) *The Ball is Round: A Global History of Football.* London: Penguin.

Jacobsen, K.H., Landais, C., and Saez, E. (2013) Taxation and international migration of superstars: evidence from the European football market. *American Economic Review*, 103, 1892–1924.

KEA and CDES (2013) *The Economic and Legal Aspects of Transfers of Players.* Study commissioned by the European Commission. [online] Retrieved from: http://ec.europa.eu/assets/eac/sport/library/documents/cons-study-transfers-final-rpt.pdf

Kesenne, S. (1997) L'affaire Bosman et l'économie du sport professionnel. *Revue du marché unique europeéen*, 1.

Kesenne, S. (2006) The Bosman case and European football. In: W. Andreff (ed.). *Handbook of Sports Economics.* Cheltenham, UK: Edward Elgar.

Lavoie, M. (2000) La proposition d'invariance dans un monde où les équipes maximisent la performance sportive. Special issue. *Reflets et Perspectives de la vie économique.*

Lanfranchi, P. and Wahl, A. (1998) La professionnalisation du football en France (1920–1939). *Modern & Contemporary France*, 6(3), 313–325.

Magee, J. and Sugden, J. (2002) The world at their feet: professional football and international labor migration. *Journal of Sport and Social Issues*, 26(4), 421–443.

Magee, J. (2006) When is a contract more than a contract? Professional football contracts and the pendulum of power. *The Entertainment and Sports Law Journal*, 4.

Milanovic, B. (2005) Globalization and goals: does soccer show the way? *Review of International Political Economy*, 12, 829–850.

Miller, D. and Shamsie, J. (1996) The resource-based view of the firm in two environments: the Hollywood firm studios from 1936 to 1965. *Academy of Management Journal*, 39, 519–543.

Morrow, S. (1999) *The New Business of Football: Accountability and Finance in Football.* Basingstoke, UK: Palgrave Macmillan.

Penrose, E.T. (1959) *The Theory of the Growth of the Firm.* New York: John Wiley.

Poli G., Semens A. and Brocard J.F. (2016) *Sports Agents and Labour Markets. Evidence from World Football.* London: Routledge.

Poli, R. and Rossi, G. (2012) *Football Agents in the Biggest Five European Football Markets. An Empirical Research Report.* Neuchâtel: CIES.

Poli, R., Besson, R., and Ravenel, L. (2016) *The Fielding of Young Footballers in Europe.* (No. 13). Neuchâtel: CIES.

Poli, R., Besson, R., and Ravenel, L. (2017) *World Expatriate Footballers.* (No. 25). Neuchâtel: CIES.

Radoman, M. (2017) Labor market implications of institutional changes in European football: the Bosman Ruling and its effect on productivity and career duration of players. *Journal of Sports Economics*, 18, 651–672.

Rosen, S. (1981) The economics of superstars. *The American Economic Review*, 71(5), 845–858.

Rossi, G. (2012) Contract duration and football player performance: the empirical evidence of serie a. In: C. Anagnostopoulos (ed.), *Contextualising Research in Sport: An International Perspective.* Athens, Atiner.

Skilton, P. (2009) Knowledge based resources, property based resources and supplier bargaining power in Hollywood motion picture projects. *Journal of Business Research*, 62, 834–840.

Sloane, P. J. (1969) The labour market in professional football. *British Journal of Industrial Relations*, 7(2), 181–199.

Szymanski, S. (2000) A market test for discrimination in the English professional soccer leagues. *Journal of Political Economy*, 108, 590–603.

Szymanski, S. and Kuypers, T. (1999) *Winners and Losers: The Business Strategy of Football*. Viking, London.

25

Value management in football

A framework to develop and analyse competitive advantage

Harald Dolles and Sten Söderman

Introduction: Management challenges in football

Why football clubs win or lose and make profits or losses are perhaps the central questions in contemporary football management research. The causes of a club's success or failure are inextricably tied to issues such as why clubs differ, how they perform on and off the pitch, and how they choose strategies and manage to enhance performance on the pitch and within the club's organisation. Given recent developments in the football industry, it has also become increasingly apparent that any quest for the reasons behind a club's success must also acknowledge the reality of international competition, the difference in governance structures of the game and the striking differences in the financial performance of clubs in different nations (see, for example, Gammelsæter and Senaux, 2011; Hamil and Chadwick, 2010; Jones and Bridge, 2017).

Yet, the question of why clubs win or lose raises a broader question. Competitive advantage in the football business cannot be examined independently from clubs' competitive scope built on creating value, with their products realised by the customer. The purpose of this chapter is, therefore, to analyse value management in football. This will be based on the introduction of a "network of value captures" framework encompassing a football club's competitive scope, defined as a number of value captures (the array of product offerings and different customer groups served), the strategic vision and the extent of coordinated strategy (see Dolles and Söderman, 2013a, 2011b, 2008 for theoretical development). A framework that has proven its relevance is being used to analyse the specific features of the Japanese professional football league (Dolles and Söderman, 2013b, 2011a, 2011b), the strategic positioning and value creation with stakeholders for the advancement of baseball (Batty, 2017), and the innovative development of floorball as a sport (Gabrielsson and Dolles, 2017); it is also being used in recent empirical research produced by the European Club Association (Jarosz, Kornakov, and Söderman, 2015).

Williams (2012) noted that sport, and professional sport leagues in particular, are unique due to the fact that individual teams, while seeking a dominant position in a winner-takes-all scenario, require competitors to provide opposition, entertainment and commercial possibilities. As such, professional sport can be a lucrative business, presenting many opportunities for revenue generation (Madichie, 2009). However, generating revenue often involves a rise in costs, frequently in the form of player recruitment and salaries for professional teams, and increasing pressure to deliver results quickly (Flint, Plumley, and Wilson, 2016). Competitive advantage for football clubs is achieved by the scope and choice of their value-capturing activities, defined as the relationship between value captures, so careful and informed selection of these activities is therefore an important undertaking for professional football club management.

The framework and its three components – eight value offerings, six customer categories, and management's tactics and strategies – will be introduced in the following section. Next, current developments and practices within the football industry will be highlighted to showcase the framework's practical relevance. Then, conclusions will be presented on how the network of value captures could be applied in a teaching context and for future research.

The network of value captures in football club management

Value, and the notion of value as something co-created, are fundamental concepts within contemporary marketing research (Pongsakornrungsilp and Schroeder, 2009). Existing literature has focused predominantly on conceptualisations of value and value-creating processes (see, for example, Grönroos, 2011; Normann and Ramírez, 1993; Prahalad and Ramaswamy, 2004; Vargo and Lusch, 2004) and on how consumers integrate resources to create value in their consumption practices (see, for example, Arnould, Price, and Malshe, 2006; Schau, Muniz Jr., and Arnould, 2009). Because of a proliferation of products and competitors, many companies are being forced to innovate beyond tangible products and commoditised services to create more value for their customers. To differentiate their offers, they are creating and managing customer experiences (Kotler and Armstrong, 2010). Pine II and Gilmore (1999) consider those experiences to be offerings that are distinct from conventional services; in their view, customer experience matters more than the economic experience. If people are able to buy goods and services at the lowest possible prices, they will seek to take their hard-earned money – and time – and spend it on more engaging, more memorable, and more highly valued experiences (Pine II, 2011). As a consequence, experiences must provide a memorable offering that remains with the consumer for a long time, but in order to achieve this, consumers must be drawn into the offering such that a sensation is felt. To feel that sensation, the consumer must participate actively. This requires highly skilled actors who can dynamically personalise each event according to the needs, responses, and behavioural traits of the consumer. Vargo and Lusch (2004) label this as a new service-dominant logic, supporting the customers' role as co-creators of our economies. Woratschek, Horbel, and Popp (2014) take it a step further, considering it the basis for relevant future research in sport management by encouraging practitioners to rethink their strategies by applying a different logic.

We might argue that the nature of football and its dependency on uncertainty complicates the analysis. Every individual sports consumer has their own thoughts, experiences, and expectations of the game or events at the match – a "something else" associated with the football experience – but there are two particular elements to consider: first, sports consumers might want different product offerings at different times under different circumstances; second, professional team sports no longer offer a single product, service, or entertainment, something that could be seen as the competitive scope of professional clubs and that will become obvious later in the chapter.

Therefore, it is the management's task to evaluate, select, bundle and utilise the club's resources (value captures). Our understanding of value captures is based on Barney's (1991) conceptualisation of resources and sustained competitive advantage. Dolles and Söderman (2011a) support this view by stating that a football club's resources can only be a source of competitive advantage when they are valuable and recognised by the customer. Resources are considered to be value captures when they enable a football club to implement strategies (value-capturing activities) that improve its efficiency and effectiveness. Valuable football club resources common to a large number of competing clubs cannot be sources of sustained competitive advantage unless clubs are differentiated by them. A football club only enjoys a competitive advantage when it implements a unique value-creating strategy combining bundles of valuable club resources (value captures) recognised and accepted by the customer (by the customer's groups).

To advance this notion, we need to understand: (1) the distinctive products and features a football club might possess; (2) the different customers or customer groups relevant for a football club; and (3) the business process, strategic vision and intent.

What is the product of a football club?

Football clubs are pluralistic organisations operating in a complex environment of many constituents (Gammelsæter, 2010) [see also Chapter 5 in this handbook]. Football's main output is a set of services surrounding a match. This set of services is provided jointly by the players of two teams and creates values for the constituents. These values are influenced by the performance of the teams during the match, win or lose. The main value created is based on the interest of most stakeholders in football as a sport. Stakeholder values are also influenced by the performance of the team over the whole season, which is defined as league performance, for example winning as many matches as possible to achieve a top position in the national league or to qualify for an international competition. A key strategic goal for a football club, then, is related to sporting performance, which is divided into match and league performance. Other values created for the stakeholders are social, originating from the interest of members, e.g., belonging to a specific group such as a fan club. The football club thus offers not one single product, service or entertainment. We can consider the following possible "offerings," termed "value captures": (1.A) team; (1.B) sporting competitions; (1.C) club; (1.D) players; (1.E) football services; (1.F) event, facilities, and arena; (1.G) merchandise; and (1.H) other commercial activities. As indicated by arrows in Figure 25.1, all value offerings are interlinked and might also be considered as bundles of a club's value captures.

Value capture 1.A: team. Various models have been proposed and explored in the literature on organisational behaviour and personnel psychology to understand work-team effectiveness in various industry settings (i.e., Campion et al., 1993). In a team sport setting such as football, it is evident that 11 skilled players do not necessarily comprise a winning team. A team with superior physical ability alone cannot beat an opponent that has good technique and a carefully planned strategy. Furthermore, without adequate training and performance techniques, even the most well-intentioned teams fail to win the match.

Value capture 1.B: sporting competitions. Football as a team sport also requires coordination amongst the contesting teams, because the game involves at least two teams. Revising the arguments for the necessary institutional features of a league (Noll, 2003a, 2003b; Smith and Westerbeek, 2004), we prefer to change perspective and to focus on the following elements of sporting competitions: (1) Distribution: How to schedule matches or tournaments; (2) Hierarchy: What are the structural pathways for players and teams to progress and regress?; (3) Multiplicity: How many leagues should be at the same level of hierarchy?; (4) Membership: What are the conditions under which a team enters and exits a league?; (5) Governance: How are league rules decided and enforced and how is the economic behaviour of its members managed?; (6) Labour: What is the structure of the transfer market and how is the level of compensation for players, coaches, and managers determined?

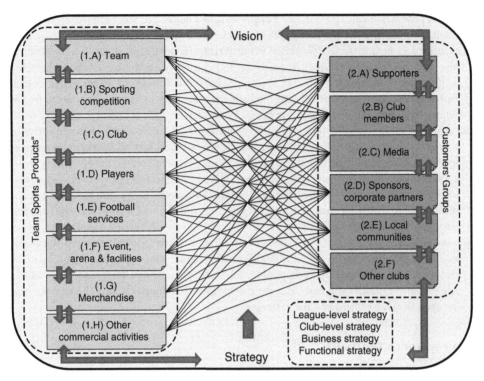

Figure 25.1 The network of value captures (Dolles and Söderman, 2013a, p. 372)

Value capture 1.C: club. Hosting a winning team has a dual meaning for professional sports organisations. Not only must the players on the sporting team be able to give their utmost to the cause of winning, but the financial and organisational structure behind it must also work closely to ensure that its business goals will be achieved (thus referring to the contextual factors of team effectiveness and the necessary prerequisites for league membership – see 1.A and 1.B).

Value capture 1.D: players. Players, and their development, are of prime concern to football managers. Football clubs send out their scouts to discover young players in the region and to sign contracts with them, as some of them might later find their way to a professional team. Driven by the rise in transfer fees of players, and the increase in value of young players, professional football clubs successfully operate youth academies, even going beyond their home region and establishing off-shore collaborations with partners in locations of strategic importance. Team members are the main service providers, creating both sporting and social values. Their main interest is to perform well in matches or in the league as a whole. There is, however, also a long-term self-interest to promote their individual careers, so matches also function as a display window for the international transfer market. Agents are often hired by players to help them promote this interest; however, agents are also characterised by players as opportunistic, because the players felt they were being treated first and foremost as a commodity (Egilsson and Dolles, 2017).

Value capture 1.E: football services. Football services cover three different areas. First, the idea of a one-stop shop for all club-related services and merchandising products (see 1.G). Second, the establishment of football youth academies as a service to recruit and retain talented young players (see also 1.D and 1.F). Third, specialised tailored services offered as a development programme for other football clubs, coaches, and players all over the world.

Value capture 1.F: event, arena, and facilities. A football match is intangible, short-lived, unpredictable, and subjective in nature. It is produced and consumed by the spectators in the arena at the same time, mostly with a strong emotional commitment. In recent years, football matches have been transformed into media events attracting millions of spectators, few of whom have the chance to watch the match in the arena.

Value capture 1.G: merchandise. In many cases, one of the key ingredients of the business of football is its local character, despite participation in a global football market; this presents special challenges to marketing the brand. Put simply, the brand represents everything about a football club, from the team to its players, and is communicated by the name and related identifiers (football merchandise). Football merchandise means goods held for resale but not manufactured by the football club, for example, flags and banners, scarves and caps, training gear, jerseys, and fleeces, etc.

Value capture 1.H: other commercial activities. Chadwick and Clowes (1998) explored the brand extension strategies of Premier League football clubs by examining the factors that led clubs to consider extending their product lines and their brands. They concluded as the key consideration for both clubs and their supporters that there is a clear and obvious link between the club's brand and the extension.

Who consumes football?

The market is paramount. Theodore Levitt's (1972) classic expression, that business is how to get and keep a customer, shows the importance of market orientation. Fans and spectators are often described as the "lifeblood" of the sports business. Without fans, there would be no live audience in the stadia, no recipients for the media, no target group for sponsors, and, therefore, no income for professional sporting organisations. Hence, fans and spectators are not only a primary customer group for sports entities, but also their most important one [see also Chapter 19 in this handbook].

Why do supporters choose one team over another? Cost is certainly not the sole argument in the football business for fans, whereas fun, excitement, skilled players, and regional embeddedness might all be good reasons for supporting a team. The bottom line may be that the corporate culture of the football club, as the underlying culture, helps to determine the value that consumers place on the football club; however, we need to recognise that every customer integrates multiple markets. Consumers want different offerings at different times under different circumstances. Consequently, the variety of offerings creates a broader consumer approach in football by addressing: (2.A) spectators and supporters (fan base); (2.B) club members (club membership); (2.C) media; (2.D) sponsors and corporate partners; (2.E) local communities; and (2.F) other clubs. As indicated by the arrows in Figure 25.1, all customer groups are interlinked and can be considered as bundles of a club's value captures.

Value capture 2.A: supporters. When it comes to "sales" in the football business, the supporters, with regard to ticket sales and merchandising, attract the main attention. Fan motivation and behaviour vary depending upon the type of fan. For our purposes, we adopt a slightly different classification by introducing the "psychic distance" dimension, defined as factors that make it difficult to understand the local embeddedness of a club: local fans versus international fans. The fans element is mainly organised into fan clubs, defined as separate social groups. A clique of "ultras" or hooligans is common within this constituent. Many fans are members, while others are outsiders. Besides the football interest, fans also have a longer-term interest in the fortunes of the club: the existence of the club itself, as a unit to which they want to belong, and with which they identify. Spectators do not take an active interest in the club, instead being passive members or watching games from the sidelines, in the stadium, or on TV. They have a short-term interest in the performance of the club, i.e., match and league performance.

Value capture 2.B: club members. The football club, as host of their teams, wants to have a sustainable stock of members, which requires an iterative approach between the product and the customer. Such approaches are covered in the vast literature on interactive marketing (Adler et al., 1996) and on relationship marketing (Bühler and Nufer, 2010; Gummesson, 2002). These are the original constituent by being the main carrier of the football interest, having a long-term interest in the fortunes of the club and being interested mainly in match and league performance.

Value capture 2.C: media. With regard to income in professional football, the media is the other main customer – or the main sales channel. A critical stakeholder, media's function is mainly for distribution of matches and communication, with interests in audience and readership numbers. The importance of football for the media business can be seen in the increasing amounts of money paid for broadcast rights to the national league or for events like the FIFA World Cup, as well as the growth in the number of sports-oriented broadcasting networks (Gratton and Solberg, 2007). Rowe (1996, 2000) notes that sport and TV have become mutually and internationally indispensable.

Value capture 2.D: sponsors and corporate partners. Football is a natural area for protection as it carries very strong images, has a mass international audience and appeals to all classes (Ferrand and Pages, 1996; Demir and Söderman, 2015). Each sponsored event is capable of reaching differently defined audiences (Meenaghan and Shipley, 1999) and thus appeals to different sponsors. Corporate partners include companies with sponsorship in kind (offering, for example, the different services needed for match-day events or to travel to away matches) and equipment manufacturers and retailers (see Gabrielsson and Dolles, 2017).

Value capture 2.E: local communities. The relationship between football clubs and their communities has been the subject of recent debate and discussion in political circles and in academic research (Dolles et al., 2016; Preuss, Könecke, and Schütte, 2010, 2012). The importance of the local community varies, usually being highest for clubs organised as public non-profit associations. For example, these clubs normally cannot afford to build their own stadium, which instead is owned by the local community, as are most facilities used by the club. The community, on the other hand, has a long-term interest in the survival of the club, since it contributes to a number of social public needs and helps to promote the community. Morrow (1999) argues that a football club's community comprises two dimensions: "first, a direct community of supporters and, second, a wider notion encompassing people and groups who can be affected either directly or indirectly by the existence and operation of a football club within a particular space, usually geographical" (Morrow and Hamil, 2003, p. 1–2).

Value capture 2.F: other football clubs. Other football clubs are of prime importance when it comes to player transfers, as well as lending players, as mentioned in the discussion of value capture (1.D). Additionally, by introducing football services as a value capture (1.E), we might also consider other football clubs – amateur as well as professional clubs; national as well as international – as potential recipients of football services. At the regional level too, clubs collaborate on player development in youth teams by providing football services in exchange.

Vision and strategy

The highest- and broadest-level business objective is the *vision of the club*. This is a statement of broad aspiration, as it deals with where the club hopes to be in the future. This is not about winning the next game; it is the attempt by club management to define where it expects the club to be at a later point in time – to win the championship; to stay in the league; to make profit; or to go international. With the exception of merchandising, the football business lacks the option of producing and storing inventory for future sale, as the main characteristic of football is its ambiguity and the uncertainty of the outcome of a game.

In order to reach the goals pertaining to the vision of where the club should be in the future, what kind of *strategies* should be applied? Strategies can be articulated for different activities within the club, where the lowest level of aggregation is one specific task, and the highest level of aggregation encompasses all activities within the club. A logical extension of this distinction is the league-level strategy.

Value management in football

Having combined the eight "offerings" with the six groups of "customers," 48 relations appear, showing the competitive scope of a football club. Each of these relations constitutes a value-capturing activity through which a football club's management can create value and competitive advantage. Value capture 1.G meets value capture 2.A when "merchandise products" are sold to "supporters." The "players" (1.D) are of interest to "sponsors and corporate partners" (2.D), and different "media" channels (2.C) are used to transmit promotional messages to local and or international fans (2.A). Good performance of the "team" (1.A) during the match (1.B) leads to enhanced interest by "other clubs" (2.F) on individual "players" (1.D), "media" (2.C), and potential "sponsors or corporate partners" (2.D). Thus, a mixture of such relations constitutes a network of value captures for the football industry, observing that not all value-capturing activities are equally important in every given situation. We also emphasise that the eight "offerings" and the six "customer groups" are interconnected. This broadens the choice of strategic options and allows strategies of bundling value captures (e.g., when "players" (1.D), the "team" (1.A), and the "club" (1.C) are presented to the "media" (2.C) or to "sponsors and corporate partners" (2.D).

Applying the framework to analyse the football industry

Value management is of increasing importance for football managers and marketers, given the increased competition from other sports for the limited time and resources of supporters, sponsors, and local communities. The "network of value captures" offers a framework in which to analyse the competitive positioning of different football clubs in the market and shows how revenues are generated from different customer groups. By looking back a few decades, for example, it becomes clear how income from ticketing (match-day income) has diversified. For example, Manchester United, the leading European club in terms of match-day revenues (total €114 million in 2016), generates 43 per cent of its income from ticket sales from the nine per cent of top-price seats. We can also identify the significance of income from sponsorship and broadcasting: €268 million and €140 million respectively (Jones and Bridge, 2016). By exploring the value-creation process, this framework offers a unique perspective on the value co-creation process, not only from the club's perspective, but also from the customer's.

Two club stories highlight value capturing (Jarosz, Kornakov, and Söderman, 2015):

1   How does KRC Genk in Belgium engage with its community (2.E)?
     Strong participation of community on match day operation, with 650 volunteers taking part (1.B and 2.E). Homeless projects support with the use of first team stars (1.D and 2.E). Selling seats with charity contribution included in the increased price (1.F and 2.A, 2.E).

2   What social and educational projects can a club pursue? (2.E)
     Real Madrid, through the Real Madrid Foundation, works in 67 countries and develops 3,000 social sports schools for kids of exclusion. With the aim of contributing to the human development of unprivileged children and youngsters aged from six to 17 (children at risk of school drop-out with family issues, behavioural problems because of being exposed to crime or drugs, disabilities, etc.), the Real Madrid Foundation tries to encourage them through regular sports participation (1.E, 1.F and 2.E).

Conclusions and implications for further research

Several ways of analysing why clubs differ have been presented in this chapter, but there is still a lot of development work to do in professional football club management. Here, we offer 13 key areas for future research:

1   Buy or train? In order to create a good player (1.D) for a team (1.A) there is a need to scout, recruit and train. The main human resource management question for the club is whether to buy from other clubs (2.F), or to train and develop, a player by using own facilities (1.F).
2   Management structure. Another urgent task is to manage a whole set of possible products and offerings. The commercialisation of the game requires management structures and techniques to manage the products and offerings at a corporate level within the limitations of current and potential financial resources (e.g., 1.G to a market 2.C and 2.D).
3   Multilevel analysis. A further application of the value-capture framework could be carried out on different levels of the football industry by, for example, comparing value capturing activities of lower leagues with top leagues, and national leagues with the Champions League (e.g., 1.B to 1.B and strategy).
4   Ownership. Another interesting aspect is how the framework can be applied within a multiple club ownership setting, with international investors and companies such as Red Bull buying clubs around the world (e.g., 1.C to 2.D and 2.F).
5   Leadership transition. How do clubs manage the process of change (i.e., football managers' transitions, succession planning and how these processes impact the club performance) (e.g., 1.C to 1.D and 2.F)?
6   Decision-making. What is the relationship between club performance outcome (i.e., winning trophies) and managerial power to make decisions on the trading and transfer of players (e.g., vision/strategy and 1.C to 1.D)?
7   Learning. What are the mechanisms to capture know-how when players move to different clubs (e.g., 1.D to 2.F)?
8   Motivation. Does the movement of players and managers between clubs influence club spirit and overall match performance (e.g., 1.D and 2.F to 1.B)?
9   Management under foreign ownership. Comparative studies of different leagues would reveal any significant differences in management structure in clubs with foreign owners in, for example, the English Premier League (Russian owners of Chelsea FC, Middle Eastern owners of Manchester City FC and US owners of Manchester United FC) (e.g., 1.H to 2.D).

10 Performance management systems. Specifically, how are bonuses and other old "command and control" metrics employed in these clubs (e.g. Strategy and 2.B to 1.C and 1.B)?

11 Consumer identification. There are many types of consumers and they are often difficult to identify. The nature of football, or professional team sport in general, and its dependency on uncertainty complicates the analysis. Every sports consumer has their own thoughts, experiences and expectations of the game or events on match day (e.g., 2.A, 2.B, 2.C, 2.D to 1.A, 1.B, 1.F).

12 Qualitative analysis. It would also be beneficial for future research to consider more qualitative factors as part of any analysis, such as fans' perceptions of the manager, the relationship between manager and owner, and the structure of the management team at boardroom level. While such variables are understandably difficult to measure, they may have a direct or indirect impact on the decision taken to change a manager and are thus important when considering a more holistic approach to investigating this field of study (e.g., 2.B and 2.D to 1.A and 1.C).

13 International transfers. Another research challenge concerns the functioning of the international transfer market and the implications for the future, for example how to conceive an overarching governance system for what Beech and Chadwick call "post commercialization" (2013, p. 8), defined as the transition of domestic transfer markets into international/foreign transfer markets. These are currently dominated by the top five European leagues (Poli, Ravenel, and Besson, 2017) in general and the English Premier League in particular (e.g., 1.B to 1.D, 1.E, 1.G and 1.H).

References

Adler, P.S., Mandelbaum, A., Nguyen, U., and Schwerer, E. (1996) Getting the most out of your product development process. *Harvard Business Review*, 74(2), 134–152.

Arnould, E.J., Price, L.L., and Malshe, A. (2006) Toward a cultural resource-based theory of the customer. In: S. Vargo and R. Lusch (eds.), *The Service-Dominant Logic of Marketing: Dialog, Debate and Directions* (pp. 320–333). Armonk, NY: ME Sharpe.

Barney, J. (1991) Firm resources and sustained competitive advantage. *Journal of Management*, 17(1), 99–120.

Batty, R. J. (2017) Loading up the bases: a case study of baseball New Zealand in the lead up to the 2020 Olympics. In: P. Sotiriadou (eds.), *Places, Events and Sport: 'Going for Gold'* (p. 53). Proceedings of the 23rd Annual SMAANZ Conference, Griffith University, Gold Coast.

Beech G. J. and Chadwick S. (2013) *The Business of Sport Management*, Revised version. Harlow: Prentice Hall.

Bühler, A. and Nufer, G. (2010) *Relationship Marketing in Sports*. Oxford: Butterworth-Heinemann.

Campion, M.A., Medsker, G.J., and Higgs, A.C. (1993) Relations between work team characteristics and effectiveness: Implications for designing effective work groups. *Personnel Psychology*, 46(4), 823–850.

Chadwick, S. and Clowes, J. (1998) The use of extension strategies by clubs in the English Football Premier League. *Managing Leisure*, 3(4), 194–203.

Demir, R. and Söderman, S. (2015) Strategic sponsoring in professional sport: a review and conceptualization. *European Sport Management Quarterly*, 15(3), 271–300.

Dolles, H., Gammelsæter, H., Solenes, O., and Straume, S. (2016) The Janus-faced relationship value of professional sports clubs: a study of Molde Football Club, Norway. *Scandinavian Sport Studies Forum*, 7(3), 47–61.

Dolles, H. and Söderman, S. (2013a) The network of value captures in football club management: a framework to develop and analyze competitive advantage in professional team sports. In: S. Söderman and H. Dolles (eds.), *Handbook of Research on Sport and Business* (pp. 367–394). Cheltenham: Edward Elgar.

Dolles, H. and Söderman, S. (2013b) Twenty years of development of the J-League: analysing the business parameters of professional football in Japan, *Soccer & Society*. 14(5), 702–721

Dolles, H. and Söderman, S. (2011a) Learning from success: implementing a professional football league in Japan. In: H. Dolles and S. Söderman (eds.), *Sport as a Business: International, Professional and Commercial Aspects* (pp. 228–250). Houndmills, Basingstoke: Palgrave Macmillan.

Dolles, H. and Söderman, S. (2011b) プロ・サッカーのマネジメントにおける経済価値獲得のネットワーク―日本プロ・サッカー・リーグ発展の分析―[The network of economic value captures in professional football management: analyzing the development of the Japanese professional soccer league]. *Shōgaku Ronsan, The Journal of Commerce*, 40(1–2), 195–232.

Dolles, H. and Söderman, S. (2008) The network of value captures: Creating competitive advantage in football management. *Wirtschaftspolitische Blätter Österreich* [Austrian Economic Policy Papers], 55(1), 39–58.

Egilsson, B. and Dolles, H. (2017). From Heroes to Zeroes' – self-initiated expatriation of talented young footballers. *Journal of Global Mobility*, 5 (2), 174–193.

Ferrand, A. and Pages, M. (1996) Image sponsoring: a methodology to match event and sponsor. *Journal of Sports Management*, 10(3), 278–291.

Flint, S.W., Plumley, D., and Wilson, R. (2016) You're getting sacked in the morning: managerial change in the English Premier League. *Marketing Intelligence & Planning*, 34(2), 223–235.

Gabrielsson, C. and Dolles, H. (2017) Value capturing in floorball: how equipment manufacturers and retailers contribute to the development of a "new" sport. *Sport Business and Management: An International Journal*, 7(5), 542–559.

Gammelsæter, H. (2010) Institutional pluralism and governance in "commercialized" sport clubs. *European Sport Management Quarterly*, 10(5) 569–594.

Gammelsæter, H. and Senaux, B. (eds) (2011) *The Organisation and Governance of Top Football across Europe.* London: Routledge.

Gratton, C. and Solberg, H.A. (2007) *The Economics of Sport Broadcasting.* London: Routledge.

Grönroos, C. (2011) Value co-creation in service logic – a critical analysis. *Marketing Theory*, 11(3), 279–301.

Gummesson, E. (2002) *Total Relationship Marketing: Rethinking Marketing Management.* Oxford: Butterworth-Heinemann.

Hamil, S. and Chadwick, S. (eds.) (2010) *Managing Football: An International Perspective.* Amsterdam: Butterworth-Heinemann.

Jarosz, O., Kornakov, K., and Söderman, S. (2015) *Club Management Guide.* Nyon: European Club Association.

Jones, D. and Bridge, T. (eds.) (2017) *Planet Football: Football Money League.* Manchester: Deloitte Sports Business Group.

Jones, D. and Bridge, T. (eds.) (2016) *Top of the Table: Football Money League.* Manchester: Deloitte Sports Business Group.

Kotler, P. and Armstrong, G. (2010) *Principles of Marketing*, 13th revised ed. International ed., Harlow: Pearson Education.

Levitt, T. (1972) The globalization of markets. *Harvard Business Review*, 61(3) 91–103.

Madichie, N. (2009) Management implications of foreign players in the English Premiership- League football. *Management Decision*, 47(1), 24–50.

Meenaghan, T. and Shipley, D. (1999) Media effect in commercial sponsorship. *European Journal of Marketing*, 33(3/4), 328–347.

Morrow, S. (1999) *The New Business of Football: Accountability and Finance in Football.* Houndmills, Basingstoke: Palgrave Macmillan.

Morrow, S. and Hamil, S. (2003) Corporate community involvement by football clubs: business strategy or social obligation?, *Stirling Research Papers in Sports Studies*, No. 1, Stirling: University of Stirling.

Noll, R. (2003a) The organization of sports leagues. *Oxford Review of Economic Policy*, 19(4), 530–551.

Noll, R. (2003b) The organization of sports leagues. *SIEPR Discussion Paper*, No 02-43, Stanford: Stanford University, Stanford Institute for Economic Policy Research.

Normann, R. and Ramírez, R. (1993) From value chain to value constellation: designing interactive strategy. *Harvard Business Review*, 71(4), 65–77.

Pine II, B.J. (2011) Memorable events are the most valuable experiences. *Harvard Business Review Online.* [online] Retrieved from: http://blogs.hbr.org/cs/2011/04/memorable_events_are_the_most.html

Pine II, B.J., and Gilmore, J.H. (1999) *The Experience Economy. Work Is Theater & Every Business a Stage.* Boston, MA: Harvard Business School Press.

Poli, R., Ravenel, L., and Besson, R. (2017) Transfer market analysis: tracking the money (2010–2017). *CIES Football Observatory Monthly Report*, 27(September). Neuchâtel: CIES.

Pongsakornrungsilp, S. and Schroeder, J. (2009) Understanding value co-creation in a co-consuming group, *Management Paper*. Exeter: The University of Exeter, Business School. [online] Retrieved from: http://business-school.exeter.ac.uk/documents/discussion_papers/management/2009/0904.pdf

Prahalad, C.K. and Ramaswamy, V. (2004) Co-creating unique value with customers. *Strategy & Leadership*, 32(3), 4–9.

Preuss, H., Könecke, T., and Schütte, N. (2012) Primäre ökonomische Auswirkungen des 1. FC Kaiserslautern für Kaiserslautern und Rheinland-Pfalz [Primary economic impacts of 1.FC Kaiserslautern for Kaiserslautern and Rhineland-Palatinate]. In: G. Trosien (ed.), *Ökonomie der Sportspiele* (pp. 205–222). Schorndorf: Hofmann.

Preuss, H., Könecke, T., and Schütte, N. (2010) Calculating the primary economic impact of a sports club's regular season competition: a first model, *Journal of Sport Science and Physical Education*, 60, 17–22.

Rowe, D. (2000) No gain, no game? Media and sport. In: J. Curran and M. Gurevitch (eds), *Mass media and society* (3rd ed.) (pp. 346–361). London: Edward Arnold.

Rowe, D. (1996) The global love-match: sport and television. *Media, Culture and Society*, 18(4), 565–582.

Schau, H., Muniz Jr, A., and Arnould, E. (2009) How brand community practices create value. *Journal of Marketing*, 73(5), 30–51.

Smith, A. and Westerbeek, H. (2004) *The Sport Business Future*. Houndmills, Basingstoke: Palgrave Macmillan.

Vargo, S.L. and Lusch, R.F. (2004) Evolving to a new dominant logic for marketing. *Journal of Marketing*, 68(1), 1–17.

Williams, P. (2012) Any given Saturday: competitive balance in elite English rugby union. *Managing Leisure*, 17(2–3), 88–105.

Woratschek, H., Horbel, C., and Popp, B. (2014) The sport value framework – a new fundamental logic for analyses in sport management, *European Sport Management Quarterly*, 14(1), 6–24.

26

Supply chain management in professional football

Birnir Egilsson

Introduction

Football has a large share of the sports industry, and at its core are professional football clubs (PFCs). Today, PFCs face a multitude of day-to-day operations. They are involved in retailing; match-day and ticketing activities; buying, developing, and selling players; and branding leisurewear or first-team kits sold through various distribution channels, to name but a few. Actually, as the product of football has turned into a commercial and global phenomenon, a growing number of PFCs have expanded commercially into multi-channel brands crossing national borders, increasing the complexity of their operations. With this development, specialised actors have emerged, forcing PFCs to relate to a number of actors on the supply side to satisfy various types of actors on the customer side. Therefore, PFC management must address many sport and non-sport challenges that engage with a variety of supply chain relationships. Management efforts within a supply chain are conceptualised as supply chain management (SCM) and this represents the integration of business processes from customers through suppliers that provide products, services, and information that add value for customers. Although there have been efforts made recently to broaden SCM research into previously unexplored industries, this stream of research has heretofore focused little attention on the sports industry in particular (Kauppi et al., 2013).

To advance both knowledge and industry practice, this chapter addresses this void by considering the importance of SCM both internally and externally and highlights how SCM practice is, and can be, utilised by PFCs. The chapter is organised as follows: first, an understanding of SCM is presented; then, the web of supply chains in which the PFCs are entangled is described; next, the few studies that have examined PFC management from a SCM perspective are reviewed. The following section presents empirical findings on, arguably, the two central supply chains of PFCs: the supply chain of talents and the match-day supply chain. The closing section explains how PFCs can realise the advantage of supply chains and their management by providing thoughts from different perspectives tailored for students, the industry, and for further research.

Supply chains and their management

The development path of SCM as an approach represents one of the most noteworthy paradigm shifts of business management by highlighting that individual businesses no longer compete as solely autonomous entities, but rather, as supply chains. The origin of SCM is difficult to pin down due to its many antecedents. SCM only emerged as an approach in the early 1980s. However, the very first fundamental assumptions on which SCM are footed can be traced back to industrial engineering (Taylor, 1914) or when scientists demonstrated the value of analytics in the study of military logistics problems (Huston, 1966). Since then, the development of the SCM approach has come a long way, having come through the technology revolution of multi-divisional mass-production corporations within the strategic integration paradigm, characterised by total quality management,[1] continuous improvement, and lean production management approaches (Bodrožić and Adler, 2017). However, SCM came to prominence within the network paradigm, linking and rationalising processes across internal and external boundaries of the firm, and, hence, redesigning business processes up and down the value chain, upgrading and bridging internal and external boundaries in the supply chain. A "value chain" is construed as the full range of activities required to bring a product or service from conception, through the different phases of production and, finally, to customers (Gereffi et al., 2001).

The term "supply chain" evolved from Porter's value chain and comprises a series of connected internal organisational value chains (Fawcett et al., 2014). A supply chain can be conceptualised as a network of organisations that are involved (through upstream and downstream linkages) in the different activities and procedures that produce value in the form of products and services for end consumers (Mentzer et al., 2001, p. 4.). A supply chain comprises the focal firm that produces the main product in the chain, its suppliers of raw materials, resources and/ or services (upstream), its distributors and dealers, and the end consumers (downstream). A close alignment and coordination of internal and external activities are referred to as "supply chain integration," and it is generally accepted that supply chain integration evolves in stages (cf. Figure 26.1). Level 1 is internal, i.e. only those activities that are internal to the focal company.

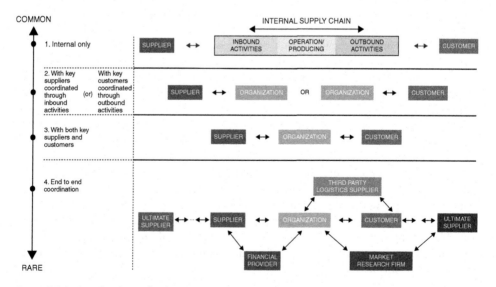

Figure 26.1 Levels of supply chain integration
Source: Adapted from Mentzer et al., 2001; Fawcett et al., 2014.

Level 2 is dyadic and represents single two-party relationships. Level 3 encapsulates the focal firm and its immediate suppliers and customers. Last, level 4 describes a network, including all organisations involved from ultimate supplier through the focal firm until the ultimate consumer is reached (Fawcett et al., 2014).

Before activities can be managed effectively up and down the supply chain, they must first be managed well *inside* a firm. This is referred to as the "internal supply chain" and represents those value chain activities within a firm that conclude with the transformational process of providing a product or service to the customer. These value chain activities fall into three internal sub-constructs for supply chain activities. The first construct is inbound activities that ensure that sourced supplies are available for operations. The second is operational practices that involve activities that convert sourced inputs into a product or a service that customers value. The third is those outbound activities that ensure that finished products or services are available when and where customers want to buy them (Fawcett et al., 2014).

It is not always possible to affirm that conscious SCM exists within those supply chains. However, management efforts by the focal firm are conceptualised as SCM. Many definitions exist (see Table 26.1). For example, Oliver and Webber (1982) viewed SCM as the planning and control of the total materials flow. Ellram (1991) considered it as an alternative form of vertical integration, while authors such as Christopher (1992) and Harland (1996) defined it as the management of complex networks of organisations or entities rather than the management of a vertical pipeline of interlinked firms. Despite their differences, these definitions share a common theme, which is the management of relations between independent organisations within a

Table 26.1 SCM definitions

Authors	Definition
Oliver and Webber (1982)	SCM covers the flow of goods from supplier through manufacturing and distribution chains to end user.
Ellram (1991)	SCM is an integrative approach to dealing with the planning and control of the materials flow from suppliers to end users.
Christopher (1992)	SCM is the management of a network of organisations that are involved, through upstream and downstream linkages, in the different processes and activities that produce value in the form of products and services in the hands of the ultimate consumer.
Harland (1996)	SCM is the management of a network of interconnected businesses involved in the ultimate provision of product and service packages required by end customers.
Lambert et al. (1998)	SCM is the integration of business processes from end customer through original suppliers that provides products, services, and information that add value for customers.
Mentzer et al. (2001)	SCM is the systemic, strategic coordination of the traditional business functions and the tactics across these business functions within a particular company and across businesses within the supply chain, for the purposes of improving the long-term performance of the individual companies and the supply chain as a whole.
CSCMP (2010)	SCM is the planning and management of all activities involved in sourcing and procurement, conversion, and all logistics management activities. Importantly, it also includes coordination and collaboration with channel partners, which can be suppliers, intermediaries, third-party service providers, and customers.

particular structure. Furthermore, they all share the belief that by understanding and managing the supply chain (internally and externally), organisations within the chain/network will enjoy commercial benefits.

SCM research is not only broad in terms of different definitions, but its research also concentrates on a handful of industry sectors. Considering this nature of the field, researchers have tried to agree on a common set of constructs to cover all aspects of SCM (e.g., Min and Mentzer, 2004). Others have attempted to define SCM practices to promote effective management of their supply chains. These practices integrate suppliers, manufacturers, distributors, and customers in order to improve the sustained performance of individual organisations and the supply chain together in a unified business model. Li et al. (2006) suggest practices covering upstream (strategic supplier partnership) and downstream (customer relationship) supply chain processes, and information flow along the supply chain (level of information sharing and quality of information sharing). Finally, researchers have attempted to categorise the SCM approach into different perspectives to see how SCM is conceptualised as a means of solving the lack of commonality. Ellram and Cooper (2014), leading SCM scholars, argue that there are three categories that add value to the practical understanding and execution of SCM: SCM as a philosophy, as a process, and as a governance structure.

SCM as a philosophy considers the way that the relationships within and across organisations come together to satisfy customers' needs from a supply chain orientation (Ellram and Cooper, 2014). According to Mentzer et al. (2001, p. 7), SCM philosophy has the following characteristics:

1 A system approach to viewing the supply chain as a whole, and to managing the total flow of goods from the supplier to the customer;
2 A strategic orientation towards cooperative efforts to synchronise and converge intra-firm and inter-firm operational and strategic capabilities into a unified goal; and
3 A customer focus to create unique and individualised sources of customer value leading to customer satisfaction.

Supply chain orientation has gestated as "the recognition by an organisation of the systemic, strategic implications of the tactical activities involved in managing the various flows in a supply chain" (Mentzer et al., 2001, p. 11). Supply chain orientation formalises an inter-organisational SCM motivation as long as that SCM happens between organisations and formalises the internal organisational SCM focus that is in harmony across other partnerships in the supply chain. This perspective is significant in understanding the value that SCM can add to competitive advantage and critical to internal integration and cross-functional understanding (Ellram and Cooper, 2014).

The *process perspective* provides understanding of how to improve activities involved in SCM (Ellram and Cooper, 2014). From this perspective, the supply chain acts as a means for linking structured activities designed to produce an output for a particular customer or market (Davenport, 1993) or as a means to coordinate processes (Fawcett et al., 2008). The importance of this perspective is that it adds insight into the relevance of linking activities and how coordination of these activities can lead to better results (Ellram and Cooper, 2014).

Different from the process perspective, *SCM as a governance structure* considers what the boundaries between organisations are, what the best types of ownership are, and seeks to identify the types of relationship involved. This perspective studies the fundamental nature of the organisation with regard to, for example, what it does itself versus what it outsources; how it treats others in the supply chain in terms of relationship issues; and who controls various aspects of SCM (e.g., Soosay et al., 2008). The governance perspective of SCM, therefore, extends beyond the firm and focuses on the supply chain relationships, how they are managed, who controls them and who sets the directions. From a practical stance, this perspective sheds light on the importance of having the right types of supply chain relationships.

PFCs entangled in a web of supply chains

In every internal supply chain process, a transformation occurs in which inputs are combined with capital to produce outputs that are then sold to customers. The same process applies to PFCs where inputs/resources (e.g., players, coaches, administration) are combined with capital (e.g., the stadium, training ground) to produce the output (e.g., the match), which is subsequently sold to customers/consumers (sponsors, ticket holders, TV providers). This implies that PFCs are involved in various supply chain relationships. In fact, the supply system is so complex that Dolles and Söderman (2013) identified eight value offerings in six customer categories representing 48 supply-chain relationships – just by focusing on the demand side only, i.e. not including suppliers and intermediaries [see Chapter 25 in this handbook]. These stakeholders may hold diverse ideas about what it is that constitutes the supply chain for them, and for PFCs it may not be obvious what their core product is and who their core customers are, which is understandable given the complex supply system (Dolles and Söderman, 2013). As mentioned, PFCs sell players, tickets, live broadcasts, and merchandising to different customers. While these sales may generate most of their income, the "products" are not easily separable. Some argue the game is the product (Sukhbinder and Baines, 2004) or the co-created experience on match day (Woratschek et al., 2014), but the game and match-day experience would not be attractive for spectators, sponsors, and media unless it was part of an extended package – the league or cup competition [see Chapter 21 in this handbook]. This means that the other clubs, their supporters, the sponsors, and the media may be seen as suppliers and co-creators of match days as well as of the larger product: the league product.

Consequently, and different from other industries, collaboration and coordination are imposed on PFCs rather than chosen strategically to create competitions. This means that PFCs are interdependent parts of a collective production system at the same time as they compete with the other parts within the same system – the parts would be worthless without the whole, and the whole would be worthless without the parts. Moreover, it is not always clear if operations are best provided by the system (the relevant league or national, regional, or international football association) or the clubs individually and, between them, clubs may have diverging interests. What is optimal for the system may sometimes be suboptimal for some of the clubs. This relates to issues such as media rights and commercialising, but it is also a matter of regulation and cost control (mechanisms such as size and composition of the roster, and UEFA's Financial Fair Play Rule and Home-grown Player Rule).

Even though the game and the match day may be seen as an experience product, that product is embedded in the league competition, so teams' performance in the league table directly influences the attraction of the game. Moreover, for many PFCs, the game is also an exhibition – it is where the club (and the players themselves) exhibit their skills in front of scouts and agents. In this sense, the game is the fare not the product; the product is the players and the chain is an ideal-typical input–output structure that starts with the process by which a player moves from being a talented amateur to a professional, and then to being promoted to other clubs and leagues. Often (and compulsory in some countries such as France and Germany), PFCs invest in football academies as a means to cultivate talent. Finally, PFCs have huge social relevance and, increasingly, they are focusing their attention on corporate social responsibility (CSR) practices, with PFC managers realising that the reach of extended supply-chain partners will help them in their endeavours, not least for value co-creation (Kolyperas et al., 2016). This complexity is mirrored in not one but a web of supply chains that are linked to the production of the match or, to be more precise, the production of the games and, hence, the competition in the league.

Research on PFC supply chains

To date, few authors have examined PFCs from a supply chain perspective (see Table 26.2). Cross and Henderson (2003) investigated the supply of players within the English Premier League, suggesting that the main source of economic rents is related to the skills of the workforce (the players). Lonsdale (2004), also with a focus on the English Premier League, provided a description of the football supply network and identified four important suppliers that clubs manage within the "talent supply network," while Egilsson and Dolles (2017) contributed by presenting the phases of the talent supply chain and the developmental challenges associated with their path from the players' perspective. Darby (2013) utilised a value chain approach, spanning different countries to analyse the production of athletes for export across international borders to provide a picture of the global distribution network of athletes, and especially how "value" is added along the way. Darby (2013) also applied a global production network approach, which supported him in demonstrating that sport entities are complex, multidirectional, and manifest themselves in heterogeneous ways. This facilitated an understanding of the ways in which the trade in football labour is both extractive, serving the interests of the developed world, and allows value to be accrued by a range of actors and stakeholders located in the developing world (Darby, 2013). Poli (2005) applied the analytic framework of the global commodity chain (Gereffi, 1996) to consider if players can be considered as a commodity and, then, as a network methodology with the aim of identifying the actors involved in the provision of African players to Europe, their ongoing relations, and the structural outcome of these relations. Relvas et al. (2010) explored internal activities of PFCs related to player development; their findings highlight an apparent lack of communication between clubs' first teams and their own youth environments, suggesting that PFC talent supply chains are not especially well integrated. This apparent gap between first teams and youth environments acts as an added barrier to player progression to the first team,

Table 26.2 Overview of SCM research within the context of football

Area	Author(s) (year)	Perspective(s)
Strategy and SCM orientation	Cross and Henderson (2003)	Football industry
Purchasing and SCM	Lonsdale (2004)	League
Retailing and SCM	Sparks (2007, 2010)	Football industry
	Szymoszowskyj et al. (2016)	PFCs
SCM	Egilsson (2017)	PFCs
Global value chain and global production networks	Darby (2013)	Countries and players
Global commodity chain	Poli (2005)	PFCs and players
Talent supply chain – internal supply chain practices	Egilsson and Dolles (2017)	PFCs and players
	Relvas et al. (2010)	PFCs
Value network	Woratschek et al. (2014)	Sport firms and stakeholders
Network of value captures	Dolles and Söderman (2013)	PFCs
Sport event management practices	Emery (2010)	Sport event organiser
Event logistics	Haugen (2011)	Event organiser

which is worrying given that all the PFCs under investigation noted that the main objective of their academy is to develop talents for their first team.

Sparks (2007, 2010) provided insights into retailing and distribution channels for sports goods and its services from a SCM perspective [see, also, Chapter 33 in this handbook]. Szymoszowskyj et al. (2016) explored the merchandising supply chain of PFCs, investigating retail branding strategies through brand equity and SCM and, thus, provided insight into the different supply-chain strategies and distribution channels utilised by PFCs. Woratschek et al. (2014) pointed out that the core product of sports is the event (the match-day experience) and the event itself is realised as service value networks (Vargo and Lusch, 2004), whereby the service concept (the requirements of the target market) and the design of the delivery system can only be achieved through the collaborative efforts of the network of stakeholders providing complementary products and services. Hence, PFCs provide the platform that enables all types of stakeholders, including fans and other spectators, to co-create the value of the match (Woratschek et al., 2014).

Haugen (2011) applied quantitative logistics concepts to events (such as forecasting, production planning, inventory management, and transport planning), predicting that the topic of supply chains in the context of football will be a source of much interesting research in event SCM. Unfortunately, a holistic understanding of event SCM is rarely considered or investigated in sports in general (Emery, 2010; Kauppi et al., 2013). A collection of empirical studies has focused on major sporting events. Still, current research focuses only on a few specialised areas such as personal volunteer management (e.g., Solberg, 2003), cost and accountability (e.g., Hanlon and Jago, 2004), event bidding (e.g., Getz, 2007) and impact, values, and outcomes of major sports events (e.g., Preuss, 2005), to name a few. Emery's (2010) empirical data showed that planning in major sporting events is mainly financial, marketing, and technical, rather than operational. Emery concluded that current management practice recognises the importance of planning but, still, the primary focus appears to be towards "getting things done" rather than achieving the quality of pre-determined and specific outcomes.

A perspective of PFCs on supply chains and their management

Assuming the importance of SCM in PFCs and the lack of comprehensive empirical studies of SCM in PFC management, I explored how PFCs relate to SCM schemes. I used sampling techniques to identify potential cases (five medium-sized European PFCs from different countries, all top clubs in their respective leagues) and the respondents (CEOs, operations managers, sports directors, and academy directors). My findings did not identify clear supply-chain philosophies within these PFCs. However, there was strong feedback from CEOs that they see their clubs entangled in a web of relationships (with various governance structures), which is challenging for them to capture within a supply-chain approach. My findings show that these PFCs invest in two entangled value chains, namely *developing talents* and *organising matches*:

> There are two [value chains], which can be broken up. Obviously, it is matches and taking part in competitions. Especially televised matches. Secondly, the production of talented players, education of players. When I say this, I mean by that, in our case, the transfer market is for us extremely important in terms of income. We are very successful in it and we are mainly successful by shaping young players … I look upon it as income for producing football actually, producing players and matches.
>
> *(CEO, PFC 1)*

As can be understood from this quote, these internal supply chains are entangled in other supply chains such as the competitive structure of football (the league or competition), as well as broadcasting and merchandising, as explained above. These insights show that even though many PFCs have enlarged commercially, resulting in wider product and service offerings, the core product of PFCs remains the production of sporting events and developing talent.

The event (match-day) supply chain

For PFCs, the match day is their ultimate *raison d'être* and a core element of their activity, it is the moment where the sporting side of their business performs after thorough preparations to ensure that the team and its players are prepared and organised to show desideratum in on-field performance. In the interim, the administrative side of the business prepares its stadium to receive supporters, the opposing team, media, sponsors, and other stakeholders that co-create the event and its atmosphere. The event itself comprises multiple layers of supply chains, and functions by utilising the connections and expertise of other supply-chain actors to ensure the event's success. Nowadays, with the commercialisation of the game and developments in stadium design, match-day operations cover various areas, including ticketing activities for different viewing areas, catering activities from standard kiosks to high-quality cuisine in the hospitality area, and accommodating VIPs where added customer value is created through better seating, restaurant-quality food and other elements of enhanced comfort, service, and exclusivity.

In addition, services related to a one-stop shop and/or various booths selling merchandise products and entertainment activities for all ages and different types of fans need to be organised alongside other support services such as Internet technology, security, logistics, and cleaning. Based on my research findings, I conceptualise the overall match-day supply chain as a network of internal and external stakeholders involved in the different activities and procedures that make it possible to organise and sell an event that is valued by customers and the stakeholders' customers. Hence, the aim is to create a platform of services that can be used by various stakeholders that interact to co-create value and determine customers' perceptions of the quality of the event. This is certainly not an easy task as PFCs depend on a large number of partners and stakeholders that not only affect the event, but who also are (or will be) affected by the impact of the event. From a process perspective, the internal match-day supply chain refers to the chain of internal activities within PFCs that concludes with delivering the match to customers and comprises three main internal activities (cf. Figure 26.2).

It can be argued that PFC matches are somehow standardised products providing the services mentioned above. However, each match-day supply chain differs from one PFC to another as

Figure 26.2 An example of a PFC's internal match-day supply chain

clubs vary in terms of, for example, size, resources, strategic orientation, and management practices. Moreover, each match needs to be prepared differently given the importance and size of the match (e.g., "derby" match, international match, cup match, or a televised match). Hence, some of the PFCs perform match-day activities in-house while others rely on third-party suppliers for those parts of the event that are not seen as core activities (e.g., security, catering, stewarding, public relations, ticketing, logistics, maintenance, etc.), either by subcontracting or outsourcing partnerships. Some PFCs choose to conduct most of these activities in-house:

> There is no strategic thinking behind the fact that we operate nearly all activities in-house. It has turned out like this because we believe that this is the cheapest solution, maybe not the most professional decision-making or the best.
>
> *(Operations manager, PFC 3)*

PFCs that choose to conduct these activities in-house therefore rely on their suppliers to provide what they need for a particular service on match day. Others elect to subcontract by hiring an external supplier to perform specific parts of the business that would be illogical for them to handle internally, and some outsource independent providers for certain activities due to a lack of expertise.

> We do not want to operate the stadium, as we do not know how to do it. … We needed to find a company that has the expertise to operate a stadium. We outsource all our activities that are not our core activities, such as operation of the stadium, security, marketing, etc.
>
> *(CEO, PFC 2)*

In some cases, clubs and suppliers operate a barter system by trading one product or service for another.

> When we negotiate with sponsors and suppliers, it is most often that they are both our sponsors and our suppliers. This means that our main sponsors have also chosen to be our suppliers and, when we negotiate, we negotiate about their roles as suppliers and our expected role to our main customers [sponsor] then.
>
> *(Operations manager, PFC 3)*

In this barter or exchange model, sponsors are both suppliers and customers, which is simultaneously interesting and complicated as processes need to be managed upstream (supplier practices) and downstream (customer service practices). The point is, each match-day strategic orientation has its roles and relationships, and without efficient operation and management of these supply chains, important opportunities to generate additional sales and brand value could be lost. Hence, the choice of suppliers and the management of their supply chains are important decisions for PFCs.

The talent supply chain

> Actually, we think of them as talents and then prospects. I would say it is a resource, for me … a player starts as a raw material and then develops into a product that we can sell or to a resource that we use.
>
> *(CEO, PFC 4)*

> [O]ur business actually relies on player development and selling players.
>
> *(CEO, PFC 3)*

Figure 26.3 The phases of the talent supply chain
Source: Dolles and Egilsson, 2017

As can been seen from the quotes above, PFCs consider football talents primarily as internal resources, instrumental to the performance on the pitch, attracting fans, sponsors, and media and, second, as commodities to trade. Different from the match-day supply chain (a network of various stakeholders co-creating the event), the talent supply chain can be seen as an ideal-typical supply-chain input–output structure, where the base of the supply chain starts with the process by which players, as "raw commodities," develop from being talented amateurs to professionals and then continue to other clubs or, perhaps, transfer to a new continent ahead of retirement (cf. Figure 26.3). Hence, the internal supply chain of talents is conceptualised as the chain of activities within PFCs that focuses on the recruitment, development and selling of sports talent.

Snell et al., (1999) proposes that organisations can enhance organisational performance and gain competitive advantage by internally developing unique and valuable employees – human resources. Therefore, if PFCs want to take advantage of the talent supply chain, attention must be devoted to those resources creating value for their organisation. While the supply chain of talents differs from sport to sport and between nations, all "sport labour production" includes the capacity of a focal firm to manage the production of labour. Therefore, each club has internal management practices that are specific and unique to the organisation that focus on the recruitment, development and selling of sports talent (cf. Figure 26.3). These internal supply-chain practices represent a holistic approach covering all areas for effective sourcing and player development.

> Our role is to develop players, providing young players the right steps to play for the club and to develop him for the next step – playing in stronger leagues. Our players are provided all the education on how to be professionals outside of training and they are given all services needed to be professionals on the pitch, for example physio, psychology, nutrition, etc.
>
> *(Sporting director, PFC 1)*

These internal practices vary amongst PFCs and it is their unique combination within individual clubs' value chains that ensures their competitive advantage. These activities fall into three activities for supply-chain activities (cf. Figure 26.4).

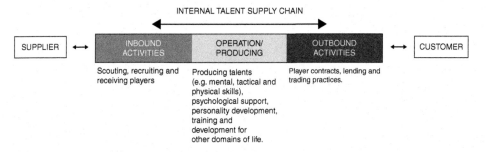

Figure 26.4 An example of a PFC's internal talent supply chain

Concluding thoughts

This chapter provides a brief introduction into supply chains and SCM from different perspectives and highlights the importance of applying SCM thinking to PFCs. It concludes that significant opportunities exist to apply SCM thinking to PFCs and, indeed, to other sports organisations. As a final point, I want to provide some closing thoughts to students, the industry and researchers.

Thoughts for students

My recommendations for future sports managers are to:

- Appreciate the importance of SCM and how it can influence PFC (and other sports) management from different stages of integration;
- Understand the internal transformation process that occurs within the internal supply chain activities in PFCs, the benefits of utilising suppliers and analysing customer needs in the wider supply network;
- Understand the complex supply networks within football and the two core PFC supply chains – managing talents and events – including their influencing factors.

Thoughts for the industry

In line with Kotzab et al. (2011), I recommend that, in the following order, PFCs:

- Develop an internal SCM philosophy by focusing on the activities and behaviours necessary to realise supply-chain flow. This includes internal supply-chain integration, and building and maintaining internal behavioural elements that facilitate relational exchange (e.g., SCM commitment, organisational compatibility, cooperative norms, and top management support). Only when internal integration has been fully embraced can activities effectively expand to include boundary-bridging processes outside the firm;
- Work with external partners on developing joint SCM efforts downstream (customers) and upstream (suppliers). This includes activities that integrate behaviour, facilitate information, risk and reward sharing, unite goals in serving customers, and create and cement long-term relationships;
- Adopt SCM-related processes that entail specific ordering of work activities across time and place, with a beginning, an end, clearly identified inputs and outputs, and a structure for action. By doing so, PFCs should be supply-chain oriented both within the firm and across other supply-chain members. Therefore, developing joint conditions and cross-functional understanding should lead to cooperation amongst three or more contiguous partners (cf. chain level in Figure 26.1).

By adopting SCM-related processes, PFCs should realise that relationships are not only output-oriented but also learning oriented, i.e. they should take the opportunity to access other organisations' core competencies through cooperative agreements as an alternative to building in-house. For instance, firms' learning in relationships enables them to enter new markets in which they can develop new relationships, giving them the platform to enter other new markets (Johanson and Vahlne, 2003). PFCs should therefore understand that by analysing their own activities and processes, the supply chain can then act as a means to access resources and competencies outside the PFC. For instance, rather than investing in internal efficacies deriving from the specific and smooth ordering of work activities across time and place (e.g. related to security, hospitality, event, and ticketing), PFCs could focus on the core activities that relate to sporting performance – the players – if that is the objective. However, talent supply-chain optimisation is challenging for different reasons. First, because there are natural restrictions on how many players clubs can keep (happy) in their roster (after all, players need to play games at the right level to develop). Second, because talent cannot be secured from one or a few suppliers (clubs) but has to be scouted and possibly acquired from across a multitude of clubs, leagues, and nations. Having said that, the industry sees examples of PFCs utilising supply-chain strategies to optimise their talent supply chain, which leads us to the final thought, from the governance structure perspective.

For their supply chains, PFCs need to address issues such as the boundaries they have with organisations, what the best type of ownership is and the type of relationships they should have in place. One interesting phenomenon growing rapidly in the football industry regarding the best type of ownership is a multi-club ownership strategy (e.g., City Group) in which an individual or private owners are growing their brands, expanding their businesses and optimising their operations and, therefore, directly influencing their supply chains. From a SCM perspective, this strategy is labelled as a vertical supply-chain strategy and is the overall scope of different business activities in a supply chain brought under the management of a single company; in the case of PFCs, vertical financial ownership. Even if all the different business activities appear to be integrated within this form of ownership structure, we still do not know for sure whether the owners are utilising supply-chain strategies to optimise their talent supply, allowing themselves to manage the production path of talents and reaping the benefits. This strategy requires investments and resources to set up a subsidiary; however, as Chadwick (2017) explains:

> Flip the coin over and think about the costs. … How do you scout around the world as quickly and cheaply as possible? Rather than having to maintain a scout network where you can always miss out, you have a franchise where you save both on intelligence and scouting acquisition costs.

Owners strategically implementing this supply strategy are bridging the cultural and operational gaps that separate the inbound (receiving talents) and outbound (trading talents) sides of their clubs, while simultaneously securing an input and output resource/price advantage within the talent supply chain. Apparently, this supports Kauppi et al.'s (2013) proposition that SCM strategies and tools could be applied to more efficiently manage the supply of talent in football. It remains to be seen if a prerequisite for such development is changing ownership structures in football, and if the football authorities will install regulations that hamper increased multi-club ownership.

Thoughts for researchers

As has been noticed in this chapter, the literature concerning SCM and PFCs is limited. Extant studies have proved fruitful; however, there remain areas within the sports industry in general and SCM and sport management research in particular in which more research of SCM topics and issues is very much needed. Further studies should address:

- The various supply chains in which PFCs are entangled, for example, the league/competition supply chain, the talent supply chain, the event supply chain, the merchandising supply chain, the supply chain of football as a broadcast entertainment and the CSR supply chain;
- Different SCM perspectives (i.e., as a philosophy, as a process, or as a governance structure) at all levels, including intra-firm, dyadic, chain and network;

- Internal SCM practices (i.e., strategic supplier management, customer relationship management, information sharing and internal processes); and
- Analysis from a league, sector, industry-level, and cross-national context for comparison.

All these are needed to further understand the importance of supply chains to delivery of the product and services of football and to advance SCM models in sports. Kauppi et al. (2013) pinpoint multiple avenues for future research to drive improved performance in various aspects of sports, both on- and off-field. It is important to highlight, though, that SCM schemes developed in other industries potentially have limited application to the football industry due to the complexity and the specific nature of the latter – but this in itself warrants in-depth study.

I challenge sports management-focused scholarly outlets to broaden their scope concerning SCM issues and topics. The same applies to standard sports management textbooks (except for retailing); event management textbooks generally provide only a brief chapter on the topic. On the other hand, operations management journals and conferences have now started calling for more research into sports operations management (e.g. the *Production and Operation Management Society*) and related topics such as club operations, sports events, sports services and *servitisation*, and on-pitch performance, as well as keeping spectators, fans, athletes, and other key stakeholders satisfied. The sports context is a fascinating one in which to further develop SCM theory in new institutional settings and/or environments.

Note

1 "Total Quality Management (TQM) is a management approach that seeks to achieve quality through the participation of all organisational members, by aiming at long-term success through customer satisfaction and benefits to all members of the organisation and society" (De Knop et al., 2004, p. 59).

References

Bodrožić, Z., and Adler, P.S. (2017) The evolution of management models: a Neo-Schumpeterian theory. *Administrative Science Quarterly*, 63(1), 85–129.

Chadwick, S (2017), in MacInnes, P. (2017) Disneyfication of clubs like Manchester City keeps showing benefits. *The Guardian*. [online] Retrieved from: https://www.theguardian.com/football/2017/aug/31/disneyfication-clubs-manchester-city-red-bull

Christopher, M.L. (1992) *Logistics and Supply Chain Management*. London: Pitman Publishing.

Cross, J., and Henderson, S. (2003) Strategic challenges in the football business: a SPACE analysis. *Strategic change*, 12(8), 409–420.

CSCMP (2017) Council of Supply Chain Management Professionals. [online] Retrieved from: https://cscmp.org/CSCMP/Educate/SCM_Definitions_and_Glossary_of_Terms/CSCMP/Educate/SCM_Definitions_and_Glossary_of_Terms.aspx

Darby, P. (2013) Moving players, traversing perspectives: global value chains, production networks and Ghanaian football labour migration. *Geoforum*, 50(Supplement c), 43–53.

Davenport, T.H. (1993) *Process Innovation: Reengineering Work Through Information Technology*. Boston, MA: Harvard Business Press.

De Knop, P., Van Hoecke, J., and De Bosscher, V. (2004) Quality management in sports clubs. *Sport Management Review*, 7(1), 57–77.

Dolles, H. and Söderman, S. (2013) The network of value captures in football club management: a framework to develop and analyze competitive advantage in professional team sports. In: H. Dolles and S. Söderman (eds.). *Handbook of Research and Sport and Business* (pp. 367–398). Cheltenham, UK: Edward Elgar.

Egilsson, B. (2017) Supply chain management practices in professional football: a single case study of Molde Football club. "*Making Knowledge Work*". EURAM conference proceedings, 21–24 June, Glasgow, Scotland.

Egilsson, B. and Dolles, H., (2017) From heroes to zeroes' – self-initiated expatriation of talented young footballers. *Journal of Global Mobility*, 5(2), 174–193.

Ellram, L. (1991) Supply chain management: the industrial organisation perspective. *International Journal of Physical Distribution & Logistics Management*, 21(1), 13–22.

Ellram, L.M., and Cooper, M.C. (2014) Supply chain management: it's all about the journey, not the destination. *Journal of Supply Chain Management*, 50(1), 8–20.

Emery, P. (2010) Past, present, future major sport event management practice: the practitioner perspective. *Sport Management Review*, 13(2), 158–170.

Fawcett, S.E., Magnan, G.M., and McCarter, M.W. (2008) Benefits, barriers, and bridges to effective supply chain management. *Supply Chain Management: An International Journal*, 13(1), 35–48.

Fawcett, S.E., Ellram, L.M., and Ogden, J.A. (2014) *Supply chain management: from vision to implementation.* Harlow: Pearsons.

Gereffi, G. (1996) Global commodity chains: new forms of coordination and control among nations and firms in international industries. *Competition and Change*, 4(1), 427–439.

Gereffi, G., Humphrey, J., Kaplinsky, R., and Sturgeon T.H. (2001) Introduction: globalisation, value chains and development. *IDS Bulletin*, 32(3), 1–8.

Getz, D. (2007) *Event Studies: Theory, Research and Policy for Planned Events.* Oxford/Burlington, MA: Butterworth–Heinemann.

Hanlon, C. and Jago, L. (2004) The challenge of retaining personnel in major sport event organisations. *Event Management*, 9(1–2), 39–49.

Harland, C. (1996) Supply chain management: relationships, chains, and networks. *British Journal of Management*, 7(s), 63–80.

Haugen, K. (2011) *Event Logistics.* Trondheim, Norway: Tapir Academic Press.

Huston, J. A. (1966) *The Sinews of War: Army Logistics; 1775–1953.* Vol. 2. Washington, DC: Government Printing Office.

Johanson, J. and Vahlne, J.E. (2003) Business Relationship Learning and Commitment in the Internationalisation Process. *Journal of International Entrepreneurship*, 1(1), 83–101.

Kauppi, K., Moxham, C., and Bamford, D. (2013) Should we try out for the major leagues? A call for research in sport operations management. *International Journal of Operations & Production Management*, 33(10), 1368–1399.

Kolyperas, D., Anagnostopoulos, C., Chadwick, S., and Sparks, L. (2016) Applying a communicating vessels framework to CSR value co-creation: empirical evidence from professional team sport organisations. *Journal of Sport Management*, 30(6), 702–719.

Kotzab, H., Teller, C., Grant, D. B., and Sparks, L. (2011) Antecedents for the adoption and execution of supply chain management. *Supply Chain Management*, 16(4), 231–245.

Lambert, D.M., Cooper, M.C., and Pagh, J.D. (1998) Supply chain management: implementation issues and research opportunities. *The International Journal of Logistics Management*, 9(2), 1–20.

Li, S., Ragu-Nathan, B., Ragu-Nathan, T.S., and Rao, S.S. (2006) The impact of supply chain management practices on competitive advantage and organisational performance. *Omega*, 34(2), 107–124.

Lonsdale, C. (2004) Player power: capturing value in the English football supply network. *Supply Chain Management: An International Journal*, 9(5), 383–391.

Mentzer, J.T., DeWitt, W., Keebler, J.S., Min, S., Nix, N.W., Smith, C.D., and Zacharia, Z.G. (2001) Defining supply chain management. *Journal of Business Logistics*, 22(2), 1–25.

Min, S. and Menzer, J.T. (2004) Developing and measuring supply chain management concepts. *Journal of Business Logistics*, 25(1), 63–99.

Oliver, R.K. and Webber, M.D. (1982) Supply-chain management: logistics catches up with strategy. *Outlook* 5(1), 42–47.

Poli, R. (2005) The football players trade as a global commodity chain. *Transnational networks from Africa to Europe,* Iwalea-Haus, Bayreuth (Vol. 4).

Preuss, H. (2005) The economic impact of visitors at major multi-sport events. *Sport Management Quarterly*, 5(3), 281–301.

Relvas, H., Littlewood, M., Nesti, M., Gilbourne, D., and Richardson, D. (2010) Organisational structures and working practices in elite European professional football clubs: understanding the relationship between youth and professional domains. *European Sport Management Quarterly*, 10(2), 165–187.

Snell, S., Lepak, D., and Yound, M. (1999) Managing the architecture of intellectual capital: implications for strategic human resource management. In: P. Wright, L. Dyer, J. Boudreau, and G. Milkovich (eds.). *Research in Personnel and Human Resources Management* (pp. 175–193). Greenwich: JAI Press.

Solberg, H.A. (2003) Major sporting events: assessing the value of volunteers' work. *Managing Leisure*, 8(1), 17–27.

Soosay, C.A., Hyland, P.W., and Ferrer, M. (2008) Supply chain collaboration: capabilities for continuous innovation. *Supply Chain Management: An International Journal*, 3(2), 160–169.

Sparks, L. (2007) Distribution channels and sport logistics. In: J. Beech and S. Chadwick (eds.). *The Marketing of Sport* (pp. 365–398). Harlow: FT Prentice Hall.

Sparks, L. (2010) Supply chain management and retailing. In: Hamil, S. and Chadwick, S. (eds.). *Managing Football an International Perspective* (pp. 151–167). Oxford: Elsevier Ltd.

Sukhbinder, S. and Baines P.R. (2004) CS7 Fulham FC: Club-supporter relationships 'COME ALL YE FAITHFUL'. In: Harris, P and McDonald, F (eds.). *European Business and Marketing* (pp. 184–194). Thousand Oaks CA: Sage.

Szymoszowskyj, A., Winand, M., Kolyperas, D., and Sparks, L. (2016) Professional football clubs retail branding strategies. *Sport, Business and Management: An International Journal*, 6(5), 579–598.

Taylor, F.W. (1914) *The Principles of Scientific Management*. New York: Harper & Brothers.

Vargo, S. L. and Lusch, R. F. (2004) Evolving to a new dominant logic for marketing. *Journal of Marketing*, 68(1), 1–17.

Woratschek, H., Horbel, C., and Popp, B. (2014) The sport value framework – a new fundamental logic for analyses in sport management. *European Sport Management Quarterly*, 14(1), 6–24.

27

Risk and crisis management

Dominic Elliott

Introduction

Nobel Prize-winning Economist Daniel Kahneman (2011) distinguishes between System 1 thinking for those activities where humans decide almost unconsciously, quickly and almost automatically and those he labels System 2, which require focused attention with continuous judgement, making sense of many variables. System 1 reflects my motorway commute to work where I often arrive almost by surprise having been lost in my thoughts and driving on autopilot, thousands of times. Compare that to motorbike racing and the degree of focus required to be successful. In April 2015 my Australian friend and colleague was killed racing in a Thundersport GB series race at Donington Park; he was the 39th racer to die in the UK since 2000. Craner Curves, the part of the track where this tragic accident occurred, is notorious, meriting a mention in Williams' (2010) book on the death of Ayrton Senna. My friend's mode of operation when racing, was very much System 2, no space for autopilot here, just focus. My colleague's death was a tragic accident and he recognised the *threat*, the *possibility*, the *chance*, the *danger* but took the *gamble* and calculated, favourably, the *probability* that his skill, that of his competitors, his machine, and the track technicians, etc. would see him through. Each of the italicised words are synonyms for risk and represent the differing ways we use the term. Risk is ubiquitous, a feature of every decision we make, albeit the consequences of a poor decision will vary significantly. Often, we increase our risk by operating in System 1 when a System 2 approach is required. Sometimes mindfulness in a System 2 context is simply not enough, but at age 48, my friend had come through many scrapes and understood the risk. Risk perception plays a vital role in identifying threats and in how to prepare for them. Thinking about how we think about risk is a vital step for each of us in minimising threats and preparing effectively to deal with them. I begin this chapter with a tragedy personal to me to emphasise that risk affects people with real consequences and can be a matter of life and death.

The death of a friend, who was a competitor in sport, is at one end of a spectrum, with the multiple deaths inside British football stadia at the other. The last such disaster in the UK, the Hillsborough Stadium Disaster (1989) where 96 spectators were crushed to death, was the subject of my doctoral research some 25 years ago. These spectators placed their trust in the hands of the police, the stadium designers, the owners' investment, and the local regulators to provide a safe environment in which they might enjoy watching a game of soccer. As I write in early 2018, the police officers involved in the incident and its aftermath are being prosecuted nearly 30 years after the event.

Fortunately, despite the opening paragraph, much of risk management is concerned with business risk and even when dealing with health and safety, the aim of risk management is to minimise failures. This chapter aims to provide sufficient content to help a manager or leader engage in an informed way with risk and associated practices and policies. Content covers an overview of key terms, the scope of risk and crisis management, and a process that may be followed from identifying potential threats through to incident management.

Sport is big business, as earlier chapters demonstrate, generating large revenues. Deloitte (2017) calculated the revenue of the European soccer industry to exceed $25 billion per annum. In addition to revenue and entertainment sport has an important, perhaps vital cultural influence too. Sport unites and divides, hence strict rules in the soccer industry on what players can wear, which meant in 2016 that British footballers were not permitted to wear a red poppy badge in memory of fallen soldiers. Symbolic actions create impact and images of African-American NFL players kneeling rather than standing during the American National Anthem in polite and silent protest concerning persistent institutionalised racism received much coverage and provoked a the US president to tweet a rebuke:

> If a player wants the privilege of making millions of dollars in the NFL, or other leagues, he or she should not be allowed to disrespect our Great American Flag (or Country) and should stand for the National Anthem.
>
> *(CNN, 2017)*

Trump added further fuel to the controversy with comments at a political rally:

> Wouldn't you love to see one of these NFL owners, when somebody disrespects our flag, to say, "Get that son of a bitch off the field right now. Out! He's fired. He's fired!"
>
> *(CNN, 2017)*

The speed and impact of so few words show the high profile of sport and the importance of social media as a communication channel.

As individuals, we make judgements involving risk every day, from deciding how to travel, where to live, and other choices such as whether to wear a cycle helmet. Sports competitors have less control and must place their trust in others – their team members, construction staff who build the facilities or the regulatory authorities. Following a death on a Luge track, the Olympic authorities had to judge whether the accident revealed a major flaw and abandon a once-in-four-years event or continue. It continued. Another Luge competitor, realising this might be his only chance of Olympic glory commented when asked what it would feel like to be the first competitor on the track following the fatal accident:

> Whatever, I could have been the first or the 10th. It's Olympic training. It's a tragedy. I can't personally deal with it until after the Games.
>
> *(Cited in Donegan, 2010a)*

Calculated risks are a part of sport, whether it is the decision on the number or timing of pit stops in Formula One, or whether a player should pass the ball or attempt to score a goal in soccer. In most cases the probabilities are uncertain and the range of outcomes unclear, although the best teams and individuals seem able to weigh up this uncertainty intuitively. Perceptions will be shaped by a host of subjective factors, including temperament, peer group, our education, to name a few. The process of risk management is vulnerable to the limitations of human judgement and although scientific tools may play a part, it is not a science.

Sport is a source of national or local pride and is often used to achieve political ends; China's massive investment in the Beijing Olympics symbolised China's emergence as a great power [see Chapter 40 in this handbook]; boycotts or bans have often been used as a means of applying pressure on some regimes; and high-profile sporting events may attract terrorists such as the suicide attacks at the Stade de France in 2015.

The degree of fanaticism of some spectators distinguishes sport from many other industries, although Apple customers may come close. The popularity of sports personalities and their place as role models secure lucrative sponsorship deals, which are vulnerable to scandals if they fail to live up to their public persona, as the ongoing coverage of the troubled golfer Tiger Woods demonstrates. Sponsors may be quick to cancel contracts to avoid tarnishing their brands by association.

Sporting events often involve large, excitable crowds, in confined spaces, and safety management must be a primary concern of event organisers. These spaces are often used infrequently, and their design often reflects this as low usage equates with low revenues. Sports stadium disasters remain a feature of sport globally, despite the large investments made in investigating failure, building safe structures, and developing management systems.

Many sports organisations have struggled to keep pace with the changing commercial opportunities open to them, reflecting the amateur origins of most sports. There has been a history of a make do approach to management, covering the basics but not recognising the necessity for sports to be led in a business-like way. This is changing and in the US NFL and baseball, and in the UK the Premier League, standout in terms of their investment in leadership, but in many cases a small group or individual, often poorly trained and overworked, is responsible for a wide range of activities, from ticket sales, contract negotiations, match arrangements, to health and safety. Within such a context, effective risk management is unlikely to receive the attention required.

In summary, although the sports industry has some unusual characteristics it shares the same issues as any other organisation. The following generic framework for considering risk and crisis through a business continuity management process is the focus of the next section of this chapter.

A business continuity approach

A Business Continuity Management (BCM) approach recognises the impact of interruptions/ failures upon a wide range of stakeholders and it seeks to avoid or else prevent incidents from escalating into crises, and increasingly, focuses upon building resilience.

Crisis management, its mother discipline, may be conceptualised as three distinct phases, as depicted in Figure 27.1 (Smith, 1990; Pauchant and Mitroff, 1992). These phases are the before, during, and after the crisis. The pre-crisis stage refers to the period in which the potential for failure is incubated. Decisions made during the months and years before an incident occurs determine the level of vulnerability of an organisation. Decisions, both formal and informal, such as the common practices might include accepting inappropriate staffing levels; ignoring or being slow to respond to health and safety reviews or near misses; poor training; too great a focus on the sports team side to the detriment of the back-office activities. These decisions reflect the core beliefs or culture of an organisation and research indicates that once embedded

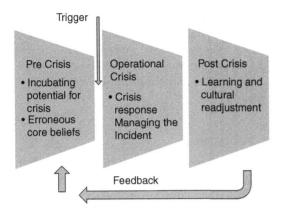

Figure 27.1 Stages of crisis model (adapted from Smith, 1990)

they become difficult to change. For example, in 2015 Sepp Blatter finally resigned as president of FIFA as pressure from sponsors including Adidas and Annheuser-Busch grew, coinciding with the arrests of several soccer officials in Switzerland (Borden, Schmidt, and Apuzzo, 2015). The pressure reflected serious concerns over the ability of a Blatter-led FIFA to respond effectively to the allegations of corruption rife within the industry. That "compulsion" was required indicates that FIFA's leadership team had lost touch with key stakeholder expectations, believed such activity was acceptable, and, quite possibly, felt itself beyond the reach of the legal authorities.

The second stage refers to the immediate incident response. A distinction must be drawn between the crisis and the trigger. The cancellation of the ITV digital contract with the Football League in 2002 triggered crises for many football clubs, especially those recently relegated but retained Premier League cost structures. The impact of this trigger was determined by the existing poor financial state of the clubs. Those that had taken such events into account within their planning scenarios were better placed to deal with the contract's cancellation than those that had not undertaken any such scenario planning. Similarly, effective crisis management may exacerbate or reduce the impact of a trigger event.

The third, and final, stage refers to the period in which an organisation seeks to consolidate and then reposition itself. Of course, phase three feeds back into phase one as organisations may or may not learn from their experiences.

A BCM approach has evolved from considering how to manage crisis incidents (i.e., phases two and three), to considering how the potential for crisis may be incubated by organisations themselves (see Pauchant and Mitroff, 1992; Elliott and Smith 1993, 1997) for a detailed sports industry case study). Here traditional risk management may play a key role in identifying the types of threat, their impacts, and how effective response may be planned and resilience developed. Core beliefs and culture are important in shaping the process, often requiring a major event to trigger real change. The death of Formula One driver Ayrton Senna whilst competing triggered a crisis of confidence in Grand Prix safety. Such crisis incidents usually possess social and technical dimensions and, in this case, the causes of Senna's crash included faulty adaptations of the steering column of Senna's vehicle alongside poor track maintenance of the San Marino track. Lovell (2003) suggests that charges against the organisers of the event and the owners of the vehicle were either dropped or "eased" because of the political connections of key personnel with senior Italian politicians. Whatever the truth, the desire to limit driver injuries and fatalities has led to vast improvements in the design of vehicles and tracks and other safety equipment, reflecting higher expectations of what is acceptable and representing a shift in core beliefs.

Effective risk management requires processes to identify and assess the source and impact of threats and their likely impact on key stakeholders. Aligned with this, organisations must develop the capability to respond to incidents and limit their impact. Although plans are one indicator of preparedness, organisations should focus on learning from the planning process, tests, and exercises to develop a competence. Further, effective risk management involves learning from near misses and the mistakes of others.

Managing risk

From a practical perspective, there are four basic steps required to manage risk effectively. Step 1 concerns identifying the range of threats. Step 2 focuses upon developing an understanding of the organisation, including its key activities and vulnerabilities, stakeholders, supply-chain dependencies, and environmental issues. Growing sensitivity to issues such as banned drugs and sexual harassment should also be included, given their impact upon victims and the potential for reputational damage. Step 3 is concerned with assessing probabilities and determining priorities. In step 4, alternative options to mitigate threats are considered, ranging from avoidance (withdrawing from an activity), deferment (wait and see), reduction (improve prevention and control measures, for example, through a continuity management process), or transfer (via insurance).

Step 1: identifying threats and hazards

Anecdotal evidence from many countries indicates that the perception of British soccer spectators as hooligans remains strong (Elliot, 1998). Although hooliganism played no part in events such as those at the Hillsborough, Bradford, and Ibrox stadia, memories of the 39 Juventus fans killed in the Heysel Stadium in Brussels live on. Although hooliganism was only one factor in Heysel, our perceptions of risk are shaped by such examples rather than by the largely passive fans in the other three incidents. Elliott and Smith (2006) argued that the persistent emphasis of police and regulators upon soccer hooliganism, when considering crowd control, is key to understanding why stadia which were unsafe continued to be designed and poorly managed. The prevailing mind-set influenced how police and security personnel repeatedly misinterpreted crowd distress as hooliganism, thereby impeding their ability to stop or slow an incident from escalating into a major disaster. For example, some police officers at Hillsborough physically forced spectators back into the crush from which they sought to escape. Such prevailing mind-sets distort our ability to judge "objective" probabilities. Individuals are more likely to die or be injured as they drive to a soccer match than die as victims of hooliganism or disaster. An essential part of the first step of this BCM process is to create a mind-set poised for objectivity, open to challenge, and thereby sensibly construct and categorise the wide range of threats organisations may face.

The scope can be narrow or broad, reflecting the managerial mind-set of an organisation. A useful way of organising and presenting the scope is via a risk register, which may be produced at a strategic level or at a more operational or micro level. The aim is to focus attention and discussion on the most salient risks facing an organisation. It is most likely to be useful when produced by a team drawn from a variety of functional areas. It may not be straightforward to quantify each risk, but if it is listed, a judgement may be made and mitigation identified. This should be reviewed regularly, at least once per year for a strategic risk register and quarterly for the operational version. Table 27.1 includes strategic and operational risks. The gaps recognise that it is not always easy to assess the likelihood of a threat nor the impact as so much is dependent upon context. What is most important is that all risks be identified and considered regardless

Table 27.1 Risk register

Category	Illustration	Example	Chance 1–5	Impact 1–5	Risk score	Possible mitigation	Risk owner	Time
Operations								
Power cut during event	Power cut in stadium during well attended evening event in winter.		1	2	3	Backup generator available. Stewards trained in evacuation procedures. Loud hailer as back up to PA system. Wind up torches for stewards and clear marking of exits with emergency lighting and marked with white paint.	Board, Stadium Manager, Chief steward	
Slip/fall hazard around stadium	Flooding, ice or uneven surface/ stairs present a trip hazard to few or many.		2	2	4	Ongoing inspection and maintenance of stadium, especially pre-match and when there are adverse weather conditions.	Board, Stadium Manager	
Succession management	Manchester United struggle to replace Alex Ferguson, with a succession of well-known coaches making unsatisfactory progress.	FC Barcelona	4	5	20	Long term plan to develop replacement, inhouse and/or manage change when right person available.	Board	
Leaks of confidential and embarrassing information	**Football leaks** – A whistleblower website reveals secret financial details /correspondence from professional soccer. Site revealed details appearing to show both Cristiano Ronaldo and Jose Mourinho moving millions of euros avoid tax. (Rengers, 2017)					First, do not behave unethically and consider how any action might viewed on the front page of a newspaper. Second, develop a crisis communications plan, identifying key stakeholders, messages, and choice of modes of communication. Build good will.	CEO, Dir. of Marketing,	

(continued)

Table 27.1 Continued

Category	Illustration	Example	Chance 1–5	Impact 1–5	Risk score	Possible mitigation	Risk owner	Time
Health and Safety	**Athletes** – Death of Luge competitor Nodar Kumaritashvili at Vancouver Olympics 2010 **Spectators** – Stadia management, disasters in Abidjan, (2009), Johannesburg (2001), Bastia (1989) Hillsborough (1989)		1	5	5	Take health and safety seriously and ensure it is adequately funded and that CEO takes leading interest, or risk corporate manslaughter. The likelihood is identified as low because this an area which receives significant attention in most professional sports.	CEO, H&S Manager	
Abuse and Harassment	Reports of sexual harassment, discrimination, homophobia and abuse of youngsters in sports training are more common and given greater credence than ten years ago, posing threats to individual victims as well as posing legal and reputational risks.		2	5	10	Appoint properly trained/empowered officers to investigate allegations promptly and thoroughly. Establish guidelines to help establish culture of dignity and respect at work. Use variety of communication channels to educate and raise awareness. Positive discrimination where appropriate.	Protection officers, Board, CEO	
Strategic								
Slow to innovate or respond to competition	In early 1970s Adidas dominated the running shoe industry. It under estimated the growth in demand for running shoes and the aggression of new rivals Nike.		3	5	15	Adidas might have reacted to protect its position by building barriers to entry, stronger promotion, sharper pricing and ongoing research and development (Hartley, 1995).	Board, CEO	
	Golf, in the US and Europe, suffers from lower engagement from younger demographic groups, in terms of participation, spectating and product purchase – reflecting ageing profile of amateur golfers and famous players.		2	5	10	Develop better understanding of customer wants, develop new products, service, promote appealing role models to grow youth and women markets.	PGA, Golf bodies	

Risk	Example / Description	Owner	L	I	Score	Response	Responsibility
Access to revenue-generating competition	For teams such as FC Barcelona, Real Madrid, Manchester Utd, Bayern Munich, Champions League revenues are a vital source of revenue, with consequences if qualification is not achieved.	Man Utd FC Barcelona	3 1	5 5	15 5	Insurance against non-qualification Different scores reflect the structure of the Premier League which creates greater uncertainty over qualification than in La Liga.	Man Utd FCB
Declining market	English and Welsh cricket suffer falling crowd attendances.	ECB	4	5	20	Creates 20-20 version and revitalises the industry.	ECB
Financial and compliance							
Cyclical risk	FIFA leads to negative cash flow in non-World Cup years.	FIFA	5	2		Budget accordingly. Develop alternative FIFA revenue-generating events.	Board, Dir. of Finance
Credit risk	Since 1992 English Football League clubs have fallen into insolvency 53 times with an estimated £200 million unpaid to creditors.	English Football League	3	5	15	Improve financial controls and competence at club level. UEFA introduce Financial Fair Play rules.	EFL, Club FDs
Abuse of position	Adamu, (VP of FIFA and Nigerian rep.) and Temarii (from Tahiti) were banned for one year when caught out in a sting by newspaper investigators pretending to buy votes for the USA's World Cup bid.		2	2	4	Poor reputationally, but this has limited impact on FIFA as a whole.	
Corruption	Former Juventus director Antonio Giraudo sentenced to three years in prison for his role in match-fixing scandal. (Guardian, 2009)		2	2	4	Very much a personal risk unlike the allegations of institutionalised corruption re football authorities.	

(continued)

Table 27.1 Continued

Category	Illustration	Example	Chance 1–5	Impact 1–5	Risk score	Possible mitigation	Risk owner	Time
Relegation and revenue	Premier League club gets relegated and loses £65 million.	Leicester City	3	4	12	Plan on basis of worst, likely, and best scenario and ensure that you have a plan for revenue/costs of worst scenario.	Board, CEO	
Political								
International relations	Threat to PyeongChang Winter Olympics (2018) with boycott/ ban of Russian team.	Korean organisers	4	2	8	Not ideal but unlikely to damage revenues and viewing figures.	None	
Equal rights	President Trump criticism of NFL players kneeling during US National Anthem to protest about mistreatment of African Americans, highlights the contrast between Black players and primarily white owners. (CNN, 2017)		?	?	?	Part of a bigger political picture. Organisations must make a judgement re. the impact of such protests in terms of ethics and then reputational/legal/ financial. Such examples are difficult to quantify, but listing them means that they will be considered.		
Equal pay	Recent research suggests that 83% of sports award equal prize money to men and women, but only one woman is in the Forbes list of the richest 100 athletes. Certain sports, including soccer and golf, retain massive pay differentials. (Perasso, 2017)	UK Soccer	5	2	10	It is difficult to see the pay gap being closed in those areas where it is widest in the short term as pay is linked to revenues earned. Only legislation is likely to effect change.		

Operational and reputational

Collective reputational risk	Rising awareness and growing capabilities to identify drugs used to enhance athlete performance have seen the World Anti-Doping Agency declare the Russian Anti-Doping Agency non-compliant and subsequent restrictions on Russian athletes' participation in the 2018 Winter Olympic Games (Press Association, 2017)	Each case is unique, and it is difficult to suggest mitigation except don't do it or ensure that drugs testing agencies are well resourced and empowered to act. Building strong links with the media and having plan to deal with media (especially social media) are vital.
Individual reputation risk	Since reports of Tiger Woods marital infidelity were widely circulated, triggering Accenture and A&T to withdraw sponsorship in 2010, Woods has not won a single major title. (see Donegan, 2010c; Finn, 2017)	There are many examples of individuals losing reputation and often this is because they fail to live up to a carefully constructed false identity or else they have a track record of misdemeanour.

of whether it is possible to allocate a weighting to them. It is a question of judgement rather than one of getting a number correct.

There is a danger that the risk register focuses solely upon physical or technical threats such as health and safety, systems failure, fire, etc. These are, of course important, but so too are the business and reputational risks and those emanating from human conduct such as corruption and sexual harassment.

Soccer stadium disasters and the well-publicised deaths of spectators and drivers in Formula One have been well reported, and even baseball has seen five spectators die since 1970. These are the most tangible of hazards. However, as the sports industry has become more professional, the threats from other categories of risk have become more obvious as Manchester United's insurance policy against non-qualification for the European Champions League indicates; it protected them when in 2016/2017 Premier League Champions Leicester City qualified and Manchester United did not.

Within the soccer industry, and in sport in general, the growing separation of coaching from business management recognises the importance of employing staff with business and other skills. In an early study of the soccer industry, Fynn and Guest (1994) identified a serious lack of business acumen. Fifteen years later, in 2010, Lord Mawhinney, the Football League chairman, observed:

> The way football clubs do business fundamentally does not work … I think people are taking this issue much more seriously now. What is given to players and agents is not sustainable. There has to be some element of control and restraint.
>
> *(see Conn, 2010)*

Organisations such as Ali Baba, Apple, Google, Ryanair, and Samsung have sustained success through ongoing market research, competitor analysis, and a sound understanding of how their competences fit with their environments and by pursuing continuous innovation. They also practice good risk management, with some success, most of the time. Although the introduction of new consumer-driven formats such as 20-20 in cricket have emerged innovation in sports, these tend to be focused upon improvements in equipment (e.g., motor racing, cycling), nutrition (athletics, cycling), or on reducing the inevitable human error of referees through video playback (rugby, cricket). Media companies often take precedence as the key customer over consumers, and sports organisations may pay too little attention to understanding their consumers and in adapting their offer to changing needs and demographic profile, as seems to be the case with golf.

Different threats may result in similar risks. For example, banned drugs, bribery, and match-fixing, and the identification of key staff as racist would all combine both legal and reputational dimensions and might benefit from a similar response. Planners are limited in terms of time and resources and cannot account for all eventualities. The case of the global soccer industry provides evidence of the failure of corporate governance to deal firmly with investigating and rooting out corruption. Law breaking, dubious ethics, tax avoidance/evasion, and reckless spending may be endemic and have been a blight on the industry for many years. The "Football Leaks" shared evidence of tax avoidance and evasion involving many players and coaches, including Barcelona's Messi, Real Madrid's Ronaldo and Manchester United's Mourinho, amongst many others (Rengers, 2017). Members of the European Parliament accuse football officials of being "enablers" of a corrupt system that permits players and agents to avoid tax (Aarons, 2017). The resignation of FIFA President Sepp Blatter in 2015 was forced through by sponsor pressure and arrests of senior figures (Borden et al., 2015).

These issues are a key part of the backdrop to FIFA facing a financial shortfall in revenues from the World Cup in Russia (2018). This shortfall emerges from the difficulties in attracting new top tier and local sponsors, with the view of FIFA as a "toxic brand". Nally (2017) asserts that unless you are from a country "where the fact FIFA is in court in New York and associated with corruption doesn't matter, no corporation is going to consider it safe to get involved with FIFA." The lack of local partners is especially worrying, both as a source of revenue and because Russian partners would help build excitement among local fans. President Putin may also have worries about being too closely associated with a team, currently 65th in world ranking (Hyde, 2017).

Where there is a perception that corruption and related behaviours are institutionalised within an industry, the consequences will be significant. Soccer's ongoing popularity has perhaps insulated it for a while, encouraging complacency and hubris with senior executives isolated from the real world and left feeling a sense of invulnerability. Parallels might be drawn with some of the worst excesses of the finance sector before the credit crunch of 2007, the effects of which are still being felt.

Macro environmental shocks may have unexpected consequences. When Britain voted for Brexit, the value of the pound sterling versus the euro fell sharply. This meant that a €40 million bid for a Spanish footballer increased from £31 million to £34 million for a British Club (Aarons, 2016). If Brexit occurs, there may be restrictions of the movement of workers, including sports coaches and players. A second consequence could be restrictions on the movement of players and coaches between the UK and its EU partners, a move, which might trigger the decline of the Premier League. Spectators will be affected too. Tennis fans travelling to Paris for the French Open or Motor-racing enthusiasts attending the German or San Marino Grand Prix will find tickets more expensive. Travellers may require visas, may lose their EU wide mobile roaming tariffs, and may no longer have access to free emergency health care. Falling land prices in London, following the 2007 monetary crisis, escalated the costs of London 2012 Olympics, by reducing the value of the post-2012 asset sale, which was to be offset against the initial investment (Taylor, 2010).

Another commonly occurring risk is the threat to reputation, as the sorry case of Tiger Woods exemplifies. In the age of social media and given the importance of media, brand, and image rights, an increasing source of revenue for sports organisations and individuals [see Chapter 9 in this handbook]. Allegations of impropriety, proven or unproven, may be highly damaging; whether they relate to infidelity (Tiger Woods), sexual harassment (Amelia Rayno), banned drug taking (Lance Armstrong), suspicions of banned drug taking (Team Sky, Bradley Wiggins), missing drug tests (Mo Farah), or result fixing, all provide a threat to the people involved and to other organisations with which they are associated, be they sponsors (see Roberts, Chadwick and Anagnostopoulos, 2017), employers, or regulators. It is not whether the allegations are true and proven which counts, rather it is the immediate, and potentially long-lasting, threat to reputation, whether fair or not. Those organisations or personalities that maintain positive relationships with the media and other key stakeholders have a real advantage over those who fail to if rumours or scandal breaks.

As these cases illustrate, the sports industry may be faced with a wide range of threats, some strategic in nature, other more operational failures but which have the potential to escalate into a crisis. The above case material also indicates warning signs in terms of overcrowded stadia, police misperceptions, and many football clubs metaphorically sailing close to the wind financially. The threats to FIFA, of business risks, low liquidity, cyclical cash flow, weak corporate governance may equally apply to other governing bodies as well as to the small and large sports businesses. Similarly, threats to spectator safety inside stadia are as apt to sports such as motor rally, Formula One, and athletics as to football (soccer).

The aim of this section has been to consider the wide range of threats to sports organisations. The frameworks provide a focus for considering the broad scope of risk and for considering which may be the most relevant for sports business. However, as the examples illustrate, threats, when realised, rarely impact upon one organisation alone, the nature of risk and crisis is that they encompass multiple stakeholders.

Step 2: identifying and assessing the risk

Two broad approaches to risk assessment have emerged, the heuristic and "scientific" approaches. The heuristic (rule of thumb approach) is qualitative and based upon judgement. The "scientific" approach utilises statistical modelling. Toft (1993) has argued that all risk assessment, no matter how sophisticated the modelling, remains inherently value-laden and is, therefore, a judgement.

Elliott et al. (2010) offer a qualitative framework for risk assessment, one emphasising the interdependence of organisations and the importance of a full stakeholder analysis. Key questions to be examined include:

- What is the potential impact upon our business and other stakeholders?
- What is the probability of a failure occurring?
- What are our key business and operational objectives?
- How do we exploit our resources to achieve our strategic objectives and create value?
- What linkages and dependencies exist within our supply network?
- What seasonal trends or critical timing issues might impact us?
- Is the threat acceptable to our stakeholders and us?
- What should be done to manage risk?

These headings (which lead to related questions) should be adapted to meet the needs of the organisation. These questions should stimulate data gatherers and managers to consider risk and how threats might affect business processes and stakeholders. Elliott et al.'s (2010) framework highlights the importance of understanding an organisation's internal and external environment. Table 27.2 highlights functional dependencies, both within an organisation and its supply chain (see Chapter 26 in this handbook]. Understanding such dependencies is crucial as no part of an organisation is an island and often it takes a crisis to highlight where the "hidden" dependencies are. There may be single points of failure not readily identifiable. A stadium control system with no proper contingency would be a single point of failure. A common example is the dominant sports club owner who insists on making all major decisions but then falls ill or loses interest. Similarly, the lack of proper succession planning for a coach might be a single point of failure.

The aim of the risk assessment stage is to better understand the degree and nature of threats in terms of severity of impact and probability of occurrence. Categorisation may occur from a simple ranking exercise using the scores from the risk register. Although risk analysis and assessment may be aided by complex mathematical modelling, these only aid judgement as they are based upon many subjective assumptions.

Step 3: risk assessment

Given the potential hazards of Formula One, safety issues receive detailed consideration, especially as new technical innovations emerge. The introduction of pit stops (1982) enabled cars to run with lighter fuel loads and softer tyres and provided an opportunity for sponsors to publicise

Table 27.2 Functional dependencies

Dependencies	Examples
Operations management and production	Sporting events require crowd management and facilities management.
	Refreshment suppliers
	Crowd monitoring systems
	Growing reliance on IS providers for core business
Information and communication technologies (ICT)	Automated crowd control systems
	CCTV
	Social media capability (technical)
Reputation	Strong media relations to build strong brand
Marketing (shared brands, marketing and promotion)	Tiger Woods loses sponsorship
	Social media capability in terms of communicating and harvesting customer data
Distribution channels (type, number and mix of wholesalers/retailers)	Increasing concentration of power in media companies with TV rights – how to respond?
Purchasing and procurement (raw materials and components from suppliers)	Collective bargaining from professional players' unions.
	Providers of key sporting venues
Logistics (whether in house or otherwise)	Ever growing online ticket and merchandise sales
Organisational support activities (such as legal, finance, etc.)	Lawyers give advice on key contractual issues

their logos. However, it increased the hazards associated with blasting fuel into tanks via pressure hoses and after an incident involving Keke Rosberg's car, it was banned until 1994. Then, Bernie Ecclestone, aware of the dramatic impact of pit stops on television, successfully advocated their reintroduction – the risk was considered worth the television entertainment value (Lovell, 2003). Risk practice results from a trade-off; in this case, driver safety versus revenue streams. The use of a safety car, in Formula One, to slow competitors following an accident reduces the need for lengthy restarts, an issue for global television companies that were concerned that long waits for restarts would encourage bored television viewers to switch channels. Drivers' concerns that the slowness of the safety car could cause the tyre pressure to drop and seriously reduce handling capability were given less consideration.

These two examples illustrate the balance that sports managers strike between conflicting objectives. The purpose of risk assessment and analysis is that such decisions are grounded in a critical evaluation of the evidence. A danger is that commercial factors outweigh health and safety, especially where threats to participants are more difficult to quantify. Risk strategies may also be evident in preparations for managing the crisis, the subject of the next section, and in the preparation of business continuity plans (BCPs).

Simply explained, a BCP is the outcome of a thorough process in which the links between an organisation's objectives, resources, environmental context, and dependencies are critically examined. The resulting plan identifies how an organisation will re-establish itself in the event of an interruption. It may include a blueprint of key personnel, contact details, equipment, activities, key deadlines, etc. in order that any business recovery can be achieved quickly (see Elliott et al., 2010 for a full discussion of BCM). The objective of BCM is to ensure that recovery occurs in an orderly manner in a way that supports the strategic objectives of an organisation.

Step 4: managing the crisis

Handling events

Major sporting events bring together thousands of people and may be characterised by dynamism, excitement, and the unfamiliarity of many spectators with their temporary surroundings. Despite the widespread understanding of how to keep crowds safe, injuries and even deaths inside sports stadia still occur at a frightening frequency. Time is likely to be of the essence in incidents where there are deaths, injury, or serious threats to property, although a longer time-frame may be more important where there is a significant threat to an organisation's reputation.

A key component of effective incident management is the crisis management team. In addition to the day-to-day structures required to implement risk management, a command and control structure for managing crisis incidents is useful. A commonly used format is a three-tier structure, as advocated by the Home Office (1997a, 1997b), mimicking the structure used by the British Police Service who label the three levels bronze, silver, and gold system (respectively tactical, operational, and strategic). This structure emerged from an attempt to encourage consistency between the emergency services and thereby minimise confusion when dealing with an incident (Flin, 1996).

The purpose of the three levels is to ensure that an organisation's response to an incident is coordinated. Bronze (operational) corresponds to the normal operational response provided by the business continuity team. The immediate response to an incident is likely to be managed at this level. For example, a sudden snowfall or build of ice outside a stadium would be dealt with by small groups of staff as a routine matter, laying salt and marking out especially slippery areas. Should there be an exceptional issue such as a major snowfall with spectators already in the ground, then a more coordinated (silver level) approach might be required to ensure that a small number of pathways through the snow might be dug, through which spectators might be guided by stewards, to ensure their safety. The event manager and team would work to ensure that this was conducted in a considered way. It is difficult to see this escalating further unless all means of transport from the stadium were closed because of the adverse weather, leaving thousands stranded. This would require escalation to the strategic (gold) level as most sports organisations would require emergency services' help to deal with thousands of people caught outside in freezing conditions with little shelter.

There is no one best way, and organisations should plan to use structures that best fit their needs and resources. The most important part of the response is effective communication, which brings together key decision-makers. The three levels identify a minimum of three roles to be undertaken when managing an incident. In smaller organisations, one team or individual may perform these distinct roles. Sport abounds with examples of task specialisation: fielders, bowlers, and wicket keepers in cricket; forwards and backs in rugby; strikers, midfielders, defenders, and goalkeepers in soccer. Individuals may switch from defence to attack depending upon need and revert as necessary. This is an apt metaphor for the crisis team. The same individual may fulfil distinct roles as necessary.

Teams are important because, generally, they outperform individuals although, as Janis' ground-breaking work identified, teams may be fallible. Errors may arise from the inadequate quality of information available, a lack of monitoring key indicators (e.g. accident statistics, budgetary controls), the cognitive abilities of the group and political differences within a group. Inevitably, political manoeuvring may reduce team effectiveness. Smart and Vertinsky (1977) identify a range of remedies to the potential difficulties of fallible teams, including the inclusion of independent experts, encouraging alternative viewpoints, protecting minority perspectives, and holding crisis simulations. Implicit in Smart and Vertinsky's analysis is the development of the critical team that continually questions decisions and information whilst possessing the mechanisms, personnel, and communication channels to support quick and effective action.

Conclusions

Risk, crisis, and BCM processes have developed rapidly during the early twenty-first century in all industry sectors. As the management of sport professionalises and moves away from its amateur roots, it too needs to meet the challenge of dealing with uncertainty and the threat of business interruptions. Indeed, the volatility of many sporting organisations' environments, with close links between performance and revenue streams, in addition to the more tangible health and safety type operational risks, highlights the relevance of risk and crisis management to this industry. It has been argued that crises impact upon a wide group of stakeholders, not simply the host organisation. A multiple stakeholder perspective is thus the starting point for effective risk management and should flow through subsequent analysis. The four-stage process outlined in this chapter provides a useful starting point and is only constrained by the imagination of the analyst.

References

Aarons, E. (2016) Brexit vote: what does it mean for professional sport in the UK?, June 24 2016 *The Guardian*. [online] Retrieved from:https://www.theguardian.com/uk-news/2016/jun/24/brexit-vote-what-does-it-mean-professional-sport-eu

Aarons, E. (2017) FIFA and UEFA accused of being 'enablers' of tax evasion in football by MEPs, September 27, 2017, *The Guardian*. [online] Retrieved from: https://www.theguardian.com/football/2017/sep/27/fifa-uefa-tax-evasion-football-meps

Berrnstein, P. (1996) *Against the Gods, the Remarkable Story of Risk*. New York: John Wiley

Borden, S, Schmidt, M.S, and Apuzzo, M. (2015) *New York Times*, June 2, 2015. [online] Retrieved from: https://www.nytimes.com/2015/06/03/sports/soccer/sepp-blatter-to-resign-as-fifa-president.html

CNN (2017) It's impossible for black athletes to leave politics off the field. [online] Retrieved from: http://edition.cnn.com/2017/09/24/politics/trump-african-american-athletes/index.htm

Conn, D. (2010) Inside Sport. *The Guardian*, 10 February. [online] Retrieved from: http://www.guardian.co.uk/football/david-conn-inside-sport-blog/2010/feb/10/portsmouth-cardiff-hmrc-winding-up

Deloittes (2017) Annual Review of Football Finance 2017. [online] Retrieved from: https://www2.deloitte.com/uk/en/pages/sports-business-group/articles/annual-review-of-football-finance.html

Donegan, L. (2010a) Luge men back on Vancouver track as IOC lets responsibilities slide. *The Observer*, 14 February, p. 1

Donegan, L. (2010b) Luge athlete's death in training casts shadow over Vancouver Olympics The Guardian, 13 February, p. 3

Elliott D. and Smith D. (1993) Learning from tragedy: sports stadia disasters in the UK. *Industrial and Environmental Crisis Quarterly*, 7(3), 205–230

Elliott, D. and Smith, D. (1997) Waiting for the next one. In: Frosdick, S. and Walley, L. (eds), *Sport and Safety Management*. Butterworth Heinemann.

Elliott, D. (1998) *Learning from Crisis*, unpublished PhD thesis, University of Durham.

Elliott, D., Swartz, E. and Herbane, B. (2010) *Business Continuity Management: A Crisis Management Approach*, (2nd ed.). London: Routledge.

Elliott, D. and Smith, D. (2006) Patterns of regulatory behaviour in the uk football industry. *Journal of Management Studies*, 43(2), 291–318.

Fenton-O'Creevey M. and Soane, E. (2001) The subjective perception of risk. In: Pickford, J. (ed.). *Mastering Risk*. London: Financial Times – Prentice Hall.

Finn, N. (2017) Tiger Woods's life hasn't been the same since his cheating scandal: all the highs and lows leading up to his DUI arrest. [online] Retrieved from: http://www.eonline.com/uk/news/858542/tiger-wood-s-life-hasn-t-been-the-same-since-his-cheating-scandal-all-the-highs-lows-leading-up-to-his-dui-arrest

Flin, R. (1996) *Sitting in the Hot Seat*. London: John Wiley.

Fynn, A. and Guest L. (1994) *Out of Time*. London: Simon and Schuster.

Hartley, R. F. (1995) *Marketing Mistakes* (6th Ed.). New York: John Wiley.

Hyde, M. (2017) Infanto busily exhibiting all the signs of a limited shelf life as the new broom at Fifa. *The Guardian*, 30 November 2017, p. 36.

Kahneman, D. (2011) *Thinking, Fast and Slow*. Allen Lane: London.

Lovell, T. (2003) *Bernie's Game*. London: Metro Publishing.

Nally, P. (2017) cited in Panja, T. (2017) As Sponsors Shy Away, FIFA faces World Cup shortfall, *New York Times*, 28 November 2017. [online] Retrieved from: https://www.nytimes.com/2017/11/28/sports/soccer/world-cup-sponsors-russia-2018.html

Pauchant, T. and Mitroff, I. (1992) *Transforming the Crisis-prone Organization*. San Francisco, California: Jossey-Bass.

Perasso, V. (2017) 100 Women: Is the gender pay gap in sport really closing? *BBC News*. [online] Retrieved from: http://www.bbc.co.uk/news/world-41685042

Press Association (2017) Russian Boycott of Winter Olympics moves step closer after Wada ruling, *The Guardian*. [online] Retrieved from: https://www.theguardian.com/sport/2017/nov/16/russia-boycott-winter-olympics-step-closer-after-wada-ruling

Rengers, M. (2017) Speaking notes. [online] Retrieved from: http://www.europarl.europa.eu/cmsdata/127803/5%20-%2001%20On%20Football%20Leaks%20-%20speaking%20notes%20Merijn%20Rengers.pdf

Roberts, S., Chadwick, S. and Anagnostopoulos, C. (2017) Sponsorship programmes and corruption in sport: management responses to a growing threat. *Journal of Strategic Marketing*, 26(1), 19–36.

Smart, C. and Vertinsky, I. (1977) Designs for crisis decision units, *Administrative Science Quarterly*, 22, 640–657.

Smith, D. (1990) Beyond contingency planning: towards a model of crisis management. *Industrial Crisis Quarterly*, 4(4), 263–275.

Taylor, M. (2010) Falling land values hit Olympic Budgets. *The Guardian*, Tuesday, 9 February, p. 3.

Toft, B (1993) Learning from Disaster, Palgrave MacMillan, London

William, R. (2010) *The Death of Ayrton Senna*. Penguin Books: London.

28

Women and football

Sue Bridgewater

Introduction

Women's football has flourished in recent years, and interest in football played by women is currently at an all-time high.

(www.FIFA.com)

While the growth in women's participation in football, attendance, and viewership of football may look like recent and very promising trends, the history of women's football is much longer, richer, and more complex. Over the past hundred years, however, the "growth in numbers has been neither steady nor unproblematic" (Williams, 2007). The ups and downs of women's football do not simply reflect interest and engagement but stem from a much more complex interplay of gender perceptions, cultural norms, and positive and negative interventions by governing bodies.

The question of whether women's football can be viewed as a globally popular sport remains the subject of much debate (Williams, 2007). In global terms, a minority of women play football, the majority do not. Both the men's and women's game of football are, however, global in scope, in their women's competitions, in participation and, increasingly, in the employment of women in the global game and business of football.

Women play a number of different roles in football, both in the women's and men's game and sometimes across both. This chapter explores the complex opportunities and challenges which face women and women's football in terms of the three areas of:

- Football participation;
- Attendance and spectatorship of football;
- Women's roles in football.

Football participation

Women's football and the elite game

When Sepp Blatter, then general secretary of football's governing body, FIFA, embraced women's football with his "future is feminine" statement in 1995, he appeared to be officially welcoming women in the football family, but in terms and in a role which remained undefined (Williams, 2007).

There had been, at this point, two successful Women's World Cup competitions: in 1991 (China) and 1995 (Sweden). Women's football would enter the Olympic Games at Atlanta in 1996. Women's football had, and has, a very promising future. By this point it also had a rich past, a heritage stretching back, in some parts of the world, for over 100 years.

Yet the story of the development of women's football has been one of ups and downs, of an evolution which has, at various points in history, been both enhanced and inhibited by the broader political and social agendas of others.

Football[1] has developed along different pathways in different regions and contexts. There are reports of women's football being played across Asia, the Americas, and Europe back into the nineteenth century (Williams, 2015). To illustrate the diversity and richness of women's football, this chapter highlights three such contexts and development pathways.

United Kingdom

When the first international match was organised between Scotland and England in 1881, football soon became mired with the suffragist[2] agenda and antagonism over the roles of women in society (Tate, 2017).

The advent of World War I, however, and an enforced move into the workplace by women as men went away to fight, resulted in the establishment of a number of successful women's football teams, predominantly in the North West of England. One of the earliest, and most successful, women's football teams, Dick, Kerr Ladies (DK Ladies), named after a munitions factory in Preston, played its first match for charity on Christmas Day against neighbouring Coulthard's factory in front of a crowd of over 10,000, with the £600[3] proceeds going to a hospital for wounded soldiers (Tate, 2017; Newsham, 2014; Jacobs, 2004).

By the 1920s, when DK Ladies played a charity match at Everton on Boxing Day, Goodison Park held a 53,000 capacity crowd, a further 14,000 people remained outside, unable to get into the ground. Pathé News, one of the biggest media players in the UK at that time, filmed these "stars" of women's football from the touchlines (Tate, 2017). In 1921, though, the Football Association (FA) began to take an interest in the finances and probity of women's football and passed resolutions that women's football should not be encouraged and that matches could not take place in football grounds without FA permission. Motivated by complex gender, political, and financial imperatives, this effectively brought about the demise of the 150 Women's football teams in existence in the UK at that time and led to the marginalisation of women's football for over 50 years (Williams, 2007).

USA

Whilst women's football in the USA began to gain popularity at the beginning of the twentieth century, the first recorded women's football league in the United States was the Craig Club Girls Soccer League: four teams in St Louis, Missouri playing 15 games per season in 1950 and 1951.

The introduction of Title IX legislation in 1972 made gender equality mandatory in education, including in collegiate athletics. More organised women's football teams and development opportunities and funding resulted. Collegiate football became more popular by the 1980s (Acosta and Carpenter, 2014). The success of the USA women's national team is attributed by Halloran (2013) to the appointment of Anson Dorrance as the team coach. Successful in collegiate football with North Carolina, Dorrance created a winning team of young players. Narcotta-Welp, in her 2016 doctoral thesis, further points to the role of such "benevolent patriarchs" in the development of successful US women's football, along with the development of opportunities in the collegiate system resulting from the Title IX legislation (Acosta and Carpenter, 2014).

The popularity of women's football in the US was, in turn, fuelled by the success of the USA women's national team in the first FIFA Women's World Cup Competition in China in 1991 (Halloran, 2013). At this time, there were still few professional opportunities for women in football in the United States, until the USL-W League was established in 1995.

PR China

In their paper on the history of women's football in China (2014), Zhao et al. describe women's football in China as having gone between the 1970s and the current time: "to the heights of international success and to the depths of ignominy. Driving the successes and failures were the national sports policies."

Some women played football in Chinese coastal cities as early as the 1920s (Fang, 2001) but women's participation in football began mainly in the early 1970s (Zhao et al., 2014). Dong and Mangan (2002) put this later, in the early 1980s: "as in 1981, the First National Women's Football Tournament took place in Guangdong. Thereafter, a number of women's football teams emerged across the country. From the mid-1980s, Chinese women took part in the Asian Women's Football Championships and dominated it in 1986."

Whilst there were 26 provincial women's football teams by 1983, the first women's professional team, Banqiu, was not established until the 1990s (Dong and Mangan, 2001). Dominating Asian football, the Chinese Women's team earned themselves the nickname of the "Steel Roses"[4] (Zhao et al., 2014) with discussion focussing on the relative burgeoning of women's football whilst the men's team languished behind. Zhao et al. identify the "zenith" of women's football in China as being in the mid-1990s when China achieved great success on an international stage. Beyond sporting success, Zhao et al. (2014) consider this very important socially and politically as China sought to establish its identity on a global stage after market reform and in the light of the relative lack of success of the Chinese men's football team.

The first FIFA Women's World Cup was hosted in China in 1991 and again in 2007, following a change of location from China for 2003 during the SARS epidemic.

By 2000, as market reforms were taking place in China, so too were changes in women's football with the development of a Professional Chinese Super League of ten teams. The relative success of women's football in China, however, has been impacted by the relatively low proportion of the budget which goes to the women's game and in that it was not self-sustaining in terms of domestic support[5] (Table 28.1).

Thirty-two countries have played in the FIFA Women's World Cup. Seven countries – the US, Germany, Norway, Japan, Brazil, Sweden, and Nigeria – have competed in all seven rounds of the competition. The first four of these have won the competition at least once. A further three countries – China, Canada, and Australia – have qualified for six of the seven editions of the competition (Table 28.2).

Table 28.1 Hosts of the Women's World Cup

Globalisation of women's elite football

Year	Host country	Number of teams competing	Tournament winner
1991	China	12	USA
1995	Sweden	12	Norway
1999	USA	16	USA
2003	USA[a]	16	Germany
2007	China	16	Germany
2011	Germany	16	Japan
2015	Canada	24	USA
2019	France	24	–

Source: FIFA.

[a] China was intended to host the 2003 FIFA Women's World Cup but a decision was taken to move this because of a SARS virus epidemic. The US hosted again and China were made hosts of the 2007 competition in compensation.

Table 28.2 Success in the FIFA Women's World Cup by confederation/region

	AFC[a]	CAF[b]	CONCACAF[c]	CONMEBOL[d]	OFC[e]	UEFA[f]
Total teams qualified	24	13	17	12	7	39
Top 8 positions	14	1	9	4	0	28
Top 4 positions	4	0	8	2	0	14
Top 2 positions	3	0	4	1	0	6
Champions	1	0	3	0	0	3

Source: FIFA.

[a] Asia
[b] Africa
[c] North, Central America and the Caribbean
[d] Latin America
[e] Oceania
[f] Europe

Whilst the FIFA Women's World Cup is clearly thriving, and expanding, and participation is spread across the range of confederations and continents, success in the competition is focused on a fairly small pool of countries. Some 177 countries have their women's teams ranked by FIFA on its website, http://www.fifa.com/fifa-world-ranking/ranking-table/women/index.html. Just 32 of 177 (18.08 per cent) have ever qualified for the FIFA Women's World Cup.[6]

Using data from the respective FIFA rankings of countries for the women's and men's football game, the following top 20 countries achieve the highest number of positions for their women's above their men's football national team (Table 28.3).

Of course, these high scores not only reflect the quality of women's football in the respective countries, they could be explained by the relatively low rank of the equivalent men's football team. Also, if a country ranks highly for both its men's and women's football teams, it will not show such a big difference. Accordingly, Table 28.4 shows the top 20 countries with the best combined FIFA ranking score for their men's and women's national team.

Table 28.3 Differences in rank between FIFA men's and women's national teams as at 29 Novermber 2017

Rank order	Country	Number of Positions by which Women's FIFA Ranking is Higher than Men's
1	Myanmar	115
2	Korea DPR	104
3	New Zealand	103
3	Thailand	103
5	Chinese Taipei	97
6	Vietnam	94
7	Canada	89
8	Jordan	57
9	Japan	47
9	China	47
11	Norway	44
11	Korea Republic	44
13	Belarus	43
14	Trinidad and Tobago	42
15	Russia	40
16	Finland	39
17	Uzbekistan	39
18	Australia	33
19	USA	23
20	Nigeria	15[a]

Source: FIFA.

[a] England would stand in 21st place with a difference of 14 places.

Women's football leagues

The structure, management, and funding of women's football leagues varies between countries. FIFA finds that all of the top FIFA ranked member associations have a women's league, whereas only 65 per cent of those who are in the bottom tier of FIFA rankings have a women's league.

Top national women's leagues are considered to be important by FIFA for the development of women's football within a country. Often such leagues are managed by member associations (national football associations), but they are not all funded entirely by the member association. Table 28.5 shows the breakdown of women's league funding as at 2014.

Football grassroots participation

Alongside the elite game, football is a very popular recreational, "grassroots" sport, which plays an important social role in health, fitness, and community engagement (www.FIFA.com).

In 2014, FIFA estimated that there were over 30 million female players; the average number of female players per member association was 168,400.

From the participation figures shown in Table 28.6, it can be seen that:

- The majority of the female football players are non-registered, i.e., playing at the grassroots level;
- 98.59 per cent of all CONCACAF players come from USA and Canada and these two account for the greatest proportion of female football[7] players;

Table 28.4 Aggregate scores for both FIFA men's and women's rankings as at 29 November 2017

Rank order	Country	Aggregate FIFA ranking scores for men's and women's football national team
1	Germany	3
2	Brazil	11
3	France	13
4	England	18
5	Spain	23
6	USA	25
7	Denmark	24
7	Switzerland	24
9	Netherlands	27
10	Belgium	28
11	Sweden	29
12	Italy	32
13	Colombia	37
13	Poland	42
13	Portugal	40
16	Mexico	42
17	Iceland	43
18	Australia	45
19	Austria	49
20	Chile	50

Table 28.5 FIFA State of the Women's Game of Football Report (2014) Breakdown of Funding for Women's Football Leagues by Confederation

Confederation	Association	Sponsors	Government	Other
AFC	19%	41%	39%	1%
CAF	89%	4%	5%	2%
CONCACAF[a]	5%	0%	95%	0%
CONMEBOL	92%	0%	8%	0%
OFC	68%	9%	0%	23%
UEFA	79%	14%	0%	7%

[a] FIFA data for CONCACAF excludes USA and Canada.

Table 28.6 FIFA State of Women's Football (2014) Data on Women's Football Participation

	Total female players	Non-registered female players	Per 10,000 inhabitants
AFC	6,327,700	6,027,585	17
CAF	1.225,400	1.171,345	14
CONCACAF	16,104,000	13,816,784	313
USA and Canada	15,877,400	13,622,366	450
Other Associations	226,600	194,418	14
CONMEBOL	256,300	230,870	6
OFC	87,200	48,468	61
UEFA	6,145,100	4,049,332	71

- The highest proportion of registered female players can be seen in Oceania (55.58 per cent of female players are non-registered, so 44.42 per cent registered), UEFA (65.9 per cent unregistered, 34.1 per cent registered), and USA and Canada (85.8 per cent unregistered, 14.2 per cent registered players).

Whilst previous data have been mixed in finding a relationship between success in elite sport and the participation levels in that sport in the respective country, Frick and Wicker (2016) study longitudinal data to discover this effect has taken place in football in Germany over an extended period. The "trickle-down effect" (Aghion and Bolton, 1997) of sport to amateur levels was studied using data on German World Cup title wins both in the men's and women's football game, and the impact on membership of sporting clubs, finding a positive relationship between the two.

Despite these positive benefits, support for women playing football is not universal. Culture, geography, and politics all place obstacles in the path of women's participation in football in some countries. Hoffmann et al. (2004) find that both political and cultural gender equality factors play a role in whether women are encouraged or inhibited from playing sport in particular cultures.

Women and football spectatorship

Women engage with sport and football in a number of ways. Together with participation in the game, women are also attending matches in growing numbers with a significant proportion also "consuming" football content via broadcast media, Internet, and mobile devices.

The case of the women's game in the UK

Football Association figures show a 5 per cent increase in attendance of Women's Super League matches from 2015 to 2016 and a 30 per cent rise in attendance for Women's Super League 2 (WSL2). Whilst these percentage increases are very encouraging, the base-line average attendance figures for 2015 were quite low. An average of 1,076 fans attended Women's Super League 1 matches in 2015 and an average of 341 for WSL2. There is clearly some way to go before the women's game attracts sufficient audiences to make it commercially attractive to sponsors or self-supporting in terms of match-day revenue (Table 28.7).

For the Women's FA Cup Final, the attendance figures have risen steeply (Table 28.8).

The Women's FA Cup Final, the top cup competition for women's football in England, has run since 1970, first as the Mitre Challenge Cup and then, since 1993, when the Football Association took over direct control for women's football, as the Women's FA Cup Final. The Women's FA Cup has often shared a sponsor with the Men's FA Cup Final competition.

If the data are limited to the last five years' attendances, a steep rise is seen from the attendance of 4,988 for the final between Arsenal and Bristol Academy in 2013 and the latest final in

Table 28.7 Increases in average attendance at WSL matches 2016 on 2015

Average attendances	2015	2016	% Increase
WSL1	1076	1128	5%
WSL2	341	443	30%

Source: The FA.

Table 28.8 Women's FA Cup Final attendance figures 2000 to date

Year	Attendance	Venue	Capacity	% Utilisation	Year on year increase %
2000	3,434	Bramall Lane	32,702	10.5%	–
2001	13,824	Selhurst Park	25,456	54.31%	302.36%
2002	10,124	Selhurst Park	25,456	39.77%	(26.77%)[a]
2003	10,389	Selhurst Park	25,456	40.81%	2.62%
2004	12,244	Loftus Road	18,439	66.4%	17.86%
2005	8,567	Upton Park	35,016	24.45%	(30.03%)
2006	13,452	New Den	20,146	66.77%	57.02%
2007	24,529	City Ground	30,445	80.57%	82.34%
2008	24,582	City Ground	30,445	80.74%	5.32%
2009	23,291	Pride Park	33,594	69.33%	(5.25%)
2010	17,505	City Ground	30,445	57.5%	(24.84%)
2011	13,885	Ricoh Arena	32,609	42.58%	(20.68%)
2012	8,723	Ashton Gate	27,000	32.31%	(37.18%)
2013	4,988	Keepmoat Stadium,	15,231	32.75%	(48.82%)
2014	15,098	Stadium MK	30,500	49.5%	202.69%
2015	30,710	Wembley	90,000	34.12%	103.4%
2016	32,912	Wembley	90,000	36.57%	7.17%
2017	35,271	Wembley	90,000	39.19%	7.17%

Sources: The FA, club websites.
[a] Brackets = minus, so a decrease on the previous year

2017 which was attended by 35,271 fans. Taking a longer timeframe, however, attendances have, in fact, fluctuated over time, perhaps influenced by the size of the support for the teams playing, the distance fans have to travel, as well as any rise and fall in popularity of the women's game. Some interesting observations on the data might be:

- Whilst there had previously been attendances above 20,000 in the mid-noughties, notably the FA Cup Final in 2008 had an attendance of 24,582 an attendance of 30,000 was not achieved until the Women's FA Cup Final moved to Wembley Stadium in 2014 and attendances had dipped steeply in the years between 2008 and 2014 (Howe 2017).
- This larger attendance might reflect the increased awareness and popularity of the women's football game in the UK since the women's team's success in the 2012 Olympics and 2015 World Cup matches. It might, also, suggest that the move to Wembley has given increased status to the Women's FA Cup match, fuelling increases in fans wishing to attend.
- It is easy to focus on the recent rise in attendance data as an indicator of a positive trend. The data, however, show that the current rising interest in women's football is not a new phenomenon. Thousands of fans have been coming together to watch women's football for decades, in the UK and beyond.

Broadcast figures

In addition to match attendance, women are increasingly engaging with sport via broadcast and social media. Martinson (2017) discusses with head of women's sport at the BBC, Barbara Slater, the growing viewership of events such as the FIFA Women's World Cup. The upward trend in viewership is seen to be largely related to on-the-pitch success – much as women's football in China and the US owed success to a virtuous cycle in which one success fuelled further successes.

Although broadcast figures have increased for some of the showcase matches, the overall picture for women's sports broadcast is mixed. In the UK, Women in Sport', who aim to increase girls and women's participation and opportunities in sport via their research and insight, show that women's sport accounts for only 7 per cent of sports coverage in the UK; 10 per cent of TV coverage, 5 per cent of radio coverage, 4 per cent of online coverage and 2 per cent of newspaper coverage (Bull, 2017).

Women in Sport (2014) found that only 0.4 per cent of all commercial investment into sport in Britain goes into women's sport. It is unclear whether sponsors won't invest because there isn't enough exposure through match attendance or broadcast viewership, or because female athletes don't get enough exposure via broadcast to create demand for women's sport.

Research has explored what underpins female viewership of both men's and women's sport (Farrell et al., 2011). First, Farrell et al. find no consensus on why women do or do not watch sport. Wann (1995) argues that men and women have different motives for watching sport, with women being more motivated by family concerns than men. Dietz-Uhler (2000) supports this viewpoint, finding that women are more motivated by family and social motivations than men who score higher for self-esteem, escapism, entertainment, and economic (gambling) motivations for sport viewership. James and Ridinger (2002), however, found no significant differences between the motives of men and women in viewing sport in relation to their highest-ranking motives of action and escapism.

Farrell et al. (2011) conclude that some of the women in the study watch men's sports in order to accommodate the interests of male partners more interested in men's sports than in women's sport, although the study is of basketball in which Sandomir (2016) says that women's basketball "struggles for relevance" and has "modest attendance and television viewership" rather than a women's sport with higher engagement.

The debate will doubtless continue, until such time as women's football generates sufficient revenue from attendances and sponsorship that it can truly be deemed self-sustaining. In many countries, even those with high levels of success in women's football, this has not, so far, been easy to achieve.

Women in football

The following section draws on research conducted by the author on behalf of the Women in Football networking group in 2016. Data are drawn from women working across the global game and business of football (Figure 28.1).

The sectors of employment with the highest levels of response are governing bodies (90 respondents), football coaching and management (82 respondents), club football (78 respondents) and media (61 respondents). These women are not all working in the women's game, 27 per cent of respondents are working in men's football, 21 per cent in women's football, and 52 per cent work across both men's and women's football. The majority of respondents working in women's football are football coaches or managers (39), players (28), or those working for governing bodies. The largest proportion of women who work in Men's Football are those working in club football (50), media (17), coaching (11), governing bodies (10), and marketing and creative (10). A large proportion of those who work across men's and women's football are in governing bodies (69), media (39), and coaching (28). Seventy-six per cent of respondents

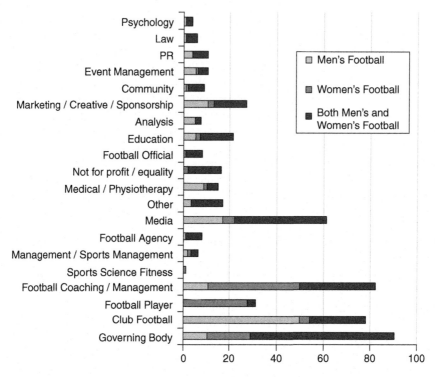

Figure 28.1   Respondents by sector of employment and whether working in men's football, women's football or both men's and women's football

work in football in England, the remaining 24 per cent are spread across football in Europe and the rest of the world.

What do women in football say?

What do you love about working in football? (Respondents rank ordered their top five.) Where one is highest, five is lowest (Table 28.9).

Overall, the highest-ranked benefit of working in football is that of being able to watch football. This also ranks highest for those working in both men's and women's football, although for those working either only in women's football or only in men's football this factor is less important. It is the second most important factor behind being part of a team atmosphere for women's football, and ranks fourth, behind "Being close to the action of a sport I love." A majority of respondents were happy with their work-life balance or neutral on this point.

How satisfied are you with your work/life balance as a woman working in football (where 1 = very dissatisfied and 5 = very satisfied) (Table 28.10 and 28.11).

The highest level of agreement is seen with the statement "my organization celebrates female talent" for which 60 per cent of respondents either agree or strongly agree. There is a split between respondents who feel supported only by women or by both men and women, with high levels of agreement and strong agreement for both statements. There are also high levels of agreement with the statements: "There are opportunities to achieve career progression" and

Table 28.9 Average rank of benefits of working in football

Rank order	Factor	Average rank both	Average rank women's	Average rank men's	Overall
1	Being able to watch football	2.29	2.32	2.87	2.44
2	Being part of a team atmosphere	2.66	2.3	2.63	2.53
3	The banter	2.45	2.56	3.02	2.56
4	Being close to the action of a sport I love	2.74	2.68	2.52	2.76
5	The high-profile nature of the football industry	2.8	2.78	3.12	2.78
6	Far-reaching industry with many possible career directions (politics, business, media, sport, education, etc.)	2.8	2.77	2.82	2.84
7	The power of football to encourage social change	2.96	3.16	2.89	3.05
8	Match-day excitement	3.52	2.68	2.64	3.07

Source: Women in Football Survey 2016.
Tables 28.9 to 28.12 are all drawn from the Women in Football 2016 Survey.

Table 28.10 Frequency table of satisfaction with work/ life balance of women working in football

Level of satisfaction	n = 468
Very satisfied	54
Satisfied	179
Neither satisfied nor dissatisfied	110
Dissatisfied	96
Very dissatisfied	29

"the language in my workplace feels inclusive." However, conversely, there are also high levels of agreement with the statement: "I feel overlooked for promotion because of my gender" (Table 28.12).

Twenty-four per cent of respondents have personally experienced bullying and 23.88 per cent have seen women barred from certain areas, whilst 19.15 per cent have personally experienced this. These proportions remain worrying; clearly further efforts are required to achieve true gender equality in the football workplace (Figure 28.2).

Overall, there is optimism among women in football about prospects for women in the football industry. More than 60 per cent of women agree or strongly agree that they are optimistic about prospects, and more than 60 per cent also agree or strongly agree that opportunities for women in the football industry are improving. Conversely, however, almost 90 per cent of women sampled agree or strongly agree (40 per cent) that more could be done to improve opportunities for women in the football industry and 70 per cent agree or strongly agree that women have to be better at their jobs than male colleagues to succeed in the football industry.

Table 28.11 Agreement or disagreement with statements on diversity of workplace

Statement	Average score	1	2	3	4	5
My organisation celebrates female talent	3.38	25	75	128	171	65
I feel supported by both men and women	3.7	12	49	80	250	76
I feel supported only by women	2.24	105	192	120	37	7
I feel supported only by men	2.05	125	208	108	18	2
My workplace feels diverse	3.22	26	111	107	177	43
The language in my workplace feels inclusive	3.36	24	67	137	192	45
There are opportunities to achieve career progression	3.16	32	114	111	168	42
I feel overlooked for promotion because of my gender	2.44	115	145	115	69	23
I feel overlooked for promotion because of other characteristics (e.g.: age, ethnicity, or other protected characteristic)	2.34	123	150	121	55	17
I believe that I am fairly remunerated compared with male colleagues	2.93	61	83	173	118	27
My appearance is judged over my ability to do my job	2.54	98	153	107	83	25
I am expected to look glamorous at work	2.25	135	167	94	54	16
I worry that getting older and changing appearance will impact my career	2.53	110	148	94	71	39

Table 28.12 Personal experience of discrimination

Type of discrimination	Yes	No
Bullying	24%	76%
Sexism	46.22%	53.78%
Sexual harassment	14.8%	85.2%
Sexist "banter" or jokes	61.88%	38.12%
Physical abuse	3.34%	96.66%
Being barred from certain areas	19.15%	80.85%
Derogatory statements on ability based on gender	38.22%	61.69%
Discrimination against a pregnant woman	5.16%	94.84%
Discrimination against a working mother	9.4%	90.6%

Conclusions: The future is feminine

If in 1995 it was not quite clear in which directions Sepp Blatter's statement would be true, now in 2018 the ways of making this a reality are much clearer. On its website, FIFA states that: "interest in football played by women is currently at an all-time high. FIFA believes that women's football still has even more potential for growth, and we actively promote women's football worldwide through major competitions and events, campaigns and development programmes." The governance of FIFA itself, with female representation now including Secretary General Fatma Samoura, and FIFA council member, including board members, including Evellina Christilin, Lydia Nsekera, Somia Bien-Aime, Maria Munoz, and Sandra Fruean, hopefully, stands as testament to a serious intent.

There remain, however, challenges ahead in maximising opportunities for all women in playing in or working in football by continuing to facilitate and support development whilst removing any remaining barriers to women around the world who are involved in the game and business of football.

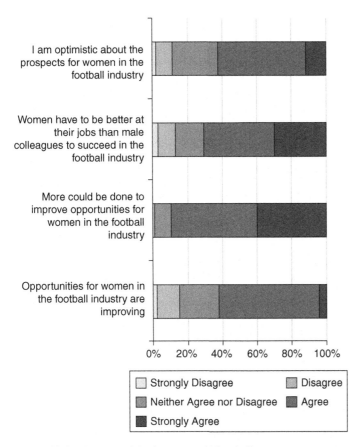

Figure 28.2 Opportunities in women's football

Notes

1 The word football will be used rather than soccer throughout this chapter for the sake of consistency.
2 Tate uses the word suffragism rather than "suffragette" to reflect the name used for the movement in 1881.
3 This would equate to £50,000 at current rates.
4 Dong and Mangan (2002) alternatively give the nickname as Iron Roses, but this is contradicted by Zhao et al. (2014).
5 The Women's Chinese Super League had run on a home and away match basis until 2005 when some teams were unable to afford the costs and it reverted to an event basis. This appeared to further impact domestic support as it took away the element of "parochial support" Zhao et al. (2014).
6 For the equivalent men's competition, 211 countries have their men's team ranked, 80 countries have ever qualified for the World Cup (37.9 per cent) but as the men's competition is of longer duration and more teams can qualify, few meaningful inferences can be drawn from this.
7 Football as in the rest of this report means soccer not American Football. The term football is used to be consistent with the rest of the chapter.

References

Acosta, R., and Carpenter, L. (2014) (1977–2014) Women in Intercollegiate Sport: A Longitudinal, National Study—A 37 Year Update. [online] Brookfield: MA. Retrieved from: http:// www.acosta carpenter.org/

Aghion and Bolton (1997) A theory of trickle-down growth and development. *Review of Economic Studies*, 64, 151–172.

Bull, A. (2017) Women's sport is coming in waves and ready to shine during biggest summer. *The Guardian*, June 23. [online] Retrieved from: https://www.theguardian.com/sport/2017/jun/23/women-sport-biggest-summer-chance-to-shine

Dietz-Uhler, B., Harrick, E., End, A.C., and Jacquemotte, L. (2000). Sex differences in sport fan behavior and reasons for being a sport fan. *Journal of Sport Behavior*, 23, 219–231.

Dong, Jinxia and J.A. Mangan, (2001) Football in the New China: political statement, entrepreneurial enticement and patriotic passion. *Soccer and Society*, 2(3) (Autumn 2001), 92.

Dong, J. and J.A. Mangan (2002) Ascending then descending? Women's soccer in modern China. *Soccer & Society*, 3(2), 1–18. DOI:10.1080/714004877

The FA (2016) [online] Retrieved from: http://www.thefa.com/news/2016/nov/07/fa-wsl-attendances-continue-to-rise-2016

Fang, D. (2001) Women's football in China: development and challenge. *Journal of Shanghai Physical Education Institute*, 25(2), 78–80.

Farrell, A., Fink, J.S., and Fields, S. (2011) Women's sport spectatorship: an exploration of men's influence" *Journal of Sport Management*, 25 190–201.

FIFA Rankings Data. [online] Retrieved from: www.fifa.com

FIFA State of the Women's Game of Football Report (2014) [online] Retrieved from: https://resources.fifa.com/mm/document/footballdevelopment/women/02/52/26/49/womensfootballsurvey2014_e_english.pdf. CIES Observatory.

Frick, B. and Wicker, P. (2016) The trickle-down effect: how elite sporting success affects amateur participation in German football. *Applied Economic Letters*, 23(4), 259–226. [online] Retrieved from: http://dx.doi.org/10.1080/13504851.2015.1068916

Frost, L., Lightbody, M., and Halabi, A. (2013) Expanding social inclusion in community sports organizations: evidence from rural Australian football clubs. *Journal of Sport Management*, 27, 453–466.

Halloran, J.D. (2013) The Rise and Rise of the United States Women's National Team. Bleacher Report. [online] Retrieved from: http://bleacherreport.com/articles/1614739-the-rise-and-rise-of-the-united-states-womens-national-team

Hoffmann, R., Ging, L.C., and Matheson, V. (2006) International women's football and gender equality. *Applied Economics Letters*, 13, 999–1001.

Howe, S. (2017) "The numbers behind the meteoric rise of women's football" Pitchero Blog [online] https://blog.pitchero.com/the-growth-of-womens-football

Jacobs, B. (2004) The Dick, Kerrs Ladies. Robinson Publishers.

James, J., and Ridinger, L. (2002) Female and male sports fans: a comparison of sport consumption motives. *Journal of Sport Behavior*, 25, 260–278.

Jinghua, L., and Liu Mingsheng (2009) On strategies for the sustainable development of women's football in China. *Journal of Shenyang Sport University*, 28(1), 102–105.

Lü Yunbao, 'Shengzhou zutan "feng xian fei"' [Phoenix flies first in China's Soccer], *Titan zhoubao* [Sports Weekly], 761 (16 Dec. 1997), *Sports Review* cited in Dong, J. and Mangan, J.A. (2002) Ascending then descending? Women's soccer in modern China" *Soccer & Society*, 3(2), 1–18. DOI:10.1080/714004877

Martinson, J. (2017) BBC Sport's Barbara Slater: "There's a transformation in women's coverage" *The Guardian* [online] Retrieved from: https://www.theguardian.com/tv-and-radio/2017/mar/05/bbc-sport-barbara-slater-transformation-in-womens-coverage

Narcotta-Welp, E.M. (2016) "The Future of Football is Feminine": A Critical Cultural History of the U.S. Women's National Soccer Team. Unpublished Doctoral Thesis. University of Iowa. [online] Retrieved from:h p://ir.uiowa.edu/etd/2125>

Newsham, G (2014) In a league of their own!: The Dick, Kerr Ladies Football Club. *The Dick, Kerr Ladies Football Team Book and website*. [online] Retrieved from: http://www.dickkerrladies.com

Sandomir, R. (2016) After two decades WBNA struggles for relevance. *New York Times*, May 28. [online] Retrieved from: https://www.nytimes.com/2016/05/28/sports/basketball/after-two-decades-wnba-still-struggling-for-relevance.html

Tate, T. (2017) *Girls with Balls: The Secret History of Women's Football*. UK Women's Sport and Fitness Foundation [online] Retrieved from: http://ukactive.com/downloads/managed/Louise_Tanner-Womens_Sport_and_Fitness_Foundation.pdf

Wann, D. (1995) Influence of identification with a sports team on objective knowledge and subjective beliefs. *International Journal of Sport Psychology*, 26, 551–567.

Williams, J. (2007) *A Beautiful Game: International Perspectives on Women's Football*. New York: Berg

Williams, J. *Sports Illustrated*. [online] Retrieved from: https://www.si.com/planet-futbol/2015/06/09/womens-soccer-world-cup-history-evolution

Women in Football (2016). Survey of opportunities and challenges for women working in football. [online] Retrieved from: https://www.womeninfootball.co.uk/assets/genericfiles/Women%20in%20Football%20Survey%20Analysis.pdf

Women in Sport (2014) Sponsorship and media. [online] Retrieved from:https://www.womeninsport.org/how-were-doing-it/sponsorship-media/

Zhao, A., Horton, P. and Liu, L. (2012) Women's football in the People's Republic of China: retrospect and prospect. *The International Journal of the History of Sport*, 29(17): Soft Power Politics – Past and Present: Football and Baseball on the Western Pacific Rim: 2372–2387.

29

Managing match officials

The influence of business and the impact of finance in an era of Premier League dominance

Tom Webb

Introduction

As one of the most marketable and commercialised sports both in a national and transnational context, association football in England has evolved and developed exponentially since the formation of the breakaway English Premier League (EPL) in 1992 from the traditional Football League to take advantage of the lucrative potential of the growing television and sponsorship market (Madichie, 2009). The success of the EPL has brought money into the clubs that constitute the EPL and also, as a consequence, the players, as the cash nexus increased wealth with each television deal, sponsorship agreement, and image rights agreement that a player or team has been given. Television rights deals now focus on both domestic and international agreements, as the international market becomes increasingly important to the continued growth of the EPL. This has meant unprecedented levels of investment, development of existing stadia and the building of new stadia, substantially increased transfer fees associated with the movement of players between clubs, and a mounting importance attached to winning and losing and the attributable success, as club owners, managers, coaches, and players ascribe elevated importance to success due to the potential consequences of failure.

Amongst all of these developments, and as a central part of the modern game, are the referees. The facilitators of the matches, the guardians of the laws of the game, and the individuals with the power to influence matches and decide the outcome of seasons with a decision, whether that decision is deemed to be correct or incorrect. The increased finance associated with the EPL, as well as the clubs and players, means that every decision is scrutinised and every incorrect judgement can potentially negatively affect the career of a player or manager. Therefore, there has been prolonged attention afforded to the professionalisation of referees in national leagues, and in the EPL in particular, with referees that officiate in the EPL made professional in 2001. Referees have never been under such scrutiny or as much a part of the media narrative as they are today, and as a consequence, the organisation, management, and training of these individuals has become a complicated business. This chapter considers the management of the match official in the highly financed and increasingly professionalised environment in which they operate, using the EPL as a starting point to examine some of the contemporary issues which concern referees, both domestically and in European and international competition. The chapter concludes with a series of policy implications and recommendations intended to increase understanding and identify areas of potential future research designed to encourage scholarship in this evolving research area.

The evolving role of the referee

The role of the referee has changed and evolved considerably over time and has inevitably been influenced by wider changes to the game of association football. Historically the movement of the referee from the side of the pitch to a central presence on the playing area was led by the developments in rule changes through the public schools and wider society (Dunning and Sheard, 2005; Harvey, 2005; Webb, 2014a). As competitions were convened, such as the Football League and the Football Association Challenge Cup, and regular competitive football was established, the requirement and necessity for a referee became evident (Webb, 2014a). By 1885 the Football Association (FA) had accepted the inevitability of the professionalisation of players and the routinisation of players being paid to play and compete with the ultimate aim of winning.

As an associated part of this process, referees were required to officiate the matches and there was also a demand that these referees operated at a certain level, given that money and financial rewards were now directly related to performance and results (Webb, 2017). Over time, the standard of the referees was questioned and improvement demanded; no longer were ad hoc training and questionable promotion pathways acceptable to the wider football community. As competition became the norm, referee promotion was introduced, as were referee classifications aimed at promoting the best and most capable match officials to league and cup matches (Webb, 2014a). These changes were not without controversy, and the introduction and implementation of referee training took a considerable time to become routinised by those that manage and organise the referees, resulting in referees playing catch-up with professional players throughout the twentieth century (Webb, 2014a; 2016).

As the influence that could be attributed to association football in English society continued to grow, so too did the demand for competent, improving referees. By the mid-twentieth century it was no longer acceptable for referees to be born into officiating, as the class structure shifted and changed within the UK, so the entrenched view of referees as societal superiors, there to supervise and control the working-class players, also changed (Mangan, 2008). Nevertheless, not only did training and effective development of referees take longer than might be expected given the advancements in the rest of the game, referees did not professionalise until 2001, as an added development associated with the formation of the EPL in 1992.

The impact and influence of the EPL on refereeing

The unprecedented growth of the EPL and the associated financial wealth which has emerged through the television rights agreements, sponsorships, and various other revenue streams that have been exploited by the league, have created one of the most successful competitions in world sport as the sport has moved from the evolutionary phase to a revolutionary phase indicating rapid and uncertain change (Beech and Chadwick, 2013). The initial TV deal signed with BskyB following the launch of the breakaway league in 1992 was worth £304 million over a five-year deal period, and the first deal of the millennium in 2002 saw the EPL television rights sold for £1.6 billion over four years (Nauright and Ramfjord, 2010). The most recent television rights are worth £8.3 billion for both domestic and overseas rights, considerably ahead of competitor football leagues in Europe (Devine, 2017; Solberg, 2017). Conservative estimates indicate that Sky will have to spend an additional £600 million annually, or £1.8 billion, over a three-year agreement, in order to maintain the television rights to the EPL in the forthcoming auction, as other potential providers such as Amazon, Google, Apple, Facebook, and Netflix emerge in the marketplace (Sweney, 2017).

An associated impact of the financial impetus which the EPL has seen has (as the league potentially enters the post-commercialisation phase (Beech and Chadwick, 2013)) been the effect that these advancements have had on the referees that officiate within the league. Over time referees became household names, as a consequence of increased television exposure of live matches and also the advancement of technology. As technology was utilised more extensively by the television companies, the pressure on referees intensified over time. The use of technology involved increasing the quality of the cameras, and therefore the television pictures, as well as an increase in the number of cameras at each Premier League match. At the same time, companies such as Sky were also developing their use of the available technology with increased slow-motion replays, and the ability for the viewer to switch camera views, as well as pause and rewind incidents from their own home. All of these developments meant that the decisions referees made during the course of a match were under greater scrutiny than had previously been evident.

The increase in technology and the focus on the decisions made by referees and also assistant referees during a match, led consumers, those involved with the organisation and management of teams and the EPL itself, to call for improved refereeing standards. In short, as technology use increased and the financial rewards became more generous, the demand grew for referees to make the right decisions. However, despite the changes to the EPL and consequently refereeing, it still took nine years for referees to become professional, or full time. This is perhaps unsurprising given the time that it took for those administrating the game to realise that referees required adequate training and development opportunities. This in itself brought some structural issues related to the funding required for these new professional match officials. This funding comes from a tripartite organisation system involving the Football Association (FA), Football League, and the Premier League, ultimately forming the Professional Game Match Officials Limited (PGMOL), which manages and trains the EPL and Football League referees (Webb, 2014b).

Leading and managing referees in the modern world

There were other aspects of the role of the referee which were trialled and changed depending on their perceived success or value to the current climate in which referees operate. For example, referees used to communicate directly with the media straight after a game, something which is not currently permitted by the PGMOL. However, there are wider issues for the managers and leaders of referees, both domestically and across transnational boundaries, when organisations such as UEFA and FIFA begin to demonstrate more involvement in governance (Beech, 2013).

Managing and leading elite referees successfully requires an understanding and comprehension of the skills associated with remote management. Referees are commonly managed and led remotely due to geographical constraints and also financial implications. Referees live in a variety of locations across any given country and therefore organising meetings and training as a group can be problematic, time consuming, and financially draining. As a result, referees meet every two weeks in England for a two-day event and spend the rest of their time working from home or working remotely. This arrangement requires referees to organise themselves and adhere to the training regimes that are prepared for them. Naturally, there are mechanisms in place to ensure that training takes place and that referees are undertaking the training to the intensity required by the sports science support staff. Moreover, referees wear heart rate monitors to measure their training sessions and they subsequently upload the data from this training session to the central support staff that manage their fitness programmes.

This means that communication is essential, as is the use of Information Communication Technology (ICT), in order to successfully manage and lead Geographically Distributed Teams (GDTs). GDTs can be defined as groups that are separated by time and/or distance, dealing with issues related to technology, teamwork, and communication (Sessa et al., 1999), although there remains limited research related to knowledge sharing and team cooperation across national and international boundaries (Hansen, Hope, and Moehler, 2012). The same can be said for referees, particularly those at the elite level. Therefore, we are still relatively unclear about models of best practice when managing or leading referees and this is compounded by the fact that each country has its own method of organising and managing their elite referees (Webb, 2017).

Working over distance, whether domestically or in international groups, presents several issues for managers or leaders, including trust, conflict, communication technology, and culture (Gerhart, 2008; Lee-Kelley and Sankey, 2008; Rosen, Furst, and Blackburn, 2007). A primary concern of both the *Fédération Internationale de Football Association* (FIFA) and the Union of European Football Associations (UEFA) is the uniformity and standardisation of referee decision-making and the refereeing systems themselves, irrespective of the country involved. Both FIFA and UEFA have a desire to move towards greater consistency (FIFA, 2012; UEFA, 2012); however, in reality, this is extremely difficult to achieve. This chapter has already considered issues related to the management and leadership of referees related to geographical distance and a reliance on home working, as well as the increased importance of technology and ICT support to ensure that there is accountability for referees when they operate from a remote location. Therefore, there are a number of barriers to effective uniformity within refereeing and as such there must be questions regarding whether uniformity or standardisation, are in fact, an achievable goal for those that manage and lead referees at domestic and international level.

Managing pressure: Dealing with increased attention and scrutiny in England

Examples of contentious episodes involving referees at football matches can be found as early as the 1880s, following codification of the laws of the game and the formation of the Football Association in 1863. Woolwich Arsenal, for example, had their ground closed for six weeks after a referee was assaulted during a match (Mason, 1980). Moreover, there were a total of 46 ground closures and 64 warnings to clubs about spectator behaviour across league and non-league football from 1895–1915, with the closure of a team's ground employed by the FA as a method of attempting to enforce and enhance respect for referees, amongst other things (Dunning, Murphy, and Williams, 1988; Lewis, 1906). By the 1930s referees were experiencing an interest in and appetite for association football alongside a sustained fascination with the referee as an increasingly central figure in the game. With this increased attention, referees became more of a focus for the media than had historically been the case; they were part of the narrative and this presented issues for those involved with refereeing (Porter, 2015; Webb, 2016a).

Difficulties begin to arise for managers and leaders when the impact of increased television exposure of both the referees themselves, and also the decisions that they make during the course of a match, are considered. Referees are now a constituent part of football commentary, highlight shows and phone-ins, as the correctness of the decisions that have been made are debated, as are the consequences of such decisions on the teams that may be affected (Webb, 2016b). It is the consequences of the decisions that referees make that are now the challenge for the referees themselves and their managers and coaches. Referees want to avoid being the subject of discussion with their decisions replayed at varying speeds and from a number of different camera angles. For those that manage and lead referees, as well as the referee coaches that help to train and develop match officials, it is about minimising the pressure that referees find themselves under and developing protocols that support the referees as much as possible.

The pressure that referees experience domestically is undoubtedly a factor which leads them to believe that it is easier to officiate in European and international fixtures rather than fixtures in their own country, with the perceived reduction in pressure when referees officiate abroad identified as a particular difference (Webb, 2017). It could be assumed that Champions League matches are actually higher-profile fixtures than those in the domestic leagues, although this is also dependent on the exposure the domestic league has negotiated through television deals. Nevertheless, referees like to be able to officiate in another country; as a consequence, they do not see any of the media or press reports which may comment on their performance and they believe that they can, as a result, evaluate their performance objectively, along with their referee coaches, following the match assessment from the observer (Webb, 2017).

It is the pressure to get decisions right and the consequences of any incorrect decisions that are aspects that have changed for the referees. The consequences of a performance which is deemed to be below the required standard is that of further and prolonged media exposure of the referee and a wider scrutiny of the refereeing system in the country in question more generally. A growing focus on referee decision-making is something that is cited as increasing within the English game, increasing pressure on referees as a consequence. There is an argument to suggest that given the number of matches shown, as well as the time and technology devoted to the analysis of matches, it is unsurprising that refereeing mistakes are being more exposed to review and criticism (Buraimo, Forrest, and Simmons, 2010; Colwell, 2000). Despite this view, research has been conducted which demonstrates that the pressure from the media in England is perhaps not as vociferous as one might expect. Twenty live EPL games were analysed in terms of the coverage related to the referee. This coverage considered any mention of the referee, whether this reference was positive, negative, questioning, or neutral in nature, with the results recorded with the use of notational analysis (Webb, 2016b). The findings demonstrated that coverage was, predominantly, positive, with the number of negative comments over the twenty live matches equating to just 10.74 per cent of the total number of comments, whereas the positive comments equated to 25.56 per cent of the total number of comments (Webb, 2016b).

Referees, management, and the approach of the media in European football

Despite these findings from the EPL, the level of media exposure is dependent on the country in which the referee officiates and this exposure varies widely. For example, although referees in the EPL receive scrutiny from the written and broadcast media through live televised matches, highlight programmes such as Match of the Day and also the sports pages of the tabloid and broadsheet newspapers, this coverage is circumspect when compared to that evident in other European countries, such as Spain and in particular Italy (Foot, 2006). In Italy, this media interest has been evident for a number of years, and much of the effect on referees can, at least in part, be attributed to historical occurrences in Italy such as the "Calciopoli" match-fixing episode. All of which has implications for the management and coordination of referees at both national and European level, and the operational environment in which referees operate.

Previous match-fixing incidents in Italy have influenced the views held by supporters, and these views can be guided by the media representation of referees and the associated analysis and discussion of referees' decisions generated on television, with public and private Italian TV channels offering a number of football-focused shows. The most important and successful among these shows are Il Processo del Lunedi ("Monday Trial") and Controcampo ("Counter-pitch"). The shows often involve verbal exchanges involving the guests as video footage related to perceived mistakes of referees are shown and discussed. The fact that referee decisions are scrutinised at such length has led to the role of the moviola (replay) being highlighted as a major reason for discontent and the destabilisation of referees in Italy (Scalia, 2009, p. 51). The gains that can be made both in monetary terms and in by-products of success, such as trophies and fame have meant that incidents such as the Italian football federation revoking the championship won by Torino Calcio as a consequence of the team's managers being found to have bribed a Juventus football player before the Turin derby in 1927 (Boeri and Severgnini, 2008). Whereas, in 1999 it was revealed that the president of Roma had sent Rolex watches to leading referees whilst other referees had enjoyed holidays paid for by Juventus (Hamil et al., 2010). Nonetheless, it was the "Calciopoli" situation in particular which revealed a complicated relationship between team managers, referees, agents, and club executives, all of whom were implicated in the match fixing of football matches, with referees and those in referee-related managerial positions procured in order to favour Juventus and AC Milan (Distaso et al., 2008; Hamil et al., 2010).

Comparatively, in Spain, the coverage of football is also extensive, and although there have not been the widespread issues acknowledged in Italian football, there have been matters which have affected the management and organisation of referees. Football in Spain is afforded almost three quarters (70.3 per cent) of the total content of all sports reported in newspapers, on the radio, and television (Gonzalez-Ramallal, 2008) and, similar to England, the number of televised games has significantly increased, increasing the exposure and coverage of referees (Garcia and Rodriguez, 2006). The rivalry between Real Madrid and Barcelona has also provided the setting for further analysis of refereeing performances and their management over time, with matches interrupted on numerous occasions, seemingly often related to refereeing decisions (McFarland, 2007).

As is the case in the EPL, the management of referees and increased role of the media can be linked to financial developments within the game, but the political climate that has historically existed within Spain creates a different setting in which referees must operate. The link between football, politics, refereeing, and the media in Spain can be traced back to the 1970s and a Spanish league referee, Antonio Camacho, who declared that Barcelona would never win the title whilst Jose Plaza, a madridista through and through, was president of the National Committee of Referees (Ball, 2003). Also, in 1970, a referee was chosen to officiate the second-leg of the 1970 cup quarter-final tie between Barcelona and Real Madrid in the Nou Camp, with Real Madrid winning on aggregate following a 2–0 victory in the first leg of the fixture. The performance of the referee fuelled Barcelona fans' notion that Real Madrid were favoured during the Franco years, by awarding the visitors a dubious and crucial penalty kick during the game, which provoked a riot and infamy in Spanish football, with the referee chased from the pitch and the police intervening (Brentnall, 2009; Burns, 2016). These incidents were inevitably covered in the media, with the gravity of the match, due to historical political issues affording intensive coverage.

Globalisation, technology, and the impact on refereeing

The influence of the media has grown as the coverage of the leagues has developed due to the technology now available to distribute the live coverage of the matches. The notion of globalisation and sport have been considered from a variety of academic disciplines; however, the link between a more globalised society and football, in particular, has been explored in some depth (see Giulianotti, 1999; Giulianotti and Robertson, 2009). The impact of the increased media exposure on the referee can be linked inextricably to globalisation, the commodification of football through the auctioning of television rights every three seasons, and the associated increased financial wealth evident at the highest levels of the game. This inevitably impacts upon the referee, those in managerial positions related to refereeing, and also the leagues which are required to evolve and adapt in a rapidly changing financial and technological environment.

The increasing ability to be able to watch and support a team irrespective of the country that one resides in, or the time differences which exist across the world, is an example of the increasingly globalised world in which association football now exists. Alongside this, managers and leaders of referees have to contend with increasing cultural diversity of referees linked to the globalised nature of the game at the highest level. Research has been conducted on the management of cultural diversity in sporting organisations, although this research is somewhat sparse (Doherty and Chelladurai, 1999). Work has also been conducted in human resource-related fields concerning managerial identities and the organisational context of the work as a senior manager, although not specifically sport related; nevertheless, these concepts can be translated and applied to the sport management subject area (Sveningsson and Alvesson, 2003).

Managers and leaders of referees are in a period of constant change and therefore adaptation is required on a frequent basis. An example of the adaptation linked to globalisation and technology for both referees and referee managers is the introduction of goal-line technology and the launch by FIFA in 2017 of a pilot project in amenable leagues with the intention of introducing Video Assistant Referees (VARs) to minimise any controversial or incorrect decisions during the course of a match. The purpose of the VAR is to intervene in four specific decisions or incidents during a match in order to assist the on-field referee. These four decisions, with three main incidents (plus one administrative incident), have been identified by FIFA as game-changing. The four areas are goals, penalty decisions, red card incidents, and mistaken identity. The use of technology has taken time in association football and yet the game is now moving at pace to try and assist referees and pacify clubs and supporters who consistently question why there is so much technology evident during live television broadcasts of matches, only for the referee to be denied the same technology during the course of a match.

The use of the VAR system in football is designed to eradicate any decisions that might be subject to question. As an incident occurs, a three-step procedure is initiated with the first phase involving a referral from the on-field referee or an interjection from the VAR; the system then progresses to offer advice to the on-field referee following the review of video footage by the VAR; finally, the on-field referee either views the incident on a monitor at the side of the pitch before deciding on any action or the on-field referee accepts the advice from the VAR and takes the appropriate decision (FIFA, n.d).

The introduction of the VAR will undoubtedly be one of the biggest changes to the structure of the game in recent times. However, at the time of writing the exact organisation, structure, and implementation of the VAR system is unknown. Trials were held across world football and FIFA launched the VAR system at the 2018 World Cup in Russia with the system available for implementation by leagues and competitions around the world, although initial uptake has been mixed. In England, the first trial of the VAR system was during the third round of the FA Cup in January 2018, and the introduction of this system will undoubtedly raise further areas of research requiring investigation, and which will have consequences for governing bodies, such as the FA, and leagues, such as the Premier League, in terms of policy implications.

Where next? Refereeing, modern football and further research

It could be argued that we have already seen the introduction of a referee transfer system through Mark Clattenburg's move from the English Premier League to Saudi Arabia to oversee their refereeing provision and structures. A job, incidentally, previously held by a former Premier League referee, Howard Webb, who is now overseeing the trial and introduction of the VAR system in Major League Soccer in America. The implications of these moves, both from a management perspective and also future research directions, should not be underestimated as refereeing enters a phase of sporting labour migration (Agergaard, 2017). Research has taken place regarding the importance of player and referee culture related to personal performance and performance within different competitions, with a significant finding identifying that referees are changing their performances and behaviour to reflect their perceptions of changing player behaviour from competition to competition (Webb and Thelwell, 2015). In terms of those leading and managing elite referees this presents some standardisation and uniformity concerns, especially when related back to the interpretation of the laws of the game.

Further questions arise related to both the leadership and management of referees in terms of uniformity and also culture when considered across transnational boundaries. Indeed, the introduction of referees moving between countries and the implications this might have in terms of their management and required understanding of referees from different cultures, such as the referees Mark Clattenburg is overseeing in Saudi Arabia, becomes even more essential. Current leaders and managers involved with elite refereeing have to contend with the leadership of referees over increasing geographical areas and a reliance on ICT in order to manage fully the referees at nationwide level or across national and international boundaries (Webb et al., 2016). Trends suggest that these issues will become exacerbated further as both active and retired referees from different countries are recruited to develop pathways for referees and to increase the quality of referees in a given country through their previous experiences as an elite referee themselves. Moreover, leagues such as the Chinese Super League are utilising high-profile foreign referees for their domestic league matches due to the controversies attached to the contentious decisions made during matches by the domestic referees (Chinese Super League: Administrators bring in foreign referees, 2017).

These changes will require a greater understanding of any differences in culture and the changes in the behaviour of players from competition to competition (Webb and Thelwell, 2015; Webb, 2017). Managers and leaders will require support and guidance in terms of training for these referees and also the club managers and players. Nevertheless, these developments also present new and novel areas of potential research, building on that which has evolved in the business and management subject area over the past four years. Research will be required to understand better the impact of culture on referees and players, the influence of the VAR system once it has been tested and subsequently implemented in leagues across the world, the continued increments associated with television rights deals, and the associated impact that these matters have on the wider game and the role of the match official in an increasingly globalised and rapidly changing operational environment.

This will present challenges for those in managerial and leadership positions related to elite refereeing, in whatever country they might be based, and also opportunities for those conducting research into subject areas related to the management, leadership, and development of referees. For example, how will the implementation of the VAR system influence or alter referee and player behaviour, will the system provide new challenges for the referees tasked with utilising it and will the system solve the issues that it is being introduced to remove? Before this can be decided there has to be a greater move towards standardisation and uniformity of refereeing systems and the training administered to referees in different countries; currently both the systems that referees operate within and the training that they receive demonstrate substantive differences and therefore these differences must be better understood and appropriate training considered in order to develop further referee support systems and in turn, increase the quality of referees across transnational boundaries.

The management of elite referees presents challenges unlike any other elite sports person; from the geographical distances involved and the remote working for a number of consecutive days to the international travel involved on a regular basis and the differences in preparation and performance required as the competition in which they officiate changes. Further understanding is required of this unique and essential workforce in modern football and the impending changes to the structure/s of the game present distinctive opportunities for researchers to advance this understanding.

References

Agergaard, S. (2017) When globalization and migration meet national and local talent development. In: U. Wagner, R. K. Storm, and K. Nielsen (eds.). *When Sport meets Business: Capabilities, Challenges and Critiques* (pp. 30–42). London: Sage.

Ball, P. (2003). *Morbo: the story of Spanish football*. London: When Saturday Comes Books.

Beech, J. (2013) Governance in sport. In: J. Beech, and S. Chadwick (eds.). *The Business of Sport Management*, (2nd ed.) (pp. 24–39). Harlow: Pearson.

Beech, J. and Chadwick, S. (2013) Introduction: the commercialisation of sport. In J. Beech, and S. Chadwick (eds), *The Business of Sport Management*, (2nd ed.) (pp. 3–23). Harlow: Pearson.

Boeri, T. and Severgnini, B. (2008) The Italian job: match rigging, career concerns and media concentration. In: Serie A. Bonn: IZA Discussion Paper.

Brentnall, R. (2009) *From a Different Corner: Exploring Spanish Football*. Leicester: Matador.

Buraimo, B., Forrest, D., and Simmons, R. (2010) The twelfth man? Refereeing dias in English and German soccer. *Journal of the Royal Statistical Society*, 173(2), 431–449.

Burns, J. (2016) *Barca: A People's Passion*, (3rd ed.). London: Bloomsbury.

Colwell, S. (2000) The "Letter" and the "Spirit": football laws and refereeing in the twenty-first century. *Soccer & Society*, 1(1), 201–214.

Chinese Super League: administrators bring in foreign referees. (2017) *BBC Sport*. [online] Retrieved from: http://www.bbc.co.uk/sport/football/41599184

Devine, J. (2017) Who is paying for the Premier League's bumper TV deal? Your local pub. *The Guardian*. [online] Retrieved from: https://www.theguardian.com/football/the-set-pieces-blog/2017/jul/13/football-watch-pub-sky-bt-cost-rise-tv-premier-league

Distaso, W., Leonida, L., Maimone, M., Patti, A., and Navarra, P. (2008) Corruption and referee bias in football: The case of Calciopoli. Economia Della Tassazione Sistemi tributari, pressione fiscale, crescita. Pavia: Universitá Pavia.

Doherty, A.J. and Chelladurai, P. (1999) Managing cultural diversity in sport organizations: a theoretical perspective. *Journal of Sport Management*, 13(4), 280–297.

Dunning, E., Murphy, P.M., and Williams, J. (1988) *The Roots of Football Hooliganism: An Historical and Sociological Study*. London: Routledge & Keegan Paul.

Dunning, E. and Sheard, K. (2005) *Barbarians, Gentlemen and Players: A Sociological Study of Rugby Football*. London: Routledge.

FIFA. (n.d) Video Assistant Referees (VAR). *FIFA*. [online] Retrieved from: https://football-technology.fifa.com/en/media-tiles/video-assistant-referees-var/

FIFA. (2012) FIFA statutes. Budapest FIFA.

Foot, J. (2006) *Calcio: A History of Italian Football*. St. Ives: Harper Perennial.

Garcia, J. and Rodriguez, P. (2006) The determinant of TV audience for Spanish football: a first approach. In: P. Rodriguez, S. Kesenne, and J. Garcia (eds.), *Sports Economics After Fifty Years: Essays in Honour of Simon Rottenberg* (pp. 147–168). Oviedo: Universidad de Oviedo.

Gerhart, B. (2008) Cross cultural management research: assumptions, evidence, and suggested directions. *International Journal of Cross Cultural Management*, 8(3), 259–274.

Giulianotti, R. (1999) *A Sociology of the Global Game*. Cambridge: Polity Press.

Giulianotti, R. and Robertson, R. (2009) *Globalization and Football*. London: Sage.

Gonzalez-Ramallal, M.E. (2008) Identity told: the information, sports around the selection, Spanish football. *Universitas humanistic*, 66, 219–238.

Hamil, S., Morrow, S., Idle, C., Rossi, G., and Faccendini, S. (2010) The governance and regulation of Italian football. *Soccer & Society*, 11(4), 373–413.

Hansen, T.S., Hope, A., and Moehler, R.C. (2012) Managing geographically dispersed teams: from temporary to permanent global virtual teams. Social Science Research Network Working Paper Series, 201–215. doi:10.2139/ssrn.2143185

Harvey, A. (2005) *Football: The First Hundred Years, the Untold Story*. London: Routledge.

Lee-Kelley, L. and Sankey, T. (2008) Global virtual teams for value creation and project success: a case study. *International Journal of Project Management*, 26(1), 51–62.

Lewis, J. (1906) The much abused referee. In: *The Book of Football: A Complete History and Record of the Association and Rugby Games* (pp. 263–264). London: The Amalgamated Press Ltd.

Nauright, J. and Ramfjord, J. (2010) Who owns England's game? American professional sporting influences and foreign ownership in the Premier League. *Soccer & Society*, 11(4), 428–441.

Madichie, N. (2009) Management implications of foreign players in the English Premiership League football. *Management Decision*, 47(1), 24–50. DOI:10.1108/00251740910929687

Mangan, J.A. (2008) Missing men: schoolmasters and the early years of association football. *Soccer & Society*, 9(2), 170–188.

Mason, T. (1980) *Association Football and English society, 1863–1915*. Brighton: Harvester Press.

McFarland, A. (2007) Building a mass activity: fandom, class and business in early Spanish football. *Soccer & Society*, 8(2–3), 205–220. http://dx.doi.org/10.1080/14660970701224418

Porter, D. (2015) Whistling his way to Wembley: Percy Harper of Stourbridge, cup final referee. *Sport in History*, 35(2), 217–240.

Rosen, B., Furst, S. and Blackburn, R. (2007) Overcoming barriers to knowledge sharing in virtual teams. *Organizational Dynamics*, 36(3), 259–273.

Scalia, V. (2009) Just a few rogues?: football ultras, clubs and politics in contemporary Italy. *International Review for the Sociology of Sport*, 44(1), 41–53.

Sessa, V.I., Hansen, M. C., Prestridge, S. and Kossler, M.E. (1999) Geographically dispersed teams: an annotated bibliography. Greensboro, NC: Center for Creative Leadership.

Solberg, H.A. (2017) The battle for media rights in European club football. In U. Wagner, R.K. Storm, and K. Nielsen (eds.). *When Sport Meets Business: Capabilities, Challenges and Critiques* (pp. 92–107). London: Sage.

Sveningsson, S. and Alvesson, M. (2003) Managing managerial identities: organizational fragmentation, discourse and identity struggle. *Human Relations*, 56(10), 1163–1193.

Sweney, M. (2017) Sky faces paying extra £1.8bn for Premier League broadcast rights. *The Guardian*. [online] Retrieved from:https://www.theguardian.com/media/2017/aug/11/premier-league-broadcast-battle-hots-up-as-sky-face-doling-out-extra-600m

UEFA. (2012) UEFA referee convention: convention on referee education and organisation. Nyon: UEFA.

Webb, T. (2014a) The emergence of training and assessment for referees in association football: moving from the side-lines, *The International Journal of the History of Sport*, 31(9), 1081–1097. DOI:.http://dx.doi.org/10.1080/09523367.2014.905545

Webb, T. (2014b) Elite refereeing structures in England: a perfect model or a challenging invention? *Soccer & Society*, 18(1), 47–62. DOI:10.1080/14660970.2014.980740

Webb, T. (2016a) "Knight of the Whistle": W.P. Harper and the impact of the media on an Association Football referee. *The International Journal of the History of Sport*, 33(3), 306–324. DOI:10.1080/09523367.2016.1151004

Webb, T. (2016b) Referees and the media: a difficult relationship but an unavoidable necessity. *Soccer & Society*. DOI:10.1080/14660970.2015.1133414

Webb, T. (2017) *Elite Soccer Referees: Officiating in the Premier League, La Liga and Serie A*. London: Routledge.

Webb, T. and Thelwell, R. (2015) "He's taken a dive": cultural comparisons of elite referee responses to reduced player behaviour in association football. *Sport, Business and Management: An International Journal*, 5(3), 242–258. [online] Retrieved from: http://dx.doi.org/10.1108/SBM-04-2014-0019.

Webb, T., Wagstaff, C., Rayner, M., and Thelwell, R. (2016) Leading elite Association Football referees: challenges in the cross-cultural organization of a geographically dispersed group. *Managing Sport and Leisure*, 21(3), 105–123. DOI:10.1080/23750472.2016.1209978

30

Perspectives on ethics and integrity in football

Simon Gardiner

Introduction

Football, at both the recreational and elite level, maintains a global appeal that is unlike any other sport. The playing rules have given football much of its accessibility and enduring appeal; they are limited in number, have been subject to limited change and are reasonably easy to understand. However, beyond the playing field, football, at the elite level, has changed dramatically over the last 50 years or so from being, in the mid-twentieth century, primarily a sporting activity that has had some limited commercial awareness and form dependent on which country the focus might be. Contemporary football is now an overtly commercialised and commodified activity that has become as much a business as a sport. During this period of change, an important discourse has been around how to engage with the problems that either have become more evident or are linked primarily to the management of the vast increase in the commercial interests of the modern game. For the purposes of this paper, these matters will be divided, firstly, into ones concerning, safety, social disorder, and racism, and, secondly, corruption of the commercial integrity at both an organisational and playing level. It is important to stress that these issues could be substituted by other ones for this analysis – the main rationale for ones chosen here is that they are ideal issues to illustrate the existence of a regulatory space concerning who should take responsibility for their management. The preference is between sporting organisations exercising the application of a traditional self-regulatory role or a form of external intervention. Furthermore, there is a choice, based on effectiveness, as to what form of regulatory mechanism will be applied: sporting rules, codes of ethics, or legal instruments.

Sporting rules within football historically have had a monopoly and dominion within and over the sport. These rules can be divided into playing rules and organisational rules. Playing rules of football, as already stated, are exemplified by their simplicity. Beyond that, they begin to become more inextricable. Football has complex playing cultures that develop to gain advantage and circumvent the formal rules (conduct that may or not be constructed as cheating), and the corresponding engagement of codes of ethics to challenge perceived deficiencies in behaviour. Codes of ethics have become widespread in football: they may be of general educative guidance as to appropriate behaviour, or they may be specifically written into the contractual terms of professional footballers.

The organisational rules of football, and its internal governance, are more complex and more contested. They include rules that focus on the labour market and act as player restraints, including the FIFA transfer system regulations and the UEFA home-grown player rule. Secondly, other rules focus on the financial market including, for example, the UEFA Club Licensing and Financial Fair Play Regulations. These rules are created at the level of leagues, national governing bodies, the regional confederations and at the apex, FIFA, as the international sports federation for football.

Increasingly, external mechanisms, primarily legal rules, have challenged this monopoly, often by invalidating sporting rules as illegal and/or forcing compliance through their reform. This process is one of *juridification* of football (Foster, 1993), where what are essentially relations between sports athletes regulated via sporting rules have become more formalised with legal intervention leading to reconstructing of the sporting rule. In essence, it has been football and its internal sporting rules framework being forced to comply with external legal norms. The danger of juridification is that what are intrinsically social relationships between individuals resolved by application of the sporting rules have become imbued with legal values and are understood as constituting legal relationships; thus, social norms become legal norms. The threat of juridification is that if a dispute then befalls the parties, a legal remedy is seen as the primary remedy and the nature and perception of the dispute and the relational connection between the parties is altered.

What has arisen in contemporary elite football (and similarly in other comparable sports) is a complex pluralistic regulatory setting. The term "normative rule milieu" (Gardiner, 2011) can be used to describe a complex amalgam and interaction of sporting rules, quasi-law and national, supranational (European Union law), and international law. Legal pluralism provides a theoretical position with which to support the view that the interventionist role of the law in sport can be too pervasive and to highlight the importance of other non-legal forms of regulation (see Santos, 1985; Teubner, 1997).

Additionally, a significant development in football has been codes or charters of ethical behaviour and fair play, stressing the need to play the game in an appropriate way (see, for example, Constandt, De Waegeneer, and Willem, 2017; Parry and McNamee, 1998; Malloy, Ross, and Zakus, 2003; McNamee, 2010). The focus on ethics in football has grown in recent years, largely due to the wide range of ethical dilemmas faced in sport including the use of violence; drug abuse; the exploitation of young athletes and a variety of forms of financial corruption. These codes target not only football participants but also administrators, coaches, spectators, and others. In terms of football participants, though, they encourage ethical behaviour within the general context of the sport.

In addition, to pressure acting in a more ethical manner, the use of the term *integrity* has, in recent years, become common currency in the football and general sports world. It is not, however, a term with a clear definition. Integrity seems to represent a central standard that sporting participants concerning a range of competition governance issues and sporting administration need to coalesce around (Gilbert and Skinner, 2015; Vanden Auweele, Cook, and Parry, 2015; Gardiner, Parry, and Robinson, 2017). However, the ubiquitous use of the term has resulted in its exhibiting both imprecision and superficiality. Different actors within and beyond the sports industry use the term "integrity of sport" in different ways. Sometimes it means simply "honesty," and other times it is used as a "catch-all" phrase for an amalgam of a range of sports-related values including the unpredictability of outcome and a promotion of a level playing field. The term "commercial integrity" is often highlighted, the need to protect the commercial structure and stakeholders in the game from outside exploitation via mechanisms such as ambush marketing. Additionally, it is used as a counter-factual, to describe desirable outcomes, such as non-corrupt administration, or non-fixed matches.

Within football, different narratives about integrity by different individuals and groups exist together with a lack of integration between the different views of integrity. This leads to the danger of imposing a narrow corporate model of behavioural-based integrity, which when applied to football-related corruption, for example, results in a limited and unsubstantiated understanding of the phenomenon being promulgated. This can be compared with an alternative model of integrity, namely a more complex inter-institutional integrity, involving individuals taking responsibility for their practice and their organisation. This emphasis on plurality and dialogue within organisations exemplifies a holistic valued-based "moral integrity." This will be exemplified in the following analysis of some of the problems facing modern football and how the discourse around ethics and integrity is visible.

Safety, social disorder, and racism in football

Football hooliganism

Elite football matches have historically attracted large levels of spectators who wish to see the attraction live "in the flesh," rather than through the variety of media available. For the football club owners and event organisers, these spectators also represent a significant income stream. The vast majority of these crowds are well ordered. However, incidents of disorder have also been a common occurrence – the term football hooliganism is one that has a strong cultural resonance; it has often been termed the "English disease." Football hooliganism is often portrayed as a modern phenomenon, which developed in the 1970s. In reality, it is likely that crowds within the era of organised football from the end of the nineteenth century have often been the locale for disorder. This has been a phenomenon in a number of parts of the world. For example, Duke and Crolley (1996) state:

> There has been a separate and distinctive evolution of football related violence in Argentina. Fighting between rival gangs of fans in Argentina developed independently and considerably in advance of the modern phenomenon of football hooliganism in Britain.

In the UK, it has been suggested that over 4,000 incidents of what one might term "football hooliganism" (rather than just individual fights) occurred in the 20 years before the First World War (Dunning et al., 1984). For example, in 1909, goalposts were torn down and over 100 people were injured in a pitched battle between fans and police after the Scottish Cup Final in Glasgow. Although only subject to specific state scrutiny in the UK over the last 30 years or so, it has existed as a social phenomenon for much longer. However, in the discourse of the media, the modern era of football hooliganism is often viewed as starting in 1961, where a major riot occurred after an equalising goal during a Sunderland versus Tottenham game. Not only has hooliganism been recognised as a national "problem" within the English game; fans travelling to see the England national side have been involved in numerous incidents. Complex issues of nationalism and national identity are being played out in football fandom, of course within the more general contemporary political and social momentum towards a more formalised integrationist Europe and the implications of Brexit.

In England, over the last 50 years or so, as far as football hooliganism is concerned, there has been a contested debate on who should bear responsibility for active engagement with the phenomenon. On the one hand, it is through self-regulation of the football authorities. On the other hand, it has been through the social policy and legal responses of the state. In England, significant amounts of legislation have been enacted, often in response to particular incidents that have led to significant media coverage. There has also been a clear conflation with football hooliganism and spectator safety issues. Two incidents in 1985 are key. The first was the fire at the Bradford City ground, which led to the deaths of 54 people. The second was the tragedy at the Heysel Stadium in Brussels at the UEFA European Cup Final, where 39 spectators died due to the collapse of a wall. Although primarily focused on the former disaster, both incidents were part of the government inquiry leading to the Popplewell Report (1986). This report made a number of recommendations concerning safety on the one hand and the consideration of a membership scheme for all football spectators on the other. Although enabling legislation was introduced in the form of the Football Spectators Act 1989, a compulsory membership scheme was never introduced.

Safety and the Hillsborough disaster

The other pivotal event involving safety was of course the Hillsborough Stadium disaster that resulted in the deaths of 96 Liverpool Football Club supporters. Although it is now recognised that this was caused primarily by safety defects and failures of policing, it was initially portrayed as being the latest manifestation of hooligan activity. Again a government inquiry took place and the subsequent Taylor Report (1990) made recommendations that were divided into ones concerning safety at stadiums and control of spectators. This included the enacting of the Football (Offences) Act 1991, which criminalised entry onto the playing area, throwing missiles, and racist chanting. Arguably, significant amounts of legislation have been passed without any real analysis of the causes of football hooliganism. The legislative response to hooligan activity has endured with the passing of the Football (Offences and Disorder) Act 1999, Football Disorder Act 2000 and the Violent Crime Reduction Act 2006 amending and strengthening many of the provisions in the earlier 1989 and 1991 Acts (Pearson and Stott, 2007). This extensive legislative framework is considered to as having "criminalised" the ordinary football fan in the UK.

Has this formal regulatory approach been successful? There is evidence that the location of hooliganism has shifted over a period of time. Whereas it "traditionally" took place in or near to stadiums, it has relocated it away from the highly regulated environment of modern football grounds to other points where rival supporters can meet. The official figures also show the increased use of domestic and international football banning orders (FBOs), which can be seen as having increasingly successfully limited the movement of and excluded (from stadiums and surrounding areas) potential offenders. The 1999, 2000, and 2006 acts have strengthened the ability for the courts to make both domestic and international banning orders when individuals are convicted of "football-related" criminal offences. It is important to note that they are essentially civil orders, but as with Anti-Social Behaviour Orders (ASBOs), their breach is a criminal offence. Their application can extend to, for example, police officers' refusing an individual fan the ability to travel abroad where the officer has "reasonable suspicion" that the individual may be involved in hooligan activity. A concern persists that the civil liberties of football supporters that may have some football-related conviction are being unfairly and unlawfully restricted (see judicial analysis in *Gough v Chief Constable of Derbyshire* [2002] 2 All ER 985) and in *R v Winkler* [2004] 168 JPN 720). Football grounds have become highly regulated areas with segregation of home and away fans, all-seater stadiums at the elite level and stewarding of the crowd at the direction of the club. It is also important to stress that football clubs have taken on more responsibility to work closely with the police and local authorities so as to manage the problem, including through educational campaigns targeting spectators.

The still ongoing consequences and aftermath of the Hillsborough disaster that occurred in 1989, provides an opportunity to develop an ethical-based comprehension around responsibility for such events (Scraton, 2016). It was not until 2012 that the Independent Panel Report provided evidence of collusion primarily on the part of the police, but also the ambulance service. The subsequent coroner inquests resulted in verdicts of unlawful killing and underlined the behaviour of the public authorities involved as an example of institutional defensiveness and a culture of denial. The football authorities, notably the FA, did not escape censure and has indisputably much to learn from this affair (Conn, 2016). The FA did not directly obfuscate the truth of what happened on that day in 1989, but it has been clear that in the preceding years it distanced itself from taking meaningful responsibility for improving safety at football matches.

One potential development that is likely to emerge from the tragedy is the creation of a so-called Hillsborough Law (Jones, 2017). This proposed legislation, which is planned to be presented to Parliament in 2018, is intended to promote ethical behaviour and create a "duty of candour" on all public officials to be open and to tell the truth. Potential criminal liability could be incurred where lying and distortion of the truth is established. Other provisions include a code of ethics supporting members of the public being able to make complaints and protection for whistleblowers. This law is designed to create the cultural environment so that events such as the protracted aftermath of Hillsborough are less likely to occur. This is also very much about the legacy of the disaster and a clear attempt to provide some form of justice for those who died and for the families of the bereaved. Openness and an effective duty of candour in a range of public (and quasi-public bodies) are honourable goals. However, it needs to be underpinned by and be part of a complex inter-institutional integrity, involving individuals taking responsibility for their practice and for the meaning and practice of their profession, their organisation, and the overall project. This emphasis on plurality and dialogue within organisations as stated earlier exemplifies a holistic valued-based "moral integrity." Although the focus is on public bodies, football authorities, both nationally and internationally as similarly closed and often opaque institutions, have plenty to gain from embracing this approach to changing cultural values. The wider picture for football from this debate around integrity highlights that football can learn by looking beyond its own experience to take cognisance of the wider debate concerning integrity and governance.

Racism and football

To conclude this section, the focus will briefly be on three expressions of racism in football. It is important to stress that players from a Black Minority and Ethnic (BME) background have historically been subject to a "racially hostile working environment" (Weaver-Williams, 1996), not only through the behaviour of spectators but also due to discriminatory actions and practice by employers and co-workers. Racist abuse by spectators has been identified as a sub-element of hooligan activity and has led to a bifurcated approach with both legal and social policy responses. First, general anti-discrimination legislation and some elements of the criminal law have been deployed within the workplace, together with the creation of football-specific criminal legislation, namely the Football Offences Act 1991, to engage with spectator racism. Secondly, a range of policy initiatives predicated on education, promotion of ethical behaviour, and raising awareness have been instigated within and outside football, including for example the "Kick it Out" campaign[4] and "Show Racism the Red Card," an anti-racism charity. The aim of both organisations has been to produce anti-racist educational resources and to engage directly with racist behaviour (see Gardiner and Welch, 2001; 2011). The FA has been active in recent years and has provided a range of methods through which players, officials, and fans can report discrimination, including speaking to the referee, speaking to a nearby steward, or email-ing the FA. There is now a reporting app from Kick It Out, football's equality and inclusion body, where reports can be made anonymously.

Racist abuse between players has also been identified as an issue to which alternative approaches can be applied. A recent research study emphasised the distinctions between two disciplinary procedures in two football codes (Gardiner, 2015). The comparison was between the procedure that operates in English football for racist abuse and the equivalent disciplinary process in Australian Rules Football. On the one hand, as seen with the English FA policy as applied to the cases of high-profile players Luis Suarez, John Terry, and Nicolas Anelka, the increasing quasi-criminal nature of sports disciplinary procedures is identified as exhibiting characteristics of formal rationality, a conflict-based process of adjudication, and being of a punitive nature. Although there is an emphasis on the application of the relevant sporting rule to the facts, and examination of the internal norms of sport, these procedures exhibit certain characteristics – such as due process, careful consideration of evidence, and use of previous cases as precedent – that are found within criminal law trials. Sporting sanctions follow where a case is proven and include increasingly lengthy playing bans, financial penalties, and putative education programmes. On the other hand, the Australian Football League (AFL), and in comparison to conflict-based and punitive responses characterised above, takes a more overtly conciliatory approach with elements of consensus-based mediation between the participants concerning the allegations of inter-player racism. The emphasis is on engaging with the ethical nature of the perpetrator's conduct and the finding of a solution not imposed from above but agreed upon between the participants that has strong elements of empowerment and justice for the victim. Such resolutions, with the emphasis on restorative justice, are ones that are likely to be lasting and require the abuser to confront not only the victim but also their own behaviour. Education programmes and club-imposed playing bans are the immediate sanctions.

Within a pluralistic model of regulation, the law has a part to play alongside sporting rules and sports-related policies that have developed to engage with manifestations of racism in sport. Non-legal models, such as that exercised in the AFL focused on conciliation, with the emphasis on consensus, victim empowerment, anti-racism awareness, and education campaigns for the abuser can be argued as having a more explicit ethical base. With significantly fewer disciplinary actions brought in the AFL compared to English football in relative terms, there appears to be more success in bringing about positive and enduring change in culture and attitudes (Gardiner, 2015).

A final matter to consider concerns more implicit forms of racism leading to lack of diversity and opportunity in terms of participation in recreational and professional football, and wider opportunities in terms of employment within coaching and administrative roles. One response has been the activity of initiatives such as that of "Sporting Equals," a charity that actively promotes greater involvement by all disengaged communities in terms of participation, especially involving the black and minority ethnic (BME) population in sport and physical activity.

In professional football, the representation of individuals from a BME background in English football is a mixed story. Over the last 40 years, indigenous players of Afro-Caribbean descent have been significantly over-represented in professional football in relation to the general population, despite having had to fight to achieve this prominence by challenging the dominant values within a football club culture that has emphasised homogeneity and replication of the familiar. This can be compared with players from other ethnic minorities, for example, those of a British Asian background, whose participation is considerably lower compared to their representation in the general population (Burdsey, 2007). This cosmopolitan makeup of players has, however, not been replicated within managerial, coaching, and administrative opportunities in the football industry. The common pathway for ex-professional players to move into management and coaching positions appears to be largely blocked for BME aspirants; BME managers in the Premier League and Football League in April 2015 occupied only 6.5 per cent of those positions available (indeed, in April 2014 it was 0 per cent, (Bradbury, 2014, p. 9)). Moreover, less than 1 per cent of senior governance and leadership roles at the English Football Association (FA), Premier and Football Leagues, and professional clubs are held by staff from a BME background (Bradbury, 2014, p. 9). This suggests that there are endemic institutional and structural obstructions in terms of work opportunities for BME individuals (Bradbury, 2013). There have been demands for a Rooney-type rule (named after a past team owner, Dan Rooney) that currently operates in American National Football League, to be introduced in the British football (Gardiner and Riches, 2016). This rule requires each shortlist for candidates to be interviewed in the hiring process for these types of positions, to include a certain quota of BME applicants. Some progress may be made with the English Football League introducing a version of the Rooney rule in 2016 (BBC, 2016), making it mandatory for clubs to interview a BME candidate for academy jobs but not first-team roles and the FA has announced that it will introduce a similar rule for coaching positions for England teams during 2018 (Burt, 2018).

The regulatory framework that has been developed around race abuse and discrimination in football over the last 25 years reflects a range of alternative mechanisms that can be applied to attempt to effectively engage with the problem. However, a persisting and fundamental question continues to relate to its impact on the identification of those who are different in terms of nationality and ethnicity: in other words, the extent to which "the fear of the other" is still prevalent.

Financial corruption

The second part of this chapter focuses on the challenges that different manifestations of financially related corruption present for modern football. The root of corruption is generally thought to be the Latin *corruptus, -a, -um,* the state of being rotten, decayed, transferable to the morally unsound state of being degenerate, decadent, and depraved. However, there is limited conceptual clarity and empirical evidence to elucidate as to how corruption in sport should be best understood and what type of conduct it encompasses (see Gorse and Chadwick, 2012; Brooks, Button, and Azeem, 2013; Gardiner, 2018). The analogy, however, with disease is clear. The concept of corruption is the antithesis of integrity (wholeness, truth), another concept widely employed in modern sport (Treagus, Cover, and Beasley, 2011; Gardiner, Parry, and Robinson, 2017). This section will chart how football, as the one truly global team sport, has been a visible location where the tensions between these two competing concepts have played out in a very public and chaotic way.

It is important to state that it was only in the 1970s and accelerating towards the end of the last century that there was formal recognition of societal-wide corruption as a problem. Similarly, after many years of cultural acceptance of corrupt activity within sport as "part of the game," the specific debate in sport in recent years has also been focused on the recurring issue of how best these nefarious corrupt activities can be challenged and attempts made to eradicate their occurrence (Chappelet, 2016; Hill, 2009). Measures have been initiated to alter the behaviour of participants in both the playing and administration of a range of sports (Condon, 2001; Gunn and Rees, 2008; Neville, 2008). The various forms of financial corruption exposed in sport in recent times has been the driver for this debate. For the purposes of this section, three forms can be identified with the focus on football.

Match fixing

First, match and so-called "spot" fixing (where a particular incident within a sports competition, in comparison with the result, is manipulated by participants for financial gain) is perhaps the phenomenon that best exemplifies corruption in contemporary professional football.

The examination of match fixing-related corruption needs to be mindful that the phenomenon exists within the interstices of the sports and gambling industries (Sorbonne/ICSS, 2012). The value of the global sports betting market is growing dramatically. One recent estimate values it at around US$1 trillion; $500 billion of this involves activity on the illegal betting market (Sportradar, 2014). It is likely that football-related betting accounts for a significant share of these figures. As with the use of prohibited performance-enhancing drugs seen as an endemic threat to the integrity of elite football, financial irregularity and match-fixing are seen as critical challenges to the wellbeing of sport and as striking at the key sporting value of "unpredictability of outcome."

A range of organisations are involved in monitoring, detecting, and attempting to manage the problem. What has emerged is a proposition that a multi-agency approach based on a holistic array of regulatory and ethically based initiatives may be effective. This can be exemplified by the Council of Europe (COE) and their recent promulgation of the "Convention on the Manipulation of Sports Competition." The convention's purpose is "to combat the manipulation of sports competitions in order to protect the integrity of sport and sports ethics in accordance with the principle of the autonomy of sport" (COE, 2014). This is an important development in the engagement with financial manipulation of sport creating certain legal obligations on signatory states (see Serby, 2015). The convention calls on governments to develop a range of provisions ranging from having relevant criminal laws in place that are fit for purpose to providing effective protection for whistleblowers. Education of players and administrators as to identifying the practice of match-fixing and recognising its corrosiveness to sport is also presented as a key requirement.

Financial impropriety

Second, irregular financial dealings have long been seen as part of professional football. English football has a long history of financial impropriety. The "bung" became part of football and public parlance in the 1990s. The bung is essentially where an undeclared payment is made to a club official to facilitate or "sweeten" a transfer deal to be completed. Two inquires under the auspices of the Premier League in the 1990s (FA Premier League, 1997) and the 2000s (Stevens, 2008) led to bans for individual managers and player agents from participating in football activities under FA rules and unsuccessful criminal prosecutions. Financial stability and accountability has been a concomitant project. At a European level, UEFA introduced club licensing in the 2004/2005 season focusing on issues such as sporting, infrastructure, legal compliance, and, vitally, financial sustainability. More recently, in 2009, UEFA introduced a set of Financial Fair Play regulations that need to be complied with, so as to facilitate eligibility to participate in competitions and promote effective financial governance. This focus is on greater financial regulation as a response to impropriety to bring about higher ethical conduct and stability within the game. The counter-argument is that, in fact, it is largely the free market rather than more regulation that has ensured sustainability. Szymanski (2009) argues that what he terms "football capitalism" – i.e., the maintenance of a free market in English football – has served football well and brought a remarkable degree of stability.

Third, evidence of bribery around the tendering process for major sporting tournaments has been uncovered. The corrupt procedures of the International Olympic Committee (IOC) were exposed as to choosing the host of the summer and winter Olympics in 1998 with the successful bid by Salt Lake City for the Winter Olympics (Jennings, 2000). More recently the focus has been on the world of football, and FIFA and its general activities – specifically the awarding of future World Cup competitions to Russia in 2018 and Qatar in 2022 (Jennings, 2006).

Organisational integrity

These various examples of financial corruption within football have been subject to an array of regulatory interventions. However, they can all be seen as symptoms of the dysfunctional activities of football governing bodies on a national, confederation, and international level. The English FA and governance in football has been a significant concern of government, resulting in recent years, in the Football Task Force (2000), the Burns Report on Football Governance (2005), and the DCMS Committee Inquiry into Football Governance (2011) (Gardiner, 2011). However, the FA continues to be subject to persistent criticism as to its failure to undergo meaningful reform (Ahmed, 2017) and illustrates the resistance of football bodies to attempts to bring about cultural change. An emerging discourse around football and other sports has been around the creation of good governance or better governance to limit the risk of external regulation (see Chappelet and Kübler-Mabbott, 2008).

At the international level, of course, FIFA cannot fail to be discussed. The crisis of governance in FIFA over the last decade has focused on lack of transparency, corruption, and lack of formal governance structures (Duval, 2016). Perhaps more fundamentally, the governance of FIFA shows a narrow view of integrity, which does not connect core values to procedures, has little space for critical deliberation and dialogue and has thus developed a blindness to the significance of actions both within the organisation and beyond (Zeidan and Fauser, 2015). "Integrity," in the first principle of the FIFA Code of Conduct, is not defined. The expression of the term, however, suggests personal integrity. The subsequent ten other principles make mention of core principles, including fairness, social responsibility, and eco-sustainability, but there is no attempt to interrogate any of these or begin to see how they connect. Hence, the FIFA Code implies a form of total integrity but does not work through the practice or how that might relate to the specific identity of football in a global context. This has led to discrete narratives around organisational sustainability and global responsibility (not least in terms of aiding football in developing nations), but not to any significant dialogue between the various stakeholders. Inevitably, this has led at different points to "moral blindness," such as initial lack of awareness of the treatment of workers by the Qatari authorities. The dominance of the organisational sustainability narrative has been further reinforced by the strong individual charismatic-style leadership focused on Sepp Blatter, and a lack of procedural integrity (what in legal or regulatory terms could be termed a lack of due process), especially around governance structures (see Tomlinson, 2014). Of course, football is not alone with this fragility around limited integrity in sport – recent reports in international cycling (Marty et al., 2015) and international athletics (Pound et al., 2016) demonstrate similar characteristics. This is of course a wider problem as evidenced in both the public sphere of the British NHS Mid-Staffs Trust (where poor levels of hospital care were identified and high mortality rates, Francis Report, 2013) and the private sphere of the German technology company Siemens (that involved widespread bribery payments by officials of the company to secure contracts, Löscher, 2012). The common feature, as within FIFA, is that there has been no space for critical dialogue or challenge to the dominant narrative.

The effect of this has been a threefold lack of responsibility: first, responsibility for ideas, values, worth, and practice (with global and national arms of FIFA unaware of the wider situation or of their mutual relationships); second, responsibility towards accountability (with little distributed leadership or space for mutually challenging dialogue); and third, responsibility for liability (shared responsibility for both global and national values of football and football governance). One attempt to address this integrity deficit has been the introduction of an aspirational ethics-based approach to adjust behaviour as found within the Transparency International Report concerning FIFA (Schenk, 2011). The report identified numerous examples of this lack of critical dialogue and a significant deficit around integrity in terms of individual responsibility for promoting the stated core values of these organisations. There has been a much publicised change of leadership at FIFA and a rather tortuous attempt to change culture and restore credibility through fundamental reform of FIFA's statutes and ethics systems. This "road map" for change is within the context of ongoing criminal investigations and prosecutions by the Federal Bureau of Investigation and the Swiss criminal authorities.

Conclusion

A number of perspectives on contemporary football have been presented in an attempt to highlight the regulatory conundrum around these issues. The regulatory space around these issues has been occupied by a complex amalgam of sporting rules, legal rules, and codes of ethics. A significant development has increasingly been on education and prevention. A clearer ethical grounding pervades the move to more nuanced and enlightened regulatory frameworks and procedures to engage with the problems discussed.

What is at the core of many problems in football, such as those presented in this chapter, is the failing of key organisations in football to reform, generate cultural change, and promote better standards of governance [see also Chapter 5 in this handbook]. The present chapter has underlined the need for effective critical dialogue and deliberation within organisations. A distinction has been made between a narrow notion of behavioural integrity that has habitually pervaded football and the need to embrace a wider value-based moral integrity where there is critical reflection on values and practice and a positive impact upon both organisational dynamics and individual behaviours. Finally, there is a need for continued empirical-based research to provide an evidence base to support these theoretical contentions.

References

Ahmed, M. (2017) UK parliament has "no confidence" in Football Association, *Financial Times*, 9 February.

FA Premier League, (1997) The Bungs Report, *The FA Premier League Inquiry into Transfers*. London: FA Premier.

Bradbury, S. (2013) Institutional racism, whiteness and the under-representation of minorities in leadership positions in football in Europe. *Soccer & Society*, 14(3), 296–331

Bradbury, S. (2014) Ethnic minorities and coaching in elite level football in England: a call to action. A report and recommendations from the sports people's think tank in Association with the FARE Network and the University of Loughborough. [online] Retrieved from: http://www.farenet.org/wp-content/uploads/2014/11/We-speak-with-one-voice.pdf

BBC, (2016) English Football League clubs approve "Rooney Rule" proposals for academies, 16 June, bbc.co.uk

Brooks, G., Button, M., and Azeem, A. (2013) *Fraud, Corruption and Sport*. Basingstoke: Palgrave.

Burdsey, D. (2007) *British Asians and Football: Culture, Identity, Exclusion*. London: Routledge.

Burt, J. (2018) Football Association to adopt the "Rooney Rule" for future England coaching, backroom and manager roles, *Daily Telegraph*, 9 January.

Chappelet and Kübler-Mabbott (2008) *The International Olympic Committee and the Olympic System: The Governance of World Sport*. London: Routledge.

Chappelet, J.L. (2016) Autonomy and governance: necessary bedfellows in the fight against corruption in sport. *Global Corruption Report: Sport*. London: Routledge.

Condon, L. (2001) *Report on Corruption in International Cricket*. London: ICC Anti-Corruption Unit.

Conn, D. (2016) Hillsborough disaster: why the FA still has serious questions to answer *The Guardian*, 10 May.

Constandt, B., De Waegeneer, E., and Willem, A. (2017) Ethical code effectiveness in football clubs: a longitudinal analysis. *Journal of Business Ethics*. [online] Retrieved from: https://doi.org/10.1007/s10551-017-3552-0

Duke, V. and Crolley, L. (1996) Football spectator behaviour in Argentina: a case of separate *Sociological Review*, 44(2), 272–293.

Dunning, E., Murphy, P., Williams, J., and Maguire, J. (1984) Football hooliganism in britain before the first world war. *International Review for the Sociology of Sport*, 19(3–4), 215–240.

Duval, A. (2016) The rules of the game: the need for transparency in sports governance. [online] Retrieved from: www.playthegame.org

Foster, K. (1993) Developments in sporting law. In: Allison, L. (ed.). *The Changing Politics of Sport*. Manchester, MUP.

Francis Report (2013) *The Mid Staffordshire Foundation Trust public enquiry*. [online] Retrieved from: www.midstaffspublicinquiry.com/

Gardiner, S. (2011) Theoretical understanding of the regulation of sport. In: Gardiner, S., O'Leary, J., Welch, R., Boyes, S. Naidoo, U. (eds.). *Sports Law*, (4th ed.). London: Routledge.

Gardiner, S. (2015) Player to Player racist hate speech in football: evaluation of alternative regulatory disciplinary mechanisms. *Sport and Society Journal*, 18(5), 552–564.

Gardiner, S. (2018) Conceptualising corruption in sport. In: Kihl, L (ed.), *Corruption in Sport*. London: Routledge.

Gardiner, S. Parry and Robinson, L. (2017) Integrity and the corruption debate in sport: where is the integrity? *European Sport Management Quarterly*, 17(1), 6–23.

Gardiner, S. and Riches, L. (2016) Racism and homophobia in English football. The equality act, positive action and the limits of law. *International Journal of Discrimination and the Law* 16(2–3), 102–121.

Gardiner, S. and Welch, R. (2001) Sport, racism and the limits of "Colour Blind" Law. In: McDonald, I. and Carrington, B. (eds.). *Racism, Sport and British Society*, (pp. 133–151). London: Routledge.

Gardiner, S. and Welch, R. (2011) Football, racism and the limits of "colour blind" law: revisited. In Burdsey, D. (ed.). *Race, Ethnicity and Football: Persisting Debates and Emergent Issues*, (pp. 222–237). London: Routledge.

Gilbert, K. and Skinner, J. (2015) Defining integrity in sport. In: *Sport and Integrity* (pp. 17–23). Lausanne: SportAccord.

Gorse, S. and Chadwick, S. (2012) Conceptualising corruption in sport: implications for sponsorship programmes. *European Business Review*, July/August, 40–45.

Gunn, B. and Rees, J. (2008) *Environmental Review of Integrity in Professional Tennis. London International Tennis Federation*. London: ITF.

Hill, D. (2009) How gambling corruptors x football matches. *European Sports Management Quarterly*, 9, 411–432.

Jennings, A. (2000) *The Great Olympic Swindle: When the World Wanted Its Games Back*. London: Simon & Schuster.

Jennings, A. (2006) *Foul! The Secret World of FIFA: Bribes, Vote Rigging and Ticket Scandals*. London: Harpers Sport.

Jones, J. (2017) *The Patronising Disposition of Unaccountable Power* A report to ensure the pain and suffering of the Hillsborough families is not repeated, London: HMSO.

Löscher, P. (2012) Löscher, the CEO of Siemens on using a scandal to drive change. *Harvard Business Review*, November.

McNamee, M. (ed.) (2010) *The Ethics of Sports [a Reader]*. London: Routledge.

Malloy, D., Ross, S., and Zakus, D., (2003) *Sports Ethics: Concepts and Cases in Sport and Recreation*. (2nd ed.). Toronto: Thompson Education.

Marty, D., Nicholson, P., and Hass, U. (2015) *Cycling Independent Reform Commission: Report to the President of the Union Cycliste Internationale*. Lausanne: UCI.

Neville, E. (2008) *The British Horseracing Authority and Integrity in Horseracing. An Independent Review*. London: BHA.

Parry, S. and McNamee, M. (1998) *Ethics and Sport* . London: Routledge.

Pearson, G. and Stott, C. (2007) *Football Hooliganism: Policing and the War on the English Disease*. London: Pennant Books.

Popplewell Final Report (1986) Final Report of the Committee of Inquiry into Crowd safety and Control on safety Grounds London: HMSO CM9710.

Pound, R., McLaren, R., and Younger, G. (2016) *The Independent Commission Report #2* Montreal: World Anti-Doping Agency.

Santos, B. (1985) On modes of production of law and social power. *International Journal of the Sociology of Law* 13, 299–307.

Scraton, P. (2016) *Hillsborough: The Truth* (Updated edition). London: Penguin Books.

Schenk, S. (2011) *Safe Hands Building Integrity and Transparency at FIFA*. London: Transparency International.

Serby, T. (2015) The Council of Europe Convention on Manipulation of Sports Competitions: the best bet for the global fight against match-fixing? *The International Sports Law Journal*, 15(1), 83–100.

Sorbonne/ICSS (2012). *Protecting the integrity of sport competition: The last bet for modern sport*. An executive summary of the Integrity Report Sport Integrity Research Programme, Paris: University of Sorbonne.

Stevens, L. (2008) *Premier League Inquiry on Football Transfers*. London: Premier League.

Szymanski, S. (2009) The reassuring stability of football capitalism. [online] Retrieved from: http://coventryuniversity.podbean.com/2009/06/10/the-reassuring-stability-of-football-capitalism-stefan-szymanski

Taylor (1990) The Hillsborough Stadium Disaster (Final Report), ("Taylor" Report) CM 962.

Teubner, G. (1997) Legal pluralism in the world society. In: Teubner, G. (ed.). *Global Law without a State*. Andover: Dartmouth.

Tomlinson, A. (2014) *FIFA: The Men, the Myths and the Money*. London: Routledge.

Treagus, M., Cover, R., and Beasley, C. (2011) *ASC's Integrity in Sport Literature Review*. Canberrra: Australian Sports Commission.

Vanden Auweele, Y., Cook, E., and Parry, J. (eds.). (2016) *Ethics and Governance in Sport: The Future of Sport Imagined*. London: Routledge.

Weaver Williams, P. (1996) Performing in a racially hostile environment. *Marquette Sports Law Journal*, 6, 287.

Zeidan, O. and Fauser, S. (2015) Corporate governance and corporate social responsibility – the Case of FIFA. *Problems and Perspectives in Management*, 13(2), 183–192.

31

Talent management

Richard P. Bailey, Rob J. Bailey, and Nick Levett

Introduction

Talent is a ubiquitous feature of contemporary sport. Recruiting, contracting, developing, supporting, and managing talent are fundamental activities of clubs, as well as the wider sports system, and the rewards for dealing with them successfully can be considerable. In some ways, talent represents the "Holy Grail" of sport: it is evasive, often mistaken, and easily lost. This chapter discusses the concept of "talent management." This is a phrase borrowed from the business world and is not currently widely used in the academic sport literature. Yet, it is, we suggest, a useful idea and is worth tentative examination. Our suggestion is that, at this embryonic phase of usage, "talent management" is understood to represent two connected contexts or paradigms. The first is the management of the talent development process (management of talent); the second is the management of talented players (management of the talented). The chapter is divided into four sections: (1) talent management as player development; (2) talent in English football, as a case study; (3) talent management as player management; and (4) talent management as human resourcing.

Talent management as player development

There have been numerous attempts to define talent. Although the term is extensively used in many areas, its specific meaning largely depends on the guiding assumption of the users. Some associate talent with some innate ability, while others stress the influences of practice, coaching, and the learning environment (Durand-Bush and Salmela, 2001). A selection of definitions is offered in the box below which demonstrates some of the competing issues in this area.

Example definitions of talent

"Talent is not properly thought of as a genetic or innate endowment, but rather as a developed set of traits that are integral to the further development of expert/elite performance."

(Ackerman, 2014, p. 11)

"Children and youth with outstanding talent perform, or show the potential for performing, at reasonably high levels of accomplishments when compared with others of their age, experience, or environment."

(Ross, 1993, p. 3)

(1) (Talent) originates in genetically transmitted structures and hence is at least partly innate. (2) Its full effects may not be evident at an early stage, but there will be some advance indications, allowing trained people to identify the presence of talent before exceptional levels of mature performance have been demonstrated. (3) These early indications of talent provide a basis for predicting who is likely to excel. (4) Only a minority are talented, for if all children were, there would be no way to predict or explain differential success. Finally, (5) talents are relatively domain-specific.

(Davidson, Howe, and Sloboda, 1998, p. 399)

"Talent refers to performance which is distinctly above average in one or more fields of human performance."

(Gagné, 2004, p. 87)

The talent development process refers to the series of activities concerned with the quest for international or professional sporting success. The timing of this process varies considerably with the sport and national traditions; in football, it typically begins during childhood and continues until early-to-mid adulthood. The absence of a universal nomenclature adds diversity to an already complex set of activities. However, two core activities: talent identification and talent development (Bailey and Morley, 2006) are prominent. Talent identification refers to strategies focused on the recognition of current players with the potential to achieve high levels of performance in a particular sport, while talent development is concerned with planning and delivering learning experiences necessary for those identified players to realise their potential.

A more nuanced way of thinking about the stages of talent development comes from football and articulates the orthogonality of developed and potential talent (Williams and Reilly, 2000). The "pursuit of excellence" model is presented in Figure 31.1.

Optimising the trajectory from talent detection to identification, through development to selection is a core feature in any sporting system. Sometimes referred to as the performance pathway, the effective management of this process is a fundamental concern for football clubs and national agencies.

The standard metaphor used to illustrate this process of talent development is a "pyramid" (Bailey and Collins, 2013) (see Figure 31.2). Simply put, the model operates as follows: a broad base of foundational participation, with increasingly higher levels of performance, engaged in by fewer and fewer people. This practical application of this model can be illustrated by considering a typical cohort of children. Physical education offers an introduction to a variety of

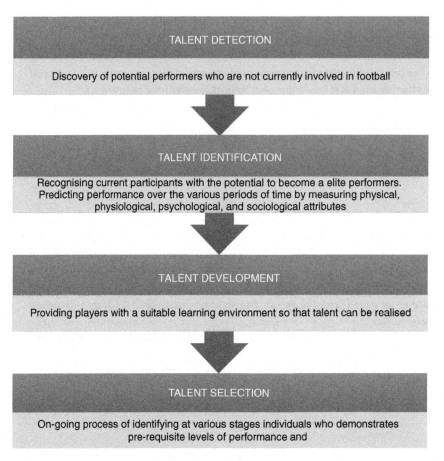

Figure 31.1 The "pursuit of excellence" model (adapted from Williams and Reilly, 2000)

sports to all children, and some of these may find they have a particular interest or ability in one or more of the sports. Some children may participate in after-school clubs and represent the school in local competitions. Either through encouragement by teachers or parents, or, less common at this stage, specialist football coaches, a small number of these children may progress to local teams and compete in more competitive events. Some of the most-able players may then be spotted by the local clubs, and, if successful in some sort of assessment, they are given the opportunity to join the clubs' programmes. And the process continues as the most-able players at each level progress further up the pyramid. Kirk, Brettschneider, and Auld (2005) argue that the influence of the pyramid metaphor can be seen in numerous international sports participation models and that "the assumptions underpinning the pyramid model continue to have a powerful residual influence on thinking about junior sport participation and sport development in sport policy" (p. 2).

Despite its wide-scale use, doubts have been raised over the scientific foundations of most talent identification programmes (Vaeyens, Lenoir, Williams et al., 2008). From the perspective of optimally effective performance pathways, the most powerful criticisms relate to their low predictive value and lack of validity (Suppiah, Low, and Chia, 2015). In other words, talent identification strategies are rarely effective ways of detecting and identifying genuine talent, with many potentially talented players being expelled from the system. There are many

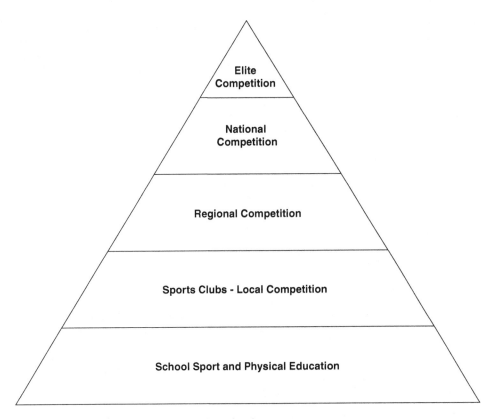

Figure 31.2 The pyramid model of talent development

reasons for this problem, but most stem from a systematic tendency to underestimate the complexity of the talent development process. For example, one of the most persistent causes of talent loss is relative age effect, whereby early birth dates in the competitive year grouping are systematically but disproportionately selected, and younger - and usually smaller and weaker – players are removed (Padrón-Cabo, Rey, García-Soidán, et al., 2016).

The best-known attempt to capture the complexity of talent is the "Differentiated Model of Giftedness and Talent" (DMGT; see Figure 3) (Gagné, 2003). This is a general theory, but its influence is evident in several sports-based models (e.g., Bailey and Morley, 2006; Vaeyens, et al., 2008). The DMGT distinguishes between *gifts* and *talents*. The former refer to outstanding natural abilities or aptitudes; the latter to the outstanding mastery of systematically developed abilities (Gagne, 2003). In simple terms, this distinction highlights the beginning and end points of the developmental process that abilities go through as they are transformed into excellence. But more importantly, the model recognises the impact that personal volition, environmental stimulation, and practice have on development. It also recognises chance as influential in the outcome of the process. Research has revealed numerous factors that can influence the emergence of talent in sport that are independent of a player's ability and effort, such as parents' background, social class, relative age, and maturity compared to peers (Baker and Horton, 2004).

The significance of a developmental model like the DMGT is that it demonstrates that the most naturally gifted are not necessarily those who progress through the different stages of the talent development pathway; commitment, opportunity, and chance always mediate that passage. Moreover, it could be argued that an effective talent development process is one that capitalises on players' physical and personal attributes through maximising practices and minimising luck (Bailey, 2007).

Talent development in football: England as a case study

Widely regarded as one of the most competitive systems in the world, talent development in English football involves transitioning 1.5 million playing the game at grassroots level to the small number selected to play at the elite level. A key element of this process is the Academy system, which involves schools for developing elite players.

The Elite Player Performance Pathway (EPPP), administered by the English Premier League, places responsibility for the development of players with professional clubs. The EPPP provides a route from players at nine years of age through, for those who remain in the system, to first team squads. Clubs are categorised into four levels, with Category 1 clubs providing an Under 9 to Under 21 programme that combines full-time education within or around the football club setting, with a day-release from the school system to train. Category 2 and 3 clubs offer a hybrid or part-time model of education and training, and have fewer requirements for full-time staffing and facilities, whilst Category 4 programmes simply provide a programme for Under 17 to Under 21 players (see www.goalreports.com/EPLPlan.pdf for a full detailed breakdown of the plan). Statistics suggest that only 180 will make it through to play in the Premier League from grassroots football (Calvin, 2017), a success rate of 0.0012 per cent of the football-playing population. The chances increase somewhat if players manage to enter the Academy system at nine years old, boosted up to 0.5 per cent.

The Academies serve a dual purpose: to develop talent drawn from the local areas, and to recruit and nurture the best young players from wider afield. They provide a range of support services to players, including personal mentoring, sports science, physiotherapy, sports medicine, psychology, nutrition, education, lifestyle management, and performance analysis. All of these aim to combine to provide an optimal pathway for young players to progress towards high levels of performance. Evidence suggests that the demands of performance within the English game are increasing, requiring high levels of endurance, motor control, power, and speed. Data suggest that the game is getting faster; with players increasing the distances travelled with and without the ball and increasing the number of high-intensity sprints during games (Minano-Espin et al., 2017). The EPPP requires clubs to track coaching hours completed by players in different activities and over time would provide a detailed database of understanding for individual player journeys.

The demands of the EPPP require a substantial investment of time, money, and energy. The 24 Category 1 Academies, mostly in the Premier League, have considerably more of all three of these, relative to Category 2, 3, or 4 Academies. This can be seen both in the number of staff available and the support offered to players (www.goalreports.com/EPLPlan.pdf). Generally speaking, however, all Academies include certain key personnel (see Table 31.1).

A common feature of the development experience of players as they progress towards elite levels is the loan system, which involves the "lending" of players from their parent club to another, often lower-ranked, club. The leading Premier League clubs have a full-time member of staff responsible for managing the loan, keeping in contact with players and ensuring they gain the most from the loan opportunity. Poorer clubs rarely have that level of support. A second core developmental activity is a comprehensive games programme. In principle, at least, this

Table 31.1 Key Academy personnel

Example roles	Brief responsibilities
Academy Manager	Oversee the strategic direction and leadership of the Academy programme, establish a Technical Control Board and link with senior management in the football club.
Head of Coaching	Manage the full- and part-time coaches that work across all age groups, work with the Academy Manager on the direction of the coaching programme and develop the individual coaches.
Foundation Phase Coach	Plan, develop, and lead coaching sessions for players aged U5 to U11, including the setting and reviewing of 12-week learning objectives. There is a focus on mastering the ball typically in this phase.
Youth Development Phase Coach	Plan, develop, and lead coaching sessions for players aged U12 to U16, including the setting and reviewing of six-week learning objectives. The aim is development of individuals in a team setting and a growing tactical awareness.
Professional Development Phase Coach	Plan, develop, and lead coaching sessions for players aged U17 to U21, including the setting and reviewing of six-week learning objectives. This phase is about ensuring the players are equipped for the transition into senior football.
Head of Sports Science and Medicine	Coordinate the science and medical programme for all players in the Academy, managing the team of staff under their stewardship.
Lead Sports Scientist and Senior Sports Physiotherapist	Coordinate the relevant programmes in their area of specialism through applied practical experiences of elite environments and appropriate qualifications and knowledge.
Head of Education	Oversee the education programme for players in the Academy and, where there is a full-time education model, liaise with schools to ensure adequate provision is available.
Performance Analysts	Work with players to ensure they are provided footage of their performances to enable individual and coach reflection for development.

programme aims to provide competition that matches the priorities within player development as they progress, affording a range of formats, from small-side to 11v11 games, futsal and international tournaments plus regular weekly fixtures.

Talent management as human resourcing

The concept of talent management in business has existed since the late-1990s when consultants McKinsey and Company identified the challenge faced by businesses of attracting and retaining key staff. They termed this as "the war for talent" (Michaels et al., 2001). Over the past two decades, there has been increasing interest in the concept of talent management as businesses and other organisations have looked at ways of trying to create competitive advantage (McDonnell et al., 2017). For example, one study found that 61 per cent of chief executive officers saw the retention of skills and talent as the key issue for the next five years, and the ability to recruit and manage talent was the second most critical issue (PwC, 2015).

Whilst talent management has become a commonly used business term, the concept lacks a standard definition. Examples of definitions of talent management, which illustrate the different interpretations of the concept.

Examples of definitions of talent management

The systematic identification of key positions which differentially contribute to the organisations sustainable competitive advantage, the development of a talent pool of high-potential and high-performing incumbents to fill these roles, and the development of a differentiated human resources architecture to facilitate filling these positions with competent incumbents, and to ensure their continued commitment to the organisation.

Collings and Mellahi, 2009, p. 304

"The process through which organizations anticipate and meet their needs for talent in strategic jobs."

(Cappelli and Keller, 2014, p. 307)

"Talent management seeks to attract, identify, develop, engage, retain and deploy individuals who are considered particularly valuable to an organization."

(Chartered Institute of Personnel Development, 2017)

"The planning, selection and implementation of development strategies for the entire talent pool to ensure that the organisation has both the current and future supply of talent to meet strategic objectives and that development activities are aligned with organisational talent management processes."

(Garavan et al., 2012, p. 6)

It is at least partly because of this lack of consensus over central concept definitions that the practical application of talent management is often messy and nuanced (Sparrow et al., 2015a). The differences in the interpretations of talent management have led to the number of important questions which impact on practical applications within businesses and other organisations, as follows (adapted from Sparrow et al., 2015b):

- Is talent management concerned with how best to handle an elite or selected group of employees who have exceptional skills?
- Should everyone within an organisation be regarded as talented, so that all employees get the same opportunity to succeed?
- Is talent management merely another term for existing Human Resource function and strategic activities such as recruitment, succession planning, and leadership development?
- Is talent management about the use of metrics which are used as evidence for the effectiveness of human resource capital (e.g., identifying the human capital needed to achieve a strategic business objective)?

The diversity of interpretations of the concept of talent management is the most plausible reason why organisations often design their own talent management systems that are unique to their organisation and the specific contexts within which they operate.Garavan et al., 2012.

A perennial problem in the business literature on talent management is that the concept is used extensively and enthusiastically, but without it being linked to scientific research and

Table 31.2 Talent management research

Category	Key findings
Management of talent	• Focuses on management of high-performing and high-potential staff regardless of position within organisation. • Promotes classification of high performers / high potentials, and that any poor performers should be managed out of the organisation. • Need to differentiate performance – and reward/compensation – amongst employees. • Key focus of the literature is on defining and effectively measuring "high performance," although an agreed definition is lacking. • Gap in knowledge as to how best to manage talented individuals, including the processes organisations use to recruit, motivate, and reward talent.
Talented individuals	• Appears to be a motivational impact on informing individuals of their talent status. • High-potential staff often report higher levels of job security and salary increases than average performers. • How "talent" is defined is widely identified as needing attention by researchers, as is the requirement to define and identity "high potential" (as the terms are often used interchangeably). • One study (Dries and Peppermans, 2012) found that learning agility is a more effective predictor of an employee being labelled as talented, than job performance. Learning agility involves willingness to learn (i.e., actively looking for novel experiences that enhance learning), emotional intelligence, and adaptability.

Source: McDonnell et al., 2017.

evidence (Lewis and Heckman, 2006). McDonnell et al. (2017) sought to begin to address the theoretical weaknesses associated with talent management through a systematic review of the scientifically based talent management literature. They found that talent management research can be classified into two broad categories, namely (1) the management of talent, which focuses on how organisations attract, recruit, retain, and reward higher performers, and the impact this has on organisational performance, and (2) the talented individuals, particularly what constitutes talent and the behaviour of talented individuals. The first of these categories (management of talent) has generated the greatest amount of academic research. Table 31.2 provides a summary of key findings from the literature within each of these categories.

There is no commonly accepted model for talent management within businesses. As mentioned, many organisations create bespoke strategies. However, Table 31.3, below, provides a summary of the questions faced by organisations when looking to develop their talent management strategies.

Talent management in business has emerged as an important issue for organisations. However, with no consensus on the precise meaning of the term, or how it should be applied, organisations are developing their own approaches to talent management, which they hope will give them a competitive advantage. Presumably, the term will move towards shared language, concepts, and values over time. However, at present the concept remains contested.

Table 31.3 Talent development and management questions faced by organisations

Dimension	Key questions
Defining talent for talent development	• What drives an organisation to nominate particular employees as talented? • Does the organisation encourage narrow or broad inclusion? • Is talent natural or developed? • Does the organisation believe in satisfying or maximising talent?
Focus on technical or generic competencies or both	• Should the talent development process focus on generic or technical competencies, or both? • When should the organisation focus on both sets of competencies? • How should both sets of competencies be developed? • Which competencies are more important for performance, potential, and career advancement?
Whose talent development needs and whose responsibility	• What needs take priority in the talent development process (organisational or individual)? • What is the proportion of organisationally driven versus self-directed development activities?
Accelerated or traditionally paced development	• What are the demands of the business strategy in respect of development? • What is the time frame required to develop talent and particularly, high potential talent? • How should development strategies be combined in both traditional and accelerated models?
The architecture of talent development	• What are the talent development needs of the organisation? • What are the key objectives of the talent development process? • How appropriate are competency models? • What sequence of experiences, exposures, and challenges are appropriate for different categories of talent? • How are talent development processes linked to talent selection, assessment and retention processes? • What is the appropriate blend of talent development programmes to achieve talent development objectives? • How customised or personalised are talent development strategies? • Does the talent development architecture provide on-time access and facilitate self-directed learning?

Source: Garavan, T.N., Carbery, R., and Rock R. (2012) Mapping talent development: definition, scope and architecture. *European Journal of Training and Development*, 36(1), 5–31.

Common concerns of the two paradigms

Professional football is a business. The Premier League alone has been estimated to be worth about 6 billion Euros in 2017 (Transmarkt: Premier League). It is surprising, therefore, that many decisions regarding the development and management of talent underpinning its success are left to tradition, "common sense," and intuition (Szymanski, 2015). Nevertheless, economic analyses have produced findings that demonstrate how the concerns of the two paradigms of talent management discussed – as talent development and human resourcing – might connect.

The potential variables associated with professional football success are, of course, numerous. However, evidence supports the claim that the most talented players represent the central human resource in the game. Four key factors seem to be predictive of success in professional football: home advantage; the general economy of the country; players' salaries; and the share of the population playing the game (Kuper and Szymanski, 2009; Dobson and Goddard, 2001). The last of these factors highlights the extent to which the talent-management-as-human-resources perspective becomes inseparable from the talent-management-as-player-development paradigm. Simply put, the efficacy of the latter is dependent on the economic processes driving the former.

The significance of the first variable associated with success in football, home-field advantage is, perhaps, the most obvious. Kuper and Szymanski's (2009) regression analyses suggest it alone "is worth a lead of about two-thirds of a goal" (p. 35). This is meaningless when applied to a single game but beginning two out of three games leading by the equivalent of a goal ought to have a powerful effect on a season's results.

The second variable is the general economy of the country. Economists have known for some time that Gross Domestic Product (GDP) is a good indicator of sporting success (Leeds and Leeds, 2009; Monks and Husch, 2009). This seems to be at least partly explainable in terms of national wealth meaning the allocation of greater resources to support the different facets of sporting success. Generally speaking, wealthy countries are better able than their competitors to fund properly resourced talent development, including facilities, scientific support, and staffing. They are also better placed to recruit and retain the best players, both locally and from around the world (Kuper and Szymanski, 2009). Specifically, when countries increase their per capita wealth they have, on average, more success in sport because they can allocate more resources to achieving this goal. An analysis of world football statistics found that the relationship between international success and national wealth was so strong that they hypothesised that FIFA rankings of national teams could be used as an indicator of national development, to complement existing measures such as GDP per capita and the World Bank's Human Development Index (Gásquez and Royuela, 2014).

The third factor, players' salaries, is perhaps more surprising. As Quirk and Fort (1999) facetiously put it: "If general managers really were perfect judges of talent, there would be no need to play the league schedule to determine the league champion – we'd simply award the title to the team with the highest payroll" (p. 85). In fact, while transfer markets are notoriously unpredictable, there is evidence that the market for players' wages is efficient, so the better a player is, the more he earns. Framed with a different focus, players' salaries in football are good predictors of competitive success (Caruso et al., 2017; Gerhards and Mutz, 2017). The recruitment and retention of talent is such an important variable in a football club's fortunes that leading teams have been forced to pay increasingly high wages in order to attract the best talent. As a consequence, the real cost of attaining success in the top leagues has risen considerably in recent years (Frick, 2013).

The final factor associated with football success relates directly to the issue of talent management. As others have argued (e.g., Bailey et al., 2010), shallow pool of socio-economic backgrounds from which British sports typically draw talent serves to restrict the pool of potential talent that enters the system. Kuper and Szymanski (2009) argue persuasively that this places the English system (insofar as it uses home-grown players) at a relative disadvantage to many of its competitors. Despite sustained efforts to address the problem of what might be called the problem of "talent exclusion," English football's "share of the soccer population changes only glacially" (ibid., p. 44).

The management of talent is a fundamental concern of any business and no less so football. These themes highlight the close parallel between the concerns of clubs regarding their talent development processes, and those of businesses, in general, with their interest in talent as a primary human resource. In practice, however, the two paradigms have barely connected.

Conclusion

The detection, identification, development, and selection of talented players is recognised as fundamental to elite sport, and the rewards for dealing with them successfully can be considerable. It is not surprising that this topic has attracted a considerable amount of research and theory-building. Talent management, however, a term widely used in business, is almost unknown in academic studies of football, despite the fact that the highest levels of the game are engaged in business. This chapter has sought to address this apparent gap. In doing so, it has offered two different, but related, paradigms. The first paradigm reflects the existing understanding of talent development. Here, talent management is a process of managing and maximising the success of the talent development pathways. The second paradigm discussed comes from the business world and refers primarily to the management of those identified as talented at the highest levels. The case study of English football suggests that the two frameworks are inextricably connected, as the benefactors of the development process join a very selective group of players requiring more personalised and differentiated management. However, empirical and theoretical research at this point of connection is currently extremely limited.

References

Ackerman, P.L. (2014) Nonsense, common sense, and science of expert performance: Talent and individual differences. *Intelligence*, 45, 6–17.

Bailey, R.P. (2007) Talent development and the luck problem. *Sports Ethics and Philosophy*, 1(3), 367–377.

Bailey, R.P. and Morley, D. (2006) Towards a model of talent development in physical education. *Sport, Education and Society*, 11(3), 211–230.

Bailey, R.P., and Collins, D. (2013) The standard model of talent development and its discontents. *Kinesiology Review*, 2(4), 248–259.

Bailey, R.P., Collins, D., Ford, P., MacNamara, A., Toms, M., and Pearce, G. (2010) Participant Development in Sport: An academic review. Leeds: Sports Coach UK Baker, J., and Horton, S. (2004) A review of primary and secondary influences on sport expertise. *High Ability Studies*, 15(2), 211–228.

Calvin, M. (2017) *No Hunger in Paradise*. London: Century.

Cappelli, P. and Keller, J.R. (2014) Talent management: conceptual approaches and practical challenges. *The Annual Review of Organizational Psychology and Organizational Behavior*, 1(1), 305–331.

Caruso, R., Di Domizio, M., and Rossignoli, D. (2017) Aggregate wages of players and performance in Italian Serie A. *Economia Politica*, 34(3), 515–531.

Chartered Institute of Personnel Development (2017) www.cipd.co.uk/knowledge/strategy/resourcing/talent-factsheet#7241

Cobley, S., Schorer, J., and Baker, J. (2012) Identification and development of sport talent: A brief introduction to a growing field of research and practice. In: J. Baker, J. Schorer, S. Cobley (eds), *Talent Identification and Development in Sport. International Perspectives* (pp. 1–10). London: Routledge.

Collings, D.G. and Mellahi, K. (2009) Strategic talent management: a review and research agenda. *Human Resource Management Review*, 19(4), 304–331.

Davidson, J.W., Howe, M.J.A., and Sloboda, J.A. (1998) Innate talents: reality of myth? *Behavioral and Brain Sciences*, 21, 399–407.

Dobson, S. and Goddard, J. (2001) *The Economics of Football*. Cambridge: Cambridge University Press.

Dries, N. and Peppermans, R. (2012) How to identify leadership potential: development and testing of a consensual model. *Human and Resource Management*, 51(3), 361–385.

Durand-Bush, N., and Salmela, J.H. (2001) The development of talent in sport. In: R.N. Singer, H.A. Hausenblas, and C.M. Janelle (eds.). *Handbook of Sport Psychology* (2nd ed.) (pp. 269–289). New York: Wiley.

Frick, B. (2013), Team wage bills and sporting performance: evidence from (major and minor) European football leagues. In: P. Rodríguez, S. Késenne, and J. García (eds.). *The Econometrics of Sport* (pp. 63–80). Northampton, MA: Edward Elgar.

Gagne, F. (2003). Transforming gifts into talents: The DMGT as a developmental theory. In N. Colangelo & G.A. Davis (eds.). *Handbook of Gifted Education* (3rd ed.). Boston: Allyn and Bacon.

Gagné, F. (2004) Giftedness and talent: Reexamining a reexamination of definitions. In: R. Sternberg (ed.). *Definitions and Conceptions of Giftedness* (pp. 79–96). Thousand Oaks, CA: Corwin Press.

Garavan, T.N., Carbery, R., and Rock R. (2012) Mapping talent development: definition, scope and architecture. *European Journal of Training and Development*, 36(1), 5–31.

Gásquez, R. and Royuela, V. (2014) Is football an indicator of development at the international level? *Social Indicators Research*, 117(3), 827–848.

Gerhards, J. and Mutz, M. (2017) Who wins the championship? Market value and team composition as predictors of success in the top European football leagues. *European Societies*, 19(3), 223–242.

Kirk, D., Brettschneider, W-D., and Auld, C. (2005) Junior sport models representing best practice nationally and internationally. Junior sport briefing papers. Canberra: Australian Sports Commission.

Kuper, S. and Szymanski, S. (2009) *Soccernomics: Why England Loses, Why Germany and Brazil Win, and Why the US, Japan, Australia, Turkey – and Even Iraq – are Destined to Become the Kings of the World's Most Popular Sport*. New York: Nation Books.

Leeds, M.A. and Leeds, E.M. (2009) International soccer success and national institutions. *Journal of Sports Economics*, 10(4), 369–390.

Lewis, R.E., and Heckman, R.J. (2006) Talent management: A critical review. *Human Resource Management Review*, 16(2), 139–154.

McDonnell, A., Collings, D. G., Mellahi, K., and Schuler, R. (2017) Talent management: A systematic review and future prospects. *European Journal of International Management*, 11(1), 86–128.

Michaels, E., Handfield-Jones, H., and Axelrod, B. (2001) *The War for Talent*. Boston, MA: Harvard Business School Press.

Miñano-Espin, J., Casáis, L., Lago-Peñas, C., and Gómez-Ruano, M.Á. (2017) High speed running and sprinting profiles of elite soccer players. *Journal of Human Kinetics*, 58(1), 169–176.

Monks, J. and Husch, J. (2009) The impact of seeding, home, continent, and hosting on FIFA World Cup results. *Journal of Sports Economics*, 10(4), 391–408.

Padrón-Cabo, A., Rey, E., García-Soidán, J.L., and Penedo-Jamardo, E. (2016) Large scale analysis of relative age effect on professional soccer players in FIFA designated zones. *International Journal of Performance Analysis in Sport*, 16(1), 332–346.

PwC (2015) 18th Annual Global Survey. London: PwC.

Quirk, J. and Fort, R. (1999) *Hard Ball: The abuse of Power in Pro Team Sports*. Princeton, NJ: Princeton University Press.

Reilly, T., Williams, A. M., Nevill, A., and Franks, A. (2000) A multidisciplinary approach to talent identification in soccer. *Journal of sports sciences*, 18(9), 695–702.

Ross, P.O. (1993) *National Excellence: A Case for Developing America's Talent*. Washington, DC: U.S. Department of Education, Office of Educational Research and Improvement.

Sparrow, P., Scullion, H., and Tarique, I. (2015) Introduction: Challenges for the field of strategic talent management. In: P. Sparrow, H. Scullion, and I. Tarique (eds.). *Strategic Talent Management: Contemporary Issues in International Context* (pp. 3–35). Cambridge: Cambridge University Press.

Sparrow, P., Scullion, H., and Tarique, I. (2015) Multiple lenses on talent management: definitions and contours of the field. In: P. Sparrow, H. Scullion, and I. Tarique (eds.). *Strategic Talent Management: Contemporary Issues in International Context* (pp. 36–69). Cambridge: Cambridge University Press.

Suppiah, H.T., Low, C.Y., and Chia, M. (2015) Detecting and developing youth athlete potential: different strokes for different folks are warranted. *British Journal of Sports Medicine*, 49(13), 878–882.

Szymanski, S. (2015) *Money and Soccer: A Soccernomics Guide*. New York: Nation Books.

Vaeyens, R., Lenoir, M., Williams, A.M., and Philippaerts, R.M. (2008) Talent identification and development programmes in sport. *Sports Medicine*, 38(9), 703–714.

32

Retailing in the football industry

Dimitrios Kolyperas and Leigh Sparks

Introduction

Over the last five decades, major changes have occurred in global sports goods retailing. The increasing globalisation of sport culture and a rise in public awareness and the media exposure of the health associations and social benefits in partaking of sports (Jarvie, 2003) in the late 1970s and 1980s were some of the main drivers of this evolution. By the late 1990s, more significant changes were occurring as affordable sportswear developed from being a functional requirement into a globally branded fashion statement. There has been a movement from "active-wear" to "casual-wear" or leisurewear, accompanied by a dramatic increase of purchasing sport-related goods, though not always for sport-specific reasons (Sparks, 2007).

Over the two last decades, celebrity endorsement and technology have helped sport as a retailing sector not only to accessorise and re-define its sport goods, but also address consumer markets not previously catered for (i.e., females, third age). The pace of change in the world of sports – by which everyday sporting goods are being connected, redeveloped, redefined, and redeployed – remains high. As new retailing channels – by which consumers can personalise or customise, add-on and experience an offering whether physical, virtual, or any and all points between – have become more popular, opportunities and challenges have expanded, whilst crossover markets between playing and fashion buying have gained in significance.

In the sport field, it is clear that consumer demands have changed in a number of ways. For example:

- The range of sports has expanded and globalised;
- Technology and safety enhancements have developed better equipment;
- Participants, consumers, and spectators have become less biased towards male and middle-age categories;
- Sport clothing (activewear) is no longer only a functional need, but in some cases, has become fashion (casual wear);
- Style has become important in sports;
- There has been an increase in both general and specific (i.e., football related, cycling, running) sport retailing specialists;

- Team/club organisation branding outlets have grown leading to retail in stadiums, and elsewhere;
- Internet-based sport goods retailing has grown dramatically;
- Fanaticism, partisanship, and overt identification with teams, individuals, events, or symbols have arisen and experiential consumption instance (i.e., real or virtual Fan Zones, fantasy leagues) have become more prominent.

The very brief description above of the changes in the sports retailing sector has focused on the broad structure and composition of the market and the ways in which the nature of sport, the consumer market (including consumers' perceptions of sport), and business practicalities have changed. We now focus our attention on the football industry and its clubs, to identify the issues in terms of retailing in football.

Issues in retailing in the football industry

Football clubs are facing a plethora of daily operational challenges. While much of this is focused on the team and players, clubs are involved in a multitude of retailing tasks that require speed, reliability, and credibility. Everyday retailing, match ticketing and match-day activities, sourcing of branded leisurewear or first team kit, branding and maximisation of media exposure are just a few of the operations that could potentially add value to the club/team organisation. Thus, retailing, distribution, and logistics in football go beyond what happens on the field.

The football industry has experienced dramatic commercial growth and rapid change. "The 20 most valuable football teams are worth an average of $1.48 billion in 2017, 3 per cent more than a year ago" (*Forbes*, 2017). The Deloitte Money League Report (2016) provides further insights into three key streams of revenue in the 20 wealthiest football clubs in the world, namely match-day revenue (gate receipts), broadcasting revenue (domestic and international), and commercial revenue (merchandise and sponsorship). Between 2004 and 2013, commercial revenues, including sponsorship and merchandise, are the only areas that demonstrate growth in terms of the overall financial performance of football clubs, compared to match-day and broadcasting revenues that remain important but rather stable. Such commercial streams include television and new (social) media rights, sponsorship and partnership generation, urban regeneration, and stadium revenue, as well as licencing and retailing of merchandise (Szymanski et al., 2016).

Directing a major football club has thus become a more complex task. While the core product of football clubs remains *within* the production of sporting events (the spectacle of the match and its uncertain dramatic outcome), secondary product categories and brand extensions have gained momentum as a result of the opportunities and variety of commercialisation and marketing activities *around* such events (Couvelaere and Richelieu, 2005). Clubs have evolved from being a one-off production spectacle (lasting 90 minutes) into multi-purpose commercial centres, or multi-channel retail brands, where consumer, cultural, political, and commercial interests interact (well beyond the 90 minutes) (see also Chapter 26 in this handbook).

The changing structure of retailing in football is a reflection of the altered nature of the sport itself, moving from a "backyard" game into a multibillion-dollar industry, the enhanced fan market, and consumers' engagement with new business opportunities. Covering all of these aspects is impossible here. The focal point of this chapter is thus on retailing of football-branded products. While academic and practical insights are available in terms of football sponsorship and other commercial revenues, it is the merchandise arm of football operations that has not yet being fully addressed. This chapter sheds light on the management of merchandise in football focusing on aspects of distribution, supply chain, and logistics. In doing so, the next section focuses on three particular aspects of football goods retailing, all of which can be broadly considered as attempts to provide alternative propositions in the market. The three topics are:

1 Retailing to the fan;
2 Channels of distribution in football;
3 Supply chains.

Retailing to the football fan

Football works in seasons and sales are heavily related to performance on the field. This brings consumer demand fluctuation on the often short-term basis (a "cup run" for example). A branded football merchandise good (i.e., a shirt) is not a simple functional product but is rather a fashion/lifestyle good (and identity statement). For this reason, football shirts are often marketed and consumed for their intangible feel-good factors (a traditional winning jersey is often more saleable) not their tangible quality characteristics (to keep us warm).

Often being utilised as a successful extension strategy to allow fan affiliation (Tapp, 2004), football shirts hold a price premium (for more on price see BBC football price survey, 2015). They appeal to different social classes (from working to upper class consumer segments) and various consumer demographics (from die-hard fans who purchase to fulfil social identity needs (Heere and James, 2007) to younger generations seeking symbols to express loyalty and a sense of belonging (Sparks, 2007), and to latent support and older "fair-weather" fans to express nostalgia (Wakefield and Wann, 2006). Different shirts can be produced for different markets in terms of cut and style, as well as the customisation of some aspects. Sales numbers are thus very high for major clubs.

Inevitably, football club merchandise can be fashion and time-dependent as well as performance-related; fans' demand may explode rapidly or disappear instantly. In addition, availability of different sizes, access to physical or virtual locations, in-store and online atmosphere, pricing and promotion, cross and within-category assortment, copyright infringements and brand dilution, as well as co-branding (with sponsors and manufactures) and (complete or partial) outsourcing of retail unit operations add to the complexity of the retail sales environment modern football clubs find themselves in (Fernie and Sparks, 2014).

Retailers in football try to attract fans to visit their stores and make purchases. There are many ways to do this. It has to be noted, however, that not all fans will be attracted to club retail stores for the same reasons. Indeed, some fans will actively neglect some retailing offers because of their approach (e.g., the in-store crowded environment on a match day or the type, range, price, and quality of the merchandise). There are trends in fans' perceptions and life stages that affect the level of loyalty and identification (Kolyperas and Sparks, 2017) and subsequently the nature of demand [see Chapter 19 in this handbook]. For example, the positive feelings towards football goods by young teenagers are remarkably strong, but these de-escalate during later teenage years as participation rates fall and other interests take over (Tinson et al., 2017). Moreover, there are gender differences which are of considerable importance given that the female football market is growing, and the pivotal role women play in the purchase of football products for and by some men.

In addition, not all fans respond to the rising cost of football products in the same way. This has a twofold implication. On the one hand, loyal fans feel neglected and left out by the over-commercialisation of their beloved team. Take for example the case of football shirts that change every year, often with a new commercial sponsor associating with the football club.

On the other hand, as prices go up, securing a season ticket (and new memorabilia) becomes more difficult for football fans. Football clubs are left to wonder if the fans dropping away are being replaced by people who just want the status of having a season ticket and they are simply picking and choosing which games to attend. This situation has spurred fan demonstrations, protests, and boycotting across various games, countries, and cultures, including silent protests in the stadia.

Case study: Leicester City (LCFC) – the story of an underdog

The remarkable underdog story of LCFC provides a useful case study for businesses as well as for smaller football club organisations. The impressive performance of the club during 2015/2016 Premier league season which they eventually won, spurred the club to enhance its commercial success. Three moves served the club particularly well:

1 **Frame the brand as an underdog** – Marketing research suggests that openly acknowledging the top dog's competitive threat can build brand support for the underdog – enhancing word of mouth and increasing sales while reducing support for the top dog. Leicester often was the highest trending topic on social media with celebrities including Tom Hanks (himself often cast as an underdog) publicly declaring their affection for the club. Leicester had entered the frame.

2 **Ride the momentum** – In February 2016, while fans of Liverpool FC staged several match-day walkouts over the spiralling cost of tickets, Leicester seized the opportunity to announce a price freeze on its 2016/2017 tickets. In other gestures, the club's owner offered home fans complimentary beer and donuts to celebrate his birthday – and announced he would donate £2 million toward building a local children's hospital. Such initiatives continued to endear the club to British soccer fans, who resoundingly voted Leicester their favourite second team, regardless of the primary team they supported.

3 **Never forget your roots** – Following its success, the club found an increasing number of fans popping up across Southeast Asia, and particularly Thailand, its owner's birthplace. To capitalise on this demand, Leicester organised a title parade in Bangkok and preseason fixtures in Asia and the United States provided opportunities for other international fans to purchase merchandise and fan club membership and to spectate at local matches. At the same time, the team had to ensure that its original fans did not feel marginalised or less valued, so a membership loyalty scheme was initiated that favoured existing supporters.

Leicester City's incredible Cinderella story has endeared the club to so many fans that the club found it difficult to accommodate the increasing demand. The club often ran out of replica kits to sell while many unlucky fans had to wait to get their hands on the shirt of their new club, as the club was unprepared. No one at the club saw it appropriate to prepare for their first Premier League title win ever, no order had been made from the beginning of the season, and thus the stock disappeared in record times. Leicester's new admirers have raided the club so much that even their online shop was struggling to quench demand with a pair of blue socks the only available apparel from the end of 2015/2016 season's kit. For the season, 2016/2017, the club sold ten times as many shirts in 24 hours as it did in the first month of past season. The sales of the club's new 2016/2017 Puma home shirt have smashed records resulting in the first delivery being sold out in small, medium, and large sizes, despite the fact that the club brought forward the launch of the new kit in an effort to have an initial delivery of shirts available to supporters in time. According to sports marketing experts, LCFC now has the opportunity of making anything between 150 million pounds ($220 million) and 250 million pounds ($365 million) from their sensational Premier League triumph.

* Before answering the questions please visit http://www.lcfcdirect.com/

Case study questions

1   What does the case of Leicester City FC entail for retailing in football?
2   What sort of supply and demand implications for management does this case reveal?

Source: Adopted from Reuters (2016), *Harvard Business Review* (2016).

Channels of distribution in football

Distribution is about making products and services available to football fans that in turn purchase, use, or consume. Making products available to a fan can occur with the simultaneous transfer of sale and ownership and thus use. However, there are now so many different products and services that football fans can benefit from, that the management of distribution channels has become a challenging task for commercial football managers. For example, a fan can buy a shirt at a club store taking physical possession of the item. In addition, the same fan could also purchase the same shirt on the Internet, perhaps customise it the way he/she wants, and then wait for delivery. The same process might be followed for the purchase of memorabilia, towels, and branded sportswear (either at the ground or via an independent online agency). These examples show the need for flows and exchanges of product and information to enable such transactions to occur.

While fans need to become aware of the offering, retailers need to be ready to accommodate dynamic demands. The flows consist of information, ownership, product elements, finance, risks, and so on, and are organised into supply chain channels (i.e., companies, individuals involved in assembling, transporting, selling football products from points of production to points of consumption). The distribution channels can thus be very simple or highly complex, taking many forms in carrying out, on the surface, these basic activities of moving product from production to consumption (Sparks, 2007). A number of key issues can be suggested as far as football products distribution is concerned:

- Channels are not static, and many football channels have been characterised by rapid change in recent years (see online retailing);
- Information is as necessary to channel functioning as is the movement of physical products;
- There has been quite considerable organisational and technological change in many channels;
- Intermediaries have become a necessity as football organisations seek to maximise revenues and minimise waste through being efficient and effective in an area of business not so closely linked to the ordinary tasks;
- Matching supply and demand is an enormously difficult exercise for managers given the performance-based element of the industry.

The next sub-sections highlight selected channel components as being amongst the most important and the most interesting (because of changes that have occurred or are underway).

Football stores/outlets/stadium

The nature of the football product is such that shops have become important factors in distribution channels. These shops may be specialised (e.g., Pro direct Soccer, Chelsea FC shop), general (e.g., Sports Direct, Nike stores), or ancillary (e.g., Asda, Wal-Mart, Debenhams). As in many channels, there is a choice to be made amongst exclusive brand-based facilities (i.e., physical club shops in stadia and airports), selective (official reseller deals) or intensive (all retailers) distribution opportunities. In a number of instances, the idea of the store as a destination is developed (e.g., the only football Niketown in Brazil, or the Manchester Centre club superstore at Old Trafford). Stores, whether real or virtual, are focusing more on the ambience (visual, aural, historical/authentic), design, and the presentation of merchandise for fans. A key theme is the idea of fan interaction and experiential consumption as part of an immersive and associative engagement.

Event-based sales

Football products are often associated with particular football games. Items such as programmes, tickets, and scarves are just a few examples of event-specific products. There are particular issues around the demand patterns and obsolescence for such items. For instance, tickets have little value after the event has taken place, whereas programmes of milestone games might be collectable years after the whistle is blown. Event-specific merchandise is growing (joint scarfs to celebrate the opponents on the field) and offers on match days are booming (concessions, etc.). Some of this merchandise is officially licenced but other sellers may be operating unofficially (e.g., street sellers) or possibly illegally. For major football events such as the World Cup, international, national, and local operations are designed for official branded merchandise to be sold directly via websites, at events, and in selected shops, and legal restrictions are often put in place and enforced strongly.

Direct selling, telephony, tablet, and mobile provision

For football organisations, which are often not the manufacturers of football products, an official shop involves sourcing products and holding stock, as well designing the atmospherics and luring in fans. Direct selling in conjunction with intermediaries to fans avoids this management effort and might reduce operating costs. By selling direct, more control is maintained, and more profit should be retained if fans can gain access to the offering. Direct mail order has been one distribution method but recently, the use of tablets and smartphones along with the Internet has opened up new opportunities for sale and potential for football clubs to build direct relationships and more personalised services with fans across a broader reach.

Online sales

A growing number of football organisations (e.g., FIFA, national leagues, clubs) have turned their attention to online sales. This approach has emerged strongly in recent years. Initially many football retailers and clubs operated informational rather than transactional websites. One argument was that the fan needed to see and touch the fabric of, for example, shirts in order to assess their quality. However, as football shirts are often being sold for their feel-good factors (intangibility aspects) and as the Internet has become more integral in our everyday lives, fans have become more adopting of the technology generally, as when they consume sports (i.e., pay-per-view) or make major purchases (season tickets). This has spurred football and club websites to enhance their transactional elements and increase their online retailing presence. Online retailing of football products also offers some additional features, or add-ons, that enhance the fans' opportunities to buy football products. Whether it is an exclusive, personalised, or hard-to-obtain football item, a web search may be a good way of tracking it down or even finding it at a cheaper price, on sale or even second hand. Some caution is needed online, however, because things may not always be what they seem. Some organisations have been less than careful in protecting their possible domain names with counterfeiting laying in wait and internet fraud is possible.

Supply chains in football

The discussion of channels of distribution provides some description of the way football products are made available. Behind the above examples, there is a process of product production and product distribution. Managerial attention in channels should be turned towards both product and information flow. To make football products (physical) and services (virtual) available, the "logistics mix," including product movement and demand management, must be considered (Table 32.1).

Distribution channels and retailing receive strategic management for football products. A multitude of issues can be identified about football product distribution but here three challenge areas are chosen for further discussion. This choice is made based on the importance of these issues for the reputation and profile management of certain football brands and illustrates the economic, social, legal, and ethical components of supply chains generally and football supply chains in particular.

First, it should become obvious by now that distribution and retailing are not neutral managerial operations but encompass aspects of value distribution, exclusivity, and ownership. One of the ways that football products are both designed and controlled is through branding and licensing, though there is an increase in counterfeit products. The licensing of football products introduces a degree of control, shared ownership or even exclusivity into distribution channels. In addition, the plethora of distribution channels (real, online) and the numerous attributes and characteristics of football products (e.g., team badge, name, sponsor, colours, symbols, numbers, images, selling price) point towards tailored channel construction and management by football clubs. This may seem a great opportunity for football organisations; however, cases of price fixing, replica shirts, and sweatshop labour exist and require managerial attention.

Second, regardless of the legal issue mentioned above, reliability and speed are pivotal in merchandise management in football. As football works in seasons and is embedded in the performance on the field, demand fluctuations are apparent (as the Leicester case shows). There are always cases where football-branded products are required at short notice, thus ensuring that all logistics are actively reactive and carefully planned is vital. However, there also lies a risk of obsolescence, as football products remain fashion based and thus time dependent. This means that branded football goods might lose their value as consumer demand might ebb and flow towards a different offering, or the new kit. Obsolescence refers to stocks and merchandise on the shelves and is a risk factor for all football organisations to some degree. For example, when a football organisation, or event (FIFA), is deciding how much to invest in a new technology or number/range of merchandise, they must ask will that retail activity remain profitable long enough for the investment to pay off, or will it become obsolete so soon that the football club (event) loses money.

Third, the economy plays a major role in determining trends in discretionary spend and there was a dramatic reduction in sports merchandising spend during the global economic downturn (PwC, 2011). Spending on football merchandising has been shown to follow two major

Table 32.1 The football logistics mix

Items	Description
Inventory control	Inventory (aka) stock is often a necessary but unloved part of the channel activities in football. As football works in cycles with new competitions kicking off, new players arriving, and new partners sponsoring, football kit runs the risk of obsolescence as stock represents capital that is tied up in unsold product. How much inventory to hold (and where) is vital part of managing channels activities. For example, back in 2004 Everton FC was found in a challenging position after the transfer of Wayne Rooney to Manchester United FC. It had £65,000 worth stock from the Rooney section of its shop that was unsold. Eventually, the club decided strategically to use the obsolete stock as a CSR mechanism sending the merchandise to needy soccer-mad youngsters in West Africa.
Storage facilities	Football stock requires being stored somewhere. The management of such facilities or locations is key in meeting both anticipated and unanticipated demand. The facilities vary from traditional warehouses to areas in the hollow bits in stadia stands. However, as the market is performance based, demands may raise and fall in an unexpected fashion. A key strategy of the football club in managing storage and inventory has been "postponement," whereby products are held in a neutral rather than finished state (perhaps with the help of intermediaries) in order to be more reactive and meet demand fluctuations in a more dynamic way.
Transportation	Most physical football products often need to be transported over considerable distances, and in the quickest possible time. Even virtual football services require a network over which to transport messages and images. Alternatively to the football team fans', players', and officials', football clubs have to deal with logistical issues when moving abroad for games or other business (e.g., different countries have legal restrictions on the weight and length of lorries and the hours for which drivers can drive). Given that a football team can also be penalised for not showing up in a game, scheduling is a major activity for football management and retailing.
Unitisation and packaging	Most products require some form of packaging. The latter can be part of the purchasing process or might be needed for protection, health and safety during transportation. Packaging also carries information important to consumers, retailers, intermediaries, and other agents and helps control the movement and time of the operation. Football clubs are challenged to operate as normal retail shops where football products tend to be purchased to small quantities but also might be found in a position to push large quantities in crowded environments during the games. Estimating the demand fluctuations and knowing the regular, consistent, known shapes, sizes, and weights allow for better planning and reduced logistical costs.
Communications	To work efficiently, channels must be constantly informed so as to be as reactive as possible. As such, and regardless of product movement, storage, and shelf time, the logistics mix is also all about information dissemination, sharing, and usage. Without good communication the house of cards can collapse, leading to higher costs and inconvenience for fans.

Source: Adapted from Sparks, L. (2007).

trends. On the one hand, there is retail in football as an entertainment, where consumers spend leisurely days at a stadium, football retailers, department stores, or high-end malls. Customer engagement, experience, and care are thus critical ingredients, with clubs competing directly with other retailers often more experienced in the areas of visual merchandising, design and experiential consumption. On the other hand, buying habits seem to migrate towards online shopping. Selling online provides the ability to engage with fans who cannot attend matches, including those who live in other countries, football clubs are given the opportunity to position their brands in those regions, build markets and demand.

Case study: Manchester United – a retail football super brand

Football clubs have become big business, but they remain comparatively small when compared to other companies (i.e., Fortune 500) or sport giants in the likes of Nike and Adidas. For instance, Adidas, one of the sponsors of Manchester United, the highest earning club in the world, will earn more in the next six months than United has earned in its whole history. However, football clubs hold something that not many companies in the world possess. Football clubs are stakeholder-embedded organisations with an enormous global reach that transcends cultural, linguistic, ethnic, and geographical boundaries (Table 32.2).

Table 32.2 The world's most valuable football brands

Rank	Brand Name	Country	Value (in millions of US dollars)
1	Manchester United	England	1733
2	Real Madrid FC	Spain	1419
3	Barcelona FC	Spain	1418
4	Chelsea FC	England	1248
5	Bayern München FC	Germany	1222
6	Manchester City FC	England	1021
7	Paris Saint-Germain FC	France	1011
8	Arsenal FC	England	941
9	Liverpool FC	England	908
10	Tottenham Hotspurs FC	England	696

Source: Statista, 2017.

Manchester United is the most successful commercially oriented football brand in the world. In doing so, Manchester United has followed four key strategies:

1 Expand portfolio of sponsors (i.e., Adidas, AON);
2 Enhance the reach and distribution of broadcasting rights (i.e., Premier League TV rights, MUTV in 136 countries);
3 Exploit new media and content opportunities (via social media, MUTV, MUapp);
4 Further develop retail, merchandising, apparel, and product licensing business.

In terms of the latter strategy, commercial operations including retail of merchandise and product licencing are now contributing more than half of the club's revenue. Manchester United market and sell sports apparel, training, and leisure wear and other clothing featuring the brand symbols on a global basis. Licensed products in the form of coffee mugs, key rings, and bedspreads, featuring the MANU trademark are also being distributed through Manchester United distribution channels worldwide, including its own Manchester United branded retail centres, e-commerce platforms, as well as partners' wholesale distribution channels. While merchandising, apparel, and product licensing revenue was £97.3 million in 2016, this has almost tripled over the last two years (£31.6 million and £37.5 million in 2015 and 2014 respectively). This growth is a result of Manchester United's successful retail strategy.

Currently, Manchester United has a ten-year agreement with Adidas with regards to global technical sponsorship and dual-branded licensing rights (such as the official shirt), which began on 1 August 2015. The agreement with Adidas does not include the rights with respect to mono-branded licensing rights or the right to create and operate Manchester United branded physical retail channels and e-commerce retail channels. These are business areas that were previously operated by Nike and the reversion of these rights to Manchester United provides increased commercial opportunities and enhanced control and ownership, spurring the club to further invest to expand its product portfolio and licensees and enhance the range of offerings available to the fans. For instance, the club has followed a mixture of global and national retail strategies. The Reds have appointed South Korean footwear brand Sbenu as the club's official footwear partner in the country. They have paired a dual-branded line of outwear gear with Columbia Sportwear so as to enhance its outdoor apparel category worldwide. In addition, they have teamed up with Kitbag (now owned by Fanatics) to efficiently operate and enhance their online and retail business. These latest deals show an opportunity to segment the different elements of the business, tailor for specific markets, as well as focus on developing these rights more proactively alone or with partners.

* Before answering the questions please visit http://ir.manutd.com/ and http://store.manutd.com to evaluate the full product range, assortment, and offerings

Case study questions

1 Discuss the strategy of Manchester United in the area of retail and merchandise. What the future holds for the club and how can Manchester United further sustain its retail success?

2 Away and third strips, as well as memorabilia, are some of the new products in common markets. However, Manchester United is facing an opportunity to tailor its product offerings for different cultures and markets. To diversify or not? To hyper-segment or standardise your offering? How do such decisions impact on aspects of retailing, distribution, and logistics?

Source: Adopted from Manchester United Website 2017, Statista (2017)

Conclusion

Football management has had to react to considerable changes in the retailing of football products, the fan market and the game itself. There has been a transformation on what we buy and where we buy it from, including a trend towards wearing football-related clothing not always for football-related reasons. While the breadth of football products available has increased, so have the challenges for directors and marketers of football organisations. The future of the football retailing market will be of considerable interest as profitability is rising, new fan markets are explored, new distribution channels are constructed, and new football talent is flourishing. Football clubs have become more sophisticated in the area of retailing.

This chapter considered retailing and distribution in football using two case studies and current practical football examples. Retailing to the fan is not an easy process as fans exhibit buying behaviours not always similar to other consumer groups. Football distribution channels thus vary from being simple to being very complex and require ongoing attention. We shed some light on certain retailing/distribution channels including official stores, direct selling, event-based sales and online sales. In order to be successful, all these operations require good management of the logistics mix, including wider matters revolving around licensing, exclusivity, integrity, ownership, speed, and social responsibility towards fans. Moving forward, students and researchers, as well as practitioners, may try addressing the following questions and/or practically deal with these points:

1 To what extent is it possible to get the "right products to the right fans and places at the right times" all the time? What is the role of the changing dynamic in how fans consume football lately?
2 Attempt to draw or map the distribution channel from production to consumption. Consider speed, range, and other design matters.
3 What changes are occurring in the football retailing market globally and in your national market?
4 What is the nature of the football product? How is this changing?

Retail in football including distribution and logistics has been an area of extreme practical development but rather minor research/academic attention. This might be the result of the market being closed-looped and somewhat secretive when it comes down to commercial operations. One thing is, however, certain; football clubs have the ability to become exclusive retail brands and retailing in football is set to grow and expand further.

References

Couvelaere, V. and Richelieu, A. (2005) Brand strategy in professional sports: the case of French soccer teams. *European Sport Management Quarterly*, 5, 23–46. Retrieved from https://doi.org/10.1080/16184740500089524

Fernie, J. and Sparks, L. (2014) *Logistics and Retail Management: Emerging Issues and New Challenges in the Retail Supply Chain*. London: Kogan page publishers.

Heere, B. and James, J.D. (2007) Sports teams and their communities: examining the influence of external group identities on team identity. *Journal of Sport Management*, 21(3), 319–337.

Jarvie, G. (2003). Internationalism and sport in the making of nations. *Identities: Global Studies in Culture and Power*, 10(4), 537–551.

Kolyperas, D. and Sparks, L. (2017) Exploring value co–creation in Fan Fests: the role of fans. *Journal of Strategic Marketing*, 26(1), 71–84.

Ozanian, M. (2017, 6 June) The world's most valuable soccer teams 2017. *Forbes* [online] Retrieved from https://www.forbes.com/sites/mikeozanian/2017/06/06/the-worlds-most-valuable-soccer-teams-2017/#1b29124477ea

PwC (2011) Changing the game. Outlook for the global sports market to 2015. [online] Retrieved from https://www.pwc.com/gx/en/hospitalityleisure/pdf/changing-the-game-outlook-for-the-global-sports-market-to-2015.pdf

Reuters (2016) Leicester stand to gain up to $365 million windfall. Yahoo! Sports [online] Retrieved fromhttps://sports.yahoo.com/news/leicester-stand-gain-365-million-windfall-151252975--sow.html

Sparks, L. (2007) Sport retailing. In: Beech, J.G. and Chadwick, S. (eds.). *The Marketing of Sport*. Essex, UK: Pearson Education.

Szymoszowskyj, A., Winand, M., Kolyperas, D., and Sparks, L. (2016) Professional football clubs retail branding strategies. *Sport, Business and Management: an International Journal*, 6(5), 579–598.

Tapp, A. (2004) The loyalty of football fans—we'll support you evermore? *Journal of Database Marketing & Customer Strategy Management*, 11(3), 203–215.

Tinson, J., Sinclair, G., and Kolyperas, D. (2017) Sport fandom and parenthood. *European Sport Management Quarterly*, 17(3), 370–391.

Wakefield, K.L. and Wann, D.L. (2006) An examination of dysfunctional sport fans: method of classification and relationships with problem behaviors. *Journal of Leisure Research*, 38(2), 168–186.

33

Sport licenced products in the football industry

Dimitra Papadimitriou and Artemisia Apostolopoulou

Introduction

A significant source of revenue for sport team and event properties around the world is the sale of official licensed merchandise. In licensing agreements, sport properties like sport governing bodies, teams at all levels, athletes, and sport events (licensors) transfer to other companies-manufacturers (licensees) the right to use their intellectual properties for commercial purposes (Covell, 2007). Those manufacturers produce, distribute, and sell products featuring the names and nicknames, logos, marks and slogans, colours and other trademarks of their sport partners and, in exchange, pay a royalty fee. It is important to note that the licensees do not own those intellectual properties; they are simply given the right to use them for the activities outlined in their licensing agreement and for the specified product categories, geographic region and length of time (Fullerton, 2010). The unauthorised use of a sport organisation's intellectual properties for licensing or other purposes is known as trademark infringement, and, if not addressed, presents a significant threat to both parties in the licensing relationship (Covell, 2007).

There is no shortage of product categories in sport licensing, ranging from the typical apparel, shoes and hats, gifts, and novelties to accessories, items for the house, office or school, trading cards, and video games. The demand for sport merchandise is driven by fans' need to feel closer to their favourite teams and athletes and to connect with other team supporters, whether they live next door or across the world (Apostolopoulou et al., 2012). According to Davis (1992; as cited in Covell, 2007, p. 192), "clothing styles are a transmitted code that can impart meanings of identity, gender, status, and sexuality." Wearing and displaying sport licensed products intensifies one's sense of belongingness with the properties they support and makes a public statement in terms of their affiliations. Sport licensed products can also serve as reminders of one's sport experience, a tangible keepsake or even a collectible item, and as a style statement (Apostolopoulou, Papadimitriou and Damtsiou, 2010; Covell, 2007). One example of this is Pharrell Williams' relationship with Adidas that produced a retro tennis collection unveiled at the 2017 US Open Tennis Championship and worn by tennis stars like Garbiñe Muguruza and Jo-Wilfried Tsonga (Yotka, 2017).

Given the significance of sport licensing agreements in contributing to the financial resources of national and international sport brands, including football clubs, we propose a chapter with the following learning goals:

- Describe the size and characteristics of the sport licensing market, including benefits and risks for licensing partners;
- Identify the unique aspects of the consumption of football licensed products;
- Discuss the various functional, experiential and symbolic meanings that give value to sport licensed products; and
- Engage in critical thinking regarding new trends and challenges for football marketers such as product and market diversification, right protection and piracy, e-commerce, and technological advancements, and innovation in sport licensing.

The market of sport licensing

Sport licensing is a growing area within the sport industry. Overall projections of future sales of sport licensed merchandise are positive, especially for North America and Asia-Pacific. In 2015, the global market for sport licensed products was valued at $27.63 billion but is expected to reach an impressive $48.17 billion by 2024 (Laster, 2016). Agreements of leagues or teams with sporting goods manufacturers lead the way, as evidenced by Adidas' ten-year shirt deals with Real Madrid and Manchester United for £850 million and £750 million, respectively (Nagle, 2017; Wilson, 2014). Mega-events are other areas of growth. Take, for instance, the 2014 World Cup held in Brazil. For that tournament, FIFA negotiated agreements with 160 licensees that sold more than 150 million licensed products in categories such as apparel, footwear and headwear, and accessories. Products were sold in 189 countries around the world through on-the-ground and online store locations (Davis, 2015a) and were, according to FIFA, designed to "help spread the excitement and to give consumers an authentic fan experience" (Retail & Merchandising, 2015). FIFA's 2014 licensing efforts were recognised as the best "Sports or Sports-Themed Entertainment Programme" by the International Licensing Industry Merchandisers' Association (2014 FIFA, 2015).

There are a number of reasons that have led to the growth of the sport licensing industry. Those include the continued popularity of sport around the world coupled with teams' and athletes' efforts to become global brands; increased interest from non-traditional sport consumer groups such as women and youth; more favourable economic conditions, especially in large markets such as China and India; the widespread availability and use of the Internet, which has provided ideal conditions for the worldwide spread of sport social media platforms, fantasy sports, and e-commerce; and technological advancements that have led to the development of innovative sport merchandise like smart clothing (Davis, 2015b; Heitner, 2014; Irwin, Sutton, and McCarthy, 2008; Laster, 2016; Olenski, 2013). A discussion on trends in this sector is presented later in the chapter.

Even though each licensing agreement is unique and customised to the needs of the partners involved in the agreement, it is important for sport marketers to be knowledgeable on how to set up a licensing program for their organisation. Fullerton (2010, p. 362) discusses a process for developing a licensing plan that includes the following steps:

i Identifying what elements from the organisation-licensor are *licensable property* (i.e., name, logo, slogan) and undergoing the process of registering those as trademarks;

ii Establishing a *fee structure* that may include an initial fixed fee, royalty payments and, in some cases, a guaranteed minimum payment to the licensor;

iii Listing *criteria* for the selection of licensees such as the quality, experience, marketability, and stability of the licensee, the potential to generate maximum sales and royalties, and the level of fit between the licensee and the licensor's goals and image;

iv Specifying the *type of agreement* with respect to the products to be manufactured, the degree of exclusivity granted to the licensee, and the geographic area (local, regional, or global) covered in the licensing agreement;

v Reviewing whether or not the licensee is in *compliance* with the terms of the licensing agreement, especially regarding the number of sales and resulting royalties that are owed to the licensor;

vi Engaging in *market surveillance* to locate counterfeit products and to identify other trademark infringement or ambush marketing activities; and

vii Conducting a *performance review* to evaluate if the terms and conditions of the agreement with respect to financial performance and product quality and availability were met.

Licensing goals

Licensing agreements present a plethora of benefits, not the least of which is the opportunity for profit for both parties involved. For licensors, in particular, allowing other companies to use their intellectual property in order to manufacture and sell products in a variety of categories can result in significant royalty revenue with minimal effort or risk (Fullerton, 2010). Local and national licensing agreements can diversify a sport property's earnings and expand its overall presence in the market, giving the property increased levels of exposure and familiarity. Sport is seasonal; the regular football season begins in August and ends in May. Licensed products can become part of one's everyday life, beyond game day and during the off-season, allowing team supporters to experience and display their connection with their favourite organisation without boundaries of time or space (Irwin et al., 2008). A football fan can enjoy their morning coffee in their Cristiano Ronaldo mug, check the time on their Lionel Messi watch, and decorate their wall with a Zlatan Ibrahimovic poster. Having a greater presence in people's lives with products in their closet, in their kitchen, in their office, and in their car keeps the sport property top of mind and strengthens fan identification levels. And given the intangible nature of sport, licensed products can provide something tangible to consumers that symbolises their bond with their favourite team or serves as a reminder of a once in a lifetime sport experience (Apostolopoulou et al., 2012).

With unlimited options for new product categories, sport organisations can use licensing partnerships to expand into areas in which they do not have the expertise (Fullerton, 2010). For example, A.C. Milan partnered with a finance company to introduce the team's inspired "CartaViva Milan" credit card, associated with a loyalty program designed for their team followers (Italian Soccer Club, n.d.). Licensing can also expand a sport property's reach into new consumer groups, especially those who may not fit the profile of the typical hard-core fan but find other reasons to follow a team (Irwin et al., 2008). And for those brands with national or global appeal, licensed products can become vehicles through which to enter new markets and connect with followers who may never have a chance to attend a game in person, further supporting internationalisation efforts of that property. Take the case of Bayern Munich, whose on-field success and commercial appeal make it one of the most highly valued soccer teams on the planet. The club has directly engaged with its fans in Asia by holding off-season matches in China and Singapore, and by opening an office in China with the goal of pursuing sponsorship and licensing partnerships (Bayern München's Bundesliga, 2017; Bayern Munich, 2017).

With respect to the licensees, official relationships with established sport properties can lead to new revenues and can, by association, elevate the profile and credibility of that manufacturer (Irwin et al., 2008). This could have a positive effect on consumers' decision to purchase other products by that licensee or could lead to even more business relationships in the future. Licensees can capitalise on championship wins and other success stories that raise sport consumers' emotional attachment to a property by introducing commemorative items to celebrate those events (Olenski, 2013). They can also benefit from the high levels of recognition and brand loyalty of sport brands that increase the likelihood that their products will be well received by distributors and customers alike. Operational and marketing efficiencies as well as the ability to negotiate greater shelf space for their products are other potential benefits for licensees (Canalichio, 2010; Fullerton, 2010).

As a word of caution, it should be noted that there are potential risks in any licensing agreement. Of those, the issue of quality control is of upmost importance. The sport property needs to ensure that, whatever product is created with their name and logo, meets high standards of quality and will lead to a positive consumer experience (Fullerton, 2010; Holland, 2016). Consider a team supporter making a significant investment in buying an official jersey of their favourite player, only to realise that it is of poor quality and construction. More likely than not, the specific consumer will blame the sport organisation (and not the manufacturer) for this unpleasant experience and may be unwilling to buy other team products in the future. Including quality control provisions in every licensing agreement with additional processes to pre-approve any product that is scheduled to enter the market is needed in order to avoid unnecessary harm to the sport brand (Seligman, 2016). Conversely, a sport property involved in a scandal can potentially taint the image of its partners. It is not uncommon to see sponsors or licensees discontinuing their partnerships with an athlete who becomes involved in some kind of questionable or illegal activity. Not being diligent in monitoring the marketplace for the sale of counterfeit products is another serious threat for both licensors and licensees as it not only takes away from their potential profits, but it could also endanger the equity of their respective brands if those products are lacking in quality (Fullerton, 2010; Seligman, 2016). Finally, overextending a sport property in too many product categories that may not seem logical for the parent brand could risk market saturation and loss of interest by consumers (Aaker, 1990). Licensing agreements, including the number of licenses to be granted, should be part of an organisation's broader marketing strategy and should be pursued only to the extent that they add value to the brand's portfolio.

Exploring the power of sport brands and the value of sport licensing

The benefits of strong sport brands

Developing a strong brand is an essential marketing activity for sport leagues and clubs. This is because branding is a strategic element in the development of fan loyalty and the overall sustainability of sport organisations. Like other mainstream brands, sport brands possess both accounting and commercial value (Keller, 1993). The accounting value reflects the asset valuation of the football clubs and is important for ownership changes, sales, or mergers. The value of Manchester United, for example, in 2017 was estimated by Forbes at $3.69 billion, giving it the top position among football clubs globally (Ozanian, 2017). The commercial value of a club stems mainly from its popularity on a national and global level, its success and the club's loyal fans and business partners.

Due to the emotional relationship with their fans, sport teams are in a more advantageous position to build brand equity using various forms of marketing communications. According to Keller (2009), "brand equity relates to the fact that different outcomes result in the marketing of the product or service because of its brand as compared to if that same product or service was not identified by the brand" (p. 140). Today, a number of football clubs, such as Manchester United, Real Madrid, and Bayern Munich, have adopted aggressive marketing strategies and have succeeded in establishing their brands at a global level. This has enabled them to strengthen their clubs' financial position and to extend well beyond the football field with new offerings.

High levels of brand equity can benefit an organisation in many ways (Gladden, 2014; Hoeffler and Keller, 2003). With respect to sport organisations, a strong brand can lead to:

- Higher levels of fan loyalty;
- Lower vulnerability to marketing crises or unsuccessful seasons;
- An inelastic response from fans to ticket price increases;
- Increased effectiveness in marketing communications efforts;
- Greater appeal for corporate partners;
- Opportunities for line and brand extensions, including sport licensed merchandise.

Depending on their marketing expertise and available resources, football clubs may vary in their potential to achieve these benefits. In general, the clubs that excel in their on-field performance and win trophies have a greater chance to enjoy all these branding benefits. However, since football is able to evoke strong emotions and offer opportunities for fan engagement even in the case of local teams, the concept of brand value creation is still relevant to lesser-known sport properties. Building a strong team brand with the appropriate knowledge structure should always be a priority for football marketing managers. A strong sport brand can be leveraged in different ways, including sponsorship and licensing programs. Sport licensing in particular, besides being a valuable revenue stream, can also serve as means by which clubs can further promote and strengthen their own brand.

Buying behaviour of consumers of sport licensed products

For sport fans there is nothing more energising than being in a stadium with thousands of other spectators celebrating together the performance of their team with chants, dances, or other special movements. They describe these moments as very powerful and emotional. Most of those fans use sport licensed products to help them feel part of a huge crowd of team supporters. In that way, licensed products contribute to broadening the value of sport event experiences (Mullin, Hardy, and Sutton, 2014). In this section we will try to answer a few questions related to the consumption of sport licensed products: What is the profile of the consumer of sport licensed merchandise? What do consumers usually buy and why? How do consumers intend to use these licensed products? And do these products hold any special meanings for their owners?

Research paints the picture of consumers of sport licensed products as younger males who spend an average of $130 per year on licensed products (Kim and James, 2016). Items bought more frequently include t-shirts, caps, jerseys, accessories, and other collectibles (Kim and James, 2016). An examination of fans of the Pittsburgh Steelers, who compete in the National Football League (NFL), offers information not only about how many and what licensed products fans buy, but also on how they use those products. Most Steelers' fans own up to 20 team licensed items, wear between three and five licensed items at the game, and use those items on occasions other than game day (Apostolopoulou et al., 2012). A more recent study with fans of the most popular football clubs in Greece, Olympiakos and Panathinaikos, reported that the two most frequently bought licensed items were team jerseys and scarves, while a smaller number of fans bought team key chains and cups (Papadimitriou and Apostolopoulou, 2016).

So far, most of the available evidence regarding the consumption of sport licensed products derives from samples in North America. Even so, the research clearly shows that licensed products are significant tools that can help a club strengthen its relationship with their fans and also extend that relationship beyond game day. Sport marketers need to have a solid understanding of all facets of sport licensing so as not to miss out on its potential to strengthen their brand and expand their fan base nationally and internationally.

Understanding the value of sport licensed products

It is not uncommon for European football clubs to use their highly recognised names to launch new product lines and create additional revenue streams in their own countries and around the world. To that end, professional clubs sign agreements with licensees from a variety of industries and operate their own on-ground and online retail outlets so as to ensure an appropriate and effective distribution strategy. However, a key parameter in succeeding in this area is an appreciation of how sport licensed products create value for their owners. Two themes are pertinent to this discussion: (a) understanding the role of team identification in the consumption of sport licensed products and (b) mapping the functional, experiential, and symbolic meanings embedded in these products that become sources of value for consumers.

The role of team identification

The concept of sport team identification has evolved as an important psychological construct through which sport marketers try to understand sport consumer behaviour. This term has been formally defined as "the extent to which individuals perceive themselves as fans of the team, are involved with the team, are concerned with the team's performance, and view the team as a representation of themselves" (Branscombe and Wann, 1992, p. 1017). Highly identified sport consumers (fans) tend to care about the performance of their favourite team, develop personal relations with their team and routinely follow that team through different media. Besides cognition, identification has also been linked to the emotional value that fans derive from their favourite teams and to meanings that fans borrow from those teams in order to construct their social self (Gwinner and Swanson, 2003). Other researchers approach team identification as membership in a social group and identity to be shared with other fans, supporters, or co-workers (Ashforth and Mael, 1989). There are well-documented differences in the consumption of sport licensed products between those with high versus low levels of team identification (Kwon and Armstrong, 2002; Kwon, Trail, and Anderson, 2006).

Buying and displaying sport licensed products can help fans strengthen their connection with their favourite team and place that team in the salient elements of their identity. This means that the functional, experiential and symbolic meanings embedded in these products can add to fans' social identity and positively influence their behaviour. Therefore, sport marketers should fully understand the centrality of meanings to sport licensed product consumption and should develop appropriate marketing and communications strategies to promote sales of those items. Select research in this area is presented in the following section.

The meanings of sport licensed products

The most recent marketing literature has widely acknowledged that many goods are purchased to satisfy needs other than the functional needs of consumers. These include emotional and symbolic needs that are significant to contemporary consumers. Sport licensing can be placed in this multi-faceted type of consumption. We know that football fans who identify highly with their favourite clubs develop strong emotional bonds with those clubs that they tend to live out in and out of the game setting. We also know that licensed products give those fans the opportunity to publicly express their feelings of love, support, and attachment and to enjoy the game atmosphere with other like-minded consumers (Apostolopoulou et al., 2012). Taken together, these highlight the idiosyncratic nature of sport licensed products and call for a greater emphasis on the meanings that add value to these products.

The Meanings of Sport Licensed Products (MSLP) scale is a measurement tool created specifically for the sport industry to help marketers capture the meanings consumers attribute to the sport licensed products they own (Papadimitriou and Apostolopoulou, 2015). The MSLP scale has five dimensions: *experience, socialisation, aesthetics, personal history*, and *locality*. Each of these serves as a source of product meaning that can guide effective promotional activities in this field. We briefly describe the five MSLP factors below and offer insights for sport marketers.

The dimension of *experience* highlights the intangible benefits of sport licensed products that relate to the emotions and feelings that fans derive from these products. Buying, displaying, or otherwise using licensed products leads fans to experience pride in and warmth toward their favourite team. It also helps them feel as if they are part of the team and enjoy the games more. Meanings capturing the aspect of *socialisation* serve the needs of fans with regards to connecting with fellow team supporters. By displaying the team's logo and colours in the products they wear and use, fans boost their image as true followers and become part of a community of team fans with a shared identity. *Aesthetics* is another prominent source of value for licensed products. Apart from any utilitarian function, fans buy licensed products because they find them attractive, authentic, and aesthetically appealing (Papadimitriou, Apostolopoulou, and Loukas, 2004). The use of the team logo and colours, but also the design and quality of the licensed products, drive sales. Lastly, the MSLP scale uncovers meanings related to one's *personal history* and *locality* that add value to sport licensed products. These products are valuable to their owners because they remind them of a special person or relationship in their life or an important sport experience and because they connect them to their roots. This is particularly evident in cases where clubs are considered identifiable icons of their city (i.e., F.C. Barcelona, A.C. Milan) and possess characteristics and associations that match the branding of that city or region.

The discussion on the meanings of sport licensed products as captured through the MSLP scale can offer valuable guidelines to marketers in the football industry. First, promotional and sales campaigns geared toward licensed products should incorporate verbal and visual stimuli that portray invigorating and emotional fan experiences. Second, those campaigns should also promote a sense of community by showing groups of fans cheering on their favourite team and celebrating together. Third, sport marketers should realise that a strong and highly identifiable brand is not adequate if the products they are offering, whether retro or modern, are not of high quality and aesthetically pleasing to consumers. Fourth, commemorative items can be used to highlight themes of history and nostalgia of past accomplishments and important moments and people in the club's life. And fifth, communications efforts promoting licensed products should include references to the club's city and region, while agreements could be sought with local manufacturers to offer licensed items inspired by the local area.

It is undeniable that European football clubs evoke very strong emotions and passion and offer multiple opportunities for the engagement of their fans. What is also true is that fans derive intangible benefits from team licensed products and that, through their interactions with team players, family members and other fans, create value for themselves and their club. Nevertheless, the spectrum of brand associations along with the value that fans attach to the licensed products they own remain rather unexplored. Relevant sport marketing research is still at an early stage.

It is our hope that the discussion that has been offered in this chapter can inform sport marketers' efforts to design, promote, and sell licensed products that fans would want to buy.

The future of sport licensing

The potential for licensing to improve the financial bottom line of sport properties in general and football clubs in particular is undeniable. Looking into the future, there are a number of emerging trends that will shape this industry for years to come. We have chosen to highlight four: a) continued product and market diversification; b) increasing levels of piracy of sport licensed products; c) the globalisation of e-commerce; and d) the expanded use of technology in licensed product design and manufacturing.

It is expected that sport properties around the world will continue to invest in identifying new product categories and new consumer groups for licensing purposes. Partnering with non-sport brands and personalities from the areas of fashion and entertainment allows sport licensors to explore new product categories and to take advantage of trends in those industries, even appeal to their customer base. One such example is the agreement between NASCAR and Nickelodeon's "Teenage Mutant Ninja Turtles" brand that included the sponsoring of a race and official licensed merchandise featuring both brands (MacKenzie, 2017). Even rethinking existing product categories could lead to increased profits from new and existing consumers. The NFL's partnership with online retailer Teespring to produce user-designed team apparel as well as offering special edition apparel in their NFL Juniors line are efforts to engage with and attract younger consumers with products that appeal to their tastes (Griffin, 2017; Konrad, 2015).

Whether it involves a pop-up shop near Old Trafford or a non-authorised e-retailer anywhere in the world, the illegal sale of counterfeit sport licensed products can be very damaging. For sport properties and their licensing partners, it could lead to loss of revenue and potential loss of goodwill. For consumers, buying a knock-off product, knowingly or unknowingly, could mean receiving a product of poor quality or not receiving a product they paid for at all (Brettman, 2013). It is almost impossible to accurately assess how much money is generated by the sale of counterfeit sport products, but what we know is that this problem affects sport properties around the world. The NFL reported that, following its 2012/2013 season, they confiscated unlicensed merchandise worth $13.6 million, while it was estimated that ten per cent of items from the 2014 Sochi Winter Olympics were unlicensed (Olenski, 2014). Sport properties would benefit from developing market surveillance processes and partnering with law enforcement or other agencies in order to identify and punish unauthorised sellers. Also, initiatives such as Premier League's 'Anti-Counterfeiting Programme' can educate consumers about the differences between authentic and counterfeit sport merchandise as well as the dangers of piracy in the sport licensing industry.

Consumers around the world are increasingly seeing e-commerce as a safe and convenient alternative to on-ground shopping. Consider the fact that in 2017, online sales in the US were 9 per cent of total retail sales and growing, while in the UK that figure reached 19.1 per cent. China is leading the way with 23 per cent of retail sales in that country in the year 2017 occurring online (E-commerce sales, 2017). As expected, this trend has also impacted the sport licensing industry, allowing local sport teams and events to sell their products to global fan bases. Within that domain, US-based sports apparel e-commerce company Fanatics is an industry leader. Labelled as "the ultimate disrupter" (p. 1), they have managed, through acquisitions and partnerships across the North American sport industry, to become a buyer, seller, and distributor of sports licensed merchandise (Lefton, 2017). Intending to gain a larger presence in the European soccer market and to grow their business globally, Fanatics bought UK online retailer

Kitbag that sold licensed merchandise of the likes of Arsenal and Real Madrid as well as products of North American properties in Europe (Del Rey, 2016).

Finally, advancements in technology and the increased use of data analytics have affected all facets of the sport licensing process from production and marketing to sale and distribution. Of particular interest is how technological innovations have inspired the design of "smart clothing." Using features such as sensors, apps, and Bluetooth, sport apparel now vibrates, tracks heart rate and stride length, connects to music and map apps, offers feedback for more efficient and injury-free workouts, even warns you if you have been sitting in the sun for too long (Laster, 2016; Sawh, 2017)! As part of their partnership with the National Basketball Association (NBA), Nike launched the "Nike NBA Connected Jersey" that not only is lighter and provides more air circulation for players, but also gives fans wearing the jersey access to player content and exclusive offers just by tapping their smartphone on a tag located on the bottom of the jersey (Moore, 2017). Technology is enabling licensors to capitalise on team/player-fan relationships in new ways by promoting personalised experiences, exclusive access, and greater connections with the sport brands that fans love to follow.

Conclusion

This chapter provided an overview of sport licensing and examined the size and characteristics of the industry and the benefits and risks for licensing partners. Beyond profit, strengthening a sport organisation's presence in fans' lives and generating goodwill are other significant benefits. Select research on the functional, experiential, and symbolic meanings of sport licensed products as well as the role of team identification in the consumption of those products, was also discussed. It is suggested that the equity of football brands provides a formidable platform for extension into new product and service categories with potential for significant financial gains. Continuing efforts of product and market diversification and taking advantage of advancements in technology and data analytics can assist sport properties in building successful and profitable licensing programs.

References

2014 FIFA World Cup Brazil wins International Licensing Award (2015)[online] Retrieved from: http://www.fifa.com/worldcup/news/y=2015/m=6/news=2014-fifa-world-cup-braziltm-wins-international-licensing-award-2647763.html

Aaker, D. (1990) Brand extensions: the good, the bad, and the ugly. *Sloan Management Review*, 31(4), 47–56.

Apostolopoulou, A., Papadimitriou, D., and Damtsiou, V. (2010) Meanings and functions in Olympic consumption: a study of the Athens 2004 Olympic licensed products. *European Sport Management Quarterly*, 10, 485–507.

Apostolopoulou, A., Papadimitriou, D., Synowka, D., and Clark, J.S. (2012) Consumption and meanings of team licensed merchandise. *International Journal of Sport Management & Marketing*, 12, 93–110.

Ashforth, B. and Mael, F. (1989) Social identity theory and the organization. *Academy o Management Review*, 14, 20–39.

Bayern München's Bundesliga World Tour trip to China and Singapore (2017) [online] Retrieved from: https://www.bundesliga.com/en/news/Bundesliga/bundesliga-world-tour-bayern-munich-2017-3.jsp

Bayern Munich (2017) [online] Retrieved from: https://www.forbes.com/teams/bayern-munich/

Branscombe, N.R. and Wann, D.L. (1992) Role of identification with a group, arousal, categorization processes, and self-esteem in sports spectator aggression. *Human Relations*, 45, 1013–1033.

Brettman, A. (2013) NFL, Nike fight to keep counterfeit products off the market. [online] Retrieved from: http://www.oregonlive.com/playbooks-profits/index.ssf/2013/11/nfl_nike_fight_to_keep_counter.html

Canalichio, P. (2010) 10 benefits of brand licensing. [online] Retrieved from: https://www.brandingstrategyinsider.com/2010/10/10-benefits-of-brand-licensing.html#.WhmNLVWnHIV

Covell, D. (2007). Licensed and branded merchandise. In: B.J. Mullin, S. Hardy, and W.A. Sutton (eds.). *Sport Marketing* (3rd ed.) (pp. 189–212). Champaign, IL: Human Kinetics.

Davis, F. (1992) *Fashion, Culture, and Identity*. Chicago, IL: The University of Chicago Press Books.

Davis, N. (2015a) Eye on the prize: a look at sports licensing in Europe. [online] Retrieved from: http://www.licensemag.com/license-global/eye-prize-look-sports-licensing-europe

Davis, N. (2015b) Sports licensing report: expanding the field of play. [online] Retrieved from: http://www.licensemag.com/license-global/sports-licensing-report-expanding-field play

Del Ray, J. (2016) Fanatics buys european online sports retailer for $17 million in big soccer push. [online] Retrieved from: https://www.recode.net/2016/2/2/11587494/fanatics-buys-european-online-sports-retailer-for-17-million-in-big

E-commerce sales as percentage of total retail sales in selected countries in 2017. (2017) [online] Retrieved from: https://www.statista.com/statistics/255083/online-sales-as-share-of-total-retail-sales-in-selected-countries/

Fullerton, S. (2010) *Sports Marketing* (2nd ed.). New York, NY: McGraw-Hill/Irwin.

Gladden, J. (2014) Managing sport brands. In: B.J. Mullin, S. Hardy, and W.A. Sutton (eds), *Sport Marketing* (4the ed.) pp. 161–178. Champaign, IL: Human Kinetics.

Griffin, C. (2017) Bringing it on home: 4 sports licensing stories to watch. *Sports Insight*, January/February, 18–20.

Gwinner, K. and Swanson, D. (2003). A model of fan identification: antecedents and sponsorship outcomes. *Journal of Services Marketing*, 17, 275–294.

Heitner, D. (2014) Sports licensing soars to $698 million in royalty revenue. [online] Retrieved from: https://www.forbes.com/sites/darrenheitner/2014/06/17/sports-licensing-soars-to-698-million-in-royalty-revenue/#3cedf77756b1

Hoeffler, S. and Keller, K.L. (2003) The marketing advantage of strong brands. *Journal of Brand Management*, 10, 421–425.

Holland, C. (2016) Trademark licensing: social media and quality control. [online] Retrieved from: https://www.knobbe.com/news/2016/04/trademark-licensing-social-media-and-quality-control-new-york-law-journal

Irwin, R.L., Sutton, W.A., and McCarthy, L.M. (2008) *Sport Promotion and Sale Management* (2nd ed.). Champaign, IL: Human Kinetics.

Italian soccer club A.C. Milan teams up with Gruppo Linea to offer credit card to fans. (n.d.) [online] Retrieved from: https://www.globalcustodian.com/Technology/Italian-Soccer-Club-A-C--Milan-Teams-Up-With-Gruppo-Linea-To-Offer-Credit-Card-To-Fans/

Keller, K.L. (1993) Conceptualizing, measuring, and managing customer-based brand equity. *Journal of Marketing*, 57, 1–22.

Keller, K.L. (2009) Building strong brands in a modern marketing communications environment. *Journal of Marketing Communications*, 15, 139–155.

Kim, M.S. and James, J. (2016) The theory of planned behaviour and intention of purchase sport team licensed merchandise. *Sport, Business and Management: An International Journal*, 6, 228–243.

Konrad, A. (2015). The NFL and Teespring team up to sell fan-created custom t-shirts for first time. [online] Retrieved from: https://www.forbes.com/sites/alexkonrad/2015/08/26/teespring-and-nfl-team-up-for-tees/#1e82164935a5

Kwon, H.H. and Armstrong, K.L. (2002) Factors influencing impulse buying of sport team license merchandise. *Sport Marketing Quarterly*, 11, 151–163.

Kwon, H., Trail, G.T., and Anderson, D.F. (2006) Points of attachment (identification) and licensed merchandise consumption among American college students. *International Journal of Sport Management*, 7, 347–360.

Laster, J. (2016). Report: global licensed sports merch to nearly double by 2024. [online] Retrieved from: https://www.sportstailgateshow.com/2016/11/report-global-licensed-sports-merch-to-nearly-double-by-2024/

Lefton, T. (2017) February 20–26. How Rubin is rocking sports licensing. [online] Retrieved from: http://www.sportsbusinessdaily.com/Journal/Issues/2017/02/20/Marketing-and-Sponsorship/Fanatics.aspx

MacKenzie, M. (2017) Cowabunga! Teenage Mutant Ninja Turtles to sponsor Chicagoland race. [online] Retrieved from: https://www.nascar.com/en_us/news-media/articles/2017/4/28/teenage-mutant-ninja-turtles-nickelodeon-return-to-chicagoland-playoff-opener.html

Moore, M. (2017). What Nike's uniform launch means for NBA, players and fans now and in the future. [online] Retrieved from: https://www.cbssports.com/nba/news/what-nikes-uniform-launch-means-for-nba-players-and-fans-now-and-in-the-future/

Mullin, B.J., Hardy, S., and Sutton, W.A. (2014) *Sport Marketing* (4th ed.). Champaign, IL: Human Kinetics.

Nagle, B. (2017) Football Leaks reveal details of Real Madrid's huge deal with adidas which will rake in £850 million for Spanish giants. [online] Retrieved from: http://www.dailymail.co.uk/sport/football/article-4479670/Details-Real-Madrid-s-huge-850m-deal-adidas.html

Olenski, S. (2013) The power of global sports brand merchandising. [online] Retrieved from: https://www.forbes.com/sites/marketshare/2013/02/06/the-power-of-global-sports-brand-merchandising/#196c44a376ac

Olenski, S. (2014) License To brand: when it comes to licensed products brands need to always be on their game. [online] Retrieved from: https://www.forbes.com/sites/steveolenski/2014/02/25/license-to-brand-when-it-comes-to-licensed-products-brands-need-to-always-be-on-their-game/#6a8b5c5d499f

Ozanian, M. (2017) The world's most valuable soccer teams 2017. [online] Retrieved from: https://www.forbes.com/sites/mikeozanian/2017/06/06/the-worlds-most-valuable-soccer-teams-2017/#6b0160f177ea

Papadimitriou, D. and Apostolopoulou, A. (2015) Capturing the meanings of sport licensed products. *Journal of Marketing Communications.* DOI:10.1080/13527266.2015.1065900

Papadimitriou, D. and Apostolopoulou, A. (2016, September). *Product meanings as drivers of sport consumer behavior: Evidence from the Greek sport industry.* Paper presented at the conference of the European Association for Sport Management, Warsaw, Poland.

Papadimitriou, D., Apostolopoulou, A., and H. Loukas, (2004) The role of perceived fit in fans' evaluation of sports brand extensions. *The International Journal of Sport Marketing & Sponsorship*, 6(1), 31–48.

Retail & Merchandising (2015) [online] Retrieved from: http://www.fifa.com/about fifa/marketing/licensing/consumer-retail.html

Sawh, M. (2017) The best smart clothing: From biometric shirts to contactless payment jackets. [online] Retrieved from: https://www.wareable.com/smart-clothing/best-smart-clothing

Seligman, D. (2016) Merchandising and licensing in football. [online] Retrieved from: https://www.cmsolicitors.co.uk/news/sports-law/merchandising-licensing-football

Wilson, B. (2014) Manchester United and Adidas in £750m deal over 10 years. [online] Retrieved from: http://www.bbc.com/news/business-28282444

Yotka, S. (2017) Pharrell Williams and Garbiñe Muguruza are bringing love to the US Open with retro Adidas outfits and a social campaign. [online] Retrieved from: https://www.vogue.com/article/pharrell-williams-garbine-muguruza-adidas-us-open

34

FIFA

Tom Bason, Paul Salisbury, and Simon Gérard

Introduction

Fédération Internationale de Football Association (FIFA) is the international governing body of world football, yet has in recent times been beset by accusations of corruption and bribery. This came to a head in 2015 with the arrest of 14 FIFA officials and the banning of president, Sepp Blatter, from football (Gibson, 2015). This resulted in FIFA introducing FIFA 2.0 in 2016, with the vision to "promote the game of football, protect its integrity, and bring the game to all" (FIFA, 2016a, p. 6).

It is not within the remit of this chapter to pass judgement on FIFA and recent allegations of corruption and bribery; it would be remiss for this crucial moment in FIFA's history to be ignored. Thus, this chapter will start by providing a brief history of FIFA, detailing the events that resulted in the implementation of FIFA 2.0. This will then be followed by a discussion of FIFA's new governance responsibilities. Next, FIFA's core business will be discussed, before consideration of FIFA's emerging business and developmental duties.

Brief overview of FIFA's history

International football predates organised club football; the first international match saw England draw 0–0 with Scotland in 1872, 16 years before the formation of the English Football League (Taylor, 2008). Over the next 30 years, international football became more popular, and it became increasingly evident that a governing body was needed to oversee world football was needed. On 21 May 1904, representatives from France, Belgium, Denmark, Netherlands, Spain, Sweden, and Switzerland met in Paris to found FIFA (Tomlinson, 2000).

The initial statutes determined by FIFA were (FIFA, n.d.(a)):

1 Reciprocal and exclusive recognition of the national associations represented and attending;
2 Clubs and players were forbidden to play simultaneously for different national associations;
3 Player suspensions would be recognised by other associations;
4 All matches would be played according to the "Laws of the Game of the Football Association Ltd."

Table 34.1 FIFA Presidents 1904–date (Tomlinson, 2000)

President	Nationality	Years
Robert Guérin	France	1904–1906
Daniel Burley Woolfall	England	1906–1918
Jules Rimet	France	1921–1954
Rodolphe Seeldrayers	Belgium	1954–1955
Arthur Drewry	England	1955–1961
Sir Stanley Rous	England	1961–1974
Dr João Havelange	Brazil	1974–1998
Sepp Blatter	Switzerland	1998–2015
Gianni Infantino	Switzerland	2016–present

The German FA joined FIFA on the same day, and over the following two years would be joined by Austria, Italy, Hungary, England, Scotland, Wales, and Ireland (FIFA, n.d.(a)). It was not until South Africa joined in 1909/10 that FIFA expanded beyond Europe, but by 1913, Argentina, Chile and the USA had all joined FIFA. At this stage, FIFA was primarily concerned with the governance of the game, and it was left to the English FA to organise the football tournaments at the 1908 and 1912 Olympic Games.

Following World War I, and the election of Jules Rimet as president, FIFA started to organise international tournaments, starting with the 1924 Olympic Games. It was the success of the 1924 and 1928 Olympic Games that led to FIFA deciding to organise its own international tournament. The first was the 1930 World Cup in Uruguay, with the trophy named after Jules Rimet, FIFA president from 1921–1954 (Tomlinson, 2000).

In the interim years, and as shown in the Table 34.1 FIFA has had nine permanent presidents (Tomlinson, 2000).

As can be seen, FIFA was dominated by European presidents until the election of Dr João Havelange in 1974. Indeed, Havelange's successful election campaign had its roots in recognition of the global game. Incumbent president Stanley Rous supported a South African football association that employed the principles of apartheid, and Havelange recognised this (Darby, 2008). Havelange rallied the African nations and became the first non-European president of FIFA. Havelange then oversaw the expansion of FIFA across the world; the 1974 World Cup had just one competitor each from the Confederation of African Football (CAF), Oceania Football Confederation (OFC) and The Confederation of North, Central American and Caribbean Association Football (CONCACAF). No Asian teams took part in the tournament (FIFA, 1976). By the 1982 World Cup, this had expanded to Kuwait (OFC), New Zealand (OFC), Algeria, and Cameroon (both CAF), and Honduras and El Salvador (both CONCACAF) (FIFA, 1982).

Havelange stepped down in 1998 and was replaced by his long-term general secretary, Sepp Blatter. Blatter continued Havelange's vision of football being the global game and was instrumental in taking the World Cup to new areas of the world. However, Blatter's time as president was mired in controversy, ultimately ending in FIFA banning Blatter from football for eight years.

2015 corruption scandal

FIFA had long been accused of underhand operations, with the bankruptcy of International Sports and Leisure (ISL) media group leading to questions of the nature of its relationship to FIFA and bribes paid to FIFA executives to secure the marketing rights for the 2002 World

Cup and 2006 World Cup (Conn, 2017; Jennings, 2006). Scrutiny into FIFA further intensified in 2010 following the decision to award the 2018 World Cup to Russia and 2022 World Cup to Qatar. Qatar's successful bid was particularly under scrutiny due to the nation's lack of football heritage (Brannagan and Rookwood, 2016). A *Sunday Times* investigation detailed bribes paid by Qatar to secure the hosting of the World Cup, including payments by Mohammed bin Hammam, a former FIFA presidential candidate (Blake and Calvert, 2015).

Following these investigations, FIFA hired an American attorney Michael Garcia to investigate. However, Garcia's report was blocked by FIFA's ethics committee, with a summary published in 2014 clearing both Russia and Qatar (Conway, 2014). Garcia distanced himself from the report and resigned as FIFA's ethics investigator, claiming that the released summary was "materially incomplete" with "erroneous representations of the facts and conclusions" (Conway, 2014). This investigation had little impact on FIFA, with many of the major power brokers staying in place, including president Sepp Blatter.

At this time, however, two FIFA executives, Jack Warner and Chuck Blazer were suspended from FIFA following accusations of bribery. Unbeknownst to FIFA, Blazer agreed to inform the FBI of FIFA practices. This led to a US FBI investigation which saw 14 FIFA officials indicted on charges of receiving more than USD 150 million in inducements and bribes (Fortunato, 2017). This included the accusation of a USD 10 million bribe in exchange for securing Jack Warner's vote for South Africa to host the 2010 World Cup (BBC News, 2015). Later in 2015, president Sepp Blatter was suspended by FIFA for eight years following revelations of a "disloyal payment" made to UEFA (Union of European Football Associations) president Michel Platini in 2011 (Gibson, 2015). In February 2016, former general secretary of UEFA, Gianni Infantino was elected as FIFA's ninth president, promising to restore FIFA's image (BBC Sport, 2016). Yet, despite these claims, FIFA has been criticised for having failed to enact any real reform (Onwumechili and Bedeau, 2017).

Reforming FIFA

In response to the numerous high-profile scandals and allegations alluded to above, in recent years FIFA has initiated and undergone major governance reforms, which can be categorised into three phases: Pre 2011; 2011–2013 and post-2016. Prior to 2011, there were several reforms that mostly focussed on transparency and financial regulations (FIFA, n.d. (b)) and these were furthered between 2011 and 2013, as detailed in Table 34.2.

The 2011–2013 reforms were designed to adhere to the previously identified priority objectives of financial transparency and ethical behaviour and they represented, in many cases, a strengthening of existing systems rather than a radical departure from what had gone before. However, the increasingly high-profile scandals, particularly the financial scandals of 2015, led to a raft of new reforms proposed by the 2016 FIFA Reform Committee and accepted by the Extraordinary FIFA Congress in Zurich on 26 February 2016 (FIFA, n.d. (c)).

The rhetoric of a reformed FIFA is clear from perusing official publications. In the 2016 FIFA Governance Report, the first such document published since the reforms were adopted, the themes of *transparency, accountability*, and a *separation of powers* are highly prominent (FIFA, 2016b). However, aside from the rhetoric there are two additional features to the reforms which perhaps were not as prominent in previous iterations. First, from the forewords provided by senior officials, there is a clear tone of acceptance of recent indiscretions. The president refers to the "events that have so tarnished the image and reputation of the organisation" (FIFA, 2016b, p. 4), while other senior officials refer to "learning from mistakes" (FIFA, 2016b, p. 5), "rebuilding trust" (FIFA, 2016b, p. 6) and "never again facing the problems of the recent past" (FIFA, 2016b, p. 6).

Table 34.2 A summary of the FIFA reform processes (adapted from FIFA, n.d. (a))

Pre-2011 Reforms	2011–2013 Reforms	2016 Reforms
Financial Controls and Transparency		
Introduction and strengthening of annual financial reporting based on International Financial Reporting Standards	Compensation sub-committee established	Separation of Political and Management Functions
Annual audits by KPMG	Best practice compliance system	FIFA Executive Committee replaced by FIFA Council (strategic function)
Internal Audit Committee established	Additional Competence of the Audit and Compliance Committee	Enhanced control of money flows
Internal Control System	Appointment of an independent chairperson	Disclosure of individual compensation of leading FIFA officials
Professional budgeting processes Tendering for major contracts	FIFA Congress to elect members of Audit and Compliance Committee	
Ethics and Integrity		
Payment controls for major development programmes	Enhanced control and disclosure of development funds	Term limits (max. 12 years)
Code of Ethics and Ethics Committee established	Two-chamber ethics committee (investigatory and adjudicatory)	Election of council members (subject to comprehensive eligibility and integrity checks).
Annual Activity Reports	Mandatory integrity checks for key officials	Sharing of good governance principles with confederations and member associations
Continuous Revision of Statutes	Revision of the Code of Ethics and a new FIFA Code of Conduct	General Secretariat (operational function)
	Introduction of a confidential reporting mechanism	
	Revised definition of bribery and corruption	
	FIFA Congress to vote on the award of the World Cup	
Other Reforms		
	Strengthening opportunities for women on the Executive Committee	Commitment to human rights enshrined in FIFA Statutes
		New Football Stakeholder Committee
	Electoral Regulations for the FIFA Presidency	Greater recognition and promotion of women in football

Second, and accompanying the rhetoric of the reform process, was a universal commitment to both the structural and cultural reform of the organisation, which is a marked departure from the theme of strengthening compliance procedures that went before. A thematic overview of the reforms is indicated in Table 34.2, but this table does not adequately address the structural reforms. Table 34.3 outlines the new post-2016 structure of FIFA and highlights significant deviations from the previous governance structure.

The dominant themes of the results of the structural reforms initiated in 2016 have been the separation of powers between the executive (FIFA Council) and operational (General Secretariat) components of the organisation and the enhancing of oversight and compliance mechanisms, represented by the Ethics Committee and newly-created Independent Audit and Compliance Committee. From a structural perspective it is also worthy of note that the previous 24-member Executive Committee has been replaced by a larger, more diverse 36-member FIFA Council. In keeping with the dilution of power away from senior individuals, the president's role has also been significantly reduced and is more akin to that of an ambassador (FIFA, 2016b).

Governing FIFA

Transparency

While the structural reforms mark a significant change from previous reforms, it should be noted that the themes of transparency and ensuring good ethical practice through good governance have continued throughout the various reform processes and are also significant aspects of the 2016 reforms. In terms of transparency, members of the FIFA Council are now required to undergo eligibility checks coordinated by an Independent FIFA Review Committee and financial compensation for the president (USD 1,513,716) and secretary general (USD 837,437), aggregated compensation for FIFA Council members (USD 13,783,841), and individual compensation for committee chairs (ranging from USD 100,000 to 1,676,353) are published annually (FIFA, 2016b)

Good governance

Good governance, aimed at combating the ethical scandals that have blighted FIFA's recent history, continued to be a core theme of the 2016 reforms and resulting FIFA Statutes that were adopted in April 2016. FIFA notes that of the 11 aspects that it considers comprise good governance (*Separation of powers; Integrity of the game; Clear roles in decision-making; Dispute resolution; Independent Audits; No conflicts of interest; Zero tolerance for discrimination; No political interference; Respect all regulations; Representative democracy; Religious and political neutrality*) (FIFA, n.d. (c)), it identified four over-arching governance priorities for the post-2016 era (FIFA, 2016b), as summarised in Table 34.4.

Compliance

One key addition to the FIFA structure in Table 34.3 is the addition of a chief compliance officer and an independent Audit and Compliance Committee, all of which were commissioned in response to the perceived expectations of external stakeholders and with the broad aims of carrying out due diligence "to prevent and detect criminal conduct" (FIFA, 2016b, p. 50). With unrestricted authority to access and inspect any component of the organisation's structure, the combined compliance "division" is charged with overseeing anti-bribery and

Table 34.3 The current structure of FIFA

FIFA Congress The supreme decision-making body. Comprised of voting members from each member association.			
Ethics Committee Split into two chambers: Investigatory (1 chair, 2 deputy chairs, 5 members) Adjudicatory (1 chair, 2 deputy chairs, 6 members)			
Political Decision-Making (Supervising)		Business Operations (Reporting)	
Body	**Composition**	**Body**	**Composition**
President	Maximum of 3 x 4 year terms in office.	**Secretary General**	Oversees the day-to-day running of the organisation
FIFA Council	36 members (maximum of 3 x 4 year terms) plus the President. Elected by the Confederations: • UEFA 9 seats • AFC 7 seats • CAF 7 seats • COCACAF 5 seats • CONMEBOL 5 seats • OFC 3 seats n.b. each confederation must elect at least one woman.	**General Secretariat**	Oversees the day-to-day running of the organisation Comprises 3 elements, split into 13 offices: Football *Human Resources; Competitions and events; Member Associations; Technical Development; Women's Football; Player and Promotion Events* Administration *Commercial; Finance; Legal and Integrity; HR and Services.* Executive *Executive Office; Compliance; Communications; Sustainability and Diversity.*
FIFA Committees	Members serve maximum of 3 x 4 years on committees. Development Committee Football Stakeholders Committee Medical Committee Organising Committee for FIFA Competitions Referees Committee Finance Committee Governance Committee and Review Committee Members Associations Committee Players' Status Committee	**Chief Compliance Officer**	Oversees good governance and imposition of reforms.
Confederations (x6) **Member Associations** (x211) **Independent Audit and Compliance Committee** (maximum 3 x year terms)			

Table 34.4 FIFA's good governance priorities (adapted from FIFA, 2016b)

Good Governance Priority	Detail
Term Limits	As indicated in Table 1.2 above, the president, members of the FIFA Council and members of the Independent Audit and Compliance Committee are limited to three terms in office of four years each.
Integration of Human Rights	In May 2017 FIFA published its new Human Rights Policy (FIFA, 2017a). In conjunction with the UN Guiding Principles on Human Rights (UNGPs) FIFA commits to *embedding* human rights into strategic and regulatory documents; *Identifying* areas where FIFA work risks adverse effects on human rights; *protecting* the human rights of all stakeholders carrying out FIFA work (and providing remedies); *engaging* external stakeholders in the area of human rights.
Inclusive Decision-Making Processes	Most notably, FIFA has established a Football Stakeholders Committee with the explicit aim of engaging the international football community more closely. These are supported by annual FIFA Executive Football Summits, which allow for member associations to meet and share good practice.
Universal Good Governance Principles	The 2016 FIFA Governance Report declared that FIFA wished to be viewed as an organisation that "is a pioneer among major sports federations" (FIFA, 2016b, 21). To achieve this bold aim, FIFA requires that confederations and member associations eventually share their good governance principles.

anti-corruption policies, monitoring the whistleblower hotline, and carrying out a range of training and employee-support duties (FIFA, 2016b).

Inclusivity

In its most recent strategy document, termed FIFA 2.0, the organisation makes the claim that one of its guiding principles is to "reflect the world and the communities in which it operates" (FIFA, 2016a, p. 28). The principle underpins the activities that are branded under the FIFA Forward banner later in this chapter, but from a governance perspective, much of the focus of inclusivity has been on increasing the number of women in senior positions, both within FIFA and in member associations and confederations. The lack of women occupying such positions was detailed in FIFA's 2014 Women's Football Survey (FIFA, 2014a), which noted that while female participation in football was experiencing steady growth, especially at youth level, with over 30,000,000 women actively playing the game, women made up less than ten per cent of executive confederation workforces. As indicated in Table 34.3, the FIFA Council now must now comprise at least one woman per confederation and FIFA has also declared the intention to encourage greater participation and diversity in decision-making though including "the promotion of women as an explicit statutory objective of FIFA to create a more diverse decision-making environment and culture" (FIFA, 2016a, p. 57).

Core business

As seen, FIFA have a wide number of responsibilities. However, as the world governing body, it earns revenue from few sources. As Figure 34.1 demonstrates, FIFA's event-related income far

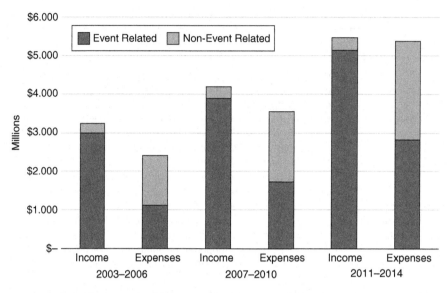

Figure 34.1 FIFA income and expenses 200314 (FIFA, 2007; 2011; 2015a)

Table 34.5 FIFA tournaments (FIFA, n.d. (d))

Men's Tournaments	Women's Tournaments
FIFA World Cup	FIFA Women's World Cup
FIFA Confederations Cup	FIFA U-20 Women's World Cup
FIFA U-20 World Cup	FIFA U-17 Women's World Cup
FIFA Club World Cup	Women's Olympic Football Tournament
FIFA Beach Soccer World Cup	Girl's Youth Olympic Football Tournament
FIFA Futsal World Cup	
Men's Olympic Football Tournament	
Boys' Youth Olympic Football Tournament	
FIFA eWorld Cup	

outweighs other sources of income. Indeed, for the 2003–2006 and 2007–2010 cycles, event-related income covered all of FIFA's expenses. Conversely, event-related costs account for a far smaller proportion of FIFA's expenses (FIFA, 2007, 2011, 2015a).

Event-related income and costs cover FIFA's portfolio of 15 tournaments. These range from the men's World Cup, one of the few global mega-events (Müller, 2014), to the Beach Soccer World Cup. FIFA has sought to open up these tournaments to new markets; these tournaments include both men and women's tournaments, youth tournaments, and even an eWorld Cup, launched in 2004 (Table 34.5).

The FIFA World Cup

The jewel in FIFA's crown is the FIFA World Cup, an international global tournament that takes place every four years. The first World Cup was played in 1930 when it was hosted and won by Uruguay. This first World Cup did not have a qualification period, and just 13 nations competed in the final tournament. Following this, the tournament was expanded to 16 teams, with nations competing with each other to qualify for the tournament. The World Cup has since grown again twice; to 24 teams in 1982, and then to 32 teams in 1998. The 2026 World Cup is set to be the first to feature 48 nations.

While only a limited number of teams can compete at the tournament itself, every nation is eligible to enter the qualification period. Over 200 nations sought to qualify for the 2010 World Cup, while 210 entered qualification for the 2018 World Cup. In comparison, the United Nations has 193-member states. Table 34.6 summarises the tournaments that have taken place.

The globalisation of the World Cup is further demonstrated by the number of regions of the world where the tournament has been hosted. The first 16 World Cup tournaments were all hosted in Europe, South America, or North America. Since then, however, Japan and South Korea (2002), South Africa (2010), and Qatar (2022) have all been awarded the rights to host the tournament. FIFA's commitment to take the World Cup to different regions was invigorated following South Africa's narrow, but controversial defeat to Germany in the bid to host the 2006 World Cup (Griffiths, 2000).

After this, FIFA decided that the World Cup would be taken to each confederation in turn, starting with the Confederation of African Football (CAF) in 2010. South Africa defeated Morocco, Egypt, Nigeria, and a joint Tunisia/Libya bid to take a sport mega-event to Africa for the first time. This initiative was short-lived, and after Brazil was effectively the only South American bidder for the 2014 World Cup, FIFA changed its regulations. Instead, a new system was introduced which ensures that any confederation who had hosted either of the previous two World Cup tournaments is ineligible to host the next.

The World Cup is FIFA's primary revenue driver. Figure 34.2 demonstrates the extent to which FIFA is reliant on the World Cup for income; over 75 per cent of FIFA's revenue in the

Table 34.6 FIFA World Cups, 1930–2018 (FIFA, n.d. (d))

	Host	Winner	Nations at the Tournament	Nations in Qualifying
1930	Uruguay	Uruguay	13	
1934	Italy	Italy	16	36
1938	France	Italy	16	37
1950	Brazil	Uruguay	15	34
1954	Switzerland	West Germany	16	37
1958	Sweden	Brazil	16	55
1962	Chile	Brazil	16	57
1966	England	England	16	70
1970	Mexico	Brazil	16	75
1974	West Germany	Germany	16	98
1978	Argentina	Argentina	16	107
1982	Spain	Italy	24	109
1986	Mexico	Argentina	24	121
1990	Italy	West Germany	24	116
1994	USA	Brazil	24	147
1998	France	France	32	174
2002	Japan/South Korea	Brazil	32	199
2006	Germany	Italy	32	197
2010	South Africa	Spain	32	205
2014	Brazil	Germany	32	203
2018	Russia	France	32	210

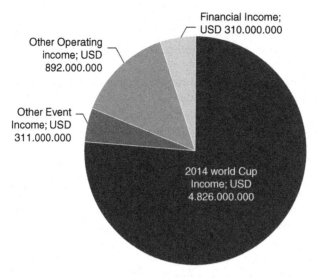

Figure 34.2   FIFA Income 2011–2014 (FIFA, 2015a)

period 2011–2014 is directly related to the 2014 World Cup, held in Brazil. However, while FIFA may have received USD 4.86 billion in income from the World Cup, its World Cup expenses are relatively little at USD 2.2 billion (FIFA, 2015a). This is due to the nature of the contract FIFA strikes with the host nation. It is specifically stated in the contract that the "host city shall be responsible to bear all costs for the fulfilment of its obligations" (FIFA, n.d.(e), p. 43). It is the responsibility of the host to ensure that the facilities and infrastructure are of a required standard; it has been estimated that the total cost of the 2014 World Cup was USD 15 billion, with USD 3.6 billion alone being spent on building new and developing existing stadia (Business Insider, 2015). As Baade and Matheson (2017, p. 304) note, FIFA's USD 2.6 billion profit equates to 72 per cent of Brazil's spending on stadia.

The profits made by FIFA on the World Cup compared to host's expenses have long been criticised, with arguments that FIFA requirements even exacerbate costs of the host nation. For example, any nation wishing to host the 2026 World Cup will need to have one stadium with a capacity of 80,000 for the opening match and final, two stadia of 60,000 for the semi-finals with further stadia of a minimum 40,000 capacity (FIFA, 2017b). It may not just be enough to have these stadia in place; FIFA requested that Cape Town build a new stadium in a more aesthetically pleasing location within the city, namely the Green Point area at the base of Table Mountain (Alegi, 2008). FIFA does not just shape decisions regarding the World Cup event itself; it has also been heavily criticised for seeking to overrule national laws (Jerabek et al., 2017). FIFA claims that hosting a World Cup can have a "huge positive impact," and that FIFA is "committed to ensuring that the FIFA World Cup leaves a tangible legacy in the host country" (FIFA, 2015b). However, these claims have long been criticised in the literature, with the benefits of hosting of World Cup tournaments often being exaggerated ex-ante (for example, Baade and Matheseon, 2002; Humphrey and Fraser, 2016; Zimbalist, 2016).

Broadcasting rights

FIFA's primary individual source of income is through the sale of broadcasting rights, and in particular, the rights to show the World Cup on television. Of FIFA's USD 5.7 billion revenue from 2011 to 2014, 42 per cent was earned from the sale of 2014 World Cup broadcasting rights (FIFA, 2015a). These rights were sold to 219 different territories across the world, netting FIFA USD 2.428 billion. The sale of these TV rights is a far cry from the first World Cup to be broadcast; the European Broadcasting Union paid USD 2,500 for the rights to show nine games of the 1954 World Cup (Tyers, 2014). This developed into 11 games being shown in 1958, but it was the 1966 World Cup in England that was the turning point. England's broadcasting infrastructure was more developed than that of Chile, hosts of the 1962 Games and, for the first time, the slow-motion replay was introduced (Chisari, 2006). The 1966 World Cup was broadcast to 75 countries, earning FIFA USD 800,000. The following World Cup (1970) was the first to be broadcast in colour, while the 1978 World Cup was seen in 100 countries across the world.

Sponsors

FIFA's second most lucrative income stream comes from their sponsors. FIFA offers three levels of sponsorship (FIFA, 2014b). At the highest level are the FIFA partners, earning FIFA USD 177 million a year prior to the 2014 World Cup (FIFA, 2015a). While FIFA note that they are prepared to have up to eight partners, there are currently seven; Adidas, Coca-Cola, Wanda Group, Gazprom, Hyundai / Kia Motors, Qatar Airways, and Visa. While FIFA does not disclose the fees that it receives from these partners, Gazprom are believed to have paid around USD 80 million to become a partner for the 2018 World Cup in Russia (Fraser, 2015). In addition to the financial benefits, partners also support FIFA's work in developing football across the world. In return, FIFA partners receive advertising opportunities, hospitality opportunities, ambush marketing protection, and the opportunity to associate themselves with FIFA and world football (FIFA, 2014b). Following the 2015 bribery scandal, FIFA had struggled to replace partners whose deal expired with the 2014 World Cup, such as Sony and Emirates, with revenue per year from partners falling from USD 177 million in 2014 to USD 136 million in 2015 and then USD 101 million in 2016 (FIFA, 2017c). As a result, FIFA's partners are from more global background, with the Wanda Group being the first Chinese organisation to partner FIFA (Homewood, 2016). While there was pressure on partners to end their association with FIFA following the 2015 scandal, none have done so as yet (Fortunato, 2017).

In addition to the partners, FIFA also offers the opportunity to be a sponsor of the World Cup and Confederations Cup. Again, FIFA wishes to have six to eight World Cup sponsors, but currently has just five; Budweiser, McDonalds, Hisense, Mengniu, and Vivo (FIFA World Cup 2018, n.d.). This list of sponsors, including three Chinese companies stands in stark contrast to the sponsors for the 2014 World Cup, which included established Western brands Castrol, Continental, and Johnson & Johnson (Wilson, 2014). In return for their sponsorship fee (Vivo are paying EUR 60–70 million per year until 2022 (Ahmed, 2017)), sponsors gain brand association with the World Cup and Confederations Cup, media exposure, and hospitality and ticketing offers during the events (FIFA, 2014b). However, as with the partners, FIFA's sponsorship revenue has fallen significantly in recent years. In the cycle leading up to the 2014 World Cup, FIFA earned USD 130 million per year from sponsors. This fell to just USD 10 million in 2015 and 2016 (FIFA, 2017c).

The final level of FIFA's sponsors are the "Regional Supporters." FIFA seeks to have four sponsors from each of Europe, North/Central America, South America, Africa/Middle East, and Asia. These sponsors have the license to associate themselves with the World Cup in their domestic markets (FIFA, 2014b). This is a new level of sponsorship introduced for the 2018 and 2022 World Cups, with the intention of attracting companies who do not wish to market themselves on a global scale (FIFA, 2014b). However, perhaps due to the issues seen with the bid process for the 2018 and 2022 World Cups, very few companies have as yet taken up this option. Russia's Alfa-Bank became the first Regional Supporter in 2016, but no other company had joined them in time for the 2017 Confederations Cup (FIFA World Cup 2018, n.d.).

Ticketing and hospitality

A key direct income surrounding FIFA events is the revenue earned from ticketing and hospitality. Prior to the 2014 World Cup, the host nation kept the net revenue from sales (FIFA, 2015a, p. 96). However, since then ticket revenue has been kept by FIFA. This amounted to USD 527 million in the 2014 World Cup, from 3,144,613 tickets sold. Of these tickets, 69 per cent were sold to the general public, including 307,000 that, due to Brazilian law, were sold at half-price to students, the elderly or part of Brazil's social welfare programme (FIFA, 2015a). FIFA earned a further USD 184 million from the sale of hospitality rights during the 2011–2014 cycle. Of these sales, less than USD 1 million related to non-World Cup events, further highlighting the importance of the World Cup to FIFA's income.

Licensing

FIFA's final income stream comes through licensing, earning FIFA USD 115 million between 2011 and 2014 (FIFA, 2015a). While this includes granting licenses for FIFA events (such as the FIFA Club World Cup), this also covers retail and merchandise licenses and brand collaborations. The retail and merchandise licenses include the selling of officially licensed products, both at the events themselves and in licensed retail outlets. Apart from in the host country, FIFA chooses to manage these licenses itself, to ensure that these fit into the long-term strategy (FIFA, n.d. (f)).

FIFA's two best-known associated brands are Panini and EA Sports (FIFA, 2014c). Panini have produced World Cup stickers and albums since 1970 but have taken on a new lease of life at recent World Cups, as social media is acting as a "virtual playground" (Topping, 2014). While the Panini license is clearly directly linked to the World Cup, arguably FIFA's most successful license is not. Electronic Arts Inc. bought the license to use the FIFA brand to launch its FIFA football video game series. The first edition, FIFA International Soccer, was released in 1993 and a version has been released every year since 1995 making it one of the longest-running sport game franchises. The current deal will see EA Sport continue to make the FIFA series until 2022. FIFA 17 was the biggest selling game console title in the world in 1996 (Electronic Arts Inc., 2016, p. 1)

Emerging business

While the previous section detailed the main streams of income for FIFA, FIFA's responsibilities to society are described below. It therefore highlights the way FIFA invest in various social development programs to build a better future (FIFA, 2015b). In 2016, FIFA spent a total of USD 428 million on development and education programs to foster new opportunities for under-privileged people and empower local communities and organisations. Among them, Football for Hope aims to improve life of youth using football, Football for Health works to develop a healthier world and prevent injury and disease while FIFA Forward, one of the most recent FIFA's football development programs, supports each of FIFA's member associations and confederations as well as several technical development projects (e.g., Youth, Women, Beach soccer, Futsal, etc.).

History of social development's initiatives at FIFA World Cup

The first coordinated FIFA social development initiatives can be traced back to the end of the 1990s, with campaigns like "My Games is Fair Play" (1997) or "Say no to racism" (2002) to tackle discriminatory and unethical behaviours. FIFA also worked in collaboration with the United Nations High Commissioner for Refugees (UNHCR) and the UN children's fund, UNICEF, to improve living conditions of refugees during the Kosovo war (1999). The ties between these organisations became stronger when the United Nations advocated for the role of sport in the achievement of the Millennium Development Goals (MDG) by establishing the Office for Sport for Development and Peace (UNOSDP) in 2008 (Suzuki, 2014).

Football-based development programs became strategic priorities in the early 2000s. This strategic shift was consecrated in 2005 with the creation of the Football for Hope initiative in partnership with Street Football World, a Non-Governmental Organisation (NGO) "that seeks to foster funding partnerships between sport for development NGOs and a range of corporations, donor agencies and operational agencies across the world" (Cornelissen, 2011, p. 521). Football for Hope aims to support responsible development projects in which football is a core part, bringing hope and positive change in the lives of people around the world. Between 2005 and 2014, the program funded more 447 social development programs in 78 countries (FIFA, 2014d).

The FIFA World Cup tournaments are key milestones to start new social initiatives or reinforce existing ones. In 2006, FIFA and the 2006 FIFA World Cup Local Organising Committee promoted social and environmental campaigns. FIFA invested EUR 400,000 in "Green Goal," the environment-oriented campaign, to reduce the carbon footprint of the World Cup. From the social campaign – called "6 villages for 2006" – ensued the construction of six villages for orphans in each continent by FIFA and the charitable organisation SOS Children's Village (FIFA, 2014d).

In the build-up to the 2010 FIFA World Cup, the sport for development sector in South-Africa was significantly boosted where long-lasting development programs were supplemented by numerous new initiatives. A myriad of actors at different levels (e.g. continental/regional, national, provincial, or local), in a variety of institutional configurations (FIFA or government-led, public-private partnerships or sport-focused CSR projects [see Chapter 10 in this handbook]) used the World Cup to foster positive social change and tackle a wide range of social issues (e.g. HIV/AIDS, poverty, racial tensions, violence). Nevertheless, the South African government and FIFA tended to be central players, by initiating or guiding most programmes (Cornelissen, 2011). Among the large-scale FIFA-led programs, Win in Africa with Africa targeted continental football development with new training and coaching programs and the creation of new pitches and facilities across the African continent. Football for Health used football to sensitise youth about healthy lifestyle and disease prevention while Football for Hope campaign associated with the 2010 FIFA World Cup aimed to build "20 centres for hope" in Africa, each centre encompassing an artificial football pitch along with a local community centre.

For the 2014 FIFA World Cup, given the central role of football in Brazilian society, FIFA massively invested a wide range of social development projects using football to get the young active, promote healthy behaviour, tackle poverty, or gender-based violence. FIFA and the local organising committee of the 2014 FIFA World Cup offered USD 8 million in grants to non-governmental organisations throughout Brazil in its sport for development framework (FIFA, 2014d). Among a large spectrum of initiatives, the Football for Hope Forum took place in 2013 to discuss football contributions to society and the Football for Hope Festival in 2014 gathered 192 young people from 26 countries to experience cultural and educational activities. For the Football for Hope campaign in Brazil, FIFA distributed USD 1,05 million to 26 football-based social development programs (FIFA, 2014d).

Building a better future

FIFA's social responsibility is not limited to FIFA World Cup programs but is also reflected in the long-term supports of organisations "who are using football as a catalyst for positive social change" (FIFA, 2016c). According to the revised budget for football development for the 2015–2018 cycle, USD 1,417 million will be spent on various social initiatives. Of this, USD 1,151 million is aimed at member associations, USD 240 million is for the confederations, and USD 26 million will go to the regional associations (FIFA, 2016d). As part of this budget, FIFA recently supported a wide range of initiatives for human development and peace such as the Diversity Award that celebrates outstanding projects promoting diversity and unity, solidarity, and equality among all people (FIFA, 2017d), an annual FIFA Conference for Equality and Inclusion, the #ENDviolence campaign to stop violence against women and children in Papua New Guinea.

Two main streams of development programs can be identified, the first one supporting football-specific development programs while the second is concerned with broader sustainability issues. In terms of sustainability, the Football for Hope programme, active since 2005, relies on a network of organisations to educate, among other things, on gender equity, discrimination, health, peace building, youth leadership, and life skills. In 2016, the FIFA for Hope programme supported 139 organisations in 58 countries for a total amount of USD 5 million (FIFA, 2016c). Football for the planet is a continuation of the programs initiated during the 2006 FIFA World Cup and aims to mitigate negative environmental consequences of FIFA activities around three key areas: carbon offsetting, sustainable stadiums, and waste management stadiums (FIFA, n.d (g)). Launched during the 1990s, initiatives to promote anti-discrimination and diversity, as well as Fairplay, in football remain the cornerstone of FIFA sustainability strategies.

FIFA also supports key educational and technical football development programmes to improve skills, knowledge, and experience of those individuals in charge of developing football around the world. Strategic investments are done in the area of grassroots football, women's football, football technology, Futsal, beach soccer, youth football, and referees. Launched in May 2016, FIFA Forward is the new leading football-specific development programme and aims to support football development in each of FIFA's 211 member associations, the six confederations, and 14 zonal/regional associations. This program centralised previous streams of funding such as the Goal programme, initiated by Sepp Blatter in 1999 to support football development worldwide, and the Performance programme that aimed to enhance administrative capabilities of member nations (FIFA, 2017c). FIFA Forward is built around three key principles: more investment, more impact, and more oversight.

The first principle – more investment – reflects FIFA increasing financial support to member associations and confederations. Approved by the FIFA Congress for the 2015–2018 budget, the FIFA Forward programme can provide each member nation with USD 5 million in development funding for the four years cycle while a budget of USD 40 million is granted to the six confederations. Various development projects are eligible for new football equipment, internships programmes, women football, or youth competitions. Funding is also available for programmes related to good governance and good managerial practices at all levels. More impact, the second key principle, aims to improve efficiency of FIFA Forward programmes to ensure long-lasting and sustainable results. Each development project is framed in a specific and tailor-made contract with agreed objectives and an implementation plan. More oversight is the last key principles and encompasses monitoring processes to guarantee transparency, accountability, and effectiveness of FIFA-supported initiatives. In 2017, 73 member associations and four confederations were reviewed by three independent auditors, resulting in several remedial measures and the limited release of funds for 22 projects (FIFA, 2017e).

By the end of 2017, 1,554 funding applications were received by the FIFA and USD 665 million in "forward-funding" were approved in several development projects worldwide. Among these projects, important financial investments were realised in South-American countries like Mexico, Colombia, Costa-Rica, and Peru, as well as in Japan, to develop youth football. A new women football league was supported in India while an overall investment of more than USD 900,000 was agreed in 2017 to support Icelandic women's football team.

Concluding comments

The FIFA 2016 reforms do appear to mark a step change in the reform process in that they build upon a frank admission of the organisation's problematic history. In addition, rather than focusing solely on strategy and policy (as could be argued with previous reforms) FIFA's 2016 reforms contained key structural changes aimed at separating its strategic and operational functions and forcing, rather than advising, confederations to be more inclusive. That said, there are issues that are still unclear in terms of the potential effectiveness of the reforms. First, the speed at which the reform process was undertaken from the 2015 scandals to the 2016 reforms has led to some confusion within the FIFA's message. In researching this chapter, it was obvious that previous iterations of strategies that often confuse and contradict the FIFA 2.0 strategy are still present on the organisation's website. Second, one key aspect of governance reform that originally appeared in the 2016 reform documents: anti-doping, remains problematic. FIFA has identified that it has a role in anti-doping, but the importance given to this area of work is questionable. Finally, while the Ethics Committee is still operational at the time of writing, the way in which it will work with the Audit and Compliance Committee is unclear. In summary, most of the critiques of FIFA's previous reforms (see for example Pielke, 2014) had criticised the organisation for attempting to reform too quickly and this certainly appears to be a theme in the 2016 reforms; however, the same critiques also point to FIFA's failure to adopt good governance practices, which does appear to have been addressed.

The issues evident in FIFA's reform have further implications. As noted, FIFA has one dominant source of income; revenues secured as part of its hosting of the World Cup. It appears that external stakeholders view these reforms with a degree of scepticism; several sponsors ended their contracts after the 2014 World Cup, and FIFA have struggled to replace them. At the time of writing, 72 days until the 2018 World Cup opens, FIFA had secured just two regional sponsors, with none from outside Russia. This lack of external faith in FIFA reforms highlights the issues facing FIFA moving forward; the first two years of the 2015–2018 World Cup cycle earned FIFA USD 1,046 million. At the same stage of the 2011–2014 World Cup cycle, FIFA's revenues were nearly double this, with revenue from marketing and broadcasting rights in 2015 and 2016 being one-third of those earned in 2011 and 2012.

However, while revenues have significantly fallen, FIFA's spending has increased over the same period to peak at USD 893 million in 2016, a 35 per cent increase in comparison to 2015. This increase in expenses is mainly due to the launch in May 2016 of the Football Forward development programme that aims to support global football development across all member associations, confederations and zonal/regional associations. In 2016, FIFA invested USD 428 million in development and education programs, that represents almost 48 per cent of its total expenses. While FIFA plans to increase its spending at least until 2018, one could question the long-term viability of these development's investments as the income's sources appear to dry up. Moreover, this level of investment was not included in the initial 2015–2018 budget cycle, which also makes uncertain the level of planning and robustness of these development initiatives.

References

Ahmed, M. (2017) FIFA nets Vivo as third Chinese World Cup sponsor with €400m deal. *Financial Times* [online] 31 May. Retrieved from: https://www.ft.com/content/b849def6-4559-11e7-8519-9f94ee97d996

Alegi, P. (2008) 'A nation to be reckoned with': the politics of World Cup stadium construction in Cape Town and Durban, South Africa. *African Studies*, 67(3), 397–422.

Baade, R. and Matheson, V. (2017) Understanding Drivers of Megaevents in Emerging Economies. In: Flyvbjerg, B. (ed.). *The Oxford Handbook of Megaproject Management*. Oxford: Oxford University Press.

Baade, R.A. and Matheson, V. (2002) Bidding for the Olympics: fool's gold?' In: Barros, C.P., Ibrahimo, M. and Szymanksi, S. (eds.). *Transatlactic Sport: The Comparative Economics of North American and European Sports* (pp. 127–151). London: Edward Elgar.

BBC News (2015) Fifa corruption crisis: Key questions answered. [online] Retrieved from: http://www.bbc.co.uk/news/world-europe-32897066

BBC Sport (2016) 'We will restore the image of Fifa'. [online] Retrieved from: http://www.bbc.co.uk/sport/football/35672725

Blake, H. and Calvert, J. (2015) *The Ugly Game: The Qatari Plot to Buy the World Cup*. London: Simon and Schuster.

Brannagan, P.M. and Rookwood, J. (2016) Sports mega-events, soft power and soft disempowerment: international supporters' perspectives on Qatar's acquisition of the 2022 FIFA World Cup finals. *International Journal of Sport Policy and Politics*, 8(2), 173–188.

Business Insider (2015) FIFA made an insane amount of money off of Brazil's $15 billion World Cup. [online] Retrieved from: http://uk.businessinsider.com/fifa-brazil-world-cup-revenue-2015-3?r=US&IR=T

Chisari, F. (2006) When football went global: televising the 1966 World Cup. *Historical Social Research*, 31(1), 42–54.

Conn, D. (2017) *The Fall of the House of FIFA*. London: Vintage.

Conway, R. (2014) *FIFA corruption report: Who is to blame and what happens now?* [online] Retrieved from: https://www.bbc.co.uk/sport/football/30042309

Cornelissen, S. (2011) More than a sporting chance? Appraising the sport for development legacy of the 2010 FIFA World Cup. *Third World Quarterly*, 32(3), 503–529.

Darby, P. (2008) Stanley Rous's 'own goal': football politics, South Africa and the Contest for the FIFA presidency in 1974. *Soccer & Society* 9(2), 259–272.

Electronic Arts Inc. (2016) *Fiscal Year 2017 Proxy Statement and Annual Report*. Redwood City: Electronic Arts Inc.

FIFA (1976) *1974 FIFA World Cup: Official FIFA-Report*. Zurich: FIFA.

FIFA (1982) *1982 FIFA World Cup in Spain: Report of FIFA*. Zurich: FIFA.

FIFA (2007) *Financial Report 2006*. [online] Retrieved from: https://resources.fifa.com/mm/document/affederation/administration/51/52/65/2006_fifa_ar_en_1766.pdf

FIFA (2011) *Financial Report 2010*. [online] Retrieved from: http://www.fifa.com/mm/document/affederation/administration/01/39/20/45/web_fifa_fr2010_eng%5B1%5D.pdf

FIFA (2014a) Women's Football Survey. [online] Retrieved from: https://img.fifa.com/image/upload/emtgxvp0ibnebltlvi3b.pdf

FIFA (2014b) FIFA World Cup Sponsorship Strategy [online] Retrieved from: http://www.fifa.com/about-fifa/marketing/sponsorship/index.html

FIFA (2014c) Brand Collaborations [online] Retrieved from: http://www.fifa.com/about-fifa/marketing/licensing/brand-collaborations.html

FIFA (2014d) *Sustainability Report: 2014 FIFA World Cup Brazil*. [online] Retrieved from: https://img.fifa.com/image/upload/educsd2hgasief3yeoyt.pdf

FIFA (2015a) *Financial Report 2014*. [online] Retrieved from: https://img.fifa.com/image/upload/e4e5lkxrbqvgscxgjnhx.pdf

FIFA (2015b) FIFA World Cup™ organisers underline sustainability efforts and detail 2014 legacy plans. [online] Retrieved from: http://www.fifa.com/worldcup/news/y=2015/m=1/news=fifa-world-cuptm-organisers-underline-sustainability-efforts-and-detai-2509097.html

FIFA (2016a) FIFA 2.0: the vision for the future. [online] Retrieved from: http://resources.fifa.com/mm/document/affederation/generic/02/84/35/01/fifa_2.0_vision_low_neu.17102016_neutral.pdf

FIFA (2016b) *Governance Report 2016*. Presented to the 67th FIFA Congress, Manama, Bahrain, 11 May 2017. [online] Retrieved from https://resources.fifa.com/mm/document/affederation/administration/02/87/89/23/gr2016env1_neutral.pdf

FIFA (2016c) FIFA extends the reach of its global social development initiative. [online] Retrieved from http://www.fifa.com/sustainability/news/y=2016/m=4/news=fifa-extends-the-reach-of-its-global-social-development-initiative-2779835.html

FIFA (2016d) *Financial and Governance Report 2015.* Zurich: FIFA.

FIFA (2017a) FIFA's Human Rights Policy. [online] Retrieved from: http://resources.fifa.com/mm/document/affederation/footballgovernance/02/89/33/12/fifashumanrightspolicy_neutral.pdf

FIFA (2017b) Guide to the Bidding Process for the 2026 FIFA World Cup. [online] Retrieved from: http://resources.fifa.com/mm/document/affederation/administration/02/91/88/61/en_guidetothe biddingprocessforthe2026fifaworldcup_neutral.pdf

FIFA (2017c) *Financial Report 2016.* [online] Retrieved from: https://resources.fifa.com/mm/document/affederation/footballgovernance/02/87/89/44/fr2016digitalen_neutral.pdf

FIFA (2017d) FIFA celebrates International Day of Sport for Development and Peace. [online] Retrieved from: http://www.fifa.com/sustainability/news/y=2017/m=4/news=fifa-celebrates-international-day-of-sport-for-development-and-peace-2878446.html

FIFA (2017e) *FIFA Activity report 2016.* [online] Retrieved from: https://resources.fifa.com/mm/document/affederation/administration/02/87/89/07/fifa_activity_report_2016_en.23052017_neutral.pdf

FIFA (n.d. (a)) History of FIFA – Foundation. [online] Retrieved from: http://www.fifa.com/about-fifa/who-we-are/history/index.html

FIFA (n.d. (b)) The reform process – chronology. [online] Retrieved from: http://www.fifa.com/governance/news/y=2016/m=1/news=the-reform-process-chronology-2756734.html

FIFA (n.d. (c)) The reform process. [online] Retrieved from: http://www.fifa.com/governance/how-fifa-works/the-reform-process.html

FIFA (n.d. (d)) FIFA tournaments. [online] Retrieved from: http://www.fifa.com/fifa-tournaments/archive/index.html

FIFA (n.d. (e)) *Host City Agreement.* Zurich: FIFA

FIFA (n.d. (f)) Retail & merchandising. [online] Retrieved from: http://www.fifa.com/about-fifa/marketing/licensing/consumer-retail.html

FIFA World Cup 2018 (n.d.) Marketing. [online] Retrieved from: https://www.fifa.com/worldcup/organisation/partners/

Fortunato, J.A. (2017) The FIFA crisis: examining sponsor response options. *Journal of Contingencies and Crisis Management,* 25(2), 68–78.

Fraser, I. (2015) FIFA's finances – where does all the money come from? *The Telegraph* [online] 29 May. Retrieved from: https://www.telegraph.co.uk/sport/football/fifa/11635985/Fifas-finances-where-does-all-the-money-come-from.html

Gibson, O. (2015) Sepp Blatter and Michel Platini banned from football for eight years by Fifa. *The Guardian* [online] 21 December. Retrieved from: https://www.theguardian.com/football/2015/dec/21/sepp-blatter-michel-platini-banned-from-football-fifa

Griffiths, E. (2000) *Bidding for Glory: Why South Africa lost the Olympic and World Cup bids, and how to win next time.* Johannesburg: Jonathan Ball Publishers.

Homewood, B. (2016) FIFA announces new sponsorship deal, says more on the way. [online] Retrieved from: https://www.reuters.com/article/us-soccer-fifa-sponsor/fifa-announces-new-sponsorship-deal-says-more-on-the-way-idUSKCN0WK1R1

Humphrey, L. and Fraser, G. (2016) 2010 FIFA World Cup stadium investment: does the post-event usage justify the expenditure? *African Review of Economics and Finance,* 8(2), 3–22.

Jennings, A. (2006) *Foul!: The Secret World of FIFA: Bribes, Vote Rigging and Ticket Scandals.* London: HarperSport.

Jerabek, M.M., Ferrerira de Andrade, A.M. and Figueroa, A.M. (2017) FIFA's hegemony: examples from World Cup hosting countries. *Global Society,* 31(3), 417–440.

Müller, M. (2014) What makes an event a mega-event? Definitions and sizes. *Leisure Studies,* 34(6), 624–642.

Onwumechili, C. and Bedeau, K. (2017) Analysis of fifa's attempt at image repair. *Communication & Sport,* 5(4), 407–427.

Pielke, R. (2014) An evaluation of the FIFA governance reform process of 2011–2013. In: Frawley S., Adair D. (eds.), *Managing the Football World Cup.* London: Palgrave Macmillan.

Suzuki, N. (2014) The FIFA World Cup 2010 and its legacy on "sport for development" practices in South African Cities. In: Kevin Young , Chiaki Okada (ed.). *Sport, Social Development and Peace* (Research in the Sociology of Sport, Volume 8) (pp. 127–145). Emerald Group Publishing Limited.

Taylor, M. (2008) *The Association Game: A History of British Football*. Londondon: Oxon.

Tomlinson, A. (2000) FIFA and the men who made it. *Soccer & Society*, 1(1), 55–71.

Topping, A. (2014) Panini World Cup sticker swaps have become a worldwide craze. *The Guardian* [online] 11 June. Retrieved from: https://www.theguardian.com/football/2014/jun/11/panini-2014-world-cup-sticker-swap-worldwide-craze

Tyers, S. (2014) How World Cup TV coverage has changed since the 1950s. *The Guardian* [online] 7 July. Retrieved from: https://www.theguardian.com/football/when-saturday-comes-blog/2014/jul/07/world-cup-tv-television-coverage-changed-1954-1958

Wilson, B. (2014) World Cup 2014 sponsors face whole new ball game [online] Retrieved from: http://www.bbc.co.uk/news/business-27667473

Zimbalist, A. (2016) *Circus Maximus: The Economic Gamble Behind Hosting the Olympics and the World Cup*. Washington: The Brookings Institution.

35

UEFA

Kenneth Cortsen

UEFA case – methodological considerations

This case study (Hamel, 1993; Stake, 1994; Maaløe, 2002; Ellet, 2007; Yin, 2008) about UEFA is under the contextual umbrella of football, business, management, and commercialisation and is grounded in symbolic interactionism (Mead and Morris, 1934; Blumer, 1986; Fast, 1996) and relevant sports management literature (Gladden, Milne, and Sutton, 1998; Cortsen, 2016b). It is supported by quantitative and qualitative desk research and accompanied by a semi-structured interview (Brinkmann and Kvale, 2007) with Frits Ahlstrøm, who is a former media director for UEFA. Ahlstrøm has been involved with UEFA since the beginning of the UEFA Champions League (UCL) in 1992 and points out that his contribution is based on "personal considerations and experiences" and that he is not commenting as an official UEFA representative. Methodologically, the contribution attempts to critically discuss and elaborate on four types of case situations (Ellet, 2007). All four situations (problems, decisions, evaluations, and rules) are subject to critical reflections on UEFA's role in the practical development of European football. Quantitative data about the economics of football helps to introduce the historic commercial development and current commercial status of European football and UEFA and to support qualitative points. The combination of quantitative and qualitative data is central to guiding the structure.

The purpose of this case study about UEFA's competitive position is to elaborate on contextual factors (Ellet, 2007) matched with theoretical frameworks that emphasise perspectives on why and how UEFA shapes the football business in a sphere of enormous spotlight, managerial complexity, stakeholder expectations, and commercialisation. The main concentration is on UEFA's premium product brand, namely, the UEFA Champions League (UCL). Moreover, the contribution seeks to inspire scholars and practitioners in the business of football to improve their football management interactions based on their aim to identify and understand vital aspects of UEFA's situation (Ellet, 2007). So, the reader should strive to read critically through the lines in order to consider how contextual factors relating to UEFA are influenced by time[1] and what implications that adds to the business of football in Europe and abroad. Hence, the learning outcome aims at engaging readers in self-guided learning in which they, through critical thinking, may be inspired to develop sustainable business models in football.

Why is UEFA and the UEFA Champions League an interesting case?

UEFA has become a global symbol of the representation of elite sporting performances at the national team and club levels and its influence on the business of football is fundamental. The cohesion between sporting and business performances in football (Cortsen, 2015) is prevailing and it consequently addresses the meaning of time and context in the business of football. The history of European football and UEFA, and thereby the decision to restructure the tournament format and the concept of the UCL, have boosted UEFA's current commercial status and will continue to do so in the years to come. Today, the practical environment of European football and UEFA is characterised by money being even more decisive in an era in which top clubs like FC Bayern Munich, Manchester United, Paris Saint-Germain, Real Madrid, and FC Barcelona are global brands (Wilkesmann, 2014). These brands are put in play in a dynamic (and to some extent interchangeable) global football marketplace where there is an ongoing flow of varied (or sometimes very contrasting) interactions with contextual factors. These factors may include Germany's "50+1 rule", UEFA Financial Fair Play, the strength of the UCL, the influence from new football states such as Qatar and China, or with commercial stakeholder groups such as fans, media, and sponsors. The result is a European football texture, which has football's passionate appeal while facing an increasing managerial complexity.

Milestones in the development of European football – vitality of the 1990s?

Professional football at the international stage went through a rapid change during the 1990s (Desbordes, 2007). Milestones in the development of the business of football in this era were especially the implementation of the UCL in 1992 and the Bosman ruling in 1995. The UCL is the pinnacle of UEFA's commercial success while the Bosman ruling refers to the judgement of the European Court of Justice concerning the Jean-Marc Bosman case. The latter resulted in enhanced mobility of football players across international borders (Simmons, 1997). The ruling also shed light on the importance of football's transfer market and its capability of transforming the sporting and business performances of European leagues and clubs due to the appeal of UEFA's high-profile leagues and clubs (Cortsen, 2014). A decisive argument for emphasising the UEFA CHL is that the tournament has profited highly from the improved supply of football superstars compared to other football tournaments and the demand seems to be insatiable at this top level, which has led to increasing commercialisation rates. Therefore, the UCL and its role as a premium sports product takes a central role in this UEFA contribution in which UEFA's progressive commercial development and professionalisation highlight the popularity of football on European soil.

The ecosystem of football

Football's ecosystem provides an optimal realm of understanding in this social science and business-oriented perspective. The ecosystem shown in Figure 35.1 has its focal point in business and stakeholder models from the economics of football (Callejo and Forcadell, 2006; Breitbarth and Harris, 2008; Demil and Lecocq, 2010; Teece, 2010; Morrow, 2013; Otto and Aier, 2013; Rossi, Thrassou, and Vrontis, 2013; Weiller and Neely, 2013; Lombardi, Manfredi, and Nappo, 2014; Foster, O'Reilly, and Dávila, 2016). The ecosystem of international football such as fans, media, sponsors, national football associations (FAs), and clubs are included to portray essential stakeholder groups in a European football context.

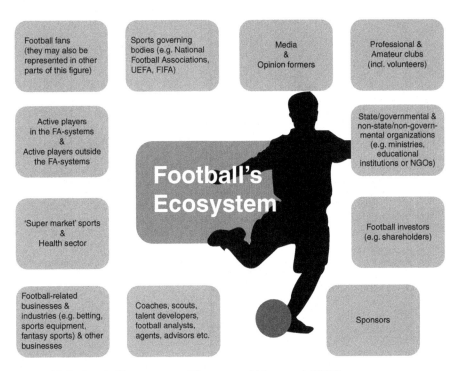

Figure 35.1   Football's ecosystem (Cortsen and Nørgaard, 2015)

However, Figure 35.1 positions football's governing bodies such as FIFA, UEFA, and national FAs without relating to the power dimension that these organisations are the governing entities at, respectively global, European, and national football level. With this in mind, the contribution's grounding in symbolic interactionism features (according to UEFA's values) the importance of acknowledging that UEFA's commercial position and that of European football is dependent on the reciprocal interaction between UEFA and other actors in football's ecosystem. In that regard, the integration of these actors determines the foundation for managerial, commercial and sporting development in European football.

The commercial appeal of football, UEFA, and the UEFA Champions League

According to Figure 35.2, UEFA has experienced significant revenue growth since the 2004/2005 season.[2] The commercial appeal of football as the most popular sport globally (Giulianotti, 1999; Giulianotti and Robertson, 2004; Kuper and Szymanski, 2012) has spilled over on UEFA's ability to generate revenue growth. UEFA's revenue generation accounted for €659.2 million in the 2004/2005 season compared to a revenue generation of €4,579.8 million in the 2015/2016 season (UEFA, 2017a).[3] The numbers showcase UEFA's impressive economic development measured on revenue growth in the past decade. That ability to monetise on football rights is a big contrast to UEFA's role in the organisation's starting phase in which UEFA according to Ahlstrøm worked as "an administrator of tournaments and regulations and so on. There were not really any finances. The only finances in UEFA came from the very little share of gate receipts from the UEFA matches at the time, i.e., club tournaments and European Championships." This commercially underdeveloped approach at the time compares poorly to

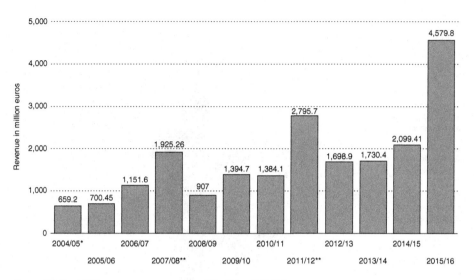

Figure 35.2 UEFA revenue generation (Statista, 2017a)

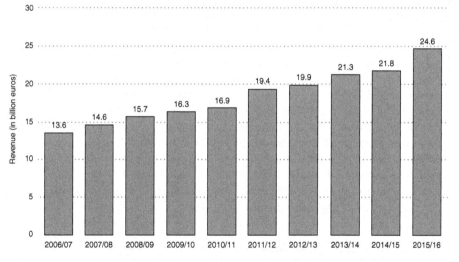

Figure 35.3 Market size of Europe's professional football market (Deloitte, 2017; Statista, 2017b)

the contemporary edition of UEFA labelled with strong capitalisation efforts. Ahlstrøm notes, "UEFA did not build fortunes or generate revenues, which like today are distributed to all the national football associations and clubs." From a critical perspective, UEFA's revenue growth is not only an illustration of UEFA's commercial strength but also a mirror of the fact that the market for professional football in Europe has grown significantly in a similar time period as seen in Figure 35.3. However, the football economy (like many other industries) depicts a market scenario where the organisations at the top of the branding hierarchy, i.e., the premium brands, have good opportunities to sustain a solid revenue generation. For instance, an American study (O'Reilly and Nadeau, 2006) has identified several factors considerably linked to revenue generation in professional sports, e.g., market support, winning, competition, market age, and heritage. While there are differences between the American and European sports model (Shropshire, 2011; Cortsen, 2016b), O'Reilly and Nadeau (2006) suggest that a strong sports product underlined by a strong legacy is vital in revenue generation. The latter supports the exemplification that UEFA's legacy and the strength of its products such as the UCL boost revenue generation in a European football context. However, a future model specifically addressed to European football should attempt to identify more football-specific variables to be operationalised and a conceptual model that accounts for indirect and direct relationships, as suggestions for future improvements to business models in football cannot be isolated from time and context.

The fact that European football is in high demand is also evidenced in the development of revenue generation of the top five European football leagues in the past two decades, cf. Figure 35.4. Though the revenue growth of the English Premier League is related to the league's global business appeal and a derived effect of the league's sales of media rights, cf. Figure 35.5. The value of the media rights of the English Premier League surpasses the value of tournaments operated by UEFA and other domestic European football leagues. Nevertheless, the English Premier League's position at top of football's broadcasting pyramid portrays an interesting commercial tendency in the European football market. This is grounded in that the cohesion between sporting and business performances (Cortsen, 2016a) in European football are manifested in the interdependencies and interactions between the Premier League and other European leagues, including UEFA as the overall governing body of European football. For instance, the portion of English clubs in top ten (six brands in top ten, led by Manchester United) of the most valuable football brands worldwide is dominant (BrandFinance, 2017; Statista, 2017e). Transfers and economic trickle-down effects (Cortsen, 2017) across European leagues have in combination with inter-European competitions in UEFA-tournaments like the UCL reinforced the fact that UEFA and the European football market takes the leading position in global football. The best and toughest leagues and clubs measured on sporting quality and business strength are in Europe and that creates a positive spiral of attracting the best players in the world to come to play in

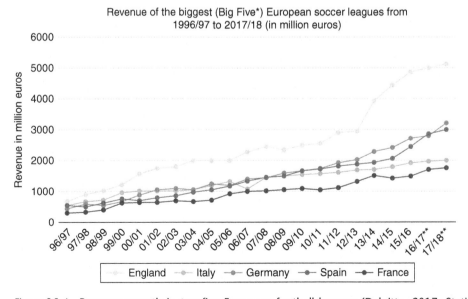

Figure 35.4 Revenue growth in top five European football leagues (Deloitte, 2017; Statista, 2017c)

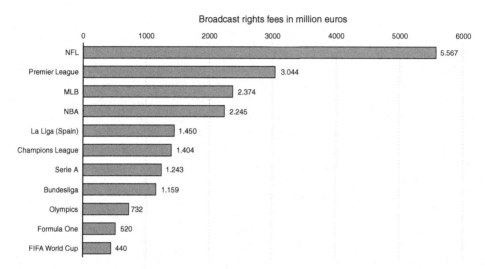

Figure 35.5 Broadcast rights fees in major professional sports leagues (Statista, 2017d)

Europe and boost the commercial potential of European football even further. This is supported by the theoretical frameworks integrated into this contribution, cf. the following sections, and in the case study methodology that emphasises that relevant case studies must strive to build a bridge between contextual factors and the applied theoretical framework (Ellet, 2007).

The branding power of football, UEFA, and the UEFA Champions League

What constitutes a strong football brand? Sports brands cannot be isolated from time and context and are dynamic phenomena that should strive to be meaningful for people "right here, right now" (Cortsen, 2016b). The same applies to football. Thus, UEFA's historic improvement measured on sporting quality and commercialisation has manifested its current brand equity and leveraged a sound platform for future progress, which is aligned with Holt's (2004) idea that brand loyalty is a product of the social network, e.g., followers. This may be relatively clarified by introducing a traditional brand management process for brand building, cf. the notions of brand awareness, brand image, brand equity, and brand loyalty (Shank and Lyberger, 2014; Smith and Stewart, 2014), and by applying a comprehensive model (Gladden, Milne, and Sutton, 1998) inspired by Aaker (1991) but for considering brand equity specifically directed at the business of sports.

Brand equity, is defined by "the 'added value' with which a brand endows a product; this added value can be viewed from the perspective of the firm, the trade or the consumer" (Farquhar, 1989), by "the difference in value between a branded product and its generic equivalent" (Shank and Lyberger, 2014) but also by "a set of assets such as name awareness, loyal customers, perceived quality and associations that are linked to a brand, its name and symbol, that add to or subtract from the value provided by a product or service" (Aaker, 1991; Gladden, Milne, and Sutton, 1998). Sports branding has its roots in classic branding theory (Kotler, 1965; Aaker, 1991; Keller, 1993) and defining a sports brand is a multidimensional and complex process (Cortsen, 2016b). Classic branding and sports branding have moved beyond the American Marketing Association's (AMA) definition from the 1960s. AMA defined a brand as something related to a name, mark, or symbol that is associated with a product or a service.[4] Critically, a brand is not as static as defined back then and UEFA's history proves it. Andersen (2007) mentions four perspectives on branding under which it is emphasised that contemporary versions of branding apply relational and cultural elements in the brand management process. Therefore, branding becomes more interactive, which helps to understand the influential brand equity of UEFA and the UCL. For instance, the UCL is a prestigious tournament and went through a remodelling from the European Cup to the UCL in 1992. This change was motivated by motives of commercialisation and to gain more branding control of the tournament (Chadwick and Holt, 2007; Cortsen, 2016b). The reinvention of the UCL tournament format in 1992 reflects viable sports business development and solid revenue generation for UEFA and its participating clubs. Former media director of UEFA Frits Ahlstrøm views the UCL as "a concept, which is sustainable and has only been enhanced through small adjustments." However, this may help to clarify why UEFA did not change the concept drastically; football fans worldwide simply adopted the sports product (UCL), which has been in increasing demand since 1992, cf. Figure 35.6. The foundation of a strong sports product is to be found in the complexity that encircles the product, e.g., sports business factors like team, organisational, and market-related antecedents (Gladden, Milne, and Sutton, 1998). For instance, Ahlstrøm points out that UCL is "incredibly well organised ... There is no one better to organise than UEFA. It is built from scratch." Considering the interplay between different groups of antecedents, UEFA benefits from the reputation of being the strongest continent in the world when it comes to club football, participation of the best teams, players, and coaches, and extensive media coverage. For instance, UEFA and its competitions led by the UCL underscore the interplay in that UCL showcases players like Messi, Neymar, Cristiano Ronaldo, and other superstars every year managed by legendary coach names such as Guardiola or Heynckes, and representing successful clubs like Real Madrid,

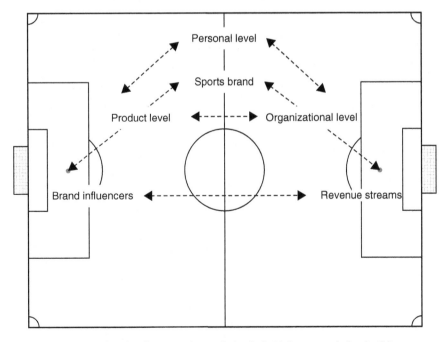

Figure 35.6 Two levels of interactions of the hybrid framework for building a sports brand (Cortsen, 2016b)

FC Barcelona, Manchester United, Liverpool FC, Juventus, Bayern Munich, or FC Barcelona. It seems like "success breeds success." These team-related antecedents have a spill-over effect on the organisation-related antecedents. Reflect on the legacy of Manchester United tracing back to the famous "Busby Babes" or the resurrection and the feeling of being "united" after the tragic plane crash in Munich in 1958 and the club's domestic and European dominance in 1999 due to a "very united" class of 92 and consider what it means for the business of the club that this happened at a time where media companies really had started to invest in European and English football. Historic football and legacies live in football clubs, e.g., Real Madrid and its reputation of pursuing the best players in the world. Players like Alfredo di Stefano, Francisco Gento, and Ferenc Puskas may thus have a connection to the "Galacticos strategy" introduced by President Perez, which brought David Beckham, Zinedine Zidane, Ronaldo (first the Brazilian and later CR7), and Luis Figo to Madrid. The strategy envisioned bringing the best players to Real Madrid. It illustrates that football has been and still is (to a higher extent) a marketing-, event- and media-driven spectacle. It has brought about the challenge that transfer amounts have been pushed to the skies when especially Real Madrid in the last decade but also other teams have broken the transfer record. However, it helps to cement the brand positioning of Real Madrid as one of (if not) the greatest club in the world with 12 European Cup/Champions League titles. Top clubs may stage specific situations like Madrid's transfer strategy in which different antecedents play together to create an offensive facilitation of commercial scoring opportunities that affect how the public eye perceives the quality of the club's brand and generate enormous exposure, a comprehensive boost of the entire business model and a better marketplace perception. It throws the brand of the club in the limelight and establishes the excitement, entertainment, and product delivery meant to encourage corporate and fan support and to positively transform the sporting and business performances of the club through the brand equity factors like perceived quality, brand awareness, brand association(s), and brand loyalty.

UEFA and the UEFA Champions League – a case of hybrid sports branding

Sports branding research (Cortsen, 2016b) takes brand building in sports a step further when illustrating "two levels of interactions of the hybrid framework for sports branding," cf. Figure 35.6. First of all, "hybrid sports branding" indicates that the three constructed sports branding levels, i.e., the personal, product, and organisational branding levels, interact.

The orchestration of the transformed UCL concept in 1992 emphasises the intersection between sports development, commercialisation, and politics and is a relevant example of hybrid sports branding, cf. Figure (F = CAP). Ahlstrøm acknowledges that former UEFA general secretary from Germany,

> Gerhard Aigner got the idea for the tournament, but what was difficult for him was that he needed political support to realize the implementation of the tournament ... Gerhard Aigner had the luck that Lennart Johansson became UEFA president. And on top of being a football man, he was also a businessman. And he had the interest to leave a mark as a president immediately and talked to Aigner about the opportunities.

Therefore, they decided to implement the new concept of the UCL based on the commercial ideas of Klaus Hempel and Jürgen Lenz from Swiss-based sports marketing agency Television Event and Media Marketing (TEAM)[5] (Chadwick and Holt, 2007). According to Ahlstrøm

"UEFA needed CHF 90 million to realise the idea. Nowadays we are talking about more than almost one and a half billion euros!" That presents a noteworthy narrative as to how European football has been commercialised since 1992. Ahlstrøm says:

> Who would make such a guarantee? The UEFA treasurer, Egidius Braun, checked with Deutsche Bank but they were not interested. Then he contacted the Kirch Group, founded by the German media entrepreneur Leo Kirch, and set up a meeting for Lennart Johansson with Dr. Helmut Thoma, the managing director of RTL Television. Football is the number one sport in Germany, he said. We have Michael Schumacher, Boris Becker, and Steffi Graf but above all in this country we have FC Bayern München. So he offered to pay CHF 70 million for the TV rights for the UEFA Champions League in Germany. Lennart Johansson is forever grateful for this.

A commercial football hybrid was formed. Ahlstrøm comments, "And it is fantastic to see how it has evolved and what it is impressive for me is the triangle with clubs, sponsors and television stations. It is the same today." The triangle reflects the "hybrid" and thus interactive branding processes that involves different brand levels from Papin, Maldini, Van Basten, Rijkaard and Baresi in the 1992/1993 season to Messi, Neymar, Cristiano Ronaldo of this year's 2017/2018 campaign at the personal branding level to the branding of the clubs or of UEFA's values (Figure 35.7) at the organisational branding level and to the events at the product branding level. Sponsors and media companies buy the rights to broadcast the spectacle of the UCL to acquire a superb show business cocktail in which the hybrid character of the branding process is intensified by how the mutually dependent brand influencers and revenue streams also influence the brand of UEFA and in particular the UCL.

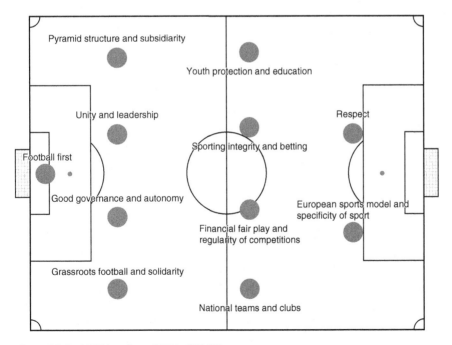

Figure 35.7 UEFA's values (UEFA, 2017b)

The hybrid nature of the UEFA and the UCL brands goes beyond top football and that's a huge strength of the UEFA system. The visions of giving back to the grassroots level and the national football associations supported Aigner and Johansson's idea regarding the UCL and Ahlstrøm supplements:

> When Lennart came in, he had no support from the Executive Committee. The conservative members couldn't follow a man with such vision although they saw as a very trustable person. Even Gerhard Aigner was a bit cautious about the economy. But, fortunately, they gave him a chance immediately because they saw that here is a man with visions and first and foremost here is a trustable person. Lennart was very honest and so was Aigner so there were no scandals, never ... and what also happened was that Aigner or Lennart never betrayed the small clubs ... of course, the UCL must be at a level; first and foremost, from a sport perspective. It must be the best teams that participate. The best teams generate the biggest revenues. But there must be room for smaller clubs to reach something, to participate. And if they are good enough, they will go far. But at the same time, they felt that they had an obligation for football in general terms, from the grassroots level and so on. And that's why a solidarity system was introduced, which is working great today. It is beyond belief how much money the UCL and the European Championships give in the form of ROIs to clubs and national associations. We are talking about many millions every year which benefit everyone.

So, UEFA and the UCL are not just about sporting success, 3–5–2 or 4–4–2 systems, but the depth of the UCL covers tactical revolutions as FC Barcelona under the leadership of Guardiola, FC Porto's CHL triumph under Mourinho, or Borussia Dortmund's revival under Jürgen Klopp to the solidarity system, which is well aligned with UEFA's values that first and foremost put "football first," cf. Figure 35.7.

However, some things in the UCL remain relatively untouched if they work, which is important in terms of brand alignment (Kunkel, Funk, and Hill, 2013). As Ahstrøm puts it:

> The logo is more or less the same. UCL has only made small adjustments. The music composed by Tony Britten is just as popular today as back then [read: in 1992] ... there are similar starting times [read: for the matches] so that people can plan ahead of time. They know that there is UCL on a particular date and that it takes place 20.45 central European time.

The amount of small adjustments in a sphere of dynamic sports branding reflects that the UCL is relatively recession-proof. This is supported by Ahlstrøm's opinion that the UCL had an extraordinary development:

> It's amazing. It gets bigger and bigger ... I don't think it is over yet ... It is the best football tournament in the world; it is also better than the World Cup and the European Championships. What happens in terms of the World Cup and the European Championships is that it is your country that plays. The team only has players from your own country and that's why it has a popularity, which actually is at the same level as the UCL although the quality on the pitch is not the same as the UCL, which has the best players ... I don't see any threats to the UCL. I see a fantastic strength in that we since 1992 have had a concept, which is sustainable and only has been improved with small adjustments. People know what they get and there has not been any erratic course.

Inspired by the need for improved commercial competencies, UEFA's hybrid approach to branding of and monetising on the UCL proved that UEFA has done a remarkable job in terms of commercialising their rights. Ahlstrøm points out:

> Team Marketing still plays a role. They have fantastic experience. They have a network because the network is so important. Personal relations are often helpful in closing deals faster and easier … They understood how to service their customers. They got the full outcome of the investment of paying so many millions for the rights.

UEFA – hybrid sports branding beats challenges

Since the UCL was revitalised in 1992, UEFA has exposed a strong belief in the concept despite various challenges. For instance, challenges revolve around the pressure from internal disagreements[6] or from Europe's top clubs regarding the wish to create their own "pirate league" to get a bigger chunk of the enormous flow of money in top flight football but none of these challenges have limited the concept and its unfolding. The strength of UEFA's and UCL's brands is manifested in the sense that sports brands are phenomena in motion but UEFA and the UCL have been capable of turning the huge global interest for football into sustainable brand development and increased monetisation. Hence, the dynamic nature of sports brands is also reflected in the examples of UEFA and UCL via enhanced profitability over the years. The pressure on UEFA from the top clubs is symbolised in that these clubs want more money to work with. However, Ahlstrøm does not perceive it to be a problem as the big clubs generate many revenues. He states: "I have never been bothered by the fact that the big clubs earn much money. These clubs also generate the money. That is, they do that because of the investments that they make." Given the flow of money in football, Ahlstrøm lists the football agents as a major challenge in that: "In terms of me having a problem with all the money that flows around in [European] football, there is too much money that goes to agents and disappears from football." The role of football agents is a potent problem for UEFA as the interests of agents do not generate the same benefits for the ecosystem as clubs reinvesting in the game on the pitch, e.g., via transfers of players or investments in infrastructure. Despite the big flow of money, Ahlstrøm believes that UEFA has been capable of maintaining a sound balance. The money flow is part of the game and he does not have a problem with that

> as long as we can be sure that it favours the sport of football and it sure does. And that is why UEFA has stood up against every attempt to create so-called piracy leagues … That will never happen. And it would be sad for the sport of football because Manchester City to take a club, which I am close to at the moment, could not at all live without playing in the [English] Premier League … You see, they would still like to play against Crystal Palace and Leicester City FC.

In a critical remark to piracy leagues, Ahlstrøm mentions the contrast between the American and European sports business models and supplements that

> withdrawing your team from the national league will be the death of football, without doubt. We are not in the US. The Americans do things their way in case of moving an entire club to a new city or selling a club to another location or another person and so on. And they play without relegation and promotion and so on. We have a very different tradition and it is so manifested that we must not touch it. That would be dangerous. And that's why I say that every time these comments occur, I don't understand why the press doesn't take it with a grain of salt.

UEFA has a solid strategic position to resist the threats from top clubs wanting to distance themselves from UEFA in hunt for more revenues. National team competitions play a central role. Ahlstrøm notes:

> that despite a few exceptions there are no one who seriously want to break out. And if there are some who break out then they won't get back. And that limits their opportunities. The players, who play for them, they also exclude themselves from the family. How things are today works well. There are always some things that can be discussed and get better. But considering the amount of money involved, there is a fine balance.

Consider how this fits the "hybrid" branding approach in that players are dependent on clubs and vice versa, and clubs are dependent on governing bodies and vice versa and the national teams play a role in this equation. Ahlstrøm says:

When clubs complain about sending players to the national teams it is a silly from my perspective. First of all, national team football is superior because in relation to national team football all the fans reflect a national identity and that's why national team football is important. If the clubs had the chance to prohibit national team football they would dig their own grave because people don't want to give up national team football. And it is also paradoxical that when clubs sell players then focus is on how many national team caps the player has played. And the higher the number of national team games, the higher the price of the player.

This conversation sparked a critical discussion about the "breading ground" of football. The foundation of football is the public, i.e., football used to be a public service product. So, with the invasion of elements like foreign ownership, increasing capital injections, and commercialisation of football over time on one side in contrast to football as the people's game on the other side, there is a need for intensified governance and accountability in European football. The level of complexity in the governance and management of football in Europe has accelerated while widening the playing field to a global market. Ahlstrøm notes that Sheikh Mansour from Abu Dhabi, who acquired Manchester City in 2008 (Manchester City, 2017), has taken the club to a new level of commercial and sporting maturity, and that

> he has sustained all the values, which were in Manchester City, and the club is one big family … he made it clear from the beginning when he acquired the club and threw all this money in the club that "you have to be good to each other and show good behaviour." Moreover, he emphasized this when he had given the club the fantastic complex they have, the academy they have.

Sheikh Mansour made sure that building the new academy did not have a negative influence on the population that was located in the area. As Ahlstrøm supplements, Mansour went to the local authorities and said: "we will offer you that I will build new housing for the people that live here in the community and they will not have to pay more than they have paid for their old ones." One problem area in European football is that ownership often comes with huge self-interest but the City example replicates a scenario of sound responsibility for the clubs' stakeholders, which is aligned with UEFA's values (UEFA, 2017b). New challenges have arrived in the wake of the FIFA corruption scandal, which have threatened the level of integrity in the global sports landscape. Other challenges, which UEFA must face like other sports and football governing bodies, include the threat of match-fixing and the role of economic responsibility (Carroll, 1979). However, Ahlstrøm notes that UEFA shows economic responsibility in his comment that: "What I may have a problem with is if the clubs spend more money than they have and go bankrupt. And that's why UEFA talks a lot about Financial Fairplay."

UEFA is held accountable by many stakeholders (Chadwick and Holt, 2007). Football is entertainment and therefore a sport with massive impassioned appeal. The entertainment happens on the pitch but also through the peripheral products, services and/or events that take place outside the pitch before, during and after the game and are put in play to entertain the football fans from various segments via more comprehensive football experiences (Pine and Gilmore, 1999). The dynamism of football is influenced by various brand influencers (Cortsen and Nørgaard, 2015; Cortsen, 2016b; Fried and Mumcu, 2016; Harrison and Bukstein, 2016) such as fans, media, sponsors, participants (players at all levels), clubs, CSR (football's ability to change the world), "big data," digitisation, increased involvement of business in football, increased need for governance, transparency, and good management practices. Football's appeal is a strong driver for UEFA's commercial development in which the UCL acts as a "cash cow" (Cortsen, 2013). It is a tendency that the European professional football landscape operates with vast sums of money when buying and selling players on the transfer market. This tendency shapes European football with the world's biggest cluster of top professional football leagues and clubs based on commercial power and sporting quality. It symbolises the meaning of cohesion between sporting quality and monetisation with the balance between sporting success and entertainment in mind (Cortsen, 2013). The relevance of a sports brand is established by what a brand means for its surrounding stakeholders. In the relational and cultural approaches to branding (Andersen, 2007; Cortsen, 2016b), there are parallels to the importance of cohesion between the sporting quality and the business performance of the UCL, e.g., fans help to determine if a sports brand is successful. Ahlstrøm mentions:

> It is important and without money you cannot improve the product. You cannot improve talent development. And that's why it is vital that the revenues are shared and I think that UEFA's template is formidable. It is clear that if we look at Denmark, no matter how much money FIFA and UEFA allocates to the Danish FA, especially UEFA, we had to close the business if we didn't have all the volunteers. They save Denmark much money … I also believe that top football has a responsibility and that is something of interest for UEFA, which pays much attention to the practice of social responsibility of national associations … In all my years, UEFA was very financially conscious … all matters were thoroughly considered before spending money because so much had to go back to football to advance the game.

Basically, good sporting quality positively reinforces the business model in football and solid business performance allows opportunities to invest in the sporting infrastructure and development. Consequently, it supports the notion that revenue streams are an inevitable part of the branding process in European football at UEFA.

European top football is a "money game" (Cortsen, 2013) and very much driven by quality sporting performances and its interdependence with commercialisation. The entire business model of UEFA has been boosted by the strength of sporting quality in UEFA competitions. In relation to the UCL, Gerhard Aigner stated, "It is senseless to try to conceal the evident fact that the significance of the continental competitions is no longer limited to questions of sporting prestige or supremacy. Money also talks and no-one who wants a successful and healthy competition can ignore that fact" (Ahlstrøm, 2002). For instance, FC Barcelona has thrilled millions of fans globally with its artistically and creatively staged football performances. However, it is a romantic misconception to acknowledge that coaches, managers, and board members in the football economy would rather entertain and lose due to tactical compromises than to win and compromise the entertainment value. Too much is at stake. Aigner mentioned, "this period [read: since the new concept of the UCL was implemented] has stirred the imagination of the players and the fans and offered the participating clubs levels of income which had hitherto never been attained in European football" (Ahlstrøm, 2002).

It speaks for the influence of revenue streams in the development of European football. Ahlstrøm describes football as "the rich market" and by that underlines the money flows in football's ecosystem and UEFA's solid economic position in top of the European football governing hierarchy. For UEFA, this works as a strong arm governing the redistribution of revenues to national football associations, clubs, and grassroots projects benefitting European football as a whole. UEFA spends massive amounts of money generated from its competitions to strengthen and favour all aspects of football from the grassroots and amateur levels to the highest professional level. This is reinforced by the solidarity payments allocated to football in the broadest sense but also in relation to top clubs participating in UEFA's international club competitions and to national football associations. So, UEFA not only governs football but also supports the growth of European football from a holistic angle. The latter refers to how the support of national team football via the national associations is capable of enhancing the sport of football in Europe. This happens due to the potential of gathering an entire nation in a sense of unity in another way than what the UCL can accomplish. From a critical perspective, the public accuses UEFA of stocking up on money, for instance, when UEFA fines a club for lighting roman candles or additional club turmoil. It should be recognised that the money generated by UEFA from disciplinary reasons goes back to the specific country.

The media play a bigger role than before in the European football economy, e.g., take a look at broadcasting deals across various European football leagues like the English Premier League or the UCL. Therefore, UEFA, via its leading competitions such as the UCL, profits from the media's increasing demand for football content. This may be in the form of sensation-oriented news, which Ahlstrøm has experienced when the media has written about the top clubs' fight for a bigger portion of the European revenue pie, e.g., "And what happens is that the media is very disposed to just quote the biggest clubs because there is a headline in it – without thinking about the consequences." This is an interesting perspective and dilemma as there is an ongoing negotiation of meaning in the football economy based on the interactions between all stakeholders in the ecosystem of football. In this system, the media companies protect their own interests and business models just like UEFA, the national football associations, and the top clubs. Ahlstrøm notes:

> The media has an obligation. I believe so. Of course, they must write the truth but I also believe that they have an obligation to choose the right side. And the right side for me is that football is for everybody. Football is the sport of the people.

However, an interesting discussion in the interview with Ahlstrøm came in relation to hybrid branding when debating the role of the media. As mentioned above, the media and thus the generation of visibility and awareness are important influencers for any sports brand along with fans, sponsors, and the integrated interactions in football's ecosystem. For instance, Ahlstrøm underscores that football should be accessible by saying:

> Manchester [read: City] keeps the ticket prices at a level, which is reasonable. It is not like the fans suddenly have to pay much more to watch players who earn so much. That's one

example. Bayern Munich has the same. There are many big clubs that know who pays for the show. And that is without discussion the football fans. They are viewers, that is television viewers, or they are radio listeners or newspaper readers because if we did not have this interest around the game, it would be impossible to finance it.

Ahlstrøm emphasised:

And that is why I say that the players should remember [read: the media] when they give various interviews because they should use the media to communicate as everybody would like to hear what he thinks about the specific situation. I miss that today. They perceive the press as an opponent whereas I think it is an obvious teammate to precisely communicate messages to those who really pay for their wages.

Today, football is "mediated content" as a central vehicle for capitalisation in the UCL.

Concluding comments

UEFA and the UCL have benefitted highly from the mutual dependence between strong sporting and business performances. Constant revitalisation of the UEFA competitions has led to more "high demand" games and increasing revenue growth; European football has become an event, marketing, media and content-driven phenomenon; e.g., this is reflected in how EURO 2020 is spread across Europe. UEFA competitions draw advantages from having the best players with the highest market value; big football stars and nations are a constant part of the European football market, which drives fan attendance, media viewership, sponsorship interest, and other means of commercialisation. As in other areas of the sports economy, there may be revenue growth but the sporting actors, e.g., players, take a huge portion of the revenues to cover their wages. Despite challenges such as the trickle-down effect from FIFA's corruption scandal, match-fixing threats, the role of agents, the difficulties of executing Financial Fair Play due to clubs' creativity in commercial set-ups, UEFA and European football are relatively recession proof. UEFA is a locomotive for the world of football and European football is financed by the enormous passion for the game worldwide. However, an interesting point in this UEFA case was the "commercial under-development" of UEFA before the 1990s. Commercial development in European football proved itself in the understanding of how and why it was possible to profit from football rights; it is not a matter of knowing that people are interested in UEFA and European football but merely about understanding why and how that understanding could be adapted to precise and popular commercial initiatives with the outcome of enhanced ROIs, ROOs, and ROEs. The strong brand equity of UEFA and the UCL is subject to a dynamic football economy in which hybrid sports branding can help to clarify how interactions between different brand levels – i.e., the personal, product, and organisational levels – and with brand influencers and revenue streams, may influence UEFA and the UCL. Time and contextual factors vary depending on the situation and affect the overall outcome.

Notes

1 The football environment is dynamic.
2 The season runs from 1 July to 30 June of the following year. The numbers for the 2004/05 season is 11 months, reflecting change in season dates. All other years are 12 months, based on a season running from the 1 July to the 30 June of the following year.
3 The numbers for the 2007/2008, 2011/2012, and 2015/2016 seasons were considerably influenced by the EURO 2008, EURO 2012, and EURO 2016 events.

Kenneth Cortsen

4 However, in the business of sports there are also experiences and transformation (Cortsen, 2016a).
5 Klaus Hempel and Jürgen Lenz were executives of International Sport and Leisure (ISL). ISL had a long-term strategic partnership with FIFA and UEFA. Hempel and Lenz left ISL to form TEAM, which then teamed up with UEFA in a strategic alliance. This alliance gave rise to the transformation of the UCL in 1992 and elevated the commercialisation of UEFA (Chadwick and Holt, 2007).
6 Not all UEFA stakeholders believed in the concept from the start, cf. earlier quote from Ahlstrøm.

References

Aaker, D.A. (1991) *Managing Brand Equity*. New York: The Free Press.
Ahlstrøm, F. (2002) *Ten Years of the UEFA Champions League*. UEFA.
Andersen, S.E. (2007) *Brands som fortællinger-fortællinger om brands: Seks teenagepigers forbrug, fortolkninger og fortællinger om brands*. Handelshøjskolen, Aarhus Universitet, Center for Virksomhedskommunikation.
Blumer, H. (1986) *Symbolic Interactionism: Perspective and Method*. Berkeley: University of California Press.
BrandFinance (2017) Football 50 2017. [online] Retrieved from http://brandfinance.com/images/upload/bf_football_2017_report_final_june_6th_1.pdf
Breitbarth, T. and Harris, P. (2008) The role of corporate social responsibility in the football business: Towards the development of a conceptual model. *European Sport Manage Quarterly*, 8(2), 179–206.
Brinkmann, S. and S. Kvale (2009) *Interviews: Learning the Craft of Qualitative Research Interviewing*. Thousand Oaks: Sage Publications.
Callejo, M.B. and Forcadell, F.J. (2006) Real Madrid Football Club: A new model of business organisation for sports clubs in Spain. *Global Business and Organisational Excellence*, 26(1), 51–64.
Carroll, A.B. (1979) A three-dimensional conceptual model of corporate performance. *Academy of management review*, 4(4), pp.497–505.
Chadwick, S. and Holt, M. (2007) Building global sports brands: key success factors in marketing the UCL. In: M. Desbordes (ed.). *Marketing and Football: An International Perspective* (pp. 21–50). Oxford: Butterworth-Heinemann.
Cortsen, K. (2013) UEFA Champions League is a Money Game. [online] Retrieved from http://kennethcortsen.com/uefa-champions-league-is-a-money-game/
Cortsen, K. (2014) Transformation, framing and the cultural DNA of football's transfer market in the postmodern era. [online] Retrieved from http://kennethcortsen.com/transformation-framing-cultural-dna-footballs-transfer-market-postmodern-era/
Cortsen, K. (2015) Key determinants for Champions League success [online] Retrieved from http://futuresport.co/key-determinants-champions-league-success/
Cortsen, K. and Nørgaard, M. (2015) ZXY-udvikling af kommercielle potentialer og skabelse af merværdi til dansk fodbold. UCN.
Cortsen, K. (2016a) Aktiviteterne I det transformationsøkonomiske transfervindue skal finde balancen mellem sund kultur og placeringsjagt. [online] Retrieved from http://kennethcortsen.com/aktiviteterne-i-det-transformationsokonomiske-transfervindue-skal-finde-balancen-mellem-sund-kultur-og-placeringsjagt/
Cortsen, K. (2016b) Strategic Sports branding at the Personal, Product and Organisational Level: Theory and Practice for Improving a Sports Brand's Interactions. Ph.D. dissertation.
Cortsen, K. (2017) Neymarketing, fodbold og geopolitik. [online] Retrieved from http://www.mediano.nu/oversigt/2017/8/31/neymarketing-fodbold-og-geopolitik
Deloitte. (2017) Annual Review of Football Finance 2017. [online] Retrieved from https://www2.deloitte.com/content/dam/Deloitte/uk/Documents/sports-business-group/deloitte-uk-annual-review-of-football-finance-2017.pdf
Demil, B. and Lecocq, X. (2010) Business model evolution: in search of dynamic consistency. *Long Range Planning*, 43(2), 227–246.
Desbordes, M. (2007) *Marketing and Football*. Routledge.
Ellet, W. (2007) *The Case Study Handbook: How to Read, Discuss, and Write Persuasively About Cases*. Harvard Business Press.
Farquhar, P.H. (1989) Managing brand equity. *Marketing research*, 1(3) 24–33.
Fast, M. (1996) *Videnskabsteori og metodologi i studier af livsverden*. Aalborg: Aalborg University.
Foster, G., O'Reilly, N., and Dávila, A. (2016) *Sports Business Management: Decision Making Around the Globe*. New York: Routledge.
Fried, G. and Mumcu, C. (eds) (2016) *Sport Analytics: A Data-driven Approach to Sport Business and Management*. New York: Taylor and Francis.

Giulianotti, R. (1999) *Football: A Sociology of the Global Game*. Oxford: Blackwell Publishing Ltd.

Giulianotti, R. and Robertson, R. (2004) The globalization of football: a study in the glocalization of the 'serious life'. *The British Journal of Sociology*, 55(4), 545–568.

Gladden, J.M., Milne, G.R., and Sutton, W.A., (1998) A conceptual framework for assessing brand equity in Division I college athletics. *Journal of sport management*, 12(1), 1–19.

Hamel, J. (1993) *Case Study Methods*. Thousand Oaks: Sage Publications.

Harrison, C.K. and Bukstein, S. (eds) (2016) *Sport Business Analytics: Using Data to Increase Revenue and Improve Operational Efficiency*. Boca Raton: CRC Press.

Holt, D.B. (2004) *How Brands Become Icons: The Principles of Cultural Branding*. Harvard Business Press.

Keller, K.L. (1993) Conceptualizing, measuring, and managing customer-based brand equity. *The Journal of Marketing*, 57(1), 1–22.

Kotler, P. (1965) Behavioral models for analyzing buyers. *The Journal of Marketing*, 29(4), 37–45.

Kunkel, T., Funk, D., and Hill, B. (2013) Brand architecture, drivers of consumer involvement, and brand loyalty with professional sport leagues and teams. *Journal of Sport Management*, 27(3), 177–192.

Kuper, S. and Szymanski, S. (2012) *Soccernomics: Why England Loses, Why Spain, Germany, and Brazil Win, and Why the US, Japan, Australia, Turkey-And Even Iraq- Are Destined to Become the Kings of the World's Most Popular Sport*. Nation Books.

Lombardi, R., Manfredi, S. and Nappo, F. (2014) Third party ownership in the field of professional football: a critical perspective. *Business Systems Review*, 3(1), 32–47.

Maaløe, Erik. (2002) *Casestudier: af og om mennesker i organisationer*. Copenhagen: Akademisk Forlag A/S.

Mead, G.H. and Morris, C. (1934) *Mind, Self, and Society: From the Standpoint of a Social Behaviorist*. Chicago, IL: University of Chicago Press.

Morrow, S. (2013) Football club financial reporting: time for a new model? *Sport, Business and Management: An International Journal*, 3(4), 297–311.

O'Reilly, N.J. and Nadeau, J.P., (2006) Revenue generation in professional sport: a diagnostic analysis. *International Journal of Sport Management and Marketing*, 1(4), 311–330.

Otto, B. and Aier, S. (2013) Business Models in the Data Economy: A Case Study from the Business Partner Data Domain. Retrieved from: https://www.alexandria.unisg.ch/220968/

Pine, B.J. and Gilmore, J.H. (1999) *The Experience Economy: Work is Theatre and Every Business A Stage*. Boston: Harvard Business Press.

Rossi, M., Thrassou, A., and Vrontis, D. (2013) Football performance and strategic choices in Italy and beyond. *International Journal of Organisational Analysis*, 21(4), 546–564.

Shank, M.D. and Lyberger, M.R. (2014) *Sports Marketing: A Strategic Perspective*. New York: Routledge.

Shropshire, K.L. (ed.) (2011) *The Business of Sports*. Sudbury: Jones and Bartlett Publishers.

Simmons, R. (1997) Implications of the Bosman ruling for football transfer markets. *Economic Affairs*, 17(3), 13–18.

Smith, A.C. and Stewart, B. (2014) *Introduction to Sport Marketing*. New York: Routledge.

Stake, R.E. (1994) Case studies. In: Denzin, N.K. and Y.S. Lincoln (eds), *Handbook of Qualitative Research* (pp. 236–224). Thousand Oaks: Sage Publications.

Statista (2017a) UEFA total revenues from 2004/05 to 2015/16. [online]. Retrieved from https://www.statista.com/statistics/279056/revenue-of-the-uefa/

Statista (2017b) Market size of the European professional football market from 2006/07 to 2015/16. [online] Retrieved from https://www.statista.com/statistics/261223/european-soccer-market-total-revenue/

Statista (2017c) Revenues of the biggest (Big Five) European soccer leagues from 1996/97 to 2017/18. [online]. Retrieved from https://www.statista.com/statistics/261218/big-five-european-soccer-leagues-revenue/

Statista (2017d) Broadcast rights fees of major professional sports leagues worldwide in 2016/2017. [online] Retrieved from https://www.statista.com/statistics/628542/tv-rights-major-sports-estimated-fees-by-league/

Statista (2017e) Most valuable football brands worldwide in 2017. [online] Retrieved from https://www.statista.com/statistics/234493/football-clubs-in-europe-by-brand-value/

Teece, D.J. (2010) Business models, business strategy and innovation. *Long Range Planning*, 43(2), 172–194.

UEFA. (2017a) UEFA Financial Report 2015/2016. [online] Retrieved from http://www.uefa.com/MultimediaFiles/Download/OfficialDocument/uefaorg/Finance/02/45/50/26/2455026_DOWNLOAD.pdf

UEFA. (2017b) UEFA's eleven values. [online] Retrieved from https://www.uefa.com/insideuefa/about-uefa/eleven-values/index.html

Kenneth Cortsen

Weiller, C. and Neely, A. (2013) Business model design in an ecosystem context. *British Academy of Management*. Working paper. Retrieved from: https://cambridgeservicealliance.eng.cam.ac.uk/resources/Downloads/ Monthly%20Papers/2013JunepaperBusinessModelDesigninEcosystemContext.pdf.

Wilkesmann, U., (2014) Geld schießt Tore? In: *Wissen–Methode–Geschlecht: Erfassen des fraglos Gegebenen* (pp. 107–124). Springer Fachmedien Wiesbaden.

Yin, Robert (2008) *Case Study Research: Design and Methods*. London: Sage Publications.

36

CONMEBOL

South American Confederation of Football

*Renan Petersen-Wagner, Alberto Reinaldo Reppold Filho,
Cássia Damiani, Felipe Magno and Felippe Marchetti*

Introduction

Association Football (hereafter football) can be considered as one of the most illuminating domains of globalisation [see Chapter 3 in this handbook], not only by its sheer worldwide diffusion as seen by the viewership numbers achieved during the 2014 FIFA World Cup finals in Brazil – 3.2 billion viewers overall and 1 billion just for the final game between Argentina and Germany (see FIFA, 2015) – but also by its inherent social, cultural, economic, and political characteristics that mimic our daily lives' experiences to a point that football can help us understand our living world (see Foer, 2010). In a sense, football is a *microcosmos* of this wider system that we call world society (Luhmann, 1997), and, by understanding it, it is possible to shed some lights on the current and historical processes that led to our contemporary world arrangements. Moreover, as argued by Ulrich Beck (2010) if we want to comprehend one cog of this machinery – for example, the business and economic aspects of football – we cannot and should not omit the other concurrent aspects as the political, social, and cultural dimensions, in a sense that disassociating them becomes impossible in our present-day cosmopolitan world (Beck, 2005). Consequently, to understand the overarching worldwide business of football, and in particular its supreme organisation – FIFA (*Fédération Internationale de Football Association*) – it is imperative to understand its parts by focusing on specific national and regional associations. Taking Pier Paolo Pasolini's (2015) opening quote, "There are two types of football, prose and poetry. European teams are prose, tough, premeditated, systematic, collective. Latin American ones are poetry, ductile, spontaneous, individual, erotic" (Pasolini, 2015), as a metaphor for football's world system it can be argued that there is a clear dichotomy that runs along the lines of the Global South and Global North divide, whereas on one side we find the somehow nostalgic and pristine football (in South America) and on the other side we encounter the somehow dirty and over-commercialised football (in Europe). The metaphor used by Pasolini (2015) to describe the two Janus-faced natures of football is also found in the writings of South American social commentators, such as the Brazilians Roberto DaMatta and Gilberto Freyre (Capraro, 2015), and the Uruguayan journalist Eduardo Galeano (1995). In theory, those two Janus-faced natures of football require each other to exist: European football is only systematic and collective if South American football is unpredictable and individualistic. In short, European and world football are what they are because of South American football. Thus, to understand the current business of world football we need to look to the concurrent cultural, political, and social processes of local and regional football, and in particular South American football.

The chapter will follow with a historical approach to the establishment of South American football in the light of CONMEBOL's (*Confederación Sudamericana de Fútbol*) foundation and development; second it will discuss the position of South American football in relation to European and world football; third, it will cover the last decade of sport mega-events in Brazil and its relationship to government initiatives to host those events, in particular, the 2014 FIFA World Cup; fourth, it will discuss one impact of the organisation of the event through the episode of the relocation of families for infrastructure construction in Porto Alegre; fifth, it will present an analysis of the economic sustainability of one of the new arenas constructed for the 2014 FIFA World Cup; and finally, it will provide some conclusions and future points for research in respect of the business of football in South America.

History of CONMEBOL

In 1910 to celebrate the centenary of the start of Argentinian independence from the Spanish Crown – the process started in 1810 with the *Revolución de Mayo* and culminated with the declaration of independence in 1816 – it was proposed by the Argentinian Football Association (AFA) that the annual international football festival between Uruguay and Argentina would also extend invitations to other South American teams, including Chile and Brazil (Mason, 1995). This incipient continental competition between the four countries was a reflection of the early football encounters between the distinct British expatriate communities in South America, in particular from the largest and most important trading route stops, such as Montevideo (Uruguay), Buenos Aires (Argentina), Rio de Janeiro and São Paulo (Brazil), and Valparaíso and Santiago (Chile). For instance, international football encounters between Argentina and Brazil started in 1907 when the former were invited for games in Brazil, whilst games between Uruguay and Argentina go back to 1888 when young British expats organised a festival to celebrate the birthday of Queen Victoria (Mason, 1995). Nevertheless, it was not 1910 that ended up being recognised as the founding year of CONMEBOL, but it was only with the centenary of the declaration of Argentinian independence that an Uruguayan – Hector R. Gómez – saw the appropriate momentum for uniting the different South American countries along one single confederation that would rule the amateur sport of football (Mason, 1995). As such, CONMEBOL is regarded as the oldest of all the continental confederations, having just national bodies and FIFA (formed in 1904) as its senior. The early task of the newly formed confederation was to organise the South American Championship (*Campeonato Sudamericano de Fútbol*) to be held in Argentina (1916), Uruguay (1917), Brazil (1919), and Chile (1920). The four first editions saw the participation of Argentina, Brazil, Chile, and Uruguay; in 1921 (Argentina) Paraguay first participated, and in 1926 (Chile) Bolivia took part, in 1927 (Peru) Peru joined, in 1939 (Peru) came Ecuador, in 1945 (Chile) Colombia, and 1967 (Uruguay) Venezuela. It was not until the 1975 edition when the competition changed its name to Copa América that all ten CONMEBOL members participated together (see CONMEBOL, 2018).

CONMEBOL was not only a pioneer in being the first continental confederation that sought to organise the sport of football, but also championed the organisation of the first FIFA World Cup finals in Uruguay in 1930. As argued by Mason (1995), Uruguay was not chosen by FIFA uniquely because of its past triumphs on the pitch – Uruguay had won the 1924 and 1928 Olympic tournaments – but because it had promised to pay travel and accommodation expenses to all participating teams, and to build a modern and larger stadium to host the competition – the Estadio Centenario (centenary) was built to celebrate the centenary of Uruguay's first constitution and also to host the 1930 FIFA World Cup finals. Moreover, Uruguay at that time in history was experiencing an unprecedented economic growth anchored in growing exports of frozen meat and wool (see Finch, 1981; Mason, 1995), whereas Europe was in its inter-war period. Another pioneering feature of CONMEBOL was the invitation of non-CONMEBOL members to take part in Copa América, as with the participation of the United States of America (USA) and Mexico in 1993 (Ecuador), and Japan in 1999 (Paraguay). Nevertheless, in a business sense it is the 2016 Copa América that can be regarded as iconic as it was the first time the competition was held outside any of the members' political national borders – it was held in the US, in a sense paving the way for the defunct proposed game 39 of the English Premier League (see Millward, 2011). In a way, as argued by Maffesoli (1988, 1990) South America, and particularly Brazil, can be considered as the laboratory of *European* modernisation where ideas and concepts are tried out before taking their *big* stages. As such, comprehending the South American experience in relation to the business of football can help us in understanding the wider processes involved with global football.

South American football as Global North and Global South

As posited previously, the social, economic, political, and cultural arrangements regarding world football in its relationship to South American football is a reflection to the wider global arrangements to a point where it becomes impossible to distinguish who reflects who – is it football that mimics the world, or is the world that mimics football? (see Giulianotti, 1999; Giulianotti and Robertson, 2004; 2009). To situate the current condition of South American football and its relationship to the global business of football it becomes imperative to look for the historical developments in the last century that shaped the processes in ways that we can understand South American football as both part of the Global North and the Global South concomitantly. As argued by Brewer (2018) the business world of football saw an increasing transformation from the mid-twentieth century onwards when there was a qualitative variation in what was the primary goal of sport. For Brewer (2018), whereas previously the commercial expansion of football was solely one of the possible means to which clubs and organisations as national associations, confederations and FIFA guided their activities, currently the commercial and businesses aspects became if not the end-in-itself, one of its primary goals. Brewer (2018) identifies the ascension of João Havelange – a Brazilian national who represented Brazil in the 1930 and 1952 Summer Olympic Games in swimming and water polo respectively – to the presidency of FIFA in 1974 as the igniter of the shifting of power within world football in what is regarded as the Global South (non-Europe) and the Global North (Europe) dynamics. The ascension of Havelange to the presidency of FIFA needs to be read in conjunction with wider social and political rearrangements that took place around that period, especially through the liberation and independence of distinct African countries (see Armstrong and Giulianotti, 2004; Said, 1994). Nevertheless, Havelange's ascension to the FIFA presidency was not the igniter of this wider change, but actually the ultimate representation of the Global North and Global South dynamics in regards to world football. Whereas in a mechanical division between Global North as the developed Europe and the Global South as the underdeveloped South America might suit some strict economic analysis (see Petersen-Wagner, 2017a; see Rosa, 2014 for a discussion on mechanical and organic Global North and Global South distinctions), it does not reflect all the distinct dimensions that are not dissociable as posited by Beck (2005). In a way, South American football was already the Global North of world football, and the ascension of Havelange to power was solely its ultimate manifestation.

As discussed previously, South American football organisation through the figure of CONMEBOL was well developed before European countries would get together to form UEFA in 1954. By the time UEFA organised its first continental championship in 1960, CONMEBOL had already hosted 27 editions of its continental competition. The prominence of South American football on the world stage by the 1960s is well documented, as by the feats of Uruguay (1930, 1950) and Brazil (1958, 1962) in the FIFA World Cup, and by the organisation of three of the seven first FIFA World Cup tournaments (Uruguay – 1930; Brazil – 1950; Chile – 1962). In respect of the cultural and social significance to the nation, football was already truly embedded in the social fabrics of Argentina (Archetti, 1999; Rein, 2015), Brazil (DaMatta et al., 1982; Freyre, 1947; Kittleson, 2014), Uruguay (Galeano, 1995), and more generally across South America (Mason, 1995) in a way that preceded the global dominance of football as a sporting practice that overcomes the strict boundaries of social class dynamics as seen in the United Kingdom example (see Baker, 1979; Mason, 1980).

Additionally, football in South America served as an expression of the nation state in a way that it became one of the key elements that glued together distinct early migrant communities who otherwise would not recognise themselves as Argentinians (see Arbena, 1995; Archetti, 1995; Gil, 2002; Rein, 2015) or Brazilians (see Bocketti, 2008; Kittleson, 2014; Mascarenhas, 2014) for example. In a way, the experience of South American football in respect of distinct first and second generation migrants during the late 1800s and early 1900s can shed light on the processes taking place in Europe at the moment. The use of football as a platform to foster a sense of national belonging was well understood by South American politicians in both positive and negative terms (see Arbena, 1990; Duke and Crolley, 2001; Rein, 1998), to a point where athletes started to gain such a popularity that raised their profile to a level where they were elected or selected for political positions (see Doidge and Almeida, 2017; Kittleson, 2014). If we understand this in light of the trend of celebrity politics (see Street, 2004, 2012; Wheeler, 2013; Zoonen, 2006), it is possible to expect this phenomenon to take hold in other spaces – at the moment of writing this chapter, George Weah, who was selected as the FIFA footballer of the year in 1995, is already the president of Liberia (*New York Times*, 2017). The centrality of players within the space of Latin American football can be understood as a manifestation of what Max Weber (2013) referred to as charismatic leadership, or what DaMatta (1997) understood as *person*. The route to *personhood* in respect of South American football follows the path described in the below quote by Eduardo Galeano (1995, p. 19):

> Al sur del mundo, Èste es el itinerario del jugador con buenas piernas y buena suerte: de su pueblo pasa a una ciudad del interior; de la ciudad del interior pasa a un club chico de la capital del paìs; en la capital, el club chico no tiene más remedio que venderlo a un club grande; el club grande, asfixiado por las deudas, lo vende a otro club más grande de un paìs más grande; y finalmente el jugador corona su carrera en Europa. [In the South of the world, this is the itinerary of the player with good legs and good luck: from his/her village to a small country town; from the small country town to a small club in the capital of the country; the small club does not have more solution than to sell to a big club; the big club asphyxiated by debts, has to sell him/her to a bigger club from a bigger country; and finally the player crowns his/her career in Europe]
>
> *(Galeano, 1995, p. 19, translated by the author)*

The migration of South American players to Europe, not only to represent club level football but also international football, has been a feature since the early 1900s especially with the return of Italian descendants from Argentina, Brazil, and Uruguay to Italy. As argued by Taylor (2006) of the over 300 foreign players playing in the Italian professional league between 1929 and 1965 half of them had come from South America, whilst over three-quarters of foreign players in the Spanish league in the 1970s were from South America. The centrality that South American footballers had in those two particular European countries highlights the idea of South America being the Global North of football within the geographical Global South. In a sense, the distinctions between European and South American football as posited by the opening quote by Pasolini (2015) are not that clear-cut, meaning that what we understand as European is to some extent already South American, and vice-versa.

A decade of mega-events in Brazil: the federal government initiatives and the 2014 FIFA World Cup

While Uruguay in the 1920s was one of the fastest-growing national economies from a worldwide perspective (see Finch, 1981), the early 2000s saw Brazil taking prominence on the world stage to a point where the acronym BRICS was coined by Jim O'Neill at Goldman Sachs (O'Neill, 2001) to represent the fast-growing economies in the world. Brazil was also featured on *The Economist*'s cover in 2009 with the heading of "Brazil takes off," where the position of Brazil in the world stage was highlighted especially by emphasising the differences between Brazil and the other BRICS economies (*Economist*, 2009). This period is also regarded as the golden decade of Brazilian sport, especially by the organisation of different mega-events, such as the Pan-American Games (2007), the World Military Games (2011), the FIFA Confederations Cup (2013), FIFA World Cup (2014), and the first Olympic Games (2016) to be held in South America. The organisation of those mega-events would not have been possible without the involvement of all spheres of Brazilian society, from local municipal governments through regional state governments, and the federal national government. In this light, this section will look at how the federal government got involved with the organisation of the 2014 FIFA World Cup, and what were its initiatives in relation to national social and economical development, and public policies in sport. In a sense, this section focuses on the public side of the business of football and how governments and public entities relate to it. This approach goes in the direction proposed by Beck (2005) in relation to the inseparability of the different aspects of world society, in a sense that to understand the private business sphere it is indispensable to understand the public government sphere.

From the first experience of organising the Pan-American Games in 2007, the Brazilian national government in its strategic agenda saw sport as one of the key factors for social and economic development of the country (Brasil, 2008, 2010, 2016). When Brazil received the rights to host the 2014 FIFA World Cup finals back on 30 October 2007 the national government perceived the event as an inductor for national development through the use of PAC (*Programa de Aceleração de Crescimento* – Program for the Acceleration of Growth) for establishing priorities in what concerned the development of the crucial infrastructure for regional and national economic growth. For this reason, the national federal government proposed changes in legislation, implemented new control and planning systems for monitoring the event's related projects, established new models for hiring, managerial monitoring, and procurement. For instance, regarding the establishment of new public procurement systems, the national federal government adopted the RDC (*Regime de Contratações Diferenciadas* – System for Special Procurement) (see Brasil, 2011) after an intense debate in the country's upper and lower chambers in order to enhance the public tender process for construction. What started as a new procurement system developed with the FIFA World Cup finals as the intended target lately became available throughout other areas of public management in Brazil. This was perceived by the national federal government as one of the legacies of hosting the competition. The organisation of the event also created a better symbiosis between the different levels of public administration in Brazil (municipal, regional, national), private companies, and civil society where for better coordination between those different entities governance committees were created under the executive coordination of the Ministry of Sport. Thematic chambers with the participation of all involved entities were created involving different areas pertinent to the organisation of the event, such as tourism; communication; doping control; public policies; intelligence, defence, and security; sustainability; accessibility; football town; culture, tourism, and Brazilian image; energy; and strategic legacy.

The national federal government in its vision perceived that hosting those sporting events, and in particular the FIFA World Cup finals, as opportunities for developing the wider and far-reaching changes they envisioned for the country. By the decision of the federal government, it was sought to install a development program through the banner of 'nationalisation of benefits' by the dissemination of investments in construction and modernisation of the sportive infrastructure beyond what those 12 host cities would get. The vision adopted by the government was that the initial development in the 12 host cities would spread and branch out to the surrounding and adjacent cities and towns in what they envisioned as a stimulant effect for both local and regional developments. For hosting the 2014 FIFA World Cup, the federal government through its development bank BNDES (*Banco Nacional de Desenvolvimento Econômico e Social* – National Bank for Economic and Social Development) had provided lines of credit of up to 3.81 billion reais (£800 million at 23 April 2018 conversation rate of 0.21), which were in accordance with market practices regarding interested rates, for mobility, ports, airports, security, telecommunications, and tourism infrastructure works. Overall, over 8 billion reais (£1.7 billion) were invested between federal, local, and regional governments, and private investments (Brasil, 2015b) for hosting the event. The broader foci of these investments was the decrease of inequalities and the generation of employment. In terms of the development of cities, the government understood the event as catalyst for wider changes in respect of urban mobility, public transportation, sewerage, and habitation. Nevertheless, as will be seen in the following section, those works were not completely without debate and political and social struggles by part of the population affected by the event. For policing, the government understood the event as catalyst for a wider integration of the three levels of police (municipal, regional, federal) and the use of a more preventive approach that focused on the community. From the social perspective, the focus was on the extension of citizenship rights and quality of public services in regard to education, health, accessibility, and security, and the valorisation of a national identity comprising multiple regional identities. In respect of local environment, sustainability was the main focus of the wider governmental investments.

Moreover, the federal government saw the 2014 FIFA World Cup also as an inductor for development of national football. The construction or refurbishment of the 12 arenas, the construction of Training Centres and Official Training Fields were perceived by the government as an indication of the desired new stage Brazilian football would achieve in the coming years. One of the first challenges envisioned by the government was how to ensure that a new management system would be in place in order to guarantee the sustainability of those new sportive spaces (see final section in this chapter). For instance, in 2015 after the FIFA World Cup finals the national federal government instituted a new law (see Brasil, 2015a) establishing the practice of fiscal responsibility in football, transparency in the business of football, and democratic principles in relation to the management of clubs and national and regional associations. Moreover, this new law introduced a special instalment plan for football clubs to repay old debts with the federal government and created the APFUT (*Autoridade Pública de Governança do Futebol* – Public

Authority for the Governance of Football). The 2014 FIFA World Cup also served as a catalyst for wider governmental initiatives to prevent violence in sport as through the *Grito pela Paz* (Cry for Peace) program that sought to prize the football spectacle and make fans aware that stadia are places for fraternisation and not of violent encounters. This federal initiative found resonance in club football by the introduction of spaces in stadia where fans from both sides can sit and watch the game together, especially at big regional derbies such as Internacional versus Grêmio in Porto Alegre (see GloboEsporte, 2015; StadiumDB, 2015).

Besides that, the 2014 FIFA World Cup in men's football has also served as a catalyst for the development of women's football with the construction of the first centre of excellence in women's football (see Itaipu, 2014) through a project within the Sport Incentive Law (*Lei de Incentivo ao Esporte*) that provides tax breaks for private investors. Moreover, the federal government through a Caixa Econômica Federal (public owned bank) sponsorship hosted the III National Women Football Championship, the II University Cup, and the II School Cup. Nevertheless, as pointed out by Damiani (2014) and Baldy dos Reis and Souza Junior (2014) the vast amount of public and private investments and media coverage still resides with men's football whilst women still experience a lower degree of professionalisation in the sport, the pay gap is still enormous, and regrettably women still face sexual and moral harassment whilst performing their roles as athletes, coaches, referees, reporters, and football managers. At the moment of writing this chapter a social movement in respect of women's space in Brazilian football has emerged under the banner of the "*Deixa ela trabalhar*" (Let her work) slogan (see BBC-Brasil, 2018).

The relocation of residents during the works for the 2014 FIFA World Cup

As mentioned in the previous section, the economic and social development project envisioned by the national federal government alongside the other two spheres of public administration in Brazil (municipal and regional) was heavily centred around the idea of using the FIFA World Cup – and also the Rio 2016 Olympic Games – as catalyst for infrastructure extension and enhancement. It was perceived by the government that because of Brazil's continental size, and its historical deficit in what regarded infrastructure foundation, this was one of the main causes for obstructing and restricting further economic and social growth (see Neto, Soares, Ferreira, Pompermayer, and Romminger, 2011). Nevertheless, for those investments in key infrastructure under the banner of "nationalisation of benefits" to take place there was an unfortunate necessity for the relocation of families where the work would take place. A particular case in question was the relocation of families in Porto Alegre – Rio Grande do Sul due to the enlargement and duplication of Avenida Moab Caldas (also known as Avenida Tronco) that would speed up the connection between the south of the city and its most densely populated areas – north and centre – and provide a ring road around the Estádio Beira-Rio (Sport Club Internacional's stadium and one of the host venues for the 2014 FIFA World Cup).

The duplication and enlargement of Avenida Tronco was featured in Porto Alegre's master plan in 1959 when it was recognised by the then mayor Leonel Brizola as a key link between the already populated areas of centre and north of the city and the growing south. Nevertheless, those works never happened and the disorderly occupation of the area that took place during 40 years led to over 1,500 families living where the road should have been standing. It was perceived by municipal managers that the less they did in relation to the area during this 40 years period, the less trouble they would create for themselves (see Magno, 2014). Nonetheless, the FIFA World Cup and the federal government incentives for infrastructure development across the country were sought as an opportunity that municipal managers could not miss in order to put into effect what Porto Alegre's master plan already proposed back in 1959. The enlargement and duplication of Avenida Tronco involved an investment of around 156 million reais (£32 million), comprising both road works (83 per cent of total costs) and also the relocation of families (17 per cent of total costs), where the former was made through financing via the federal-owned bank – Caixa Economica Federal – and the latter invested by the municipal government (see PMPA, 2018). The history of the disorderly growth of the area and further occupation of where Avenida Tronco stands is related to the construction of the new horse-racing track in Porto Alegre during the 1950s, when it moved from a central location (Moinhos de Vento neighbourhood) to the south of the city (Cristal neighbourhood), and attracted a large contingency of manual labourers from the countryside, Santa Catarina (the closest regional state to Rio Grande do Sul), and Uruguay and Argentina. Those manual labourers worked at the horse-racing track, but with the economic decline of horse racing during the next decades those individuals without jobs still decided to stay in the surrounding areas of the track. Moreover, those spaces also served as attracting poles for the huge influx of countryside individuals in the 1960s, and historically the periphery was also the space where the early liberated slaves (late 1800s and early 1900s) sought to settle.

Nevertheless, the decision-making process taken by the public municipal managers for duplicating Avenida Tronco that involved the relocation of families was seen by residents as top-down, generating further setbacks that prevented the works from occurring at the desired pace. Porto Alegre is widely recognised by its experience in participatory budgeting (see Gilman, 2016; Santos, 1998), where inhabitants can make direct decisions on how to allocate part of the budget for investments. In a sense, the experience of participatory budgeting in Porto Alegre that started back in 1989 with then-mayor Olivio Dutra serves as a backdrop for understanding the processes around the relocation of families during the construction and duplication of Avenida Tronco. Whereas initially the municipal government had agreed to relocate families to surrounding areas to their original location, with the proximity of the FIFA World Cup the municipal council passed a complementary law in 2010 releasing it from the obligation to spend the allocated resources from the national federal government program (*Minha Casa, Minha Vida* – My House, My Life – PMCMV) for the construction of new houses in the same surrounding location. This decision by the municipal council and the mayor at the time – José Fortunati – caused further setbacks in talks with residents, leading the municipal government to approach the relocation through two other legal procedures available: house payment bonus (*bonus moradia*) and social rent (*aluguel social*). In the former case, individuals could decide to find houses they wished to buy up to a limit imposed by the government, who would subsidise that negotiation in order for those individuals to move from their original home (up to 52,000 reais – £10,000). In the latter case, the municipal government would pay rent for individuals until the new houses outside the surrounding areas were ready through the PMCMV (up to 500 reais monthly – £105 monthly). Until July 2014, when the FIFA World Cup started, there were 708 families who had been relocated; 402 opted for house payment bonus, 108 received indemnities that were higher than the bonus, and 180 families decided for social rent. The rest of the families decided to resist and stayed in the region while they waited for the PMCMV houses to be completed. The latter resistance movement was known as "key for key" (*chave por chave*) where residents would only give up their house keys when they would get their hands on the new house keys. In a way, the public municipal managers found themselves in a situation where they were engaging in talks with two further connected social movements who provided support for the residents' concerns: the *Comitê Popular da Copa em Porto Alegre* (World Cup Popular Committee) and the *Ponto de Cultura Quilombo*[1] *do Sopapo* (the Quilombo do Sopapo Cultural Centre). At the time of writing, the duplication and enlargement of Avenida Tronco has not been completed (see CMPA, 2017); nevertheless, because of this work not featuring in the official works related to the FIFA World Cup, it is not regarded as a failure in hosting the event.

In a sense, when looking at the business aspect of football and in particular when analysing the hosting of a mega-event such as the FIFA World Cup, it is inherently necessary to look at interconnected dimensions such as social and public management and policies. What the example above shows is that whilst the business and economic dimension of the event might have been planned for providing a platform for economic and social growth under the banner of "nationalisation of benefits," on the local social level those plans had completely unintended consequences that generated further struggles. For anyone seeking to understand the business aspect of football, it becomes absolutely necessary to also look at the local social consequences of those decisions.

The new football arenas in Brazil: Possibilities for economic sustainability

The hosting of sport mega-events in what could be considered the economic and social Global South is becoming a late trend for both FIFA – South Africa (2010), Brazil (2014), Russia (2018), Qatar (2022) – and the IOC – Beijing (2008), Sochi (2014), Rio (2016), Beijing (2022) – and one of the recurrent themes in international media outlets is the question of whether all the stadia constructed for the event would be used afterwards, or would they become white elephants (see Manfred, 2015; Pearson, 2014). In a way media discourse in a dialogical fashion (see Foucault, 1969) constructs "reality," which in turn frames those discourses to a point where we can understand the collection of those discourses as the *épistèmé* of the event, or what Petersen-Wagner (2017c) conceptualised as symbolic footprints. Nevertheless, discourses are not "reality," neither deos the "real" reality frame discourses. As such, in this section we will analyse the economic sustainability of one of the 12 arenas redeveloped or build specifically for the 2014 FIFA World Cup in Brazil – the Estádio Beira-Rio in Porto Alegre – by delving into the financial reports of Sport Club Internacional (the owner of the stadium), BRio (the holding company that co-manages the stadium), and interviews with the club's vice-president and two senior managers from BRio. Our analysis centres around eight main areas for income generation for the club and the stadium: ticket sales; catering; VIP areas; advertising; events; commercial centre; parking; and tour guides and museum.

According to a report by Delloite (2011) football clubs in Europe generated between 42 per cent and 8 per cent of their operational income through sales of match-related tickets. Sport Club Internacional in the 2015 season reported an income of 26.7 million reais (£5,600,000) through sales of match-related tickets, which corresponds to 12.2 per cent of their overall operational income (217.8 million reais – £45,738,000) (see Internacional, 2015). Nevertheless, one of the main concerns by the international media when "Global South" countries host mega-events is that initially stadia would be unable to attract crowds, and, secondly, the possibility of gentrification of the stadia by increase in ticket prices and upscaling the installations by removing old popular areas. Historically, Brazil had an occupation rate of its stadia around 41 per cent according to a report by Pluri Consultoria (2014), whereas what was seen in regards to Sport Club Internacional and its Beira-Rio stadium was a total occupation rate of 37 per cent in the 2015 Brazilian League. Some of the possible reasons for a decline in occupation across the country (there was an increase of attendance of 234 per cent and income generation of 392 per cent), and specifically with Sport Club Internacional, was that many stadia increased their capacity after their renovation or construction. In respect of Sport Club Internacional, its occupation rate varied across the different tournaments it played during the 2015 season. For instance, at Brazilian Cup games it had an average occupation of 62 per cent, whereas in the Brazilian League it was of 37 per cent; at the State Championship it was 37 per cent, and with the Copa Libertadores it was 81 percent. Overall, the average occupation rate for 2015 for Sport Club Internacional was of 45.4 per cent, still well below the occupation rates found in Europe. Nevertheless, just with the income generated by match-related tickets, Sport Club Internacional can cover the maintenance costs of the stadium that are calculated to be around 18,000,000 reais (£3,780,000) per year (see Internacional, 2015). Sport Club Internacional decided to licence the use of its catering spaces (66 in total) to five local companies that would in turn pay a percentage or fixed rent for the club. The information regarding the rent or percentage is omitted in the financial report of Sport Club Internacional, but we can estimate based on the figures released by FIFA in regards to fan spending during the games at Beira-Rio in the World Cup that a fan would spend around 7 reais (£1.50) per game, with a total attendance of 840,000 for the 2015 year, catering would have accounted for an income of 5,930,000 reais (£1,245,000).

Estádio Beira-Rio has 70 VIP-boxes (allowing 14 to 18 fans to attend) and 55 Skyboxes (up to 24 fans), where the monthly rent per fan of those spaces varies between $760 reais (£160) and 1,375 reais (£288) depending on the location in the stadium. At the moment, Sport Club Internacional has 50 per cent of those spaces rented out, which account for an income of 14,400,000 reais (£3,000,000) per season (see Internacional, 2015). In respect of advertising, which is still in control of clubs (pitch-side boards are owned by the broadcasters), Sport Club Internacional could have generated through naming rights over 4,500,000 reais (£945,000) per season according to the current market prices paid for the naming rights of Arena Fonte Nova (Bahia) and Arena Pernambuco (Recife) that are both under a deal with the Itaipava brewery, and so known as Itaipava Arena Fonte Nova and Itaipava Arena Pernambuco respectively. Nevertheless, the approach taken by Rede Globo (the broadcasting rights owner) and other mainstream media, not to mention the naming rights owners in their broadcasting or reports, prevents other companies from sponsoring stadia. Moreover, another source of income for Estádio Beira-Rio is the rent of its area for events such as major music shows. At the moment, the stadium has four distinct areas that can be used for events, ranging from the whole stadium, one side of the stadium (amphitheatre), sunset area, and the Arthur Dallegrave events centre (CEAD). It is estimated by the senior managers at BRio that Estádio Beira-Rio can host two full stadium events (estimated public of over 50,000), with a rent of 500,000 reais (£105,000) per event; eight amphitheatre events (estimated public of up to 12,000), with a rent of 150,000 reais (£31,500); 52 sunset events, with a rent of 15,000 reais (£3,150); and 52 CEAD events, with a rent of 14,000 reais (£2,940) per year. At the time of our analysis in 2015, the stadium has hosted one full-size event (Rolling Stones concert), one amphitheatre event (Los Hermanos), and thirty sunset events (bike fairs, beer festivals, and parties). Similarly to the occupation rate for football games, Estádio Beira-Rio occupation with regards to events is below 50 per cent but it still generates over 1,800,000 reais (£378,000) per financial year. Besides events, Estádio Beira-Rio has a commercial centre with over 44 distinct spaces and an area of 6,000 square metres that is rented out at a market price of 140,00 reais (£30) per square meter. At the time of our analysis, 40 per cent of those spaces are rented out, accounting for an extra income of 4,000,000 reais (£840,000). Estádio Beira-Rio has two distinct parking areas with over 5,000 spaces that are market at $30 reais (£6.3); its occupation rate for major events (50 in total for football games, full stadium or amphitheater events) is estimated by BRio senior managers to be around 60 per cent.

Parking therefore generates an extra 4,600,000 reais (£966,000) per financial year. For its tour and museum, Sport Club Internacional receives around 350 and 200 daily visits respectively that are marketed at 10 reais each (£2.1), generating over 1,600,000 reais (£336,000) per financial year (see Internacional, 2015).

As our analysis showed, Sport Club Internacional and BRio, the holding company that manages Estádio Beira-Rio, can cover the maintenance costs of the stadium just through gate receipts for the football games. At the same time, the stadium does generate surplus with regards to its maintenance costs even without achieving its full commercial potential, contradicting the widely perceived image from the international media that stadia in "Global South" countries are doomed to become white elephants.

Conclusion

In this chapter, we sought to present an analysis of the current condition of South American football, and in particular its business side. As we argued throughout the chapter, to understand the current business condition of South American football we need to direct our gaze not solely to this aspect but especially to the concomitant dimensions as social and political. Moreover, to understand the current condition it is imperative that we take an historical approach in order to demonstrate how the world structures have been shaped or are shaping our focus of analysis. The first argument that we put forward in this chapter was that South American football should not be understood as in opposition to European or world football, in a way that for us the historical interconnections, cultural, economic, and social exchanges from the incipience of football in the late 1800s and early 1900s had configured South American and European or world football as sides of the same coin. As such, South American football should not be mechanically understood as Global South because it is the generative force behind the mechanically understood Global North (Europe). In a way, the historical experience of the organisation of South American football in light of CONMEBOL, the prominence of football in the national imaginary across South America, and its links to how first and second generation migrant communities related to the nation and to the continent can shed light and provide clues to how Europe and world football can and should take initiatives to tackle difficult issues, such as racial discrimination and violence. Moreover, what our particular analysis of Brazil reinforced was the absolute necessity to look at the concomitant dimensions to understand the business of football, as not only the political aspect but also the social struggles can have a determinant effect in how matters take place. Besides that, our chapter, by looking at the financial and economic sustainability of a particular stadium in Brazil, sought to counterbalance the dominant perspective in the world media that "Global South" experiences in hosting mega-events are doomed to fail and the sportive equipment is doomed to become white elephants. Nevertheless, South American football still faces major "threats" to its businesses especially by the historical movement of its best players to more dominant leagues in the world that can have potentially a detrimental effect on the occupation rate as seen in our analysis. Furthermore, the wide diffusion of new information and communication technologies and the ability to constantly follow foreign clubs through social media as described by Petersen-Wagner (2017a, 2017b) might become a further point of contention for South American clubs in order to keep their fans for themselves. In a sense, the physical mobility of players might be matched by the metaphysical mobility of fans paving the way for the impoverishment of South American football culture.

Note

1 Quilombos are the original settlements by slaves and freed-slaves (see Reis and Gomes, 1996).

References

Arbena, J. (1990) Generals and goles: assessing the connection between the military and soccer in Argentina. *International Journal of the History of Sport*, 7(1), 120–130.

Arbena, J. (1995) Nationalism and sport in Latin America, 1850–1990: the paradox of promoting and performing "European" sports. *International Journal of the History of Sport*, 12(2), 220–238.

Archetti, E. (1995) In search of national identity: Argentinian football and Europe. *International Journal of the History of Sport*, 12(2), 201–219.

Archetti, E. (1999) *Masculinities: Football, Polo and the Tango in Argentina*. Oxford: Berg.

Armstrong, G. and Giulianotti, R. (eds) (2004) *Football in Africa: Conflict, Conciliation and Community*. London: Palgrave Macmillan.

Baker, W.J. (1979) The making of a working-class football culture in Victorian England. *Journal of Social History*, 13(2), 241–251.

Baldy-dos-Reis, H.H. and Souza-Junior, O.M.d. (2014) A invisibilidade e a trajetória das mulheres no futebol brasileiro. *Revista do Observatório Brasil de Igualdade de Gênero*, 4(6), 25–35.

BBC-Brasil. (2018) Tim Vickery: A importância do "Deixa Ela Trabalhar" e de enxergar além da sexualidade. [online] Retrieved from: http://www.bbc.com/portuguese/blog-tim-vickery-43747081

Beck, U. (2005) The cosmopolitan state: redefining power in the global age. *International Journal of Politics, Culture & Society*, 18, 143–159. doi:10.1007/s10767-006-9001-1

Beck, U. (2010) *Cosmopolitan Vision* (C. Cronin, Trans. 3rd ed.) Cambridge: Polity.

Bocketti, G.P. (2008) Italian immigrants, Brazilian football, and the dilemma of national identity. *Journal of Latin American Studies*, 40(2), 275–302.

Brasil. (2008) Presidente Luis Inacio da Silva (2007) Mensagem ao Congresso, 2008. [online] Retrieved from: http://www2.planalto.gov.br/acompanhe-o-planalto/mensagem-ao-congresso

Brasil. (2010) Presidente Luis Inacio da Silva (2007) Mensagem ao Congresso, 2010. [online] Retrieved from http://www2.planalto.gov.br/acompanhe-o-planalto/mensagem-ao-congresso

Brasil. (2011) *Lei N 12.462, de 4 de Agosto de 2011*. Brasilia: Casa Civil. [online] Retrieved from http://www.planalto.gov.br/ccivil_03/_ato2011-2014/2011/lei/l12462.htm.

Brasil. (2015a) *Lei N 13.155, de 4 de Agosto de 2015*. Brasilia Casa Civil. [online] Retrieved from: http://www.planalto.gov.br/ccivil_03/_ato2015-2018/2015/lei/l13155.htm.

Brasil. (2015b) *Ministerio do Esporte: Matriz de Responsabilidade Consolidada*. Brasilia [online] Retrieved from: http://www.esporte.gov.br/arquivos/assessoriaespecialfutebol/copa2014/matriz_consolidada_dez_2014.pdf.

Brasil. (2016) Presidenta Dilma Vana Roussef (2011) Mensagem ao Congresso, 2016. [online] Retrieved from: http://www2.planalto.gov.br/acompanhe-o-planalto/mensagem-ao-congresso

Brewer, B.D. (2018) The commercial transformation of world football and the North-South divide: a global value chain analysis. *International Review for the Sociology of Sport*, 1–21.

Capraro, A.M. (2015) Diz-me como jogas e te direis quem és..: estilos de jogar futebol em Pasolini, Freyre e DaMatta. *História Unisinos*, 19(3), 283–292.

CMPA. (2017) Câmera Municipal de Porto Alegre - Após cinco anos, apenas 30% das obras da Avenida Tronco estão concluídas [Press release]. [online] Retrieved from: http://www.camarapoa.rs.gov.br/noticias/apos-cinco-anos-apenas-30-das-obras-na-avenida-tronco-estao-concluidas

CONMEBOL. (2018) Copa América. História. [online] Retrieved from: http://www.conmebol.com/es/copa-america-2015/historia

DaMatta, R. (1997) *A Casa & A Rua: Espaço, Cidadania, Mulher e Morte* (5th ed.). Rio de Janeiro: Rocco.

DaMatta, R., Flores. L. Guedes, S., and Vogel, A. (eds.) (1982) Universo do Futebol: Esporte e Sociedade Brasileira. Rio de Janeiro: Pinakotheke.

Damiani, C. (2014) Avanço da participação das mulheres nas políticas públicas de esporte. *Revista do Observatório Brasil de Igualdade de Gênero*, 4(6), 44–52.

Delloite. (2011) Football Money League. [online] Retrieved from: http://www.delloite.com/assets/Dcom-chile/local%20assets/documents/nuevos/c1%28es%29_fml2011_140211.pdf

Doidge, M., and Almeida, B.S.D. (2017) From goalscorer to politician: the case of Romário and football politics in Brazil. *International Review for the Sociology of Sport*, 52(3), 263–278.

Duke, V. and Crolley, L. (2001) Fútbol, politicians and the people: populism and politics in Argentina. *International Journal of the History of Sport*, 18(3), 93–116.

Economist, T. (2009) Brazil Takes Off. *The Economist*.

FIFA (2015) 2014 FIFA World Cup reached 3.2 billion viewers, one billion watched final. [online] Retrieved from: http://www.fifa.com/worldcup/news/y=2015/m=12/news=2014-fifa-world-cuptm-reached-3-2-billion-viewers-one-billion-watched--2745519.html

Finch, M.H.J. (1981) *A Political Economy of Uruguay since 1870* (1st ed.). London: Macmillan.

Foer, F. (2010) *How Soccer Explains the World: An Unlikely Theory of Globalization*. New York: Harper Perennial.

Foucault, M. (1969) *L'Archeologie du Savoir*. Paris: Gallimard.

Freyre, G. (1947) Prefácio. In M.R. Filho (ed.). *O Negro no Futebol Brasileiro*. Rio de Janeiro: Mauad.

Galeano, E. (1995) *El Futbol: A Sol Y Sombra Y Otros Escritos*. Buenos Aires: Siglo XXI Editores.

Gil, G.J. (2002) Soccer and kinship in Argentina: the mother's brother and the heritage of identity. *Soccer & Society*, 3(3), 11–25.

Gilman, H.R. (2016) *Engaging Citizens: Participatory Budgeting and the Inclusive Governance Movement within the United States*. Cambridge, MA: Harvard Kennedy School.

Giulianotti, R. (1999) *Football: A Sociology of the Global Game*. London: Polity Press.

Giulianotti, R. and Robertson, R. (2004) The globalization of football: a study in the glocalization of the "serious life". *British Journal of Sociology*, 55(4), 545–568. doi:10.1111/j.1468-4446.2004.00037.x

Giulianotti, R. and Robertson, R. (2009) *Globalization and Football* (1st ed.) London: Sage.

GloboEsporte. (2015) Torcida mista se consolida apos novo sucesso e conquista "Familia Gre-Nal". [online] Retrieved from: http://globoesporte.globo.com/rs/futebol/campeonato-gaucho/noticia/2015/04/torcida-mista-se-consolida-apos-novo-sucesso-e-conquista-familia-gre-nal.html

Internacional. (2015) Site Oficial. [online] Retrieved from: http://www.internacional.com.br

Itaipu. (2014) Foz terá primeiro centro de excelência de futebol feminino. [online] Retrieved from: https://www.itaipu.gov.br/sala-de-imprensa/noticia/foz-tera-primeiro-centro-de-excelencia-de-futebol-feminino

Kittleson, R. (2014) *The Country of Football: Soccer and the Making of Modern Brazil*. Berkeley: University of California Press.

Luhmann, N. (1997) Globalization or world Society: how to conceive of modern society? *International Review of Sociology: Revue Internationale de Sociologie*, 7(1), 67–79.

Maffesoli, M. (1988) *Le Temps des Tribus: Le déclin de l'individualisme dans les sociétés postmodernes* (3rd ed.). Courtry: La Table Ronde.

Maffesoli, M. (1990) *Au creux des apparences: Pour une éthique de l'esthétique* (3rd ed.). Paris: La Table Ronde.

Magno, F. (2014) A Copa do Mundo de Futebol em Porto Alegre: A relocação dos moradores afetados pela duplicação da Avenida Tronco. (MPhil in Human Movement Sciences), Federal University of Rio Grande do Sul, Porto Alegre.

Manfred, T. (2015) Brazil's $3 billion World Cup stadiums are becoming white elephants a year later. *Business Insider*. [online] Retrieved from: http://uk.businessinsider.com/brazil-world-cup-stadiums-one-year-later-2015-5

Mascarenhas, G. (2014) The adoption of soccer in southern Brazil: the influences of international boundaries immigrants. *Soccer & Society*, 15(1), 29–35.

Mason, T. (1980) *Association Football and English Society: 1863–1915* (1st ed.). Sussex: The Harvester Press.

Mason, T. (1995) *Passion of the People? Football in South America*. London: Verso.

Millward, P. (2011) *The Global Football League: Transnational Networks, Social Movements and Sport in the New Media Age* (1st ed.). New York: Palgrave.

Neto, C.C., Soares, R., Ferreira, I., Pompermayer, F., and Romminger, A. (2011) Gargalos e Demandas da Infraestrutura Rodoviária e os Investimentos do PAC: Mapeamento IPEA de Obras Rodoviárias. (1592) [online] Retrieved from: http://repositorio.ipea.gov.br/bitstream/11058/1637/1/TD_1592.pdf

NYT. (2017) George Weah Wins Liberia Election. [online] Retrieved from: https://www.nytimes.com/2017/12/28/world/africa/george-weah-liberia-election.html

O'Neill, J. (2001) Building Better Global Economic BRICs. *Global Economic Paper* 66, 1–16.

Pasolini, P.P. (2015) *Sobre el deporte*. Barcelona: Contra.

Pearson, S. (2014) Brazil faces problem of "white elephant cities" after World Cup. *Financial Times*. [online] Retrieved from: https://www.ft.com/content/7c207b1e-dfff-11e3-b709-00144feabdc0

Petersen-Wagner, R. (2017a) Cultural consumption through the epistemologies of the South: "humanization" in transnational football fan solidarities. *Current Sociology*, 65(7), 953–970.

Petersen-Wagner, R. (2017b) The football supporter in a cosmopolitan epoch. *Journal of Sport & Social Issues*, 41(2), 133–150.

Petersen-Wagner, R. (2017c) Symbolic footprints: media representations of host countries. In L.J. Mataruna-dos-Santos and B.G. Pena (eds), *Mega Events Footprints: Past, Present and Future*. Rio de Janeiro: Engenho, pp. 319–344.

Pluri Consultoria (2014) O Impacto das novas arenas sobre o público e a renda do campeonato. [online] Retrieved from: http://www.pluriconsultoria.com.br/uploads/relatorios/pluri%20especial%20-%20 aumento%20de%20publico%20novas%20arenas%202014.pdf

PMPA. (2018) Portal da Transparência e Acesso a Informação – Copa do Mundo FIFA 2014 – Sede Porto Alegre. [online] Retrieved from: http://www2.portoalegre.rs.gov.br/transparencia/default. php?p_secao=28

Rein, R. (1998) "El primer deportista": the political use and abuse of sport in peronist Argentina. *International Journal of the History of Sport*, 15(2), 54–76.

Rein, R. (2015) *Fútbol, Jews, and the making of Argentina* (M. Grenzeback, Trans.) Stanford: Stanford University Press.

Reis, J.J., and Gomes, F.d.S. (Eds.) (1996) *Liberdade por um fio: História dos quilombos no Brasil*. São Paulo: Cia das Letras.

Rosa, M. (2014) Theories of the South: limits and perpectives of an emergent movement in social sciences. *Current Sociology Review*, 62(6), 851–867.

Said, E.W. (1994) *Culture and Imperialism* (2nd ed.) London: Vintage Books.

Santos, B.d.S. (1998) Participatory budgeting in Porto Alegre: towards a redistributive justice. *Politics and Society*, 26(4), 461–510.

StadiumDB. (2015) Brazil: a completely different derby experience. [online] Retrieved from: http://www. stadiumdb.com/news/2015/11/brazil_a_completely_different_derby_experience

Street, J. (2004) Celebrity politicians: popular culture and political representation. *British Journal of Politics and International Relations*, 6(4), 435–452.

Street, J. (2012) Do celebrity politics and celebrity politicians matter? *British Journal of Politics and International Relations*, 14(3), 346–356.

Taylor, M. (2006) Global Players? Football, Migration and Globalization, c. 1930-2000. *Historical Social Research*, 31(1), 7–30.

Weber, M. (2013) *Economy and Society*. Berkeley: University of California Press.

Wheeler, M. (2013) *Celebrity Politics: Image and Identity in Contemporary Political Communication*. London: Polity.

Zoonen, L.v. (2006) The personal, the political and the popular: a woman's guide to celebrity politics. *European Journal of Cultural Studies*, 9(3), 287–301.

37

Asian Football Confederation

N. David Pifer

Introduction

The Asian Football Confederation (AFC) serves as FIFA's governing body for association football in Australia and most of Asia. The only exceptions to this classification are certain nations (i.e., Azerbaijan, Georgia, Kazakhstan, Russia, Turkey, Armenia, and Israel) that lie on the borders between Europe and Asia, in which case they have been classified with Europe's governing body, the Union of European Football Associations (UEFA). As of 2017, the AFC was comprised of 46 member associations and one associate member (the Northern Mariana Islands). A complete list of the member nations and states can be seen in Table 37.1.

The AFC was formed in 1954 in Manila and officially sanctioned in June of that same year by FIFA (AFC, 2018a). Founding members included Afghanistan, Myanmar, China, Hong Kong, India, Israel, Indonesia, Japan, South Korea, Pakistan, Philippines, Singapore, and Vietnam. South Korea is the most successful nation in the AFC in terms of FIFA World Cup appearances, having qualified for the tournament on ten occasions. The South Koreans have also advanced further than any other Asian nation at the tournament, making it to the semi-finals and finishing in fourth place as joint hosts of the competition in 2002. Japan, with six appearances, is the second most successful side. Australia, which did not join the AFC until 2006, Saudi Arabia, and Iran, have each qualified for the tournament on five occasions. These figures account for the fact that all five of the nations mentioned above qualified for the 2018 FIFA World Cup in Russia.

In addition to being members of the broader AFC, the nations' individual federations are further grouped within one of five regional associations: the West Asian Football Federation (WAFF), the ASEAN (Association of South East Asian Nations) Football Federation (AFF), the East Asian Football Federation (EAFF), the South Asian Football Federation (SAFF), and the Central Asian Football Association (CAFA). The WAFF and AFF are the largest federations with 12 members each. The EAFF contains ten members, while the SAFF and CAFA are the two smallest divisions with seven and six members, respectively (AFC, 2018b).

The main international-level football event organised and operated by the AFC is the AFC Asian Cup, which crowns the winning nation as the Asian champion. Started in 1956, the competition is the second-oldest continental football championship in the world behind only South America's Copa America. Like many other major football tournaments, it is staged on a

Table 37.1 Asian Football Confederation members and statistics

Nation	Member since	Avg. FIFA rank (2014–2017)	World Cup appearances / last appearance (through 2018)	
Afghanistan	1954	148	0	–
Australia	2006	62	5	2018
Bangladesh	1973	182	0	–
Bahrain	1969	124	0	–
Bhutan	1993	191	0	–
Brunei	1969	189	0	–
Cambodia	1954	175	0	–
China	1974	80	1	2002
Guam	1991	173	0	–
Hong Kong	1954	143	0	–
Indonesia	1954	169	1	1938
India	1954	144	0	–
Iran	1954	41	5	2018
Iraq	1970	98	1	1986
Jordan	1970	97	0	–
Japan	1954	49	6	2018
Kyrgyzstan	1993	126	0	–
South Korea	1954	55	10	2018
Saudi Arabia	1972	75	5	2018
Kuwait	1964	155	1	1982
Laos	1968	167	0	–
Lebanon	1964	128	0	–
Macau	1978	186	0	–
Malaysia	1954	164	0	–
Maldives	1984	150	0	–
Mongolia	1993	198	0	–
Myanmar	1954	153	0	–
Nepal	1954	184	0	–
Northern Mariana Islands*	2009	NA	0	–
Oman	1980	107	0	–
Pakistan	1954	193	0	–
Philippines	1954	126	0	–
Palestine	1995	116	0	–
North Korea	1974	128	2	2010
Qatar	1974	91	0	–
Singapore	1954	161	0	–
Sri Lanka	1954	190	0	–
Syria	1970	112	0	–
Thailand	1954	135	0	–
Tajikistan	1993	134	0	–
Turkmenistan	1993	131	0	–
East Timor	2002	185	0	–
Chinese Taipei	1954	166	0	–
United Arab Emirates	1974	71	1	1990
Uzbekistan	1993	72	0	–
Vietnam	1978	135	0	–
Yemen	1980	153	0	–

Note: The Northern Mariana Islands are not members of FIFA, so they do not have a FIFA ranking; data obtained from www.the–afc.com

four-year cycle with rotating hosts. The latest edition of the tournament was held, and won, by Australia in 2015. The AFC also helps manage the Asian Ladies Football Confederation (ALFC), which oversees the women's game in the region and the AFC Women's Asian Cup tournament. Each AFC region also organises its own periodic tournaments for its respective nations to compete in. As of 2017, South Korea (EAFF), India (SAFF), Thailand (AFF), and Qatar (WAFF) were the reigning champions in these regional competitions. The CAFA is slated to host its first regional tournament in 2018.

In addition to staging events for its national team federations, the AFC also oversees the club scenes across Asia and Australia. Its premier competition in this regard is the AFC Champions League, an annual continental football tournament that pits the most successful clubs from the AFC's top leagues, based on their finishing positions in the prior season, against one another in a 32-club tournament that begins with a group stage and advances to a series of knockout rounds. The most successful club to date has been the Pohang Steelers, a team from South Korea's top club league, the K League. The Steelers have won the competition three times, with their most recent victory coming in 2009. Eleven other clubs have won the competition twice, including the 2017 champion Urawa Red Diamonds of Japan's J1 League (AFC, 2018c).

Like its counterparts on other continents, the AFC Champions League uses historical performance data and other criteria such as league marketability and stadia infrastructure to determine which leagues will be represented more prominently in the competition. The higher a league's ranking in relation to these criteria, the greater the number of clubs that can directly qualify for the competition via their domestic performances. Table 37.2 lists all of the current member

Table 37.2 AFC Champions League qualification spots and champion nations (2010–17)

	2010	2011	2012	2013	2014	2015	2016	2017
East Asia								
Australia	2	2	3	1	3*	2	2	3
China	4	4	3	4*	4	4*	4	3
Hong Kong	0	0	0	0	0	0	0	1
Indonesia	1	1	0	0	0	0	0	0
Japan	4	4	4*	4	4	4	4	4*
South Korea	4*	4	4	4	4	4	4*	4
Singapore	1	0	0	0	0	0	0	0
Thailand	0	0	1	1	1	1	1	1
Vietnam	0	0	0	0	0	1	1	0
West Asia								
Bahrain	0	0	0	0	0	0	0	0
Iran	4	4	3	3	4	4	3	4
Iraq	0	0	0	0	0	0	0	0
Kuwait	0	0	0	0	0	0	0	0
Qatar	2	3*	4	4	4	2	2	2
Saudi Arabia	4	4	3	4	4	4	4	4
Syria	0	0	0	0	0	0	0	0
Turkmenistan	0	0	0	0	0	0	0	0
UAE	4	4	4	4	3	2	3	4
Uzbekistan	2	2	3	2	1	4	4	2

Note: *Indicates that season's AFC Champions League winner came from that league; data obtained from www. the-afc.com nations that have supplied a team to the AFC Champions League in the past, along with the number of direct qualification spots they are currently awarded. Countries that had a team win the AFC Champions League from 2010 to 2017 are also identified in the table. Thanks in part to a host of sponsorship agreements and increased broadcast rights deals, the tournament is able to award clubs $50,000 for every group stage win they secure, in addition to a $3 million purse for the winner of the tournament and a $1.5 million prize for the runner-up. The annual winners of the tournament also gain entry into the FIFA Club World Cup, the yearly event that plays host to the winners of each governing body's continental competition. Though Asian clubs have finished in third place at the competition on six occasions, only one – the J1 League's Kashima Antlers in 2016 – has ever made it through to the finals (FIFA, 2018a).

Chinese football: The next frontier?

Beginning with a look at China is only fitting given that FIFA credits the world's most populous nation with football's ancient origins. Indeed, the Han Dynasty's primitive version of the sport, known as *Tsu' Chu*, required players to fend off opponents while manoeuvring (without the use of their hands) a leather ball stuffed with feathers and hair through a small opening on the opposite end of the playing field (FIFA, 2018b). A couple of millennia and the English transformation of the game later, it is perhaps surprising that the modern version of the sport has not become a mainstay in Chinese society. Though football is popular and upwards of 26 million people – the most of any country – are said to play the game in a nation that contains nearly 1.4 billion inhabitants (FIFA, 2006), China's obsession with individual sports and Olympic glory have remained at the forefront of its sporting culture in recent decades [see also Chapter 40 in this handbook]. In a phenomenon not dissimilar to other populous countries like India and the United States, participation at the grassroots level has not translated into sustained success at the higher levels of the game.

This could all change, though, given the recent emphasis that was placed on football by Chinese authorities, the least of whom was President Xi Jinping. Xi, a self-proclaimed fan of the sport, who has frequently called for China to revamp its youth development systems and playing standards in order to enhance the game for future generations of Chinese footballers. In 2015, Xi created a special cabinet with the purposes of articulating a strategic plan for the development of football in China; in 2016, the cabinet and Chinese Football Association released an ambitious list of goals and target dates that included putting 70,000 football pitches into service, training 10,000 coaches, doubling the number of specialised academies to 20,000, producing two to three first-class clubs, and increasing its football-playing population from 26 million to 50 million by 2020. According to Xi, the purpose is to "strive to realise the goal of becoming a first-rate major footballing power, realise the all-around development of Chinese football, fulfil the football dreams of the sons and daughters of China, and fulfil our obligations to world football" (*Japan Times*, 2016, para. 5). Also included in the cabinet's release were the longer-term goals of having its men's national team become the best team in Asia and the women's national team return to its prior status as a world power by 2030. The plan further stated that it intended for the men's team to rank among the world's elite by 2050 (Mai, 2016).

As of January 1, 2018, the Chinese men were ranked No. 71 in FIFA's world rankings, sixth-best among all AFC national teams. The women were ranked No. 16. This, however, is not to say that China is stalling in its attempts to get the figurative ball rolling. The Chinese Super League (CSL), the top men's league in China's club system, spent $451.3 million during the 2017 transfer windows on mostly foreign talent (FIFA TMS, 2017). That figure, alone, was 344% per cent higher than the rest of the AFC clubs' expenditures combined. Many of the big names that were brought in had been members of, or targets for, Europe's elite. Meanwhile, the women's national team responded almost simultaneously to Xi's calls for reform, putting together a relatively impressive quarterfinal showing at the 2015 FIFA Women's World Cup after failing to qualify for the tournament for the first time in 2011.

Is, however, any of this evidence of Xi's plan taking hold? Is China set to become a dominant force in world football in the not-to-distant future? While the nation's footballing goals were clearly outlined in its plans for reform, and there is surface evidence of these changes being enacted, questions remain as to whether or not China and its current strategies are on the right track. In this regard, researchers have already begun examining and offering their opinions on a number of these topics. For starters, Andrei Markovits, a professor of comparative politics at the University of Michigan, has doubts that China will be able to implement its plans over the long term because the nation is still playing catch-up to the football superpowers. "It is very hard to buy success in a team sport, not only football, because such sports are deeply rooted in popular culture and have everything to do with little kids playing them from when they start to walk," noted Markovits. "In other words, one cannot plan these things from above like one can individual sports" (*Japan Times*, 2016, para. 12). There are also questions about whether Chinese parents will buy into the plan's philosophy of treating football as an important educational function when team sports rely heavily on elements external to the individual's talent.

Nonetheless, while it may be difficult for a country and its inhabitants to plan or buy success for their children in a team sport like football, or for a culture not immersed in the sport to find its legs in a decent period of time, it is perhaps possible at the higher levels for clubs and club owners to purchase success. Indeed, much has been made across world football of the relationship between player acquisition costs (i.e., wages and transfer fees) and where clubs tend to finish in the league standings. Generally, the evidence has suggested that there is a positive correlation between how much clubs spend on players and where they finish in a given league's table (Hall, Szymanski, and Zimbalist, 2002; Tomkins, Riley, and Fulcher, 2010). This is particularly evident in the more free-market, open leagues that operate throughout Europe. Recently, clubs in the CSL seem to have taken a page from this book, splashing the cash on expensive foreign players without hesitation. The numbers reported in Figure 37.1 show just

CSL TRANSFER SPENDING (2014–2017)

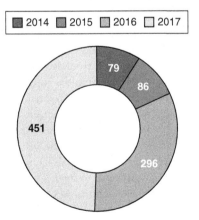

Figure 37.1   A comparison of Chinese Super League transfer spending from 2014–2017; all numbers are reported in millions (USD); data obtained from the FIFA Transfer Matching System (www.fifatms.com/data-reports/)

how much the league's expenditures on transfer fees have grown over the past few seasons (FIFA TMS, 2016; 2017).

The surge in transfer fees being paid by CSL clubs for foreign players occurred shortly after the release of China's plans for football supremacy. In the 2015–2016 transfer window, for example, CSL clubs spent nearly $296 million on transfer fees (FIFA TMS, 2016). Comparatively, the world's wealthiest and most popular footballing league, the English Premier League (EPL), spent $181 million in that same window. Jiangsu Suning FC, a generally mid-level CSL team, ignited the spending spree with the $32 million acquisition of Brazilian midfielder Ramires from Chelsea FC of the EPL. They were outdone shortly thereafter by Guangzhou Evergrande's $48 million payment for Alex Teixeira of Shakhtar Donetsk (Ukraine) in a move that reportedly offered the Brazilian $11.5 million a year over the duration of a four-year contract. In the summer of 2016, Shanghai SIPG paid approximately $58 million for FC Porto's (Portugal) Brazilian forward Hulk and returned again in January of that season to sign Oscar from Chelsea for nearly $63 million. That same winter, Argentinian striker Carlos Tevez was bought from Boca Juniors (Argentina) for $11 million by Shanghai Shenhua and made the highest paid player in the world, with some reports suggesting that his wages were in excess of $750,000 per week (Doyle, 2017).

The money being spent on players has also coincided with some of the world's premier managers arriving in China, as the likes of Andre Villas-Boas, Fabio Capello, and Manuel Pellegrini have all plied their trade in the CSL at various points in time. Even so, the league's history of translating foreign star power into long-term success is shaky at best. After all, a smaller version of this strategy was attempted by the CSL's Shanghai Shenhua in 2012 when former Chelsea teammates Didier Drogba and Nicolas Anelka were brought into the fold in big money moves. The catalytic transfers did not go as expected, however, with Drogba opting to return to Europe after just half a season following claims of lacklustre football and unpaid wages. Many within China regarded the failure to retain his services as a national embarrassment (Ramzy, 2013). In January 2018, misfortune struck again for Shanghai Shenhua after it was reported that Tevez would be leaving the club after one injury-plagued season that included just 16 league appearances and four goals. "His performances were disappointing for many Chinese fans and I'm not really sure what he did that was good for the club or for football in China," noted one of China's leading football journalists. "I think he thought it would be easy and he said some things that weren't good for the club as well … He got so much money, but he didn't prove he deserved it" (Church, 2018, para. 10).

These cash outlays and examples of failure in the transfer market raise interesting questions as to whether or not the CSL's current strategy of spending money on foreign talent is the best method of boosting football in China as a whole. While one line of thought entertains the possibility that China's domestic players will benefit from being surrounded by world-class opponents, teammates, and coaches, the other suggests that their opportunities and growth may be stifled by the continuous arrival of foreign imports. Furthermore, the money being invested in inflated player wages and transfer fees could be invested in other, more sustainable areas. This is certainly akin to the arguments so frequently cited in England, where fans of the English national team highlight the EPL's reliance on foreign talent as a reason for the national team having not won a World Cup title since 1966. Perhaps unsurprisingly, the CSL has now limited the number of foreign players who can take the pitch in a given match to three. The league also revised a previous policy whereby clubs were allowed to field an additional AFC (non-Chinese) player in the line-up, changing the rule to read that teams must now include a Chinese player under the age of 23 (Church, 2017).

All of this has done little, though, to alter the perceptions of the league's current and potential viewers. The clubs are majority owned by Chinese companies that see their investments in football as a way to gain favouritism in Xi's eyes (Price, 2017). As such, the associated government influence and corporate kickbacks have not helped the image of a brand already tarnished by subpar play and the prior failures to keep some of its biggest stars happy. Previous studies have shown that there is indeed a general distrust of the CSL's operations as viewers have struggled to overcome negative perceptions of match-fixing and poor match quality (Gong et al., 2015). Better marketing has also been cited as a necessary pre-requisite for increased satisfaction. Perhaps if the league can continue to free itself from controversy, bureaucratic mishandlings, and failed player transfers, it could fulfil Xi's goals of competing with the world's elite. In the meantime, researchers would be wise to take a long look at the impact, both positive and negative, that the CSL is having on Chinese football across the board, and whether or not the strategy of spending for success is optimal and sustainable. It is also worth examining what is required to market and manage the league in a way that befits Xi's agenda and the ultimate advancement of the game.

South Korea and Japan: The standard bearers

While football in China is still overcoming some of its internal and rudimentary challenges, the nations and leagues on the other side of the Yellow Sea have experienced more fundamental and consistent success. On the international stage, South Korea and Japan have histories of advancing to the knockout rounds of the FIFA World Cup. China, on the other hand, has only qualified for the tournament on one occasion. Japan's women's national team also won the FIFA Women's World Cup in 2011, becoming the first Asian nation to ever do so. Japan and South Korea were also the first Asian countries awarded the rights to host a FIFA World Cup when they joint-hosted the event in 2002. By most accounts, the event was a veritable success. Lee and Taylor (2005) noted that the tournament provided the nations with a unique opportunity to showcase their skills and abilities, develop business contacts, partner with investors, and promote international awareness. They also noted the positive, social legacy that was left with the locals as the success of the teams, and in particular, South Korea provided the countries with immeasurable feelings of national pride and unity. From a structural capital perspective, the stadia and infrastructure developed for the tournament remained in use in the years that followed, allowing the nations' domestic leagues and clubs to play in state-of-the-art facilities. It is perhaps no surprise, then, that both South Korea's K League and Japan's J1 League have managed to sustain operations in the years that have followed.

However, it cannot be said that these leagues have reached their full potential. After all, much like the United States and other countries where football is not the primary sport, the best Korean and Japanese players (e.g., Hidetoshi Nakata, Kazu Miura, Keisuke Honda, Shunsuke Nakamura, Shinji Kagawa, and Shinji Okazaki of Japan; Park Ji-Sung, Ki Sung-yueng, and Son Heung-min of South Korea) tend to migrate to European clubs during the peak years of their careers. This, in addition to the general levels of global popularity carried by the non-Asian, superstar players and clubs, means that the European version of the sport remains more desirable across much of East Asia. In response, many EPL teams embark on preseason tours across the continent for the purposes of bolstering their fan bases in these previously untapped market areas. While good for the game as a whole, this could be part of the reason why researchers have found that K League and J1 League spectators do not identify heavily with the local clubs (Won and Kitamura, 2006). Seeing as there is still room for attendance to grow in both of these competitions, marketers, and managers in these leagues would be wise to foster higher levels of team identification among current and potential supporters.

While the operations of these leagues have held steady on the surface, their revenue streams have started to show signs of weakness in recent seasons. This is particularly true with some of the K League's smaller market clubs, where unpaid wages and the withdrawal of certain bankrolling companies have left a handful of teams in flux (Williams, 2016). The K League's image has also been tarnished in recent years by its own match-fixing scandals, political owner-ship motivations, and poor play. As a result, recent broadcast deals for the K League have not been up to global or even Asian standards, with the latest deal reportedly worth just $5 million a season. By comparison, the J1 League has a $20 million-a-season deal in place, Australia's A-League earns approximately $29 million a season, and the CSL – fresh off its transfer spending sprees and corporate investments – recently garnered a staggering $250 million a season from the sale of its broadcast rights. Large Korean corporations such as Samsung have also pulled their financial backing away from clubs as shrinking tax benefits and financial struggles have limited their sporting contributions. The subsequent lack of commercial and broadcast funding means the clubs must rely more heavily on ticket sales and local revenues, but such funding can be hard to come by when clubs lack star power and are more closely associated with privatised compa-nies than the cities that host them (Williams, 2016).

As the revenues flee to other areas of Asia, many of the top domestic players find it in their best interests to play abroad. One such expatriate, Lee Young-pyo, formerly of Borussia Dortmund (Germany) and Tottenham (England), said:

> It is certainly true that there are many people who are concerned about the absence of elite players in the K League. The elite players will be staying in the market with a strong financial base and it is not easy to change this pattern.
>
> *(Williams, 2016, para. 42)*

Speaking further about the K League, South Korea's Ki Sung-yueng, who also left his homeland to play in England, noted that "there are many people who put in their best effort to improve the [K League] and achieve some improvement, but there is still a long way to go" (para. 25). Ki even went so far as to note that he "doubts what would change" in the long-term if he, and some of his expatriate teammates, were to return toward the end of their careers (para. 26).

While such information suggests that the near-term future looks more promising for the CSL from a financial standpoint, it is the J1 League and K League clubs that the CSL will likely have to overcome if it wants to monopolise the AFC Champions League and other regional competitions. As Table 37.3 shows, South Korean clubs have 11 AFC Champions League titles,

Table 37.3 AFC Champions League title winners by nation

Nation	Champions	Finalists	Last champion
South Korea	11	6	2012
Japan	6	3	2017
Saudi Arabia	4	9	2005
Iran	3	4	1993
China	3	2	2015
Israel*	3	1	1971
Qatar	2	1	2011
Thailand	2	1	1994
UAE	1	3	2003
Australia**	1	1	2014

Notes: *Israel left the AFC in 1974; **Australia joined in 2006; data obtained from www.the-afc.com

Table 37.4 Demographic statistics of AFC Champions League winners (2013–2017)

Year	Club	Nation	Age	Total Value	Foreign
2013	Guangzhou Evergrande	China	26.455	18.920	66.6%
2014	West Sydney Wanderers	Australia	26.818	0.000	0.0%
2015	Guangzhou Evergrande	China	26.273	33.475	66.6%
2016	Jeonbuk Hyundai Motors	S. Korea	27.727	1.850	100.0%
2017	Urawa Red Diamonds	Japan	28.000	0.200	0.0%

Notes: Age is expressed as an average of the 11 players with the most minutes played in AFC Champions League competition; *Total Value* denotes the reported value, in transfer fee expenditures, of the 11 players with the most minutes played; *Foreign* is expressed as the percentage of the transfer expenditures (*Total Value*) that was invested in foreign players; all data was obtained from www.transfermarkt.com.

more than any other Asian nation, while Japan is second with six. It is also the Japanese and Korean leagues that have managed to operate relatively smoothly since 1993 and 1983, respectively. Their recent moves away from in-depth corporate and government involvement further show that they are capable of innovating, which is something the CSL will likely have to do if it also wishes to prosper in the long run. In the absence of revenues that are capable of attracting domestic, European, or South American superstars, Japanese and Korean clubs have flipped the script and begun plucking marquee talent from some of the AFC's more obscure nations. This, in turn, has not only provided them with skilful players, but also newfound followings in countries such as Vietnam where the sport is still growing (Williams, 2016).

How they can capitalise on their innovations and continue competing in a setting where China is attempting to become a world power will be interesting to examine in the years ahead. Researchers have mentioned how analytics are helping to shape the footballing landscape [see also Chapter 20 in this handbook], particularly in leagues and clubs where funds are limited (Pifer et al., 2018). Small market teams and AFC Champions League competitors from less-populated nations could certainly benefit from having proper data and data analysts in place. From player scouting networks to studies of opponents' strengths and weaknesses, properly guided data can help level the playing field in a setting where money has traditionally dominated. Looking at the demographics of the AFC Champions League winners over the past five seasons (2013–2017) in Table 37.4, there does not appear to be a consistent strategy in terms of how the winning clubs spent their money in the transfer market. Some of the title winners, such as the A-League's West Sydney Wanderers and Japan's Urawa Red Diamonds, spent little to nothing in terms of transfer fees for their starters, while Chinese club Guangzhou Evergrande invested considerably more, mostly in foreign talent. If success on the pitch is the primary motivation, managers would be wise to examine those strategies that have proven successful, relative to the financial standings of their clubs and the competition. On the other hand, if a club is simply looking to boost its reputation and awareness, it could spend the money on star players regardless of what ends up happening on the field of play. Ultimately, the underlying motivations help determine what data are useful and how the decisions should be made.

Looking Ahead: Qatar 2022, the AFC's second World Cup

While Japan and South Korea's hosting of the 2002 FIFA World Cup was regarded by many as a success for Asian football, Qatar's hosting of the 2022 edition of the tournament will be hard-pressed to live up to its continent's previous standards. This, of course, will likely not be due to the show that Qatar – a wealthy oil nation – will put on, the quality of play on the pitch, or the state-of-the-art stadia that will be erected for play in a suboptimal, desert climate. Rather, it will be the allegations of corruption, bribery, and human rights violations that have overshadowed Qatar's bidding and preparation processes that will make it hard for Asia's second hosting of the games to live up to the initial billing.

On 2 December 2010, it was announced that Qatar had been awarded the 2022 FIFA World Cup ahead of countries such as Japan, South Korea, and the United States. Almost immediately, questions arose as to how a nation with a population of just 2.57 million and an average summer temperature of 120 degrees Fahrenheit (48.89 degrees Celsius) could host such a spectacle. It was also puzzling to some that Qatar, rather than some of West Asia's historically more successful nations such as the UAE and Saudi Arabia, was elected to serve as host of the event. Qatar had never qualified for a FIFA World Cup in the past, and its history of club footballing success at the time was rather limited. Fast forward to May 2011, and allegations of bribery among FIFA officials began to surface within some of FIFA's poorer nations. The claims stated that under-the-table payments had been made to these officials in exchange for them voting for Qatar as the recipient of the 2022 tournament. In the media and legal storms that followed, former FIFA President Sepp Blatter was forced to step down, and several of the involved officials faced criminal prosecution for racketeering and money laundering. Nonetheless, with the investigations ongoing, Qatar retained the rights to the tournament, and for the time being has continued to prepare for 2022. This, however, has not ended the controversies, as reports of slave labour and construction-related deaths continue to position the nation's preparations in a negative light (Manfred, 2015).

Assuming Qatar can overcome these negative, preliminary issues and host the games without any major problems, the tournament will be a hallmark event for West Asia and the Middle East. For starters, Qatar is expected to introduce the footballing world to new technologies such as solar powered and air-conditioned stadia that could help expand the sport into previously uncharted territories and leave a positive legacy for those with environmental concerns. Qatari officials are pledging that this will be one of the most environmentally friendly World Cups ever hosted, with some of the completed venues already receiving the Global Sustainability Assessment System's four-star rating (FIFA, 2017a). Indeed, the 40,000-seat Khalifa International Stadium is the first in the world to receive four-star certification, doing so on the back of energy efficient cooling technology, lighting systems, and plumbing fixtures. The stadium will also feature a sensory room to which spectators with cognitive and learning disabilities can escape should the sights and sounds of the games overtake them (FIFA, 2017b). Marketing itself as "a football experience for all," the 2022 World Cup in Qatar could set a new benchmark in the areas of inclusion and sustainability should the plans to host remain in place.

Conclusion

While there is still much work to be done on and off the pitch if the AFC and its member clubs and nations hope to become recognised forces in the world of football, the prior evidence indicates that the region is taking various steps in the right direction. With large economies and emerging fan bases, the AFC could one day serve as host to some of the world's elite players and teams. *Soccernomics* authors Simon Kuper and Stefan Szymanski note that, "To win at sports, you need to find, develop, and nurture talent. Doing that requires money, know-how, and some kind of administrative infrastructure" (2012, p. 353). The duo's findings of a correlation between nations' places in the United Nations' development index and their athletic success demonstrate the importance of wealth and infrastructure in establishing a national sport. Japan and South Korea already have many of these measures in place, and China's economic growth in recent decades may just tilt the bar in its favour as it moves ahead with plans to dominate the football landscape. Similarly, AFC countries that are able to host a World Cup may find themselves endowed with the infrastructures and inspired populations that can help them create and maintain footballing success. As further noted by Kuper and Szymanski, experience will also prove pivotal to long-term success, as talented coaches, players, tactics, and training methods disseminate from their European centres to the rest of the world. Some might say this is already happening in Asia. Others might argue that millions of dollars in foreign transfer fees and wages could help pave the way. Regardless, the *Soccernomics'* authors envision a future where an AFC nation wins the World Cup: "The best bets for the future are probably Japan, the U.S., or China: the three largest economies on Earth" (p. 409). With the right resources and leadership in place, it will be interesting to see what these countries can accomplish moving forward.

References

AFC, (2018a) The Asian Football Confederation. [online] Retrieved from: http://www.the-afc.com/about-afc_1/

AFC, (2018b) Member Associations. [online] Retrieved from: http://www.the-afc.com/about-afc_1/memberassociations/

AFC, (2018c) Archive. [online] Retrieved from: http://www.the-afc.com/competitions/afc-champions-league/archive/

Church, M. (2017) Chinese FA confirms limit on foreign players for Super League clubs. [online] Retrieved from: http://www.espn.com/soccer/chinese-super-league/story/3039771/chinese-fa-confirms-limit-on-foreign-players-for-super-league-clubs

Church, M. (2018) Carlos Tevez departs China under a cloud to return to Boca Juniors. [online] Retrieved from: http://www.espn.com/soccer/chinese-super-league/0/blog/post/3340945/carlos-tevez-departs-china-under-a-cloud-to-return-to-boca-juniors

Doyle, M. (2017) CSL the world's highest-spending league in 2017. [online] Retrieved from: http://www.goal.com/en-us/news/china-spend-whopping-330m-in-2017-transfer-window/mezho0jgfhzm1bbyseb59p780

FIFA, (2006) 265 million playing football. [online] Retrieved from: https://www.fifa.com/mm/document/fifafacts/bcoffsurv/emaga_9384_10704.pdf

FIFA, (2017a) Khalifa International Stadium receives major sustainability award. [online] Retrieved from: http://www.fifa.com/worldcup/news/y=2017/m=11/news=khalifa-international-stadium-receives-major-sustainability-award-2921733.html

FIFA, (2017b) A football experience for all, at Qatar 2022. [online] Retrieved from: http://www.fifa.com/worldcup/news/y=2017/m=12/news=a-footballing-experience-for-all-at-qatar-2022-2923861.html

FIFA, (2018a) FIFA Club World Cup. [online] Retrieved from: http://www.fifa.com/fifa-tournaments/statistics-and-records/clubworldcup/index.html

FIFA, (2018b) History of football: The origins. [online] Retrieved from: http://www.fifa.com/about-fifa/who-we-are/the-game/index.html

FIFA TMS, (2016) Monthly insights: China PR. [pdf] Zurich, Switzerland: FIFA Transfer Matching System. Retrieved from: https://www.fifatms.com/data-reports/

FIFA TMS, (2017) Global transfer market report 2017. [pdf] Zurich, Switzerland: FIFA Transfer Matching System. [online] Retrieved from: https://www.fifatms.com/data-reports/

Gong, B., Pifer, N. D., Wang, J.J., Kim, M., Kim, M., Qian, T.Y., and Zhang, J.J. (2015) Fans' attention to, involvement in, and satisfaction with professional soccer in China. *Social Behavior and Personality: An International Journal*, 43(10), 1667–1682.

Hall, S., Szymanski, S., and Zimbalist, A.S. (2002) Testing causality between team performance and payroll: the cases of Major League Baseball and English soccer. *Journal of Sports Economics*, 3(2), 149–168.

Japan Times, (2016) China announces ambitious plan to join world soccer elite [online] Retrieved from: https://www.japantimes.co.jp/sports/2016/04/12/soccer/china-announces-ambitious-plan-join-world-soccer-elite/#.Wl8PqainFPa

Kuper, S. and Szymanski, S. (2012) *Soccernomics: Why England Loses, Why Spain, Germany, and Brazil Win, and Why the US, Japan, Australia, Turkey—and Even Iraq—Are Destined to Become The Kings of The World's Most Popular Sport.* New York: Nation Books, pp. 353–409.

Lee, C.K. and Taylor, T. (2005) Critical reflections on the economic impact assessment of a mega event: the case of 2002 FIFA World Cup. *Tourism Management*, 26(4), 595–603.

Mai, J. (2016) China sets out grand plan to become world's soccer superpower by 2050. [online] Retrieved from: http://www.scmp.com/news/china/policies-politics/article/1935166/china-sets-out-grand-plan-become-worlds-soccer

Manfred, T. (2015) 14 reasons the Qatar World Cup is going to be a disaster. [online] Retrieved from: https://sports.yahoo.com/news/14-reasons-qatar-world-cup-174400894.html

Pifer, N.D., Wang, Y., Scremin, G., Pitts, B.G., and Zhang, J.J. (2018) Contemporary global football industry: an introduction. In: J.J. Zhang and B.G. Pitts, (eds.). *The Global Football Industry: Marketing Perspectives*, (1st ed.) (pp. 3–35). New York: Routledge.

Price, S. (2017) Why Chinese clubs are breaking transfer records—and why players are wise to go. [online] Retrieved from: https://www.theguardian.com/football/these-football-times/2017/jan/05/china-chinese-super-league-oscar-carlos-tevez

Ramzy, A. (2013) Didier Drogba leaves China: Inside a failed football experiment. [online] Retrieved from: http://keepingscore.blogs.time.com/2013/01/30/didier-drogba-leaves-china-inside-a-failed-soccer-experiment/

Tomkins, P., Riley, G., and Fulcher, G. (2010) *Pay as You Play: The True Price of Success in the Premier League Era*. United Kingdom: GPRF Publishing, pp. 1–340.

Williams, P. (2016) Struggling K-League turning to Southeast Asia for assistance. [online] Retrieved from: https://www.fourfourtwo.com/sg/features/struggling-k-league-turning-southeast-asia-assistance.

Won, J.U. and Kitamura, K. (2006) Motivational factors affecting sports consumption behavior of K-League and J-League spectators. *International Journal of Sport and Health Science*, 4, 233–251.

38

Confederation of African Football

Michael M. Goldman and Mlondi Mashinini

Introduction

History and organisation of CAF

Before the establishment of the Confederation of African Football (CAF) in 1957, football management in Africa had been a colonial endeavour, driven by missionaries and colonial governments. By 1954, Egypt, Sudan, Ethiopia, and South Africa had joined FIFA and were represented at the 29th FIFA Congress in Switzerland. Africa was recognized as a FIFA zonal group that year, with Egyptian Abdelaziz Abdallah Salem being elected to represent Africa on the executive committee until a confederation was established. Representatives of Egypt, Sudan, and South Africa met at the 1956 FIFA Congress in Portugal to develop the statutes and regulations for the new confederation and for an Africa Cup of Nations (AFCON). In early 1957, representatives from Ethiopia joined the group for the first Constitutional Assembly of CAF, which was immediately followed by the first AFCON on February 10 (CAF, 2007).

Although football as a "European cultural form" had been used by Christian missionaries, colonial governments, and industrialists to encourage discipline, maintain order, and occupy workers' free time, the game had also been used as part of the resistance to colonial rule (Fletcher, 2017). Football and CAF membership were "vehicles for pan-Africanism" in postcolonial Africa (Fletcher, 2017). National independence in Ghana, Uganda, Nigeria, Kenya, and Zambia was marked by football tournaments featuring their new national teams. For example, Kwame Nkrumah, the first independent president of Ghana, actively used football to promote national and African unity. In this way, the nation-football nexus played an important part of forming a post-colonial identity across Africa. More recently, the "African World Cup" narrative surrounding the 2010 FIFA World Cup in South Africa™ reinforced the use of football to advance a pan-Africanist cause (Alegi, 2010). The formation of CAF also saw the emergence of a "politically vociferous African constituency" within FIFA (Darby, 2003).

South Africa was represented at the 1957 founding gathering of CAF by the whites-only Football Association of South Africa (FASA), which had been formed in 1892 as the South African Football Association (SAFA). The racial segregation of sport had been in place in South Africa before the National Party instituted their Apartheid policy of separate development, although the Apartheid government made this segregation explicit under the law. SAFA was

485

the first association in Africa to become affiliated to FIFA in 1910. The anti-Apartheid South African Soccer Federation (SASF) applied for FIFA membership in 1954, arguing that SAFA/FASA did not represent the whole of South African football. Although FIFA agreed with this argument, it rejected SASF's application because there were no white clubs or players included, and confirmed SAFA/FASA's view that segregation was a traditional practice (Fletcher, 2017).

South Africa did not participate in the first Africa Cup of Nations in 1957 and was formally expelled from CAF by 1960 after refusing to send a racially integrated team. Fighting Apartheid thus became part of the pan-African identity of CAF (Fletcher, 2017). By 1960, pressure was building on FASA for their refusal to field non-white players, and in September 1961, FASA was suspended from FIFA. After FIFA reinstated FASA's membership, CAF lobbied the Soviet and Asian National Associations, and South Africa was suspended again in 1964. CAF successfully applied pressure again in 1973, this time on Joao Havelange, the head of the Brazilian Football Association, to withdraw the Brazilian team from that year's South Africa Games. Havelange also echoed the "clarion call of African football," to ostracise Apartheid South Africa in his successful FIFA presidential campaign (Darby, 2003).

By early 2018, CAF had 56 members, including Zanzibar and Reunion, that were not yet members of FIFA. CAF therefore had the most members of FIFA's continental confederations. Zanzibar formally submitted their application for FIFA membership in mid-2017, which if accepted would make them the 212th member association. The membership of CAF was structured into six smaller regional zones, covering North Africa, Central Africa, West Africa, East Africa, and Southern Africa. CAF's official languages are French, English, and Arabic, while Portuguese is also an official language of CAF's General Assembly.

CAF's influence within FIFA increased as more countries gained their independence, and the organisation grew to 35 members by 1975, the same number as UEFA at that time. By 2000, CAF had passed 50 members. CAF's successful support for Brazilian Joao Havelange for FIFA President in 1974 also reinforced their growing influence and a shift in power away from Europe. African members of FIFA were responsible for the presidential election of Sepp Blatter in 1998 as the champion of African football, and his re-election in 2002, in spite of the official CAF endorsement of his opponents on both occasions. The 1970 FIFA World Cup saw the first guaranteed place for an African country. By 1998, Africa had five guaranteed berths. After South Africa controversially lost out to Germany to host the 2006 World Cup, a continental rotation system was introduced, resulting in Africa hosting the 2010 tournament.

On the continent, CAF holds the exclusive rights to organise a number of competitions for national teams and club teams. These include:

- the Africa Cup of Nations (AFCON) for national men's teams;
- the African Nations Championship for national men's teams comprised of domestic-based players only;
- the Women's Africa Cup of Nations;
- Futsal Africa Cup of Nations;
- Beach Soccer Africa Cup of Nations; and
- U-23, U-20, and U-17 competitions for men's and women's national sides.

At a club level, CAF hosts the African Champions League, as well as the Confederations Cup for domestic cup winners. Winners of both competitions complete in a one-off match for the CAF Super Cup.

The hosting of AFCON in January and February every second year has created a difficult club-versus-country conflict, as African athletes playing in Europe are forced to decide between staying with their league club for important mid-season games or responding positively to their call-up to play for their national team. The 2017 tournament in Gabon saw seven Cameroon players ignoring their country's call, while 12 English Premier League clubs lost over 20 players during the period (BBC, 2017). CAF, under the previous president Issa Hayatou, had argued that the weather in different parts of the continent made a mid-year tournament impossible, although some questioned whether this decision was driven more by not wanting to bow to European pressure (BBC, 2017). The new CAF president, Ahmad, supported the idea of shifting the biennial tournament to June and July, and aligned African football more with the European schedule. This change was confirmed by the CAF Executive Committee in July 2017.

Commercialisation of football in Africa

> Football is the only way that we make a living, and we expect that when we play for our countries, we should get a fair share of whatever revenue comes as a result. If the administrators of football fail to recognize this fact, things will not run smoothly. Football is not a pastime for us. It's big business.
>
> *(Lucas Radebe, former captain of South Africa and Leeds United)*

Since the mid-1980s, individuals, clubs, national associations, and CAF have increasingly prioritised financial profits (Alegi, 2010). In 1984, private sponsors and commercial advertisements were allowed for the first time in the African Nations Cup. Cameroonian Issa Hayatou's election as CAF president in 1988 increased commercialisation of the game in Africa, with FIFA partners adidas and Coca-Cola joining the newly opened categories of alcohol and tobacco (Alegi, 2010). Since then, CAF has enjoyed the support of a number of leading African and global brands, including South Korea's Samsung, Japan's Nissan, and South Africa's Standard Bank.

Corporate partnerships

In 2016, CAF signed an eight-year deal with the French multinational Total, to replace the French mobile operator Orange as the title sponsor of the Africa Cup of Nations. Orange had sponsored the Africa Cup of Nations four times since 2010, offering its African customers exclusive mobile and web content. Total's sponsorship covers all CAF's inter-club and national competitions, as the international oil and gas company aims to become the local services champion on the continent. According to Jacques-Emmanuel Saulnier, Total's Senior Vice-President of Corporate Communications:

> Africa is a cornerstone of our global presence and a keystone of our 20-year ambition. …
> Today, more than 10,000 people work in all of Total's African businesses … each day, we serve two million customers in our 4,200 retail outlets across the continent.
>
> *(Chibelushi, 2017)*

Corporate sponsorship has played an important role in the development of football in Africa, including incentivising players competing in FIFA and CAF tournaments. For example, each member of the Cameroon team participating in the 2002 World Cup received £5,000 for qualifying from Guinness Cameroon. The brewer also offered £1,000 for the best player in each match, and another £5,000 for the team if they progressed past the first round (Schatzberg, 2006).

Outside of the traditional energy, financial services, telecommunications, and consumer goods brands that have invested in football across the continent, online sports betting companies have also recently become more prominent. The most active of these has been SportPesa, a Kenyan company founded in 2014 by local and international investors, including the CEO, Captain Ronald Karauri, the former chairman of the Kenya Airline Pilots Association. By early 2018, the company operated in Kenya, Tanzania, South Africa, Italy, and the United Kingdom. SportPesa's association with African football began with a $4.36 million title sponsorship of the Kenyan Premier League in 2015, followed by deals with the Kenyan Football Federation as well as two of the biggest clubs in Kenyan football, Gor Mahia and AFC Leopards. The company also sponsors Simba SC and Singida United of the Tanzanian Premier League, and the South African football club Cape Town City FC. SportPesa became the first Kenyan company to sponsor an English Premier League team when it announced a three-year sponsorship deal with Hull City in 2016, which was the most lucrative in the club's 112-year history. This deal was followed by agreements with Southampton FC and Everton Football Club. SportPesa's sponsorships in Kenya were called into question in June 2017, however, when Kenyan President Uhuru Kenyatta signed a new finance bill into law, which included a new 35 per cent tax rate on all gambling revenue, in addition to the existing 30 per cent corporate tax. SportPesa responded by withdrawing all sports sponsorships of Kenyan teams in January 2018, although returned as title sponsor of the Kenyan Premier League five months later.

Private capital has also introduced new entrepreneurs and business leaders to the administration of football in Africa. In Cameroon, for example, Coton Sport FC de Garoua was founded in 1986 as a workers' social team for Societe de Developpement du Coton (Sodecoton), Cameroon's state enterprise to manage the cotton sector. Since joining Cameroon's first division in 1993, the club has dominated the domestic tournament, winning 14 national championships, six Cameroon Cups, and being runners-up in the CAF Cup in 2003 and CAF Champions League in 2008. Coton Sport enjoyed the financial and management support of Sodecoton until new leadership questioned the role of for-profit sports activities in 2014. An employee-owned mutual association with a board of directors and executive office was subsequently set up to manage the club, which operates with monthly financial contributions from employees.

Alegi (2010) highlighted the role of South African Patrice Motsepe, a lawyer turned entrepreneurial mining magnate, who bought Mamelodi Sundowns FC in 2003. The club was founded in 1970 by a group of young local footballers, and competed modestly in racially segregated domestic leagues before being signed up for the new multi-racial National Soccer League in 1985 by their new owner, Zola Mahobe. Thirty-one-year-old Mahobe, then a flamboyant black businessman (known as "Mr. Cool"), bought the struggling team for R100,000 (US$50,000 at the time) and then spent approximately US$1 million signing record player and coaching deals, developing appealing media brands for his players and the club, and incentivising his team with expensive gifts and trips (Marsh, 1992). Within three years, Mamelodi Sundowns had won the league title and two cup competitions. Mahobe nurtured his image with a "flashy dress sense: afro, open neck shirts, rings and gold necklaces" (Jacobs, 2014), which would eventually contribute to his undoing when he and his mistress Snowy Moshoeshoe were found guilty of more than US$3 million in bank fraud in 1989. When the club was repossessed by Standard Bank, which Mahobe had defrauded, it was bought by gambling tycoon Abe Krok, with the support of the Greek immigrant football couple Anastasia and Angelo Tsichlas. During the following 14 years, Sundowns continued to dominate domestic league and cup competitions, and reached the final of the CAF Champions League in 2001. In 2003, Patrice Motsepe bought the club and "tried to bring back the Mahobe glory days" (Jacobs, 2014). Some reports suggested Mahobe was actually a "silent director" at the club after his release from prison, with Motsepe stating in December 2013 that Sundowns "will be eternally grateful to Mahobe" (Jacobs, 2014).

Since Motsepe bought Sundowns, the club has won the domestic league title another four times, earned seven additional cup trophies, and in 2016 won their first CAF Champions League title, followed in 2017 with their first CAF Super Cup title.

Media rights

After Cameroon's impressive quarter-final appearance at the 1990 FIFA World Cup in Italy, CAF changed their TV broadcast rights strategy. The association went from making the broadcasts of the Africa Cup of Nations and African Champions League available to African public broadcasters for a nominal fee, to selling these rights to the highest bidder (Alegi, 2010). CAF selected Frenchman Jean-Claude Darmon and his MediaFoot agency to manage the sale of TV rights for the Africa Cup of Nations, and then later also the TV and marketing rights for the African Champions League. The latter deal saw over $2 million of guaranteed prize money available in 1997, partly to incentivise the best local footballers to stay in Africa. Television deregulation and technology improvements across Africa contributed to the commercial development of football (Alegi, 2010), with direct broadcast satellite technologies broadening the base of television viewers, while providing access to additional commercial channels and offerings.

The initial TV rights deal with Jean-Claude Darmon in 1990 was extended in 1997, and then renewed until 2008 through a new $50 million contract. Darmon merged with Canal Plus and RTL to form Sportfive in 2002, and guaranteed CAF a minimum of almost $140 million from 2008 to 2016. In mid-2015, CAF extended their marketing and media rights deal with Sportfive until 2028. The new deal guaranteed $1 billion to CAF, and covered the Africa Cup of Nations, the African Nations Champions, the CAF Champions' League, the Confederations Cup, the Super Cup, and the African U-20 and U-23 championships.

Although CAF's new media rights strategy resulted in additional resources and private investment, it meant that many football viewers missed out on seeing their clubs and national teams competing. For example, millions of viewers in Guinea Bissau, Malawi, and the Republic of Congo could not watch the 2006 Africa Cup of Nations when their state broadcasters were unable to pay the higher provider fees (Alegi, 2010). In this way, African football experienced both the positive and negative impacts of the "international media-business-sport alliance" that characterises the business of football (Cornelissen, 2010).

Another example of this media-driven alliance is SuperSport International, which was established in South Africa in 1988 as the sports segment of M-Net, the country's first pay TV channel. Initially the content focus was on rugby, along with cricket, golf, boxing, cycling, and English Premier League football, but in 1994 M-Net bought Pretoria City Football Club and rebranded the team SuperSport United FC. In 2007, SuperSport, then a multichannel pay TV network within Multichoice South Africa, won the rights to the South African Premier Soccer League (PSL) in a five-year deal worth $200 million. The broadcast deal did require some football games to be broadcast on SABC, the domestic free-to-air channel, however. Given the commercial success of the deal for Multichoice's new more-affordable Compact package, the PSL deal was renewed in 2011 for $277 million until the 2017/2018 season. By December 2017, the tender process for the next set of rights was still under consideration. The chairperson of the PSL, Dr Irvin Khoza, reflected on the ten-year partnership:

> The relationship was a defining moment for the industry in this country. It's been far more than a mere investment in the PSL. Development has benefitted too, with club academies producing top players. I commend SuperSport for their courage, for being so

single-minded, for understanding .... They had the inner spirit to help bring out the best of the immense talent available in our country.

(SuperSport, 2017)

SuperSport reportedly funded approximately 70 per cent of all sub-Saharan sport, including purchasing broadcast rights, upskilling league administrators and production crews in each territory, as well as improving facilities and helping federations acquire sponsors (Naspers, 2014). For example, the Multichoice Diski Challenge PSL Reserve League (MDC), a multi-pronged corporate social responsibility program, was launched in South Africa in August 2014. The MDC comprised a league competition for the PSL academy clubs; player life skills and development; player scholarships for study purposes; an internship programme to develop broadcasting skills among youth; and the broadcast of MDC matches on community TV channels available on Multichoice. In January 2017, the PSL chairman, Irvin Khoza, reported that 23 players had advanced from the MDC to the PSL. Additionally, South African PSL clubs earned a monthly grant of $100,000 directly from the SuperSport broadcast deal, while national First Division teams earned $40,000 monthly.

Beyond South Africa, SuperSport acquired the broadcasting rights of Africa's most popular domestic leagues in Nigeria, Ghana, Kenya, Zambia, and Zimbabwe. Yet despite being seen as having a symbiotic relationship with football in Africa, in November 2016 the broadcaster declined to renew its sponsorship of the Ghana Premier League. After ten years of involvement, SuperSport also terminated its contract with the Kenyan Premier League (KPL) in March 2017, due to a dispute between the KPL and Football Kenya Federation about which was recognised by FIFA to administer professional football in Kenya (Kwalimwa, 2017). In April 2017, SuperSport also terminated its broadcast deal with Nigeria's Professional Football League organisers, League Management Company, citing a breach of contract as the reason for the termination. League officials later suggested that the breach was due to a lack of foreign exchange and the weakness of the Nigerian naira against the US dollar.

The development of football media rights in Africa and abroad therefore impacted domestic fandom and viewership both positively and negatively (Frimpong, 2014). Analysts suggested that the appeal of European leagues lay in the level of elite on-field performance, the television production quality, the entertainment atmosphere in iconic sporting facilities, and the participation of many of the best footballers in the world (Alegi, 2010). In this sense, the extensive broadcasts of European football in Africa served as a form of "electronic colonialism" (Gerard Akindes in Alegi, 2010), which contributed to the substitution of domestic attendance and viewership with European viewership (Bankole, Olaniyan, Babatunde, and Nghargbu, 2012). For example, SuperSport paid four times as much for English Premier League (EPL) rights in sub-Saharan Africa than it paid to broadcast domestic South African Premier Soccer League games. By early 2018, SuperSport was the English Premier League's longest-serving international partner, and had signed on until the end of the 2021/22 season. In 2004, EPL sponsor Barclays attracted 24,000 people to watch a live game on a big screen in South Africa, which was four times the average attendance at domestic league matches.

Political and social dimensions of football management in Africa

Alegi (2010) highlighted the negative impacts of privatisation of African football, including the intensifying competitive imbalances, accelerating migration abroad, and increasing corruption. After independence, African countries unsuccessfully attempted to end the migration of their best players to Europe. Previously, European countries, especially France, Portugal and Belgium, had transferred players from their colonies to club and sometimes national teams in Europe.

This trend continued after the end of colonial rule in Africa, with an estimated 350 Africans playing first or second division football in Europe by 1995 (Darby, Akindes, and Kirwin, 2007). That year's Bosman ruling in Europe relaxed the quota on foreign players in European leagues, which saw this number grow to 571 players in Europe by 2009 (Besson, Poli, and Ravenel, 2010). By October 2015, over 3,700 African expatriate footballers were playing for one of the world's 6,135 clubs, making up almost 20 per cent of expatriate footballers at the time. Nigeria provided the largest number of African players in other leagues (596), followed by Senegal (377), Cote d'Ivoire (370), Cameroon (366), and Ghana (365), together contributing 24 per cent of the top 15 exporter countries (Poli, Ravenel, and Besson, 2015). Over 35 per cent of the combined squads of France and Portugal competing in the Euro 2016 final featured players with African roots (Aarons, 2016).

In 2003, Sepp Blatter expressed a view about football migration from Africa that numerous scholars had previously argued, describing the European clubs that benefited as:

> neo-colonialists who don't give a damn about heritage and culture, but engage in social and economic rape by robbing the developing world of its best players. Dignity and integrity tend to fall by the wayside in what has become a glorified body market.
>
> *(Bradley, 2003)*

Given his ethics violations and subsequent banning from all football-related activities in 2015, ironically Blatter also added: "If we are not careful, football may degenerate into a game of greed - a trend I will vigorously oppose" (Bradley, 2003). The United Nations Commission on Human Rights highlighted the "danger of effectively creating a modern day 'slave trade'" (Bale, in Darby et al., 2007) in their study of the migration, and sometimes illegal abandonment, of younger African footballers. Darby et al. (2007) argued that football migration has been:

> interpreted as a form of neocolonial exploitation in that it involves the sourcing, refinement and export of raw materials … for consumption and wealth generation in the European **core** and that this process results in the impoverishment of the African **periphery** (emphasis in the original).

The difficult socioeconomic and political environments facing many African countries have also hampered efforts by some well-organised professional African clubs and leagues to provide the regular, guaranteed salaries and labour protection promised in Europe. The very substantial differences in club budgets and player salaries between African clubs and those in Europe increase the appeal for talented footballers.

CAF initially responded by banning players from competing in the Africa Cup of Nations if they played internationally. Issa Hayatou believed that the African Champions League also created economic incentives to retain African talent, although he argued in 1999:

> CAF cannot do anything. It is the responsibility of the national federations to come up with some kind of legislation to regulate this process. CAF cannot intervene in this matter, but we could advise them to avoid the exploitation of African talents to enrich the football of the countries above our continent.
>
> *(Darby et al., 2007)*

FIFA's Regulations for the Status and Transfer of Players (RSTP) in 2001 included a provision that only allowed European countries to sign players under the age of 18 if the player moved to Europe for reasons unrelated to football, and made provision for clubs involved in the training and education of players between the ages of 12 and 23 to receive compensation from the buying club (Lembo, 2011). Besides the illegal practices of European clubs creating jobs for parents in order to bypass the regulations, clubs also used a 2009 Court for the Arbitration of Sport ruling, which allows the transfer of minors if an exchange agreement is in place with a foreign club. This has resulted in partnerships between European clubs and African clubs, which is the second of the four broad types of academies that Darby et al. (2007) identified.

Football academies in Africa

Darby et al. (2007) classify African academies into four main types. First, African academies that are similar to those in Europe but are organised and run by African club teams or national federations. Second, Afro-European academies, which are partnerships between an existing African academy and European club, or where the partnership is developed through the European club's acquisition of the African club. Third, well-established corporate-sponsored academies supported by private individuals or companies. Finally, "non-affiliated, improvised" ad hoc academies that lack well-qualified staff or proper facilities (Darby et al., 2007).

MimoSifcom, the successful academy of Association Sportive des Employes de Commerce (ASEC) Mimosas in Cote d'Ivoire, is a well-known example of the first type of academy, although it was originally set up as a joint venture with AS Monaco (Alegi, 2010). As one of the first structured football academies in sub-Saharan Africa, MimoSifcom provided players between the ages of 13 and 17 with both a football and an academic education (Darby et al., 2007). Although the goal was to produce elite players for ASEC Mimosas' professional team and the Ivorian national team (Alegi, 2010), the academy also sold their most talented players to European teams to recoup the costs involved in training and educating the players (Darby et al., 2007). These players include Salomon Kalou of Feyenoord, Chelsea, Lille, and Hertha; Yaya Toure of Olympiacos, Monaco, Barcelona, and Manchester City; and his brother Kolo Toure of Arsenal, Manchester City, Liverpool, and Celtic, who reflected: "I feel very lucky to have been part of the academy, because for Africa, the facilities were very good. It formed me a lot as a player, and as an adult" (World Soccer, 2008).

In neighbouring Ghana, the Dutch club Feyenoord partnered with the Ghanian Sports Ministry and local tribal chiefs in the Gomoa Fetteh area to establish the Feyenoord Fetteh Football Academy in 1999. As suggested by this second category of academies, its purpose was to provide a steady stream of raw talent to the Dutch club (Darby et al., 2007), although by 2009 only one player had signed with Feyenoord (Alegi, 2010). That same year, Wienco, a Dutch-Ghanian agricultural company, took over the management of the academy, and in 2014, the academy changed its name to the West Africa Football Academy when it acquired the Red Bull Academy in Ghana.

Nogoom El Mostakbal FC is a privately owned Egyptian professional football club that was founded in 2007. The club is an example of Darby et al.'s (2007) third category of academy, as it developed out of a PepsiCo corporate social responsibility project, known as the Pepsi School League. Spain's La Liga partnered with the Pepsi School League and Nogoom El Mostakbal FC in 2015 to send the best 23 young Egyptian players to participate in a Royal Andalusian Football Federation camp. By 2015, the project had involved 800,000 students from 7,500 schools in Egypt, with 60 Egyptian professional players having graduated to local and international clubs (Ayyad, 2015). For example, Mohamed Salah made his professional debut for Cairo-based El Mokawloon in 2010 before playing for Basel, Chelsea, and Roma, and then signed a €50 million deal to join Liverpool in mid-2017. Nogoom El Mostakbal FC was created to accommodate talented players from the Pepsi School League who were not recruited by other professional teams, and by the end of 2017, the Pepsi-sponsored club was competing in the second division league.

The final category of academies in Africa operate outside of the legal and administrative regulations designed to safeguard young players from unscrupulous agents, and have been established with the primary interest of personal financial gain rather than football or educational development (Darby et al., 2007). Players identified by noncertified agents at these academies are not required to obtain an official letter from their national federation, while the agents are not required to pay a bond to take the players abroad for trial.

Illegal practices

Alegi (2010) argued that some football administrators in Africa were motivated to create and maintain patronage networks and launch political careers, the opportunities for which increased with privatisation. He pointed to "greed, shoddy organisation, and callous indifference towards spectator safety" that partly led to the stadium disasters in Ghana, Cote d'Ivoire, South Africa, and the Democratic Republic of the Congo between 2001 and 2009. At a higher level, African football administrators have also been caught up in the illegal practices related to World Cup bidding. As part of the US Department of Justice indictment of FIFA officials in 2015, former FIFA Executive Committee member Chuck Blazer testified that bribes were paid in order to vote for numerous World Cup tournaments, including the Morocco bids for the 1998 and 2010 tournaments, and the South African bid for 2010 (Gibson and Lewis, 2015). According to US prosecutors, South Africa paid $10 million to CONCACAF president Jack Warner in exchange for votes. The head of the South African 2010 Local Organising Committee, Danny Jordaan, confirmed that $10 million was paid to CONCACAF, via FIFA, as a contribution to their football development fund, but denied that this was a bribe (Motale, 2015). Officials related to Egypt's bid for the 2010 World Cup also claimed that Warner had solicited $1 million for each of the seven votes he promised to deliver, but that they refused to pay (Brown and Randall, 2015).

Club and league-level sponsorship rights in Africa have provided additional opportunities for illegal practices. For example, a joint $50 million sponsorship deal between South Africa's Football Association, the professional league, banking group ABSA, and South African Breweries attracted negative attention when it emerged that five of the football administrators involved in negotiating the deal received $5 million commission. The chairman of the Premier Soccer League and vice-president of SAFA defended the payment, suggesting that the administrators "deserve to be rewarded … They have done the best for football … and have acted in the best interest of the PSL" (Cornelissen, 2010).

Alegi (2010) argued that South Africa's new World Cup stadiums could help "debunk stereotyped images of Africa as a primitive, tribal, wild, sick, conflict-ridden, chaotic place populated by kleptocratic tyrants and faceless victims in need of Western help." The unfortunate reality, however, was that the stadiums presented opportunities for large established local firms to participate in illegal practices. Collusion by World Cup stadium construction companies was estimated to have added $1 billion to the costs. By February 2017, seven construction companies had been fined over $100 million in competition penalties, and had agreed to contribute another $100 million to promote black South African ownership in the construction sector (SA News, 2017). In April 2017, the City of Cape Town won a judgement against WBHO Construction (previously Wilson Bayly Holmes (Pty) Limited) in its efforts to recover more than $40 million in damages from construction companies that were found guilty of collusion (Etheridge, 2017).

Another illegal issue that football administrators have had to deal with across the continent is the perception of sorcery. For some fans, players, and administrators, the performance of their club or national team depended on the extent to which "juju", "witchcraft", or "black magic" had been used by the teams. For example, South Africa's Sports Minister in 2002, Ngconde Balfour, approved "traditional healers" travelling with the team to that year's World Cup, arguing: "If the Bafana Bafana players believe the efforts of the inyangas help them to play better, they should be assisted by their special doctors … This is a cultural expression" (Schatzberg, 2006). CAF did not want to present a "Third-World" image, and banned all "team advisors", "wise men", "counsellors", "technical consultants", and "morale officers" from any role within the participating teams. African Player of the Year and Bayern Munich's Samuel Kuffour echoed this view, suggesting: "It is an old belief that has no place in modern football … Juju can never help a player become a superstar. Only hard work, training and discipline will do that" (Schatzberg, 2006). Following a 2003 AFCON qualifier between Rwanda and Uganda, which involved a well-publicised incident of perceived sorcery, the Federation of Uganda Football Association (FUFA) committed to "trying to find a way in which we will educate fans and all those concerned that juju does not work in football" (Schatzberg, 2006).

Recommendations and implications

Madichie (2010) lamented the lack of scholarship on football's contribution to economic development in Africa. Beyond this topic, academic research at the intersection of football, business, and management is limited, especially in quality peer-reviewed publications. An opportunity exists for scholars across Africa's three main languages, French, English, and Arabic, to collaborate on research projects to investigate a range of important questions. This chapter points to the need to further investigate the relationship between organisational design and leadership practices, and the development of the game. With the recent realignment of African football to the European schedule, it may be important to examine the impact on African players at home and abroad. Although some initial analysis has taken place to understand the substitution effect of international football media, limited guidance exists on appropriate mitigation strategies or policy options. Lastly, the difficult issues of migration and the role of football academies demands further research, especially in terms of ethical and sustainable practices.

The chapter's implications for football administrators and related managers are to consider the diversity and complexity of Africa's 56 football territories. As demonstrated by the experiences of previous FIFA presidential candidates, viewing the continent as a single entity is dangerous. Industry practitioners should also take note of the limited published resources related to the business of football in Africa, suggesting a need to build quality business relationships in order to more deeply understand the local dynamics. A final implication of this exploration of African football is that the game engages a substantial majority of the continent's population, and therefore presents compelling partnership opportunities.

References

Aarons, E. (2016) France's and Portugal's colonial heritage brings African flavor to Euro 2016. *The Guardian*, [online]. Available at https://www.theguardian.com/football/2016/jul/09/france-portugal-colonial-history-african-flavour-euro-2016

Alegi, P. (2010) *African Soccerscapes: How a Continent Changed the World's Game*. Athens: Ohio University Press.

Ayyad, M. (2015) PepsiCo considers developing Pepsi league for students in Egypt: Ahmed El-Sheikh. *Daily News Egypt*, [online]. Available at https://dailynewsegypt.com/2015/01/25/pepsico-considers-developing-pepsi-league-students-egypt-ahmed-el-sheikh/

Bankole, A., Olaniyan, O., Babatunde, M.A., and Nghargbu, R. (2012) Does cross-border broadcast of foreign football change the demand pattern of domestic recreation? Empirical study of imports of audiovisual services through digital satellite television. *Journal of International Trade Law and Policy*, 11(2), pp. 191–211.

BBC. (2017) Africa Cup of Nations: CAF considers June or July move. [online] Available at http://www.bbc.com/sport/football/40645125

Besson, R., Poli, R., and Ravenel, L. (2010) *Demographic Study of Footballers in Europe.* [online] Neuchâtel: CIES. Available at http://www.footballfordevelopment.net/uploads/tx_drblob/storage/Poli_migration-of-African-football-players_01.pdf

Bradley, M. (2003) Blatter takes swipe at G-14 "colonialists." *The Guardian*, [online]. Available at https://www.theguardian.com/football/2003/dec/18/newsstory.sport8

Brown, L. and Randall, N. (2015) Fifa corruption: "Morocco won 2010 World Cup vote – not South Africa" – as it happened. *The Telegraph*, [online]. Available at http://www.telegraph.co.uk/sport/football/fifa/11657595/Fifa-corruption-Morocco-2010-World-Cup-vote-live.html

CAF. (2007) *CAF Official Magazine: Special Edition.* Egypt: Nubar Cairo.

Chibelushi, W. (2017) Talking to Total: Africa Cup of Nations sponsorship 2017. *African Business Review*, [online]. Available at http://www.africanbusinessreview.co.za/finance/2708/Talking-to-Total:-African-Cup-of-Nation-sponsorship-2017

Cornelissen, S. (2010) Football's tsars: proprietorship, corporatism and politics in the 2010 FIFA World Cup. *Soccer & Society*, 11(1–2), pp. 131–143.

Darby, P. (2003) Africa, the FIFA Presidency, and the Governance of World Football: 1974, 1998, and 2002. *Africa Today*, pp. 3–24.

Darby, P., Akindes, G., and Kirwin, M. (2007) Football academies and the migration of African football labor to Europe. *Journal of Sport & Social Issues*, 31(2), pp. 143–161.

Etheridge, J. (2017) Court rules in Cape Town's favour in stadium collusion case. *News24*, [online]. Available at https://www.news24.com/SouthAfrica/News/court-rules-in-cape-towns-favour-in-stadium-collusion-case-20170402

Fletcher, M. (2017) Confederation of African Football. In: J. Hughson, K. Moore, R. Spaaij, and J. Maguire, eds., *Routledge Handbook of Football Studies*, 1st ed. London: Routledge, pp. 423–431.

Frimpong, K. (2014) Wooing fans back into Ghana stadia – in the wake of globalization of football. *Emerald Emerging Markets Case Studies*, 4(4), pp. 1–17.

Gibson, O. and Lewis, P. (2015) Fifa informant Chuck Blazer: I took bribes over 1998 and 2010 World Cups. *The Guardian*, [online]. Available at https://www.theguardian.com/football/2015/jun/03/fifa-chuck-blazer-bribes-world-cup

Jacobs, S. (2014) *Mr Big Bucks and the Mamelodi Sundowns.* [online] Roads & Kingdoms. Available at http://roadsandkingdoms.com/2014/mr-big-bucks-and-the-mamelodi-sundowns/

Kwalimwa, D. (2017) SuperSport, Kenyan Premier League end partnership. *Daily Nation*, [online]. Available at http://www.nation.co.ke/sports/football/SuperSport-KPL-end-partnership/1102-3881134-iy09kyz/index.html

Lembo, C. (2011) FIFA transfer regulations and UEFA player eligibility rules: major changes in European Football and the negative effect on minors. *Emory International Law Review*, [online] 25(1), pp. 539–585. Available at http://law.emory.edu/eilr/content/volume-25/issue-1/comments/fifa-transfer-regulations-uefa-eligibility-rules-european-football-minors.html

Madichie, N.O. (2010) Giving the beautiful game a "pretty bad name": a viewpoint on African football. *African Journal of Business and Economic Research*, 5(1), 135–151.

Marsh, R. (1992) *Famous South African Crimes: An investigation into 26 of South Africa's most famous crimes 1900 – 1988*, [online] Cape Town: Struik Publishers. Available at www.africacrime-mystery.co.za/books/fsac/chp23.htm

Motale, P. (2015) Danny: Yes, we paid R120m. *The Sunday Independent*, [online]. Available at https://www.iol.co.za/sport/soccer/danny-yes-we-paid-r120m-1865523#.VWr72M_BzRY

Naspers (2014) *Pay Television.* [online] Available at http://www.naspers-reports.com/2014/per-op-pay.php

Poli, R., Ravenel, L., and Besson, R. (2015) *Exporting countries in world football. CIES Football Observatory Monthly Report No. 8.* [pdf] Neuchâtel: CIES. Available at http://www.football-observatory.com/IMG/pdf/mr08_eng.pdf

SA News. (2017) *Collusion implicated construction companies making amends.* [online] Available at http://www.bizcommunity.com/Article/196/494/157626.html

Schatzberg, M. G. (2006) Soccer, science, and sorcery: Causation and African football. *Afrika Spectrum*, 41(3), pp. 351–369.

SuperSport. (2017) SuperSport, PSL celebrate 10-year partnership. [online] Available at https://www.supersport.com/football/absa-premiership/news/170130/supersport_psl_celebrate_10year_partnership

World Soccer. (2008) Kolo Toure on his African Nations adventure. [online] Available at http://www.worldsoccer.com/features/kolo-toure-on-his-african-nations-adventure-174537

39

CONCACAF

Dr Joel Rookwood and Dr Glaucio Scremin

Introduction

The Confederation of North, Central and Caribbean Association Football (CONCACAF) is one of six FIFA confederations, which are organised on a loosely continental basis. There are certain exceptions to this, with strategic (re)positioning usually relating to political expediency or football development. For instance, Israel are under the auspices of UEFA and Australia are now a member of the Asian Football Confederation (having moved from the Asian and Oceanian confederations in 1991 and 2006 respectively), and the three smallest mainland South American entities are longstanding members of CONCACAF: Guyana, French Guiana, and Suriname. (Burks, Goldman, and Agha, 2017). CONCACAF membership is held by the three most populous North American states, namely Canada, the US, and Mexico, as well as seven Central American nations and 31 "Caribbean countries," including the three Guianas.

As the administrative organisation for 41 members (25 of which are UN member states) CONCACAF governs more than quadruple the number of national associations than the equivalent South American governing body CONMEBOL. However, the two confederations oversee collective territories that are more equal in terms of population, land mass, and population density. They also represent contrasting entities and offer interesting frames of reference in relation to the culture, governance, and gendered impact of football. Nine of the 20 Men's FIFA World Cup tournaments have been won by a South American team, whereas CONCACAF has only had one representative in a semi-final, that coming at the inaugural 13-team event in 1930. Conversely, the seven FIFA Women's World Cups have all had CONCACAF representation at the semi-final stage, three of which culminated in tournament victories (all for the US), whereas CONMEBOL teams have only competed in two semi-finals, and no South American team has won the event.

The varying degrees of relative success have impacted upon the commercial activities of individual member organisations and domestic leagues and teams therein (Shobe and Gibson, 2017). Competitive balance is more equitable amongst CONMEBOL associations, compared to their CONCACAF counterparts where population variance is more extreme, featuring the least and most populous entities across both football confederations of the Americas (Montserrat with 5,000 inhabitants and the US with 323.1 million). Every CONMEBOL member has competed in a Men's World Cup except Venezuela, whereas only 11 CONCACAF national teams have qualified for the event, six of them doing so only once. Similarly, no CONCACAF team has ever reached the final of the FIFA World Club Cup, whereas 12 of the 15 events have featured a COMNEBOL finalist.

Despite the challenges of variance and polarisation in population, culture, competition, and infrastructure, the popularity and commercial impact of football in the CONCACAF region – which includes the USA as the largest and most competitive sports market in the world – has grown exponentially in recent years (Markovits and Green, 2016). This chapter examines the socio-cultural and structural organisation of sport and football in North America, partly set in the wider context of the Americas and beyond. It then addresses CONCACAF's competitions, mission, governance, and corporate structure, as well as the recent corruption scandals and reform framework.

Sport and football in North America

Football is a sport growing in popularity and economic viability across many areas of the North American continent. However, it has long been a significant cultural and commercial component of Latin America (Yoder, 2016). It is firmly established and widely recognised as the dominant sport of South America, where historically, advanced continental governance and demand for a greater global influence helped shape the creation of UEFA and provide an organisational model for international football in Europe (Vonnard and Quin, 2017). The codification of rules, formation of national governing bodies, creation of clubs, and the introduction of competitions in the nineteenth century is most readily attributed to and associated with British football (Rookwood and Hughson, 2017). However, at confederation level governing bodies were not established until the period between 1954 and 1966, in Asia (1954), Europe (1954), Africa (1957), North America (1961) and Oceania (1966); but the administrative body of football in South America was formed in 1916 and has since staged 45 South American championships (Asia, Europe, North America, and Oceania have staged 55 events between them). This extensive legacy has impacted upon the organisation, governance, culture, and financial framework of football in North America (Coates, Frick, and Jewell, 2016).

The three North American countries with the highest populations – the US, Mexico, and Canada – have also significantly shaped the culture, business, and management of sport in the CONCACAF region, reflecting both differentiation and commonalities. With a national average yearly temperature of -5°C, Canadian sport has often been impacted by and responsive to its climate, with ice hockey firmly established as the dominant sport in terms of recreational participation, cultural significance, professional prevalence, and revenue generation (Kitchen and Chowhan, 2016). Mexican sport, politics, and economics have produced different forms of development. In the 1940s and 1950s Mexico experienced a dynamic economy, characterised by extensive government investment in infrastructure, and relative political stability in contrast to the Latin American tendency towards military dictatorships (Brewster and Brewster, 2010). Domestic football was established in Mexico in 1902 and professionalised in 1943. In transnational sporting contexts Mexico hosted the 1968 Olympics at a significantly contentious phase for international relations and civil rights. However, this was staged against the emergence of significant turmoil in domestic politics, evidenced by the massacre of several hundred protesting students ten days before the opening ceremony (Sheppard, 2016). Despite political and economic difficulties Mexico subsequently represented CONCACAF as hosts of the 1970 and 1986 FIFA World Cup tournaments, which both reflected and reinforced the place of football in the country and Latin America (Moreno-Brid and Ros, 2009).

The "athletic system" in the USA has been dominated by sports invented in and by Americans. Collegiate sport occupies a connected and central component of the structure, culture, and economy of its national sporting model. Eight of the nine largest sport stadiums in the world, all with a capacity of over 100,000, are used primarily by American university football teams. Of the globe's top five professional sporting leagues in terms of revenue production, four of them are based and played primarily in the USA and/or Canada (Hillman, 2016). The National Football League, Major League Baseball (MLB), and the National Basketball Association are the most profitable domestic sports leagues in the world; the National Hockey League is fifth behind English football's Premier League (Leeds and Von Allmen, 2016). Football is often referred to as the world's most popular sport, and global broadcasting figures and participation rates would testify to this (Rookwood and Hughson, 2017). In North America, however, the popularity and financial significance of football is not ranked as highly, especially when considered in the context of key metrics such as participation figures, broadcasting revenues, sponsorship agreements, and other commercial practices (Smolianov et al., 2015).

The historical preference for American football and relative resistance to association football in the US – also seen in parts of Ireland and Australia with their more dominant national variants of football – has led to the term "soccer" being deployed (having possibly taken its name from the "soc" in association) in reference to the sport, its domestic governing body and national league (Collins, 2015). CONCACAF is the only FIFA confederation with the named reference to "association football" to differentiate it from other codes. Football has often been overshadowed by other key sports in the US where hand-eye rather than foot-eye coordination dominates the technical and tactical components and related talent profiling and recruitment strategies (Rothschadl and Nunes, 2016). The relative success of the American women's game has helped grow the sport in the US (Madden, 2015), but it has also proliferated the view of soccer as a female sport, which has also served to intensify cultural resistance in some contexts (Sveinson and Hoeber, 2016; Kristiansen, Broch, and Pedersen, 2014).

In Central America (usually understood as the seven geographically connected nation states situated between Mexico and Colombia), baseball, boxing, and basketball are often perceived as popular and commercially viable sports, although football is usually considered the dominant sport in the region (Brown, 2014). A CONCACAF World Cup qualifier between El Salvador and neighbouring Honduras in 1969 led to a short but brutal conflict in which 3,000 soldiers and civilians died, in what some have retrospectively termed the "Football War" (Moore, 2017). The conflict followed a series of political tensions and was not caused by the tie, but the fixture did serve as a trigger for the ensuing war (Spaaij, 2014). Although this example has often been employed to denote the historical relationship between sport and conflict, football in Central America has not typically been characterised by civil unrest and social disorder (Duke and Crolley, 2014). All seven countries feature functioning domestic leagues, most of which are well established whilst being subject to financial restrictions shaped by limited broadcasting and commercial revenues (Campomar, 2014). Football governance in the region is overseen by *Unión Centroamericana de Fútbol*, which organises club and international competitions that usually serve as qualifiers for respective CONCACAF tournaments.

Sport in the Caribbean is subject to considerable variance in relation to cultural engagement, participation and performance, organisational governance, and commercial and broadcasting investment and revenue. The focus of recent business management-related research in the region has ranged from elite performance involving globally iconic and successful sportspersons and their impact on place branding and public diplomacy (Johnson, 2014), to the programming and monitoring of burgeoning sport-for-development initiatives often framed as responses to contexts at the other end of the socio-economic spectrum (Kaufman, Rosenbauer, and Moore, 2013).

Sporting culture in the island nations of the Caribbean usually reflects but sometimes withstands socio-economic, political and/or (post)colonial interests. For instance, in Cuba, situated

90-miles from the Florida coast, baseball has long been one of the most popular sports – cutting across race and class – with matches organised from the 1870s (Carter, 2014). This predates the period of American intervention and the subsequent Cuban Revolution which has shaped the consumption, production, and financial structure of sports including baseball (Klein and Marcus, 2016). A drain on the talent pool, partly caused by a steady stream of defectors to MLB has limited its development, whilst financial and technical sports aid from political allies has helped sustain a sporting industry suffering from the effects of an American blockade (Pye and Pettavino, 2016). Despite being a national pastime, commercial development has been resisted in Cuban baseball, which is organised and played with minimal or no advertisement, sponsorship, or significant salaries. Conversely, athletics dominates the modern sporting culture of Jamaica which has sought to harness the economic potential of its athletes, notably its world-renowned sprinters (Robertson-Hickling, 2015). This represents a key element of its nation branding approach which is aligned to that which is presented as distinctively, successfully, and creatively Jamaican (Hankinson, 2009; Hanna and Rowley, 2011).

The Caribbean Basin, which includes island countries and three major archipelagos of the Greater Antilles, Lesser Antilles, and Bahama archipelago, is often referred to as the West Indies. The multi-national cricket team of the same name represents a chain of 15 mainly English-speaking Caribbean territories. Representative teams have competed internationally since the 1890s, shaped by experience of and resistance to colonisation and slavery; a region which has since become virtually synonymous with cricket (Yelvington, 1995; McCree, 2017). Britain's Caribbean colonies were sites of exploitation rather than development so when the professional football league started in England this professionalism was not diffused to the Caribbean (Charles, 2015). Conversely, between the 1970s and 1990s the composite team dominated world cricket, winning both the World Cup and World Twenty20 twice. The relatively advanced levels of infrastructure developed on several Caribbean islands, with modern stadia and broadcasting and sponsorship deals, came to reflect the post-Westernisation of cricket and the shift in administrative power away from England (Rumford, 2007).

The investment of resources and experience of sporting prowess and related cultural and commercial activities centred on particular sports in specific regions of the North American continent have often served to marginalise and stifle football development in those locations. Simultaneously however, the impact of Latin American football culture, combined with diasporas and migration and fused with the globalisation and broadcasting of European football leagues and international tournaments, has led to increased interest in football. In some cases, this has been shaped by pioneering and successful North American exports migrating into European leagues, together with national team appearances at mega events. Dwight Yorke, for instance, won numerous honours particularly at Manchester United from the mid-1990s, and helped Trinidad and Tobago qualify for its first World Cup in 2006 (Charles, 2015). More recently, Costa Rica excelled in reaching the 2014 World Cup quarterfinals (Wilson, 2015) and Panama qualified for the 2018 World Cup for the first time at the expense of USA who missed out for the first time since 1986. As football has become more ubiquitous across North America, CONCACAF has emerged as a more significant administrative body overseeing competitions with increasing global recognition and commercial potential.

Key CONCACAF competitions

The first Pan-North American international football competition was instituted as the CONCACAF Championship in 1963, shortly after the confederation was formed as a merger of the *Confederación Centroamericana y del Caribe de Fútbol* (founded in 1938), and the North

American Football Confederation (established in 1946). The competition was rebranded as the Gold Cup in 1991, with 13 of the 14 modern events won by either Mexico or USA. The most prestigious club competition in the continent is CONCACAF Champions League, which was known as the Champions Cup from 1962 until its rebranding in 2008, inspired by the remodelling of the lucrative trans-European equivalent (Jewell, 2014). Qualification processes and formats have varied during the various stages of its development, with the current structure involving 16 teams (nine from the North American Zone, five from the Central American Zone, one from the Caribbean football championship, and one from either the Caribbean or Central American Zone) competing in an annual event. The tournament has been dominated by Mexican clubs who have won more titles collectively (33) than every other competing country combined (21).

There are 40 domestic leagues spread throughout the continent, and although the vast majority are amateur or semi-professional, the Mexican Liga MX and Major League Soccer (MLS) in USA and Canada are the most lucrative and globally recognised professional domestic leagues in CONCACAF. The Liga MX has five levels and operates with the promotion and relegation system developed and adopted in European football. MLS was formed in 1993 as a condition of hosting the 1994 FIFA Men's World Cup held in the US – the third of three editions of the global event to be staged by CONCACAF. Prior to this the North American Soccer League (NASL) operated in its original format from 1968–1984, a league which attracted some high-profile players, yet proved a structural, commercial, and developmental failure. Despite attendances averaging 13,000 with matches broadcast on network television in the late 1970s, the initial popularity was not sustained, ratings decreased rapidly and investments were subsequently terminated (Smith and Clinton, 2016).

Various American sporting entertainment and commercial practices were unsuccessfully introduced into the NASL – many of which were countercultural for football – such as halting play to allow for advertisement breaks. The league was effectively rejected by America's sporting communities, with a model of foreign players earning high salaries playing in front of small crowds in large rented stadiums proving financially unsustainable (Francis, 2011). The league adopted other practices common across or interpretive of mainstream American sports, such as countdown clocks, penalty shootouts for drawn league matches and bonus points awarded for goals scored. Ultimately, the lack of interest, poor viewer ratings, and attendances, together with the relatively high proportion of league revenues being spent on player salaries and the overall lack of commercial activity led to a collapse in investment which saw the league disbanded (Armstrong and Rosbrook-Thompson, 2010).

It took time for the MLS to become a recognised component of the American sporting system, partly due to the widespread appeal and commercial success of other established leagues (Elliott and Harris, 2011; Jewell, 2014). The "national" competitions of baseball, basketball, and ice hockey are played in both USA and Canada; whereas the National Football League (NFL) is based in the contiguous United States, although matches have been played in England's Wembley stadium as part of the NFL International Series, and other dominant sporting leagues have also staged or proposed holding matches abroad (Rookwood and Chan, 2011; Macintosh and Harris, 2017). Certain key elements of the membership and governance structure of these sports have essentially been adopted in the MLS, and differ to how football is organised in Latin America and Europe.

In the aforementioned North American sports, rather than a governing body, the respective league determines the rules and scoring and the conditions by which players sign for and transfer between teams. The league owns all broadcast and intellectual property rights and its partners (franchise investor-operators) share certain sources of revenue. The member clubs are corporate entities separate from the leagues in which they compete, but they operate solely under league auspices (Massey and Thaler, 2013). In closed membership systems, the league's franchises are not promoted from or relegated to subsequent tiers. New teams proposed by potential investors enter the league only by a vote of existing members. Franchises have territorial rights and usually cover major metropolitan areas to avoid having local competition and rivalries. Professional teams are not bound to specific communities, however, and can move cities to increase revenues or chances of success. This first occurred in 1902, and since 1966 there have been 33 franchise relocations across the four major sports leagues (Kitchens, 2015). The services of players are acquired through draft systems (such as the Entry Draft which typically involves college graduates), intended to maintain competitive balance in a given league and to avoid expensive and unsustainable bidding wars for players (Reynolds et al., 2015).

The MLS operates with a structural system far closer to other American sports than other national football leagues. It began tentatively with ten clubs but has since expanded to 22 members, split into Western and Eastern Conferences. Various developments were initially introduced such as timed shootouts and All-star games; however, the current match structure essentially reflects that adopted by other FIFA and CONCACAF-affiliated leagues (Jewell, 2014). Each club can register a total of 30 players to its roster, with an annual salary cap of $3.845 million – not including salaries for designated players (Celik and Ince-Yenilmez, 2017). Players can be signed from other clubs such as those in Europe, with an additional Super Draft system for recruitment of college graduates and other players signed by the league.

Most MLS franchises are based in separate metropolitan areas, with the 22 clubs spread across 20 states, provinces, and districts. Additional memberships are awarded by vote. According to FIFA's (2017) Annual Global Football Report, 84.5 per cent of the world's top-tier professional football competitions operate with a system of promotion and relegation, and the MLS is a notable representative of the minority. In August 2017, two American teams competing in secondary but disconnected leagues (Miami FC of the North American Soccer League and Kingston Stockdale FC of the National Premier Soccer League North Atlantic Conference) lodged a claim to the Court of Arbitration for Sport against the United States Soccer Federation, CONCACAF, and FIFA for allowing MLS to operate a closed league system preventing other clubs from earning promotion to it based on merit (Reuters, 2017).

Therefore, in some respects the MLS represents both a bridge between and clash of organisational and economic sporting systems. Together with the performance of the Men's and Women's national teams, the league has helped football achieve and consolidate a position as a mainstream sport in the largest and most competitive sports market in the world. From a business management perspective, there are a number of key contemporary issues concerning CONCACAF and football in North America some of which are examined in the subsequent sections of this chapter. The remainder of this section focuses upon the confederation's corporate structure and model of football governance, its organisational structure, the 2015 corruption scandals involving CONCACAF officials and the related reform framework.

CONCACAF: Mission, governance and organisational structure

CONCACAF is a non-profit organisation incorporated in Nassau, Bahamas, and headquartered in Miami, Florida (USA). It has satellite offices in both Guatemala City (Guatemala) to support the *Unión Centroamericana de Fútbol* (UNCAF) members and the operation of the CONCACAF Champions League tournaments, and Kingston (Jamaica) to support and allocate funds to the largest but least developed CONCACAF region – the Caribbean Football Union (CFU). The ONE CONCACAF financial assistance programme currently allocates 80 per cent of its funds to CFU member unions, with plans to treble its current financial investments in Caribbean football (CONCACAF, 2017). CONCACAF's mission is to "develop, promote and manage football throughout the region with integrity, transparency, and passion in order to inspire participation in the game" (CONCACAF Mission Statement, 2017).

To focus its strategic efforts and investments in light of this mission, the CONCACAF Council developed 14 organisational objectives. These include: improving the game by unifying educational, cultural, and humanitarian values particularly through youth and development programs; promoting, regulating, and controlling the game; ensuring that all CONCACAF stakeholders observe the statutes, regulations, decisions, disciplinary code, and code of ethics of FIFA and CONCACAF; instituting strong measures and campaigns against racism, discrimination, bribery, corruption, and match-fixing; and organising and managing international competitions at all levels of and variants of football across North America (CONCACAF, 2016). There are not many of these objectives that have not been called into question in some capacity through the conduct of particular CONCACAF personnel over the past two decades (Sugden and Tomlinson, 2017).

There is a lack of available academic and critical analysis of CONCACAF's organisational and governance structures, and meaningful published critiques of the confederation are relatively few in number. However, the confederation promotes details of its structure and professes to facilitate governance through five independent but interrelated branches with distinct areas of authority and responsibility. The Congress is the legislative branch of CONCACAF, which is comprised of up to three delegates from each of the confederation's 41 full member associations, with one delegate from each member association afforded voting rights (Burks et al., 2017). The Congress represents the overall authority within the CONCACAF governance structure. The scope of power and responsibilities of the Congress includes: enacting or amending CONCACAF statutes, electing the members of the CONCACAF Council, granting full membership, suspending or expelling a member association, approving reports, and reviewing the recommendations of the CONCACAF Council, appraising the audited financial statements and the annual CONCACAF budget, and sanctioning or dismissing members of CONCACAF standing and ad-hoc committees (CONCACAF, 2016).

The Council branch serves as the regulatory and strategic arm of CONCACAF, overseeing the implementation of CONCACAF statues, polices, regulations, and objectives. The Council also operates as an organisational liaison by reviewing, approving, or reporting the recommendations made by the confederation's committees and the general secretary of its Congress (Apostolov, 2017). This Council is composed of a president, three vice-presidents, three member-association members, up to three independent members, four CONCACAF representatives to the FIFA Council, and one female member. All Council members are elected by the Congress to serve a four-year term. CONCACAF Council members are eligible for re-election but can only serve up to 12 years, as three terms of four years, whether consecutive or otherwise. At least one vice-president and one member-association delegate from each of the three CONCACAF Unions – the CFU, the North American Football Union (NAFU) and the UNCAF – represent their respective Unions in the CONCACAF Council. Presently this equates to eleven Council members (CONCACAF, 2016).

The executive branch of CONCACAF is formed by the General Secretariat, a team of remunerated staff working under the leadership of the general secretary. The General Secretariat assumes the operational and administrative responsibilities of CONCACAF. In contrast to Congress and Council memberships, the general secretary (whose role is comparable to that of a CEO) is appointed by CONCACAF, which also set the terms of employment for the post. The general secretary is responsible for: managing CONCACAF's finances, ensuring that decisions made by the Congress are implemented, managing the confirmation's properties, and representing its interests in relations with FIFA, other regional confederations, member associations, and commercial establishments (CONCACAF, 2016).

The disciplinary, appeals and ethics committees act collectively as the judicial branch of CONCACAF. Each committee is led by a chairperson and a deputy chairperson appointed by the Council then sanctioned by the Congress to serve a four-year term. A valid and current license to practice law is a prerequisite to serve as a chairperson or a deputy chairperson in any of the three judicial committees. The CONCACAF Disciplinary Code and the Code of Ethics govern the charges of the three judicial committees. In response to any complaints filed with the general secretary, the ethics committee is mandated to investigate potential breaches in the CONCACAF Code of Ethics and either dismiss or adjudicate the case (CONCACAF, 2014). The ethics committee is awarded autonomy and power to impose sanctions to those in breach of any provision stipulated in the CONCACAF Code of Ethics. The disciplinary committee undertakes similar responsibilities to the ethics equivalent, managing issues pertaining to the CONCACAF Disciplinary Code. The appeals committee is responsible for hearing appeals against decisions from both the disciplinary and ethics committees (CONCACAF, 2016).

The CONCACAF standing and ad-hoc committees assume advisory roles within the organisation, reporting directly to the CONCACAF Council and advising on matters concerning their scope of responsibilities (CONCACAF, 2016). CONCACAF currently has nine standing committees, namely, those relating to associations, audit and compliance, compensation, finance, football, governance, medicine, referees, and the organisation of competitions within the confederation. Ad-hoc committees are occasionally formed to tackle specific or significant issues. The integrity committee for instance, was established in 2012 to investigate the allegations of corruption and misconduct by former CONCACAF administrations, and played a key role in the resultant organisational reform implemented between 2012 and 2014. After what was purported to be a thorough investigation, the committee produced significant incriminating evidence against former CONCACAF president Jack Warner and former general secretary Chuck Blazer, concluding that both violated several FIFA and CONCACAF statutes, codes, and regulations, whilst committing fraud and misappropriating funds from both organisations (CONCACAF Integrity Committee, 2013).

Post-corruption scandals of 2015 and reform framework

Corruption allegations levied against CONCACAF executives have plagued the organisation since the 1980s (Sugden and Tomlinson, 2017). Although numerous claims have been made about combatting the corruption of CONCACAF officials during this period, arguably the first decisive (although not necessarily effective) anti-corruption institutional initiative was established in 2012. This followed the suspension of its former president and FIFA vice-president Jack Warner by FIFA's Ethics Committee, which prompted his resignation from the positions he occupied in FIFA and CONCACAF. Demonstrating the reputational damage to the confederation, and linked to its mission, an "integrity committee" was thereby formed tasked with investigating the corruption allegations made against CONCACAF executives (CONCACAF Integrity Committee, 2013).

Warner had resided as the confederation's president since 1990 and had also served on FIFA's Executive Committee since 1983. His removal from all positions in international football provided potential opportunities for the redevelopment of CONCACAF's ethical procedures and organisational structure (*The Guardian*, 2016). However, what followed "hardly led to a reformed CONCACAF" according to renowned organisational corruption scholars Sugden and Tomlinson (2017, p. 213). Nevertheless, a movement for reform did gather momentum amongst CONCACAF stakeholders. Jeffrey Webb, the president of the Cayman Islands Football Association, was unanimously elected by the CONCACAF Congress in 2012 to lead the reform. A new Code of Ethics and Code of Conduct were instituted during Webb's tenure as president (Tomlinson, 2016; Sheu, 2016). However, despite claiming to represent the image of a new transparent organisation devoid of corrupt practices, Webb was arrested in May 2015 on charges of racketeering, wire fraud, and money laundering conspiracy (Clifford and Apuzzo, 2015). Webb pleaded guilty to those charges and received a life ban from football activity by the FIFA Ethics Committee (Bean, 2015). A year after the dismissal of Jeffrey Webb from FIFA and CONCACAF, Victor Montagliani assumed the presidency of CONCACAF. As president of the Canadian Soccer Association, Montagliani helped enact a comprehensive package of legislative and organisational governance reforms at confederation level. Those reforms were presented as the CONCACAF Reform Framework and voted unanimously at the CONCACAF's Extraordinary Congress in February 2016 (*The Guardian*, 2016).

The key reforms include the creation of standing and independent committees to oversee compensation, governance, compliance, and finance. Also, eligibility checks were established to be conducted by the independent ethics committee for all candidates to the CONCACAF Council, CONCACAF presidency, standing committee members, members of judicial bodies, and senior officials. In addition, a 12-year term limit (consecutive or otherwise) was imposed for all elected CONCACAF officials, to help avoid an organisational equivalent of the kind of dictatorial system that often pervades countries with long-serving leaders (Johnston, 2017). Furthermore, in order to test the legitimacy of the use of funds and enhance the transparency of the system, the right to audit any member association or union was introduced for those receiving CONCACAF funds for a specific purpose. Finally, in relation to compensation packages awarded to its delegates, the CONCACAF Congress was awarded the authority to undertake an annual review and approval of the remuneration of CONCACAF Council members, CONCACAF representatives before FIFA, the chairpersons of standing and ad-hoc committees, and senior officials including the general secretary, chief financial officer, and chief legal and compliance officer (CONCACAF, 2016).

As Johnston (2017, p. 3) argues, however, "too many anti-corruption efforts take the form of process-orientated institutional changes", with best practice assumed to require the emulation of democratic institutions in which corruption has "apparently been brought under control"; and yet corruption control could instead be considered an outcome or by-product of "broad-based contention over power and justice, not of amassing reform 'solutions'" (ibid). The pattern of positive internal accounts of apparently rigorous and transparent practices is evident in how CONCACAF officials describe their Reform Framework, which is framed as representative of: "fundamental change to the governance structure of football in the region and sets new standards for accountability and transparency within international sports organizations" (CONCACAF, 2016). Those reforms are also presented as incorporating essential principles of good governance and compliance within CONCACAF's statutes. If implemented transparently, such reforms could ensure that decisions regarding CONCACAF's operations are made in the best interest of its member associations in partial fulfilment of its mission.

On one hand, the reform package passed and implemented since 2013 appears a positive step towards the making of a transparent confederation unencumbered by corruption. Entrenched cultures of corruption and poor sports governance, however, can take time to change (Cashmore and Cleland, 2014), and CONCACAF as an organisation has yet to meaningfully represent every aspect of its own mission. The complexities associated with the unique nature of non-governmental sport governance entities such as CONCACAF can also prove a difficult climate in which to operate. As Pielke argues in relation to such organisations:

> They are not governmental, not intergovernmental, not corporations and not international bodies like the United Nations or World Health Organization. It is, arguably, this special, non-profit status that is at the heart of challenges to hold such bodies accountable to the same rules and norms that govern other international bodies.
>
> *(2015, p. 5)*

The unusual transnational and organisational structure and corporate climate in which confederations such as CONCACAF operate therefore can foster the conditions for malpractice and poor governance, potentially leading to and becoming manifest in reduced accountability, a lack of transparency, and ultimately to fraud and corruption. CONCACAF promotes various aspects of its governance and organisational structure but does not for instance openly publish remuneration details for its high-ranking executives. As a frame of reference, the salary of the CEO of Ford Motor Company is published online: $1.8 million in 2016 (Lawrence, 2017). Such disparity in transparency practices reflects the reality that mechanisms of accountability built into organisations including Ford, have limited influence on football confederations like CONCACAF where the consequences for the lack of transparency in such instances are relatively minimal (DiCenso, 2017; Pielke, 2015). As a summation that has been applied across innumerable economic, political, and organisational contexts: football often plays by its own rules.

Conclusion

As the body responsible for the governance of football in North America, CONCACAF is engaged in a complicated undertaking, representing what is often perceived to be a polarised continent in terms of scale, wealth, economic capacity, and sporting culture. With the US – the largest sports market in the world – dominated by four major leagues, football has previously been marginalised. It is now, however, showing signs of sustained growth. The MLS is developing in terms of its franchise base, fan support, commercial dealings, and revenue generation. For instance, Atlanta United were founded in 2014 and became an MLS team in 2017 and have already developed four identified fan groups and recorded the highest attendance for an MLS match with over 70,000 attendees in September 2017.

Such rapid and widespread engagement – fusing American, Latin, and European cultures and practices – is likely to see increased investment and broadcasting and commercial revenues, impacting upon existing and subsequent franchises. This could also enhance the level of competition with other CONCACAF leagues, notably in Latin America, such as the Mexican Liga MX through the CONCACAF Champions League. International football has a somewhat different profile, with a notable gendered division. With the women's game having considerable success, men's international football, in particular, might actually benefit from closer ties to COMNEBOL competitions. The quadrennial international tournament Copa America for instance typically has invited participation from countries such as Japan. Incorporating CONCACAF teams through a permanent allocation of places could promote football development in North America and drive commercial and broadcasting revenues. The 2016 centenary version which was held in the US and included six CONCACAF entrants provided a useful model in this respect.

Aside from its competitions, CONCACAF has endured significant problems with governance and corruption as identified in this chapter. With more than four times the number of member associations as COMNBOL it also has more transnational layers of complexity. Future work should examine the nature and impact of international relations within CONCACAF, and the degree of transparency in the organisation and its acquisition and use of funds. Voting practices and associated politics and consequences would also represent a useful study. Marketing, broadcasting, and commercial practices should also be investigated, as relatively little is known about the confederation in such contexts. This is particularly evident outside the dominant competitions of the MLS, Liga MX, Champions League, and Gold Cup. Future work could also examine the structure of North America's various regional subdivisions of transnational football associations. Such work would be facilitated by any positive ongoing developments in CONCACAF's post-corruption reform. Recent work from scholars such as Sugden and Tomlinson (2017), Burks et al., (2017) and DiCenso (2017) represents a critical and at times understandably sceptical view in this regard. However, the current CONCACAF president and FIFA council member Victor Montagliani has sought to acknowledge and address the concerns relating to the confederation and stressed the developmental nature of the game in North America:

> I totally get the skepticism from the public about reform and I think everyone at Fifa gets it … We are starting to see a bit of humbleness from the sport's leaders and that is a good thing. The one thing that people have to realize is that as much as there has been a bit of a shitstorm here in the past few years, the game itself is in good shape.
>
> *(The Guardian, 2016)*

References

Apostolov, S. (2017) USA v Mexico: history, geopolitics and economics of one of the world's oldest rivalries in soccer. *Soccer & Society*, 19(2), 1–15.

Armstrong, G. and Rosbrook-Thompson, J. (2010) Coming to America: historical ontologies and United States soccer. *Global Studies in Culture and Power*, 17(4), 348–371.

Bean, B. W. (2015) An interim essay on FIFA's World Cup of corruption: the desperate need for international corporate governance standards at FIFA. *ILSA J. Int'l & Comp. L.*, 22, 367.

Brown, M. (2014) *From Frontiers to Football: An Alternative History of Latin America since 1800*. London: Reaktion Books.

Brewster, C. and Brewster, K. (2010) *Representing the Nation: Sport and Spectacle in post-Revolutionary Mexico*. New York: Routledge.

Burks, A., Goldman, A.M., and Agha, N. (2017) Strategic repositioning of CONCACAF: rebuilding trust in 'the beautiful game'. In: SD. Arthur and J. Beech (eds), *International Cases in the Business of Sport* (pp. 97–113). London: Routledge.

Campomar, A. (2014) *¡Golzalo! A History of Latin American Football*. London: Quercus Books.

Cashmore, E. and Cleland, J. (2014) *Football's Dark Side: Corruption, Homophobia, Violence and the Beautiful Game*. Palgrave: Basingstoke.

Carter, T. (2014) Game changer: the role of sport in revolution. *The International Journal of the History of Sport*, 31(7), 735–746.

Celik, O.N. and Ince-Yenilmez, M. (2017) Salary difference under the salary cap in Major League Soccer. *International Journal of Sports Science & Coaching*, 12(5), 623–634.

Charles, C. (2015). *Perspectives on Caribbean Football*. London: Hansib Publications.

Clifford, S. and Apuzzo, M. (2015) After indicting 14 soccer officials, US vows to end graft in FIFA. *New York Times*, 27. [online] Retrieved from: https://www.nytimes.com/2015/05/28/sports/soccer/fifa-officials-arrested-on-corruption-charges-blatter-isnt-among-them.html

Coates, D., Frick, B., and Jewell, T. (2016) Superstar salaries and soccer success. The impact of designated players in Major League Soccer. *Journal of Sports Economics*, 17(7), 76–735.

Collins, T. (2015) Early football and the emergence of modern soccer, c.1840–1880. *The International Journal of the History of Sport*, 32(9), 1127–1142.

CONCACAF (2016a, February 25) Member associations pass statutes reforms. Retrieved from: http://www.concacaf.com/article/concacaf-member-associations-unanimously-pass-landmark-statutes-reforms

CONCACAF (2014) CONCACAF Code of Ethics Edition 2014. Retrieved from: http://www.concacaf.com/concacaf-code-of-ethics

CONCACAF (2017, February 28) CONCACAF opens new office in Caribbean to support growth [Press release]. Retrieved from: http://www.concacaf.com/article/concacaf-opens-new-office-in-caribbean-to-support-growth

CONCACAF Integrity Committee (2013, April 18) Integrity Committee Report of Investigation. Retrieved from: http://www.guardian.co.tt/sites/default/files/story/FinalReport.PDF

CONCACAF Mission Statement (2017) Retrieved from: http://www.concacaf.com/concacaf

DiCenso, M.B. (2017) A long-awaited reboot: the FIFA scandal and its repercussions for football's governing body. *Boston College International & Comparative Law Review*, 40, 115.

Duke, V. and Crolley, L. (2014) *Football, Nationality and the State*. London: Routledge.

Elliott, R. and Harris, J. (2011) Crossing the Atlantic from football to soccer: preliminary observations on the migrations of English players and the internationalization of Major League Soccer. *Journal of Labor and Society*, 14(4), 557–570.

FIFA (2017) Global Club Football Report. Retrieved from: https://resources.fifa.com/mm/document/footballdevelopment/proffootballdept/02/90/12/72/clubfootballreport_29.6.2017_neutral.pdf

Francis, J.D. (2011) Learning from failure: Is Major League Soccer repeating the mistakes of the North American Soccer League? In: H. Dolles and S. Söderman (eds), *Sport as a Business* (pp. 213–227). Palgrave Macmillan, London..

Hankinson, G. (2009) Managing destination brands: establishing a theoretical foundation. *Journal of Marketing Management*, 25(1/2), 97–115.

Hanna, S. and Rowley, J. (2011) Towards a strategic place brand-management model. *Journal of Marketing Management*, 27 (5–6), 458–476.

Hillman, C. (2016) *American Sports in an age of Consumption: How Commercialization is Changing the Game*. Jefferson, NC: McFarland and Company.

Jewell, T. (2014) Major League Soccer in the USA. In: J. Goddard and P. Sloane (eds), *Handbook on the Economics of Professional Football* (pp. 351–367). Cheltenham: Edward Elgar Publishing.

Johnson, H.N. (2014) Jamaica: A Famous, strong but damaged brand. *Brand Placing and Public Diplomacy*, 10(3), 199–217.

Johnston, M. (2017) Reform, rebooted: building long-term resistance to corruption. *Georgetown Journal of International Affairs*, 18(2), 3–9.

Kaufman, Z., Rosenbauer, B.P., and Moore, G. (2013) Lessons learned from monitoring and evaluating sport-for-development programmes in the Caribbean. In: N. Schulenkorf and D. Adair (eds.), *Global Sport-for-Development: Critical Perspectives* (pp. 173–193). (New York: Palgrave Macmillan).

Kitchen, P. and Chowhan, K. (2016) Forecheck, backcheck, health check: the benefits of playing recreational ice hockey for adults in Canada. *Journal of Sports Sciences*, 34(21), 2121–2129.

Kitchens, C.T. (2015) Are winners promoted too often? Evidence from the NFL Draft 1999–2012. *Economic Inquiry*, 53(2), 1317–1330.

Klein, A. and Marcus, J. (2016) United States-Cuba normalized relations and the MLB influence: the Baseball Coalition Committee. *University of Miami Inter-American Law Review*, 258–315.

Kristiansen, E., Broch, T.B., and Pedersen, P.M. (2014) Negotiating gender in professional soccer: an analysis of female footballers in the United States. *Choregia*, 10, 5–27.

Lawrence, E.D. (2017, May 24) New Ford CEO Jim Hackett's salary to be $1.8 million. Detroit Free Press. Retrieved from: https://www.freep.com/story/money/cars/ford/2017/05/24/new-ford-ceo-jim-hacketts-salary-1-8-million/343248001/

Leeds, M. and Vol Allmen, P. (2016) *Economics of Sports*. Routledge: London.

Macintosh, E. and Harris, J. (2017) The global sport environment. In T. Bradbury and I. O'Boyle (eds), *Understanding Sport Management: International Perspectives* (pp. 58–71). Routledge: London.

Madden, K. (2015) Hegemonic masculinity and women footballers. In C.A.D. Charles (ed.), *Perspectives on Caribbean Football* (pp. 47–72). Hertford: Hansib Publications.

Markovits, A.S. and Green, A.I. (2016) FIFA, the video game: a major vehicle for soccer's popularization in the United States. *Sport in Society*, 20(5–6), 716–734.

Massey, C. and Thaler, R.H. (2013) The loser's curse: decision making and market efficiency in the National Football League Draft. *Management Science*, 59(7), 1479–1495.

McCree, R. (2017) Caribbean sport sociology: The ongoing journey. In: K. Yound (ed.). *Reflections on Sociology of Sport* (pp. 119–133). Bingley: Emerald Publishing Limited.

Moore, C. (2017) Football unity during the Northern Ireland troubles? *Soccer & Society*, 18(5–6), 663–678.

Moreno-Brid, J.C. and Ros, J. (2009) *Development and Growth in the Mexican Economy: A Historical Perspective*. Oxford: Oxford University Press.

Office of Public Affairs – US Department of Justice. (2015, May 27) Nine FIFA officials and five corporate executives indicted for racketeering conspiracy and corruption [Press release]. Retrieved from: https://www.justice.gov/opa/pr/nine-fifa-officials-and-five-corporate-executives-indicted-racketeering-conspiracy-and

Pielke Jr, R. (2015) Obstacles to accountability in international sports governance. Global Corruption Report: Sport. Retrieved from: http://sciencepolicy.colorado.edu/admin/publication_files/2015.19.pdf

Pye, G. and Pettavino, P. (2016) Sport policy in Cuba. In: G. Bravo., R. López de D'Amico and C. Parrish (eds.). *Sport in Latin America: Policy, Organization, Management* (pp. 89–102). New York: Routledge.

Reuters (2017) Lower-tier U.S. teams take promotion/relegation fiht to CAS. Retrieved from: https://www.reuters.com/article/us-soccer-usa-cas/lower-tier-u-s-teams-take-promotion-relegation-fight-to-cas-idUSKBN1AJ2YL

Reynolds, Z., Bonds, T., Thompson, S., and LeCrom, C.W. (2015) Deconstructing the draft: An evaluation of NFL draft as a predictor of team success. *Journal of Applied Sport Management*, 7(3), 74–89.

Rookwood, J. and Chan, N. (2011) 'The 39th Game' – Fan responses to the Premier League's proposal to globalise English football. *Soccer & Society*, 12(6), 897–913.

Rookwood, J. and Hughson, J. (2017) Historical context: cultures, consumption and commerce. In: R. Elliott (ed.). *The English Premier League: A Socio-Cultural Analysis*. Routledge: London.

Rothschadl, A.M. and Nunes, C.M. (2016) Organized play through youth sports: a four-tier system. In: R.L. Clements and L. Fiorentino (eds.)., *The Child's Right to Play: A Global Approach* (pp. 137–143). Westport, CT: Praeger.

Rumford, C. (2007) More than a game: Globalization and the post-Westernization of world cricket. *Global Networks*. 7(2), 202–214.

Sheppard, R. (2016) *A Persistent Revolution: History, Nationalism, and Politics in Mexico since 1968*. Albuquerque: University of New Mexico.

Sheu, V. (2016) Corrupt Passions: An Analysis of the FIFA Indictments. Tex. Rev. *Ent. & Sports L.*, 18, 65.

Shobe, H. and Gibson, G. (2017) Place, nation and the Mexico-US soccer rivalry: dual citizenship, home stadiums, and hosting the Gold Cup. In: J.W. Kassing, and L.J. Meân (eds.). *Perspectives on the US-Mexico Soccer Rivalry: Passion and Politics in Red, White, Blue and Green* (pp. 49–72). Cham, Switzerland: Palgrave Macmillan.

Smith, S.D. and Clinton, S.R. (2016) Exploring factors that led to people watching professional soccer on television. *Journal of Electronic Commerce in Organizations*, 14(4), 66–95.

Smolianov, P., Murphy, J., McMahon, S.G., and Naylor, A.H. (2015) Comparing the practices of US Soccer against a global model for integrated development of mass and high-performance sport. *Managing Sport and Leisure*, 20(1), 1–21.

Spaaij, R. (2014) Football-related violence and the impact of political conflicts. *Panorama: Insights into Asian and European Affairs*, 5(1), 71–74.

Sveinson, K. and Hoeber, L. (2016) Female sports fans' experiences or marginlisation and empowerment. *Journal of Sport Management*, 30(1), 8–21.

Sugden, J. and Tomlinson, A. (2017) *Football, Corruption and Lies: Revisiting Badfellas, the Book FIFA Tried to Ban*. Routledge: London.

The Guardian (2016) Concacaf president Victor Montagliani: 'There has been a shitstorm here'. Retrieved from: https://www.theguardian.com/football/2016/sep/05/concacaf-president-vincent-montagliani-interview-fifa-corruption

Tomlinson, A. (2016) The world governing body's escalating crisis of credibility. In: A. Bairner, J. Kelly and J.W. Lee (eds.). *Routledge Handbook of Sport and Politics*. New York, NY: Routledge.

Vonnard, P. and Quin, G. (2017) Did South America foster European football? Transnational influences on the continentalization of FIFA and the creation of UEFA, 1926–1959. *Sport in Society*, 20(10), 1424–1439.

Wilson, B. (2015) Social unrests and the 2014 World Cup in Brazil: lessons for the Caribbean. In C.A.D. Charles (ed.). *Perspectives on Caribbean Football*. Hertford: Hansib Publications, pp. 89–102.

Yellvington, K.A. (1995) Cricket, colonialism, and the culture of Caribbean politics. In M.A. Malec (ed.). *The Social Roles of Sport in Caribbean Societies* (pp. 13–52). Routledge: New York.

Yoder, A. (2016) Sport policy and political regimes in Latin America. In: G. Bravo., R. López de D'Amico, and C. Parrish (eds.)., *Sport in Latin America: Policy, Organization, Management* (pp. 65–76). New York: Routledge.

40

Oceania Football Confederation

Geoff Dickson and Sean Phelps

Introduction

This chapter provides a critical analysis of role of the Oceania Football Confederation (OFC) in the business and management of football. In the first section, we introduce the region of Oceania, the OFC members, and the organisation's origins. In the next section we describe the quality of play, governance issues, qualification standards for FIFA tournaments, and the performance of OFC teams at FIFA tournaments. We conclude that the OFC has four main legitimacy deficiencies when compared to FIFA's other continental confederations: low quality of play; small number of influential/prominent members; low qualification standards for FIFA tournaments; and poor performance of OFC teams at FIFA tournaments. In the third section, we review the OFC's social responsibility initiatives, media and communications strategies, technical and development initiatives, and their competitions and administrative structures. In the fourth section, we conclude with an examination of OFC's future, including how the OFC might be reconfigured as part of a restructured network of continental confederations.

Oceania

The Oceania region spans both the eastern and western hemispheres, and incorporates Melanesia, Micronesia, Polynesia, and Australasia. Oceania is the smallest continental grouping in land area and, with approximately 40 million inhabitants, is the second smallest in population after Antarctica. The OFC nations have "widely varying socio-economic and cultural contexts, poised between small Pacific islands nations and the former white-settler colony of New Zealand" (Falcous 2017, p. 445).

OFC membership

The OFC is one of the six continental confederations of the *Fédération Internationale de Football Association* (FIFA). OFC is comprised of 11 full member associations and three associate members. The full members are Football Federation American Samoa (FFAS), Cook Islands Football Association (CIFA), Fiji Football Association (FFA), *Fédération Calédonienne de Football* (FCF)

(New Caledonia), New Zealand Football (NZF), Papua New Guinea Football Association (PNGFA), Football Federation Samoa (FFS), Solomon Islands Football Federation (SIFF), *Fédération Tahitienne de Football* (FTF) (Tahiti), Tonga Football Association (TFA), and Vanuatu Football Federation (VFF). The associate members are Kiribati Islands Football Association, Niue Island Soccer Association, and Tuvalu National Football Association.

Several sovereign states or dependencies in Oceania have national football federations that have no affiliation to the OFC and FIFA. These include the Federated States of Micronesia Football Association, Palau Football Association, *Fédération de Ligue de Football de Wallis et Futuna*. Nauru, Marshall Islands, Tokelau, Norfolk Island, and the Pitcairn Islands are all without a national football federation. There are sovereign states and dependencies with territory in Oceania, but their national football federation is not affiliated to OFC. For example, Football Federation Australia, Guam Football Association, and the Northern Mariana Islands Football Association are all affiliated to the AFC.

OFC history

The OFC is the youngest, smallest, and most geographically isolated of all the FIFA confederations (Dickson et al., 2010). Declined the opportunity to affiliate with the Asian Football Confederation (AFC), Australia and New Zealand developed a proposal for the OFC. FIFA approved the proposal in 1966 with four founding member nations: Australia, Fiji, New Zealand, and Papua New Guinea. In 1996, the OFC acquired full confederation status, meaning that OFC now had a representative on the FIFA executive. Former members of OFC are Australia (1966–1972, 1978–2006), Chinese Taipei (1967–1989), and the Northern Mariana Islands (1998–2009). Israel participated in some OFC competitions throughout the 1970s and 1980s, but they were never OFC members.

The disaffiliation of the Football Federation of Australia in 2006 was a seismic moment in the OFC's history. With it, the OFC lost its strongest and most powerful member association in terms of on-field success, overall player memberships, number of referees, and country of origin for the professional A-League (Dempsey, 2006). Australia has the region's largest population and economy (OECD, 2013). Additionally, the OFC lost a powerful asset in terms of both the administrative (i.e., officials, coaches, administrators) and playing strength. For many stakeholders this meant that the OFC would be unable to be recognised as a legitimate confederation within

Table 40.1 OFC membership and year of FIFA and OFC affiliation

OFC Member	Founded	Year of FIFA Affiliation	Year of OFC Affiliation
American Samoa	1984	1998	1998
Cook Islands	1971	1994	1994
Fiji	1938	1964	1966
New Caledonia	1928	2004	1966
New Zealand	1891	1948	1966
Papua New Guinea	1962	1966	1966
Samoa	1968	1986	1986
Solomon Islands	1979	1988	1988
Tahiti	1989	1990	1990
Tonga	1965	1994	1994
Vanuatu	1934	1988	1988

the FIFA network. In March 2005, the then New Zealand Soccer chief executive Graham Seatter indicated strong opposition to the move, saying it would damage the OFC's position in the game (Australia hoping to opt out of Oceania, 2005). He commented, "We have suffered by being in the weakest FIFA confederation. Without Australia we would be further weakened and we will suffer more" (Soccer: Oceania unaware of Australian shift, 2005).

With disaffiliation it was posited by members in the media that the remaining OFC member associations should also affiliate with the AFC (Brown, 2005). This would end the OFC. The OFC has always struggled to make its presence felt in the "world's game" (Vrooman, 2007, p. 314). This lack of profile and influence exists despite football being the number one sport in the majority of the OFC's member nations and providing a tool for social development and hope amongst its citizens (Waugh et al., 2014). Given FIFA's proclamation of being "for the world" (FIFA, 2010), it was important for the OFC to at least maintain its status within the football community.

Legitimacy issues

Legitimacy refers to "generalised perception or assumption that the actions of an entity are desirable, proper, or appropriate within some socially constructed systems of norms, values, beliefs, and definitions" (Suchman, 1995, p. 574). Organisations are oriented towards attaining, maintaining, and protecting legitimacy (Kumar and Das, 2007). Legitimacy is a consequence of complying with industry norms and broader societal expectations (Lounsbury and Glynn, 2001). Waugh, Dickson, and Phelps (2014) concluded that the FFA's disaffiliation exacerbated a number of pre-existing OFC legitimacy deficiencies: low quality of play; small number of influential/prominent members; low qualification standards for FIFA tournaments; poor performance of OFC teams at FIFA tournaments; and small participation numbers. These themes are used to structure this overview of the OFC.

Quality of play

Absolute quality of play reflects the standard of athletic talent. There are many indicators of absolute quality of play. The FIFA World Rankings indicate that only New Zealand approaches the Top 100 football nations. The New Zealand women's team is much more competitive internationally. No other OFC women's team is ranked by FIFA. Sepp Blatter's assertion that the future of football is feminine has not been heard in the Pacific Islands. In this case, the quality of play is a significant difference in on-field capability. In the four years after the FFA's disaffiliation, New Zealand won all 12 of the OFC championship events (excluding Futsal events). It was not uncommon for the score difference between two teams to be greater than ten goals. OFC competitions are now dominated by New Zealand, whereas prior to the FFA disaffiliation they were dominated by Australia and New Zealand. Whilst other confederations also have strong and weak teams, the difference between the strong and weak teams in the OFC is perceived to be greater. Also, in other confederations, there will be more than one strong team.

The OFC Champions League, informally known as the O-League, is the premier men's club football competition. The O-League was introduced in 2007, succeeding the Oceania Club Championship. Australia or New Zealand clubs have won all but one of the 17 competitions. The qualification of Hekari United from Papua New Guinea was the first time that a club from Australia and New Zealand did not participate at a FIFA club football tournament at any level.

New Zealand dominates OFC tournaments. Auckland City FC are the current OFC Champions League winner, and their national teams are the titleholders in both the men's and women's Champions Cup, Under 17, Under 20 championships. New Zealand was the OFC representative

Table 40.2 OFC and FIFA ranking of OFC affiliates

OFC Ranking	Men's Football		Women's Football	
	Country	FIFA ranking	Country	FIFA ranking
1	American Samoa	122	New Zealand	19
2	Cook Islands	148	Papua New Guinea	*
3	Fiji	150	Fiji	*
4	New Caledonia	152	Tonga	*
5	New Zealand	159	New Caledonia	*
6	Papua New Guinea	175	Tahiti	*
7	Samoa	188	Cook Islands	*
8	Solomon Islands	193	Solomon Islands	*
9	Tahiti	193	Vanuatu	*
10	Tonga	193	Samoa	*
11	Vanuatu	206	American Samoa	*

Sources: http://www.fifa.com/fifa-world-ranking/ranking-table/men/ofc.html and http://www.fifa.com/fifa-world-ranking/ranking-table/women/ofc.html Data accurate as of October 2017.

* Inactive for more than 18 months and therefore not ranked

in women's football at the 2016 Olympics. The New Zealand men's team was disqualified from the Olympic qualifying tournament for playing an ineligible player. Fiji defeated Vanuatu in the final (Johnstone, 2016). It has been said "Oceania means New Zealand" (D. Waugh et al., 2014, p. 547). New Zealand has been called the "the local bully" within the OFC (Bennett, 2013).

Prior to the FFA's disaffiliation, New Zealand could counter some of the dominance of Australia. With their departure, New Zealand is the proverbial big fish in a small pond. Other FIFA confederations are not dominated by single nation in this way. In other FIFA confederations the social and economic resources are more equally distributed. By comparison, the Union of European Football Associations (UEFA) has member organisations from a number of football powerhouses (i.e., England, France, Germany, Italy, The Netherlands, and Spain).

Governance issues

Historically, the OFC was dominated on and off the field by the Football Federation of Australia (FFA). Their dominance ended on 1 January 2006, when the FFA disaffiliated from the OFC and subsequently affiliated with the Asian Football Confederation (AFC). OFC representatives serve on a wide variety of FIFA standing committees and judicial bodies. The OFC is structured around five pillars: growing the game, promoting their elite, ensuring financial sustainability, professionalising the management, and making the Pacific a better place (Oceania Football Confederation, 2011). In 2012, a women's representative was placed permanently on the executive committee. FIFA's senior vice-president is from Papua New Guinea. David Chung was the president of the Papua New Guinea Football Association in 2004. He became the OFC's senior vice-president in 2007 before being elected its president in 2011. He has been a FIFA council member since 2011.

OFC stakeholders in FIFA-related corruption scandals

There is considerable variation as to the extent to which corruption pervades the OFC nations. Three OFC nations are ranked in the 2016 Corruptions Perceptions Index produced by

Transparency International (1 equals least corrupt, 176 equals most corrupt): New Zealand (1), the Solomon Islands (72) and Papua New Guinea (136). Match-fixing, money-laundering, kick-backs, extortion, and bribery are well established features of the international football industry (Bayle and Rayner, 2016; Boudreaux et al., 2016; Dorsey, 2015). The OFC is not immune to these problems.

Charlie Dempsey. Dempsey led the Oceania Football Confederation from 1982 to 2000. Dempsey is best known for his decision to abstain from the voting in the third round of voting to award hosting rights for the 2006 FIFA World Cup. As Oceania's representative, Dempsey was under instruction to support the South African bid, once England had dropped out of the ballot. Having voted for England in the first two rounds, Dempsey's abstention effectively handed victory to Germany. The reason for the abstention was never explained fully, but Dempsey did refer to "intolerable pressure" by supporters of the competing bids, including attempts to bribe him. His abstention prompted some to question his integrity and rumours of bribes were never far from the surface. Within weeks, Dempsey resigned as OFC president, two years before his term expired. No corruption charges were ever laid, let alone sustained against Dempsey.

Reynald Temarii. In 2015, Temarii was banned from any kind of football-related activity at national and international level for a period of eight years. The FIFA Ethics Committee determined that the former minister for youth and sport in French Polynesia had violated a number of FIFA Code of Ethics articles related to rules of conduct, loyalty, confidentiality, conflicts of interest, and offering and accepting gifts and other benefits. Temarii had previously accepted money from Qatari powerbroker Mohamed bin Hammam to pay legal costs in a corruption case linked to the 2022 World Cup vote. Bin Hamman's aim was to ensure that Temarii stayed in office so that he could vote for Qatar to host the 2022 World Cup. In 2010, Temarii had been banned for one year amid allegations that he asked for money for votes as part of the bidding process for the 2018 and 2022 World Cup finals.

Ahongalu Fusimalohi. Fusimalohi was a member of the OFC executive committee and the FIFA Olympic Tournaments Committee. In 2010, a hidden camera filmed Fusimalohi when he was meeting with an undercover newspaper journalist. The journalist was posing as a lobbyist working on behalf of the United States football federation's bid for the 2018 and 2022 FIFA World Cups. This "sting" also exposed Temarii. Despite the fake lobbyist revealing his intentions to corrupt members of the FIFA executive, Fusimalohi offered his assistance. In rejecting Fusimalohi's appeal, the Court of Arbitration for Sport (2011, p.79) concluded that Fusimalohi was "willing to engage in this illicit activity and his conduct was obviously motivated by the pursuit of personal benefit and gain" (Court of Arbitration for Sport, 2011).

David Chung. Malaysian born, but based in Papua New Guinea (PNG), Chung became the OFC president in 2010 when Temarii was forced to resign. In 2016, Chung faced a contested election to remain president of the PNGFA. The election was postponed from August until late December. Chung's opponents claim that the meeting was postponed when it became clear that the majority of PNG's 18 local associations were planning to support Chung's rival John Kapi Natto. Between the postponement of the election and the eventual 28 December Congress, the OFC Ethics Committee suspended seven of the 12 associations that were supporting Kapi Natto. In a decision subsequently endorsed by FIFA and the PNG High Court, the members were found not to be compliant to their member obligations in accordance with the PNGFA Statutes. The seven suspensions pushed the voting balance in Chung's favour, and he won by a single vote. Chung also refuted allegations that he used FIFA funds to incentivise votes for his candidacy.

Qualification standards for FIFA tournaments

The competitive imbalance problem within the OFC permits the OFC champion to enter FIFA tournaments without a rigorous confederation qualifying competition. There have been some occasions at the youth level when the OFC nominated a team *without* a tournament. Prior to the FIFA World Cup 2010, a South African journalist wrote about New Zealand's inclusion: "No disrespect to the Kiwis, but competing against obscure names such as the Cook Islands, Fiji, Vanuatu, Samoa, Tahiti, and Tonga does not inspire much confidence in football circles" (Moyo, 2009). Ironically, New Zealand was the only undefeated team at the FIFA World Cup 2010. They drew all three pool games and even Spain, the winner of the event, lost a pool game.

Reflecting the dearth of high-level competition within the OFC itself, it is the only FIFA confederation whose champion team is not provided with direct entry into world championship events. For example, the OFC winner (New Zealand) played the fifth place South American finisher (Peru) for entry into the 2018 FIFA World Cup. For the FIFA World Cup 2014, New Zealand played Mexico, the fourth-placed team from the Confederation of North, Central American and Caribbean Association Football qualifying matches. In other confederations, national teams compete in highly competitive qualifying tournaments just to earn the right to participate at FIFA tournaments. Without these, the OFC must contend with the perception that their teams do not deserve their place at FIFA tournaments. This criticism is not extended to teams representing other FIFA confederations.

Performance of OFC teams at FIFA tournaments

Oceania is the only FIFA confederation whose affiliated members have not won a single international title (i.e., World Cup, Olympic). New Zealand has only qualified for the men's World Cup in 1982 (finishing 23rd) and 2010 (finishing 22nd). When Australia was a member, the Socceroos qualified in 1974 and in 2006, where they made the Round of 16. The OFC has had large participation gaps over its history. No men's teams qualified in 1966, '70, '78, '86, '90, '94, '98, '02, '14, and '18.

For the men's Under 20 group, New Zealand qualified for the tournament in '07, '11, '13, '15 (host nation), and '17. Tahiti qualified in '09 while Fiji qualified in '15 and Vanuatu in '17. No OFC team has made it past the second round in the men's U-20 competition. In the men's Under 17 tournament, New Zealand qualified in '97, '07, '09, '11, '13, '15, and '17. Australia dominated this division from 1983–05, with the exception of 1997.

New Zealand's women's team qualified for the FIFA World Cup in 1991, 2007, '11, and '15. In the Under 20 division, New Zealand qualified in '06, '08, '10, '12, '14,'16, and '18. The New Zealand Under 17 teams qualified in'08 (as host nation), '10, '12, '14, and '16, but have never advanced past the Group Stage in any of the FIFA tournaments. Across all competitions ranging from Word Cup to Under 20, Under 17, Futsal, and Beach Soccer, the participating OFC countries rarely progress beyond the Group Stage.

OFC initiatives

Social responsibility programmes

Just Play is a sport for social development programme designed for children aged 6–12 years. Just Play was launched in 2009 "as a grassroots initiative which promotes physical activity for primary-aged children while encouraging community involvement and healthy living"

(Oceania Football Confederation, 2013, p.10). The program is delivered by primary school teachers (during school hours) and by community volunteers (after school hours). The development outcomes are healthy lifestyles, support and encouragement for gender equality, and increased school and community engagement. Just Play is managed by the OFC, with support from the Australian Government, the Football Federation of Australia, the New Zealand Government, Special Olympics New Zealand, UNICEF, and the Union of European Football Association (through the UEFA Foundation for Children). The involvement of UNICEF and the Australian and New Zealand governments is unsurprising. Many Pacific Island nations are dependent upon foreign-aid, more formally known as Official Development Assistance (ODA). ODA is higher in the Pacific than in any other region on a per capita basis (Dornan and Pryke, 2017).

The OFC also positions itself as a catalyst or facilitator for post-disaster recovery programs in the Pacific Islands. In times of devastation and destruction "sport is an effective to help communicate messages of emergency preparedness and response in fun and interactive way" (Oceania Football Confederation, 2015, p.15). The statement is important because in 2015 Severe Tropical Cyclone Pam cyclone tore through OFC member nations Kiribati, Solomon Islands, Tuvalu, and Vanuatu. Pam was the second most intense tropical cyclone of the South Pacific Ocean in terms of sustained winds. FIFA, using its Humanitarian Fund, allocated US$200,000 to help with disaster relief. UNICEF directly received $100,000 to help children cope with the storm's aftermath. Through these partnerships the OFC was able to deliver much-needed support to citizens of its member nations. Sports organisations seem to do well in areas of tangible and emotional support in the aftermath of tragedies (Inoue and Havard, 2015). Direct funds help rebuild infrastructure (tangible) while football camps and clinics help provide a distraction in the aftermath of the storm (emotional).

Additionally, the Pacific Youth and Sport Conference, which began in 2010 and was hosted in Auckland, New Zealand, is another initiative the OFC is involved in throughout the Pacific. New Caledonia hosted in 2013.

Media and communications strategies

With the OFC's large geographic footprint (not just multiple time zones but also the International Dateline) and sparse population, there are no large-scale media companies interested in bidding for the media rights to the various competitions. In 2011, the OFC brought all media operations in house (Oceania Football Confederation 2011) after having previously used external partners to facilitate broadcasts (Oceania Football Confederation 2009). Live streaming of events is one way in which the confederation facilitates broadcasting of its key tournaments (Oceania Football Confederation 2012). Additionally, member football associations often produce specific football-related content for their own domestic use.

Also part of its OFC TV strategy is the use of social media (as well as the organisation's website). The OFC has a presence on Twitter, Facebook, Instagram, and a YouTube channel. These platforms are "all being harnessed to deliver key news items across the Oceania region and wider world" (Oceania Football Confederation, 2015, p. 15) without the need for the traditional infrastructure needed for over-the-top broadcasts of its competitions. However, metrics used to measure reach and impact are rudimentary with the total number of matches being streamed, increased Facebook traffic, increased Twitter usage, and increased readership of the *OFC Insider Magazine* (Oceania Football Confederation, 2015). The magazine was published on quarterly basis via the OFC's website but no issues have been posted since 2016.

Technical and development initiatives

The OFC did not have a full-time technical director until 2006 (Oceania Football Confederation, 2009). Its Referee Assistance Program was created in 2008. By 2009, the Technical Department began to deliver courses pertaining to coaches, referees, and a variety of other stakeholders in the confederation. In 2011, the Technical Department instituted a new, and more formalised, process for coaches to upgrade their certifications which covered all areas and forms of the game (Oceania Football Confederation, 2011). The requirements from moving from a D license to A license were more clearly defined. The OFC's first B license course was held in 2012 at the OFC Academy in Auckland with 19 coaches attending (Oceania Football Confederation, 2012). By 2013, the OFC looked to focus on the long-term development and education of coaches within its member nations. The OFC trained over 800 coaches that year with 117 being women (Oceania Football Confederation, 2013). In 2015 the OFC proposed a new mixed "Member Association/OFC accreditation system" whereby each member nation would be "responsible for awarding Grassroots, Youth, Senior, Laws of the Game and Goalkeeping Certificates. From there, those coaches can then progress to completing the OFC coaching accreditation" (Oceania Football Confederation, 2015).

While the OFC's member nations struggled to make an impact at the international level, 14 officials were assigned to FIFA events in 2009 (Oceania Football Confederation, 2009). The referees program has been able to place OFC officials at the highest level of FIFA competitions. At the 2010 FIFA World Cup in South Africa, the OFC had two trios of officials assigned. This was followed up with OFC-based referees assigned to the 2010 Women's U-17 tournament, the Youth Olympic Games in Singapore, and the FIFA Club World Cup in the UAE. In 2011 there were OFC referees assigned to the FIFA U-17, U-20, Women's World Cup, Club World Cup, and the Beach Soccer World Cup (Oceania Football Confederation, 2011). At the London Olympic Games, a trio of OFC officials worked that competition. Additionally, OFC referees were assigned to the 2012 Club World Cup, U-17 Women's World Cup, as well as to the Futsal World Cup (Oceania Football Confederation, 2012). By 2014, a full-time referee development officer was hired and OFC officials were present at the FIFA World Cup, Women's U-20, Men's U-17, and the Youth Olympic Games (Oceania Football Confederation, 2014). In 2015, the OFC let the member associations begin training and working with referees before graduating to the OFC-sanctioned courses and accreditation. Similar to the coaching accreditation pathway, the OFC has ceded some of its power and authority back to its members. Once again, OFC referees were assigned to a variety of international competitions such as the FIFA Women's World Cup, U-17 and U-20 tournaments, FIFA Club World Cup, and the Beach Soccer World Cup (Oceania Football Confederation, 2015).

The OFC's vision statement for women's football is "to lead and inspire our Member Associations to provide an environment where girls and women of Oceania access all aspects of football, aspiring to be competitive and successful" (Oceania Football Confederation, 2015). Women's football within the OFC hit a high point at the 2011 Women's World Cup in Germany. New Zealand's Football Ferns "confirmed themselves as a force on the international stage with a pair of creditable losses and a first ever World Cup point" (Oceania Football Confederation, 2011, p.17). The following year at the London Games New Zealand's women qualified for the quarter-finals before being eliminated by the US 2–0 (Oceania Football Confederation, 2011). In 2014, the OFC announced that from 2010–14 over 5,000 new girls began playing football (Oceania Football Confederation, 2014).

Competitions and administrative structures

The OFC hosts a variety of domestic competitions similar to other FIFA confederations. The Nation's Cup (for both men and women) is the inter-confederation tournament among members, as are the U-17 and U-20 tournaments for both men and women. Futsal and beach soccer are also played with the Solomon Islands being the dominant force in both competitions. There are no OFC women's Futsal tournaments. In Futsal, the Solomon Islands won titles in '08, '09, '10, '11, and '16. Australia won the first four OFC Futsal championships in '92, '96, '99, and '04. Australia also won the OFC title as an invited guest to the Auckland-hosted tournament in 2013.

Beach soccer did not begin until 2006 within the OFC. The Solomon Islands have won four tournaments ('06, '07, '09, and '13). They were runner-ups in 2011. Additionally, they were selected by the OFC as its World Cup representative in '08 when that tournament was cancelled. Tahiti won in 2011 and represented the OFC at the World Cup in '15 and '17 due to cancelled tournaments. Just as there are no OFC Futsal tournaments for women, there are also no OFC women's beach soccer events.

Only two members of the OFC have hosted in any type of FIFA-branded tournament. PNG hosted the women's Under 20 tournament in 2016. New Zealand hosted the women's Under 17 tournament in 2008, the men's Under 20 tournament in 2015, and the men's Under 17 competition in 1999. Prior to leaving the OFC, Australia hosted the FIFA men's World Youth Championships in 1981 and 1993.

Concluding thoughts: OFC's future

Both Australia and New Zealand are engaging more with Asian markets, having relinquished their cultural and economic ties with traditional trading partners. Sport organisations in both countries are also following this strategy (Dickson and Stewart, 2007). The economic opportunities afforded by the Asian football market are significantly greater than those available within Australia, New Zealand, and the wider Oceania region. It is this growing football economy which threatens to dominate, and at worst, decimate the OFC. The future of the OFC is anything but guaranteed. Earlier, we highlighted four legitimacy deficiencies – low quality of play; small number of influential/prominent members; low qualification standards for FIFA tournaments; and poor performance of OFC teams at FIFA tournaments.

New Zealand football has on many occasions made public their interest in joining the AFC. Enthusiasm to do so accelerated after the success of the FFA's entry into the AFC. If New Zealand Football were to leave the OFC, the already tiny confederation would struggle to survive. There is already a move to combine the OFC and AFC in a single Asia-Pacific confederation. In 2005, a ten-year plan to establish a new Asia-Pacific confederation was mooted (Cockerill, 2005). The plan was to split the AFC either through South Asia or Indochina. The 20 nations east of Bangladesh would combine with the 12 OFC nations (including Australia) to form an Asia-Pacific confederation. Japan was considered to be especially keen on dividing Asia into two distinct confederations, but the Middle East nations were less than enthusiastic. Over ten years later, the same concept was being debated in the same newspaper. Lynch (2015) wrote:

> … it's worth asking once more whether it is time for FIFA to look seriously at splitting up the AFC and in the same breath fix up the anomaly that is Oceania. Why not fold Oceania into this huge block, and then split it in two so we have a genuine West and Central Asian Confederation and an East Asian and Oceania Confederation?

However, whilst an OFC–AFC merger remains theoretically possible, the practicalities remain problematic. Duerden (2015) wrote: "There is little appetite in an already unwieldy Asian confederation for absorbing the 13 far-flung and sparsely populated island nations that make up the rest of the group." A more likely, though still not likely, scenario is to split the AFC into two, and align the OFC members with an Asia-Pacific confederation.

Whilst these options would effectively dissolve the OFC, this is not problematic because the OFC was established to serve the interests of its member associations. Should another organisation be able to serve the member associations better, does not mean that the OFC has failed. Just as in the game of football itself, the key is to pass the ball to a player in a better position. The FFA's disaffiliation has started a slow, domino-like process that may allow for the assimilation of the OFC into a new Asia-Pacific confederation, thus ensuring the survival of all its members. This is more important than the survival of the OFC itself.

References

Bayle, E. and Rayner, H. (2016) Sociology of a scandal: the emergence of "FIFAgate." *Soccer & Society*, 1–19.

Bennett, R. (2013) Tahiti a triumph for football's everyman. *espnfc.com*. [online] Available at: http://espnfc.com/blog/ _/name/relegationzone/id/908?cc=3436.

Boudreaux, C.J., Karahan, G., and Coats, M. (2016) Bend it like FIFA: corruption on and off the pitch. *Managerial Finance*, 42(9), 866–878.

Brown, M. (2005) Soccer: Asia rocks Australia as Kiwis follow lead. *New Zealand Herald*. March 13. Retrieved from http://www.nzherald.co.nz/sport/news/article.cfm?c_id=4&objectid=10114999

Cockerill, M. (2005) New boundaries may put Oceania in Asia. *Sydney Morning Herald*. [online] Available at: http://www.smh.com.au/news/Football/New-boundaries-may-put-Oceania-in-Asia/2005/03/15/1110649200137.html.

Court of Arbitration for Sport (2011) *CAS 2011 / A / 2425 Ahongalu Fusimalohi v / FIFA*.

Dickson, G., Phelps, S., and Waugh, D. (2010) Multi-level governance in an international strategic alliance: the plight of the Phoenix and the Asian football market. *Asia Pacific Journal of Marketing and Logistics*, 22(1), 111–124.

Dickson, G. and Stewart, B. (2007) Crystal-ball gazing: The future of football. In B. Stewart (Ed.). *The Games are not the Same: The Political Economy of Football in Australia* (pp. 332–348). Melbourne: Melbourne University Press.

Dornan, M. and Pryke, J. (2017) Foreign aid to the Pacific: trends and developments in the twenty-first century. *Asia & the Pacific Policy Studies*, 4(3), 386–404. Available at: http://doi.wiley.com/10.1002/app5.185.

Dorsey, J.M. (2015) Asian Football: A cesspool of government interference, struggles for power, corruption, and greed. *International Journal of the History of Sport*, 32(8), 1001–1015.

Duerden, J. (2015) Games with New Zealand are distant possibilities. *New York Times*.

Falcous, M. (2017) Oceania: Football at the Pacific periphery. In: J. Hughson et al. (eds), *Routledge Handbook of Football Studies*. London: Taylor & Francis, pp. 445–456.

Inoue, Y. and Havard, C.T. (2015) Sport and disaster relief: a content analysis. *Disaster Prevention and Management: An International Journal*, 24(3), 355–368. Available at: http://www.emeraldinsight.com/doi/10.1108/DPM-12-2014-0276.

Johnstone, D., 2016. New Zealand Football's Olympics eligibility appeal to Oceania fails. *stuff.co.nz*. [online] Available at: http://www.stuff.co.nz/sport/football/73317334/New-Zealand-Footballs-Olympics-eligibility-appeal-to-Oceania-fails

Kumar, R. and Das, T.K. (2007) Interpartner legitimacy in the alliance development process. *Journal of Management Studies*, 44(8), 1425–1453.

Lounsbury, M. and Glynn, M.A. (2001) Cultural entrepreneurship: stories, legitimacy, and the acquisition of resources. *Strategic Management Journal*, 22(6–7), 545–564.

Lynch, M. (2015) Should Asia be split in two? *Sydney Morning Herald*. [online] Available at: http://www.smh.com.au/news/Football/New-boundaries-may-put-Oceania-in-Asia/2005/03/15/1110649200137.html.

Moyo, P. (2009) Black record for All Whites. *Mail and Guardian*. [online] Available at: http://mg.co.za/article/2009-05-19-black-record-for-all-whites.

Oceania Football Confederation (2009) *Activity Report 2009*, Auckland, New Zealand.

Oceania Football Confederation (2011) *Activity Report 2011*, Auckland, New Zealand.

Oceania Football Confederation (2012) *Activity Report 2012*, Auckland, New Zealand.

Oceania Football Confederation (2013) *Activity Report 2013*, Auckland, New Zealand.

Oceania Football Confederation (2014) *Activity Report 2014*, Auckland, New Zealand.

Oceania Football Confederation (2015) *Activity Report 2015*, Auckland, New Zealand.

Suchman, M.C. (1995) Managing legitimacy: Strategic and institutional approaches, 20(3), 571–610.

Vrooman, J. (2007) Theory of the beautiful game: The unification of European football. *Scottish Journal of Political Economy*, 54(3), 314–354. doi:10.1111/j.1467-9485.2007.00418.x

Waugh, D., Dickson, G., and Phelps, S. (2014) The impact of member disaffiliation on the internal legitimacy of a federated network. *European Sport Management Quarterly*, 14(5), 538–555.

41

Football in China

Simon Chadwick and Jonathan Sullivan

Introduction

Over the past three years, the Chinese government has used a series of official documents to set out a blueprint for the transformation of Chinese sport, particularly football. Among the state's ambitions are to build one of the world's largest domestic sport economies and become a "major footballing nation." The latter is an expression of the "Chinese football dream" (中國足球夢) that President Xi Jinping first expressed in 2009. To achieve this ambition, the state plans to popularise the sport by investing in infrastructure and nurturing a "football culture" at the grass-roots, while at the same time promoting developments at the elite level of the game. The plans call for re-animating the domestic league, working towards hosting the male FIFA World Cup and improving performances in international competition by strengthening the national team structure. Indeed, Xi's vision is for China's male national team to have won the World Cup by 2050. Given China's lowly current-status in the football world (the women's national team is an exception), Xi's vision will require a substantial, if not near complete, overhaul of the game in the People's Republic of China (PRC). That process has already started. Immediately pursu-ant to the promulgation of the state's reform plans, Chinese football clubs, investors, and related authorities launched an intense, if largely uncoordinated, series of initiatives that have already made a substantial impact on the domestic and global football industry. This is hardly surprising: the goals that Xi's administration has set, and the resources made available to pursue them, are on a unique, unprecedented scale, and represent a new confidence and ambition to engage globally.

Evolution of football in the PRC

Within two years of the establishment of the PRC in 1949, the six administrative regions plus the Army and Railways sent teams to participate in the first National Football Championships. A squad of 30 players was selected to received specialist training in advance of representing the nation, marking "the beginning of "centralised" (state-organised) football training in China" (Dong and Mangan, 2001). Region-based specialist teams followed, setting up across the country to participate in the first two-division national league established in 1956. By the end of the dec-ade, China was a football power in Asia, but advances were negated by the Great Leap Forward and Cultural Revolution. With domestic football shut down, and absent from the organised international scene from 1958 to 1974 due to FIFA's recognition of the Republic of China (ROC), Chinese football was set back decades. Domestic football institutions, infrastructure, and training were disrupted beyond recognition, setting the national team up for decades of subsequent futility. At the start of the reform era, football, like the media and other sectors, underwent processes of institutional reform, commercialisation and professionalisation. In 1984 Baiyunshan, a Guangzhou-based state-owned pharmaceutical company and pioneer of commercial advertising in the reform era (Sullivan and Kehoe, forthcoming), agreed to fund the Guangzhou football club. Other professional clubs came into being in the same way, like the Liaoning club sponsored by another state-owned pharmaceutical company to the tune of half a million RMB in 1988. Between 1987 and 1993, a mix of professional and semi-professional clubs (including the Army team) competed in the top division of a national league sponsored by Goldlion. The league was dominated by the professionals from Liaoning who won the league six out of seven seasons.

With its 1993 document "Suggestions on Moving Further Ahead in Sports Reformation," the Sports Ministry "officially announced a market economy-oriented reform policy" (Lu and Hong, 2013). This reform had three parts: the establishment of a new professional league, commercialisation of the league's image, marketing and naming rights, and the opening-up of clubs to private capital investment. The new league, consisted of two divisions with promotion and relegation between them, but teams in the lower tier were conceived as a training ground for first division teams and thus foreigners were banned and there was a quota on young players. The first division secured a title sponsor in the form of Philip Morris International and was known as the Marlboro Jia-A (邁寶路甲级A组联赛). The Chinese Football Association (CFA) then signed a $9 million five-year deal with International Management Group (IMG), the American global sports company, giving it the marketing rights to the league (Tan et al., 2016). The final piece of the commercialisation puzzle was the separation of clubs from local government ownership through the legalisation of private and collectively owned clubs ahead of the inaugural Jia-A season. Shanghai Shenhua became the first collectively owned club in Jan 1994, splitting from the Shanghai Sports Bureau. Soon after, the former Dalian Dockyard team was bought by Wang Jianlin's Wanda corporation, becoming the first fully privately owned club. Dalian Wanda went on to win seven Jia-A titles between 1993 and 2004, and established Wang, one of Chinese richest entrepreneurs, as a major figure in the development of Chinese soccer.

As the state reduced its subsidies to the CFA, the league and the new professional clubs were forced to seek investment and sponsorship as their main revenue streams. By the end of the first Jia-A season, however, the 12 competing clubs had all survived through a combination of their own income and a share of the CFA's commercial income. The league expanded from eight teams to 12 in its second season, and the competition resonated with Chinese fans as shown by average attendances set out in Figure 41.1. When Marlboro's sponsorship ended with the ban on tobacco advertising in professional sports in 1998, Pepsi paid significantly more for the title sponsorship rights ($10 million per season compared with Marlboro's $8 million over five years). The incremental professionalisation of the newly expanded 14-team league continued with regulations passed in 1999 forcing professional clubs to establish independent companies with business plans and transparent ownership, followed in 2002 with the requirement for clubs to secure a business license and meet other commercial operating standards.

Notwithstanding advances in the institutionalisation of the league structure, the Jia-A league suffered numerous ailments. The most serious was the influence of organised crime, widespread bribery of referees, players, and coaches conspiring to fix the outcome of matches, and underground gambling. When it became obvious that fans could not trust the fairness of what they

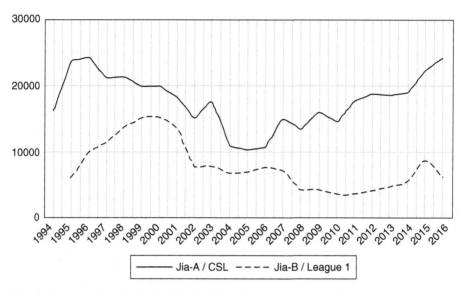

Figure 41.1 Average attendance in Divisions 1 and 2 over time

were witnessing on the pitch, they stopped attending games. The decision to abandon watching matches was made easier since most clubs had not invested in creating fan communities and consolidating bonds, a problem exacerbated by clubs changing location, name, and colours as owners and sponsors changed. Clubs were criticised of short-term instrumentality, paying (relatively) exorbitant salaries to players and refusing to invest in youth development. The public was unhappy about the lack of improvement in the national team and the arrogance and bad behaviour of spoilt professional players, prompting the CFA to introduce maximum wages and transfer fees in 2001. When Pepsi stood down early from its sponsorship (replaced by Siemens for one year at half the rate) in 2003, it was obvious that the Jia-A was in trouble. The authorities' solution was to rebrand Jia-A the Chinese Super League (CSL), but aside from reducing the number of teams, major problems were not addressed.

The new CSL continued to be plagued by suspect refereeing, whether the result of incompetence or nefarious arrangements. A season-long series of incidents in 2014 came to a head when the match between Beijing Hyundai and Shenyang Ginde was abandoned when the Beijing team walked off the pitch and refused to continue in protest at a refereeing decision to award a penalty. Although the CFA fined the referee involved, it also awarded the match to Shenyang, leading Beijing to threaten to quit the league. Seven-time Jia-A champion Dalian Shide said that the league should be run by the clubs, and seven clubs (the G-7) threatened to break away from the CSL. In the end, the CFA succumbed to the G-7's proposals, agreeing to disclose financial statements and implement more transparent practices. This stop gap measure did not help, and with poor quality play, declining attendances and the continuing spectre of corruption, the CSL suddenly faced the loss of IMG as marketing partner and Siemens as league sponsor when both pulled out at the end of the season. In 2005, CSL had no title sponsor leading several clubs to experience financial difficulties. The problems were met with apathy as Chinese sports publications shut down and Chinese TV stopped broadcasting domestic matches in favour of showing European league matches.

Facing an ailing CSL and clubs in strife, the General Administration of Sport (GAS) stepped in to enforce one of the reforms the clubs had been asking for, the establishment of the Chinese

Super League Company (CSLC) as commercial manager of the CSL. The 16 CSL clubs split 64 per cent of the shares in the company, with the CFA taking the remaining 36 per cent. Clubs thus had a literal stake in managing and making a success of the league. Yet even this incentive failed to curb the bribery and corruption that continued to dominate the sport as sponsors and fans fled. The situation became so serious that in 2009 the Ministry of Public Security was compelled to launch an anticorruption campaign across the football industry. Large numbers of players, referees, coaches, and CFA officials were arrested. The Control, Ethics and Disciplinary Committee of National Football Leagues (CEDCNFL) was founded under the direction of Xi Jinping, led by the GAS and several ministries, as an institutional measure to reduce the problem of match fixing, bribing, gambling and organised crime involvement in elite football. Continuing through 2011, the campaign to clean up Chinese football re-established investor and fan confidence. Sponsors returned and attendances recovered, and as clubs began making money again there was an influx of foreign players and coaches. The league has not looked back since.

When looking to explain China's "sudden" interest in football, unfamiliar journalists are quick to remark on Xi Jinping's love for the game (for example, see Wan, 2015). Xi is indeed a life-long enthusiast and has revealed his passion and ambition on numerous occasions. He first revealed his ambitions for Chinese football on a visit to Germany in 2009, and announced his FIFA World Cup goals for the country (to qualify, host, and eventually win the tournament) when meeting with Korean politicians in 2011. It is, however, in three formal documents that the parameters and pathways for Xi's 'football dream' are established.

In 2014, the State Council issued its opinions on "Accelerating the Development of the Sports Industry to Promote Sport Consumption" (国务院关于加快发展体育产业促进体育消费的若干意见). The document set out an industrial vision for Chinese sport, which foresaw a domestic sport economy that will be worth up to US$800 billion+ by 2025 (Goddard, 2014). This remains a bold, ambitious vision (Chadwick, 2015b) as even the most optimistic estimates of current global industry size range from as little as US$145 billion (PWC, 2011) to around US$1.3 trillion (Plunkett Research, 2017). The United States sport economy currently dominates global industrial landscape, accounting for approximately 41 per cent of the total industry size. Clearly though, Xi's proclamation was intended as a prelude to China challenging the existing industrial order.

It was followed by "The Overall Reform Plan to Boost the Development of Football in China" (中国足球改革发展总体方案) issued in 2015. Among the reforms in this plan were greater autonomy for the CFA planning and operations. Then, in 2016, the Chinese government published its long-term football ambitions in its "Long Term Development Plan 2016–50" (中国足球中长期发展规划 2016—2050年). The plan set out ambitious targets. By 2020, i.e., just four years after the plan was promulgated, 20,000 specialist football schools would have been created, along with 70,000 new football pitches, and between 30 million and 50 million primary and middle school students would be regularly playing football. By 2030, 50,000 specialist football schools would have been created, China's male football team would be ranked as one of the best in Asia, and the women's football team would be ranked one the world's best. By 2050, China would have become a first-class football superpower, ranked among FIFA's top-20 teams and to have hosted and won the World Cup. Given the difficulties Chinese football has faced in the past 70 years, these are hugely ambitious targets, and to pursue them the Ministry of Education, Ministry of Finance, Development and Reform Commission of the State Council, SAPPRT, GAS, Communist Youth League and significant private capital have been corralled. Since 2015 the Chinese Football Leading Small Group (中国足球改革领导小组) has been led by Politburo member Liu Yandong (刘延东).

Motivations – why football, why now?

As mentioned earlier, China's football ambitions are longstanding. Notwithstanding Xi Jinping's evident enthusiasm for the game, the motivations for the latest iteration of China's "football dream" are the result of multiple factors and rationales. Though they often overlap, there are domestic and international considerations, including nationalism, the economy, diplomacy and soft power. The connection between national pride and sporting performance has been made explicit since the founding of the PRC. At a time when China has re-emerged as a global power, and the inculcation of nationalism has become a major pillar of the regime's legitimacy, the continuing futility of the national football team is incongruous, particularly considering recent Olympic successes. The Beijing Olympics, underwritten by a $45 billion state investment in flawless infrastructure, stunning opening ceremony, and decade-long strategic investment in specific sports led to China's dominance of the medal table. Despite disruption to the torch relay, and criticism over heavy-handed urban redevelopment and freedom of speech (Economy and Segal, 2008), the Games were generally regarded in China as a successful contribution to the "national pride" narrative underpinning the popularisation of nationalism (Mangan and Dong, 2013). As one of the two pillars of party legitimacy post-1989 (the other being economic growth; Gries, 2004; Rosen, 2009), appeals to national pride have been structured by the education and media systems reinforced by the authoritarian information regime (Zhao, S., 1998; Zhao, Y., 1998). There is little doubt that hosting international sports events and performing well on the international sporting stage are conceived by the party–state as a further means to nourishing regime-supportive feelings of national pride (Dong and Mangan, 2008; Xu, 2009). It is not surprising then that "patriotism and nationalism" are constant themes in the "education of elite athletes" (Tan and Bairner, 2010, p. 596).

Projecting, however, strong nationalist feelings onto sports is a double-edged sword, producing adulation for "winners" like Olympic gold medallist Liu Xiang and anger for "losers" (Lovell, 2008). Disappointing performances by the men's football team have led to rioting by frustrated supporters, from World Cup qualifying losses to Hong Kong in 1985 and Syria in 2016 to the Asian Cup final loss to Japan in 2004 (Bridges, 2008). While the women's side won the Asian Cup in 1997 and finished second in the World Cup in 1999, the men's national representative teams have not been a source of national pride. The Republican era dominance of the now defunct Far Eastern Games, when the ROC won nine consecutive times between 1915 and 1934, has never been repeated in the PRC. The men's national team has qualified for the Olympics just twice (1988 in Seoul and 2008 in Beijing) and the World Cup once (2002 in Korea/Japan). In all three tournaments China failed to win a match, and indeed in nine matches it scored a solitary goal. Taking second place in the 1984 and 2004 Asian Cup and a silver medal at the Asian Games in 1994 hardly compensates for an almost continuous stream of disappointing performances and failure to qualify for major international tournaments. Furthermore, these disappointments have been punctuated by periodic humiliations, like the "615 Massacre," a 5:1 defeat to Thailand in a June 2015 friendly match. At time of writing in June 2017, the men's team is ranked 81st in the FIFA world rankings, immediately behind the Faroe Islands and Benin, China's average FIFA ranking between 1993 and 2017 is 72.6, and the highest ranking is 37th achieved for a single month in 1998.

At this stage in China's development, there are sensible economic reasons for developing the domestic football sector. As China attempts to recalibrate its economic model away from low-end manufacturing toward services and greater consumption, an established sports economy with its associated entertainment products and opportunities for consumption, has the potential to generate enormous revenues. It remains unclear how large the Chinese domestic

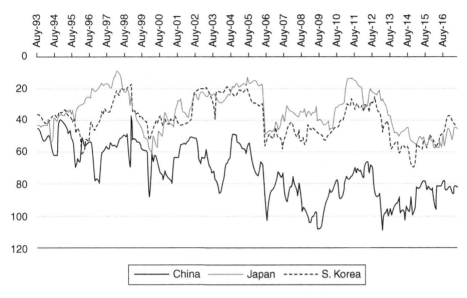

Figure 41.2 FIFA World Rankings over time

sport economy currently is, principally because reliable public data is unavailable. Investment in sport does have a tangible impact upon national income, job creation, and tax contributions. As a point of reference, it is worthwhile noting that English football's Premier League reportedly makes an annual £3.4 billion contribution to British Gross Domestic Product; pays £2.4 billion in taxation to the government and maintains almost 104,000 jobs (Ernst and Young, 2015). Attending football matches, buying merchandise, and watching games on TV and online generate huge sums for economies across the world.

As prosperity becomes increasingly widespread, greater numbers of Chinese people are choosing and spending on leisure activities. Some of these activities promote healthy living, others less so, like the phenomenon of "internet addiction" frequently mentioned in state media. China is faced with serious public health issues, including rapidly increasing levels of obesity and high rates of tobacco use. The popularisation of football as a participatory sport for young people has been advanced with public health in mind in addition to improving elite performance. In other parts of the world, Qatar being one example, football has been commonly used to improve public health. This has often been a response in countries where unhealthy diet and sedentary lifestyles have become significant challenges for government authorities. China's football reform plan makes explicit reference to such concerns, emphasising how the sport will be expected to contribute to an overall improvement in the country's public health. As the work undertaken by Jiang et al. (2009) has shown, only 9.4 per cent of boys and 1.9 per cent of girls in China meet an expected standard of 60 minutes moderate or vigorous exercise each day. Hence, the unprecedented, ambitious target to create thousands of school football pitches over the ten years is as much about domestic health and lifestyle as it is about elite professional team success.

There has always been an international dimension to China's engagement with sport. The PRC has a history of using sport as a vehicle for diplomacy. The most famous episode was the "ping-pong diplomacy" that broke the ice in US-China relations and paved the way for President Nixon's visit to China in 1972. Beijing has also engaged in 'stadium diplomacy' as a means of securing access to resources and markets (Chadwick, 2016a). For example, for football's 2010 African Cup of Nations in Angola, the Chinese government gifted the country four stadiums worth US$500 million. In subsequent years, China became the biggest export market for Angolan oil, as well as its biggest export market (US$27 billion, five times the value of exports Angola makes to the United States) (Chadwick, 2017). This form of diplomacy has continued, the Gabonese hosts of 2017's African Cup of Nations having reached similar such agreements with China. As these examples suggest, sport is part of China's "soft power" repertoire. Responding to critical narratives about its intentions and the nature of its global engagement, the Chinese government explicitly acknowledged in 2006 the importance of its international image and building "soft power" as part of the nation's "comprehensive power" (*zonghe guoli*综合国力) (Li, 2008).

It has subsequently made substantial investments in international media operations to counter negative narratives, and significantly increased its "cultural footprint" abroad through public diplomacy efforts, cultural exhibitions, student exchanges, and the establishment of Confucius Institutes (Hartig, 2012). Chinese "soft power" initiatives have mostly been top-down, i.e., led by the state, and it is no secret that they have not yielded the hoped-for results (Gill and Huang, 2006) with many Chinese cultural products "lost in translation" (Keane, 2013). Given these results, it is easy to appreciate the attraction of football as a potential "soft power" vehicle. Football requires no cultural interpretation and is particularly popular in regions where China's global engagement is most intense – Africa, South America, and Europe. Indeed, football is often referred to as the global game or the people's game (Morrow, 2003), with good reason. FIFA estimated in 2006 that upwards of 260 million people worldwide play football and almost 3.2 billion people worldwide watched the 2014 World Cup Final on television (Kunz, 2007). The potential for a country to achieve global visibility is therefore immense.

As Ginesta and San Eugenio (2014) have noted, the opportunity for a country to utilise a high profile in football as a means of building a nation's brand, improving its reputation and establishing a global position are widely accepted. Equally, Grix and Houlihan (2014) have observed the continuing importance of football as a soft power instrument. Winning the World Cup is one way of establishing positive associations with a country in the minds of fans. However, there are numerous other ways in which football can enable soft power influence to be asserted. For instance, as Chadwick (2016b) highlighted, the English Premier League is employed as a means of engaging trade partners, teaching English to overseas students and enabling people to engage with British culture. The role of sport as a focal point of socio-cultural, political, and economic activity has been widely documented (Eitzen, 2000). The prevailing discourse about sport is characterised by its power and the positive impact it can have (Armour et al., 2013; Coates and Humphreys, 2003; Spaaij, 2009). Football, therefore, occupies a prominent and influential global position, which has led nations across the world to formulate strategies for using it as a means of achieving socio-cultural, political, and economic ambitions (Gratton and Henry, 2002), including China (Dong and Mangan, 2001). As a "soft power" resource, football has a distinguished history. Brazil's national image is inseparable from its football culture, while England makes much of its footballing tradition and countries with popular domestic leagues like Spain, Italy, and Germany have dedicated followings around the world.

Implementing China's soccer dream

Since Xi's announcement, various individuals and organisations from China have engaged in activities ranging from signing sponsorship agreements with high-profile sports properties to the acquisition of professional football clubs. As an emergent strategy for its transformational change, China's latest football reform plan is a hybrid model drawing on the US, Japanese, and European experience as reference points.

- United States: a significant characteristic of US sport is the role played by college sports. Most of the country's leading athletes are drawn from colleges via a draft system, which is one of the fundamental principles of US sports leagues and competitions (Berri et al., 2011). Many of the athletes who are selected for sports (e.g., National Basketball Association (NBA)) are recruited by colleges via scholarship schemes that fund students to study for a degree whilst playing sport. Given the aspirations (and concerns) of Chinese parents for their children (Riordan and Jones, 1999), engaging in professional sport is often dismissed as a career option. This is a potential impediment to the sustainable development of football, hence China is examining US campus-style models as a basis for reconciling the state's football needs with the hopes and ambitions of parents (Chadwick, 2016c);
- Europe: the continent's national teams are among the most successful in international competitions, having won a majority of the World Cup tournaments held to date. Its club sides routinely win the World Cup championship, while the continent's club competition (the UEFA Champions League) is among the most valuable sports properties in the world (Ozanian, 2016). In addition, its leagues are often acknowledged as the biggest in the world, while its teams are routinely identified as the richest (Chapman, 2017). As a performance benchmark, European football will therefore serve an important purpose for China. At the same time, Europe has developed a strong and deeply engrained fan culture that underpins attendances, affiliations and commercial activity (Brown, 1998), which also provides important lessons for China to learn from;
- Japan: over the last two decades, Japan has made great strides in football, its women's national team winning the World Cup in 2011 and its men's team routinely qualifying for the men's World Cup. The country's club sides have also performed well in international competition, winning the Asian Football Confederation's (AFC) Championship several times in recent years. Yet the J-League (Japan's top division) was formed just over 20 years ago (in 1993), making the country's achievements especially notable. From a Chinese perspective, the way in which Japan has enabled cultural change and organised its football is important. The clubs of which the J-League is comprised were largely established and are run as collaborative ventures between industrial corporations and local prefectures (Manzenreiter and Horne, 2005). As such, the Japanese have sought to reconcile commercial performance with local identity, whilst at the same time aligning football with local rather than central government. This is something China also appears to be doing which is particularly important as FIFA regulations prohibit central government interference in domestic football associations. This is an important detail with which China needs to comply, if it is to successfully bid to host the World Cup.

In the context of this hybrid model and the transformational change being executed by the CFA, the state and local government, commercial partners, and other stakeholders, there appear to be five key operating principles underpinning China's football strategy: top-down investment; bottom-up investment; external acquisition; network influence; football diplomacy; and entertainment. In seminal work on strategy, Burgelman (1983) distinguished between top-down and bottom-up approaches to strategy formulation and implementation, a combination of which the Chinese appear to be using in football. At the elite professional level, Chinese organisations have engaged in a programme of investment whose principle goal appears to have initially been learning and competence acquisition. Most notably in football, this has resulted in high-profile player transfers (for example, the likes of Brazilian internationals Oscar and Hulk), and overseas club acquisitions (Suning's purchase of Italian club Inter Milan arguably being the highest-profile purchase thus far).

By signing players and buying clubs, China is not only acquiring productive investments that may generate an economic return, they are also acquiring expertise from which to learn – how to manage a club, how to develop talent, how to construct successful teams, and so forth. Growing transfer fees and large wages have inevitably caught the attention of observers. However, Chinese football's failure to create its own heroes and icons has undermined its attempts to build a culture of football fandom. As the sport marketing literature demonstrates (e.g., Mueller and Sutherland, 2010), heroes and icons are a key factor in stimulating fan engagement. Until such time as Chinese players are globally prominent, the strategy will continue to import players. This assessment helps explain and justify China's bottom-up investment strategy whereby resources are being channelled into grassroots football projects. The Evergrande Real Estate Corporation had already created China's largest training facility (combining football pitches and academic programmes) even prior to Xi's 2014 proclamation (Sevastopoulos, 2014). Now though, other corporations have followed suit, whilst local governments have set about creating sports campuses similar to those in the United States and mentioned above (Chongqing sports campus being one example of this). Given the magnitude of China's football goals, inward investment has been needed to pump-prime grassroots projects (Phillips, 2017). This has resulted in the likes of Spain's FC Barcelona establishing academies, and coaches such as former Italian national team coach Marcello Lippi being recruited. Such investments are nevertheless long-term ones, as talent development in football is accompanied by long lead times, hence the short-term measures involving the acquisition of overseas players.

While Wang and other entrepreneurs have responded enthusiastically to Xi's urging, their responses are not necessarily altruistic. Wanda has a rapidly proliferating portfolio consisting either of entertainment businesses, or else businesses connected to the entertainment industry. Indeed, when the company purchased a 20 per cent stake in Spanish La Liga football club Atletico Madrid, Wang spoke of his desire to create a global entertainment axis stretching from Beijing, through Madrid, to Hollywood (Chadwick, 2015a). He has followed through on that statement by, among other things, buying mid-sized Hollywood studio Legendary as well as Dick Clark productions (owners of the Golden Globe awards). Crucially though, Wang's thinking, as well as that of other businesses such as Fosun, Alibaba, and Suning, appears to see football as an entertainment commodity and source of social media content. In his keynote to the Caixin Summit in 2016, Wang claimed that the sports industry needs to "integrate with business, media, tourism, and urban development," which coincides with Wanda's diverse range of businesses. Table 41.1, setting out the business interests of CSL and League One club owners in the 2017 season, suggests particular concentrations in property development and real estate. China Fortune Land Development, Evergrande, and R&F for instance are construction and real estate companies that have invested in Guangzhou and Hebei football clubs, with local governments granting land for development of football and related facilities. With China's housing bubble, land in urban areas is a valuable commodity that may be exploited for commercial purposes. Buying a football club can thus be a valuable equity investment, in addition to generating useful political capital with municipal and provincial governments keen to demonstrate their commitment to implementing Xi's football development plans.

China is currently one of the most dynamic social media and digital environments in the world (Chiu et al., 2012), with large numbers of people thought to be using platforms such as "We Chat" and Sina Weibo; indeed, some estimates indicate that there are more than 500 million users (Incitez, 2016). In turn, it appears sport, particularly football, is one of the reasons why

Table 41.1 Ownership and business interests of CSL and League One clubs, 2017

Club	Owners	Business interests
Beijing Sinobo Guoan	Sinobo Group; CITIC	Real estate; SOE steel & property
Changchun Yatai	Chanchun Jisheng Investment	Property development & financial
Chongqing Dangdai Lifan	Desports; Lifan Group	Sports marketing; Autos
Guangzhou Evergrande Taobao	Evergrande; Alibaba	Real estate; E-commerce
Guangzhou R&F	Guangzhou R&F Properties Co.	Property development
Guizhou Hengfeng Zhicheng	Zhicheng; Hengfeng Group; Guizhou Provincial Sports Bureau	Real estate; financial; local state
Hebei CFFC	China Fortune Land Development	Real estate
Henan Jianye	Henan Haolin Investment	Real estate
Jiangsu Suning	Suning Appliance Group	Home appliances & retail
Liaoning Whowin	Whowin; Liaoning Sport College	Real estate, finance; local state
Shandong Luneng Taishan	Luneng Group	State utility
Shanghai Greenland Shenhua	Greenland Group	Property development
Shanghai SIPG	Shanghai International Port Group	Shanghai govt; port operator
Tianjin Quanjian	Quanjian Natural Medical Group	Pharmaceuticals
Tianjin Teda	TEDA Investment Holding Co.	SOE financial
Yanbian Funde	Funde Sino Life; Yanbian SMC	Insurance; local state
Baoding Yingli Yitong	Baoding City Real Estate Group	Real estate
Beijing BG	Beijing Enterprises Holdings	Food
Beijing Renhe	Renhe Commercial Holdings	Property development
Dalian Transcendence	Zhao Yang	Publicly listed football club
Dalian Yifang	Dalian Yifang Group	Real estate
Hangzhou Greentown	Greentown China Holdings	Real estate
Qingdao Huanghai	Huanghai Pharmaceutical	Pharmaceuticals
Meizhou Kejia	Meizhou municipal govt; Wei Real Estate Development	Local state; Real estate
Shanghai Shenxin	Hengyuan Corporation	Real estate
Shenzhen F.C.	Kaisa Group	Property development
Shijiazhuang Ever Bright	Yongchang Real Estate	Real estate
Inner Mongolia Zhongyou	Hohhot Sports Bureau; Shanghai Zhongyou Real Estate Group	Local state; Real estate
Wuhan Zall	Zall Development	Financial
Xinjiang Tianshan Leopard	China-Kyle Special Steel Corp	Steel
Yunnan Lijiang	Minjian Mechanical & Electrical; Lijiang Materials; Taihe Group.	State; Steel
Zhejiang Yiteng	Yiteng Group	Property development

users engage with social media in China (Nielsen, 2016). Overseas football players such as Real Madrid's Cristiano Ronaldo routinely garner massive online support among Chinese fans, something that presents a range of potential commercial opportunities (e.g., by selling exclusive content). In the medium- to long-term however, China is keen to develop its own football icons. This will not only deliver economic and commercial benefits, but also enable China to exert soft power influence.

Preliminary assessment of Xi's reforms

The major ambitions contained in Xi's plans require long-term investment and will not deliver results for many years. However, we can already perceive effects in China and internationally. On the field, the CSL is buoyant, enjoying its highest ever attendances, access to global TV audiences and an influx of high-quality foreign coaches and players. The most potent symbol of this has arguably been the acquisition of high-quality overseas playing talent, with some estimates indicating that Chinese clubs have spent almost £500 million on such talent (Ahmed, 2016), making China's Super League one of the world's largest spenders on football player transfers (Rumsby, 2017). This expenditure has nevertheless been widely criticised, with many observers noting that it is creating a bubble effect of artificially high transfer fees and wages in the football player labour market (Romero, 2017). Otherwise, critics have questioned the commitment of foreign signings, suggesting that Chinese football is of poor quality and that overseas players are more interested in the financial returns of playing in China than in developing its football (Aarons, 2017). Figure 41.3, which sets out the frequency of select terms in UK media reports on the CSL, shows that these player transactions, including the fees and wages involved, are the major pre-occupation for outside observers. Notwithstanding, buying-in expensive recruits has paid off for some, notably six-time reigning CSL champion Guangzhou Evergrande Taobao. In 2010 Xu Jiayin of Evergrande bought the Guangzhou team that had just been relegated for $14 million. He then invested huge sums to attract China's best players. It paid off: they were promoted at the first time of asking and went on to win the CSL six times in a row, the Asian Champions League in 2013 and 2015, and reached the semi-final of the FIFA Club World Cup. It is an investment that paid off financially: Xu sold half his shares to Ma Yun's Alibaba group in 2014 for nearly $200 million. It has rapidly become China's most valuable club (Klebinikov, 2016) and appears on the verge of becoming Asian football's first super club.

Yet such has been the voracity of player and club spending overseas that the Chinese state has now made moves intended to address the challenges the spending has created. The football authorities have announced measures designed to limit the number of players signing for Chinese clubs, moving from the previous '4+1' model to a new '3+1' model (Porteous, 2017). This means clubs can only have four overseas squad members, of which only three can be on

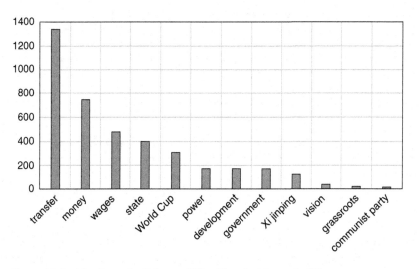

Figure 41.3 Number of articles on CSL with select terms in UK newspapers

the field of play at any one time. This move coincided with a stern rebuke issued to investors by central government, for the extravagance of their overseas expenditure. Later, the government enforced a taxation rule upon CSL clubs whereby overseas player signings were subjected to the imposition of a 100 per cent tax, with consequent revenues in turn being allocated to developmental activities in Chinese football (de Menezes, 2017). At one level, this is consistent with concerns about external currency outflows and consequent liquidity problems that have characterised other Chinese industrial sectors (Balding, 2017), which has resulted in similar rebukes and controls being introduced. However, at another level, the hawkish behaviour of football intermediaries, the global focus on international players in China, the potential loss of Chinese identity, and raised concerns about the re-emergence of corruption in football are also likely to have contributed to the state's intervention (Porteous, 2016).

In addition, interventions by these various actors has already resulted in several significant outcomes for global football, such as inflating player transfer fees and challenging the existing governance system. Alongside player acquisitions, Chinese investors have also been predominantly acquiring ownership of overseas clubs. In some cases, such as at England's Aston Villa and France's Nice, investors have bought clubs outright. In other cases, such as Spain's Atletico Madrid and Italy's Inter Milan, Chinese investors have bought stakes (of 20 per cent in the case of Atletico and 70 per cent in the case of Inter). Some people have questioned investors' motives for engaging in such investments (Gibson, 2016), although it seems likely that club ownership yields benefits ranging from competence acquisition through to building some control over football's supply chains. High-street electrical retailer and e-commerce platform Suning has acquired the CSL club Jiangsu and Italian club Inter Milan, while also reportedly having expressed an interest in purchasing player agency business Stellar (Jourdan, 2016). One possible outcome of this could be that Suning might own the buying and selling clubs in a player transaction, as well as the intermediary involved in brokering it. This form of supply-chain control is unprecedented in world football, may be in breach of FIFA regulations, and could pose some significant governance challenges for world football.

In addition to players and clubs, over the last three-years Chinese investors have also spent heavily on acquiring other football-related properties. Most notably, Wanda signed a deal with FIFA to sponsor the World Cup until 2030, while also buying Switzerland's Infront Sports and Media (which owns the media rights to the 2018 and 2022 World Cup, having acquired them from FIFA). This not only diversifies Wanda's sports industry portfolio, it may also enable China to exert political pressure on FIFA in respect of its 2026 and 2030 World Cup hosting decisions. Standards of governance in football can sometimes be opaque (Jackson, 2010), but with China now embarked upon programmes of multiple club ownership alongside a strategy of soft power influence, football's over-dependence on Chinese money could compromise governance and ethics within the sport. Recent developments have suddenly raised China's footballing profile in the global consciousness, highlighting its multifaceted ambitions and the substantial resources at its disposal. Figure 41.4, showing the number of articles in UK newspapers about the CSL over time, highlights the sudden interest in Chinese football.

The unprecedented scale of China's investment in football has been such that it has not only attracted scrutiny but also raised expectations, particularly from the country's own population. Unfulfilled expectations almost inevitably result in cognitive dissonance, which both Chinese football and the government are now confronted with. Following poor national team performances during 2018 World Cup qualifying games, large crowds gathered in some Chinese cities to protest at the poor return the country is achieving on its football investments. Widespread public dissent could be one unintended consequence, anathema to the party and state. The rapid response of China's football authorities to the national team's abject performances (in this

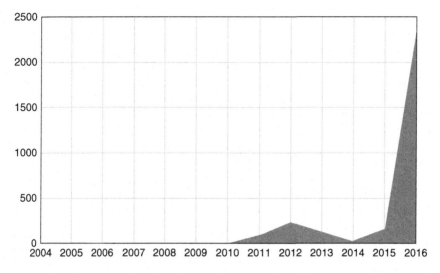

Figure 41.4 Number of articles mentioning CSL in UK newspapers

case, sacking the incumbent and replacing him at great expense with Italian World Cup winning manager Marcello Lippi) raises some concerns about China's commitment to its football strategy. While investing top-down and bottom-up suggests an appreciation of the roles elite professional and grassroots football play, strategic drift may become an issue for Chinese football. Building a sustainable football culture requires decades rather than years, however, if the state and football authorities respond to populist demands and the need to save face, the sport's strategic direction and coherence may be undermined.

Conclusions

Some commentators in China itself have long observed that the country is the home of football, claiming that the game was invented there 2,000 years ago. Whether this was the case will remain a moot point, though China has clearly discovered a new appetite for football. Recent developments have followed-on from several false starts in recent decades, notably the hype following China's qualification for the 2022 World Cup and the moves of Nicholas Anelka and Didier Drogba from English Premier League Chelsea to Shanghai in 2012. However, with President Xi Jinping having assumed presidential office in late 2012, football appears to have taken on a new impetus and a new role in China. Indeed, from the outset, the self-avowed football fan has placed the sport centre-stage in sporting, political, socio-cultural, and economic terms.

As a result, China has launched a football development strategy, investments in the sport have been made at home and abroad, and both the grassroots and elite professional levels of football have been subject to regulatory interventions by the Chinese government. Given Xi's and China's long-term goals – to become a leading FIFA nation and win the World Cup – we should expect further such interventions in the future, especially as the vision is of securing football's most important trophy by 2050. Furthermore, with President Xi seemingly intent on strengthening his position as president, possibly even beyond his allotted term in office, we should not expect China to significantly deviate away from pursuing its football vision.

Domestically, there have already been several developments in football, notably the implementation of school strategies aimed at promoting the sport among young people. At the same time, several initiatives such as the creation of football towns, restructuring of the country's football leagues, and the import of overseas talent has taken place to promote change in Chinese football. Internationally, China has used football both as a means of building its role in world football, and of extending its influence. An example of the former is Chinese corporation Wanda's multi-million-dollar sponsorship deal with football's world governing body, FIFA. An example of the latter is the way in which China has continued to use stadium diplomacy as a means of securing access to natural resources by building venues in return (the African Cup of nations being one example of this).

Such is the profound nature of China's growing interest in football that it is inevitably posing some challenges for the sport. At a fundamental level, it raising questions regarding the nature and purpose of football. What was once simply a game, is rapidly being turned by the Chinese into a highly political and industrial activity [see also Chapter 5 in this handbook for a theoretical reasoning about all this]. This raises all manner of questions ranging from the sport's governance through to marketing of the sport. Yet the way in which China appears to view football as a diplomatic and soft power tool, as a basis for nation branding, and as a basis for addressing its health and soft skills deficiencies (for example, decision-making, working in teams), also suggests that football's stakeholders may have to reappraise their views as the country's relentless march towards 2050 continues.

References

Aarons, E. (2017) Agents and players the real winners in Chinese Super League's spending spree. *The Guardian*. [online] Available from https://www.theguardian.com/football/blog/2017/jan/08/chinese-super-league-spending-materialism-extravagance

Ahmed, M. (2016) China spree pushes football transfer spending to record $4.8bn. *Financial Times*. [online] Available from https://www.ft.com/content/f976aaae-e31f-11e6-8405-9e5580d6e5fb

Armour, K., Sandford, R., and Duncombe, R. (2013) Positive youth development and physical activity/sport interventions: mechanisms leading to sustained impact. *Physical Education and Sport Pedagogy*, 18(3), 256–281.

Balding, C. (2017) China Finally Halts Outflows. Now What? *Bloomberg*. Available from: https://www.bloomberg.com/view/articles/2017-04-10/china-finally-stems-capital-outflows-now-what

Berri, D.J., Brook, S.L., and Fenn, A.J. (2011) From college to the pros: predicting the NBA amateur player draft. *Journal of Productivity Analysis*, 35(1), 25–35.

Bridges, B. (2008) Football, nationalism, and fan violence in China. *Journal of Current Chinese Affairs-China aktuell* 37(2), 60–82.

Brown, A. (ed.) (1998) *Fanatics!: Power, Identity, and Fandom in Football*. Oxford, Psychology Press.

Burgelman, R.A. (1983) Corporate entrepreneurship and strategic management: Insights from a process study. *Management Science*, 29(12), 1349–1364.

Chadwick, S. (2015) Football's bamboo revolution. *Asia and the Pacific Policy Forum*. [online] Available from: https://www.policyforum.net/footballs-bamboo-revolution/

Chadwick, S. (2015) China's financial muscle makes its mark on the global sport industry. *The Conversation*. [online] Available from: https://theconversation.com/chinas-financial-muscle-makes-its-mark-on-the-global-sport-industry-36750

Chadwick, S. (2016a) China and Qatar's stadium diplomacy. *Asia and the Pacific Policy Forum*. [online] Available from: https://www.policyforum.net/china-qatars-stadium-diplomacy/

Chadwick, S. (2016b) How football is becoming a major player for British soft power. *Newsweek*. [online] Available from: http://www.newsweek.com/football-uk-brexit-soft-power-arsenal-premiere-league-527228

Chadwick, S. (2016c) How China is moving the goalposts. *Asia and the Pacific Policy Forum*. [online] Available from: https://www.policyforum.net/how-china-is-moving-the-goalposts/

Chadwick, S. (2017) How China is fuelling the African Cup of Nations. *Asia and the Pacific Policy Forum*. [online] Available from: https://www.policyforum.net/china-fuelling-african-cup-nations/ [Accessed 13 November 2017].

Chapman, B. (2017) Manchester United overtake Real Madrid to become Europe's most valuable football club. *The Independent*. [online] Available from: http://www.independent.co.uk/news/business/news/manchester-united-overtake-real-madrid-europes-most-valuable-football-club-kpmg-champions-league-a7764776.html [Accessed 13 November 2017].

Chiu, C., Ip, C., and Silverman, A. (2012) Understanding social media in China. *McKinsey Quarterly*. [online] Available from: http://www.mckinsey.com/business-functions/marketing-and-sales/our-insights/understanding-social-media-in-china [Accessed 13 November 2017].

Coates, D. and Humphreys, B.R. (2003) The effect of professional sports on earnings and employment in the services and retail sectors in US cities. *Regional Science and Urban Economics*, 33(2),175–198.

De Menezes, J. (2017) Chinese Super League transfer plans hit by new tax law meaning Diego Costa could cost as much as £180m. *The Independent*. [online] Available from: http://www.independent.co.uk/sport/football/transfers/chinese-super-league-transfer-news-diego-costa-tax-law-rule-180m-wayne-rooney-a7755406.html [Accessed 13 November 2017].

Dong, Jinxia, and Mangan, J.A. (2001) Football in the new China: political statement, entrepreneurial enticement and patriotic passion. *Soccer & Society*, 2(3), 79–100.

Dong, Jinxia, and Mangan, J.A. (2008) Beijing Olympics legacies: Certain intentions and certain and uncertain outcomes. *The International Journal of the History of Sport*, 25(14), 2019–2040.

Economy, E.C. and Segal, A. (2008) China's Olympic nightmare: what the games mean for Beijing's future. *Foreign Affairs*, 87(4), 47–56.

Eitzen, D.S. (ed.) (2000) *Sport in Contemporary Society: An Anthology*. Oxford, Macmillan.

Ernst and Young (2015) The Economic Impact of the Premier League. [online] Available from: http://www.ey.com/Publication/vwLUAssets/EY_-_The_economic_impact_of_the_Premier_League/$FILE/EY-The-economic-impact-of-the-Premier-League.pdf [Accessed 13 November 2017].

Gibson, O. (2016) The Great Windfall of China: a football revolution that may lead to World Cup. *The Guardian*. [online] Available from: https://www.theguardian.com/football/blog/2016/feb/06/china-football-revolution-world-cup [Accessed 13 November 2017].

Gill, B. and Huang, Y. (2006) Sources and limits of Chinese 'soft power', *Survival* 48(2), 17–36.

Ginesta, X. and de San Eugenio, J. (2014) The use of football as a country branding strategy. Case study: Qatar and the Catalan sports press, *Communication & Sport*, 2(3), 225–241.

Goddard, E. (2014) China reveals multi-billion dollar investment in sport *Inside the Games*. [online] Available from: http://www.insidethegames.biz/articles/1023349/china-reveals-multi-billion-dollar-investment-plan-for-sport [Accessed 13 November 2017].

Gratton, C. and Henry, I. (2002) *Sport in the City: The Role of Sport in Economic and Social Regeneration*. (eds.), Oxford: Routledge.

Gries, P.H. (2004) *China's New Nationalism: Pride, Politics and Diplomacy*, Los Angeles: University of California Press, 2004.

Grix, J. and Houlihan, B. (2014) Sports mega-events as part of a nation's soft power strategy: the cases of Germany (2006) and the UK (2012). *The British Journal of Politics and International Relations*, 16(4), 572–596.

Hartig, F. (2012) Confucius Institutes and the rise of China. *Journal of Chinese Political Science* 17(1), 53–76.

Incitez (2016) 482 million Chinese Visited Social Media per Month in 2015. [online] Available from: https://www.chinainternetwatch.com/17191/481-5-million-chinese-social-media-month-2015/ [Accessed 13 November 2017].

Jackson, J. (2010) Football Association condemn Fifa as 'opaque' after 2018 bid humiliation. *The Guardian*. [online] Available from: https://www.theguardian.com/football/2010/dec/05/football-association-fifa-opaque-humiliation [Accessed 13 November 2017].

Jiang, C.M., Zhang, Y.F, Cai, R., Zhang, Y.M, Wang, M., Meng, Y.Z., Zhang, M., and Zou, J.H. (2009) Analysis on current condition of participating in physical exercise for both urban and rural residents in China in 2007. *China Sport Science* 29(3), 9–19.

Jourdan, A. (2016) China's Suning leads race for soccer 'super agent' Stellar – source. *Reuters*. [online] Available from: http://www.reuters.com/article/us-soccer-china-stellar/chinas-suning-leads-race-for-soccer-super-agent-stellar-source-idUSKCN0YN3T2 [Accessed 13 November 2017].

Keane, M. (2013) *Creative Industries in China: Art, Design and Media*. Hoboken: John Wiley & Sons, 2013.

Klebnikov, S. (2016) China's ten most valuable soccer teams are led by Guangzhou Evergrande at $282 million. *Forbes*. [online] Available from: https://www.forbes.com/sites/sergeiklebnikov/2016/08/10/chinas-ten-most-valuable-soccer-teams-are-led-by-guangzhou-evergrande-at-282-million/#3c7fbfd43dfa [Accessed 13 November 2017].

Kunz, M. (2007) 265 million playing football. *FIFA Magazine.* [online] Available from: https://www.fifa.com/mm/document/fifafacts/bcoffsurv/emaga_9384_10704.pdf [Accessed 13 November 2017].

Li, Mingjiang (2008) China debates soft power. *The Chinese Journal of International Politics,* 2(2), 287–308.

Lovell, Julia (2008) Prologue: Beijing 2008–the mixed messages of contemporary Chinese nationalism. *The International Journal of the History of Sport,* 25(7), 758–778.

Lu, Z. and Hong, F. (2013) *Sport and Nationalism in China.* Routledge.

Mangan, J.A. and Dong, J. (2013) *Beijing 2008: Preparing for Glory: Chinese Challenge in the 'Chinese Century'.* Oxford: Routledge.

Manzenreiter, W. and Horne, J. (2005) Public policy, sports investments and regional development initiatives in Japan. In: *The Political Economy of Sport.* Oxford, Palgrave Macmillan UK, pp. 152–182.

Morrow, S. (2003) *The People's Game? Football, Finance and Society.* Berlin, Springer.

Mueller, T.S. and Sutherland, J.C. (2010) Heroes and villains: increasing fan involvement in pursuit of the elusive fan. *Journal of Applied Sport Management,* 2(1).

Nielson (2016) [online] Available from: http://nielsensports.com/wp-content/uploads/2014/12/2016-Nielsen-Sports-China-and-Football.pdf [Accessed 13 November 2017].

Ozanian, M. (2016) Forbes Fab 40: the world's most valuable sports brands. Available from: https://www.forbes.com/sites/mikeozanian/2016/10/24/forbes-fab-40-the-worlds-most-valuable-sports-brands/ [Accessed 13 November 2017].

Philips, T. (2017) China aims for football glory with academy based on Barcelona's. [online] Available from: https://www.theguardian.com/world/2017/mar/06/china-to-open-football-academy-modelled-on-barcelonas-la-masia [Accessed 13 November 2017].

Plunkett Research (2017) Sports Industry statistic and market size overview, business and industry statistics. [online] Available from: https://www.plunkettresearch.com/statistics/Industry-Statistics-Sports-Industry-Statistic-and-Market-Size-Overview/ [Accessed 13 November 2017].

Porteous, J. (2016) Why glamorous big-money signings won't be enough to fix Chinese football's corruption problems. *South China Morning Post.* [online] Available from: http://www.scmp.com/sport/china/article/1920960/why-glamorous-big-money-signings-wont-be-enough-fix-chinese-footballs [Accessed 13 November 2017].

Porteous, J. (2017) Have shock new rules on foreign players burst Chinese football's transfer bubble? *South China Morning Post.* [online] Available from: http://www.scmp.com/sport/soccer/article/2062455/have-shock-new-rules-foreign-players-burst-chinese-footballs-transfer [Accessed 13 November 2017].

PWC (2011) Changing the game – outlook for the global sports market to 2015. [online] Available from: https://www.pwc.com/gx/en/hospitality-leisure/pdf/changing-the-game-outlook-for-the-global-sports-market-to-2015.pdf [Accessed 13 November 2017].

Riordan, J. and Jones, R.E. (eds) (1999) *Sport and Physical Education in China.* Oxford: Taylor & Francis.

Romero, V. (2017) Chinese football bubble set to burst. *Marca.* [online] Available from: http://www.marca.com/en/football/international-football/2017/07/26/5978aed022601d25568b45c1.html [Accessed 13 November 2017].

Rosen, S. (2009) Contemporary Chinese youth and the state, *The Journal of Asian Studies* 68(2), 359–369.

Rumsby, B. (2017) Chinese Super League clubs among top five biggest spenders in world football. [online] Available from: http://www.telegraph.co.uk/football/2017/01/27/chinese-super-league-clubs-among-top-five-biggest-spenders-world/ [Accessed 13 November 2017].

Sevastopoulos, D. (2014) China's Evergrande academy sets sights on World Cup. [online] Available from: https://www.ft.com/content/80286618-83c0-11e3-86c9-00144feab7de [Accessed 13 November 2017].

Spaaij, R. (2009) The social impact of sport: diversities, complexities and contexts. *Sport in Society,* 12(9), 1109–1117.

Sullivan, J. and Kehoe S. (forthcoming), "Truth, good and beauty:" politics of celebrity in China. *The China Quarterly.*

Tan, T.C. and Bairner, A. (2010) Globalization and Chinese sport policy: the case of elite football in the People's Republic of China. *The China Quarterly,* 203, 581–600.

Tan, T.C., Huang, H.C., Bairner, A., and Chen, Y.W. (2016) Xi Jin-Ping's World Cup dreams: from a major sports country to a world sports power. *The International Journal of the History of Sport,* 33(12), 1449–1465.

Wan 2015 [online] Available from: http://www.independent.co.uk/news/world/asia/chinas-xi-jinping-loves-football-so-much-hes-put-it-on-the-national-curriculum-but-can-he-secure-the-10071110.html [Accessed 13 November 2017].

Xu, Guoqi (2009) *Olympic Dreams: China and Sports, 1895–2008*. Cambridge MA, Harvard University Press.

Zhao, S. (1998) A state-led nationalism: The patriotic education campaign in post-Tiananmen China, *Communist and Post-Communist Studies*, 31(3), 287–302.

Zhao, Yuezhi (1998) *Media, Market, and Democracy in China: Between the Party Line and the Bottom Line*. Vol. 114. Champaign: University of Illinois Press.

42

Business and governance of football in Qatar

Mahfoud Amara and Ahmed Al-Emadi

Introduction

One of the milestones in Qatar's international strategy in sport was the 2006 Asian Games. The Games considered to be the second largest sporting event after the Summer Olympic Games, in terms of number of sports and number of participants. The Asian Games positioned Qatar as an ambitious nation, with sport as significant to its strategy for development and diplomacy. To date, Qatar has engaged in international sport in a number of venues, with an average of 50 international events organised on yearly basis. For some the "over" visibility of Qatar in sporting events is driven more by political agenda than rational business model. Although one would ask the same question about private investments in sport in general, and whether it is possible to neutralise politics from sport as business investors have to deal with governments and public authorities as well as adapting to different political contexts. For others having a country like Qatar or China investing in sport in times of austerity is an opportunity to seek other financial resources in a globalised sport industry, with new emerging centres.

Business model of Qatar's investment in football

Qatar is engaged in sport using both direct and indirect investment. The approach is to establish an international network and alliances as well as bringing more international visibility to local companies/sectors involved in the economic diversification of Qatar's economy, including the development of retail, tourism, and hospitality as well as other services such as banking, education and technology (Amara, 2013; Chavannat, 2017). Qatar's sport investment can be categorised under the following pillars: sponsorship, direct investment, and sport TV broadcasting.

Sponsorship

Qatari companies such as Qatar Airways, Qatar National Bank, and Oreedoo have been active lately in the sponsoring of sport events and clubs. These companies are expanding their market internationally. In 2018 Qatar Airways currently has a fleet of more than 300 airplanes reaching every continent and turning Hamad Airport to a hub for international flights, thus competing with Emirates Airlines in the region, and other international airline companies. Oreedoo is also investing in telecommunication (telephone, Internet, and Cable TV) in 12 countries in Africa and in Asia. The purpose of sponsorship associated with global sport arena is to increase brand awareness about Qatari companies and products, as well as Qatar/Doha as a tourist destination, competing with other cities in the region such as Dubai, Abu Dhabi, Manama, Muscat, in attracting tourists and travellers transiting through the region.

Direct investment

The takeover of Paris Saint-Germain (PSG) by Qatar Sport Investment (QSI) in 2011 has been so far a landmark in terms of sport investment and positioning of Qatar on the world stage. The ambition of Qatar is to make PSG one of the most successful French clubs and one of the top football clubs not only in Europe, but also internationally. Although PSG has dominated the French league in the last few years, so far the club is still chasing the Champion's League title despite significant investment in the club. According to some estimates, the current team value of PSG is 775 million euros, including revenue of 521 million euros (Forbes, 2017). The spectacular signing of Brazilian Neymar in the summer of 2017 for nearly 200 million euros from FC Barcelona is a case in point. This has put the club and Qatar further under the international spotlight, particularly during Qatar's political crisis with its neighbouring countries. Somehow, the signing became a political defiance against the blockade imposed on Qatar by the UAE, Saudi Arabia, Bahrain, and Egypt. The signing has also put the club under the scrutiny of European football authority in relation to question of fair play (discussed further in the subsequent section on principals of good governance).

Qatar is also involved in other ventures in European sport. Aspire Academy to sustain its elite football development and offer graduates from the academy an opportunity to play professionally in Europe took over the Belgian Football Club, KAS Eupen, in 2012 when it was in the 2nd division. Qatar is also present through private investment in Malaga Football Club in Spain owned by member of the Qatari royal family, Sheikh Abdullah Bin Nassar Al-Thani. He owns a number of ventures, including hotel chains, shopping centres, mobile phone companies, and car dealerships (Reuters, 2010). Qatar, represented by Qatar Sport Investment (QSI), has also invested in another lucrative sector, that of sport goods industry, through the development of its own sport brand, Burdda Sports. It is now the official supplier of a number of local sport clubs in Qatar, including Aspire Sport Academy, as well as foreign teams including Tunisian Football National Team, Watford FC, Hull FC, British and the US National Handball Teams, Toulon Rugby, to name but a few.

Sport TV broadcasting

One of the most notable of Qatar's investments in the sport industry is obviously Aljazeera Sport, which was rebranded as BeIN Sports in 2012 and moved recently under the management of BeIN Media Group. Interestingly the chairman of BeIN Media Group, Nasser Al-Khelaifi, is also the chairman of QSI, and is also the president of Qatar Tennis Federation and, more importantly, the chief executive of PSG. The investment in BeIN Sports is also economically beneficial to French football and thus directly or indirectly to other football clubs in the professional league. The launch of BeIN Sports has completely changed the sport broadcasting industry in the MENA region, including viewers' expectations in terms of accessing quality service in exchange for a subscription fee, which is relatively new in the MENA region where state-owned TV had control for decades over the broadcasting of domestic leagues and matches involving national teams. State-owned TV channels in the region used to form a coalition through the Union of Arabsat Broadcasting, or in partnership with Eurovision, to minimise the cost and to secure large access. The acquisition by Aljazeera Sport in 2009 of ART (Arab Radio and Television) Sport, previously owned by Salah Kamel, a rich businessman from Saudi Arabia, and with it the broadcasting rights of major football leagues and competitions, has given a competitive advantage to Qatar over other state-owned TV channels, including in neighbouring oil-rich Gulf countries. There was a time where the UAE via its Abu Dhabi or Dubai Sport TV Networks could compete to certain extent over a few leagues, such as the English Premier League and German Bundesliga; however, these channels and others in the region soon found themselves only with the right to broadcast minor leagues such as those from Switzerland, Belgium, and the Netherlands. They are obliged to negotiate with BeIN Sports to broadcast their national teams on terrestrial channels only. During high-profile tournaments, to protect its investment, BeIN Sports is even intervening with other local European satellite channels (available in Astra and Hotbird) to crypt their free to air signal within their national territories. BeIN Sports would argue that it is offering value for money for its services in comparison to other giant sport TV networks. When first launched in France, BeIN Sports was charging 11 euros per month in comparison to Canal Plus (Vivendi group) which was charging 30–60 euros for its full entertainment package. Over time, there have been tentative attempt for Canal Plus and BeIN Sports to join efforts to reduce inflation of sport TV rights in France to compete against new emerging actors in the industry, including live streaming platforms such as Netflix and Amazon. Moreover, BeIN Sports is changing its business model from sport to include other entertainment packages to minimise its deficit and to seek other opportunities to generate revenues. Thus, taping into different categories of viewers who are not necessarily sport fans.

World Cup and reform in Qatari football

Qatari authorities, including local stakeholders of national sport, football in particular, have engaged in a number of reforms to respond to national and international demands.

International perspective

The hosting of the 2022 World Cup has put Qatar under the spotlight and scrutiny of a number of sport and non-sport governing bodies and the so-called international community. Qatar to sustain (and for some to defend) its legitimacy and ambition as partner and investor in international sport business has had to respond to a number of criticisms, particularly in relation to issues of principles of good governance. This includes questions of transparency in relation to the principle of Financial Fair Play (FFP) in Europe. In particular, the distinction between Qatar state's finance and investment in PSG and the protection of fair competition between clubs in the league, which do not have necessarily the financial back up of other governments or public entities. Hence, they cannot afford to run a deficit or to inflate their revenues, as "clubs cannot make losses of over 30 million euros (£27 million) for any given three-year "assessment period" (Shilton, 2017). PSG leadership's response was that the club "increased through ticketing, sponsoring, merchandising, match day and TV rights from 90 million euros (£81m) to approximately 500 million euros (£453m), with the last two seasons running profits" (Shilton, 2017). The club is counting on the popularity of Neymar and the impact this is having on the PSG brand and the selling of its products internationally (including in Brazil). Furthermore, the club's ultimate ambition is to finally win the Champions League trophy which would transform PSG into one of the top European football clubs, hence improving the ranking of the French

League in Europe and internationally. The signing of Neymar from FC Barcelona, followed by the emerging star of French football Mbappe from Monaco, are also having an impact on ticket sales for both home and away games. Fans of other French clubs want to see PSG football stars playing in their home pitch, even if the final score is not to the advantage of their home team. The signing is also impacting the visibility of PSG in social media. According to estimates, the club went from 500,000 followers in 2011/12 to 48 million in 2018. In terms of tax revenue and other social charges, it is estimated that the state would receive 37.5 million euros per year (total of 300 million euros) from Neymar's lucrative salary (Poingt, 3 August 2017).

The other principle is that of accountability – Qatar's accountability to the international football community, including of course FIFA and its business partners. We argued elsewhere how Qatar has relaxed its legislation to find some acceptable solutions (culturally and religiously) to preserve the interest of alcohol beverage companies such as Budweiser, which is one of the top sponsor of FIFA, with a strong brand association particularly in Europe and elsewhere with football culture (Bodet and Amara, 2015). Alcohol, which is forbidden in public spaces in Qatar, will be allowed for consumption in "designated areas." One would argue that the issue of alcohol is somehow over-emphasised by international media when it comes to Qatar to promote the idea that alcohol drinking associated with football culture is incompatible with having the World Cup organised by an Arab and Muslim country. This is illustrated in the following headline in an Australian online newspaper (News.come.au)

"Come and camp in the desert": Qatar addresses concerns about 2022 World Cup

THE decision to award Qatar the 2022 World Cup continues to upset football fans. The tiny nation wants visitors to camp in the desert.

(Murray, 2017 [emphasis added by the author])

Interestingly, Australia has put new legislation in place to regulate alcohol commercials during televised sport events at certain times of the day, following calls by medical experts for alcohol advertising and sponsorship to be simply "phased out of live sports broadcasts" (Kozaki, 2016).

The other important agenda that Qatar as future host of the FIFA World Cup has had to work on is that of workers' rights, following a number of reports in international media and by international workers unions and human rights organisations. The Supreme Committee for the Delivery and Legacy (henceforth SC) supervising the preparation for the mega-event in terms of the construction of football stadia and other logistics has developed new guidelines to monitor Workers' Welfare Standards. The implementation of those guidelines is monitored by Workers' Welfare Department in partnership with international agencies such as Building and Wood Workers' International and Impactt Ltd[1]:

A set of mandatory, contractually binding rules which ensure that companies working on SC projects operate in line with our values. The standards clearly set out the SC's requirements regarding the recruitment, employment, living and working conditions for everyone engaged on an SC project … We hold ourselves and our partners accountable to our Workers' Welfare Standards, regularly monitoring adherence to them, and we immediately address any cases where a party falls short.

(Supreme Committee webpage)

To improve the working condition of workers, SC teamed up with Weill Cornell Medicine in Qatar to develop Nutrition Program designed to identify prevalent health risks and to raise awareness of healthy eating among workers and contractors. SC is also working on improving safety measures in response to the alarming reports by human rights groups such as Human Rights Watch (HRW). HRW stated in a recent report that "many thousands of migrant workers on construction sites in Qatar, including those building stadiums for the 2022 World Cup, are being subjected to potentially life-threatening heat and humidity, according to new research on the extreme summer conditions in the Gulf". The same report suggested that:

> In August 2017, Qatari authorities responded to Human Rights Watch with information on migrant worker deaths at the workplace resulting from injuries. This information indicates that 35 migrant workers died in 2016 as a result of serious injuries, most of them apparently sustained in the course of construction work.
>
> *(Human Rights Watch, 2017)*

In response, SC indicated "to date there have been two work-related fatalities and nine non-work related deaths of workers engaged on our projects" (Supreme Committee, 2017). The government established a support centre and helpline for domestic workers, including construction workers. The purpose of the centre is to protect vulnerable employees from abuses that include violence, long working hours, non-payment of wages, and wage deductions. SC announced a new measure recently, which is to pay compensation for contract fees (total amount reaching 19 million QR), to reduce workers exploitation by agencies specialised in recruitment and transfer of workers to the region.

Understanding the importance of promoting its image as the first Arab and Muslim country to host the FIFA World Cup, and to protect its economy because of the recent blockade by neighbouring countries, the state of Qatar has implemented a range of reforms. This concerns changes to its Kafala (sponsorship) system to allow workers freedom to leave the country and change jobs without their employer's permission. Furthermore, the state established a minimum wage and a fund to guarantee late wages, as well as a method of salary payment via bank accounts to measure monthly payment of salaries including those of unskilled workers. In August 2018 HH the Emir Sheikh Tamim bin Hamad Al-Thani approved a new labour (Law No. 13 of 2017) to establish a Labour Dispute Resolution Committee that allows employees to circumvent the court system.

Qatar has also been active in recent years, represented by the International Centre of Sport Security (ICSS), which has now branches in Washington and in London, in the moral ground around sport, particularly in relation to sport integrity and sport for development. This reflects what Houlihan and Zheng (2015, p. 7) refer to as small states strategy, to counter their vulnerability (due to their small geography and population size) and to engage with NGOs and sport policy regimes (such as those of anti-doping, integrity, and child protection). The goal is to pursue their sport and non-sport objectives, including developing a stronger global profile and a greater scope for the exercise of influence.

National perspective

The controversial case of French-Algerian football player Zahir Belounis has shed light on the question of professional football contracts in Qatar and exposed the country to criticism by international media and non-governmental organisations. Belounis, who played for El Jaish Sports Club, eventually returned to France in November 2013 after he was prevented from leaving Qatar for two years due to dispute with his club (sponsor) over his contract. Since then a number of reforms have been implemented to bring Qatar's football system in line with international norms in relation to mobility of players, their salaries, their representation in decision-making, as well as their right to education and retirement. There have been also other decisions about the structure of the league itself and the competition system to make it more sustainable in terms of balancing competition level of clubs and maintaining the uncertainty of outcome. Hence making the league more attractive to spectators. Qatar has been criticised for being the host of the FIFA World Cup while having empty stadia, as the average number spectators per match can be low (in comparison to other countries in the region such as the Kingdom of Saudi Arabia and in North Africa). Although one should consider looking at numbers in relative terms considering the local demography and not necessarily comparing local football culture with other nations with a bigger fan base.

Qatar football has undergone a number of changes in recent years in reforming its football, commencing with the launch of the professional league in 2003 and then the Qatar Stars League in 2010. Over the last few years, the Qatar Stars League, which initially included ten teams, was expanded to 12 teams and then to 14 teams to meet the requirements of the Asian Football Confederation. In 2017, Qatar Stars League returned to a system of 12 teams. One of its goals is to offer players on the Qatar national team the opportunity to take part in many competitions and matches over the year (including the Qatar Cup, QSL Cup and the Emir Cup).

There is also the launch of the Qatar Stars League Management (QSLM), an independent body that organises the professional league, which is the longest tournament that runs in any given season. QSLM is the body that operates the licensing process and grants the licenses as per Club Licensing Regulations. The purpose of the licensing system is to reinforce conduct compliance and audits as per Qatar Football Association regulations, the highest football authority in the country, which represents the interest of AFC and FIFA. As indicated in the Club Licensing Regulations, requirements to be fulfilled by the license applicant (the club), are divided into six categories:

> Sporting, Infrastructure, Personnel and Administrative, Legal, Financial and Business being split into 3 grades: A,B and C" (…) License may be withdrawn during the relevant Sporting Season by the relevant decision-making bodies if: a) any of the conditions for the issuing of the License are no longer satisfied; or b) the Licensee violates any of its obligations under the present Regulations.[2]

The criteria for licensing is for the club to have football development pathways, including

(a) at least three age group squads below the first team; (b) at least two of the above squads must be Under 15 (U-15) and Under 18 (U-18); (c) each squad must have a minimum of 18 players to prepare a team ready for participation in an age-group or open competition.

The development pathway of local talents is strengthen by the signing of a number of big names in the world of coaching to develop the football system in Qatar and the senior stars such as Xavi (Al-Sadd), who has been nominated as ambassador of a number of Corporate Social Responsibility initiatives. To secure equal chances between clubs, the QFA implemented new rules about the signing of foreign players. Each club in the league can register up to 26 players, including three foreigners, one Asian player, and one resident. In 2017, the Qatar Football Association (QFA) announced the introduction of a new league competition for U-23 teams, as part of the development of second tier football in the country. More recently, new measures were taken to reduce the cost of running professional leagues and clubs. The merger between Al-Jaish club (the army club) and Lakhwiya (the police club), although both successful, was the most significant example. The merger formed a new club with the name of Duhail Club. The move has been criticised as reinforcing the dominance of a few clubs, resulting in the creation of another entity even stronger and more dominant in comparison to other clubs with smaller budget. The Ministry of Culture and Sport had to recently intervene to cover the deficit in terms of players' salaries, some of them international players who did not receive their salary for few months. One of the reasons for the non-payment of salaries is the consequence of so-called informal contracts agreed between the club and non-accredited football managers.[3] Furthermore, it was announced that according to article No (28) Rules and Regulations of the QFA a player's contract would be deemed terminated for "just cause" in case that:

> The club fails to pay the player for 60 days. If a player does not get paid on time, he has the right to notify the club of the negligence and can demand payment "within a period of 10 days". A final five-day notice will be a prelude to effectively terminating the contract without any consequences. If the club does not comply with FIFA's decision to compensate the players, the club will face an immediate ban on transfers.

To protect the rights of players, the first union of football players, Qatar Players Association, was established in 2015 to be the first entity representing football players in the State of Qatar. The union of Qatari players signed an agreement with FIFPro, the International Association of Professional Footballers, aimed at aligning the QPA with FIFPro-approved standards on how to best represent players. To this end a new retirement fund was put in place by QSL to deduct pension contributions (6 per cent) directly from players' salaries to be paid back during retirement in addition to end-of-service bonus.

Conclusion

To conclude, the FIFA 2022 World Cup despite all challenges, exasperated recently by the political situation and the blockade on Qatar (still ongoing at the time of writing), and criticism over Qatar's readiness (including culturally) to host this mega-event and thus to meet its promise, has also been somehow advantageous in advancing a number of reforms in the country. These include working toward meeting international standards for labour rights (including those of professional athletes), raising awareness about the working conditions of construction workers, and developing the sport industry around the FIFA 2022 World Cup which brings together different sectors: sport broadcasting, sport event management, sport sciences training in general, sport tourism and hospitality, to name but a few.

Qatar has move a long way to involve in its reform of national sport system more scrutiny over the principles of good governance and financial auditing. There are also other legitimate questions to be raised about return on investment regarding the acquisition of PSG and other sport-related ventures. The move of BeIN TV Network to include other entertainment channels (including cinema, series, documentary, cooking, and travel) is an indicator that the strategy of positioning in international sport business market (i.e., to get recognition as a serious contender), is now paralleled with a strategy justified by business rationale and a more economically viable approach. The country has to overcome other challenges in relation to the legacy of the 2022 FIFA World Cup, including the cost of maintaining newly built football stadia and the sustainability of the transportation system (metro and rail) connecting different World Cup venues inside and outside Doha. However, a challenge can also be an opportunity to reform and to tackle issues that have not been fully addressed in the past. The hosting of the FIFA World Cup has contributed in pushing high up the agenda issues around labour rights, including athletes' rights, and women's participation in sport, which were previously silent or perceived as low priority.

Notes

1 The BWI is the Global Union Federation grouping free and democratic unions with members in the Building, Building Materials, Wood, Forestry and Allied sectors. Impactt describes itself as an award-winning ethical trade consultancy with a vision to improve workers' livelihoods in a way that benefits businesses and workers.
2 A, B, C criteria involve Infrastructures, Player Development Structures, Youth Development Program, Grassroots, Youth Academy, Medical support, Educational Program, Social Responsibility, Racial Equality (Gender equality not mentioned), professional management.
3 In a press conference the head of QSL, Selman Al-Ansari, declared that there are only seven accredited football managers, among them three are Qataris (Al-Arab, 1 November 2016).

References

Amara, M. (2013) The pillars of Qatar's international sport strategy. [online] Retrieved from http://www.e-ir.info/2013/11/29/the-pillars-of-qatars-international-sport-strategy/ [Accessed 29 November 2013].

Bodet, G. and Amara, M. (2015) *Islam, Sport and Marketing or Sport Marketing in Muslim cultures, in Testa and Amara, Sport in Islam and in Muslim Communities.* London: Routledge.

Chanavat, N. (2017) French football, foreign investors: global sports as country branding. *Journal of Business Strategy*, 38(6), 3–10.

Forbes Magazine (2017) The business of Soccer, 2017 ranking. [online] Retrieved from https://www.forbes.com/teams/paris-saint-germain/ [Accessed 5 November 2017].

Houlihan, B. and Zheng, J. (2015) Small states: sport and politics at the margin. *International Journal of Sport Policy and Politics*, 7, 329–344.

Human Rights Watch (2017, 27 September) Qatar: Take Urgent Action to Protect Construction Workers. FIFA, National Associations Should Press Qatar on Heat Risks, Preventable Deaths, Human Rights Watch. [online] Retrieved from: https://www.hrw.org/news/2017/09/27/qatar-take-urgent-action-protect-construction-workers [Accessed 27 September 2017].

Kozaki, D. (2016, 30 May) Alcohol advertising during live sports broadcasts "should be phased out". ABC News [online] Retrieved from http://www.abc.net.au/news/2016-05-30/state-of-origin-alcohol-advertising-live-sport-phased-out-call/7458584 [Accessed 5 June 2017].

Murray, O. (2017, 11 February) "Come and camp in the desert": Qatar addresses concerns about 2022 World Cup. News.come.au [online] Retrieved from: http://www.news.com.au/sport/football/world-cup/come-and-camp-in-the-desert-qatar-addresses-concerns-about-2022-world-cup/news-story/d3b484bc6878b5fb2ed5efdcfe16d31c [Accessed 2 January 2017].

Poingt, G. (2017, 3 August), Neymar tout proche du PSG : l'État pourrait toucher près de 300 millions d'euros. *Le Figaro* [online] Retrieved from http://www.lefigaro.fr/conjoncture/2017/07/28/20002-20170728ARTFIG00019-si-neymar-debarque-au-psg-l-etat-pourrait-toucher-le-jackpot.php [Accessed 2 April 2018].

Reuters, (2010, 26 June) Soccer-Qatari Sheikh Al-Thani buys Malaga football club. [online] Retrieved from https://uk.reuters.com/article/soccer-spain-malaga/soccer-qatari-sheikh-al-thani-buys-malaga-football-club-idUKLDE65P06420100626 [Accessed 3 January 2018].

Shilton, A. (2017, 12 September). "WE HAVE A YEAR" Neymar and Kylian Mbappe deals did NOT break Financial Fair Play rules, insists PSG president Nasser al-Khelaifi. *The Sun* [online] Retrieved from https://www.thesun.co.uk/sport/football/4445044/neymar-kylian-mbappe-ffp-psg-nasser-al-khelaifi/ [Accessed 15 September 2017].

The Supreme Committee (2017) SC statement on Human Rights Watch report. [online] Retrieved from https://www.sc.qa/en/news/sc-statement-on-human-rights-watch-report [2 December 2017].

43

Football in Brazil

Leonardo José Mataruna-Dos-Santos, Daniel Range, André Luiz Pereira Guimarães, Luis Antonio Verdini de Carvalho, and Carlos Eugenio Zardini Filho

Introduction

Brazil is the largest country in South America, and the only one with Portuguese as its official language. The country is officially divided into five geographic regions: North, Northeast, Center-West, Southeast and South, and from there further subdivided into 26 states and the federal districts. Brazil has long been viewed as a significant emerging economy and is part of the BRICS (Brazil, Russia, India, China, and South Africa) and Mercosul economic blocs (Brazil, Argentina, Uruguay, Paraguay, Chile, Peru, Bolivia, Colombia, Ecuador, and Venezuela).

According to IBGE (2018), the Gross Domestic Product (GDP) in Brazil was worth 1796.19 billion US dollars (USD) in 2016. The GDP value of Brazil represents 2.9 per cent of the world economy. GDP in Brazil averaged USD 634.46 billion from 1960 to 2016, reaching an all-time high of USD 2616.20 billion in 2011 and a record low of USD 15.17 billion in 1960 (Tradingeconomics, 2018). Though GDP and GDP per capita have both grown in Brazil, poverty is still rife and income inequality, even in large international facing cities such as Rio de Janeiro, is amongst the highest in the world. The net income generated by the Brazilian Football Confederation was USD 175 million in 2016 (CBF, 2018). The Sports Sector GDP observed by Kasznar, Graça and Ary (2012), represents 2 per cent of Brazil's GDP from 2003 to 2010. "Therefore, it turns out that the football business, especially the Brazilian Championship, rests on three major institutional support systems – the economy, the market (the sports industry) and the media" (Reis et al, 2014).

Many of Brazil's greatest footballers and sportspeople came from the poorest areas of the country and, even today, football is seen as the most likely route out of poverty for many. Social projects are a pathway used for social inclusion, and sport is a central instrument for people to leave poverty. In Brazil, one such instrument is the "*Taça das Favelas*" (Favelas[1] Football Tournament) organised by CUFA (*Unique Centre of Favelas*). It is a NGO institution with social responsibility to help the people from favelas to reveal talents in football through this tournament.

Football in Brazil

Football is played across Brazil, formally and informally, everywhere. Parks, schools, academies, universities, and open spaces are dominated by the sport. Sometimes a ball is not even used to play the game. The children often use empty candy packets, fruit, plastic bottles, or even a shoe in place of a ball. The goal is marked by stone or flip flops and it is from these humble beginnings that many players emerge. However, the formal base for the sport in Brazil is usually through clubs maintaining dedicated schools for players associated with the club to play and train. However, there are other environments that provide the required facilities for the sport, including, sports schools maintained by educational institutions; private schools; universities; sports centres maintained by the federation; and states or town halls (Ciampa, Leme, and de Souza, 2016). Sport academies are used in Brazil for the big teams to hone and pick the talented players and to sign them to their first contracts. Yet, the actual playing fields, at the beginning of twentieth century, has declined. Indeed, industrialisation and the urbanisation of the new cities have reduced the number of public pitches considerably.

Following this reduction of accessible leisure space, widely acknowledged as fundamental for involvement in sport, the rates for physical inactivity in the country have increased dramatically. Indeed, 122.9 million people aged 15 years or over did not engage in any kind of sport or physical activity in 2015, equivalent to 76 per cent of the whole population in this age group, according IBGE (2015). This data is part of the study Pnad 2015: Sports Practice and Physical Activity Survey, which the Brazilian Institute of Geography and Statistics (IBGE) released, in Rio de Janeiro, with data extracted from the National Household Sample Survey (Pnad) of that year (IBGE, 2015). The Pnad shows that, in 2015, 61.3 million people aged 15 years or more – equivalent to 37.9 per cent of the total 161.8 million people in this age group – participated in some kind of sport or physical activity. From these 53.9 per cent were men and 46.1 per cent women, with football selected as the most popular physical practice in the country. Yet football remains the heart of the nation.

How football developed in Brazil gives an important insight into how it came to dominate the sporting and cultural landscapes of the country. It was at the end of the nineteenth century that the practice of football began in Brazil, having been brought to the country from Europe, and mainly England. It is believed that the first organised game in Brazil took place in 1895. Football, a typical product of English culture, has hit different parts of the globe, including Brazil (Alcântara, 2006). Football was initially an elite sport and was brought from England by university students who made up the bourgeoisie. Later, in the 1930s soccer began to be played across the whole country and all social classes. Brazilian football reached a resounding national success at that time, escaping the control of club officers, directors of foreign schools and factory owners to be practiced on the beaches, in the *várzea* field, and all over the country (Alcântara, 2006).

> The history of Brazilian football is also a history of social struggle in the biggest South American country, so that it now carries a special sociological meaning. Football offers access to the fundamental dimensions of Brazil's social life. Here, football is more than just a game for the masses, it is a metaphor of social life par excellence. The early history of Brazilian football, with its tension between being a sport for the elites and fun for the masses, also marked the beginning of a popularisation process, in whose course football developed into the most powerful expression of the so-called popular culture of the country. This development may be divided into several stages: Between 1910 and 1920, football found a new home in Brazil, the sport entered the clubs in the twenties, and in the fifties, its popularisation and "democratisation" was complete. The country's poor classes gave football its "Brazilian" character. What is expressed in football is a cultural identity inherited from the Indian and black population.
>
> *(Murad, 2018)*

The first Brazilian football clubs formalised in the 1910s. Several people involved with the management of the teams and federations were drawn from the military leagues such as the Football League of the Army (1914) and the Navy Sport League in 1915 (Cancella and Mataruna, 2012). The Brazilian Football Federation founded later carried on the legacy of the military as a vehicle for organised sport and it is considered one of the first sport organisations in Latin-America. The football federations of Argentina, Chile, and Uruguay are older than the Brazilian organisation but they are contemporary institutions.

Within a few years' people began to associate with particular clubs and they bought a passion and an audience to the game. Indeed, football came to symbolise what it was to be Brazilian and part of one's central identity:

> Example of the popularity of football is the loyalty of the fans to their teams. Although the phase is not good or that the team falls to the second division, the fan does not change team. Suffer with him, believing in successful days, becoming even more fanatical. In Brazil, this fidelity comes from the day of birth, when the boy receives a name, a religion and a soccer team for which he will cheer his whole life. Loyalty that is expressed in the door of the maternity room, when parents hang a pair of cleats and a miniature uniform, representing the family football team. Throughout childhood, there is a continuous process of inculcating positive values and habits about the family team and negatives towards opposing teams.
>
> *(Alcântara, 2006)*

Consumer relations and teams

The match-day experience for spectators in Brazil is very different to those in many other countries. In Brazil alcohol is forbidden around and inside the stadium, in part to avoid hooliganism, which is prominent in the game since 2003. For the FIFA 2014 the president Dilma Rousseff signed a law in 2012 to permit alcohol commercialisation inside the stadiums during the event only. Since then, however, there has been continuous pressure from the beer industry on the politicians to maintain this law. The conflict among football gangs is rife with rival gangs pre-arranging fights and confrontations. Sometimes these happen between supporters of the same team from different gangs and often these gangs are connected with narcotics, organised crime, samba clubs/groups, or leaders of militias. The group of fans (gangs) are legally and formally known in Brazil as "*torcida organizada*". The word "torcida" come from the verbs "to root for", "to wring" or "to twist", during the late 1930s when people went to the stadium to support the team and had the behaviour of twisting their own t-shirts.

The fans and gangs consume official and pirated products (non-official) from the clubs. Pirated sport products are a very serious problem in Brazil. In addition to loss of sales to manufacturers who own the brands, taxes are not collected by the government, and the profit from pirated products is often linked to other crimes, such as money laundering. However, here, at least in football, the situation seems to be changing. According to Stochos Sports & Entertainment (2013), in the last two years, there has been a 7 per cent reduction in the number of fans who buy pirated products from their team and an increase in those who prefer to buy only official items. The survey, which was administered between March 2011 and March 2013, points out that 77 per cent of respondents purchase only official uniforms of the teams they support as opposed to 23 per cent who refuse to buy genuine products and who prefer to buy pirated produce. The main reason for the proliferation of piracy in Brazil is the prices. While an original t-shirt may cost around USD 85–130, a pirated one can cost USD 10–25.

However, there has been awareness raising campaigns of the consequences of piracy and, as such, the consumption of official products, which help to support the finances of clubs are increasing every year.

With more professional management of the clubs and an increasing focus on their supporters, the main Brazilian teams have been achieving record revenues in recent years. The amount among the top 20 Brazilian clubs has already surpassed USD 1 billion per year, according to a recent analysis of Club Federations. Generally, the organised fan gangs and groups receive free tickets to watch the games.

In 2018, Globo TV will distribute among the 18 clubs the highest fixed revenue in Brazilian football history, worth approximately USD 500 million. This figure does not include the increasing pay-per-view market either, with 380 games now shown on Premiere (private cable TV channel). Brazilian clubs have grown their revenues, mainly through these TV rights and sales. For example, in 2017, the Flamengo Club grossed and Corinthians Club grossed USD 28 million for each team from Globo TV investments (Zirpoli, 2017). Most income from clubs is now not from match-day ticket revenue and in stadium sales.

The first national entity that directed football in Brazil was the CBD (Brazilian Confederation of Sports) created in 1916 and which ceased to operate in 1979 with the creation of the Brazilian Football Confederation (CBF). From 1980, the CBF began to organise the Brazilian Football Championship and the Brazilian national soccer team. Nowadays, the professional clubs are seen as the main actors which support and maintain the Brazilian football championships and national team. Though nearly all of the stars of the Brazilian national team play their club football outside of Brazil, their education and development is firmly rooted in the country.

After decades as an amateur activity, the Law n. 8.672 of 1993 (known as "Zico Law") was the first federal movement towards the professionalisation of the football clubs in the country. Nowadays, the clubs of Series A and B face huge challenges and contrasts, involving huge debts and revenues (Cunha, Santos, and Haveroth, 2017). Sabino (2017) comments that in 2016, the top 20 Brazilian clubs, 17 from Serie A and the others in Serie B, had a gross revenue of R$ 4.86 billion. This is equivalent to USD 1.42 billion as of 30 December 2016 (National Brazilian Bank – Banco do Brasil). However, on top of this, in 2017, the Serie A clubs also had around 2.5 billion euros in debts and outstanding funds to the Brazilian government (Sabino, 2017). Based on Cunha, Santos, and Haveroth (2017), as business, the Brazilian football clubs have been facing problems such as late (and sometimes non-existent) salary payments, corruption, money laundering, poor managerial qualifications, issues around tax payments, and other administrative problems. These are, generally, not well-governed bodies. The series are divided at the national level for tournaments from March to November in four different levels illustrated in Figure 43.1. The regional cups involve two or more states in the same region: for example, the Rio-São Paulo Tournament, the Green Cup with teams from the North, Centre-West and Espirito Santo, and the Northeast Cup. The champions go directly into the Brazilian Cup. In the state competitions, the clubs are geographically localised in the same state. The division level is variable between two or four degrees, depending of the number of clubs in each state. São Paulo has 16 clubs but Rondônia has only eight clubs.

In recognition of this and in order to help the football clubs, the Brazilian government has recently tried to promote initiatives aimed at decreasing the taxes and labour debts of professional clubs. Indeed, in 2008 a national lottery called "Timemania" was created, using the brands of the football clubs as an asset, to generate revenue to be used to decrease the total debts of the clubs which took part in the lottery program within the Brazilian state (Pazzi Junior, 2008). Furthermore, in 2016 the Brazilian government created a federal organisation (APFUT) to monitor and regulate a federal program known as PROFUT (re-launched in 2015), which

Figure 43.1   National tournaments

* *Clubs in the semi-final go for the next level Serie C. Nobody lower from this Serie.*
** *Clubs in the semi-final go for the next level Serie B and the two last clubs in the rank lower from this Serie D.*
*** *Four Clubs come from the Serie C and four clubes go for the Serie A.*
**** *Four clubs lower for Serie B.*

has as its main goal the refinancing of the debts of professional football clubs to the Brazilian government (Brazil, 2016). Clearly the Brazilian government recognises that issues exist and is working to mitigate these as much as possible, in order that debts are repaid. This is situation is indicative of the message that Brazilian football has been coping with countless challenges in terms of maintaining a healthy club system.

Current structure

In 2014, there were 29,208 football teams and 2,100,000 football players registered in the federations spread across the country (Brasil, 2014). In 2016, CBF figures show that there were 776 professional clubs, 435 amateur, and 27 formation. There is an imbalance between the number of players and the investments in men's and women's soccer in Brazil. Only in 1965 were women allowed to play organised soccer in Brazil (Goellner, 2005). The somewhat arcane structure of Brazilian domestic football sees three pyramid structures running simultaneously. These are: (1) national, (2) regional, and (3) state-level, all being organised by different bodies, see Figure 43.2.

In Brazil, unlike most other countries there are national, regional and state championships. The Nationals, denominated by Brasileirões, are organised by the CBF in four series – A, B, C, and D – where the clubs ascend or descend from one to another according to their classifications at the end of each of these competitions. There is also the Brazil Cup, where all regional federations are present.

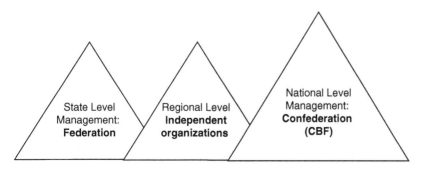

Figure 43.2   The Brazilian football pyramid model

In relation to the Regionals, the Northeast Cup and the Green Cup are regularly played, with the participation of teams from the North and Centre-West regions (CBF, 2016). In addition, Brazilian football also has the State Championships where most of the federations organize in more than one series. In relation to the annual calendar, the states are played in the first four months of the year, the Brazil Cup from February to December, and the Brazilian Championships from May to December.

The diversity is not only in relation to the types of competition but also to the ages. Regarding the age groups for official men's football competitions, the following categories are divided: Professional, sub 23, sub 20, sub 17, sub 15, and sub 13. The CBF has professional competitions, sub 20 and sub 17; the state federations also organise championships for the sub 15, sub 14, sub 13, sub 12, and sub 11. All of this adds up to a huge amount of football, played in various formats and across a number of different tournaments and times. It is confusing for many fans and doubtlessly baffling to follow for all but the most informed casual observers.

The first league in Brazil was created in 2016 with clubs from the South region, namely Rio de Janeiro and Minas Gerais. They organised a competition called Cup of First League or South-Minas-Rio Cup with 25 teams. The first phase is a group round and the second round comprises eliminatory games. For decades Globo TV has controlled the broadcasting rights of the sport event including the top Brazilian soccer league.

As football is part of the popular culture of the country and, as such, has drawn the attention of major investors. The most popular manifestation of investment in the country involves the private sector, primarily through sponsorship and direct investments in the clubs. Traditionally, the clubs are private companies that use the pyramidal management system. They are administrated by presidential system, with the president elected by the fans associated and registered in a branch bank (or club membership) system. Some clubs had very real plans to enter in the Brazilian stock market. However, the instability of the clubs and the lack of proper management and accounting practices saw them avoided by serious investors with long-term perspectives.

The management of the biggest clubs in the southeast region of the country has been praised, attracting investment from large companies. However, this is not true for the country as a whole and there is a recognised lack of qualified managers and administrators. The CBF does provide courses for coaches, managers, referees, and others but this is not enough to bring the clubs up to strength.

In Brazil, in addition to the CBF, each state has its own football federation. The Brazilian state federations have different peculiarities in each of the five regions in the country. This is due, in part, to the continental dimensions of the country. Many of the Brazilian states cover larger geographical areas than major European countries. The practice of professional football in all federal units has different weight, values and importance. In some regions, such as Southeast, Northeast, and South the football is stronger than in other areas. In other parts around the world, there is only the national championship, but in Brazil there are state championships and regional championships, which makes the process of management by the clubs much more complicated and creates a troubled calendar and many different negotiations with sponsors. Due to this, Brazilian teams are obliged to participate in a large number of games per season. For example, in 2017 the Corinthians Club in São Paulo were crowned national champions, having played played 71 official matches in the year.

Another peculiarity of Brazil is that CBF takes direct responsibility for the national teams and for the domestic club competitions. It is administering the national competitions and sponsoring the regional ones in each state of the country. On a professional level in Brazil, there is only one national competition that is not organised by the organisation. The event called Rio / São

Paulo / Minas Cup is organised by the participating clubs themselves, and this takes a league format. The league system is not the conventional one of the soccer sports organisation management in Brazil. Traditionally the model is used where the state entities, the federations, organise the regional championships and the Brazilian Confederation of Soccer, a national organisation, organises the national competitions.

How football is offered

In Brazil, as in many other countries, children often playing soccer or, more uniquely to Brazil, futsal, either in their schools or specialised football or futsal academies. The clubs too have teams for ages seven and upwards and these are where the children with the most talent are bought to play. Brazil is not unique in that players recruited during childhood; however, the esteem in which the game is held in Brazil coupled with high inequality and poor prospects for many makes the competition, even at these ages, fierce. "The recognition of the most talented football players is directly related to the increasingly precocious development of the potential presented by the athlete" (Paoli, Silva, and Soares, 2013).

International football clubs such as Paris Saint-Germain, Barcelona, Real Madrid, Inter Milan, Roma, and others have started their own football academies and franchises in Brazil. In the early 2000s, the private companies that bought the rights to use the brand of international clubs, charged each child an average of USD 250, around 900 reais in Rio de Janeiro and São Paulo, to train with and play for these academies. More than 3,000 children are involved in international academies. The national clubs and the private schools (extra class activities) offer football constantly for youth and teenagers in different parts of the country, as we can see on from table 43.1 and 43.2. The local teams have been organising their own football academies, where they scout for talent and future professional players.

As mentioned previously, to understand Brazil one must understand that football is a social and cultural manifestation present across the whole country. However, this is not what we found in our studies on the location of birth of male soccer players selected to play for the Brazilian national team. We find an imbalance in relation to the birth of the players within one of the regions; the Southeast recorded a much larger number than the other geographical regions of the country. We also found 96.82 per cent of occurrences in the Eastern region of the country (Verdini, 2017). This concentration of player birth coincides with the most economically

Table 43.1 Ranking of fans according teams

Ranking	Clubs	Participation	Fans
1.	Flamengo	16.2%	32.5 Mi
2.	Corinthians	13.6%	27.3 Mi
3.	São Paulo	6.8%	13.6 Mi
4.	Palmeiras	5.3%	10.6 Mi
5.	Vasco	3.6%	7.2 Mi
6.	Atlético - MG	3.5%	7.0 Mi
7.	Cruzeiro	3.1%	6.2 Mi
8.	Grêmio	3.0%	6.0 Mi
9.	Internacional	2.8%	5.6 MI
10.	Santos	2.4%	4.8 Mi
–	–	60,3%	120.8 Mi

Source: IBGE/O Lance (2014).

Table 43.2 Ticket sales, attendance figures and income in Brazil 2018

Final Rank	Team	Total of tickets sold	Average Ticket Sold per Game	Number of Games in the Season	Average Filled Space	Total of Stadium Incoming USD	Average Price for Ticket USD
1.	Palmeiras	239.518	29.939	8	69%	4.331.663,48	17,98
2.	Corinthians	250.144	27.793	9	62%	3.895.153,41	15,50
3.	Cruzeiro	188.667	23.583	8	38%	1.018.622,80	5,27
4.	São Paulo	167.094	18.566	9	27%	1.418.820,71	8,37
5.	Grêmio	128.714	18.387	7	33%	1.765.829,13	13,64
6.	Atlético-MG	118.367	14.795	8	64%	497.364,00	4,03
7.	Internacional	115.300	14.412	8	32%	1.256.882,91	10,85
8.	Santos	109.339	12.148	9	47%	1.122.105,45	10,23
9.	Fortaleza	108.767	12.085	9	18%	316.832,40	2,79
10.	Remo	95.637	11.954	8	28%	722.709,22	7,44
11.	Flamengo	75.389	9.423	8	23%	745.846,36	9,61
12.	Paysandu	72.254	9.031	8	49%	576.379,90	7,75
13.	Vasco	65.297	8.162	8	30%	942.399,38	14,26
14.	Fluminense	78.415	7.841	10	18%	909.211,40	11,47
15.	Bahia	66.527	7.391	9	15%	262.208,23	3,72
16.	Botafogo-SP	51.216	7.316	7	29%	646.805,70	12,40
17.	Atlético Paranaense	76.836	6.985	11	17%	537.436,15	6,82
18.	Vila Nova	61.065	6.785	9	23%	237.735,90	3,72
19.	Chapecoense	59.232	6.581	9	29%	398.968,45	5,89
20.	Coritiba	50.345	6.293	8	15%	398.968,45	7,75
21.	Vitória	60.565	6.056	10	17%	221.430,21	3,41
22.	CSA	52.721	5.857	9	33%	221.430,21	3,41
23.	CRB	44.680	5.585	8	31%	265.398,44	4,96
24.	Figueirense	59.600	5.418	11	27%	381.140,97	6,51
25.	Sport	356.993	5.284	7	16%	225.763,70	5,89
26.	Botafogo-PB	52.577	5.257	10	26%	279.367,04	5,27
27.	Ceará	47.468	4.746	10	8%	83.221,98	1,55
28.	Avai	37.694	4.711	8	26%	250.923,92	6,51
29.	Náutico	53.531	4.460	12	9%	26.636,44	8,06
30.	Botafogo-RJ	25.202	4.200	6	9%	149.875,70	5.90

Source: Globoesporte.com (March, 2018).

and financially developed regions of the country. The states with the highest incomes and best economic conditions are better able to provide and maintain the facilities and opportunities to develop football players.

How Brazilian clubs survive

The global demand for elite-level football players is high and the demand far outstrips supply. It is here that many Brazilian clubs have found their place in the market. "Brazil stands out in the global labour market by supplying Brazilian football professionals, especially players, to the entire world" (Soares, 2010).

Sport Club Corinthians Paulista published its financial report for 2017 and its biggest source of financial income revenues generated from the sale and loans of economic rights of players. This outstrips the money made from competing, from TV rights and from sponsors and came to a total of USD 46,102,000 (Corinthians, 2018). That this is the main source of income for one of the most popular clubs of the country emphasises the importance of the training, developing and selling new players to the Brazilian clubs.

The number of transfers of Brazilian players to the international soccer markets shows that Brazilian clubs are major suppliers to external markets; Once again, in 2014, Brazil was the most active country in the transfer market with 1,335 international transfers (FIFA/TMS, 2016). The soccer business has considerable weight in Brazilian exports. Sales of players are among the services exported by the country that increased 34 per cent in 2005 (about USD 6 billion). This group of services represents 40 per cent of Brazilian exports "all Brazilian exports of services generated USD 16 billion in 2005" (Daolio, 2010). The volume of transfers creates a constant production line, or chain, where space for new soccer players appears with the exit of others. This, naturally, leads to questions around the long-term capacity of Brazil to continue to develop players at this rate and around the standards of the players in, and emerging in, the domestic leagues.

Nonetheless, most (if not all) of the professional football clubs in Brazil depend on the financial resources from broadcasting rights. In the last 30 years, this dependency has been exponentially growing; Serie A clubs nowadays see more than 81 per cent of their revenues coming only from TV agreements (Cara, 2017). Moreover, over the last 20 years, the TV channel, Globo TV has developed a semi-monopoly of the main Brazilian championships (Serie A and Copa do Brasil). Table 43.3 highlights figures from 2016, which illustrate the importance, influence and soft power of the TV rights and the companies which purchase the rights.

The Brazilian (national) team

The Brazilian Confederation of Soccer has several teams for male and female players. These are Principal, Olympic, sub 20 and sub 17; with sub 15 only in for male players. The main competition in international football is the men's FIFA World Cup, which has its regionalised elimination phase in relation to the continental confederations and its final phase in a unique tournament in which in 2014 32 teams classified in the continental phases participated. For the final tournament, 13 places were initially reserved for the European continent, five for Africa, four for South America, four for Asia and three for Central and North America; in addition to the seat of the host country and two places were filled in repêchage tournaments between fifth place in Asia, fifth place in South America, fourth place in CONCAF and first in Oceania (FIFA, 2016)

Brazil has been hugely successful on the international stage, claiming five world cups. Brazilian titles were won in 1958 in Sweden; 1962 in Chile; 1970 in Mexico; 1994 in the United

Table 43.3 2016 Serie A clubs revenue

Clubs in the Serie A	2016 – Revenues from					
	TV Rights	Transfer of Players	Sponsorships	Memberships	Tickets	Others
Flamengo	58%	2%	13%	16%	8%	3%
Corinthians	47%	30%	15%	6%	0%	2%
Palmeiras	27%	11%	19%	19%	15%	9%
São Paulo	33%	28%	9%	12%	8%	10%
Grêmio	62%	5%	11%	16%	0%	6%
Atlético MG	41%	25%	10%	9%	9%	6%
Santos	50%	25%	8%	6%	5%	6%
Fluminense	60%	18%	5%	8%	4%	5%
Internacional	53%	7%	12%	22%	4%	2%
Cruzeiro	55%	12%	11%	7%	13%	2%
Vasco	77%	0%	6%	7%	2%	8%
Atlético PR	34%	20%	5%	15%	5%	21%
Botafogo	63%	6%	6%	10%	5%	10%
Bahia	75%	3%	7%	5%	8%	2%
Vitória	81%	2%	8%	4%	2%	3%
Coritiba	52%	8%	9%	16%	10%	5%
Goiás	65%	28%	3%	3%	1%	0%
Chapecoense	41%	8%	9%	9%	3%	30%
Figueirense	59%	18%	10%	9%	2%	2%

Source: Adapted from Cara (2017).

Table 43.4 TV budget incoming from the broadcast rights in 2018 per each Top club

Clubs	Budget in BRL Real Currency	Budget in USD Currency
Corinthians and Flamengo	170 Mi	52.7 Mi
São Paulo	110 Mi	34.1 Mi
Palmeiras e Vasco da Gama	100 Mi	31 Mi
Santos	80 Mi	24.8 Mi
Atlético-MG, Botafogo, Cruzeiro, Fluminense, Grêmio e Internacional	60 Mi	18.6 Mi
Atlético-PR, Bahia, Sport and Vitória	35 Mi	10.85 Mi
Chapecoense	32 Mi	9.92 Mi
América-MG, Ceará e Paraná	28 Mi	8.68 Mi

Source: Zirpoli (2017), Globoesporte.com (2018).

States; and 2002 in Korea/Japan. The Brazilian national team is the only nation to have won titles on all the continents in which the competition was held.

In continental competitions, Brazil has won the Copa America eight times. This is behind the most prolific winner Uruguay (15 titles), and Argentina (14). However, it is ahead of Peru and Paraguay with two titles each and Bolivia, Colombia and Chile as winners in one tournament each. The Copa America is the oldest competition in the world; it had its first match in 1916 in Argentina (CONMEBOL, 2016).

With regard to football in the Olympics, where FIFA restricts the participation of the main selections of its member countries in the Olympic soccer tournament by creating regulations related to age or participation in World Cup tournaments as limiting players, the Brazilian men's soccer team won a gold medal in 2016 in Rio de Janeiro; three silver medals; and one bronze medal. (IOC, 2016). In junior tournaments, Brazil has been crowned five times sub 20 World Champions; the highest holder of titles in this category is Argentina, which won six of the 20 competitions held since 1977 – the competition is held every two years. The other junior (men's) competition organised by FIFA, also every two years, for the junior categories is the sub 17 World Cup, where Brazil has won three of 15 competitions (FIFA, 2016).

In the South American Football Championships for the junior categories, Brazil holds the supremacy of titles in both the sub 20 category where it won 11 of the 27 tournaments held, as well as in the sub 17 category with the Brazilian national team being the winner of 11 of the 16 editions (CAF, 2016).

Brazilian football clubs and governance

According to Moresco and Silva (2017), the main features of good governance practices are related to transparency, accountability, and responsibility. In Brazil, legal frameworks, such as the Law 9.615/98 (called Pelé Law), provide mandatory governance practices to be implemented by football clubs. The same law also provides articles 18 and 18A which obligate clubs to chance or amend their statutes and financial policies in order to be able to receive federal funding and incentives.

Even with these very specific laws, Oliveira et al. (2018) point out that the main Brazilian clubs are often reckless about avoiding conflicts of interest, for example, involving statutory members and their professional activities or companies being hired by their respective clubs and no articles around financial responsibility of the club management. In terms of transparency, it is clear that official information from the clubs needs to be better documented and detailed in their financial accounting (Moresco and Silva, 2017). Even with soft regulation allowing those "resumed" financial statements, the Brazilian football clubs should proactively improve their transparency initiatives not only to make their brand more attractive to the market, but also to create a better relationship with fans and members. In this sense, another professional figure has become essential to the management of professional football teams: the accountant (Moresco and Silva, 2017).

Football in Brazil is closely linked to the entertainment industry, which generates direct and indirect jobs. This means that people rely on football clubs and associated bodies for their employment and livelihoods and so the clubs also bear social responsibilities. As such they need to be correctly managed to keep them financially healthy and sustainable. Moreover, in an "industry" with countless competitors, it is vital to apply more modern and innovative practices so as to improve commercial value and output. As demonstrated by Moresco and Silva (2017), old fashioned, conservative and questionable models of governance are pillars that block the Brazilian clubs from opening their capital to the stock market.

Indeed, there is a consensus that the whole structure of governance used by Brazilian clubs has to be improved. Undoubtedly, statutory and financial gaps result in questions and uncertainties which affect investment in football clubs (Oliveira et al., 2018). However, the recent decade has witnessed clubs striving for more professional administration. One way that this has happened is through the hiring of professional executives to lead their football departments.

One aspect that has not yet been resolved is the administration of the Brazilian national team and the associated football businesses. These have been heavily criticised by the social sectors and widely publicised by the media and have been the target of lengthy CPIs (Concerning the Parliamentary Inquiry) in the Federal Senate. The results are alarming with irregularities in the sale of players, use of brand, expenses, selections and championships, sponsors, excessive expenses in the construction of stadiums, and myriad other issues. The most influential processes investigated were: the parliamentary committee to determine the regularity of the agreement between CBF and NIKE (2001); the Football Mafia CPI created on the basis of Application No. 616 (2015) established one year after the World Cup was held in Brazil. The government tried to follow transactions and paper trails but had a huge problem in accessing data and agreements. It is commonly thought that the information was hidden to avoid transparency in the transactions. Brazilian legislation obliges the annual disclosure of the balance sheets of sports entities, but crucially it does not establish how the document should be set out and this gives licence for some to fudge or obscure facts. Some football clubs do not even divulge their expenses with professional football on the balance sheet.

Verdini (2017) investigated the top ten football clubs in the 2012 Season with a focus on transparency, accountability, and auditor actions. The chaotic situation of economic transparency is a reflection of the other institutions in Brazilian society. In Brazilian football there is little transparency about player transfers, early career contracts, fee payments, and financial reports. Regarding these issues, it is suggested that there is unduly strong interference from the sponsors, especially TV, in the scheduling of games, refereeing assignments, and other potentially dubious practices. The author investigated the publicly available data and found real issues regarding transparency. He found that the accounts of just 50 per cent of the clubs presented the money earned, budget designated for the season, and the expenses associated with professional and amateurs' players. Only 10 per cent of clubs presented the prize money and the amounts collect from the various lotteries. In Brazil the game is supported by the government through a lottery system.

It is easily seen that the amount awarded to football is the second highest amount from the lottery. However, for the FIFA World Cup 2014 the amount awarded hugely exceeded the planned budget (Mataruna and Pena, 2017). Also, the amount for the Olympic and Paralympic committee is unusually high because of the Rio 2016 Games. The Brazilian government invested large sums in an attempt to assure the country's best results in the Games. This level of spending on Olympic-related activities will certainly not be sustained. It is important to mention that the CBF, Brazilian Olympic Committee, and Brazilian Paralympic Committee are private organisations and that they each have several different incomes sources. Sponsorship is one of the more obvious, and lucrative, sources of these incomes. In the Olympic Games or FIFA

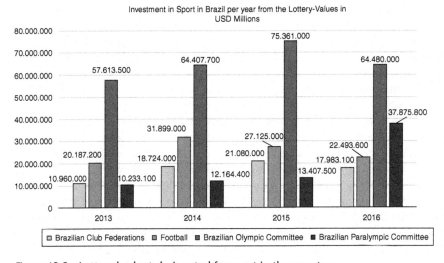

Figure 43.3 Lottery budget designated for sport in the country
Source: Adapted from Caixa (2018).

World Cup, the rules governing sponsorship are extremely prescriptive. In contrast, the national, regional, state, or international tournaments in Brazilian football have more flexibility and far fewer regulations. Often too when rules are broken or flouted, a small fine is the only penalty and so there is little disincentive for pushing boundaries and bending rules around sponsorship in Brazilian football.

Sponsorship in t-shirts

The Brazilian market for sponsorship in t-shirts has recently gone far beyond what has been seen in most other countries with the maximum number of sponsors being crammed into a small space on a t-shirt. For example, Corinthians and Santos openly broke the rules by using up a great deal of space on the shirt. Many fans have reacted negatively, both in person at the stadia and through social media about the proliferation of sponsorship deals on club shirts.

Sometimes too protests on the field have been directed at the brands sponsoring clubs. For example, it is a normal and friendly practice after the match that the players swap shirts. However, during a match between Palmeiras and Portuguesa, Cesar of Palmeiras threw the Portuguesa t-shirt on the grass and stamped on it. At this time, the main sponsor of Palmeiras was Parmalat, a company that sells milk and other food produce. Many fans of Portuguesa are bakers and supermarket owners of Portuguese descent and, because of Cesar's actions, they boycotted Parmalat products for two weeks and caused significant financial damage to the company. Cesar was eventually persuaded to publicly apologise to the fans and players of Portuguesa.

An emerging, and growing, trend in Brazilian football is for marketing teams to flood the field of play after the game has ended to bring t-shirts and caps for the players to wear whilst being interviewed and celebrating. This materiel is, naturally, covered in highly visible sponsor logos.

In some regions of the country, it is usual to find just two strong teams. However, this has created a situation where when one company signs a sponsorship contract with one of those clubs, they generally also sign with the rival as well. This is so that fans of the rival team do not boycott their products or services. A perfect example is where two teams from the South (Grêmio and Internacional) and two from the North East (Bahia and Vitoria) have seen the same sponsor invest in both teams.

After analysing the sponsorship of the main 21 teams in Brazil, we have found a diversity of sport goods companies sponsoring the teams. The Bank Caixa is a government company and has sponsored the 70 per cent of the clubs whilst 10 per cent of clubs received funds from other banks. That one bank sponsors 70 per cent of the major teams in a country is most unusual. The alcohol and tobacco industries are not allowed to sponsor teams in Brazil and players are not allowed to promote products from these industries either. This is one piece of regulation that appears to be firmly adhered to by all.

To illustrate this phenomena of temporary advertisement and overuse of sponsors in Brazilian football we present the case study below.

Temporary advertisement on the t-shirt

One common practice in the country is for small clubs gets new sponsorship deals upon qualification for or entry into the national tournament *Copa do Brasil*. Sometimes a small or local company advertises with the club in the hope that on-pitch success will see their product or services reaching a national audience. Income for the clubs here though is generally small as it reflects the risk that sponsors are undertaking. However, should a club perform well having settled for a small deal, then they have sold their advertising spaces at a lower than market rate value and so they lose out. Here the case of Botafogo is interesting.

Botafogo innovate in sponsorship and they adopted an approach of taking on a new sponsor for every new game with the space on the back of the shirt being used to swap the sponsors. In the last Carioca (regional competition), Botafogo had the following different sponsors occupy the same spot on their shirt in different games: "Casa & Video," "Ricardo Eletro," "99 Taxis," "Netshoes," "Zeex," "Naveg," "Supermercados Unidos." This is seven different sponsors.

The values earned here are not usually high through this format: for two classics last year, Botafogo earned USD 60,000 with the sale of the same spot on the shirt to five different companies. To put this in perspective, the team's star player, Jefferson, earns around USD 80,000 per week. The club admitted at the time that it had little to gain financially from marketing its advertising space in this way, but believed that the good performance of the team and subsequent good publicity and exposure would be enough to boost their next, longer-term sponsorship deal. The values of the current partnership were not disclosed, but it is speculated that Botagato will receive from the "Casa & Video" by the shirt and shorts for two games USD 50,000.

The "Casa & Video" sponsorship was especially novel in that it featured a hair dryer with a promotional price on the back of the shirt, but the chosen piece was reduced in intervals throughout the match: from R\$ 49 (BRL Real, approximately USD 15) to R\$ 39 (BRL Real, approximately USD 12). On the sponsorship bar was a sticker that is applied to the uniform in the locker room and thus allowed the advertisement to be changed at half time to show the new advert and lower price. This caused significant controversy at the time with a politician condemning the strategy and threatening to lodge a complaint with the Procon (Consumer Protection and Defense Authority). However, the advertisement was merely a promotion on the grounds that anyone who phoned to buy the product in the first half was not harmed as they were only charged the same amount of money as those who purchased during the final stage of the match. In other games they advertised mobile phones and other products.

With no master partner a year ago, the priority of Botafogo continues to be to attract long-term, fixed sponsors. To help attract investors, Botafogo has already begun to count on the help of a professional marketing company and has since ceased this aggressive strategy. Now the team has support and sponsorship of a government, state-owned bank as well. However, the political crisis in the country makes this challenging and slows down the process because it is a state bank. A similar strategy was also used by ASA de Arapiraca. They put an advertisement on the club shirt of cars for sale without much information regarding the cars or their price. Any fans or spectators of the game who took an interest found that the shirt was promoting a virtual store that sells cars. In the second half, the team entered with another t-shirt informing fans and spectators that the cars are sold.

In another innovative twist, Corinthians, perhaps mindful of the criticism of their cluttered shirts of previous seasons, kicked off the 2018 season in a relatively plain white shirt with no major sponsor on the front. This would have been extremely unusual anywhere in the modern game but, as we have seen, even more so in Brazil. However, the shirts hid a logo of a Unilever brand product which only emerged onto the shirt as players began to perspire. Fan and media reaction to this gimmick was mixed but it did make international news. In the same week that Corinthians launched this shirt, the Italian club Internazionale (Inter Milan) played an Italian Cup game with the players' social media profile names on the backs of shirts as opposed to the players' surnames or given names. Reaction to this was almost universally negative, but social media appears to be an untapped frontier for Brazilian clubs and so it is surely only a matter of time before similar is seen, and monetised, in the Brazilian game.

Concluding remarks

Football in Brazil is in many ways reflective of the country as a whole. It is growing and generating more income than ever; however, it is also producing larger inequalities than ever and is poorly administrated and often run for the personal gain of those at the top. This is at the expense of many of the players, fans and clubs themselves.

Brazilian football is now potentially at a crossroads and needs to ensure that it takes the right path. There has been unprecedented investment in football and other sports across the whole nation over the last decade because of the Rio Games and the 2016 World Cup. How much of this investment has been misappropriated or squandered is still to be determined. This coupled with the internationalisation of football means that the production line of talent in Brazil could be under threat and clubs that rely on player sales to foreign teams may soon find this avenue exhausted. Many of the major European clubs are opening academies in the country and it is easy to see that top Brazilian talent will be poached by them before they have ever kicked a ball or signed a contract for a Brazilian club. A talent drain at a time when football is available on TV screens, tablets, and smartphones from all over the world could set off a negative spiral in the Brazilian game that sees fans turn away from the familial traditions of supporting a particular team.

The novel uses of sponsorship in the Brazilian game coupled with the nous around ambush marketing tactics and the use of social media demonstrate that there is potential for the clubs to be a success and to bring new ideas to the table. Ideas that will doubtlessly be emulated for far greater profit elsewhere too. This all strengthens the case for better regulation and administration of football clubs in Brazil. They could be vibrant and successful organisations if they were run for the benefit of the clubs themselves. Demand for this change is not going to come from the voices in charge of the clubs, for it is they who have the most to lose from it. It is hoped that this chapter can provide a degree of optimism to the Brazilian game and be used as a starting point for further research.

Note

1 According Matos (2010), circa 11,400,000 of people living in favelas in Brazil. In the Brazilian Portuguese language favela is define for slum. It is a low-income historically area, informal urban area in Brazil. The first favela, now known as *Providência* in the center of Rio de Janeiro, appeared in the late 19th century, built by soldiers who had nowhere to live following the *Canudos* War. Some of the first settlements were called *bairros africanos* (African neighborhoods).

References

Alcântara H. (2006) A magia do futebol. Estudo Av. 20(57):297–313.

Brasil. (2016) *DECRETO Nº 8.642, DE 19 DE JANEIRO DE 2016*. Acesso em 02 de 04 de 2018, disponível em Presidência da República Casa Civil Subchefia para Assuntos Jurídicos: http://www.planalto.gov.br/ccivil_03/_ato2015-2018/2016/decreto/D8642.htm

CAF. Member Associations. [accessed on 10 de agosto de 2016]. Available at: http://www.cafonline.com/en-us/memberassociations

CAIXA. Investimentos da Loteria no Brasil. Available: www.caixa.gov.br

Cancella, K. and Mataruna, L. (2012) Gestão do esporte militar no Brasil: uma análise histórica do primeiro modelo de gestão adotado pela Liga de Sports da Marinha (1915–1919). *PODIUM: Sport, Leisure and Tourism Review* 07/2012b; 1(2):123–147. DOI:10.5585/podium. v1i2.30.

Cara, T. (2017) TV despeja R$ 2,4 bilhões para clubes faturarem como nunca e irem na contramão do país em 2016. Acesso em 02 de 04 de 2018, disponível em ESPN: http://www.espn.com.br/noticia/691384_tv-despeja-r-24-bilhoes-para-clubes-faturarem-como-nunca-e-irem-na-contramao-do-pais-em-2016

CBF (2018) Balanço Financeiro. Available at: https://cdn.cbf.com.br/content/201704/ 20170420183312_0. pdf

CBF (2016) Apresentação. Available at: http://www.cbf.com.br

Conmebol (2016) The history of football. La Paz: Commebol.

Corinthians. (2018) *Sport Club Corinthians Paulista*. Acesso em 02 de 04 de 2018, available at: http://www. futebolpaulista.com.br/Repositorio/Institucional/2017/SCCP2017-Corinthians-10-04-2018.pdf

Cunha, P. R., Santos, C.A., and Haveroth, J. (2017) Fatores Contábeis Explicativos da Política de Estrutura de Capital dos Clubes de Futebol Brasileiros. *Podium Sport, Leisure and Tourism Review*, v. 6, n. 1, Janeiro – Abril.

Ciampa A.C., Leme C,G., and de Souza R.F. Considerações sobre a formação e transformação da identidade profissional do atleta de futebol no Brasil. Divers 17949998 [Internet]. 2010 [citado 10 de agosto de 2016];6(1) Available at: http://search.ebscohost.com/login.aspx?direct=true&profile=ehos t&scope=site&authtype=crawler&jrnl=17949998&AN=54855112&h=46BJZOTRzJPQI4UCowwE ZtLMchq76%2BBz1tv%2FGyEmw2Ibb%2BcGrFhSlQ55YGazDlh9vxNHi2eC28s4z5%2Ff6JNVZA %3D%3D&crl=c.

Daolio J. (2010) As contradições do futebol brasileiro. Futeb Paixão E Política Rio Jan DPA. 2000; 29–44.

De Oliveira, M.C., Borba, J.A., Ferreira, D.D.M., and Lunkes, R.J. (2018) Características da estrutura organizacional dos clubes de futebol brasileiros: o que dizem os estatutos? *Revista de Contabilidade e Organizações*, 11(31), 47–57.

Equipes - Campeonato Brasileiro de Futebol - Série A 2016 - Confederação Brasileira de Futebol [Internet]. Confereção Brasileira de Futebol. [citado 10 de agosto de 2016]. Available at: http://www. cbf.com.br/competicoes/brasileiro-serie-a/equipes/2016.

FIFA, Associations and Confederations [Internet]. FIFA.com. [citado 10 de agosto de 2016]. Available at: http://www.fifa.com/associations/index.html

Globoesporte.com. (2018) O público nos estádios de futebol em 2018. Available at: http://app. globoesporte.globo.com/futebol/publico-no-brasil/

Goellner, S. V. (2005) Mulheres e futebol no Brasil: entre sombras e visibilidades. *Revista Brasileira de Educação Física e Esporte*, 19(2), 143–151.

IBGE. O Lance. As maiores torcidas do futebol brasileiros Available at: http://globoesporte.globo.com/ futebol/noticia/2014/08/pesquisa-fla-tem-maior-torcida-mas-corinthians-encurta-distancia.html.

IBGE (2018) http://www.ibge.gov.br/home/geociencias/cartografia/default_territ_area.shtm ´[accessed on 28 de January 2018]. Available at: http://www.ibge.gov.br

IBGE (2015) Brazil. [accessed on 28 de January 2018]. Available at: http://www.ibge.gov.br

Justo, W.R, Neto R da M.S. Quem são e para onde vão os migrantes no Brasil? O perfil do migrante interno brasileiro. Rev ABET [Internet]. 2009 [citado 10 de agosto de 2016];8(1). Available at: http:// www.ies.ufpb.br/ojs/index.php/abet/article/view/15262.

Kasznar, I.K., Graça F., and Ary S. (2012) A indústria do esporte no Brasil: Economia, PIB e Evolução Dinâmica. São Paulo: M. Books do Brasil.

Mattos, R.C. (2010) Aldeias do mal. Rio de Janeiro: Wayback Machine.

Mataruna-Dos-Santos, LJ, Pena, BG (2017) Mega Events Footprints: past, present and future. Rio de Janeiro. Engenho.

Member Associations | AFC [Internet]. [citado 10 de agosto de 2016]. Available at: http://www.the-afc. com/member-associationx

Member Associations – CONCAF [Internet]. CONCACAF. [citado 10 de agosto de 2016]. Available at: http://www.concacaf.com/member-associations

Moresco, E. and Silva, R. (2017) Avaliação da governança corporativa nos clubes de futebol profissional da série "a" do campeonato brasileiro de 2015, classificados até a 8ª colocação. *Revista Gestão Premium*, 5(1), 64–92.

Murad, M. (2018) Football and society in Brazil. Access in 1 Apr 2018. Available on: http://www.kas.de/ wf/doc/kas_9018-544-2-30.pdf?060830124836

Oceania Football Confederation [Internet]. [citado 10 de agosto de 2016]. Available at: http://www. oceaniafootball.com/ofc/MemberAssociations

Paoli, P.B, Silva, C.D, Soares, A.J.G. Tendência atual da detecção, seleção e formação de talentos no futebol brasileiro. Rev Bras Futeb Braz J. Soccer Sci. 2013; 1 (2):38–52.

Pazzi. Jr, M. (2008) *Entenda o que é a Timemania, nova loteria do futebol*. Acesso em 02 de 04 de 2018, disponível em Estadão: http://esportes.estadao.com.br/noticias/futebol,entenda-o-que-e-a-timemania-nova-loteria-do-futebol,126620

Reis, R.M., Remédios, J.L., Telles, S.C.C., and DaCosta, L.P. (2014) The football business in Brazil: Connections between the economy, market and media. *Motriz: Revista de Educação Física*, 20(2), 120–130. https://dx.doi.org/10.1590/S1980-65742014000200001

Rinaldi, W. Futebol: manifestação cultural e ideologização. Revista Educação Física UEM. 2008; 11(1):167–72.

Rodrigues C. Olhares sobre a cidade: reflexos das alterações urbanas na formação do jogador de futebol ao longo do século XX. Horiz Científico. 2008; 2:1–30.

Sabino, A. (2017) *Com refinanciamento, dívida de clubes da Série A do Brasileiro cai 63%*. Acesso em 02 de 04 de 2018, disponível em Folha de São Paulo: http://www1.folha.uol.com.br/esporte/2017/09/1921733-com-refinanciamento-divida-de-clubes-da-serie-a-do-brasileiro-cai-63.shtml

Soares, D.A.J. (2010) A pátria de chuteiras está desaparecendo? 2010 [citado 10 de agosto de 2016]; Available at: http://www.scielo.br/pdf/rbce/v32n1/v32n1a02.

TaskFleet GmbH. Data and Reports – Insights for success. FIFA TMS GmbH [Internet]. FIFA TMS GmbH. [accessed on 10 de agosto de 2016]. Available at: https://www.fifatms.com/data-reports/.

Torneos | Conmebol.com [Internet]. [citado 10 de agosto de 2016]. Available at: http://www.conmebol.com/es/content/torneos

Tradingeconomics. (2018) Brazil GDP 1960–2018. Accessed on 20 March 2018. Available at: https://tradingeconomics.com/brazil/gdp-growth

UEFA. Federações-membro - Ligas e taças europeias [Internet]. UEFA.com. [citado 10 de agosto de 2016]. Available at: http://pt.uefa.com/memberassociations/leaguesandcups/index.html

UN. Países-membros – ONU [Internet]. ONU Brasil. 2014 [citado 10 de agosto de 2016]. Available at: https://nacoesunidas.org/conheca/paises-membros/

Verdini, L. (2017) Distribuição geográfica do nascimento dos jogadores de futebol de campo. Master Thesis. Rio de Janeiro: EEFD/UFRJ.

Zirpoli, C. (2017) A distribuição dos milhões das cotas de televisão nas Séries A e B de 2017. Acesso em 01 de 04 de 2018, Pernanbuccom: Available at: http://blogs.diariodepernambuco.com.br/esportes/2017/12/04/a-distribuicao-das-cotas-de-televisao-na-serie-a-2018-com-bolo-de-r-13-bilhao/

44

Football in Turkey

Cem Tinaz, Emir Güney, and Ahmet Talimciler

Introduction

Football began gaining popularity in Turkey at the beginning of the twentieth century and remains the most popular sport in the country today. Football in Turkey can be seen as a model of Turkish society, and the developmental history of the game is closely related to the country's economic and political history. Football's relationship with politics was established during the Ottoman Empire, grew during the foundation of the Republic, and persists today; despite Turkey's turbulent history, this relationship has never weakened.

Relations between football and politics have mutual functional characteristics. Political support is imperative for football clubs, especially in regards to solving economic bottlenecks and tax problems. On the other side, the public's interest in football has held great importance for politicians in terms of earning votes. Although Turkish football as we know it was born in Izmir, it spread all across Turkey under the leadership of the Istanbul clubs. Roughly 90 per cent of football fans in Turkey align themselves with Beşiktaş, Galatasaray, or Fenerbahçe teams (called the Big Three); these teams' fan distribution is unprecedented globally.

The transformation of world football since the 1990s has closely affected Turkish football, leaving a profound impact on managerial processes, first and foremost, and on the media and fans' perceptions. Thus, the subject of football in Turkey grows continuously contentious. As the industrialisation of football has come to the forefront, fans have been transformed into consumers and the clubs into companies. Despite Turkish football's huge popularity, targeted success has never been achieved due to managerial problems. Following the match-fixing scandal on 3 July 2011, football (and especially fan culture) suffered a heavy blow. The scandal both increased tensions and strengthened the ties between football and politics.

The purpose of this chapter, divided into three subchapters, is to evaluate Turkish football from different angles. The first subchapter will look at Turkish football from the socio-political perspective, shedding light on the historical development of the game. The second subchapter will focus on the present management structure, while the last subchapter will evaluate the commercial potential and structure of the football sector as a business field.

A socio-political analysis of football in Turkey

Football was first played in 1890 on Ottoman territory at Izmir Bornova by Levantine families. From Izmir, it came to Istanbul and from there spread over the country (Ertuğ, 1977). In Turkey, football held a political identity from the beginning, and its connections to politics have survived regardless of changing ruling powers. For example, the aims of the founders of the Galatasaray Club at Galatasaray Lycée in 1905 were defined as "playing collectively like the Englishmen, possessing a color and a name, [and] defeating the teams who were not Turkish" (Gökaçtı, 2008). Even for Turkish teams who played games at Izmir, though they aimed to underscore their Turkish and Muslim identities, the main goal was to defeat Greek teams. During that period, when competitor teams were losing strength, the teams who the ruling powers favoured could very easily become champions. The relation established between football and the political body would continue its existence in a different form during the occupation years. Games played at this time would take the form of face-to-face settlements in which nationalist fervour reached its peak (Irak, 2013).

Studying football in Turkey consequently implies a review of the social, economic, and communal history of the country. Thus, the period between the formation of the Republic and 1950, the year in which the multi-party system was adopted, can be defined as the single-party years of football. The period between 1950 and 1980, when football expanded across Anatolia through local leagues, can be defined as the period of football club formation and countrywide expansion. From 1980 through to today can be evaluated as the stage in which football was given particular attention by the ruling political powers and the media.

Football's position in the single-party years (1923–1950)

Three days prior to the formation of the Republic in 1923, Turkey played its first national game against the Romanian national team. With the establishment of the Turkish Football Federation (TFF), the start of the national games, and later the organisation of the national league, the nationalisation of football was made complete (Gökaçtı, 2008).

Amateur leagues organised by the Turkish Union of Training Associations (TICI), the first Turkish sports organisation, started to play as of the 1923/1924 season in Istanbul, Ankara, Izmir, Eskişehir, Adana, and Trabzon. Parallel to the organisation of these leagues, a public interest in Turkish football was increasing exponentially (Bora and Erdoğan, 2015). Between 1923 and 1937, apart from the football matches played in the abovementioned counties, private matches, played by the Turkish national team and teams such as Galatasaray, Fenerbahçe, and Beşiktaş contributed considerably to the public's growing interest.

The Republican government evaluated sports as a mass transformative tool early on. In part, it was through settling disputes arising on (and off) the football fields during this time that the government was able to "insert itself" into the sport. For example, in the case of the Galatasaray–Güneş clashes of 1937, Prime Minister İsmet İnönü vehemently condemned all those involved in the violence:" … For our party and our government sports education is a basic education; we will never permit anything to deviate it from the correct direction" (Atabeyoğlu, 1985).

According to the decision taken by the TFF in 1936, as of the 1937 season, the "National Division" games began playing with the participation of the first four teams in the Istanbul league and the first two teams of the Ankara and Izmir leagues, respectively. The National Division games continued until 1950 and were important for the yet-to-be-founded "National League" organization. However, due to economic problems and post-war difficulties, the National Division organization was dismantled and games continued according to the previous league order.

During this period, despite football's popularity in comparison to other sports, it was not considered the most prominent sport by the government. As a matter of fact, the clubs were on shaky ground; consequently, the regional chairman of the Cumhuriyet Halk Party (CHP) was appointed as chairman of the provincial sports departments, a decision which first and foremost impacted Izmir; a number of teams were merged in order for Izmir to be able to compete properly with the Istanbul teams in the National League. The newly formed clubs' offices were opened in CHP buildings (Akın; 2004). It could be argued that as a result of this loss of independence clubs in Izmir and elsewhere lost some vitality; Beşiktaş, Fenerbahçe, and Galatasaray were able to assume pioneering roles in the institutionalisation and popularisation of football.

Club formation and countrywide expansion (1950–1980)

The year 1950 carries significance in Turkish history as the end of the single-party ruling period and the beginning of a new stage. The world of football was about to change dramatically as a consequence of shifts in political power. As a result of developments in Turkey's foreign policy following the country's entry into The North Atlantic Treaty Organisation (NATO), Turkish football took its place in the European group, and on 10 February 1962, Turkey became a member of the Union of European Football Associations (UEFA). Professionalism in sports was approved in 1951, and in 1952, the professional league competition started in Istanbul with the participation of eight teams. The Istanbul league would be followed by the formation of Ankara, Izmir, and Adana professional leagues, but the most remarkable development would be the formation of the Turkish "National League" in 1959. According to Fişek, "the single division "National League" [was] the concrete expression [that] economic integration in Turkey had been completed to a large extent and that football, having entered the contemporary phase, [had] been professionalized." A planned development phase started in 1963, and "conditions [became] suitable for inter-city competition" (Fişek, 1985).

The second football league of Turkey was organised in the 1963/1964 season with the third in 1967/1968. The organisation of these leagues would increase football activity and raise public interest even more. For fans, football had become an indispensable source of pride and entertainment, and the power of football to excite the public continued to catch the attention of both civil and well as military governments. The Turkish Armed Forces who took power in the 27 May 1960 coup accorded utmost importance to the first national game. In fact, at the time, Chief of General Staff Cemal Gürsel explained personally to the national team players how important this game was for the prestige of his management.

Parallel to the increase in the number of teams playing in the Turkish leagues, the demands of the deputies for their regions would increase in kind. These demands can be enumerated on a large scale, ranging from "special" applications for regional teams to tax amnesty of clubs. The primary favour on the demand list requested by the deputies was the removal of divisional disqualification "for one season," first put into force during the 1962/1963 season upon an order given by Prime Minister Ismet Inönü.

The connection between the close relations of the ruling Adalet Party to the Anatolian bourgeoisie and the consolidation of football illustrates football-politics relations in the 1960s. Those in top management positions of the Big Three had been selected from persons close to the ruling party. Faruk Ilgaz, for example, chairman of Fenerbahçe for three consecutive terms, was the Adalet Party regional chairman. Talat Asal, chairman of Beşiktaş, and Suphi Batur, chairman of Galatasaray, were elected as deputies of the Adalet Party and appointed as ministers.

The inseparable alliance between football and politics, the economy, and the media (post-1980)

As for other spheres, 1980 was a milestone year for football in Turkey. After 1980 military rulers, and later the Turgut Özal government, fully realised the cultural importance of football, and accordingly, paid closer attention to the game in order to take full advantage of its societal influence. Football became a valuable component of the "peaceful and reliable" atmosphere the government was attempting to foster in the country; football as entertainment contributed to the de-politicisation process and maintained the social order (Gökaçtı, 2008). Methods for the maintenance of social harmony made their way into the stadiums and football fields; fans' behaviour in the stands and even players' haircuts were closely monitored. It was during this period when the Ankaragücü team was accepted into the first league according to the president and 1980 coup leader Kenan Evren's instruction.

Undoubtedly, Turkish football during the 1980s was affected by shifting global economic and political conditions as well as by the inextricable association established between football and the media. A growing public interest in the sport would lead to the creation of a football media, who kept close contact with football clubs and played a part in reshaping football culture as much if not more so than the teams themselves (Talimciler, 2014).

Together with private TV channels broadcasting in the 1990s, football would contribute to the proliferation of the pay-to-watch system, and as the game became more closely associated with the media, stadiums and the sport in general would adopt a new appearance. During this transformation process, the Twelve Men concept would be created to position fans into consumer positions, and from this point forward, expectations of fans would not be limited to their attendance of the games. Apart from this, they were expected to contribute to football consumption extensively, from purchasing the official products of their teams to buying decoders. Fans' lives and identities became intrinsically connected to their teams; fans became, in essence, "part of" the game (Talimciler, 2015).

As the amount of money circulating in Turkish football increased, bets and match arrangements would be discussed more frequently. On 3 July 2011, the country was shocked by the biggest match-fixing investigation in Turkey's history. During this period, the "necessity to separate persons from institutions" was an idea gaining ground. At the same time, interestingly, all decisions concerning the teams were made with regards to the football economy.

The fact that fans have reflected the public's reactions to the politicisation of football deserves further social study. At present, we are passing through a phase in which stadiums are popping up in every corner of the country and live broadcasting tender values are steadily increasing; however, standards of team success are not being achieved. Moreover, actors in football are contributing, at least as much as politicians are, to the politicisation of football every passing day. Though these close ties between Turkish politics and football could invite scrutiny, one could look at things another way. Turkey is one of the few countries which directly supports its teams; the government funds the building of new stadiums, for example, a job usually designated to individual municipalities in other countries. The following sections will now take a closer look at the internal legal and structural governance of Turkish football.

Legal status of the Turkish Football Federation

The Turkish Football Federation (TFF) became a member of *Fédération Internationale de Football Association* (FIFA) in 1923, becoming its 26th member. TFF then became a member of the Union of European Football Associations (UEFA) in 1962 (Tff.org, 2017). TFF is the only football federation in the world founded by a law of the state. Although the federation was established in 1923, in 1992 The Law of Establishment and Duties of the Turkish Football Federation (Law 3813, 1992) was entered into force by the Turkish government to separate football from all other sports federations by making it a formal, autonomous entity. In 2009, Law 3813 was replaced by Law 5894 (2009), which had the same name but with updated articles. According to Law 5894 Article 1, all football activities and bodies are to be established, run, structured, and improved by the TFF. All other sports federations are governed under the authority of the Youth and Sports Ministry.

Football's global governing body, FIFA, encourages national football federations under its realm to be private non-governmental institutions rather than public governmental institutions. Articles 14, 15, and 19 of the FIFA Statutes (2016) state that member associations are obliged to manage their affairs independently, away from undue interference from political bodies or third-parties. The independence issue was raised, for example, in the 2014 Nigerian Football Federation (NFF) case in which the NFF was suspended by FIFA on account of government interference in the election of the federation's president and executive body (Fifa.com, 2014).

In the case of Turkey, there is continuous debate over the status of the TFF as a public or private institution. According to Özelçi (2010), although Law 3813 Article 1 clearly states that the TFF "is subject to private law provisions," the public legislative body has the right to establish a legal entity in order to perform public services that require expertise and technical competence, such as the governance of football. Thus, the abovementioned article is not enough to compensate for the fact that the TFF carries the responsibility of providing public services, such as organising sports events and competitions, and improving football in Turkey as a whole; it thus continues to operate as a public rather than private legal entity. From a different angle, Petek and Ertaş (2011) suggest that the TFF cannot be considered purely a public or a private entity and should instead be understood as an institution with its own, unique structure, a *sui generis* entity.

Domestic structure and the organisation of football

This distinction of originality bears importance when considered with the fact that the decision-making bodies (i.e., general assembly and executive committee) and legal committees with sporting and economic disciplinary sanctioning powers (i.e., disciplinary bodies, the Arbitration Committee, and Club Licensing Committee) are influential in the management and governance of Turkish football. Their legal and structural establishment methods confirm their level of impartiality from government influence and intervention.

Macro-level management issues aside, it is also essential to analyse the micro-level governance rules and applications of a federation to understand the logic behind business decisions made by the executive and disciplinary bodies. According to Statutes Article 21(a) (Turkish Football Federation, 2008), the general assembly is the highest authority in the decision-making process within the TFF. Article 9 of the Statutes states that the members of the general assembly are as follows: clubs that compete in the professional football leagues of Turkey; the Confederation of Turkish Amateur Sports Clubs; the Professional Footballers Association; the Association of Football Coaches; the Association of Active Football Referees and Observers; disabled sports federations that have football activities in their structures; individuals who have duties at FIFA or UEFA executive committees; individuals who have worked at FIFA or UEFA committees for over ten years; previous presidents of the Turkish Football Federation; and individuals who would be accepted as members of the general assembly.

Although members of the TFF general assembly cover a broad range of the stakeholders, delegate numbers and their voting power vary considerably. This list of delegates shows an irrationally high distribution of voting power among the top-level clubs and for the professional clubs in general. For example, according to the Article 22, six delegates from the general assembly and the president of each club from the Turkish professional league top level (TFF Super League) hold a 42 per cent voting power percentage, whereas all other general assembly members hold between 1 per cent and 18 per cent (Turkish Football Federation, 2008).

Excepting decisions to change the statutes (which require two-thirds of the total votes), all decisions made by the TFF general assembly are made by simple majority. According to Article 23 (Turkish Football Federation, 2008), these decisions may include approving the budget, financial reports, or annual reports prepared by the executive committee, or giving authorisation to the executive committee to buy/sell assets belonging to the federation. When this voting power distribution is considered, it can be seen that these financial and administrative decisions must always be in line with the top two professional leagues' wishes, since together they have more than enough votes to pass or block a decision proposed within the general assembly. This improper distribution of power, given to a total of only 34 clubs, causes an elitist approach to be taken toward TFF decision-making; conversely, a "public-benefit approach" would make the improvement and reach of football countrywide a top priority. It seems that the only way to redistribute voting power is to change the statutes from which the assembly draws its professional clubs' power.

The only association that holds influence regarding Super League issues but is not represented in the general assembly as an institution is the Union of Clubs. Although the name of the institution suggests a union of all clubs, membership is exclusive to the 18 Super League clubs represented by their respective presidents. The union's influence comes from the fact that in 2015 the board of directors decided to incorporate the union and, with the approval of the TFF, gain control of the Super League using a similar model to the English Premier League (TTF.org, 2015). This decision has yet to materialise.

Legal and administrative decision-making processes of the federation

The highest decision-making authority of the TFF may be the general assembly, though smaller, 15-member executive committees are elected every four years to run the daily and short-term administrative processes (Art. 27). The elected executive committee votes to elect a president during their first meeting (Art. 34). The president has the power to choose individually the members of the disciplinary bodies, the Arbitration Committee, the Club Licensing Committee, the Ethics Committee, and the presidential committee of the Dispute Resolution Chamber, and approves the arbitrators that are offered to the chamber (Art. 35.1y). These legal bodies of the TFF are responsible for ensuring that the system runs smoothly. Each committee has regulations which circumscribe the range of its jurisdiction and functions. The statutes give each of these legal committees the power to work independently but also enforce the terms of office, limiting them to those of the executive committees (Art. 55, 57, 59, 60, and 61). For example, in the case of a resignation within the executive committee or the term of office ends for an executive committee member, these legal bodies' terms of office also end. This interconnectedness raises the question of a lack of independence regarding decision-making processes since these bodies have jurisdiction over the federation committees' decisions as well as those of the executive committee.

A significant discussion arises around the Arbitration Committee of the TFF. In 2011 a clause was added to Article 59 of the Constitution of the Turkish Republic which stated that "only mandatory arbitration can be used regarding the administrative and disciplinary decisions on the sports activities of the sports federations ….” It also stated that the decisions made by the arbitration bodies were final and could not be appealed in a court of law (Constitution of Turkish Republic, 1982). Essentially, this clause grants uncontrolled and unsupervised judiciary power to a disciplinary body of a sports federation that is not elected but assigned by an individual, namely the federation president. The only protection given to the legal committee members is that a member may not be relieved of duty unless that member resigns or withdraws voluntarily.

The league and club structures

Turkish professional football has four league divisions: the Super League with 18 clubs; the First Division with 18 clubs; the Second Division with two groups (Red Group and White Group) with 18 clubs; and the Third Division with three groups (Group 1, 2, and 3), each consisting of 18 clubs. Each league has its annual statutes which lay out the rules and regulations of how it should be run. Below the professional levels is the national amateur level, called the Regional Amateur League. Below that exist leagues for each city, depending on a city's population and the number of teams per district in a town. Besides professional and amateur football leagues, there is also the Turkish Cup, the Super Cup, the U-21 League, the Development League, the Women's League, the Beach Football League, and the Futsal League. None of these leagues is a formal legal entity but rather a competition run by the TFF on an annual basis. Therefore, any administrative or commercial decisions about these leagues are made by the TFF's executive committee and related sub-committees.

Football clubs in Turkey are founded as associations and are subject to the Associations Law. Similar to the TFF, all football clubs have general assemblies that elect executive committees to run the club. According to Devecioğlu et al. (2012), due to the fast-growing nature of the sports industry, it was not feasible for associations to manage the budgets, and, therefore, led clubs to form commercial entities within their associations. Devecioğlu suggests that the most important reason for the clubs to go public was to sell shares to garner funds. Historically, the four most prominent and successful clubs – Beşiktaş, Fenerbahçe, Galatasaray, and Trabzonspor – have been quoted on the Istanbul Stock Exchange.

The demand for football in Turkey

The fact that in Turkey, during the period before the Republic, young people's growing interest in football resulted in the foundation of the first clubs and mass participation provided football a crucial competitive advantage over other sports. Football has always been the most popular sport in Turkey. On the other hand, compared with leading football countries such as Germany, Italy, and England, total participation in Turkish football could be considered low. The latest numbers according to the TFF (2012–2013) reveal that the total number of licenced football players under the age of 19 is 205,656 whereas the total number of licenced players above the age of 19 is 67,726; Turkey's total population is around 80 million with more than 25 million people younger than 25 (TTF.org, 2013). These 273,382 players are representatives of 4,973 football clubs; the clubs have 12,878 teams in different age groups.

The “Football Professionalism Regulations,” which paved the way toward professionalism in Turkish football, were compiled and administered in 1951. Starting in the 1958/1959 season, all leagues of the TFF began to be organised and played within the framework of these regulations (Devecioğlu, 2008). The football leagues have acquired a completely professional structure since the 1960s. This transformation has further crystallised the difference between professional and amateur clubs. As a result, the expansion of the infrastructure to a broad base and the decrease of the number of teams parallel to the age increase, as seen in Europe, reveal a contrary develop-ment trend in Turkey. The number of teams with professional status in Turkey is more than three times higher than the number of professional teams in Germany. This situation reveals that, in fact, professionalism was misunderstood in Turkish football. The fact that neo-liberal policies adopted after 1980 especially have also been approved by Turkish football leagues has expedited free market and industrialisation processes in football. As a consequence of this transformation, amateur football teams, which were providers of opportunity for the greater public and crucial for the expansion of football, were not able to continue their activities (Gökaçtı, 2008). The constriction encountered at the primary level of football was reflected in the upper structures as well; it became difficult to find a sufficient number of qualified Turkish football players; profes-sional football teams proceeded, then, to recruit players from foreign countries. The efforts on the part of the TFF to find a solution to this problem, led to the signing of highly controver-sial decisions. The TFF, which on the one hand has prioritised individual team infrastructure-building in order to strengthen competition between national teams, and on the other hand aims to improve Turkey's standing internationally, has changed regulations regarding the participation of foreign football players nine times over the past 12 years (Altinordu, 2017). Currently, there is no limit on how many foreign players can be on the pitch at one time. In October 2017, for example, in a Galatasaray-Konyaspor match, all of Galatasaray's starting 11 were foreign players (Eurosport.com.tr, 2017). This practice of recruiting players from abroad has brought financial borrowing along with it, which will be further discussed in the next section.

Income streams

According to some analysts, from the financial value point of view, Turkish football is one of the outstanding leagues of Europe. In its 2016 football research, the TAVAK Foundation pointed out that the size of the football sector in Turkey is at almost 1 billion Euro (Fortuneturkey.com, 2016). This size calculation took into consideration TV broadcasting rights, sponsorship revenues, gate revenues, and bets revenues. However, it is obvious that these calculations were done without taking into account current club debts. Lately, even though broadcasting revenues especially are increasing remarkably, the borrowing increase remains higher than the revenue increase. This issue and Turkish professional football's sources of revenue will be evaluated in the following section.

Football broadcasting in Turkey and media rights

The Super League games began in the 1959/1960 season and have maintained their status until today. The 1971 match between Karşıyaka and Istanbulspor, broadcasted by TRT, was the first live match to be aired on Turkish television. Until the pool system had been appro-priately implemented, some clubs aired their matches within the frame of their contracts with broadcasting companies (Aljazeera.com.tr, 2016). The broadcast sales model became dominant as the pool system was implemented for the first time in 1996 through a three-year contract offer submitted by Cine 5, a private broadcast company, on the initiative of the TFF. The chan-nel bought the broadcast rights to the Turkish league for that season, and the pool system was implemented. For three consecutive years, Cine 5 broadcasted matches by paying $40, million, $45 million, and $50 million, respectively. Through the last tender, which was made on November 2nd, 2016, Turkey's largest pay-tv operator Digiturk acquired Turkish league football broadcasting rights for a five-year period. Digiturk won the bid for the mobile broadcast rights of both the Super League and the TFF 1st League by paying $500 million per year for five seasons, starting with the 2017/2018 season. Digiturk pays yearly $600 million (including 18 per cent VAT) for the acquisition of the rights between 2017 and 2022. Since Digiturk was the one and only bidder for the available "A Package" (which includes the right to broadcast live all Super League matches and sell these broadcasts on the international market), the tender lasted only ten minutes with no auction (Hürriyetdailynews.com, 2016). As a result of the amount paid for the broadcasting rights, the revenue of the clubs increased by 321 per cent compared to the last tender in 2009; consecutively the Super League became the sixth most expensive league in Europe (Turan, 2017).

At this point it should also be mentioned that in 2015 BeIn Media Group, the sports arm of Al Jazeera, bought Digiturk. In the past, Cukurova Group owned 53 per cent of Digiturk, but its shares were seized by Turkey's Savings Deposit Insurance Fund in 2013 over unsettled debts (*Financial Times*, 2015). According to calculations made by football economist Tuğrul Akşar based on Digiturk's subscriber numbers and prices paid by users for football content, membership revenues are estimated to reach a total of $450 million against the paid amount of $600 million (Akşar, 2016). When advertising and sponsorship revenues are added to this figure, the total revenue is estimated to reach approximately $500 million. BeIn Sports, with a network encompassing almost 40 countries, would provide additional revenues by selling broadcasting rights of the Turkish Super League overseas.

Match-day income

A new ticketing system was introduced in Turkey during the 2014/2015 season as a result of Law no. 6222 on the prevention of violence and unethical behaviour in sports. This system uses a card called "Passolig" in place of traditional tickets. All football fans including seasonal cardholders must have this card to enter the stadiums. Unfortunately, Super League crowds were heavily impacted by the new controversial system, which was met with resistance from a significant number of fans. On the other hand, the aims of the new system were declared by the government as the following:

- Prevention of violence among fans;
- Acknowledgment of violent fans and limiting of their access to the stadiums;
- Increasing the number of women and children in the stadiums;
- Ending the ticketing black–market.

No one can deny that the Turkish Super League is dominated by the Big Three teams (Beşiktaş, Fenerbahçe, and Galatasaray) in both sportive and financial aspects. There are plenty of reasons why these teams dominate the league and why their revenues differ considerably from those of the other teams. These reasons could include sportive history and success, the conditions of the stadiums, squad depth, and so on.

In the 2014/2015 season, 104,000 season ticket holders filled stadiums to watch the Super League games; that number dropped to 77,500 in the 2015/2016 season. Regarding average attendance, Fenerbahçe ranked first with an average attendance number of 24,958 followed by Galatasaray with an average of 18,745. Similarly, in the 2015/2016 season. Fenerbahçe received the highest match revenue ($31.2 million) followed by Galatasaray ($30.6 million). Beşiktaş followed these clubs with an income of $15.5 million. However, the team following the Big Three (Atiker Konyaspor) received only $2 million (Ekolig, 2016). These numbers prove the dramatic difference in success between the Big Three and other teams in the Super League.

Sponsorships

As a result of their popularity and success, the Big Three receive the highest share of sponsorship income. However, clubs such as Antalyaspor, Atiker Konyaspor, and Medipol Basakşehir FK increase their commercial revenues by stadium renovation, high performance in the league, and increased spectator attendance numbers. As stated in the Ekolig Report (2016), in 2014/2015 season, four of the 18 clubs in the Super League had a naming sponsor (Caykur Rizespor, Kardemir Karabukspor, Medipol Basakşehir FK, Atiker Konyaspor) and three clubs acquired a sponsor for stadium naming rights (Turk Telekom Arena, Vodafone Arena, Torku Arena). In the 2015/2016 season, four clubs had a naming sponsor (Caykur Rizespor, Medicana Sivasspor, Medipol Basakşehir FK, Atiker Konyaspor), while five clubs acquired a sponsor for stadium naming rights (Turk Telekom Arena, Vodafone Arena, Ulker Stadium Fenerbahçe Sukru Saracoğlu Sports Complex, Torku Arena, Didi Stadium).

The sponsorship deal between Beşiktaş and Vodafone is worth closer examination. It is reported that Vodafone is paying $145 million in total to Beşiktaş for the stadium naming rights sponsorship (10+5 years) and shirt sponsorship (3+2 years). On the other hand, the total of the stadium naming rights agreement executed by and between Fenerbahçe and Ulker in the 2015/2016 season (in effect for ten years) is $90 million. Galatasaray acquires $6.5 million per year through a stadium naming right sponsorship agreement with Turk Telekom Arena, which entered into force as of the season 2009/2010 and will be in effect for 10 years (Ekolig, 2016).

Infrastructure and stadia development

As a result of the social, political, and economic potential of football, the current AK Party (AKP) government is putting tremendous effort into the construction of new football stadiums. At this point Turkey has no confirmed plans to host any high-profile international football competitions in the near future, although it did bid (along with Germany) to host Euro 2024. Nevertheless, AKP is funding the construction of 25 football stadiums in 23 different cities around the country with a total budget around $1 billion (Aksan, 2014). In a country in which football spectatorship is suffering, one could speculate that Turkey's stadia development is intended to invigorate fan culture, boost capacity, and prepare for the hosting of international events down the road.

Financial wealth

Financial indicators denote that despite the increase of revenues during the last period, the borrowing level of Turkish football has reached an almost unmanageable level. As mentioned in the Football Productivity Report prepared by Turan (2017), even the income obtained by selling all assets of the 18 Super League teams would cover only 55 per cent of total team debt. The yearly loss of the Turkish football clubs, which was 41 million euro in 2011, increased five-fold in four years, reaching 204 million euro in 2015. On the other hand, the risk of debt increase has been present for years. According to the UEFA's inspection, in 2011, due to having violated Article 65 of the UEFA Club License and Fair Play stating that "football clubs should not have delayed debts," and Article 66 which states that "there should be no delayed debts to the employees and/ or tax offices," Beşiktaş was sent to the disciplinary council and was afterwards disqualified from the European Cups for one year; in addition, the team had to pay indemnities for having violated the Financial Fair Play rules. The main reason behind the teams' such high level of borrowing is the fact that their player profiles are based on player transfer (Altinordu, 2017). According to the Sefton (2015), the testimonials and salaries paid by the Turkish clubs represent 89 per cent of their total revenues. Thirteen of the 18 clubs participating in the Super League are facing loss of revenue, and, with taxes included, this loss reaches 30 per cent. At this point, the government may intervene, and there are likely to occur actions which warrant discussion. For example, through tax amnesty (regularly implemented by the government), Galatasaray's tax debt of $43.6 million was reduced to $1.79 million in 2011; $66.4 million was reduced to $6.64 million in 2016; $86.3 million in tax debt was reduced to $5.4 million in 2017 (Sözcü.com.tr, 2017).

In spite of tax amnesty, various sponsorships, and the Financial Fair Play Rules implemented by the UEFA, the three biggest Turkish teams' debt (that of Galatasaray, Beşiktaş, Fenerbahçe) continues to increase. Given the data provided by the clubs' council sessions and the Public Enlightenment Platform (KAP), the total debt of these clubs is around 1.25 billion euro (t24.com.tr, 2017).

At this point, developments made by Beşiktaş in 2012 (one year following its ban from the European Cups) represent a positive example. Beşiktaş was able to reach financial stability due to the management model it was obliged to adopt, and new transfer policies maintained a low rate of revenue for football player salaries (Forbes, 2017). When adding a stadium project sponsored by the government, two consecutive championships, and a sponsorship agreement with Vodafone to these developments, Beşiktaş succeeded for the first time to get out of debt deadlock. However, there is one point worth considering noted in the club's 2017 KAP report: "As of May 31st, 2017, the short-term obligations of the Group are exceeding the short-term assets by $150,5 million; the equity is negative $145,5, and that according to Article 376 of the Turkish Trade Law, having negative equity is considered being 'deep in debt'." These circumstances reveal that there are important uncertainties which may create serious doubts regarding the sustainability of the Group (BJK Futbol Konsolide, 2017).

Conclusion

Turkish football has a deeply rooted history stretching over 100 years. Teams Galatasaray and Fenerbahçe were founded in the early part of the century and are continuously supported by political powers, followed by team Beşiktaş; each team has an extensive fan base practically unparalleled in the world. The economic and social dynamics existent in 1900, when the first football clubs were founded, made it imperative for clubs to become dependent on government subvention for survival. On the other hand, political powers, having noticed the effects of football on the populace, were inclined from time to time to use football as a means of reaching different targets. This situation led to the creation of a relationship between political powers and football institutions, a relation beyond sports and one based on mutual interests. Endless fluctuations in the course of the social, political, and economic life of Turkey necessitated the continuance of this relation.

The formation of teams in Anatolia and football's expansion over the country dates back to the 1960s. The divide between professional and amateur sports clubs widened, especially after 1970. The adoption of a neo-liberal approach in Turkish football was parallel to world developments after 1980: capital dependency and the commercialisation of football became all-important. Professionalism standards adopted by Turkish football in line with world football also brought along structural deterioration.

In the 1990s revenues began to increase. However, despite the fact that broadcasting, advertising, sponsorships, and tribune income provided essential opportunities for the sport, football's structural system deficiencies made possible the inefficient use of this income and enabled poor management, pushing Turkish football to a level of debt from which it has been nearly impossible to recover (Akşar, 2013). Although according to some analysts the financial value of the Super League and some Turkish teams seem to be up to European standards, the bottleneck of amateur football, attachment of football to political agendas, and dependency of professional teams on overseas availabilities are collectively dragging Turkish football closer to a severe crisis. It is necessary at this time to halt structural changes and, as some teams have done, revise management strategies.

References

Akın,Y. (2004) *Yavuz ve Gürbüz Evlatlar*, Istanbul: İletişim Publications.

Aksan, S. (2014) *23 Şehir, 25 Süper Stadyum*. [online] Retrieved from: http://www.gsb.gov.tr/HaberDetaylari/1/15020/23-sehir-25-super-stadyum.aspx

Aksar, T. (2016) *Digitürk bu parayı bu lig'den nasıl çıkartacak?* [online] Retrieved from: https://www.dunya.com/kose-yazisi/digiturk-bu-parayi-bu-ligden-nasil-cikartacak/341448

Akşar, T. (2013) *Krizdeki Futbol*. Istanbul: Literatür Publications.

Aljazeera.com.tr, (2016) *1996'dan 2016'ya Türk futbolunun yayıncılık tarihi*. [online] Retrieved from: http://www.aljazeera.com.tr/haber/1996dan-2016ya-turk-futbolunun-yayincilik-tarihi

Altınordu, A. (2017) Yabancı Sınırı. *Sokrates Dergi*, (31), 51–57.

Atabeyoğlu, C. (1985) Cumhuriyet Döneminde Spor Politikası. In: *Cumhuriyet Dönemi Türkiye Ansiklopedisi*. Istanbul: İletişim Publications,Vol. 8, 2187–2197.

BJK Futbol Konsolide, (2017) *Beşiktaş Futbol Yatırımları Sanayi ve Ticaret A.Ş. ve Bağlı Ortaklıkları 31 Mayıs 2017 tarihi itibariyle konsolide finansal tablolar ve bağımsız denetçi raporu*. [online] Available at: https://www.kap.org.tr/tr/sirket-bilgileri/genel/4028e4a241a25fcb0141a276cda10189

Bora, T., Erdoğan, N. (2015) Dur Tarih, Vur Türkiye. In: R. Horak, W. Reiter, T. Bora (eds), *Futbol ve Kültürü*, 8th ed. Istanbul: İletişim Publications, pp. 223–242.

Constitution of Turkish Republic. (1982) *Article No. 59*. [online] Available at: http://www.anayasa.gov.tr/icsayfalar/mevzuat/1982anayasas%C4%B1.html

Devecioğlu, S. (2008) Türkiye'de Futbolun Kurumlaşması. *Gazi Üniversitesi İletişim Kuram ve Araştırma Dergisi*, 26, 373–396.

Devecioğlu, S., Çoban, B., Karakaya, Y., and Karataş, Ö. (2012) Türkiye'de Spor Kulüplerinin Şirketleşmeye Yönelimlerinin Değerlendirilmesi. *Beden Eğitimi ve Spor Bilimleri Dergisi*, [online] 10(2), 36–38. Available at: http://dergiler.ankara.edu.tr/dergiler/17/1770/18731.pdf

Ekolig (2016) *Football Economy Report for 2014-2015 / 2015-2016 Seasons*. [online] Istanbul: Aktif Bank, Available at: http://www.aktifbank.com.tr/tr/hakkimizda/basinodasi/ekolig

Ertuğ, A.R. (1977) *Türkiye Futbol Tarihi: 1890–1923*. Ankara: Beden Terbiyesi Bölge Müdürlüğü Publications, pp. 54–60.

Eurosport.com (2017) *Galatasaray'da tarihe geçen kadro*. [online] Available at: http://tr.eurosport.com/futbol/super-lig/2017-2018/galatasaray-da-tarihe-gecen-kadro_sto6366690/story.shtml

FIFA (2016) *FIFA Statutes*. [online] Available at: http://resources.fifa.com/mm/document/affederation/generic/02/78/29/07/fifastatutsweben_neutral.pdf

FIFA.com (2014) *FIFA Emergency Committee suspends Nigeria Football Federation*. [online] Available at: http://www.fifa.com/governance/news/y=2014/m=7/news=keep-pending-fifa-emergency-committee-suspends-nigeria-football-federa-2402265.html

Financial Times (2015) *Al-Jazeera's Bein buys Turkish pay-TV network Digiturk*. [online] Retrieved from: https://www.ft.com/content/d524cdce-2a17-11e5-acfb-cbd2e1c81cca

Fişek, K. (1985) *100 Soruda Türkiye Spor Tarihi*. İstanbul: Gerçek Publications, pp. 146–149.

Fortuneturkey.com (2016) *Türkiye'de futbol ekonomisi 1 milyar euroya yakın*. [online] Available at: http://www.fortuneturkey.com/turkiyede-futbol-ekonomisi-1-milyar-euroya-yakin-28264#popup

Gökaçtı, M.A. (2008) *Bizim için oyna: Türkiye'de Futbol ve Siyaset*. Istanbul: İletişim Publications.

Hurriyetdailynews.com (2016) *Digitürk wins giant tender for Turkish football broadcasting rights for five years*. [online] Available at: http://www.hurriyetdailynews.com/digiturk-wins-giant-tender-for-turkish-football-broadcasting-rights-for-five-years.aspx?pageID=238&nID=106363&NewsCatID=345

Irak, D. (2013) *Hükmen Yenik! Türkiye'de ve İngiltere'de futbolun sosyo-politiği*. Istanbul: Evrensel Print.

Law 3813 (1992) *The Law of Establishment and Duties of the Turkish Football Federation*. [online] Available at: http://www.hukuki.net/kanun/3813.15.text.asp

Law 5894 (2009) *The Law of Establishment and Duties of the Turkish Football Federation*. [online] Available at: http://www.tff.org/Resources/TFF/Documents/TFF-KANUN-STATU/TFF-Kurulus-ve-Gorevleri-Hakkinda-Kanun.pdf

Özelçi, A. (2010) *Türkiye Futbol Federasyonu'nun Türk hukukundaki yeri*. Ankara: Seçkin Publications, p. 97.

Petek, H. and Ertaş, Ş. (2011) *Spor Hukuku*. Ankara: Yetkin Publications, p. 197.

Sefton, P. (2015) *The European Club Footballing Landscape: Club Licensing Benchmarking Report Financial Year 2015*. [online] Available at: http://www.uefa.com/MultimediaFiles/Download/Tech/uefaorg/General/02/42/27/91/2422791_DOWNLOAD.pdf

Sozcu.com.tr (2017) *Beşiktaş ve Fenerbahçe de vergi indiriminden faydalandı*. [online] Available at: http://skor.sozcu.com.tr/2017/03/28/besiktas-ve-fenerbahce-de-vergi-indiriminden-faydalandi-606855/

Turkish Football Federation (2008) *Statutes* [online] Available at: http://www.tff.org/Resources/TFF/Documents/TFF-KANUN-STATU/TFF-Statusu.pdf

T24.com.tr (2017) *Dört büyüklerin borcu 6,5 milyar liraya dayandı*. [online] Available at: http://t24.com.tr/haber/dort-buyuklerin-borcu-65-milyar-liraya-dayandi,405675

Talimciler, A. (2014) *Türkiye'de Futbol Fanatizmi ve Medya İlişkisi*. İstanbul: Bağlam Publications.

Talimciler, A. (2015) *Sporun Sosyolojisi Sosyolojinin Sporu*. İstanbul: Bağlam Publications.

TFF.org (2013) *Faal lisanslı amatör futbolcu sayısı yüzde 18 arttı*. [online] Available at: http://www.tff.org/default.aspx?pageID=470&ftxtID=18363

TFF.org (2017) *TFF Tarihçesi 2*. [online] Available at: http://www.tff.org/default.aspx?pageID=294

TFF.org (2015) *TFF ile Kulüpler Birliği toplandı*. [online] Available at: http://www.tff.org/default.aspx?pageID=285&ftxtID=22513

Turan, Ö. (2017). Futbol Verimlilik Raporu: Gizli İflas. *Forbes Türkiye*, (10), pp. 22–38.

45

Management of football in India

Gautam Ahuja and Eric C. Schwarz

Background

Football in India has had a continuous history that goes back to the nineteenth century. During colonial rule, the British regimental team and missionaries introduced the game in India. As Calcutta was the capital at the time, the game became immensely popular in the Eastern Metropolis regions (Kapadia, 2001). The All India Football Federation (AIFF) was established in 1937 with the objective of shifting the emphasis from local to national, as well as to create standards for practice and competition (Dimeo, 2001).

At the international level, the Indian national team started touring in the 1930s. They qualified for and participated in all Olympic Games until the 1960s, finishing a respectable fourth in the 1956 Olympics. India also qualified for the 1950 Brazil World Cup but the long sea journey and issue of barefoot players forced India to pull out of the tournament (Kapadia, 2001). At the Asian level, India was among the top three during this era, including winning Gold at the Asian Games in 1951 and 1962.

The period from 1948 to 1962 provided many highlights to demonstrate that India had the potential to realise its footballing vision. Thereafter, India's football fortunes took a turn for the worse. The AIFF failed to establish any national unity with equal representation to all states being problematic. The political and economic changes in the country along with traditionalism was responsible for holding back the progress of the sport (Dimeo, 2001). As many of the footballers were from marginalised backgrounds, there was a lack of scientific consciousness among them and even the coaches or administrators made no concrete efforts to remain afloat with the modern game developments. This combined with the rapid improvement in the efficiency of other Asian countries made the sport competitive at the Asian level. Many of these countries adopted a professional setup and heavily invested in infrastructure and coaching. The supremacy of these countries made it difficult for an old powerhouse such as India to maintain a competitive edge. All these practices were a reflection of amateurism that strictly viewed football as a pastime.

The AIFF was unable to adopt modern sport management practices. The 50-minute match rule for the domestic league during the 1950s made the team unsuitable for foreign competitions. India's insistence on playing barefoot at the World Cup in 1950 was a major setback for the sport in the country. From a management perspective, there was little formalisation or adoption of legal restrictions and protections. Despite a popular club culture, there was little accountability, which inevitably led to the serious accusation of irregularities. As the AIFF failed to take concrete steps to spread football throughout the country, the BCCI (parent body for cricket) established the National Cricket Academy to improve the grassroots setup in the country. The success at the 1983 Cricket World Cup was a watershed moment for sports in the country, resulting in a cricket revolution.

In the early 1980s, the AIFF attempted to improve the footballing standard and the most noteworthy event was the inauguration of the Nehru Cup in 1982. The event attracted participation from full-strength teams from around the world; however, the move gradually faded owing to the lack of funds and planning. India's quest for foreign coaches without far-sighted planning added to footballing woes in India (Ray, 2006). With the arrival of television in the 1980s, Indian fans were for the first time exposed to foreign football, which highlighted the poor standard of football in the country. This gradually resulted in declining interest from spectators towards the national team and domestic league.

Football and globalisation

The 1990s saw the further decline of the national team with no substantial achievement. With the introduction of FIFA rankings and the introduction of satellite television, the gap between India and the rest of the world became apparent. This situation led to the fading of the popularity of football in the country. However, what followed in 1995 was a process to work towards reinventing Indian domestic football starting with the development of the National Football League (NFL), the birth of the I-League, the development of the AIFF-IMG Reliance Deal, and the creation of the Indian Super League.

National Football League

The 1990s was the era of corporate involvement in domestic football. In 1995, the FIFA inspection committee visited India and recommended the establishment of the National Football League (NFL) as a step towards professionalisation. In 1996, the national league began with much fanfare, a major sponsor, and a major television broadcaster. This triggered positive development with the establishment of professional clubs and a state league in a few states (Ray, 2006). Major corporate houses including United Breweries and Zee Group made significant investments in sponsoring clubs and the leagues. This move towards professionalisation witnessed a departure from the old system of employment of players in the Public Sector Unit to the players being able to focus on football full-time. This meant the players on contracts became eager to earn as much as possible in a particular season. Inflated wages and the instant stardom attached to domestic football superseded that of the national team, resulting in the importance of the national team taking a backseat (Rodrigues, 2001).

The NFL brought many positive developments, especially with clubs outside Kolkata (earlier Calcutta) recruiting better players; this was evident with JCT Phagwara, a club from Punjab winning the inaugural league, beating the likes of traditional powers such as East Bengal and Mohun Bagan. In line with increased player salaries was a significant increase in the salaries received by coaches.

The positive trend continued only for a few years, however; a sudden downward trend was brought about by a realistic return on investment. Despite entering into an agreement with the premium broadcaster ESPN-Star, the AIFF backed out of the contract and provided rights to the government-owned public broadcaster Doordarshan. This breach of contract resulted in Philips withdrawing sponsorship from the national league, citing poor returns and lack of exposure in the media (Rodrigues, 2001). The company thereafter returned to cricket and made use of international events to market itself. Other corporations also complained of poor publicity return for the television coverage of the game.

At the same time, the cost of operations for the clubs went up significantly. In 1996, the operation of a club was around INR (Indian rupee) 35–50 lakhs (100,000–140,000 USD/75,000–110,000 euro) annually. This went up by four times by 2001, with the cost increasing to around INR 2 crore (420,000 USD/460,000 euro) annually. Despite the heavy investment, the returns were significantly low and the prize money for the domestic event was negligible. With the focus of the teams on winning the league, the majority of the investment concentrated on the top tier with negligible investment in the youth setup (Ugra, 2001). The poor management of the league resulted in troubled period for the AIFF, which resulted in nine of the ten NFL teams boycotting football in 2000 to protest against inadequate resources and inept marketing of the league (Dimeo, 2001). Many clubs failed to obtain sponsorship, which eventually further negatively affected the standard of football in the country.

As the NFL struggled, many corporate sponsors withdrew their financial support and there was a significant reduction in the budgets of the clubs. Many clubs were critical of the functioning of AIFF and blamed the poor organisation of the league as the major reason why the sponsors quickly lost interest in football. For instance, the Bengal Mumbai Football Club complained of poor scheduling and discriminatory policies of the federation, which resulted in a loss of INR 1.5 million for the club. The regional bodies were also unable to meet the professional expectations of the sponsors. The Western Indian Football Association lost Gulf Oil as their sponsor, as the company became disillusioned by the controversies surrounding the association. At the same time, the popularity of cricket and its lure as a publicity vehicle dominated the sports industry. Cricket made inroads into the two strongholds of Indian football (Goa and Bengal), which displaced many of the traditional football supporters (Dimeo, 2001). Quite simply then, at the end of the 2000s, football found itself in an uneasy state between the forces of old and new. While the sport witnessed commercialisation and modernisation, traditional measures of amateurism affected its continued growth.

Birth of the I-League

The NFL continued to struggle and despite being in existence for ten years, only 12 teams were a part of the competition, with the majority being from Calcutta and Goa. The clubs struggled with infrastructure as all matches were played in the municipal stadium that was leased out to the clubs. The attendance for the matches was low, 6,000 people on average.

In response to these concerns, the AIFF signed a ten-year deal with Zee Sports worth 70 million USD in 2005–2006, which led to the rebranding of NFL as I-League. Indian football moved from INR 10 crores (2.2 million USD/1.9 million euro) to approximately INR 274 crores (41.1 million USD/38.36 million euro) over the ten years. As a result of the deal, the Zee Group, who were also responsible for attracting new sponsorship for the game, won the telecast rights of Indian football. In addition, AIFF also signed a seven-year deal with Nike to supply apparel, footwear, etc. for the national team (Banerjee, 2017).

The inaugural I-League consisted of eight teams along with two promoted teams from the second division. ONGC was the sponsor of the league; it incidentally was the sponsor for the last season of the NFL as well. The league sought to introduce professionalism to football in India. The objective of the I-league was to develop Indian football and place itself on the world map.

Learning from history, the AIFF introduced a number of incentives to ensure the success of the league (Banerjee, 2017):

- Subsidies were provided to the clubs for the appointment of administrative staff in order to bring in professionalism in management and administration structures;
- To encourage the clubs to increase their marketing activities and provide financial stability, 90 per cent of the revenue from the sale of tickets was to be kept by the clubs;
- A considerable increase in match prize money and bonuses including the money for overall winners and runners-up was implemented;
- Enhanced advertising opportunities were provided for the clubs with billboard ownership in and around the stadiums.

In order to improve the viewer experience, the Zee Group reached out to foreign commentators who worked within the production of various European Leagues. Unlike previous years, the organisers released the full schedule in one go. The aim of the organisers was to have 16 teams in the top division, with representation from different parts of the country (Press Trust of India, 2007).

The Federation Cup was the first tournament broadcasted as a part of the deal. This was one of the better-organised tournaments that Indian football had seen to date. The Goa stadium was upgraded, floodlights were added, and cheerleaders introduced. Nearly 12,000 people witnessed the match with supporters in open jeeps with flags and trumpets. The signs were encouraging with quality foreign players and an electrifying atmosphere; Indian football seemed on the rise again (de Sousa, 2016).

The momentum, however, could not be sustained and the league ran into trouble when in late 2010, despite having a contract for ten years, extendable for another ten years, the Zee Group and the AIFF parted company. This was prompted by a five-year review clause. The AIFF felt the I-League was unable to get the desired publicity or coverage. Delayed payments were another factor (Basu, 2010). The broadcaster Zee Sports demanded INR 70 crore (15.4 million USD/11.9 million euro) as compensation from the AIFF after it decided to terminate the ten-year deal (Press Trust of India, 2010)

Unlike European clubs, the clubs in India do not rely on the income from the merchandise or ticket sales and rely predominately on sponsorship. Further, many of the clubs in India were termed institutional teams. These teams represent a company rather than a city/district and are merely a social undertaking for the benefit of their employees. The players were required to work a full-time job outside of the game; this was the same model used before the introduction of J-League in Japan. The biggest drawback for such clubs was the limitation to spectatorship and fan following, which was restricted to a few thousand (Banerjee, 2017). These factors made the marketing of the league a difficult undertaking; this affected the financial stability of the clubs. Further setbacks awaited the league and post-2010 the domestic league went sponsor-less until 2013 with the deal with ONGC not being renewed.

AIFF-IMG Reliance deal

In 2010, AIFF and Zee Sports reached an amicable agreement and terminated the old contract. AIFF decided to sign a contract with IMG Reliance, similar to the one signed with the Zee Group. The 15-year agreement with IMG-Reliance sought to maximise the potential of football in India from the grassroots to the professional level and develop a sustainable sporting model. Importantly, the agreement provided IMG-Reliance with the mandate to alter the structure of football in India with the objective of developing and popularising the game.

The overall deal was worth INR 700 crores (154 million USD/112 million euro) which was the biggest outside of cricket. As a part of the agreement, IMG-Reliance was to make a one-off payment to the Zee Group for early termination of the agreement for INR 70 crore to exit from the agreement five years before expiry (Basu, 2010). The deal with IMG-Reliance was a huge relief for the AIFF, as Zee was unable to raise the money it had promised, which resulted in the AIFF going through an economically challenging period.

Thereafter, the AIFF was to receive around INR 25 crores (5.5 million USD/4 million euro) annually for the next five years. Despite the engagement of IMG-Reliance, the league continued to suffer from lack of financial stability. Two years into the agreement, despite the hype, the progress was rather slow with little clarity on the future roadmap of Indian Football. Aside from the traditional clubs from Kolkata and Goa, the I-League continued to struggle, with many clubs failing to attract more than 100 spectators to home games. In an interview with the *Economic Times*, a club official laments the lack of buzz or hype around the league. With a lack of marketing being undertaken, the visibility of the league suffered. The biggest criticism involved the broadcasting of the league, as the league was considered commercially unattractive and many of the private channels did not bid for the television rights. In 2012, a week before the commencement of the Federation Cup, a FA Cup-styled tournament, IMG-Reliance sold the TV rights for the I-League to Ten Group and Bengal Media (regional broadcaster) and Nehru Cup (invitational international tournament) to NEO Sports. The value of these rights was less than INR 34 crores (6.3 million USD/4.8 million euro), which was the amount being paid to the AIFF by IMG-Reliance (Prabhakar, 2012). Though there is no official confirmation as per various sources, the regional broadcaster is said to have paid a higher amount than the national broadcaster TEN (Santikari, 2012).

However, despite the agreement, the Federation Cup commenced without a broadcaster as contractual issues between TEN and IMG-Reliance led to the former withdrawing from the agreement. With IMG-Reliance unable to find a replacement, AIFF signed a television rights deal with the public broadcaster Doordarshan to broadcast the Federation Cup (Soccerex, 2012). A Hindu newspaper reported the unease between the federation and the commercial partner, leading to the AIFF considering the activation of an exit clause. The efforts of IMG-Reliance to market the league and competition were not deemed satisfactory.

Financially, the clubs struggled to survive. In an interview with the *Economic Times*, a Pune FC (an I-League club) official estimated that the clubs were exhausting INR 150 crores (27.8 million USD/21 million euro) a year and in return, only a subsidy of INR 7 crores (1.3 million USD/1 million euro) was provided as a share in the sponsorship or broadcasting revenue. This revenue covered only 30–40 per cent of the costs for a small club. The AIFF, however, questioned the viability of EPL-style revenue distribution model in the wake of the domestic league being unmarketable. As the sale of the broadcast rights was insufficient to cover the expenses, the AIFF argued the clubs be required to bear losses as well (Prabhakar, 2012). By 2013, four clubs had disbanded their operations since the commencement of the league in 2007. JCT Phagwara, the winner of the first NFL in 1996 cited lack of credible exposure and money as the major reason for folding. In response, from 2015 onwards, IMG-Reliance guaranteed AIFF at least INR 50 crore (11 million USD/8 million euro) or 20 per cent of the net revenue, whichever was more for the next ten years. The deal brought financial stability to AIFF.

Indian Super League

In 2012, under criticism from various quarters over lack of action to improve football in the country, the AIFF planned an Indian Premier League styled league to run parallel to the

I-League. This agreement allowed IMG-Reliance to start a franchise-based league to popularise and improve the sport (Indian Television, 2012).

In 2013, the Indian Super League (ISL) was conceptualised to foster the local talent and attract international stars. The ISL was to run for three months and consist of eight city-based teams. The league aimed to engage in various football development projects and create an infrastructure for identification of local talent and coaches (Indian Television, 2013). As a strategy to ensure the success of the league, the franchisee-based club would be required to partner with a European club for technical assistance and engage popular players on the verge of retirement (Bali, 2012).

The proposed league, however, ran into trouble and met resistance from the Indian Professional Football Clubs Association (IPFCA) – the union of I-League clubs. The clubs unanimously decided not to release or sign any player contracted with IMG-Reliance. The player-transfer and club registration rules mandated the registration of players only with state association; hence, for ISL, the players could only be taken on loan from the I-League clubs (News18, 2013). The clubs expressed their displeasure and questioned the necessity of another league. The clubs instead wanted the focus to be on improving the I-League and making it into a separate legal entity for effective functioning. Through a separate legal entity, the club owners would become stakeholders and be more actively involved in running the league. It would be in the interest of the clubs to shift their focus from short-term targets and work towards the development of the league (Bali, 2013). This was critical as more than 90 per cent of the club's budget was reinvested in the I-League with the little amount being invested for the development of the youth. On an average, an Indian club spent anywhere between Rs 3 crores to Rs 15 crores on the wages of the players and operations. This leaves a little amount to be invested in the development of youth (Sharma, 2016).

However, cracks emerged in the IPFCA when Mohammedan Sporting went against the unanimous decision to boycott the IMG-Reliance and signed five players for I-League on loan (*The Times of India*, 2013). Following this move, Rangdajied United became the second club to break away from IPFCA and sign players on loan. Both Mohammedan Sporting and Rangdajied United made up the two teams that qualified for I-League from Division 2. In the meanwhile, the ISL partnered with Star India (television broadcaster) and signed famous footballers like Robert Pires, Louis Saha, and Fredrik Ljungberg. IMG-Reliance also signed 72 uncontracted players that included the likes of Indian international Subrata Pal, Syed Rahim Nabi, and Nirmal Chhetri among others. Despite the above, the league was postponed, as the right mix of Indian players was not available to participate in the ISL due to the reluctance of the I-League clubs to loan their players. The postponement of the league left the contracted players out-of-action from competitive football for over a year.

By June 2014, the organisers of ISL managed to convince five I-Leagues clubs to release their star players for the tournament. This was a departure from the initial stand adopted by the IPFCA to not release any player, as the viability of I-League would be affected. Two I-League club owners became the proprietors of the ISL clubs themselves. The agreement with the clubs was critical considering the clubs were required to have an adequate quota of players, i.e., 84 to choose from in the player draft (Jitendran, 2014). In July 2014, the ISL took its first step towards realisation when 84 players were drafted into eight franchisees. The event provided a glimpse into how IMG-Reliance, Star, and the AIFF would radically change the way football was viewed in India.

The league structure included:

- A conscious attempt was made to ensure pan-Indian representation. Bids were invited from nine specific cities with a focus not just on the financial competence but also the long-term vision of the applicant;

- A commitment to grassroots programming was a prerequisite to becoming an owner of a franchise;
- The introduction of a cap on expenditure by the clubs including the salary was added to ensure the focus remains on the development of local talent rather than international signing.

The marketing roadmap for the league included (Dhar, 2014):

- Star value: ISL signed well-known names like Henry Crespo, Luis Garcia, and Mikael Sylvestre, who were retired or nearing the end of their career. These stars were to give the required push to the league.
- Promotion: IMG and Star make a formidable team to promote the league. IMG – with operational and execution experience – and Star – the strongest sports broadcaster in India – pumped in the money to come up with a radical concept to revolutionise football.
- Focus on stadium experience: Efforts were made to ensure a comfortable experience for the fans; packed stadiums would attract higher advertising revenue.
- Player draft system: The system was devised around the Major League Soccer draft system to ensure hefty salaries for the month-long competition, as well as participation in the I-League. The players were to benefit from matches with the likes of Atletico Madrid, Fiorentina, and other global football clubs.

The ISL commenced in October 2014, with the very first game attracting a record 65,000 fans to the stadium, larger than many of the English Premier League turnouts. Such was the success of the league, as when the league concluded it had become the fourth biggest league in the world. The clubs followed the international model and operated with a professional setup with clear plans and budgets. The focus was on injury prevention and fitness became the focus of the team, something that was neglected in the I-League. With a bigger budget, it was possible for the clubs to afford the facilities, staff, and other matter that had not largely been used before. Fan engagement and marketing was also focused on, and departments like venue management, ticketing, and marketing gained importance in the process (Chidananda, 2015).

Future roadmap

As per the FIFA statue, every member nation can have only one recognised domestic league. The ISL was birthed with special permission from FIFA on the condition that in the next four years, there be a merger between the ISL and the I-League. To avoid conflict, the ISL was scheduled at the beginning of September and the I-League was moved to the January slot and was considerably shortened. Officially, the AIFF and FIFA supported the I-League as the premier football competition in the country considering the Indian representatives for the Asian Football Confederation (AFC) Cup and AFC Champions League were to be selected from I-League. Nonetheless, the AIFF acknowledged the long-term need of merging the two leagues and creating a more sustainable product with the focus being on much longer and competitive league (Mishra, 2015).

In 2016, the AIFF and IMG-Reliance consortium presented a roadmap for Indian football with the merger between the two leagues taking a backseat. The following critical points emerged (Bali, 2016):

- Indian football to have three leagues with ISL becoming the premier competition in the country. The I-League was christened as League One and I-League Division II as

League Two. The ISL was to have no promotion or relegation while the League One and League Two incorporated the system.

- The three leagues were to run concurrently from November to March over a period of five months. Thereafter, the league shall run from September to March after completion of U-17 World Cup.
- The ISL clubs and League One clubs were to fulfil the AIFF licensing criteria, which is in consonance with the licensing regulations of the AFC. Meanwhile, the League Two was also required to fulfil the criteria but not to the fullest.
- As an effort towards building a fan base, the League One was to be broadcasted over Star channels, while League Two was to be streamed digitally.
- The AIFF guaranteed larger financial assistance to the League One and League Two teams.

The proposed roadmap had serious implications with two Goan teams pulling out from the I-League. The decision came after the clubs failed to find a common ground and agree on the proposed structure. In the following month, another club (Dempo FC) also shut operations leaving no representation from Goa for the first time in the history of Indian football. After the closure of Pune FC, Royal Wahingdoh, and Bharat FC in the previous years, only eight teams remained in the I-League at the start of 2017. Meanwhile, the I-League clubs also demanded their share in the ISL with East Bengal and Mohun Bagan, the two most prominent clubs, being the most vocal. However, the ISL lured only Bengaluru FC, the current I-League champions with a better marketing coverage, to ditch I-League.

The breakthrough was finally achieved in June 2017 when I-League clubs agreed to a compromised solution in a meeting with the AIFF. As per the agreement, both leagues were to run simultaneously from November with winners of each obtaining a continental berth. While the I-League champion is eligible for an Asian Champions League playoff spot, the winners of ISL would compete in AFC Cup playoffs. This was made possible after the AFC, with an exception to global norms, agreed to two national leagues. The decision was a departure from FIFA's policy of recognising one top-tier domestic league. This, however, is a short-term solution with the focus being on the merger in the next 2–3 years (Vasavda, 2017).

FIFA and the AIFF

FIFA has long felt that India is the sleeping giant of world football. To awaken the dormant potential of the country, the international body has worked closely with the AIFF on various programs and activities. In this regard, FIFA and the AIFF signed a ten-year strategic and technical assistance pact for developing football in the country in 2012. Both parties agreed that the focus needed to be on developing grassroots programs and the infrastructure. The main objective of the memorandum of understanding (MOU) was India hosting the U-17 World Cup in 2017 and qualification for the 2022 World Cup (FIFA, 2012). Before any discussion on U-17 World Cup and its ramification on the footballing landscape in the country, it was important to revisit the various development projects undertaken that eventually led to India being awarded the rights for the U-17 World Cup. The pattern shows the long-term vision with which the AIFF and FIFA (and also the AFC) operated, including how a grassroots culture was to be created.

AFC Vision Asia Project

In 2002, the AFC president, with the backing from FIFA, launched the "Vision Asia" project. The main objective was to prepare Asian countries in the best possible environment to finish on the podium at the FIFA World Cup. Under this project, in each of the pilot project countries, the 11 key elements to football were to be developed. In India, Manipur and Delhi were selected as part of the pilot project by the AFC in 2004 (Unnikrishnan, 2006). The emphasis of the project was youth development and, with this vision, Manipur adopted some key elements of Vision India project. The success of Manipur in establishing a state league and starting various grassroots programs eventually led to the expansion of the program to include other states like Kerala and Tamil Nadu (Mykhel, 2007). However, in 2010, the AFC scrapped its program in Delhi and Tamil Nadu due to inaction. Despite the failures at some levels, the success of Manipur on its way to becoming a powerhouse highlighted the significance of a strong youth development program. The key elements that ensured the success of the project in Manipur included:

- The implementation of Vision India's program in schools with the initial selection of four districts for the project. The boys trained in school until age 13 and were later picked up by local clubs to undergo further training until age 18. The objective was to have a well-developed structure starting with the U-13 festival for boys and girls and then U-16 and U-19 tournaments.
- The establishment of the Manipur State League played an important role in the development of football in Manipur. The objective of the league was to introduce elite competition in the state through a well-structured club approach with the highest standard of players, infrastructure, coaches, and referees.

Regional and elite academies

In 2011, as an exercise towards solving the infrastructure at the grassroots level, FIFA set up four regional academies in phase 1 of the project. Each academy was to house 30–35 budding footballers that were selected in the age group 13/14 after a thorough scouting process. The selected kids were to undergo two years of training where food, accommodation, and education were provided. Thereafter, the boys from the age group 16 were to be selected into elite academies until age 18, from where they could move towards clubs. As a step towards success, the AIFF hired experts related to providing guidance towards successful implementation of the program (Chaudhuri, 2017). Despite setbacks, the success of the academies is evidenced by the fact that majority of the present U-17 squad participating at the World Cup 2017 were picked in 2013 for the AIFF Elite Academy when Manipur won the first U-14 National Championships (Selvaraj, 2017).

U-17 World Cup

In 2013, FIFA awarded the host rights for the 2017 U-17 World Cup to India. This decision came as no surprise, as it was clear after the secretary general's visit to India in 2012 that FIFA's focus was on India. This was the first time that India hosted and participated in a FIFA tournament. Many consider this World Cup as a game changer for Indian football for multiple reasons:

- Bidding: The path was anything but easy because in January 2013 India's bid was rejected as a result of insufficient insurance from the central government. However, in June 2013, the government assured its support and committed INR 95 crores (16.15 million USD/12.35 million euro) for the event to develop the infrastructure and INR 25 crores (4.25 million USD/3.25 million euro) was kept as a contingency to ensure smooth execution of the event (FiRSTpost, 2013). For this event, three other countries (Ireland, South Africa, and Uzbekistan) also showed interest. India's final bid was submitted in November 2013 with the submission of written guarantees pertaining to tax exemptions for broadcasters, foreign exchange remittance, security, transport, and accommodation, among others. On 5 December 2013, FIFA awarded the hosting rights to India over the other countries (Basu, 2013).

- Infrastructure: For hosting of the games, the AIFF initially proposed five states, from which eight cities were short-listed and eventually six cities were selected based on their capability of being the host city as per the requirement of FIFA. These venues were selected to ensure a country-wide presence of the game across India. The biggest legacy of this World Cup was the facility infrastructure. Prior to the conducting of the event, India had only three stadiums capable of holding a World Cup match. Some 80 per cent of the club matches were played in only three stadiums, eight of the 14 clubs in the I-League were from Goa and Kolkata. The World Cup provided an opportunity to develop football infrastructure in the country that would have a long-term impact on Indian football (Mittal, 2014). It is estimated the total cost of the infrastructure renovation has been INR 600 crores (102 million USD/78 million euro). The focus was on making structural changes to the stadiums and preparing practice pitches. As a result of the World Cup, the country now has six World Class stadiums and 24 internationally approved training grounds (Sen, 2017).

- Youth development: The government of India, recognising the U-17 World Cup as the turning point, created a pioneering programme called Mission XI Million that intended to bring 11 million school kids to actively participate in football prior to the commencement of the event. The program, which was the largest school contact programme in the country, aimed to make football as the sport of choice among the youth. The school network and facilities were utilised to encourage children to play the game. The scheme was spread across 36 cities and eventually reached out to 15,000 schools and over 11 million children. Adidas supported the programme by providing a significant amount of high-quality football gear, as well as the operation of exclusive master classes at the various festivals across the country (FIFA, 2017).

- Future of U-17 team: Despite the mediocre performance of the Indian team at the World Cup, the Indian U-17 stars attracted considerable interest from clubs, both domestic and international. However, the AIFF, with a long-term aim of qualifying for the 2018 AFC U-19 Championship and FIFA U-20 World Cup, is keen to continue developing the group. In this regard, AIFF has offered a three-year contract extension to these footballers and has doubled their wages (Bharali, 2017). As a result, the U-17 team shall be competing in the I-League to ensure the players collectively graduate to the next level. The team will also include players from the U-19 side and be based in Delhi. This decision was arrived at in consideration of the limited playing time these players would have had with other clubs.

- Tournament response: Despite India's early exit from the tournament, the U-17 World Cup was a watershed moment for Indian sports. The Indian teams inspired performance drew a huge number of fans. Such has been the success of the tournament and it has become one of the biggest events in FIFA's U-17 history. India is only the third country to register attendance of over one million spectators after China and Mexico.

AIFF election

Days after the successful hosting of the U-17 World Cup in late October 2017, the AIFF was dealt with a heavy blow by the Delhi High Court. The 2016 election of the president and the executive council was deemed invalid for being non-compliant with the nomination procedures provided in the National Sports Code (Joseph, 2017) issued by the Ministry of Youth Affairs and Sports under the government of India. The president and the 16 other members of the executive council were removed from their positions (Joseph, 2017) and Justice S.Y Qureshi, the former chief election commissioner, was appointed as the administrator with the direction to hold "fresh elections within five months" (ESPN Staff, 2017). The AIFF has approached the Supreme Court regarding this matter.

Though it is unlikely that the present ruling will affect the daily functioning of football in the country, the administrative mess could seriously impact the plans that the AIFF boasted during the U-17 World Cup, including the aspiration of hosting the U-20 World Cup. The new election could also have serious implications for the proposed merger of the I-League and the ISL in 2018. The biggest concern for the AIFF will be the judicial interference. As per the FIFA statutes, a member association should be free from legal and political interference. Previously, many associations have been banned for similar situations. In early November 2017, taking note of the situation, FIFA wrote to AIFF to seek more details of the ruling and its impact including the steps undertaken by the federation in the said matter (ESPN Staff, 2017). Looking ahead, 2018 will be a critical year for football in the country to see if it can maintain the positive momentum from recent years.

Conclusion

Indian football is passing through a restructuring phase with a focus on multiple elements that influence the overall development of the sport in the country. The senior national team qualified for the 2019 AFC Asian Cup and reached a high of 96 in FIFA rankings in July 2017, its highest ranking in 20 years. With the success of hosting the U-17 World Cup in India, the focus has rightly shifted to grassroots development to ensure long-term success. The AIFF is focused on retaining the core nucleus of the squad and ensuring the best possible environment for future editions of Olympics, Asian Cup and World Cup.

On the domestic front, the recognition of two official leagues has thrown an interesting challenge for the AIFF. Facing severe criticism from both FIFA and the AFC for the dual-league structure, the AIFF has been under pressure to effect a merger between the two. However, after one year of trying for a merger, the decision was delayed in 2017 for another 2–3 years. The main opposition to this has come from the two most popular clubs in India (Mohun Bagan and East Bengal) who disagree with certain points contained in the draft contract offered. These include giving up intellectual property rights such as the name of the club, the colour of the jersey, and the emblem to the new promoter for 30 years, as well as issues concerning the sharing of profit and investment (Sharma, 2017). The resistance has grown further with Aizwal FC, the winners of I-League 2016/2017, being in danger of being relegated if the ISL is made the top league. For an effective merger, AIFF would be required to ensure a fine balance between the traditional clubs and the financial strength of the ISL clubs.

When the discussion about mergers continues, the AIFF very well may look to leagues with no relegation system and an 8–9-month season, such as Major League Soccer (MLS) in the United States and the A-League in Australia, as potential models to incorporate. Also, the AIFF will need to walk a fine line to ensure that a battle between the two leagues does not escalate to the level of the Super League War in Australian rugby during the 1990s. While that dispute did result in a merger into what is now the National Rugby League (NRL), the process is something that the AIFF will want to avoid. In addition, the importance of connecting all levels of football in India – from grassroots to supporters to professional leagues to the national team program – is vital to the continued growth of the sport in India. Without a strategic plan that has all levels of the sport working in synergy with each other, the likelihood of growth and success will not be possible. Finally, overcoming the invalidated election of the AIFF board from 2016 and the resulting judicial inquiry ongoing at the time of writing will also play a key role in the future of football in India.

References

Banerjee, D. (2017) The I-League as a product. *Scribd*. [online] Retrieved from: https://www.scribd.com/document/48796334/THe-I-league-as-a-product

Bali, R. (2016) Indian football: Roadmap for future of Indian Super League and I-League explained - Goal.com. *Goal.com*. [online] Retrieved from: http://www.goal.com/en-india/news/7083/isl/2016/05/17/23620432/indian-football-roadmap-for-future-of-indian-super-league

Bali, R. (2013) Nandan Piramal calls for I-League to be made a separate legal entity - Goal.com. *Goal.com*. [online] Retrieved from: http://www.goal.com/en-india/news/1064/i-league/2013/07/17/4122878/nandan-piramal-calls-for-i-league-to-be-made-a-separate

Bali, R. (2012) IMG-Reliance keen to start an eight team franchisee competition, I-League likely to follow the MLS model - Goal.com. *Goal.com*. [online] Retrieved from: http://www.goal.com/en-india/news/136/india/2012/07/19/3250992/img-reliance-keen-to-start-an-eight-team-franchisee?ICID=AR_RS_4

Basu, S. (2013) India wins bid to host U-17 football World Cup - Times of India. *The Times of India*. [online] Retrieved from: https://timesofindia.indiatimes.com/sports/football/top-stories/India-wins-bid-to-host-U-17-football-World-Cup/articleshow/26923547.cms

Basu, M. (2010) IMG Reliance in deal for Indian football rights. Livemint. [online] Retrieved from: http://www.livemint.com/Home-Page/KqWdJwiVnuydSRHFKoUgFP/IMG-Reliance-in-deal-for-Indian-football-rights.html

Bharali, A. (2017) FIFA U17 World Cup: 3x money from ISL, I-League clubs turns India U17s' heads. Sportskeeda. [online] Retrieved from: https://www.sportskeeda.com/football/fifa-u17-world-cup-3x-money-from-isl-i-league-clubs-turns-india-u17s-heads

Chidananda, S. (2015) A leg-up for Indian football. *The Hindu*. [online] Retrieved from: http://www.thehindu.com/sunday-anchor/indian-super-league-a-legup-for-indian-football/article7774805.ece

Chaudhuri, A. (2017) AIFF and FIFA to set up elite camp; regional academies in India. *Sportskeeda*. [online] Retrieved from: https://www.sportskeeda.com/general-sports/aiff-fifa-to-set-up-elite-regional-academies-in-india

de Sousa, J. (2016) Decoding the I-League and Indian Super League merger. *Zee News*. [online] Retrieved from: http://zeenews.india.com/sports/football/decoding-the-i-league-and-indian-super-league-merger_1920310.html

Dhar, P. (2014) 10 takeaways from the Indian Super League's draft. *FiRStpost*. [online] Retrieved from: http://www.fiRStpost.com/sports/10-takeaways-indian-super-leagues-draft-1631003.html

Dimeo, P. (2001) Contemporary developments in Indian football. *Contemporary South Asia*, 10(2), 251–264.

ESPN Staff. (2017) FIFA "requests" more info from AIFF on Praful Patel case. *ESPN.com*. [online] Retrieved from: http://www.espn.in/football/india/story/3257610/fifa-seeks-more-information-from-aiff-on-delhi-hc-decision-setting-aside-election-of-praful-patel

FIFA. (2017) Mission XI Million set to boost India's football growth. [online] Retrieved from: http://www.fifa.com/u17worldcup/news/y=2017/m=2/news=mission-xi-million-set-to-boost-india-s-football-growth-2868816.html

FIFA. (2012) FIFA sets the development of football in India as priority objective. [online] Retrieved from: http://www.fifa.com/development/news/y=2012/m=9/news=fifa-sets-the-development-football-india-priority-objective-1696734.html

FiRStpost. (2013) Govt gives go ahead to India's FIFA U-17 World Cup bid. [online] Retrieved from: http://www.fiRStpost.com/sports/govt-gives-go-ahead-to-indias-fifa-u-17-world-cup-bid-868369.html

Indian Television. (2013) Reliance, Star India, IMG brings Indian Super League for football to India. [online] Retrieved from: http://www.indiantelevision.com/headlines/y2k13/oct/ oct98.php

Indian Television. (2012) AIFF, IMG Reliance plan to launch IPL-style football league. [online] Retrieved from: http://www.indiantelevision.com/headlines/y2k12/july/july88.php

Jitendran, N. (2014) IMG-Reliance reach pact with five clubs – report – Goal.com. *Goal.com*. [online] Retrieved from: http://www.goal.com/en-india/news/1064/i-league/2014/06/13/4879290/img-reliance-reach-pact-with-five-clubs-report/b%3E-mohun-bagans-ban

Joseph, R.J. (2017) Explained: What is the ongoing AIFF crisis? *Theweek.in*. [online] Retrieved from: http://www.theweek.in/news/sports/explainer-aiff-crisis-fifa-praful-patel.html [Accessed 9 November 2017].

Kapadia, N. (2001) Triumphs and Disasters: The Story of Indian Football, 1889–2000. In: P. Dimeo and J. Mills (eds), *Soccer in South Asia: Empire, Nation, Diaspora*, (1st ed.) (pp.17–40). London: Frank Cass.

Mishra, S. (2015) Two leagues one goal: should India's two leagues merge to improve Indian football? *LawInSport*. [online] Retrieved from: https://www.lawinsport.com/features/item/two-leagues-one-goal-should-india-s-two-leagues-merge-to-improve-indian-football

Mittal, V. (2014) Expected event legacies from FIFA's 2017 U-17 World Cup in India. [online] Retrieved from: https://brage.bibsys.no/xmlui/bitstream/handle/11250/ 225769/master_mittal.pdf?sequence=1

Mykhel. (2007) AFC selects Kerala, Tamil Nadu for Vision India project. [online] Retrieved from: https://www.mykhel.com/football/afc-selects-kerala-tamil-nadu-for-vision-india-project-029773.html

News18. (2013) IPL-style football league: an AIFF dream fair distance away. [online] Retrieved from: http://www.news18.com/news/sports/ipl-style-football-league-an-aiff-dream-fair-distance-away-614173.html

Prabhakar, B. (2012) I-League struggling to woo sponsors: IMG Reliance facing difficulties in promoting football. *Economic Times*. [online] Retrieved from: https://economictimes.indiatimes.com/industry/services/advertising/i-league-struggling-to-woo-sponsoRS-img-reliance-facing-difficulties-in-promoting-football/articleshow/msid-17079345,curpg-2.cms?from=mdr

Press Trust of India (2010) Zee Sports demands RS 70 crore as compensation from AIFF. [online] Retrieved from: http://www.sify.com/sports/zee-sports-demands-RS-70-crore-as-compensation-from-aiff-news-football-kk0qC5edeahsi.html

Press Trust of India (2007) AIFF's I-League to have 10 teams. [online] Retrieved from: http://www.rediff.com/sports/report/aiff/20071121.htm

Ray, S. (2006) The decline of Indian football: a critical narrative. *Soccer & Society*, 7(4), 508–519.

Rodrigues, M. (2001) The corporates and the game: football in India and the conflicts of the 1990s. *Soccer & Society*, 2(2), 105–127.

Santikari, S. (2012) Football fans deprived of Federation Cup telecast. *India Today*. [online] Retrieved from: http://indiatoday.intoday.in/story/football-fans-deprived-of-federation-cup-telecast/1/221647.html

Selvaraj, J. (2017) How 14,000 became 21: the story of India's history boys. *ESPN*. [online] Retrieved from: http://www.espn.in/football/u-17-world-cup/story/3218395/how-14,000-became-21-the-story-of-indias-history-boys

Sen, D. (2017) "Most important to bring about a football revolution" – Ceppi. *ESPN*. [online] Retrieved from: http://www.espn.in/football/u-17-world-cup/story/3217014/most-important-to-bring-about-a-football-revolution-javier-ceppi

Sharma, N. (2016). Financial sustainability crucial for taking Indian football forward: a blueprint. catchnews.com. [online] Retrieved from: http://www.catchnews.com/football-news/financial-sustainability-crucial-for-taking-indian-football-forward-a-blueprint-1464178031.html

Soccerex. (2012) AIFF and IMG-Reliance partnership on the rocks. [online] Retrieved from: https://www.soccerex.com/insight/articles/2012/aiff-and-img-reliance-partneRShip-on-the-rocks-report

The Times of India. (2013) Md Sporting snap ties with IPFCA - Times of India. [online] Retrieved from: https://timesofindia.indiatimes.com/sports/football/i-league/Md-Sporting-snap-ties-with-IPFCA/articleshow/24893031.cms

Ugra, S. (2001) Alive and kicking. *India Today*. [online] Retrieved from: http://indiatoday.intoday.in/story/business-houses-come-up-with-big-time-sponsoRShips-of-top-football-clubs/1/233145.html

Unnikrishnan, M. (2006) The Tribune – Magazine section - Saturday Extra. *Tribuneindia.com*. [online] Retrieved from: http://www.tribuneindia.com/2006/20060603/ saturday/main1.htm

Vasavda, M. (2017) In compromise solution, I-League and ISL to share space. *The Indian Express*. [online] Retrieved from: http://indianexpress.com/article/sports/football/isl-i-league-merge-aiff-in-compromise-solution-isl-and-i-league-to-share-space-4728407

46

Soccer in the United States

Clinton J. Warren and Kwame J.A. Agyemang

Introduction

In the United States, soccer is a sport of growing popularity. There are more than three million youth players registered with United States Youth Soccer (US Youth Soccer, 2017), and there are countless others who play for unregistered youth teams and recreationally at the local level. The top division of professional soccer in the US, Major League Soccer (MLS), has helped build an infrastructure of professional teams, soccer stadiums, and fan bases in an ever increasing number of markets across the country. Americans have begun consuming soccer matches, media, and merchandise at unprecedented levels. In the US, Saturdays and Sundays in the fall are no longer reserved exclusively for American football games. For an increasingly large number of sport fans, these days start in the early hours of the morning when the first Premier League fixture of the day kicks off. The US Women's National Team (USWNT) has won the FIFA World Cup three times, and the National Women's Soccer League (NWSL) appears to be on the strongest footing of any women's professional league in the country's history. Further, the diversity of the US has lent itself to successfully hosting international friendlies between foreign nations that routinely draw more than 50,000 spectators. The majority of what has been written about the history of American soccer has chronicled the litany of short-term organisational successes followed by significant failures (Wangerin, 2011). Moreover, scholars have explored the role of broader American culture in the creation of a uniquely American soccer culture that is closed off from the rest of the world (Collins, 2009; Foer, 2006; Markovitz and Hellerman, 2001). However, the US is no longer the global soccer backwater it was assumed to have been when FIFA awarded the nation with hosting rights to the 1994 World Cup. While there are still other sports that can claim greater popularity in the US, it appears soccer is outgrowing its niche status in America.

In this chapter we give a brief overview of the history, organisational structure, and business dynamics of soccer in the US. Due to the unique nature of the sport's governance structure in the US, significant attention is paid to the United States Soccer Federation's (USSF) approach to sanctioning leagues and teams throughout its closed pyramid system. Additional attention is paid to league and team structures at the professional level, with a decided emphasis on MLS. Further, this chapter discusses the role of Soccer United Marketing (SUM) as a third-party company that has worked on behalf of the USSF, MLS, and other soccer entities to sell and market the sport throughout the country. Finally, the chapter describes the emergence of American soccer supporter culture and lays out a series of future challenges and opportunities that exist for soccer in the US.

Origins of the game in the US

The roots of soccer in the US are entangled with those of American football. November 6, 1869 is often considered the date on which the first American football game was played between Princeton University and Rutgers University. However, that game was played using rules developed by the London FA (Wangerin, 2006). From that date onward, soccer and American football began to take divergent paths within the American sporting lexicon. Both sports continued to develop in the context of the US collegiate system with the Ivy League schools of Harvard, Yale, and Princeton creating the rules of game play and providing the initial teams that would compete in each sport. However, in 1884 the American Football Association (AFA) was formed to govern the sport of soccer in a manner that was consistent with the English game. The AFA created the first national competition for club teams in the US. The America Cup was a competition that mirrored the English FA Cup and allowed any professional or amateur club to compete for a national championship. Club teams were born in the country's most densely populated regions of New York, Massachusetts, New Jersey, Pennsylvania, and even as far west as St. Louis, Missouri. A litany of regional and city leagues were formed in the early 1900s with US's first notably successful clubs like Bethlehem Steel, Fall River Marksmen, and St. Louis Athletic Club winning trophies with regularity. However, the emergence of a competing soccer association, the United States Football Association (USFA), and the mounting wartime pressures on the economy saw soccer fall behind baseball and American football in terms of American sporting interests (Wangerin, 2006). Soccer in the US has seen this pattern of success and failure repeat itself for more than 100 years.

Emergence of the national team and its accomplishments

Founded in 1913, the USFA was the federation that has come to be known as the USSF (US Soccer, 2017). The USSF was one of the first FIFA-affiliated soccer governing bodies, and it continues to govern soccer in the US. The USSF established the National Challenge Cup (now called the US Open Cup) in 1914, and it is the longest running national soccer competition in the US (Hakala, 2015). In 1916, the US men's national team (USMNT) played its first sanctioned international matches in a tour of Scandinavia that saw the team play Norway and Sweden. The US was one of the 13 nations to compete in the first ever FIFA World Cup hosted by Uruguay in 1930, and the country finished third at the inaugural tournament. In the period of time from 1954 to 1990, the US did not qualify for the World Cup, and since that time, the best finish for the USMNT was when it reached the quarterfinals of the World Cup in 2002 (US Soccer, 2017). In total, the USMNT has qualified for the World Cup ten times, and its primary success has come in regional competitions having won the CONCACAF Gold Cup six times. Most recently, the USMNT failed to qualify for the 2018 World Cup in Russia. This failure led to a significant backlash among media and fans of the national team and put pressure on USSF to re-evaluate its governance structure from youth through to the professional ranks (Wahl, 2017).

International success for the USSF has come overwhelmingly on the women's side of the game. The US women's national team (USWNT) has appeared in seven World Cup tournaments and has won the tournament three times (1991, 1999, and 2015). Additionally, the

USWNT has appeared in eight CONCACAF Gold Cup tournaments, and it has won that tournament seven times. The US women have also won Olympic gold four times. On the heels of such international success, players on the women's national team pushed for fairer and more equitable treatment by the USSF. In 2016, the USWNT filed a complaint against the USSF with the Equal Employment Opportunities Commission (EEOC) alleging wage discrimination. One year after the complaint was filed; the USSF and USWNT entered into a labour agreement that led to a sizable increase in wages for the players (Das, 2017).

Turbulent history of professional leagues

Just as international success has generally eluded the USMNT, professional soccer in the US has experienced a tumultuous history. While large flashes of success have been seen in American professional soccer, the sports failures have gained the most significant attention. The American Soccer League (ASL) and American Professional Soccer League (APSL) competed with one another for status as the country's top professional league through the 1920s and early 1930s, but neither league was able to fully survive the Great Depression and its aftermath (Wangerin, 2006). Throughout the 1940s, 1950s, and 1960s, professional soccer in the US saw leagues make attempts at providing national competitions in both outdoor and indoor iterations (Wangerin, 2011). However, it was not until the North American Soccer League (NASL) began play in 1968 that the US had a stable first division of professional soccer. The NASL experienced modest success at the gate in its early years, and the league grew tremendously when stars like Pele, Franz Beckenbauer, George Best, and Johan Cruyff arrived in the US. At its peak, the NASL played games in front of as many as 70,000 spectators, and its championship was broadcast on major television networks, CBS and ABC (Francis and Zheng, 2010). However, the success of the league's largest clubs did not transfer to its smaller clubs. The rapid folding of clubs as a result of increasing player wages and lagging team revenues led to the NASL's suspension of operations in 1985. For more than a decade, the US did not have a sanctioned first division of professional soccer. When FIFA awarded the US hosting rights for the 1994 World Cup, the USSF agreed to assist in the launch of a new first division professional league. On 17 December 1993, MLS was founded, and the league began play in the spring of 1996 (Dure, 2010). Since that time, MLS has been the USSF sanctioned first division of professional soccer in America.

Governance structure of soccer in the US

The European model of sport is often described as a pyramid with vertical channels of authority and governing bodies situated at each level of the pyramid. This pyramid structure allows for a clear hierarchy and governance structure in which the regulatory system and sport policies tend to be unified from the top of the pyramid to the bottom. The governance of soccer throughout Europe has served as a classic example of the European model for sport. However, recent European Union policy, court rulings, and the emergence of power among commercial entities external to sport have challenged this status quo (Garcia, 2011). The North American model of sport does not exhibit this same unified pyramidal structure. While sports in North America are still governed by international and national sport federations, the manner by which professional and amateur sport is governed is far more fragmented. The professional leagues in North America operate as closed systems for which franchise operations are licensed to individual team owners. This structure originated with the formation of baseball's National League in 1876, and it has served as the template for professional sport in North America since that time (Szymanski, 2015). Governance of North American professional leagues was established by a collective bargaining agreement between franchise owners and players on each team in the league. While professional franchises may have units or departments within their business structure that focus on youth sport development and community outreach, the primary objective of professional sport teams in North America are profit making and team success within their league. Most professional leagues in North America have chosen to utilise playing rule structures for their sports that are consistent with international sport federation standards as their professional athletes compete at the international level in their sports. With regard to soccer, the USSF has sought to create a pyramid structure of governance while working within the context of North American professional sport (Hums and MacLean, 2013).

The USSF states that its purposes are: (1) to promote, govern, coordinate, and administer the growth and development of soccer in all its recognised forms in the US for all persons of all ages and abilities, including national teams and international games and tournaments, (2) to provide for the continued development of soccer players, coaches, referees, and administrators, (3) to provide for national cup competitions, and 4) to provide for the prompt and equitable resolution of grievances. The federation is governed by bylaws and procedures that are adopted by a board of directors and a national council. Most recently, the USSF Board of Directors consisted of 17 members (15 with voting privileges) made up of players, coaches, and administrators representing professional, amateur, and youth soccer. The National Council is considered to be representative of the USSF membership and has voting rights related to amending bylaws, electing the USSF president and vice president, and other policies that affect the membership. The USSF Board of Directors and National Council have created a series of 12 committees and task forces that are responsible for oversight and policy development related to their wide-ranging focal areas (US Soccer, 2017).

In the context of regulating the levels of professional soccer in America, the USSF has established a divisional structure that is meant to be consistent with the FIFA Laws of the Game. The federation sanctions three competitive divisions of professional soccer, Division I, Division II, and Division III. Unlike other nations, teams that participate in professional play in the US are not eligible for performance-based promotion and/or relegation from one division to another. Instead, the USSF asserts professional teams must be certified by the Board of Directors and authorised to participate in a professional league in accordance with the rules and regulations of that professional league (United States Soccer Federation, 2017). At present, MLS is the USSF sanctioned Division I league in the US. Below MLS in the divisional structure, professional soccer in the US has exhibited a near constant state of change. Since MLS began to play several different professional leagues have held a spot as the US's Division II league and a number of other leagues have been sanctioned as USSF Division III. From 1996–2004 the A-League was considered the US second division by the USSF with the United Soccer Leagues (USL) operating as a sanctioned third division. Then, following the collapse of the A-League, the USL split to form the USL First Division (USL-1) and USL Second Division (USL-2). The USSF sanctioned these leagues as Division II and Division III respectively. This structure endured until the end of the 2009 soccer season. In an effort to remain financially solvent, USL-1 and USL-2 rebranded themselves as USL and applied for sanctioning solely as a USSF Division III league. Upon granting that sanctioning for the 2010 season, the USSF operated an unbranded Division II league until a new iteration of the NASL began to play in 2011. The new NASL held second division status according to USSF from 2011 until 2017. During that time the USL operated as the nation's third division of professional soccer. However, prior to the start of the 2017 season, the USL challenged the NASL's position as the country's second division league and applied for Division II sanctioning. The USSF jointly sanctioned the NASL and USL to serve as Division II leagues for the 2017 season. Following the conclusion of the 2017 NASL season, the USSF made the determination to revoke the NASL's Division II status as a result of the league's failure to meet the USSF requirements to participate as Division II. Subsequently, the NASL filed a lawsuit against the USSF alleging antitrust violations that included the USSF and MLS conspiring to force NASL to fail while favouring USL (McCann, 2017). Upon publication of this chapter, the lower division structure of soccer in the US was still in a state of flux as a result of this legal challenge.

The organisational structure of Major League Soccer

While the organisation of soccer in the US has seen upheaval in the lower divisions since MLS began to play, the league itself has been generally stable for more than 20 years. MLS has maintained its stability by implementing a slow and sustained growth strategy that has been enacted through the creation of strict player acquisition policies, roster management rules, and capital structures that are centralised and operationalised with the league office (Francis and Zheng, 2010). Players who join MLS sign playing contracts with the league rather than individual clubs. However, the teams within the league cooperate via a system of unique rules and regulations that allow for the acquisition of players who have signed with the league. For example, MLS uses a collegiate draft similar to those used in other American professional sports. Players that enter the draft sign with the league and have little choice over where they will pursue their professional career if they play in MLS. More recently, MLS has created other player acquisition mechanisms such as the designated player rule, a re-entry draft for current players, a waiver draft, allocation money that may be traded among teams, and expansion drafts for new franchises entering the league. Most of these rules are unique to MLS, and these regulations create a complicated system in which player movement within the league is controlled by the league office.

MLS operates as a single-entity business in which franchise owners are granted a license to operate their teams. In 2017, there were 22 owner operated teams that played in MLS. As a result of the large geography of the US, teams in MLS are divided into geographical conferences. Both the Eastern and Western Conference consisted of 11 teams in 2017. Table 46.1 includes a complete list of MLS teams that participated in the league competition in 2017 with corresponding stadium and attendance information. In 2018, the Western Conference will add a new expansion franchise, Los Angeles Football Club.

MLS awards a series of trophies upon the culmination of its league season. The team with the most total points throughout the regular season of competition is awarded the Supporter's Shield. Following the conclusion of the regular season, the six teams from each conference with the most points qualify for a playoff tournament. The tournament is structured based on the league's geographical conferences. The two teams that advance to the playoff final, MLS Cup, each win a trophy as their respective conference champions. The MLS Cup Final is considered the league's most prestigious prize and is awarded to the playoff champion. This championship structure is common in American professional sports.

Commercial structure and strategy in US soccer

In addition to the unique competition structure of soccer in the US, the marketing and management of soccer in America includes some unique features. First, SUM is a for-profit business that operates as the marketing division of MLS and as an exclusive marketing partner of the USSF. Additionally, SUM serves as a marketing partner for the Mexican national team, and the company worked with CONCACAF and CONMEBOL to secure hosting rights for the US

Table 46.1 2017 Major League Soccer teams, stadiums, and average attendance data

Team	Stadium	Capacity	Attendance
Atlanta United FC	Mercedes-Benz Stadium	42,500^	48,200
Chicago Fire	Toyota Park*	20,000	17,383
Colorado Rapids	Dick's Sporting Goods Park*	18,061	15,322
Columbus Crew SC	Mapfre Stadium*	19,968	15,439
D.C. United	RFK Stadium	20,000^	17,904
FC Dallas	Toyota Stadium*	20,500	15,122
Houston Dynamo	BBVA Compass Stadium*	22,039	22,039
LA Galaxy	Stub Hub Center*	27,167	22,246
Minnesota United FC	TCF Bank Stadium	22,649^	20,538
Montreal Impact	Stade Saputo*	20,801	20,046
New England Revolution	Gillette Stadium	20,000^	19,367
New York City FC	Yankee Stadium	27,470^	22,643
New York Red Bulls	Red Bull Arena*	24,219	21,175
Orlando City SC	Orlando City Stadium*	25,500	25,028
Philadelphia Union	PPL Park*	18,500	16,812
Portland Timbers	Providence Park*	21,144	21,144
Real Salt Lake	Rio Tinto Stadium*	20,213	18,781
San Jose Earthquakes	Avaya Stadium*	18,000	19,875
Seattle Sounders	CenturyLink Field	40,000^	43,666
Sporting Kansas City	Children's Mercy Park*	18,467	19,537
Toronto FC	BMO Field*	30,000	27,647
Vancouver Whitecaps FC	BC Place	22,120^	21,416

* Soccer-specific stadium.
^ Represents an artificially reduced capacity for soccer that may be oversold for more popular matches.
Data compiled from official MLS box scores (2017).

for the 2016 Copa America Centenario. Since its founding in 2002, SUM has been a catalyst for the commercial growth of professional and international soccer in the US.

Despite the extensive professional sports infrastructure in the US, professional soccer teams have typically operated as secondary tenants of other sporting facilities. However, the opening of Crew Stadium (now Mapfre Stadium) in Columbus, Ohio in 1999 began a movement of soccer infrastructure construction. As of 2017, MLS boasted 14 soccer-specific stadiums (SSS) for its 22 franchises. The league projects at least 17 SSS will be operational by 2019. Investment in SSS for MLS teams has allowed team front offices to market a unique in-game experience for its spectators and have greater control in the ticket, sponsorship, and premium seating revenues yielded by these specialised venues. Table 46.1 includes designations of the SSS in MLS with corresponding venue capacities and average attendance figures for the 2017 season.

In general, SSS in MLS have a smaller overall venue capacity when compared to the clubs who share their facility with other professional sport teams. For example, in 2017 five teams shared facilities with NFL or Canadian Football League (CFL) franchises. In some cases, these American football stadiums are capable of seating in excess of 70,000 spectators; however, it is common for these venues to artificially reduce their total capacity in an effort to enhance the stadium atmosphere for MLS matches. SSS in MLS typically offer venue capacities near 20,000 spectators.

While MLS still lags well behind the other major professional sports in North America with regard to total attendance, MLS has surpassed the National Basketball Association (NBA) and

Table 46.2 Professional League attendance data 2016–2017

League	Total Attendance	Avg. Attendance
Major League Baseball	73,158,044	30,168
National Basketball Association	21,972,129	17,884
National Hockey League	21,451,041	17,501
National Football League	17,468,825	69,325
Premier League	13,851,829	36,452
Bundesliga	13,249,778	43,300
La Liga	10,703,881	28,168
Serie A	8,604,537	22,199
Liga MX	8,506,812	25,557
Ligue 1	7,970,815	20,976
Major League Soccer	7,375,144	21,692
Primera Division	6,999,924	18,817
Eredivisie	5,940,000	18,744
2. Bundesliga	5,861,328	17,667
Chinese Super League	5,798,135	24,159
J1 League	5,452,311	17,818

Data compiled from ESPN Attendance Reports (2017), official MLS box scores (2017), and worldfootball.net (2017).

National Hockey League (NHL) in terms of average per game attendance. Additionally, MLS has managed to break into the top ten of global soccer leagues with regard to both total attendance and average match attendance. Table 46.2 includes a list of the top ten global soccer leagues as well as the four major North American sports leagues and their corresponding attendance figures.

These statistics indicate MLS seems to be gaining a foothold with regard to spectator popularity, when compared to other professional leagues domestically and globally. In addition to this emerging success, MLS has shown a general trajectory of attendance growth since it began play in 1996. In its inaugural season, MLS drew a total of 2,785,001 spectators to its 160 matches. In 2017, MLS teams saw a total of 8,270,187 spectators attend their 374 matches. It is clear the addition of more franchises, and thus more matches, to the league schedule has been the primary contributor to such significant growth. However, Figure 46.1 shows this total attendance growth trajectory for MLS from 1996 to 2017.

Another critical catalyst for the growth of soccer in the US has been the emergence of television broadcast rights fees and expanded television viewing options for global soccer properties. In 2006, SUM secured a joint broadcasting agreement with ESPN, NBC Sports Network, and Univision that generated a reported $20 million for the league annually. That agreement expired in 2014 and led to a landmark deal in US soccer broadcasting. SUM bundled the rights to MLS and USSF matches to secure a joint media partnership with ESPN, Fox Sports, and Univision worth a reported $720 million over eight years (Ourand and Botta, 2014). MLS commissioner, Don Garber, stated the media deal "represents the most comprehensive US media rights arrangement in the history of soccer in our country" (Tannenwald, 2014).

In addition to this tremendous growth in revenue and media coverage for domestic soccer in the US, soccer supporters in America are consuming global soccer media at increasing rates. NBC Sports entered into a three-year, $250 million broadcast partnership with the Premier League in 2013. NBC's corresponding commitment to marketing this broadcasting relationship and emphasis on the development of ancillary Premier League programming

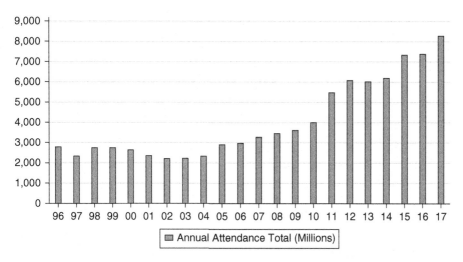

Figure 46.1 Major League Soccer annual total match attendance. Data compiled from official MLS box scores (2017)

has helped the league further establish itself in the US. The network followed this initial three-year agreement with a new six-year deal worth a reported $1 billion that began in 2016 (Sandomir, 2015). As a result, the Premier League has become a significant player in the American sporting landscape.

The rise of soccer supporters in the US

The increase in media attention for and spectator attendance at domestic soccer matches in the US has come in part as a result of a growing soccer supporter culture in America. While the presence and significance of groups supporting global soccer properties and national teams other than the US should not go unmentioned, the growth of a supporter's culture for domestic teams and the US national team has been critical to the growth of soccer in America. The American Outlaws were established in 2007 in Lincoln, Nebraska and have the state mission "to support the United States National Soccer Teams through a unified and dedicated group of supporters. Creating a community locally and nationally to Unite and Strengthen U.S. Soccer fans from all parts of this country" (American Outlaws, 2017). As of 2017, the American Outlaws reported 191 official chapters of the organisation spread throughout the US with a total of more than 30,000 members. The growth of this supporters group has brought a new energy and enthusiasm to US national team matches both in the America and abroad.

In addition to the growth of a supporters movement for the US national teams, recent MLS expansion franchises have brought regional American soccer cultures to the league with tremendous popularity. The two newest MLS franchises in 2017, Atlanta United FC and Minnesota United FC each introduced unique supporter movements to the league. In Atlanta, the team has seen its attendance exceed 70,000 people at times through mass marketing and high profile player and manager acquisitions that have engaged a new group of soccer fans. While in Minnesota, the team brought a unique group of lower division soccer supporters to the league. The Dark Clouds, supporters of Minnesota United FC, are a good example of the growing emphasis on social responsibility, diversity, and inclusion that has become a hallmark of soccer supporter groups in the United States.

The most recent expansion franchises serve as great examples of the growth of American soccer fandom and supporter culture. However, MLS has used the Pacific Northwest as its case study for what domestic soccer support can be. The league has featured the engaged stadium atmospheres, large attendance figures, and strong television viewership ratings for Seattle Sounders FC, Portland Timbers FC, and Vancouver Whitecaps FC in a great deal of its digital marketing. From the years 2009 to 2011, MLS added these three franchises with deep histories of soccer supporter engagement that can be traced to the 1970s (Dure, 2010). As a result, these teams have brought a unique, long-standing rivalry dynamic to MLS with the team's supporters groups, the Emerald City Supporters, Timbers Army, and the Southsiders, awarding the team with the most points in head-to-head competition among the three the Cascadia Cup. Continued MLS expansion initiatives have sought to identify markets with this type of soccer history and tradition to ensure greater franchise stability and financial solvency.

Future challenges and opportunities for soccer in the US

Soccer in the US is experiencing a period of growth and stability unlike anything it has seen in the past. However, there are several emerging challenges and opportunities for those interested in making an impact in American soccer. First, with the sport's growth, has come an increasing number of criticisms related to the quality of soccer that is played in the US and the lack of success of the USMNT. Following the USMNT failure to qualify for the 2018 World Cup in Russia, a social media-fuelled backlash toward USSF gained momentum. Mainstream media outlets like Sports Illustrated, ESPN, and Fox Sports provided pointed, critical analysis, and in some cases, pundits suggested massive changes to the US soccer governance and player development system. This type of critical commentary, while common in much of the world, was a new phenomenon for soccer in the US. The USMNT failure has created an opportunity for those working in the business of soccer management in the US and scholars of soccer business and management to comprehensively assess the structure of soccer in the US Researchers and practitioners would be well-served to apply existing theories of governance and policy for elite sport development to the USMNT problem of lacking international success.

Second, domestic soccer in the US still does not draw strong television viewership. The SUM contract for MLS and the USSF has brought significant revenues to soccer in the US; however, television ratings have generally remained stagnant. In 2017, ESPN averaged 272,000 viewers for its regular-season broadcasts, Fox Sports averaged 236,000 viewers, and Univision averaged 250,000 viewers for its Spanish-language broadcasts (AP, 2017). The shortcomings of domestic soccer on television in America, represents a critical opportunity and area for potential growth.

Finally, the quality of soccer in the US is generally believed to be below the standard of other predominant global leagues. Whether this issue is systemic, or more directly, a matter of increasing financial investment in players is a matter of ongoing debate. Researchers and soccer management executives should work to understand what role a change in the US soccer system would play in facilitating player development. Specifically, research should be conducted to ascertain the relevance and potential success of a promotion and relegation system in professional soccer in the US. Additionally, further analysis is needed to determine if MLS is in a strategic position to considerably relax its strict player acquisition policies to allow for greater spending by teams. While the league has added policies like the Designated Player Rule and has allocated league resources to clubs interested in adding more expensive talent, player earnings in MLS lag well behind many top professional leagues worldwide. Overall, the business of soccer in the US serves as a unique example of how globalisation is creating pressure on the North American professional sport system. It is quite possible that this pressure will serve to benefit soccer in the US in the future.

References

American Outlaws (2017) About. [online] Retrieved from: https://www.theamericanoutlaws.com/about

AP (2017) Major League Soccer attendance is up, but TV ratings lag as US Soccer mulls future. *USA Today*. [online] Retrieved from: https://www.usatoday.com/story/sports/mls/2017/11/17/mls-attendance-up-tv-ratings-lag-as-us-mulls-future/107770250/

Collins, S. (2009) National sports and other myths: the failure of US soccer. In: Bandyopadhyay, K. and Mallick, S. (eds), *Fring Nations in World Soccer*, (1st ed.) (pp. 197–207). New York: Routledge.

Das, A. (2017) Long Days, Google Docs and Anonymous Surveys: How the US Soccer Team Forged a Deal. *New York Times*. [online] Retrieved from: https://www.nytimes.com/2017/04/05/sports/soccer/uswnt-us-soccer-labor-deal-contract.html?smid=tw-share&_r=0

Dure, B. (2010) *Long-Range Goals*. Washington DC: Potomac Books, Inc.

ESPN. (2017). MLB Attendance Report. [online] Available at: http://www.espn.com/mlb/attendance

ESPN. (2017). NBA Attendance Report. [online] Retrieved from: http://www.espn.com/nba/attendance

ESPN. (2017). NFL Attendance Report. [online] Retrieved from: http://www.espn.com/nfl/attendance

ESPN. (2017). NHL Attendance Report. [online] Retrieved from: http://www.espn.com/nhl/attendance

Foer, F. (2006) *How Soccer Explains the World: An Unlikely Theory of Globalization*. New York: Harper Perennial.

Francis, J. and Zheng, C. (2010) Learning vicariously from failure: the case of Major League Soccer and the collapse of the North American Soccer League. *Group & Organization Management*, 35(5), 542–571.

Garcia, B. (2011) The influence of EU policy on the governance of football. In: H. Gammelsaeter and B. Senaux (eds.). *The Organisation and Governance of Top Football Across Eurpoe: An Institutional Perspective*, (1st ed.) (pp. 32–45). New York: Routledge.

Hakala, J. (2015) US Open Cup, National Challenge Cup history: year-by-year. *TheCup.us*. [online] Retrieved from: http://thecup.us/2015/05/15/us-open-cup-national-challenge-cup-history-year-by-year/

Hums, M. and MacLean, J. (2013) *Governance and Policy in Sport*, (3rd ed.). Scottsdale, AZ: Holcomb Hathaway, Publishers.

Major League Soccer. (2017). Official Box scores. [online] Retrieved from: http://www.mlssoccer.com

Markovitz, A. and Hellerman, S. (2001) *Offside: Soccer and American Exceptionalism*. Princeton, N.J.: Princeton University Press.

McCann, M. (2017) Answers to 5 Key Questions in the NASL's Lawsuit vs. US Soccer. *Sports Illustrated*. [online] Retrieved from: https://www.si.com/soccer/2017/09/25/nasl-us-soccer-lawsuit-questions-fifa-kessler

Ourand, J. and Botta, C. (2014) MLS's Big Play. *Sports Business Daily*. [online] Retrieved from: http://www.sportsbusinessdaily.com/Journal/Issues/2014/05/12/Media/MLS-TV.aspx

Tannenwald, J. (2014) MLS, US Soccer officially announce new TV deal with ESPN, Fox, Univision. *The Philadelphia Inquirer*. [online] Retrieved from: http://www.philly.com/philly/blogs/thegoalkeeper/Live-MLS-US-Soccer-officially-announce-new-TV-deal-with-ESPN-Fox-Univision.html

Sandomir, R. (2015) TV networks bank on future of M.L.S. *The New York Times*. [online] Retrieved from: https://www.nytimes.com/2014/05/13/sports/soccer/tv-networks-bank-on-future-of-mls.html?partner=rss&emc=rss

Szymanski, S. (2015). Economics and (modern) sports history. *The International Journal of Sports History*, 32(15), 1775–1777.

United States Soccer Federation. (2017) *Bylaws of the United States Soccer Federation*. Chicago: USSF, pp. 1–18.

US Soccer (2017) History: Timeline. [online] Retrieved from: https://www.ussoccer.com/about/history/timeline

US Soccer (2017) Governance. [online] Retrieved from: https://www.ussoccer.com/about/governance

US Youth Soccer (2017) What is US Youth Soccer? [online] Retrieved from: http://www.usyouthsoccer. org/aboutus/WhatIsYouthSoccer/

Wahl, G. (2017) USA's haunting World Cup qualifying failure emits blame, shock, and calls for change. *Sports Illustrated.* [online] Retrieved from: https://www.si.com/soccer/2017/10/11/usa-world-cup-qualifying-failure-us-soccer-gulati-arena

Wangerin, D. (2011) *Distant Corners: American Soccer's History of Missed Opportunities and Lost Causes.* Philadelphia: Temple University Press.

Wangerin, D. (2006) *Soccer in a football world.* London: WSC Books, Ltd.

Worldfootball.net. (2017). Attendance. [online] Retrieved from: http://www.worldfootball.net/attendance

47

The rise and rise of the world's favourite sport

Simon Chadwick, Daniel Parnell, Paul Widdop, and Christos Anagnostopoulos

Introduction

At its very heart, football is simply a game played between two competing teams, from which a victor emerges. Strip the game back even further and there are thousands, possibly millions, of kids who enjoy nothing more than kicking a ball against a wall. Whatever the contents of this book, one should not forget the simple basis for a sport that has become the world's favourite, which some oft-quoted individuals have labelled as being beautiful and a matter more important than life or death. Perhaps its simplicity and purity has allowed football to capture the world's affections, like no other form of popular culture.

However, as the twenty-first century matures, it is increasingly obvious that football has changed and continues to do so, possibly at a faster pace than ever before. Though still a sport, it is now seen by many as an industry, a business, a form of diplomacy, a way to improve national well-being and so forth. Football drives massive investments (Qatar is spending US$240 billion on preparations for the 2022 World Cup); it attracts some of the world's largest television audiences (the World Cup reaches 3.5 billion people); it is played by iconic celebrities (Cristiano Ronaldo is believed to earn almost US$100 million a year); it is associated with powerful brands (FC Barcelona is estimated to be worth US$3.6 billion); and it draws record-breaking sponsorship deals (Manchester United is paid £53 million a year by its shirt sponsor Chevrolet).

This raises all manner of issues for those working in sport, notably various groups of managers and directors. Yet there are people coaching teams at the grassroots level; politicians sat in cabinet rooms across the world; and media observers generating insights, all of whom also need to understand the issues and challenges facing football. We hope that, in compiling this book, we have addressed, analysed, and drawn conclusions about the most pertinent matters of business and management facing football today.

Being a football fan can often be an exhilarating experience (although many would surely argue that it is sometimes negatively so), thus we hope the book also proves to be appealing to the people who watch the game. The academic foundations of our work cannot be denied; indeed, students, academics, and practitioners are the main targets of this text. However, football fans should ideally be aware of the context within which their favourite sport is now being played. Many people were shocked when Brazilian international Neymar made his world record-breaking transfer from Spain's FC Barcelona to France's Paris Saint-Germain. At the same time, these same people were probably either supporting professional clubs owned by overseas entrepreneurs or else left wondering what the future might hold for their lower league, financially impoverishment local team. There were some important issues behind the Neymar transfer, as there are with most players, clubs, competitions, and representative associations. As such, our belief is that fans too should be able to derive some benefit by reading this book, even if just in certain sections. One goal of the handbook has been to demystify some of football's most significant issues. We will therefore consider the chapters presented here as having been a success if students and academics across the world are using it as a reference; if managers and directors in football utilise it as an important source of information; and if fans see it as important background reading for the sport they love.

With a book of this scale and nature, it is somewhat challenging to identify the major themes running through it. Moreover, establishing and explaining the connections between the different subjects addressed here suggests a hugely complex exercise. There are hence some important discussions that are likely to emerge about the nature of analyses undertaken here. Indeed, we invite those who read this book to appropriately comment and debate, perhaps via the editors' social media channels. In the meantime, for the purposes of brevity, we identify five key issues that not only pervade throughout this text but are also likely to shape the future of football:

- Formats and entertainment;
- Governance, ethics, and social responsibility;
- Glocalisation;
- Digitalisation and data;
- Talent and teams.

These issues are not necessarily presented in order of importance, though we feel the fundamental nature of football and the way the sport is run is especially pertinent. In addition, we implore readers not to see each of these five issues as being mutually exclusive as there are multiple ways in which they interact and shape one another.

Formats and entertainment

The basic format of a professional football game is established, well known, and largely accepted. There have been some variations to it, notably following the development of futsal and the popularity of five-a-side football. However, there are growing challenges to the game as we know it, especially due to changing consumption habits. Broader societal changes have left many people time impoverished, whilst others now prefer to consume sport in short segments (typically via an online platform). In turn, there are further issues pertaining to consumer experiences, service expectations and so forth. Such matters are influenced by, and exert influence on, for example, media coverage of football. Whilst globalisation has engaged large audiences with football, bringing with it sometimes vastly different sets of wants. Consequently, there have been some profound changes in the scheduling of matches – the English Premier League and Spain's La Liga are two notable examples of this. With the growth of social media platforms too, we should expect further challenges to tradition and convention, particularly as some commentators have observed that television audience figures are falling in some countries. Football is also increasingly having to confront the fact that while in some countries the sport is part of a nation's socio-cultural fabric, in others it is an entertainment product akin to Hollywood blockbuster franchises. From a business and management perspective, this raises some interesting philosophical, ideological, and practical issues.

Governance, ethics, and social responsibility

When, where, how, and why football matches are played, and whom they involve, at one level are existential issues the sport is now being forced to confront. At the forefront of this debate are the systems of governance and sets of associated standards that are in place across football. FIFA has largely borne the brunt of criticism of and debate about standards of governance in the game. However, the responsibility for upholding good governance standards extends way beyond the Switzerland-based world governing (albeit that they need to be led and moderated by FIFA). As football changes – especially given the large influx of money and the current shifting balance of the world game – governance will remain at the top of the sport's agenda. An important element of future football governance issues is the ethical standards that are developed and applied. Once more, this is not simply about, say, the conduct of FIFA board members. Rather, it embraces everything from the human rights records of countries now investing heavily in football and the role that fans could or should play, through to the on- and off-field activities of players and the way in which a club manages its talent. To retain credibility, legitimacy, authority, and relevance, it is imperative that football is alert to the ethical challenges it faces, and that it responds to them in a robust, timely fashion. Consequently, overt social-responsibility actions that football clubs implement to demonstrate CSR (such as community programmes) are not commensurate with the socially irresponsible actions that have plagued many (or even the very same) football organisations. As such, the idea that a football club that possesses a community programme (see CSR) is somehow socially responsible is no more logical than a drug dealer who recycles. One action or programme does not represent the general responsibility of a football club, particularly when that action is not core to that club's operational functions.

Glocalisation

A mantra from many traditional football club fans could be "this is a local club for local people." The ongoing strength and relevance of football is, in many ways, underpinned by such a mantra. The heritage of football is embedded in community and identity, European football and clubs' connections to towns, cities, industry, and politics is notable in this context. The established underpinnings of fandom have therefore sometimes been as much about one's place of birth as about the football itself. However, this notion of fandom is increasingly being juxtaposed alongside a much broader notion of where fans (some might even refer to customers) were born and reside. Indeed, it is not uncommon now for fans of Real, AC Milan, and Bayern to live thousands of miles away from Madrid, Milan, and Munich. Reconciling the disparate needs of locals and *globals* is thus a major challenge for organisations in football, and understanding how to address it is something that preoccupies many working in the sport. At the same time, an influx of international owners and investors into football has similarly posed issues of legitimacy and identity. Italy's Roma, the Czech Republic's Slavia Prague, and Australia's Melbourne City are all owned by "foreigners," who are perhaps motivated more by commercial returns and political influence than an affinity with local communities. What's more, with the likes of global media corporations, Asian governments, and super agents exercising an ever stronger influence on football, issues around managing in the context of glocalisation will continue to press.

But on the flipside to globalisation is the idea of localisation. Major urban areas continue to swell, creating mega cities, such as London, Paris, Beijing, Guangzhou, Istanbul, etc., which swallow up talent and resources. This exponential growth of mega cities leaves behind an often improvised, poorly resourced hinterland of small cities and towns. It is increasingly becoming apparent that in these places football is often the only identity left, playing a vital role in local economics. Therefore, at the local level economic and political developments must put football clubs at the heart of policymaking. There are examples of good practice around the world, such as the role of football clubs in Columbia, but too few. Policymakers, academics, and football clubs must come together at this local level to create hope and prosperity.

Digitalisation and data

Some commentators assert that we are currently living through a new industrial revolution, which is characterised by the digitalisation of industry and the generation, collection, and analysis of data. So profound are some of the changes taking place that football cannot not avoid being affected. In fact, dating from the mid-90s dot-com boom, when many clubs first launched websites, the pace of digitalisation has only been strengthening. In this book, several chapters directly address what is happening; for example, those on analytics and social media. Analytics is not just having an impact upon players and teams, but also upon relationships with fans and customers. So too social media, where the likes of Manchester City's "Cityzens" platform and the club's tie-up with Tinder suggest a future that is some considerable distance away from the origins of most football clubs. In one sense, the implication is that technology is changing consumer behaviour, though so empowering has technology become that consumers are also driving the demand for new digital platforms, technologies, and the products delivered through them. Indeed, some have cynically observed that football is rapidly moving from 90 minutes to 90 seconds, as younger audiences adopt You Tube as their preferred medium of consumption. At the same time, the development of virtual technology and artificial intelligence poses some opportunities and threats for the sport. Already, video-assisted refereeing has been introduced into football, to a mixed reception. However, this is likely to be only the beginning of such developments, which, as the impact of technology becomes normalised, is likely to change the face of the game most of us have known up until now.

Talent and teams

Constructing a winning team is the very essence of football, and most aficionados of the sport inevitably have lists of their all-time favourite players and teams. Managing the flow of talent has always been an issue for clubs to manage, though over the last decade or two it has become an increasingly sophisticated phenomenon. Nowadays, it is cast in terms of human resource acquisition, development, and retention. Rather this than it being conceived of as a scouting exercise, it is now a talent-spotting strategy, often using global networks. There have already been some interesting developments, of which Arsene Wenger's African connections and some Middle Eastern countries' player harvesting activities are two examples. More recent developments suggest new and different strategies are now being formulated including *inter alia*: multi-club ownership models (through which players are often shared); links between agents and clubs (of which Jorge Mendes' relationship with Fosun, owners of Wolverhampton Wanderers, is an example); and an increasingly judicious use of the player loan system (of which Chelsea appears to be a particularly accomplished exponent). The same "arms race" for talent also now seems to be pervading the offices and boardrooms of football. At one time, working in football was hardly the most lucrative or the most enriching career move. However, as football has managerialised, commercialised, and industrialised, so the demand for top people (many of whom are now entering the industry from other sectors) has grown. This is a trend that will continue and is a narrative into which this book generally plays.

Wherever a reader of this book is in the world, we join them in celebrating a sport that never seems to weaken. Football is as popular today as it has been for decades; indeed, one might argue that the sport is as popular, diverse, and successful as it has ever been. However, this should not gloss over the fact that football faces some major challenges to its existence, its nature, and its future. In reading this book, the editors believe that we have made a contribution not only to assessing the nature of football today, but also to helping us understand where football goes from here. We hope you have benefited from reading the first ever *Handbook of Football Business and Management*.

Index

3 + 2 rule 296
3 × 3 strategic growth matrix for European football clubs 10

Aaker, D.A. 89, 91, 92
Abramovich, R. 192
abuse of social media 107–8
academies, EPPP (Elite Player Performance Pathway) 392
acceleration of migrations 300–1
Accion Diablos Rojos Casa Hogar 122
accounting 187–96
Ackerman, P.L. 389
action plans, creating 181–2
Adaptive Bracket 261
Adidas 408–9, 412–13
administrative structures, OFC (Oceania Football Confederation) 519
ADR (alternative dispute resolution) 75
advertisements, t-shirts, Brazil 560–1
AFA (American Football Association) 591
AFA (Argentinian Football Association) 460
AFC (Asian Football Confederation) 473–83; Vision Asia project 584–5
AFC Ajax 23
AFC Asian Cup 285–6, 289, 473
aficionados 239
AFL (Australian Football League) 381
Africa, football academies 492–3 see also CAF (Confederation of African Football)
Africa Cup of Nations 487
agents 131–41, 299–300
Agle, B. 283
Ahlstrom, F. 441, 448–51, 453–6
AIFF (All India Football Federation) 577–88
Aigner, G. 448, 450
Ajax Cape Town 23
Alarcón, F. 266
alcohol: Brazil 549; Qatar 542
Alegi, P. 488–90, 493
ALFC (Asian Ladies Football Confederation) 475
Alfred McAlpine stadium 204

Aljazeera Sport 540–1
Al-Khelaifi, N. 40, 540
All India Football Federation see AIFF (All India Football Federation)
allegiance, PCM (Psychological Continuum Model) 235
Allianz 201
alternative dispute resolution (ADR) 75
AMA (American Marketing Association) 446–7
Amazon, broadcasting 27
American Football Association (AFA) 591
American Outlaws 597
American Professional Soccer League (APSL) 592
American Soccer League (ASL) 592
Amir, E. 191
Ammirante, J. 28–9
amortisation 192
Anagnostopoulos, C. 109
analysis: performance analysis 175–6; situational analysis 175–6; strategic management 173–5
analytics 246–55
Anelka, N. 381, 478
ANFP (Chile's Professional Football Association) 266
anti-brand communities 104
anti-doping 52
The Anti-Doping Convention 83
Anti-Social Behaviour Orders (ASBOs) 379
APFUT (Public Authority for the Governance of Football) 464–5
Appeals Body 75
APSL (American Professional Soccer League) 592
arenas: Brazil 467–9; value management 312
Argentinian Football Association (AFA) 460
Aronshtam, L. 262
Arsenal FC 11, 27; reactions to corporate stadium names 202
Arsenal Innovation Lab 11–12, 27
AS Roma 24
ASBOs (Anti-Social Behavior Orders) 379
ASEC (Association Sportive des Employes de Commerce) 492

Asian Football Confederation (AFC) 473–83;
  Vision Asia project 584–5
Asian Games 540
Asian Ladies Football Confederation (ALFC) 475
ASL (American Soccer League) 592
Aspire Academy 540
assessing risk 346–7
assessing strengths and weaknesses, external analysis
  178–80
asset valuation of players 190–2
Association Sportive des Employes de Commerce
  (ASEC) 492
Athletic Club Bilbao 11
Atlanta United FC 597
attachment, PCM (Psychological Continuum
  Model) 235
attendance: in Brazil 554–5; in China 524–5;
  MLS (Major League Soccer), USA 597; at
  professional leagues, USA 596; at women's
  football games 357–8
attraction, PCM (Psychological Continuum
  Model) 235
attractiveness of the game, future of football
  28–9
Auld, C. 390
Australia 512–3; event leveraging 282–3; social
  benefits 289
Australian Football League (AFL) 381
Austrian Bundesliga 203
Avenida Tronco 465–7
awareness, PCM (Psychological Continuum
  Model) 235
Ayers, R. 105–7

Baade, R.A. 432
Babiak, K. 115
Backhaus, C. 201
Bacon, N. 223
Baek, S.K. 261
Baiyunshan 523
balance constraints 266
balance sheets 189
Baldwin, R. 20
Balfour, N. 494
Bank Caixa 559
Banqiu 353
Barajas, A. 267
Barça Innovation Hub 27
Barney, J. 309
Barton, J. 107
baseball, analytics 252–3
basketball, plus-minus ratings 255
basking in reflected glory (BIRG) 237
Bayern Munich 103, 414, 448
BBAG (Bundesbehindertenfanarbeitsge
  meinschaft) 35
BBC, broadcasting 22–3

BCM (Business Continuity Management) 336–8;
  crisis management 348–9; identifying and
  assessing risk 346; identifying threats and
  hazards 338–46; risk assessment 346–7
BCPs (business continuity plans) 347
beach soccer 519
Beane, B. 246
Beck, U. 459
Beech, N. 221, 224
behaviour of: fans 234–5; spectators 238–40
Beijing Olympics 336, 526
BeIN Sports 540–1, 572
Belounis, Z. 543
Bernard case 81
Besiktas 574
Besson, R. 300
Bevington, A. 62
Bingham, J. 275
BIRG (basking in reflected glory) 237
Black Minority and Ethnic (BME)
  background 380
Blatter, J. 77
Blatter, S. 52, 337, 344, 352, 362, 384, 424,
  425, 491
Blazer, C. 425, 493
BME (Black Minority and Ethnic)
  backgrounds 380
Bolton Wanderers Football Club 226
Borussia Dortmund 11, 201
Bosman, J-M. 46
Bosman case 35, 80, 134, 441–2
Botafogo 560
Boyd, J. 200, 202
Brailsford, D. 246
brand associations 90–1
brand awareness 90
brand communities 104
brand consistency of EPL's foreign markets 96–7
brand equity 89, 416; UEFA 446–8
Brand Finance 93
brand identity 95–6
brand image 95–6
brand loyalty 91–3
branding power, UEFA 446–8
brands, benefits of 415–16
Brannagan, P. 290
Braun, E. 449
Brazil 259–60, 464–6, 547–9, 561; broadcasting
  23; clubs 555; consumer relations 549–1;
  current structure 551–3; governance of clubs
  557–9; national team 555–7; new arenas 467–9;
  raising football players 553–5; relocation of
  residents during World Cup 465–7; sponsorship
  in t-shirts 559–60; teams 549–51; temporary
  advertisements on t-shirts 559–60
Brazil Cup 551–3
Brazilian Football Confederation (CBF) 265, 550

Brazilian League, scheduling optimisation 264–5
breaks, scheduling constraints 262–3
Brettschneider, W-D. 390
Breuer, C. 61
Brewer, B.D. 461
Brexit 345
bribery 383
Bridgewater, S. 92, 156
BRio 467–9
British NHS Mid-Staffs Trust 384
British Universities and Colleges Sport (BUCS) 64
Brizola, L. 465
broadcast figures for women's football 358–9
broadcast rights fees, EPL (English Premier League) 95
broadcasting 22–3; European football industry 4; Premier League 27
broadcasting rights: CAF (Confederation of African Football) 488–9; FIFA 432–4; Qatar 540–1; Turkey 571–2; UEFA 445
Brouwer, A.E. 263
Brown, S.P. 90
BskyB 242, 367
BUCS (British Universities and Colleges Sport) 64
budgets: of CSR-football programmes 118; strategic planning 182
Budweiser 28
Bundesliga 262
Burgelman, R.A. 529
business, football as 50–1
Business Continuity Management *see* BCM (Business Continuity Management)
business continuity plans (BCPs) 347
business proximity, GS (Growth Strategy) framework 8

Cadbury 221–2
Cadbury, E. 222
CAF (Confederation of African Football) 485–94
CAFÉ (Center for Access to Football in Europe) 35
Calciopoli match-fixing episode 370
calculating means, analytics 249–50
Caldwell 78
Calico, T. 371
Camacho, A. 371
Cameroon 488
capabilities, analysing 178
Cape Town, World Cup 432
capitalisation 192
Cappelli, P. 394
Caribbean 499–500
Caribbean Basin 500
Caribbean Football Union (CFU) 502–4
Carr, C.T. 107
carry-over effect, scheduling constraints 263–4
CAS (Court of Arbitration for Sport) 75–7, 302

Casa & Video 560
case studies: brand consistency of EPL's foreign markets 96–7; CSR implementation 120–7; EPL (English Premier League) 94–5; Leicester City (LCFC) 403–4; Manchester United, retailing 408–9; PAM (Performance Assessment Model) 195–6; Real Oviedo 237; talent development 392–3; transfer of Neymar Jr. 40–1
cases: Bernard case 81; Bosman case 80; Caldwell 78; Condon v Basi 78; Eastham v Newcastle United FC 80; FA v Balotelli 72–4; FA v Sagbo 72–4; FA v Terry 73; FA v Thatcher 73, 79; Lehtonen case 81; Meca-Medina 81; Mutu v Switzerland 83; R v Barnes 79; Smoldon v Whitworth & Nolan 78; Stevenage Borough Football Club v Football League Ltd 79; Walrave 80; Watson v British Boxing Board of Control 78; X v Netherlands 83
casual fans 239
Catalonnia, soft power 290
CBF (Brazilian Football Confederation) 259, 550
CEDCNFL (Control, Ethics and Disciplinary Committee of National Football Leagues) 525
Celtic FC Foundation 122
Center for Access to Football in Europe (CAFÉ) 35
Central America 499
Cervone, D. 255–6
CFA (Chinese Football Association) 523
CFCB (Club Financial Control Body) 75
CFU (Caribbean Football Union) 502–4
Chadwick, S. 101, 312, 330, 528
challenges of: fans, keeping 241–3; performance support programmes 149–51
champ followers 239
Champions League (CL), UEFA 4, 370, 441–2; AFC (Asian Football Confederation) 475
changing commercial relationships, future of football 26–7
changing media landscape, future dynamics of global football 27
channels, social media 104
channels of distribution, retailing 404–6
characteristics of CSR 115
charitable foundations, CSR (corporate social responsibility) 119
Chatterjee, S. 14
Chelsea FC 11, 192
China 140, 476–9, 522, 534–5; assessment of reforms 532–4; Beijing Olympics 336, 526; evolution of football 522–5; implementing the dream 529–32; motivations for football 526–28; women's football 353–4
Chinese Football Association (CFA) 523
Chinese Super League (CSL) 29, 476–9, 524, 532–4

Chinese Super League Company (CSLC) 525
Chopping, D. 187
CHP (Cumhuriyet Halk Party) 566
Christopher, M.L. 321
Chung, D. 514–5
Cissé, P. 28
CL (Champions League), UEFA 4, 35,
    267, 370, 441–2; AFC (Asian Football
    Confederation) 475
classic games 265
Clattenburg, M. 373
Clavio, G. 102
Clowes, J. 312
Club Financial Control Body (CFCB) 75
Club Licensing and Fair Play Regulations 75
Club Licensing System 34
club members, value management 313
Cohen, H. 262
collaboration 123–4
collaborative projects 120
Collings, D.G. 394
Colorado Rapids 203
commercial activities, value management 312
commercial appeal of UEFA 443–6
commercial globalisation 22–3
commercial integrity 377
commercial structure, USA 594–7
commercialisation of football in Africa 488–91
committed causal fans 239
communicating, strategic plans 183
communication strategies, OFC (Oceania Football
    Confederation) 517
compact schedules 260
competition 258, 269–70; CONCACAF 500–2;
    design of 260–2; geographical issues 259–60;
    OFC 519; quest for the best tournament
    266–9; scheduling constraints 262–4; scheduling
    optimisation 264–6; value management 310
competitive advantage 309
compliance, FIFA 427–8
CONCACAF (Confederation of North, Central
    and Caribbean Association Football) 493,
    497–507
CONCACAF Champions League 501
concessions 214
Condon v Basi 78
Confederaçao Brasileira de Futebol (CBF) 259
Confederation of African Football (CAF) 485–94
Confederation of North, Central and Caribbean
    Association Football (CONCACAF) 493,
    497–507
CONMEBOL (South American Football
    Confederation) 266, 459–69
connected stadiums 109–10
constraints: influences on sport consumption 238;
    scheduling 262–4
consumer demands 400–1

consumer relations, Brazil 549–51
consumers 232; buying behaviours 416–7; value
    management 312–3
Conte, A. 227–9
content, social media 104–5
contention, CSR (corporate social responsibility)
    implementation 126–7
continental football law 74–5
Controcampo ("Counter-pitch") 371
Control, Ethics and Disciplinary Body 74–5
Control, Ethics and Disciplinary Committee of
    National Football Leagues (CEDCNFL) 525
*The Convention on the Manipulation of Sports
    Competitions* (2014) 83, 383
coordination, strategic management 173
core business, FIFA 429–34
core close-by strength strategy 11
core global ambition strategy 11
core national power strategy 11
CORF (cutting off reflected failure) 237
Corinthians 559–60
Corporate Governance Code 189
corporate naming rights, sponsorship fit 203–4
corporate partnerships: CAF (Confederation
    of African Football) 487–9; value
    management 313
corporate social responsibility (CSR) 35
corporations 210
corruption 382–3; CONCACAF 504–6; FIFA
    424–5; OFC 514–15
Costa, C.A. 275
Costa Rica 500
Coton Sport FC de Garoua 488
Council of Europe (COE), *The Convention on the
    Manipulation of Sports Competitions* (2014) 383
Court of Arbitration for Sport (CAS) 302
Craig Club Girls Soccer League 352
Crew Stadium 595
crisis management 336, 348–9
Croci, O. 28–9
Crolley, L. 378
Cross, J. 324
crowding out 286
Cry for Peace (Grito pela Paz) 465–6
CSCMP (Council of Supply Chain Management
    Professionals) 321
CSL (Chinese Super League) 476–9, 524, 532–4
CSLC (Chinese Super League Company) 525
CSR (corporate social responsibility) 35, 114–15,
    127; developments in the field of football-
    related CSR 115–20; implementation 120–7
Cuba 499–500
cultural battles within the playground of
    football 28
Cumhuriyet Halk Party (CHP) 566
Cuskelly, G. 225
Custodio, M. 286

customers 38, 232
cutting off reflected failure (CORF) 237

Dalian Wanda 523
DaMatta, R. 462
Darby, P. 324, 492
Dark Clouds 597
Darmon, J-C. 489
data 604
Dauncey, H. 289
Davidson, J.W. 389
Davis, N. 412
De Bosscher, V. 275
De Knop, P. 275
De Werra, D. 262
debt, Turkish football clubs 573–4
decision-making support, strategic management
    172–3
delivery of performance services 151–4
Deloitte 36, 335
demographics, changing demographics of fans 241
Dempsey, C. 515
Denmark 453
dependencies 346–7
DePodesta, P. 246
design of competition 260–2
designing: individual performance appraisal
    and incentive systems 183–4; organisational
    structures 183
developing talents, value chains 325–8
Dick, Kerr Ladies (DK Ladies) 352
Dick's Sporting Goods 203
Dickson, G. 278
die-hard fans 239
Differentiated Model of Giftedness and Talent
    (DMGT) 391–2
digital fanbase 106
digital globalisation 23–4
digital media 101–4, 110–1
digital natives 6
digitalisation 3, 605; European football
    industry 5–6
Digiturk 572–3
direct investment, Qatar 540
direct selling, retailing 405
direction, strategic management 172
directors' valuation model 191
DIS Group 304
distribution of merchandise 404–6
diversification 6–10
diversification paths, GS (Growth Strategy)
    framework 12–13
DK Ladies 352
DMGT (Differentiated Model of Giftedness and
    Talent) 391–2
Dodson, S. 296
Doeringer, P.B. 294

Dolles, H. 309, 323, 324
domain mapping 176–7
domestic football law 71–4
Dong, J. 353
Dorrance, A. 353
Drogba, D. 478
Duerden, J. 520
Duke, V. 378
Durán, G. 266
Dutch Football League, scheduling 264
Dutra, O. 466

EA Sports 434
EA SPORTS Player Performance Indicator 221
earnings multiplier model 191
Eastham, G. 133
Eastham v Newcastle United FC 80
Easton, K. 263
ECA (European Club Association) 35, 116, 128n1;
    budgets of CSR-football programmes 118
Ecclestone, B. 347
ECF (European Club Forum) 35
ECHR (European Convention on Human
    Rights) 83
economic impact, event leveraging 284–5
ecosystem of football 442–3
EFL (English Football League) 72; fees paid to
    agents 138
Egilsson, B. 324
elections, AIFF (All India Football Federation)
    586–7
Electronic Arts Inc. 434
electronic colonialism 490
Element 12
Elite Player Performance Pathway (EPPP) 392–3
Elliott, D. 338, 346
Ellram, L. 321
emerging business, FIFA 434
Emery, P. 325
Emirates 200
emotions 237
endorsements 24
England: CSR (corporate social responsibility) 116;
    Futsal 63–5; grassroots football 59–63; national
    football law 77–80; sporting directors 157
English disease 378
English football, talent development 392–3
English Football Association (FA) 72, 295
English Football League (EFL) 72; fees paid to
    agents 138
English Player's Union 295–6
English Premier League see EPL (English Premier
    League)
entertainment 237, 602
entrepreneurship 184–5
EPL (English Premier League) 4, 72, 366, 445; brand
    consistency of EPL's foreign markets 96–7;

broadcasting 27; fees paid to agents 138;
on-field/off-field performance 193; financial
impropriety 383; marketing management 94–5;
perceived quality 92; referees 367–8; television
rights 367–8; TPO (Third-Party Ownership)
303–4; worth of 396
EPPP (Elite Player Performance Pathway) 392–3
Eredivise 262
ESPN, Ref Cam 25
e-sports 11, 243
Estadio Beira-Rio 467–9
Estadio Bernabeu, hospitality and VIP
management 217
Estadio Centenario 461
ethics 376–7, 603; financial corruption 382–3;
organisational integrity 384–5
EU (European Union): changes in structures and
policies in European football 34; governance
50–1
EU football law 80–2
Euro 2004 284, 286
Euro 2016 102
Europe, system of sport 529
European Club Association (ECA) 35, 116
European Club Forum (ECF) 35
European Commission 80–2
European Convention on Human Rights
(ECHR) 83
European Convention on Spectator Violence 83
European football clubs 445; ownership and
management models 37–8
European football industry 4–6; changes in
structures and policies 34–8; strategic growth
matrix 10
European Super League 267
European Union (EU): changes in structures and
policies in European football 34; governance 50–1
evaluating success, venue management 217–18
event leveraging 282–90
event planning, venue management 214–15
event supply chain 326–8
event-based sales, retailing 405
events, value management 312
EVP (expected value of possession) 255–6
expansion of, transfer market 296–7
expected goals, analytics 253–5
expected value of possession (EVP) 255–6
expenses, FIFA 430
external analysis, strategic management 176–80
external factors, influences on sport consumption
237–8
external products 212
external services 212
externalities 247

FA (English Football Association) 72
FA (Football Association), labour markets 295

"The FA Charter Standard Clubs" 58
FA Premier League, grassroots football 60
FA v Balotelli 74
FA v Sagbo 74
FA v Terry 73
FA v Thatcher 73, 79
Facebook 102, 107; broadcasting 27
facilities, value management 312
fair play 49
fan segmentation, social media 105–6
fanatical fans 239
Fanatics 419
fans 232–4; behaviour of 234–5; future challenges
for 241–3; reactions to corporate stadium
names 201–2; relationships 35–40; retailing to
402–4; sport consumption 235–8
Farrell 359
FASA (Football Association of South Africa) 486
Fawbert, J. 91, 92
FBOs (football banning orders) 379
FC Barcelona 11, 27, 109; rivalries 28
FC Brest Armorique 303
FC United of Manchester 242
Federation Cup 580
Federation of International Football Associations
see FIFA (Federation of International Football
Associations)
fees paid to agents, EPL (English Premier
League) 138
Ferdinand, A. 73
Ferdinand, R. 107
Ferguson, A. 220, 227, 228
Feyenoord Fetteh Football Academy 492
FFA (Football Federation of Australia) 512, 514
FFP (financial fair play) 72, 193–4
FIFA (Federation of International Football
Associations) 259, 345, 436, 603; agents 134;
AIFF (All India Football Federation) 584–7;
broadcasting rights 432–3; CAF (Confederation
of African Football) 486; Code of Conduct
384; Conference of Equality and Inclusion 435;
core business 430–34; corruption scandal 2015
424–5; emerging business 434; global football
law 75–7; governing 427–9; grassroots football
56; history of 423–4; income 432; ISL (Indian
Super League) 581–4; licensing agreements 434;
licensing efforts 413; licensing system 135–6;
OFC (Oceania Football Confederation) 511–12;
organisational integrity 384–5; qualification
standards for tournaments 516; referees 369;
reforming 425–7; RWI (Regulations Working
with Intermediaries) 141; social development
initiatives 435; social responsibility 436–7;
sponsors 433–4; ticketing 434; TPO (Third-Party
Ownership) 303–4; U-17 World Cup 585–6;
Women's World Cup 353–5; World Cup 430–4;
World Cup of 2022 545; world rankings 527

FIFA Forward 436
FIFPro 305
finalising strategic plans 182
financial corruption, ethics 382–3
Financial Fair Play (FFP) 34–8, 47, 72
financial impropriety 383
financial information 187–9
financial management 212
Financial Reporting Standard (FRS) 188
financialisation of labour markets 301–4
Fixed Bracket 261
flaneur 238
flow chart of three-stage decomposition
approach 265
Football (Offences) Act 1991 379–80
Football + Foundation 122
football academies in Africa 492–3
Football and Social Responsibility (FSR) 123
Football Association (FA), labour markets 295
Football Association Judicial Panel 72–4
Football Association of South Africa (FASA)
485–6
Football Association Regulatory
Commission 72–4
football banning orders (FBOs) 379
football business networks 276
Football Federation of Australia 512, 514
Football for Health, FIFA 434
Football for Hope 434–6
football goods consumers 232
football hooliganism 378–9
football law 71–83
Football League 22–3
Football Leaks 344
football managers 227–9
football participants and volunteers 232
football performance 144; performance support
programmes 145–6
Football Research in an Enlarged Europe
(FREE) 33
football services, value management 311–12
football services consumers 232
football stores, retailing 405
football supporters 232
Football Supporters' Association (FSA) 39
Football War 499
Footbonaut 11
formats 603
Formula One 346–7
Fort, R. 397
Fortunati, J. 466
FPs (foundational premises) 277
FREE (Football Research in an Enlarged
Europe) 33
free advertising 90
Frelot, P. 140
French Professional League (LFP) 303

Frick, B. 301, 357
FRS (Financial Reporting Standard) 188
FRS 10 188–9
FSA (Football Supporters' Association) 39
FSR (Football and Social Responsibility) 123
Fullerton, S. 413
functional dependencies 346–7
funding for grassroots football in England 59–60
Funk, D. 234
Fusimalohi, A. 515
Futsal 63–5
future dynamics of global football 25–9

G7 20
Gagné, F. 389
Galacticos strategy 448
Galatasaray Club 565
Galeano, E. 459, 462
Garavan, T.N. 394
Gasparetto, T. 267
Gazprom 433
GB (cycling) 246
GDTs (Geographically Distributed Teams) 369
Generali 203
geographic diversification, GS (Growth Strategy)
framework 9–10
geographical globalisation 22
geographical issues, competition 259–60
geographical reach of CSR-football
programmes 117
Geographically Distributed Teams (GDTs) 369
German clubs, ownership management models
37–8
Germany 284–9
Gerrard, B. 190
Gestifute 140
Geunes, J. 262
Ghana 485, 490–3
Ghemawat, P. 21, 23
Giggs, R. 228
Gilmore, S. 226
Gilmore, J.H. 309
Ginesta, X. 528
Glazer family 195
Glickman, M. 261
global fans, social media 106–7
global football law 75–7
Global North 461–3
global outlook with fidelity to local roots, future
of football 25–6
Global South 461–3
globalisation 20–5; refereeing 371–2
glocalisation 603–4
goals: analytics 253–5; for organisations 181
Goddard, J. 296
Gold Cup 501
Gómez, H. 460

good governance, FIFA 427, 429
goodwill 190
Goossens, D. 262, 264
governance 46–8, 603; Brazilian football
  clubs 557–9; under competing logics
  52–3; CONCACAF (Confederation of
  North, Central and Caribbean Association
  Football) 502–4; FIFA 427–9; OFC
  (Oceania Football Confederation) 514; SCM
  (supply chain management) 322; strategic
  management systems 184; USA 592–4; venue
  governance 210
governance by trust 210
government 46
Grand Prix 337
Grassroots Charter 58
grassroots football 56–66; women's football 355–7
Grayson, E. 71
Griffiths, M. 107
Griggs, T.S. 260
Grito pela Paz (Cry for Peace) 465
Grix, J. 290, 528
GS (Growth Strategy) framework 4, 7–14
Guajardo, M. 266
Guangzhou football club 523
Guardiola, P., 227–9
Guedes, A.C.B. 264
Guesgen, H.W. 263

Habibi, M.R. 104
Hakes, J. 252
Hall, E. 135
Halloran, J.D. 353
Hamil, S. 122
Hardy, L. 161
Hare, G. 289
Harland, C. 321
Haselhoff, V. 201
Haugen, K. 325
Havelange, J. 424, 461
Hayatou, I. 487
Hayes, R.A. 107
hazards, identifying 338–46
head coaches 158
Hempel, K. 448
Henderson, S. 324
Hennessy, J. 261
Hertha BSC 28
Heysel tragedy 38–9, 83, 338, 379
Hicks, Muse, Tate & Furst 23
Hillsborough Law 380
Hillsborough Stadium Disaster 334–5, 338, 379–80
historical cost model 191
Hoehn, T. 267
Hoffmann, R. 357
Holmes, J. 135
hooliganism 338, 378–9

Horbel, C. 309
hospitality management 217
Houlihan, B. 528, 543
Howe, M.J.A. 389
Hoyer, W.D. 90
HR Information Systems (HRISs) 225–7
HRM (human resource management) 220–9
HRW (Human Rights Watch) 543
human activity 45–6
human resource management (HRM) 220–9
human resourcing, talent management 393–6
Human Rights Watch (HRW) 543
Husted, B.W. 119–20, 124
hybrid sports branding, UEFA 448–55
Hyundai 108–9

IASB (International Accounting Standards
  Board) 187
ICSS (International Centre of Sport Security) 543
ICT (Information Communication Technology)
  20, 369
identifying risk 346
identity 25–6
IESR (Independent European Sport Review),
  34, 37
IFRSs (International Financial Reporting
  Standards) 187
Il Processo del Lunedì ("Monday Trial") 371
I-League, India 579–80
illegal practices, CAF (Confederation of African
  Football) 493–4
image enhancement, event leveraging 287–8
IMG (International Management Group) 523
IMG-Reliance, India 580–1
impact of regulatory framework on football 188–9
implementation: of CSR and football 118–19; of
  strategic management systems 173, 182–4
importance-performance matrix 179
IMUSA (Independent Manchester united
  Supporters Association) 242
incentive systems, designing 183–4
inclusivity, FIFA 429
income: FIFA 430, 432; Turkey 571; UEFA 444,
  451 see also revenues
income statements 189
Independent European Sport Review (IESR) 34
Independent Manchester United Supporters
  Association (IMUSA) 242
Independent Supporters Associations (ISAs) 39
India 29, 577–88
Indian Super League (ISL) 581–4
individual performance appraisal, designing 183–4
Industrial Training Act (1964) 222
Industrial Tribunals 223
Industrial Welfare Department 222
Infantino, G. 425
influencers 108

Information Communication Technology (ICT)
20, 369
infrastructure, Turkey 573
in-house, CSR, RBFA (Royal Belgian Football
Association) 122–3
innovation 184–5
Inönü, I. 566
in-season programming 148
Instagram 102
Institute of Personnel and Development (IPD) 224
Institute of Personnel Management (IPM) 224
Institute of Training and Development (ITD) 224
institutional logics 48–53
institutional organisation, human activity 45–6
intangible assets 190
integrity 380; organisational integrity 384–5
integrity of sport 377–8
intellectual properties 412
intermediaries 131–8, 300; RWI (Regulations
Working with Intermediaries) 141
intermediation: on behalf of clubs 132–3; labour
markets 299–300
internal products 212
internal services 212
internal supply chains 321
International Accounting Standards Board
(IASB) 187
International Centre of Sport Security (ICSS) 543
International Financial Reporting Standards
(IFRSs) 187
international football law 82–3
International Management Group (IMG) 523
international networks 278
International Sports and Leisure (ISL) 424
international tours 10
international transfers 298
internationalisation 300–1
inter-organisational networks 273, 276
intra-organisational networks 273, 276
Inverting the Pyramid (Wilson) 251
investment: in Brazilian football 558; event
leveraging 285–6
IPD (Institute of Personnel and Development) 224
IPM (Institute of Personnel Management) 224
ISAs (Independent Supporters Associations) 39
ISL (Indian Super League) 581–4
ISL (International Sports and Leisure) 424
Italy, referees 370–1
ITD (Institute of Training and Development) 224

James, B. 225, 234
James, M. 82–3
Jansen, R. 140
Japan 480–2; economic impact 284; system of
sport 529
Jia-A league 5243
Jiang, C.M. 527

J-League 529
Johanson, J. 9
Johansson, L. 448
Johnston, M. 505
juridification 377
Just Play 516–17
Just Sports 303

K League 475, 479–80
Kahneman, D. 334
Kantar Media 90, 105
Karauri, R. 488
Kasparov, G. 228
Kauppi, K. 330–1
Keller, J.R. 394
Keller, K.L. 89, 91, 416
Kelly, J.E. 223
Kenyatta, U. 488
key for key 466
key performance indicators (KPIs) 217
key success factor 177
Kharrat, K. 254, 255
Khoza, I. 489–90
Kick It Out 380
Kim, B.J. 261
Kirk, D. 390
Kitbag 420
Klopp, J. 227–9
Kluivert, P. 24
Kluivert, S. 24
knockout 261–2
"Know the Fan" 102
knowledge-based resource 302
Koenigstorfer, J. 117
Kolamo, S. 200
Kolyperas, D. 116, 119, 122, 127, 278
Kotzab, H. 329
KPIs (key performance indicators) 217
Krok, A. 488
Kuffour, S. 494
Kulczycki, W. 117
Kumar, M.S. 8
Kuper, S. 397
Kuypers, T. 301

L Marks 11, 27
La Liga 109
labour markets 294–303
labour mobility 300–1
Lambert, D.M. 321
landscape advertisements 200
leadership style, HRM (human resource
management) 227–9
League of Legends 12
Lee, C.K. 479
legal requirements, accounting 187–9
legislation regarding football 379

Lehtonen case 81
Leicester City 253; retailing 403–4
Lembrechts, E. 264
Lenz, J. 448
level of diversification 7
Level Playing Field (LPF) 35
leveraging events 282–90
Levitt, T. 312
Lewis, M. 246, 247
lex sportiva 76
LFP (French Professional League) 303
Li, S. 322
Liaoning club 523
Liasko, R. 109
Liberty City 203
licensing agreements 412–20
licensing goals 414–15
licensing of merchandise 406
licensing plans 414
licensing system, FIFA 135–6
limited liability companies 50
Line 107
Livne, G. 191
loan system, EPPP (Elite Player Performance
    Pathway) 392
local communities, value management 313
logistics management 212–13
logistics of retailing 407
long-ball 251–2
Lonsdale, C. 324
Lopez-Pena, J. 254, 255
Lovell, T. 337
loyalty 240
LPF (Level Playing Field) 35
luge 335
lurkers on social media 106–7
Lusch, R.F. 309
Lynch, M. 520

MacDonald, B. 255
machine learning 250
Madichie, N.O. 494
Maffesoli, M. 461
Mahobe, Z. 488
Major League Soccer (MLS) 260, 503, 593–4
Malyon, E. 41
Mamelodi Sundowns FC 488
management: BCM (Business Continuity
    Management) 336–8; crisis management 336,
    348–9; HRM (human resource management)
    220–9; marketing management 93–7; strategic
    management 173–84; talent management
    388–98; value management 308–16; venue
    management 209–16
Management by Objectives (MBO) 183–4
management models 37–8

managing: grassroots football 57–9; referees 368–9
managing up 158
Manchester City 192, 254, 226, 454, 604
Manchester United 90–1, 194, 195, 314, 344,
    448; core global ambition strategy 11; retailing
    408–9; Sky TV 242; sponsorships 199; worth
    of 416
Manchester United Foundation 120
Manchester United Foundation Trading 120, 192
Mangan, J.A. 353
Mansour, Sheikh 452
Maracana stadium (Brazil) 26
marginal gains 246
market concentration in the representation market
    138–41
market size: European football clubs 452;
    UEFA 444
marketing 88–93, 97–8
marketing management 93–7; venue
    management 216
marketing mix 89
Markov Game models 250
Marlboro Jia-A 523
Martinson, J. 358
Mascherano, J. 303
Mason, T. 460
match fixing 382–3
match preparation 147
match-day income, Turkey 572
match-day supply chain 326–8
Matheson, V. 432
Matsui, T. 264
Matuzalem, Mr. 77
Mawhinney, Lord 344
MBO (Management by Objectives) 183–4
McCarthy, J.E. 89, 107
McDonnell, A. 395
McGarry, T. 269
McGovern, P. 133
McHale, I. 221, 254, 255
McKenna, B. 107, 221, 224
McLaren, D. 105
Mclean, R. 107
MDC (Multichoice Diski Challenge) 490
Meanings of Sport Licensed Products (MSLP)
    418–19
measuring success, venue management 217–18
Meca-Medina 81
media 456; changing media landscape 27;
    marketing management 95; OFC (Oceania
    Football Confederation) 518; referees 370–1;
    Turkey 571–2; value management 313 see also
    digital media
media framing 287–8
media rights, CAF (Confederation of African
    Football) 489–90 see also broadcasting rights

Media Sport Investments 303
MediaFoot 489
Mediaset 267
Mellahi, K. 394
membership in OFC (Oceania Football Confederation) 512–13
memory places 202
Mendes, J. 140–1
Mendes, P. 73
Mennerich, Stefan 103
Mentzer, J.T. 321, 322
merchandise: channels of distribution 404–6; retailing to fans 402–4; supply chains 406–9; value management 312
Messi, L. 90
Mexico 498
Middlesbrough Football Club 227
migration of players 22
migrations, acceleration of 300–1
Milan, A.C. 414
Milanovic, B. 301
millennial fans 108–9
MimoSifcom 492
Ministry of Munitions 222
Minnesota United FC 597
Mintzberg, H. 155–6, 162, 168
misconduct 72–4
mission, CONCACAF 502–4
mission statements 181
Mitchell, R. 283–4
Miyashiro, R. 264
MLS (Major League Soccer) 260, 503, 593–4
M-Net 489
Mobile Sports Report 109
mode of diversification 7
modern portfolio theory (MPT) 6–7
modes of CSR implementation 119–20, 124–7
Mondial Promotion 140
Moneyball 246, 252–3
Montagliani, V. 505
moral blindness 384
moral integrity 380
Moreno, R. 304
Moresco, E. 557
Morgan, J. 225
Morrow, S. 115, 122, 188, 190
Motsepe, P. 488–9
Mount, J. 248
Mourinho, J. 227
MPT (modern portfolio theory) 6–7
MSI (Media Sport Investments) 303
MSLP (Meanings of Sport Licensed Products) 418–19
Muller, M. 285
Multichoice Diski Challenge (MDC) 490
multiple player evaluation model 191

Muniz, A.M. 104
Mutu v Switzerland 83

Nadeau, J.P. 445
NADS 35
Nafziger, J.A.R. 82–3
Nally, P. 345
naming rights 199–204
Narcotta-Welp, E.M. 353
NASCAR 419
NASL (North American Soccer League) 592–4
National Basketball Association (NBA) 420
national football law 77–80
National Football League (NFL) 335; India 578–9; Pittsburgh Steelers 417; sport licensing 419
national football teams 453
Nations League, UEFA 268–9
nature of sport 49
NBA (National Basketball Association) 420
Neale, W.C. 258
Nemhauser, G. 263
Net Book Value 189
network of value captures 314
networks 273–9
New Castle United Football Club 188; naming rights sponsorship 199–200
New England Patriots 200
New Public Management 59
New York Convention on the Recognition and Enforcement of Foreign Arbitral Awards 1958 75
New Zealand 513–14, 516
Newcastle United Football Club 28, 199
Neymar Jr. 24, 106, 304; transfer of, 40–1, 601–2
NFL (National Football League) 335; India 578–9; Pittsburgh Steelers 417; sport licensing 419
Nickelodeon 419
Nielsen Sport 90, 109
Nigeria 492
Nike 24, 420
Nissen, R. 158
Niven, M. 221
Nkrumah, K. 485
Nogoom El Mostakbal FC 492–3
noise 247
Noll, R. 258
non-profit governance 210
normative rule milieu 377
North America 498–500
North American Soccer League (NASL) 501, 592

O2 Arena 202
Oakland Athletics 246, 252
objectives: for organisations 181; role of finance linked to strategy 192–3
obsolescence, merchandise 405–6

Oceania 512
Oceania Football Confederation (OFC) 511–20
ODA (Official Development Assistance) 517
OFC (Oceania Football Confederation) 511–20
OFC Champions League 513
O'Guinn, T.C. 104
Ohmann, S. 289
O-League 513
Oliver, R.K. 321
OLS (ordinary least squares) 190
Olson, J. 135
Olympic Games 102
Olympique de Marseille 11
on-base percentages, baseball 252
on-field/off-field performance 193–4
ONGC 579–80
online sales, retailing 405–6
Open Stadium 122
operations management 213–14
OPTA 221
optimal bracket 261
optimisation, scheduling 264–6
Orange 109, 487
Ordinary Arbitration Procedure 76
ordinary least squares (OLS) 190
Ordonez, J.G. 237
Oreedoo 539–40
O'Reilly, N.J. 445
organisational activation 183
organisational integrity 384–5
organisational management 211
organisational rules 376–7
organisational structures: CONCACAF
    (Confederation of North, Central and
    Caribbean Association Football) 502–4;
    designing 183; European football 34–8; MLS
    (Major League Soccer) 594; TFF (Turkish
    Football Federation) 568–9; United States
    soccer 592–4
organising matches 325–8
outlets, retailing 405
ownership, European football clubs 37–8
ownership structures, venue management 210–11
Özelçi, A. 568

PAC (Program for the Acceleration of
    Growth) 463
PAM (Performance Assessment Model) 195–6
Panini 434
Parganas, P. 109
Paris Saint-Germain (PSG) 193, 540
Park, H.J. 261
Parkes-Nield, C. 105
parking 213–14
Parklife Project 60–1
Parmalat 559
participation, grassroots football in England 62–3

partnerships 210; changing commercial
    relationships 26–7; UEFA 123
Pasolini, P. 459
passing sequences, analytics 251
passionate partisans 239
Passolig 572
Path 1, diversification paths 12
Path 2, diversification paths 12
PCM (Psychological Continuum Model) 234
Penrose, E.T. 301
people analytics 221
People's Republic of China see China
Pepsi 523–4
Pepsi School League 492
perceived quality 92
performance 144–6; on-field/off-field
    performance 193–4; team performance 156
performance analysis 175–6
Performance Assessment Model (PAM) 195–6
performance directors 152–4
performance measurement 194–6
performance of OFC teams at FIFA
    tournaments 517
performance pathway 389
performance specialists 149
performance support programmes 145–51
Perna, F. 286
personal factors, influences on sport
    consumption 236
personhood 462
personnel 222–3
Petersen-Wagner 467, 469
PFCs (professional football clubs) 319, 329–30;
    SCM (supply chain management) 323–8
Philip Morris International 523
Philips 579
Pielke, R. 506
Pine II, B.J. 309
Piore, M.J. 294
Pittsburgh Steelers 417
planning 180–3
Platini, M. 52, 77, 425
player agents 299–300
player development 388–92
players: migration of 22; as resources 301–2; value
    management 311
Players' Status Committee (PSC) 75
playing rules 376
plus-minus ratings 255
Poli, R. 22, 135, 300–1, 324
policies, changes in structures and policies in
    European football 34–8
political dimensions of football in Africa 490–2
Popp, B. 309
Popplewell Report 379
portfolio growth options, GS (Growth Strategy)
    framework 11–12

Porto Alegre 465–7
Portugal, image enhancement 287
Portuguese Primeira Liga 300–1
positive interest principle 77
Post, G. 263
PRC (People's Republic of China) *see* China
Premier League, broadcasting 27
Premiere Soccer League (PSL), South Africa 489
pre-season 147
pressure on referees 369–70
Prince, M. 262
private venue governance 210
Pro League, RBFA (Royal Belgian Football
    Association) 123
process perspective, SCM (supply chain
    management) 322
professional football clubs *see* PFCs (professional
    football clubs)
Professional Football League, influencers 108
professional staff 211
professionalisation of agents 134–6
profit-making 50–1
Program for the Acceleration of Growth
    (PAC) 463
property-based resources 302
prosumers 243
PSC (Players' Status Committee) 75
PSG (Paris Saint-Germain) 193, 540
PSL (South African Premier Soccer League) 489
PSV 23
Psychological Continuum Model (PCM) 234
psychological factors, influences on sport
    consumption 237
Public Authority for the Governance of Football
    (APFUT) 464
public football facilities 210
pursuit of excellence model 390
Putin, V. 345
pyramid model of talent development 391

Qatar 425, 539–45; World Cup of 2022 481–2, 545
Qatar Airways 539–40
Qatar Football Association (QFA) 544–5
Qatar Sport Investment (QSI) 540
Qatar Stars League 544
Qatar Stars League Management (QSLM) 544
QFA (Qatar Football Association) 544–5
QSI (Qatar Sport Investment) 540
QSLM (Qatar Stars League Management) 544
quality, sport licensing 415
Quirk, J. 397

R v Barnes 79
racism 380–2
Radebe, L. 487
Randomly Generated Bracket 262
Rasmussen, R. 260, 263

ratio analysis 194
Ravenel, L. 300
RB Leipzig 11
RB Salzburg 11
RBFA (Royal Belgian Football Association)
    122–3
RBV (resource-based view) 136, 190, 302
RDC (System for Special Procurement) 463
reactions to corporate stadium names 201–2
Real Madrid 28, 109, 217, 448
Real Oviedo 237
reclusive partisans 239
Reep, C. 251
Ref Cam, ESPN 25
refereeing 371–4
referees 366–71
Reform Framework, CONCACAF
    (Confederation of North, Central and
    Caribbean Association Football) 505
reforming
    China's football programs 532–4
    CONCACAF 504–6
    FIFA 425–7
    football in Qatar 541–5
regional academies, AIFF (All India Football
    Federation) 585
regional games 265
regional supporters 433
regionality, GS (Growth Strategy) framework 9
Regis, C. 135
regression 250
regulation of labour market 295–6
regulations, anti-doping 52
Regulations on the Status and Transfer of Players
    (RSTP) 75, 302
Regulations Working with Intermediaries (RWI),
    FIFA 136
regulatory frameworks, accounting 187–9
related close-by strength strategy 11
related diversification 8–9
related geographic diversification 9–10
related global ambition strategy 11
related national power strategy 11
relationships, fans 35–40
relocation of residents, World Cup of 2014 465–7
Relvas, H. 162, 163, 324
representation market, market concentration
    138–41
representation of football players, agents and
    intermediaries 133–4
resource leverage, analysing 180
resource requirements, strategic planning 182
resource-based view (RBV) 190
resources: analysing 178; players as 301–2
Resultsports 103
retailing 400–10
retain-and-transfer system 133, 295–6

revenues: impact from fans 233–4; retailing
    400–10; UEFA 444
Ribeiro, C.C. 263–5
Riddle, P.J. 263
Rimet, J. 424
risk 334–5 *see also* crisis management
risk assessment 346–7; venue management 215–16
risk management: crisis management 348–9;
    identifying and assessing risk 346; identifying
    threats and hazards 338–6; risk assessment
    346–7
risk register 339–3
rivalries 28
role of finance linked to strategy 192–4
role of referees 367
role of sporting directors 161–7
Ronaldo, C. 90, 106
Rooney, W. 227
Rooney rule 382
Rosa, A. 260
Rosberg, K. 347
Rosen, S. 299
Ross, S.F. 82–3, 389
round robin plus playoffs 262
round robin (RR) 260
Rous, S. 424
Rousseff, Dilma 21, 549
Rowles, D. 104
Rowntree, S. 222
Rowntrees 221–2
Royal Belgian Football Association (RBFA) 122–3
Royal Dutch Football Association 264
RR (round robin) 260
RSTP (Regulations on the Status and Transfer of
    Players) 75, 302
rules 376–7
Russell, K.G. 263
Russia, economic impact 285
Ruta, D. 224–5
RWI (Regulations Working with Intermediaries),
    FIFA 136, 141

Sabermetrics 225–6
Sabino, A. 550
SAD (Sociedades Anónimas Deportivas) 37
SAFA (South African Football Association) 485
safety 378–80
Sala, I. 224–5
Salah, M. 492
salaries, European leagues 298–9
salva calcio decree 188
Samoura, F. 362
San Eugenio, J. 528
SASF (South African Soccer Federation) 486
SASP (Société Anonyme Sportive
    Professionnelle) 37
Sauer, R. 252

Saulnier, J-E. 487
Sauré, D. 266
Sbenu 409
Schaefer Brewing Company 200
Schalke 04 12
scheduling 258–66
Schreuder, J.A.M. 264
Schulte, O. 250
Schutz, R. 269
SCM (supply chain management) 319–23; PFCs
    (professional football clubs) 325–30
SCM philosophy 322
Scottish football, Celtic FC Foundation 122
scouting, agents 132–3
SDL (service dominant logic) 276–7
Searle, J. 108
seasonal staff 211
Seatter, G. 514
second screen viewing 101
security planning, venue management 215–16
segmentation of labour market 298–9
selling home 200
Semens, A. 135
Senna, Ayrton 334, 337
serendipitous networks 277–9
service dominant logic (SDL) 276–7
Shangai Foyo 140
Shanghai Shenhua 479
Shepherd, F. 199
Shibli, S. 275
Shrot, T. 262
Siemens 384, 524
Sierra Leone, grassroots football 65–6
Silkman, B. 135
Silva, R. 557
single round robin (SRR) 260
situational analysis 175–6
Sky TV 242, 367–8
Slater, B. 358
Sloane, P.J. 294
Sloboda, J.A. 389
slugging percentages, baseball 252
small-sided games, grassroots football 62–3
Smart, C. 348
Smith, A.C. 224, 338
Smith, J.C. 262
Smoldon v Whitworth & Nolan 78
SNA (Social Network Analysis) 274, 277–8
Snapchat 102
Snell, S. 328
soccer-specific stadiums (SSS) 595
social benefits, event leveraging 289
social development initiatives, FIFA 435
social dimensions, of football in Africa 490–2
social factors, influences on sport
    consumption 236
social globalisation 24–5

social identity theory 201
social media 23, 24, 101–111
Social Network Analysis (SNA) 274, 277–8
social responsibility 604; FIFA 436–7; OFC
   (Oceania Football Confederation) 516–17
social spheres 46
Société Anonyme Sportive Professionnelle
   (SASP) 37
SociOL Room, Olympique Lyonnais 108–9
Söderman, S. 323
soft power: China 528; event leveraging 289–90
sole proprietorship 210
Solomon Islands 519
Sondaal, T. 25
South Africa 284–90, 485–6; PSL (South African
   Premier Soccer League) 489–90
South African Football Association (SAFA) 485–6
South African Soccer Federation (SASF) 486
South American football 461–3
South American World Cup qualifiers 266
South Korea 286–7, 479–81
Spain, referees 371
Sparks, L. 116, 325
spectators 109, 232–3; behaviour of 238–40;
   women 357–8
Spieksma, F. 262, 264
sponsors, value management 313
sponsorship fit, corporate stadium naming rights
   and sponsorships 203–4
sponsorships 199, 204–5; Brazil, t-shirts 5659; FIFA
   433–4; grassroots football in England 61–2;
   Qatar 539–40; social media 108–9; Turkey 573
spontaneous group association 102
sport business networks 274–5
Sport Club Internacional 467–9
sport clusters 275
sport consumption, factors of 235–8
Sport England, grassroots football 59
sport event networks 275
sport incubators 275
sport licensed products, meanings of 417–19
sport licensing 412–20
sport scientists 146
sport tourism networks 275
sport value framework (SVF) 276–7
Sportfive 489
sporting competitions, value management 310
sporting directors 156–67
SportPesa 488
Sport-Promotion 140
sports, HRM (human resource management)
   224–6
sports analytics 250
sports branding, UEFA 446–55
Sports Direct Arena 199
SRR (single round robin) 260
SSS (soccer-specific stadiums) 596

St James' Park 199
stadia naming rights 199–200
stadiums, retailing 405
staffing structures 151
stages of crisis model 336–8
stakeholder theory 283
stakeholders, event leveraging 283–4
Statement of Principles 187
states 51
Stevenage Borough Football Club v Football
   League Ltd 79
Stewart, B. 224
Still, A. 135
strategic analysis 174–5
strategic growth matrix: diversification paths 13;
   European football industry 10
strategic management 172–3; innovation and
   entrepreneurship 184–5
strategic management systems 173–84
strategic networks 278
strategic planning 180–3
strategies, value management 314
Stray, S. 92
strengths, assessing 178–80
structures see organisational structures
Suarez, L. 381
success of venue management, measuring 217–18
success factors 177
SUM 594–5
Sunday Times 425
Suning 533
SuperSport International 489–90
superstars, following 6
supply chain integration 320–1
supply chain management see SCM (supply chain
   management)
supply chain orientation 322
supply chains 213, 320; event supply chain
   326–8; PFCs (professional football clubs) 323–5;
   retailing 406–9
supporter model 238
supporters 38; value management 312–13
Supreme Committee for the Delivery and Legacy
   (SC) 542
survival analysis 250
SVF (sport value framework) 276–7
symmetry, round robin (RR) 261
System 1 334
System 2 334
System for Special Procurement (RDC) 463
Szymanski, S. 267, 301, 383, 397

tables: 2016 Series A clubs revenue 556; AFC
   Champions League qualification spots and
   champion nations (2010–2017) 475; AFC
   Champions League title winners by nation
   480; Aggregate scores for both FIFA men's and

women's rankings as at 29 November 2017 356;
Agreement or disagreement with statements
on diversity of workplace 362; Asian Football
Confederation members and statistics 474;
Average OPS for all clubs 1992–2013 196;
Average rank of benefits of working in football
361; Categorisation of football fans 240; The
current structure of FIFA 428; Demographic
statistics of AFC Champions League winners
(2013–2017) 481; Differences in rank between
FIFA men's and women's national teams
as at 29 November 2017 355; Examples of
domains 177; FIFA Presidents 1904-date 424;
FIFA State of the Women's Game of Football
Report (2014) 356; FIFA State of Women's
Football (2014) Data on Women's Football
Participation 356; FIFA tournaments 430; FIFA
World Cups, 1930-2018 431; FIFA's good
governance priorities 429; The football logistics
mix 407; Forms of football business networks
depending on the type of network and the
type of network formation 274; Frequency
table of satisfaction with work/life balance of
women working in football 361; Functional
dependencies 347; Hosts of the Women's World
Cup 354; Increases in average attendance at
WSL matches 2016 on 2015 357; Key Academy
personnel 393; Key issues on the three modes
of CSR implementation 125–6; Major League
Soccer teams, stadiums, and average attendance
595; OFC and FIFA ranking of OFC affiliates
514; OFC membership and year of FIFA and
OFC affiliation 512; Overall Performance
Score: a hypothetical example 195; Overview
of SCM research within the context of football
324; Ownership and business interests of CSL
and League One clubs 2017, 531; Personal
experience of discrimination 362; Possible
examples of weekly in-season training schedules
for a team that pays one game per week 148;
Professional League attendance data 2016-2017
596; Ranking of fans according to teams 553;
Risk register 339–43; SCM definitions 321;
Success in the FIFA Women's World Cup by
confederation/region 354; A summary of the
FIFA reform processes 426; Symmetry schemes
in a double round robin league with n=20 261;
Talent development and management questions
faced by organisations 396; Talent management
research 395; Ticket sales, attendance figures
and income in Brazil 2018 554; Top 10 football
agencies with the highest market power 140;
Top 10 football agencies with the highest
market shares 139; TV budget incoming from
the broadcast rights in 2018 per each Top club
556; Typical resources football organisations
possess 178; Women's FA Cup Final attendance
figures 2000 to date 358; The world's most
valuable football brands 408
Tacon, R. 116
Talen Energy 203
talent 389, 604
talent analytics 221
talent development 388–93
talent management 388–98
talent supply chain 328
talent supply network 324
target population of CSR-football
programmes 117
tax evasion 188
Taylor, T. 479
Taylor, M. 22
Taylor Report 379
team identification 417
team loyalty 240
team managers 156–7
team performance 156
Team Sky 246
teams 605; crisis management 348–9; value
management 310
Tebas, J. 109
technology: impact on fans 242; impact on
refereeing 371–2; sport licensing 419–20
Teece, D.J. 8
telephony, retailing 405
television rights, EPL (English Premier League)
367–8
Temarii, R. 515
temporary advertisements on t-shirts 559–60
Tencent 107
terrorist attacks in Paris, France (15 November
2015) 215–16
Terry, J. 73, 381
Tévez, C. 303, 478
Tévez-Mascherano case 303
TFF (Turkish Football Federation) 565–71
Thatcher, B. 73
theatergoers 239–40
themes of CSR-football programmes 116
Third Party Entitlement (TPE) 135–8
third screen viewing 101
Third-Party Ownership (TPO) 302–3
Thorpe, R.T. 148
threats, identifying 338–46
TICI (Turkish Union of Training Associations) 565
ticketing: FIFA 434; Turkey 572
ticketing operations 213
time switching 286
Title IX (USA) 353
titles for sporting directors 159–61
TMS (Transfer Matching System) 295
Total 487
Total Quality Management (TQM) 156, 213
Tottenham Hotspur 11

Totti, Francesco 24
tourism, event leveraging 286–7
tournaments: Brazil 551; FIFA 430; qualification standards for FIFA tournaments 516 *see also* competition
tours 10
TPE (Third Party Entitlement) 135–8
TPO (Third-Party Ownership) 302–3
TQM (Total Quality Management) 156, 213
trade, event leveraging 285–6
trade unions 223
trademark infringement 412
training, performance support priorities during 147–9
transfer fees 35–6, 40–1, 297; CSL (Chinese Super League) 478
transfer market 132; expansion of 296–7; tax evasion 188; UK 134
Transfer Matching System *see* TMS (Transfer Matching System) 136
transfer of Neymar Jr., 40–1
transparency, FIFA 427
travel distances, scheduling constraints 263
Trick, M. 260, 263
trickle-down effect 357
trolling, social media 107–8
Trump, Donald 335
TSG Hoffenheim 11
t-shirts, Brazil 559–60
Tuckman, B. 227
Turkey 564–75; decision-making processes of TFF 569–70; growth after 1980 567
Turkish Football Federation (TFF) 565–71
Turkish Union of Training Associations (TICI) 565
Twitter 102, 106–7; broadcasting 27
type of diversification 7

U-17 World Cup, India 585–6
UCL (UEFA Champions League) 441–8; hybrid sports branding, 448–55
UEFA (Union of European Football Association) 4, 225, 441–2; branding power 446–8; broadcasting rights 446; CFCB (Club Financial Control Body) 75; changes in structures and policies in European football 34–8; CL (Champions League) 4, 35, 267, 442; Club Licensing and Fair Play Regulations 75; commercial appeal 443–6; continental football law 74–5; CSR (corporate social responsibility) 123–4; ecosystem of football 442–3; FFP (financial fair play) 193–4; Financial Fair Play 47; grassroots football 56, 58; hybrid sports branding 448–55; Nations League 268–9; partnerships 124; referees 369; revenues 444; round robin plus playoffs 262; values 449
UK (United Kingdom): agents 132–3; transfer market 134; Women in Sport 359; women's football 352

underdogs, Leicester City 403–4
UNICEF 517
Union of European Football Association *see* UEFA (Union of European Football Association)
United States Football Association (USFA) 591
unrelated close-by chance strategy 12
unrelated diversification 8–9
unrelated geographic diversification 9–10
unrelated global opportunity strategy 12
unrelated national power strategy 12
Urrutia, S. 263, 265
Uruguay 460–1
US men's national team (USMNT) 591–2, 598
USA (United States of America) 498–9, 590–9; system of sport 529; women's football 352–3
USFA (United States Football Association) 591
USMNT (US men's national team) 591–2, 598
USSF (US Soccer) 590–2
Uthus, D.C. 263

Vachani, S. 9
Vahlne, J.-E. 9–10
valuation of players 190–2
valuations of football clubs 106–7
value captures 309–15
value chains 320
value creation in football club networks 277–9
value management 308–16
value of licensed products 417–19
values, UEFA 449
van Bottenburg, M. 275
Van der Heijden, L. 229
Vargo, S.L. 309
VARs (Video Assistant Referees) 372
VContact 107
venue management 209–16
venue operations 209
Verdini, L. 558
Vertinsky, I. 348
VfB Stuttgart 277
video, social media 104–5
Video Assistant Referees (VARs) 372
VIP management 217
vision: for organisations 181; value management 314
Vision Asia project 584–5
Vitesse Arnheim 11
Vodafone 573
volunteers 211; grassroots football 59
Vrooman, J. 267
Vuolteenaho, J. 200

WADA (World Anti-Doping Agency) 52, 83
wages 397; English football 298–9
Walrave case 80
Walters, G. 116
Walvin, James 57
Wanda 530, 533

Wang, M. 531
Warner, J. 425, 493, 504
Wasserman, C. 140
Watson v British Boxing Board of Control 78
Watts, M. 139
"We Are Social" 102
Weah, G. 462
weaknesses, assessing 178–80
Webb, H. 373
Webb, J. 505
Webber, M.D. 321
Weber, M. 462
Weed, M. 101–2
weekly wages, English football 298–9
Weibo 107
Weimar, D. 253
Wernerfelt, B. 14
West Africa Football Academy 492
West Ham United 254, 303
Wicker, P. 61, 253, 357
Williams, P. 308, 412, 480
Wilson, J. 251
WMG 139–40
Woeginger, G. 263
Woisetschläger, D. 201
Wolfe, R. 115, 225
women 351–62; as fans 241
Women in Sport 359
Women's FA Cup Final, spectators 357
women's football 352–63, 518
Women's Super League 357
Women's World Cup 352–5
Wonga 28
Wonga.com 199
Wood, D. 283

Wood, M. 222
Wood, S. 223
Woodman, T. 161
Woods, T. 336, 345
Woolwich Arsenal 369
Woratschek, H. 277, 309, 325
working conditions 35
World Anti-Doping Agency (WADA) 83
World Cup: FIFA 430–4; South American
    qualifiers 266; ticketing 434
World Cup of 1930 22
World Cup of 1998 289
World Cup of 2002 284
World Cup of 2006 284, 289
World Cup of 2010 284–5
World Cup of 2014 21, 241, 435, 463–5; relocation
    of residents, 465–7
World Cup of 2018 285
World Cup of 2022 481–2, 541–5

X v Netherlands 83
Xi Jinping 97, 476, 522, 525
Xu Jiayin 532

Yi, I.G. 261
Yorke, Dwight 500
youth development 176
Youtube 102, 105, 108

Zee Sports 579–80
zero sum characteristic 49
Zhao, A. 353
Zheng, J. 543
Ziakas, V. 275
Zumel, N. 248

Printed in the United States
by Baker & Taylor Publisher Services